The **Shelly Cashman** Series®

Microsoft® Office 365®
Excel® 2021

Comprehensive

Cengage

Australia • Brazil • Canada • Mexico • Singapore • United Kingdom • United States

Cengage

Shelly Cashman Series® Microsoft® Office 365® & Excel® 2021 Comprehensive
Steven M. Freund

SVP, Product: Erin Joyner

VP, Product: Thais Alencar

Product Director: Mark Santee

Senior Product Manager: Amy Savino

Product Assistant: Ciara Horne

Learning Designer: Zenya Molnar

Senior Content Manager: Anne Orgren

Digital Delivery Quality Partner: Jim Vaughey

Developmental Editor: Barbara Clemens

VP, Product Marketing: Jason Sakos

Director, Product Marketing: Danaë April

Executive Product Marketing Manager: Jill Staut

IP Analyst: Ann Hoffman

IP Project Manager: Ilakkiya Jayagopi

Production Service: Lumina Datamatics, Inc.

Designer: Erin Griffin

Cover Image Source: 819825958 -
Credit: Nagy/Getty Images

Library of Congress Control Number: 2022905502

Student Edition ISBN: 978-0-357-67697-4
Looseleaf available as part of a digital bundle

Cengage
5191 Natorp Boulevard
Mason, OH 45040
USA

Cengage is a leading provider of customized learning solutions. Our employees reside in nearly 40 different countries and serve digital learners in 165 countries around the world. Find your local representative at: **www.cengage.com.**

To learn more about Cengage platforms and services, register or access your online learning solution, or purchase materials for your course, visit **www.cengage.com.**

Printed at CLDPC, USA, 1-26

Brief Contents

Excel 2021

Contents

MODULE FOUR

Financial Functions, Data Tables, and Amortization Schedules

The
Shelly Cashman
Series®

Microsoft® Office 365®
Excel® 2021

Comprehensive

Getting to Know Microsoft Office Versions

Cengage is proud to bring you the next edition of Microsoft Office. This edition was designed to provide a robust learning experience that is not dependent upon a specific version of Office.

Microsoft supports several versions of Office:

- **Office 365:** A cloud-based subscription service that delivers Microsoft's most up-to-date, feature-rich, modern productivity tools direct to your device. There are variations of Office 365 for business, educational, and personal use. Office 365 offers extra online storage and cloud-connected features, as well as updates with the latest features, fixes, and security updates.
- **Office 2021:** Microsoft's "on-premises" version of the Office apps, available for both PCs and Macs, offered as a static, one-time purchase and outside of the subscription model.
- **Office Online:** A free, simplified version of Office web applications (Word, Excel, PowerPoint, and OneNote) that facilitates creating and editing files collaboratively.

Office 365 (the subscription model) and Office 2021 (the one-time purchase model) had only slight differences between them at the time this content was developed. Over time, Office 365's cloud interface will continuously update, offering new application features and functions, while Office 2021 will remain static. Therefore, your onscreen experience may differ from what you see in this product. For example, the more advanced features and functionalities covered in this product may not be available in Office Online or may have updated from what you see in Office 2021.

For more information on the differences between Office 365, Office 2021, and Office Online, please visit the Microsoft Support site.

Cengage is committed to providing high-quality learning solutions for you to gain the knowledge and skills that will empower you throughout your educational and professional careers.

Thank you for using our product, and we look forward to exploring the future of Microsoft Office with you!

Using SAM Projects and Textbook Projects

SAM Projects allow you to actively apply the skills you learned live in Microsoft Word, Excel, PowerPoint, or Access. Become a more productive student and use these skills throughout your career.

To complete SAM Textbook Projects, please follow these steps:

SAM Textbook Projects allow you to complete a project as you follow along with the steps in the textbook. As you read the module, look for icons that indicate when you should download your SAM Start file(s) and when to upload the final project file to SAM for grading.

Everything you need to complete this project is provided within SAM. You can launch the eBook directly from SAM, which will allow you to take notes, highlight, and create a custom study guide, or you can use a print textbook or your mobile app. Download IOS or Download Android.

To get started, launch your SAM Project assignment from SAM, MindTap, or a link within your LMS.

Step 1: Download Files

- Click the "Download All" button or the individual links to download your **Start File** and **Support File(s)** (when available). You must use the SAM Start file.
- Click the Instructions link to launch the eBook (or use the print textbook or mobile app).
- Disregard any steps in the textbook that ask you to create a new file or to use a file from a location outside of SAM.
- Look for the SAM Download icon to begin working with your start file.
- Follow the module's step-by-step instructions until you reach the SAM Upload icon.
- Save and close the file.

Step 2: Save Work to SAM

- Ensure you rename your project file to match the Expected File Name.
- Upload your in-progress or completed file to SAM. You can download the file to continue working or submit it for grading in the next step.

Step 3: Submit for Grading

- Upload the completed file to SAM for immediate feedback and to view the available Reports.
    - The **Graded Summary Report** provides a detailed list of project steps, your score, and feedback to aid you in revising and resubmitting the project.
    - The **Study Guide Report** provides your score for each project step and links to the associated training and textbook pages.
- If additional attempts are allowed, use your reports to assist with revising and resubmitting your project.
- To re-submit the project, download the file saved in step 2.
- Edit, save, and close the file, then re-upload and submit it again.

<u>For all other SAM Projects, please follow these steps:</u>

To get started, launch your SAM Project assignment from SAM, MindTap, or a link within your LMS.

Step 1: Download Files

- Click the "Download All" button or the individual links to download your **Instruction File**, **Start File**, and **Support File(s)** (when available). You <u>must</u> use the SAM Start file.
- Open the Instruction file and follow the step-by-step instructions. Ensure you rename your project file to match the Expected File Name (change _1 to _2 at the end of the file name).

Step 2: Save Work to SAM

- Upload your in-progress or completed file to SAM. You can download the file to continue working or submit it for grading in the next step.

Step 3: Submit for Grading

- Upload the completed file to SAM for immediate feedback and to view available Reports.
  - The **Graded Summary Report** provides a detailed list of project steps, your score, and feedback to aid you in revising and resubmitting the project.
  - The **Study Guide Report** provides your score for each project step and links to the associated training and textbook pages.
- If additional attempts are allowed, use your reports to assist with revising and resubmitting your project.
- To re-submit the project, download the file saved in step 2.
- Edit, save, and close the file, then re-upload and submit it again.

For additional tips to successfully complete your SAM Projects, please view our Common Student Errors Infographic.

1 Creating a Worksheet and a Chart

Objectives

After completing this module, you will be able to:

- Start an app
- Identify the components of the Microsoft Office ribbon
- Describe the Excel worksheet
- Enter text and numbers
- Use the Sum button to sum a range of cells
- Enter a simple function
- Copy the contents of a cell to a range of cells using the fill handle
- Apply cell styles
- Format cells in a worksheet
- Create a pie chart
- Change a worksheet name and sheet tab color
- Change document properties
- Preview and print a worksheet
- Use the AutoCalculate area to display statistics
- Correct errors on a worksheet
- Use Microsoft Office Help

Introduction

Almost every organization collects vast amounts of data. Often, data is consolidated into a summary so that people in the organization better understand the meaning of the data. An Excel worksheet allows data to be summarized and charted easily. A **chart** is a graphic element that illustrates data. In this module, you will create a worksheet that includes a chart. The data in the worksheet and chart comprise a budget that contains monthly estimates for each income and expense category.

Project: Real Estate Budget Worksheet and Chart

The project in this module follows proper design guidelines and uses Excel to create the worksheet and chart shown in Figure 1–1a and Figure 1–1b. The worksheet contains budget data for Frangold Real Estate. Mrs. Frangold has compiled a list of her projected expenses and sources of income and wants to use this information to create an easy-to-read worksheet. In addition, she would like a pie chart to show her estimated monthly expenses by category.

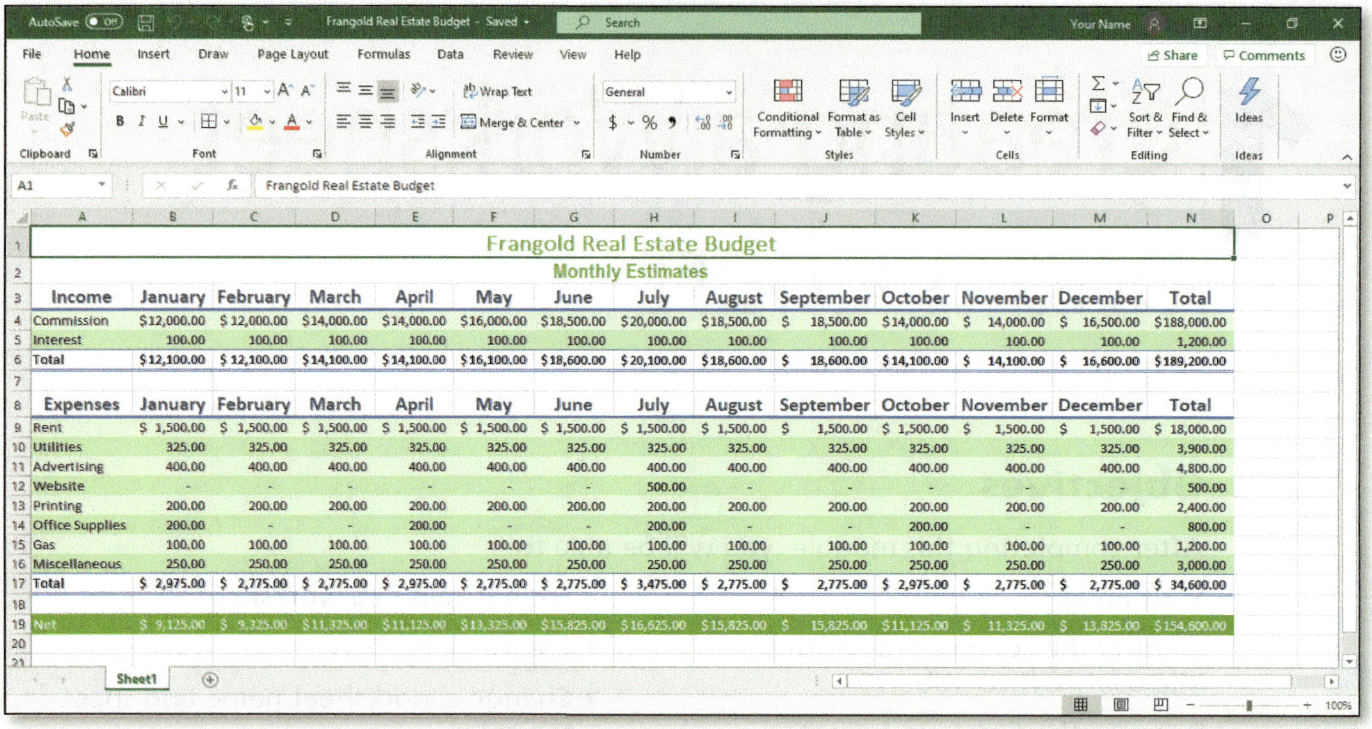

(a) Real Estate Budget Worksheet

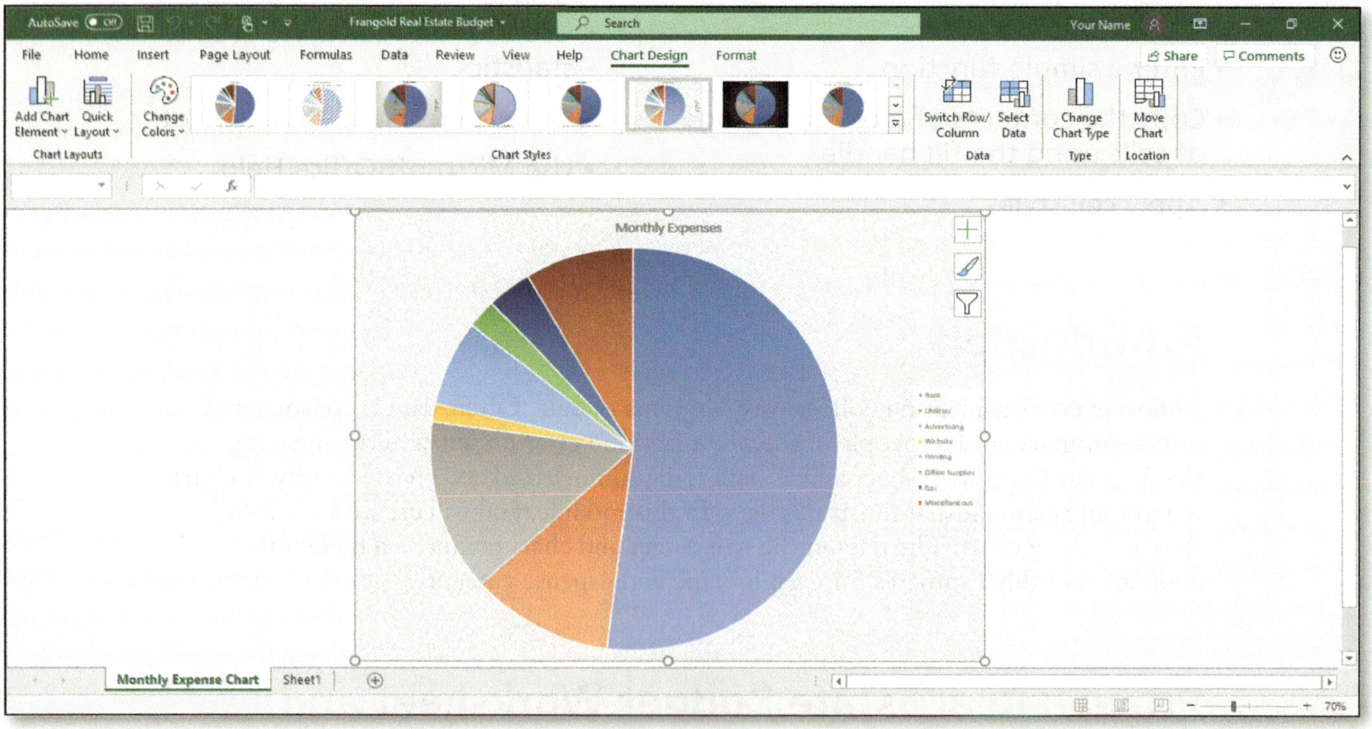

(b) Pie Chart Showing Monthly Expenses by Category

Figure 1–1

The first step in creating an effective worksheet is to make sure you understand what is required. The person or persons requesting the worksheet may supply their requirements in a requirements document, or you can create one. A requirements document includes a needs statement, a source of data, a summary of calculations, and any other special requirements for the worksheet, such as charting and web support. Figure 1–2 shows the requirements document for the new workbook to be created in this module.

Worksheet Title	Frangold Real Estate Budget
Need	A yearly projection of Frangold Real Estate's budget
Source of data	Data supplied by Madelyn Frangold includes monthly estimates for income and expenses
Calculations	The following calculations must be made: 1. For each month, a total for income and expenses 2. For each budget item, a total for the item 3. For the year, total all income and expenses 4. Net income = Total income - Expenses

Figure 1–2

Consider This

Why is it important to plan a worksheet?

The key to developing a useful worksheet is careful planning. Careful planning can reduce your effort significantly and result in a worksheet that is accurate, easy to read, flexible, and useful. When analyzing a problem and designing a worksheet solution, what steps should you follow?

1. Define the problem, including need, source of data, calculations, charting, and web or special requirements.
2. Design the worksheet.
3. Enter the data and formulas.
4. Test the worksheet.

After carefully reviewing the requirements document (Figure 1–2) and making the necessary decisions, the next step is to design a solution or draw a sketch of the worksheet based on the requirements, including titles, column and row headings, the location of data values, and the pie chart, as shown in Figure 1–3. The dollar signs and commas that you see in the sketch of the worksheet indicate formatted numeric values.

sketch of worksheet and chart

Real Estate Budget Worksheet

Income	January	December	Total
Commission	$99,999.99	$99,999.99	$99,999.99
Interest			
Total	$99,999.99	$99,999.99	$99,999.99
Expenses	**January**	**December**	**Total**
Rent	$99,999.99	$99,999.99	$99,999.99
Utilities			
Advertising			
Website			
Printing			
Office Supplies			
Gas			
Miscellaneous			
Total	$99,999.99	$99,999.99	$99,999.99
Net	$99,999.99	$99,999.99	$99,999.99

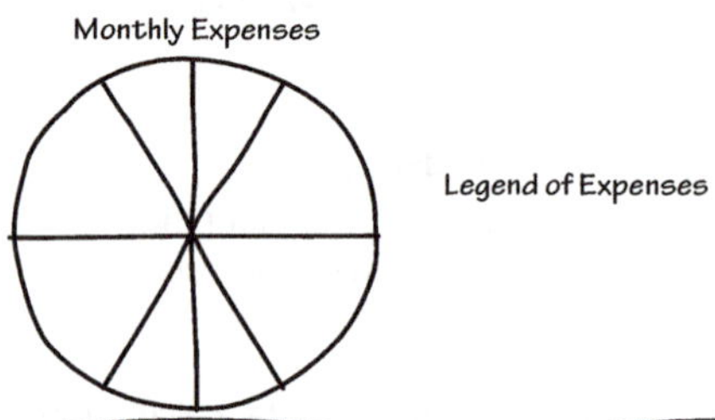

Figure 1–3

With a good understanding of the requirements document, an understanding of the necessary decisions, and a sketch of the worksheet, the next step is to use Excel to create the worksheet and chart.

Starting and Using Excel

What Is Excel?

Microsoft Excel 365 is a powerful spreadsheet app that allows users to organize data, complete calculations, make decisions, graph data, develop professional-looking reports, publish organized data to the web, and access real-time data from websites. The four major parts of Excel are as follows:

- **Workbooks and Worksheets:** A workbook is like a notebook. Inside the workbook are sheets, each of which is called a worksheet. A **worksheet** is a single sheet in a workbook file that lets you enter and manipulate data, perform calculations with data, and analyze data. Thus, a workbook is a collection of worksheets. Worksheets allow users to enter, calculate, manipulate, and analyze data, such as numbers and text. The terms "worksheet" and "spreadsheet" are interchangeable.
- **Charts:** Excel can draw a variety of charts, such as column charts and pie charts.
- **Tables:** Tables organize and store data within worksheets. For example, once a user enters data into a worksheet, an Excel table can sort the data, search for specific data, and select data that satisfies defined criteria.

- **Web Support:** Web support allows users to save Excel worksheets or parts of a worksheet in a format that a user can view in a browser, so that a user can view and manipulate the worksheet using a browser. Excel web support also provides access to real-time data, such as stock quotes, using web queries.

To Start Excel and Create a Blank Workbook

Across the bottom of the Windows desktop is the taskbar. The taskbar contains the **Start button**, a clickable button at in the lower-left corner of the Windows 10 screen that you click to open the Start menu. The **Start menu** provides access to all programs, documents, and settings on the computer. The Start menu may contain one or more folders, and these folders can be used to group related apps together. A **folder** is an electronic container that helps you organize your computer files, like a manilla folder on your desk; it can contain subfolders for organizing files into smaller groups.

The Start menu allows you to start programs, store and search for documents, customize the computer or mobile device, and sign out of a user account or shut down the computer or mobile device. A **menu** is a list of related items, including folders, programs, and commands. Each **command** on a menu performs a specific action, such as saving a file or obtaining help. **Why?** Commands are one of the principal ways you communicate with an app so you can tell it what you want it to do.

The following steps, which assume Windows is running, use the Start menu to start Excel and create a blank workbook based on a typical installation. You may need to ask your instructor how to start Excel on your computer.

1

- **sam** Click the Start button on the Windows taskbar to display the Start menu containing a list of apps installed on the computer or mobile device.
- If necessary, scroll to display Excel (Figure 1–4).

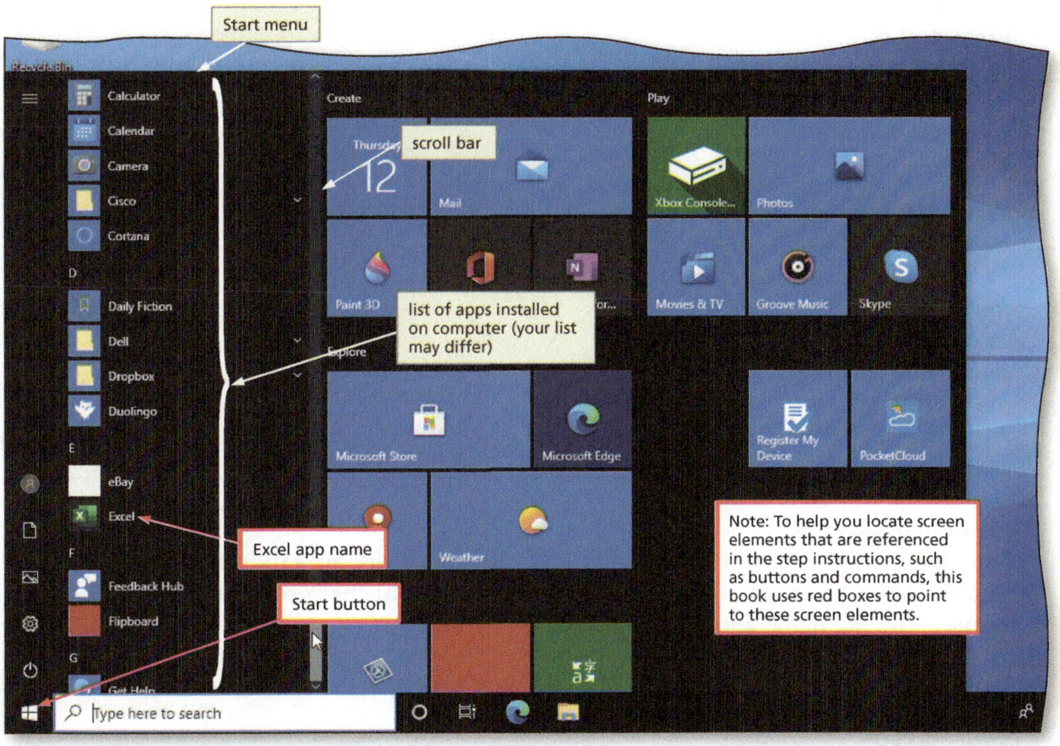

Figure 1–4

2

- Click Excel to start the app (Figure 1–5).

Q&A **Why does my screen look different?**
Although you will always have an option to create a blank workbook, additional thumbnails may differ based on your software version or how you use Excel.

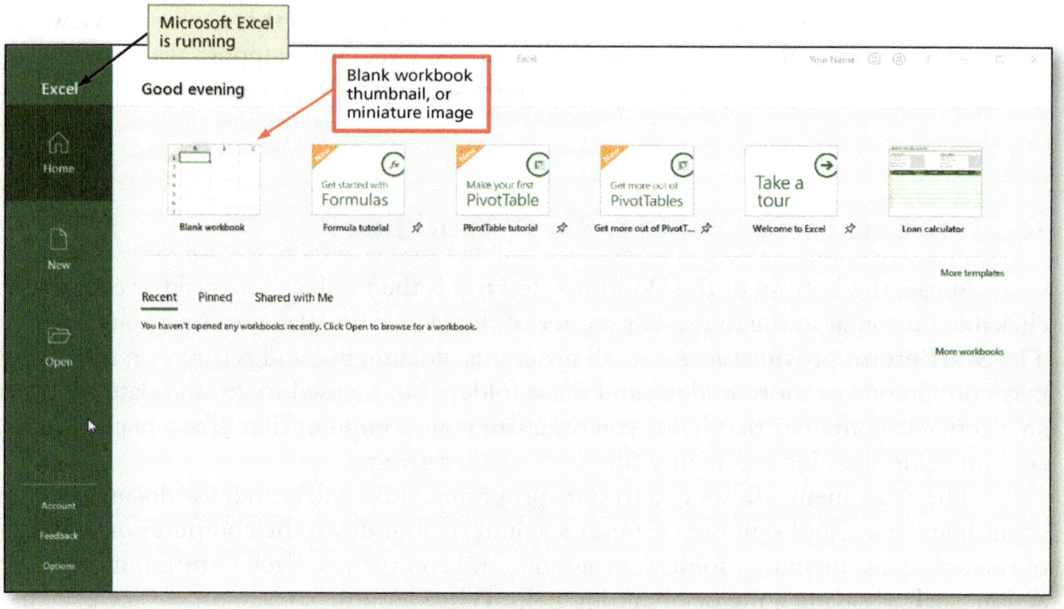

Figure 1–5

3

- Click the Blank workbook thumbnail on the Excel start screen to create a blank Excel workbook in the Excel window (Figure 1–6).

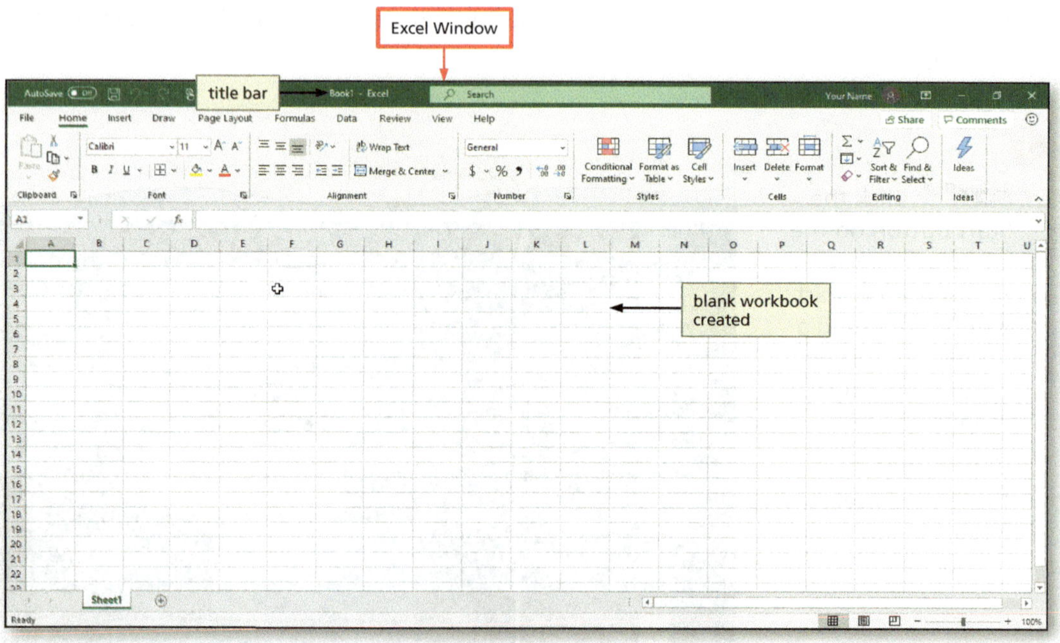

Figure 1–6

Q&A **What happens when I start Excel?**
Excel provides a means for you to create a blank document, as shown in Figure 1–5. After you click the Blank workbook thumbnail, the Excel window shown in Figure 1–6 opens. A **window** is a rectangular-shaped work area that displays an app or a collection of files, folders, and Windows tools. A window has a **title bar**, an area at the top of a document window or app window that displays the file name and program name.

Other Ways

1. Type app name in search box, click app name in results list
2. Double-click file created in app you want to start

The Excel Window

The Excel window consists of a variety of components to make your work more efficient and worksheets more professional. These include the worksheet window, ribbon, Search box, Quick Access Toolbar, and Microsoft Account area.

Excel opens a new workbook with one worksheet. If necessary, you can add additional worksheets. Each worksheet has a sheet name that appears on a **sheet tab**, an indicator at the bottom of the window that identifies a worksheet. For example, Sheet1 is the name of the active worksheet displayed in the blank workbook shown in Figure 1–7. You can add more sheets to the workbook by clicking the New sheet button.

Worksheet The worksheet is organized into a rectangular grid containing vertical columns and horizontal rows. A column letter in a box above the grid, also called the **column heading**, appears above each worksheet column to identify it. A row number in a box on the left side of a worksheet row, also called the **row heading**, identifies each row.

The intersection of each column and row is a cell. A **cell** is the box, formed by the intersection of a column and a row, where you enter data. Each worksheet in a workbook has 16,384 columns and 1,048,576 rows for a total of 17,179,869,184 cells. Only a small fraction of the active worksheet appears on the screen at one time.

A cell is referred to by its unique address, or **cell reference**, which is the column letter and row number location that identifies a cell within a worksheet, such as A1. To identify a cell, specify the column letter first, followed by the row number. For example, cell reference D5 refers to the cell located at the intersection of column D and row 5 (Figure 1–7).

One cell on the worksheet, designated the **active cell**, is the worksheet cell into which you are entering data. The active cell in Figure 1–7 is A1. The active cell is identified in three ways. First, a heavy border surrounds the cell; second, the active cell reference shows immediately above column A in the Name box; and third, the column heading A and row heading 1 are highlighted so that it is easy to see which cell is active (Figure 1–7).

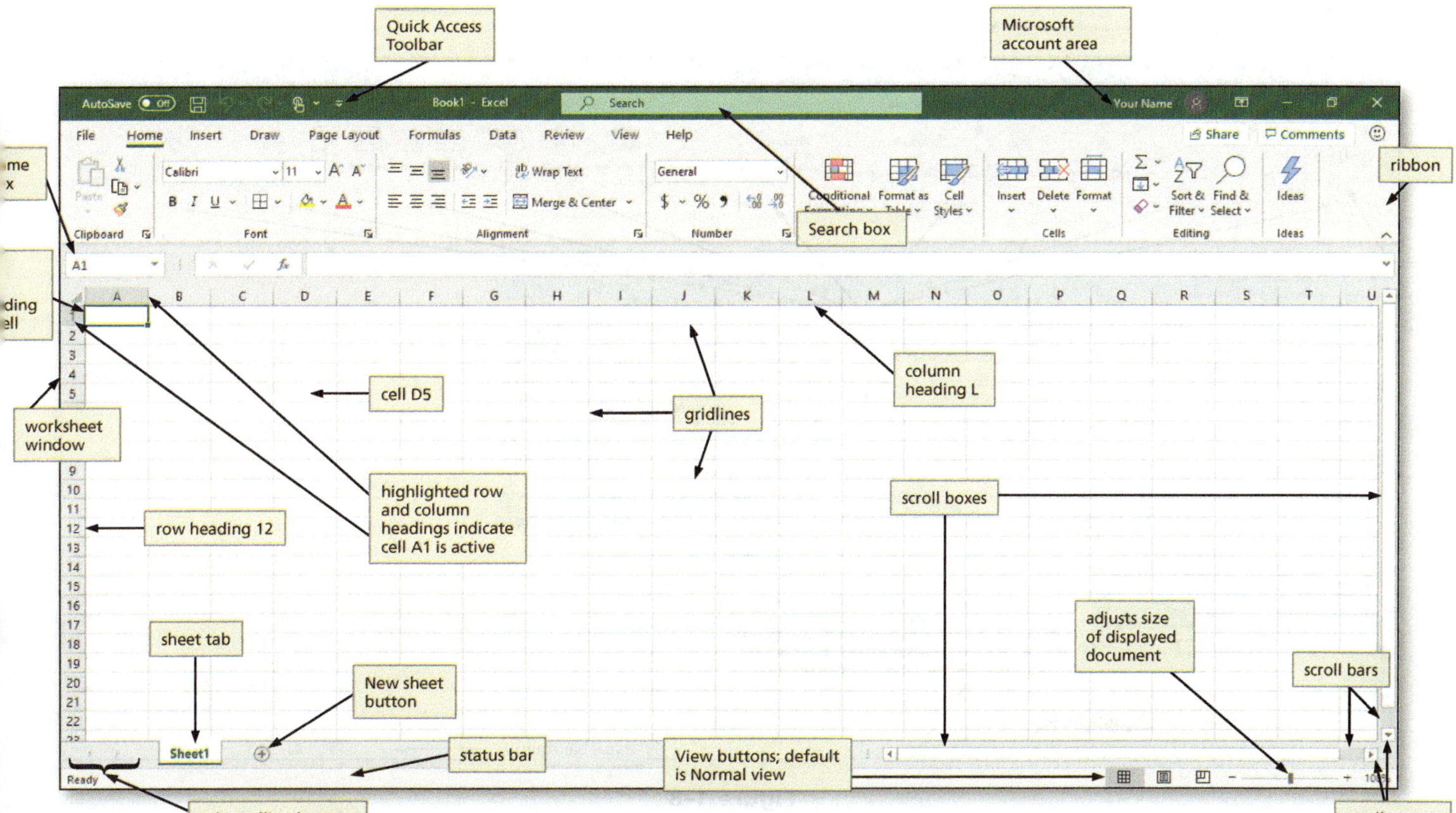

Figure 1–7

The evenly spaced horizontal and/or vertical lines used in a worksheet or chart are called **gridlines**. Gridlines make a worksheet easier to read. If desired, you can turn the gridlines off so that they do not show on the worksheet. While learning Excel, gridlines help you to understand the structure of the worksheet.

The pointer appears as a block plus sign whenever it is located in a cell on the worksheet. Another common shape of the pointer is the block arrow. The pointer turns into the block arrow when you move it outside the worksheet or when you drag cell contents between rows or columns.

Scroll Bars **Scroll bars** on the right edge (vertical scroll bar) and bottom edge (horizontal scroll bar) of a document window let you view a document that is too large to fit on the screen at once. You use a scroll bar to display different portions of a document in the document window. On a scroll bar, the position of the scroll box reflects the location of the portion of the document that is displayed in the document window.

Status Bar The **status bar** is the gray bar at the bottom of the Excel window that shows status information about the currently open worksheet, as well as view buttons and zoom controls. As you type text or perform certain tasks, various indicators and buttons may appear on the status bar. The right side of the status bar includes buttons and controls you can use to change the view of a document and adjust the size of the displayed document.

Ribbon The **ribbon** (shown in Figure 1–7) is a horizontal strip near the top of the window that contains tabs (pages) of grouped command buttons that you click to interact with the app. Each **tab** in the ribbon contains a group of related commands and settings. Each **group** is a tab element on the ribbon that contains related commands. When you start an Office app, such as Excel, it initially displays several main tabs, also called default or top-level tabs. All Office apps have a Home tab, which contains the more frequently used commands. When you start Excel, the ribbon displays 10 main tabs: File, Home, Insert, Draw, Page Layout, Formulas, Data, Review, View, and Help. (If you are using a desktop computer, you might not see the Draw tab.)

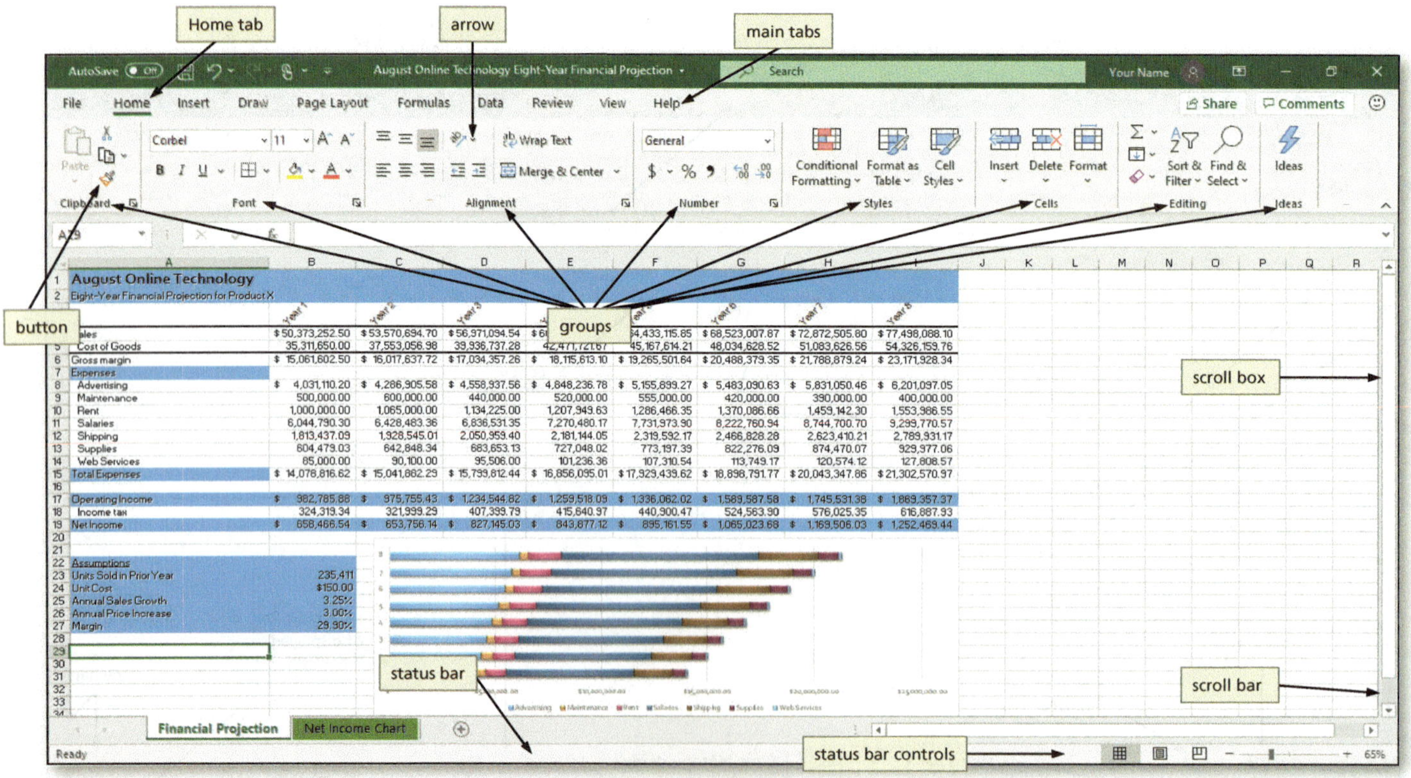

Figure 1–8

In addition to the main tabs, Excel displays other tabs, called **contextual tabs** (Figure 1–9), tabs that appear in addition to the main tabs on the ribbon when you perform certain tasks or work with objects, such as pictures or tables. If you insert a chart in an Excel workbook, for example, the Chart Design tab and Format tab appear. When you are finished working with the chart, the Chart Design and Format tabs disappear from the ribbon. Excel determines when contextual tabs should appear and disappear based on tasks you perform.

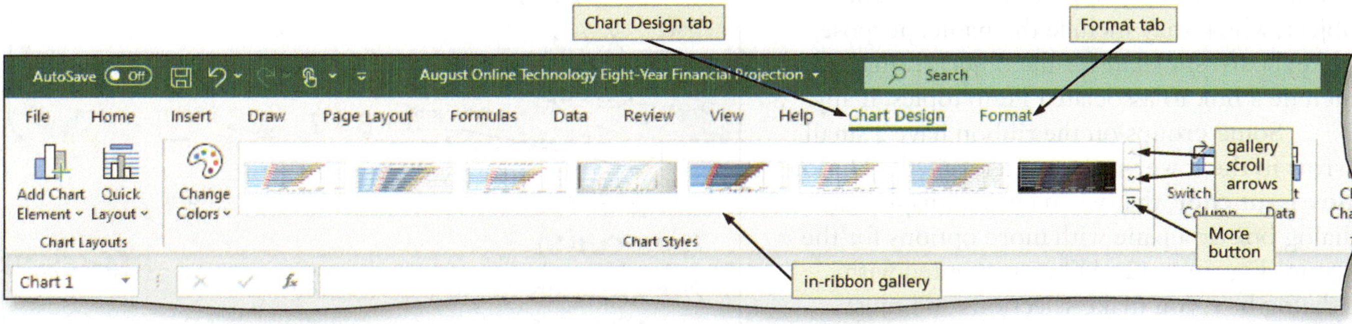

Figure 1–9

Items on the ribbon include buttons and galleries (shown in Figures 1–8 and 1–9). A **gallery** is a collection of choices, arranged in a grid or list, that you can browse through before making a selection of items such as fonts. You can scroll through choices in a gallery by clicking its scroll arrows. Or, you can click a gallery's More button to view more gallery options on the screen at a time.

Some buttons and boxes have arrows that, when clicked, also display a gallery; others always cause a gallery to be displayed when clicked. Most galleries support **live preview**, an Office feature that shows the results that would occur in your file, such as the effects of formatting options on a document's appearance, if you clicked the option you are pointing to (Figure 1–10). Live preview works only if you are using a mouse; if you are using a touch screen, you will not be able to view live previews.

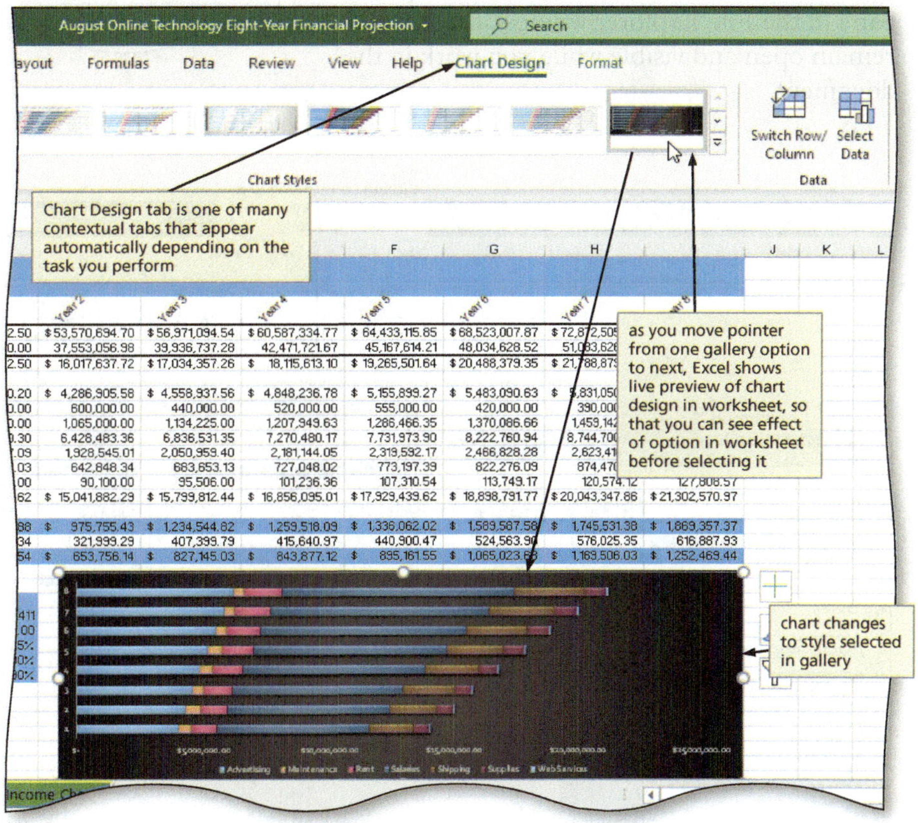

Figure 1–10

Some commands on the ribbon display an image to help you remember their function. When you point to a command on the ribbon, all or part of the command glows in a darker shade of gray, and a ScreenTip appears on the screen. A **ScreenTip** (Figure 1–11) is a label that appears when you point to a button or object, which may include the name, purpose, or keyboard shortcut for the object. It may also include a link to associated Help topics, if any.

Some groups on the ribbon have a small arrow in the lower-right corner, called a **Dialog Box Launcher**, that when clicked displays a dialog box or a pane with more options for the group (Figure 1–12). When presented with a dialog box, you make selections and must close the dialog box before returning to the document. A **pane**, in contrast to a dialog box, is a section of a window, such as the navigation pane in the File Explorer window, that can remain open and visible while you work in the document.

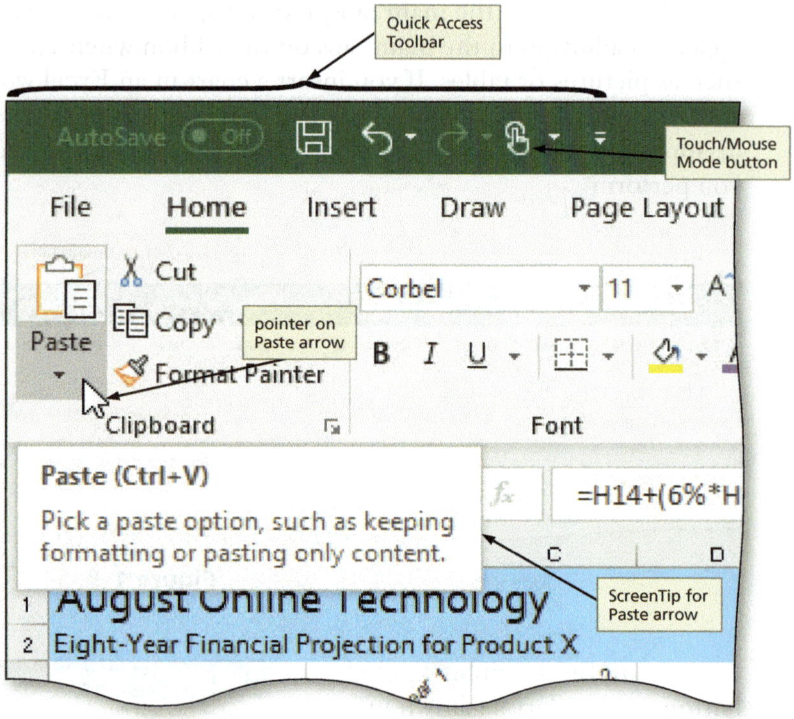

Figure 1–11

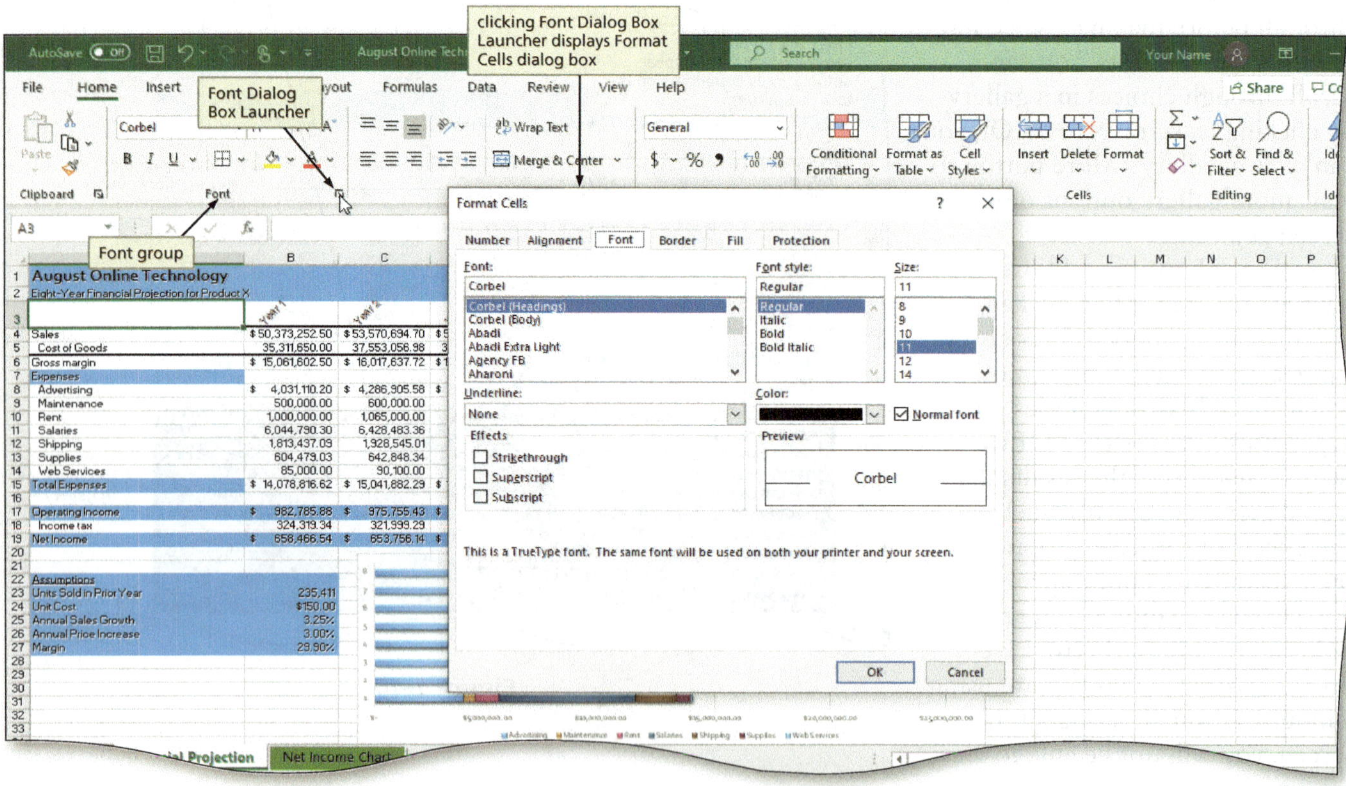

Figure 1–12

Mini Toolbar The **Mini toolbar** is a small toolbar that appears automatically next to selected text and that contains the most frequently used text formatting commands, such as bold, italic, font color, and font size

(Figure 1–13). If you do not use the Mini toolbar, it disappears from the screen. The buttons, arrows, and boxes on the Mini toolbar may vary, depending on whether you are using Touch mode versus Mouse mode. If you right-click an item in the document window, Excel displays both the Mini toolbar and a shortcut menu, which is discussed in a later section in this module.

All commands on the Mini toolbar also exist on the ribbon. The purpose of the Mini toolbar is to minimize hand or mouse movement.

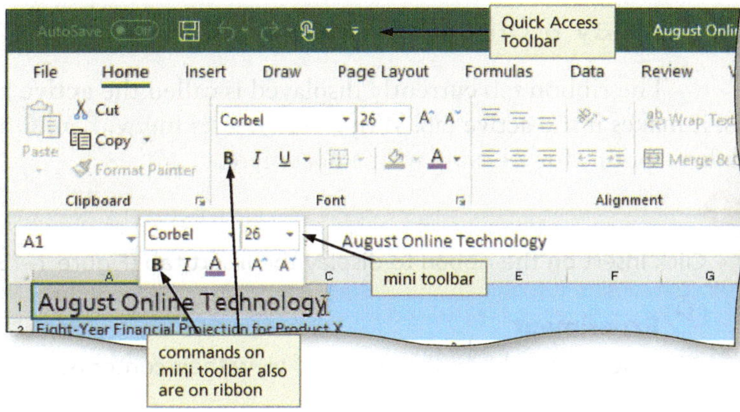

Figure 1–13

Quick Access Toolbar The **Quick Access Toolbar** (shown in Figure 1–13) is a customizable toolbar at the left edge of the title bar that contains buttons you can click to perform frequently used commands. The commands on the Quick Access Toolbar always are available, regardless of the task you are performing. If your computer or mobile device has a touch screen, the Touch/Mouse Mode button will appear on the Quick Access Toolbar and will allow you to switch between Touch mode and Mouse mode. If you are primarily using touch gestures, Touch mode will add more space between commands on menus and on the ribbon so that they are easier to tap. While touch gestures are convenient ways to interact with Office apps, not all features are supported when you are using Touch mode. If you are using a mouse, Mouse mode will not add the extra space between buttons and commands. The Quick Access Toolbar is discussed in more depth later in the module.

KeyTips If you prefer using the keyboard instead of the mouse, you can display KeyTips for certain commands (Figure 1–14). **KeyTips** are labels that appear over each tab and command on the ribbon when the ALT key is pressed. To select a command using the keyboard, press the letter or number displayed in the KeyTip, which may cause additional KeyTips related to the selected command to appear. To remove KeyTips from the screen, press the ALT key or the ESC key until all KeyTips disappear, or click anywhere in the app window.

Formula Bar As you type, Excel displays your entry in the **formula bar**, the area above the worksheet grid where you enter or edit data in the active cell (Figure 1–14). You can make the formula bar larger by dragging the bottom of the formula bar or clicking the expand button to the right of the formula bar. Excel also displays cell information in the **Name box**, a box to the left of the formula bar that shows the cell reference or name of the active cell.

Search Box The **Search box** is a text box on the title bar that is used to find a command or to access the Office Help system (Figure 1–14). As you type in the Search box, Excel displays search results that are refined as you type. For example, if you want to center text in a cell, you can type "center" in the Search box and then select the appropriate command. The Search box also lists related commands and/or the last five commands accessed from the box.

Microsoft Account Area In the **Microsoft Account area**, an area on the right side of the title bar, you can use the Sign in link to sign in to your Microsoft account (Figure 1–14). Once signed in, you will see your account information.

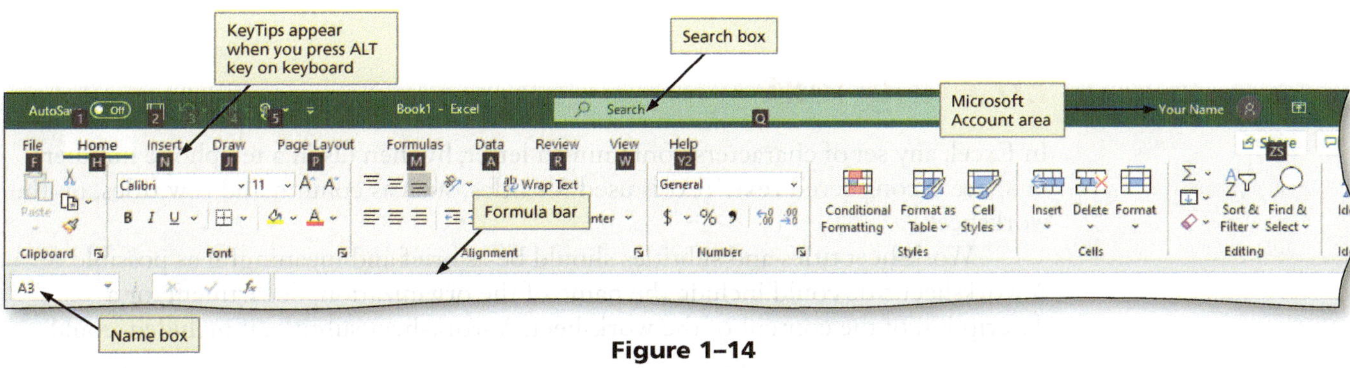

Figure 1–14

To Display a Different Tab on the Ribbon

The ribbon tab currently displayed is called the **active tab**. The following step displays the Insert tab; that is, it makes it the active tab. **Why?** When working with an Office app, you may need to switch tabs to access other options for working with a document.

1

- Click Insert on the ribbon to display the Insert tab (Figure 1–15).

Experiment

- Click the other tabs on the ribbon to view their contents.
- Click the View tab, click the Page Layout tab, and then click the Insert tab again.

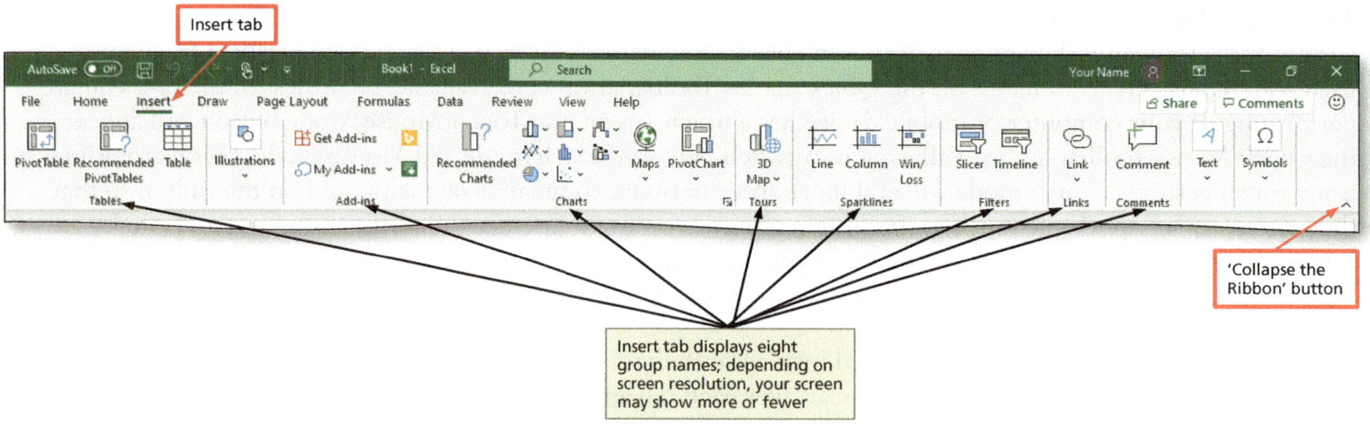

Figure 1–15

Other Ways

1. Press ALT, press letter corresponding to tab to display

Selecting a Cell

BTW
Touch Mode Differences
The Office and Windows interfaces may vary if you are using touch mode. For this reason, you might notice that the function or appearance of your touch screen differs slightly from this module's presentation.

To enter data into a cell, you first must select it. The easiest way to **select** a cell (to make it active) is to use the mouse to move the block plus sign pointer to the cell and then click.

An alternative method is to use the arrow keys that are located on a standard keyboard. An arrow key selects the cell adjacent to the active cell in the direction of the arrow on the key.

You know a cell is selected, or active, when a heavy border surrounds the cell and the active cell reference appears in the Name box on the left side of the formula bar. Excel also changes the color of the active cell's column and row headings to a darker shade.

Entering Text

In Excel, any set of characters containing a letter, hyphen (as in a telephone number), or space is considered **text**. Text is used for titles, such as column and row titles, on the worksheet.

Worksheet titles and subtitles should be as brief and meaningful as possible. A worksheet title could include the name of the organization, department, or a description of the content of the worksheet. A worksheet subtitle, if included, could include a more detailed description of the content of the worksheet. Examples of worksheet titles are January 2025 Payroll and Year 2025 Projected Budget, and examples of subtitles are Finance Department and Monthly Projections, respectively.

As shown in Figure 1–16, data in a worksheet is identified by row and column titles so that the meaning of each entry is clear. Rows typically contain information such as categories of data. Columns typically describe how data is grouped in the worksheet, such as by month or by department.

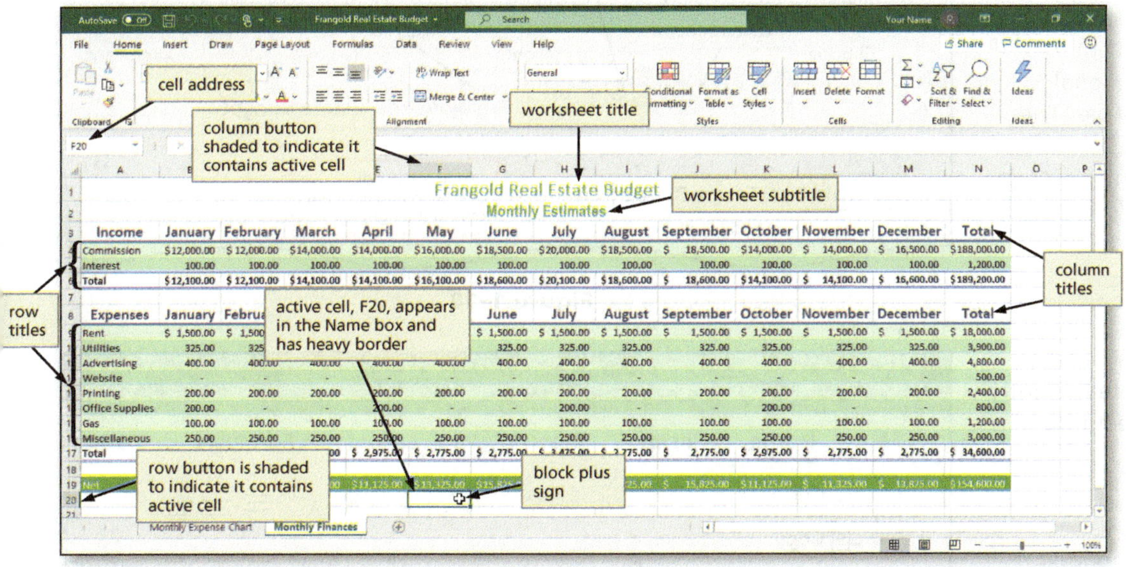

Figure 1–16

BTW

Screen Resolution

If you are using a computer to step through the project in this module and you want your screens to match the figures in this book, you should change your screen's resolution to 1366 × 768.

To Enter the Worksheet Titles

As shown in Figure 1–16, the worksheet title, Frangold Real Estate Budget, identifies the purpose of the worksheet. The worksheet subtitle, Monthly Estimates, identifies the type of data contained in the worksheet. **Why?** A title and subtitle help the reader to understand clearly what the worksheet contains. The following steps enter the worksheet titles in cells A1 and A2. Later in this module, the worksheet titles will be formatted so that they appear as shown in Figure 1–16.

1

- Click Home on the ribbon to display the Home tab.
- If necessary, click cell A1 to make cell A1 the active cell (Figure 1–17).

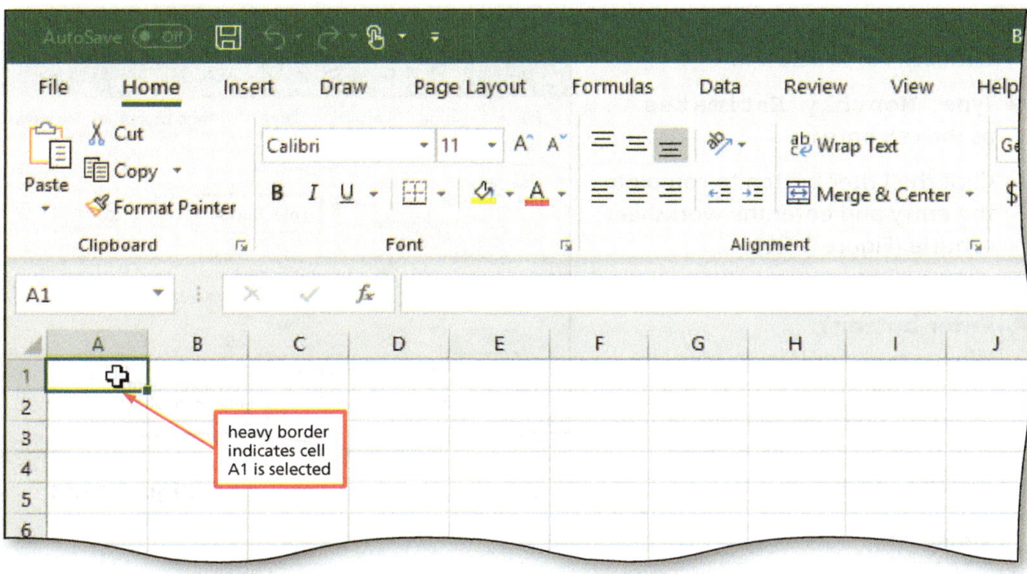

Figure 1–17

2

- Type **Frangold Real Estate Budget** in cell A1 (Figure 1–18).

Q&A **Why did the appearance of the formula bar change?**
Excel displays the title in the formula bar and in cell A1. When you begin typing a cell entry, Excel enables two additional buttons in the formula bar: The Cancel button and the Enter button. Clicking the Enter button completes an entry. Clicking the Cancel button cancels an entry.

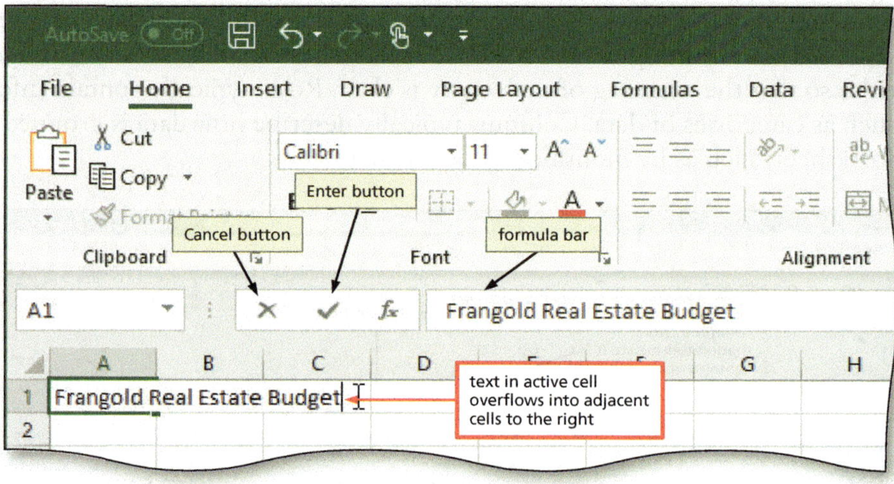

Figure 1–18

3

- Click the Enter button in the formula bar to complete the entry and enter the worksheet title (Figure 1–19).

Q&A **Why does the entered text appear in three cells?**
When the typed text is longer than the width of a cell, Excel displays the overflow characters in adjacent cells to the right as long as those adjacent cells contain no data. If the adjacent cells contain data, Excel hides the overflow characters. The overflow characters are visible in the formula bar whenever that cell is active.

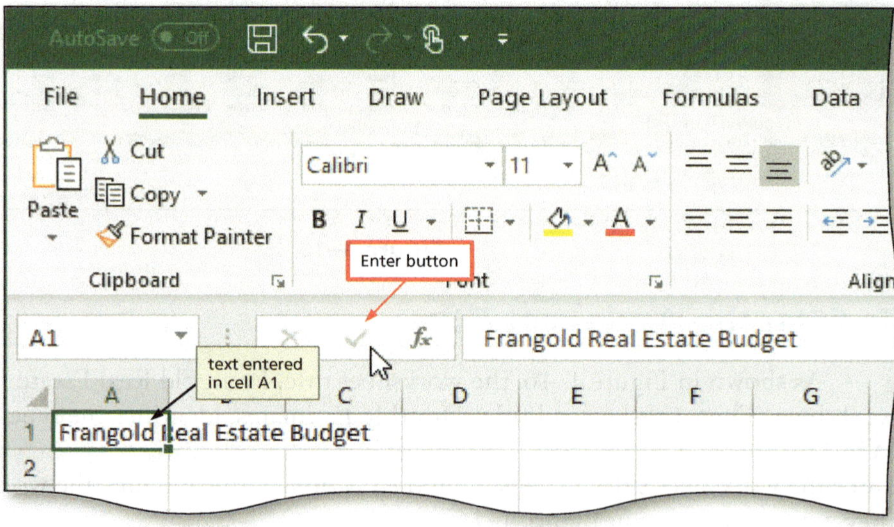

Figure 1–19

4

- Click cell A2 to select it.
- Type **Monthly Estimates** as the cell entry.
- Click the Enter button to complete the entry and enter the worksheet subtitle (Figure 1–20).

Q&A **What happens when I click the Enter button?**
When you complete an entry by clicking the Enter button, the insertion point disappears and the cell in which the text is entered remains the active cell.

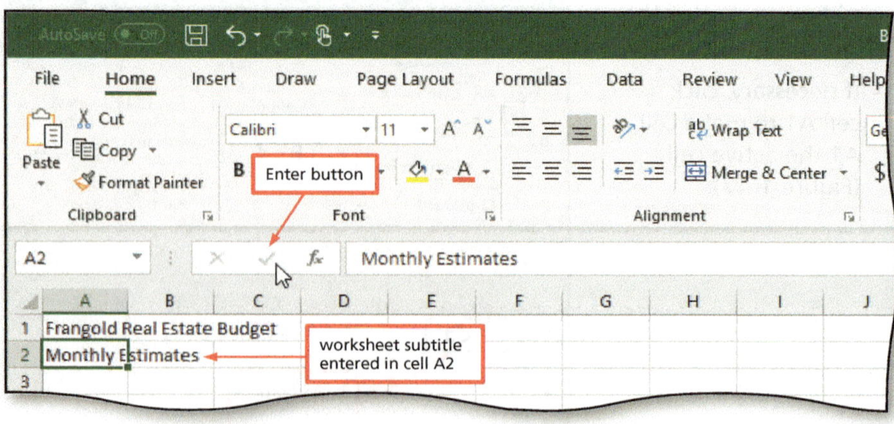

Figure 1–20

Other Ways

1. Click any cell other than active cell
2. Press ENTER
3. Press HOME, PAGE UP, PAGE DOWN, END, UP ARROW, DOWN ARROW, LEFT ARROW, or RIGHT ARROW

Consider This

Why is it difficult to read the text on my screen?
If you are having trouble reading the cell values in your spreadsheet, you can zoom in to make the cells larger. When you zoom in, fewer columns and rows display on your screen, and you might have to scroll more often. To zoom in, drag the zoom slider on the right side of the status bar, or click the plus button on the zoom slider, until you reach your desired zoom level. You also can zoom by clicking the Zoom button (View tab | Zoom group), selecting a desired zoom percentage (Zoom dialog box), and then clicking OK (Zoom dialog box).

AutoCorrect

The **AutoCorrect** feature of Excel works behind the scenes, where it automatically detects and corrects typing errors. AutoCorrect makes three types of corrections for you:

1. Corrects two initial uppercase letters by changing the second letter to lowercase.
2. Capitalizes the first letter in the names of days.
3. Replaces commonly misspelled words with their correct spelling. For example, it will change the misspelled word recieve to receive when you complete the entry. AutoCorrect will correct the spelling of hundreds of commonly misspelled words automatically.

BTW
Ribbon and Screen Resolution
Excel may change how the groups and buttons within the groups appear on the ribbon, depending on the screen resolution of your computer. Thus, your ribbon may look different from the ones in this book if you are using a screen resolution other than 1366 × 768.

To Enter Column Titles

The worksheet is divided into two parts, income and expense, as shown in Figure 1–16. Grouping income and expense data by month is a common method for organizing budget data. The column titles shown in row 3 identify the income section of the worksheet and indicate that the income values will be grouped by month. Likewise, row 8 is clearly identified as the expense section and similarly indicates that the expense values will be estimated on a per-month basis. The following steps enter the column titles in row 3. **Why?** Data entered in columns should be identified using column titles to identify what the column contains.

1

- Click cell A3 to make it the active cell.
- Type **Income** to begin entry of a column title in the active cell (Figure 1–21).

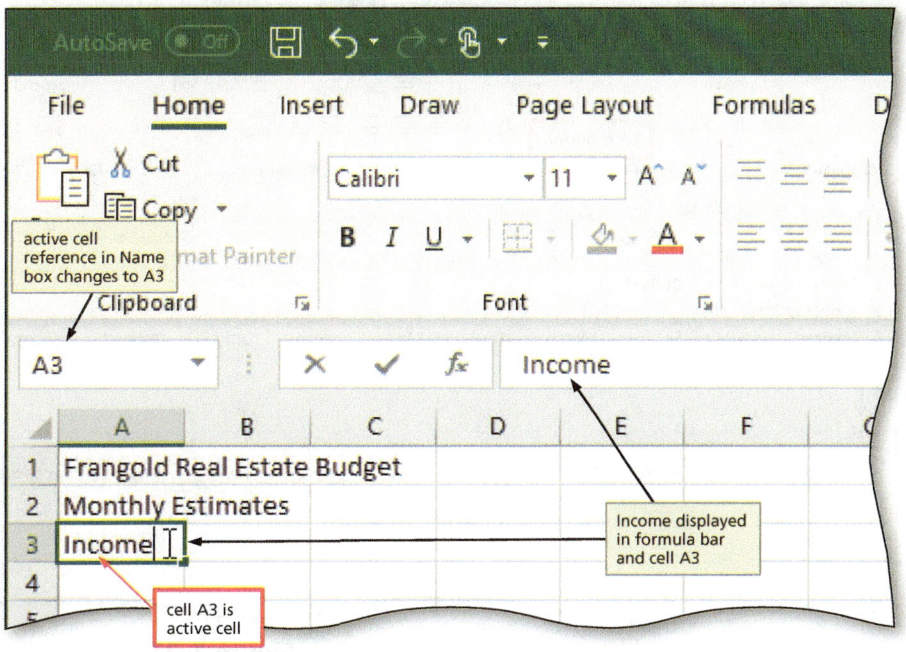

Figure 1–21

2

- Press the RIGHT ARROW key to enter the column title and make the cell to the right the active cell (Figure 1–22).

Q&A

Why is the RIGHT ARROW key used to complete the entry in the cell?
Pressing an arrow key to complete an entry makes the adjacent cell in the direction of the arrow (up, down, left, or right) the next active cell. However, if your next entry is in a nonadjacent cell, you can complete your current entry by clicking the next cell in which you plan to enter data. You also can press ENTER and then click the appropriate cell for the next entry.

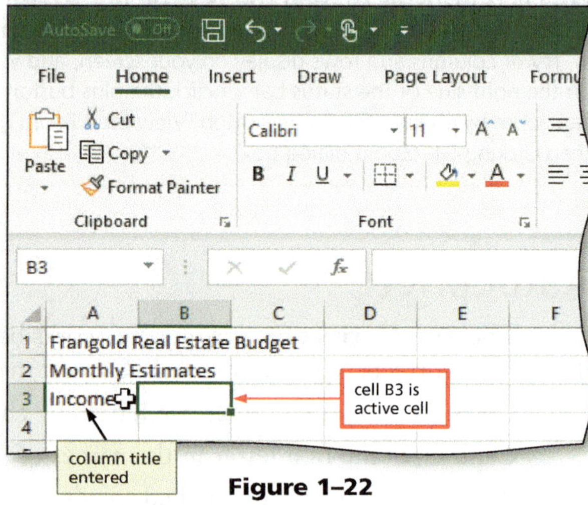

Figure 1–22

3

- Repeat Steps 1 and 2 to enter the remaining column titles; that is, enter **January** in cell B3, **February** in cell C3, **March** in cell D3, **April** in cell E3, **May** in cell F3, **June** in cell G3, **July** in cell H3, **August** in cell I3, **September** in cell J3, **October** in cell K3, **November** in cell L3, **December** in cell M3, and **Total** in cell N3 (complete the last entry in cell N3 by clicking the Enter button in the formula bar).
- Click cell A8 to select it.
- Repeat Steps 1 and 2 to enter the remaining column titles; that is, enter **Expenses** in cell A8, **January** in cell B8, **February** in cell C8, **March** in cell D8, **April** in cell E8, **May** in cell F8, **June** in cell G8, **July** in cell H8, **August** in cell I8, **September** in cell J8, **October** in cell K8, **November** in cell L8, **December** in cell M8, and **Total** in cell N8 (complete the last entry in cell N8 by clicking the Enter button in the formula bar) (Figure 1–23).

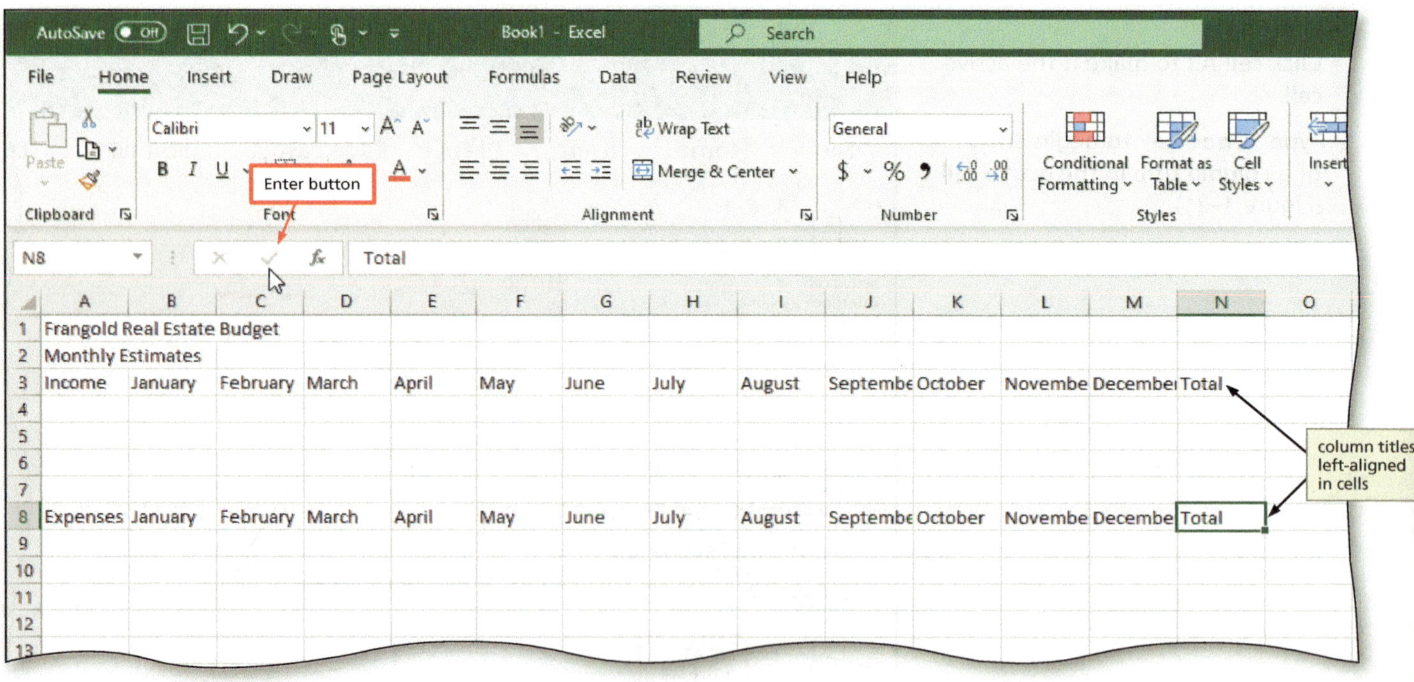

Figure 1–23

To Enter Row Titles

The next step in developing the worksheet for this project is to enter the row titles in column A. For the Frangold Real Estate Budget worksheet data, the row titles contain a list of income types and expense types. Each income or expense item should be placed in its own row. **Why?** Entering one item per row allows for maximum flexibility, in case more income or expense items are added in the future. The following steps enter the row titles in the worksheet.

1

- Click cell A4 to select it.
- Type **Commission** and then click cell A5 or press the DOWN ARROW key to enter a row title (Figure 1–24).

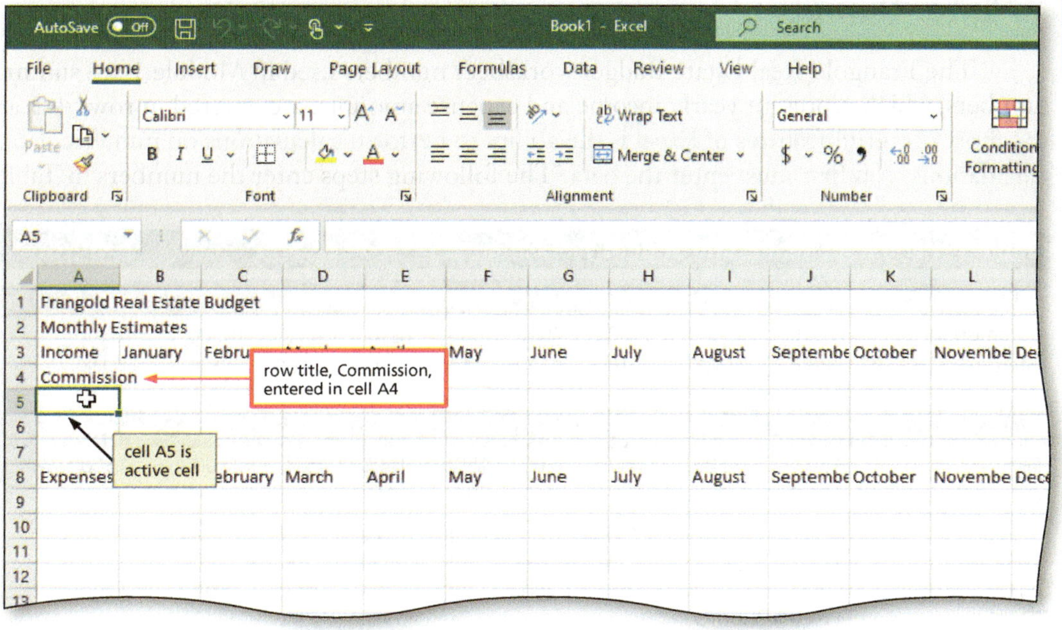

Figure 1–24

2

- Repeat Step 1 to enter the remaining row titles in column A; that is, enter **Interest** in cell A5, **Total** in cell A6, **Rent** in cell A9, **Utilities** in cell A10, **Advertising** in cell A11, **Website** in cell A12, **Printing** in cell A13, **Office Supplies** in cell A14, **Gas** in cell A15, **Miscellaneous** in cell A16, **Total** in cell A17, and **Net** in cell A19 (Figure 1–25).

Q&A **Why is the text left-aligned in the cells?**
Excel automatically left-aligns the text in the cell. Excel treats any combination of numbers, spaces, and nonnumeric characters as text. For example, Excel would recognize the following entries as text: 401AX21, 921–231, 619 321, 883XTY. How to change the text alignment in a cell is discussed later in this module.

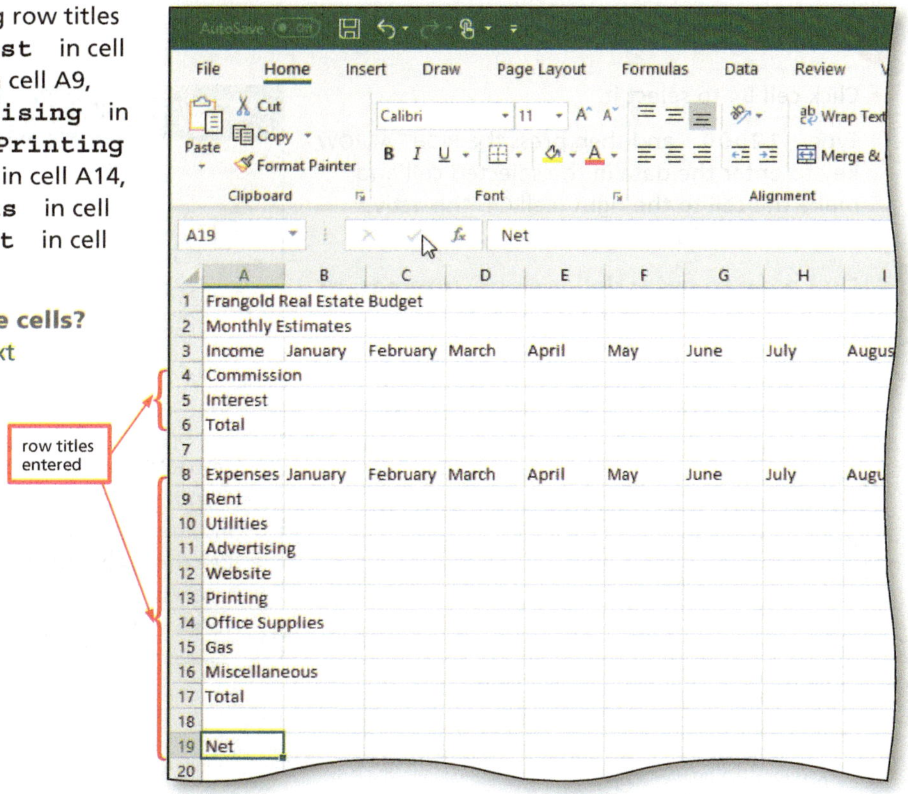

Figure 1–25

Entering Numbers

In Excel, you enter a number into a cell to represent an amount or value. A **number** is an amount or value using any of the following characters: 0 1 2 3 4 5 6 7 8 9 + - ( ) , / . $ E e. The use of special characters is explained when they are used in this book. If you are entering numbers that will not be used in a calculation, you should format those numbers as text. You can format numeric data as text by typing an apostrophe before the number(s).

To Enter Numbers

The Frangold Real Estate Budget worksheet numbers used in Module 1 are summarized in Table 1–1. These numbers, which represent yearly income and expense amounts, are entered in rows 4–5 and 9–16. **Why?** One of the most powerful features of Excel is the ability to perform calculations on numeric data. Before you can perform calculations, you first must enter the data. The following steps enter the numbers in Table 1–1 one row at a time.

Table 1–1 Frangold Real Estate Budget Worksheet

Income	January	February	March	April	May	June	July	August	September	October	November	December
Commission	12000	12000	14000	14000	16000	18500	20000	18500	18500	14000	14000	16500
Interest	100	100	100	100	100	100	100	100	100	100	100	100

Expenses	January	February	March	April	May	June	July	August	September	October	November	December
Rent	1500	1500	1500	1500	1500	1500	1500	1500	1500	1500	1500	1500
Utilities	325	325	325	325	325	325	325	325	325	325	325	325
Advertising	400	400	400	400	400	400	400	400	400	400	400	400
Website	0	0	0	0	0	0	500	0	0	0	0	0
Printing	200	200	200	200	200	200	200	200	200	200	200	200
Office Supplies	200	0	0	200	0	0	200	0	0	200	0	0
Gas	100	100	100	100	100	100	100	100	100	100	100	100
Miscellaneous	250	250	250	250	250	250	250	250	250	250	250	250

1

- Click cell B4 to select it.
- Type `12000` and then press the RIGHT ARROW key to enter the data in the selected cell and make the cell to the right (cell C4) the active cell (Figure 1–26).

Q&A **Do I need to enter dollar signs, commas, or trailing zeros for the amounts?**
You are not required to type dollar signs, commas, or trailing zeros. When you enter a dollar value that has cents, however, you must add the decimal point and the numbers representing the cents. Later in this module, you will learn how to format numbers with dollar signs, commas, and trailing zeros to improve their appearance and readability.

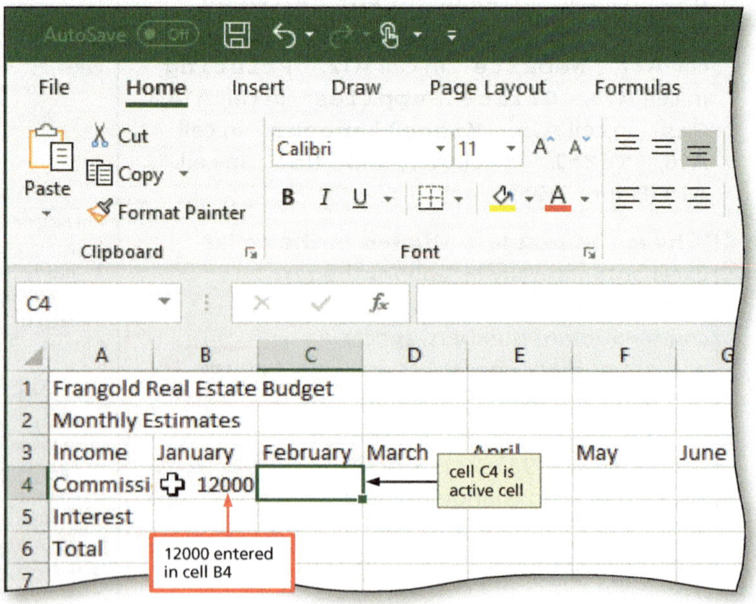

Figure 1–26

2

- Refer to Table 1–1 and enter the appropriate values in cells C4, D4, E4, F4, G4, H4, I4, J4, K4, L4, and M4 to complete the first row of numbers in the worksheet (Figure 1–27).

Q&A **Why are the numbers right-aligned?**
When you enter numeric data in a cell, Excel recognizes the values as numbers and automatically right-aligns the values in order to vertically align decimal and integer values.

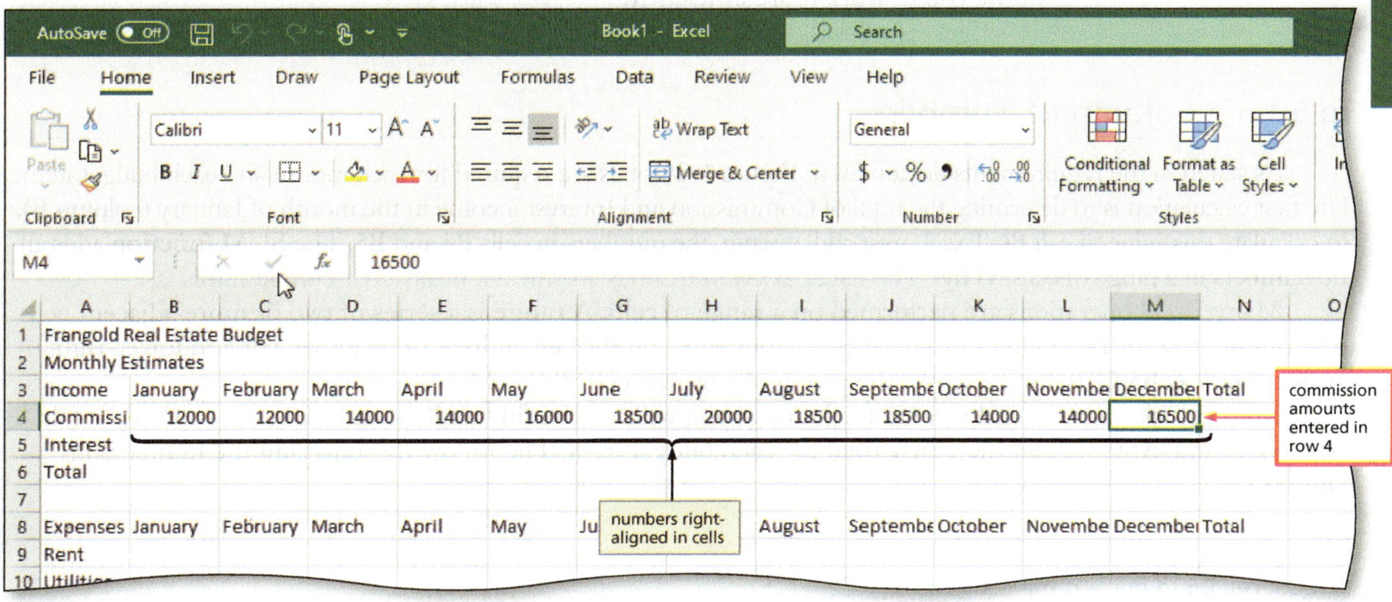

Figure 1–27

3

- Click cell B5 to select it and complete the entry in the previously selected cell.
- Enter the remaining numbers provided in Table 1–1 for each of the nine remaining budget items in row 5 and rows 9–16 (Figure 1–28).

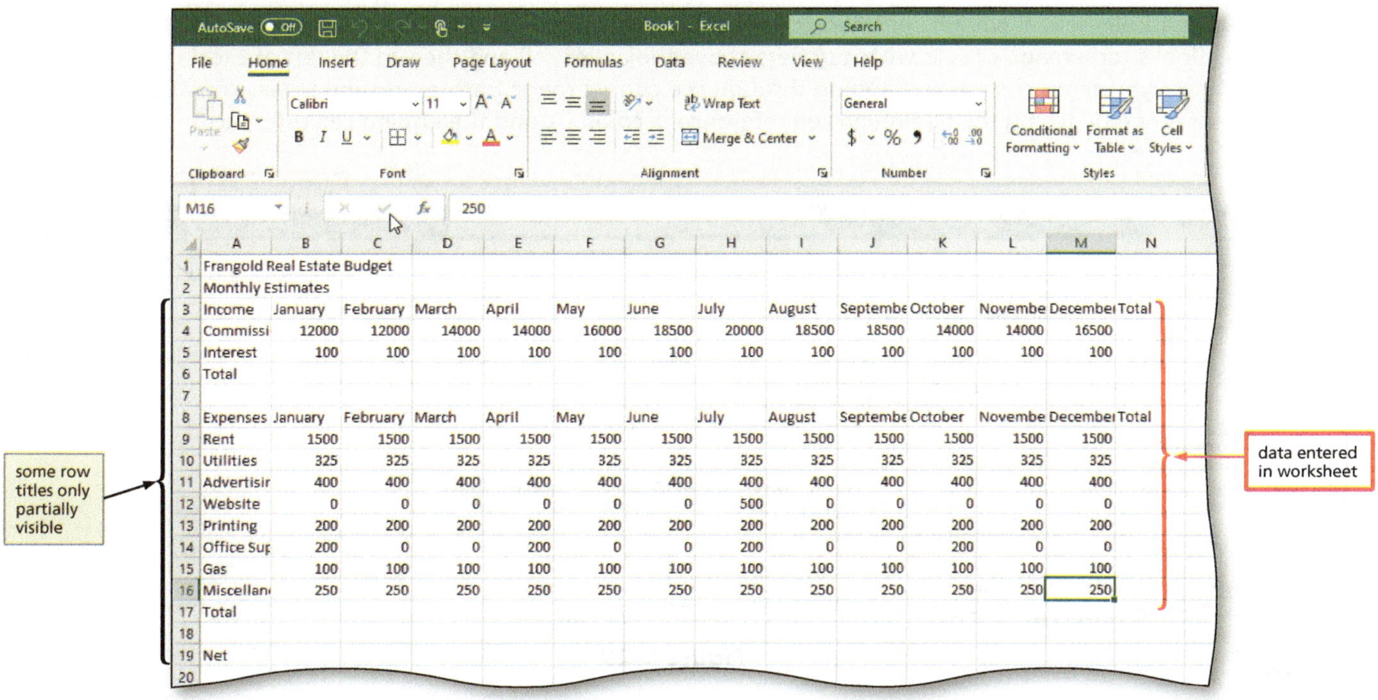

Figure 1–28

Calculating Sums and Using Formulas

The next step in creating the worksheet is to perform any necessary calculations, such as calculating the column and row totals. In Excel, you can easily perform calculations using a function. A **function** is a special, predefined formula that provides a shortcut for a commonly used calculation, for example, SUM or COUNT. When you use functions, Excel performs the calculations for you, which helps to prevent errors and allows you to work more efficiently.

To Sum a Column of Numbers

As stated in the requirements document in Figure 1–2, totals are required for each month and each budget item. The first calculation is to determine the total of Commission and Interest income in the month of January (column B). To calculate this value in cell B6, Excel must add, or sum, the numbers in cells B4 and B5. The **SUM function** adds all the numbers in a range of cells. **Why?** The Excel SUM function is an efficient means to accomplish this task.

Many Excel operations are performed on a range of cells. A **range** is a series of two or more adjacent cells in a column, row, or rectangular group of cells, notated using the cell address of its upper-left and lower-right corners, such as B5:C10. For example, the group of adjacent cells B4 and B5 is a range.

After calculating the total income for January, you will use the fill handle to calculate the monthly totals for income and expenses and the yearly total for each budget item. The following steps sum the numbers in column B.

1

- Click cell B6 to make it the active cell.
- Click the AutoSum button (Home tab | Editing group) to enter a formula in the formula bar and in the active cell (Figure 1–29).

Q&A

What if my screen displays the Sum menu?
If you are using a touch screen, you may not have a separate AutoSum button and AutoSum arrow. In this case, select the desired option (Sum) on the AutoSum menu.

How does Excel know which cells to sum?
Excel automatically selects what it considers to be your choice of the range to sum. When proposing the range, Excel first looks for a range of cells with numbers above the active cell and then to the left. If Excel proposes the wrong range, you can correct it by dragging through the correct range before pressing ENTER. You also can enter the correct range by typing the beginning cell reference, a colon (:), and the ending cell reference.

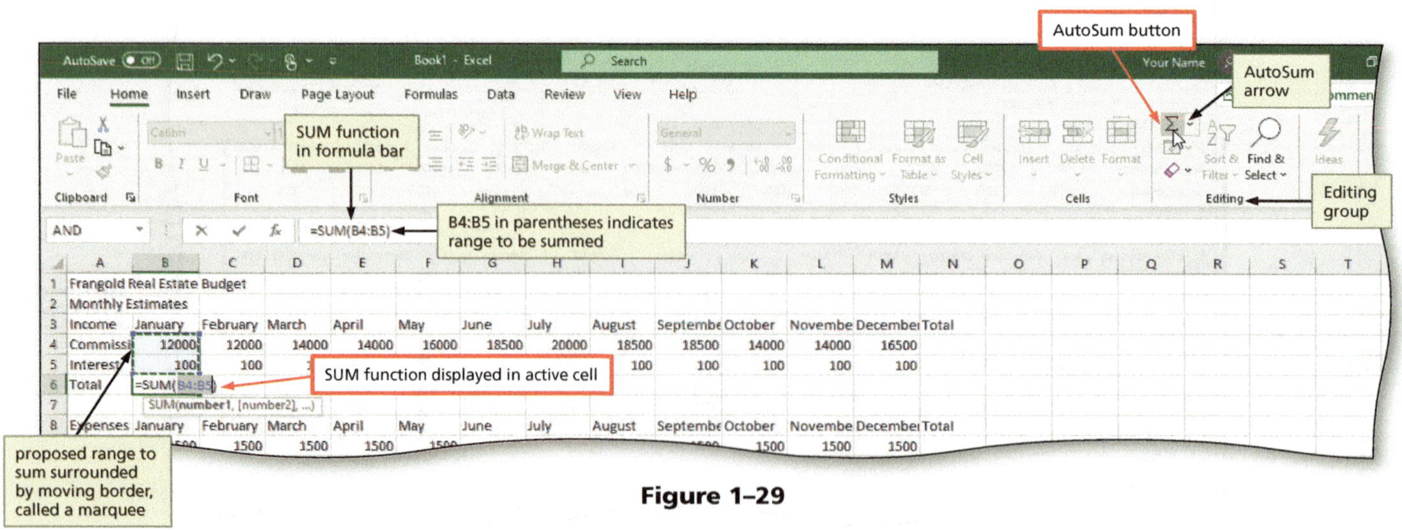

Figure 1–29

2

- Click the Enter button in the formula bar to enter the sum in the active cell.

Q&A

What is the purpose of the arrow next to the AutoSum button on the ribbon?
The AutoSum arrow (shown in Figure 1–29) displays a list of functions that allow you to easily determine the average of a range of numbers, the number of items in a selected range, or the maximum or minimum value of a range.

3

- Repeat Steps 1 and 2 to enter the SUM function in cell B17 (Figure 1–30).

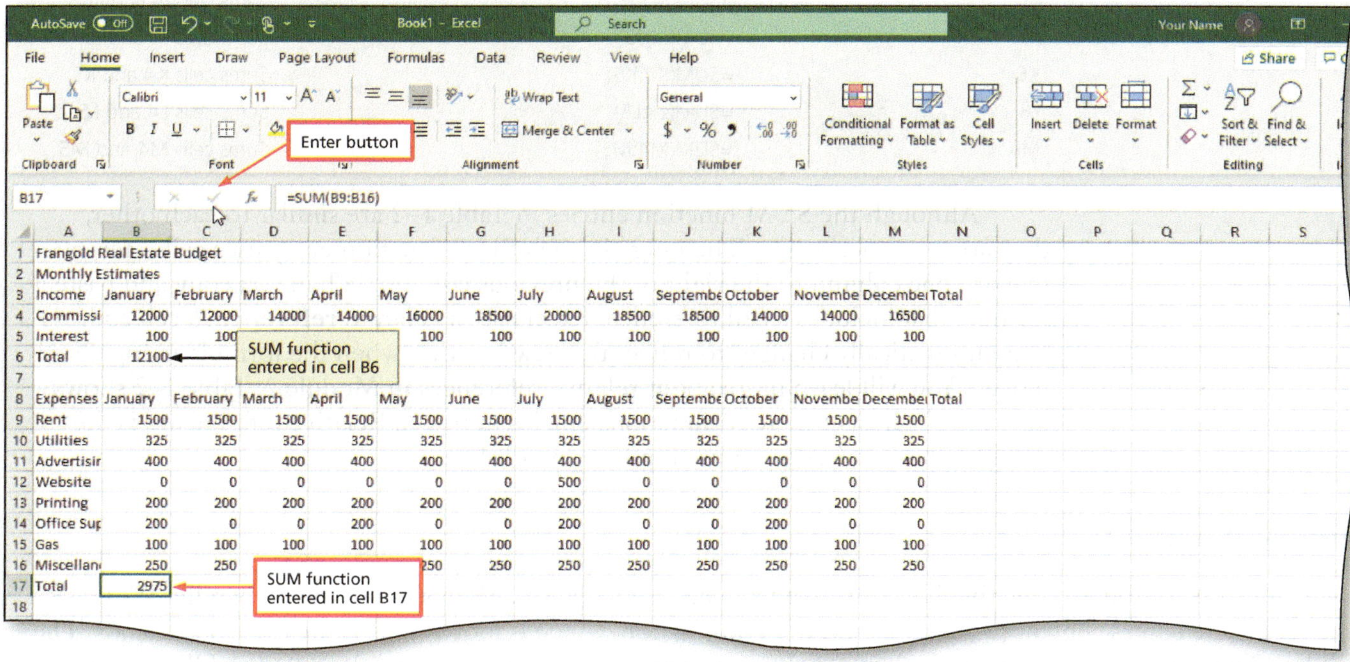

Figure 1–30

Other Ways

1. Click Insert Function button in formula bar, select SUM in Select a function list, click OK (Insert Function dialog box), click OK (Function Arguments dialog box)
2. Click AutoSum arrow (Home tab | Editing group), click More Functions in list, scroll to and then click SUM (Insert Function dialog box), click OK, select range (Function Arguments dialog box), click OK
3. Type **=S** in cell, select SUM in list, select range, click Enter button
4. Press ALT+EQUAL SIGN (=) twice

Using the Fill Handle to Copy a Cell to Adjacent Cells

You want to calculate the income totals for each month in cells C6:M6. Table 1–2 illustrates the similarities between the function and range used in cell B6 and the function and ranges required to sum the totals in cells C6, D6, E6, F6, G6, H6, I6, J6, K6, L6, and M6.

To calculate each total for each range across the worksheet, you could follow the same steps shown previously in Figure 1–29 and Figure 1–30. A more efficient method, however, would be to copy the SUM function from cell B6 to the range C6:M6. A range of cells you are cutting or copying is called the **source area** or **copy area**. The range of cells to which you are pasting is called the **destination area** or **paste area**.

Table 1–2 Sum Function Entries in Row 6

Cell	SUM Function Entries	Result
B6	=SUM(B4:B5)	Sums cells B4 and B5
C6	=SUM(C4:C5)	Sums cells C4 and C5
D6	=SUM(D4:D5)	Sums cells D4 and D5
E6	=SUM(E4:E5)	Sums cells E4 and E5
F6	=SUM(F4:F5)	Sums cells F4 and F5
G6	=SUM(G4:G5)	Sums cells G4 and G5
H6	=SUM(H4:H5)	Sums cells H4 and H5
I6	=SUM(I4:I5)	Sums cells I4 and I5
J6	=SUM(J4:J5)	Sums cells J4 and J5
K6	=SUM(K4:K5)	Sums cells K4 and K5
L6	=SUM(L4:L5)	Sums cells L4 and L5
M6	=SUM(M4:M5)	Sums cells M4 and M5

Although the SUM function entries in Table 1–2 are similar to each other, they are not exact copies. The range in each SUM function entry uses cell references that are one column to the right of the previous column. When you copy and paste a formula that includes a cell reference, Excel uses a **relative reference**, a cell address that automatically changes to reflect the new location when the formula is copied or moved. You will learn more about relative references in Module 2. Table 1–2 shows how Excel adjusts the SUM functions entries in row 6. Relative referencing is the default type of referencing used in Excel worksheets.

To Copy a Cell to Adjacent Cells in a Row

The easiest way to copy the SUM formula from cell B6 to cells C6:M6 is to use the fill handle. **Why?** Using the fill handle copies content to adjacent cells using one action, which is more efficient than other methods. The **fill handle** is a box that appears in the lower-right corner of a selected cell or range. It is used to fill adjacent cells with duplicate or similar data. The following steps use the fill handle to copy cell B6 to the adjacent cells C6:M6.

1

- With cell B6 active, point to the fill handle; your pointer changes to a crosshair (Figure 1–31).

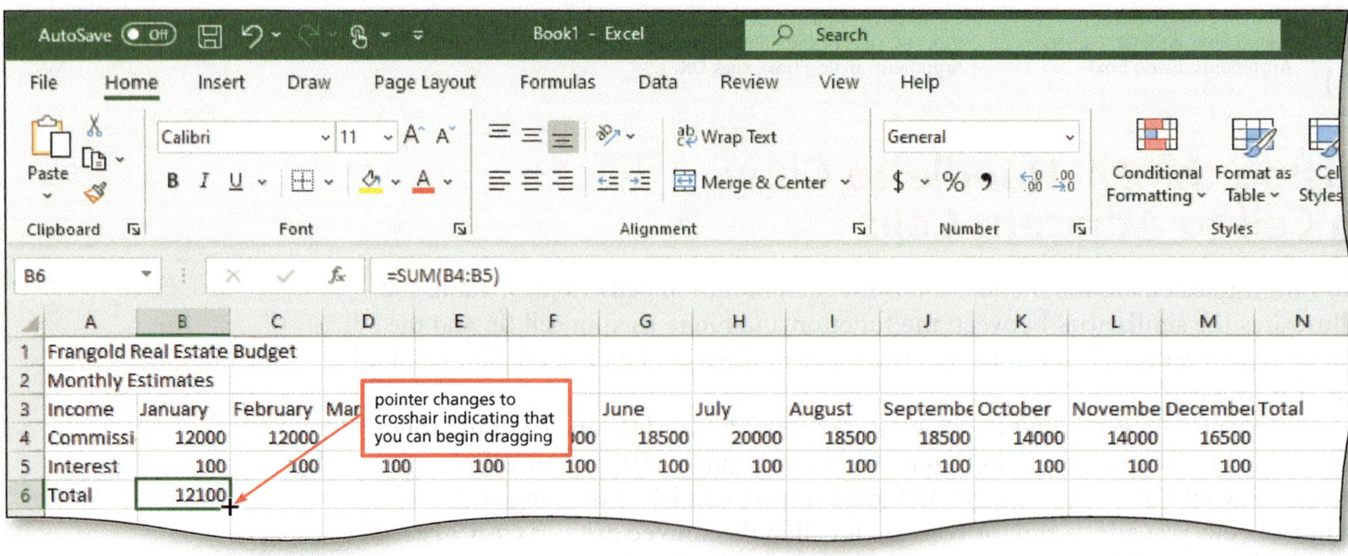

Figure 1–31

2

- Drag the fill handle to select the destination area, the range C6:M6, which will draw a heavy green border around the source area and the destination area (Figure 1–32). Do not release the mouse button.

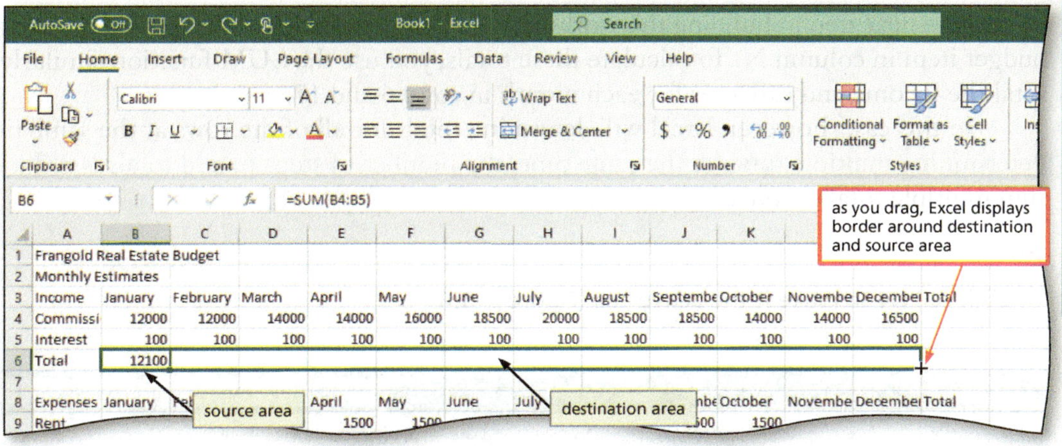

Figure 1–32

3

- Release the mouse button to copy the SUM function from the active cell to the destination area and calculate the sums (Figure 1–33).

Q&A

What is the purpose of the Auto Fill Options button?

The Auto Fill Options button allows you to choose whether you want to copy the values from the source area to the destination area with the existing formatting, without the formatting, or with the formatting but without the functions.

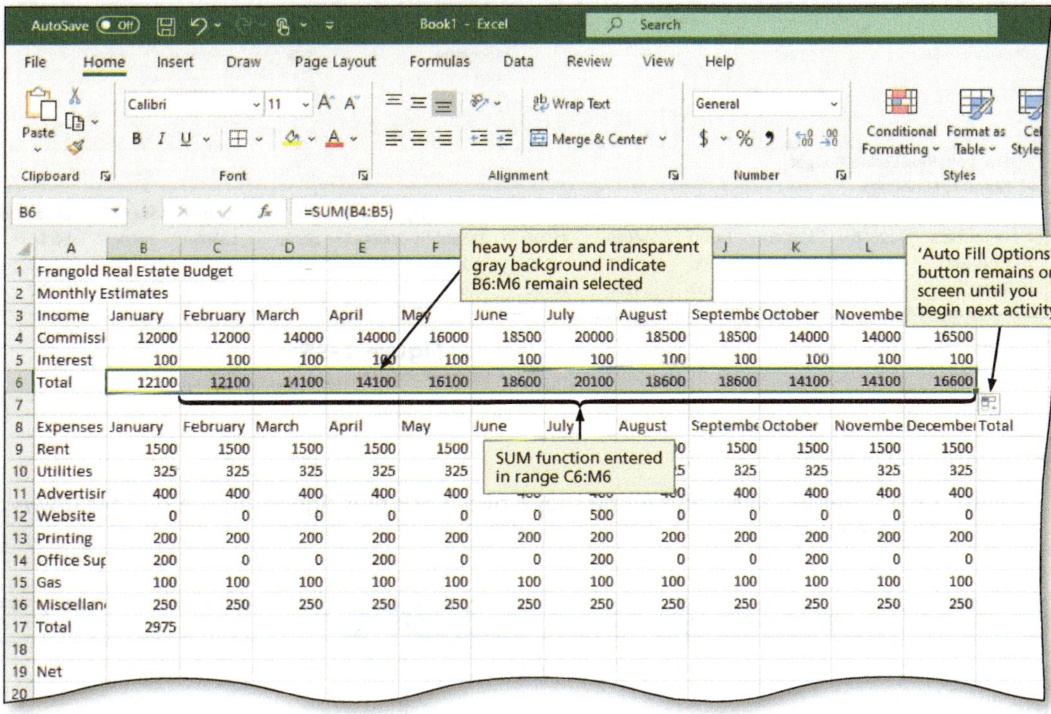

Figure 1–33

4

- Repeat Steps 1–3 to copy the SUM function from cell B17 to the range C17:M17 (Figure 1–34).

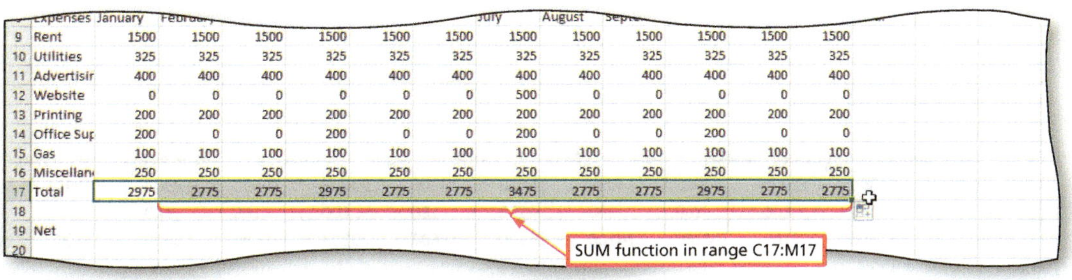

Figure 1–34

Other Ways

1. Select source area, click Copy button (Home tab | Clipboard group), select destination area, click Paste button (Home tab | Clipboard group)
2. Right-click source area, click Copy on shortcut menu, select and right-click destination area, click Paste on shortcut menu
3. Select source and destination areas, click Fill arrow (Home tab | Editing group), click Sum

To Calculate Multiple Totals at the Same Time

The next step in building the worksheet is to determine the total income, total expenses, and total for each budget item in column N. To calculate these totals, you use the SUM function similarly to how you used it to total the income and expenses for each month in rows 6 and 17.

In this case, however, Excel will determine totals for all of the rows at the same time. **Why?** By determining multiple totals at the same time, the number of steps to add totals is reduced. The following steps sum multiple totals at once.

1

- Click cell N4 to make it the active cell (Figure 1–35).

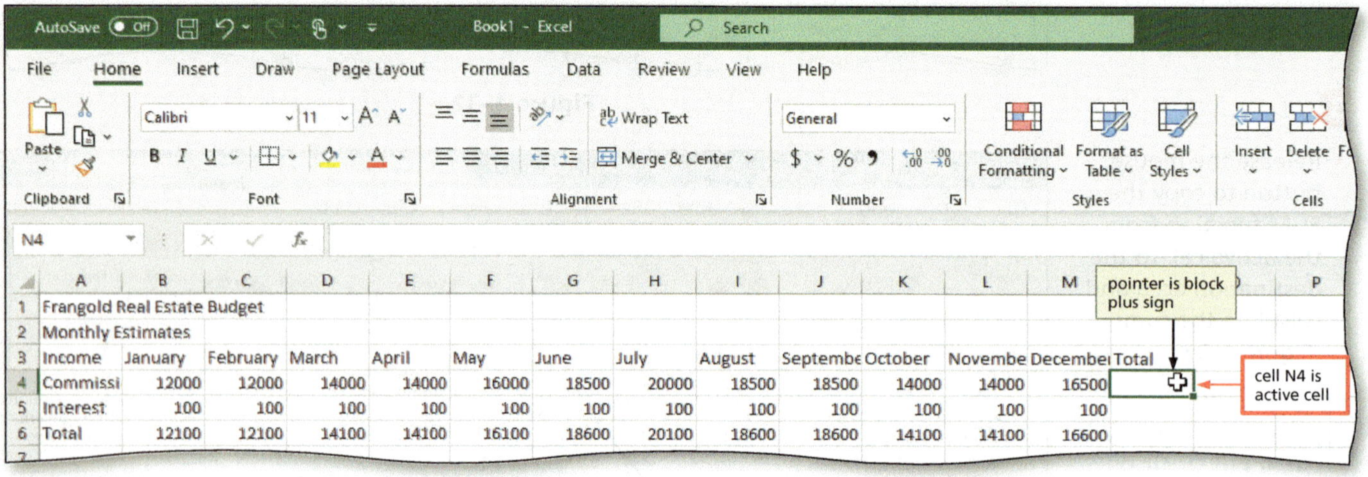

Figure 1–35

2

- With the pointer in cell N4 and in the shape of a block plus sign, drag the pointer down to cell N6 to select the range (Figure 1–36).

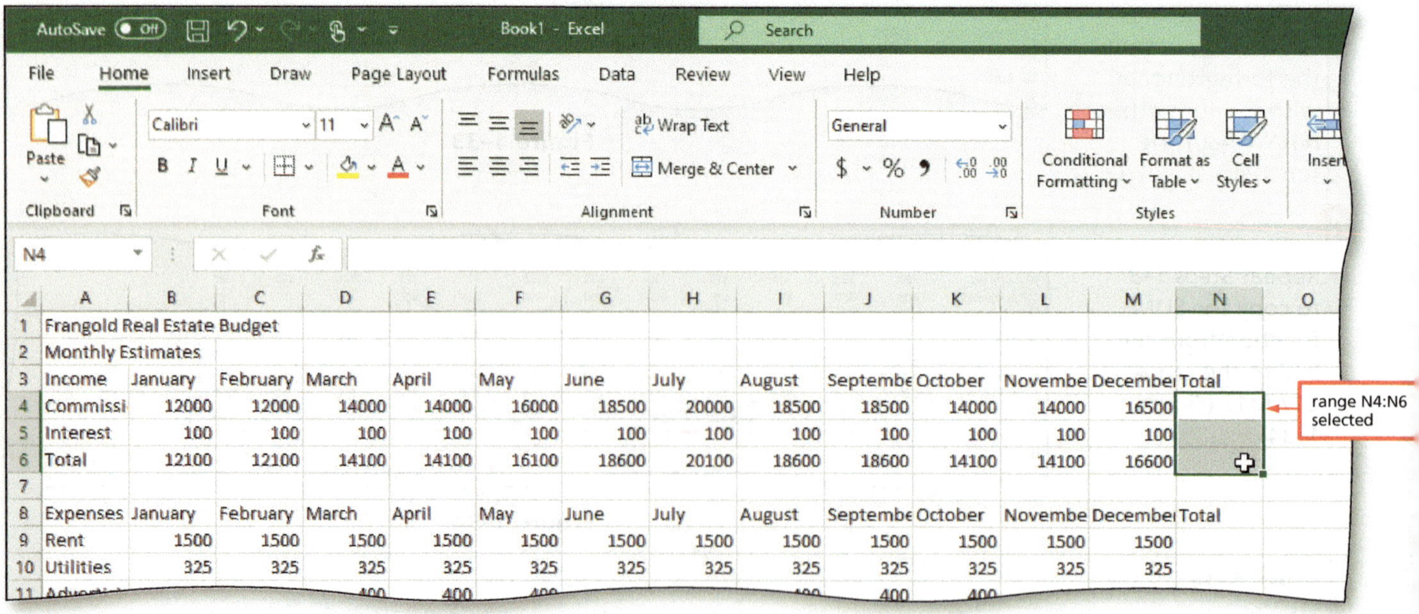

Figure 1–36

3

- Click the AutoSum button (Home tab | Editing group) to calculate the sums of all three rows (Figure 1–37).

Q&A

How does Excel create unique totals for each row?
If each cell in a selected range is adjacent to a row of numbers, Excel assigns the SUM function to each cell when you click the Sum button.

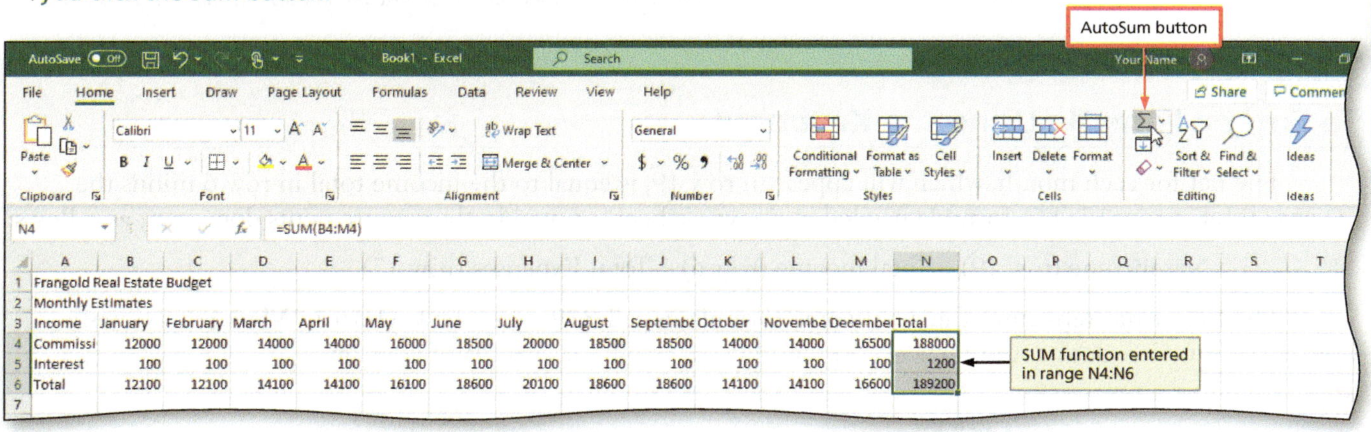

Figure 1–37

4

- Repeat Steps 1–3 to select cells N9 to N17 and calculate the sums of the corresponding rows (Figure 1–38).

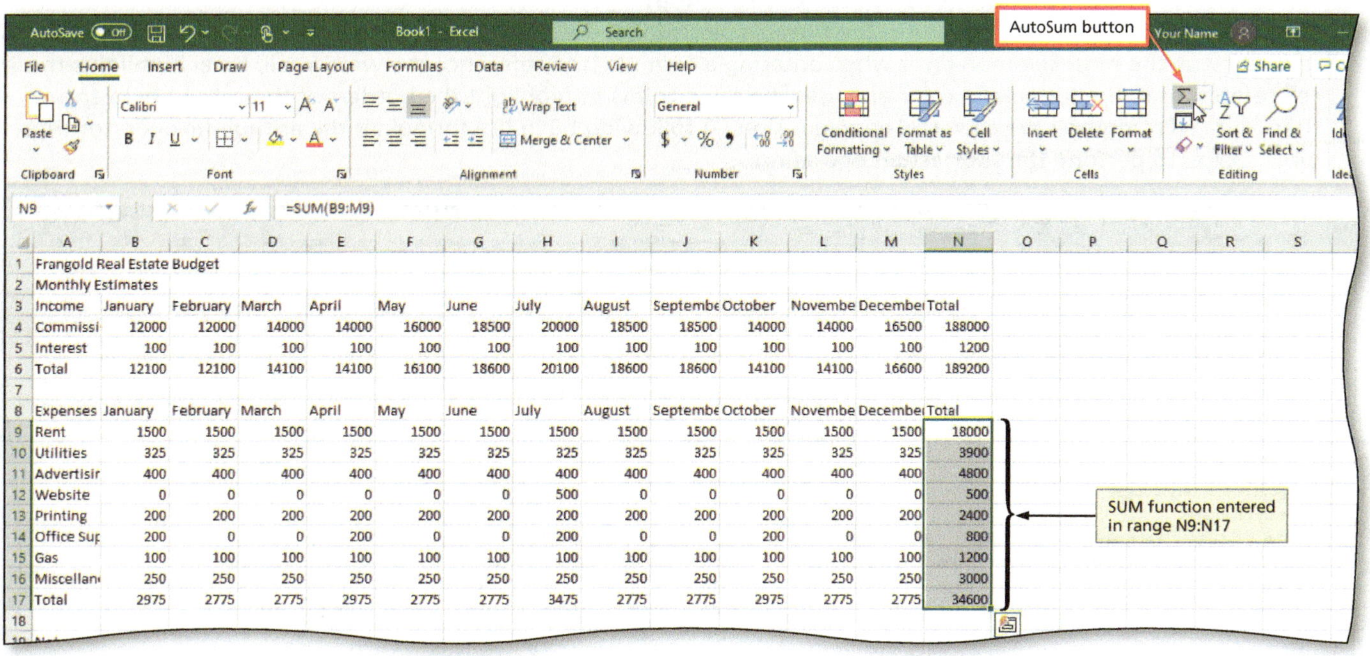

Figure 1–38

Calculating Average, Maximum, and Minimum Values

As you learned earlier in this module, the AutoSum list lets you calculate not only sums but also the average, the number of items, or the maximum or minimum value of a range. You can calculate these using three additional functions: AVERAGE, MAX, and MIN. The AVERAGE function calculates the average value in a range of cells, the MAX function calculates the maximum value in a range of cells, and the MIN function calculates the minimum value in a range of cells. Table 1–3 shows examples of each of these functions.

Table 1–3 AVERAGE, MAX, and MIN Functions	
Function	**Result**
=AVERAGE(H1:H5)	Determines the average of the values in cells H1, H2, H3, H4, and H5
=MAX(H1:H5)	Determines the maximum value entered in cells H1, H2, H3, H4, and H5
=MIN(H1:H5)	Determines the minimum value entered in cells H1, H2, H3, H4, and H5

To Enter a Formula Using the Keyboard

The net for each month, which will appear in row 19, is equal to the income total in row 6 minus the expense total in row 17. The formula needed in the worksheet is noted in the requirements document as follows:

Net income (row 19) = Total income (row 6) – Total Expenses (row 17)

The following steps enter the net income formula in cell B19 using the keyboard. **Why?** Sometimes a predefined function does not fit your needs; therefore, you enter a formula of your own.

1

- Select cell B19 to deselect the selected range.
- Type **=b6-b17** in the cell. The formula is displayed in the formula bar and the current cell, and colored borders are drawn around the cells referenced in the formula (Figure 1–39).

Q&A

What occurs on the worksheet as I enter the formula?

The equal sign (=) preceding b6–b17 in the formula alerts Excel that you are entering a formula or function and not text. Because the most common error when entering a formula is to reference the wrong cell, Excel highlights the cell references in the formula in color and uses the same colors to highlight the borders of the cells to help ensure that your cell references are correct. The minus sign (–) following b6 in the formula is the arithmetic operator that directs Excel to perform the subtraction operation.

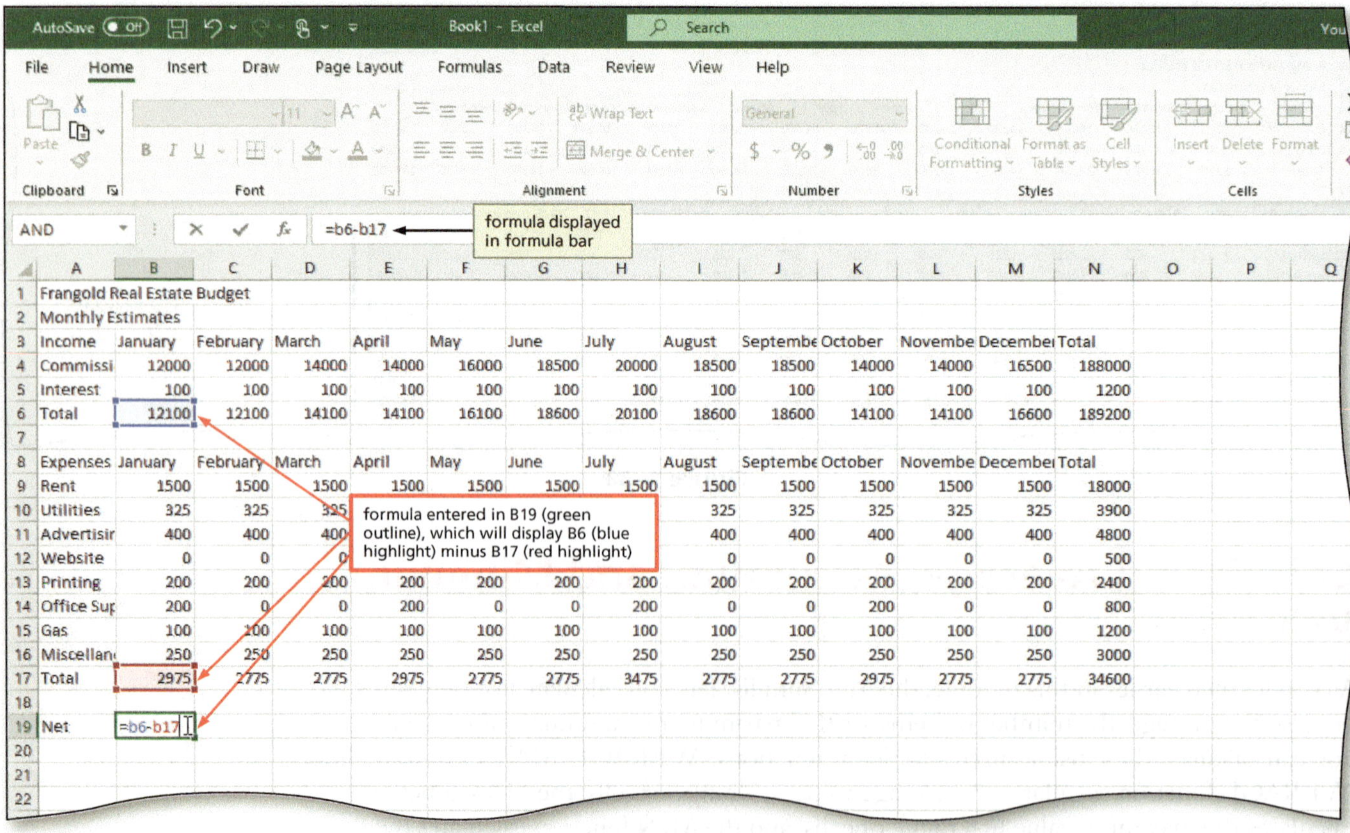

Figure 1–39

2

- Click cell C19 to complete the arithmetic operation, display the result in the worksheet, and select the cell to the right (Figure 1–40).

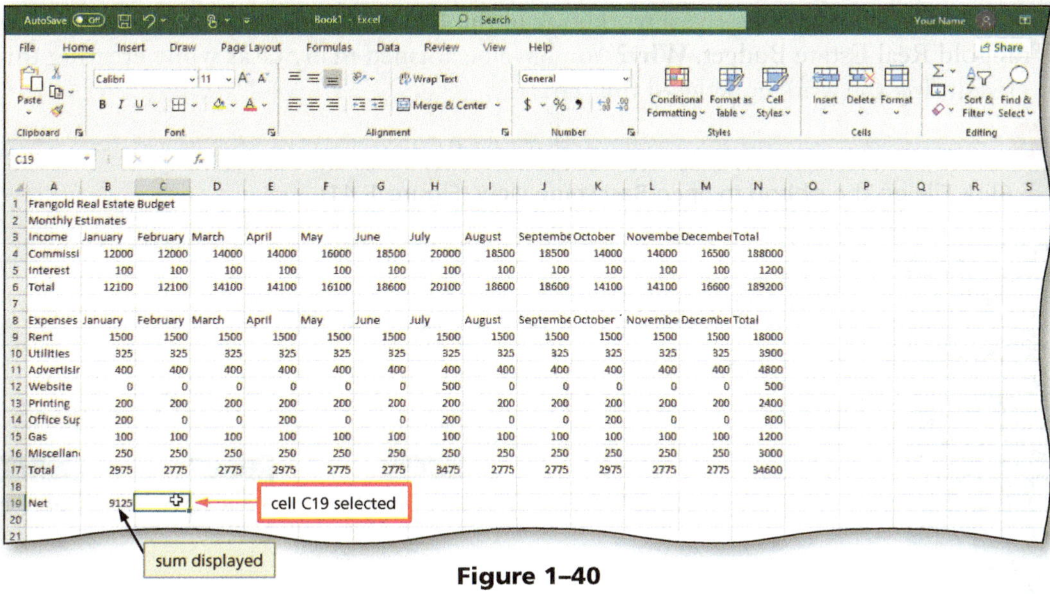

Figure 1–40

To Copy a Cell to Adjacent Cells in a Row Using the Fill Handle

The easiest way to copy the SUM formula from cell B19 to cells C19, D19, E19, F19, G19, H19, I19, J19, K19, L19, M19, and N19 is to use the fill handle. The following steps use the fill handle to copy the formula in cell B19 to the adjacent cells C19:N19.

1. Select cell B19.
2. Drag the fill handle to select the destination area, range C19:N19, which highlights and draws a border around the source area and the destination area. Release the mouse button to copy the function from the active cell to the destination area and calculate the results.

Saving the Project

While you are building a worksheet in a workbook, the computer stores it in memory. When you save a workbook, the computer places it on a storage medium such as a hard drive, USB flash drive, or online using a service such as OneDrive. A saved workbook is called a **file**. A **file name** is the name assigned to a file when you save it. It is important to save the workbook frequently for the following reasons:

- The worksheet in memory will be lost if the computer is turned off or you lose electrical power while Excel is open.
- If you run out of time before completing your workbook, you may finish your worksheet at a future time without starting over.

BTW

Organizing Files and Folders

You should organize and store files in folders so that you can easily find the files later. For example, if you are taking an introductory technology class called CIS 101, a good practice would be to save all Excel files in an Excel folder in a CIS 101 folder.

Consider This

Where should you save the workbook?

When saving a workbook, you must decide which storage medium to use:

- If you always work on the same computer and have no need to transport your projects to a different location, then your computer's hard drive will suffice as a storage location. It is a good idea, however, to save a backup copy of your projects on a separate medium, such as an external drive, in case the file becomes corrupted or the computer's hard drive fails. The workbooks used in this book are saved to the computer's hard drive.
- If you plan to work on your workbooks in various locations or on multiple computers or mobile devices, then you should save your workbooks on a portable medium, such as a USB flash drive. Alternatively, you can save your workbooks to an online cloud storage service such as OneDrive.

To Save a Workbook

The following steps save a workbook in the Documents library on the hard drive using the file name, Frangold Real Estate Budget. **Why?** You have performed many tasks while creating this project and do not want to risk losing the work completed thus far.

1

- Click File on the ribbon to open Backstage view (Figure 1–41).

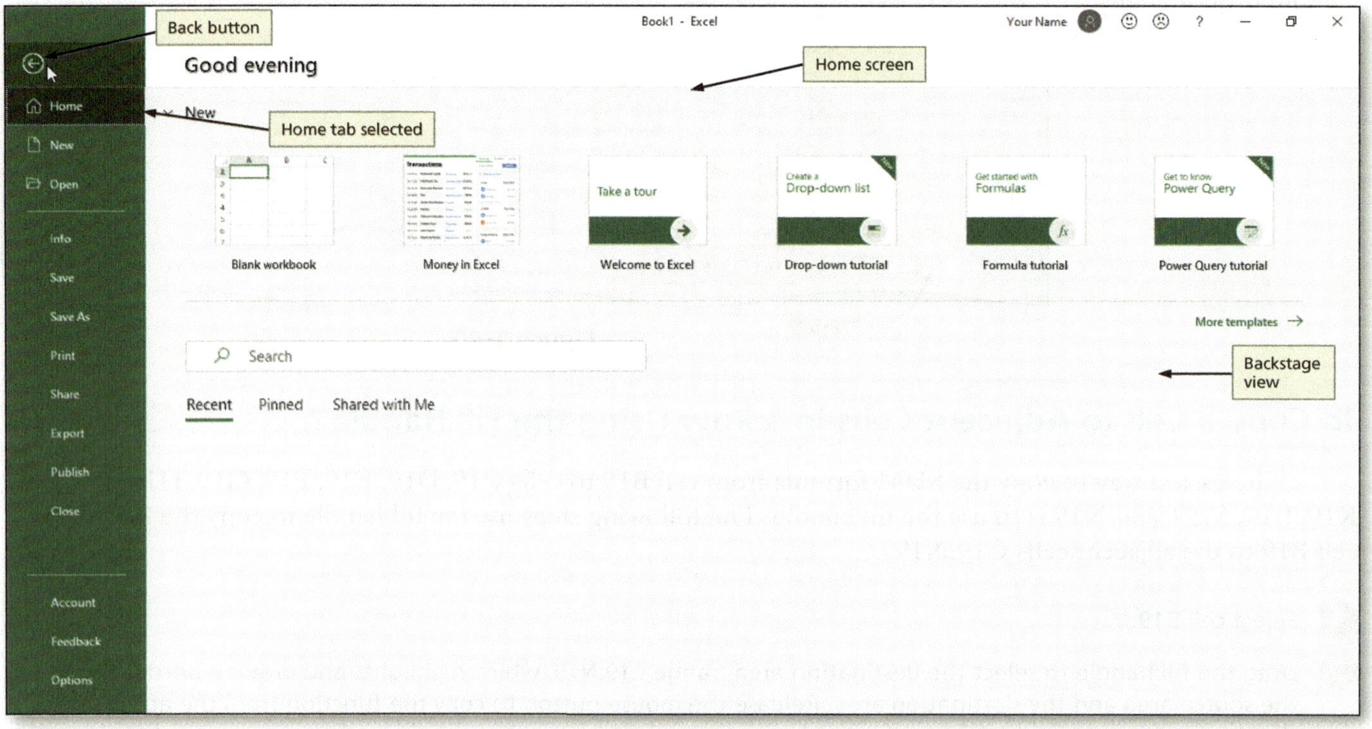

Figure 1–41

2

- Click Save As in Backstage view to display the Save As screen (Figure 1–42).

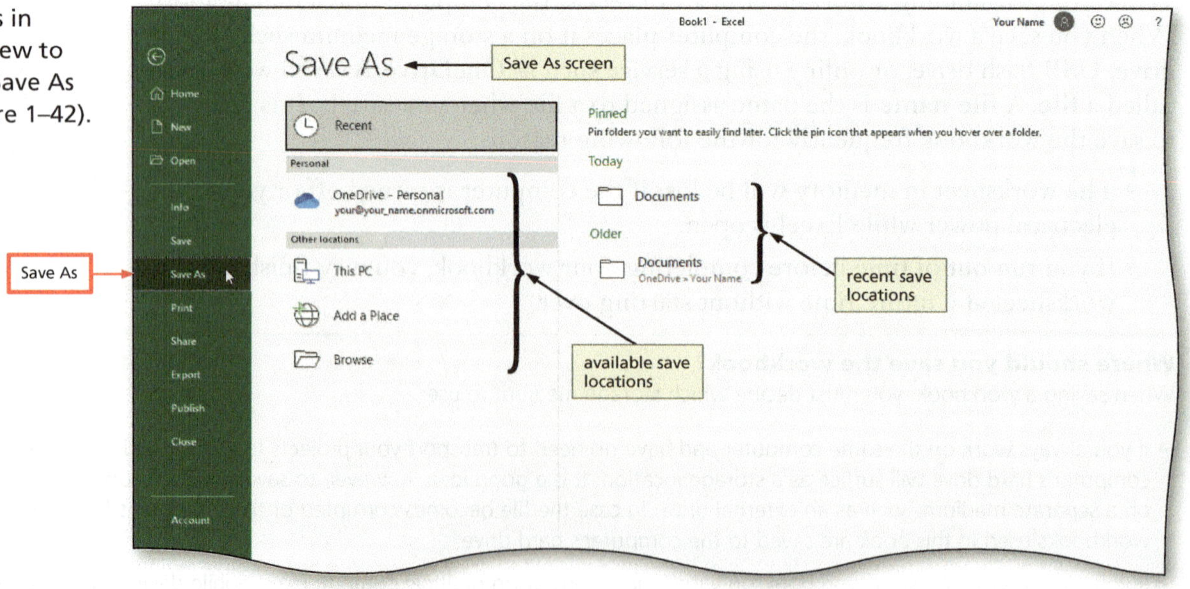

Figure 1–42

3

- Click This PC in the Other locations section to display the default save location on the computer or mobile device (Figure 1–43).

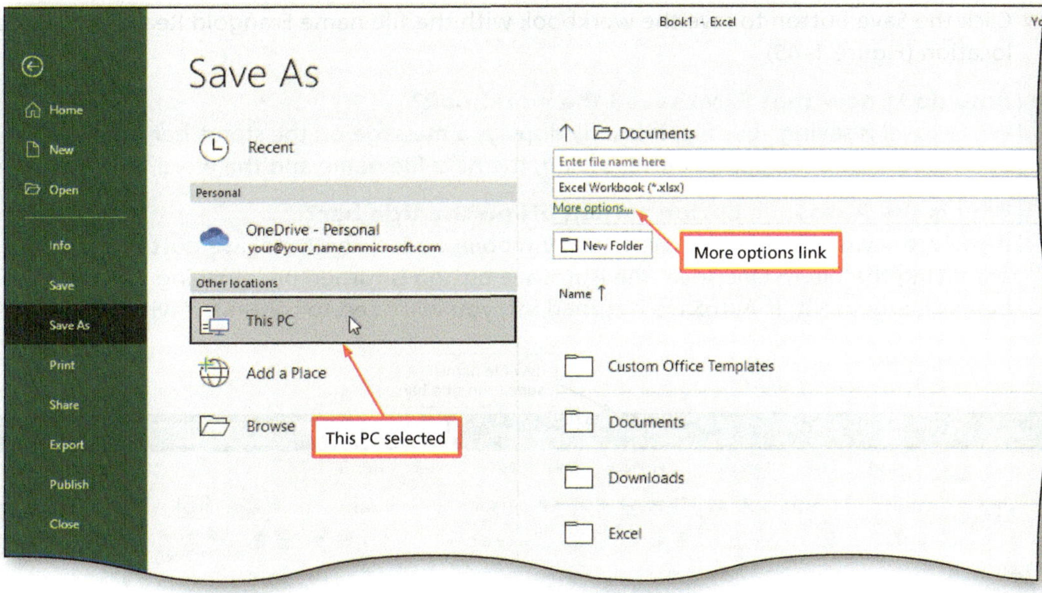

Figure 1–43

Q&A **How can I save a file to OneDrive?**
To save a new workbook to OneDrive, click the Save button on the Quick Access Toolbar. To save an existing workbook with the same name while changing the location to OneDrive, click the file name in the title bar, and then click Upload. In both cases, Excel turns on the AutoSave button on the title bar and saves the workbook as you make changes to it.

4

- Click the More options link to display the Save As dialog box.
- If necessary, click Documents in the Navigation pane to select the Documents library as the save location.
- Type **Frangold Real Estate Budget** in the File name text box to specify the file name for the workbook (Figure 1–44).

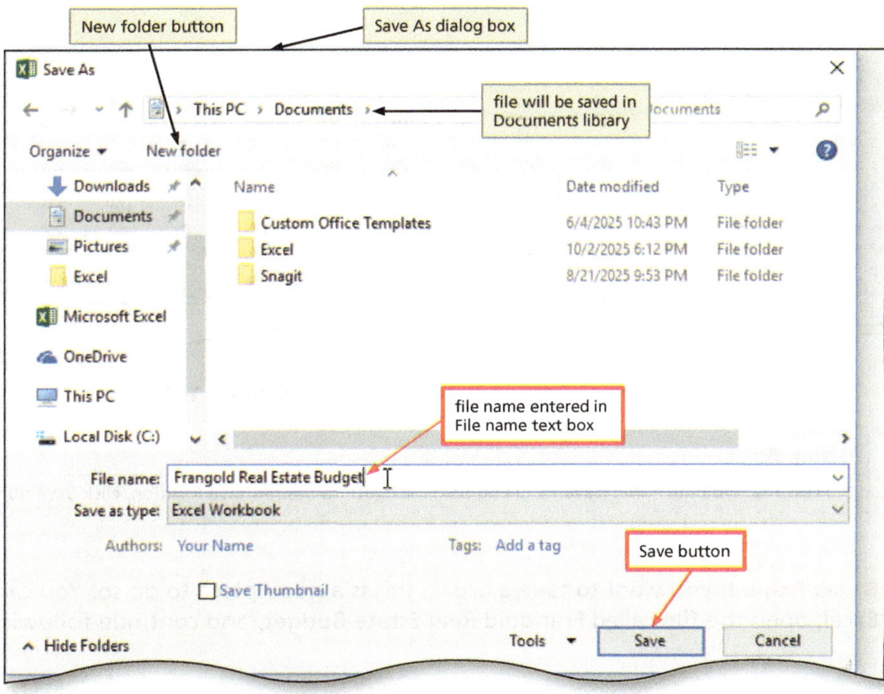

Figure 1–44

Q&A **Do I have to save to the Documents library?**
No. You can save to any device or folder. A folder is a specific location on a storage medium. You can save to the default folder or a different folder. You also can create your own folders by clicking the New folder button shown in Figure 1–44. To save to a different location, navigate to that location in the Navigation pane instead of clicking Documents.

What characters can I use in a file name?
The only invalid characters are the backslash (\), slash (/), colon (:), asterisk (*), question mark (?), quotation mark ("), less than symbol (<), greater than symbol (>), and vertical bar (|).

Why is my list of files, folders, and drives arranged and named differently from those shown in the figure?
Your computer or mobile device's configuration determines how the list of files and folders is displayed and how drives are named. You can change the save location by clicking links in the Navigation pane.

5

- Click the Save button to save the workbook with the file name Frangold Real Estate Budget to the default save location (Figure 1–45).

Q&A

How do I know that Excel saved the workbook?
While Excel is saving your file, it briefly displays a message on the status bar indicating the amount of the file saved. When the workbook appears after saving, the new file name and the word, Saved, appear in the title bar.

Why is the AutoSave button turned off on the title bar?
If you are saving the file to a computer or mobile device, the AutoSave button on the title bar is turned off. If you are saving the file to OneDrive, the AutoSave button is turned on, allowing Excel to save the workbook as you make changes to it. If AutoSave is turned off, you will need to continue saving your changes manually.

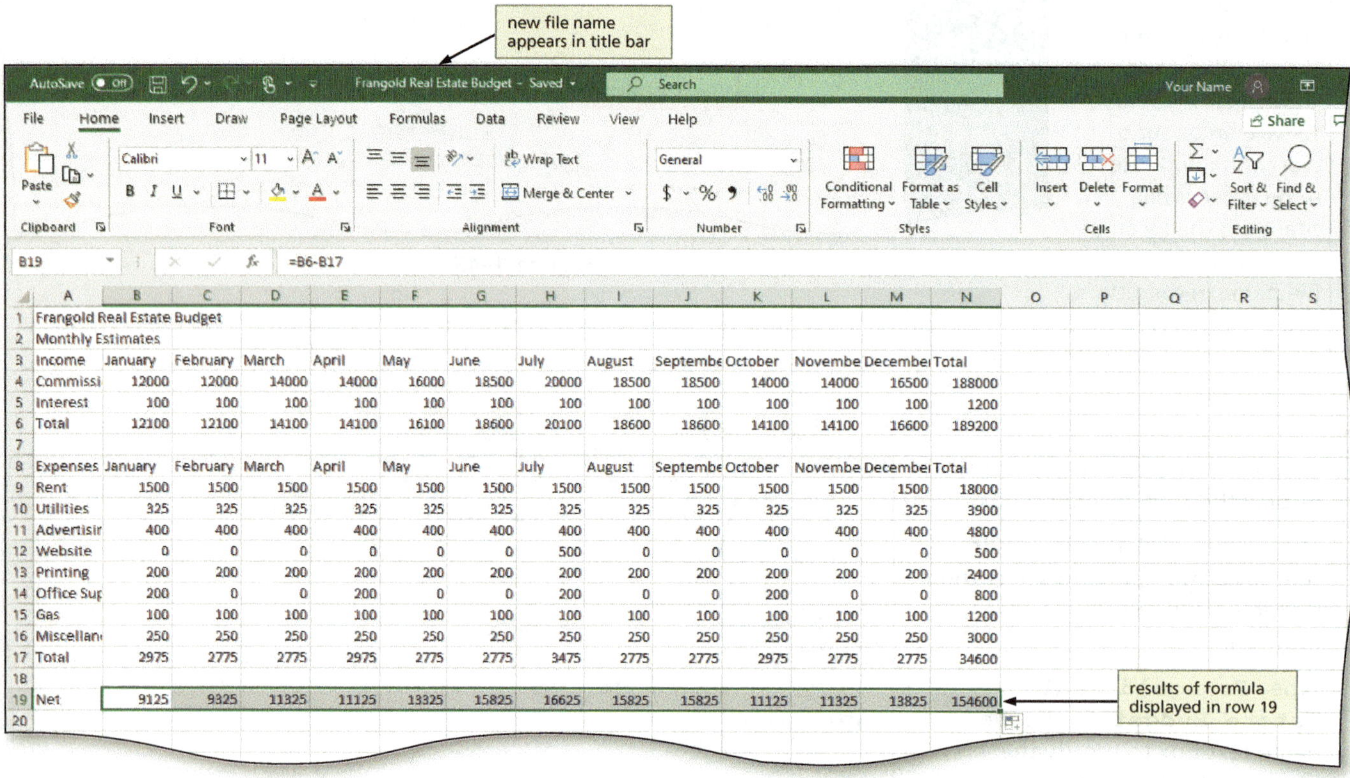

Figure 1–45

Other Ways

1. Press F12, type file name (Save As dialog box), navigate to desired save location, click Save button

Break Point: If you want to take a break, this is a good place to do so. You can exit Excel now. To resume later, start Excel, open the file called Frangold Real Estate Budget, and continue following the steps from this location forward.

Formatting the Worksheet

The text, numeric entries, and functions for the worksheet now are complete. The next step is to format the worksheet. You **format** a worksheet to enhance the appearance of information by changing its font, size, color, or alignment.

Figure 1–46a shows the worksheet before formatting. Figure 1–46b shows the worksheet after formatting. As you can see from the two figures, a worksheet that is formatted not only is easier to read but also looks more professional.

Consider This

What steps should you consider when formatting a worksheet?

The key to formatting a worksheet is to consider the ways you can enhance the worksheet so that it appears professional. When formatting a worksheet, consider the following steps:

- Identify in what ways you want to emphasize various elements of the worksheet.
- Increase the font size of cells.
- Change the font color of cells.
- Center the worksheet titles, subtitles, and column headings.
- Modify column widths to best fit text in cells.
- Change the font style of cells.

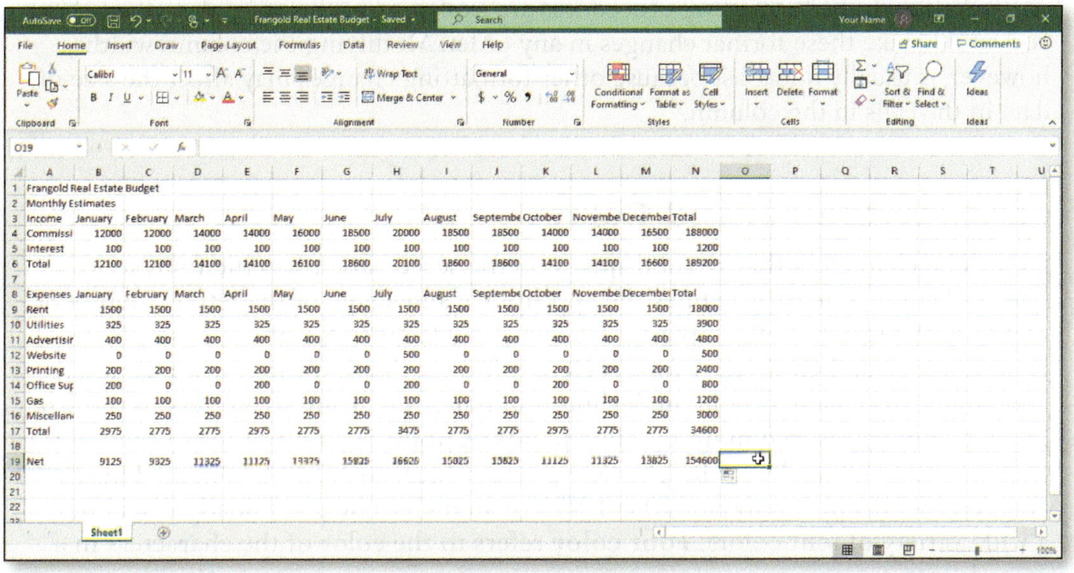

(a) Unformatted Worksheet

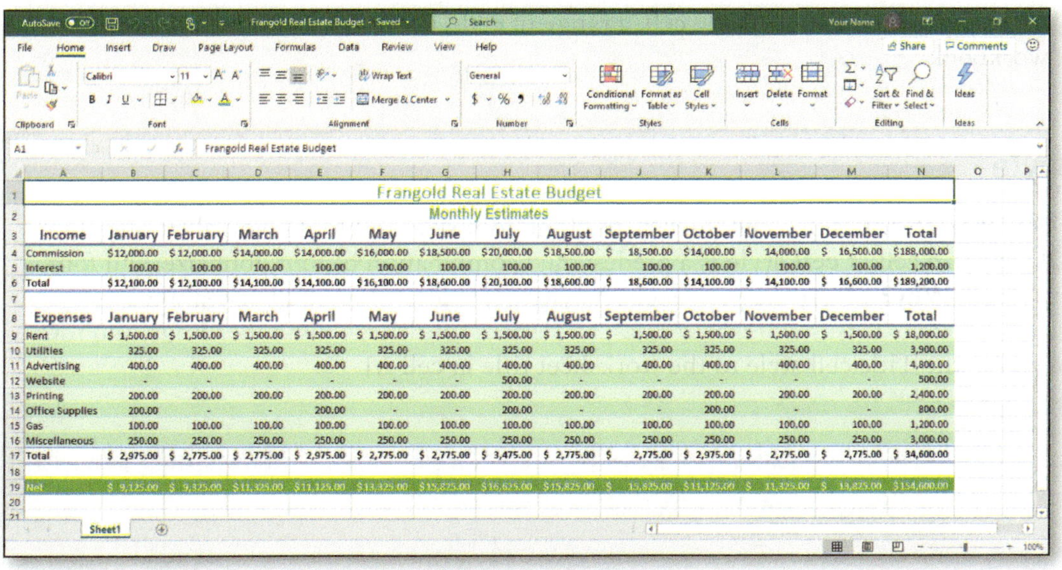

(b) Formatted Worksheet

Figure 1–46

To change the unformatted worksheet in Figure 1–46a so that it looks like the formatted worksheet in Figure 1–46b, the following tasks must be completed:

1. Change the font, change the font style, increase the font size, and change the font color of the worksheet titles in cells A1 and A2.
2. Center the worksheet titles in cells A1 and A2 across columns A through N.
3. Format the body of the worksheet. The body of the worksheet, range A3:N19, includes the column titles, row titles, and numbers. Formatting the body of the worksheet changes the numbers to use a dollars-and-cents format, with dollar signs in rows 4 and 9 and in the total rows (row 6 and 17); changes the styles of some rows; adds underlining that emphasizes portions of the worksheet; and modifies the column widths to fit the text in the columns and make the text and numbers readable.

Although the formatting procedures are explained in the order described above, you could make these format changes in any order. Modifying the column widths, however, is usually done last because other formatting changes may affect the size of data in the cells in the column.

Font Style, Size, and Color

The characters that Excel displays on the screen are a specific font, style, size, and color. The **font** defines the appearance and shape of the letters, numbers, and special characters. Examples of fonts include Calibri, Cambria, Times New Roman, Arial, and Courier. A **font style** is a format that indicates how characters are emphasized, such as bold, underline, and italic. The **font size** refers to the size of characters, measured in units called points. A **point** is a unit of measure used for font size and, in Excel, row height; one point is equal to 1/72 of an inch. Thus, a character with a **point size** of 10 is 10/72 of an inch in height. Finally, Excel has a wide variety of font colors. **Font color** refers to the color of the characters in a spreadsheet.

When Excel first starts, the default font for the entire workbook is Calibri, with a font size, font style, and font color of 11-point regular black. You can change the font characteristics in a single cell, a range of cells, the entire worksheet, or the entire workbook.

To Change a Cell Style

You can change several characteristics of a cell, such as the font, font size, and font color, all at once by assigning a predefined cell style to a cell. A **cell style** is a predesigned combination of font, font size, and font color that you can apply to a cell. **Why?** Using the predesigned styles provides a consistent appearance to common portions of your worksheets, such as worksheet titles, worksheet subtitles, column headings, and total rows. The following steps assign the Title cell style to the worksheet title in cell A1.

1

- Click cell A1 to make cell A1 the active cell.
- Click the Cell Styles button (Home tab | Styles group) to display the Cell Styles gallery (Figure 1–47).

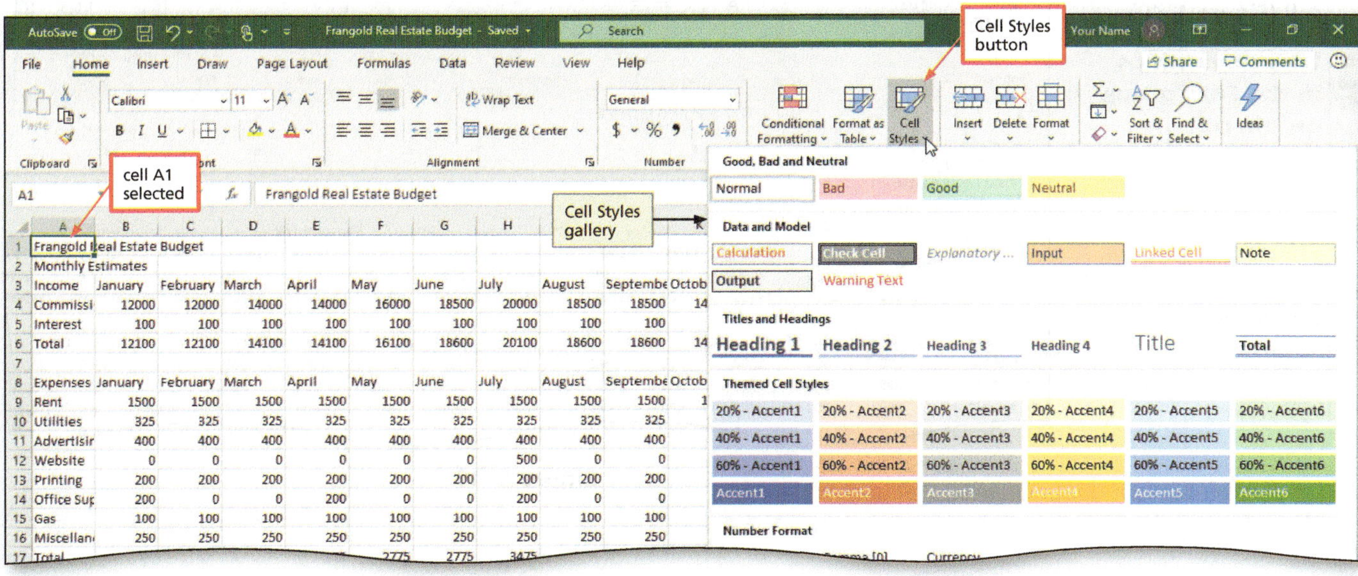

Figure 1–47

2

- Point to the Title cell style in the Titles and Headings area of the Cell Styles gallery to see a live preview of the cell style in the active cell (Figure 1–48).

Experiment

- If you are using a mouse, point to other cell styles in the Cell Styles gallery to see a live preview of those cell styles in cell A1.

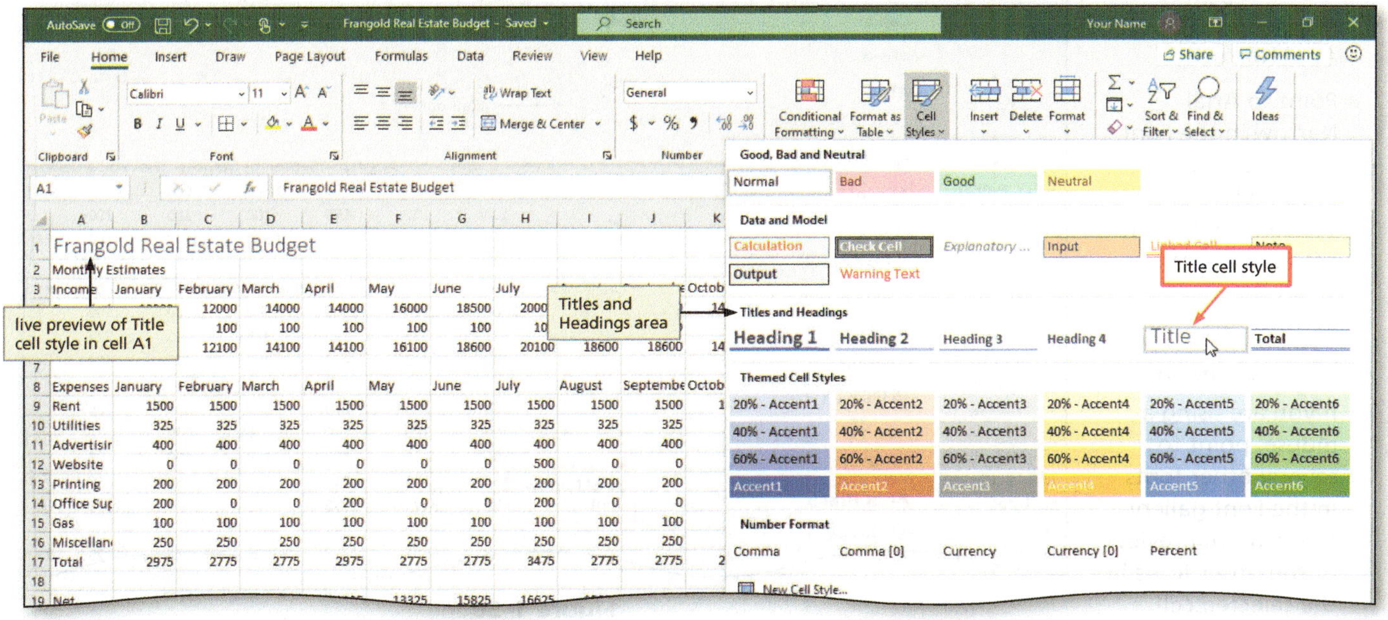

Figure 1–48

3

- Click the Title cell style to apply the cell style to the active cell (Figure 1–49).

Q&A **Why do settings in the Font group on the ribbon change?**
The font and font size change to reflect the font changes applied to the active cell, cell A1, as a result of applying the Title cell style.

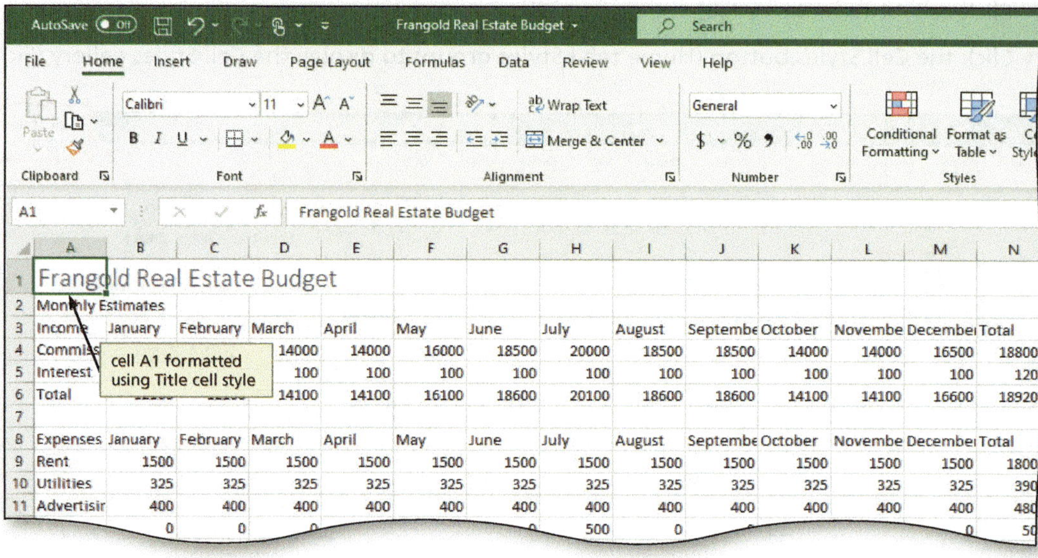

Figure 1–49

To Change the Font

Why? Different fonts are often used in a worksheet to make it more appealing to the reader and to relate or distinguish data in the worksheet. The following steps change the worksheet subtitle's font to Arial Narrow.

1

- Click cell A2 to make it the active cell.
- Click the Font arrow (Home tab | Font group) to display the Font gallery. If necessary, scroll to Arial Narrow.
- Point to Arial Narrow in the Font gallery to see a live preview of the selected font in the active cell (Figure 1–50).

Experiment

- If you are using a mouse, point to several other fonts in the Font gallery to see a live preview of the other fonts in the selected cell.

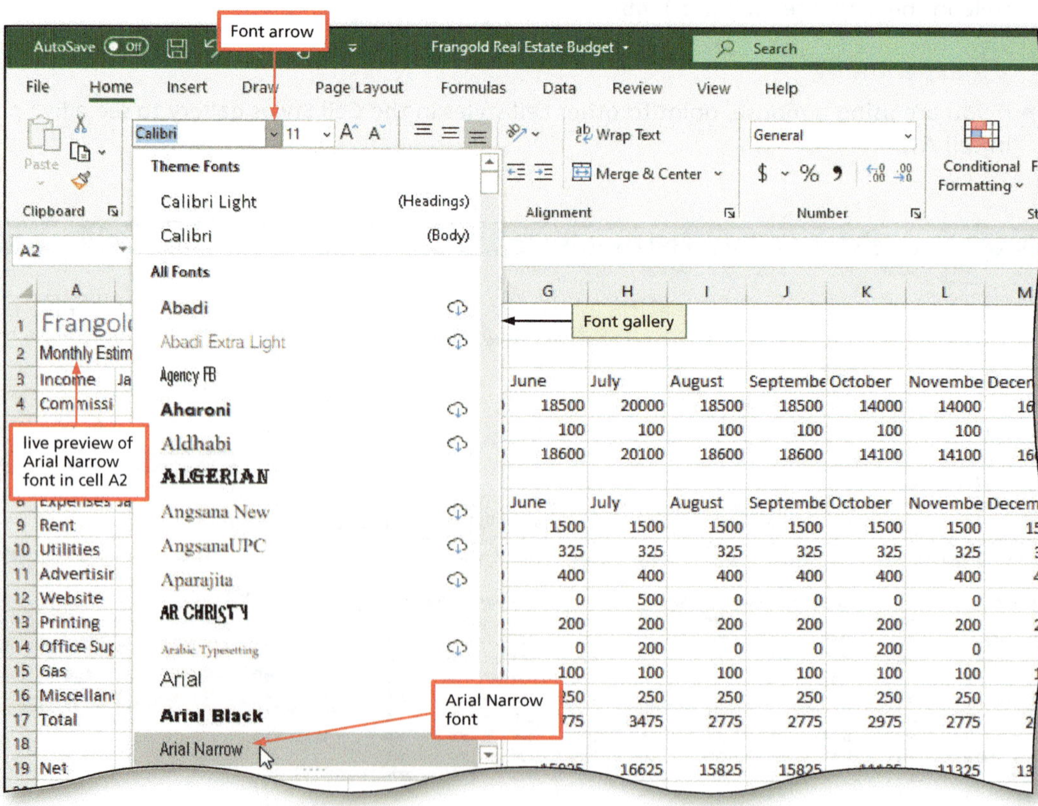

Figure 1–50

2

- Click Arial Narrow in the Font gallery to change the font of the worksheet subtitle to Arial Narrow (Figure 1–51).

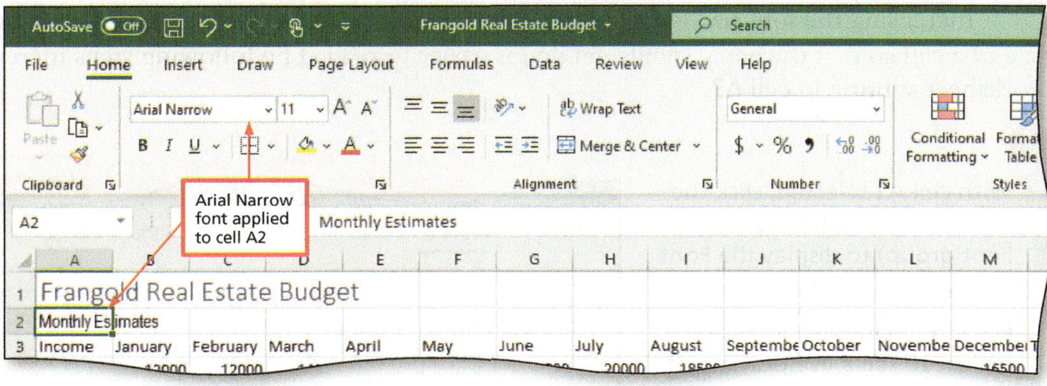

Figure 1–51

Other Ways

1. Click Font Settings Dialog Box Launcher, click Font tab (Format Cells dialog box), click desired font in Font list, click OK
2. Right-click the cell to display Mini toolbar, click Font arrow on Mini toolbar, click desired font in Font list
3. Right-click selected cell, click Format Cells on shortcut menu, click Font tab (Format Cells dialog box), click desired font in Font list, click OK

To Apply Bold Style to a Cell

Bold, or boldface, text has a darker appearance than normal text. **Why?** You apply bold style to a cell to emphasize it or make it stand out from the rest of the worksheet. The following steps apply bold style to the worksheet title and subtitle.

1

- Click cell A1 to make it active and then click the Bold button (Home tab | Font group) to change the font style of the active cell to bold (Figure 1–52).

Q&A

What if a cell already has the bold style applied?
If the active cell contains bold text, then Excel displays the Bold button with a darker gray background.

How do I remove the bold style from a cell?
Clicking the Bold button (Home tab | Font group) a second time removes the bold style.

2

- Repeat Step 1 to bold cell A2.

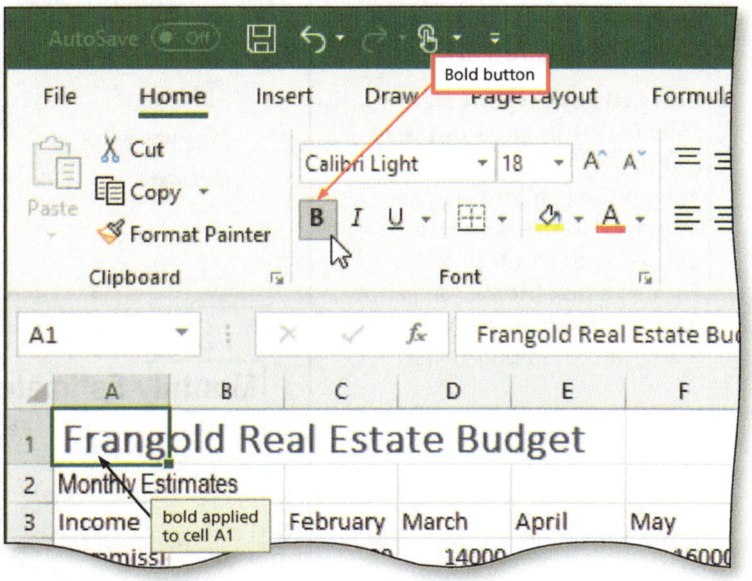

Figure 1–52

Other Ways

1. Click Font Settings Dialog Box Launcher, click Font tab (Format Cells dialog box), click Bold in Font style list, click OK
2. Right-click selected cell, click Bold button on Mini toolbar
3. Right-click selected cell, click Format Cells on shortcut menu, click Font tab (Format Cells dialog box), click Bold in Font style list, click OK
4. Press CTRL+B

To Increase the Font Size of a Cell Entry

Increasing the font size is the next step in formatting the worksheet subtitle. **Why?** You increase the font size of a cell so that the entry stands out and is easier to read. The following steps increase the font size of the worksheet subtitle in cell A2.

1

- With cell A2 selected, click the Font Size arrow (Home tab | Font group) to display the Font Size gallery.
- Point to 16 in the Font Size gallery to see a live preview of the active cell with the selected font size (Figure 1–53).

Experiment

- If you are using a mouse, point to several other font sizes in the Font Size list to see a live preview of those font sizes in the selected cell.

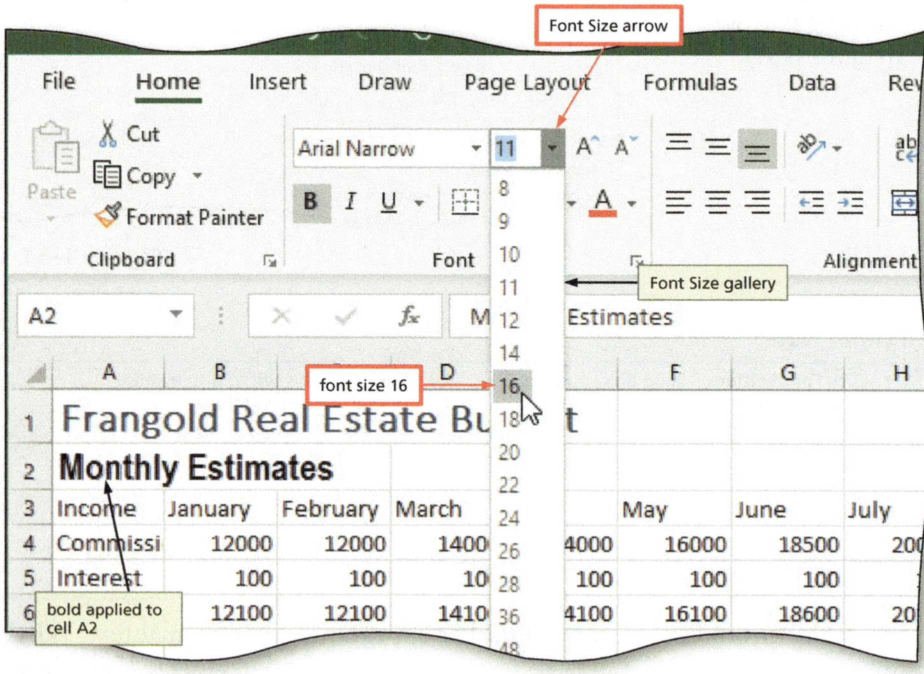

Figure 1–53

2

- Click 16 in the Font Size gallery to change the font size in the active cell (Figure 1–54).

Q&A

Can I choose a font size that is not in the Font Size gallery?
Yes. To select a font size not displayed in the Font Size gallery, such as 13, click the Font Size box (Home tab | Font group), type the font size you want, and then press ENTER.

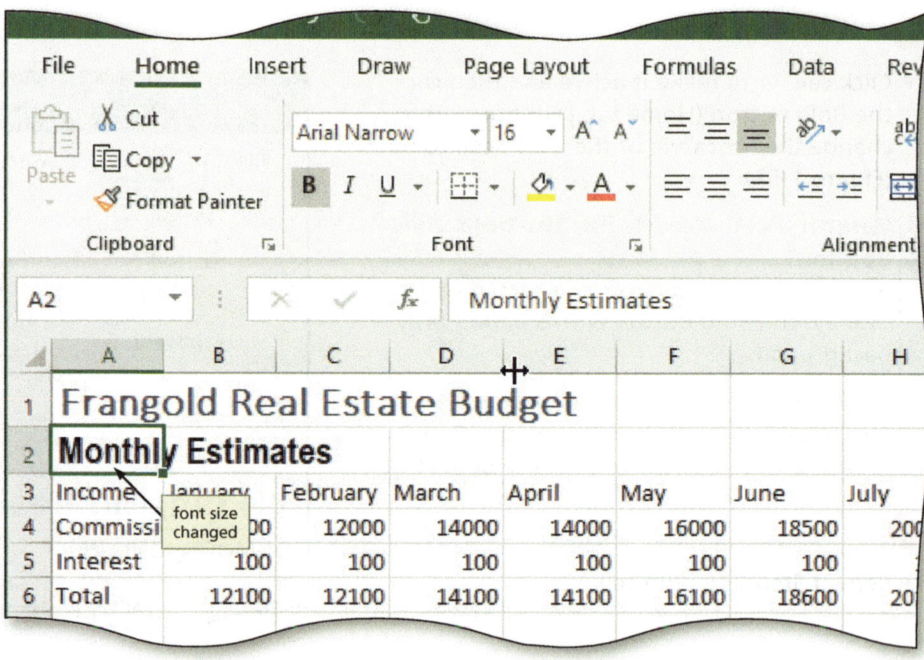

Figure 1–54

Other Ways

1. Click 'Increase Font Size' button (Home tab | Font group) or 'Decrease Font Size' button (Home tab | Font group)
2. Click Font Settings Dialog Box Launcher, click Font tab (Format Cells dialog box), click desired size in Size list, click OK
3. Right-click cell to display Mini toolbar, click Font Size arrow on Mini toolbar, click desired font size in Font Size gallery
4. Right-click selected cell, click Format Cells on shortcut menu, click Font tab (Format Cells dialog box), select font size in Size box, click OK

To Change the Font Color of a Cell Entry

The next step is to change the color of the font in cells A1 and A2 to green. **Why?** Changing the font color of cell entries can help the text stand out more. You also can change the font colors to match a company's or product's brand colors. The following steps change the font color of a cell entry.

1

- Click cell A1 and then click the Font Color arrow (Home tab | Font group) to display the Font Color gallery.
- If you are using a mouse, point to Green, Accent 6 (column 10, row 1) in the Theme Colors area of the Font Color gallery to see a live preview of the font color in the active cell (Figure 1–55).

Experiment

- Point to several other colors in the Font Color gallery to see a live preview of other font colors in the active cell.

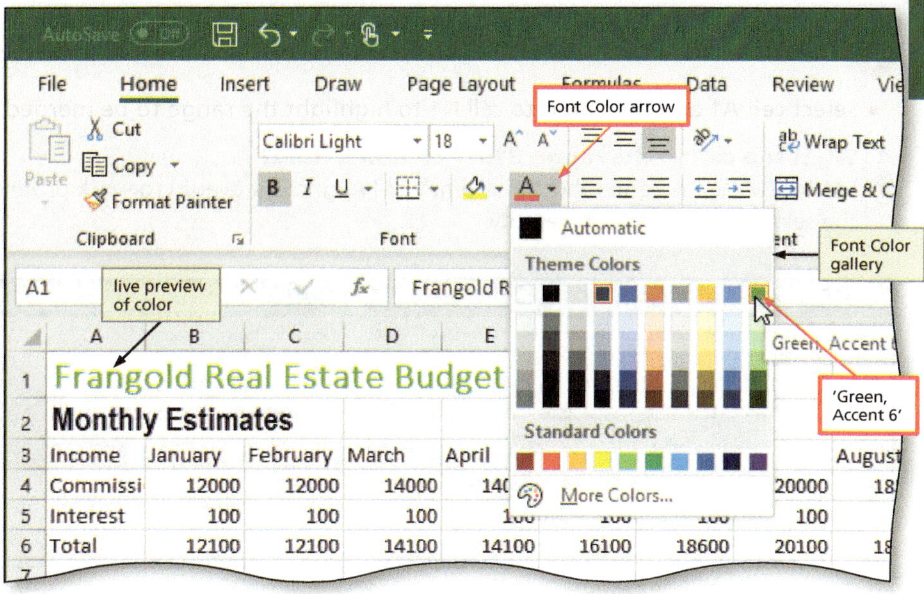

Figure 1–55

Q&A **How many colors are in the Font Color gallery?**
You can choose from approximately 70 different font colors in the Font Color gallery. Your Font Color gallery may have more or fewer colors, depending on the color settings of your operating system. The Theme Colors area contains colors that are included in the current workbook's theme.

2

- Click Green, Accent 6 (column 10, row 1) in the Font Color gallery to change the font color of the worksheet title in the active cell (Figure 1–56).

Q&A **Why does the Font Color button change after I select the new font color?**
When you choose a color in the Font Color gallery, Excel changes the Font Color button (Home tab | Font group) to your chosen color. Then when you want to change the font color of another cell to the same color, you need only to select the cell and then click the Font Color button (Home tab | Font group).

Figure 1–56

3

- Click cell A2.
- Click the Font Color button to apply Green, Accent 6 (column 10, row 1) to cell A2.

Other Ways

1. Click Font Settings Dialog Box Launcher, click Font tab (Format Cells dialog box), click desired font color in Color list, click OK
2. Right-click cell to display Mini toolbar, click Font Color arrow on Mini toolbar, click desired color in Font Color gallery
3. Right-click selected cell, click Format Cells on shortcut menu, click Font tab (Format Cells dialog box), click Color arrow, click desired color, click OK

To Center Cell Entries across Columns by Merging Cells

The final step in formatting the worksheet title and subtitle is to center them across columns A through N. **Why?** Centering a title across the columns used in the body of the worksheet improves the worksheet's appearance. To do this, the 14 cells in the range A1:N1 are combined, or merged, into a single cell that is the width of the columns in the body of the worksheet. The 14 cells in the range A2:N2 are merged in a similar manner. When you **merge** cells, you combine multiple adjacent cells into one larger cell. To unmerge cells, you **split** them to display the original range of cells. The following steps center the worksheet title and subtitle across columns by merging cells.

1

- Select cell A1 and then drag to cell N1 to highlight the range to be merged and centered (Figure 1–57).

Q&A

What if a cell in the range B1:N1 contains data?
For the 'Merge & Center' button (Home tab | Alignment group) to work properly, all the cells except the leftmost cell in the selected range must be empty.

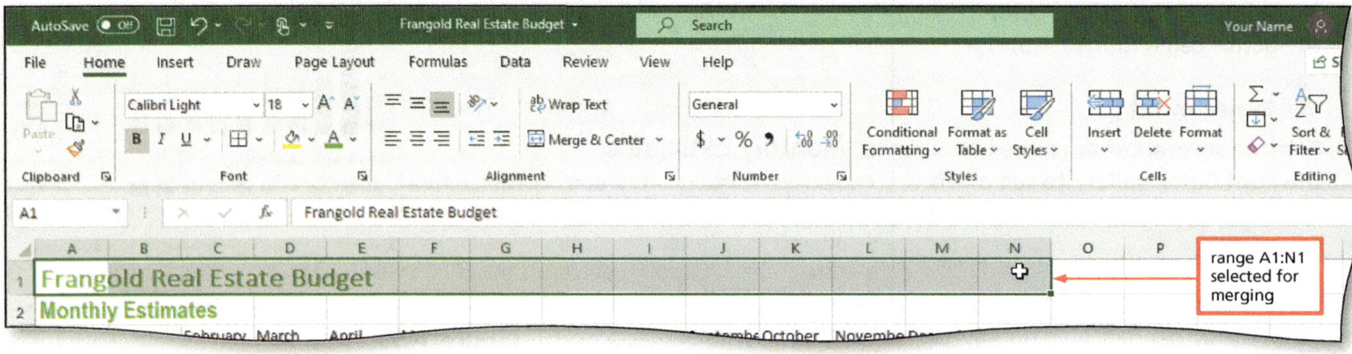

Figure 1–57

2

- Click the 'Merge & Center' button (Home tab | Alignment group) to merge cells A1 through N1 and center the contents of the leftmost cell across the selected columns (Figure 1–58).

Q&A

What if my screen displays a Merge & Center menu?
If you are using a touch screen, Excel might display a Merge & Center menu. Select the desired option on the Merge & Center menu if you do not have a separate 'Merge & Center' button and 'Merge & Center' arrow.

What happened to cells B1 through N1?
After the merge, cells B1 through N1 no longer exist. The new cell A1 now extends across columns A through N.

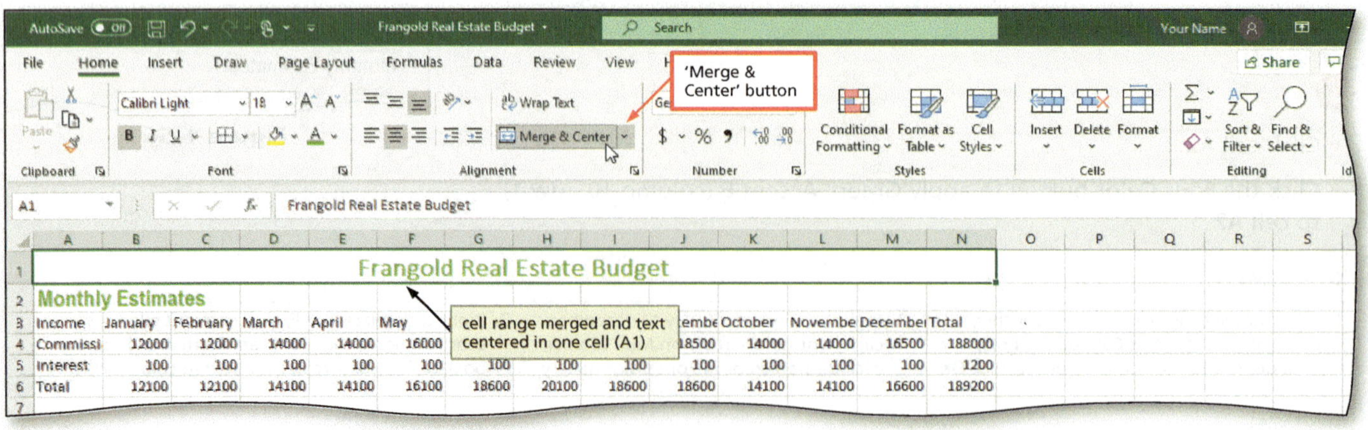

Figure 1–58

3

- Repeat Steps 1 and 2 to merge and center the worksheet subtitle across cells A2 through N2 (Figure 1–59).

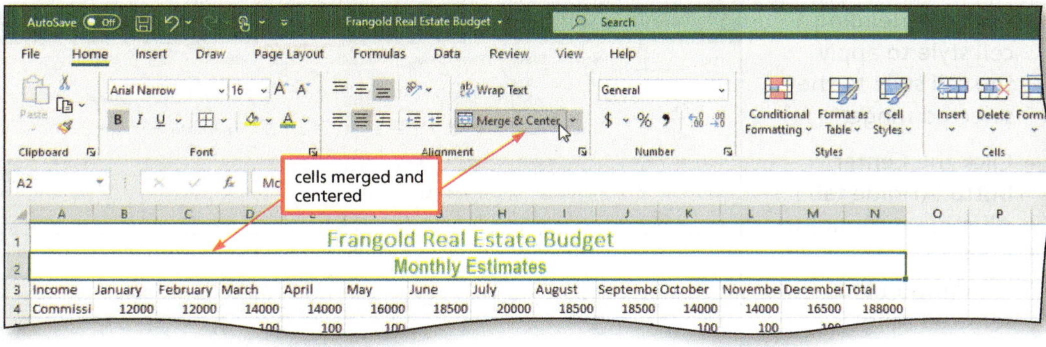

Figure 1–59

Q&A **Are cells B1 through N1 and B2 through N2 lost forever?**
No. You can split a merged cell to redisplay the individual cells. You split a merged cell by selecting it and clicking the 'Merge & Center' button. For example, if you click the 'Merge & Center' button a second time in Step 2, it will split the merged cell A1 into cells A1, B1, C1, D1, E1, F1, G1, H1, I1, J1, K1, L1, M1, and N1, and move the title to its original location in cell A1.

Other Ways

1. Right-click selection, click 'Merge & Center' button on Mini toolbar
2. Right-click selected cell, click Format Cells on shortcut menu, click Alignment tab (Format Cells dialog box), select 'Center Across Selection' in Horizontal list, click OK

To Format Rows Using Cell Styles

The next step to format the worksheet is to format the rows. **Why?** Row titles and the total row should be formatted so that the column titles and total row can be distinguished from the data in the body of the worksheet. Data rows can be formatted to make them easier to read as well. The following steps format the column titles and total row using cell styles in the default worksheet theme.

1

- Click cell A3 and then drag to cell N3 to select the range.
- Click the Cell Styles button (Home tab | Styles group) to display the Cell Styles gallery.
- Point to the Heading 1 cell style in the Titles and Headings area of the Cell Styles gallery to see a live preview of the cell style in the selected range (Figure 1–60).

Experiment

- If you are using a mouse, point to other cell styles in the Titles and Headings area of the Cell Styles gallery to see a live preview of other styles.

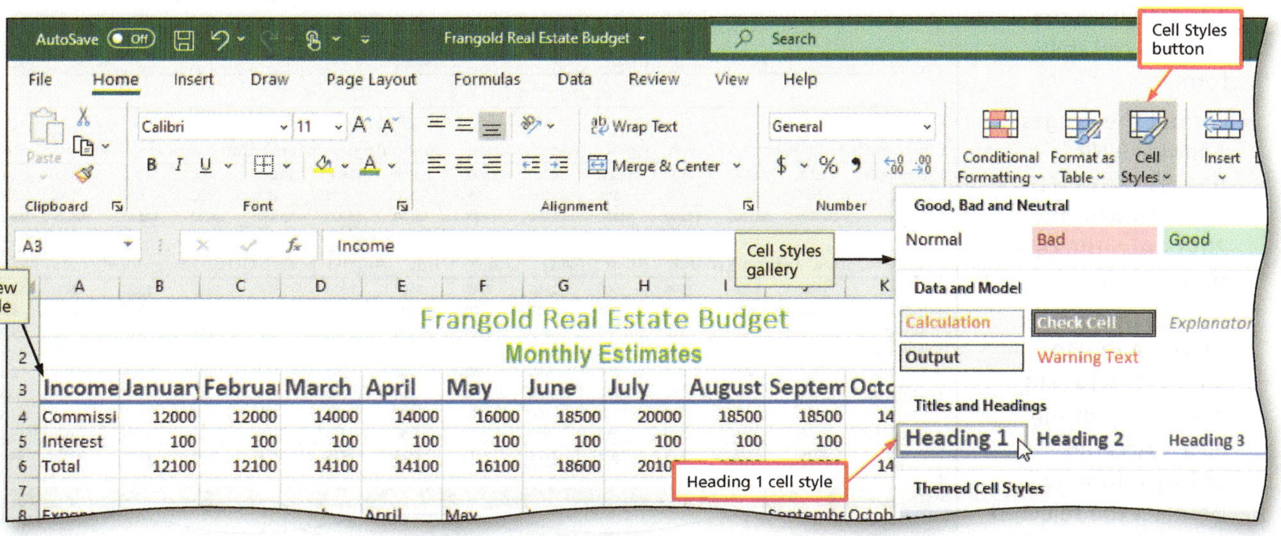

Figure 1–60

2

- Click the Heading 1 cell style to apply the cell style to the selected range.
- Click the Center button (Home tab | Alignment group) to center the column headings in the selected range.
- Select the range A8 to N8 (Figure 1–61).

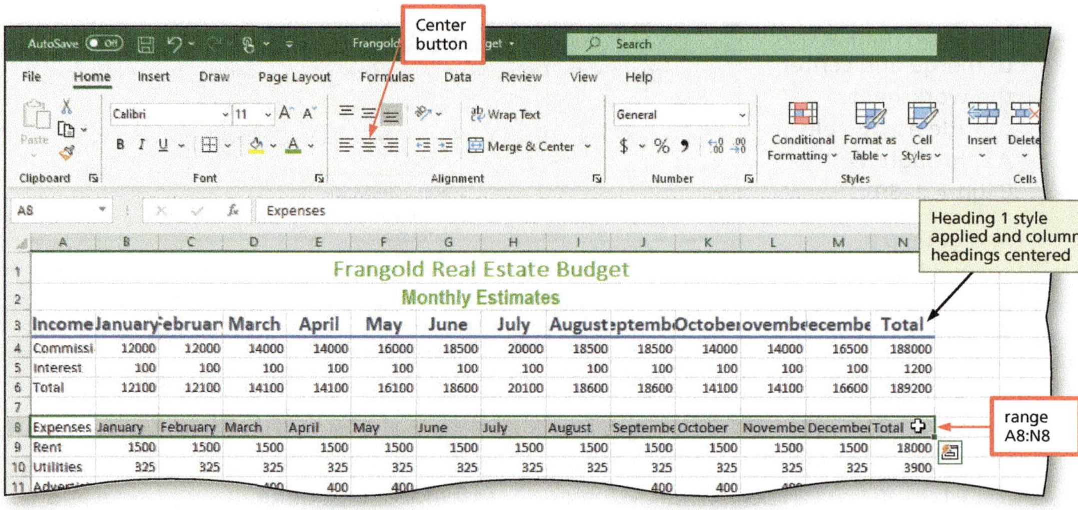

Figure 1–61

3

- Apply the Heading 1 cell style format and then center the headings (Figure 1–62).

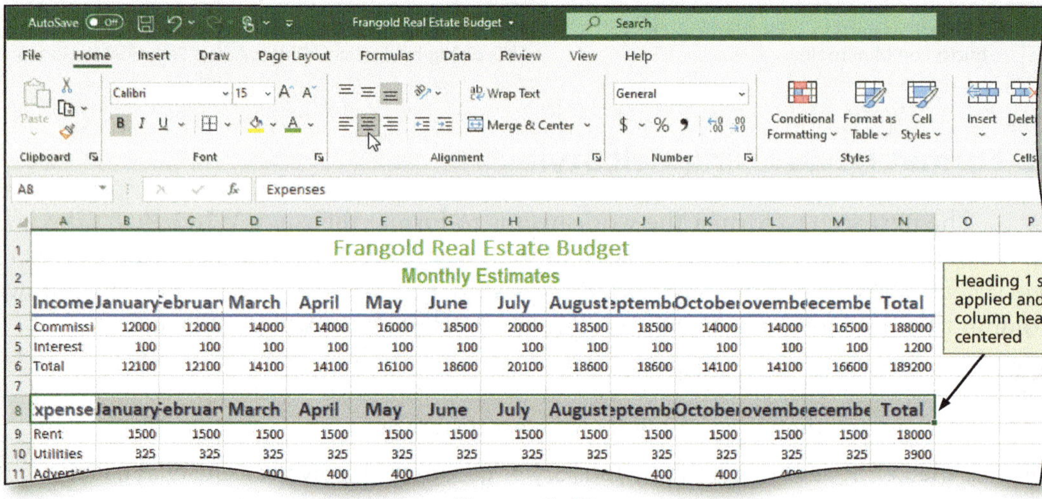

Figure 1–62

4

- Format the ranges A6:N6 and A17:N17 with the Total cell style format.
- Format the range A19:N19 with the Accent6 cell style format.
- Format the ranges A4:N4, A9:N9, A11:N11, A13:N13, A15:N15 with the 20% - Accent6 cell style format.
- Format the ranges A5:N5, A10:N10, A12:N12, A14:N14, A16:N16 with the 40% - Accent6 cell style format. Deselect the selected ranges (Figure 1–63).

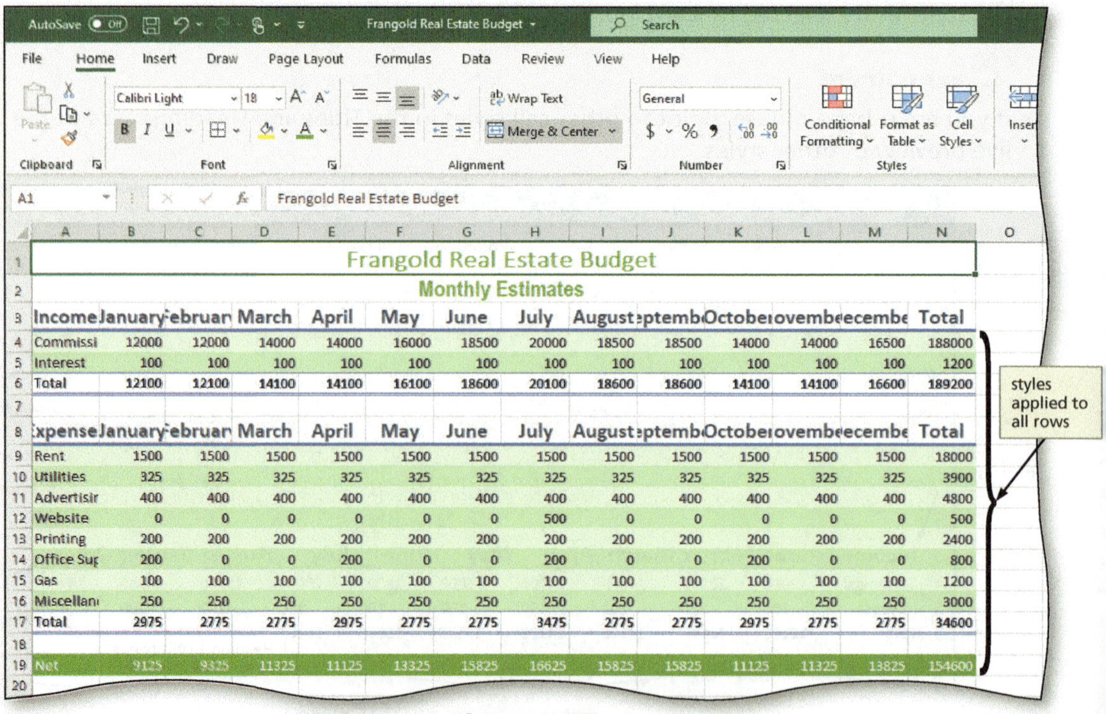

Figure 1–63

To Format Numbers in the Worksheet

The requirements document requested that numbers in the first row and last row of each section should be formatted to use a dollar-and-cents format, while other numbers receive a comma format. **Why?** Using a dollar-and-cents format for selected cells makes it clear to users of the worksheet that the numbers represent dollar values without cluttering the entire worksheet with dollar signs, and applying the comma format makes larger numbers easier to read. Excel allows you to apply various number formats, many of which are discussed in later modules. The following steps use buttons on the ribbon to format the numbers in the worksheet.

1

- Select the range B4:N4.
- Click the 'Accounting Number Format' button (Home tab | Number group) to apply the accounting number format to the cells in the selected range.
- Select the range B5:N5 (Figure 1–64).

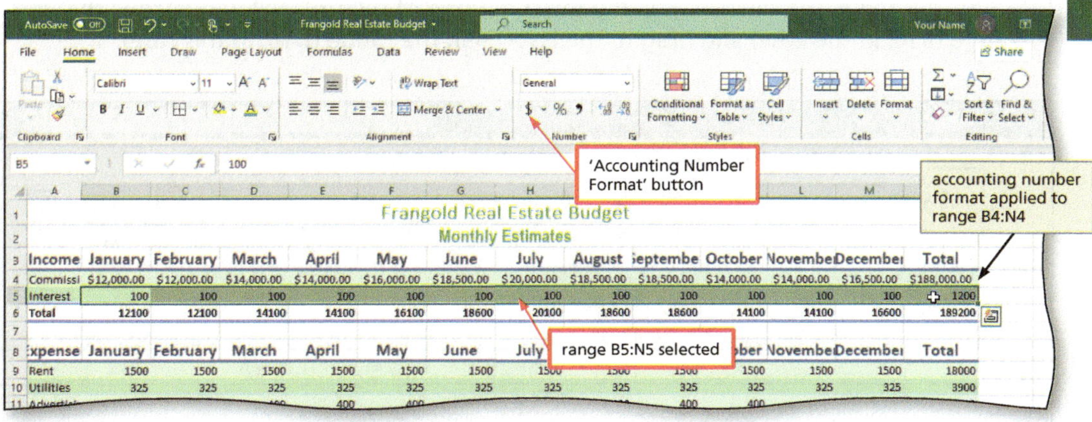

Figure 1–64

Q&A **What if my screen displays an Accounting Number Format menu?**
If you are using a touch screen, you may not have a separate 'Accounting Number Format' button and 'Accounting Number Format' arrow. In this case, select the desired option on the Accounting Number Format menu.

What effect does the accounting number format have on the selected cells?
The accounting number format causes numbers to be displayed with two decimal places and to align vertically. Cell widths are adjusted automatically to accommodate the new formatting.

2

- Click the Comma Style button (Home tab | Number group) to apply the comma style format to the selected range.

Q&A **What effect does the comma style format have on the selected cells?**
The comma style format formats numbers to have two decimal places and commas as thousands separators.

- Select the range B6:N6 to make it the active range (Figure 1–65).

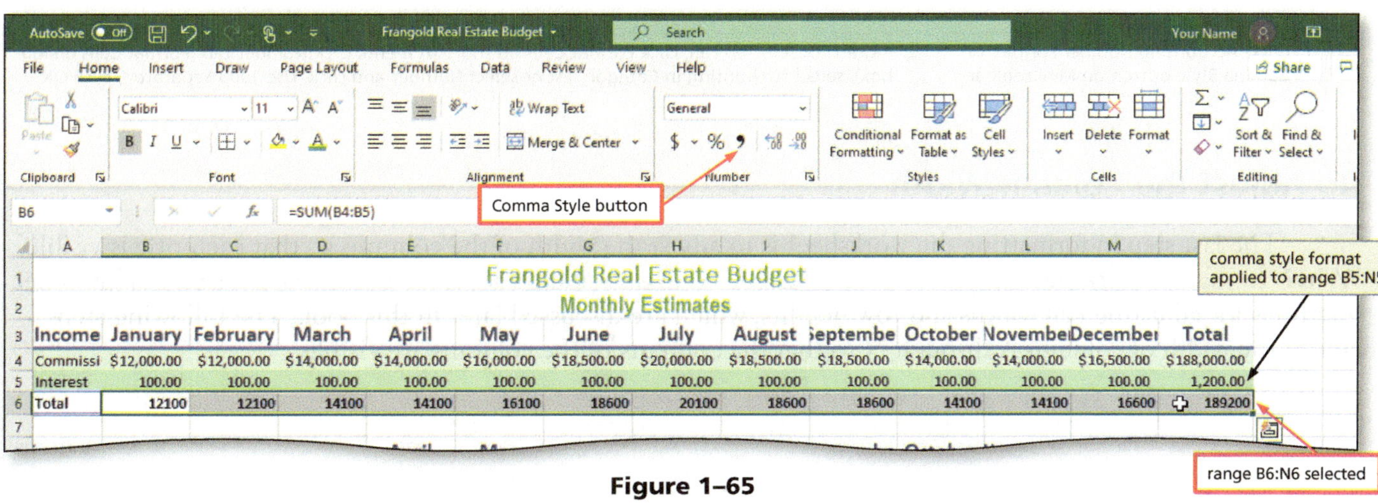

Figure 1–65

3

- Click the 'Accounting Number Format' button (Home tab | Number group) to apply the accounting number format to the cells in the selected range.

4

- Format the ranges B9:N9, B17:N17, and B19:N19 with the accounting number format.
- Format the range B10:N16 with the comma style format. Click cell A1 to deselect the selected ranges (Figure 1–66).

Q&A
How do I select the range B10:N16?
Select this range the same way as you select a range of cells in a column or row; that is, click the first cell in the range (B10, in this case) and drag to the last cell in the range (N16, in this case).

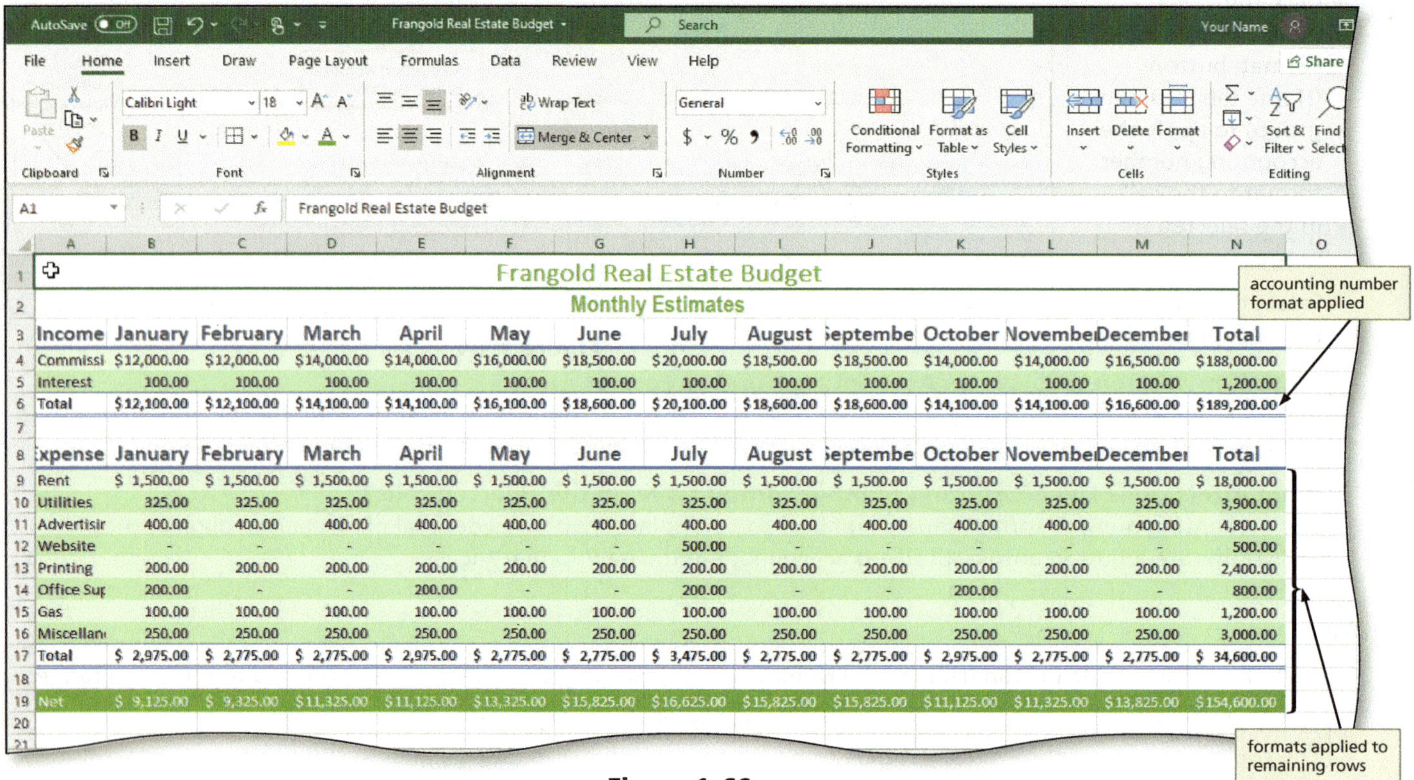

	A	B	C	D	E	F	G	H	I	J	K	L	M	N
3	Income	January	February	March	April	May	June	July	August	Septembe	October	Novembe	December	Total
4	Commissi	$12,000.00	$12,000.00	$14,000.00	$14,000.00	$16,000.00	$18,500.00	$20,000.00	$18,500.00	$18,500.00	$14,000.00	$14,000.00	$16,500.00	$188,000.00
5	Interest	100.00	100.00	100.00	100.00	100.00	100.00	100.00	100.00	100.00	100.00	100.00	100.00	1,200.00
6	Total	$12,100.00	$12,100.00	$14,100.00	$14,100.00	$16,100.00	$18,600.00	$20,100.00	$18,600.00	$18,600.00	$14,100.00	$14,100.00	$16,600.00	$189,200.00
7														
8	xpense	January	February	March	April	May	June	July	August	Septembe	October	Novembe	December	Total
9	Rent	$ 1,500.00	$ 1,500.00	$ 1,500.00	$ 1,500.00	$ 1,500.00	$ 1,500.00	$ 1,500.00	$ 1,500.00	$ 1,500.00	$ 1,500.00	$ 1,500.00	$ 1,500.00	$ 18,000.00
10	Utilities	325.00	325.00	325.00	325.00	325.00	325.00	325.00	325.00	325.00	325.00	325.00	325.00	3,900.00
11	Advertisir	400.00	400.00	400.00	400.00	400.00	400.00	400.00	400.00	400.00	400.00	400.00	400.00	4,800.00
12	Website	-	-	-	-	-	-	500.00	-	-	-	-	-	500.00
13	Printing	200.00	200.00	200.00	200.00	200.00	200.00	200.00	200.00	200.00	200.00	200.00	200.00	2,400.00
14	Office Sup	200.00	-	-	200.00	-	-	200.00	-	-	200.00	-	-	800.00
15	Gas	100.00	100.00	100.00	100.00	100.00	100.00	100.00	100.00	100.00	100.00	100.00	100.00	1,200.00
16	Miscellan	250.00	250.00	250.00	250.00	250.00	250.00	250.00	250.00	250.00	250.00	250.00	250.00	3,000.00
17	Total	$ 2,975.00	$ 2,775.00	$ 2,775.00	$ 2,975.00	$ 2,775.00	$ 2,775.00	$ 3,475.00	$ 2,775.00	$ 2,775.00	$ 2,975.00	$ 2,775.00	$ 2,775.00	$ 34,600.00
18														
19	Net	$ 9,125.00	$ 9,325.00	$11,325.00	$11,125.00	$13,325.00	$15,825.00	$16,625.00	$15,825.00	$15,825.00	$11,125.00	$11,325.00	$13,825.00	$154,600.00

Figure 1–66

Other Ways

1. Click 'Accounting Number Format' or Comma Style button on Mini toolbar
2. Right-click selected cell, click Format Cells on shortcut menu, click Number tab (Format Cells dialog box), select Accounting in Category list or select Number and click 'Use 1000 Separator', click OK

To Adjust the Column Width

The last step in formatting the worksheet is to adjust the width of the columns so that each title is visible. **Why?** To make a worksheet easy to read, the column widths should be adjusted appropriately. Excel offers other methods for adjusting cell widths and row heights, which are discussed later in this book. The following steps adjust the width of columns A through N so that the contents of the columns are visible.

1

- Point to the boundary on the right side of the column A heading above row 1 to change the pointer to a split double arrow (Figure 1–67).

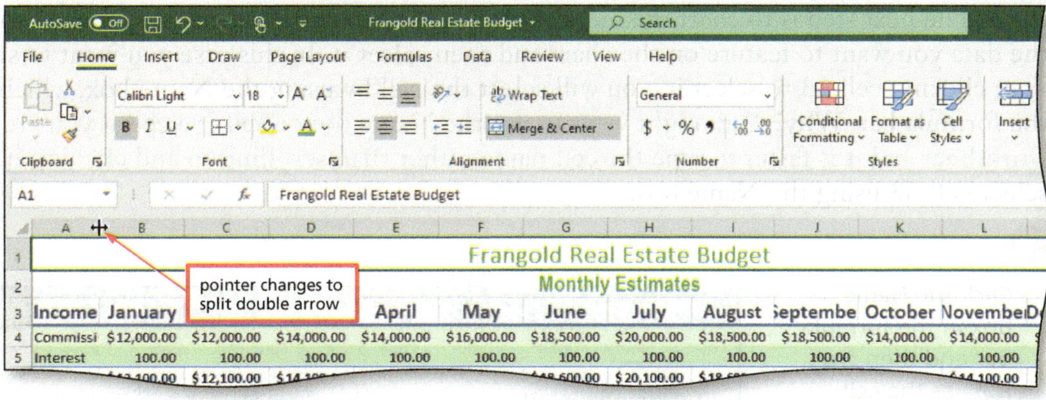

Figure 1–67

2

- Double-click the boundary to adjust the width of the column to accommodate the width of the longest item in the column (Figure 1–68).

Q&A **What if all of the items in the column are already visible?**
If all of the items are shorter in length than the width of the column and you double-click the column boundary, Excel will reduce the width of the column to the width of the widest entry.

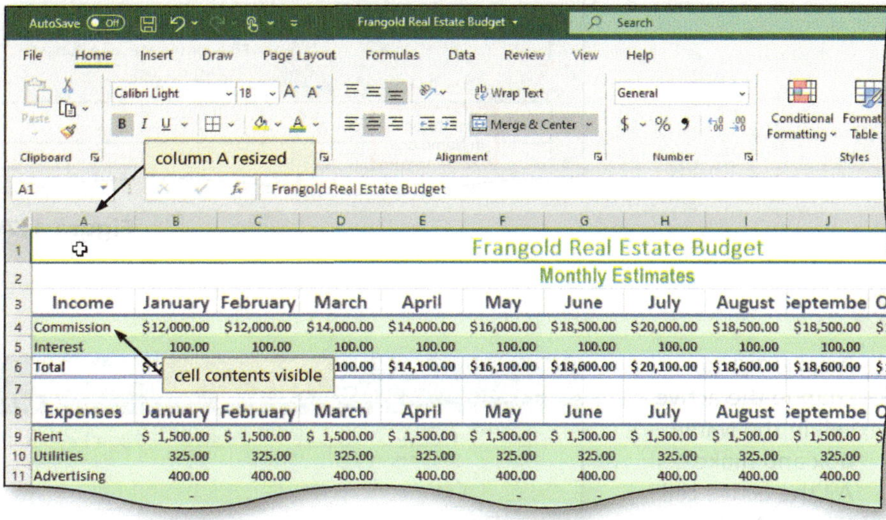

Figure 1–68

3

- Repeat Steps 1 and 2 to adjust the column width of columns B through N (Figure 1–69).

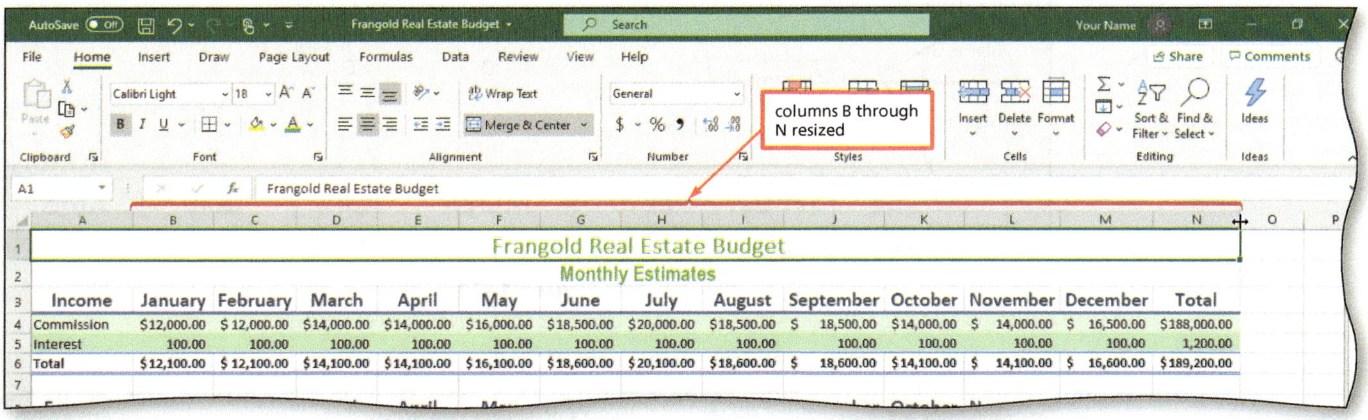

Figure 1–69

Other Ways

1. Select column heading, click Format (Home tab | Cells group), click AutoFit Column Width

To Use the Name Box to Select a Cell

The next step is to chart the monthly expenses. To create the chart, you need to identify the range of the data you want to feature on the chart and then select it. In this case you want to start with cell A3. Rather than clicking cell A3 to select it, you will select the cell by using the Name box, which is located to the left of the formula bar. **Why?** You might want to use the Name box to select a cell if you are working with a large worksheet and it is faster to type the cell name rather than scrolling to and clicking it. The following steps select cell A3 using the Name box.

1

- Click the Name box in the formula bar and then type **a3** as the cell you want to select (Figure 1–70).

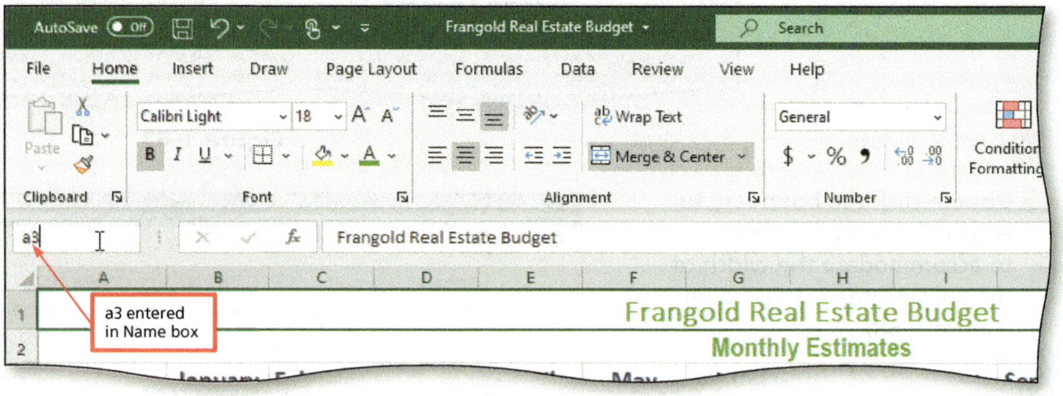

Figure 1–70

2

- Press ENTER to change the active cell in the Name box and make cell A3 the active cell (Figure 1–71).

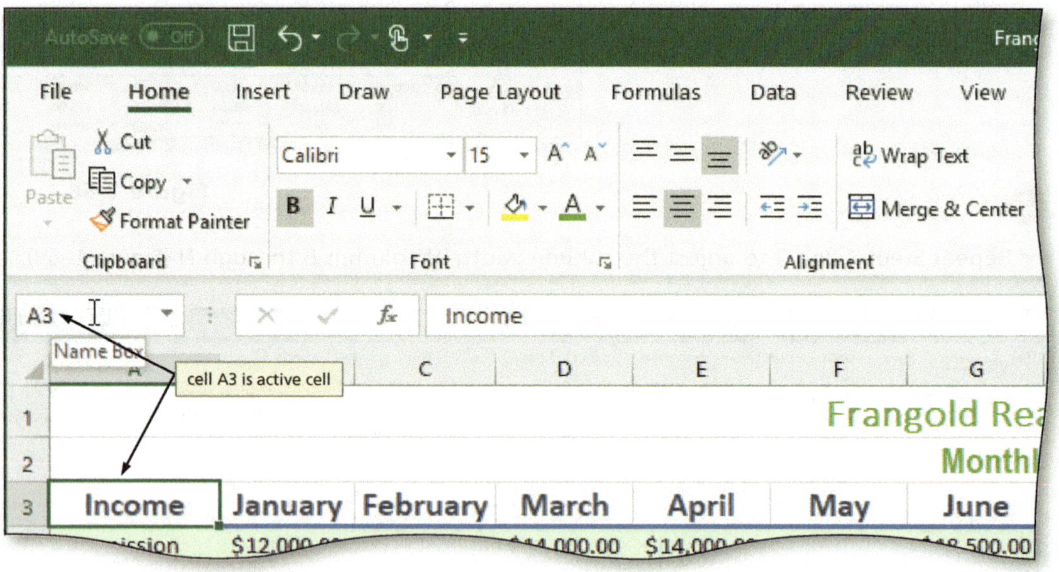

Figure 1–71

Other Ways to Select Cells

As you will see in later modules, in addition to using the Name box to select any cell in a worksheet, you also can use it to assign names to a cell or range of cells. Excel supports several additional ways to select a cell, as summarized in Table 1–4.

Table 1–4 Selecting Cells in Excel

Key, Box, or Command	Function
ALT+PAGE DOWN	Selects the cell one worksheet window to the right and moves the worksheet window accordingly.
ALT+PAGE UP	Selects the cell one worksheet window to the left and moves the worksheet window accordingly.
ARROW	Selects the adjacent cell in the direction of the arrow on the key.
CTRL+ARROW	Selects the border cell of the worksheet in combination with the arrow keys and moves the worksheet window accordingly. For example, to select the rightmost cell in the row that contains the active cell, press CTRL+RIGHT ARROW. You also can press END, release it, and then press the appropriate arrow key to accomplish the same task.
CTRL+HOME	Selects cell A1 or the cell one column and one row below and to the right of frozen titles and moves the worksheet window accordingly.
Find command on Find & Select menu (Home tab | Editing group) or SHIFT+F5	Finds and selects a cell that contains specific contents that you enter in the Find and Replace dialog box. If necessary, Excel moves the worksheet window to display the cell. You also can press CTRL+F to display the Find and Replace dialog box.
Go To command on Find & Select menu (Home tab | Editing group) or F5	Selects the cell that corresponds to the cell reference you enter in the Go To dialog box and moves the worksheet window accordingly. You also can press CTRL+G to display the Go To dialog box and its Special button to go to special worksheet elements, such as formulas.
HOME	Selects the cell at the beginning of the row that contains the active cell and moves the worksheet window accordingly.
Name box	Selects the cell in the workbook that corresponds to the cell reference you enter in the Name box.
PAGE DOWN	Selects the cell down one worksheet window from the active cell and moves the worksheet window accordingly.
PAGE UP	Selects the cell up one worksheet window from the active cell and moves the worksheet window accordingly.

Break Point: If you want to take a break, this is a good place to do so. Be sure to save the Frangold Real Estate Budget file again, and then you can exit Excel. To resume later, start Excel, open the file called Frangold Real Estate Budget, and continue following the steps from this location forward.

Adding a Pie Chart to the Worksheet

Excel includes 17 chart types from which you can choose, including column, line, pie, bar, area, X Y (scatter), map, stock, surface, radar, treemap, sunburst, histogram, box & whisker, waterfall, funnel, and combo. The type of chart you choose depends on the type and quantity of data you have and the message or analysis you want to convey.

A column chart is a good way to compare values side by side. A line chart is often used to illustrate changes in data over time. Pie charts show the contribution of each piece of data to the whole, or total, of the data. A pie chart can go even further in comparing values across categories by showing each pie piece in comparison with the others. Area charts, like line charts, illustrate changes over time but are often used to compare more than one set of data, and the area below the lines is filled in with a different color for each set of data. An X Y (scatter) chart is used much like a line chart, but each piece of data is represented by a dot and is not connected with a line. Scatter charts are typically used for viewing scientific, statistical, and engineering data. A map chart depicts data based on geographic location. A stock chart provides a number of methods commonly used in the financial industry to show fluctuations in stock market data. A surface chart compares data from three columns and/or rows in a 3-D manner. A radar chart can compare aggregate values of several sets of data in a manner that resembles a radar screen, with each set of data represented by a different color. A funnel chart illustrates values during various stages. A combo chart allows you to combine multiple types of charts.

As outlined in the requirements document in Figure 1–2, the budget worksheet should include a pie chart to graphically represent the yearly expense totals for each item in Frangold Real Estate's budget. The pie chart shown in Figure 1–72 is on its own sheet in the workbook. The pie chart resides on a separate sheet, called a chart sheet. A **chart sheet** is a separate sheet in a workbook that contains only a chart, which is linked to the workbook data.

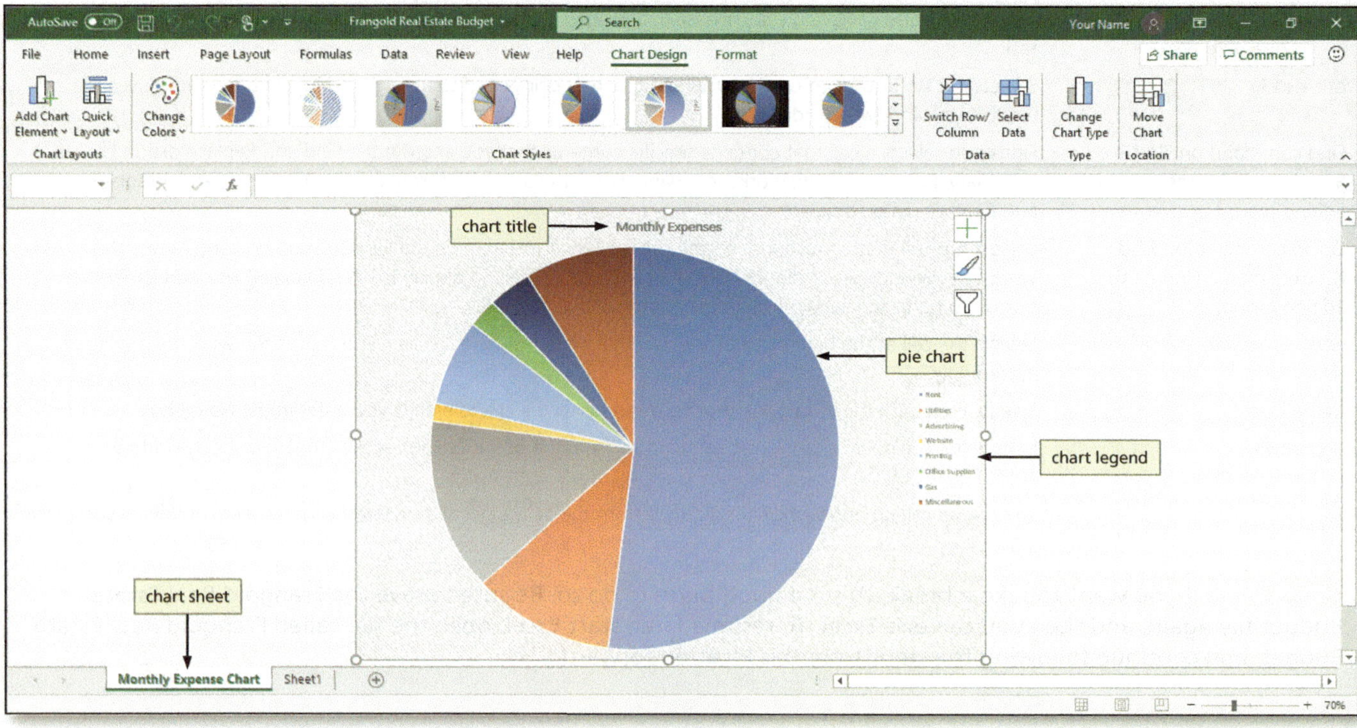

Figure 1–72

In this worksheet, the ranges you want to chart are the nonadjacent ranges A9:A16 (expense titles) and N9:N16 (yearly expense totals). The expense titles in the range A9:A16 will identify the slices of the pie chart; these entries are called category names. The range N9:N16 contains the data that determine the size of the slices in the pie; these entries are called the data series. A **data series** is a column or row in a datasheet and also the set of values represented in a chart. Because eight budget items are being charted, the pie chart contains eight slices.

To Add a Pie Chart

Why? When you want to see how each part relates to the whole, you use a pie chart. The following steps draw the pie chart.

1

- Select the range A9:A16 to identify the range of the category names for the pie chart.
- While holding down CTRL, select the nonadjacent range N9:N16.
- Click Insert on the ribbon to display the Insert tab.
- Click the 'Insert Pie or Doughnut Chart' button (Insert tab | Charts group) to display the Insert Pie or Doughnut Chart gallery (Figure 1–73).

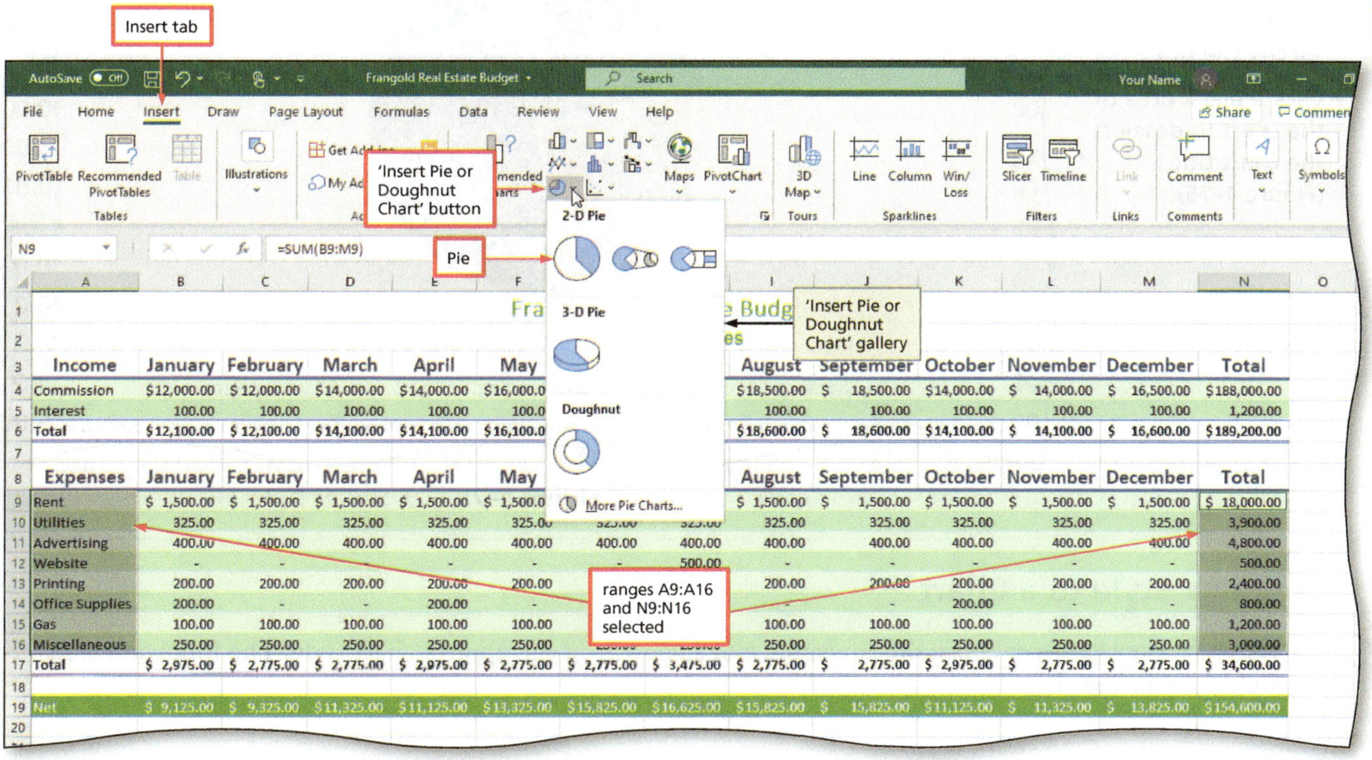

Figure 1–73

2

- Click Pie in the 2-D Pie category of the Insert Pie or Doughnut Chart gallery to insert the chart in the worksheet (Figure 1–74).

Q&A

Why have new tabs appeared on the ribbon?
The new tabs provide additional options and functionality when you are working with certain objects, such as charts, and only display when you are working with those objects.

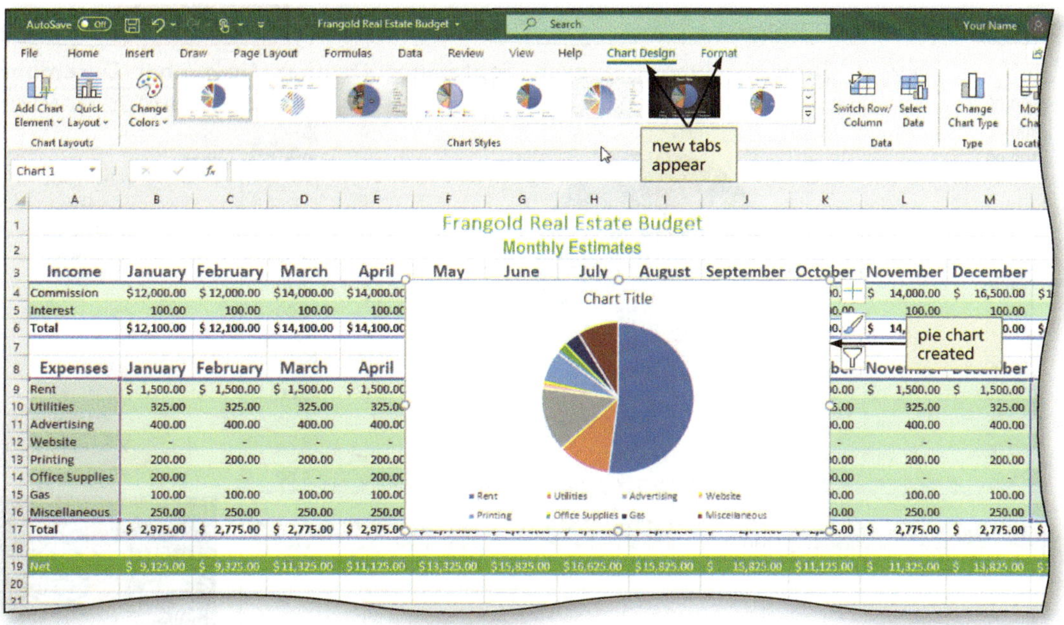

Figure 1–74

3

- Click the chart title to select it.
- Click and drag to select all the text in the chart title.
- Type `Monthly Expenses` to specify the title.
- Click a blank area of the chart to deselect the chart title (Figure 1–75).

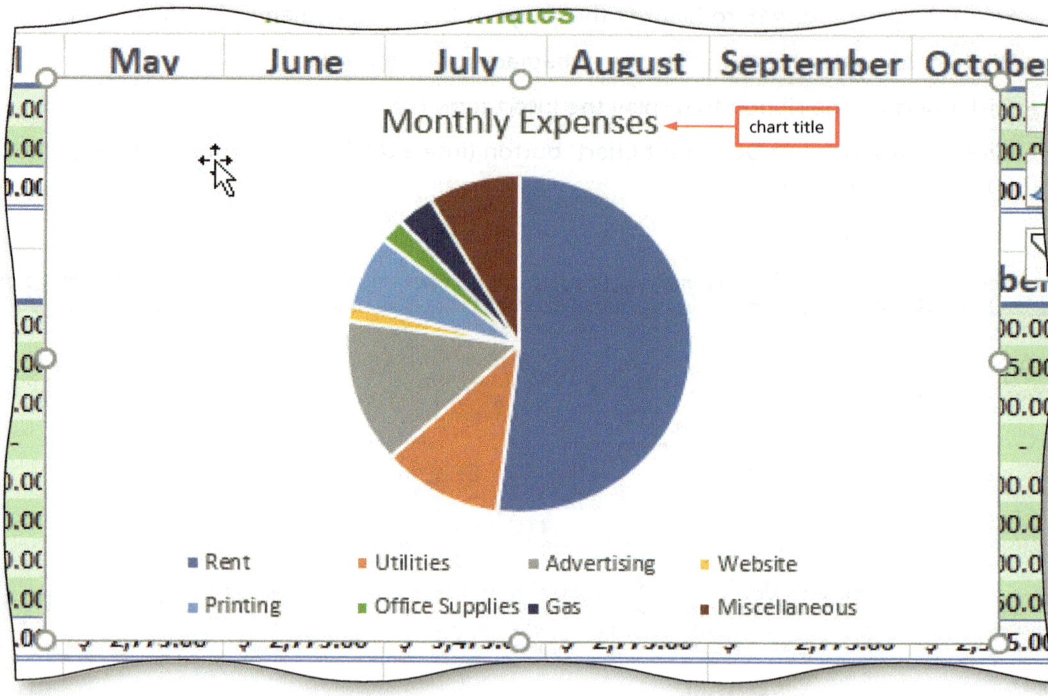

Figure 1–75

To Apply a Style to a Chart

Why? If you want to enhance the appearance of a chart, you can apply a chart style. The following steps apply Style 6 to the pie chart.

1

- Click the Chart Styles button to the right of the chart to display the Chart Styles gallery.
- Scroll in the Chart Styles gallery to display the Style 6 chart style (Figure 1–76).

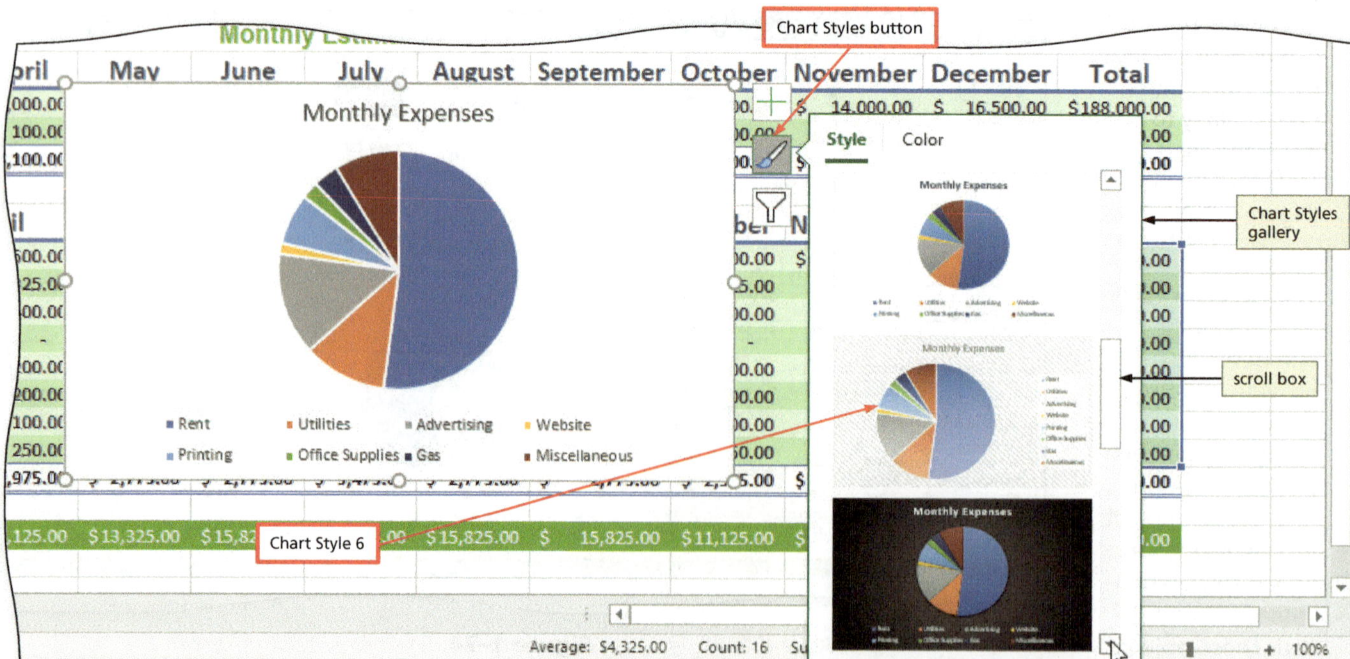

Figure 1–76

2

- Click Style 6 in the Chart Styles gallery to change the chart style to Style 6 (Figure 1–77).

3

- Click the Chart Styles button to close the Chart Styles gallery.

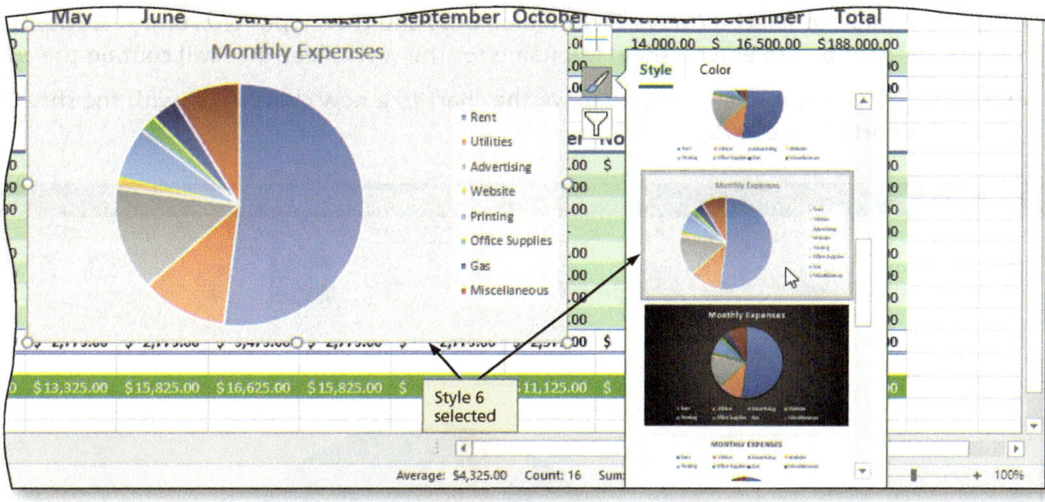

Figure 1–77

Changing the Sheet Tab Names and Colors

The sheet tabs at the bottom of the window allow you to navigate between any worksheet in the workbook. You click the sheet tab of the worksheet you want to view in the Excel window. By default, the worksheets are named Sheet1, Sheet2, and so on. The worksheet names become increasingly important as you move toward more sophisticated workbooks, especially workbooks in which you place objects such as charts on different sheets, which you will do in the next section, or you reference cells between worksheets.

BTW

Exploding a Pie Chart

If you want to draw attention to a particular slice in a pie chart, you can offset the slice so that it stands out from the rest. A pie chart with one or more slices offset is referred to as an exploded pie chart. To offset a slice, click the slice two times to select it (do not double-click) and then drag the slice outward.

To Move a Chart to a New Sheet

Why? By moving a chart to its own sheet, the size of the chart will increase, which can improve readability. The following steps move the pie chart to a chart sheet named Monthly Expenses.

1

- Click the Move Chart button (Chart Design tab | Location group) to display the Move Chart dialog box (Figure 1–78).

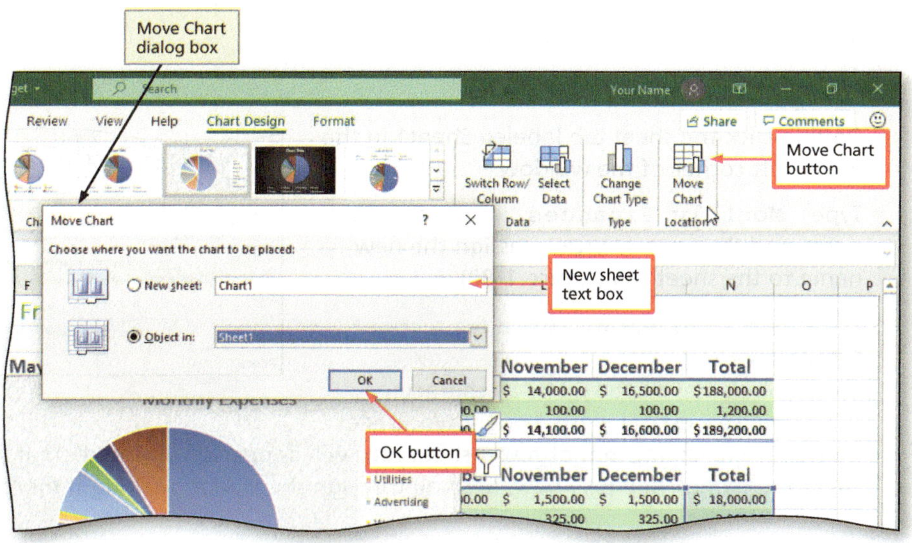

Figure 1–78

2

- Click New sheet to select it (Move Chart dialog box) and then type `Monthly Expense Chart` in the New sheet text box to enter a sheet tab name for the worksheet that will contain the chart.
- Click OK (Move Chart dialog box) to move the chart to a new chart sheet with the sheet tab name, Monthly Expense Chart (Figure 1–79).

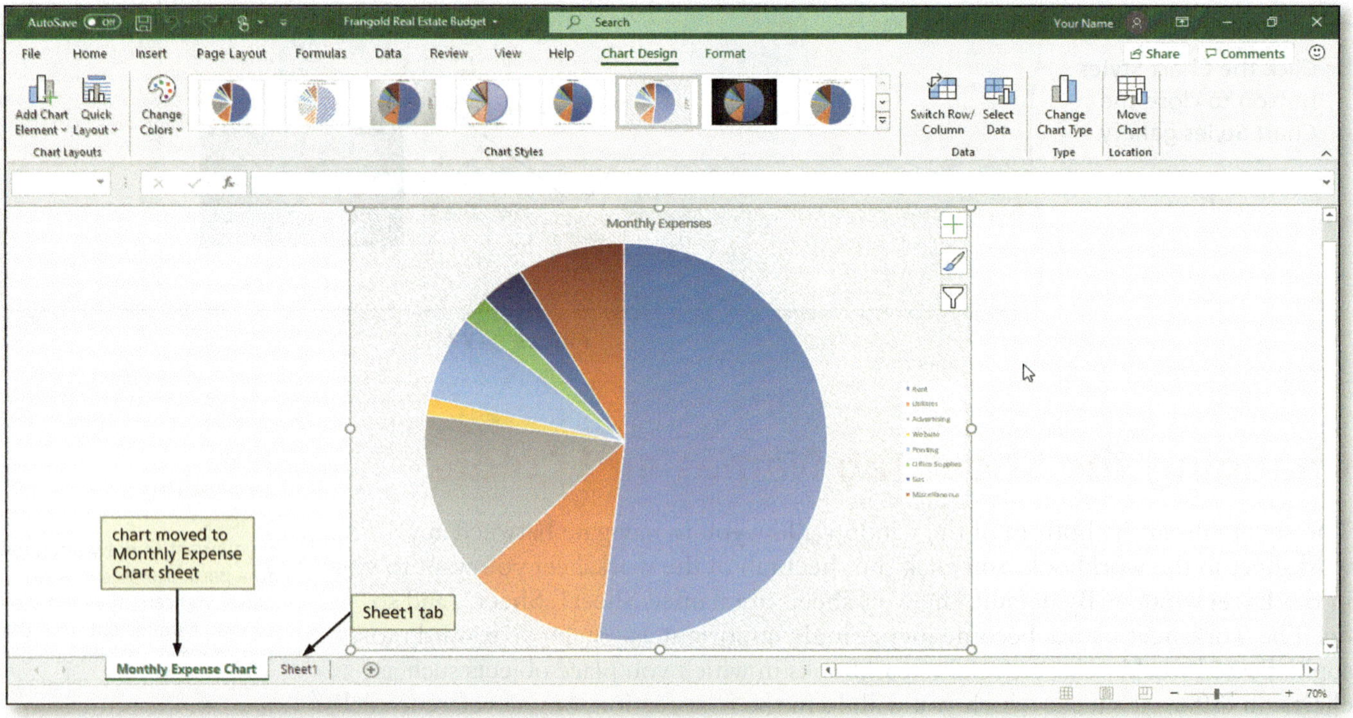

Figure 1–79

To Change the Sheet Tab Name and Color

You decide to change the name and color of the Sheet1 tab to Monthly Finances. **Why?** Use simple, meaningful names for each sheet tab. Sheet tab names often match the worksheet title. If a worksheet includes multiple titles in multiple sections of the worksheet, use a sheet tab name that encompasses the meaning of all of the sections. Changing the tab color also can help uniquely identify a sheet. The following steps rename the sheet tab and change the tab color.

1

- Double-click the sheet tab labeled Sheet1 in the lower-left corner of the window.
- Type `Monthly Finances` as the sheet tab name and then press ENTER to assign the new name to the sheet tab (Figure 1–80).

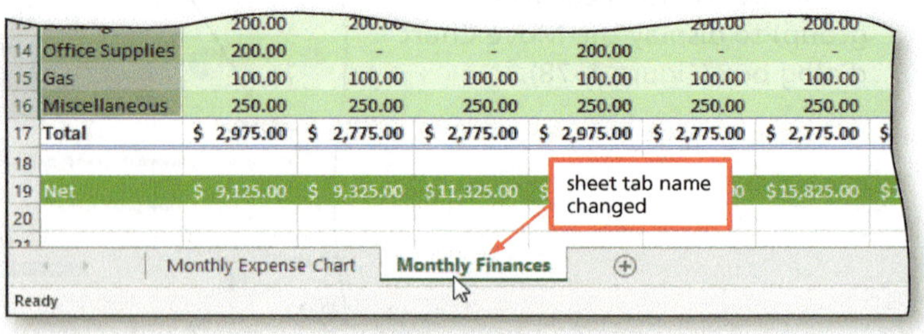

Figure 1–80

Q&A **What is the maximum length for a sheet tab name?**

Sheet tab names can be up to 31 characters (including spaces) in length. Longer worksheet names, however, mean that fewer sheet tabs will appear on your screen. If you have multiple worksheets with long sheet tab names, you may have to scroll through sheet tabs, making it more difficult to find a particular sheet.

2

- Right-click the sheet tab labeled Monthly Finances, in the lower-left corner of the window, to display a shortcut menu.
- Point to Tab Color on the shortcut menu to display the Tab Color gallery (Figure 1–81).

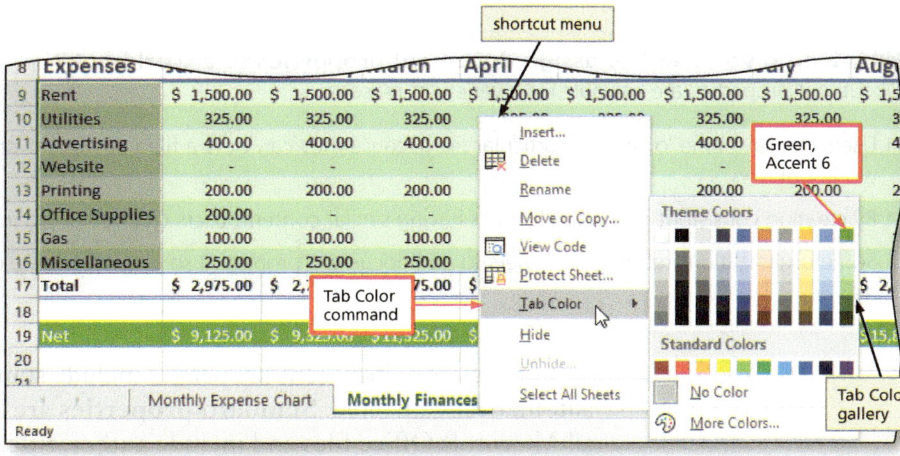

Figure 1–81

3

- Click Green, Accent 6 (column 10, row 1) in the Theme Colors area to change the color of the tab (Figure 1–82).
- If necessary, click Home on the ribbon to display the Home tab.
- Click the Save button on the Quick Access Toolbar to save the workbook again on the same storage location with the same file name.

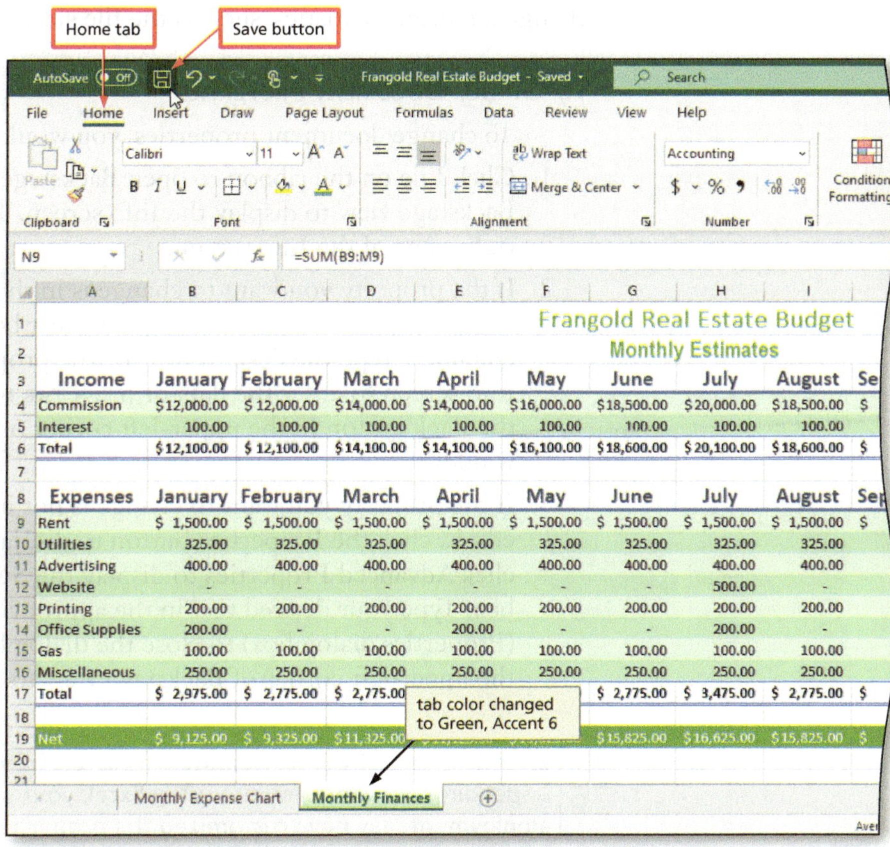

Figure 1–82

Q&A

Why should I save the workbook again?
You have made several modifications to the workbook since you last saved it. Thus, you should save it again.

What if I want to change the file name or storage location when I save the workbook?
Click Save As in Backstage view and follow the "To Save a Workbook" steps earlier in this module to specify a different file name and/or storage location.

Document Properties

Excel helps you organize and identify your files by using **document properties**, which are the details about a file such as the project author, title, and subject. For example, you could use the class name or topic to describe the workbook's purpose or content in the document properties.

Consider This

Why would you want to assign document properties to a workbook?
Document properties are valuable for a variety of reasons:

- Users can save time locating a particular file because they can view a file's document properties without opening the workbook.
- By creating consistent properties for files having similar content, users can better organize their workbooks.
- Some organizations require Excel users to add document properties so that other employees can view details about these files.

Common document properties include standard properties and those that are automatically updated. **Standard properties** are document properties associated with all Microsoft Office files and include author, title, and subject. **Automatically updated properties** are file system or document properties, such as the date you create or change a file, and statistics, such as the file size.

To Change Document Properties

To change document properties, you would follow these steps.

1. Click File on the ribbon to open Backstage view and then click the Info tab in Backstage view to display the Info screen. The Properties list is located in the right pane of the Info screen.
2. If the property you want to change is in the Properties list, click to the right of the property category to display a text box. (Note that not all properties are editable.) Type the desired text for the property and then click anywhere in the Info screen to enter the data or press TAB to navigate to the next property. Click the Back button in the upper-left corner of Backstage view to return to the Excel window.
3. If the property you want to change is not in the Properties list or you cannot edit it, click the Properties button to display the Properties menu, and then click Advanced Properties to display the Summary tab in the Properties dialog box. Type your desired text in the appropriate property text boxes. Click OK (Properties dialog box) to close the dialog box and then click the Back button in the upper-left corner of Backstage view to return to the workbook.

Q&A

Why do some of the document properties in my Properties dialog box contain data?
Depending on where you are using Excel, your school, university, or place of employment may have customized the properties.

Printing a Worksheet

After creating a worksheet, you may want to preview and print it. A **preview** is an onscreen view of your document prior to printing, to see exactly how the printed document will look. Printing a worksheet enables you to distribute the worksheet to others in a form that can be read or viewed but not edited. It is a good practice to save a workbook before printing a worksheet, in the event you experience difficulties printing.

Consider This

What is the best method for distributing a workbook?

The traditional method of distributing a workbook uses a printer to produce a hard copy. A **hard copy** or **printout** is information that exists on paper. Hard copies can be useful for the following reasons:

- Some people prefer proofreading a hard copy of a workbook rather than viewing it on the screen to check for errors and readability.
- Hard copies can serve as a backup reference if your storage medium is lost or becomes corrupted and you need to recreate the workbook.

Instead of distributing a hard copy of a workbook, users can distribute the workbook as an electronic image that mirrors the original workbook's appearance. An electronic image of a workbook is not an editable file; it simply displays a picture of the workbook. The electronic image of the workbook can be sent as an email attachment, posted on a website, or copied to a portable storage medium such as a USB flash drive. Two popular electronic image formats, sometimes called fixed formats, are PDF by Adobe Systems and XPS by Microsoft. In Excel, you can create electronic image files through the Save As dialog box and the Export, Share, and Print tabs in Backstage view. Electronic images of workbooks, such as PDF and XPS, can be useful for the following reasons:

- Users can view electronic images of workbooks without the software that created the original workbook (e.g., Excel). Specifically, to view a PDF file, you use a program called Adobe Acrobat Reader, which can be downloaded free from the Adobe website. Similarly, to view an XPS file, you use a program called XPS Viewer, which is included in the latest version of Windows.
- Sending electronic workbooks saves paper and printer supplies. Society encourages users to contribute to **green computing**, which involves reducing the electricity consumed and environmental waste generated when using computers, mobile devices, and related technologies.

To Preview and Print a Worksheet in Landscape Orientation

With the completed workbook saved, you may want to print it. **Why?** A printed copy is sometimes necessary for a report delivered in person.

An on-screen preview of your worksheet lets you see each page of your worksheet in the current orientation. **Portrait orientation** describes a printed copy with the short (8½") edge at the top of the printout; the printed page is taller than it is wide. **Landscape orientation** describes the page orientation in which the page is wider than it is tall. The print settings allow you to change the orientation as well as the paper size, margins, and scaling. **Scaling** determines how the worksheet fits on the page. You may want to adjust scaling to ensure that your data fits on one sheet of paper. **Why?** A printed worksheet may be difficult to read if it is spread across more than one page. The following steps print one or more hard copies of the contents of the worksheet.

1

- Click File on the ribbon to open Backstage view.
- Click Print in Backstage view to display the Print screen (Figure 1–83).

Q&A

How can I print multiple copies of my worksheet?
Increase the number in the Copies box on the Print screen.

What if I decide not to print the worksheet at this time?
Click the Back button in the upper-left corner of Backstage view to return to the workbook window.

Why does my Print screen look different?
Depending on the type of printer you select, your Print screen may display different options.

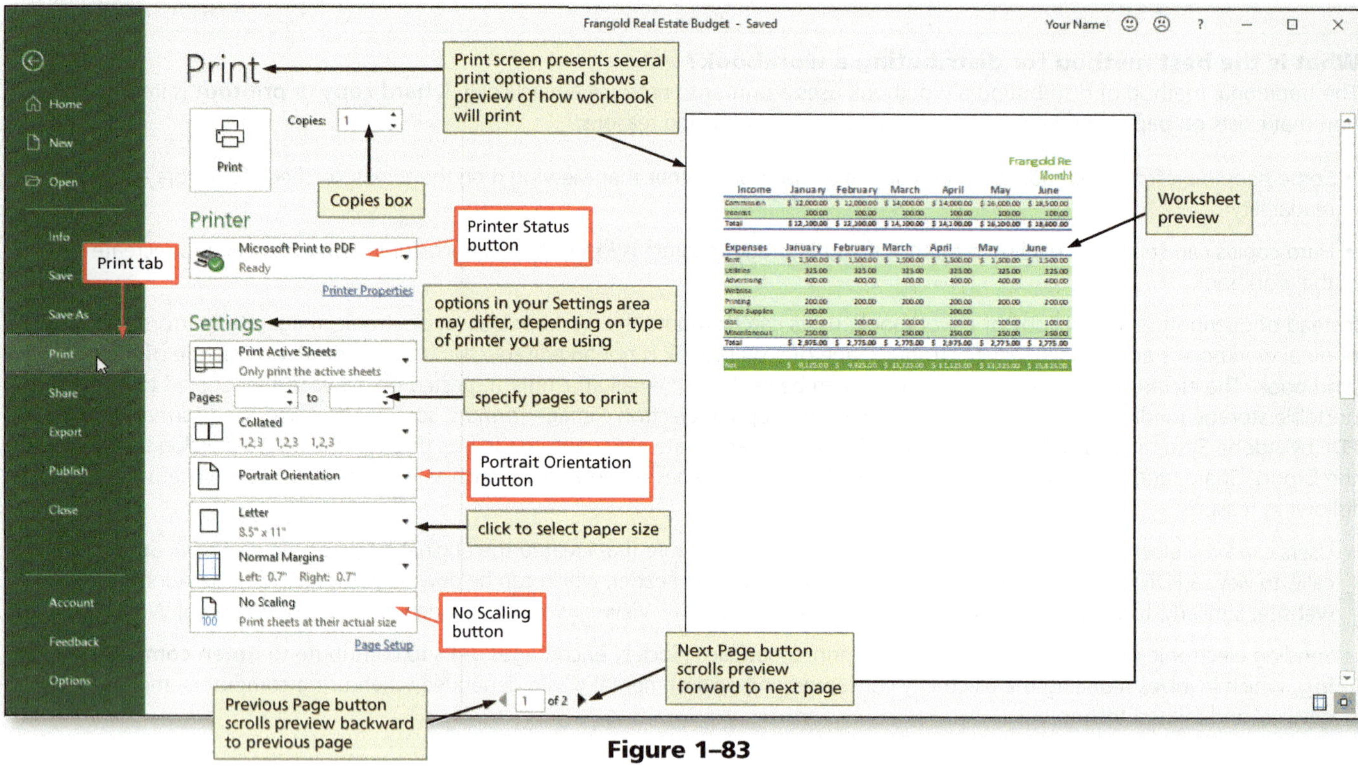

Figure 1–83

2

- Verify that the printer listed on the Printer Status button is the printer you want to use. If necessary, click the Printer Status button to display a list of available printer options and then click the desired printer to change the currently selected printer.
- If you want to print more than one copy, use the Copies up arrow to increase the number.
- If you want to change the paper size, use the paper size arrow (which currently reads Letter 8.5" × 11") to view and select a different one.

3

- Click the Portrait Orientation button in the Settings area and then select Landscape Orientation to change the orientation of the page to landscape.
- Click the No Scaling button and then select 'Fit Sheet on One Page' to print the entire worksheet on one page (Figure 1–84).

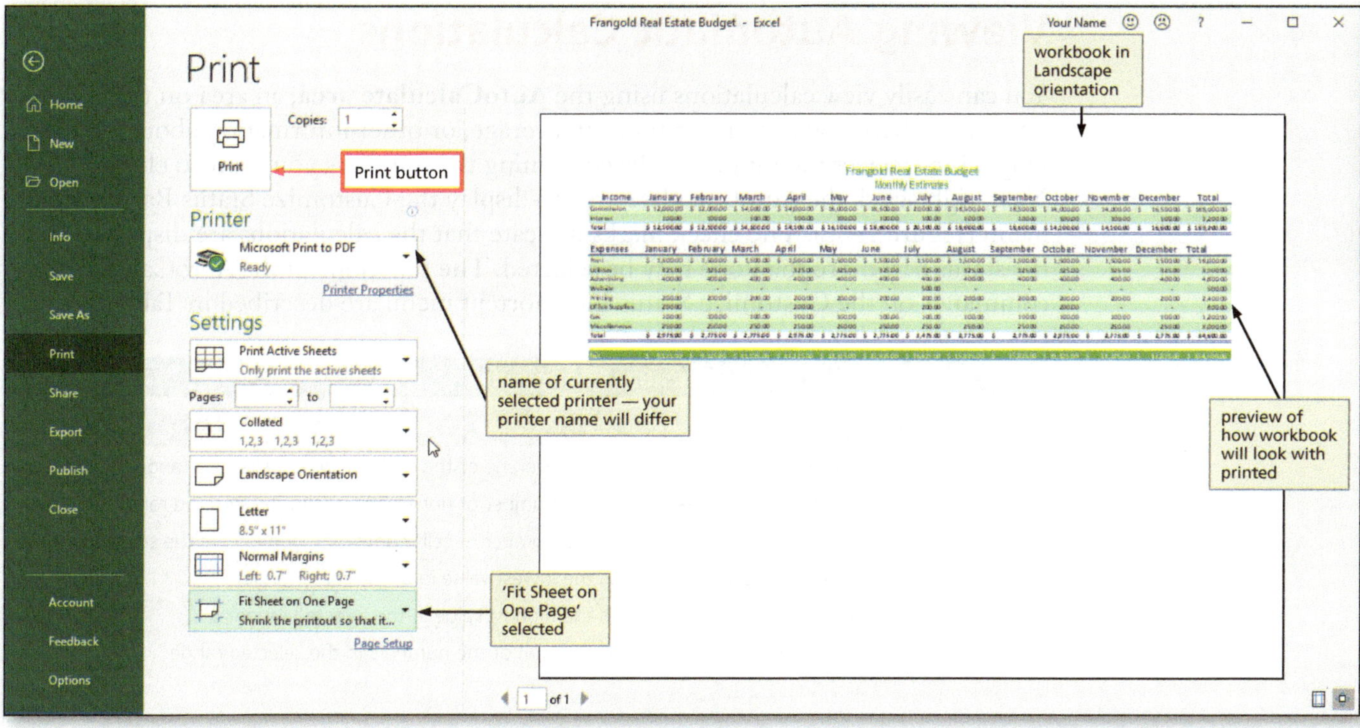

Figure 1–84

4

- Click the Print button on the Print screen to print the worksheet in landscape orientation on the currently selected printer.
- When the printer stops, retrieve the hard copy (Figure 1–85).

Q&A

Do I have to wait until my worksheet is complete to print it?
No, you can print a document at any time while you are creating it.

Frangold Real Estate Budget
Monthly Estimates

Income	January	February	March	April	May	June	July	August	September	October	November	December	Total
Commission	$ 12,000.00	$ 12,000.00	$ 14,000.00	$ 14,000.00	$ 16,000.00	$ 18,500.00	$ 20,000.00	$ 18,500.00	$ 18,500.00	$ 14,000.00	$ 14,000.00	$ 16,500.00	$ 188,000.00
Interest	100.00	100.00	100.00	100.00	100.00	100.00	100.00	100.00	100.00	100.00	100.00	100.00	1,200.00
Total	**$ 12,100.00**	**$ 12,100.00**	**$ 14,100.00**	**$ 14,100.00**	**$ 16,100.00**	**$ 18,600.00**	**$ 20,100.00**	**$ 18,600.00**	**$ 18,600.00**	**$ 14,100.00**	**$ 14,100.00**	**$ 16,600.00**	**$ 189,200.00**

Expenses	January	February	March	April	May	June	July	August	September	October	November	December	Total
Rent	$ 1,500.00	$ 1,500.00	$ 1,500.00	$ 1,500.00	$ 1,500.00	$ 1,500.00	$ 1,500.00	$ 1,500.00	$ 1,500.00	$ 1,500.00	$ 1,500.00	$ 1,500.00	$ 18,000.00
Utilities	325.00	325.00	325.00	325.00	325.00	325.00	325.00	325.00	325.00	325.00	325.00	325.00	3,900.00
Advertising	400.00	400.00	400.00	400.00	400.00	400.00	400.00	400.00	400.00	400.00	400.00	400.00	4,800.00
Website	-	-	-	-	-	-	500.00	-	-	-	-	-	500.00
Printing	200.00	200.00	200.00	200.00	200.00	200.00	200.00	200.00	200.00	200.00	200.00	200.00	2,400.00
Office Supplies	200.00	-	-	200.00	-	-	200.00	-	-	200.00	-	-	800.00
Gas	100.00	100.00	100.00	100.00	100.00	100.00	100.00	100.00	100.00	100.00	100.00	100.00	1,200.00
Miscellaneous	250.00	250.00	250.00	250.00	250.00	250.00	250.00	250.00	250.00	250.00	250.00	250.00	3,000.00
Total	**$ 2,975.00**	**$ 2,775.00**	**$ 2,775.00**	**$ 2,975.00**	**$ 2,775.00**	**$ 2,775.00**	**$ 3,475.00**	**$ 2,775.00**	**$ 2,775.00**	**$ 2,975.00**	**$ 2,775.00**	**$ 2,775.00**	**$ 34,600.00**
Net	$ 9,125.00	$ 9,325.00	$ 11,325.00	$ 11,125.00	$ 13,325.00	$ 15,825.00	$ 16,625.00	$ 15,825.00	$ 15,825.00	$ 11,125.00	$ 11,325.00	$ 13,825.00	$ 154,600.00

Figure 1–85

Other Ways

1. Press CTRL+P to open the Print screen, press ENTER

Viewing Automatic Calculations

You can easily view calculations using the **AutoCalculate area**, an area on the Excel status bar where you can view a total, an average, or other information about a selected range. First, select the range of cells containing the numbers you want to check. Next, right-click the AutoCalculate area to display the Customize Status Bar shortcut menu (Figure 1–86). The check marks indicate that the calculations are displayed in the status bar; more than one may be selected. The functions of the AutoCalculate commands on the Customize Status Bar shortcut menu are described in Table 1–5.

Table 1–5 Commonly Used Status Bar Commands

Command	Function
Average	AutoCalculate area displays the average of the numbers in the selected range
Count	AutoCalculate area displays the number of nonempty cells in the selected range
Numerical Count	AutoCalculate area displays the number of cells containing numbers in the selected range
Minimum	AutoCalculate area displays the lowest value in the selected range
Maximum	AutoCalculate area displays the highest value in the selected range
Sum	AutoCalculate area displays the sum of the numbers in the selected range

To Use the AutoCalculate Area to Determine a Maximum

The following steps determine the largest monthly total in the budget. **Why?** Sometimes, you want a quick analysis, which can be especially helpful when your worksheet contains a lot of data.

1

- Select the range B19:M19. Right-click the status bar to display the Customize Status Bar shortcut menu (Figure 1–86).

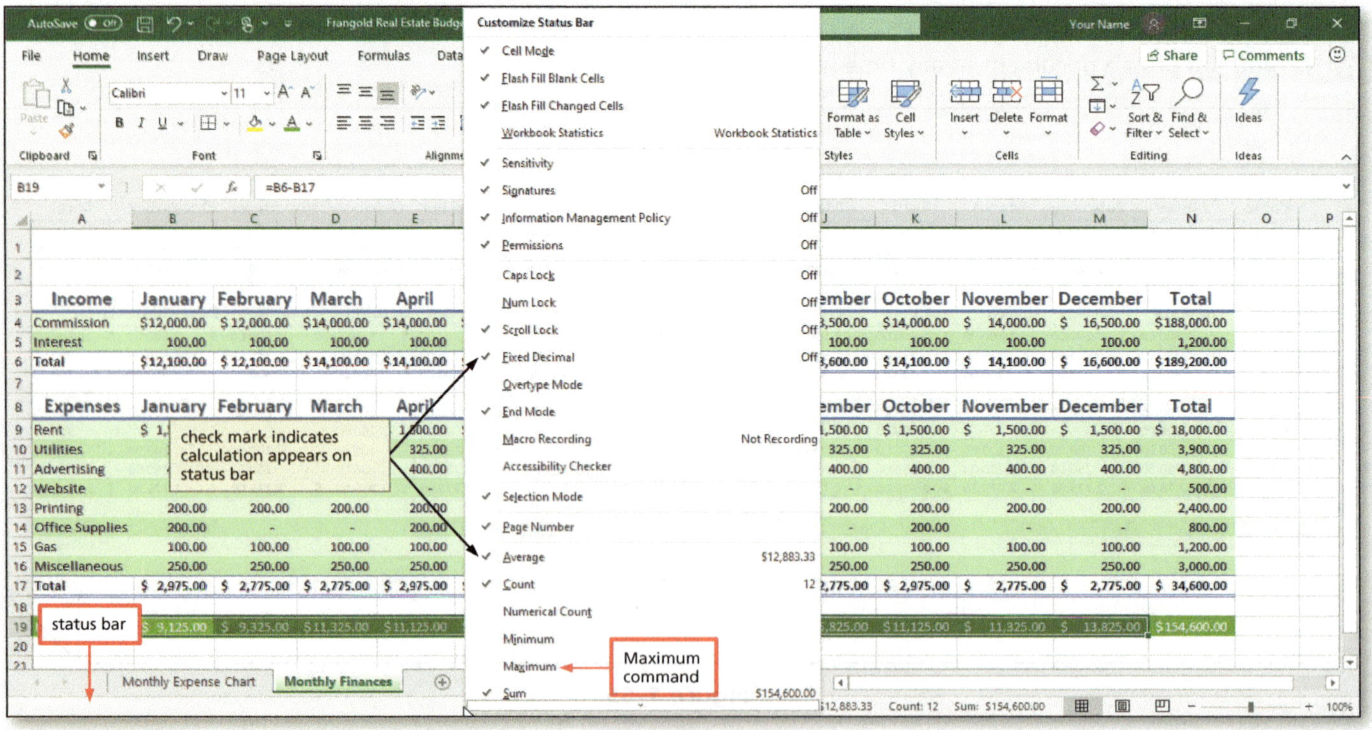

Figure 1–86

2

- Click Maximum on the shortcut menu to display the Maximum value in the range B19:M19 in the AutoCalculate area of the status bar.
- If necessary, click anywhere on the worksheet to close the shortcut menu (Figure 1–87).

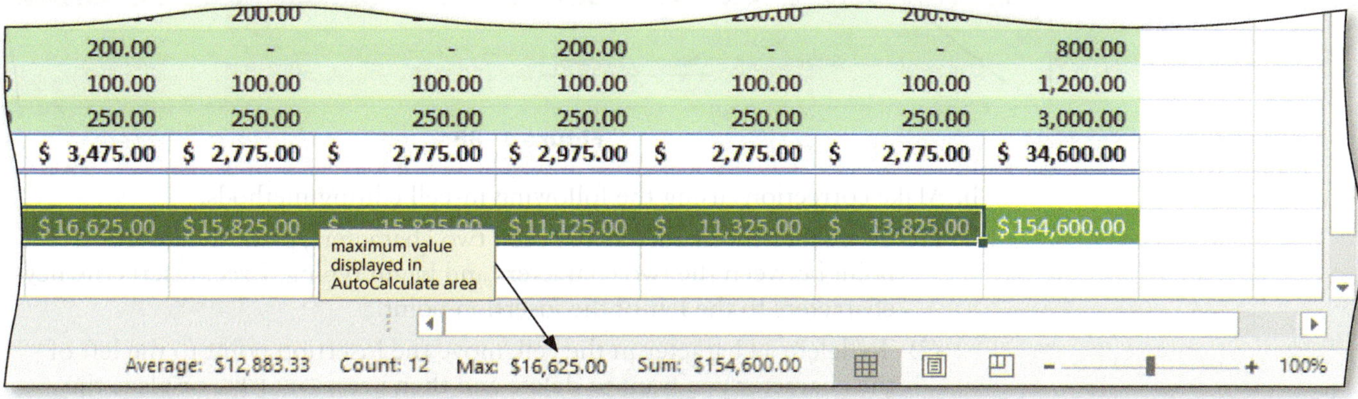

Figure 1–87

3

- Right-click the AutoCalculate area and then click Maximum on the shortcut menu to deselect it. The Maximum value will no longer appear on the status bar.
- If necessary, close the shortcut menu.

Correcting Errors

You can correct data entry errors on a worksheet using one of several methods. The method you choose will depend on the extent of the error and whether you notice it while entering the data or after you have entered the incorrect data into the cell.

Correcting Errors while Entering Data into a Cell

If you notice an error while you are entering data into a cell, press BACKSPACE to erase the incorrect character(s) and then enter the correct character(s). If the error is a major one, click the Cancel box in the formula bar or press ESC to erase the entire entry and then reenter the data.

Correcting Errors after Entering Data into a Cell

If you find an error in the worksheet after entering the data, you can correct the error in one of two ways:

1. If the entry is short, select the cell, retype the entry correctly, and then click the Enter button or press ENTER. The new entry will replace the old entry.
2. If the entry in the cell is long and the errors are minor, using Edit mode may be a better choice than retyping the cell entry. In **Edit mode**, a mode that lets you perform in-cell editing, Excel displays the active cell entry in the formula bar and a flashing insertion point in the active cell. There you can edit the contents directly in the cell — a procedure called **in-cell editing.**
   a. Double-click the cell containing the error to switch Excel to Edit mode (Figure 1–88).

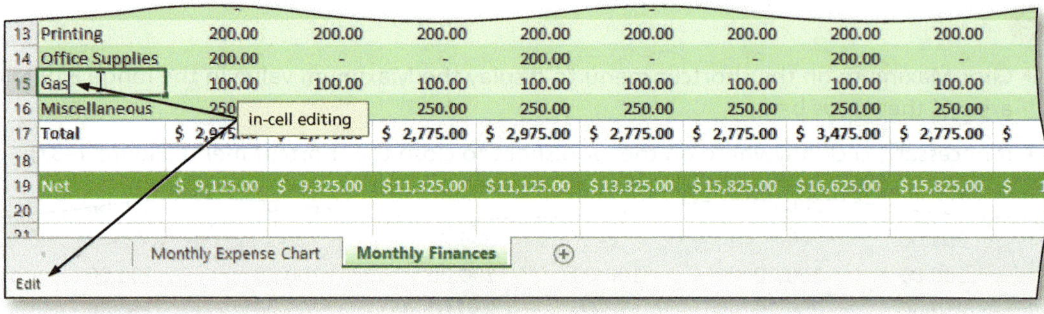

Figure 1–88

b. Make corrections using the following in-cell editing methods.

(1) To insert new characters between two characters, place the insertion point between the two characters and begin typing. Excel inserts the new characters to the left of the insertion point.

(2) To delete a character in the cell, move the insertion point to the left of the character you want to delete and then press DELETE, or place the insertion point to the right of the character you want to delete and then press BACKSPACE. You also can drag to select the character or adjacent characters you want to delete and then press DELETE or CTRL+X or click the Cut button (Home tab | Clipboard group).

(3) When you are finished editing an entry, click the Enter button or press ENTER.

There are two ways to enter data in Edit mode: Insert mode and Overtype mode. **Insert mode** is the default Excel mode that inserts a character and moves all characters to the right of the typed character one position to the right. You can change to Overtype mode by pressing INSERT. In **Overtype mode**, Excel replaces, or overtypes, the character to the right of the insertion point. The INSERT key toggles the keyboard between Insert mode and Overtype mode.

While in Edit mode, you may want to move the insertion point to various points in the cell, select portions of the data in the cell, or switch from inserting characters to overtyping characters. Table 1–6 summarizes the more common tasks performed during in-cell editing.

Table 1–6 Summary of In-Cell Editing Tasks

	Task	Mouse Operation	Keyboard
1.	Move the insertion point to the beginning of data in a cell.	Point to the left of the first character and click.	Press HOME.
2.	Move the insertion point to the end of data in a cell.	Point to the right of the last character and click.	Press END.
3.	Move the insertion point anywhere in a cell.	Point to the appropriate position and click the character.	Press RIGHT ARROW or LEFT ARROW.
4.	Highlight one or more adjacent characters.	Drag through adjacent characters.	Press SHIFT+RIGHT ARROW or SHIFT+LEFT ARROW.
5.	Select all data in a cell.	Double-click the cell with the insertion point in the cell if the data in the cell contains no spaces.	
6.	Delete selected characters.	Click the Cut button (Home tab | Clipboard group).	Press DELETE.
7.	Delete characters to the left of the insertion point.		Press BACKSPACE.
8.	Delete characters to the right of the insertion point.		Press DELETE.
9.	Toggle between Insert and Overtype modes.		Press INSERT.

Undoing the Last Cell Entry

The Undo button on the Quick Access Toolbar (Figure 1–89) allows you to erase recent cell entries. Thus, if you enter incorrect data in a cell and notice it immediately, click the Undo button and Excel changes the cell entry to what it was prior to the incorrect data entry.

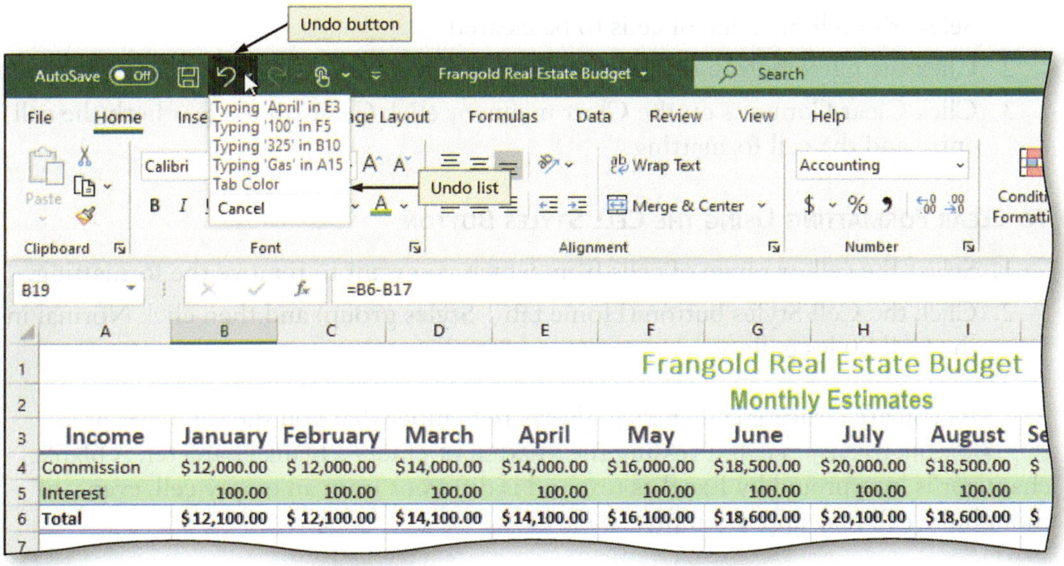

Figure 1–89

Excel remembers the last 100 actions you have completed. Thus, you can undo up to 100 previous actions by clicking the Undo arrow to display the Undo list and then clicking the action to be undone (Figure 1–89). You can drag through several actions in the Undo list to undo all of them at once. If no actions are available for Excel to undo, then the dimmed appearance of the Undo button indicates that it is unavailable.

The Redo button, next to the Undo button on the Quick Access Toolbar, allows you to repeat previous actions; that is, if you accidentally undo an action, you can use the Redo button to perform the action again.

Clearing a Cell or Range of Cells

If you enter data into the wrong cell or range of cells, you can erase, or clear, the data using one of the first four methods listed below. The fifth method clears the formatting from the selected cells. To clear a cell or range of cells, you would perform the following steps:

To Clear Cell Entries Using the Fill Handle

1. Select the cell or range of cells and then point to the fill handle so that the pointer changes to a crosshair.
2. Drag the fill handle back into the selected cell or range until a shadow covers the cell or cells you want to erase.

To Clear Cell Entries Using the Shortcut Menu

1. Select the cell or range of cells to be cleared.
2. Right-click the selection.
3. Click Clear Contents on the shortcut menu.

To Clear Cell Entries Using the Delete Key

1. Select the cell or range of cells to be cleared.
2. Press DELETE.

To Clear Cell Entries and Formatting Using the Clear Button

1. Select the cell or range of cells to be cleared.
2. Click the Clear button (Home tab | Editing group).
3. Click Clear Contents on the Clear menu, or click Clear All to clear both the cell entry and the cell formatting.

To Clear Formatting Using the Cell Styles Button

1. Select the cell or range of cells from which you want to remove the formatting.
2. Click the Cell Styles button (Home tab | Styles group) and then click Normal in the Cell Styles gallery.

As you are clearing cell entries, always remember that you should never press the SPACEBAR to clear a cell. Pressing the SPACEBAR enters a blank character. A blank character is interpreted by Excel as text and is different from an empty cell, even though the cell may appear empty.

Clearing the Entire Worksheet

If the required worksheet edits are extensive or if the requirements drastically change, you may want to clear the entire worksheet and start over. To clear the worksheet or delete an embedded chart, you would use the following steps.

To Clear the Entire Worksheet

1. Click the Select All button on the worksheet. The Select All button is located above the row 1 identifier and to the left of the column A heading.
2. Click the Clear button (Home tab | Editing group) and then click Clear All on the menu to delete both the entries and formats.

The Select All button selects the entire worksheet. To clear an unsaved workbook, click the Close Window button on the workbook's title bar or click the Close button in Backstage view. Click the No button if the Microsoft Excel dialog box asks if you want to save changes. To start a new, blank workbook, click the New button in Backstage view.

Using Excel Help

Once an Office app's Help window is open, you can use several methods to navigate Help. You can search for help by using the Help pane or the Search box.

To Obtain Help Using the Search Text Box

Assume for the following example that you want to know more about functions. The following steps use the Search text box to obtain useful information about functions by entering the word, functions, as search text. **Why?** You may not know the exact help topic you are looking to find, so using keywords can help narrow your search.

1

- Click Help on the ribbon to display the Help tab (Figure 1–90).

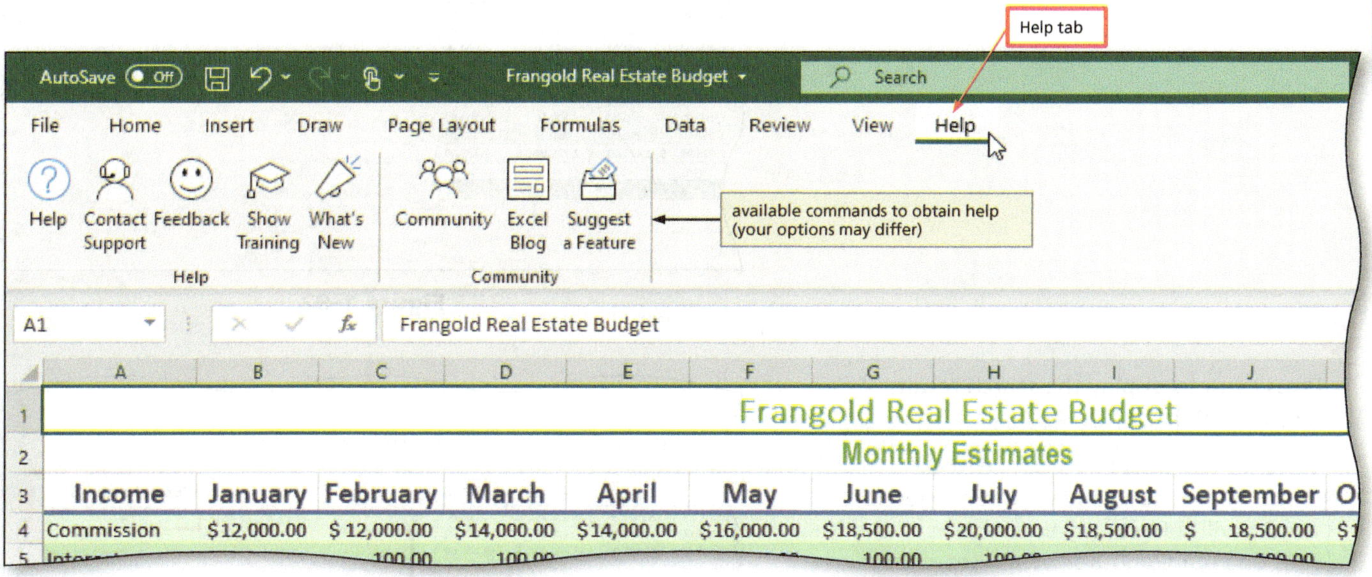

Figure 1–90

2

- Click the Help button (Help group) to display the Help pane (Figure 1–91).

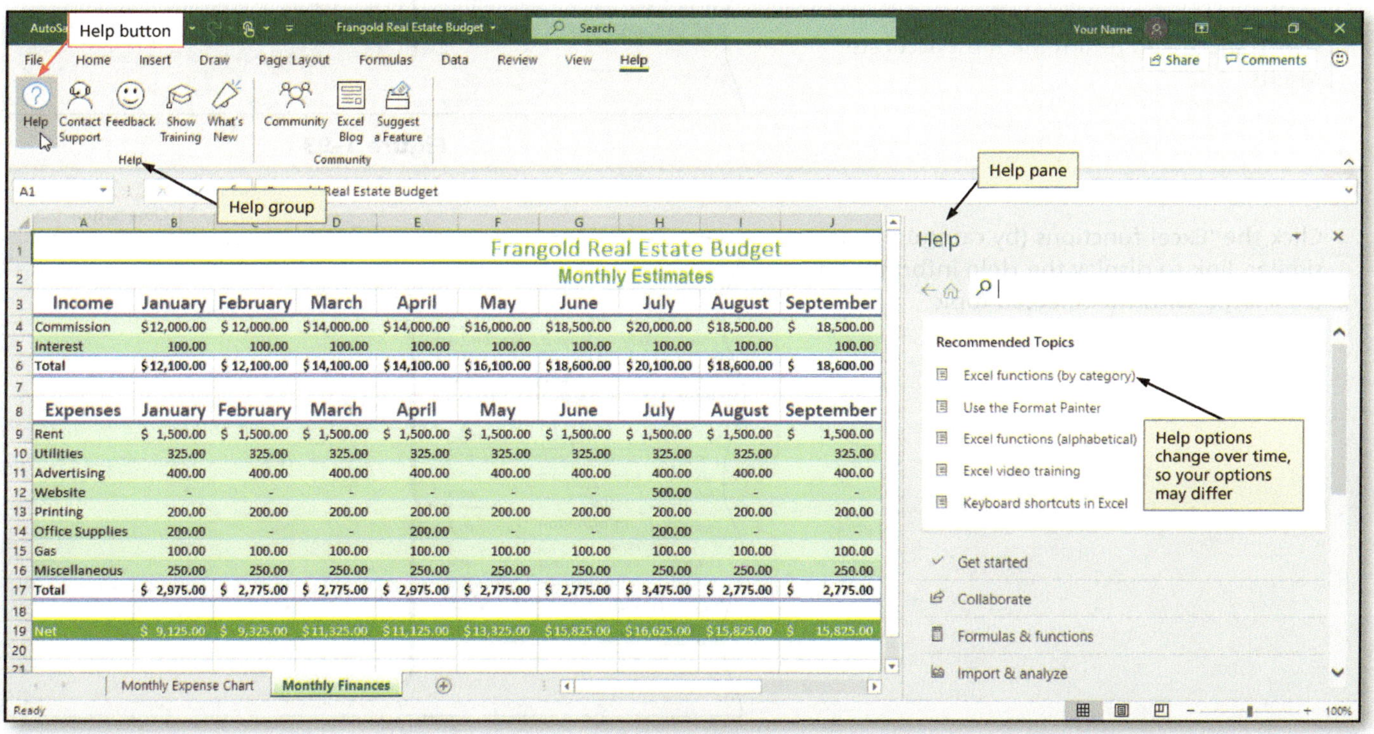

Figure 1–91

3

- Type **`functions`** in the Search help box at the top of the Help pane to enter the search text (Figure 1–92).

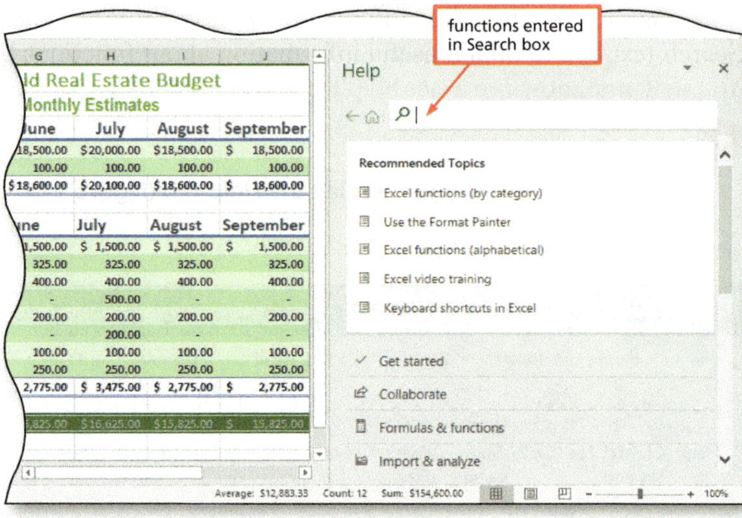

Figure 1–92

4

- Press ENTER to display the search results (Figure 1–93).

Q&A

Why do my search results differ?
If you do not have an Internet connection, your results will reflect only the content of the Help files on your computer. When searching for help online, results also can change as content is added, deleted, and updated on the online Help webpages maintained by Microsoft.

Why were my search results not very helpful?
When initiating a search, be sure to check the spelling of the search text; also, keep your search specific to return the most accurate results.

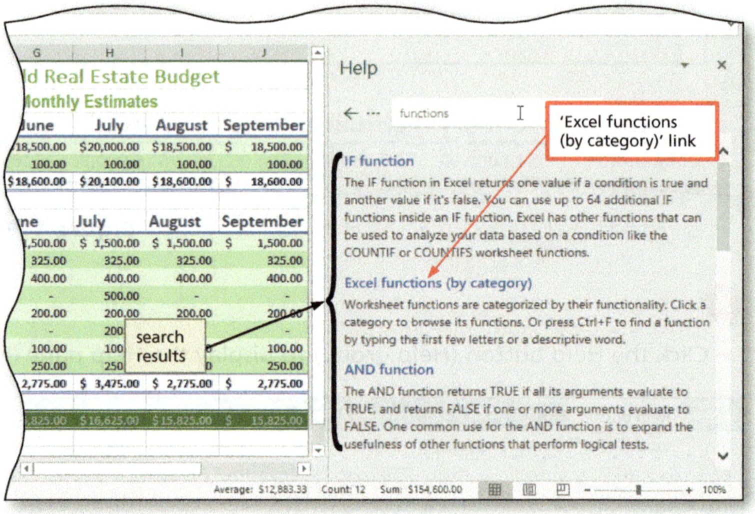

Figure 1–93

5

- Click the 'Excel functions (by category)', or similar, link to display the Help information associated with the selected topic (Figure 1–94).

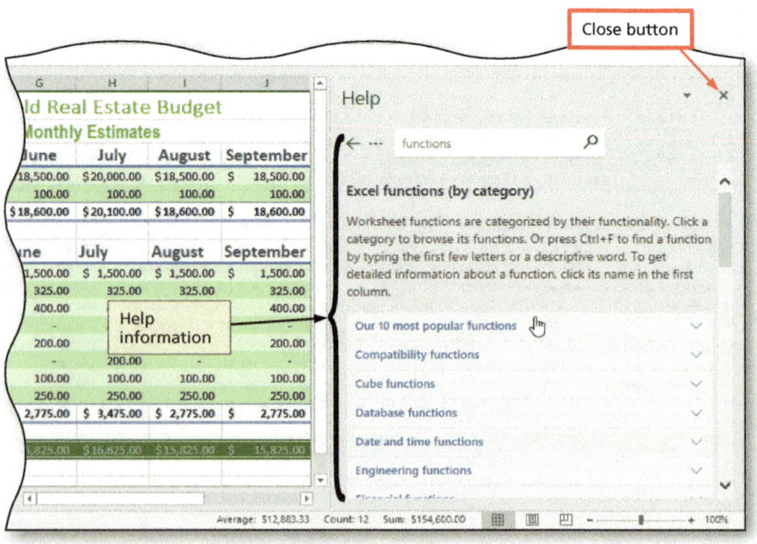

Figure 1–94

6

- Click the Close button in the Help pane to close the pane.
- Click Home on the ribbon to display the Home tab.

Obtaining Help while Working in an Office App

You also can access the Help functionality without first opening the Help pane and initiating a search. For example, you may be confused about how a particular command works, or you may be presented with a dialog box that you are not sure how to use.

If you want to learn more about a command, point to its button and wait for the ScreenTip to appear, as shown in Figure 1–95. If the Help icon and 'Tell me more' link appear in the ScreenTip, click the 'Tell me more' link (or press F1 while pointing to the button) to open the Help window associated with that command.

Dialog boxes also contain Help buttons, as shown in Figure 1–96. Clicking the Help button (or pressing F1) while the dialog box is displayed opens a Help window, which will display help contents specific to the dialog box, if available. If no help file is available for that particular dialog box, then the window will display the Help home page.

As mentioned previously, the Search box is integrated into the title bar in Excel and most other Office apps and can perform a variety of functions, including providing easy access to commands and help content as you type.

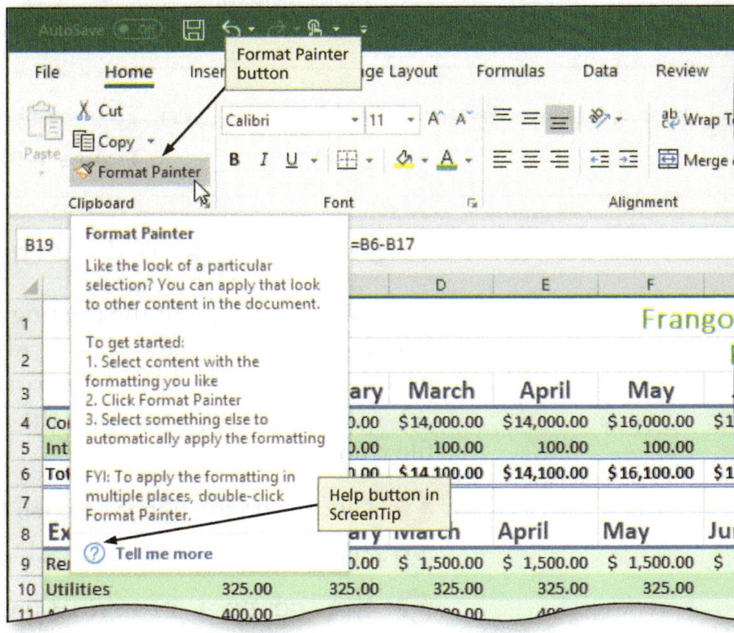

Figure 1–95

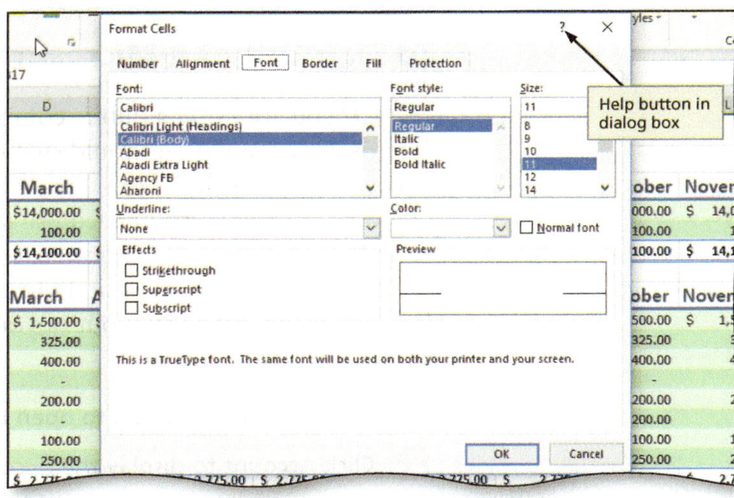

Figure 1–96

To Obtain Help Using the Search Box

If you are having trouble finding a command in Excel, you can use the Search box to search for the function you are trying to perform. As you type, the Search box will suggest commands that match the search text you are entering. **Why?** You can use the Search box to access commands quickly you otherwise may be unable to find on the ribbon. The following steps find commands related to headers and footers.

1

- Type `header and footer` in the Search box and watch the search results appear (Figure 1–97).

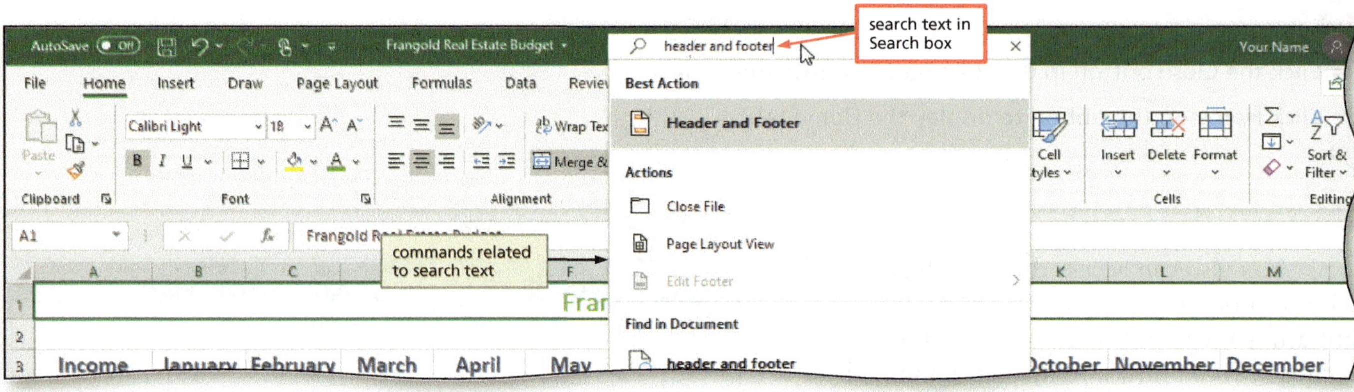

Figure 1–97

To Save a Workbook with a Different File Name

To save a copy of the existing file, you can save the file with a new file name. **Why?** You have finished working on the Frangold Real Estate Budget workbook and would like to save a copy of the workbook with a new file name.

The following steps save the Frangold Real Estate Budget workbook with a new file name.

1. Click File on the ribbon to open Backstage view.
2. Click Save As in Backstage view to display the Save As screen.
3. Type `SC_EX_1_Frangold` in the File name text box, replacing the existing file name.
4. Click the Save button to save the workbook with the new name.

To Sign Out of a Microsoft Account

If you are using a public computer or otherwise want to sign out of your Microsoft account, you should sign out of the account from the Accounts screen in Backstage view. **Why?** For security reasons, you should sign out of your Microsoft account when you are finished using a public or shared computer. Staying signed in to your Microsoft account might enable others to access your files.

The following steps sign out of a Microsoft account and exit the Excel program. If you do not want to sign out of your Microsoft account or exit Excel, read these steps without performing them.

1. Click File on the ribbon to open Backstage view.
2. Click Account to display the Account screen (Figure 1–98).
3. Click the Sign out link, which displays the Remove Account dialog box. If a Can't remove Windows accounts dialog box appears instead of the Remove Account dialog box, click OK and skip the remaining steps.

Q&A **Why does a Can't remove Windows accounts dialog box appear?**
If you signed in to Windows using your Microsoft account, then you also must sign out from Windows rather than signing out from within Excel. When you are finished using Windows, be sure to sign out at that time.

4. Click the Yes button (Remove Account dialog box) to sign out of your Microsoft account on this computer.

Q&A **Should I sign out of Windows after removing my Microsoft account?**
When you are finished using the computer, you should sign out of Windows for maximum security.

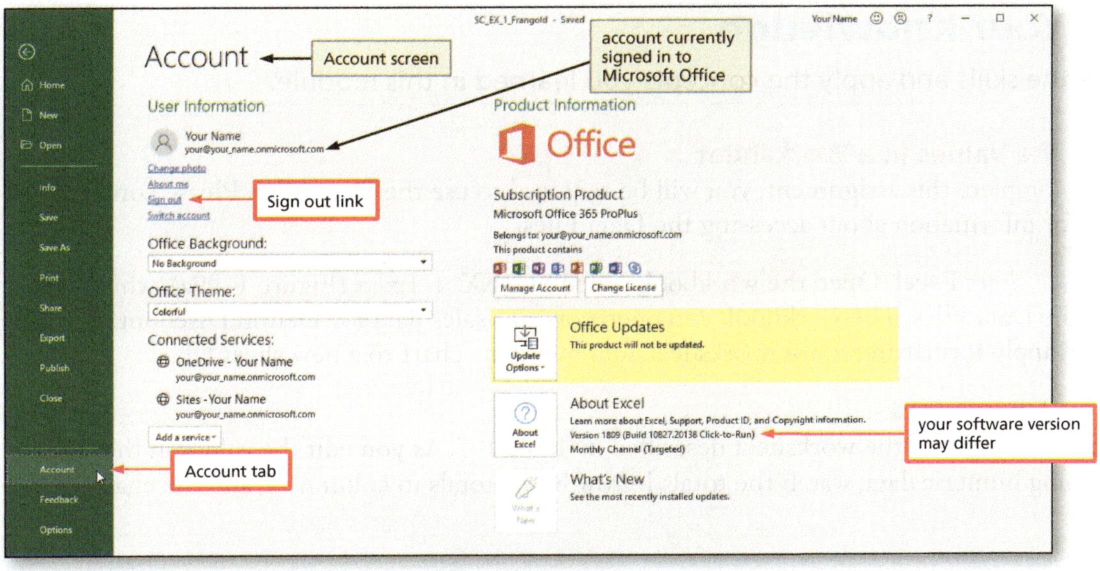

Figure 1–98

5. Click the Back button in the upper-left corner of Backstage view to return to the document.
6. sam Click the Close button to close the workbook and exit Microsoft Excel. If you are prompted to save changes, click Yes.

Summary

In this module you have learned how to create a real estate budget worksheet and chart. Topics covered included starting Excel and creating a blank workbook, selecting a cell, entering text, entering numbers, calculating a sum, using the fill handle, formatting a worksheet, adding a pie chart, changing sheet tab names and colors, printing a worksheet, using the AutoCalculate area, correcting errors, and obtaining help.

Consider This: Plan Ahead

What decisions will you need to make when creating workbooks and charts in the future?

Use these guidelines as you complete the assignments in this module and create your own spreadsheets outside of this class.

1. Determine the workbook structure.
   a) Determine the data you will need for your workbook.
   b) Sketch a layout of your data and your chart.
2. Create the worksheet.
   a) Enter titles, subtitles, and headings.
   b) Enter data, functions, and formulas.
3. Format the worksheet.
   a) Format the titles, subtitles, and headings using styles.
   b) Format the totals.
   c) Format the numbers.
   d) Format the text.
   e) Adjust column widths.
4. Create the chart.
   a) Determine the type of chart to use.
   b) Determine the chart title and data.
   c) Determine the chart location
   d) Format the chart.

Apply Your Knowledge

Reinforce the skills and apply the concepts you learned in this module.

Changing the Values in a Worksheet

Note: To complete this assignment, you will be required to use the Data Files. Please contact your instructor for information about accessing the Data Files.

Instructions: Start Excel. Open the workbook called SC_EX_1-1.xlsx (Figure 1–99a), which is located in the Data Files. The workbook you open contains sales data for Delton Discount. You are to edit data, apply formatting to the worksheet, and move the chart to a new sheet tab.

Perform the following tasks:

1. Make the changes to the worksheet described in Table 1–7. As you edit the values in the cells containing numeric data, watch the totals in row 8, the totals in column H, and the chart change.

Table 1–7 New Worksheet Data

Cell	Change Cell Contents To
A2	Monthly Departmental Sales
B5	13442.36
C7	115528.13
D5	24757.85
E6	39651.54
F7	29667.88
G6	19585.46

2. Change the worksheet title in cell A1 to the Title cell style and then merge and center it across columns A through H.
3. Use buttons in the Font group on the Home tab on the ribbon to change the worksheet subtitle in cell A2 to 14-point font and then merge and center it across columns A through H. Change the font color of cell A2 to Blue, Accent 1, Darker 50%.
4. Name the worksheet, Department Sales, and apply the Blue, Accent 1, Darker 50% color to the sheet tab.
5. Move the chart to a new sheet called Sales Analysis Chart. Change the chart title to MONTHLY SALES TOTALS.

   If requested by your instructor, on the Department Sales worksheet, replace Delton in cell A1 with your last name.
6. Save the workbook with the file name, SC_EX_1_Delton, and submit the revised workbook (shown in Figures 1–99b and 1–99c) in the format specified by your instructor and exit Excel.
7. Besides the styles used in the worksheet, what other changes could you make to enhance the worksheet?

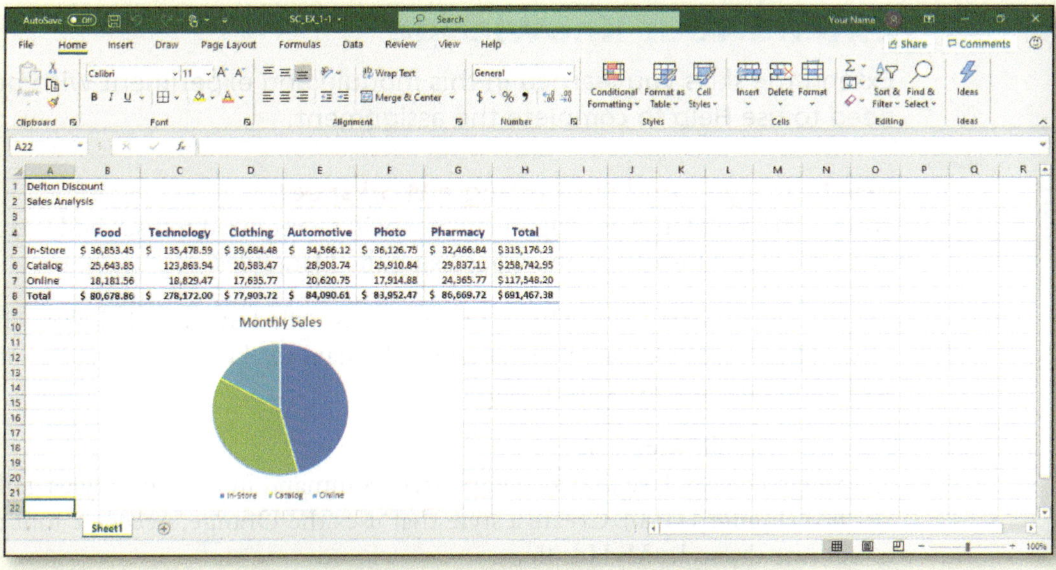

(a) Worksheet before Formatting

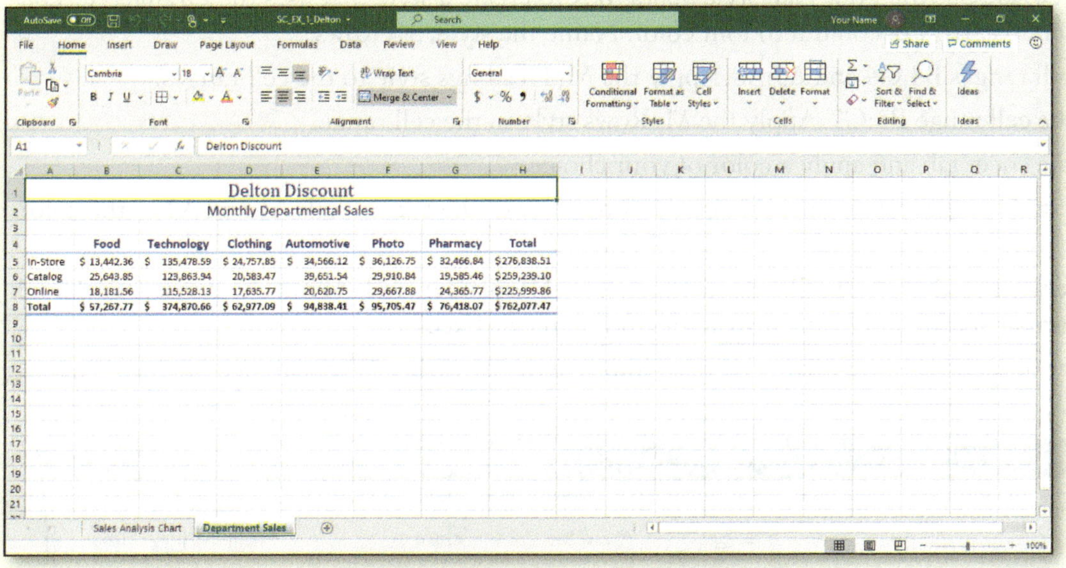

(b) Worksheet after Formatting

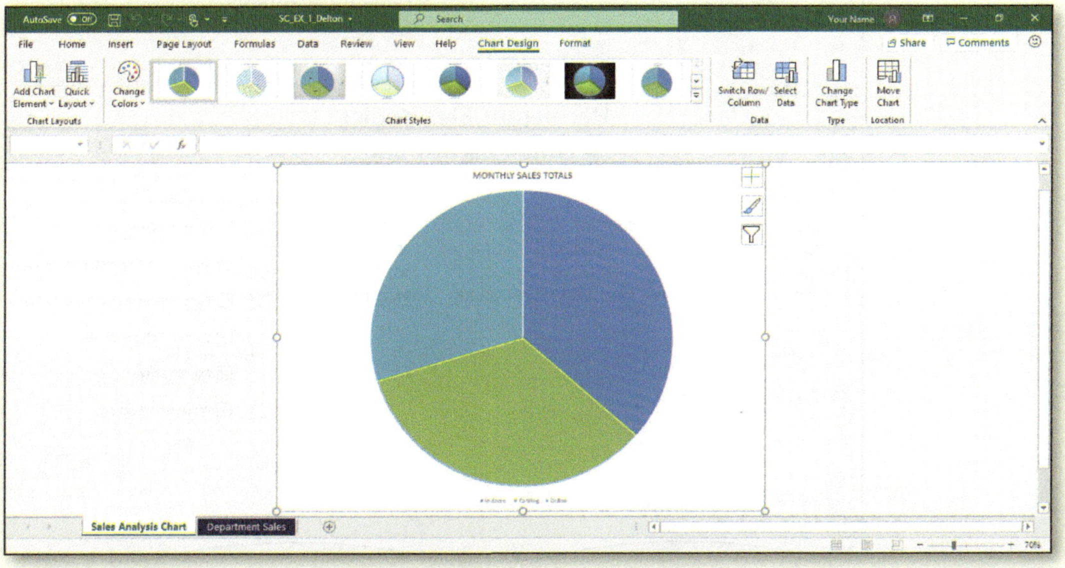

(c) Pie Chart on Separate Sheet

Figure 1–99

Extend Your Knowledge

Extend the skills you learned in this module and experiment with new skills. You may need to use Help to complete the assignment.

Creating Styles and Formatting a Worksheet

Note: To complete this assignment, you will be required to use the Data Files. Please contact your instructor for information about accessing the Data Files.

Instructions: Start Excel. Open the workbook called SC_EX_1-2.xlsx, which is located in the Data Files. The workbook you open contains sales data for Harolamer Electronics. You are to create styles and format a worksheet using them.

Perform the following tasks:

1. Select cell A4. Use the New Cell Style command in the Cell Styles gallery open the Style dialog box (Figure 1-100). Create a style that uses the Orange, Accent 2 font color (row 1, column 6). Name the style, MyHeadings.
2. Select cell A5. Use the New Cell style dialog box to create a style that uses the Orange, Accent 2, Darker 50% (row 6, column 6) font color. Name the style, MyRows.
3. Select cell ranges B4:G4 and A5:A8. Apply the MyHeadings style to the cell ranges.
4. Select the cell range B5:G7. Apply the MyRows style to the cell range.
5. Name the sheet tab and apply a color of your choice.

   If requested by your instructor, change the font color of the text in cells A1 and A2 to the color of your eyes.
6. Save the workbook with the file name, SC_EX_1_Harolamer, and submit the revised workbook in the format specified by your instructor, and then exit Excel.
7. What other styles would you create to improve the worksheet's appearance?

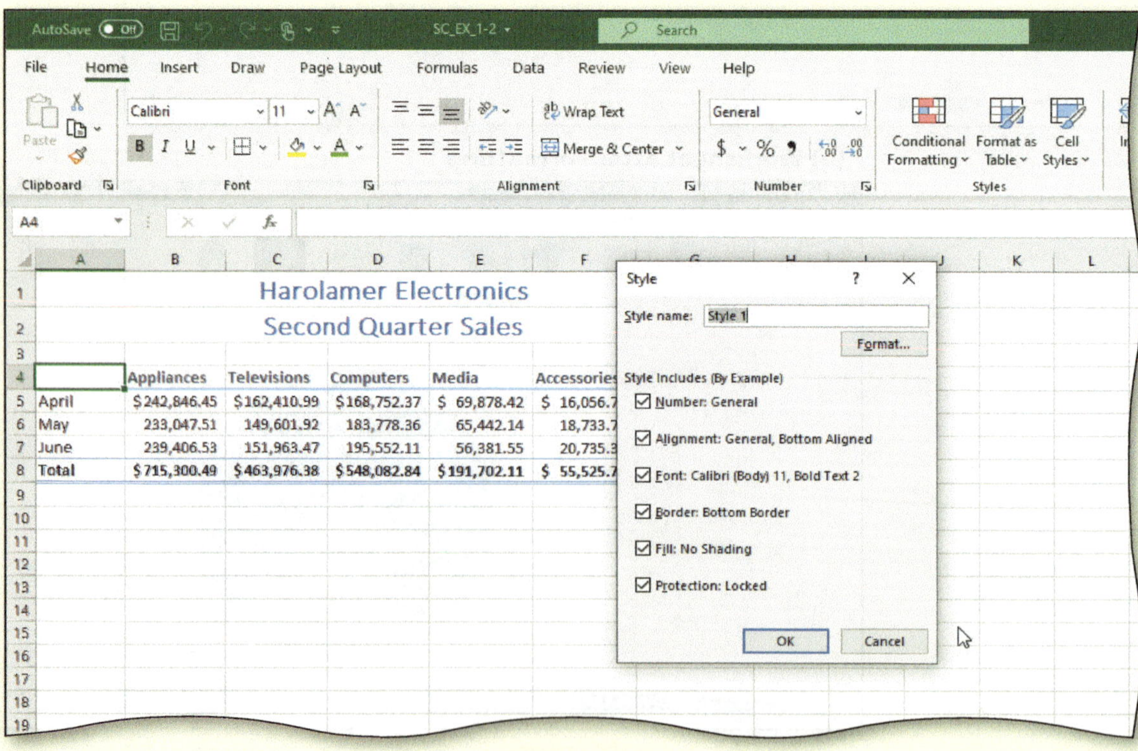

Figure 1–100

Expand Your World

Create a solution that uses cloud or web technologies by learning and investigating on your own from general guidance.

Loan Calculator

Instructions: Start Excel. You are to determine how long it will take you to pay back a loan. You decide to download and use one of the Excel templates to create your worksheet.

Perform the following tasks:

1. Click New in Backstage view and then search for and click a template that can calculate loans for an item you choose, such as a vehicle, mortgage, or general loan.
2. Enter fictitious (but realistic) information for a loan, including loan number, lender, loan amount, annual interest rate, beginning date, and length (in years). If the template you chose does not include a place for this information, add the information in an appropriate location. Search the web to examine current interest rates and typical loan durations.
3. Save the file as SC_EX_1_LoanCalculator, print the worksheet, and submit the assignment in the format specified by your instructor and then exit Excel.
4. Which template would you use if you wanted to plan and keep track of a budget for a wedding?

In the Lab

Design and implement a solution using creative thinking and problem-solving skills.

Create a Worksheet Comparing Laptops

Problem: You are shopping for a new laptop and want to compare the prices of three laptops. You will compare laptops with similar specifications, but where the brands and/or models are different.

Perform the following tasks:

Part 1: Create a worksheet that compares the type, specifications, and the price for each laptop, as well as the costs to add an extended warranty. Use the concepts and techniques presented in this module to calculate the average price of a laptop and average cost of an extended warranty and to format the worksheet. Include a chart to compare the different laptop costs. Submit your assignment in the format specified by your instructor.

Part 2: You made several decisions while creating the worksheet in this assignment: how to organize the data, how to display the text, which calculations to use, and which chart to use. What was your rationale behind each of these decisions?

2 Formulas, Functions, and Formatting

Objectives

After completing this module, you will be able to:

- Use Flash Fill
- Enter formulas using the keyboard
- Enter formulas using Point mode
- Apply the MAX, MIN, and AVERAGE functions
- Verify a formula using Range Finder
- Apply a theme to a workbook
- Apply a date format to a cell or range
- Add conditional formatting to cells
- Change column width and row height
- Check the spelling on a worksheet
- Change margins and headers in Page Layout view
- Preview and print versions and sections of a worksheet

Introduction

In Module 1, you learned how to enter data, sum values, format a worksheet to make it easier to read, and draw a chart. This module continues to illustrate these topics and presents some new ones.

The new topics covered in this module include using formulas and functions to create a worksheet. Recall from Module 1 that a function is a special, predefined formula that provides a shortcut for a commonly used calculation. Other new topics include using option buttons, verifying formulas, applying a theme to a worksheet, adding borders, formatting numbers and text, using conditional formatting, changing the widths of columns and heights of rows, checking spelling, generating alternative worksheet displays and printouts, and adding page headers and footers to a worksheet. One alternative worksheet display and printout shows the formulas in the worksheet instead of the values. When you display the formulas in the worksheet, you see exactly what text, data, formulas, and functions you have entered into it.

Project: Worksheet with Formulas and Functions

The project in this module follows proper design guidelines and uses Excel to create the worksheet shown in Figure 2–1. Every two weeks, the owners of Klapore Engineering create a salary report by hand, where they keep track of employee payroll data. Before paying employees, the owners must summarize the hours worked, pay rate, and tax information for each employee to ensure that the business properly compensates its employees. This report includes the following information for each employee: name, email address, number of dependents, gross pay, deductions, net pay, and hire date. As the complexity of creating the salary report increases, the owners want to use Excel to make the process easier.

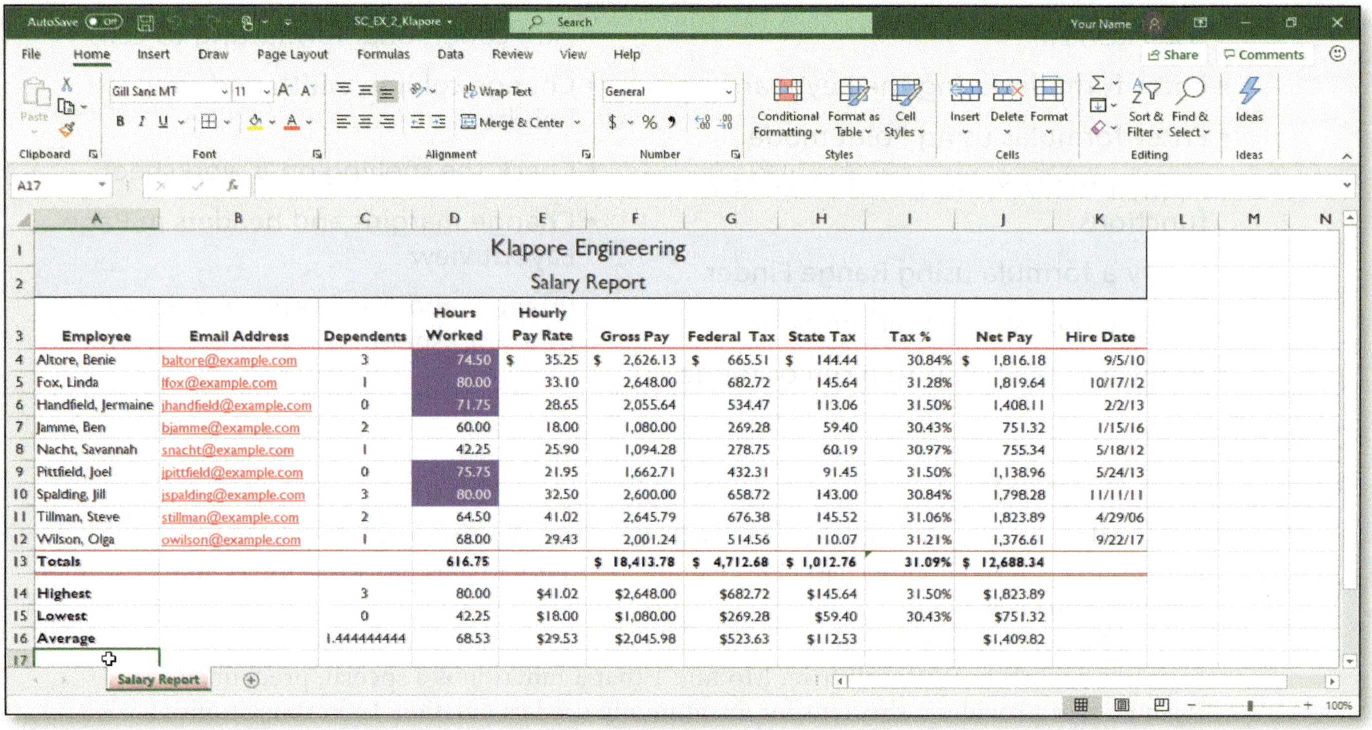

Employee	Email Address	Dependents	Hours Worked	Hourly Pay Rate	Gross Pay	Federal Tax	State Tax	Tax %	Net Pay	Hire Date
Altore, Benie	baltore@example.com	3	74.50	$ 35.25	$ 2,626.13	$ 665.51	$ 144.44	30.84%	$ 1,816.18	9/5/10
Fox, Linda	lfox@example.com	1	80.00	33.10	2,648.00	682.72	145.64	31.28%	1,819.64	10/17/12
Handfield, Jermaine	jhandfield@example.com	0	71.75	28.65	2,055.64	534.47	113.06	31.50%	1,408.11	2/2/13
Jamme, Ben	bjamme@example.com	2	60.00	18.00	1,080.00	269.28	59.40	30.43%	751.32	1/15/16
Nacht, Savannah	snacht@example.com	1	42.25	25.90	1,094.28	278.75	60.19	30.97%	755.34	5/18/12
Pittfield, Joel	jpittfield@example.com	0	75.75	21.95	1,662.71	432.31	91.45	31.50%	1,138.96	5/24/13
Spalding, Jill	jspalding@example.com	3	80.00	32.50	2,600.00	658.72	143.00	30.84%	1,798.28	11/11/11
Tillman, Steve	stillman@example.com	2	64.50	41.02	2,645.79	676.38	145.52	31.06%	1,823.89	4/29/06
Wilson, Olga	owilson@example.com	1	68.00	29.43	2,001.24	514.56	110.07	31.21%	1,376.61	9/22/17
Totals			**616.75**		**$ 18,413.78**	**$ 4,712.68**	**$ 1,012.76**	**31.09%**	**$ 12,688.34**	
Highest		3	80.00	$41.02	$2,648.00	$682.72	$145.64	31.50%	$1,823.89	
Lowest		0	42.25	$18.00	$1,080.00	$269.28	$59.40	30.43%	$751.32	
Average		1.444444444	68.53	$29.53	$2,045.98	$523.63	$112.53		$1,409.82	

Figure 2–1

Recall that the first step in creating an effective worksheet is to make sure you understand what is required. The people who request the worksheet usually provide the requirements. The requirements document for the Klapore Engineering Salary Report worksheet includes the following needs: source of data, summary of calculations, and other facts about its development (Figure 2–2).

Worksheet Title	Klapore Engineering Salary Report
Needs	An easy-to-read worksheet that summarizes the company's salary report (Figure 2–3). For each employee, the worksheet is to include the employee's name, email address, number of dependents, hours worked, hourly pay rate, gross pay, federal tax, state tax, total tax percent, net pay, and hire date. The worksheet also should include the total pay for all employees, as well as the highest value, lowest value, and average for each category of data.
Source of Data	Supplied data includes employee names, email addresses, number of dependents, hours worked, hourly pay rate, and hire dates.
Calculations	The following calculations must be made for each of the employees: 1. Gross Pay = Hours Worked * Hourly Pay Rate 2. Federal Tax = 0.26 * (Gross Pay – Number of Dependents * 22.16) 3. State Tax = 0.055 * Gross Pay 4. Tax % = (Federal Tax + State Tax) / Gross Pay 5. Net Pay = Gross Pay – (Federal Tax + State Tax) 6. Compute the totals for hours worked, gross pay, federal tax, state tax, and net pay 7. Compute the total tax percent 8. Use the MAX and MIN functions to determine the highest and lowest values for number of dependents, hours worked, hourly pay rate, gross pay, federal tax, state tax, total tax percent, and net pay 9. Use the AVERAGE function to determine the average for number of dependents, hours worked, hourly pay rate, gross pay, federal tax, state tax, and net pay

Figure 2–2

In addition, using a sketch of the worksheet can help you visualize its design. The sketch for the Klapore Engineering Salary Report worksheet includes a title, a subtitle, column and row headings, and the location of data values (Figure 2–3). It also uses specific characters to define the desired formatting for the worksheet, as follows:

1. The row of Xs below the leftmost column heading defines the cell entries as text, such as employee names.

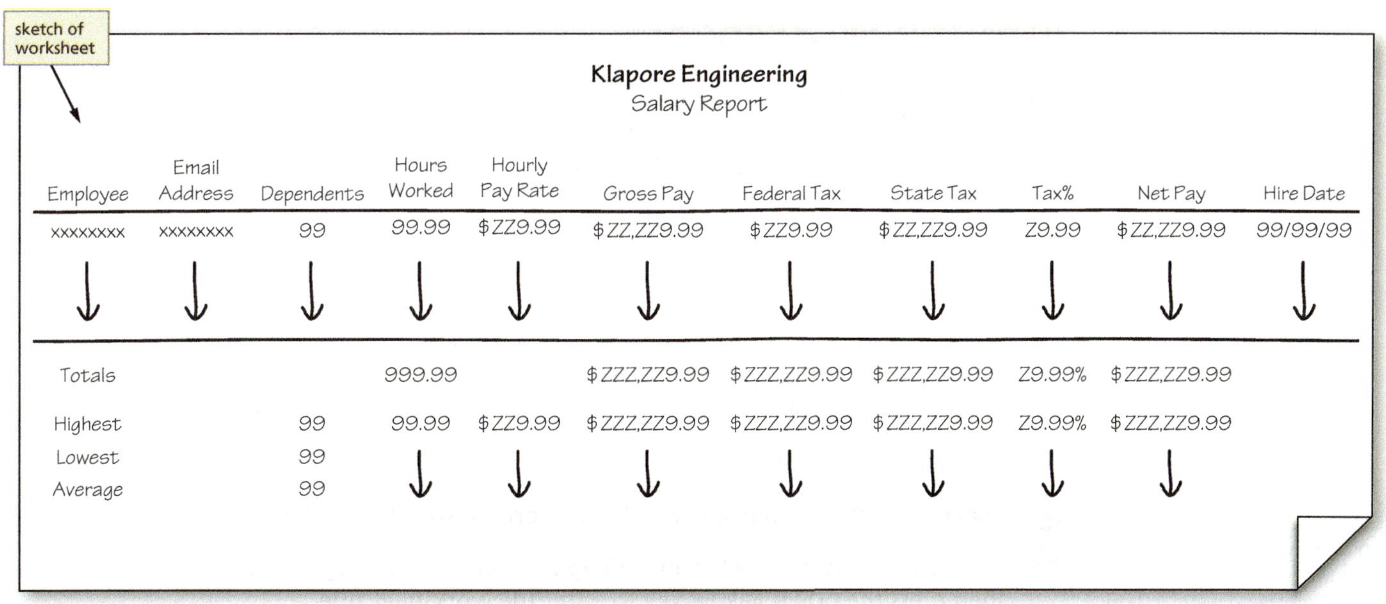

Figure 2–3

2. The rows of Zs and 9s with slashes, dollar signs, decimal points, commas, and percent signs in the remaining columns define the cell entries as numbers. The Zs indicate that the selected format should instruct Excel to suppress leading 0s. The 9s indicate that the selected format should instruct Excel to display any digits, including 0s.
3. The decimal point means that a decimal point should appear in the cell entry and indicates the number of decimal places to use.
4. The slashes in the last column identify the cell entry as a date.
5. The dollar signs that are adjacent to the Zs below the totals row signify a floating dollar sign, or one that appears next to the first significant digit.
6. The commas indicate that the selected format should instruct Excel to display a comma separator only if the number has sufficient digits (values in the thousandths) to the left of the decimal point.
7. The percent sign (%) in the Tax % column indicates a percent sign should appear after the number.

Consider This

What is the function of an Excel worksheet?

The function, or purpose, of a worksheet is to provide a user with direct ways to accomplish tasks. In designing a worksheet, functional considerations should supersede visual aesthetics. Consider the following when designing your worksheet:

- Avoid the temptation to use flashy or confusing visual elements within the worksheet.
- Understand the requirements document.
- Choose the proper functions and formulas.

BTW
Touch Mode Differences
The Office and Windows interfaces may vary if you are using touch mode. For this reason, you might notice that the function or appearance of your touch screen differs slightly from this module's presentation.

BTW
Excel Help
At any time while using Excel, you can find answers to questions and display information about various topics through Excel Help. Used properly, this form of assistance can increase your productivity and reduce your frustrations by minimizing the time you spend learning how to use Excel.

Entering the Titles and Numbers into the Worksheet

The first step in creating the worksheet is to enter the titles and numbers into the worksheet. The following sets of steps enter the worksheet title and subtitle and then the salary report data shown in Table 2–1.

To Enter the Worksheet Title and Subtitle

With a good comprehension of the requirements document, an understanding of the necessary decisions, and a sketch of the worksheet, the next step is to use Excel to create the worksheet. The following steps enter the worksheet title and subtitle into cells A1 and A2.

1. sam Start Excel and create a blank workbook in the Excel window.
2. If necessary, select cell A1. Type **`Klapore Engineering`** in the selected cell and then press the DOWN ARROW key to enter the worksheet title.
3. Type **`Salary Report`** in cell A2 and then press the DOWN ARROW key to enter the worksheet subtitle.

To Enter the Column Titles

The column titles in row 3 begin in cell A3 and extend through cell K3. The employee names and the row titles begin in cell A4 and continue down to cell A16. The employee data is entered into rows 4 through 12 of the worksheet. The remainder of this section explains the steps required to enter the column titles, payroll data, and row titles, as shown in Figure 2–4, and then to save the workbook. The following steps enter the column titles.

1. With cell A3 selected, type `Employee` and then press the RIGHT ARROW key to enter the column heading.
2. Type `Email Address` in cell B3 and then press the RIGHT ARROW key.
3. In cell C3, type `Dependents` and then press the RIGHT ARROW key.
4. In cell D3, type `Hours` and then press ALT+ENTER to enter the first line of the column heading. Type `Worked` and then press the RIGHT ARROW key to enter the column heading.

Q&A **Why do I use ALT+ENTER?**
You press ALT+ENTER in order to start a new line in a cell. The final line can be completed by clicking the Enter button, pressing ENTER, or pressing one of the arrow keys. When you see ALT+ENTER in a step, press ENTER while holding down ALT and then release both keys.

5. Type `Hourly` in cell E3, press ALT+ENTER, type `Pay Rate,` and then press the RIGHT ARROW key.
6. Type `Gross Pay` in cell F3 and then press the RIGHT ARROW key.
7. Type `Federal Tax` in cell G3 and then press the RIGHT ARROW key.
8. Type `State Tax` in cell H3 and then press the RIGHT ARROW key.
9. Type `Tax %` in cell I3 and then press the RIGHT ARROW key.
10. Type `Net Pay` in cell J3 and then press the RIGHT ARROW key.
11. Type `Hire Date` in cell K3 and then press the RIGHT ARROW key.

BTW
Screen Resolution
If you are using a computer to step through the project in this module and you want your screens to match the figures in this book, you should change your screen's resolution to 1366 × 768.

BTW
Wrapping Text
If you have a long text entry, such as a paragraph, you can instruct Excel to wrap the text in a cell. This method is easier than pressing ALT+ENTER to end each line of text within the paragraph. To wrap text, right-click in the cell, click Format Cells on a shortcut menu, click the Alignment tab, and then click Wrap text. Excel will increase the height of the cell automatically so that the additional lines will fit. If you want to control where each line ends in the cell, rather than letting Excel wrap the text based on the cell width, you must end each line with ALT+ENTER.

To Enter the Salary Data

The salary data in Table 2-1 includes a hire date for each employee. Excel considers a date to be a number, and, therefore, it displays the date right-aligned in the cell. The following steps enter the data for each employee, except their email addresses, which will be entered later in this module.

1. Select cell A4. Type `Altore, Benie` and then press the RIGHT ARROW key two times to enter the employee name and make cell C4 the active cell.
2. Type `3` in cell C4 and then press the RIGHT ARROW key.
3. Type `74.50` in cell D4 and then press the RIGHT ARROW key.

BTW

Two-Digit Years

When you enter a two-digit year value (xx) that is less than 30, Excel changes that value to 20xx; when you enter a value that is 30 or greater (zz), Excel changes the value to 19zz. Use four-digit years, if necessary, to ensure that Excel interprets year values the way you intend.

Q&A **Why did 74.50 change to 74.5 when I pressed the RIGHT ARROW key?**
Depending on the number format applied to the cell, Excel might remove trailing zeros from a cell value.

4. Type `35.25` in cell E4.
5. Click cell K4 and then type `9/5/10`.
6. Enter the payroll data in Table 2–1 for the eight remaining employees in rows 5 through 12. Click the Enter button when you have finished entering the value in the last cell.

Q&A **In Step 5, why did the date change from 9/5/10 to 9/5/2010?**
When Excel recognizes a date in mm/dd/yy format, it formats the date as mm/dd/yyyy. Many professionals prefer to view dates in mm/dd/yyyy format as opposed to mm/dd/yy format to avoid confusion regarding the intended year. For example, a date displayed as 3/3/50 could imply a date of 3/3/1950 or 3/3/2050.

Table 2–1 Klapore Engineering Salary Report Data

Employee	Email Address	Dependents	Hours Worked	Hourly Pay Rate	Hire Date
Fox, Linda		1	80.00	33.10	10/17/12
Handfield, Jermaine		0	71.75	28.65	2/2/13
Jamme, Ben		2	60.00	18.00	1/15/16
Nacht, Savannah		1	42.25	25.90	5/18/12
Pittfield, Joel		0	75.75	21.95	5/24/13
Spalding, Jill		3	80.00	32.50	11/11/11
Tillman, Steve		2	64.50	41.02	4/29/06
Wilson, Olga		1	68.00	29.43	9/22/17

BTW

The Ribbon and Screen Resolution

Excel may change how the groups and buttons within the groups appear on the ribbon, depending on the screen resolution of your computer. Thus, your ribbon may look different from the ones in this book if you are using a screen resolution other than 1366 × 768.

Flash Fill

When you are entering data in a spreadsheet, occasionally Excel will recognize a pattern in the data you are entering. **Flash Fill** is an Excel feature that looks for patterns in the data and automatically fills or formats data in remaining cells based on those patterns. For example, if column A contains a list of 10 phone numbers without parentheses around the area code or dashes after the prefix, Flash Fill can help automatically create formatted phone numbers with parentheses and dashes with relative ease. To use Flash Fill, simply start entering formatted phone numbers in cells next to the unformatted numbers. After entering a few formatted phone numbers, Flash Fill will suggest similarly formatted phone numbers for the remaining cells in the column. If you do not want to wait for Excel to offer suggestions, type one or two examples and then click the Flash Fill button (Data tab | Data Tools group). Flash Fill will autocomplete the remaining cells. If Flash Fill makes a mistake, simply click the Undo button, enter a few more examples, and try again. In addition to formatting data, Flash Fill can perform tasks such as concatenating data from multiple cells and separating data from one cell into multiple cells.

To Use Flash Fill

In the Klapore Engineering Salary Report worksheet, you can use Flash Fill to generate email addresses using first and last names from another column in the worksheet. **Why?** The Flash Fill feature is a convenient way to avoid entering a lot of data manually. The following steps use Flash Fill to generate employee email addresses using the names entered in column A.

1

- Click cell B4 to select it.
- Type **baltore@example.com** and then press the DOWN ARROW key to select cell B5.
- Type **lfox@example.com** and then click the Enter button to enter Linda Fox's email address in cell B5 (Figure 2–4).

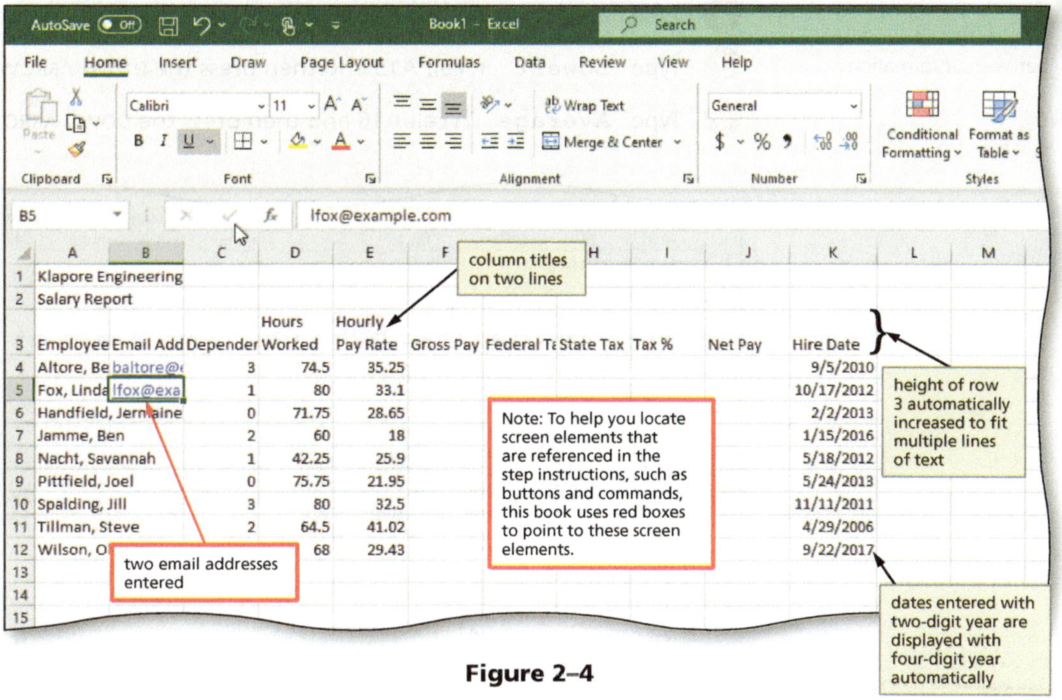

Figure 2–4

2

- Select the range B4:B12.
- Click Data on the ribbon to select the Data tab.
- Click the Flash Fill button (Data tab | Data Tools group) to enter similarly formatted email addresses in the range B6:B12.
- If necessary, remove any entries from cells B1 and B2 (Figure 2–5).

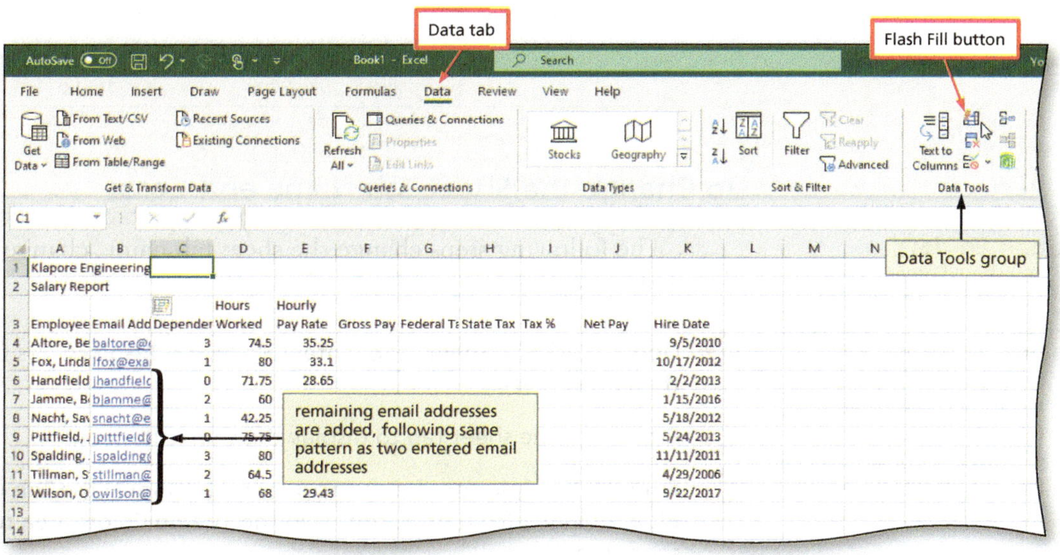

Figure 2–5

Q&A

Why was I unable to click the Flash Fill button after entering the first email address?
One entry might not have been enough for Excel to recognize a pattern. For instance, Flash Fill might have used the letter b before each last name in the email address instead of using the first initial and last name.

What would have happened if I kept typing examples without clicking the Flash Fill button?
As soon as Excel recognized a pattern, it would have displayed suggestions for the remaining cells. Pressing ENTER when the suggestions appear will populate the remaining cells.

BTW
Formatting Worksheets
With early spreadsheet programs, users often skipped rows to improve the appearance of the worksheet. With Excel it is not necessary to skip rows because you can increase row heights to add white space between information.

To Enter the Row Titles

The following steps add row titles for the rows that will contain the totals, highest, lowest, and average amounts.

1. Select cell A13. Type `Totals` and then press the DOWN ARROW key to enter a row header.
2. Type `Highest` in cell A14 and then press the DOWN ARROW key.
3. Type `Lowest` in cell A15 and then press the DOWN ARROW key.
4. Type `Average` in cell A16 and then press the DOWN ARROW key (Figure 2–6).

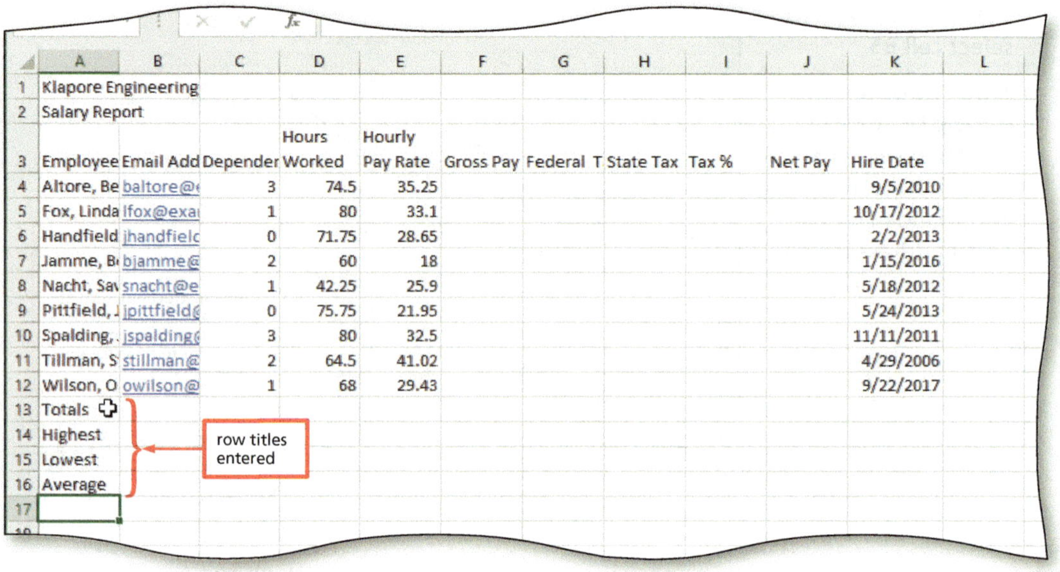

Figure 2–6

BTW
Organizing Files and Folders
You should organize and store files in folders so that you can easily find the files later. For example, if you are taking an introductory technology class called CIS 101, a good practice would be to save all Excel files in an Excel folder in a CIS 101 folder.

To Change the Sheet Tab Name and Color

The following steps change the sheet tab name, change the tab color, and save the workbook.

1. Double-click the Sheet1 tab, enter `Salary Report` as the sheet tab name and then press ENTER.
2. Right-click the sheet tab to display the shortcut menu.
3. Point to Tab Color on the shortcut menu to display the Tab Color gallery. Click Blue, Accent 1 (column 5, row 1) in the Theme Colors area to apply the color to the sheet tab.
4. Save the workbook using SC_EX_2_Klapore as the file name.

Q&A
Why should I save the workbook at this time?
You have performed many tasks while creating this workbook and do not want to risk losing work completed thus far.

Entering Formulas

One of the reasons Excel is such a valuable tool is that you can assign a formula to a cell, and Excel will calculate the result. A **formula** is a mathematical statement in a spreadsheet or table cell that calculates a value using cell references, numbers, and arithmetic operators such as +, –, *, and /. Consider, for example, what would happen if you had to multiply 74.50 by 35.25 and then manually enter the product for Gross Pay, 2,626.13, in cell F4. Every time the values in cells D4 or E4 changed, you would have to recalculate the product and enter the new value in cell F4. By contrast, if you enter a formula in cell F4 to multiply the values in cells D4 and E4, Excel recalculates the product whenever new values are entered into those cells and displays the result in cell F4.

In a spreadsheet, an error that occurs when one of the defining values in a cell is itself is called a **circular reference.** Excel warns you when you create circular references. In almost all cases, circular references are the result of an incorrect formula. A circular reference can be direct or indirect. For example, placing the formula =A1 in cell A1 results in a direct circular reference. A **direct circular reference** occurs when a formula refers to the same cell in which it is entered. An **indirect circular reference** occurs when a formula in a cell refers to another cell or cells that include a formula that refers back to the original cell.

BTW
Entering Numbers in a Range
An efficient way to enter data into a range of cells is to select a range and then enter the first number in the upper-left cell of the range. Excel responds by accepting the value and moving the active cell selection down one cell. When you enter the last value in the first column, Excel moves the active cell selection to the top of the next column.

To Enter a Formula Using the Keyboard

The formulas needed in the worksheet are noted in the requirements document as follows:

1. Gross Pay (column F) = Hours Worked × Hourly Pay Rate
2. Federal Tax (column G) = 0.26 × (Gross Pay – Dependents × 22.16)
3. State Tax (column H) = 0.055 × Gross Pay
4. Tax % (column I) = (Federal Tax + State Tax) / Gross Pay
5. Net Pay (column J) = Gross Pay – (Federal Tax + State Tax)

The gross pay for each employee, which appears in column F, is equal to hours worked in column D times hourly pay rate in column E. Thus, the gross pay for Benie Altore in cell F4 is obtained by multiplying 74.50 (cell D4) by 35.25 (cell E4) or = D4 × E4. The following steps enter the initial gross pay formula in cell F4 using the keyboard. **Why?** In order for Excel to perform the calculations, you must first enter the formulas.

1

- With cell F4 selected, type **=d4*e4** in the cell to display the formula in the formula bar and the current cell and to display colored borders around the cells referenced in the formula (Figure 2–7).

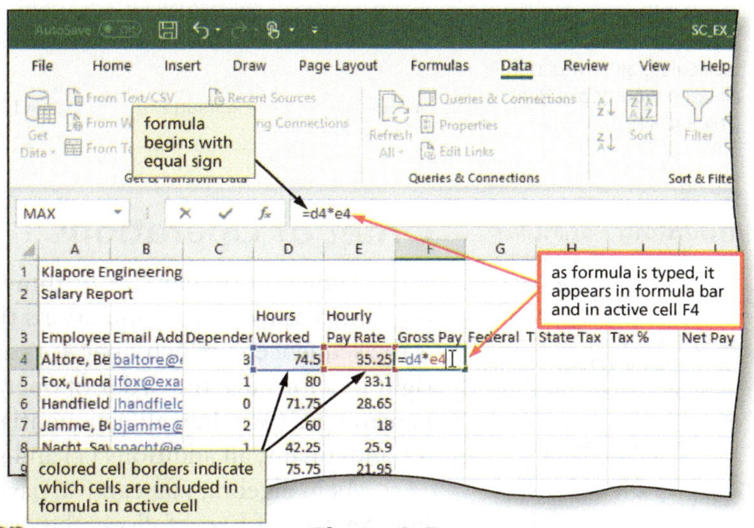

Figure 2–7

Q&A

What happens when I enter the formula?
The **equal sign** (=) preceding d4*e4 alerts Excel that you are entering a formula or function — not text. Because the most common error when entering a formula is to reference the wrong cell, Excel colors the cells referenced in the formula. The colored cells help you determine whether the cell references are correct. The asterisk (*) following d4 is the arithmetic operator for multiplication.

Is there a function, similar to the SUM function, that calculates the product of two or more numbers?
Yes. The **PRODUCT function** calculates the product of two or more numbers. For example, the function, =PRODUCT(D4,E4) will calculate the product of cells D4 and E4.

2

- Press TAB to complete the arithmetic operation indicated by the formula, display the result in the worksheet, and select the cell to the right (Figure 2–8). The number of decimal places on your screen may be different from that shown in Figure 2–8, but these values will be adjusted later in this module.

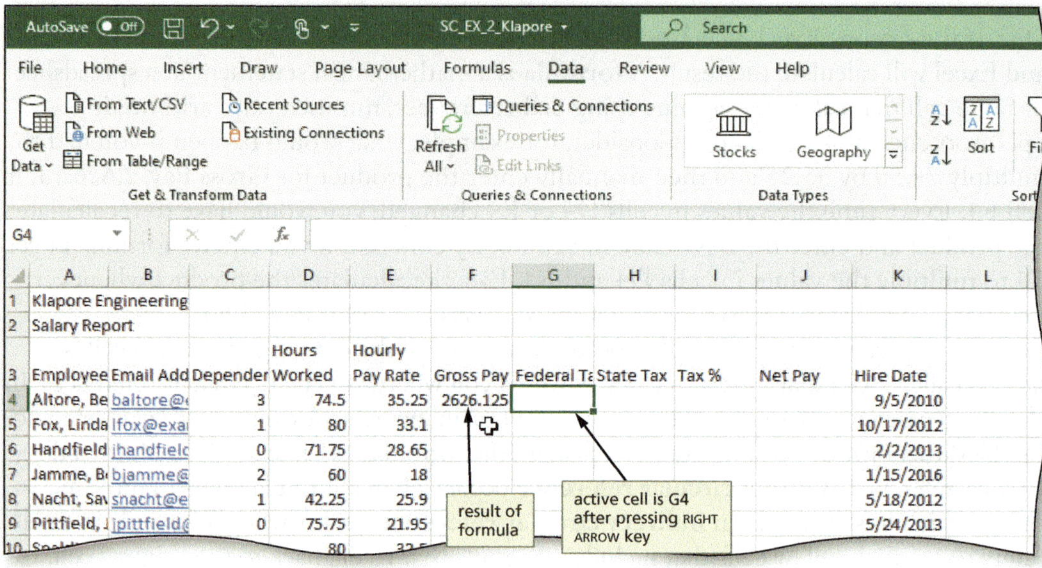

Figure 2–8

BTW
Automatic Recalculation
Every time you enter a value into a cell in the worksheet, Excel automatically recalculates all formulas. You can change to manual recalculation by clicking the Calculation Options button (Formulas tab | Calculation group) and then clicking Manual. In manual calculation mode, pressing F9 instructs Excel to recalculate all formulas on all worksheets. Press SHIFT+F9 to recalculate the active worksheet. To recalculate all formulas in all open workbooks, press CTRL+ALT+F9.

Arithmetic Operations

Excel provides powerful functions and capabilities that allow you to perform arithmetic operations easily and efficiently. Table 2–2 describes multiplication and other valid Excel arithmetic operators, listed in the order in which Excel performs them.

Table 2–2 Arithmetic Operations Listed in Order of Operations

Arithmetic Operator	Meaning	Example of Usage	Result
–	Negation	–78	Negative 78
%	Percentage	=23%	Multiplies 23 by 0.01
^	Exponentiation	=3 ^ 4	Raises 3 to the fourth power
*	Multiplication	=61.5 * C5	Multiplies the contents of cell C5 by 61.5
/	Division	=H3 / H11	Divides the contents of cell H3 by the contents of cell H11
+	Addition	=11 + 9	Adds 11 and 9
–	Subtraction	=22 – F15	Subtracts the contents of cell F15 from 22

BTW
Troubling Formulas
If Excel does not accept a formula, remove the equal sign from the left side and complete the entry as text. Later, after you have entered additional data in the cells reliant on the formula or determined the error, reinsert the equal sign to change the text back to a formula and edit the formula as needed.

Order of Operations

When more than one arithmetic operator is involved in a formula, Excel follows the same basic order of operations that you use in algebra. The **order of operations** is the sequence in which operators are applied in a calculation. Moving from left to right in a formula, the order of operations is as follows: first negation (–), then all percentages (%), then all exponentiations (^), then all multiplications (*) and divisions (/), and, finally, all additions (+) and subtractions (–).

As in algebra, you can use parentheses to override the order of operations. For example, if Excel follows the order of operations, 8 * 3 + 2 equals 26. If you use parentheses, however, to change the formula to 8 * (3 + 2), the result is 40, because the parentheses instruct Excel to add 3 and 2 before multiplying by 8. Table 2–3 illustrates several examples of valid Excel formulas and explains the order of operations.

Table 2–3 Examples of Excel Formulas

Formula	Result
=G15	Assigns the value in cell G15 to the active cell.
=2 ^ 4 + 7	Assigns the sum of 16 + 7 (or 23) to the active cell.
=100 + D2 or =D2 +100 or =(100 + D2)	Assigns 100 plus the contents of cell D2 to the active cell.
=25% * 40	Assigns the product of 0.25 times 40 (or 10) to the active cell.
– (K15 * X45)	Assigns the negative value of the product of the values contained in cells K15 and X45 to the active cell. *Tip:* You do not need to type an equal sign before an expression that begins with a minus sign, which indicates a negation.
=(U8 – B8) * 6	Assigns the difference between the values contained in cells U8 and B8 times 6 to the active cell.
=J7 / A5 + G9 * M6 – Z2 ^ L7	Completes the following operations, from left to right: exponentiation (Z2 ^ L7), then division (J7 / A5), then multiplication (G9 * M6), then addition (J7 / A5) + (G9 * M6), and finally subtraction (J7 / A5 + G9 * M6) – (Z2 ^ L7). If cells A5 = 6, G9 = 2, J7 = 6, L7 = 4, M6 = 5, and Z2 = 2, then Excel assigns the active cell the value –5; that is, 6 / 6 + 2 * 5 – 2 ^ 4 = –5.

BTW

Parentheses

Remember that you can use parentheses to override the order of operations. You cannot use brackets or braces in place of parentheses in arithmetic operations.

To Enter Formulas Using Point Mode

The sketch of the worksheet in Figure 2–3 calls for the federal tax, state tax, tax percentage, and net pay for each employee to appear in columns G, H, I, and J, respectively. All four of these values are calculated using formulas in row 4:

Federal Tax (cell G4) = 0.26 × (Gross Pay – Dependents × 22.16) or = 0.26 * (F4 – C4 * 22.16)
State Tax (cell H4) = 0.055 × Gross Pay or = 0.055 * F4
Tax % (cell I4) = (Federal Tax + State Tax) / Gross Pay or = (G4 + H4) / F4
Net Pay (cell J4) = Gross Pay – (Federal Tax + State Tax) or = F4 – (G4 + H4)

An alternative to entering the formulas in cells G4, H4, I4, and J4 using the keyboard is to enter the formulas using the pointer and Point mode. **Point mode** allows you to select cells for use in a formula by using the pointer or a screen tap. The following steps enter formulas using Point mode. **Why?** Using Point mode makes it easier to create formulas without worrying about typographical errors when entering cell references.

1

- With cell G4 selected, type **=0.26*(** to begin the formula and then click cell F4 to add a cell reference in the formula (Figure 2–9).

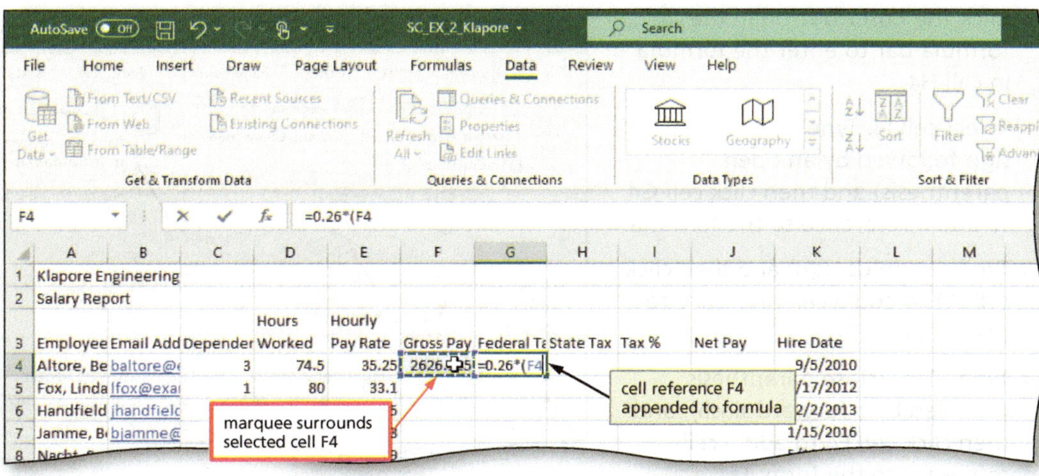

Figure 2–9

2

- Type `–` (minus sign) and then click cell C4 to add a subtraction operator and a reference to another cell to the formula.
- Type `*22.16)` to complete the formula (Figure 2–10).

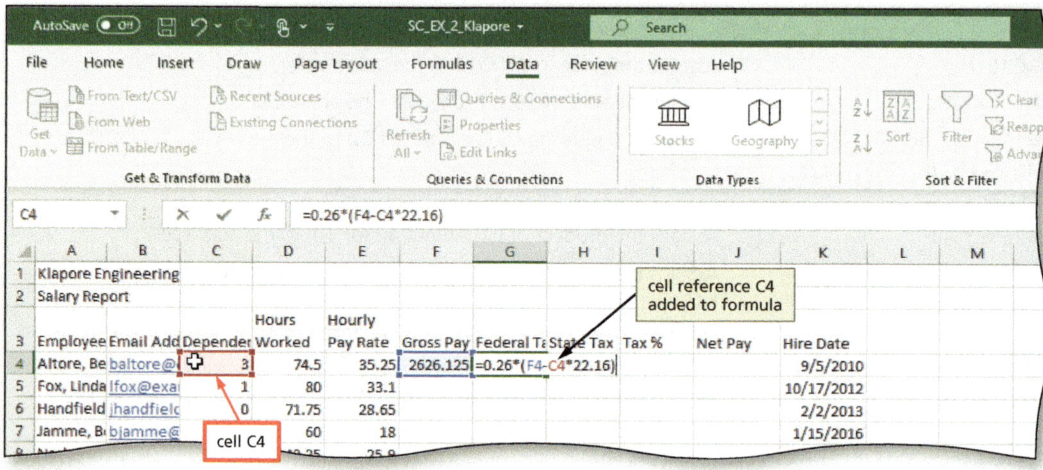

Figure 2–10

3

- Click the Enter button in the formula bar and then select cell H4 to prepare to enter the next formula.
- Type `=0.055*` and then click cell F4 to add a cell reference to the formula (Figure 2–11).

Q&A **Why should I use Point mode to enter formulas?**
Using Point mode to enter formulas often is faster and more accurate than using the keyboard, but only when the cell you want to select does not require you to scroll. In many instances, as in these steps, you may want to use both the keyboard and pointer when entering a formula in a cell. You can use the keyboard to begin the formula, for example, and then use the pointer to select a range of cells.

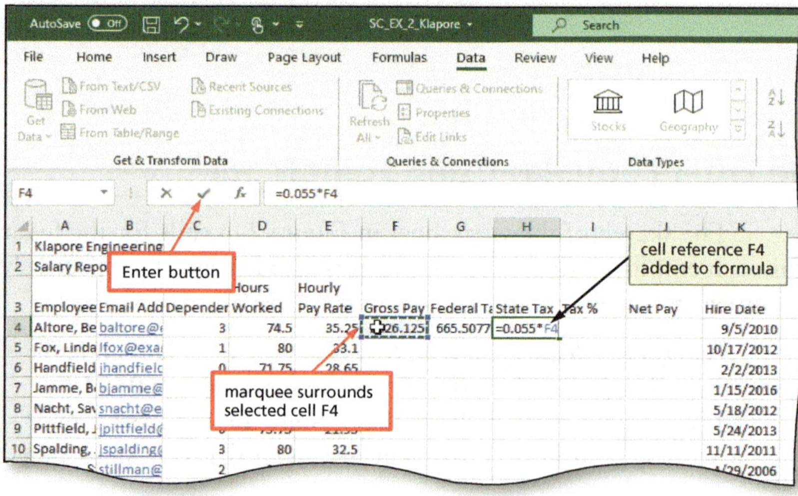

Figure 2–11

4

- Click the Enter button in the formula bar to enter the formula in cell H4.
- Select cell I4. Type `=(` (equal sign followed by an open parenthesis) and then click cell G4 to add a reference to the formula.
- Type `+` (plus sign) and then click cell H4 to add a cell reference to the formula.
- Type `)/` (close parenthesis followed by a forward slash), and then click cell F4 to add a cell reference to the formula.
- Click the Enter button in the formula bar to enter the formula in cell I4 (Figure 2–12).

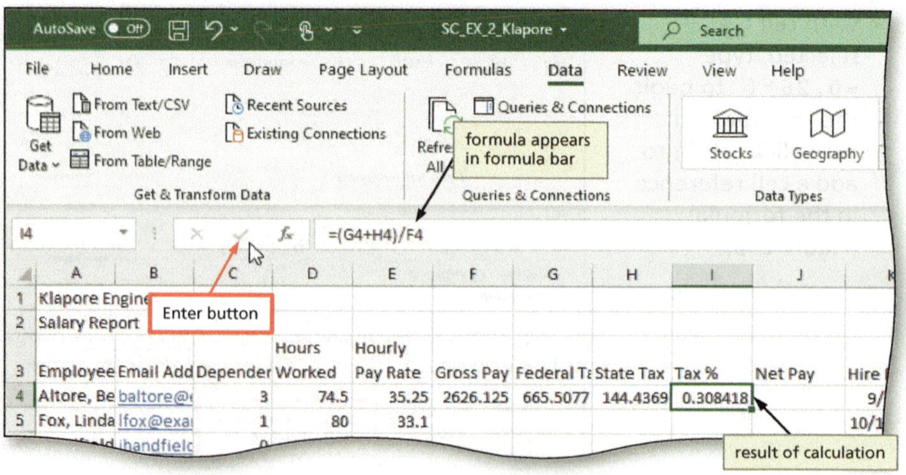

Figure 2–12

5

- Click cell J4, type = (equal sign) and then click cell F4.
- Type –((minus sign followed by an open parenthesis) and then click cell G4.
- Type + (plus sign), click cell H4, and then type) (close parenthesis) to complete the formula (Figure 2–13).
- Click the Enter button.

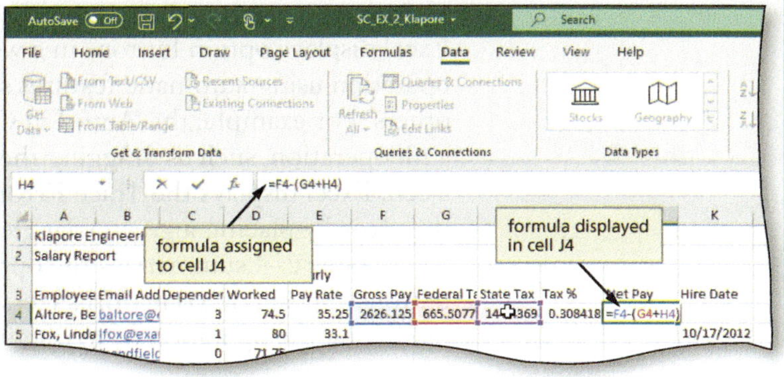

Figure 2–13

To Copy Formulas Using the Fill Handle

The five formulas for Benie Altore in cells F4, G4, H4, I4, and J4 now are complete. The next step is to copy them to the range F5:J12. When copying formulas in Excel, the source area is the cell, or range, from which data or formulas are being copied. When a range is used as a source, it sometimes is called the **source range**. The destination area is the cell, or range, to which data or formulas are being copied. When a range is used as a destination in a data exchange, it sometimes is called the **destination range**. When you copy a formula, Excel adjusts the cell references so that the new formulas contain new cell references corresponding to the new locations and perform calculations using the appropriate values. Thus, if you copy downward, Excel adjusts the row portion of the cell references relative to the source cell. If you copy across, then Excel adjusts the column portion of the cell references to the source of the cell. Cells that automatically change to reflect the new location when the formulas are copied or moved are called **relative references**. Recall from Module 1 that the fill handle is a small square in the lower-right corner of the active cell or active range. The following steps copy the formulas using the fill handle.

1 Select the source range, F4:J4 in this case, point to the fill handle, drag the fill handle down through cell J12, and then continue to hold the mouse button to select the destination range.

2 Release the mouse button to copy the formulas to the destination range (Figure 2–14).

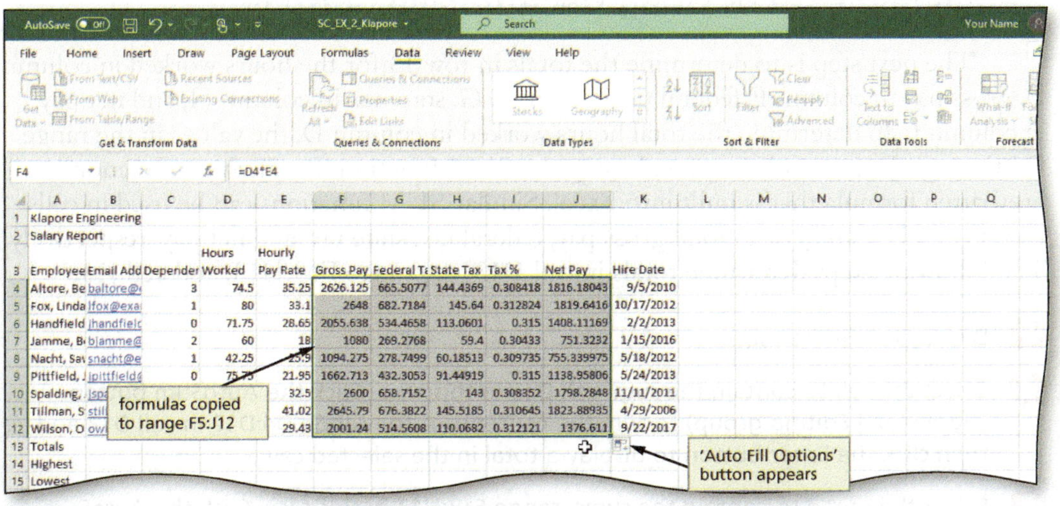

Figure 2–14

Option Buttons

Excel displays option buttons in a worksheet to indicate that you can complete an operation using automatic features such as AutoCorrect, Auto Fill, error checking, and others. For example, the 'Auto Fill Options' button shown in Figure 2–14 appears after a fill operation, such as dragging the fill handle. When an error occurs in a formula in a cell, Excel displays the Trace Error button next to the cell and identifies the cell with the error by placing a green triangle in the upper left of the cell.

Table 2–4 summarizes the option buttons available in Excel. When one of these buttons appears on your worksheet, click its arrow to produce the list of options for modifying the operation or to obtain additional information.

Table 2–4 Option Buttons in Excel

Name	Menu Function
Auto Fill Options	Provides options for how to fill cells following a fill operation, such as dragging the fill handle
AutoCorrect Options	Undoes an automatic correction, stops future automatic corrections of this type, or causes Excel to display the AutoCorrect Options dialog box
Insert Options	Lists formatting options following an insertion of cells, rows, or columns
Paste Options	Specifies how moved or pasted items should appear (for example, with original formatting, without formatting, or with different formatting)
Trace Error	Lists error-checking options following the assignment of an invalid formula to a cell

Consider This

Why is the Paste Options button important?

The Paste Options button provides powerful functionality. When performing copy and paste operations, the button allows you great freedom in specifying what it is you want to paste. You can choose from the following options:

- Paste an exact copy of what you copied, including the cell contents and formatting.
- Copy only formulas.
- Copy only formatting.
- Copy only values.
- Copy a combination of these options.
- Copy a picture of what you copied.

BTW

Selecting a Range

You can select a range using the keyboard. Press F8 and then use the arrow keys to select the desired range. After you are finished, make sure to press F8 to turn off the selection process or you will continue to select ranges.

To Determine Totals Using the AutoSum Button

The next step is to determine the totals in row 13 for the hours worked in column D, gross pay in column F, federal tax in column G, state tax in column H, and net pay in column J. To determine the total hours worked in column D, the values in the range D4 through D12 must be summed using the SUM function. Recall that a function is a prewritten formula that is built into Excel. Similar SUM functions can be used in cells F13, G13, H13, and J13 to total gross pay, federal tax, state tax, and net pay, respectively. The following steps determine totals in cell D13, the range F13:H13, and cell J13.

1. Display the Home tab.
2. Select the cell to contain the sum, cell D13 in this case. Click the AutoSum button (Home tab | Editing group) to sum the contents of the range D4:D12 in cell D13 and then click the Enter button to display a total in the selected cell.
3. Select the range to contain the sums, range F13:H13 in this case. Click the AutoSum button (Home tab | Editing group) to display totals in the selected range.

4 Select the cell to contain the sum, cell J13 in this case. Click the AutoSum button (Home tab | Editing group) to sum the contents of the range J4:J12 in cell J13 and then click the Enter button to display a total in the selected cell (Figure 2–15).

Q&A **Why did I have to click the Enter button?**
When you click the AutoSum button to calculate the sum of a single cell, the formula to calculate the sum appears in that cell. If you want Excel to display the results of the formula, you should click the Enter button.

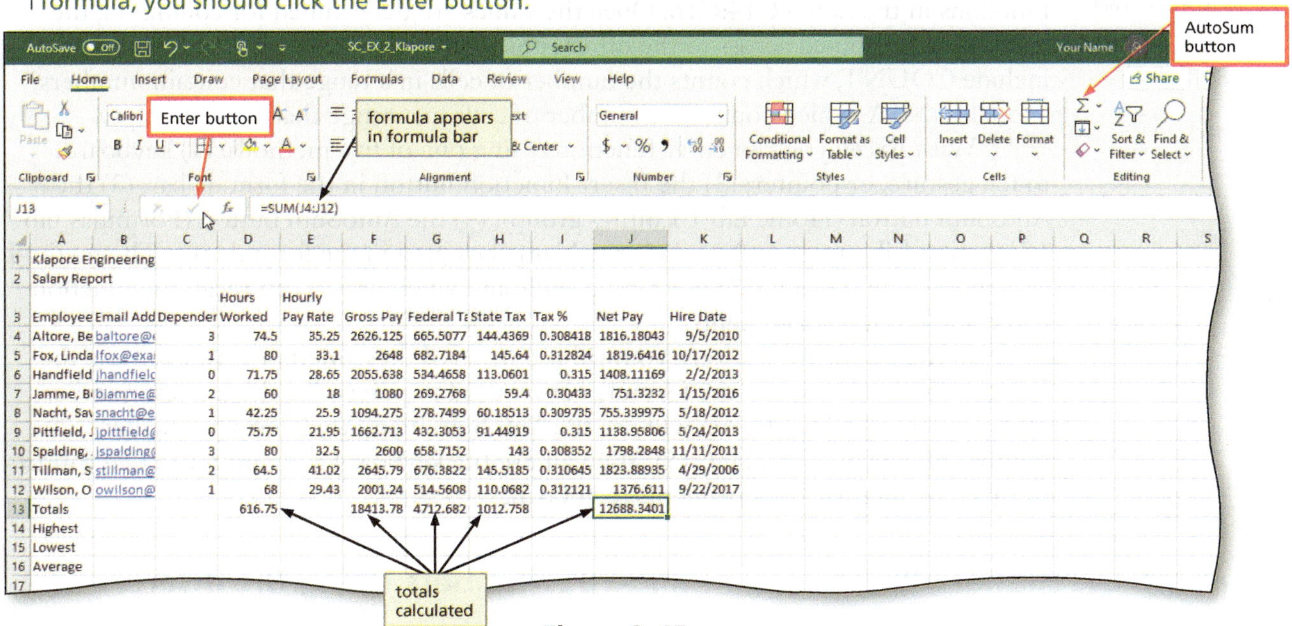

Figure 2–15

To Determine the Total Tax Percentage

With the totals in row 13 determined, the next step is to copy the tax percentage formula in cell I12 to cell I13. The following step copies the tax percentage formula.

1 Select the cell to be copied, I12 in this case, and then drag the fill handle down through cell I13 to copy the formula (Figure 2–16).

Q&A **Why was the SUM function not used for tax percentage in I13?**
The total tax percentage is calculated using the totals of the Gross Pay, Federal Tax, and State Tax columns, not by summing the tax percentage column.

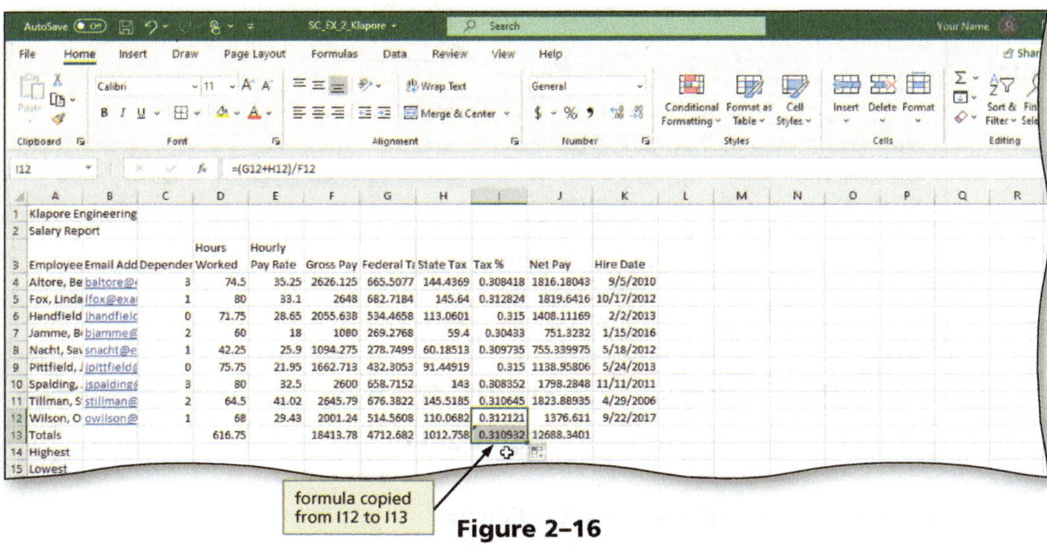

Figure 2–16

BTW

Statistical Functions

Excel usually considers a blank cell to be equal to 0. The statistical functions, however, ignore blank cells. Excel thus calculates the average of three cells with values of 10, blank, and 8 to be 9 [(10 + 8) / 2] and not 6 [(10 + 0 + 8) / 3].

Using the AVERAGE, MAX, MIN, and Other Statistical Functions

The next step in creating the Klapore Engineering Salary Report worksheet is to compute the highest value, lowest value, and average value for the number of dependents listed in the range C4:C12 using the MAX, MIN, and AVERAGE functions in the range C14:C16. Once the values are determined for column C, the entries can be copied across to the other columns. Other useful statistical functions include COUNT, which counts the number of cells in a range that contain numbers, and COUNTA, which counts the number of cells in a range that are not empty.

With Excel, you can enter functions using one of five methods: (1) keyboard, touch gesture, or pointer; (2) the Insert Function button in the formula bar; (3) the AutoSum button (Home tab | Editing group); (4) the AutoSum button (Formulas tab | Function Library group); and (5) the Name box area in the formula bar. The method you choose will depend on your typing skills and whether you can recall the function name and required arguments.

In the following sections, you will use three of these methods. You will use the Insert Function button in the formula bar method to determine the highest number of dependents (cell C14). You will use the AutoSum menu to determine the lowest number of dependents (cell C15). You will use the keyboard and pointer to determine the average number of dependents (cell C16).

To Determine the Highest Number in a Range of Numbers Using the Insert Function Dialog Box

The next step is to select cell C14 and determine the highest (maximum) number in the range C4:C12. As discussed in Module 1, Excel includes a function called the **MAX function** that displays the highest value in a range. The following steps use the Insert Function dialog box to enter the MAX function. **Why?** Although you could enter the MAX function using the keyboard and Point mode as described previously, an alternative method to entering the function is to use the Insert Function button in the formula bar to display the Insert Function dialog box. The Insert Function dialog box is helpful if you do not remember the name of a function or need to search for a particular function by what it does.

1

- Select the cell to contain the maximum number, cell C14 in this case.
- Click the Insert Function button in the formula bar to display the Insert Function dialog box.
- Click MAX in the Select a function list (Insert Function dialog box; Figure 2–17). You may need to scroll.

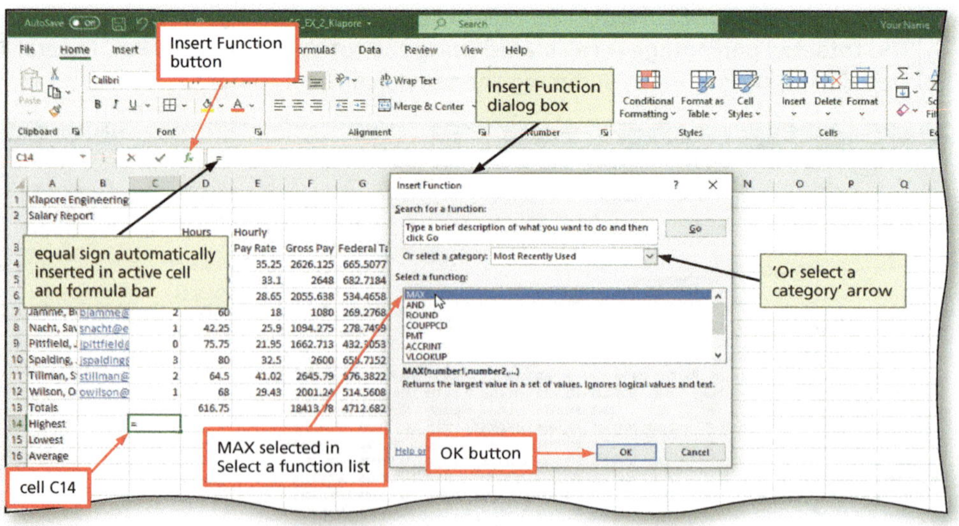

Figure 2–17

Q&A **What if the MAX function is not in the Select a function list?**

Click the 'Or select a category' arrow to display the list of function categories, select All, and then scroll down and select the MAX function in the Select a function list.

Q&A **How can I learn about other functions?**
Excel has more than 400 functions that perform nearly every type of calculation you can imagine. These functions are categorized in the Insert Function dialog box shown in Figure 2–17. To view the categories, click the 'Or select a category' arrow. Click the name of a function in the Select a function list to display a description of the function.

2

- Click OK (Insert Function dialog box) to display the Function Arguments dialog box.
- Replace the text in the Number1 box with the text, **`c4:c12`** (Function Arguments dialog box) to enter the first argument of the function (Figure 2–18).

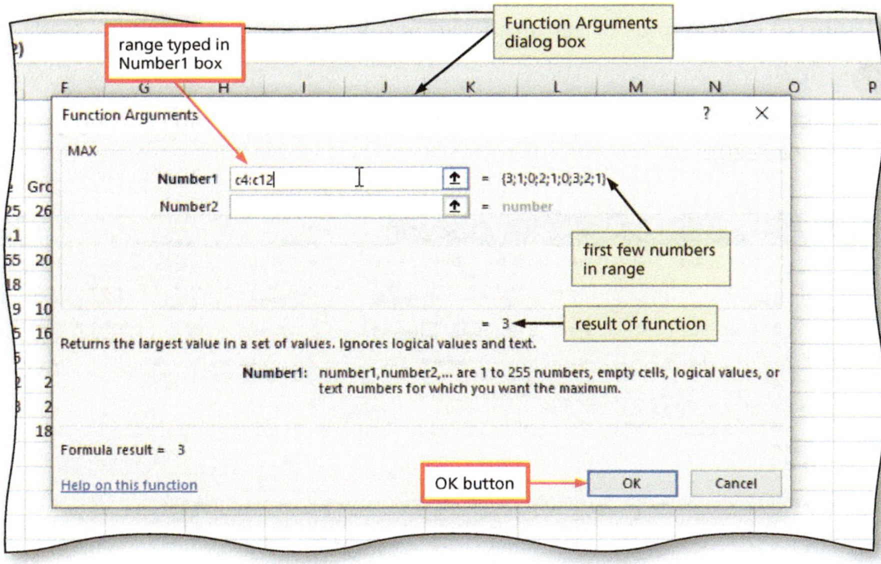

Figure 2–18

Q&A **What are the numbers that appear to the right of the Number1 box in the Function Arguments dialog box?**
The numbers shown to the right of the Number1 box are the values in the selected range (or if the range is large, the first few numbers only). Excel also displays the value the MAX function will return to cell C14 in the Function Arguments dialog box, shown in Figure 2–18.

3

- Click OK (Function Arguments dialog box) to display the highest value in the chosen range in cell C14 (Figure 2–19).

Q&A **Why should I not just enter the highest value that I see in the range C4:C12 in cell C14?**
In this example, rather than entering the MAX function, you could examine the range C4:C12, determine that the highest number of dependents is 3, and manually enter the number 3 as a constant in cell C14. Excel would display the number similar to how it appears in Figure 2–19. However, because C14 would then contain a constant, Excel would continue to display 3 in cell C14 even if the values in the range change. If you use the MAX function, Excel will recalculate the highest value in the range each time a new value is entered.

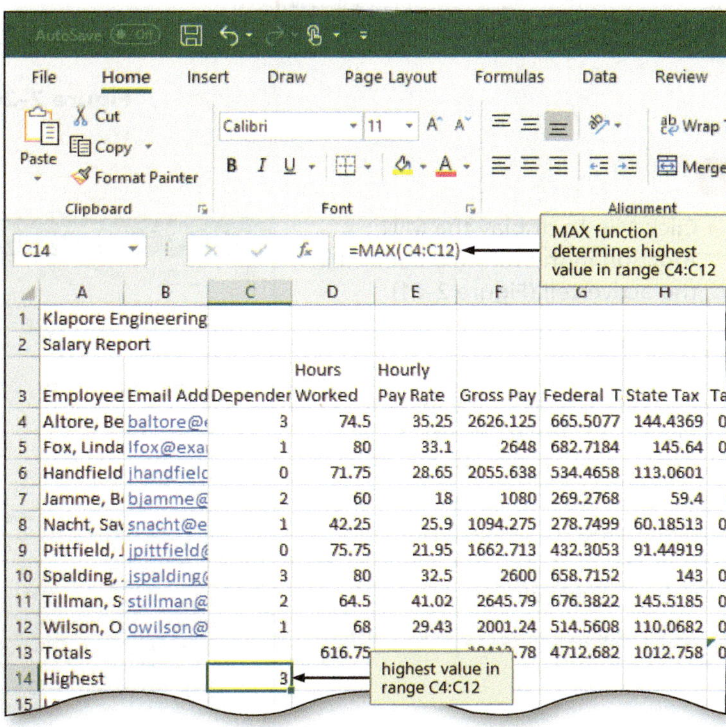

Figure 2–19

Other Ways

1. Click AutoSum arrow (Home tab | Editing group), click Max
2. Click AutoSum arrow (Formulas tab | Function Library group), click Max
3. Type **=MAX(** in cell, specify range, type)

To Determine the Lowest Number in a Range of Numbers Using the Sum Menu

The next step is to enter the **MIN function** in cell C15 to determine the lowest (minimum) number in the range C4:C12. Although you can enter the MIN function using the method used to enter the MAX function, the following steps illustrate an alternative method using the AutoSum button (Home tab | Editing group). **Why?** Using the AutoSum menu allows you quick access to five commonly used functions, without having to memorize their names or required arguments.

1

- Select cell C15 and then click the AutoSum arrow (Home tab | Editing group) to display the AutoSum menu (Figure 2–20).

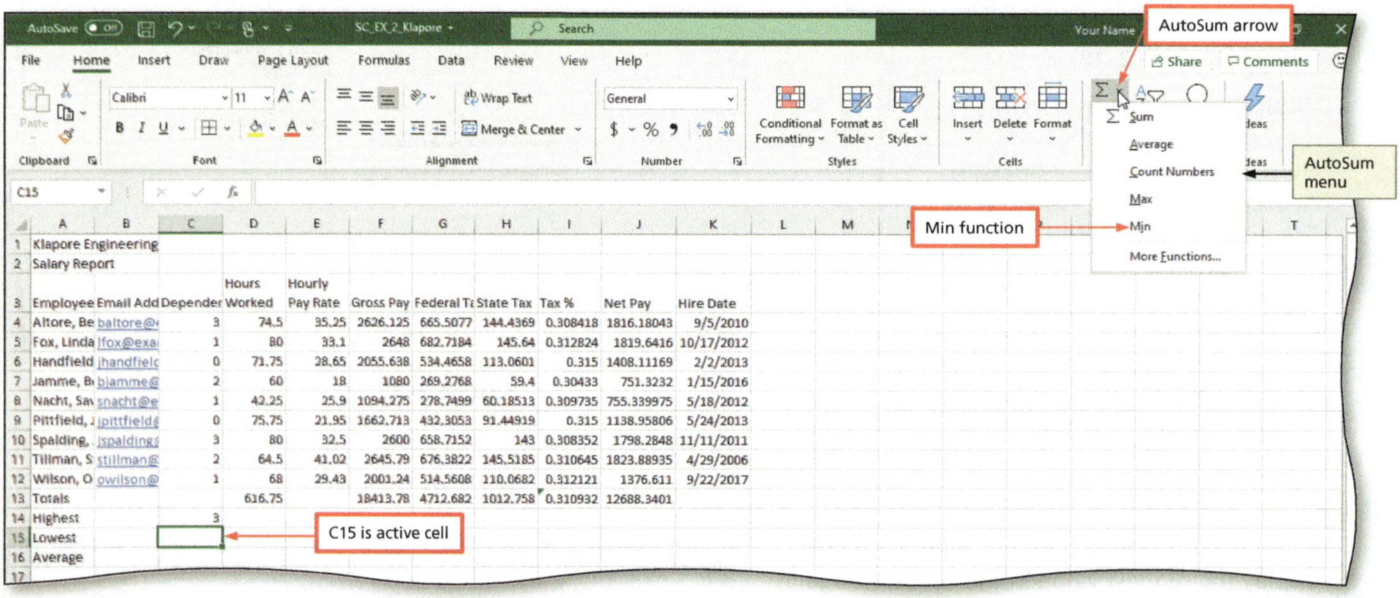

Figure 2–20

2

- Click Min to display the MIN function in the formula bar and in the active cell (Figure 2–21).

Q&A

Why does Excel select the incorrect range?

The range selected by Excel is not always the right one. Excel attempts to guess which cells you want to include in the function by looking for ranges containing numeric data that are adjacent to the selected cell.

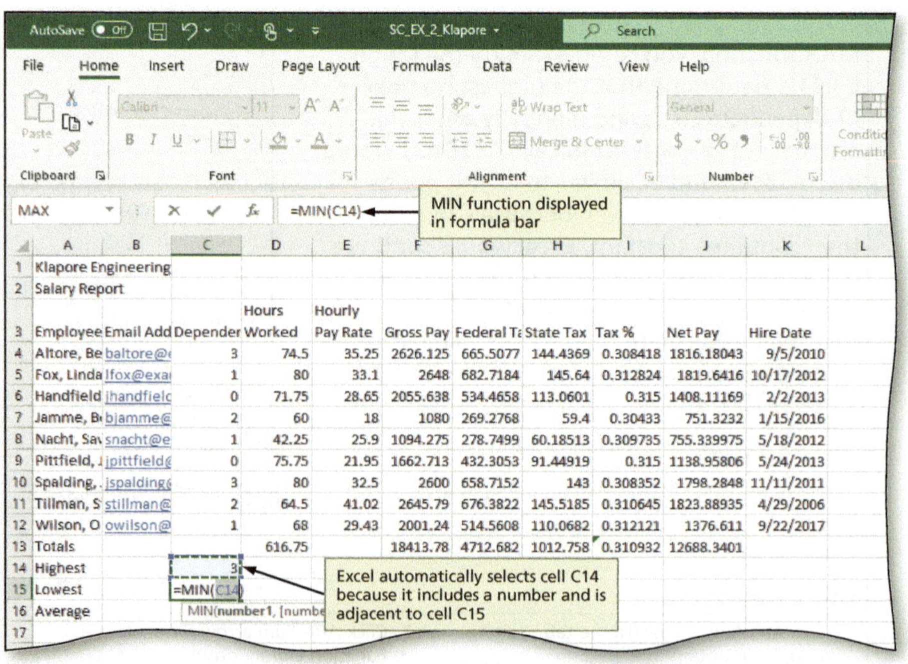

Figure 2–21

3

- Click cell C4 and then drag through cell C12 to update the function with the new range (Figure 2–22).

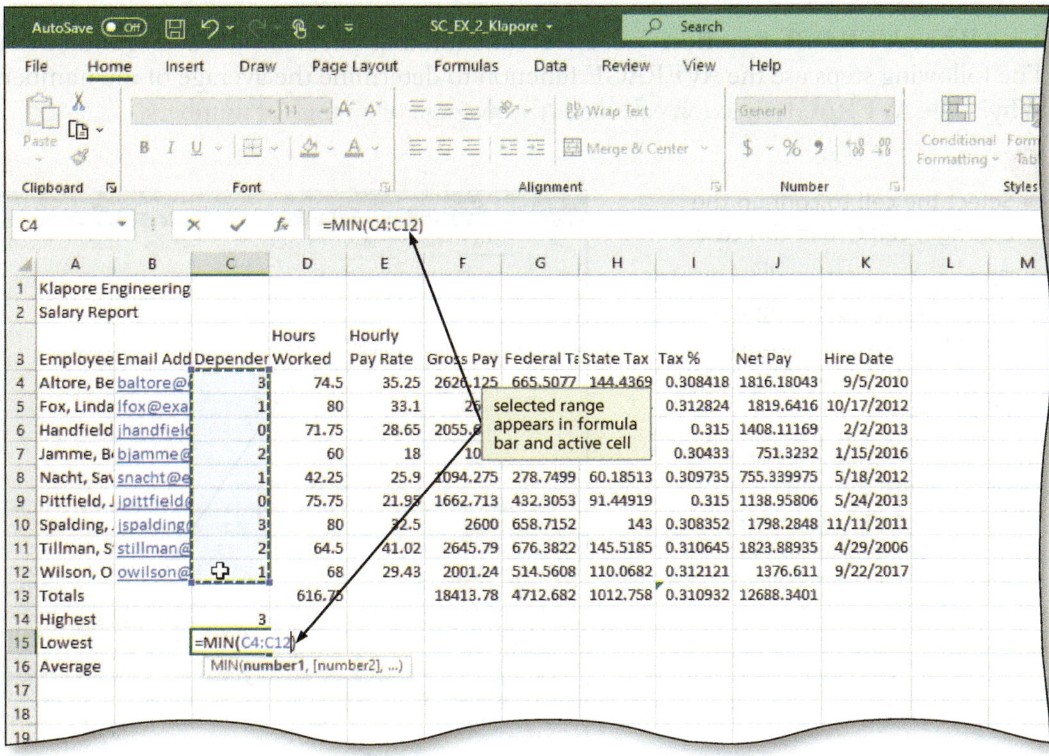

Figure 2–22

4

- Click the Enter button to determine the lowest value in the range C4:C12 and display the result in cell C15 (Figure 2–23).

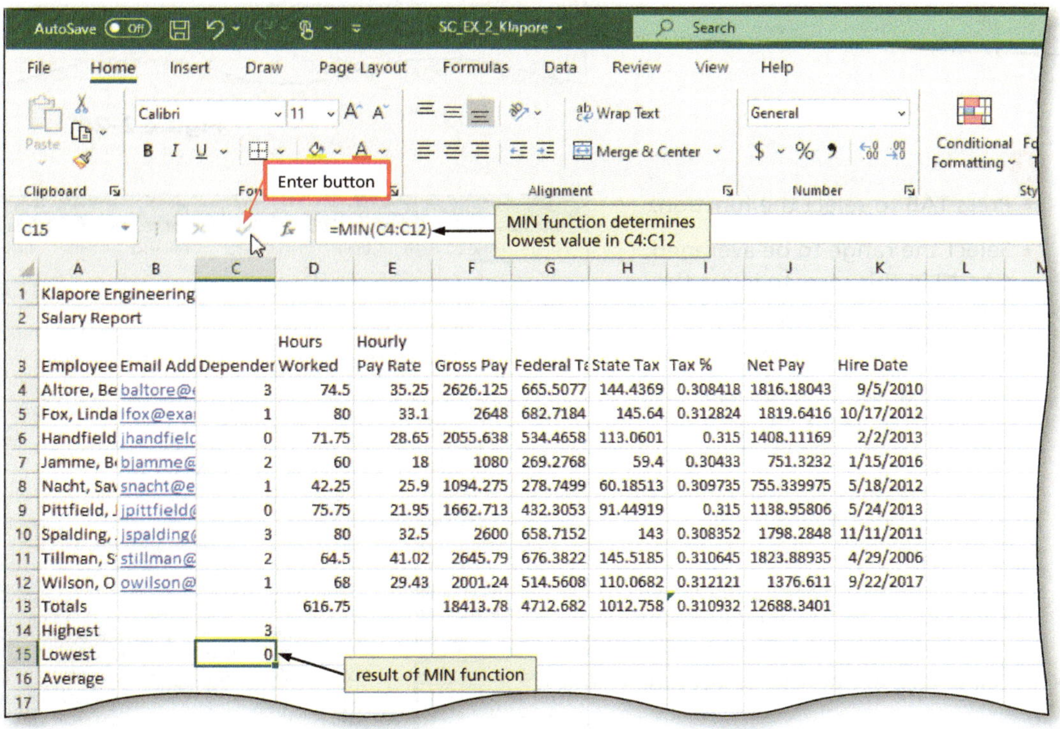

Figure 2–23

Other Ways

1. Click Insert Function button in formula bar, select Statistical category if necessary, click MIN, specify arguments
2. Click AutoSum arrow (Formulas tab | Function Library group), click Min
3. Type `=MIN(` in cell, fill in arguments, type `)`

To Determine the Average of a Range of Numbers Using the Keyboard

The **AVERAGE function** is an Excel function that calculates the average value of a collection of numbers. The following steps use the AVERAGE function to determine the average of the numbers in the range C4:C12. **Why?** The AVERAGE function calculates the average of a range of numbers.

1

- Select the cell to contain the average, cell C16 in this case.
- Type **=av** in the cell to display the Formula AutoComplete list. Press the DOWN ARROW key to highlight the AVERAGE function (Figure 2–24).

Q&A **What is happening as I type?** As you type the equal sign followed by the characters in the name of a function, Excel displays the Formula AutoComplete list. This list contains those functions whose names match the letters you have typed.

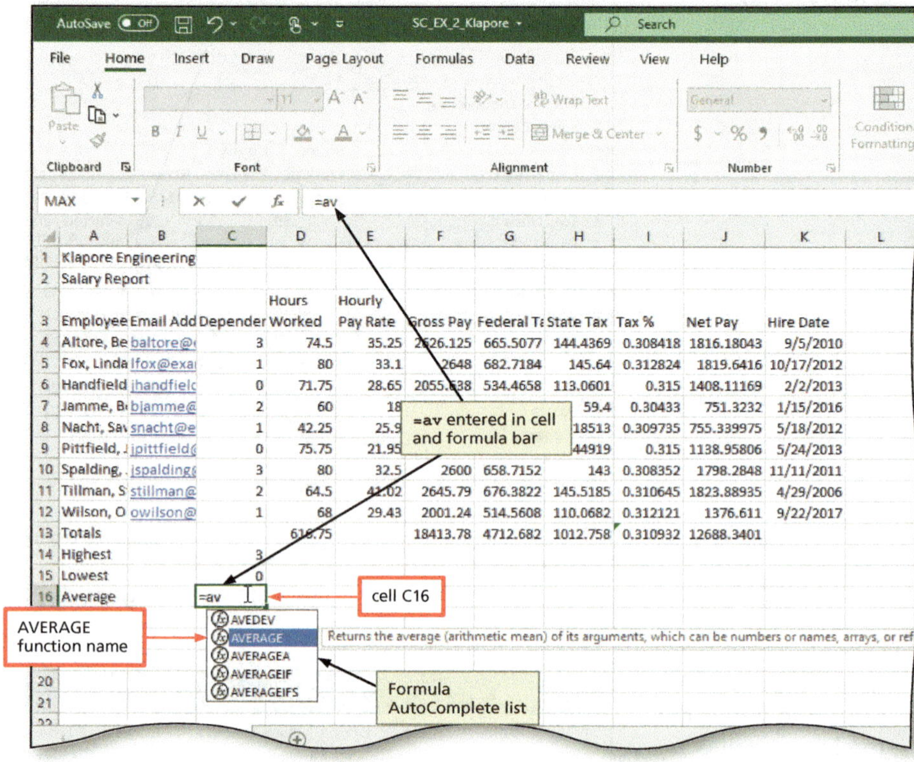

Figure 2–24

2

- Press TAB to select the function.
- Select the range to be averaged, C4:C12 in this case, to insert the range as the argument to the function (Figure 2–25).

Q&A **As I drag, why does the function in cell C16 change?** When you click cell C4, Excel surrounds cell C4 with a marquee and appends C4 to the left parenthesis in the formula bar. When you begin dragging, Excel appends to the argument a colon (:) and the cell reference of the cell where the pointer is located.

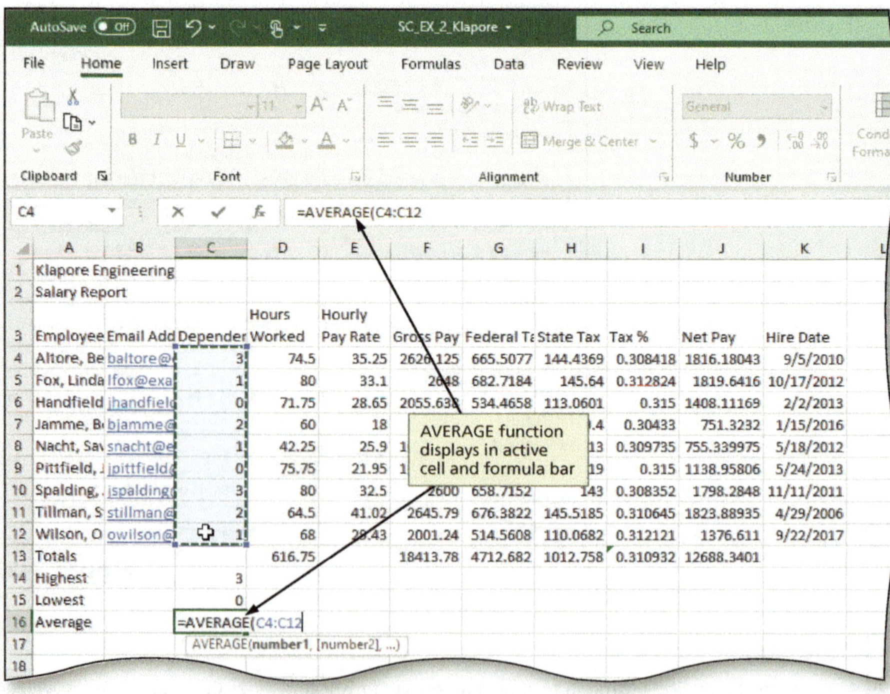

Figure 2–25

3

- Click the Enter button to compute the average of the numbers in the selected range and display the result in the selected cell (Figure 2–26).

Q&A

Can I use the arrow keys to complete the entry instead?
No. While in Point mode, the arrow keys change the selected cell reference in the range you are selecting instead of completing the entry.

What is the purpose of the parentheses in the function?
Most Excel functions require that the argument (in this case, the range C4:C12) be included within parentheses following the function name. In this case, Excel appended the right parenthesis to complete the AVERAGE function when you clicked the Enter button.

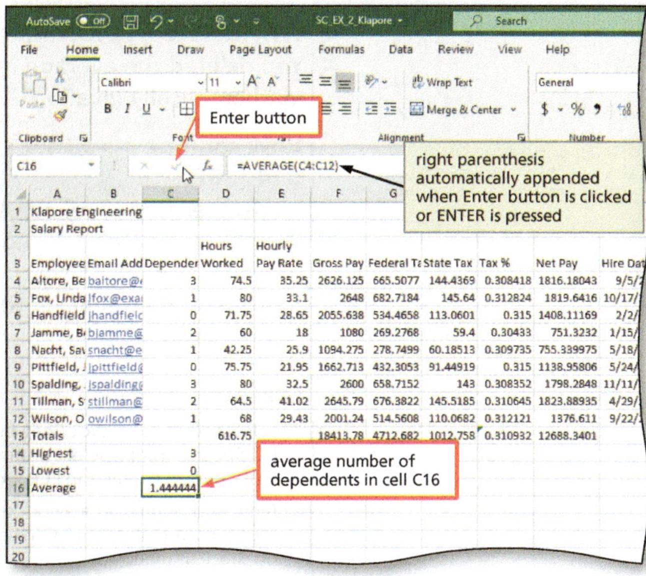

Figure 2–26

To Copy a Range of Cells across Columns to an Adjacent Range Using the Fill Handle

The next step is to copy the AVERAGE, MAX, and MIN functions in the range C14:C16 to the adjacent range D14:J16. The following steps use the fill handle to copy the functions.

1 Select the source range from which to copy the functions, in this case C14:C16.

2 Drag the fill handle in the lower-right corner of the selected range through cell J16 to copy the three functions to the selected range.

3 Select cell I16 and then press DELETE to delete the average of the Tax % (Figure 2–27).

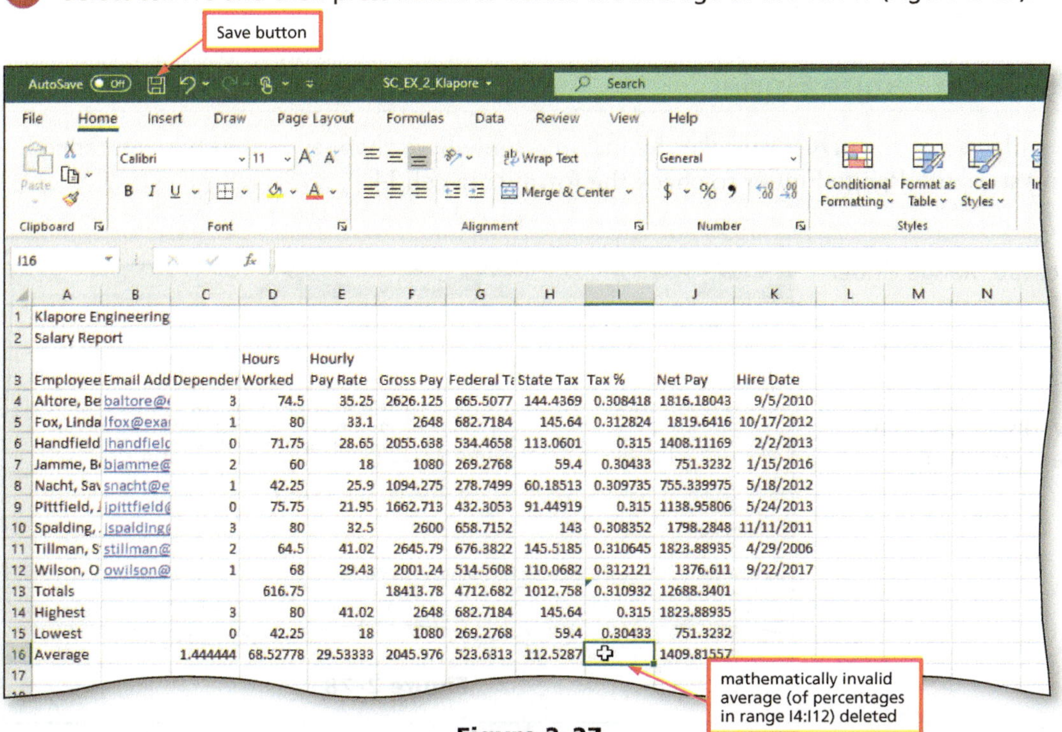

Figure 2–27

4. Save the workbook again with the same file name.

Q&A

Why delete the formula in cell I16?
You deleted the average in cell I16 because averaging this type of percentage is mathematically invalid.

How can I be sure that the function arguments are correct for the cells in range D14:J16?
Remember that Excel adjusts the cell references in the copied functions so that each function refers to the range of numbers above it in the same column. Review the functions in rows 14 through 16 by clicking on individual cells and examining the function as it appears in the formula bar. You should see that the functions in each column reference the appropriate ranges.

Other Ways

1. Select source area, click Copy button (Home tab | Clipboard group), select destination area, click Paste button (Home tab | Clipboard group)
2. Right-click source area, click Copy on shortcut menu; right-click destination area, click Paste icon on shortcut menu
3. Select source area and then point to border of range; while holding down CTRL, drag source area to destination area
4. Select source area, press CTRL+C, select destination area, press CTRL+V

Break Point: If you want to take a break, this is a good place to do so. You can exit Excel now. To resume later, start Excel, open the file called SC_EX_2_Klapore, and continue following the steps from this location forward.

Verifying Formulas Using Range Finder

One of the more common mistakes made with Excel is to include an incorrect cell reference in a formula. An easy way to verify that a formula references the cells you want it to reference is to use Range Finder. **Range Finder** checks which cells are referenced in the formula assigned to the active cell.

To use Range Finder to verify that a formula contains the intended cell references, double-click the cell with the formula you want to check. Excel responds by highlighting the cells referenced in the formula so that you can verify that the cell references are correct.

To Verify a Formula Using Range Finder

Why? Range Finder allows you to correct mistakes by making immediate changes to the cells referenced in a formula. The following steps use Range Finder to check the formula in cell I4.

1
- Double-click cell I4 to activate Range Finder (Figure 2–28).

2
- Press ESC to quit Range Finder and then click anywhere in the worksheet, such as cell A18, to deselect the current cell.

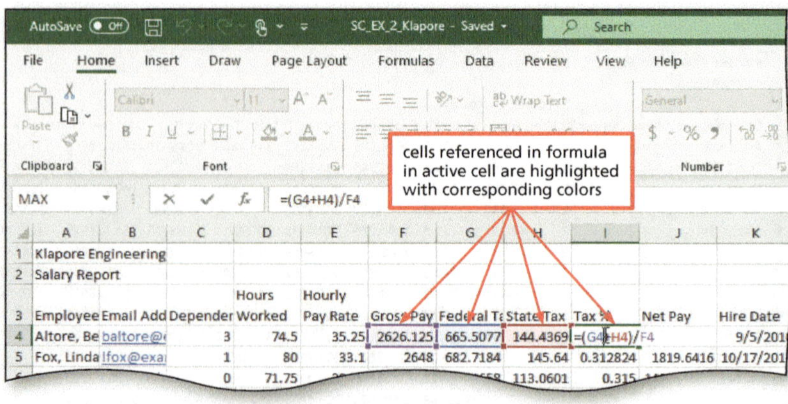

Figure 2–28

Formatting the Worksheet

Although the worksheet contains the appropriate data, formulas, and functions, the text and numbers need to be formatted to improve their appearance and readability.

In Module 1, you used cell styles to format much of the worksheet. This section describes how to change the unformatted worksheet in Figure 2–29a to the formatted worksheet in Figure 2–29b using a theme and other commands on the ribbon. A **theme** formats a worksheet by applying a collection of fonts, font styles, colors, and effects to give it a consistent appearance.

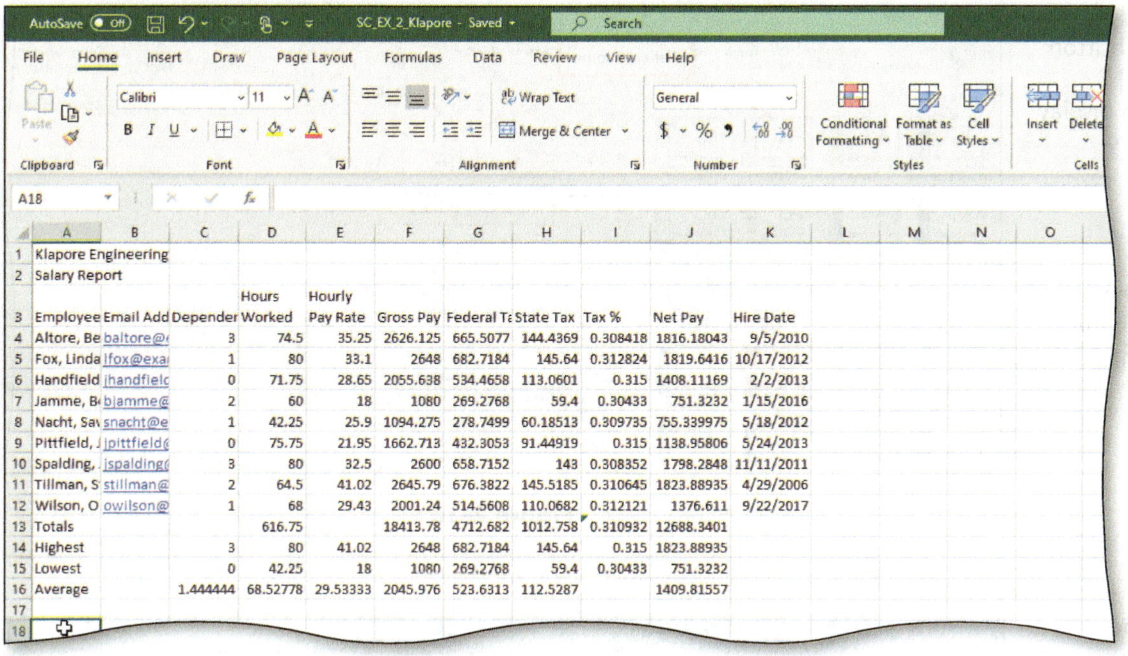

(a) Unformatted Worksheet

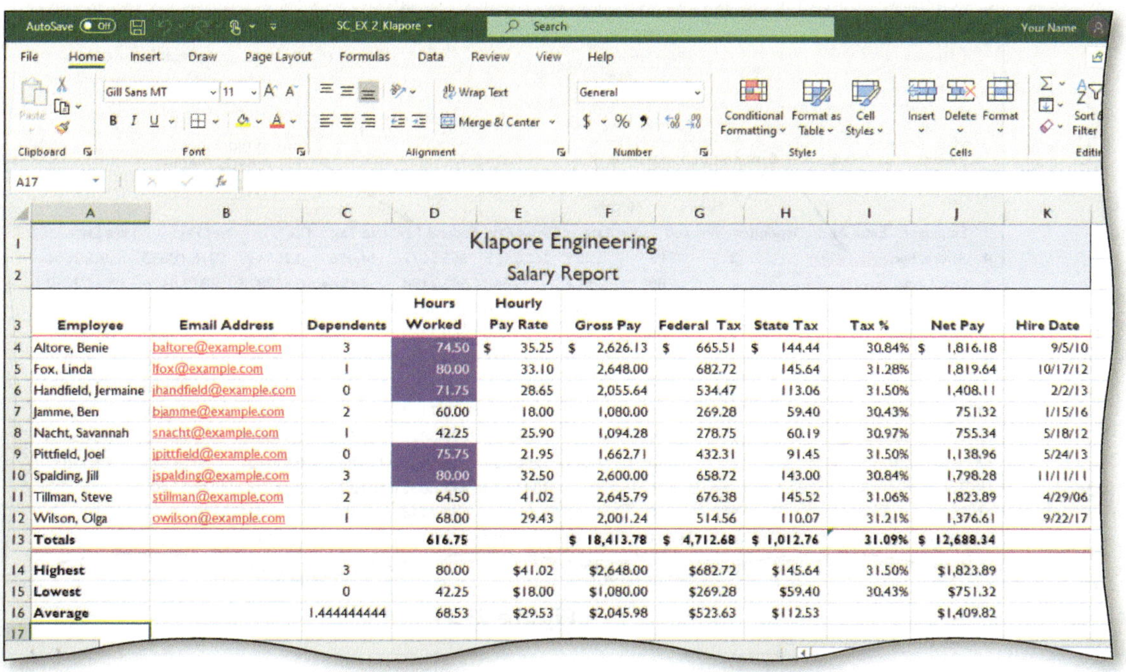

(b) Formatted Worksheet

Figure 2–29

To Change the Workbook Theme

Why? A company or department may choose a specific theme as their standard theme so that all of their documents have a similar appearance. Similarly, you may want to have a theme that sets your work apart from the work of others. Other Office programs, such as Word and PowerPoint, include the same themes so that all of your Microsoft Office documents can share a common look. The following steps change the workbook theme to the Gallery theme.

1

- Click Page Layout to display the Page Layout tab.
- Click the Themes button (Page Layout tab | Themes group) to display the Themes gallery (Figure 2–30).

Experiment

- Point to several themes in the Themes gallery to preview the themes.

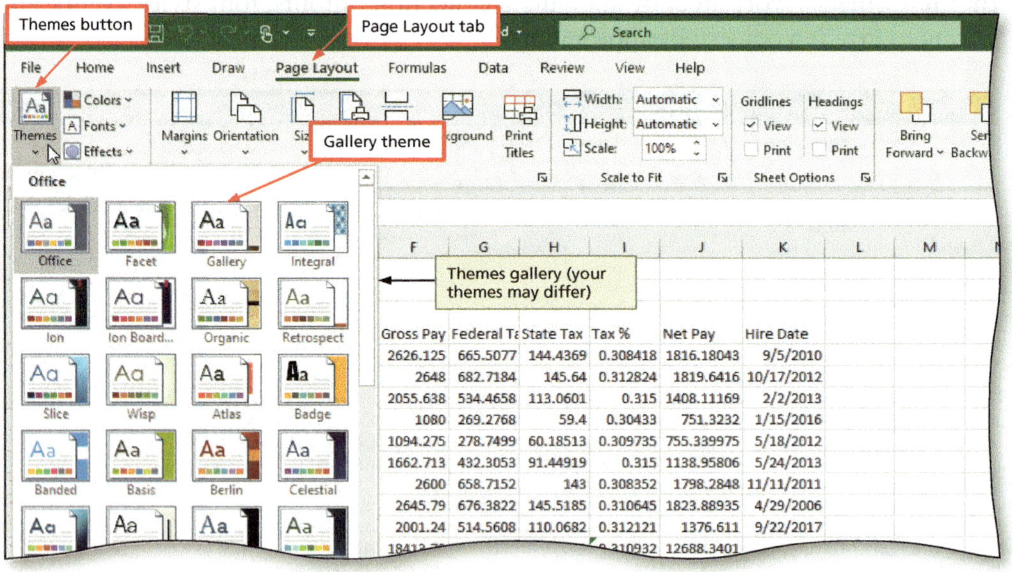

Figure 2–30

2

- Click Gallery in the Themes gallery to change the workbook theme (Figure 2–31).

Q&A

Why did the cells in the worksheet change?
Originally, the cells in the worksheet were formatted with the default font of the default Office theme. The Gallery theme has a different default font than the Office theme, so when you changed the theme, the font changed. If you had modified the font for any cells, those cells would not have changed to the default font of the Gallery theme.

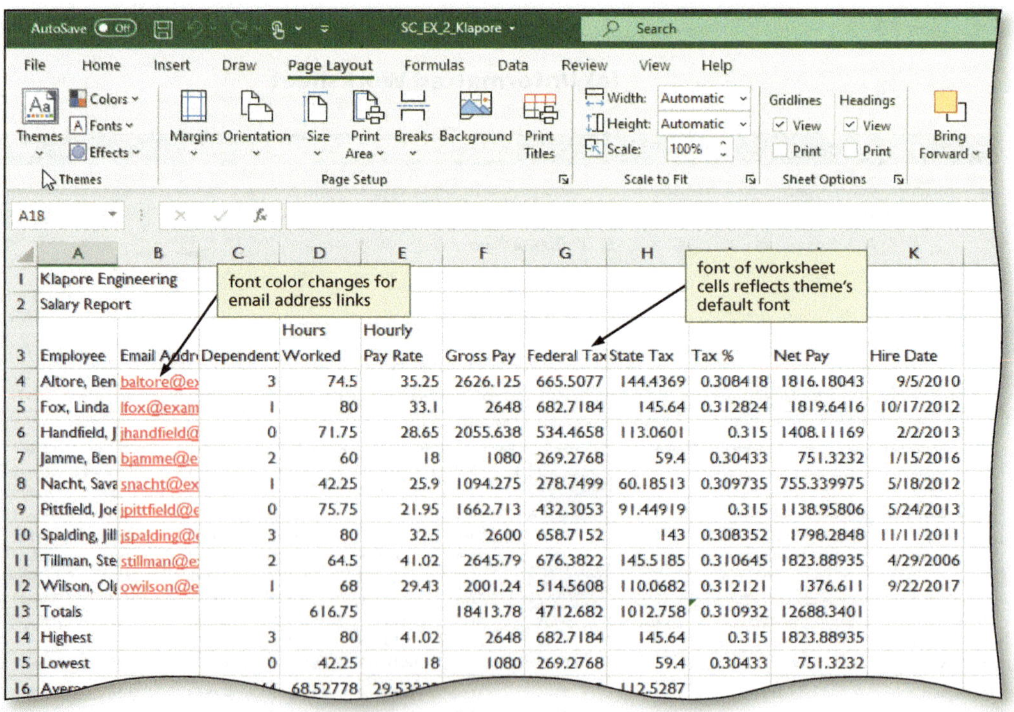

Figure 2–31

To Format the Worksheet Titles

The following steps merge and center the worksheet titles, apply the Title cells style to the worksheet titles, and decrease the font of the worksheet subtitle.

1. Display the Home tab.
2. Select the range to be merged, A1:K1 in this case, and then click the 'Merge & Center' button (Home tab | Alignment group) to merge and center the text in the selected range.
3. Select the range A2:K2 and then click the 'Merge & Center' button (Home tab | Alignment group) to merge and center the text.
4. Select the range to contain the Title cell style, in this case A1:A2, click the Cell Styles button (Home tab | Styles group) to display the Cell Styles gallery, and then click the Title cell style in the Titles and Headings group in the Cell Styles gallery to apply the Title cell style to the selected range.
5. Select cell A2 and then click the 'Decrease Font Size' button (Home tab | Font group) to decrease the font size of the selected cell to the next lower font size (Figure 2–32).

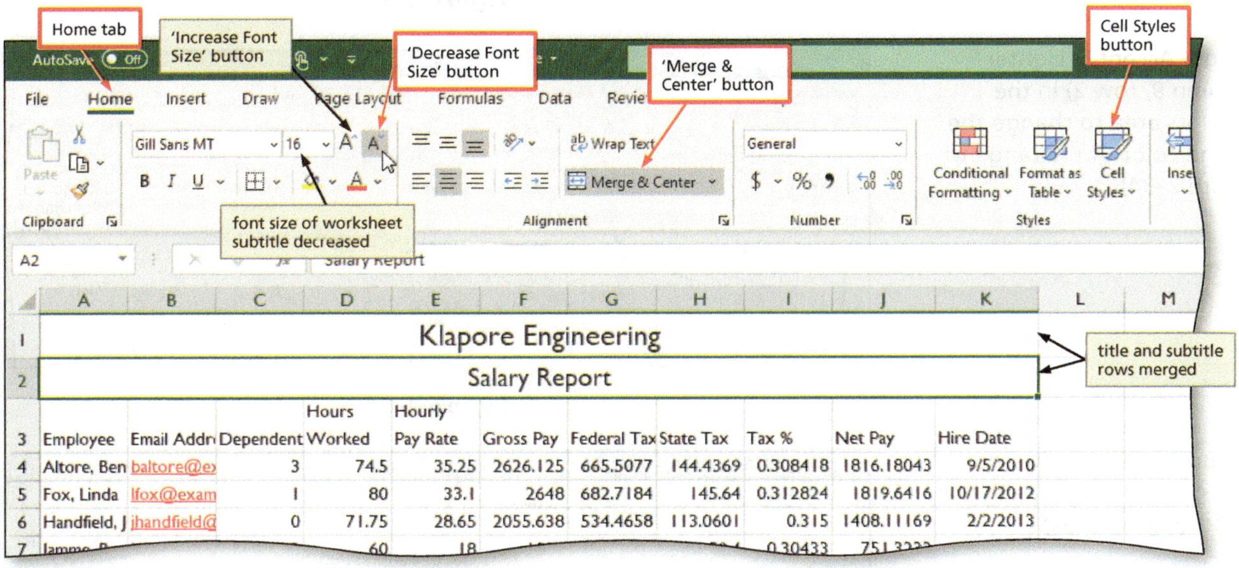

Figure 2–32

Q&A

What happens when I click the 'Decrease Font Size' button?
When you click the 'Decrease Font Size' button, Excel assigns the next smaller font size in the Font Size gallery to the selected range. The 'Increase Font Size' button works in a similar manner, assigning the next larger font size in the Font Size gallery to the selected range.

Consider This

Which colors work best when formatting your worksheet?
Knowing how people perceive colors can help you focus attention on parts of your worksheet. For example, warmer colors (red and orange) tend to reach toward the reader. Cooler colors (blue, green, and violet) tend to pull away from the reader.

To Change the Background Color and Apply a Box Border to the Worksheet Title and Subtitle

Why? A background color and border can draw attention to the title of a worksheet. The final formats assigned to the worksheet title and subtitle are the blue-gray background color and thick outside border. The following steps complete the formatting of the worksheet titles.

1

- Select the range A1:A2 and then click the Fill Color arrow (Home tab | Font group) to display the Fill Color gallery (Figure 2–33).

Experiment

- Point to a variety of colors in the Fill Color gallery to preview the selected colors in the range A1:A2.

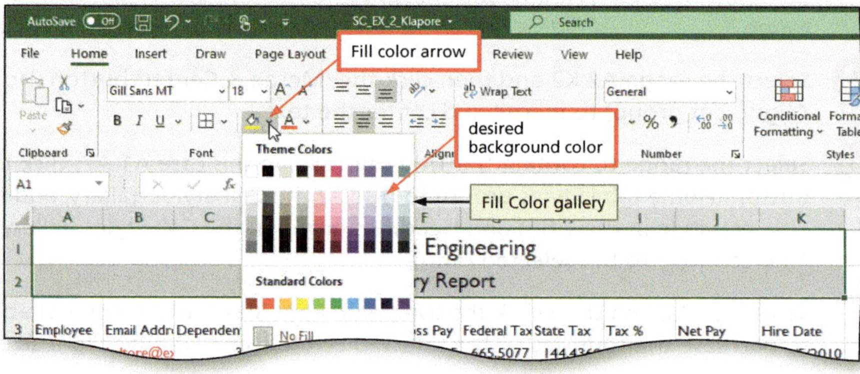

Figure 2–33

2

- Click Indigo, Accent 5, Lighter 80% (column 9, row 2) in the Theme Colors area to change the background color of the range of cells (Figure 2–34).

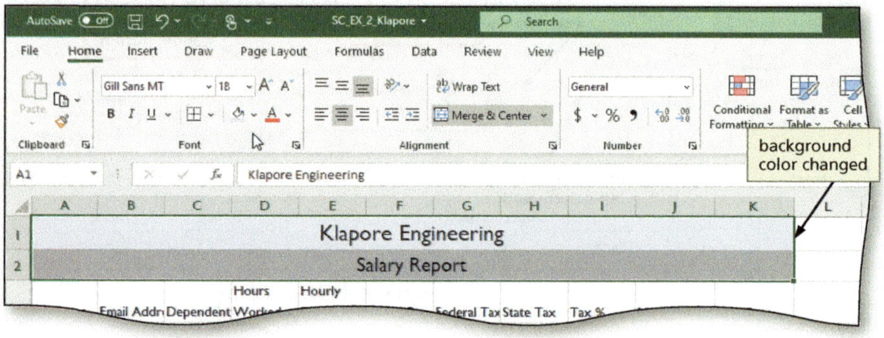

Figure 2–34

3

- Click the Borders arrow (Home tab | Font group) to display the Borders list (Figure 2–35).

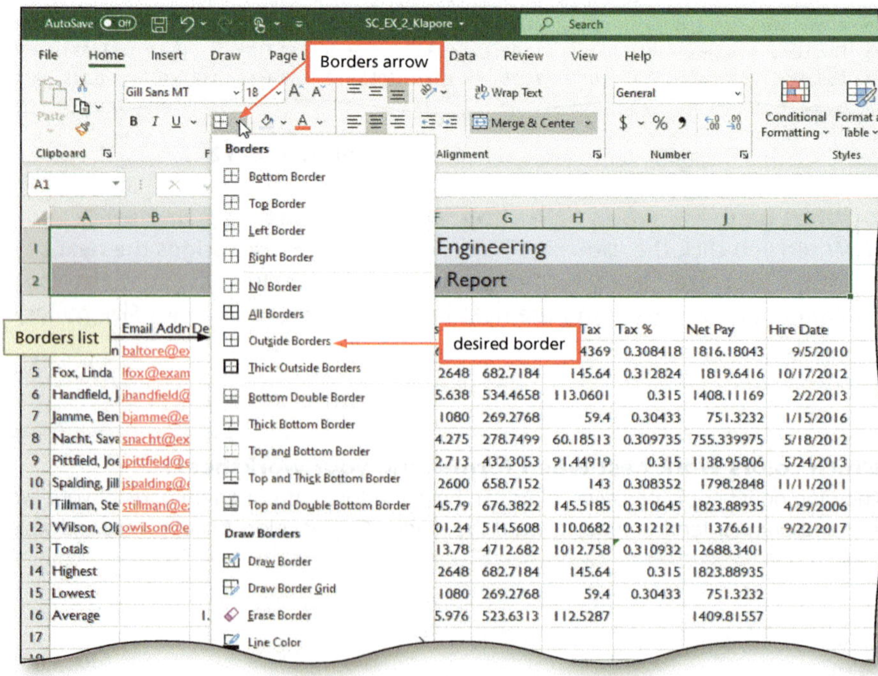

Figure 2–35

4

- Click 'Outside Borders' in the Borders gallery to create an outside border around the selected range.
- Click anywhere in the worksheet, such as cell A17, to deselect the current range (Figure 2–36).

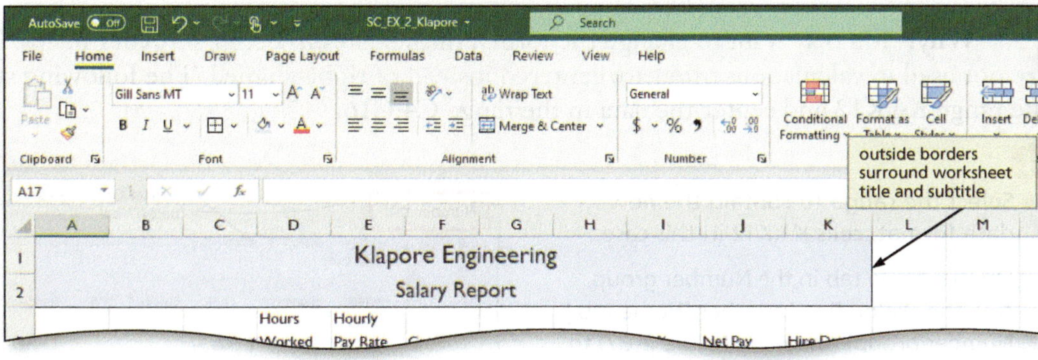

Figure 2–36

Other Ways

1. Click Font Settings Dialog Box Launcher (Home tab | Font group), click Fill tab (Format Cells dialog box), click desired fill, click OK
2. Right-click range, click Format Cells on shortcut menu, click Fill tab (Format Cells dialog box), click desired fill, click OK
3. Press CTRL+1, click Fill tab (Format Cells dialog box), click desired fill, click OK

To Apply a Cell Style to the Column Headings and Format the Total Rows

As shown in Figure 2–29b, the column titles (row 3) should have the Heading 3 cell style and the totals row (row 13) should have the Total cell style. The headings in the range A14:A16 should be bold. The following steps assign these styles and formats to row 3, row 13, and the range A14:A16.

BTW
Color Selection
Bright colors jump out of a dark background and are easiest to see. White or yellow text on a dark blue, green, purple, or black background is ideal for highlighting.

1. Select the range to be formatted, cells A3:K3 in this case.
2. Use the Cell Styles gallery to apply the Heading 3 cell style to the range A3:K3.
3. Click the Center button (Home tab | Alignment group) to center the column headings.
4. Apply the Total cell style to the range A13:K13.
5. Bold the range A14:A16 (Figure 2–37).

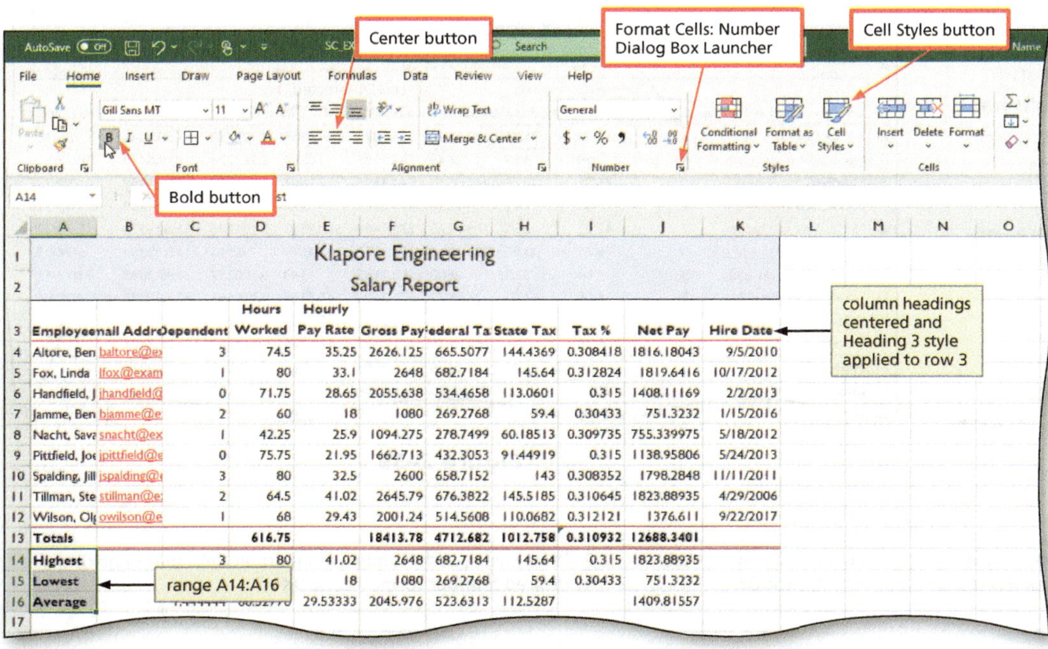

Figure 2–37

BTW
Background Colors
The most popular background color is blue. Research shows that the color blue is used most often because this color connotes serenity, reflection, and proficiency. Use color in spreadsheets to highlight data or to format worksheet elements such as titles. In most cases, colors should not be used for numbers because it may make them less visible.

To Format Dates and Center Data in Cells

Why? You may want to change the format of the dates to better suit your needs. In addition, numbers that are not used in calculations often are centered instead of right-aligned. The following steps format the dates in the range K4:K12 and center the data in the range C4:C16.

1

- Select the range to contain the new date format, cells K4:K12 in this case.
- On the Home tab in the Number group, click the Dialog Box Launcher (Home tab | Number group) (shown in Figure 2–37) to display the Format Cells dialog box.
- If necessary, click the Number tab (Format Cells dialog box), click Date in the Category list, and then click 3/14/12 in the Type list to choose the format for the selected range (Figure 2–38).

2

- Click OK (Format Cells dialog box) to format the dates in the current column using the selected date format style.

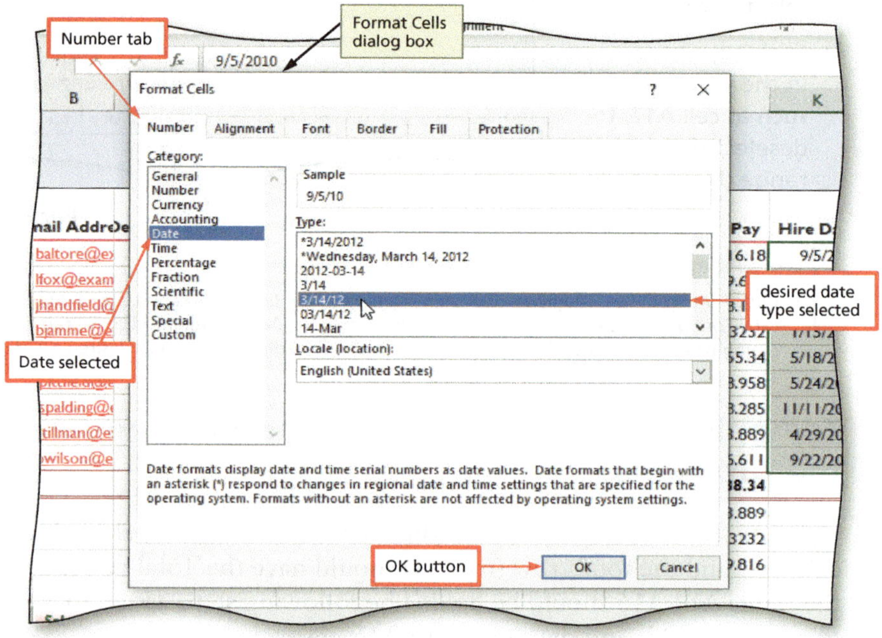

Figure 2–38

3

- Select the range C4:C16 and then click the Center button (Home tab | Alignment group) to center the data in the selected range.
- Select cell E4 to deselect the selected range (Figure 2–39).

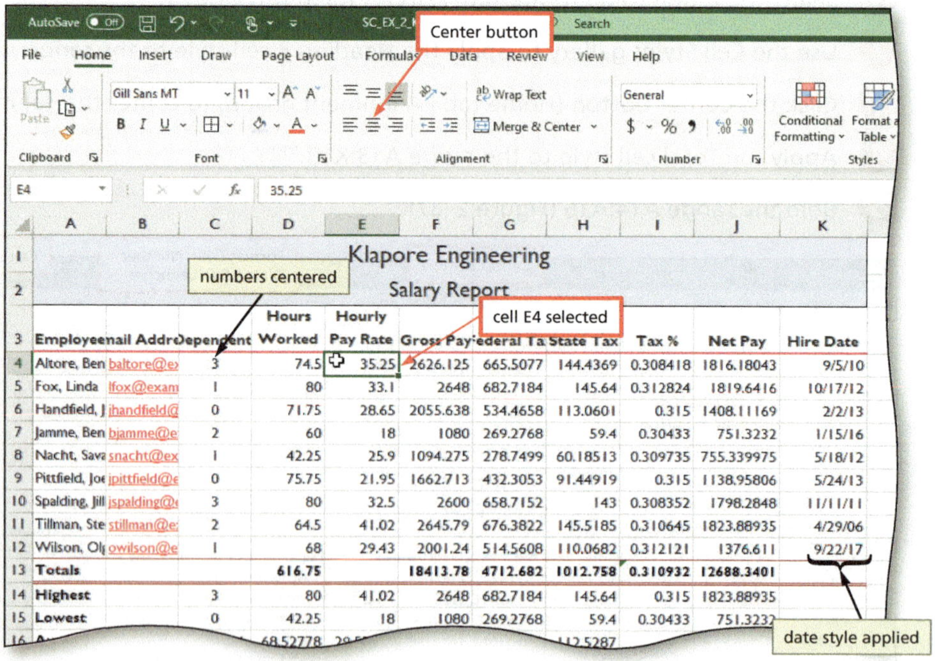

Figure 2–39

Q&A

How can I format an entire column at once?

Instead of selecting the range C4:C16 in Step 3, you could have clicked the column C heading immediately above cell C1, and then clicked the Center button (Home tab | Alignment group). In this case, all cells in column C down to the last cell in the worksheet would have been formatted to use center alignment. This same procedure could have been used to format the dates in column K.

Other Ways

1. Right-click range, click Format Cells on shortcut menu, click Number tab (Format Cells dialog box), click desired number format, click OK
2. Press CTRL+1, click Number tab (Format Cells dialog box), click desired number format, click OK

To Apply an Accounting Number Format and Comma Style Format Using the Ribbon

As shown in Figure 2–29b, the worksheet is formatted to resemble an accounting report. In columns E through H and J, the numbers in the first row (row 4), the totals row (row 13), and the rows below the totals (rows 14 through 16) have dollar signs, while the remaining numbers (rows 5 through 12) in columns E through H and column J do not. The following steps assign formats using the 'Accounting Number Format' button and the Comma Style button. **Why?** This gives the worksheet a more professional look.

1. Select the range to contain the accounting number format, cells E4:H4 in this case.
2. While holding down CTRL, select cell J4, the range F13:H13, and cell J13 to select the nonadjacent ranges and cells.
3. Click the 'Accounting Number Format' button (Home tab | Number group) to apply the accounting number format with fixed dollar signs to the selected nonadjacent ranges.

Q&A

What is the effect of applying the accounting number format?
The 'Accounting Number Format' button assigns a fixed dollar sign to the numbers in the ranges and rounds the figure to the nearest 100th. A fixed dollar sign is one that appears to the far left of the cell, with multiple spaces between it and the first digit in the cell.

4. Select the ranges to contain the comma style format, cells E5:H12 and J5:J12 in this case.
5. Click the Comma Style button (Home tab | Number group) to assign the comma style format to the selected ranges.
6. Select the range D4:D16 and then click the Comma Style button (Home tab | Number group) to assign the comma style format to the selected range (Figure 2–40).

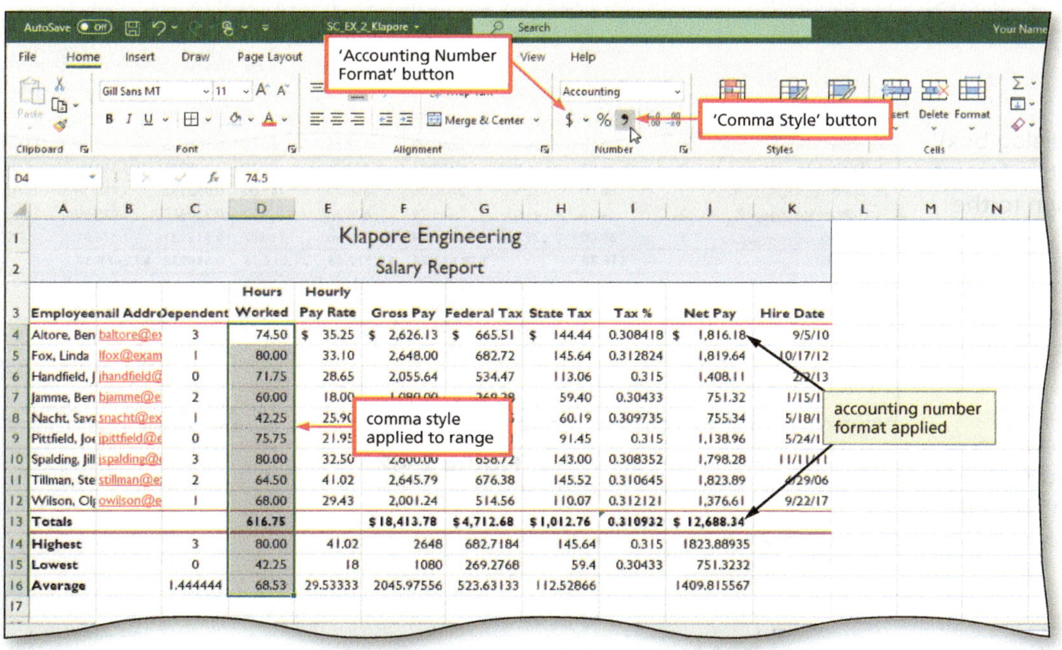

Figure 2–40

To Apply a Currency Style Format with a Floating Dollar Sign Using the Format Cells Dialog Box

Why? The Currency format places dollar signs immediately to the left of the number (known as floating dollar signs, as they change position depending on the number of digits in the cell) and displays a zero for cells that have a value of zero. The following steps use the Format Cells dialog box to apply the currency style format with a floating dollar sign to the numbers in the ranges E14:H16 and J14:J16.

1

- Select the ranges (E14:H16 and J14:J16) and then on the Home tab in the Number group, click the Dialog Box Launcher to display the Format Cells dialog box.
- If necessary, click the Number tab to display the Number sheet (Format Cells dialog box).
- Click Currency in the Category list to select the necessary number format category and then click the third style ($1,234.10) in the Negative numbers list to select the desired currency format for negative numbers (Figure 2–41).

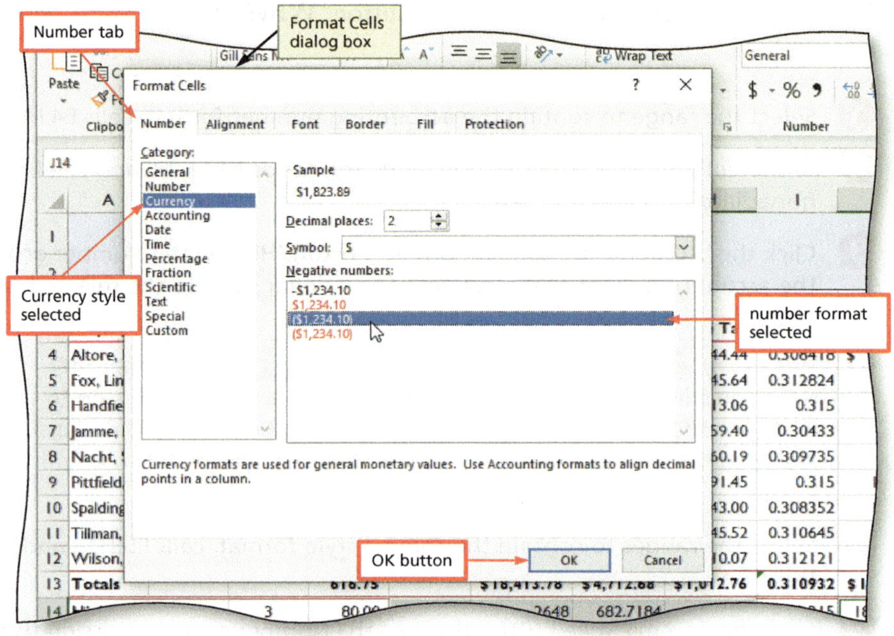

Figure 2–41

Q&A **How do I decide which number format to use?**
Excel offers many ways to format numbers. Once you select a number category, you can select the number of decimal places, whether to include a dollar sign (or a symbol of another currency), and how negative numbers should appear. Selecting the appropriate negative numbers format is important, because some formats add a space to the right of the number in order to align numbers in the worksheet on the decimal points and some do not.

2

- Click OK (Format Cells dialog box) to assign the currency style format with a floating dollar sign to the selected ranges (Figure 2–42).

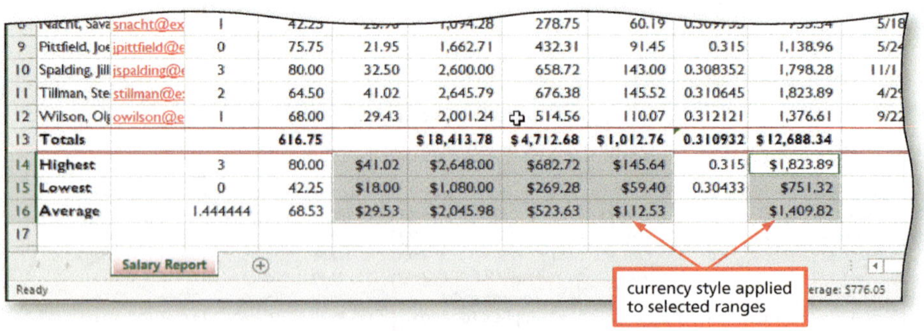

Figure 2–42

Q&A **What is the difference between using the accounting number style and currency style?**
When using the currency style, recall that a floating dollar sign always appears immediately to the left of the first digit. With the accounting number style, the fixed dollar sign always appears on the left side of the cell.

Other Ways

1. Press CTRL+1, click Number tab (Format Cells dialog box), click Currency in Category list, select format, click OK
2. Press CTRL+SHIFT+DOLLAR SIGN ($)

To Apply a Percent Style Format and Use the Increase Decimal Button

The next step is to format the tax percentage in column I. **Why?** Currently, Excel displays the numbers as decimal fractions when they should appear as percentages. The following steps format the range I4:I15 to the percent style format with two decimal places.

1

- Select the range to format, cells I4:I15 in this case.
- Click the Percent Style button (Home tab | Number group) to display the numbers in the selected range as a rounded whole percent.

Q&A

What is the result of clicking the Percent Style button?

The Percent Style button instructs Excel to display a value as a percentage, which is determined by multiplying the cell entry by 100, rounding the result to the nearest percentage, and adding a percent sign. For example, when cell I4 is formatted using the Percent Style buttons, Excel displays the actual value 0.308418 as 31%.

2

- Click the Increase Decimal button (Home tab | Number group) two times to display the numbers in the selected range with two decimal places (Figure 2–43).

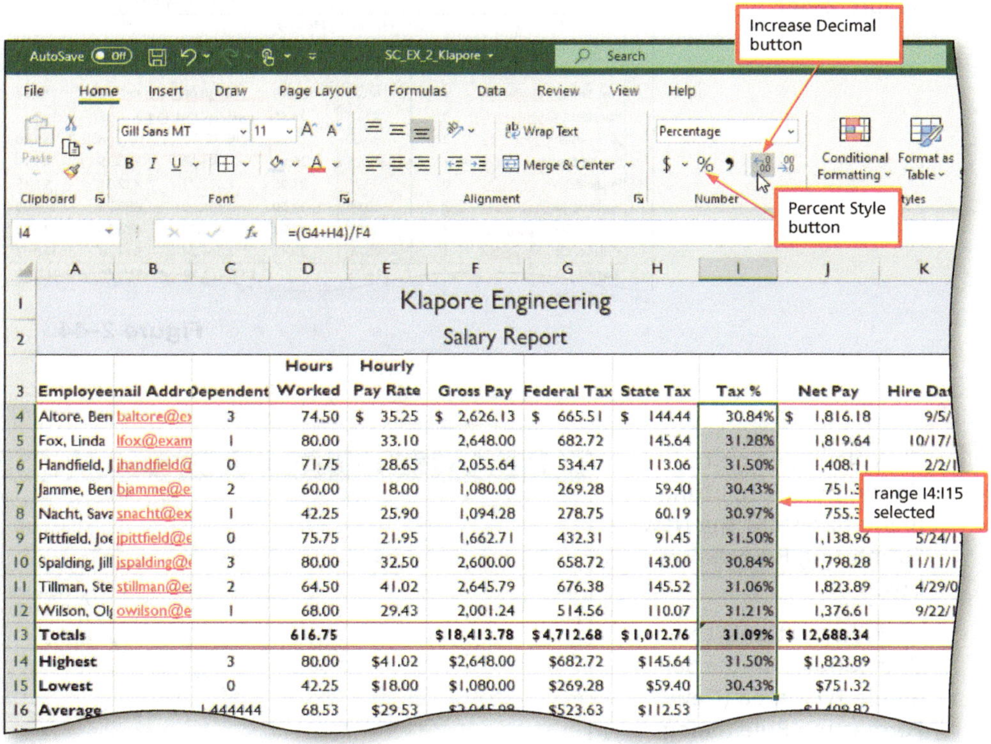

Figure 2–43

Other Ways

1. Right-click selected range, click Format Cells on shortcut menu, click Number tab (Format Cells dialog box), click Percentage in Category list, select format, click OK
2. Press CTRL+1, click Number tab (Format Cells dialog box), click Percentage in Category list, select format, click OK button
3. Press CTRL+SHIFT+PERCENT SIGN (%)

Conditional Formatting

Conditional formatting is special formatting — the font, font color, background fill, and other options — that is applied if cell values meet specified criteria. Excel offers a variety of commonly used conditional formatting rules, along with the ability to create your own custom rules and formatting. The next step is to emphasize the values greater than 70 in column D by formatting them to appear with a purple background and white font color.

BTW

Conditional Formatting

You can assign any format to a cell, a range of cells, a worksheet, or an entire workbook conditionally. If the value of the cell changes and no longer meets the specified condition, Excel suppresses the conditional formatting.

To Apply Conditional Formatting

The following steps assign conditional formatting to the range D4:D12. **Why?** After formatting, any cell with a value greater than 70 in column D will appear with a purple background and a white font.

1

- Select the range D4:D12.
- Click the Conditional Formatting button (Home tab | Styles group) to display the Conditional Formatting menu (Figure 2–44).

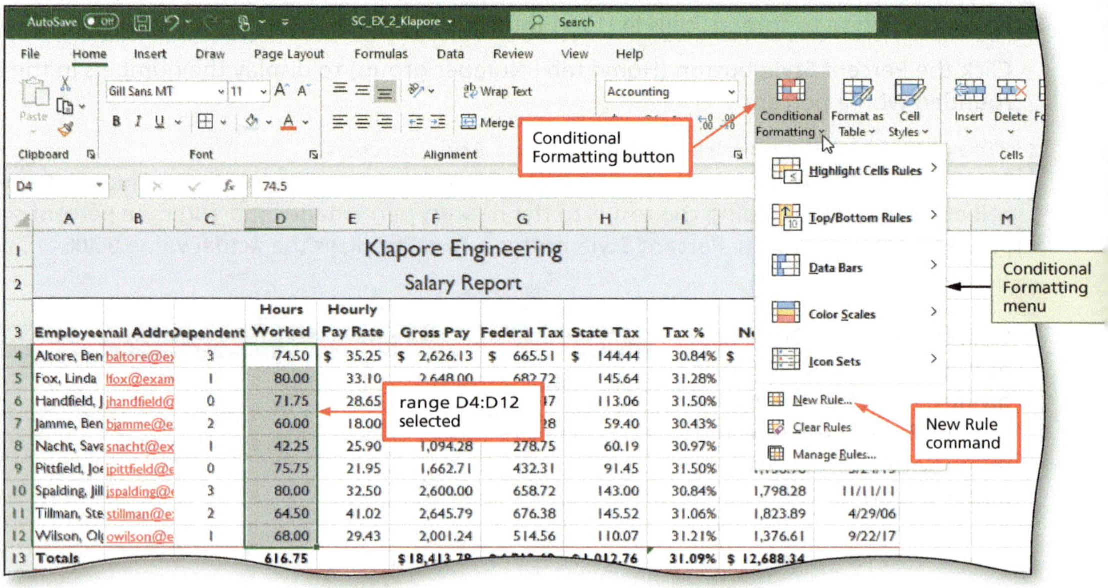

Figure 2–44

2

- Click New Rule on the Conditional Formatting menu to display the New Formatting Rule dialog box.
- Click 'Format only cells that contain' in the Select a Rule Type area (New Formatting Rule dialog box) to change the Edit the Rule Description area.
- In the Edit the Rule Description area, click the arrow in the relational operator box (second box) to display a list of relational operators, and then select greater than to select the desired operator.

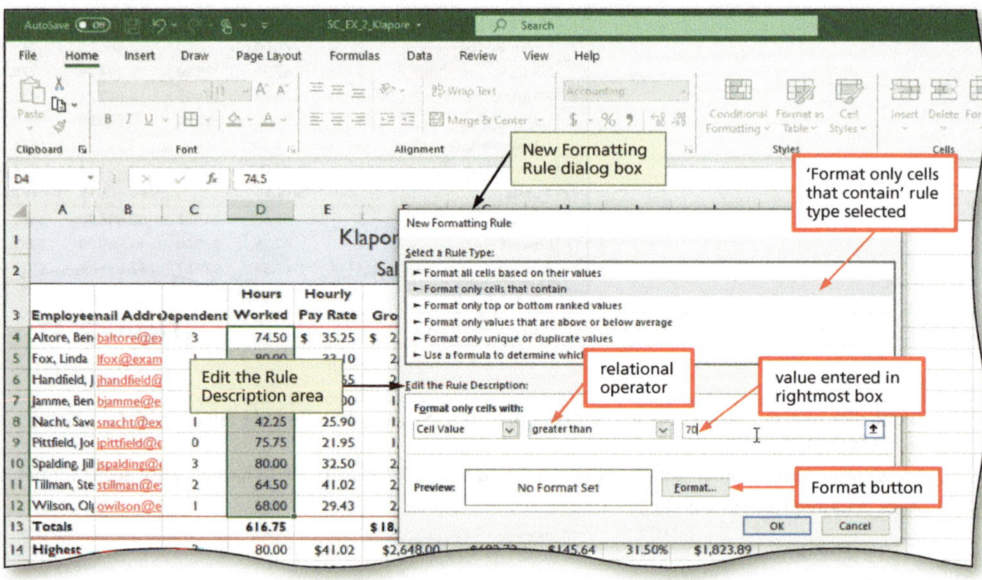

Figure 2–45

- Click in the rightmost box, and then type `70` to enter the value of the rule description (Figure 2–45).

Q&A **What do the changes in the Edit the Rule Description area indicate?**
The Edit the Rule Description area allows you to view and edit the rules for the conditional format. In this case, the rule indicates that Excel should format only those cells with cell values greater than 70.

3

- Click the Format button (New Formatting Rule dialog box) to display the Format Cells dialog box.
- If necessary, click the Font tab (Format Cells dialog box) to display the Font sheet. Click the Color arrow to display the Color gallery and then click White, Background 1 (column 1, row 1) in the Color gallery to select the font color (Figure 2–46).

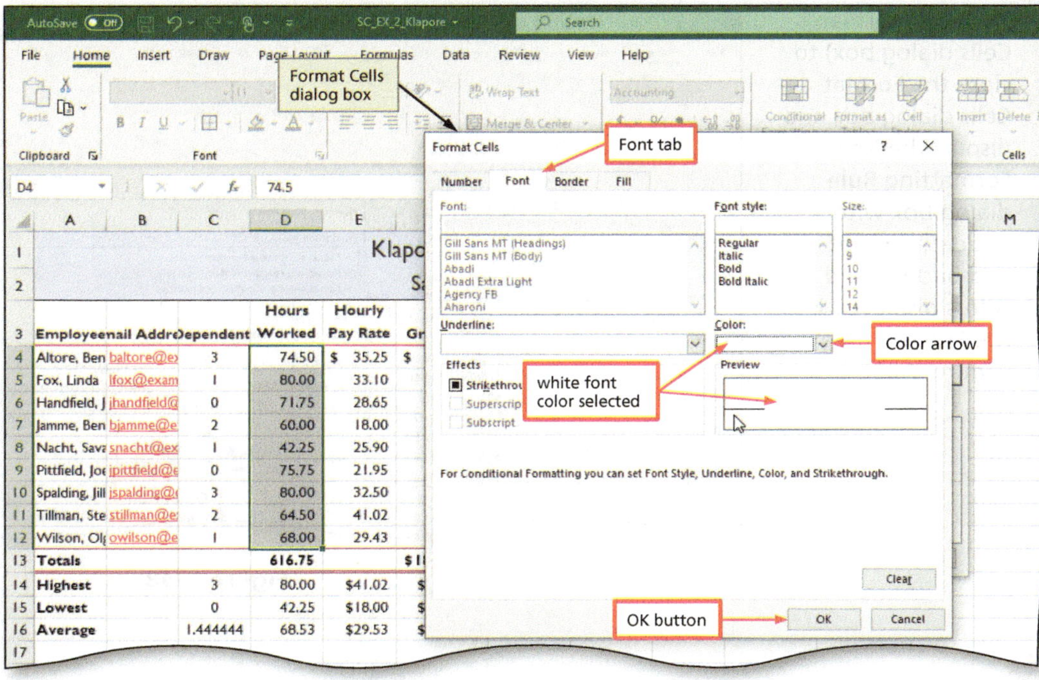

Figure 2–46

4

- Click the Fill tab (Format Cells dialog box) and then click the purple color in column 8, row 1 to select the background color (Figure 2–47).

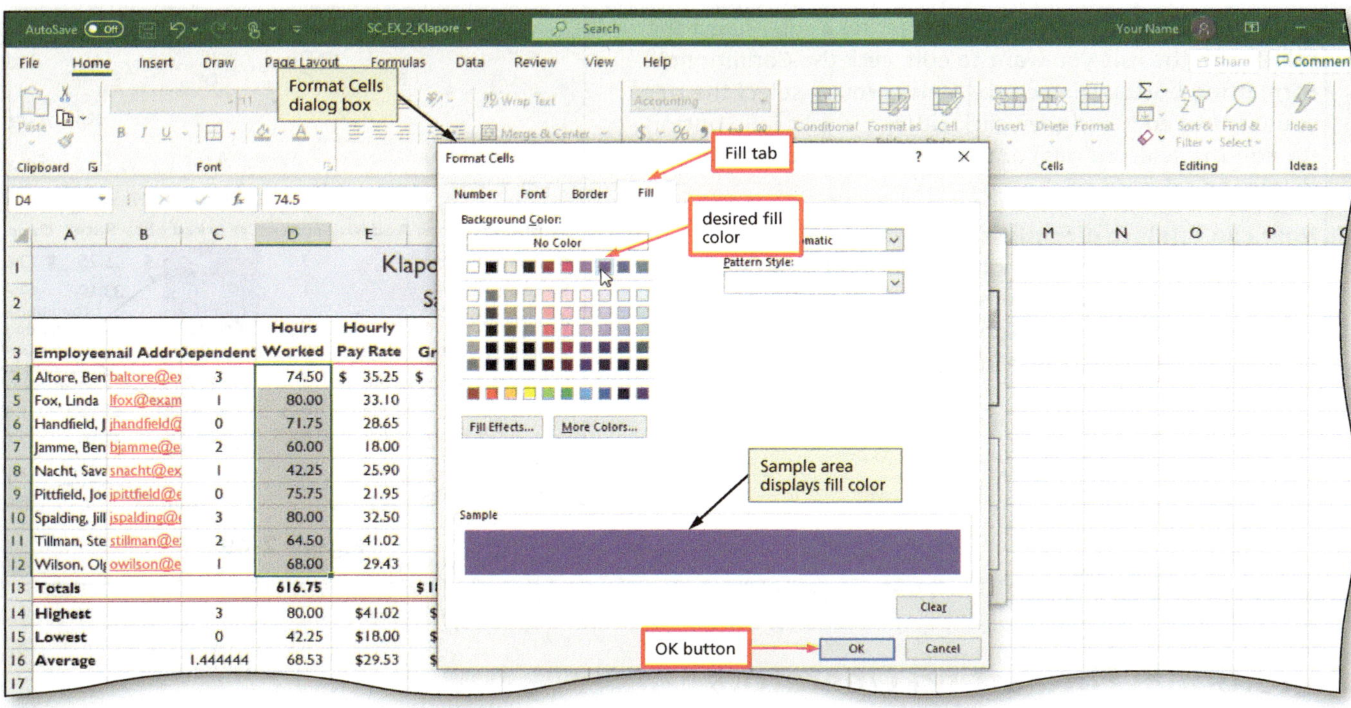

Figure 2–47

5

- Click OK (Format Cells dialog box) to close the Format Cells dialog box and display the New Formatting Rule dialog box with the desired font and background colors displayed in the Preview area (Figure 2–48).

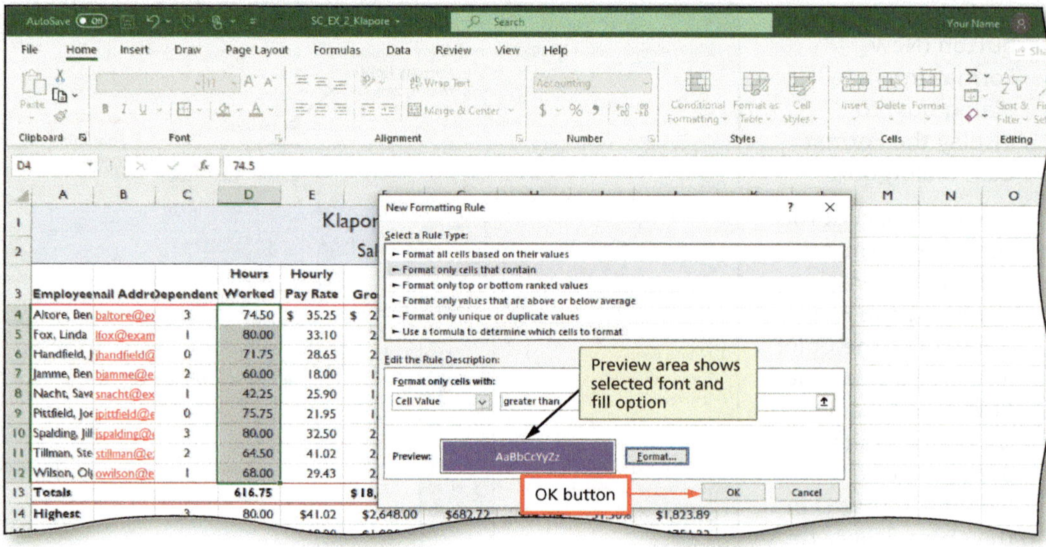

Figure 2–48

6

- Click OK (New Formatting Rule dialog box) to assign the conditional format to the selected range.
- Click anywhere in the worksheet, such as cell A17, to deselect the current range (Figure 2–49).

Q&A

What should I do if I make a mistake setting up a rule?
If after you have applied the conditional formatting you realize you made a mistake when creating a rule, select the cell(s) with the rule you want to edit, click the Conditional Formatting button (Home tab | Styles group), select the rule you want to edit, and then click either the Edit Rule button (to edit the selected rule) or the Delete Rule button (to delete the selected rule).

How can I delete a conditional formatting rule?
If you no longer want a conditional formatting rule applied to a cell, select the cell or cells, click the Conditional Formatting button (Home tab | Styles group), click Clear Rules, and then select Clear Rules from Selected Cells.

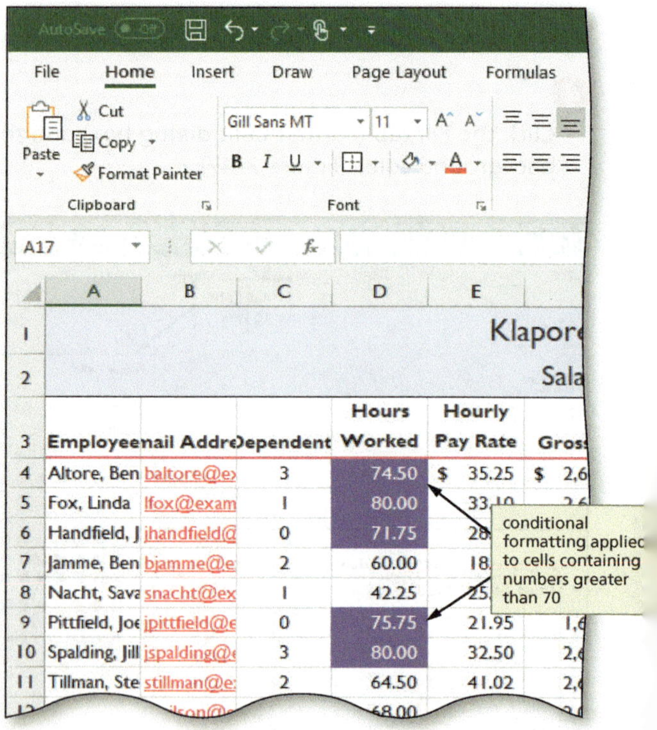

Figure 2–49

Conditional Formatting Operators

As shown in the New Formatting Rule dialog box, when the selected rule type is "Format only the cells that contain," the second text box in the Edit the Rule Description area allows you to select a relational operator, such as greater than, to use in the condition. The eight different relational operators from which you can choose for conditional formatting are summarized in Table 2–5.

Table 2–5 Summary of Conditional Formatting Relational Operators

Relational Operator	Formatting Will Be Applied If...
between	cell value is between two numbers
not between	cell value is not between two numbers
equal to	cell value is equal to a number
not equal to	cell value is not equal to a number
greater than	cell value is greater than a number
less than	cell value is less than a number
greater than or equal to	cell value is greater than or equal to a number
less than or equal to	cell value is less than or equal to a number

Changing Column Width and Row Height

You can change the width of the columns or height of the rows at any time to make the worksheet easier to read or to ensure that an entry fits properly in a cell. By default, all of the columns in a blank worksheet have a width of 8.43 characters, or 64 pixels. This value may change depending on the theme applied to the workbook. For example, when you applied the Gallery theme to the workbook in this module, the default width of the columns changed to 8.38 characters. A **character** is defined as a letter, number, symbol, or punctuation mark. An average of 8.43 characters in 11-point Calibri font (the default font used by Excel) will fit in a cell.

The default row height in a blank worksheet is 15 points (or 20 pixels), which easily fits the 11-point default font. Recall from Module 1 that a point is equal to 1/72 of an inch. Thus, 15 points is equal to about 1/5 of an inch.

Another measure of the height and width of cells is pixels. A **pixel**, which is short for picture element, is an individual point of color on a display screen or printout. The size of the dot is based on your screen's resolution. At the resolution of 1366 × 768, for example, 1366 pixels appear across the screen and 768 pixels appear down the screen for a total of 1,049,088 pixels. It is these 1,049,088 pixels that form the font and other items you see on the screen.

In addition to changing column width and row heights, you also can hide columns and rows so that they temporarily do not appear. The values in the columns and rows will remain, but they will not appear on the screen. To hide a column or row, right-click the column letter or row number and then click hide. To unhide a hidden column or row, select the columns to the left and right of the hidden column, right-click the column heading, and then click Unhide. To unhide a hidden row, select the rows above and below the hidden row, right-click the row numbers, and then click Unhide.

BTW

Hidden Rows and Columns

For some people, trying to unhide a range of columns using the mouse can be frustrating. An alternative is to use the keyboard: select the columns to the right and left of the hidden columns and then press CTRL+SHIFT+) (RIGHT PARENTHESIS). To use the keyboard to hide a range of columns, press CTRL+0 (zero). You also can use the keyboard to unhide a range of rows by selecting the rows immediately above and below the hidden rows and then pressing CTRL+SHIFT+((LEFT PARENTHESIS). To use the keyboard to hide a range of rows, press CTRL+9.

To Change Column Width

When changing the column width, you can set the width manually or you can instruct Excel to size the column to best fit. **Best fit** is an Excel feature that automatically increases or decreases the width of a column so that the widest entry will fit. **Why?** Sometimes, you may prefer more or less white space in a column than best fit provides. To change the white space, Excel allows you to change column widths manually.

When the format you assign to a cell causes the entry to exceed the width of a column, Excel changes the column width to best fit. If you do not assign a format to a cell or cells in a column, the column width will remain 8.43 characters. Recall from Module 1 that to set a column width to best fit, double-click the right boundary of the column heading above row 1. The following steps change the column widths.

1

- Drag through column headings A, B, and C above row 1 to select the columns.
- Point to the boundary on the right side of column heading C to cause the pointer to become a split double arrow (Figure 2–50).

Q&A **What if I want to make a large change to the column width?**
If you want to increase or decrease column width significantly, you can right-click a column heading and then use the Column Width command on the shortcut menu to change the column's width. To use this command, however, you must select one or more entire columns.

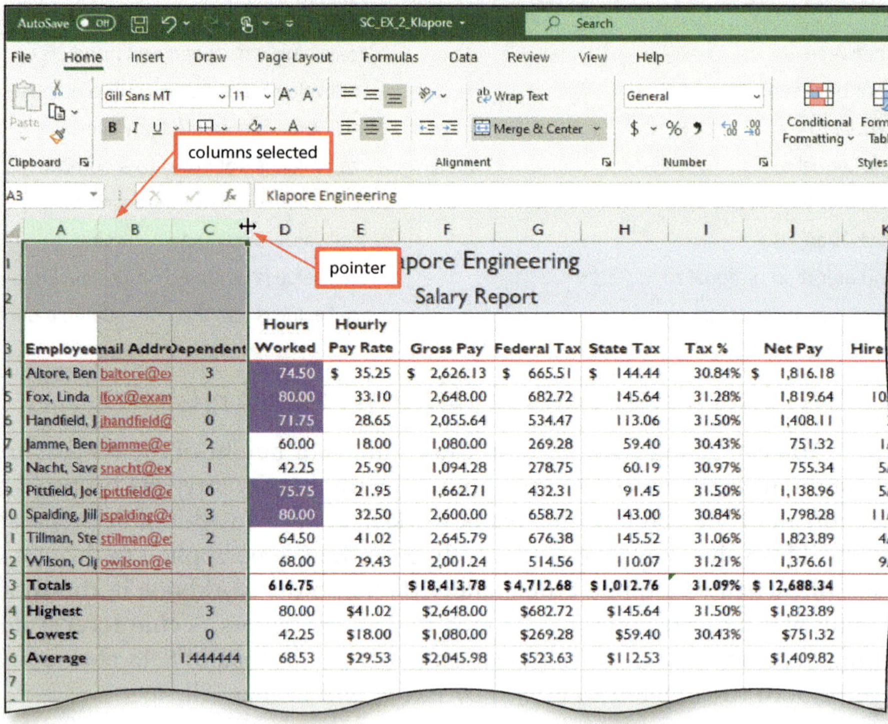

Figure 2–50

2

- Double-click the right boundary of column heading C to change the width of the selected columns to best fit.
- Point to the right boundary of the column H heading above row 1.
- When the pointer changes to a split double arrow, drag until the ScreenTip indicates Width: 10.38 (88 pixels). Do not release the mouse button. If you are unable to drag and reach the specified width, double-click the right boundary of column heading H to change the width of the column to best fit (Figure 2–51).

Q&A **What happens if I change the column width to zero (0)?**
If you decrease the column width to 0, the column is hidden. Hiding cells is a technique you can use to hide data that might not be relevant to a particular report. To instruct Excel to display a hidden column, position the mouse pointer to the right of the column heading boundary where the hidden column is located and then drag to the right.

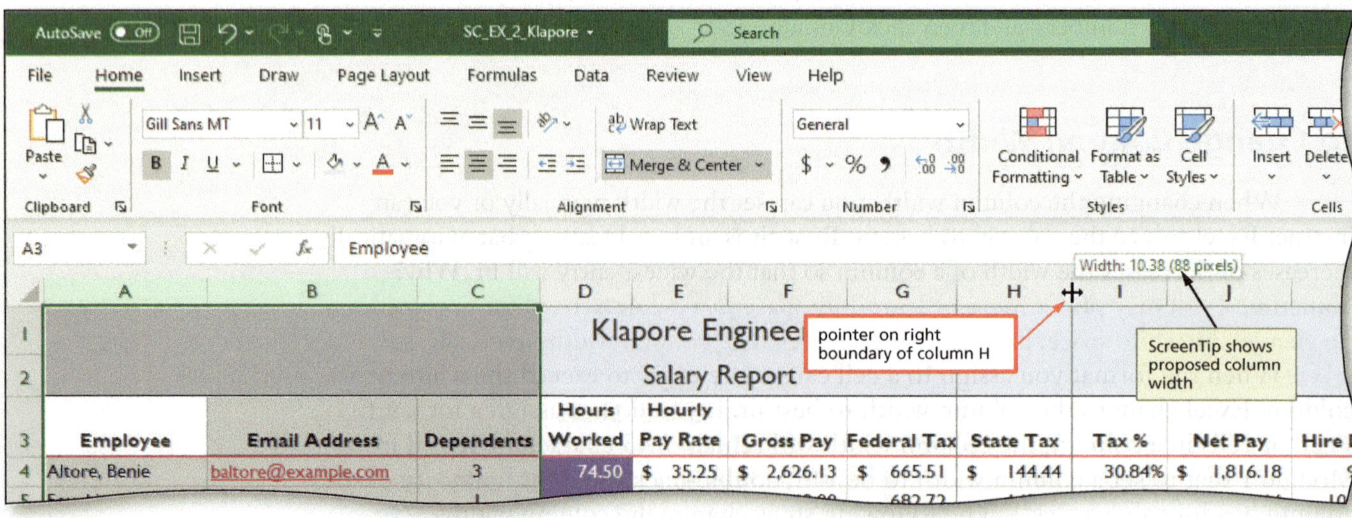

Figure 2–51

3

- Release the mouse button to change the column width.
- Click the column D heading above row 1 to select the column.
- While holding down CTRL, click the column E heading and then the column I heading above row 1 so that nonadjacent columns are selected.
- Point to the boundary on the right side of the column I heading above row 1.
- Drag until the ScreenTip indicates Width: 10.50 (89 pixels). Do not release the mouse button. If you are unable to drag and reach the specified width, double-click the right boundary of column heading I to change the width of the columns to best fit (Figure 2–52).

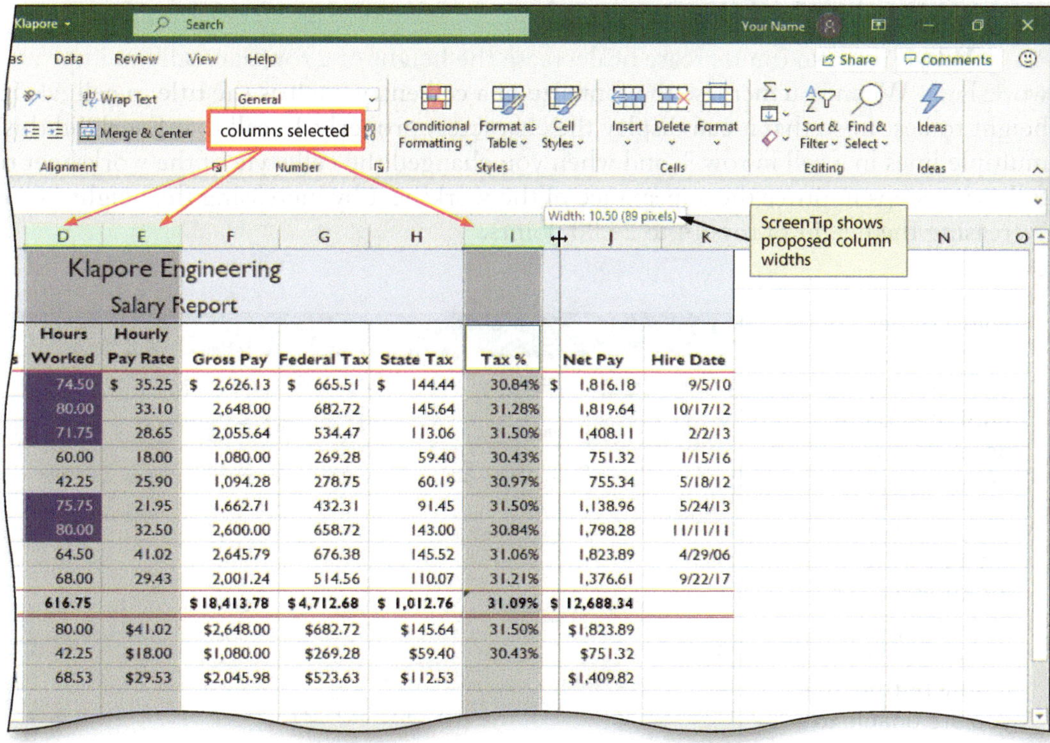

Figure 2–52

4

- Release the mouse button to change the column widths.
- Click the column F heading and drag to select the column G heading.
- While holding down CTRL, click the column J heading and drag to select the column K heading above row 1 so that nonadjacent columns are selected.
- Drag the right boundary of column G until the ScreenTip indicates Width: 11.13 (94 pixels). Release the mouse button to change the column widths. If you are unable to drag and reach the specified width, double-click the right boundary of column heading G to change the width of the columns to best fit

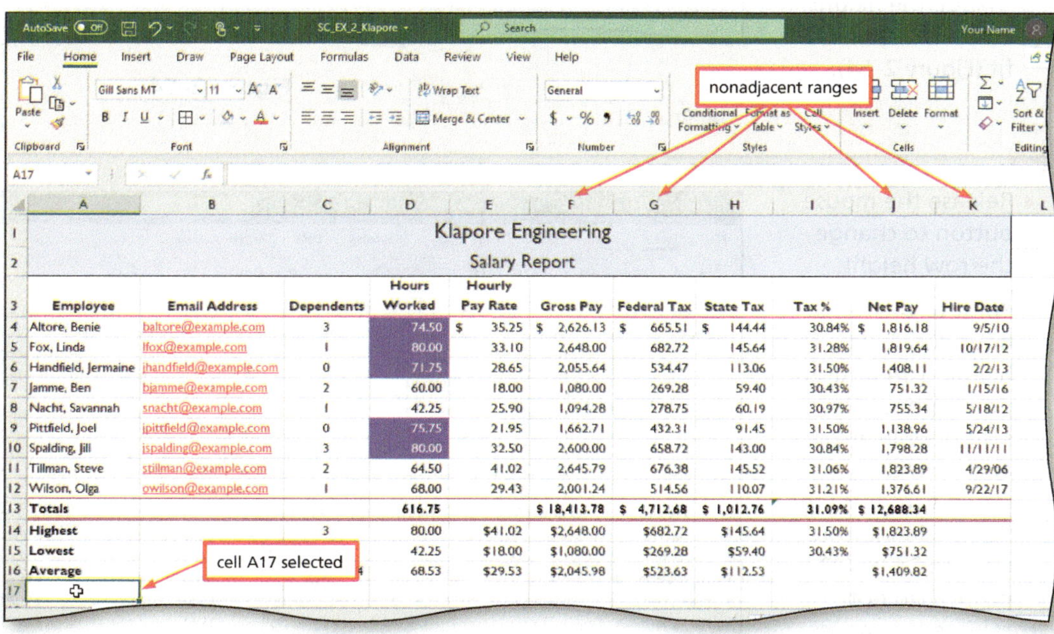

Figure 2–53

- Click anywhere in the worksheet, such as cell A17, to deselect the columns (Figure 2–53).

Other Ways

1. Click column heading or drag through multiple column headings, right-click selected column, click Column Width on shortcut menu, enter desired column width, click OK

To Change Row Height

Why? You also can increase or decrease the height of a row manually to improve the appearance of the worksheet. When you increase the font size of a cell entry, such as the title in cell A1, Excel increases the row height to best fit so that it can display the characters properly. Recall that Excel did this earlier when you entered multiple lines in a cell in row 3, and when you changed the cell style of the worksheet title and subtitle. The following steps improve the appearance of the worksheet by increasing the height of row 3 to 39.00 points and increasing the height of row 14 to 24.00 points.

1

- Point to the boundary below row heading 3 until the pointer becomes a split double arrow.
- Drag down until the ScreenTip indicates Height: 39.00 (52 pixels). Do not release the mouse button. If you are unable to drag to reach the specified height, double-click the bottom boundary of row heading 3 to change the height of the row to best fit (Figure 2–54).

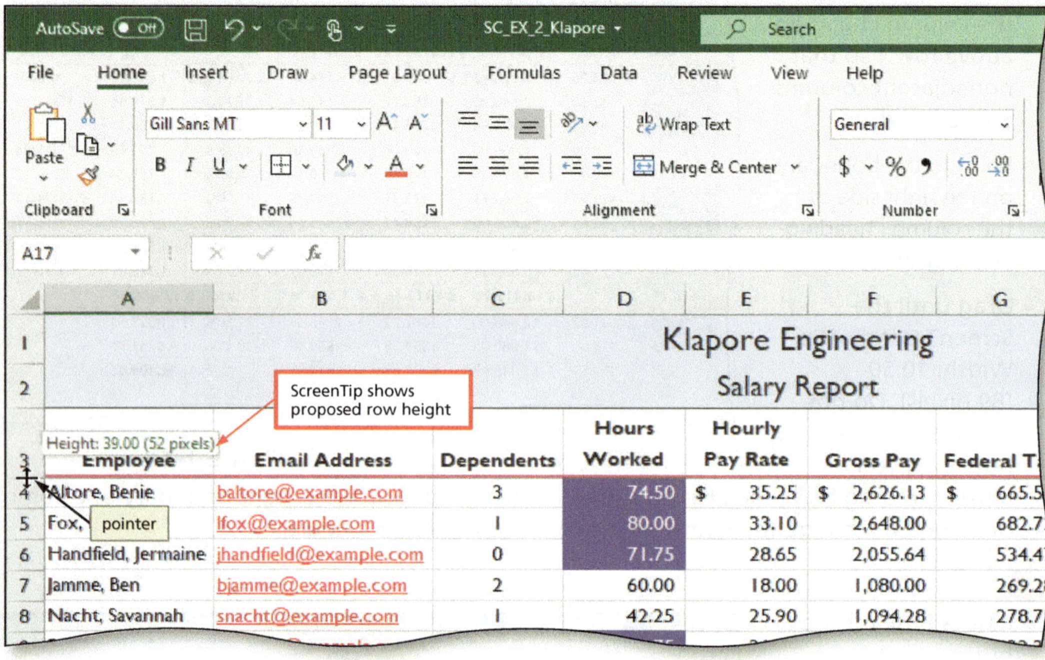

Figure 2–54

2

- Release the mouse button to change the row height.
- Point to the boundary below row heading 14 until the pointer becomes a split double arrow and then drag downward until the ScreenTip indicates Height: 24.00 (32 pixels). Do not release the mouse button (Figure 2–55).

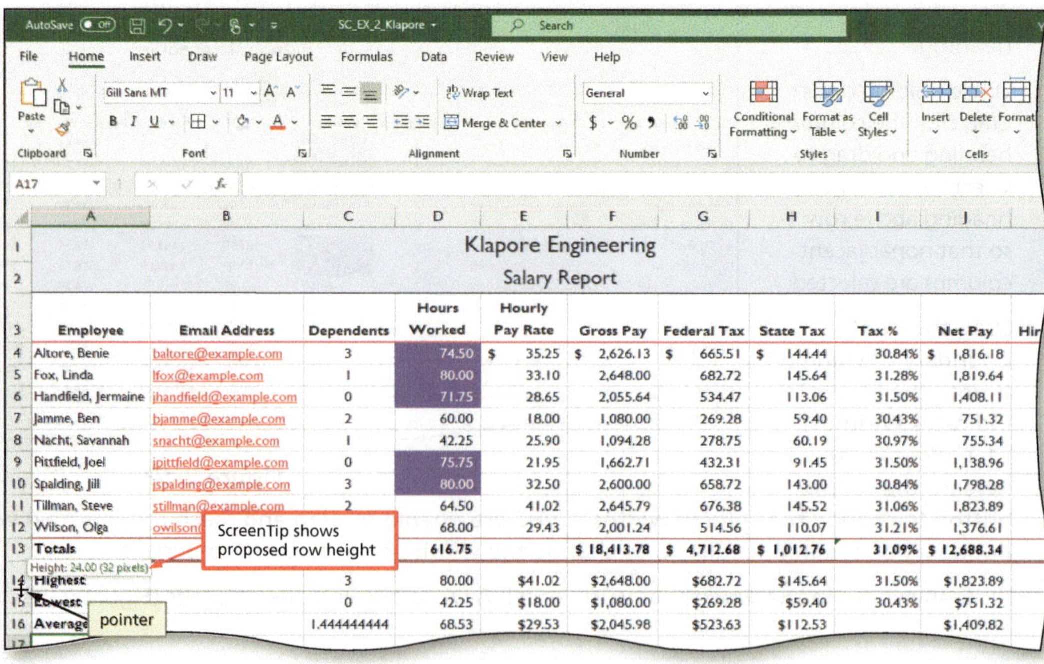

Figure 2–55

3

- Release the mouse button to change the row height.
- Click anywhere in the worksheet, such as cell A17, to deselect the current cell (Figure 2–56).

Q&A

Can I hide a row?

Yes. As with column widths, when you decrease the row height to 0, the row is hidden. To instruct Excel to display a hidden row, position the pointer just below the row heading boundary where the row is hidden and then drag downward. To set a row height to best fit, double-click the bottom boundary of the row heading. You also can hide and unhide rows by right-clicking the row or column heading and selecting the option to hide or unhide the cells.

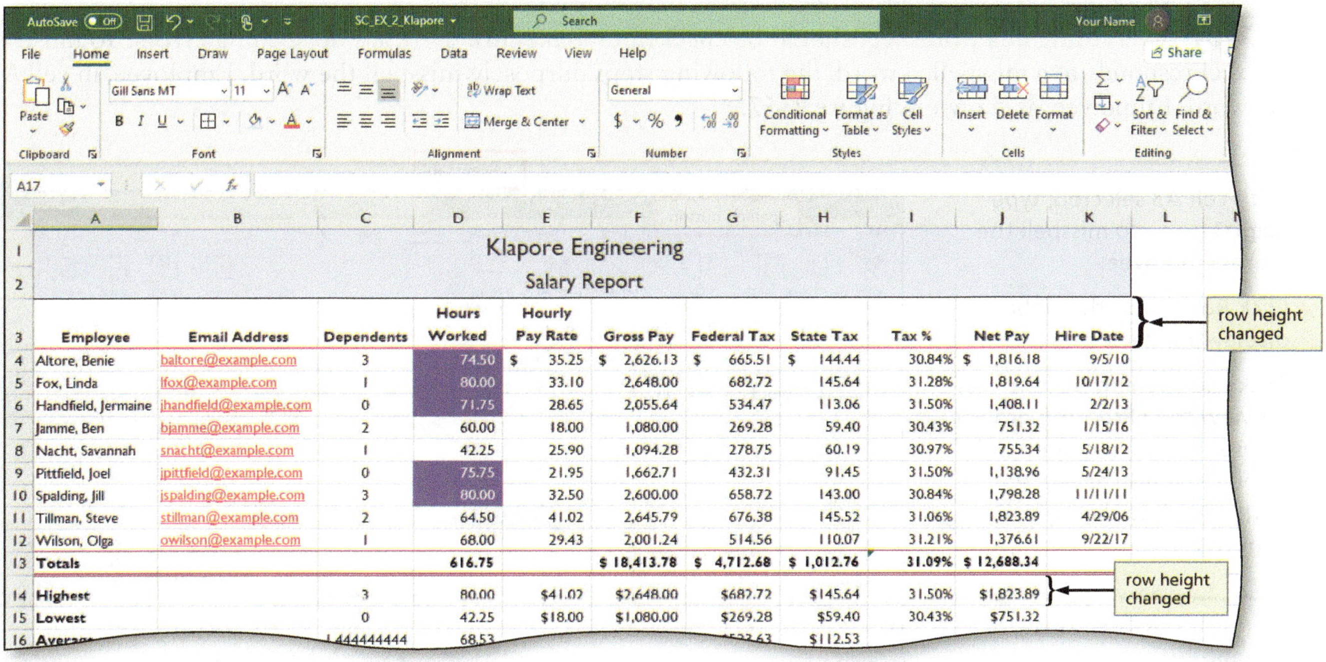

Figure 2–56

Other Ways

1. Right-click row heading or drag through multiple row headings, right-click selected heading, click Row Height on shortcut menu, enter desired row height, click OK

Break Point: If you want to take a break, this is a good place to do so. Be sure to save the SC_EX_2_Klapore file again and then you can exit Excel. To resume later, start Excel, open the file called SC_EX_2_Klapore, and continue following the steps from this location forward.

Checking Spelling

Excel includes a **spelling checker** you can use to check a worksheet for spelling errors. The spelling checker looks for spelling errors by comparing words on the worksheet against words contained in its standard dictionary. If you often use specialized terms that are not in the standard dictionary, you may want to add them to a custom dictionary using the Spelling dialog box. When the spelling checker finds a word that is not in either dictionary, it displays the word in the Spelling dialog box. You then can correct it if it is misspelled.

Consider This

Does the spelling checker catch all spelling mistakes?
While Excel's spelling checker is a valuable tool, it is not infallible. You should proofread your workbook carefully by pointing to each word and saying it aloud as you point to it. Be mindful of misused words such as its and it's, through and though, your and you're, and to and too. Nothing undermines a good impression more than a professional report with misspelled words.

To Check Spelling on the Worksheet

Why? Everything in a worksheet should be checked to make sure there are no spelling errors. To illustrate how Excel responds to a misspelled word, the following steps purposely misspell the word, Employee, in cell A3 as the word, Empolyee, as shown in Figure 2–57.

1

- With cell A3 selected, type **`Empolyee`** to misspell the word, Employee.
- Click Review on the ribbon to display the Review tab.
- Click the Spelling button (Review tab | Proofing group) to use the spelling checker to display the misspelled word in the Spelling dialog box (Figure 2–57).

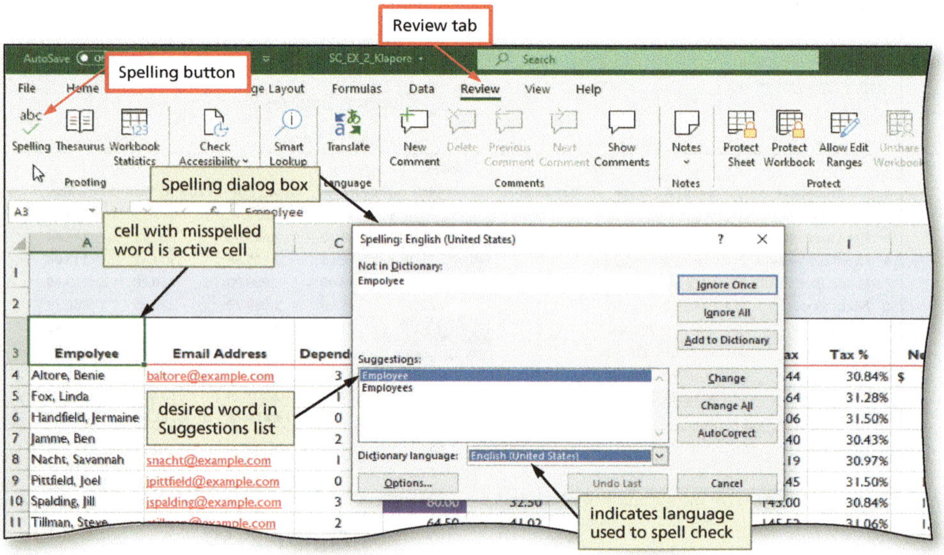

Figure 2–57

Q&A **What happens when the spelling checker finds a misspelled word?**
When the spelling checker identifies that a cell contains a word not in its standard or custom dictionary, it selects that cell as the active cell and displays the Spelling dialog box. The Spelling dialog box displays the word that was not found in the dictionary and offers a list of suggested corrections (Figure 2–58).

2

- Verify that the word highlighted in the Suggestion area is correct.
- Click the Change button (Spelling dialog box) to change the misspelled word to the correct word (Figure 2–58).
- Click the Close button to close the Spelling dialog box.
- If a Microsoft Excel dialog box is displayed, click OK.

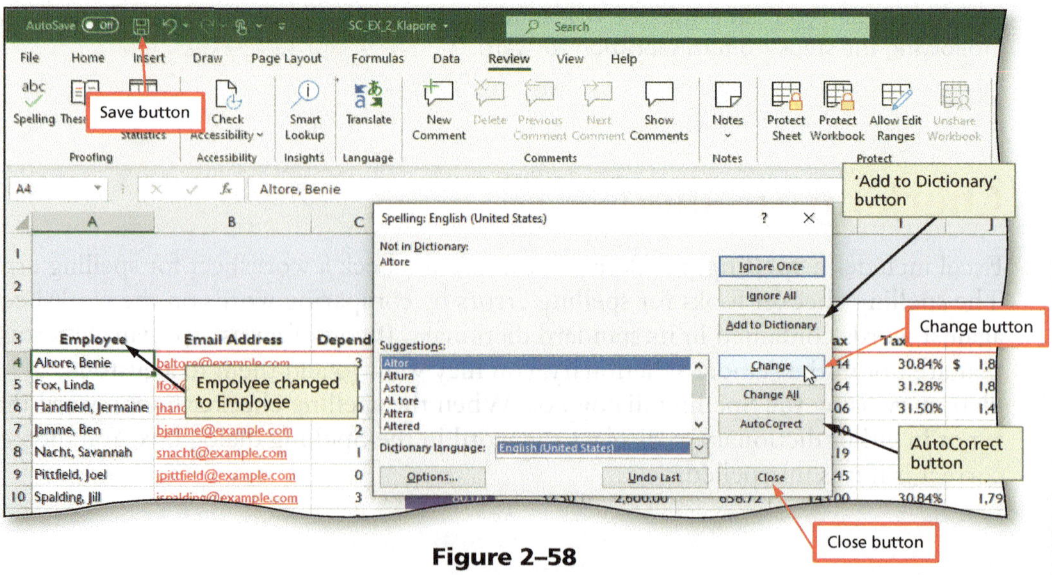

Figure 2–58

3

- Click anywhere in the worksheet, such as cell A17, to deselect the current cell.
- Display the Home tab.
- Save the workbook again on the same storage location with the same file name.

Q&A **What other actions can I take in the Spelling dialog box?**
If one of the words in the Suggestions list is correct, select it and then click the Change button. If none of the suggested words are correct, type the correct word in the 'Not in Dictionary' text box and then click the Change button. To change the word throughout the worksheet, click the Change All button instead of the Change button. To skip correcting the word, click the Ignore Once button. To have Excel ignore the word for the remainder of the worksheet, click the Ignore All button.

Other Ways

1. Press F7

Additional Spelling Checker Considerations

Consider these additional guidelines when using the spelling checker:

- To check the spelling of the text in a single cell, double-click the cell to make the formula bar active and then click the Spelling button (Review tab | Proofing group).
- If you select a single cell so that the formula bar is not active and then start the spelling checker, Excel checks the remainder of the worksheet, including notes and embedded charts.
- If you select a cell other than cell A1 before you start the spelling checker, Excel displays a dialog box when the spelling checker reaches the end of the worksheet, asking if you want to continue checking at the beginning.
- If you select a range of cells before starting the spelling checker, Excel checks the spelling of the words only in the selected range.
- To check the spelling of all the sheets in a workbook, right-click any sheet tab, click 'Select All Sheets' on the sheet tab shortcut menu, and then start the spelling checker.
- To add words to the dictionary, such as your last name, click the 'Add to Dictionary' button in the Spelling dialog box (shown in Figure 2–58) when Excel flags the word as not being in the dictionary.
- Click the AutoCorrect button (shown in Figure 2–58) to add the misspelled word and the correct version of the word to the AutoCorrect list. For example, suppose that you typically misspell the word, do, as the word, dox. When the spelling checker displays the Spelling dialog box with the correct word, do, in the Suggestions list, click the AutoCorrect button. Then, any time in the future that you type the word, dox, Excel will change it to the word, do.

BTW
Error Checking
Always take the time to check the formulas of a worksheet before submitting it to your supervisor. You can check formulas by clicking the Error Checking button (Formulas tab | Formula Auditing group). You also should test the formulas by employing data that tests the limits of formulas. Experienced spreadsheet specialists spend as much time testing a workbook as they do creating it, and they do so before placing the workbook into production.

BTW
Distributing a Workbook
Instead of printing and distributing a hard copy of a workbook, you can distribute the workbook electronically. Options include sending the workbook via email; posting it on cloud storage (such as OneDrive) and sharing the file with others; posting it on social media, a blog, or other website; and sharing a link associated with an online location of the workbook. You also can create and share a PDF or XPS image of the workbook, so that users can view the file in Acrobat Reader or XPS Viewer instead of in Excel.

Printing the Worksheet

Excel allows for a great deal of customization in how a worksheet appears when printed. For example, the margins on the page can be adjusted. A header or footer can be added to each printed page as well. A **header** is text and graphics that print at the top of each page. Similarly, a **footer** is text and graphics that print at the bottom of each page. When you insert a header or footer in a workbook, they can display the same on all pages, you can have a different header and footer on the first page of the workbook, or you can have different headers and footers on odd and even pages. With the header or footer area selected on the Header & Footer tab, click the desired check box in the Options group. Excel also has the capability to alter the worksheet in Page Layout view. **Page Layout view** provides an accurate view of how a worksheet will look when printed, including headers and footers. The default view that you have worked in up until this point in the book is called Normal view.

To Change the Worksheet's Margins, Header, and Orientation in Page Layout View

The following steps change to Page Layout view, narrow the margins of the worksheet, change the header of the worksheet, and set the orientation of the worksheet to landscape. **Why?** You may want the printed worksheet to fit on one page. You can do that by reducing the page margins and changing the page orientation to fit wider printouts across a sheet of paper. You can use the header to identify the content on each page. **Margins** are the space between the page content and the edges of the page. The current worksheet is too wide for a single page and requires landscape orientation to fit on one page in a readable manner.

1

- Click the Page Layout button on the status bar to view the worksheet in Page Layout view (Figure 2–59).

Q&A **What are the features of Page Layout view?**
Page Layout view shows the worksheet divided into pages. A gray background separates each page. The white areas surrounding each page indicate the print margins. The top of each page includes a Header area, and the bottom of each page includes a Footer area. Page Layout view also includes rulers at the top and left margin of the page that assist you in placing objects on the page, such as charts and pictures.

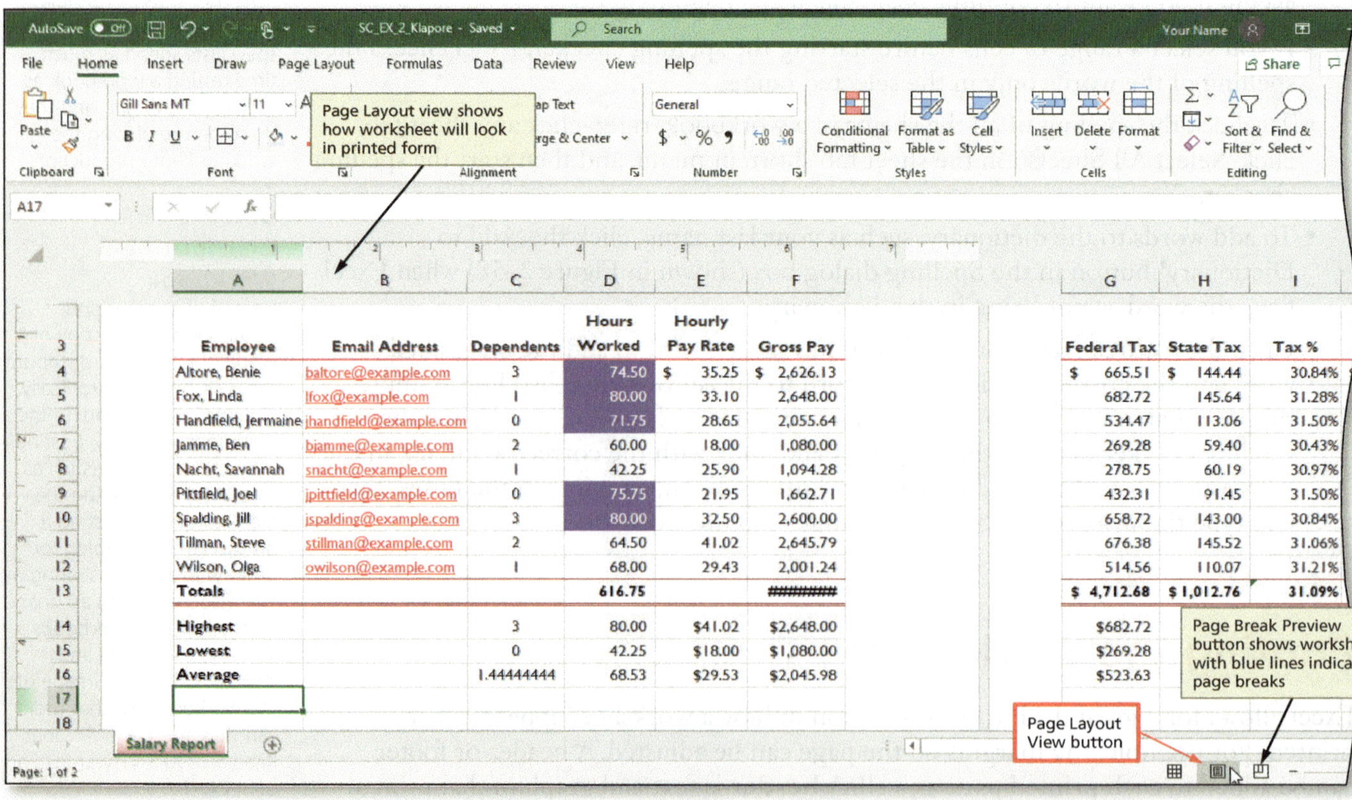

Figure 2–59

2

- Display the Page Layout tab.
- Click the Margins button (Page Layout tab | Page Setup group) to display the Margins gallery (Figure 2–60).

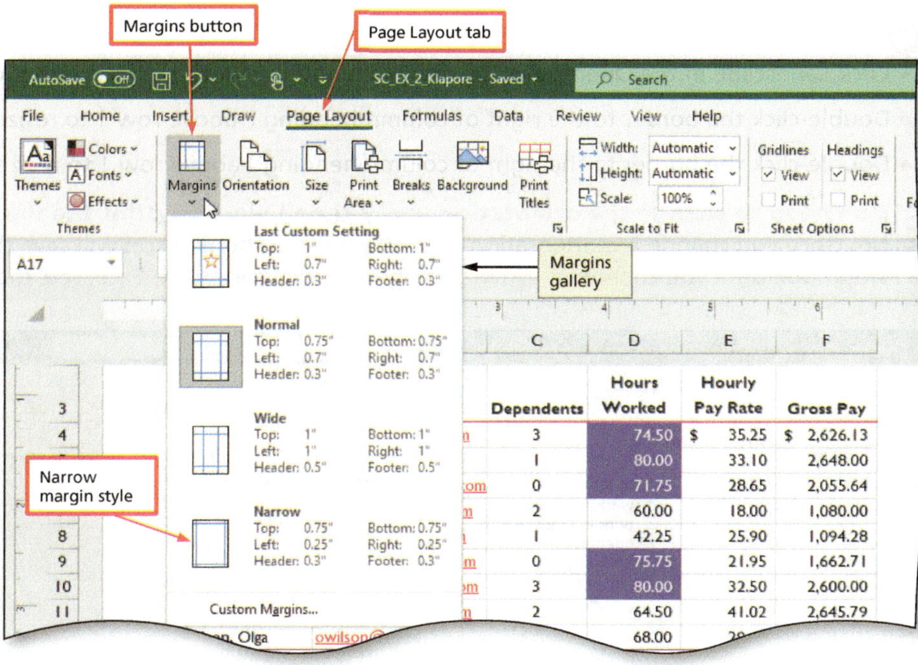

Figure 2–60

3

- Click Narrow in the Margins gallery to change the worksheet margins to the Narrow margin style.
- If necessary, scroll up to display the Header area.
- Click the center of the Header area above the worksheet title.
- Type **Madelyn Samuels** and then press ENTER. Type **Chief Financial Officer** to complete the worksheet header (Figure 2–61).

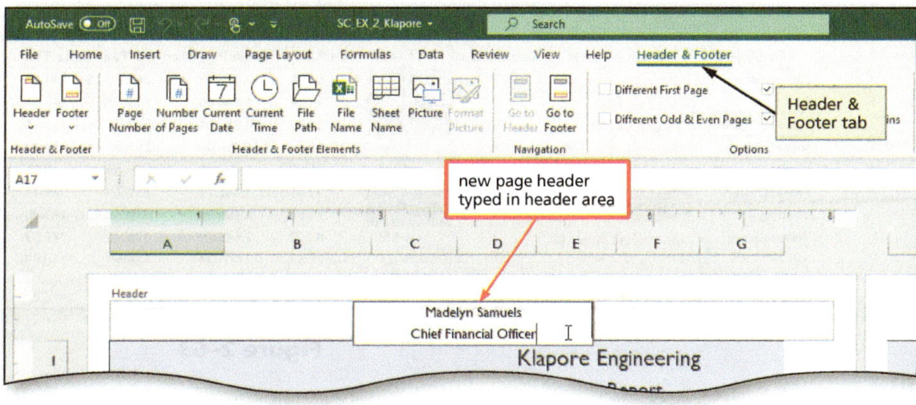

Figure 2–61

- If requested by your instructor, type your name instead of Madelyn Samuels.
- Select cell A6 to deselect the header.

Q&A **What else can I place in a header?**
You can add additional text, page number information, date and time information, the file path of the workbook, the file name of the workbook, the sheet name of the workbook, and pictures to a header.

4

- Display the Page Layout tab.
- Click the Orientation button (Page Layout tab | Page Setup group) to display the Orientation gallery (Figure 2–62).

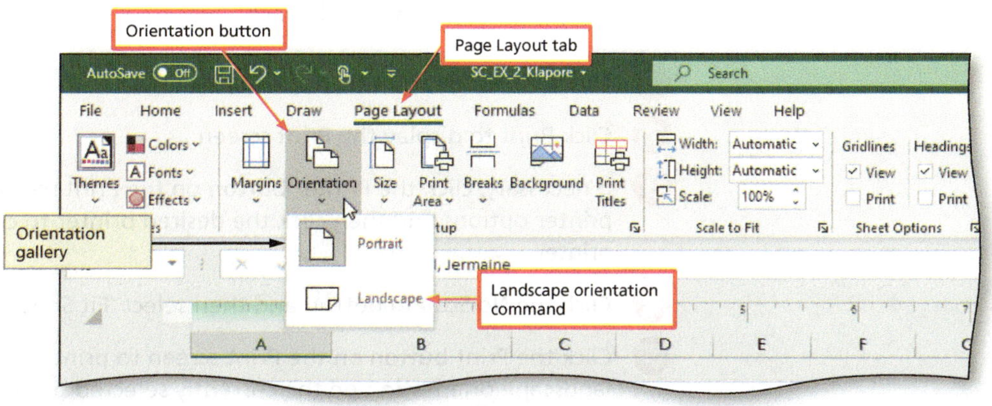

Figure 2–62

5

- Click Landscape in the Orientation gallery to change the worksheet's orientation to landscape.
- Double-click the border to the right of column heading F above row 1 to resize the column to best fit.
- Double-click the border to the right of column heading J above row 1 to resize the column to best fit (Figure 2–63).

Q&A **Do I need to change the orientation every time I want to print the worksheet?**
No. Once you change the orientation and save the workbook, Excel will save the orientation setting for that workbook until you change it. When you open a new workbook, Excel sets the orientation to portrait.

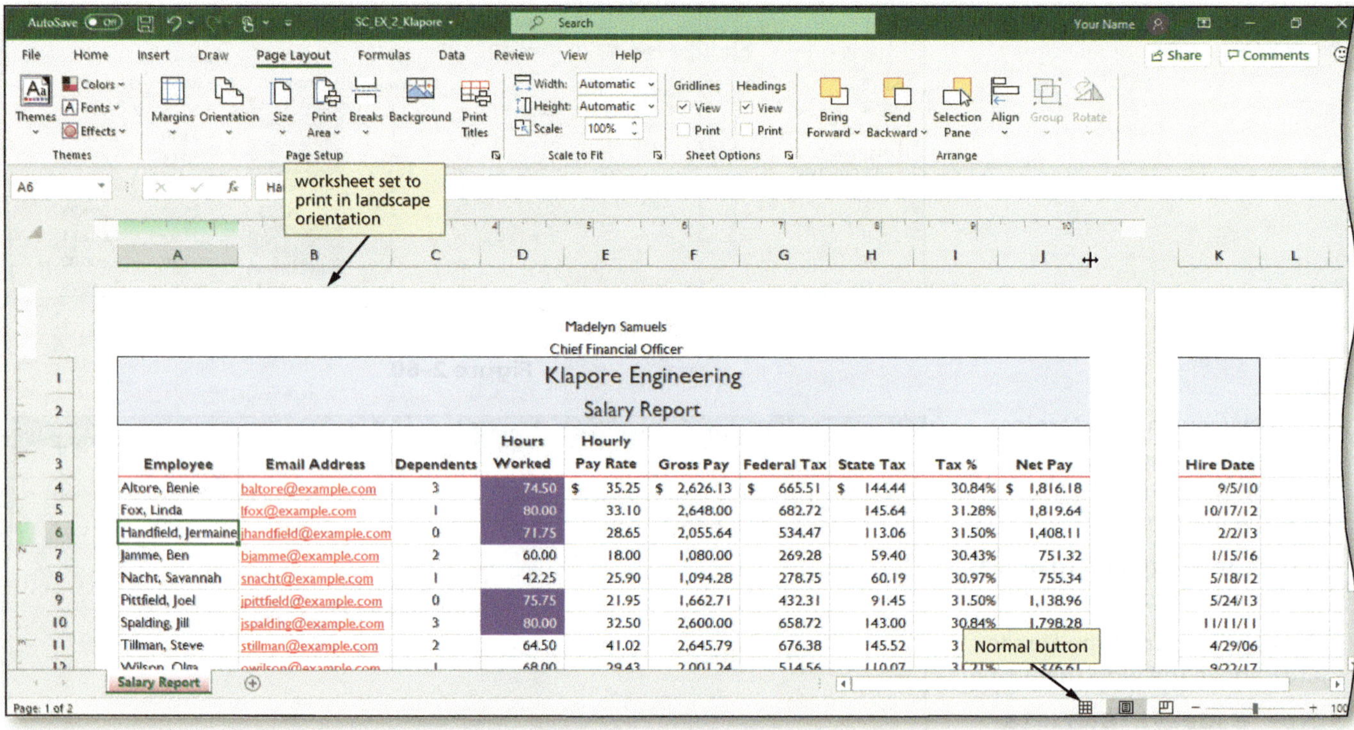

Figure 2–63

Other Ways

1. Click Page Setup Dialog Box Launcher (Page Layout tab | Page Setup group), click Page tab (Page Setup dialog box), click Portrait or Landscape, click OK

To Print a Worksheet

Excel provides multiple options for printing a worksheet. In the following sections, you first print the worksheet and then print a section of the worksheet. The following steps print the worksheet.

1. Click File on the ribbon to open Backstage view.
2. Click Print to display the Print screen.
3. If necessary, click the Printer button on the Print screen to display a list of available printer options and then click the desired printer to change the currently selected printer.
4. Click the No Scaling button and then select 'Fit Sheet on One Page' to select it.
5. Click the Print button on the Print screen to print the worksheet on one page in landscape orientation on the currently selected printer.

6 When the printer stops, retrieve the hard copy (Figure 2–64).

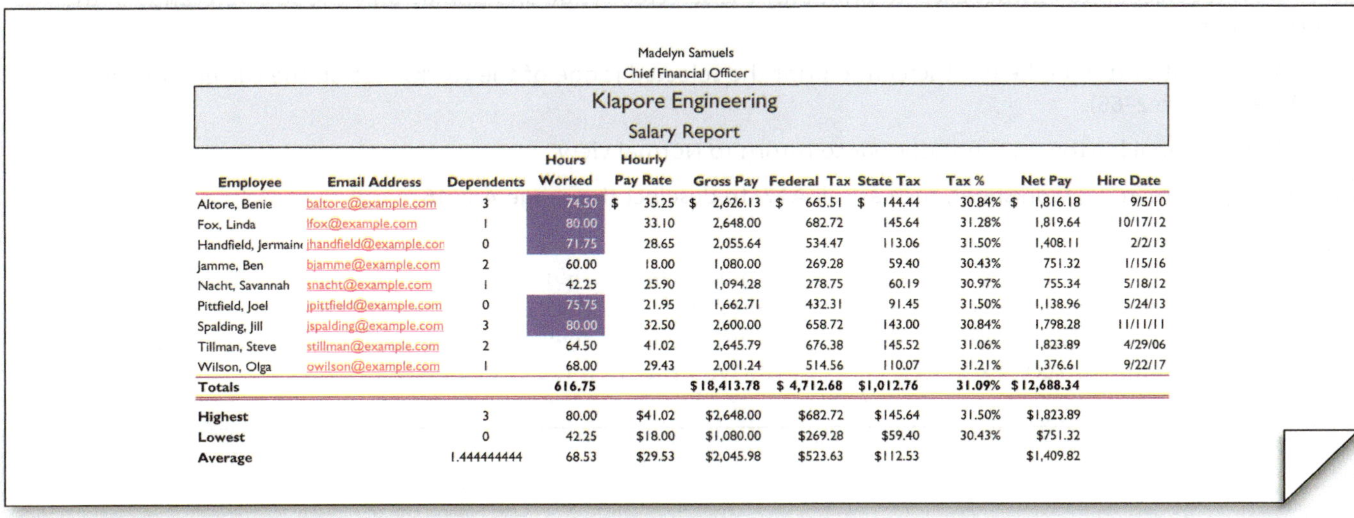

Madelyn Samuels
Chief Financial Officer

Klapore Engineering
Salary Report

Employee	Email Address	Dependents	Hours Worked	Hourly Pay Rate	Gross Pay	Federal Tax	State Tax	Tax %	Net Pay	Hire Date
Altore, Benie	baltore@example.com	3	74.50	$ 35.25	$ 2,626.13	$ 665.51	$ 144.44	30.84%	$ 1,816.18	9/5/10
Fox, Linda	lfox@example.com	1	80.00	33.10	2,648.00	682.72	145.64	31.28%	1,819.64	10/17/12
Handfield, Jermain	jhandfield@example.cor	0	71.75	28.65	2,055.64	534.47	113.06	31.50%	1,408.11	2/2/13
Jamme, Ben	bjamme@example.com	2	60.00	18.00	1,080.00	269.28	59.40	30.43%	751.32	1/15/16
Nacht, Savannah	snacht@example.com	1	42.25	25.90	1,094.28	278.75	60.19	30.97%	755.34	5/18/12
Pittfield, Joel	jpittfield@example.com	0	75.75	21.95	1,662.71	432.31	91.45	31.50%	1,138.96	5/24/13
Spalding, Jill	jspalding@example.com	3	80.00	32.50	2,600.00	658.72	143.00	30.84%	1,798.28	11/11/11
Tillman, Steve	stillman@example.com	2	64.50	41.02	2,645.79	676.38	145.52	31.06%	1,823.89	4/29/06
Wilson, Olga	owilson@example.com	1	68.00	29.43	2,001.24	514.56	110.07	31.21%	1,376.61	9/22/17
Totals			**616.75**		**$18,413.78**	**$ 4,712.68**	**$1,012.76**	**31.09%**	**$12,688.34**	
Highest		3	80.00	$41.02	$2,648.00	$682.72	$145.64	31.50%	$1,823.89	
Lowest		0	42.25	$18.00	$1,080.00	$269.28	$59.40	30.43%	$751.32	
Average		1.444444444	68.53	$29.53	$2,045.98	$523.63	$112.53		$1,409.82	

Figure 2–64

To Print a Section of the Worksheet

You can print portions of the worksheet by selecting the range of cells to print and then clicking the Selection option button in the Print what area in the Print dialog box. **Why?** To save paper, you only want to print the portion of the worksheet you need, instead of printing the entire worksheet. The following steps print the range A3:F16.

1

- Select the range to print, cells A3:F16 in this case.
- Click File on the ribbon to open Backstage view.
- Click Print to display the Print screen.
- Click 'Print Active Sheets' in the Settings area (Print screen | Print list) to display a list of options that determine what Excel should print (Figure 2–65).

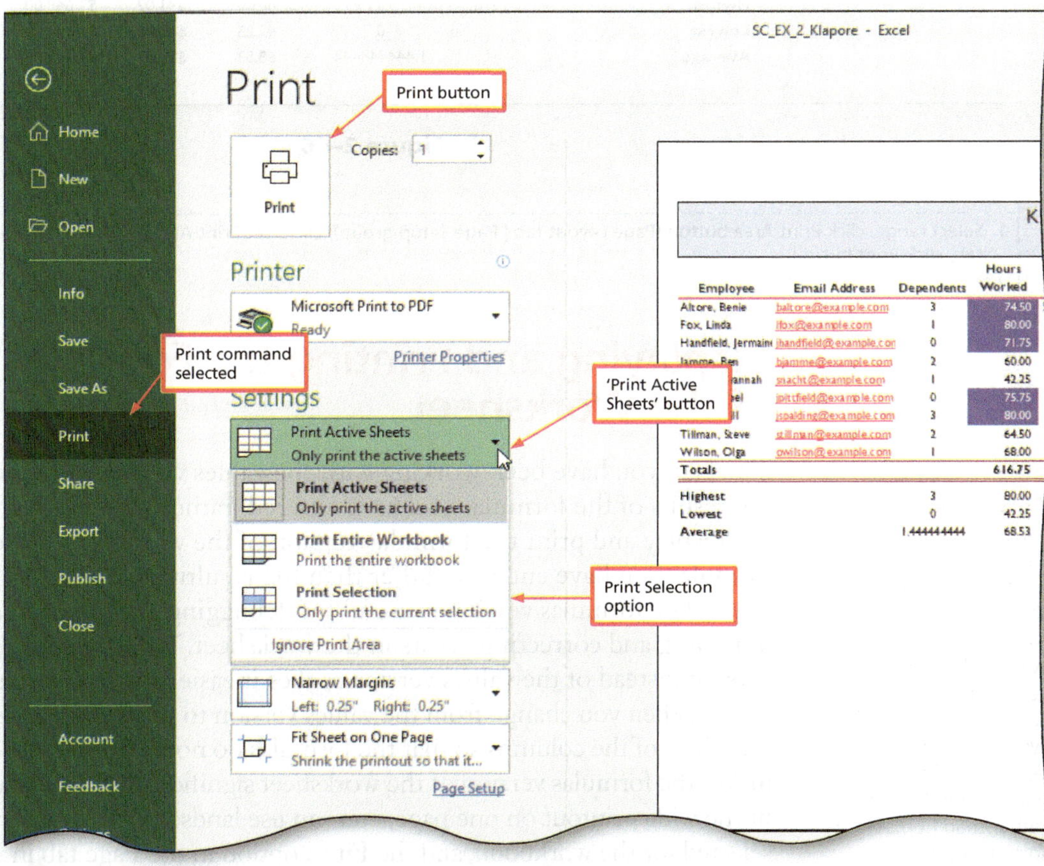

Figure 2–65

2

- Click Print Selection to instruct Excel to print only the selected range and display only the selected range in the preview area.
- Click the Print button in the Print screen to print the selected range of the worksheet on the currently selected printer (Figure 2–66).
- Click the Normal button on the status bar to return to Normal view.
- Click anywhere in the worksheet, such as cell A17, to deselect the range A3:F16.

Q&A

What can I print?

Excel includes three options for selecting what to print (Figure 2–65). As shown in the previous steps, the Print Selection option instructs Excel to print the selected range. The 'Print Active Sheets' option instructs Excel to print the active worksheet (the worksheet currently on the screen) or selected worksheets. Finally, the 'Print Entire Workbook' option instructs Excel to print all of the worksheets in the workbook.

Madelyn Samuels
Chief Financial Officer

Employee	Email Address	Dependents	Hours Worked	Hourly Pay Rate	Gross Pay
Altore, Benie	baltore@example.com	3	74.50	$ 35.25	$ 2,626.13
Fox, Linda	lfox@example.com	1	80.00	33.10	2,648.00
Handfield, Jermain	jhandfield@example.con	0	71.75	28.65	2,055.64
Jamme, Ben	bjamme@example.com	2	60.00	18.00	1,080.00
Nacht, Savannah	snacht@example.com	1	42.25	25.90	1,094.28
Pittfield, Joel	jpittfield@example.com	0	75.75	21.95	1,662.71
Spalding, Jill	jspalding@example.com	3	80.00	32.50	2,600.00
Tillman, Steve	stillman@example.com	2	64.50	41.02	2,645.79
Wilson, Olga	owilson@example.com	1	68.00	29.43	2,001.24
Totals			**616.75**		**$18,413.78**
Highest		3	80.00	$41.02	$2,648.00
Lowest		0	42.25	$18.00	$1,080.00
Average		1.444444444	68.53	$29.53	$2,045.98

Figure 2–66

Other Ways

1. Select range, click Print Area button (Page Layout tab | Page Setup group), click 'Set Print Area', click File tab to open Backstage view, click Print tab, click Print button

Displaying and Printing the Formulas Version of the Worksheet

BTW

Values versus Formulas

When completing class assignments, do not enter numbers in cells that require formulas. Most instructors will check both the values version and the formulas version of your worksheets. The formulas version verifies that you entered formulas, rather than numbers, in formula-based cells.

Thus far, you have been working with the values version of the worksheet, which shows the results of the formulas you have entered, rather than the actual formulas. Excel also can display and print the formulas version of the worksheet, which shows the actual formulas you have entered, rather than the resulting values.

The formulas version is useful for debugging a worksheet. **Debugging** is the process of finding and correcting errors in the worksheet. Viewing and printing the formulas version instead of the values version makes it easier to see any mistakes in the formulas.

When you change from the values version to the formulas version, Excel increases the width of the columns so that the formulas do not overflow into adjacent cells, which makes the formulas version of the worksheet significantly wider than the values version. To fit the wide printout on one page, you can use landscape orientation, which already has been selected for the workbook, and the Fit to option in the Page tab in the Page Setup dialog box.

To Display the Formulas in the Worksheet and Fit the Printout on One Page

The following steps change the view of the worksheet from the values version to the formulas version of the worksheet and then print the formulas version on one page. **Why?** Printing the formulas in the worksheet can help you verify that your formulas are correct and that the worksheet displays the correct calculations.

1

- Press CTRL+ACCENT MARK (`) to display the worksheet with formulas.
- Click the right horizontal scroll arrow until column K appears (Figure 2–67).

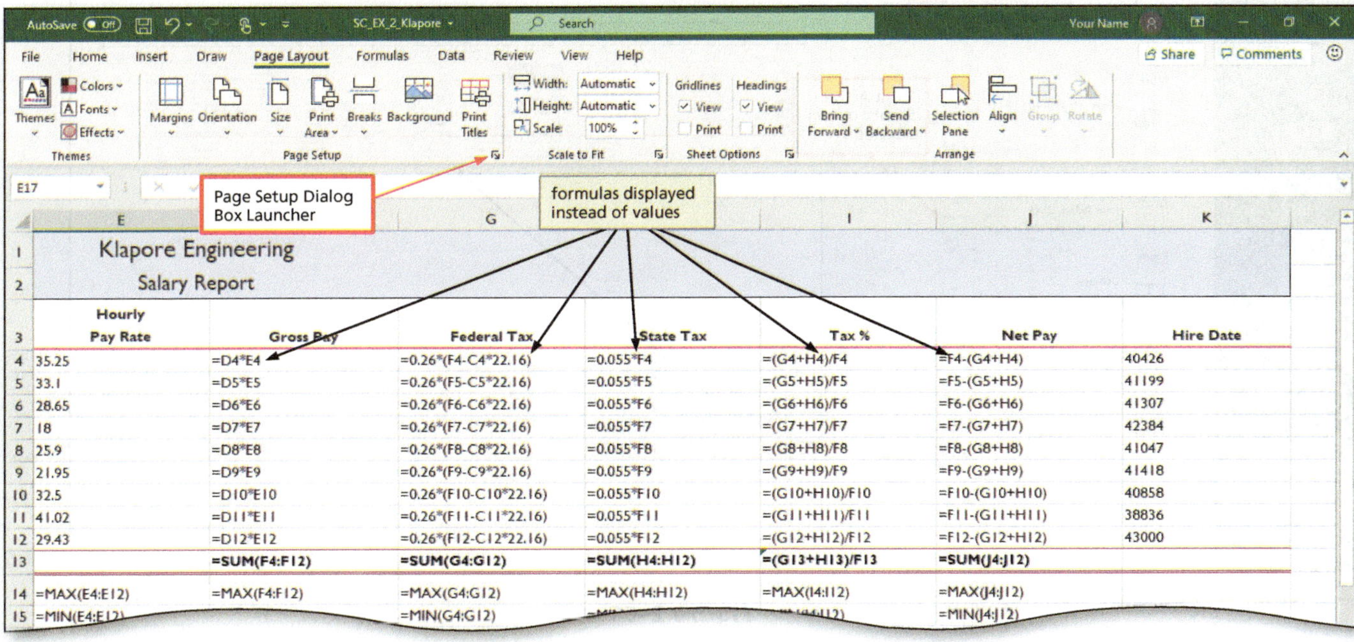

Figure 2–67

2

- Click the Page Setup Dialog Box Launcher (Page Layout tab | Page Setup group) to display the Page Setup dialog box (Figure 2–68).
- If necessary, click Landscape in the Orientation area in the Page tab to select it.
- If necessary, click the Fit to option button in the Scaling area to select it.

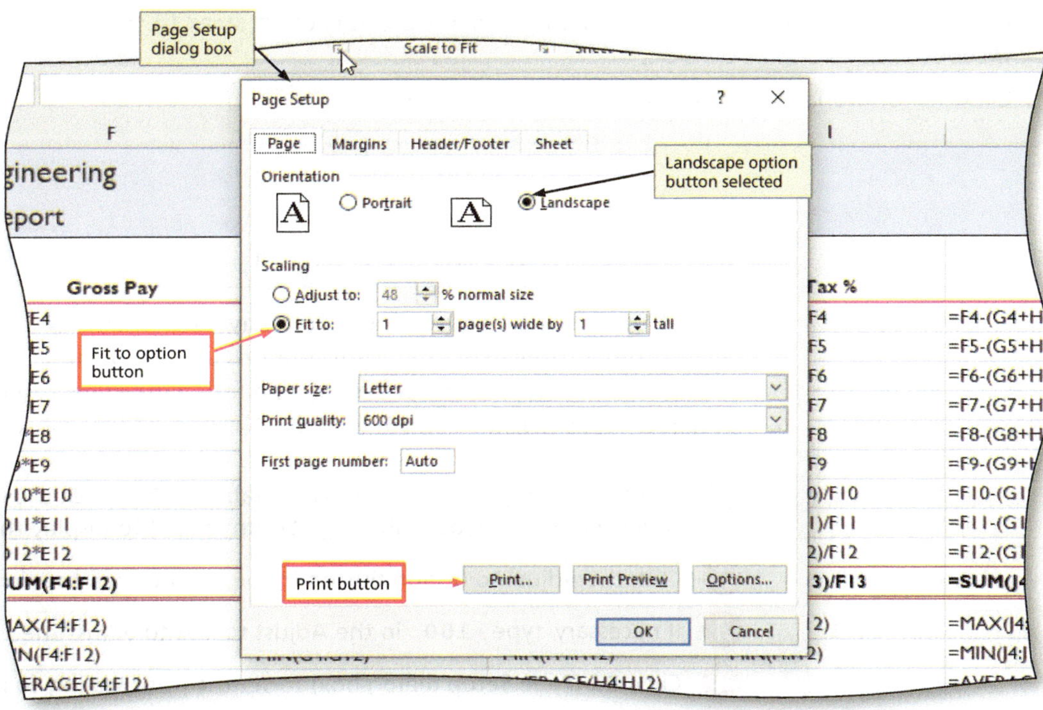

Figure 2–68

3

- Click the Print button (Page Setup dialog box) to open the Print screen in Backstage view. In Backstage view, select the Print Selection button in the Settings area of the Print gallery and then click Print Active Sheets (Figure 2–69).
- Click the Print button to print the worksheet.

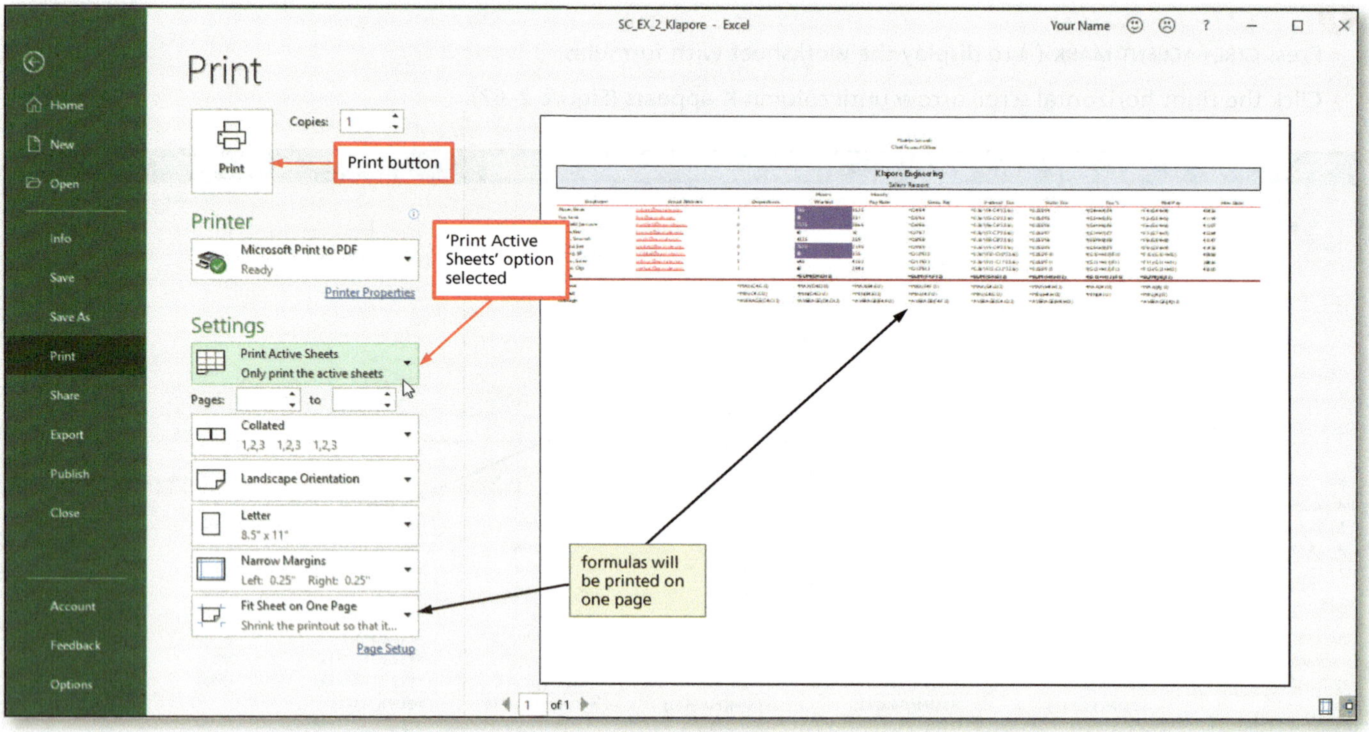

Figure 2–69

4

- After viewing and printing the formulas version, press CTRL+ACCENT MARK (`) to instruct Excel to display the values version.
- Click the left horizontal scroll arrow until column A appears.

To Change the Print Scaling Option Back to 100%

Depending on your printer, you may have to change the Print Scaling option back to 100% after using the Fit to option. Doing so will cause the worksheet to print at the default print scaling of 100%. The following steps reset the Print Scaling option so that future worksheets print at 100%, instead of being resized to print on one page.

1. If necessary, display the Page Layout tab and then click the Page Setup Dialog Box Launcher (Page Layout tab | Page Setup group) to display the Page Setup dialog box.
2. Click the Adjust to option button in the Scaling area to select the Adjust to setting.
3. If necessary, type `100` in the Adjust to box to adjust the print scaling to 100%.
4. Click OK (Page Setup dialog box) to set the print scaling to normal.

5. Display the Home tab.
6. Save the workbook again on the same storage location with the same file name.
7. If desired, sign out of your Microsoft account.
8. **sam** Exit Excel.

Q&A **What is the purpose of the Adjust to box in the Page Setup dialog box?**
The Adjust to box allows you to specify the percentage of reduction or enlargement in the printout of a worksheet. The default percentage is 100%. When you click the Fit to option button, this percentage changes to the percentage required to fit the printout on one page.

Summary

In this module you have learned how to enter formulas, calculate an average, find the highest and lowest numbers in a range, verify formulas using Range Finder, add borders, align text, format numbers, change column widths and row heights, and add conditional formatting to a range of numbers. In addition, you learned how to use the spelling checker to identify misspelled words in a worksheet, print a section of a worksheet, and display and print the formulas version of the worksheet using the Fit to option.

Consider This: Plan Ahead

What decisions will you need to make when creating workbooks in the future?

1. Determine the workbook structure.
   a) Determine the formulas and functions you will need for your workbook.
   b) Sketch a layout of your data and functions.
2. Create the worksheet.
   a) Enter the titles, subtitles, and headings.
   b) Enter the data, desired functions, and formulas.
3. Format the worksheet.
   a) Determine the theme for the worksheet.
   b) Format the titles, subtitles, and headings using styles.
   c) Format the totals, minimums, maximums, and averages.
   d) Format the numbers and text.
   e) Resize columns and rows.

STUDENT ASSIGNMENTS

Apply Your Knowledge

Reinforce the skills and apply the concepts you learned in this module.

Cost Analysis Worksheet

Note: To complete this assignment, you will be required to use the Data Files. Please contact your instructor for information about accessing the Data Files.

Instructions: Start Excel. Open the workbook called SC_EX_2-1.xlsx, which is located in the Data Files. The workbook you open contains information about vehicles driven for Prontix Courier Services. You are to enter and copy formulas and functions and apply formatting to the worksheet in order to analyze the costs associated with a bus company's fleet of vehicles, as shown in Figure 2–70.

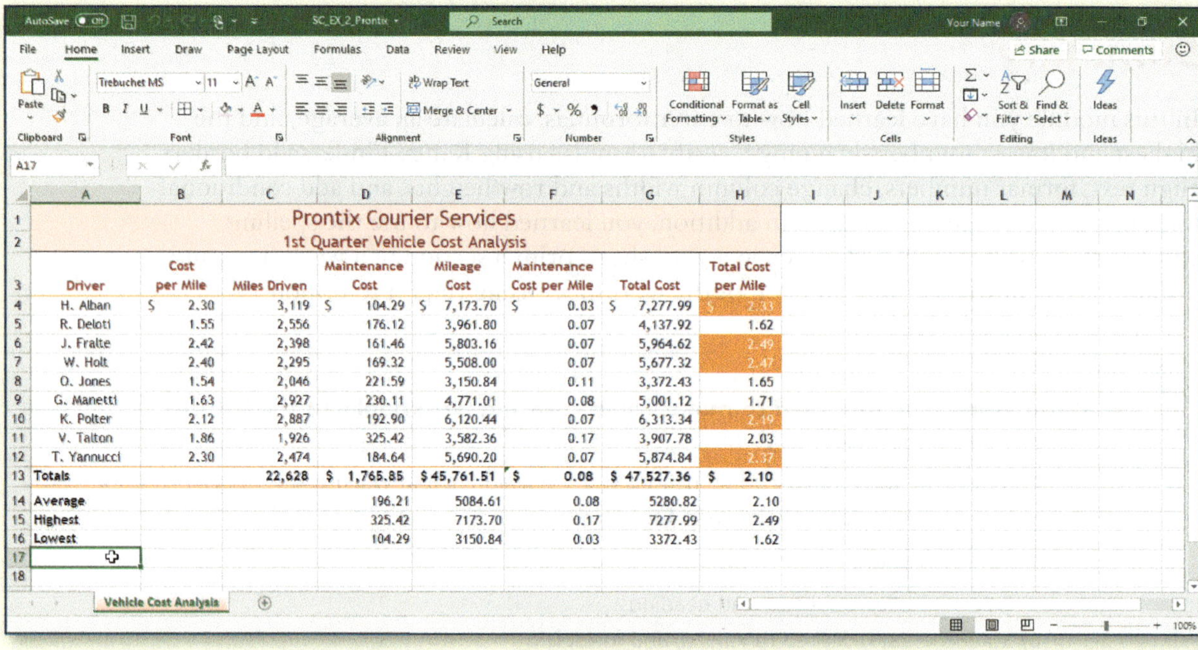

Figure 2–70

Perform the following tasks:

1. Use the following formulas in cells E4, F4, G4, and H4:
   Mileage Cost (cell E4) = Cost per Mile * Miles Driven or = B4 * C4
   Maintenance Cost per Mile (cell F4) = Maintenance Cost / Miles Driven or = D4 / C4
   Total Cost (cell G4) = Maintenance Cost + Mileage Cost or = D4 + E4
   Total Cost per Mile (cell H4) = Total Cost / Miles Driven or = G4 / C4
   Use the fill handle to copy the four formulas in the range E4:H4 to the range E5:H12.
2. Determine totals for the miles driven, maintenance cost, mileage cost, and total cost in row 13. Copy the formula in cell F12 to F13 to assign the formula in cell F12 to F13 in the total line. Copy the formula in cell H12 to H13 to assign the formula in cell H12 to H13 in the total line. Reapply the Total cell style to cells F13 and H13.
3. In the range D14:D16, determine the average value, highest value, and lowest value, respectively, for the values in the range D4:D12. Use the fill handle to copy the three functions to the range E14:H16.
4. Format the worksheet as follows:
   a. Change the workbook theme to Berlin by using the Themes button (Page Layout tab | Themes group)
   b. Cell A1: change to Title cell style
   c. Cell A2: change to Title cell style and a font size of 14

d. Cells A1:A2: Rose, Accent 6, Lighter 80% fill color and add outside borders
e. Cells B4, D4:H4, and D13:H13: accounting number format with two decimal places and fixed dollar signs by using the 'Accounting Number Format' button (Home tab | Number group)
f. Cells B5:B12 and D5:H12: comma style format with two decimal places by using the Comma Style button (Home tab | Number group)
g. Cells C4:C13: comma style format with no decimal places
h. Cells H4:H12: apply conditional formatting so that cells with a value greater than 2.15 appear with an orange background color and White, Background 1 font

5. If necessary increase the size of any columns that do not properly display data.
6. Switch to Page Layout view. Enter your name, course, and any other information, as specified by your instructor, in the header area.
7. Preview and print the worksheet in landscape orientation so that it appears on one page. Save the workbook using the file name, SC_EX_2_Prontix.
8. Use Range Finder to verify the formula in cell H13.
9. Print the range A3:D16. Press CTRL+ACCENT MARK (`) to change the display from the values version of the worksheet to the formulas version. Print the formulas version in landscape orientation on one page by using the Fit to option in the Page tab in the Page Setup dialog box. Press CTRL+ACCENT MARK (`) to change the display of the worksheet back to the values version. Close the workbook without saving it.
10. Submit the workbook in the format specified by your instructor and exit Excel.
11. Besides adding a header to your document, can you think of anything else that could be added when printing the worksheet?

Extend Your Knowledge

Extend the skills you learned in this module and experiment with new skills. You may need to use Help to complete the assignment.

Creating a Customer Tracking Worksheet for Kalto Security Outlet

Note: To complete this assignment, you will be required to use the Data Files. Please contact your instructor for information about accessing the Data Files.

Instructions: Start Excel. Open the workbook SC_EX_2-2.xlsx, which is located in the Data Files. The workbook you open contains vendor information for Kalto Security Outlet. You are to apply Flash Fill and four types of conditional formatting to cells in a worksheet.

Perform the following tasks:

1. Add the account identifiers to the cells in the range E4:E16. The account identifier is determined by taking the first initial of the vendor's first name, the first initial of the vendor's last name, followed by the entire vendor number. For example, the account identifier for John Abrahms is JA28689. Continue entering two or three account identifiers, then use Flash Fill to complete the remaining cells. Add the thick bottom border back to cell E16 (Figure 2–71).
2. Select the range F4:F16. Click the Conditional Formatting button (Home tab | Styles group) and then click New Rule on the Conditional Formatting menu. Select 'Format only top or bottom ranked values' in the Select a Rule Type area (New Formatting Rule dialog box).
3. If requested by your instructor, enter 35 in the Edit the Rule Description (New Formatting Rule dialog box) area, and then click the '% of the selected range' check box to select it.
4. Click the Format button, and choose a light orange background on the Fill tab to assign this conditional format. Click OK in each dialog box and view the worksheet.

Continued >

Extend Your Knowledge *continued*

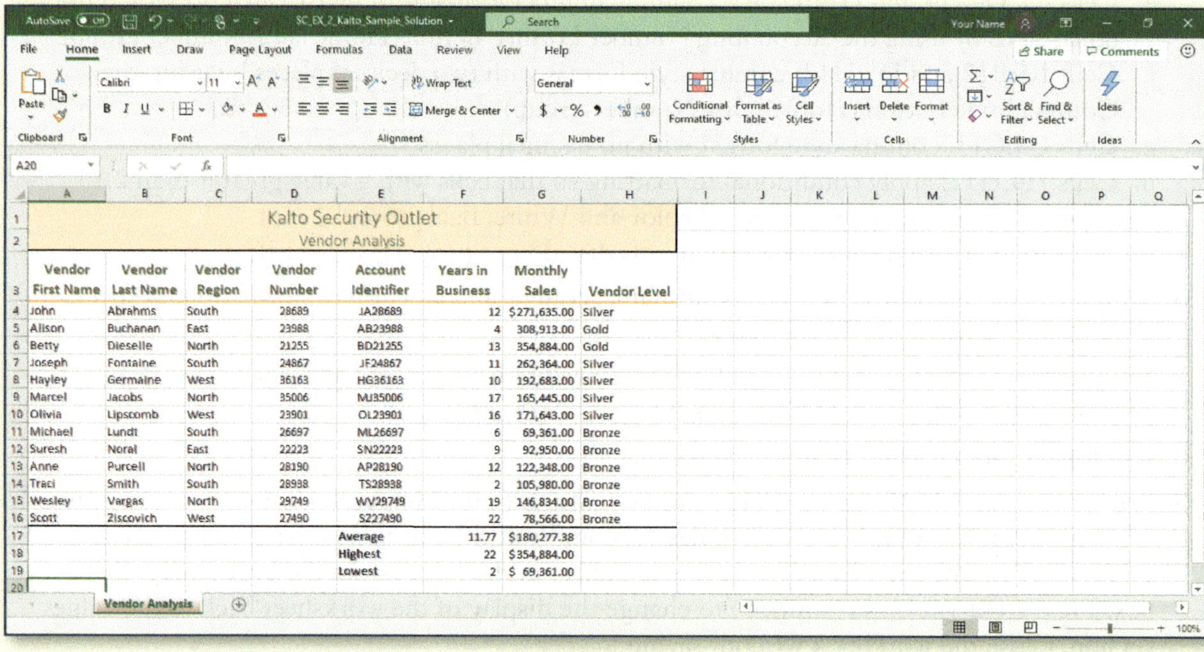

Kalto Security Outlet							
Vendor Analysis							
Vendor First Name	Vendor Last Name	Vendor Region	Vendor Number	Account Identifier	Years in Business	Monthly Sales	Vendor Level
John	Abrahms	South	28689	JA28689	12	$271,635.00	Silver
Alison	Buchanan	East	23988	AB23988	4	308,913.00	Gold
Betty	Dieselle	North	21255	BD21255	13	354,884.00	Gold
Joseph	Fontaine	South	24867	JF24867	11	262,364.00	Silver
Hayley	Germaine	West	36163	HG36163	10	192,683.00	Silver
Marcel	Jacobs	North	35006	MJ35006	17	165,445.00	Silver
Olivia	Lipscomb	West	23901	OL23901	16	171,643.00	Silver
Michael	Lundt	South	26697	ML26697	6	69,361.00	Bronze
Suresh	Noral	East	22223	SN22223	9	92,950.00	Bronze
Anne	Purcell	North	28190	AP28190	12	122,348.00	Bronze
Traci	Smith	South	28938	TS28938	2	105,980.00	Bronze
Wesley	Vargas	North	29749	WV29749	19	146,834.00	Bronze
Scott	Ziscovich	West	27490	SZ27490	22	78,566.00	Bronze
				Average	11.77	$180,277.38	
				Highest	22	$354,884.00	
				Lowest	2	$ 69,361.00	

Figure 2–71

5. With range F4:F16 selected, apply a conditional format to the range that uses a light red fill with dark red text to highlight cells with scores that are below average. Hint: Explore some of the preset conditional rules to assist with formatting this range of cells.
6. With range G4:G16 selected, apply a conditional format to the range that uses a light blue background to highlight cells that contain a value between 150,000 and 299,999.
7. With range H4:H16 selected, apply a conditional format to the range that uses a background color of your choice to highlight cells that contain Silver and another background color of your choice for cells that contain Gold. (Hint: You need to apply two separate formats, one for Silver and one for Gold.)
8. Save the file with the file name, SC_EX_2_Kalto, and submit the revised workbook in the format specified by your instructor.
9. Why did you choose the background colors for the Silver and Gold loyalty levels in Step 7?

Expand Your World

Create a solution that uses cloud or web technologies by learning and investigating on your own from general guidance.

Four-Year College Cost Calculator

Instructions: You are to create an estimate of the cost for attending your college for four years. You decide to create the worksheet using Excel Online so that you can share it with your friends online.

Perform the following tasks:

1. If necessary, sign in to your Microsoft account on the web and start Excel Online.
2. Create a blank workbook. In the first worksheet, use column headings for each year of college (First Year, Second Year, Third Year, and Fourth Year). For the row headings, use your current expenses (such as car payment, rent, utilities, tuition, and food).

3. Enter expenses for each year based upon estimates you find by searching the web.
4. Calculate the total for each column. Also determine highest, lowest, and average values for each column.
5. Using the techniques taught in this module, create appropriate titles and format the worksheet accordingly.
6. Save the file with the file name, SC_EX_2_CollegeExpenses, and submit the workbook in the format specified by your instructor.
7. When might you want to use Excel Online instead of the Excel app installed on your computer?

In the Lab

Design and implement a solution using creative thinking and problem-solving skills.

Create a Cell Phone Service Summary

Problem: You and your friends have decided to sign up for new cell phone service. You would like to maximize services while keeping costs low.

Perform the following tasks:

Part 1: Research and find three cell phone providers in your area. If you cannot find three providers in your area, you can research three providers in another area of your choosing. For each company, find the best service package as well as the basic service package. Using the cost figures you find, calculate the cost per month for each service for a year. Include totals, minimum, maximum, and average values. Use the concepts and techniques presented in this module to create and format the worksheet.

Part 2: You made several decisions while creating the worksheet in this assignment: how to display the data, how to format the worksheet, and which formulas to use. What was the rationale behind each of these decisions?

3 Working with Large Worksheets, Charting, and What-If Analysis

Objectives

After completing this module, you will be able to:

- Rotate text in a cell
- Create a series of month names
- Copy, paste, insert, and delete cells
- Format numbers using format symbols
- Enter and format the system date
- Use absolute and mixed cell references in a formula
- Use the IF function to perform a logical test
- Create and format sparkline charts
- Change sparkline chart types and styles
- Use the Format Painter button to format cells
- Create a clustered column chart on a separate chart sheet
- Use chart filters to display a subset of data in a chart
- Change the chart type and style
- Reorder sheet tabs
- Change the worksheet view
- Freeze and unfreeze rows and columns
- Answer what-if questions
- Goal seek to answer what-if questions
- Use Smart Lookup
- Understand accessibility features

Introduction

This module introduces you to techniques that will enhance your ability to create worksheets and draw charts. This module also covers other methods for entering values in cells, such as allowing Excel to automatically enter and format values based on a perceived pattern in the existing values. In addition, you will learn how to use absolute cell references and how to use the IF function to assign a value to a cell based on a logical test.

When you set up a worksheet, you should use cell references in formulas whenever possible, rather than constant values. The use of a cell reference allows you to change a value in multiple formulas by changing the value in a single cell. The cell references in a formula are called assumptions. **Assumptions** are cell values that you can change to determine new values for formulas. This module emphasizes the use of assumptions and shows how to use assumptions to answer what-if questions, such as what happens to the six-month operating income if you decrease the Marketing expenses assumption by 5%. Being able to analyze the effect of changing values in a worksheet is an important skill in making business decisions.

Worksheets are normally much larger than those you created in the previous modules, often extending beyond the size of the Excel window. When you cannot view the entire worksheet on the screen at once, working with a large worksheet can be frustrating. This module introduces several Excel commands that allow you to control what is displayed on the screen so that you can focus on critical parts of a large worksheet. One command allows you to freeze rows and columns so that they remain visible, even when you scroll. Another command splits the worksheet into separate panes so that you can view different parts of a worksheet on the screen at once. Another changes the magnification to allow you to see more content, albeit at a smaller size. This is useful for reviewing the general layout of content on the worksheet.

From your work in Module 1, you know how easily you can create charts in Excel. This module covers additional charting techniques that allow you to convey meaning visually, such as by using sparkline charts or clustered column charts. This module also introduces the Accessibility checker.

Project: Financial Projection Worksheet with What-If Analysis and Chart

The project in this module uses Excel to create the worksheet and clustered column chart shown in Figures 3–1a and 3–1b. Manola Department Stores, Incorporated, operates a store in Manchester, New Hampshire. The store has multiple departments such as electronics, clothing, appliances, and toys. Each December and June, the chief executive officer projects monthly sales revenues, costs of goods sold, gross margin, expenses, and operating income for the upcoming six-month period, based on figures from the previous six months. The CEO requires an easy-to-read worksheet that shows financial projections for the upcoming six months to use for procuring partial financing and for determining staffing needs. The worksheet should allow for quick analysis when projected numbers change, such as the percentage of expenses allocated

BTW

Screen Resolution

If you are using a computer to step through the project in this module and you want your screens to match the figures in this book, you should change your screen's resolution to 1366 × 768.

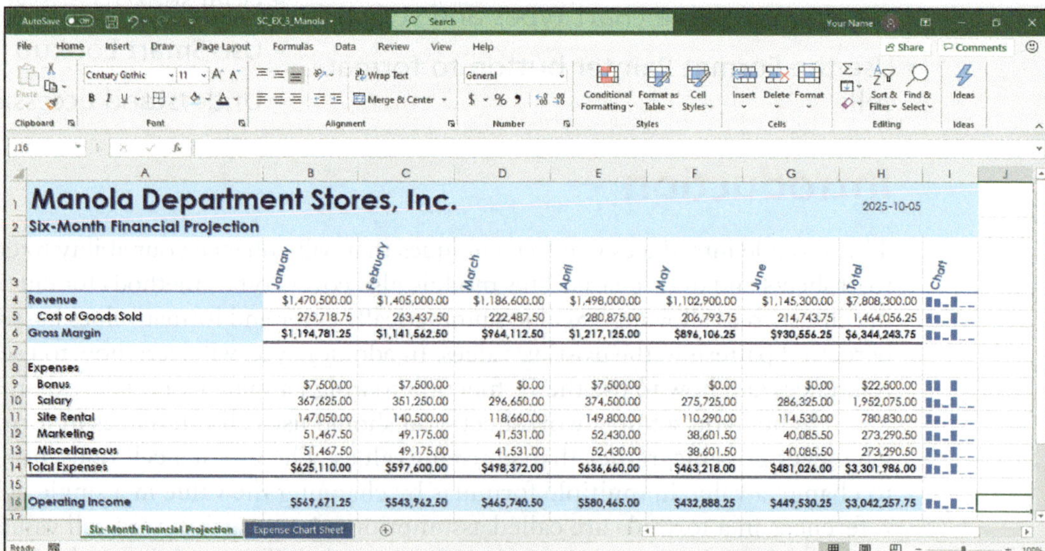

(a) Worksheet

Figure 3–1

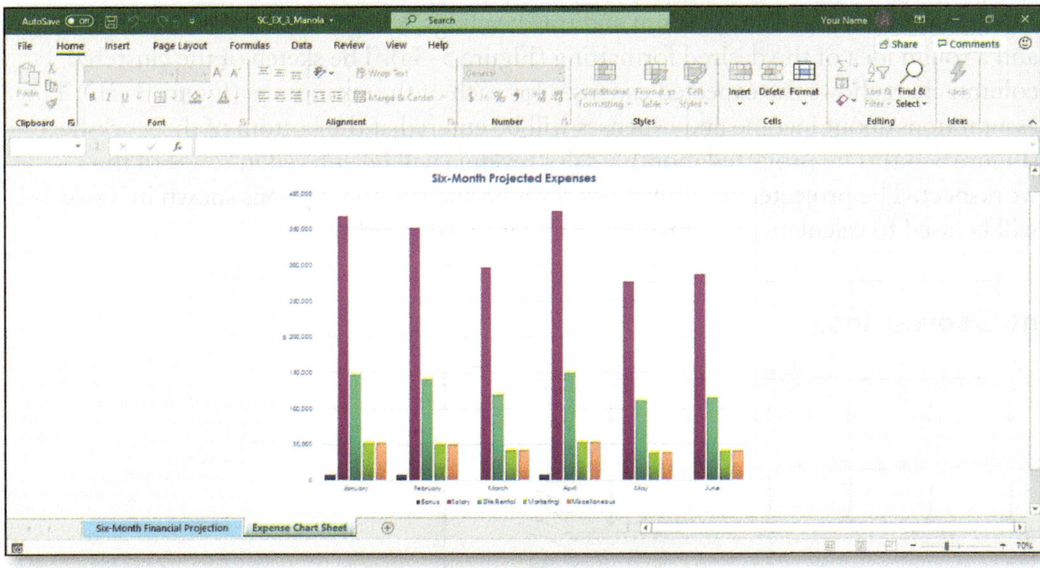

(b) Clustered Column Chart

Figure 3–1 (Continued)

to commission or the cost of miscellaneous expenses. In addition, you need to create a column chart that shows the breakdown of expenses for each month in the period.

The requirements document for the Manola Department Stores, Inc. Six-Month Financial Projection worksheet is shown in Figure 3–2. It includes the needs, source of data, summary of calculations, and chart requirements.

Worksheet Title	Manola Department Stores, Inc. Six-Month Financial Projection
Needs	• A worksheet that shows Manola Department Stores, Inc.'s projected monthly sales revenue, cost of goods sold, gross margin, expenses, and operating income for a six-month period. • A clustered column chart that shows the expected contribution of each expense category to total expenses.
Source of Data	Data supplied by the business owner includes projections of the monthly sales and expenses based on prior year figures (see Table 3–1). Remaining numbers in the worksheet are based on formulas.
Calculations	The following calculations are needed for each month: • Cost of Goods Sold = Revenue * (1 – Margin) • Gross Margin = Revenue – Cost of Goods Sold • Bonus expense = Predetermined bonus amount if Revenue exceeds the Revenue for Bonus, otherwise Bonus = 0 • Salary expense = Revenue × Salary percentage • Site Rental expense = Revenue × Site Rental percentage • Marketing expense = Revenue × Marketing percentage • Miscellaneous expense = Revenue × Miscellaneous expense percentage • Total expenses = Sum of all expenses • Operating Income = Gross Margin – Total expenses
Chart Requirements	• Show sparkline charts for revenue and each of the items noted in the calculations area above. • Show a clustered column chart that shows the contributions of each month's expense categories to the total monthly expense figure.

Figure 3–2

BTW

Touch Mode Differences

The Office and Windows interfaces may vary if you are using Touch Mode. For this reason, you might notice that the function or appearance of your touch screen differs slightly from this module's presentation.

Using a sketch of the worksheet can help you visualize its design. The sketch of the worksheet consists of titles, column and row headings, location of data values, calculations, and a rough idea of the desired formatting (Figure 3–3a). The sketch of the clustered column chart shows the expected expenses for each of the six months (Figure 3–3b). The assumptions about income and expenses will be entered at the bottom of the worksheet (Figure 3–3a). The projected monthly sales revenue will be entered in row 4 of the worksheet. The projected monthly sales revenue and the assumptions shown in Table 3–1 will be used to calculate the remaining numbers in the worksheet.

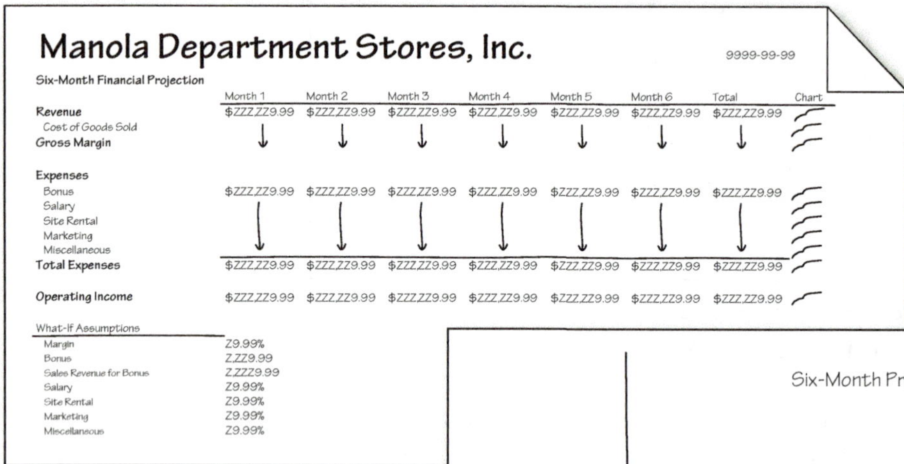

(a) Worksheet

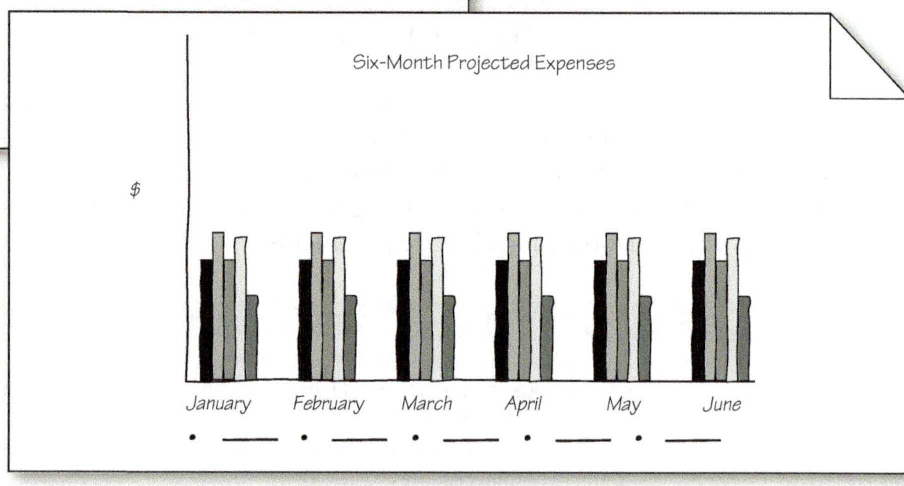

(b) Clustered Column Chart

Figure 3–3

Table 3–1 Manola Department Stores, Inc. Six-Month Financial Projections Data and What-If Assumptions

Projected Monthly Total Sales Revenues	
January	1,470,500.00
February	1,405,000.00
March	1,186,600.00
April	1,498,000.00
May	1,102,900.00
June	1,145,300.00
What-If Assumptions	
Margin	81.25%
Bonus	$5,000.00
Sales Revenue for Bonus	1,250,000.00
Salary	20.00%
Site Rental	10.00%
Marketing	3.50%
Miscellaneous	5.00%

With a solid understanding of the requirements document, an understanding of the necessary decisions, and a sketch of the worksheet, the next step is to use Excel to create the worksheet.

BTW

Excel Help

At any time while using Excel, you can find answers to questions and display information about various topics through Excel Help. Used properly, this form of assistance can increase your productivity and reduce your frustrations by minimizing the time you spend learning how to use Excel.

To Enter the Worksheet Titles and Apply a Theme

The worksheet contains two titles in cells A1 and A2. In the previous modules, titles were centered across the worksheet. With large worksheets that extend beyond the size of a window, it is best to leave titles left-aligned, as shown in the sketch of the worksheet in Figure 3–3a, so that the worksheet will print the title on the first page if the worksheet requires multiple pages. This allows the user to easily find the worksheet title when necessary. The following steps enter the worksheet titles and change the workbook theme to Slice.

BTW

Ribbon and Screen Resolution

Excel may change how the groups and buttons within the groups appear on the ribbon, depending on the screen resolution of your computer. Thus, your ribbon may look different from the ones in this book if you are using a screen resolution other than 1366 × 768.

1. sam Start Excel and create a blank workbook in the Excel window.
2. Select cell A1 and then type `Manola Department Stores, Inc.` as the worksheet title.
3. Select cell A2, type `Six-Month Financial Projection` as the worksheet subtitle, and then press ENTER to enter the worksheet subtitle.
4. Apply the Slice theme to the workbook.

Rotating Text and Using the Fill Handle to Create a Series

The data on the worksheet, including month names and the What-If Assumptions section, now can be added to the worksheet.

BTW

Rotating Text in a Cell

In Excel, you use the Alignment sheet in the Format Cells dialog box (shown in Figure 3–5) to position data in a cell by centering, left-aligning, or right-aligning; indenting; aligning at the top, bottom, or center; and rotating.

Consider This

What should you take into account when planning a worksheet layout?

Using Excel, you can change text and number formatting in many ways, which affects the visual impact of the worksheet. Rotated text often provides a strong visual appeal. Rotated text also allows you to fit more text into a smaller column width. When laying out a worksheet, keep in mind the content you want to emphasize and the length of the cell titles relative to the numbers.

To Rotate Text in a Cell

The design of the worksheet calls specifically for data for the six months of the selling season. Because there always will be only six months of data in the worksheet, place the months across the top of the worksheet as column headings rather than as row headings. Place the income and expense categories in rows, as they are more numerous than the number of months. This layout allows you to easily navigate the worksheet. Ideally, a proper layout will create a worksheet that is longer than it is wide.

When you first enter text, its angle is zero degrees (0°), and it reads from left to right in a cell. Excel allows you to rotate text in a cell counterclockwise by entering a number between 1° and 90°. If you specify an exact value by entering 90 in the Degrees box in the Orientation area, the text will appear vertically and read from bottom to top in the cell. **Why?** Rotating text is one method of making column headings visually distinct. The following steps enter the month name, January, in cell B3 and format cell B3 by rotating the text.

1

- If necessary, click the Home tab and then select cell B3 because this cell will include the first month name in the series of month names.
- Type `January` as the cell entry and then click the Enter button.
- On the Home tab in the Alignment group, click the Dialog Box Launcher to display the Format Cells dialog box (Figure 3–4).

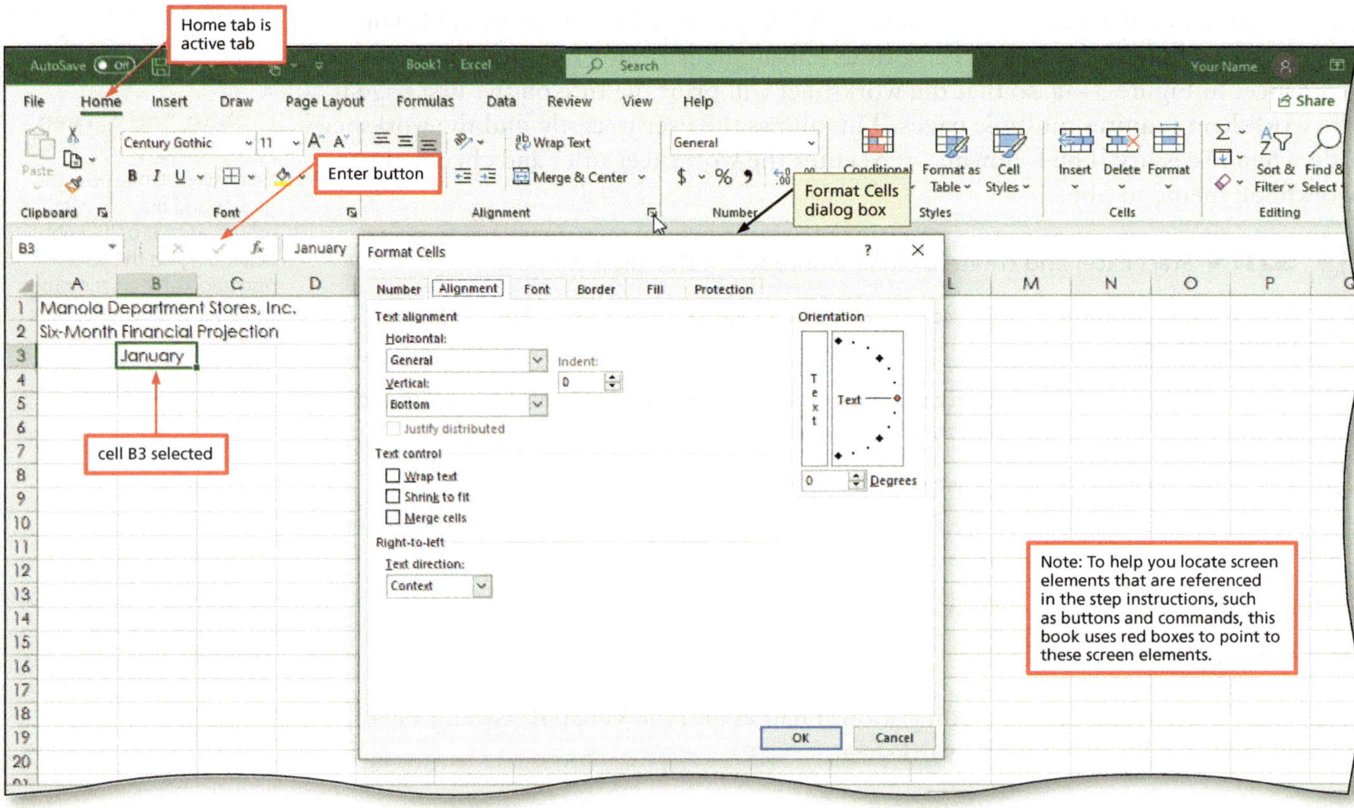

Figure 3–4

2

- Click the 75° point in the Orientation area (Format Cells dialog box) to move the indicator in the Orientation area to the 75° point and display a new orientation in the Degrees box (Figure 3–5).

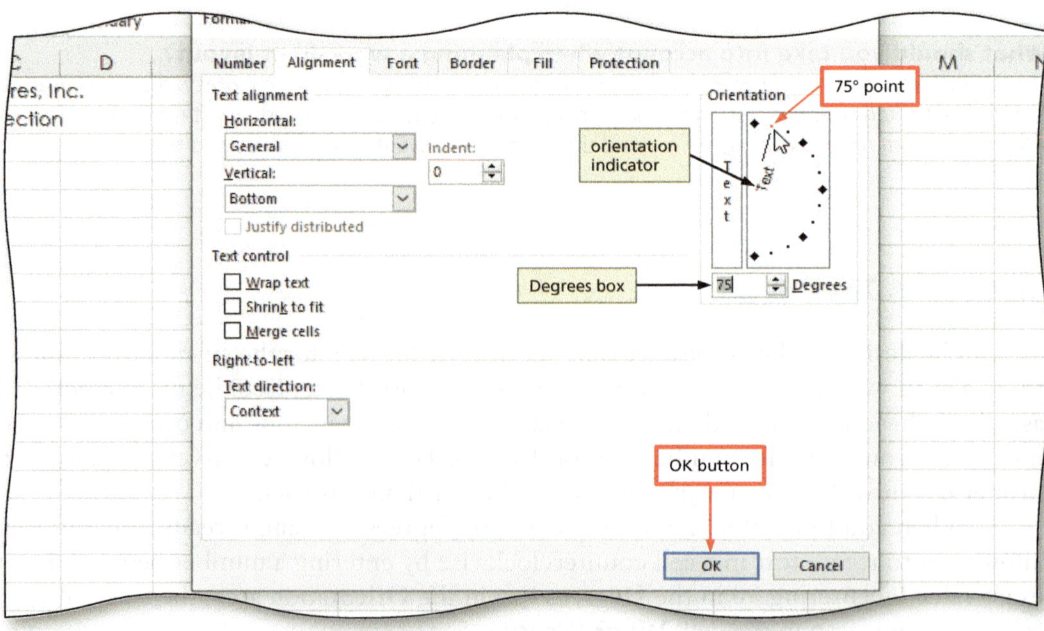

Figure 3–5

3

- Click OK (Format Cells dialog box) to rotate the text to the preset angle in the active cell and increase the height of the current row to best fit the rotated text (Figure 3–6).

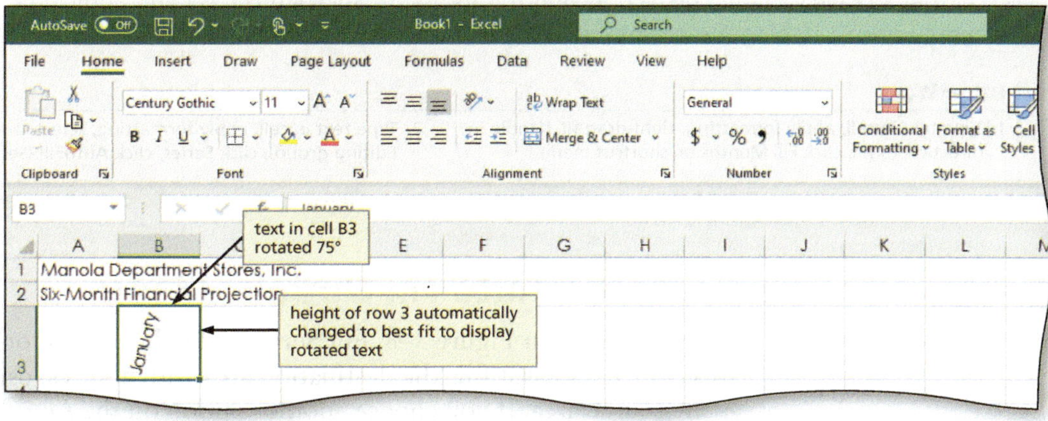

Figure 3–6

Other Ways

1. Right-click selected cell, click Format Cells on shortcut menu, click Alignment tab (Format Cells dialog box), click 75° point, click OK

To Use the Fill Handle to Create a Series of Month Names

Why? Once the first month in the series has been entered and formatted, you can complete the data series using the fill handle rather than typing and formatting all the entries. The following steps use the fill handle and the entry in cell B3 to create a series of month names in cells C3:G3.

1

- Drag the fill handle on the lower-right corner of cell B3 to the right to select the range to fill, C3:G3 in this case. Do not release the mouse button (Figure 3–7).

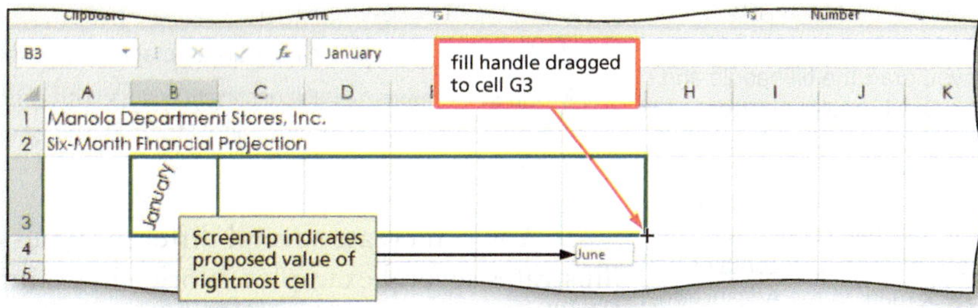

Figure 3–7

2

- Release the mouse button to create a month name series in the selected range and copy the format of the selected cell to the selected range.
- Click the 'Auto Fill Options' button below the lower-right corner of the fill area to display the Auto Fill Options menu (Figure 3–8).

Q&A **What if I do not want to copy the format of cell B3 during the auto fill operation?**
In addition to creating a series of values, dragging the fill handle instructs Excel to copy the format of cell B3 to the range C3:G3. With some fill operations, you may not want to copy the formats of the source cell or range to the destination cell or range. If this is the case, click the 'Auto Fill Options' button after the range fills and then select the desired option on the Auto Fill Options menu (Figure 3–8).

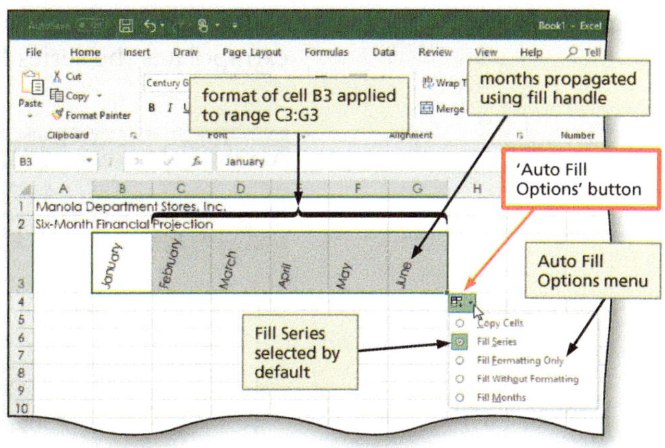

Figure 3–8

3

- Click the 'Auto Fill Options' button to hide the Auto Fill Options menu.
- Select cell H3, type `Total,` and then press the RIGHT ARROW key to enter a column heading.
- Type `Chart` in cell I3 and then press the RIGHT ARROW key.

Q&A

Why is the word, Total, formatted with a 75° rotation?

Excel tries to save you time by recognizing the format in adjacent cell G3 and applying it to cell H3. Such behavior also occurs when typing the column heading in cell I3.

Other Ways

1. Type text in cell, apply formatting, right-drag fill handle in direction to fill, click Fill Months on shortcut menu
2. Type text in cell, apply formatting, select range, click Fill button (Home tab | Editing group), click Series, click AutoFill (Series dialog box), click OK

BTW

The Fill Handle

If you drag the fill handle up or to the left, Excel will decrement the series rather than increment the series. To copy a word, such as January or Monday, which Excel might interpret as the start of a series, hold down CTRL while you drag the fill handle to a destination area. If you drag the fill handle back into the middle of a cell, Excel erases the contents of the cell.

BTW

Auto Fill Options Button

If you drag the fill handle and the Quick Analysis button appears instead of the Auto Fill Options button, make sure the 'Show Paste Options button when content is pasted' check box contains a check mark in the Advanced options.

Using the Auto Fill Options Menu

As shown in Figure 3–8, Fill Series is the default option that Excel uses to fill an area, which means it fills the destination area with a series, using the same formatting as the source area. If you choose another option on the Auto Fill Options menu, Excel changes the contents of the destination range. Following the use of the fill handle, the 'Auto Fill Options' button remains active until you begin the next Excel operation. Table 3–2 summarizes the options on the Auto Fill Options menu.

Table 3–2 Options Available on the Auto Fill Options Menu

Auto Fill Option	Description
Copy Cells	Fill destination area with contents using format of source area. Do not create a series.
Fill Series	Fill destination area with series using format of source area. This option is the default.
Fill Formatting Only	Fill destination area using format of source area. No content is copied unless fill is series.
Fill Without Formatting	Fill destination area with contents, without applying the formatting of source area.
Fill Months	Fill destination area with series of months using format of source area. Same as Fill Series and shows as an option only if source area contains the name of a month.

You can create several different types of series using the fill handle. Table 3–3 illustrates several examples. Notice in examples 4, 7, 9, and 11 that, if you use the fill handle to create a series of nonsequential numbers or months, you must enter the first item in the series in one cell and the second item in the series in an adjacent cell, and then select both cells and drag the fill handle through the destination area. Excel extrapolates the series based on the previous input.

Table 3–3 Examples of Series Using the Fill Handle

Example	Contents of Cell(s) Copied Using the Fill Handle	Next Three Values of Extended Series
1	4:00	5:00, 6:00, 7:00
2	Qtr2	Qtr3, Qtr4, Qtr1
3	Quarter 1	Quarter 2, Quarter 3, Quarter 4
4	22-Jul, 22-Sep	22-Nov, 22-Jan, 22-Mar
5	2020, 2021	2022, 2023, 2024
6	1, 2	3, 4, 5
7	625, 575	525, 475, 425
8	Mon	Tue, Wed, Thu
9	Sunday, Tuesday	Thursday, Saturday, Monday
10	4th Section	5th Section, 6th Section, 7th Section
11	2205, 2208	2211, 2214, 2217

You can create your own custom fill sequences for use with the fill handle. For example, if you often type the same list of products or names in Excel, you can create a custom fill sequence. You then can type the first product or name and then use the fill handle to automatically fill in the remaining products or names. To create a custom fill sequence, display the Excel Options dialog box by clicking Options in Backstage view. Click the Advanced tab (Excel Options dialog box) and then click the 'Edit Custom Lists' button in the General section (Excel Options dialog box).

To Increase Column Widths

Why? In Module 2, you increased column widths after the values were entered into the worksheet. Sometimes, you may want to increase the column widths before you enter values and, if necessary, adjust them later. You can resize columns to exact widths using dragging, as described below. You can also resize columns to an approximate value by dragging until the cell contents are displayed in a visually pleasing way, without regard for the numbers displayed. The following steps increase the column widths to specific values.

1

- Move the pointer to the boundary between column heading A and column heading B so that the pointer changes to a split double arrow in preparation for adjusting the column widths.
- Drag the pointer to the right until the ScreenTip displays the desired column width, Width: 38.50 (313 pixels) in this case. Do not release the mouse button. If you are unable to drag and reach the specified width, get as close as you can, or double-click the right boundary of column heading A to change the width of the column to best fit (Figure 3–9).

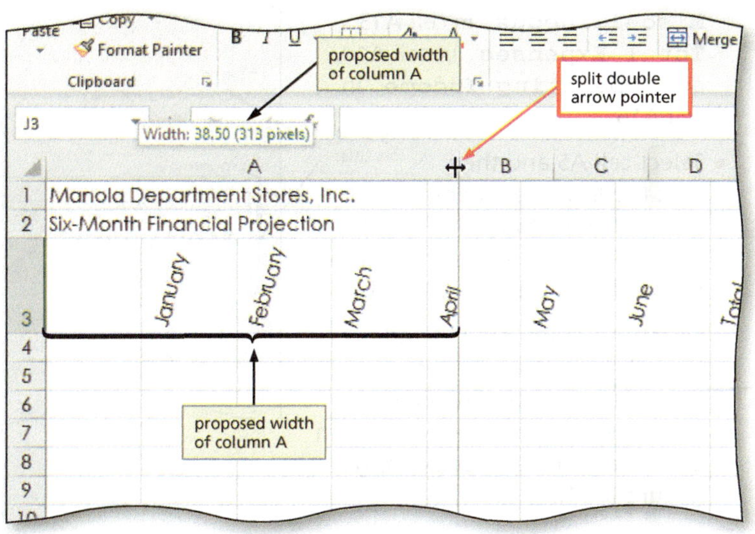

Figure 3–9

2

- Release the mouse button to change the width of the column.
- Click column heading B to select the column and then drag through column heading G to select the range in which to change the widths.
- Move the pointer to the boundary between column headings B and C in preparation for resizing column B and then drag the pointer to the right until the ScreenTip displays the desired width, Width: 15.00 (125 pixels) in this case. Do not lift your finger or release the mouse button (Figure 3–10).

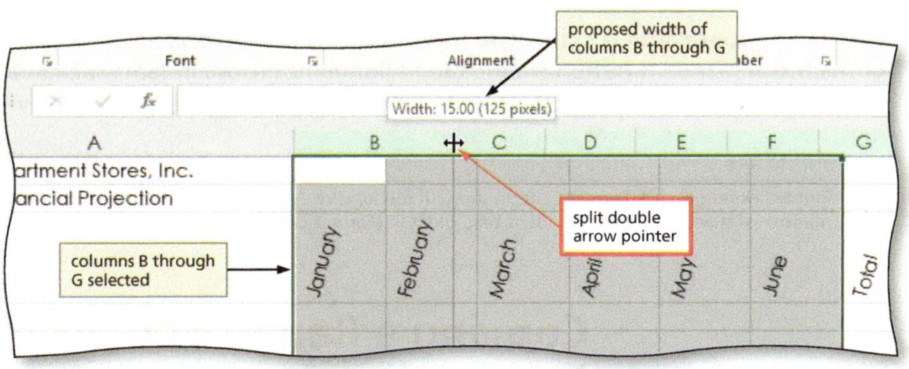

Figure 3–10

3

- Release the mouse button to change the width of the selected columns.
- If necessary, scroll the worksheet so that column H is visible and then use the technique described in Step 1 to increase the width of column H to 18.00 (149 pixels).

To Enter and Indent Row Titles

Excel allows you to indent text in cells. The following steps enter the row titles in column A and indent several of the row titles. **Why?** Indenting rows helps you create a visual hierarchy by indenting some of the row titles, like in an outline or table of contents.

1

- If necessary, scroll the worksheet so that column A and row 4 are visible and then enter `Revenue` in cell A4, `Cost of Goods Sold` in cell A5, `Gross Margin` in cell A6, `Expenses` in cell A8, `Bonus` in cell A9, `Salary` in cell A10, `Site Rental` in cell A11, `Marketing` in cell A12, `Miscellaneous` in cell A13, `Total Expenses` in cell A14, and `Operating Income` in cell A16.
- Select cell A5 and then click the Increase Indent button (Home tab | Alignment group) to increase the indentation of the text in the selected cell.
- Select the range A9:A13 and then click the Increase Indent button (Home tab | Alignment group) to increase the indentation of the text in the selected range (Figure 3–11).

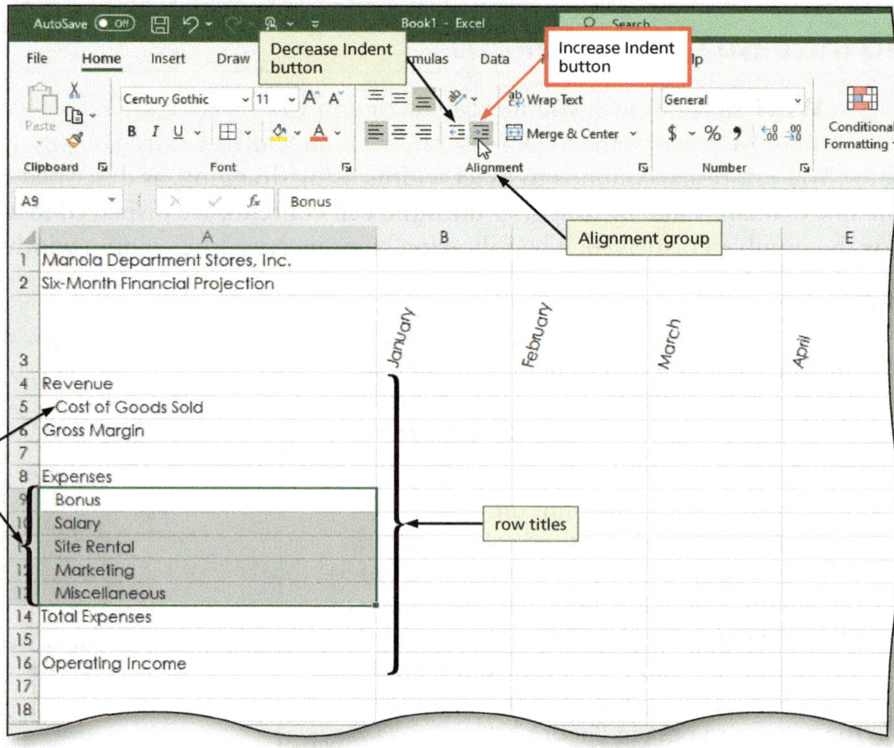

Figure 3–11

2

- Select cell A18 to finish entering the row titles and deselect the current cell.

Q&A

What happens when I click the Increase Indent button?

The Increase Indent button (Home tab | Alignment group) indents the contents of a cell two spaces to the right each time you click it. The Decrease Indent button decreases the indent by two spaces each time you click it.

Other Ways

1. Right-click range, click Format Cells on shortcut menu, click Alignment tab (Format Cells dialog box), click Left (Indent) in Horizontal list, type number of spaces to indent in Indent box, click OK (Format Cells dialog box)

Copying a Range of Cells to a Nonadjacent Destination Area

The What-If Assumptions section should be placed in an area of the worksheet that is accessible yet does not impair the view of the main section of the worksheet. As shown in Figure 3–3a, the What-If Assumptions will be placed below the calculations in the worksheet. This will allow the reader to see the main section of the worksheet when first opening the workbook. Additionally, the row titles in the Expenses area are the same as the row titles in the What-If Assumptions table, with the exception of the two additional entries in cells A19 (Margin) and A21 (Sales Revenue for Bonus). Hence, the row titles in the What-If Assumptions table can be created by copying the range A9:A13 to the range A19:A23 and then inserting two rows for the additional entries in cells A19 and A21. You cannot use the fill handle to copy the range because the source area (range A9:A13) is not adjacent to the destination area (range A19:A23).

A more versatile method of copying a source area is to use the Copy button and Paste button (Home tab | Clipboard group). You can use these two buttons to copy a source area to an adjacent or nonadjacent destination area.

BTW

Fitting Entries in a Cell

An alternative to increasing column widths or row heights is to shrink the characters in a cell to fit the current width of the column. To shrink to fit, on the Home tab in the Alignment group, click the Dialog Box Launcher and then place a check mark in the 'Shrink to fit' check box in the Text control area (Format Cells dialog box).

To Copy a Range of Cells to a Nonadjacent Destination Area

The Copy button copies the contents and format of the source area to the **Office Clipboard**, a temporary storage area in the computer's memory that allows you to collect text and graphics from any Office document and then paste them into almost any other type of document; the Office Clipboard can hold a maximum of 24 items. The Paste button pastes a copy of the contents of the Office Clipboard in the destination area. **Why?** Copying the range of cells rather than reentering the content ensures consistency within the worksheet. The following steps enter the What-If Assumptions row heading and then use the Copy and Paste buttons to copy the range A9:A13 to the nonadjacent range A19:A23.

1

- With cell A18 selected, type **`What-If Assumptions`** as the new row title and then click the Enter button.
- Select the range A9:A13 and then click the Copy button (Home tab | Clipboard group) to copy the values and formats of the selected range, A9:A13 in this case, to the Office Clipboard.
- If necessary, click the down scroll arrow to display cell A19, and then select cell A19, the top cell in the destination area (Figure 3–12).

Q&A **Why do I not select the entire destination area?**

You are not required to select the entire destination area (A19:A23) because Excel only needs to know the upper-left cell of the destination area. In the case of a single column range, such as A19:A23, the top cell of the destination area (cell A19) also is the upper-left cell of the destination area.

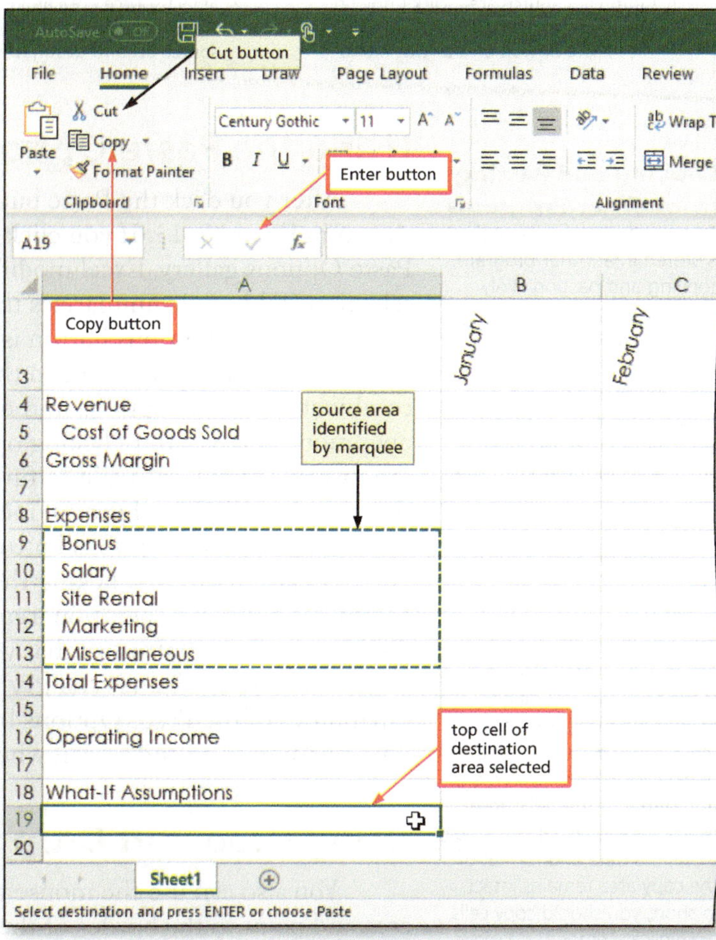

Figure 3–12

2

- Click the Paste button (Home tab | Clipboard group) to copy the values and formats of the last item placed on the Office Clipboard, range A9:A13, to the destination area, A19:A23. If necessary, scroll down to see the complete destination area (Figure 3–13).

Q&A **What if there was data in the destination area before I clicked the Paste button?**
Any data contained in the destination area prior to the copy and paste would be lost. When you complete a copy, the values and formats in the destination area are replaced with the values and formats of the source area. If you accidentally delete valuable data, click the Undo button on the Quick Access Toolbar or press CTRL+Z.

3

- Press ESC to remove the marquee from the source area and deactivate the Paste button (Home tab | Clipboard group).

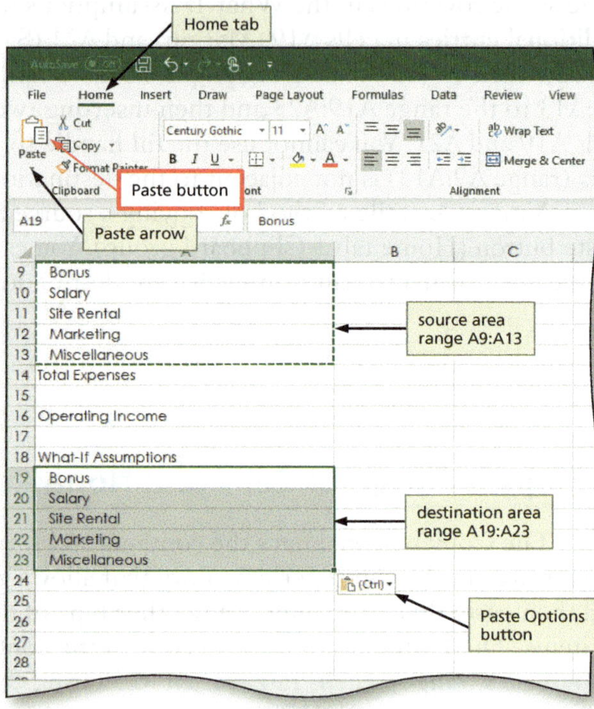

Figure 3–13

Other Ways

1. Right-click source area, click Copy on shortcut menu, right-click destination area, click Paste button on shortcut menu
2. Select source area and point to border of range; while holding down CTRL, drag source area to destination area
3. Select source area, press CTRL+C, select destination area, press CTRL+V

BTW
Copying and Pasting from Other Programs
If you need data in Excel that is stored in another program, copying and pasting likely will help you. You might need to experiment before you are successful, because Excel might attempt to copy formatting or other information that you did not intend to paste from the other program. Trying various Paste Option buttons will solve most of such problems.

BTW
Move It or Copy It
Contrary to popular belief, move and copy operations are not the same. When you move a cell, the data in the original location is cleared and the format of the cell is reset to the default. When you copy a cell, the data and format of the copy area remains intact. In short, you should copy cells to duplicate entries and move cells to rearrange entries.

Using the Paste Options Menu

After you click the Paste button, Excel displays the Paste Options button, as shown in Figure 3–13. If you click the Paste Options arrow and select an option in the Paste Options gallery, Excel modifies the most recent paste operation based on your selection. Table 3–4 summarizes the options available in the Paste Options gallery. When the Paste Options button is visible, you can use keyboard shortcuts to access the paste commands available in the Paste Options gallery. Additionally, you can use combinations of the options in the Paste Options gallery to customize your paste operation. That is, after clicking one of the buttons in the Paste Options gallery, you can display the gallery again to further adjust your paste operation. The Paste button (Home tab | Clipboard group) includes an arrow that, when clicked, displays the same options as the Paste Options button.

An alternative to clicking the Paste button is to press ENTER. Pressing ENTER completes the paste operation, removes the marquee from the source area, and disables the Paste button so that you cannot paste the copied source area to other destination areas. The ENTER key was not used in the previous set of steps so that the capabilities of the Paste Options button could be discussed. The Paste Options button does not appear on the screen when you use ENTER to complete the paste operation.

Using Drag and Drop to Move or Copy Cells

You also can use the mouse to move or copy cells. First, you select the source area and point to the border of the cell or range. You know you are pointing to the border of the cell or range when the pointer changes to a four-headed arrow. To move the selected cell or cells, drag the selection to the destination area. To copy a selection,

Table 3–4 Paste Gallery Commands

Paste Option Button	Paste Option	Description
	Paste	Copy contents and format of source area. This option is the default.
	Formulas	Copy formulas from the source area, but not the contents and format.
	Formulas & Number Formatting	Copy formulas and format for numbers and formulas of source area, but not the contents.
	Keep Source Formatting	Copy contents, format, and styles of source area.
	No Borders	Copy contents and format of source area, but not any borders.
	Keep Source Column Widths	Copy contents and format of source area. Change destination column widths to source column widths.
	Transpose	Copy the contents and format of the source area, but transpose, or swap, the rows and columns.
	Values	Copy contents of source area but not the formatting for formulas.
	Values & Number Formatting	Copy contents and format of source area for numbers or formulas, but use format of destination area for text.
	Values & Source Formatting	Copy contents and formatting of source area but not the formula.
	Formatting	Copy format of source area but not the contents.
	Paste Link	Copy contents and format and link cells so that a change to the cells in source area updates the corresponding cells in destination area.
	Picture	Copy an image of the source area as a picture.
	Linked Picture	Copy an image of the source area as a picture so that a change to the cells in source area updates the picture in destination area.

hold down CTRL while dragging the selection to the destination area. You know Excel is in Copy mode when a small plus sign appears next to the pointer. Be sure to release the mouse button before you release CTRL. Using the mouse to move or copy cells is called **drag and drop**.

Using Cut and Paste to Move Cells

Another way to move cells is to select them, click the Cut button (Home tab | Clipboard group) (Figure 3–12) to remove the cells from the worksheet and copy them to the Office Clipboard, select the destination area, and then click the Paste button (Home tab | Clipboard group) or press ENTER. The cell(s) you move using the Cut command either can contain a static value or a formula. You also can use the Cut command on the shortcut menu instead of the Cut button on the ribbon.

BTW

Cutting

When you cut a cell or range of cells using the Cut command on a shortcut menu or Cut button (Home tab | Clipboard group), Excel copies the cells to the Office Clipboard; it does not remove the cells from the source area until you paste the cells in the destination area by either clicking the Paste button (Home tab | Clipboard group) or pressing ENTER. When you complete the paste, Excel clears the cell's or range of cell's entries and their formats from the source area.

Inserting and Deleting Cells in a Worksheet

At any time while the worksheet is on the screen, you can insert cells to enter new data or delete cells to remove unwanted data. You can insert or delete individual cells; a range of cells, rows, or columns; or entire worksheets. As you insert cells into your worksheet, making the worksheet larger, it may print on multiple pages. If you want to indicate where one page should stop and the next page should start, you can insert a page break. To insert a page break, first select the cell immediately below where you want to insert the page break. Next, click the Breaks button (Page Layout tab | Page Setup group) and then click Insert Page Break. If you want to remove a page break, you should instead click the 'Remove Page Break' command. To remove all page breaks from a worksheet, click the 'Reset All Page Breaks' command.

To Insert a Row

Why? According to the sketch of the worksheet in Figure 3–3a, two rows must be inserted in the What-If Assumptions table, one above Bonus for the Margin assumption and another between Bonus and Salary for the Sales Revenue for Bonus assumption. The following steps insert the new rows into the worksheet.

1

- Right-click row heading 20, the row below where you want to insert a row, to display the shortcut menu and the mini toolbar (Figure 3–14).

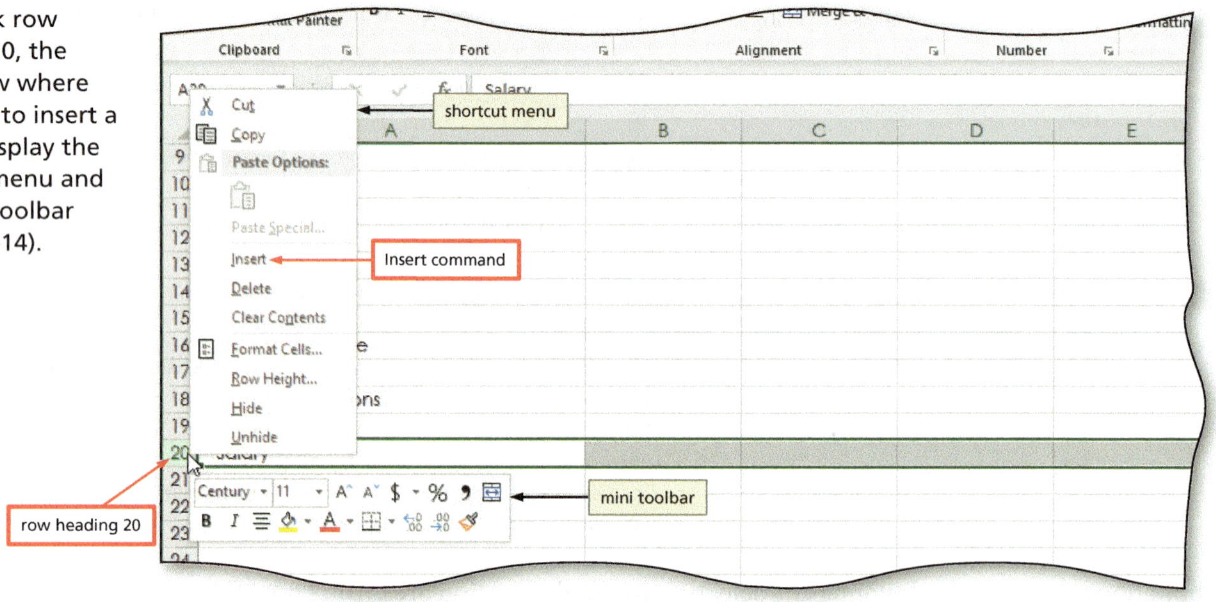

Figure 3–14

2

- Click Insert on the shortcut menu to insert a new row in the worksheet by shifting the selected row and all rows below it down one row.
- Select cell A20 in the new row and then type `Sales Revenue for Bonus` to enter a new row title (Figure 3–15).

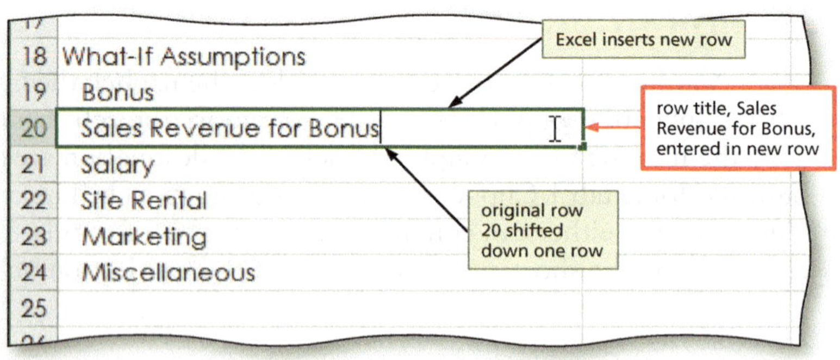

Figure 3–15

Q&A **What is the resulting format of the new row?**

The cells in the new row inherit the formats of the cells in the row above them. You can change this behavior by clicking the Insert Options button that appears below the inserted row. Following the insertion of a row, the Insert Options button allows you to select from the following options: (1) 'Format Same As Above', (2) 'Format Same As Below', and (3) Clear Formatting. The 'Format Same As Above' option is the default. The Insert Options button remains active until you begin the next Excel operation. Excel does not display the Insert Options button if the initial row does not contain any formatted data.

3

- Right-click row heading 19, the row below where you want to insert a row, to display the shortcut menu and the mini toolbar.
- Click Insert on the shortcut menu to insert a new row in the worksheet.
- Click the Insert Options button below row 19 (Figure 3–16).
- Click 'Format Same As Below' on the menu.
- Select cell A19 in the new row and then enter **`Margin`** as a new row title.

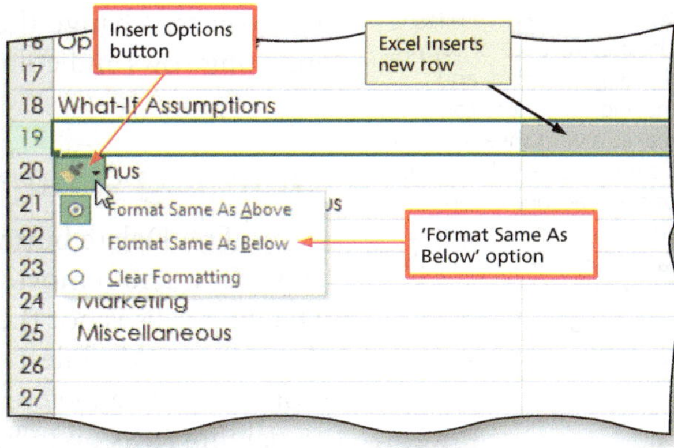

Figure 3–16

Q&A **What would happen if cells in the shifted rows were included in formulas?**
If the rows that shift down included cell references in formulas located in the worksheet, Excel would automatically adjust the cell references in the formulas to their new locations. Thus, in Step 2, if a formula in the worksheet referenced a cell in row 19 before the insert, then Excel would adjust the cell reference in the formula to row 20 after the insert.

4

- Save the workbook using **`SC_EX_3_Manola`** as the file name.

Other Ways

1. Click Insert Cells arrow (Home tab | Cells group), click 'Insert Sheet Rows'
2. Press CTRL+SHIFT+PLUS SIGN, click Entire row (Insert dialog box), OK

BTW
Inserting Multiple Rows
If you want to insert multiple rows, you have two choices. You can insert a single row by using the Insert command on the shortcut menu and then repeatedly press F4 to continue inserting rows. Alternatively, you can select a number of existing rows equal to the number of rows that you want to insert. For instance, if you want to insert five rows, select five existing rows in the worksheet, right-click the selected rows, and then click Insert on the shortcut menu.

Inserting Columns

You insert columns into a worksheet in the same way you insert rows. To insert columns, select one or more columns immediately to the right of where you want Excel to insert the new column or columns. Select the number of columns you want to insert, click the Insert arrow (Home tab | Cells group), and then click 'Insert Sheet Columns' in the Insert list; or right-click the selected column(s) and then click Insert on the shortcut menu. The Insert command on the shortcut menu requires that you select an entire column (or columns) to insert a column (or columns). Following the insertion of a column, Excel displays the Insert Options button, which allows you to modify the insertion in a fashion similar to that discussed earlier when inserting rows.

Inserting Single Cells or a Range of Cells

You can use the Insert command on the shortcut menu or the Insert Cells command on the Insert menu—produced by clicking the Insert button (Home tab | Cells group)—to insert a single cell or a range of cells. You should be aware that if you shift a single cell or a range of cells, however, it no longer lines up with its associated cells. To ensure that the values in the worksheet do not get out of order, spreadsheet experts recommend that you insert only entire rows or entire columns. When you

BTW
Dragging Ranges
You can move and insert a selected cell or range between existing cells by holding down SHIFT while you drag the selection to the gridline where you want to insert the selected cell or range. You also can copy and insert by holding down CTRL+SHIFT while you drag the selection to the desired gridline.

BTW
Ranges and Undo
The incorrect use of copying, deleting, inserting, and moving cell ranges can makes a worksheet incorrect. Carefully review the results of these actions before continuing on to the next task. If you are not sure the result of the action is correct, click the Undo button on the Quick Access Toolbar.

BTW
Organizing Files and Folders
You should organize and store files in folders so that you easily can find the files later. For example, if you are taking an introductory technology class called CIS 101, a good practice would be to save all Excel files in an Excel folder in a CIS 101 folder.

insert a single cell or a range of cells, Excel displays the Insert Options button so that you can change the format of the inserted cell, using options similar to those for inserting rows and columns.

Deleting Columns and Rows

The Delete button (Home tab | Cells group) or the Delete command on the shortcut menu removes cells (including the data and format) from the worksheet. Deleting cells is not the same as clearing cells. The Clear Contents command,. described in Module 1, clears the data from the cells, but the cells remain in the worksheet. The Delete command removes the cells from the worksheet and shifts the remaining rows up (when you delete rows) or shifts the remaining columns to the left (when you delete columns). If formulas located in other cells reference cells in the deleted row or column, Excel does not adjust these cell specifically references. Excel displays the error message **#REF!** in those cells to indicate a cell reference error. For example, if cell A7 contains the formula =A4+A5 and you delete row 5, Excel assigns the formula =A4+#REF! to cell A6 (originally cell A7) and displays the error message, #REF!, in cell A6. Excel also displays an Error Options button when you select the cell containing the error message, #REF!, which allows you to select options to determine the nature of the problem.

To Enter Numbers with Format Symbols

The next step in creating the Financial Projection worksheet is to enter the what-if assumptions values in the range B19:B25. The numbers in the table can be entered and then formatted using techniques from Modules 1 and 2, or each number can be entered with **format symbols**, which assign a format to numbers as they are entered. When a number is entered with a format symbol, Excel displays it with the assigned format. Valid format symbols include the dollar sign ($), comma (,), and percent sign (%).

If you enter a whole number, it appears without any decimal places. If you enter a number with one or more decimal places and a format symbol, Excel displays the number with two decimal places. Table 3–5 illustrates several examples of numbers entered with format symbols. The number in parentheses in column 4 indicates the number of decimal places.

Table 3–5 Numbers Entered with Format Symbols

Format Symbol	Typed in Formula Bar	Displays in Cell	Comparable Format
,	374,149	374,149	Comma(0)
	5,833.6	5,833.60	Comma(2)
$	$58917	$58,917	Currency(0)
	$842.51	$842.51	Currency(2)
	$63,574.9	$63,574.90	Currency(2)
%	85%	85%	Percent(0)
	12.80%	12.80%	Percent(2)
	68.2242%	68.2242%	Percent(4)

Why? In some cases, using a format symbol is the most efficient method for entering and formatting data. The following step enters the numbers in the What-If Assumptions table with format symbols.

1

- Enter the following values, using format symbols to apply number formatting: **81.25%** in cell B19, **5,000.00** in cell B20, **1,250,000.00** in cell B21, **20.00%** in cell B22, **10.00%** in cell B23, **3.50%** in cell B24, and **5.00%** in cell B25 (Figure 3–17).

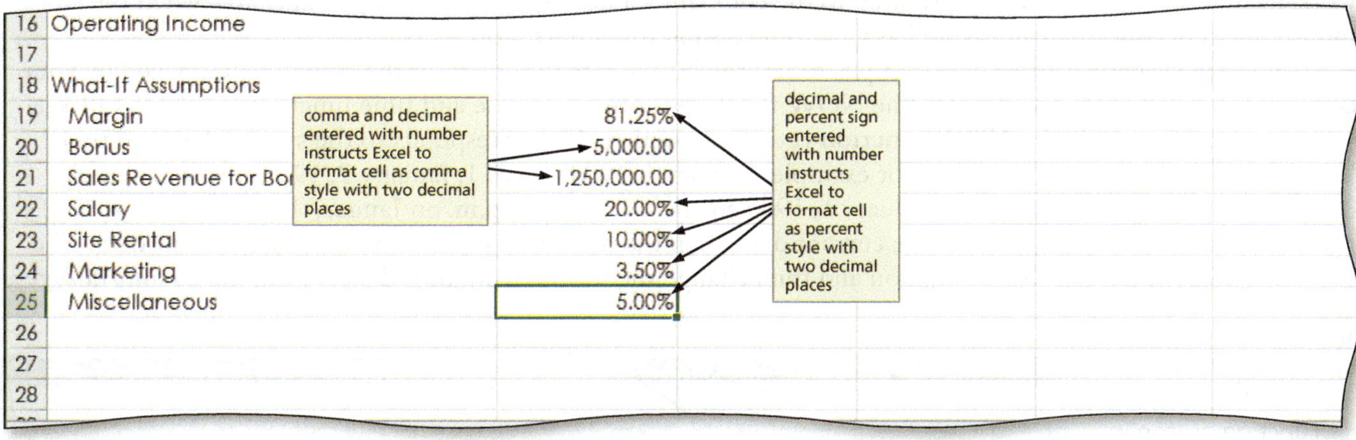

Figure 3–17

Other Ways

1. Right-click range, click Format Cells on shortcut menu, click Number tab (Format Cells dialog box), click category in Category list, select desired format, click OK
2. Press CTRL+1, click Number tab (Format Cells dialog box), click category in Category list, select desired format, click OK

To Enter the Projected Monthly Sales

The following steps enter the projected revenue, listed previously in Table 3–1, in row 4 and compute the projected six-month revenue in cell H4.

1. If necessary, display the Home tab.
2. Enter **1,470,500.00** in cell B4, **1,405,000.00** in cell C4, **1,186,600.00** in cell D4, **1,498,000.00** in cell E4, **1,102,900.00** in cell F4, and **1,145,300.00** in cell G4.
3. Select cell H4 and then click the Auto Sum button (Home tab | Editing group) twice to create a sum (7,808,300.00) in the selected cell (Figure 3–18).

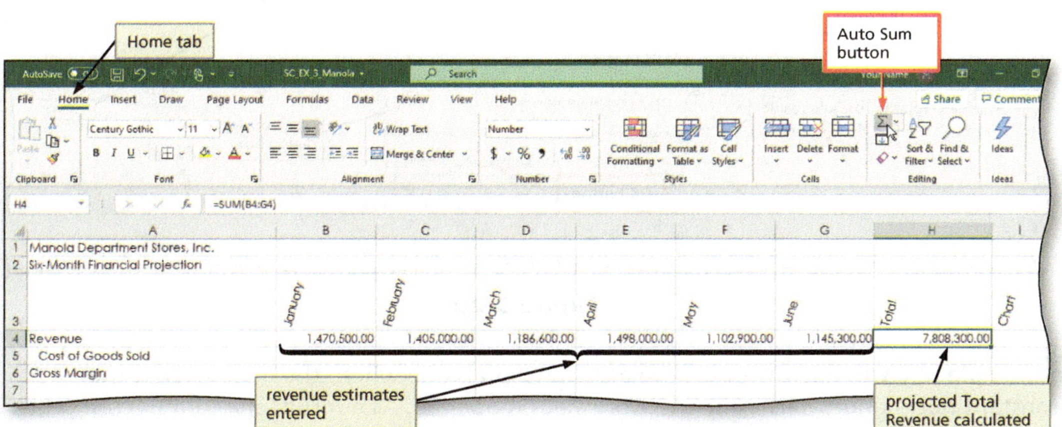

Figure 3–18

To Enter and Format the System Date

Why? The sketch of the worksheet in Figure 3–3a includes a date stamp on the right side of the heading section. A date stamp shows the date a workbook, report, or other document was created or the time period it represents. In business, a report is often meaningless without a date stamp. For example, if a printout of the worksheet in this module were distributed to the company's analysts, the date stamp could show when the six-month projections were made, as well as what time period the report represents.

A simple way to create a date stamp is to use the NOW function to enter the system date tracked by your computer in a cell in the worksheet. The NOW function is one of 24 date and time functions available in Excel. When assigned to a cell, the **NOW function** returns a number that corresponds to the system date and time beginning with December 31, 1899. For example, January 1, 1900 equals 1, January 2, 1900 equals 2, and so on. Noon equals .5. Thus, noon on January 1, 1900 equals 1.5 and 6:00 p.m. on January 1, 1900 equals 1.75. If the computer's system date is set to the current date, then the date stamp is equivalent to the current date. The following steps enter the NOW function and then change the format from mm/dd/yyyy hh:mm to mm/dd/yyyy.

1

- Select cell H1 and then click the Insert Function button in the formula bar to display the Insert Function dialog box.
- Click the 'Or select a category' arrow (Insert Function dialog box) and then select 'Date & Time' to populate the 'Select a function' list with date and time functions.
- Scroll down in the 'Select a function' list and then click NOW to select the required function (Figure 3–19).

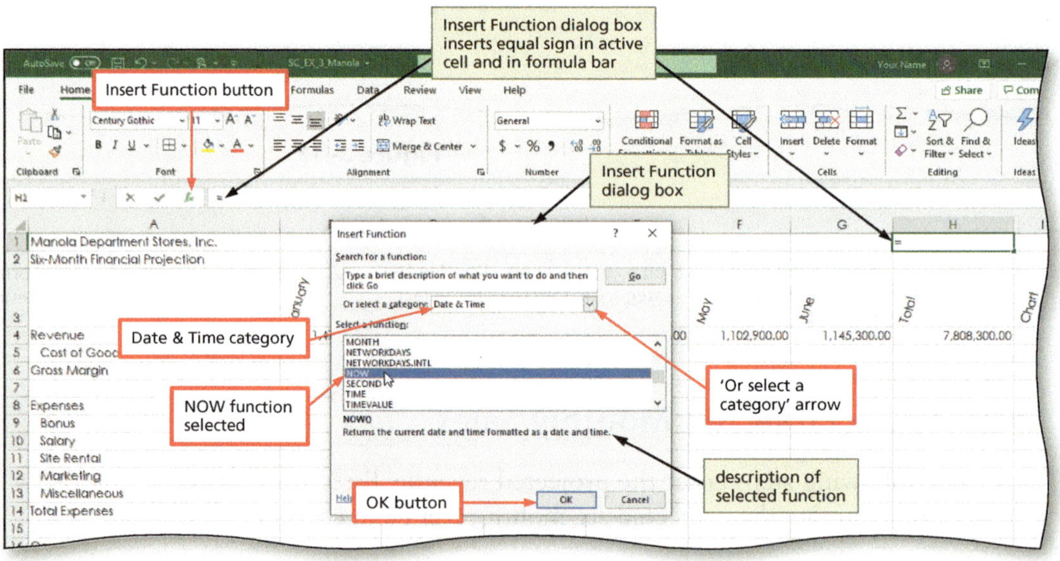

Figure 3–19

2

- Click OK (Insert Function dialog box) to close the Insert Function dialog box and display the Function Arguments dialog box (Figure 3–20).

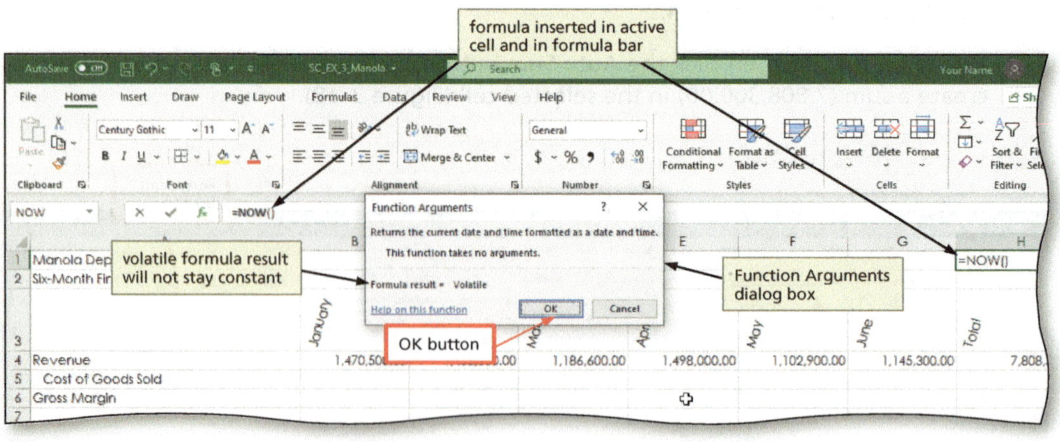

Figure 3–20

Q&A **What is meant by 'Formula result = Volatile' in the Function Arguments dialog box?**

The NOW function is an example of a volatile function. A **volatile function** is one where the number that the function returns is not constant but changes each time the worksheet is opened. As a result, any formula using the NOW function will have a variable result.

3

- Click OK (Function Arguments dialog box) to display the system date and time in the selected cell, using the default date and time format, which is mm/dd/yyyy hh:mm.

Q&A **What does the mm/dd/yyyy hh:mm format represent?**
The mm/dd/yyyy hh:mm format can be explained as follows: the first mm is the two-digit month, dd is the two-digit day of the month, yyyy is the four-digit year, hh is the two-digit hour of the day, and the second mm is the two-digit minutes past the hour. Excel applies this date and time format to the result of the NOW function.

- Right-click cell H1 to display a shortcut menu and mini toolbar.
- Click Format Cells on the shortcut menu to display the Format Cells dialog box.
- If necessary, click the Number tab (Format Cells dialog box) to display the Number sheet.
- Click Date in the Category list (Format Cells dialog box) to display the date format options in the Type list. Click 2012-03-14 to display a sample of the data in the Sample area in the dialog box (Figure 3–21).

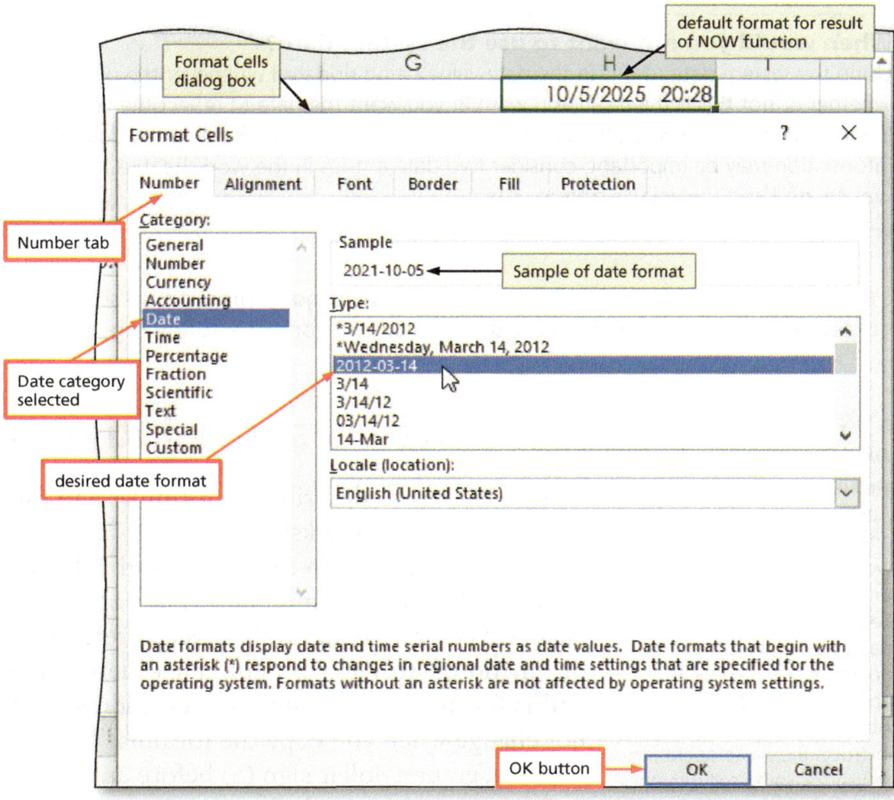

Figure 3–21

Q&A **Why do the dates in the Type box show March 14, 2012, instead of the current date?**
March 14, 2012, is just used as a sample date in this version of Office.

4

- Click OK (Format Cells dialog box) to display the system date (the result of the NOW function).
- Double-click the border between columns H and I to change the width of the column to best fit (Figure 3–22).
- Save the workbook again on the same storage location with the same file name.

Q&A **Why should I save the workbook again?**
You have made several modifications to the workbook since you last saved it. Thus, you should save it again to make sure all your changes become part of the saved file.

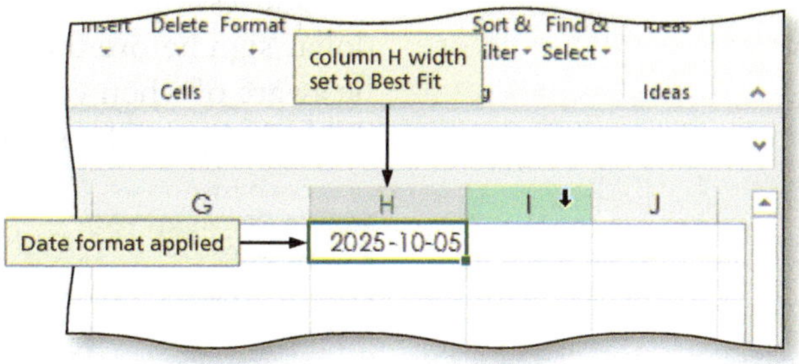

Figure 3–22

Other Ways

1. Click 'Date & Time' button (Formulas tab | Function Library group), click NOW
2. Press CTRL+SEMICOLON (this enters the date as a static value, meaning the date will not change when the workbook is opened at a later date)
3. Press CTRL+SHIFT+# to format date as day-month-year

Consider This

When would you not want to use the system date?

Using the system date results in the date value being updated whenever the worksheet is opened. Think carefully about whether or not this is the result you want. If you want the date to reflect the current date, using the system date is appropriate. If you want to record when the worksheet was created, using a hard-coded date makes more sense. If both pieces of information may be important, consider two date entries in the worksheet: a fixed entry identifying the date the worksheet was created and the volatile system date.

Break Point: If you want to take a break, this is a good place to do so. You can exit Excel now. To resume later, start Excel, open the file called SC_EX_3_Manola, and continue following the steps from this location forward.

BTW

Absolute Referencing

Absolute referencing is one of the more difficult worksheet concepts to understand. One point to keep in mind is that the paste operation is the only operation affected by an absolute cell reference. An absolute cell reference instructs the paste operation to use the same cell reference as it copies a formula from one cell to another.

Absolute versus Relative Addressing

The next sections describe the formulas and functions needed to complete the calculations in the worksheet.

As you learned in Modules 1 and 2, Excel modifies cell references when copying formulas. However, sometimes while copying formulas you do not want Excel to change a cell reference. To keep a cell reference constant when copying a formula or function, Excel uses a technique called absolute cell referencing. An **absolute cell reference** in a formula is a cell address that refers to a specific cell and does not change when you copy the formula. To specify an absolute cell reference in a formula, enter a dollar sign ($) before any column letters or row numbers you want to keep constant in formulas you plan to copy. For example, $B$4 is an absolute cell reference, whereas B4 is a relative cell reference. Both reference the same cell. The difference becomes apparent when they are copied to a destination area. A formula using the absolute cell reference $B$4 instructs Excel to keep the cell reference B4 constant (absolute) in the formula as it is copied to the destination area. A formula using the relative cell reference B4 instructs Excel to adjust the cell reference as it is copied to the destination area. A **relative cell reference** is a cell address in a formula that automatically changes to reflect the new location when the formula is copied or moved. This is the default type of referencing used in Excel worksheets and is also called a relative reference. When a cell reference combines both absolute and relative cell addressing, it is called a **mixed cell reference.** A mixed cell reference includes a dollar sign before the column or the row, not before both. When planning formulas, be aware of when you might need to use absolute, relative, and mixed cell references. Table 3–6 provides some additional examples of each of these types of cell references.

Table 3–6 Examples of Absolute, Relative, and Mixed Cell References

Cell Reference	Type of Reference	Meaning
$B$4	Absolute cell reference	Both column and row references remain the same when you copy this cell, because the cell references are absolute.
B4	Relative cell reference	Both column and row references are relative. When copied to another cell, both the column and row in the cell reference are adjusted to reflect the new location.
B$4	Mixed reference	This cell reference is mixed. The column reference changes when you copy this cell to another column because it is relative. The row reference does not change because it is absolute.
$B4	Mixed reference	This cell reference is mixed. The column reference does not change because it is absolute. The row reference changes when you copy this cell reference to another row because it is relative.

Figure 3–23 illustrates how the type of cell reference used affects the results of copying a formula to a new place in a worksheet. In Figure 3–23a, cells D6:D9 contain formulas. Each formula multiplies the content of cell A2 by 2; the difference between formulas lies in how cell A2 is referenced. Cells C6:C9 identify the type of reference: absolute, relative, or mixed.

Figure 3–23b shows the values that result from copying the formulas in cells D6:D9 to ranges E6:E9, F7:F10, and G11:G14. Figure 3–23c shows the formulas that result from copying the formulas. While all formulas initially multiplied the content of cell A2 by 2, the values and formulas in the destination ranges illustrate how Excel adjusts cell references according to how you reference those cells in original formulas.

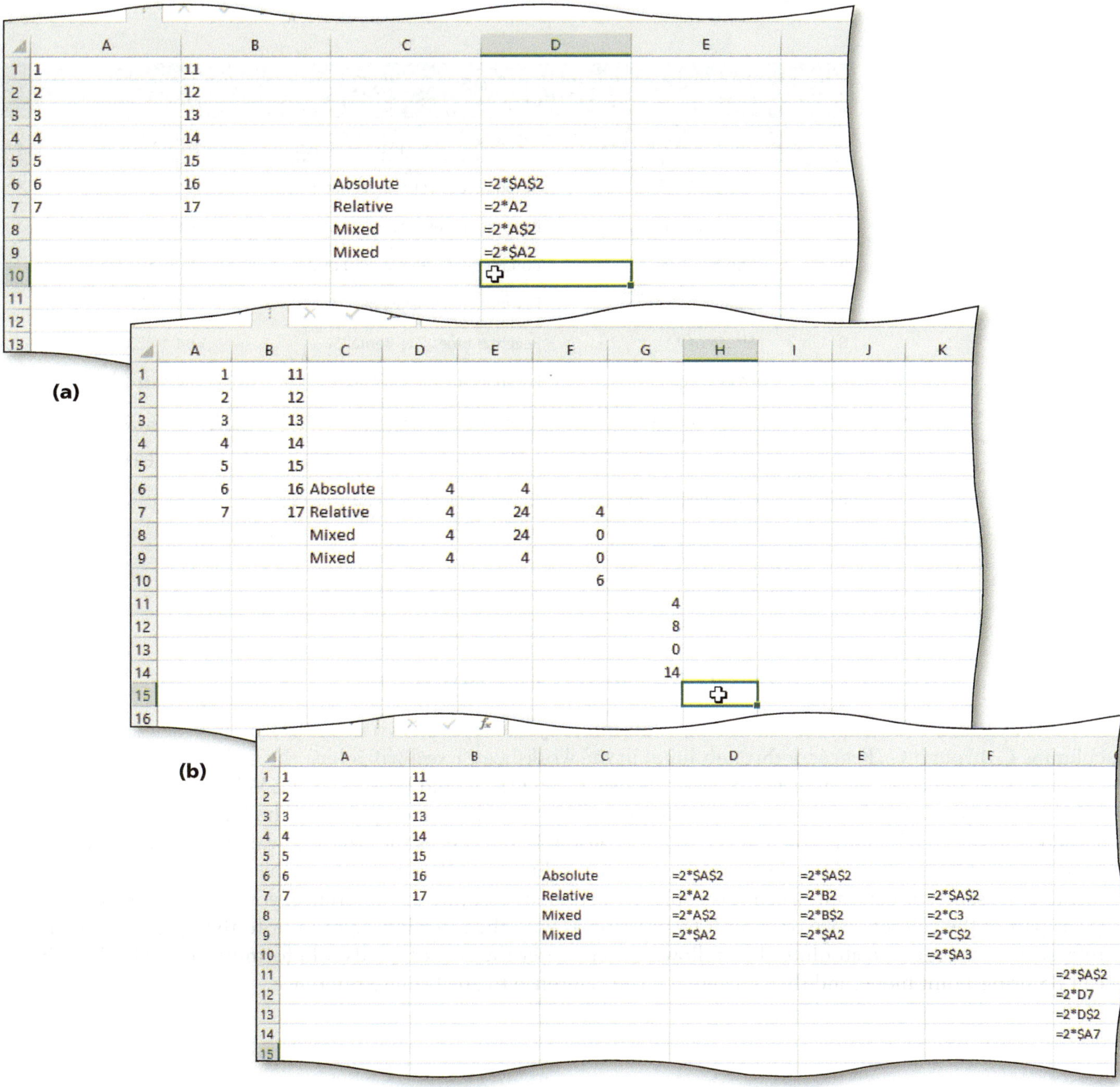

(a)

(b)

(c)

Figure 3–23

In the SC_EX_3_Manola worksheet, you need to enter formulas that calculate the following values for January: cost of goods sold (cell B5), gross margin (cell B6), expenses (range B9:B13), total expenses (cell B14), and operating income (cell B16). The formulas are based on the projected monthly revenue in cell B4 and the assumptions in the range B19:B25.

The calculations for each column (month) are the same, except for the reference to the projected monthly revenue in row 4, which varies according to the month (B4 for January, C4 for February, and so on). Thus, the formulas for January can be entered in column B and then copied to columns C through G. Table 3–7 shows the formulas for determining the January cost of goods sold, gross margin, expenses, total expenses, and operating income in column B.

Table 3–7 Formulas for Determining Cost of Goods Sold, Gross Margin, Expenses, Total Expenses, and Operating Income for January

Cell	Row Title	Calculation	Formula
B5	Cost of Goods Sold	Revenue times (1 minus Margin %)	=B4 * (1 – B19)
B6	Gross Margin	Revenue minus Cost of Goods Sold	=B4 – B5
B9	Bonus	Bonus equals value in B20 or 0	=IF(B4 >= B21, B20, 0)
B10	Salary	Revenue times Salary %	=B4 * B22
B11	Site Rental	Revenue times Site Rental %	=B4 * B23
B12	Marketing	Revenue times Marketing %	=B4 * B24
B13	Miscellaneous	Revenue times Miscellaneous %	=B4 * B25
B14	Total Expenses	Sum of all expenses	=SUM(B9:B13)
B16	Operating Income	Gross Margin minus Total Expenses	=B6 – B14

To Enter a Formula Containing Absolute Cell References

Why? As the formulas are entered in column B for January, as shown in Table 3–7, and then copied to columns C through G (February through June) in the worksheet, Excel will adjust the cell references for each column. After the copy, the February Salary expense in cell C10 would be =C4 * C22. While the cell reference C4 (February Revenue) is correct, the cell reference C22 references an empty cell. The formula for cell C10 should read =C4 * B22, rather than =C4 * C22, because B22 references the Salary % value in the What-If Assumptions table. In this instance, you must use an absolute cell reference to keep the cell reference in the formula the same, or constant, when it is copied. To enter an absolute cell reference, you can type the dollar sign ($) as part of the cell reference or enter it by pressing F4 with the insertion point in or to the right of the cell reference to change it to absolute. The following steps enter the cost of goods sold formula =B4 * (1 – B19) in cell B5 using Point mode, and then change the cell reference to an absolute reference.

1

- Click cell B5 to select the cell in which to enter the first formula.
- Type = (equal sign), select cell B4, type `*(1-B19` to continue entering the formula, and then press F4 to change the cell reference from a relative cell reference to an absolute cell reference. Type) (closing parenthesis) to complete the formula (Figure 3–24).

Q&A **Is an absolute reference required in this formula?**

No, a mixed cell reference also could have been used. The formula in cell B5 will be copied across columns, rather than down rows. So, the formula entered in cell B5 in Step 1 could have been entered as =B4*(1–$B19) using a mixed cell reference, rather than =B4*(1–$B$19), because when you copy a formula across columns, the row does not change. The key is to ensure that column B remains constant as you copy the formula across columns. To change the absolute cell reference to a mixed cell reference, continue to press F4 until you achieve the desired cell reference.

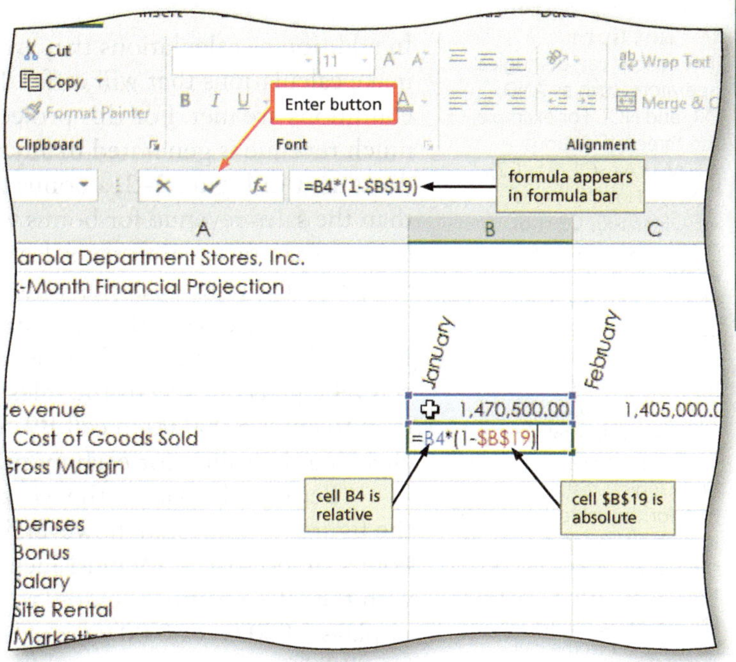

Figure 3–24

2

- Click the Enter button in the formula bar to display the result, 275718.75, instead of the formula in cell B5 (Figure 3–25).

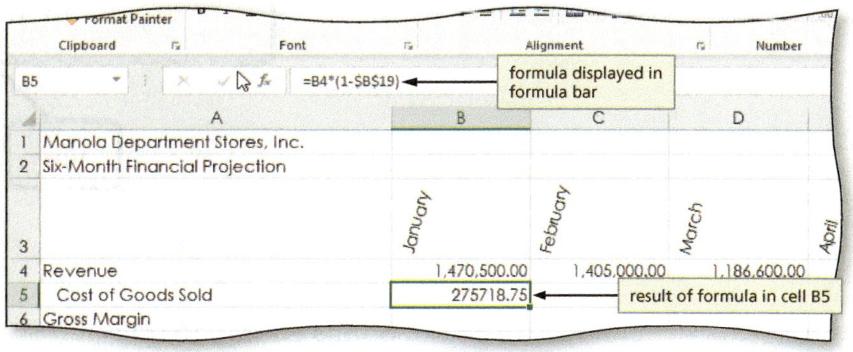

Figure 3–25

3

- Click cell B6 to select the cell in which to enter the next formula, type = (equal sign), click cell B4, type – (minus sign), and then click cell B5 to add a reference to the cell to the formula.
- Click the Enter button in the formula bar to display the result in the selected cell, in this case gross margin for January, 1,194,781.25, in cell B6 (Figure 3–26).

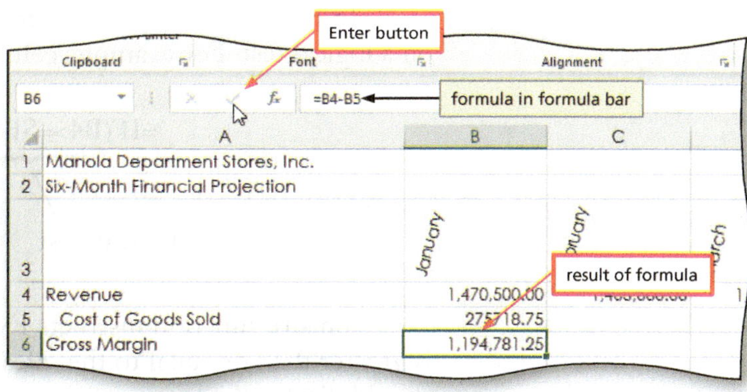

Figure 3–26

BTW

Logical Operators in IF Functions

IF functions can use logical operators, such as AND, OR, and NOT. For example, the three IF functions =IF(AND(A1>C1, B1<C2), "OK", "Not OK") and =IF(OR(K5>J5, C3<K6), "OK", "Not OK") and =IF(NOT(B10<C10), "OK", "Not OK") use logical operators. In the first example, both logical tests must be true for the value_if_true OK to be assigned to the cell. In the second example, one or the other logical tests must be true for the value_if_true OK to be assigned to the cell. In the third example, the logical test B10<C10 must be false for the value_if_true OK to be assigned to the cell.

Making Decisions—The IF Function

In addition to calculations that are constant across all categories, you may need to make calculations that will differ depending on whether a particular condition or set of conditions are met. For this project, you need to vary compensation according to how much revenue is generated in any particular month. According to the requirements document in Figure 3–2, a bonus will be paid in any month where revenue is greater than the sales revenue for bonus value. If the projected January revenue in cell B4 is greater than or equal to the sales revenue for bonus in cell B21 (1,250,000.00), then the projected January bonus value in cell B9 is equal to the bonus value in cell B20 (5,000.00); otherwise, the value in cell B9 is equal to 0. One way to assign the projected January bonus value in cell B9 is to manually check to see if the projected revenue in cell B4 equals or exceeds the sales revenue for the bonus amount in cell B21 and, if so, then to enter 5,000.00 in cell B9. You can use this manual process for all six months by checking the values for each month.

Because the data in the worksheet changes each time a report is prepared or the figures are adjusted, however, it is preferable to have Excel calculate the monthly bonus. To do so, cell B9 must include a function that compares the projected revenue with the sales revenue required to generate a bonus (Sales Revenue for Bonus), and displays 5,000.00 or 0.00 (zero), depending on whether the projected January revenue in cell B4 is greater than, equal to, or less than the sales revenue for bonus value in cell B21. This decision-making process is a **logical test**. It can be represented in diagram form, as shown in Figure 3–27.

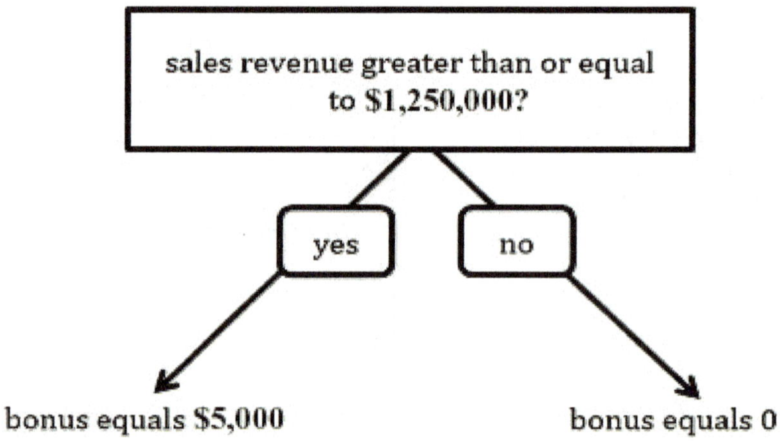

Figure 3–27

In Excel, you use the **IF function** when you want to assign a value to a cell based on a logical test. For example, cell B9 can be assigned the following IF function:

=IF(B4>=$B$21, $B$20, 0)

logical_test — value_if_true — value_if_false

This IF function instructs Excel that if the projected January revenue in cell B4 is greater than or equal to the sales revenue for bonus value in cell B21, then Excel should display the bonus value found in cell B20 in cell B9. If the projected January revenue in cell B4 is not greater than or equal to the sales revenue for bonus value in cell B21, then Excel should display a 0 (zero) in cell B9.

The general form of the IF function is:

=IF(logical_test, value_if_true, value_if_false)

The argument, logical_test, is made up of two expressions and a comparison operator. Each expression can be a cell reference, a number, text, a function, or a formula. In this example, the logical test compares the projected revenue with the Sales Revenue for Bonus amount, using the comparison operator greater than or equal to. Valid comparison operators, their meanings, and examples of their use in IF functions are shown in Table 3–8. The argument, value_if_true, is the value you want Excel to display in the cell when the logical test is true. The argument, value_if_false, is the value you want Excel to display in the cell when the logical test is false.

Table 3–8 Comparison Operators

Comparison Operator	Meaning	Example
=	Equal to	=IF(A1=A2, "True", "False")
<	Less than	=IF(A1<A2, "True", "False")
>	Greater than	=IF(A1>A2, "True", "False")
>=	Greater than or equal to	=IF(A1>=A2, "True", "False")
<=	Less than or equal to	=IF(A1<=A2, "True", "False")
<>	Not equal to	=IF(A1<>A2, "True", "False")

To Enter an IF Function

Why? Use an IF function to determine the value for a cell based on a logical test. The following steps assign the IF function =IF(B4>=$B$21,$B$20,0) to cell B9. This IF function determines whether or not the worksheet assigns a bonus for January.

1

- Click cell B9 to select the cell for the next formula.
- Click the Insert Function button in the formula bar to display the Insert Function dialog box.
- Click the 'Or select a category' arrow (Insert Function dialog box) and then select Logical in the list to populate the 'Select a function' list with logic functions.
- Click IF in the 'Select a function' list to select the required function (Figure 3–28).

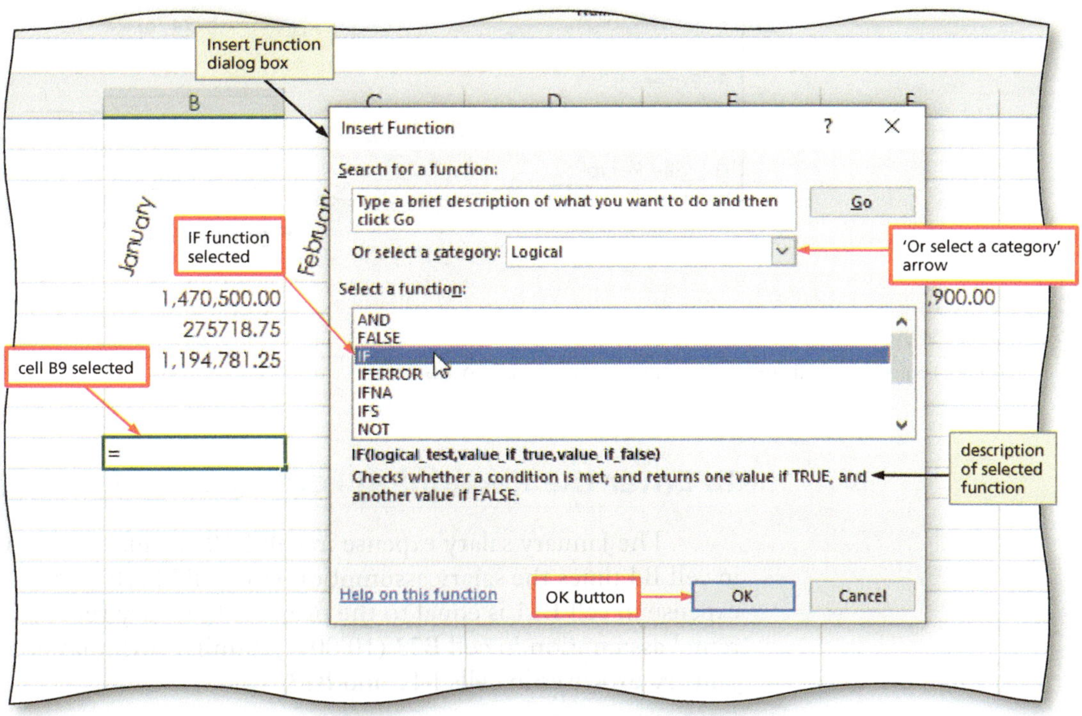

Figure 3–28

2

- Click OK (Insert Function dialog box) to display the Function Arguments dialog box.
- Type **b4>=b21** in the Logical_test box to enter a logical test for the IF function.
- Type **b20** in the Value_if_true box to enter the result of the IF function if the logical test is true.
- Type **0** (zero) in the Value_if_false box to enter the result of the IF function if the logical test is false (Figure 3–29).

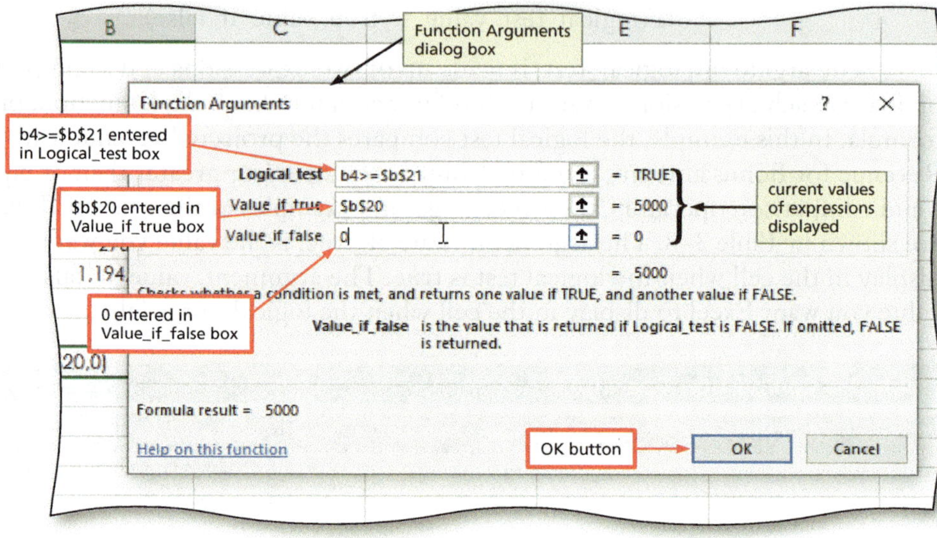

Figure 3–29

3

- Click OK (Function Arguments dialog box) to insert the IF function in the selected cell (Figure 3–30).

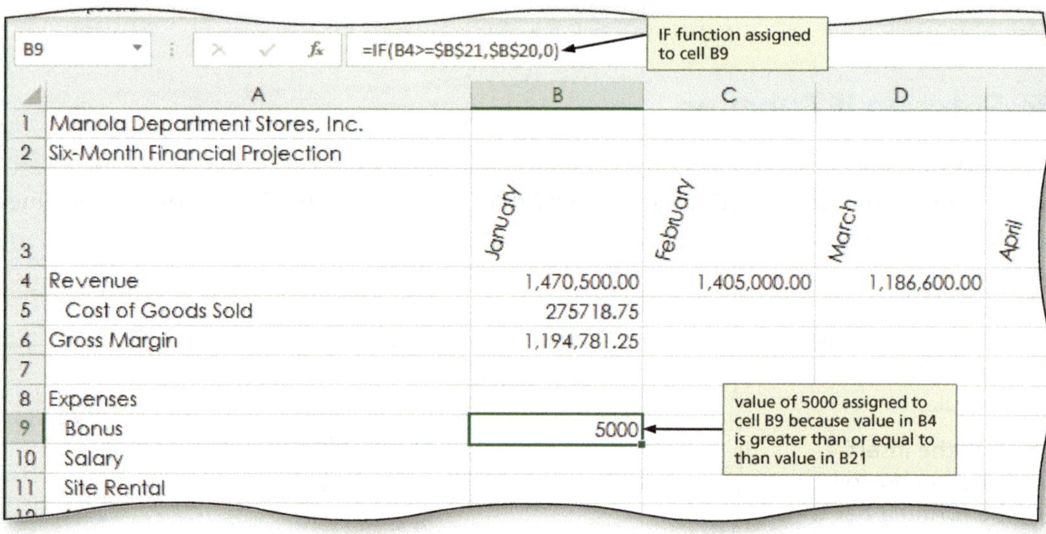

Figure 3–30

Other Ways

1. Click Logical button (Formulas tab | Function Library group), click IF

To Enter the Remaining Formulas for January

The January salary expense in cell B10 is equal to the projected January revenue in cell B4 times the salary assumption in cell B22 (20.00%). The January site rental expense in cell B11 is equal to the projected January revenue in cell B4 times the site rental assumption in cell B23 (10.00%). Similar formulas determine the remaining January expenses in cells B12 and B13.

The total expenses value in cell B14 is equal to the sum of the expenses in the range B9:B13. The operating income in cell B16 is equal to the gross margin in cell B6 minus the total expenses in cell B14. Because the formulas are short, you will type them in the following steps, rather than using Point mode.

1. Select cell B10. Type **=b4*b22** and then press the DOWN ARROW key to enter the formula in the selected cell. Type **=b4*b23** and then press the DOWN ARROW key to enter the formula in cell B11. Type **=b4*b24,** press the DOWN ARROW key, type **=b4*b25,** and then press the DOWN ARROW key again.
2. With cell B14 selected, click the Auto Sum button (Home tab | Editing group) twice to insert a SUM function in the selected cell. Select cell B16 to prepare to enter the next formula. Type **=b6-b14** and then press ENTER to enter the formula in the selected cell.
3. Press CTRL+ACCENT MARK (`) to display the formulas version of the worksheet (Figure 3–31).
4. When you are finished viewing the formulas version, press CTRL+ACCENT MARK (`) again to return to the values version of the worksheet.

Q&A **Why should I view the formulas version of the worksheet?**
Viewing the formulas version (Figure 3–31) of the worksheet allows you to check the formulas you entered in the range B5:B16. Recall that formulas were entered in lowercase. You can see that Excel converts all the formulas from lowercase to uppercase.

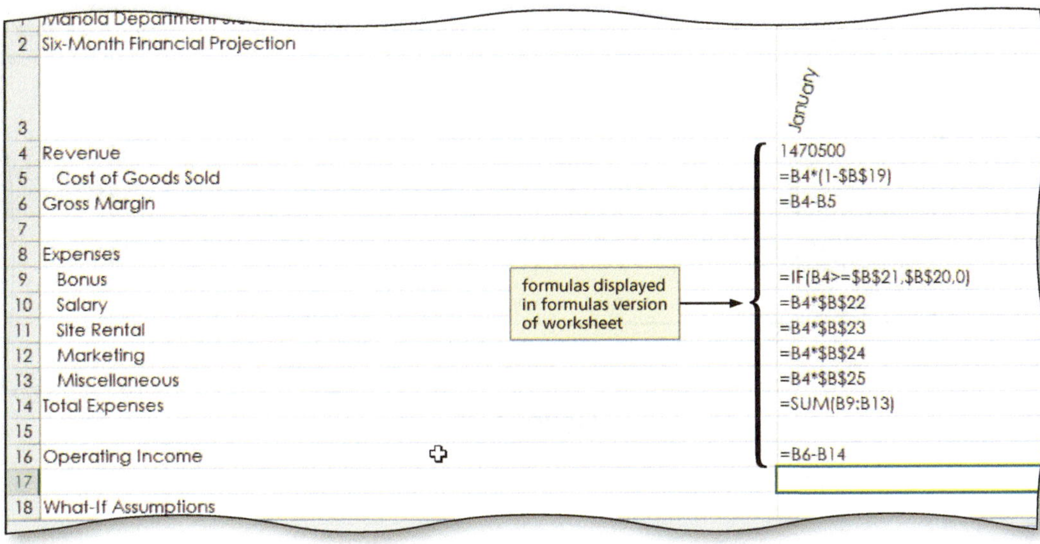

Figure 3–31

BTW

Replacing a Formula with a Constant

Using the following steps, you can replace a formula with its result so that the cell value remains constant: (1) click the cell with the formula; (2) press F2 or click in the formula bar; (3) press F9 to display the value in the formula bar; and (4) press ENTER.

BTW

Error Messages

When Excel cannot calculate a formula, it displays an error message in a cell. These error messages always begin with a number sign (#). The more commonly occurring error messages are as follows: #DIV/0! (tries to divide by zero); #NAME? (uses a name Excel does not recognize); #N/A (refers to a value not available); #NULL! (specifies an invalid intersection of two areas); #NUM! (uses a number incorrectly); #REF (refers to a cell that is not valid); #VALUE! (uses an incorrect argument or operand); and ##### (refers to cells not wide enough to display entire entry).

To Copy Formulas with Absolute Cell References Using the Fill Handle

Why? Using the fill handle ensures a quick, accurate copy of the formulas. The following steps use the fill handle to copy the January formulas in column B to the other five months in columns C through G.

1

- Select the range B5:B16 and then point to the fill handle in the lower-right corner of the selected cell, B16 in this case, to display the crosshair pointer (Figure 3–32).

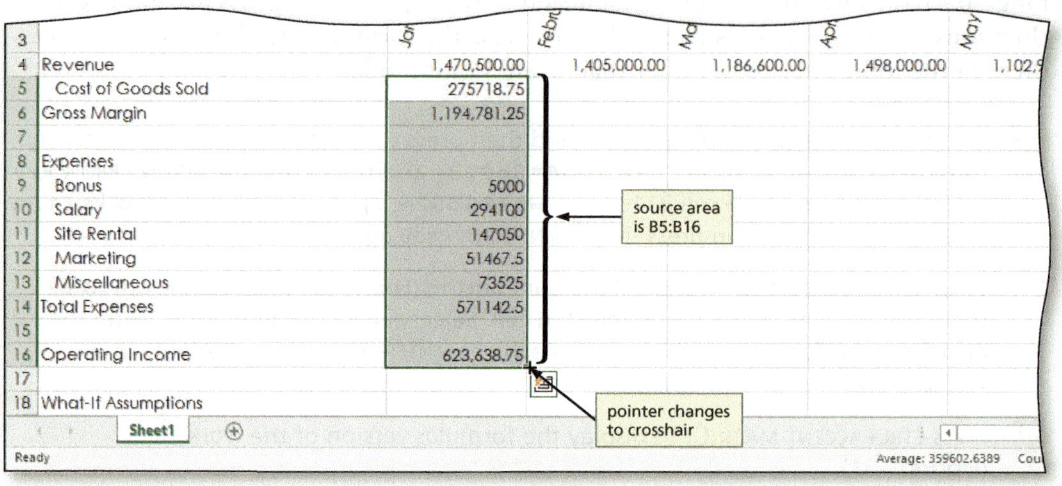

Figure 3–32

2

- Drag the fill handle to the right to copy the formulas from the source area, B5:B16 in this case, to the destination area, C5:G16 in this case, and display the calculated amounts (Figure 3–33).

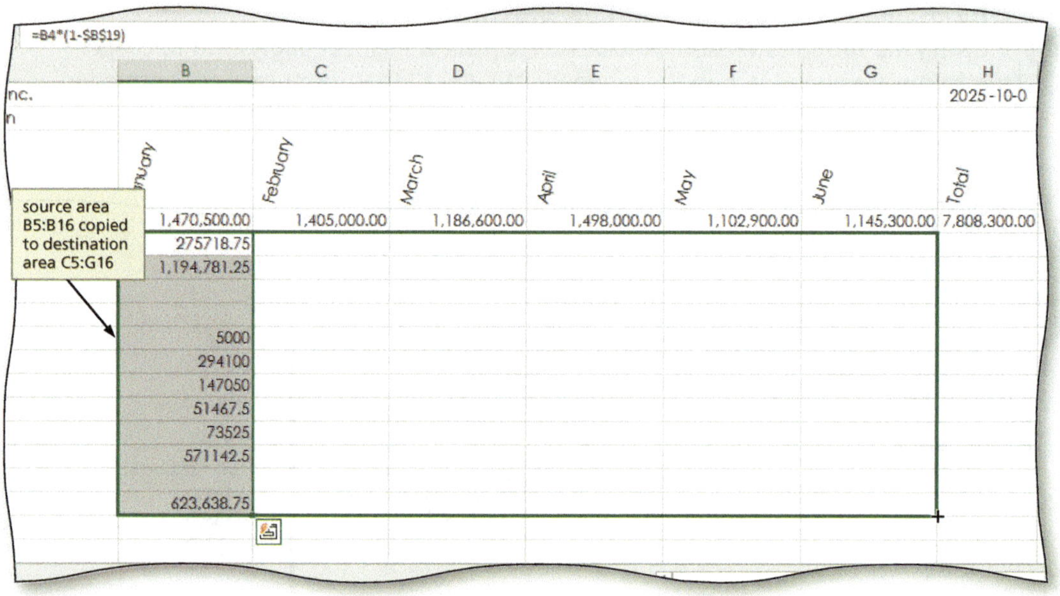

Figure 3–33

Q&A **What happens to the formulas after performing the copy operation?**
Because the formulas in the range B5:B16 use absolute cell references, when they are copied to the range C5:G16, they still refer to the values in the What-If Assumptions table.

To Determine Row Totals in Nonadjacent Cells

The following steps determine the row totals in column H. To determine the row totals using the Sum button, select only the cells in column H containing numbers in adjacent cells to the left. If, for example, you select the range H5:H16, Excel will display 0s as the sum of empty rows in cells H7, H8, and H15.

1 Select the range H5:H6. While holding down CTRL, select the range H9:H14 and cell H16, as shown in Figure 3–34.

2 Click the Auto Sum button (Home tab | Editing group) to display the row totals in the selected ranges (Figure 3–34).

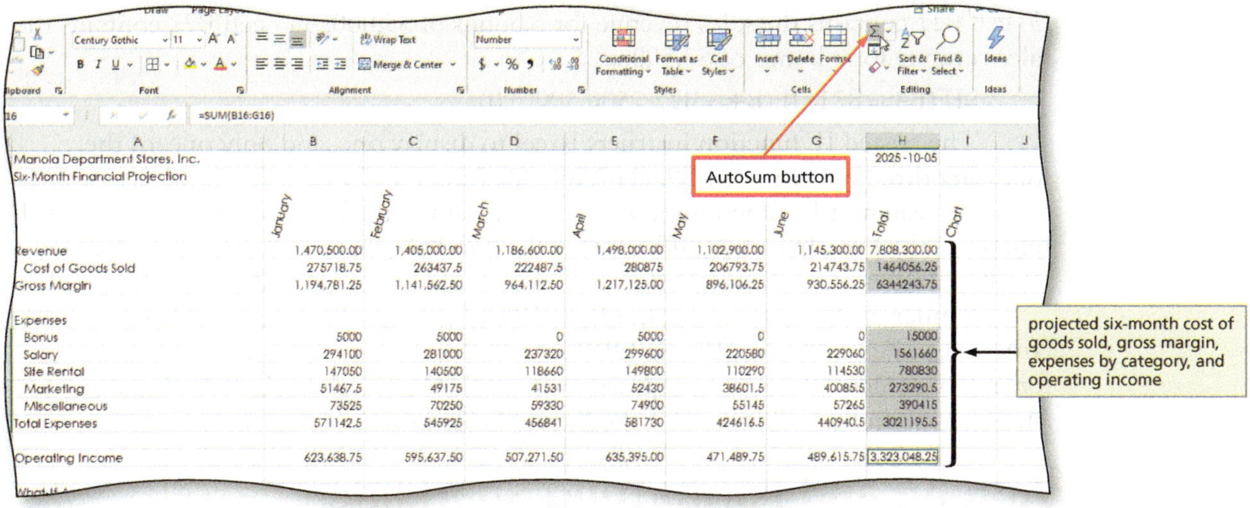

Figure 3–34

3. Save the workbook again in the same storage location with the same file name.

Nested Forms of the IF Function

A **nested IF function** is one in which the action to be taken for the true or false case includes another IF function. The second IF function is considered to be nested, or layered, within the first. You can use a nested IF function to add another condition to the decision-making process. Study the nested IF function below, which would add another level of bonus to the compensation at Manola Department Stores. In this case, Manola's assigns a bonus for sales of $1,250,000 and above. For months where sales make that level, additional bonus money is available for sales of $1,450,000 and above. In this case, three outcomes are possible, two of which involve paying a bonus. Figure 3–35 depicts a decision tree for this logical test.

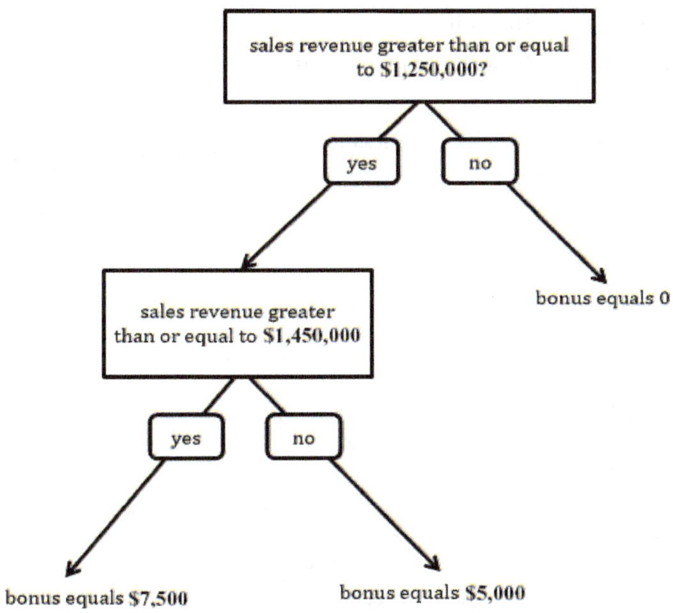

Figure 3–35

Assume the following in this example: (1) the nested IF function is assigned to cell B9, which will display one of three values; (2) cell B4 contains the sales revenue;

(3) cell B21 contains the sales revenue for a bonus of $5,000; and cell B22 contains the sales revenue for a bonus of $7,500.

=IF(B4>=B21, IF(B4>=B22,7500,5000),0)

The nested IF function instructs Excel to display one, and only one, of the following three values in cell B9: (1) 7,500, (2) 5,000, or (3) 0.

You can nest IF functions as deep as you want, but after you get beyond three IF functions, the logic becomes difficult to follow, and alternative solutions, such as the use of multiple cells and simple IF functions, should be considered.

Similar to the IF function, the IFERROR function checks a formula for correctness. For example, =IFERROR(formula, "Error Message") examines the formula argument. If an error appears (such as #N/A), Excel displays the Error Message text in the cell instead of the Excel #N/A error.

Adding and Formatting Sparkline Charts

Sometimes you may want to condense a range of data into a small chart in order to show a trend or variation in the range, and Excel's standard charts may be too large or extensive for your needs. A sparkline chart provides a simple way to show trends and variations in a range of data within a single cell. Excel includes three types of sparkline charts: line, column, and win/loss. Because sparkline charts appear in a single cell, you can use them to convey succinct, eye-catching summaries of the data they represent.

To Add a Sparkline Chart to the Worksheet

Each row of monthly data, including those containing formulas, provides useful information that can be summarized by a line sparkline chart. **Why?** A line sparkline chart is a good choice because it shows trends over the six-month period for each row of data. The following steps add a line sparkline chart to cell I4 and then use the fill handle to create line sparkline charts in the range I5:I16 to represent the monthly data shown in rows 4 through 16.

1

- If necessary, scroll the worksheet so that both columns B and I and row 3 are visible on the screen.
- Select cell I4 to prepare to insert a sparkline chart in the cell.
- Display the Insert tab and then click the Line button (Insert tab | Sparklines group) to display the Create Sparklines dialog box (Figure 3–36).

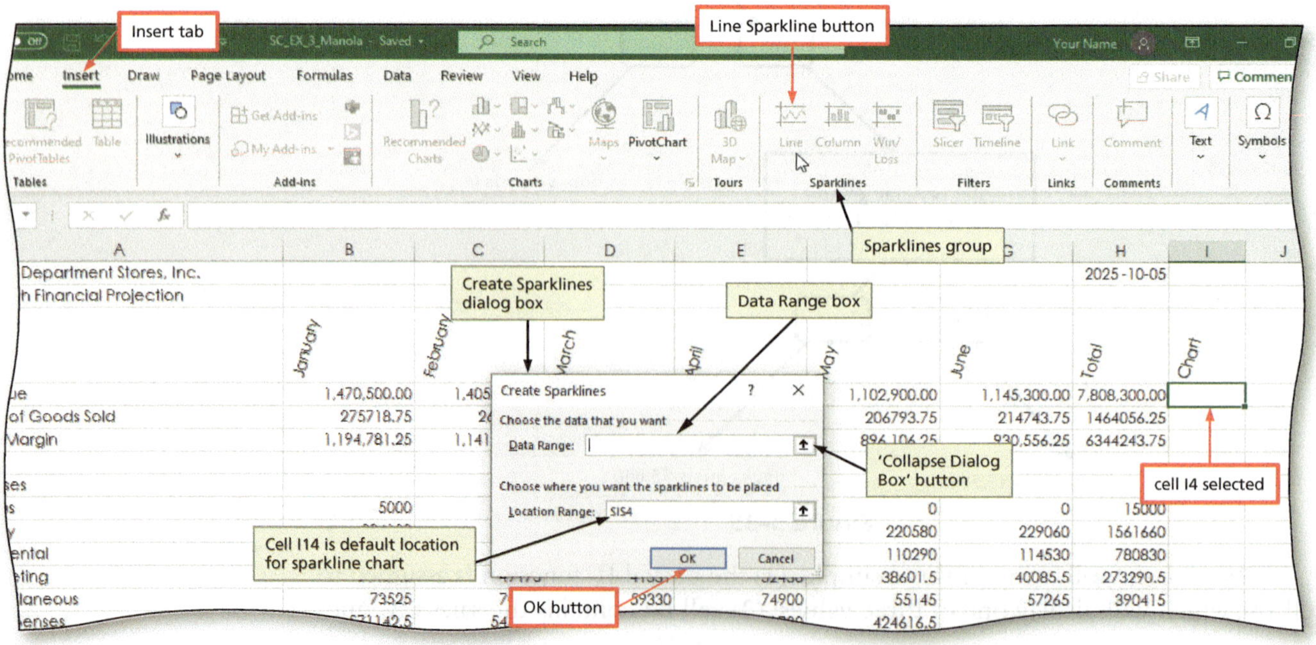

Figure 3–36

2

- Drag through the range B4:G4 to select the range. Do not release the mouse button (Figure 3–37).

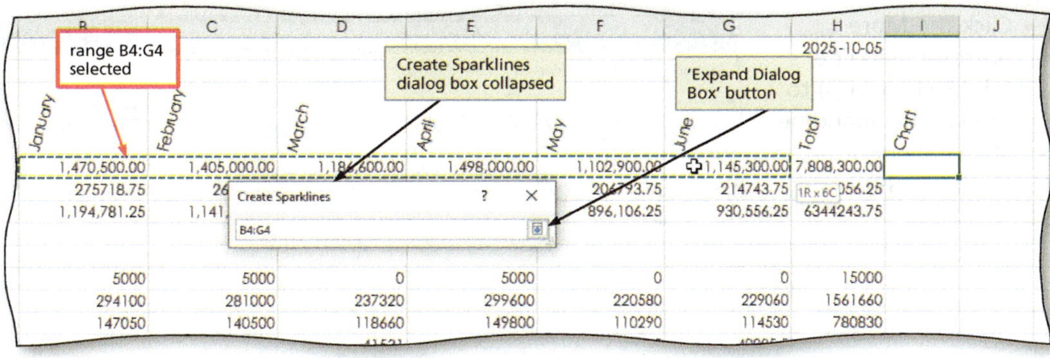

Figure 3–37

Q&A **What happened to the Create Sparklines dialog box?**

When a dialog box includes a 'Collapse Dialog Box' button (Figure 3–36), selecting cells or a range collapses the dialog box so that only the current text box is visible. This allows you to select your desired range without the dialog box getting in the way. Once the selection is made, the dialog box expands back to its original size. You also can click the 'Collapse Dialog Box' button to make your selection and then click the 'Expand Dialog Box' button (Figure 3–37) to expand the dialog box.

3

- Release the mouse button to insert the selected range, B4:G4 in this case, in the Data Range box.
- Click OK as shown in Figure 3–36 (Create Sparklines dialog box) to insert a line sparkline chart in the selected cell and display the Sparkline tab (Figure 3–38).

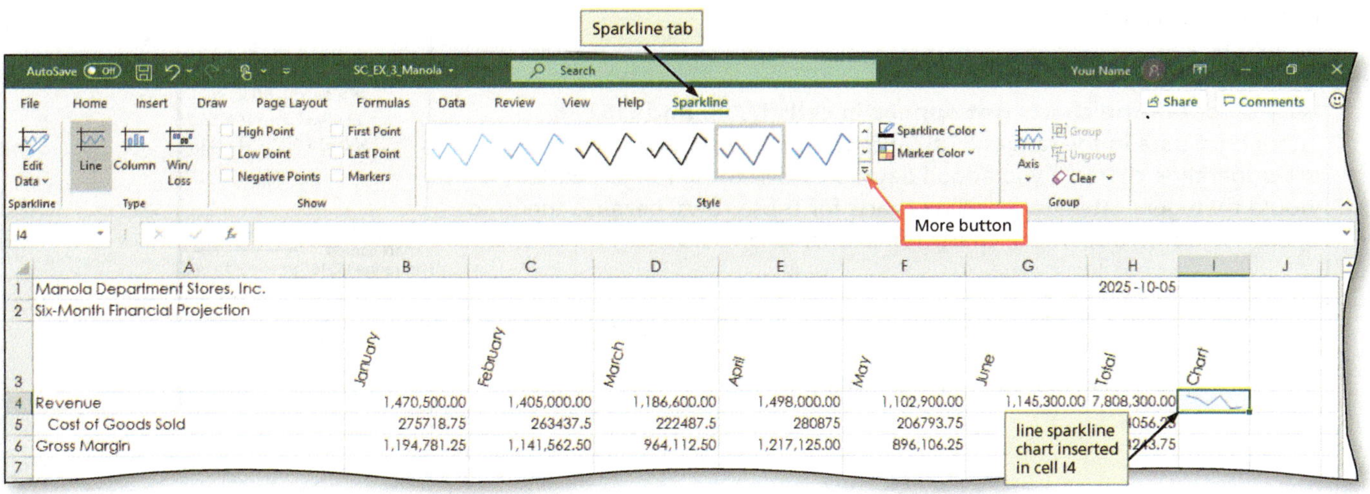

Figure 3–38

To Change the Sparkline Style and Copy the Sparkline Chart

Why? The default style option may not provide the visual impact you seek. Changing the sparkline style allows you to alter how the sparkline chart appears. The following steps change the sparkline chart style.

1

- Click the More button (Sparkline tab | Style group) to display the Sparkline Style gallery (Figure 3–39).

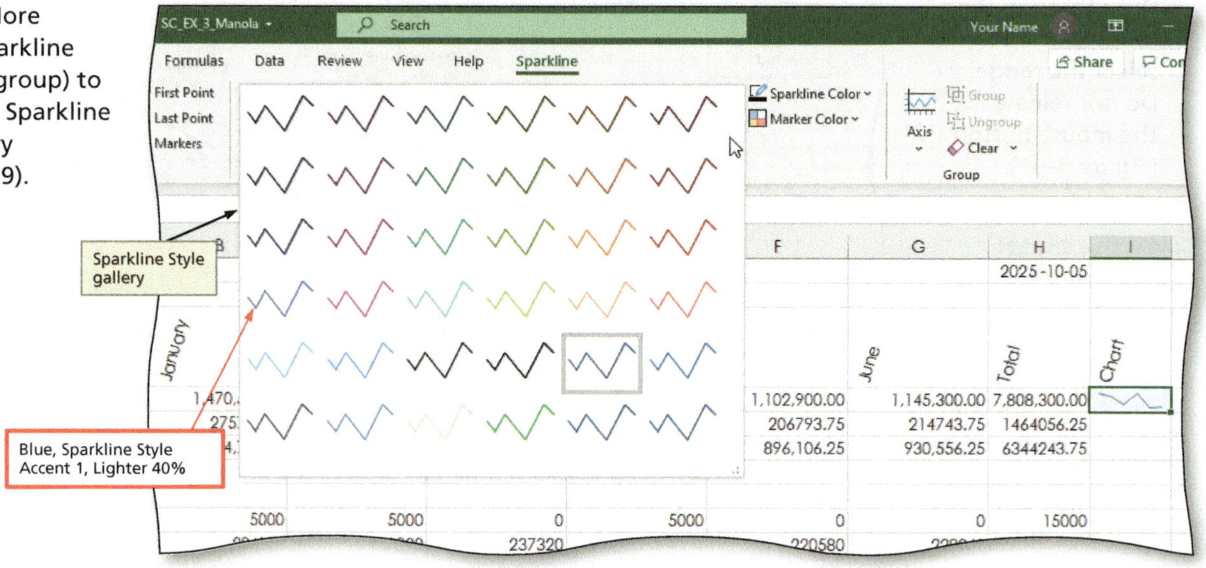

Figure 3–39

2

- Click 'Blue, Sparkline Style Accent 1, Lighter 40%' in the Sparkline Style gallery to apply the style to the sparkline chart in the selected cell, I4 in this case.
- Point to the fill handle in cell I4 and then drag through cell I16 to copy the line sparkline chart.
- Select cell I18 (Figure 3–40).

Q&A

Why do sparkline charts not appear in cells I7, I8, and I15?
There is no data in the ranges B7:G7, B8:G8, and B15:G15, so Excel cannot draw sparkline charts. If you added data to cells in those ranges, Excel would then generate line sparkline charts for those rows, because the drag operation defined sparkline charts for cells I7, I8, and I15.

How can I remove a sparkline chart?
To remove a sparkline chart from a worksheet, you should clear it. To clear a sparkline chart, select the cell(s) containing the sparkline(s) to clear, and then click Clear (Sparkline tab | Group group).

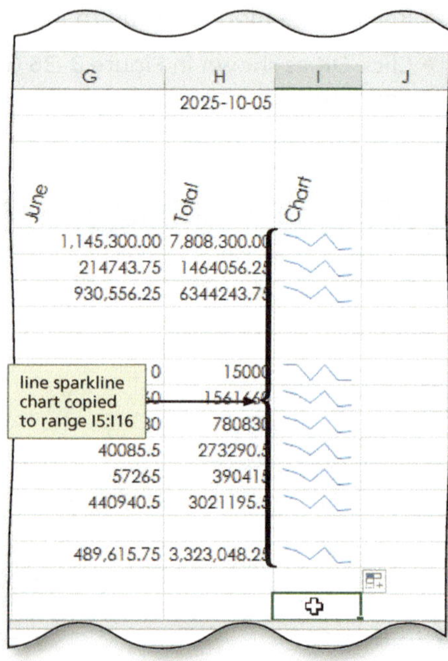

Figure 3–40

To Change the Sparkline Type

In addition to changing the sparkline chart style, you also can change the sparkline chart type. **Why?** You may decide that a different chart type will better illustrate the characteristics of your data. As shown in Figure 3–40, most of the sparkline charts look similar. Changing the sparkline chart type allows you to decide if a different chart type will better present your data to the reader. The following steps change the line sparkline charts to column sparkline charts.

1

- Select the range I4:I16 to select the sparkline charts.
- Click the Sparkline tab to make it the active tab.

- Click the Column button (Sparkline tab | Type group) to change the sparkline charts in the selected range to the column type (Figure 3–41).

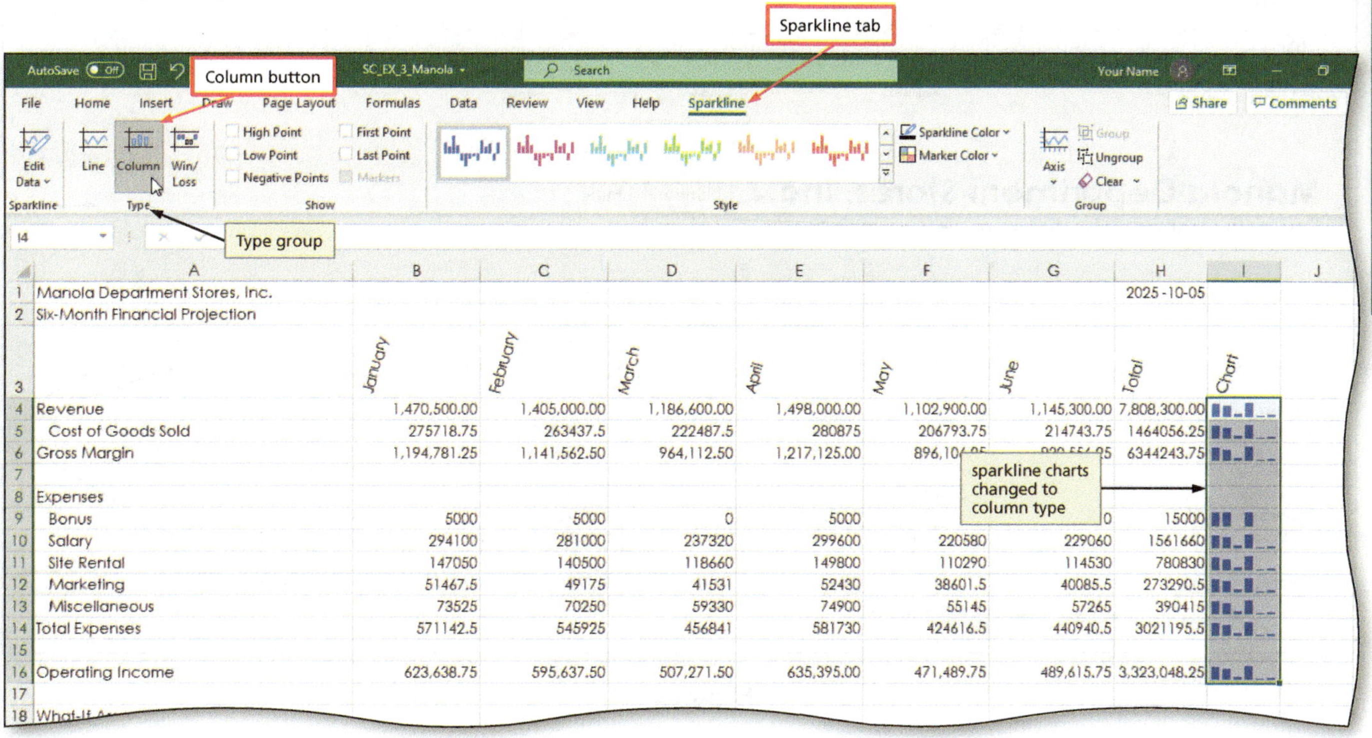

Figure 3–41

2

- Select cell I18.
- Save the workbook again in the same storage location with the same file name.

Customizing Sparkline Charts

You can customize sparkline charts using commands on the Sparkline tab. To show markers on specific values on the sparkline chart, such as the highest value, lowest value, any negative numbers, the first point, or the last point, use the corresponding check boxes in the Show group. To show markers on all line sparkline points, select the Markers check box in the Show group. You can change the color of sparklines or markers by using the Sparkline Color and Marker Color buttons in the Style group. You can group sparklines so changes apply to all sparklines in the group by using the Group command in the Group group.

Formatting the Worksheet

The worksheet created thus far shows the financial projections for the six-month period from January to June. Its appearance is uninteresting, however, even though you have performed some minimal formatting earlier (formatting assumptions numbers, changing the column widths, formatting the date, and formatting the sparkline chart). This section completes the formatting of the worksheet by making the numbers easier to read and emphasizing the titles, assumptions, categories, and totals, as shown in Figure 3–42.

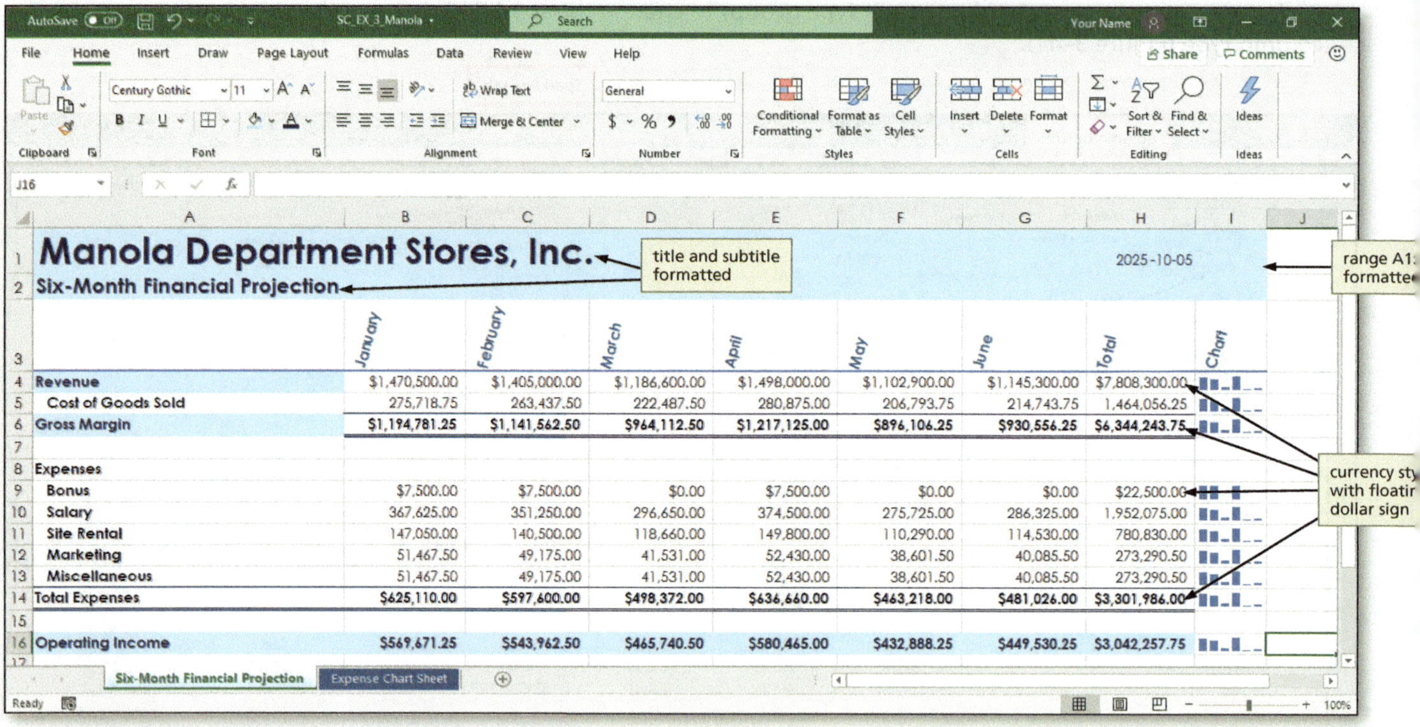

Figure 3–42

Consider This

How should you format various elements of the worksheet?

A worksheet, such as the one presented in this module, should be formatted in the following manner: (1) format the numbers; (2) format the worksheet title, column titles, row titles, and total rows; and (3) format the assumptions table. Numbers in heading rows and total rows should be formatted with a currency symbol. Other dollar amounts should be formatted with a comma style. The assumptions table should be diminished in its formatting so that it does not distract from the main data and calculations in the worksheet. Assigning a smaller font size to the data in the assumptions table would visually illustrate that it is supplementary information and set it apart from other data formatted with a larger font size.

To Assign Formats to Nonadjacent Ranges

The following steps assign formats to the numbers in rows 4 through 16. **Why?** These formats increase the readability of the data.

1

- Select the range B4:H4 as the first range to format.
- While holding down CTRL, select the nonadjacent ranges B6:H6, B9:H9, B14:H14, and B16:H16, and then release CTRL to select nonadjacent ranges.
- On the Home tab in the Number group, click the Dialog Box Launcher to display the Format Cells dialog box.
- Click Currency in the Category list (Format Cells dialog box), if necessary select 2 in the Decimal places box and then select $ in the Symbol list to ensure a dollar sign shows in the cells to be formatted, and select the red font color ($1,234.10) in the Negative numbers list to specify the desired currency style for the selected ranges (Figure 3–43).

Q&A

Why was this particular style chosen for the negative numbers?

In accounting, negative numbers often are shown with parentheses surrounding the value rather than with a negative sign preceding the value. Although the data being used in this module contains no negative numbers, you still must select a negative number format. It is important to be consistent when selecting negative number formats if you are applying different formats in a column; otherwise, the decimal points may not line up.

Q&A

Why is the Format Cells dialog box used to create the format for the ranges in this step?

The requirements for this worksheet call for a floating dollar sign. You can use the Format Cells dialog box to assign a currency style with a floating dollar sign, instead of using the 'Accounting Number Format' button (Home tab | Number group), which assigns a fixed dollar sign.

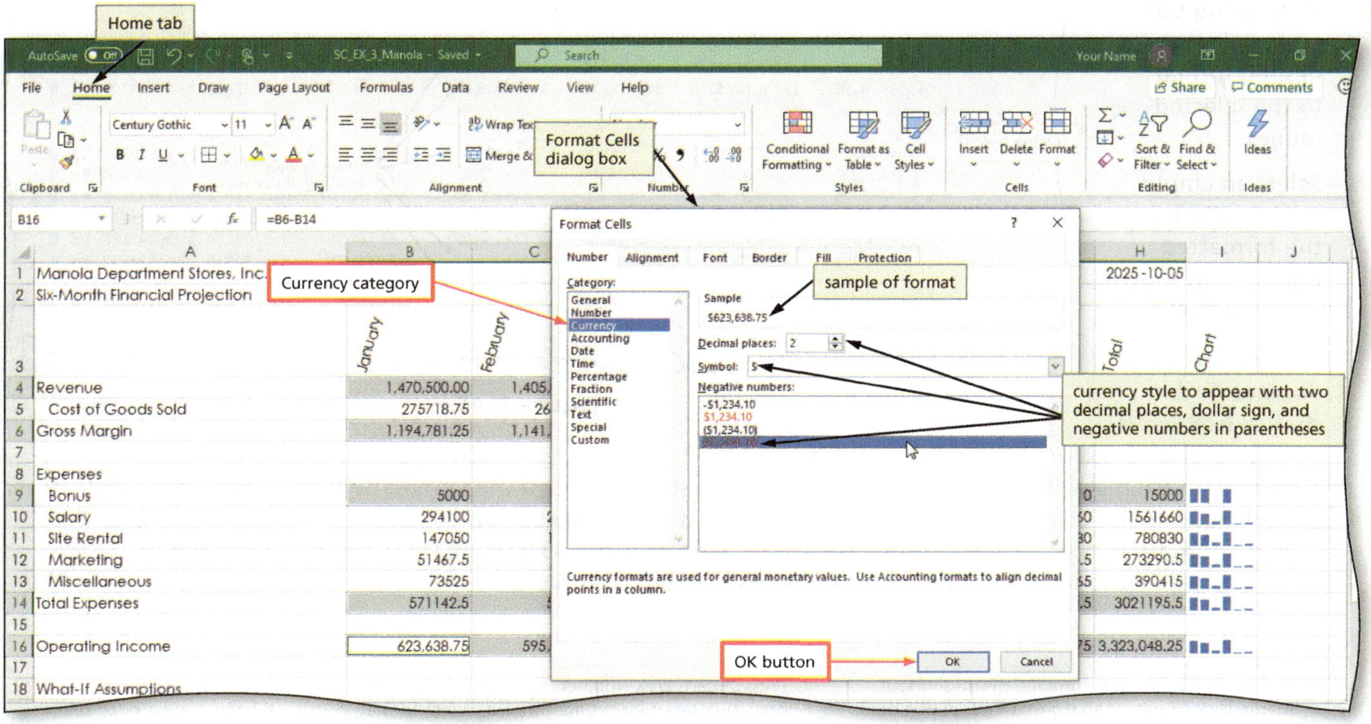

Figure 3–43

2

- Click OK (Format Cells dialog box) to close the Format Cells dialog box and apply the desired format to the selected ranges.
- Select the range B5:H5 as the next range to format.
- While holding down CTRL, select the range B10:H13, and then release CTRL to select nonadjacent ranges.
- On the Home tab in the Number group, click the Dialog Box Launcher to display the Format Cells dialog box.
- Click Currency in the Category list (Format Cells dialog box), if necessary select 2 in the Decimal places box, select None in the Symbol list so that a dollar sign does not show in the cells to be formatted, and select the red font color (1,234.10) in the Negative numbers list (Figure 3–44).

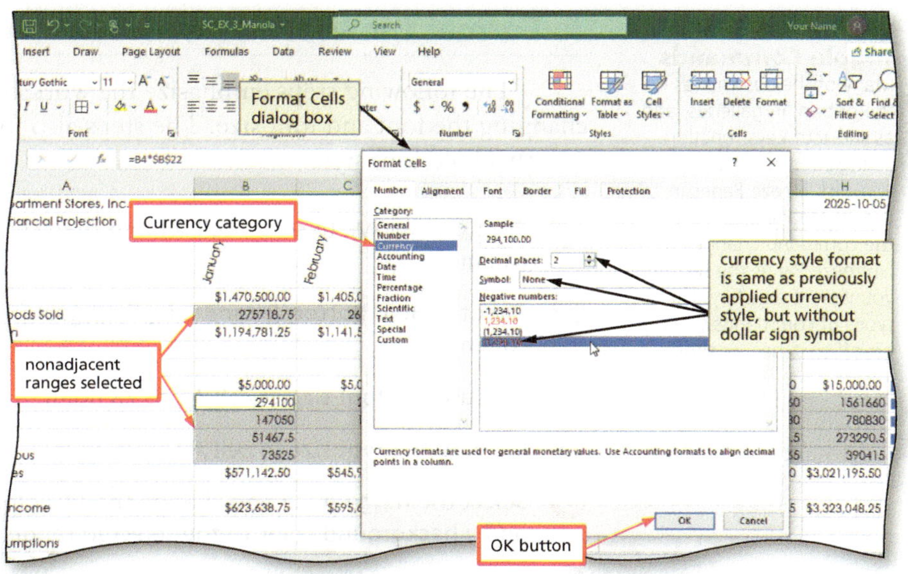

Figure 3–44

3

- Click OK (Format Cells dialog box) to close the Format Cells dialog box and apply the desired format to the selected ranges.
- Select an empty cell and display the formatted numbers, as shown in Figure 3–45.

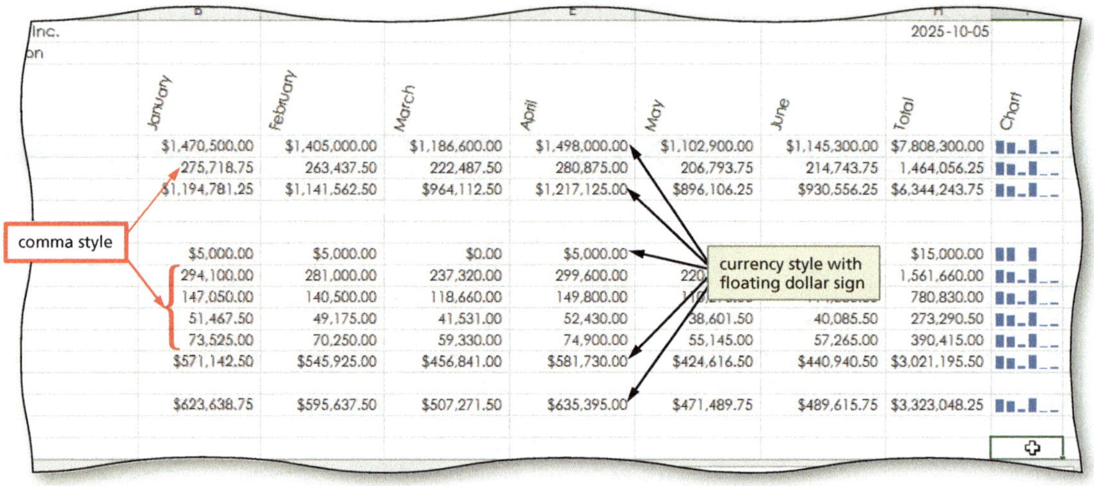

Figure 3–45

Q&A **Why is the Format Cells dialog box used to create the style for the ranges in Steps 2 and 3?**
The Format Cells dialog box is used to assign the comma style instead of the Comma Style button (Home tab | Number group), because the Comma Style button assigns a format that displays a dash (–) when a cell has a value of 0. The specifications for this worksheet call for displaying a value of 0 as 0.00 (see cell D9 in Figure 3–45) rather than as a dash. To create a comma style using the Format Cells dialog box, you use a currency style with no dollar sign.

Other Ways

1. Right-click range, click Format Cells on shortcut menu, click Number tab (Format Cells dialog box), click category in Category list, select format, click OK (Format Cells dialog box)
2. Press CTRL+1, click Number tab (Format Cells dialog box), click category in Category list, select format, click OK (Format Cells dialog box)
3. Click Currency arrow (Home tab | Number group), select desired format

BTW
Toggle Commands
Many of the commands on the ribbon, in galleries, and as shortcut keys function as toggles. For example, if you click Freeze Panes in the Freeze Panes gallery, the command changes to Unfreeze Panes the next time you view the gallery. These types of commands work like on-off switches, or toggles.

To Format the Worksheet Titles

The following steps emphasize the worksheet titles in cells A1 and A2 by changing the font and font size. The steps also format all of the row headers in column A with a bold font style.

1. Press CTRL+HOME to select cell A1 and then click the column A heading to select the column.
2. Click the Bold button (Home tab | Font group) to bold all of the data in the selected column.
3. Increase the font size in cell A1 to 28 point.
4. Increase the font size in cell A2 to 16 point.
5. Select the range A1:I2 and change the fill color to Dark Blue, Text 2, Lighter 80% to add a background color to the selected range.
6. With A1:I2 selected, change the font color to Dark Blue, Accent 1.
7. Click an empty cell to deselect the range (Figure 3–46).

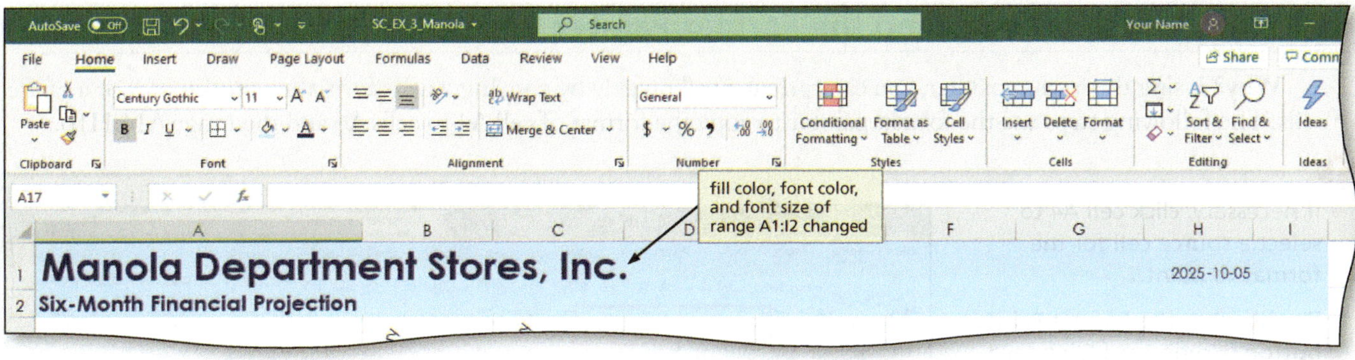

Figure 3–46

Other Ways

1. Right-click range, click Format Cells on shortcut menu, click Fill tab (Format Cells dialog box) to color background (or click Font tab to color font), click OK
2. Press CTRL+1, click Fill tab (Format Cells dialog box) to color background (or click Font tab to color font), click OK

To Assign Cell Styles to Nonadjacent Rows and Colors to a Cell

The following steps improve the appearance of the worksheet by formatting the headings in row 3 and the totals in rows 6, 14, and 16. Cell A4 also is formatted with a background color and font color.

1. Select the range A3:I3 and apply the Heading 3 cell style.
2. Select the range A6:H6 and while holding down CTRL, select the ranges A14:H14 and A16:H16.
3. Apply the Total cell style to the selected nonadjacent ranges.
4. Select cell A4 and click the Fill Color button (Home tab | Font group) to apply the last fill color used (Dark Blue, Text 2, Lighter 80%) to the cell contents.
5. Click the Font Color button (Home tab | Font group) to apply the last font color used (Dark Blue, Accent 1) to the cell contents (Figure 3–47).

BTW

The Fill and Font Color Buttons

You may have noticed that the color bar at the bottom of the Fill Color and Font Color buttons (Home tab | Font group) (Figure 3–46) changes to the most recently selected color. To apply this same color to a cell background or text, select a cell and then click the Fill Color button to use the color as a background or click the Font Color button to use the color as a font color.

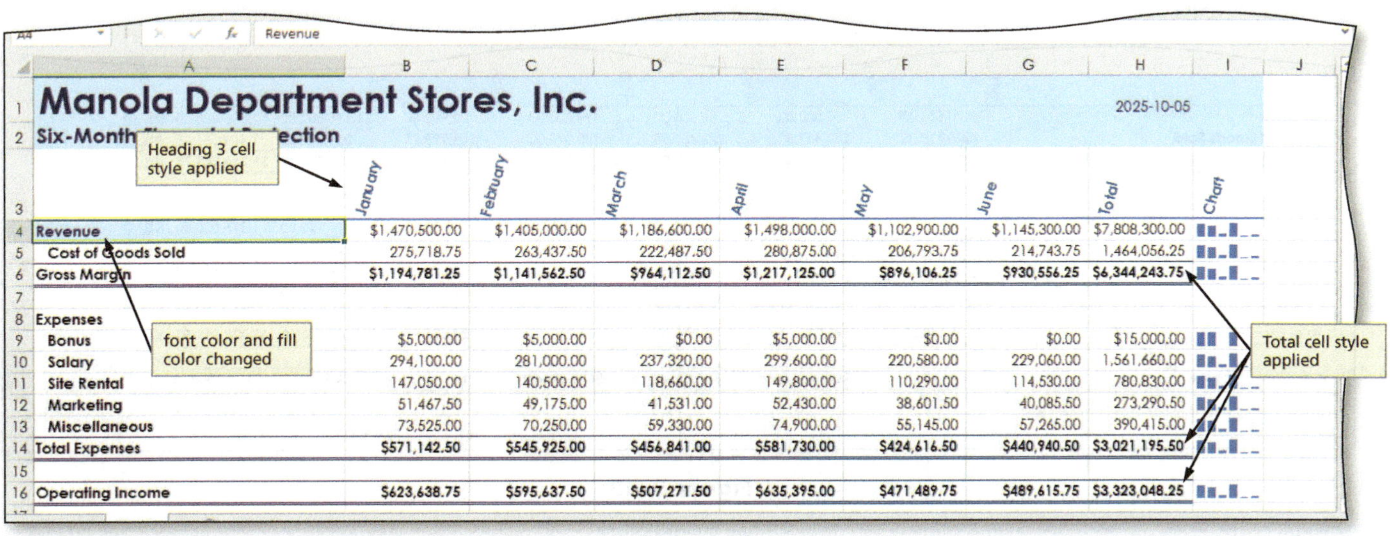

Figure 3–47

To Copy a Cell's Format Using the Format Painter Button

Why? Using the format painter, you can format a cell quickly by copying a cell's format to another cell or a range of cells. The following steps use the format painter to copy the format of cell A4 to cells A6 and the range A16:H16.

1

- If necessary, click cell A4 to select a source cell for the format to paint.
- Double-click the Format Painter button (Home tab | Clipboard group) and then move the pointer onto the worksheet to cause the pointer to change to a block plus sign with a paintbrush (Figure 3–48).

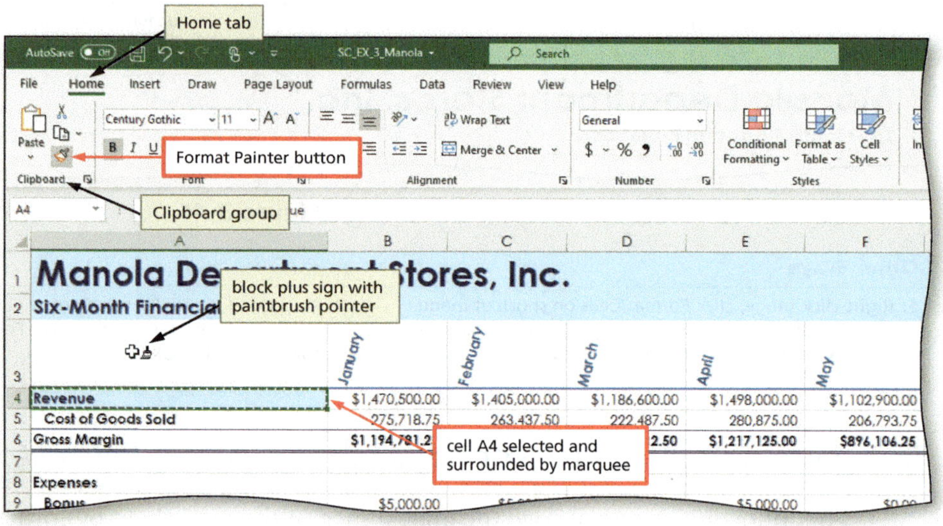

Figure 3–48

2

- Click cell A6 to assign the format of the source cell, A4 in this case, to the destination cell, A6 in this case.
- With the pointer still a block plus sign with a paintbrush, drag through the range A16:H16 to assign the format of the source cell, A4 in this case, to the destination range, A16:H16 in this case.
- Click the Format Painter button or press ESC to turn off the format painter.
- Apply the currency style to the range B16:H16 to cause the cells in the range to appear with a floating dollar sign and two decimal places (Figure 3–49).

Q&A **Why does the currency style need to be reapplied to the range B16:H16?**
Sometimes, the use of the format painter results in unintended outcomes. In this case, changing the background fill color and font color for the range B16:H16 resulted in the loss of the currency style because the format being copied did not include the currency style. Reapplying the currency style to the range results in the proper number style, fill color, and font color.

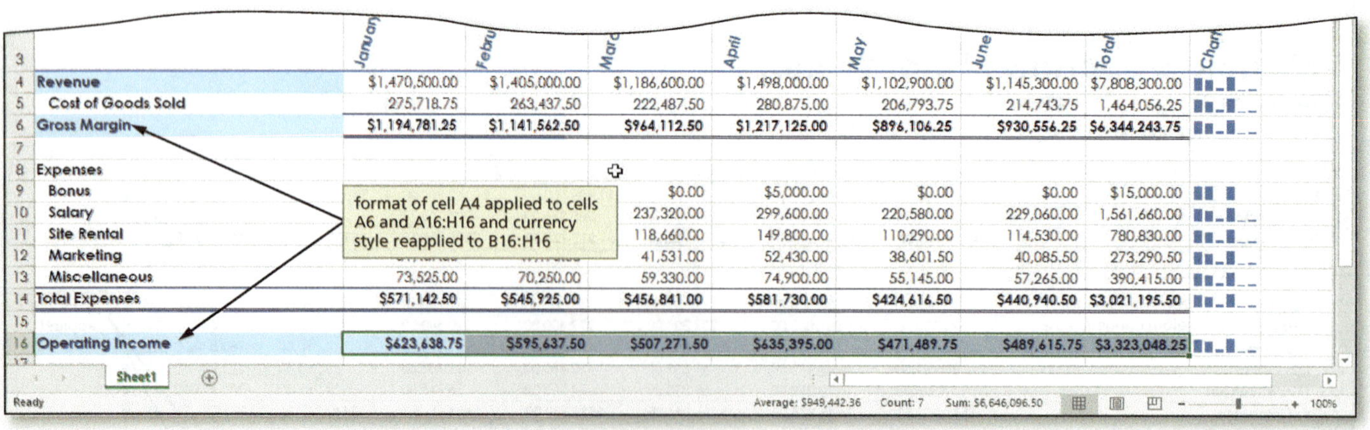

Figure 3–49

Other Ways

1. Click Copy button (Home tab | Clipboard group), select cell, click Paste arrow (Home tab | Clipboard group), click Formatting button in Paste gallery
2. Right-click cell, click Copy on shortcut menu, right-click cell, click Formatting button on shortcut menu

To Format the What-If Assumptions Table

The following steps format the What-If Assumptions table, the final step in improving the appearance of the worksheet.

1. Select cell A18.
2. Change the font size to 9 pt.
3. Italicize and underline the text in cell A18.
4. Select the range A19:B25, and change the font size to 9 pt.
5. Select the range A18:B25 and then click the Fill Color button (Home tab | Font group) to apply the most recently used background color to the selected range.
6. Click the Font Color button (Home tab | Font group) to apply the most recently used font color to the selected range.
7. Deselect the range A18:B25 and display the What-If Assumptions table, as shown in Figure 3–50.
8. Save the workbook on the same storage location with the same file name.

Q&A **What happens when I click the Italic and Underline buttons?**
When you assign the italic font style to a cell, Excel slants the characters slightly to the right, as shown in cell A18 in Figure 3–50. The underline format underlines only the characters in the cell, rather than the entire cell, as is the case when you assign a cell a bottom border.

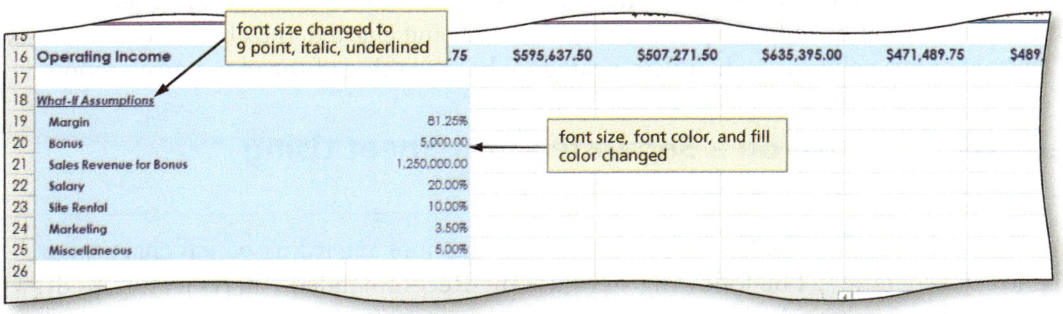

Figure 3–50

BTW
Painting a Format to Nonadjacent Ranges
Double-click the Format Painter button (Home tab | Clipboard group) and then drag through the nonadjacent ranges to paint the formats to the ranges. Click the Format Painter button again to deactivate it.

BTW
Selecting Nonadjacent Ranges
One of the more difficult tasks to learn is selecting nonadjacent ranges. To complete this task, do not hold down CTRL when you select the first range because Excel will consider the current active cell to be the first selection, and you may not want the current active cell in the selection. Once the first range is selected, hold down CTRL and drag through the nonadjacent ranges. If a desired range is not visible in the window, use the scroll arrows to view the range. You need not hold down CTRL while you scroll.

Break Point: If you want to take a break, this is a good place to do so. You can exit Excel now. To resume later, start Excel, open the file called SC_EX_3_Manola, and continue following the steps from this location forward.

Adding a Clustered Column Chart to the Workbook

The next step in the module is to create a clustered column chart on a separate sheet in the workbook, as shown in Figure 3–51. Use a clustered column chart to compare values side by side, broken down by category. Each column shows the value for a particular category, by month in this case.

The clustered column chart in Figure 3–51 shows the projected expense amounts, by category, for each of the six months. The clustered column chart allows the user to see how the various expense categories compare with each other each month, and across months.

The clustered column is a two-dimensional chart. Excel also lets you create three-dimensional charts, but some experts feel that three-dimensional charts are more difficult to read and may not represent certain types of data accurately.

Recall that charts can either be embedded in a worksheet or placed on a separate chart sheet. The clustered column chart will reside on its own sheet, because if placed on the worksheet, it would not be visible when the worksheet first opens and could be missed.

BTW

Charts

When you change a value on which a chart is dependent, Excel immediately redraws the chart based on the new value.

BTW

Chart Items

When you rest the pointer over a chart item, such as a legend, bar, or axis, Excel displays a chart tip containing the name of the item.

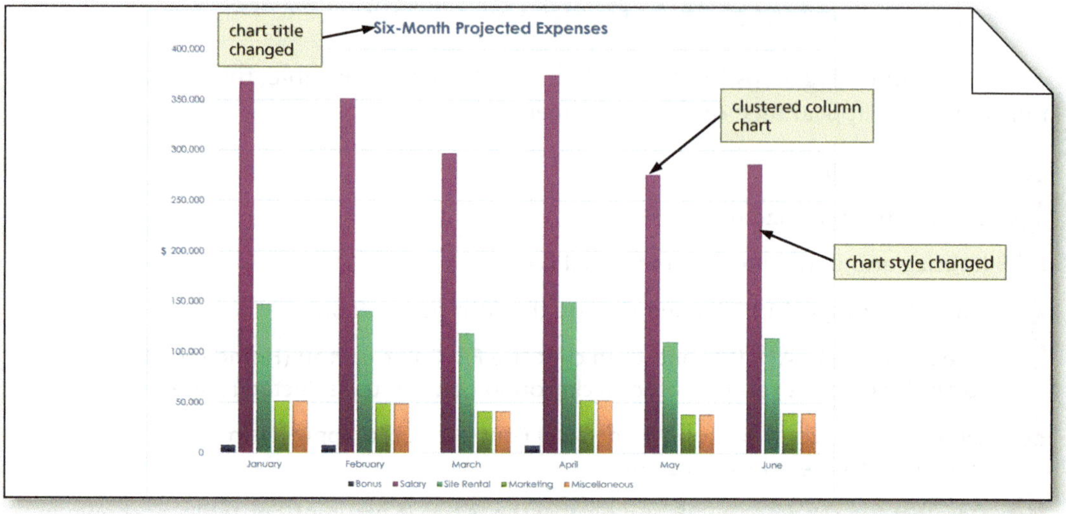

Figure 3–51

In this worksheet, the ranges to chart are the nonadjacent ranges B3:G3 (month names) and A9:G13 (monthly projected expenses, by category). The month names in the range B3:G3 will identify the major groups for the chart; these entries are called **category names.** The range A9:G13 contains the data that determines the individual columns in each month cluster, along with the names that identify each column; these entries are called the **data series**, which is the set of values represented in a chart. Because six months of five expense categories are being charted, the chart will contain six clusters of five columns each, unless a category has the value of zero for a given month.

To Draw a Clustered Column Chart on a Separate Chart Sheet Using the Recommended Charts Feature

Why? This Excel feature evaluates the selected data and makes suggestions regarding which chart types will provide the most suitable representation. The following steps use the Recommended Charts feature to draw the clustered column chart on a separate chart sheet.

1

- Select the range A3:G3 to identify the range of the categories.
- Hold down CTRL and select the data range A9:G13.
- Display the Insert tab.
- Click the Recommended Charts button (Insert tab | Charts group) to display the Insert Chart dialog box with the Recommended Charts tab active (Figure 3–52).

Experiment

- Click the various recommended chart types, reading the description for each of its best use and examining the chart preview.

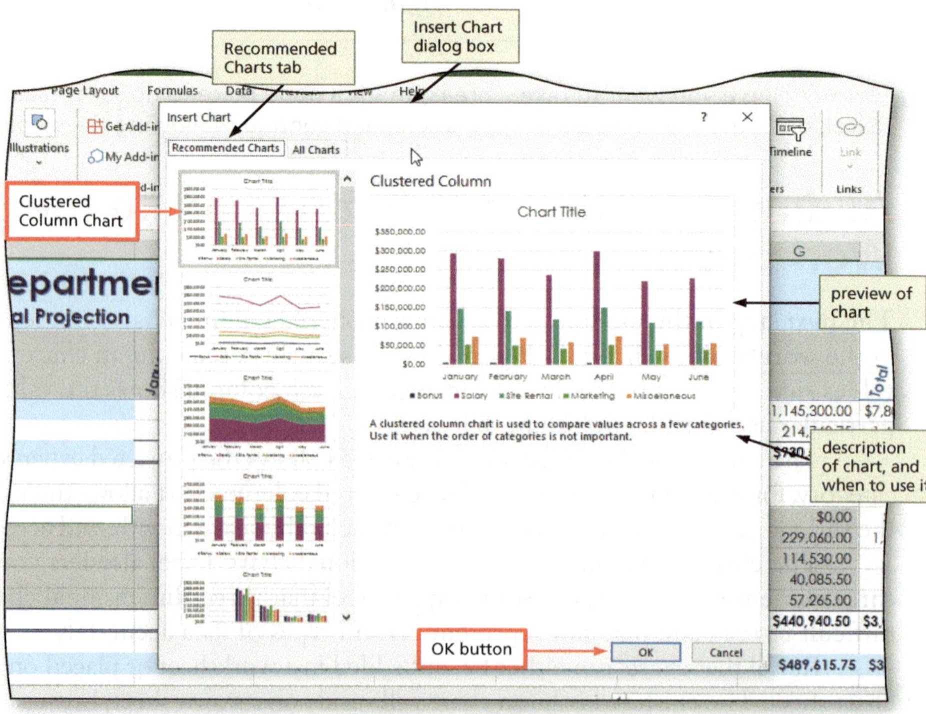

Figure 3–52

2

- If necessary, click the first Clustered Column recommended chart to select it and then click OK (Insert Chart dialog box).
- After Excel draws the chart, click the Move Chart button (Chart Design tab | Location group) to display the Move Chart dialog box.
- Click the New sheet option button (Move Chart dialog box) and then type **`Expense Chart Sheet`** in the New sheet text box to enter a sheet tab name for the chart sheet (Figure 3–53).

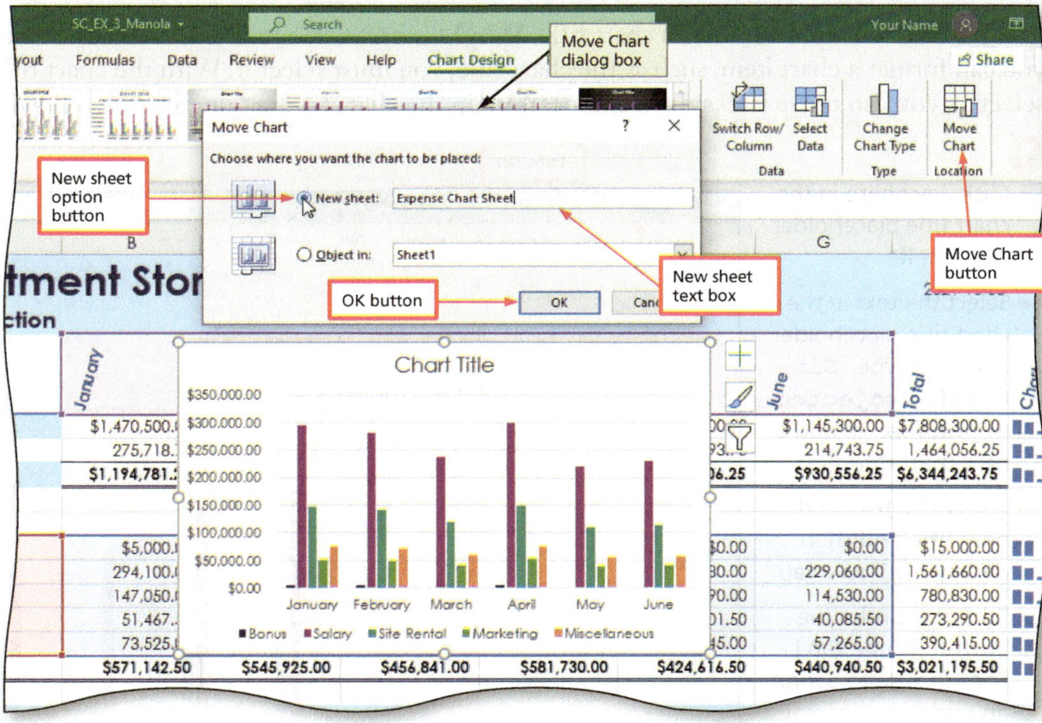

Figure 3–53

3

- Click OK (Move Chart dialog box) to move the chart to a new chart sheet with a new sheet tab name, Expense Chart Sheet (Figure 3–54).

Q&A

Why do March, May, and June have only four columns charted?
March, May, and June have a value of $0 for the Bonus category. Values of zero are not charted in a column chart, so these three months have one fewer column than the other months.

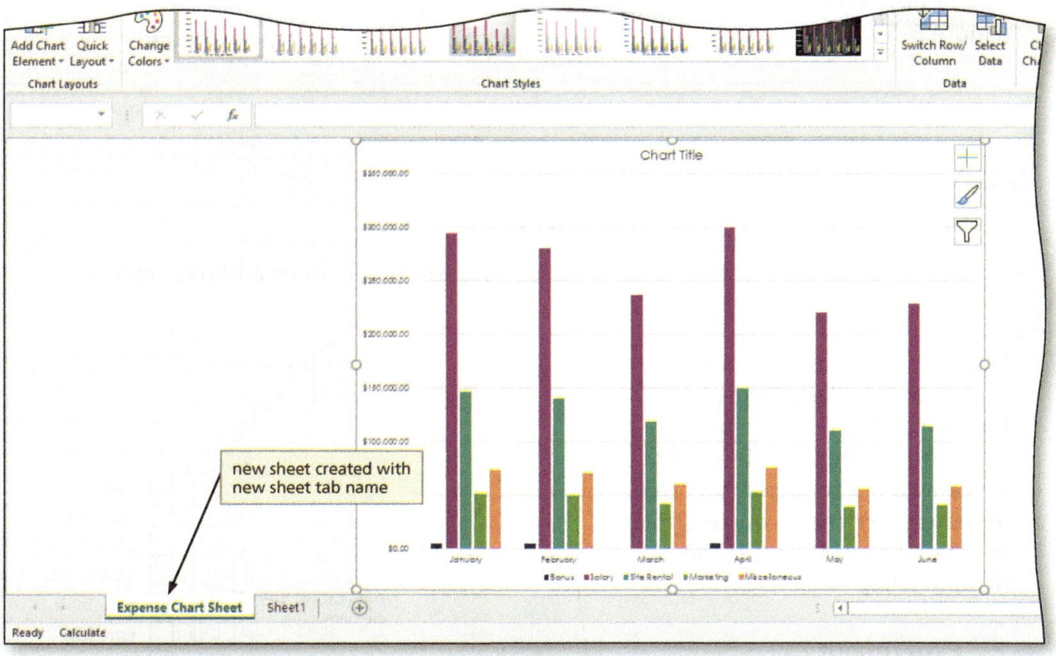

Figure 3–54

Other Ways

1. Select range to chart, press F11

To Insert a Chart Title

The next step is to insert a chart title. **Why?** A chart title identifies the chart content for the viewer. Before you can format a chart item, such as the chart title, you must select it. With the chart title or other chart element selected, you can move it to a different location on the chart by dragging it. The following step inserts a chart title.

1

- Click anywhere in the chart title placeholder to select it.
- Select the text in the chart title placeholder and then type `Six-Month Projected Expenses` to add a new chart title.
- Select the text in the new title and then display the Home tab.
- Click the Underline button (Home tab | Font group) to assign an underline format to the chart title.
- Click anywhere outside of the chart title to deselect it (Figure 3–55).

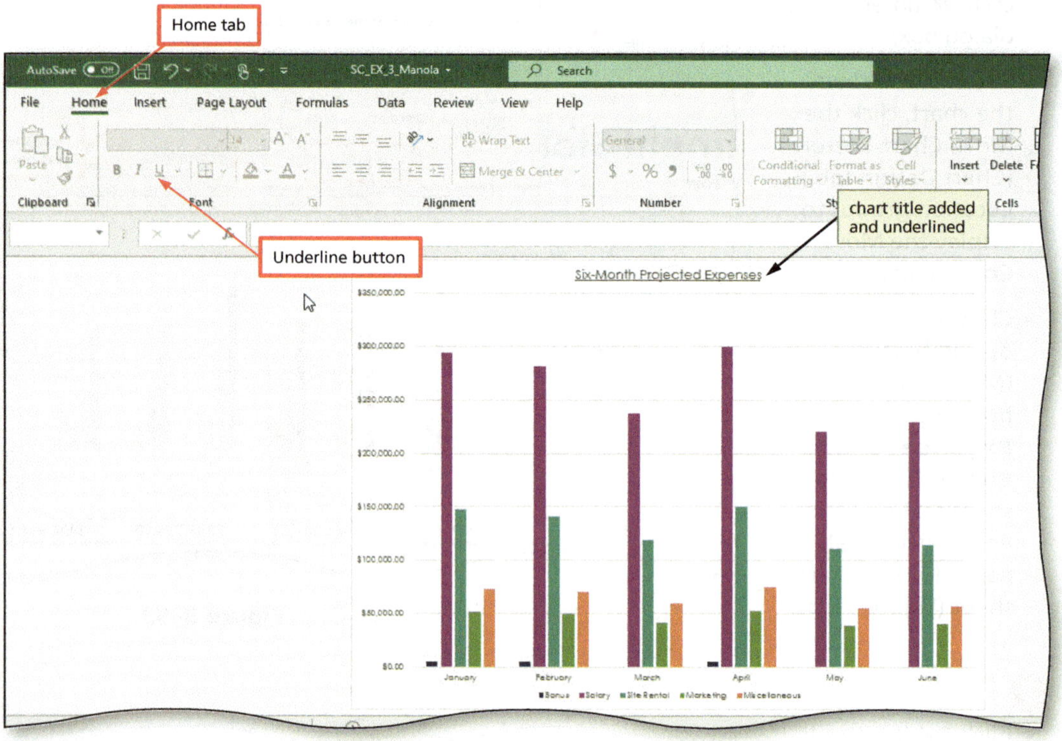

Figure 3–55

To Add Data Labels

The next step is to add data labels. **Why?** Data labels can make a chart more easily understood. You can remove them if they do not accomplish that. The following steps add data labels.

1

- Click the chart to select it and then click the Chart Elements button (on the chart) to display the Chart Elements gallery. Point to Data Labels to display an arrow and then click the arrow to display the Data Labels fly-out menu (Figure 3–56).

Experiment

- If you are using a mouse, point to each option on the Data Labels fly-out menu to see a live preview of the data labels.

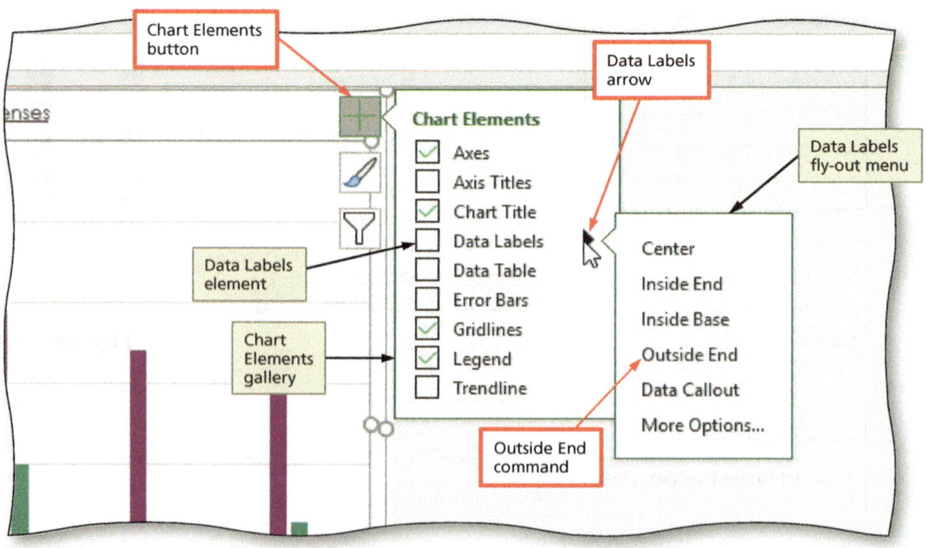

Figure 3–56

2

- Click Outside End on the Data Labels fly-out menu so that data labels are displayed outside the chart at the end of each column.
- Click the Chart Elements button to close the gallery (Figure 3–57).

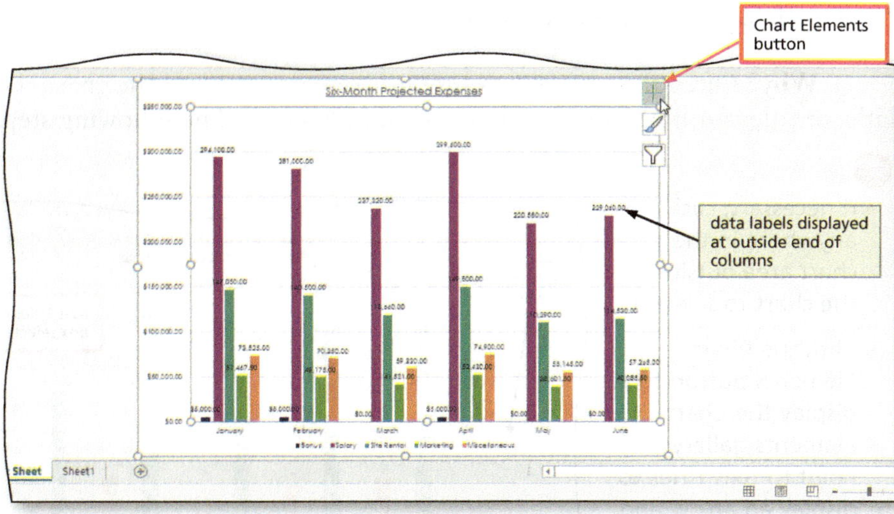

Figure 3–57

To Apply Chart Filters

Why? With some data, you may find that certain data series or categories make it difficult to examine differences and patterns between other series or categories. Excel allows you to easily filter data series and categories to allow more in-depth examinations of subsets of data. In this case, filters can be used to temporarily remove the compensation categories Bonus and Salary from the chart, to allow a comparison across the noncompensation expenses. The following steps apply filters to the clustered column chart.

1

- Click the Chart Filters button (on the chart) to display the Chart Filters gallery.
- In the Series section, click the Bonus and Salary check boxes to remove their check marks and then click the Apply button to filter these series from the chart (Figure 3–58).

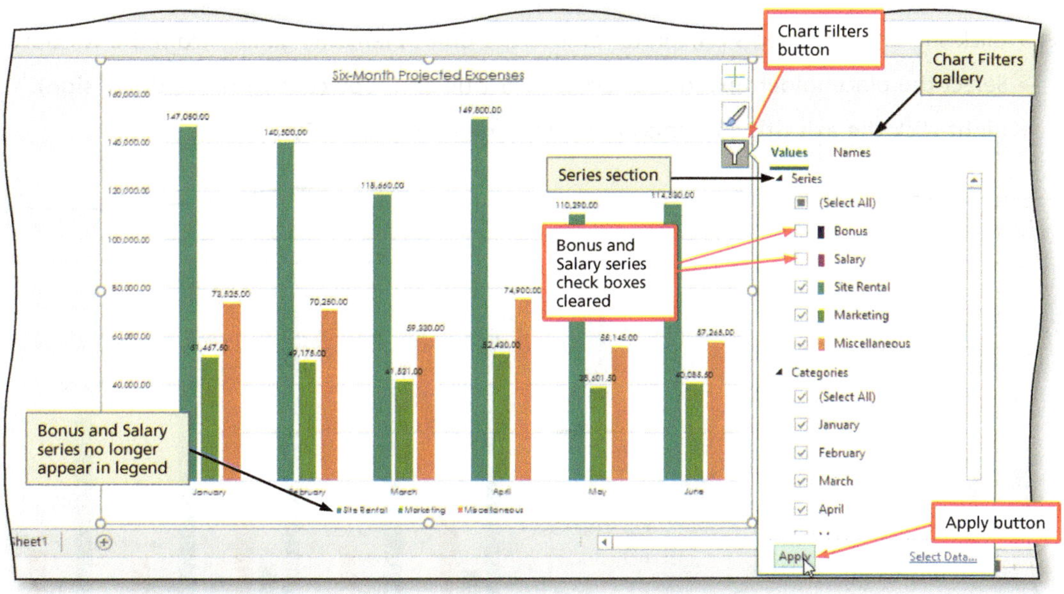

Figure 3–58

Q&A **What happens when I remove the check marks from Bonus and Salary?**
When you remove the check marks from Bonus and Salary, Excel filters the Bonus and Salary series out and redraws the chart without them.

2

- Click the Chart Filters button to close the gallery.

To Add an Axis Title to the Chart

Why? Often the unit of measurement or categories for the charted data is not obvious. You can add an axis title, or titles for both axes, for clarity or completeness. The following steps add an axis title for the vertical axis.

1

- If necessary, click anywhere in the chart area outside the chart to select it.
- Click the Chart Elements button to display the Chart Elements gallery. Point to Axis Titles to display an arrow and then click the arrow to display the Axis Titles fly-out menu.

Experiment

- Point to each option on the fly-out menu to see a live preview of the axes' titles.

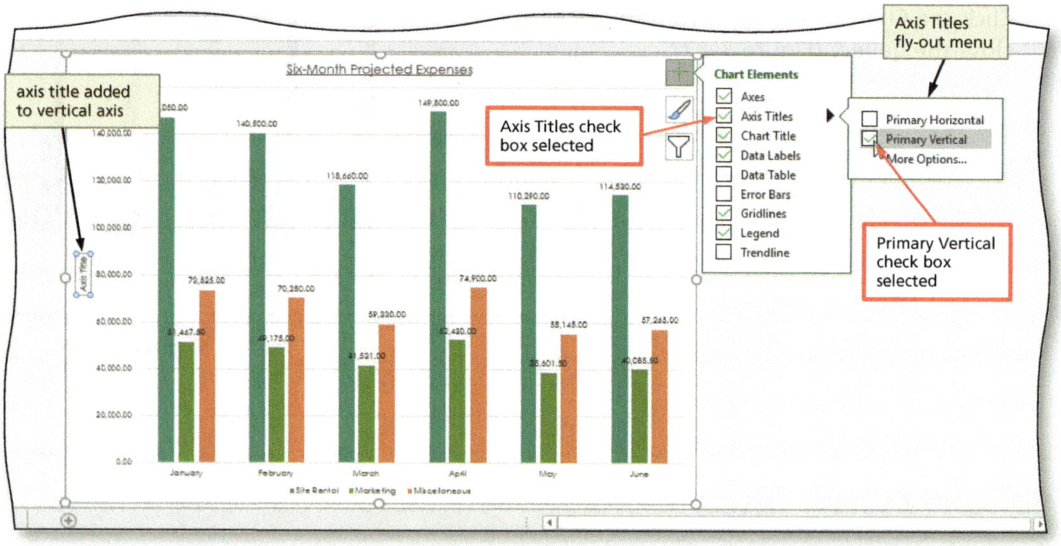

Figure 3–59

- Click Primary Vertical on the Axis Titles fly-out menu to add an axis title to the vertical axis (Figure 3–59).

2

- Click the Chart Elements button to remove the Chart Elements gallery from the window.
- Select the placeholder text in the vertical axis title and replace it with $ (a dollar sign).
- Right-click the axis title to display a shortcut menu (Figure 3–60).

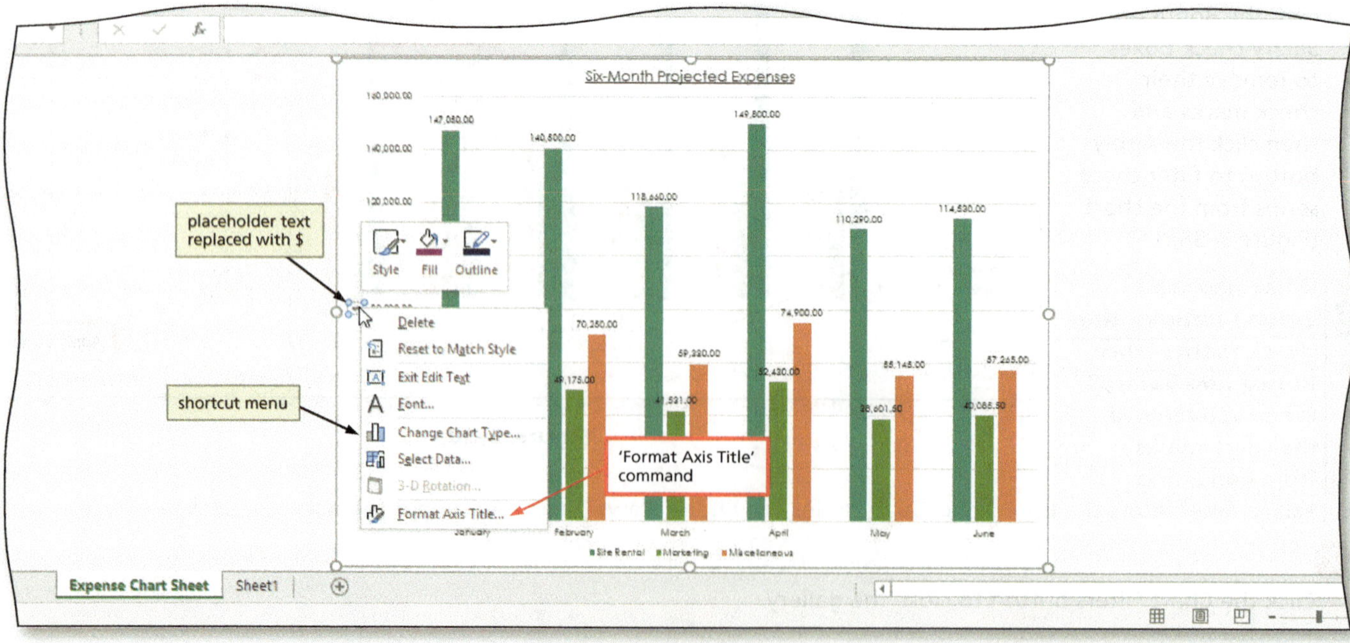

Figure 3–60

3

- Click 'Format Axis Title' on the shortcut menu to open the Format Axis Title pane.
- If necessary, click the Title Options tab, click the 'Size & Properties' button, and then, if necessary, click the Alignment arrow to expand the Alignment section.
- Click the Text direction arrow to display the Text direction list (Figure 3–61).
- Click Horizontal in the Text direction list to change the orientation of the vertical axis title.
- Click the Close button (shown in Figure 3–61) on the pane to close the Format Axis Title pane.

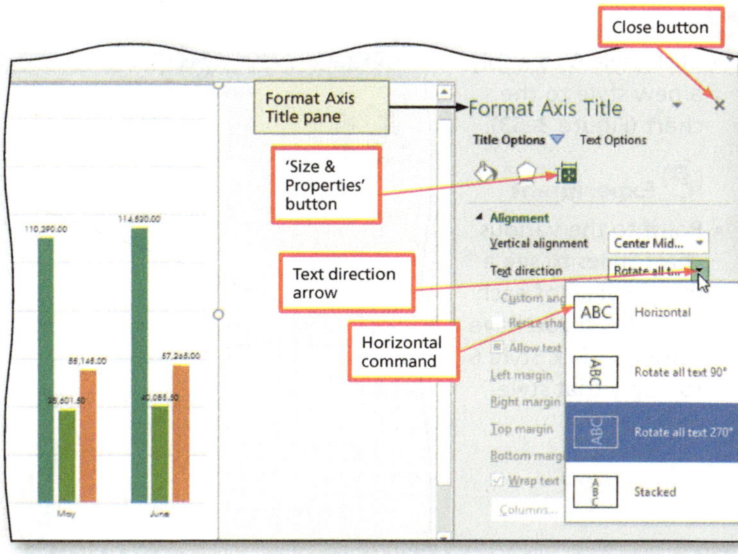

Figure 3–61

To Change the Chart Style

Why? You decide that a chart with a different look would better convey meaning to viewers. The following steps change the chart style.

1

- Display the Chart Design tab and then click the More button (Chart Design tab | Chart Styles group) to display the Chart Styles gallery (Figure 3–62).

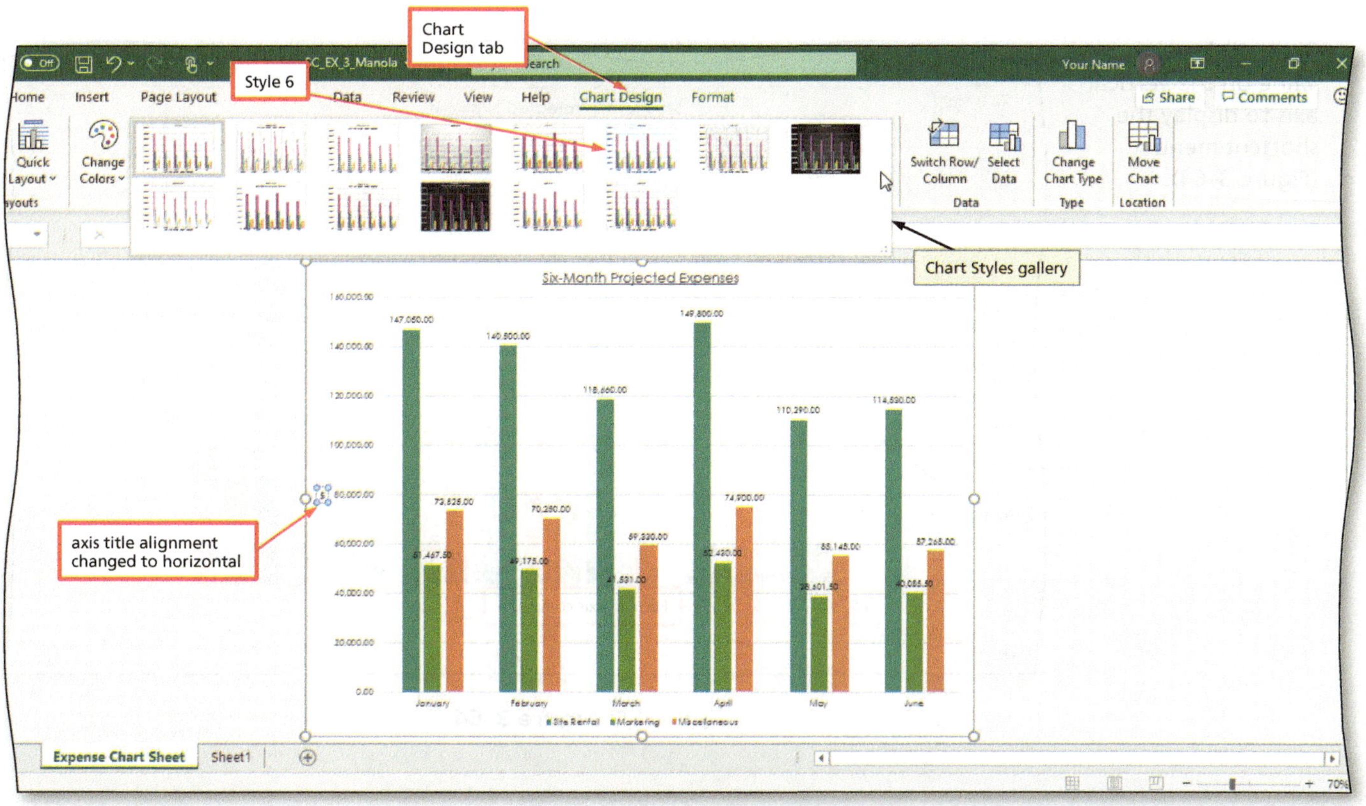

Figure 3–62

2

- Click Style 6 to apply a new style to the chart (Figure 3–63).

Experiment

- Point to the various chart styles to see a live preview of each one. When you have finished, click Style 6 to apply that style.

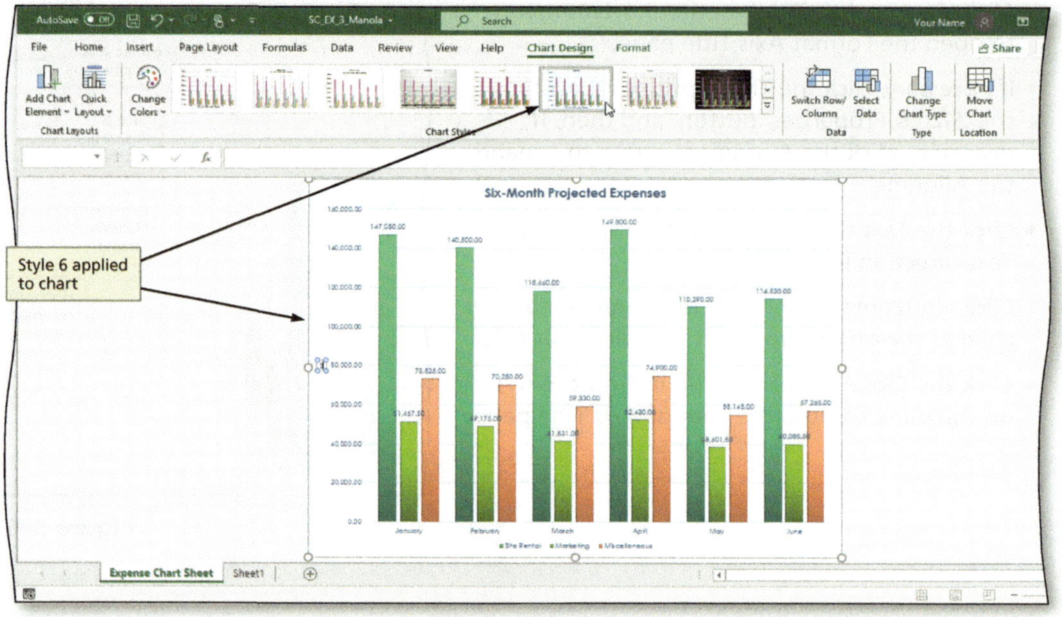

Figure 3–63

To Modify the Chart Axis Number Format

Why? The two decimal places in the vertical chart axis numbers are not necessary and make the axis appear cluttered. The following steps format the numbers in the chart axis to contain no decimal places.

1

- Right-click any value on the vertical axis to display the shortcut menu (Figure 3–64).

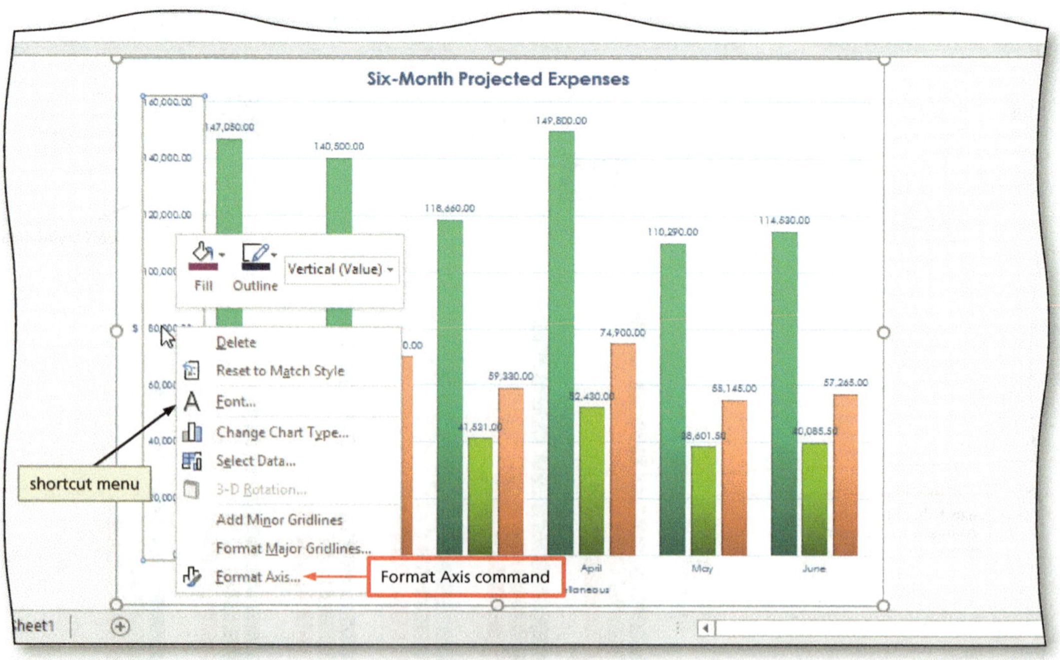

Figure 3–64

2

- Click Format Axis on the shortcut menu to open the Format Axis pane.
- If necessary, click the Axis Options tab in the Format Axis pane and then scroll until Number is visible. Click the Number arrow to expand the Number section and then scroll to review options related to formatting numbers.
- Change the number in the Decimal places text box to 0 (Figure 3–65).

Q&A

Can I change the minimum and maximum bounds displayed on the axis?

Yes. In the Format Axis pane, expand the Axis Options area and then enter the desired values in the Minimum and Maximum text boxes.

3

- Close the Format Axis pane.

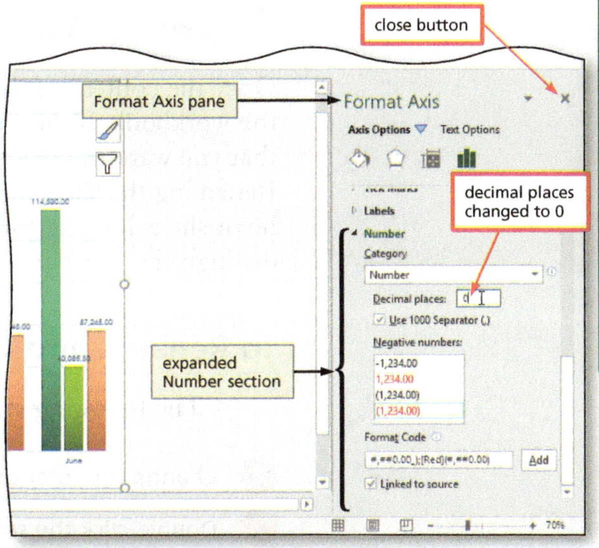

Figure 3–65

To Remove Filters and Data Labels

You decide that the data labels on the bars are distracting and add no value to the chart. You decide to remove the data labels and filters so that all expense data is once again visible. You also can experiment with various chart layouts that specify which chart elements display and where they display. To change the layout of a chart, click the Quick Layout button (Chart Design tab | Chart Layouts group) and then select the desired layout. You also can change the chart type by selecting the chart, clicking the 'Change Chart Type' button (Chart Design tab | Type group), and then selecting the desired chart in the Change Chart Type dialog box. The following steps remove the data labels and the filters.

1. Click the Chart Elements button to display the Chart Elements gallery.
2. Click the Data Labels check box to remove the check mark for the data labels.
3. Click the Chart Elements button again to close the gallery.
4. Click the Chart Filters button to display the Chart Filters fly-out menu.
5. In the Series section, click Bonus and then Salary, click the Apply button to add the compensation data back into the chart, and then click the Chart Filters button again to close the menu (Figure 3–66).

BTW

Chart Templates

Once you create and format a chart to your liking, consider saving the chart as a template so that you can use it to format additional charts. Save your chart as a chart template by right-clicking the chart to display the shortcut menu and then selecting 'Save as Template' from that shortcut menu. The chart template will appear in the Templates folder for Charts. When you want to use the template, click the Templates folder in the All Charts sheet (Insert Chart dialog box) and then select your template.

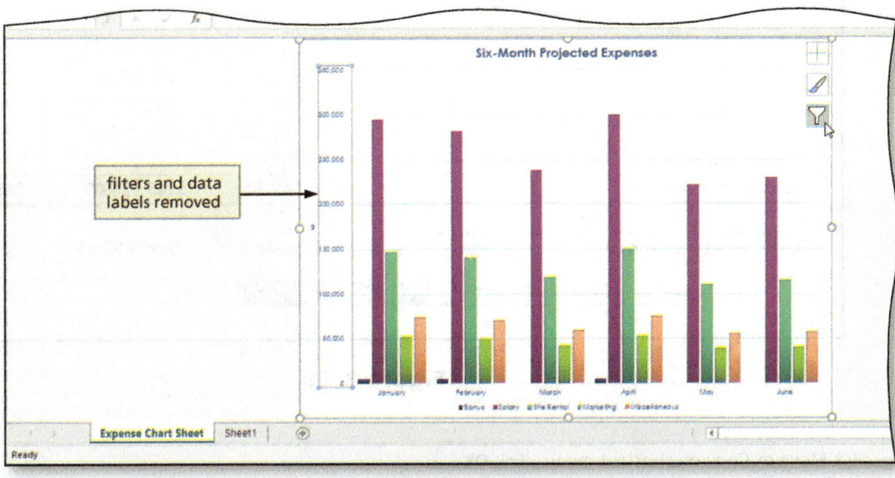

Figure 3–66

Organizing the Workbook

Once the content of the workbook is complete, you can address the organization of the workbook. If the workbook has multiple worksheets, place the worksheet on top that you want the reader to see first. Default sheet names in Excel are not descriptive. Renaming the sheets with descriptive names helps the reader find information that he or she is looking for. Modifying the sheet tabs through the use of color further distinguishes multiple sheets from each other.

To Rename and Color Sheet Tabs

The following steps rename the sheets and color the sheet tabs.

1. Change the color of the Expense Chart Sheet tab to Dark Blue, Text 2 (column 4, row 1).
2. Double-click the sheet tab labeled Sheet1 at the bottom of the screen.
3. Type `Six-Month Financial Projection` as the new sheet tab name and then press ENTER.
4. Change the sheet tab color of the Six-Month Financial Projection sheet to Light Turquoise, Background 2 (column 3, row 1) and then select an empty cell (Figure 3–67).

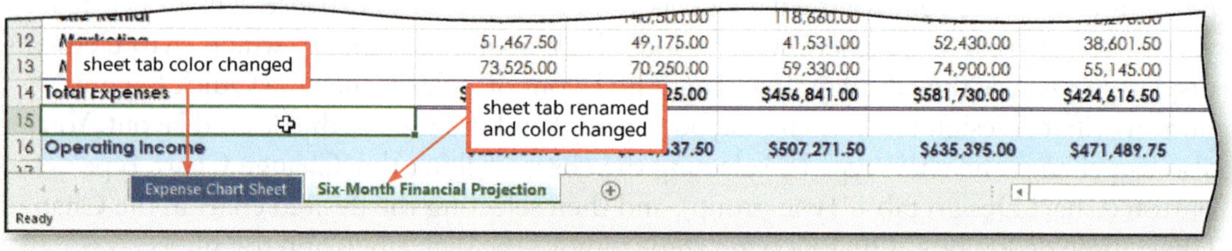

Figure 3–67

To Reorder the Sheet Tabs

Why? You want the most important worksheets to appear first in a workbook, so you need to change the order of sheets. The following step reorders the sheets so that the worksheet precedes the chart sheet in the workbook.

1

- Drag the Six-Month Financial Projection tab to the left so that it precedes the Expense Chart sheet tab to rearrange the sequence of the sheets (Figure 3–68).

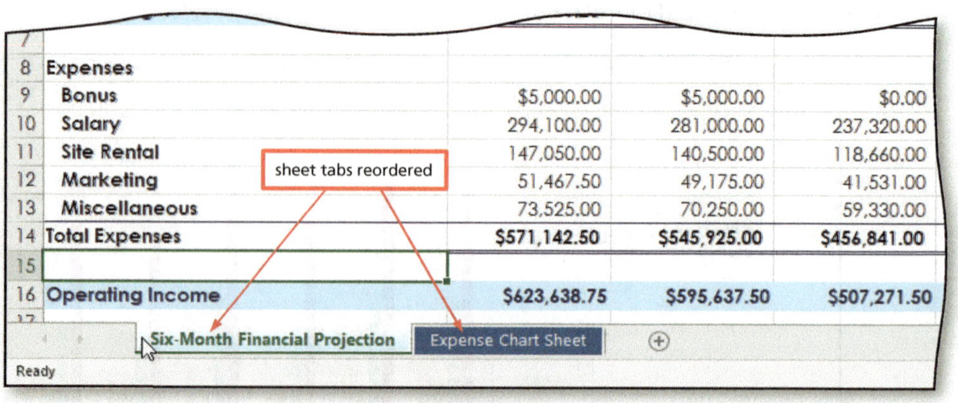

Figure 3–68

Other Ways

1. To move sheet, right-click sheet tab, click Move or Copy on shortcut menu, click OK

To Check Spelling in Multiple Sheets

By default, the spelling checker reviews spelling only in the selected sheets. It will check all the cells in the selected sheets unless you select a range of two or more cells. Before checking the spelling, the following steps select both worksheets in the workbook so that both are checked for any spelling errors.

1. With the Six-Month Financial Projection sheet active, press CTRL+HOME to select cell A1. Hold down CTRL and then click the Expense Chart Sheet tab to select both sheets.
2. Display the Review tab and then click the Spelling button (Review tab | Proofing group) to check spelling in the selected sheets.
3. Correct any errors and then click OK (Spelling dialog box or Microsoft Excel dialog box) when the spelling checker is finished.

BTW

Checking Spelling

Unless you first select a range of cells or an object before starting the spelling checker, Excel checks the entire selected worksheet, including all cell values, cell comments, embedded charts, text boxes, buttons, and headers and footers.

To Preview and Print the Worksheet

After checking the spelling, the next step is to preview and print the worksheets. As with spelling, Excel previews and prints only the selected sheets. In addition, because the worksheet is too wide to print in portrait orientation, the orientation must be changed to landscape. The following steps adjust the orientation and scale, preview the worksheets, and then print the worksheets.

1. If both sheets are not selected, hold down CTRL and then click the tab of the inactive sheet.
2. Click File on the ribbon to open Backstage view.
3. Click Print in Backstage view to display the Print screen.
4. Click the Portrait Orientation button in the Settings area and then select Landscape Orientation to select the desired orientation.
5. Click the No Scaling button in the Settings area and then select 'Fit Sheet on One Page' to cause the worksheets to print on one page.
6. Verify that the desired printer is selected. If necessary, click the printer button to display a list of available printer options and then click the desired printer to change the currently selected printer.
7. Click the Print button in the Print gallery to print the worksheet in landscape orientation on the currently selected printer.
8. When the printer stops, retrieve the printed worksheets (shown in Figure 3–69a and Figure 3–69b).
9. Right-click the Six-Month Financial Projection tab, and then click Ungroup Sheets on the shortcut menu to deselect the Expense Chart Sheet tab.
10. Save the workbook again in the same storage location with the same file name.

BTW

Distributing a Workbook

Instead of printing and distributing a hard copy of a workbook, you can distribute the workbook electronically. Options include sending the workbook via email; posting it on cloud storage (such as OneDrive) and sharing the file with others; posting it on social media, a blog, or other website; and sharing a link associated with an online location of the workbook. You also can create and share a PDF or XPS image of the workbook, so that users can view the file in Acrobat Reader or XPS Viewer instead of in Excel.

Manola Department Stores, Inc.
Six-Month Financial Projection
2025-10-05

	January	February	March	April	May	June	Total	Chart
Revenue	$1,470,500.00	$1,405,000.00	$1,186,600.00	$1,498,000.00	$1,102,900.00	$1,145,300.00	$7,808,300.00	
Cost of Goods Sold	275,718.75	263,437.50	222,487.50	280,875.00	206,793.75	214,743.75	1,464,056.25	
Gross Margin	$1,194,781.25	$1,141,562.50	$964,112.50	$1,217,125.00	$896,106.25	$930,556.25	$6,344,243.75	
Expenses								
Bonus	$5,000.00	$5,000.00	$0.00	$5,000.00	$0.00	$0.00	$15,000.00	
Salary	294,100.00	281,000.00	237,320.00	299,600.00	220,580.00	229,060.00	1,561,660.00	
Site Rental	147,050.00	140,500.00	118,660.00	149,800.00	110,290.00	114,530.00	780,830.00	
Marketing	51,467.50	49,175.00	41,531.00	52,430.00	38,601.50	40,085.50	273,290.50	
Miscellaneous	73,525.00	70,250.00	59,330.00	74,900.00	55,145.00	57,265.00	390,415.00	
Total Expenses	$571,142.50	$545,925.00	$456,841.00	$581,730.00	$424,616.50	$440,940.50	$3,021,195.50	
Operating Income	$623,638.75	$595,637.50	$507,271.50	$635,395.00	$471,489.75	$489,615.75	$3,323,048.25	

What-If Assumptions	
Margin	81.25%
Bonus	5,000.00
Sales Revenue for Bonus	1,250,000.00
Salary	20.00%
Site Rental	10.00%
Marketing	3.50%
Miscellaneous	5.00%

(a)

(b)

Figure 3–69

Changing the View of the Worksheet

With Excel, you easily can change the view of the worksheet. For example, you can magnify or shrink the worksheet on the screen. You also can view different parts of the worksheet at the same time by using panes.

To Shrink and Magnify the View of a Worksheet or Chart

You can magnify (zoom in) or shrink (zoom out) the appearance of a worksheet or chart by using the Zoom button (View tab | Zoom group). **Why?** When you magnify a worksheet, Excel enlarges the view of the characters on the screen but shows fewer columns and rows. Alternatively, when you shrink a worksheet, Excel is able to display more columns and rows. Magnifying or shrinking a worksheet affects only the view; it does not change the window size or the size of the text on the worksheet or chart. If you have a range of cells selected, you can click the 'Zoom to Selection' button (View tab | Zoom group) to zoom the worksheet so that the selected range fills the entire window. The following steps shrink and magnify the view of the worksheet.

1

- If cell A1 is not active, press CTRL+HOME.
- Display the View tab and then click the Zoom button (View tab | Zoom group) to display a list of magnifications in the Zoom dialog box (Figure 3–70).

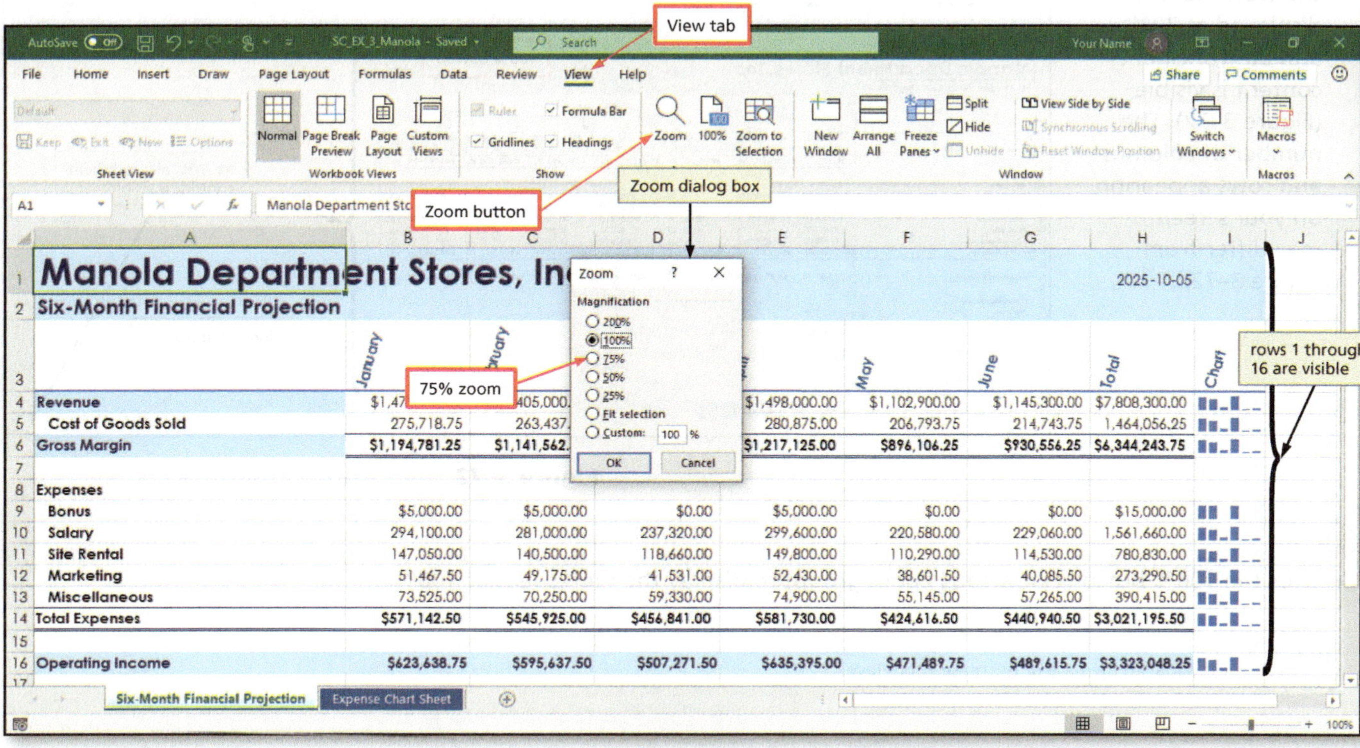

Figure 3–70

2

- Click 75% and then click OK (Zoom dialog box) to shrink the display of the worksheet (Figure 3–71). The number of columns and rows appearing on your screen may differ from Figure 3–71.

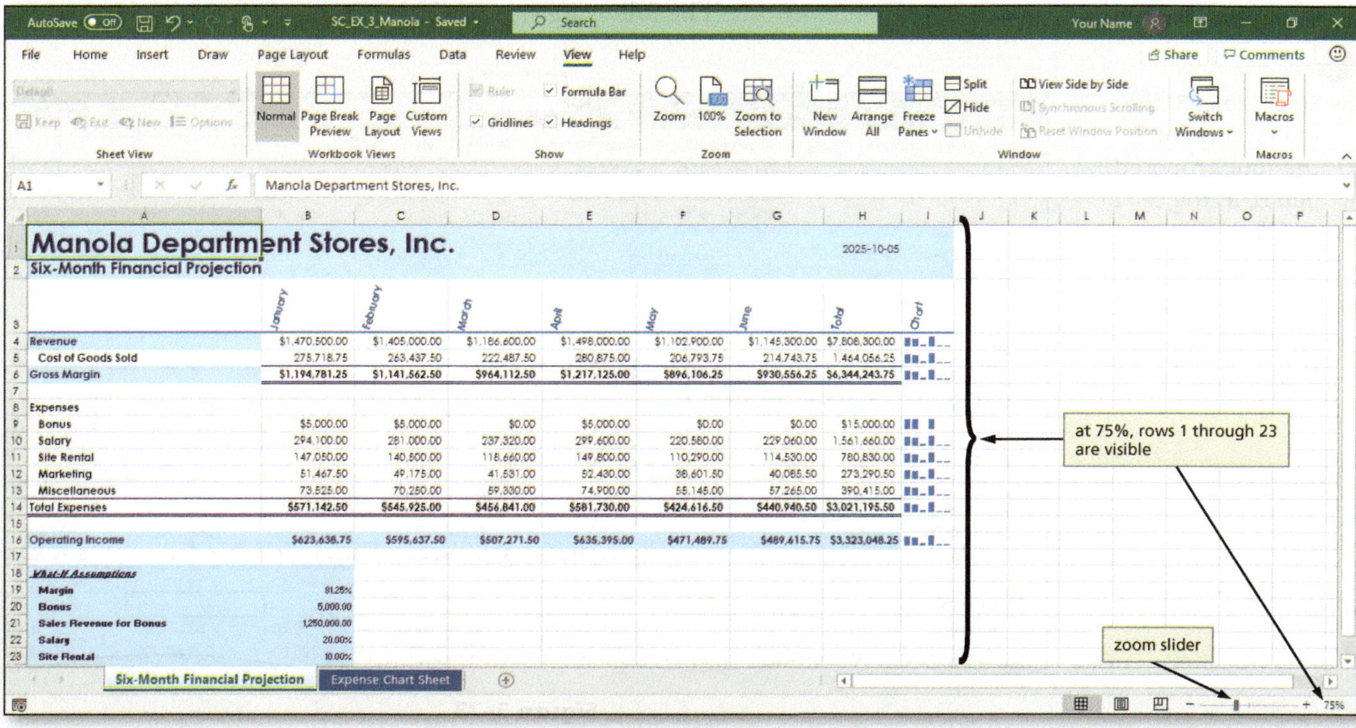

Figure 3–71

3

- Click the Zoom Out button on the status bar until the worksheet is displayed at 70% and all worksheet content is visible (Figure 3–72). The number of columns and rows appearing on your screen may differ from Figure 3–72.

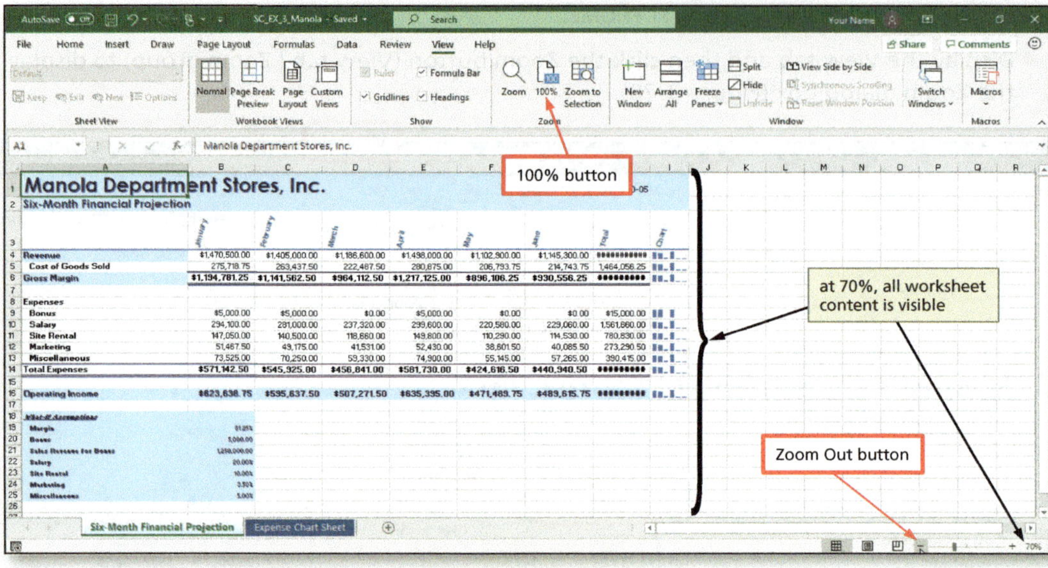

Figure 3–72

4

- Click the 100% button (View tab | Zoom group) to display the worksheet at 100%.

Other Ways

1. Drag zoom slider to increase or decrease zoom level

To Split a Window into Panes

When working with a large worksheet, you can split the window into two or four panes to view different parts of the worksheet at the same time. **Why?** Splitting the Excel window into four panes at cell E8 allows you to view all four corners of the worksheet simultaneously. The following steps split the Excel window into four panes.

1

- Select cell E8, the intersection of the four proposed panes, as the cell at which to split the window.
- If necessary, display the View tab (Figure 3–73).

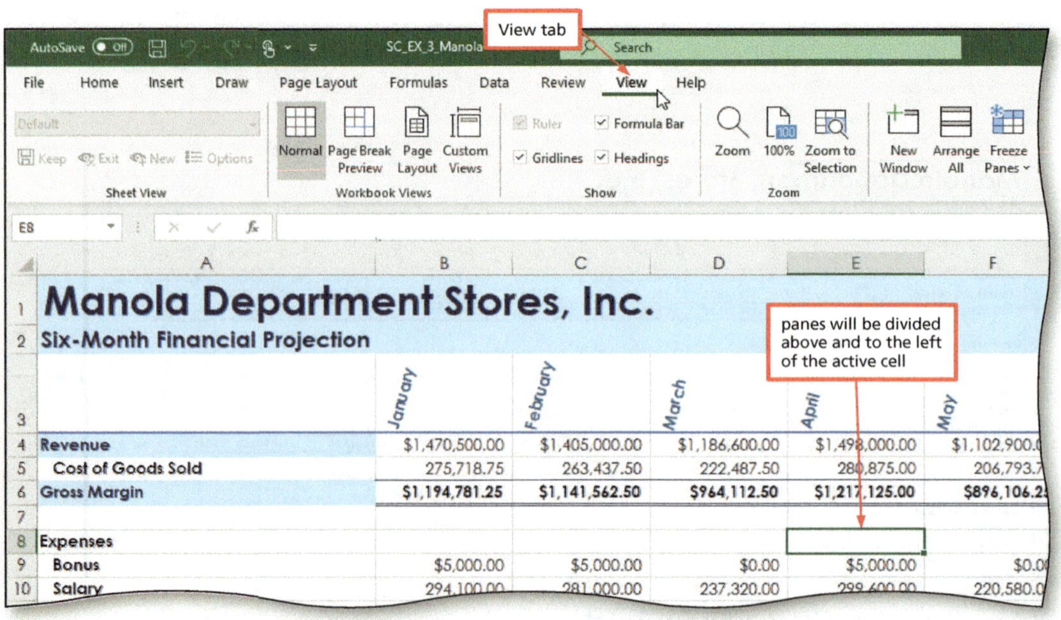

Figure 3–73

2

- Click the Split button (View tab | Window group) to divide the window into four panes.
- Use the scroll arrows to show the four corners of the worksheet at the same time (Figure 3–74).

Q&A **What is shown in the four panes?**
The four panes in Figure 3–74 show the following: (1) range A1:D7 in the upper-left pane; (2) range E1:J7 in the upper-right pane; (3) range A17:D25 in the lower-left pane; and (4) range E17:J25 in the lower-right pane. The vertical split bar is the vertical bar running up and down the middle of the window. The horizontal split bar is the horizontal bar running across the middle of the window. If you use the scroll bars below the window, you will see that the panes split by the horizontal split bar scroll together horizontally. The panes split by the vertical split bar scroll together vertically when using the scroll bars to the right of the window. To resize the panes, drag either split bar to the desired location.

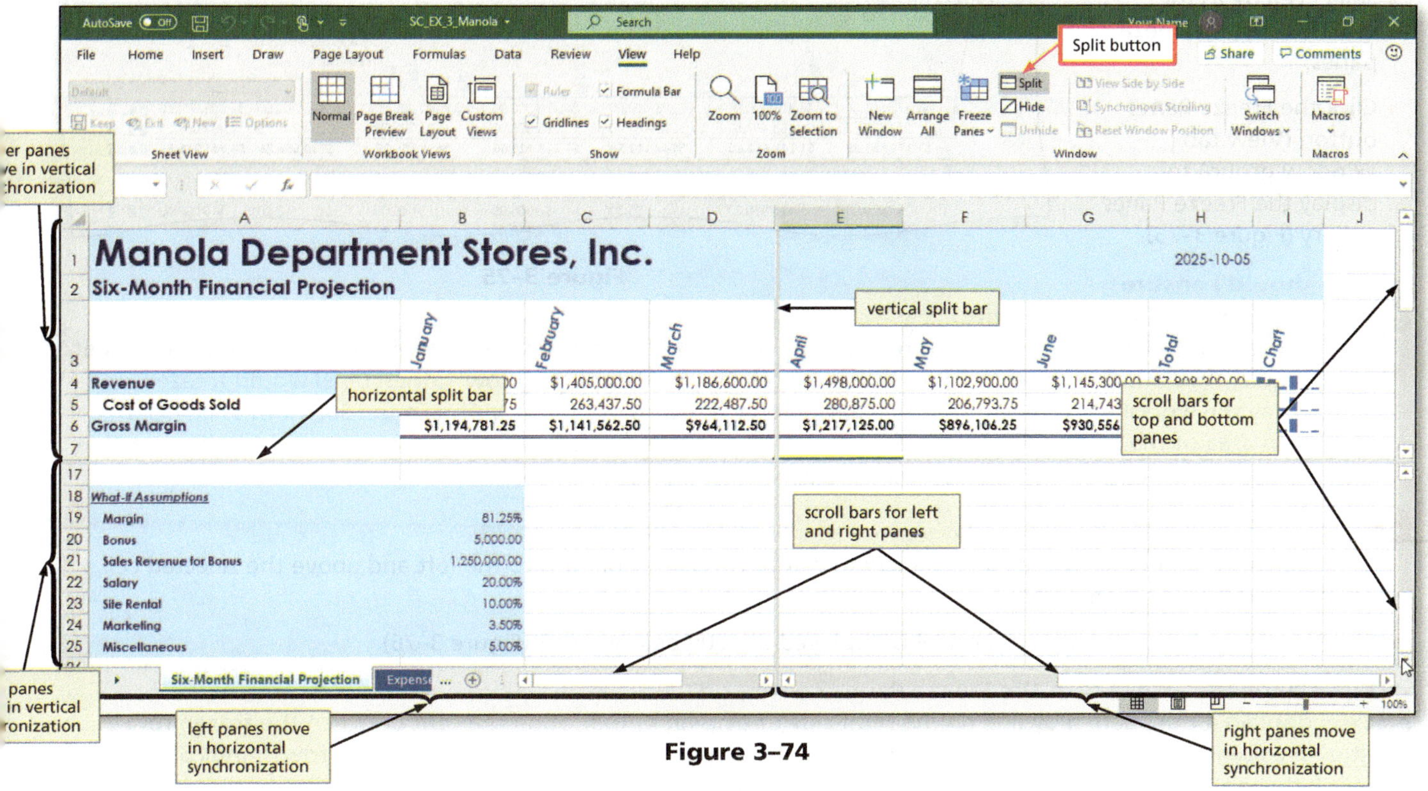

Figure 3–74

To Remove the Panes from the Window

The following step removes the panes from the window.

1 Click the Split button (View tab | Window group) to remove the four panes from the window.

Other Ways

1. Double-click intersection of horizontal and vertical split bars

To Freeze Worksheet Columns and Rows

Why? Freezing worksheet columns and rows is a useful technique for viewing large worksheets that extend beyond the window. Normally, when you scroll down or to the right, the column content in the top rows and the row content in the leftmost columns no longer appear on the screen. When the content of these rows and/or columns helps to identify or define other content still visible on the worksheet, it can make it difficult to remember what the numbers in the visible cells represent. To alleviate this problem, Excel allows you to freeze columns and rows, so that their content, typically column or row titles, remains on the screen, no matter how far down or to the right you scroll. You also may wish to keep numbers visible that you need to see when making changes to content in another part of the worksheet, such as the revenue, cost of goods sold, and gross margin information in rows 4 through 6. The following steps use the Freeze Panes button (View tab | Window group) to freeze the worksheet title and column titles in row 3, and the row titles in column A.

1

- Scroll the worksheet until Excel displays row 3 as the first row and column A as the first column on the screen.
- Select cell B4 as the cell on which to freeze panes.
- Click the Freeze Panes button (View tab | Window group) to display the Freeze Panes gallery (Figure 3–75).

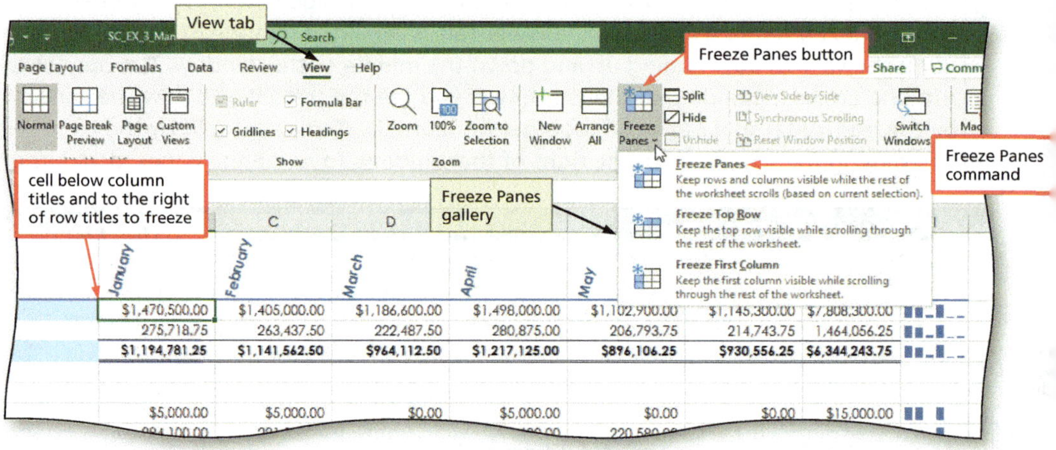

Figure 3–75

Q&A **Why should I ensure that row 3 is the first row visible?**
Before freezing the titles, it is important to align the first row that you want frozen with the top of the worksheet. For example, if you used the Freeze Panes button in cell B4 while displaying row 1, then Excel would freeze and display the worksheet title and subtitle, leaving only a few rows of data visible in the Six-Month Financial Projection area of the worksheet. To ensure that you can view as much data as possible, always scroll to a row that maximizes the view of your important data before freezing panes.

2

- Click Freeze Panes in the Freeze Panes gallery to freeze rows and columns to the left and above the selected cell, column A and row 3 in this case.
- Scroll down in the worksheet until row 9 is displayed directly below row 3 (Figure 3–76).

Q&A **What happens after I click the Freeze Panes command?**
Excel displays a thin, dark gray line on the right side of column A, indicating the split between the frozen row titles in column A and the rest of the worksheet. It also displays a thin, dark gray line below row 3, indicating the split between the frozen column titles in row 3 and the rest of the worksheet. Scrolling down or to the right in the worksheet will not scroll the content of row 3 or column A off the screen (Figure 3–76).

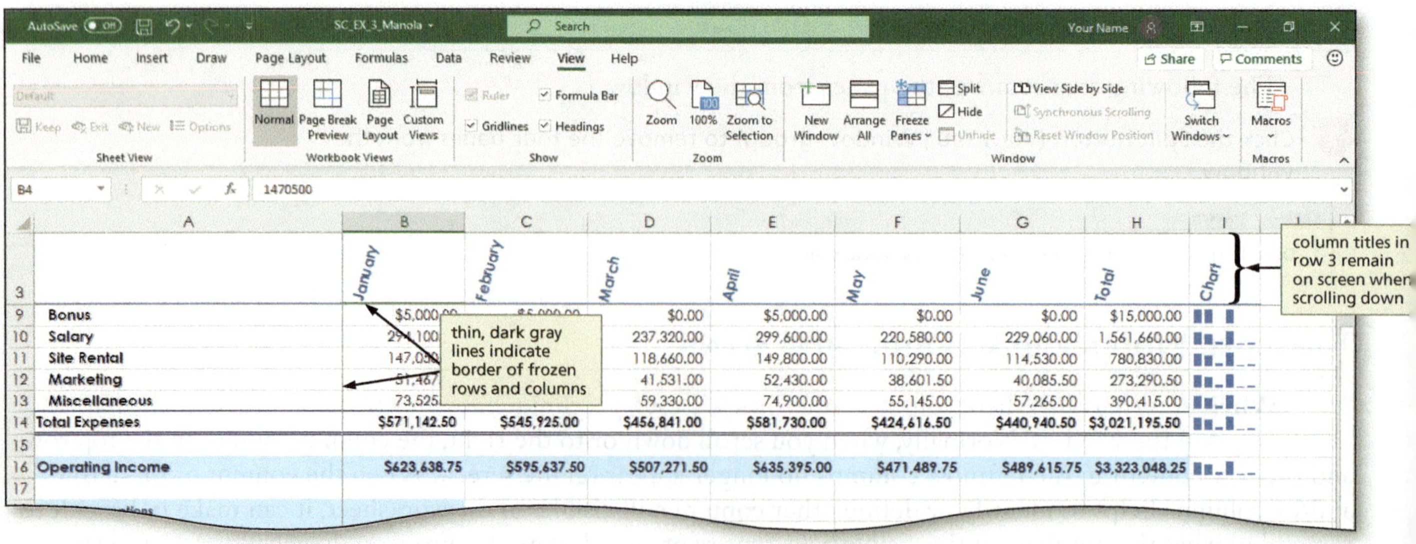

Figure 3–76

To Unfreeze the Worksheet Columns and Rows

Why? When you no longer need to view frozen columns and rows at all times, you should unfreeze them so that all columns and rows are displayed. The following steps unfreeze the titles in column A and row 3 to allow you to work with the worksheet without frozen rows and columns, or to freeze the worksheet at a different location.

1. Press CTRL+HOME to select cell B4 and view the upper-left corner of the screen.
2. Click the Freeze Panes button (View tab | Window group) to display the Freeze Panes gallery.
3. Click Unfreeze Panes in the Freeze Panes gallery to unfreeze the frozen columns and rows.
4. Save the workbook again in the same storage location with the same file name.

Q&A **Why does pressing CTRL+HOME select cell B4?**
When the titles are frozen and you press CTRL+HOME, Excel selects the upper-leftmost cell of the unfrozen section of the worksheet. For example, in Step 1 of the previous steps, Excel selected cell B4. When the titles are unfrozen, pressing CTRL+HOME selects cell A1.

BTW
Freezing Titles
If you want to freeze only column headings, select the appropriate cell in column A before you click the Freeze Panes button (View tab | Window group). If you want to freeze only row titles, select the appropriate cell in row 1 before you click the Freeze Panes button. To freeze both column headings and row titles, select the cell that is the intersection of the column and row titles before you click the Freeze Panes button.

What-If Analysis

The automatic recalculation feature of Excel is a powerful tool that can be used to analyze worksheet data. **What-if analysis** is a decision-making tool in which changing input values recalculate formulas, in order to predict various possible outcomes. When new data is entered, Excel not only recalculates all formulas in a worksheet but also redraws any associated charts.

In the workbook created in this module, many of the formulas are dependent on the assumptions in the range B19:B25. Thus, if you change any of the assumption values, Excel recalculates all formulas. Excel redraws the clustered column chart as well, because it is based on these numbers.

To Analyze Data in a Worksheet by Changing Values

Why? The effect of changing one or more values in the What-If Assumptions table—essentially posing what-if questions—allows you to review the results of different scenarios. In this case, you are going to examine what would happen to the six-month operating income (cell H16) if the following changes were made in the What-If Assumptions table: Bonus $5,000.00 to $7,500.00; Salary 20.00% to 25.00%; Miscellaneous 5.00% to 3.50%. To answer a question like this, you need to change only the second, fourth, and seventh values in the What-If Assumptions table. The following step splits the screen, which allows you to view income and expense figures simultaneously, and then changes values in the worksheet to answer a what-if question. When a new value is entered, Excel recalculates the formulas in the worksheet and redraws the clustered column chart to reflect the new data.

1.
- Scroll the worksheet so that row 4 is the first row visible on the worksheet.
- Click in cell A7 to select the row above which to split the window.
- Click the Split button (View tab | Window group) to split the window after row 6.
- Use the scroll arrows in the lower pane to scroll the window content until row 9 is the first row visible in the lower part of the screen, as shown in Figure 3–77.

- Enter **7,500** in cell B20, **25.00%** in cell B22, and **3.50%** in cell B25 (Figure 3–77), which causes the six-month operating income in cell H16 to decrease from $3,323,048.25 to $3,042,257.75.
- Save the workbook again on the same storage location with the same file name.

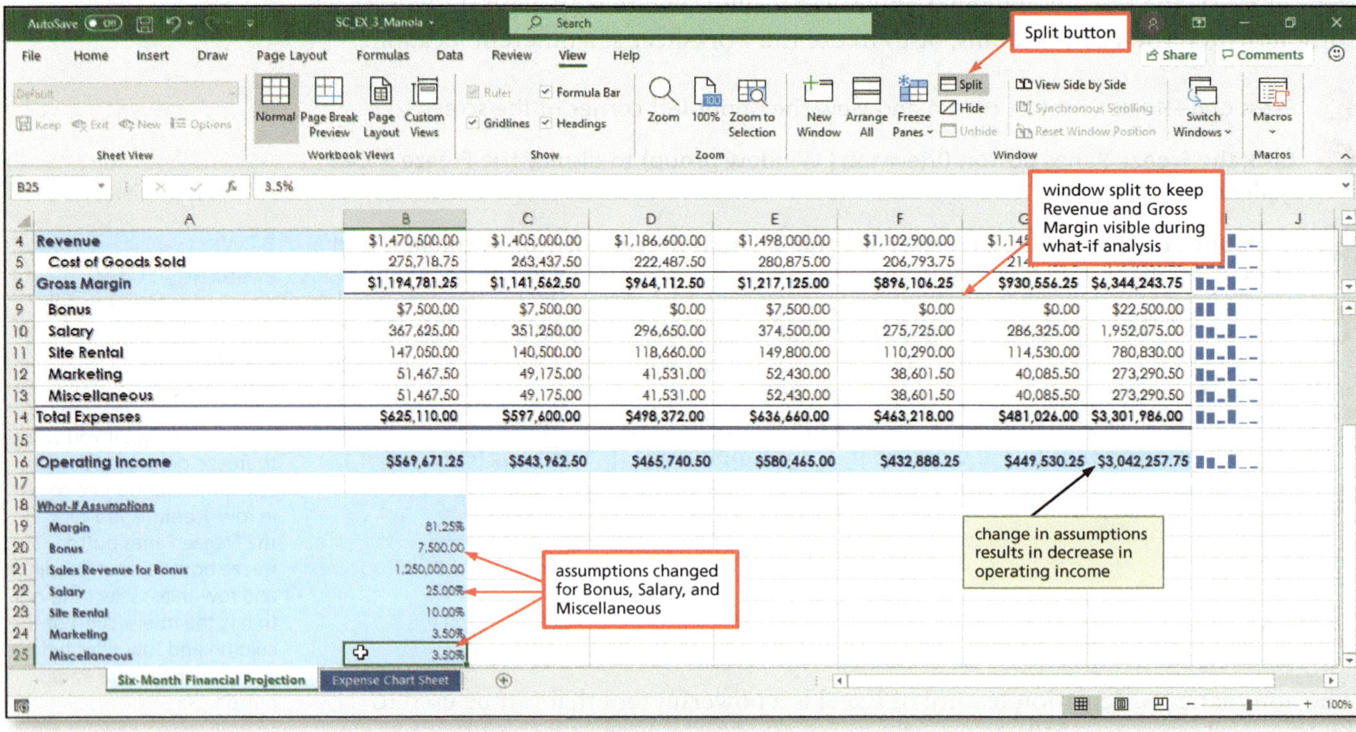

Figure 3–77

Goal Seeking

Goal seek is a problem-solving method in which you specify a solution and then find the input value that produces the answer you want. In this example, to change the six-month operating income in cell H16 to $3,500,000.00, the Site Rental percentage in cell B23 must decrease by 5.86% from 10.00% to 4.14%.

You can see from this goal seeking example that the cell to change (cell B23) does not have to be referenced directly in the formula or function. For example, the six-month operating income in cell H16 is calculated by the function =SUM(B16:G16). Cell B23 is not referenced in this function. Instead, cell B23 is referenced in the formulas in row 11, on which the monthly operating incomes in row 16 are based. By tracing the formulas and functions, Excel can obtain the desired six-month operating income by varying the value for the Site Rental assumption.

To Goal Seek

Why? If you know the result you want a formula to produce, you can use goal seeking to determine the value of a cell on which the formula depends. The previous step, which made changes to the What-If Assumptions table, resulted in an operating income that approaches but does not reach $3,500,000.00. The following steps use the Goal Seek command (Data tab | Forecast group) to determine what Site Rental percentage (cell B23), in conjunction with the earlier changes in assumptions, will yield a six-month operating income of $3,500,000.00 in cell H16, rather than the $3,042,257.75 calculated in the previous set of steps.

1

- If necessary, use the scroll arrows in the lower pane to ensure that you can view all of the What-If Assumptions table and the Operating Income figures.
- Select cell H16, the cell that contains the six-month operating income.
- Display the Data tab and then click the 'What-If Analysis' button (Data tab | Forecast group) to display the What-If Analysis menu (Figure 3–78).

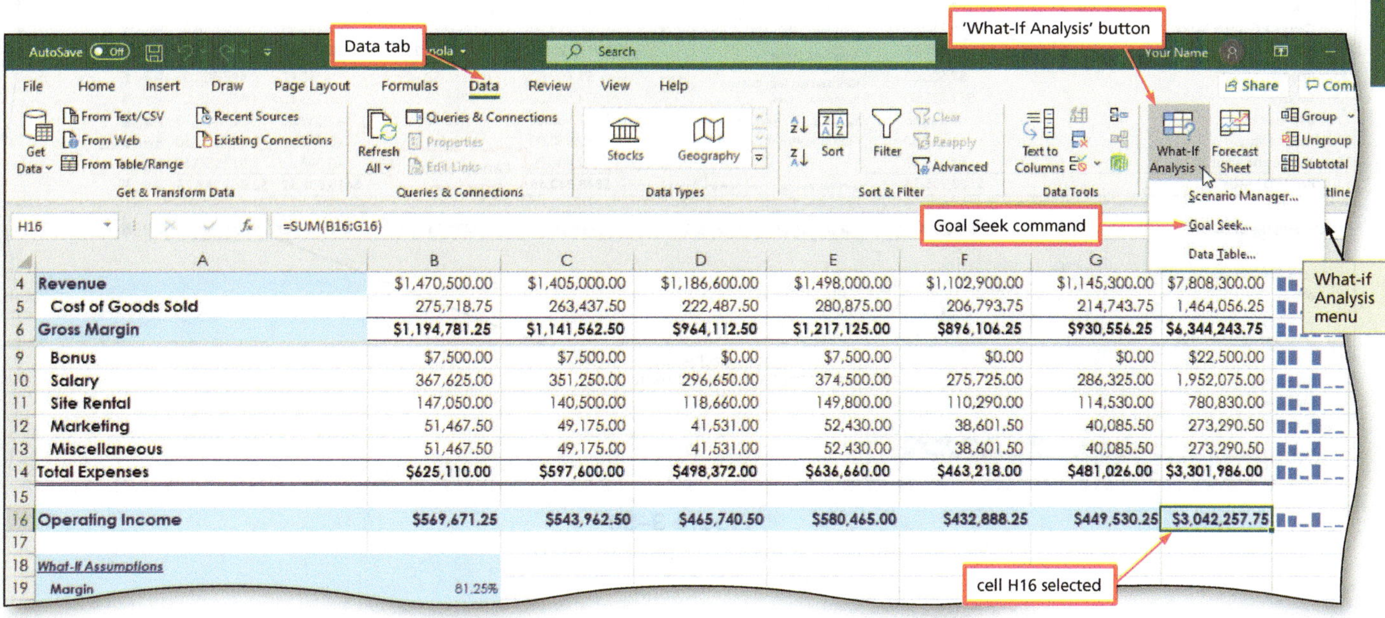

Figure 3–78

2

- Click Goal Seek to display the Goal Seek dialog box with the Set cell box set to the selected cell, H16 in this case.
- Click the To value text box, type `3,500,000` and then click the 'By changing cell' box to select it.
- Click cell B23 on the worksheet to assign the current cell, B23 in this case, to the 'By changing cell' box (Figure 3–79).

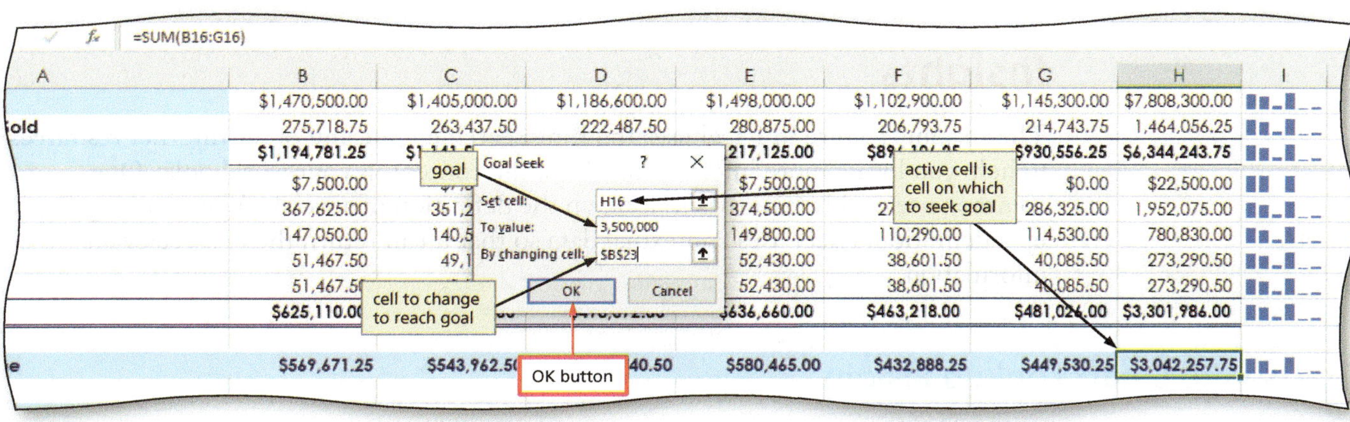

Figure 3–79

3

- Click OK (Goal Seek dialog box) to goal seek for the sought-after value in the To value text box, $3,500,000.00 in cell H16 in this case (Figure 3–80).

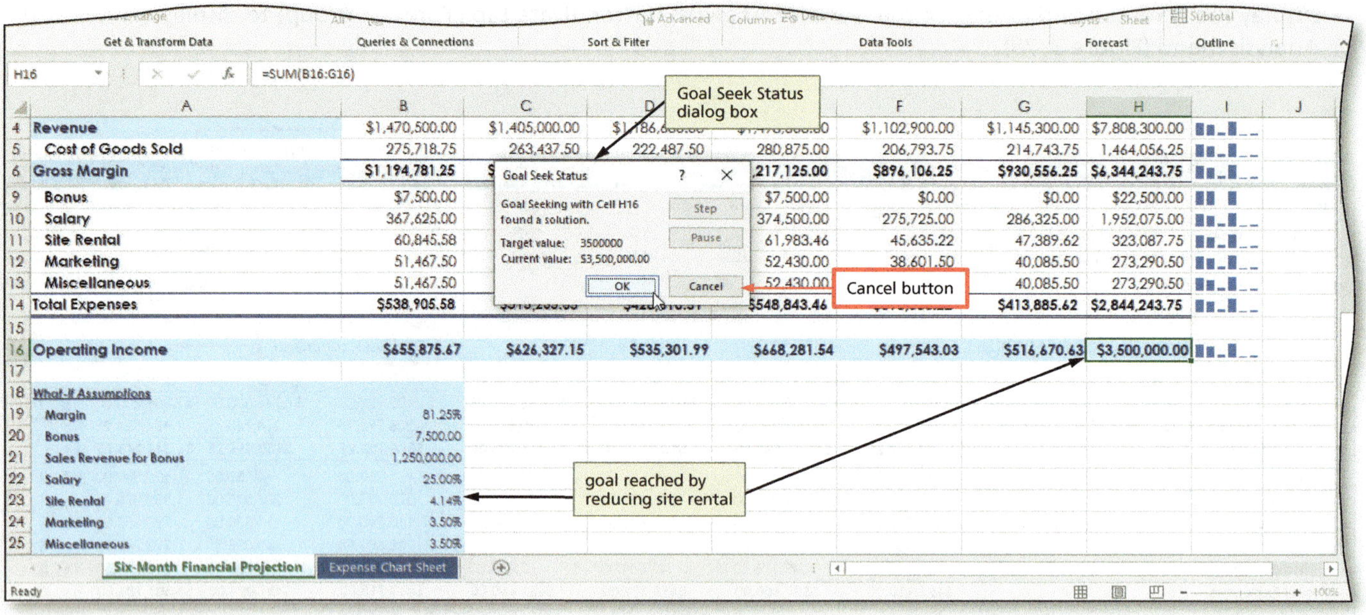

Figure 3–80

Q&A **What happens when I click OK?**
Excel changes cell H16 to the desired value of $3,500,000.00. More importantly, Excel changes the Site Rental assumption in cell B23 to 4.14% (Figure 3–80). Excel also displays the Goal Seek Status dialog box. If you click OK, Excel keeps the new values in the worksheet. If you click the Cancel button, Excel redisplays the original values.

4

- Click the Cancel button in the Goal Seek Status dialog box to redisplay the original values in the worksheet.

5

- Click the Split button (View tab | Window group) to remove the two panes from the window.

Insights

The Insights feature in Excel uses the Bing search engine and other Internet resources to help you locate more information about the content in your workbooks. One common use of this feature is to look up the definition of a word. When looking up a definition, Excel uses contextual data so that it can return the most relevant information.

To Use the Smart Lookup Insight

Smart Lookup locates useful information about text in your spreadsheet and then displays that information in the Search pane. **Why?** You want to locate additional information about the contents of your worksheet. The following steps use Smart Lookup to look up information about the text in cell A6.

1

- Select cell A6.
- Display the Review tab and then click Smart Lookup (Review tab | Insights group) to display the Search pane containing information about the text in the selected cell. If necessary, click the Turn on button to turn on intelligent services (Figure 3–81).

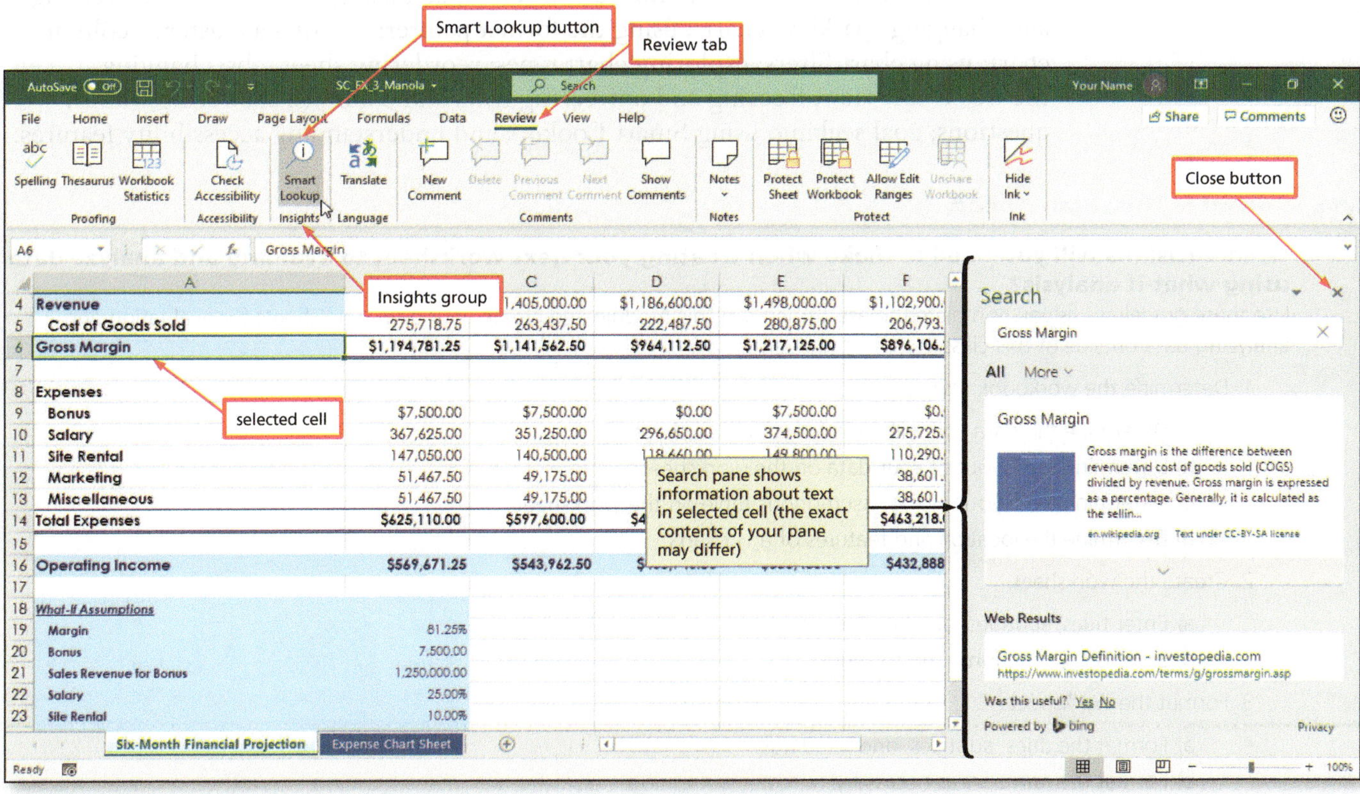

Figure 3–81

2

- **sam** Click the Close button on the Search pane to close the pane.
- If desired, sign out of your Microsoft account.
- Exit Excel.

Accessibility Features

Excel provides a utility that can be used to check a workbook for potential issues related to accessibility. **Accessibility** refers to the practice of removing barriers that may prevent individuals with disabilities from interacting with data or an app. To use the Check Accessibility command, click File on the ribbon to open Backstage view, click Info, click the 'Check for Issues' button, and then click Check Accessibility. Excel will check your workbook for content that could prove difficult for people with disabilities to read, either alone or with adaptive tools. The resulting report (Figure 3–82 shows an example) will identify issues and offer suggestions for addressing the reported issues.

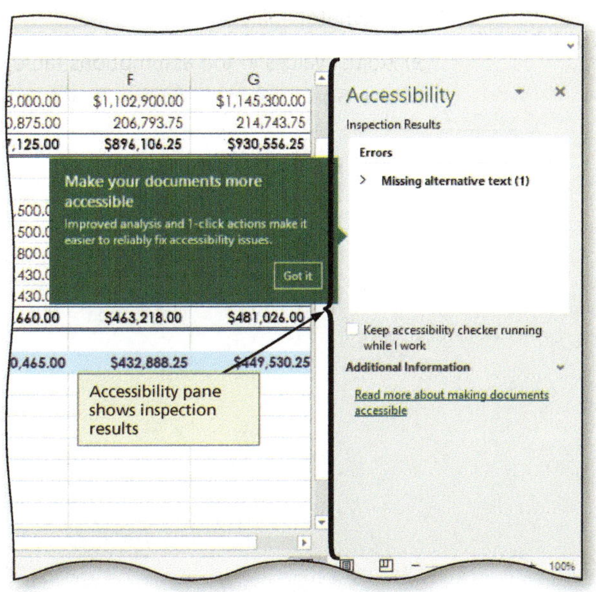

Figure 3–82

Summary

In this module, you learned how to use Excel to create a six-month financial projection workbook. Topics covered included rotating text in a cell; creating a series of month names; copying, pasting, inserting, and deleting cells; entering and formatting the system date; using absolute and mixed cell references; using the IF function; creating and changing sparkline charts; using the format painter; creating a clustered column chart; using chart filters; exploring chart types; reordering sheet tabs; changing the worksheet view; freezing and unfreezing rows and columns; answering what-if questions; goal seeking; using Smart Lookup; and understanding accessibility features.

Consider This: Plan Ahead

What decisions will you need to make when creating your next worksheet to evaluate and analyze data using what-if analysis?

Use these guidelines as you complete the assignments in this module and create your own worksheets for evaluating and analyzing data outside of this class.

1. Determine the workbook structure.
   a) Determine the data you will need for your worksheet.
   b) Determine the layout of your data on the worksheet.
   c) Determine the layout of the assumptions table on the worksheet.
   d) Determine the location and features of any charts.
2. Create the worksheet.
   a) Enter titles, subtitles, and headings.
   b) Enter data, functions, and formulas.
3. Format the worksheet.
   a) Format the titles, subtitles, and headings.
   b) Format the numbers as necessary.
   c) Format the text.
4. Create and use charts.
   a) Select data to chart.
   b) Select a chart type for selected data.
   c) Format the chart elements.
   d) Filter charts if necessary to view subsets of data.
5. Perform what-if analyses.
   a) Adjust values in the assumptions table to review scenarios of interest.
   b) Use Goal Seek to determine how to adjust a variable value to reach a particular goal or outcome.

Apply Your Knowledge

Reinforce the skills and apply the concepts you learned in this module.

Understanding Logical Tests and Absolute Cell Referencing

Note: To complete this assignment, you will be required to use the Data Files. Please contact your instructor for information about accessing the Data Files.

Instructions Part 1: For each of the following logical tests, indicate whether an IF function in Excel would return a value of True or False; given the following cell values: C2 = 41; H12 = 13; L3 = 32; M14 = 125; and G4 = 2.

1. C2 < H12 Returned value: ____________________
2. L3 = G4 Returned value: ____________________
3. M14 + 15 * H12 / 10 <= L3 Returned value: ____________________
4. M14 + G4 < H12 / C2 Returned value: ____________________
5. (C2 + H12) * 2 >= L3 – (L3 / 4) * 2 Returned value: ____________________
6. L3 + 300 > H12 * G4 + 10 Returned value: ____________________
7. G4 * M14 >= 2 * (M14 – 25) Returned value: ____________________
8. H12 = 10 * (C2 + 8) Returned value: ____________________

Instructions Part 2: Write cell L23 as a relative reference, absolute reference, mixed reference with the column varying, and mixed reference with the row varying.

____________ ____________ ____________ ____________

Instructions Part 3: Start Excel. Open the workbook called SC_EX_3-1.xlsx. The workbook you open contains sample data that you will reference to create formulas. You are to re-create the numerical grid pictured in Figure 3–83.

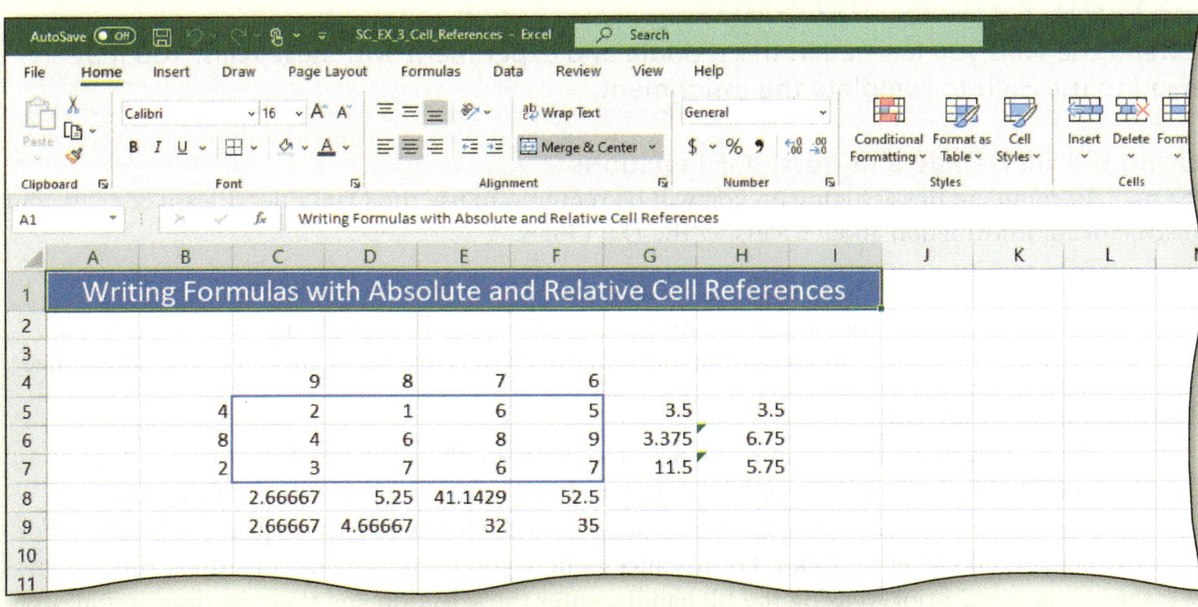

Figure 3–83

Continued >

Apply Your Knowledge *continued*

Perform the following tasks:

1. Enter a formula in cell G5 that divides the sum of cells C5 through F5 by cell B5. Write the formula so that when you copy it to cells G6:G7, Excel adjusts all the cell references according to the destination cells. Verify your formula by checking it against the values found in cells G5, G6, and G7 in Figure 3–83.
2. Enter a formula in cell C8 that divides the product of cells C5 through C7 by cell C4. Write the formula so that when you copy the formula to cells D8:F8, Excel adjusts all the cell references according to the destination cells. Verify your formula by checking it against the values found in cells C8, D8, E8, and F8 in Figure 3–83.
3. Enter a formula in cell C9 that divides the product of cells C5 through C7 by cell C4. Write the formula using an absolute cell reference so that when you copy the formula to cells D9:F9, cell C4 remains absolute. Verify your formula by checking it against the values found in cells C9, D9, E9, and F9 in Figure 3–83.
4. Enter a formula in cell H5 that divides the sum of cells C5:F5 by cell B5. Write the formula using an absolute cell reference so that when you copy the formula to cells H6 and H7, cell B5 remains absolute. Verify your formula by checking it with the values found in cells H5, H6, and H7 in Figure 3–83.
5. Apply the worksheet name, Cell References, to the sheet tab and apply the Blue, Accent 1, Darker 25% Theme color to the sheet tab.

   If requested by your instructor, add a dash followed by your name to the worksheet title in cell A1.
6. Save the revised workbook (shown in Figure 3–83) using the file name, SC_EX_3_Cell_References. Submit the revised workbook as specified by your instructor.
7. Exit Excel.
8. How would you rewrite the formula in cell H5 using relative and mixed cell references only, to come up with the same result as shown in Figure 3–83, and to produce the results currently shown in cells G6 and G7 in cells H6 and H7 when the formula in cell H5 is copied to those cells?

Extend Your Knowledge

Extend the skills you learned in this module and experiment with new skills. You may need to use Help to complete the assignment.

Using the Fill Handle and Nested IF Functions

Note: To complete this assignment, you will be required to use the Data Files. Please contact your instructor for information about accessing the Data Files.

Instructions Part 1: Start Excel. Open the workbook SC_EX_3-2.xlsx, which is located in the Data Files. The workbook you open contains starter data you will use to complete the workbook. You are to use the fill handle and enter functions as directed. If necessary, make Fill the active sheet.

Perform the following tasks:

1. Use the fill handle on one column at a time to propagate the 12 series through row 14, as shown in Figure 3–84. (Hint: Search in Help to learn more about the fill handle and Auto Fill.) In cells O2:O13, indicate the actions used with the fill handle to propagate the series. For instance, in cell O2, enter **`Drag`**. For instances where you need to select something other than the cell in row 2 prior to using the fill handle, enter the selection and then the drag action, **`A2:A3 Drag`** for example.

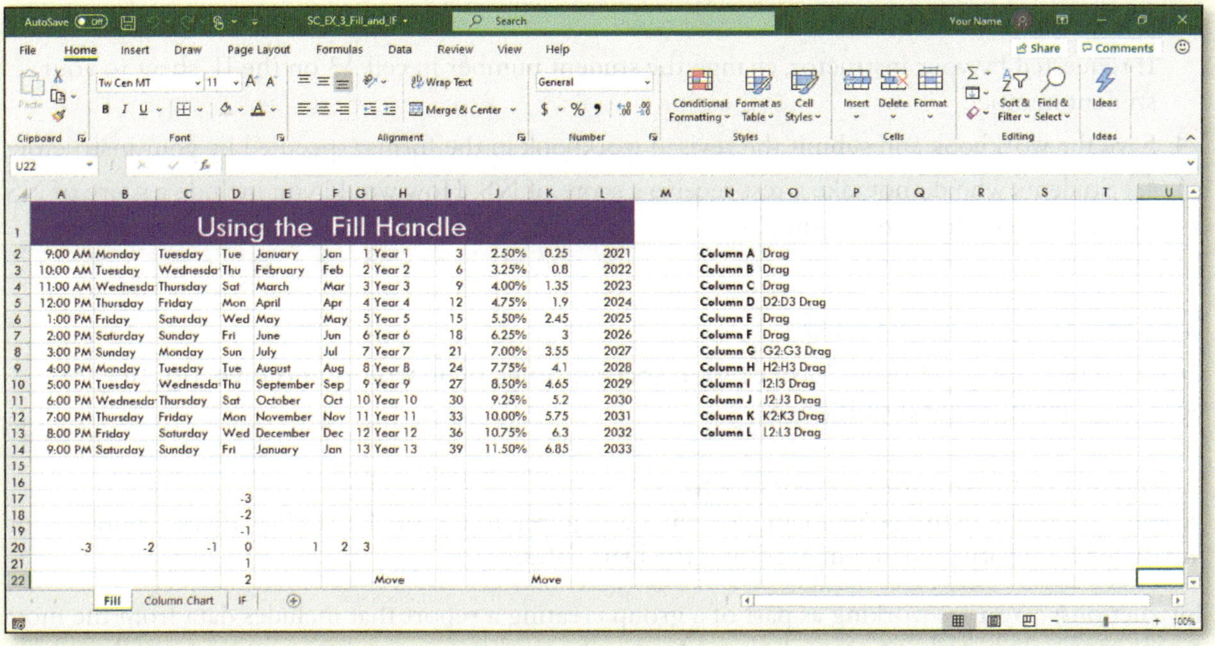

Figure 3–84

2. Select cell D20. While holding down CTRL, one at a time drag the fill handle three cells to the right, to the left, up, and down to generate four series of numbers beginning with zero and incremented by one.
3. Select cell H20. Point to the cell border so that the pointer changes to a plus sign with four arrows. Drag the pointer down to cell H22 to move the contents of cell H20 to cell H22.
4. If necessary, select cell H22. Point to the cell border so that the pointer changes to a plus sign with four arrows. While holding down CTRL, drag the pointer to cell K22 to copy the contents of cell H22 to cell K22.
5. Select cell K20. Drag the fill handle in to the center of cell K20 until that the cell is shaded and the cell contents are deleted.
6. Select cell range H2:I14, and insert a 3-D clustered column chart on a new sheet.
7. Change the chart title to Annual Breakdown.
8. Add a data table with legend keys to the chart. Change the chart colors to Colorful Palette 4.
9. Name the chart sheet, Column Chart, and move the sheet to follow the Fill sheet.
10. Save the workbook using the file name, SC_EX_3_Fill_and_IF.

Instructions Part 2: Switch to the IF sheet in the SC_EX_3_Fill_and_IF workbook.

1. Write an IF function in cell C3 that assigns a grade of "Pass" if the score in cell B3 is above 70, and a grade of "Fail" if the score in cell B3 is 70 or below. Copy this function to cells C4:C19.
2. Write a nested IF function in cell D3 that assigns a grade of A for scores between 90 and 100, a grade of B for scores between 80 and 89, a grade of C for scores between 70 and 79, and a grade of F for scores below 70. (Hint: Search in Help for nested IF when constructing your function.) Copy this function to cells D4:D19.
3. Calculate the average grade in cell B21. In cells C21 and D21, use a formula to determine whether the average grade is a passing grade, and the overall grade achieved by the class.

Continued >

Extend Your Knowledge *continued*

If requested by your instructor, change the student number in cell A3 on the IF sheet to your student number.

4. Save the workbook and submit the revised workbook in the format specified by your instructor.
5. Students who do not take a test receive a score of NS. How would you include a score of NS as a grade in each of Steps 1 and 2?

Expand Your World

Create a solution that uses cloud or web technologies by learning and investigating on your own from general guidance.

Analyzing and Graphing Census Data

Note: To complete this assignment, you will be required to use the Data Files. Please contact your instructor for information about accessing the Data Files.

Instructions: You are working as part of a group creating a report that includes data from the most recent census. Your task is to complete and format the worksheet using information from the census.gov website, chart the data, and make the chart available to your group using OneDrive. Start Excel. Open the workbook called SC_EX_3-3.xlsx, which is located in the Data Files. This workbook contains a basic structure to represent data from the last census.

Perform the following tasks:

1. Save the workbook using the file name, SC_EX_3_Census.
2. Identify three U.S. cities of your choice and enter the city and state names in cells A4, A5, and A6.
3. Open a web browser and navigate to the data.census.gov website. Use the most recent census data to locate the population, median age, number of housing units, and median income for each city. Enter the information into the respective cells in the worksheet, as shown in Figure 3–85 but using cities of your own choosing. If you are unable to locate the necessary data, either choose a different city or perform a search for another website containing the necessary data.

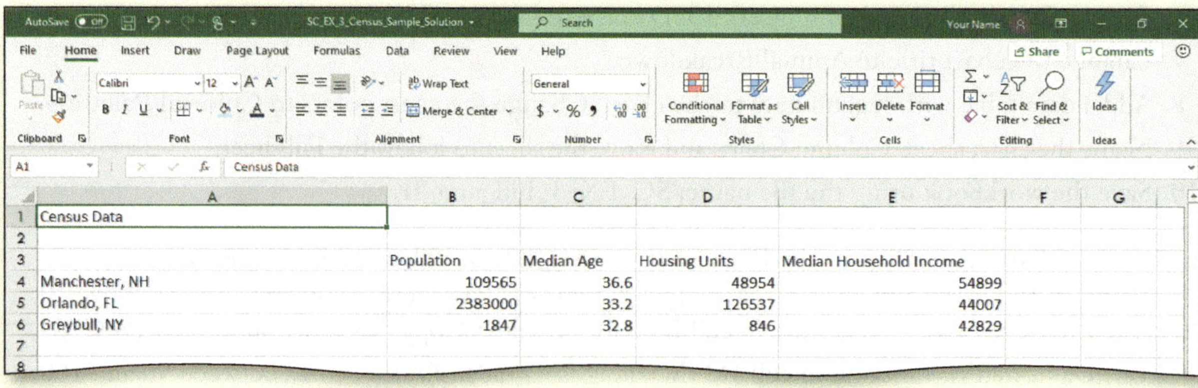

Figure 3–85

4. Format the worksheet using techniques you have learned to present the data in a visually appealing form.
5. Create charts that present the data for each of the four categories of data. Decide which chart types will best present the data. (Hint: If you are not sure which types to use, consider selecting

the data and using the Recommended Chart button to narrow down and preview suitable choices.) Place each chart on a separate sheet and format the charts to best present the data in a clear, attractive format.

6. Give each worksheet a descriptive name and color the tabs using theme colors. Reorder the sheets so that the data table appears first, followed by the charts.
7. If requested by your instructor, export the file to OneDrive.
8. Submit the revised workbook as specified by your instructor.
9. Justify your choice of chart types in Step 5. Explain why you selected these types over other suitable choices.

In the Lab

Design and implement a solution using creative thinking and problem-solving skills.

Comparing Transportation Costs

Problem: You are thinking about buying a new vehicle, and you want to make sure that you buy one that offers the highest fuel savings. You decide to research hybrid cars as well as gas-only cars. Your friends are also interested in your results. Together, you decide to research the fuel costs associated with various types of vehicles.

Perform the following tasks:

Part 1: Research the gas mileage for eight vehicles: four should run only on gas, and the others should be hybrid vehicles, combining gas and battery power. After you find the gas mileage for each vehicle, you will use formulas to calculate the fuel cost for one month, six months, and two years. Assume that in a typical month, you will drive 1,250 miles. Develop a worksheet following the general layout in Table 3–9 that shows the fuel cost analysis. Use the formulas listed in Table 3–10 and the concepts and techniques presented in this module to create the worksheet. You will need to find the average price of gas for your market. Add a chart showing the cost comparisons as an embedded chart.

Table 3–9 Fuel Cost Analysis

Vehicle	Miles Per Gallon	Fuel Cost 1 Month	Fuel Cost 6 Months	Fuel Cost 2 Years
Gas 1		Formula A	Formula B	Formula C
Gas 2		—	—	—
Gas 3		—	—	—
Gas 4		—	—	—
Hybrid 1		—	—	—
Hybrid 2		—	—	—
Hybrid 3		—	—	—
Hybrid 4		—	—	—
Assumptions				
Distance per Month	1,250			
Price of Gas				

Continued >

In the Lab *continued*

Table 3–10 Fuel Cost Analysis Formulas
Formula A = (Distance per Month / Miles per Gallon) * Price of Gas
Formula B = ((Distance per Month / Miles per Gallon) * Price of Gas) * 6
Formula C = ((Distance Per Month / Miles per Gallon) * Price of Gas) * 24

Part 2: You made several decisions while creating the workbook for this assignment: how to lay out the data in the worksheet and which chart types to use. What was the rationale behind each of these decisions? What other costs might you want to consider when making your purchase decision?

4 Financial Functions, Data Tables, and Amortization Schedules

Objectives

After completing this module, you will be able to:

- Assign a name to a cell and refer to the cell in a formula using the assigned name
- Determine the monthly payment of a loan using the financial function PMT
- Understand the financial functions PV (present value) and FV (future value)
- Create a data table to analyze data in a worksheet
- Create an amortization schedule
- Control the color and thickness of outlines and borders
- Add a pointer to a data table
- Analyze worksheet data by changing values
- Use range names and print sections of a worksheet
- Set print options
- Protect and unprotect cells in a worksheet
- Hide and unhide worksheets and workbooks
- Use the formula checking features of Excel

Introduction

Two of the more powerful aspects of Excel are its wide array of functions and its capability of organizing answers to what-if questions. In this module, you will learn about financial functions such as the PMT function, which allows you to determine a monthly payment for a loan, and the PV function, which allows you to determine the present value of an investment.

In earlier modules, you learned how to analyze data by using the Excel recalculation feature and goal seeking. This module introduces an additional what-if analysis tool, called a data table. A **data table** is a range of cells that shows the resulting values when one or more input values are varied in a formula. You use a data table to automate data analyses and organize the results returned by Excel. Another important loan analysis tool is an amortization schedule. An **amortization schedule** is a schedule that shows loan balances and the payment amounts applied to the principal and interest for each payment period.

In previous modules, you learned how to print in a variety of ways. In this module, you will learn additional methods of printing using range names and a print area.

Finally, this module introduces you to cell protection, hiding and unhiding worksheets and workbooks, and formula checking. **Cell protection** ensures that users do not inadvertently change values that are critical to the worksheet. Hiding portions of a workbook lets you show only the parts of the workbook that the user needs to see. The **formula checker** examines the formulas in a workbook in a manner similar to the way the spelling checker examines a workbook for misspelled words.

Project: Mortgage Payment Calculator with Data Table and Amortization Schedule

The project in this module follows proper design guidelines and uses Excel to create the worksheet shown in Figure 4–1. Cranford Credit Union provides mortgages (loans) for homes and other types of property. The credit union's chief financial officer has asked for a workbook that loan officers and customers can use to calculate mortgage payment information, review an amortization schedule, and compare mortgage payments for varying annual interest rates. To ensure that the loan officers and customers do not delete the formulas in the worksheet, they have asked that cells in the worksheet be protected so that they cannot be changed accidentally.

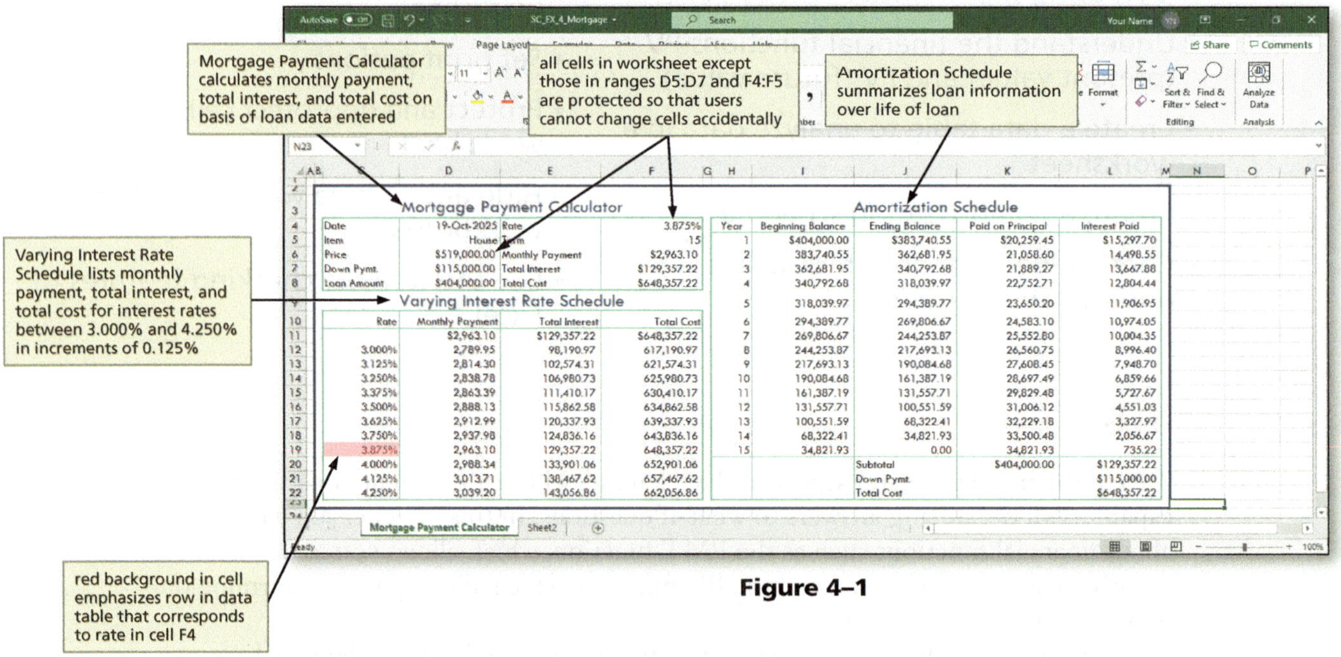

Figure 4–1

The requirements document for the Cranford Mortgage Payment Calculator worksheet is shown in Figure 4–2. It includes the needs, source of data, summary of calculations, and special requirements.

Worksheet Title	Cranford Mortgage Payment Calculator
Needs	An easy-to-read worksheet that 1. Determines the monthly payment, total interest, and total cost for a mortgage. 2. Shows a data table that answers what-if questions based on changing interest rates. 3. Highlights the rate in the data table that matches the actual interest rate. 4. Shows an amortization schedule that lists annual summaries of interest paid, principal paid, and balance on principal.
Source of Data	Data supplied by the credit union includes interest rate and term of mortgage. Data supplied by the customer includes item to be purchased, price, and down payment. All other data is calculated or created in Excel.
Calculations	1. The following calculations must be made for each mortgage: a. Mortgage Amount = Price – Down Payment b. Monthly Payment = PMT function c. Total Interest = 12 × Term × Monthly Payment – Loan Amount d. Total Cost = 12 × Term × Monthly Payment + Down Payment 2. The Amortization Schedule involves the following calculations: a. Beginning Balance = Loan Amount b. Ending Balance = PV function or zero c. Paid on Principal = Beginning Balance – Ending Balance d. Interest Paid = 12 × Monthly Payment – Paid on Principal or 0 e. Paid on Principal Subtotal = SUM function f. Interest Paid Subtotal = SUM function
Special Requirements	1. Assign names to the ranges of the three major worksheet components separately and together to allow the worksheet components to be printed separately or together easily. 2. Use locked cells and worksheet protection to prevent loan officers and customers from inadvertently making changes to formulas and functions contained in the worksheet.

Figure 4–2

In addition, using a sketch of the worksheet can help you visualize its design. The sketch of the worksheet consists of titles, column and cell headings, the location of data values, and a general idea of the desired formatting (Figure 4–3).

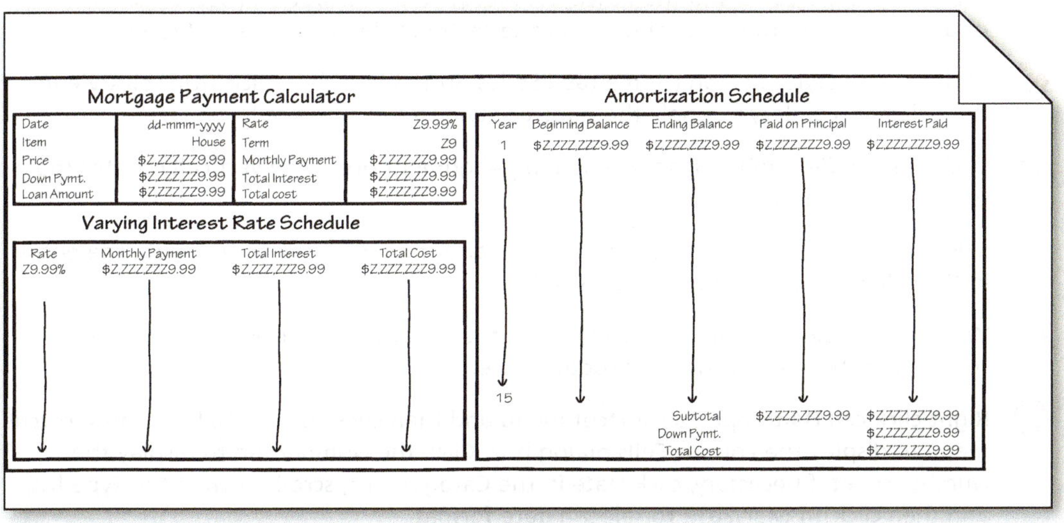

Figure 4–3

BTW
Good Worksheet Design
Consider creating worksheets with an eye toward reusing them in the future. Carefully design worksheets as if they will be on display and evaluated by your fellow workers. Smart worksheet design starts with visualizing the results you need. A well-designed worksheet often is used for many years.

As shown in the worksheet sketch in Figure 4–3, the three basic sections of the worksheet are the Mortgage Payment Calculator on the upper-left side, the Varying Interest Rate Schedule data table on the lower-left side, and the Amortization Schedule on the right side. The worksheet will be created in this order.

With a good understanding of the requirements document, an understanding of the necessary decisions, and a sketch of the worksheet, the next step is to use Excel to create the worksheet.

In this module, you will learn how to create and use the workbook shown in Figure 4–1.

BTW
Ribbon and Screen Resolution
Excel may change how the groups and buttons within the groups appear on the ribbon, depending on the screen resolution of your computer. Thus, your ribbon may look different from the ones in this book if you are using a screen resolution other than 1366 x 768.

To Apply a Theme to the Worksheet

The following steps apply the Droplet theme to the workbook.

1. sam Start Excel and create a blank workbook in the Excel window.
2. Apply the Droplet theme to the workbook.

To Enter the Section and Row Titles and System Date

BTW
Global Formatting
To assign formats to all the cells in all the worksheets in a workbook, click the Select All button, right-click a sheet tab, and click 'Select All Sheets' on the shortcut menu. Next, assign the formats. To deselect the worksheets, hold down SHIFT and click the Sheet1 tab or select Ungroup sheets on the shortcut menu. You also can select a cell or a range of cells and then select all worksheets to assign formats to that cell or a range of cells on all worksheets in a workbook.

The next step is to enter the Mortgage Payment Calculator section title, row titles, and system date. The Mortgage Payment Calculator section title also will be changed to the Title cell style and vertically middle-aligned. The following steps enter the section title, row titles, and system date.

1. Select cell C3 and then enter `Mortgage Payment Calculator` as the section title.

   Q&A **Why did I not begin creating the worksheet in cell A1?**
   Two rows at the top of the worksheet and two columns on the left of the worksheet will be left blank to provide a border around the worksheet.

2. Select the range C3:F3 and then click the Merge & Center button (Home tab | Alignment group) to merge and center the section title in the selected range.
3. Click the Cell Styles button (Home tab | Styles group) and then click Title cell style in the Cell Styles gallery to apply the selected style to the active cell.
4. Click the Middle Align button (Home tab | Alignment group) to vertically center the text in the selected cell.
5. Select cell C4, type `Date` as the row title, and then press TAB to complete the entry in the cell and select the cell to the right.
6. With cell D4 selected, type `=NOW()` and then click the Enter button to add a function to the cell that displays today's date.
7. Right-click cell D4 to open a shortcut menu and then click Format Cells on the shortcut menu to display the Format Cells dialog box. Click the Number tab to display the Number sheet if necessary, click Date in the Category list, scroll down in the Type list, and then click 14-Mar-2012 to select a date format.
8. Click OK (Format Cells dialog box) to close the Format Cells dialog box.
9. Enter the following text in the indicated cells:

BTW
Touch Mode Differences
The Office and Windows interfaces may vary if you are using touch mode. For this reason, you might notice that the function or appearance of your touch screen differs slightly from this module's presentation.

Cell	Text	Cell	Text
		E4	Rate
C5	Item	E5	Term
C6	Price	E6	Monthly Payment
C7	Down Pymt.	E7	Total Interest
C8	Loan Amount	E8	Total Cost

To Adjust the Column Widths and Row Heights

To make the worksheet easier to read, the width of columns A and B will be decreased and used as a separator between the left edge of the worksheet and the row headings. Using a column(s) as a separator between sections on a worksheet is a technique used by spreadsheet specialists. The width of columns C through F will be increased so that the intended values fit. The height of row 3, which contains the title, will be increased so that it stands out. The height of rows 1 and 2 will be decreased to act as visual separators for the top of the calculator.

1. Click column heading A and then drag through column heading B to select both columns. Position the pointer on the right boundary of column heading B and then drag to the left until the ScreenTip indicates Width: 0.85 (11 pixels) to change the width of both columns.

Q&A **What if I am unable to drag to set the exact column widths and row heights specified?** Depending on your display settings, you may be unable to set the exact column widths and row heights by dragging. In this case, right-click the column or row heading to resize, click Column Width (for columns) or Row Height (for rows) to display the Column Width or Row Height dialog box, type the exact column width or row height, and then click OK.

2. Position the pointer on the right boundary of column heading C and then drag to the right until the ScreenTip indicates Width: 12.00 (101 pixels) to change the column width.

3. Click column heading D to select it and then drag through column headings E and F to select multiple columns. Position the pointer on the right boundary of column heading F and then drag until the ScreenTip indicates Width: 16.00 (133 pixels) to change multiple column widths.

4. Click row heading 1 to select it and then drag through row heading 2 to select both rows. Position the pointer on the bottom boundary of row heading 2 and then drag until the ScreenTip indicates Height: 8.25 (11 pixels).

5. Select an empty cell to deselect the selected rows (Figure 4–4).

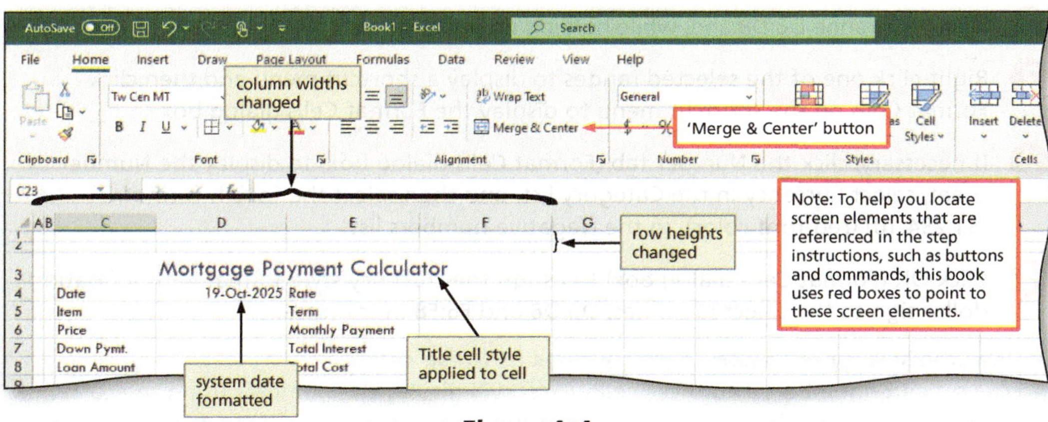

Figure 4–4

To Change the Sheet Tab Name

The following steps change the Sheet1 sheet tab name to a descriptive name and then save the workbook.

1. Double-click the Sheet1 tab and then enter `Mortgage Payment Calculator` as the sheet tab name.

2. Save the workbook on your hard drive, OneDrive, or location that is most appropriate to your situation using `SC_EX_4_Mortgage` as the file name.

Q&A **Why should I save the workbook at this time?**
You have performed many tasks while creating this workbook and do not want to risk losing work completed thus far.

Creating Cell Names

A **cell name** is a name you assign to a cell or range. You can then use that name in formulas in place of the cell or range address. Using names instead of addresses makes formulas easier to understand. Using names also lets you build formulas more quickly because you can select them quickly using the Name box (shown in Figure 4–7). Clicking the name will select the corresponding cell or range, and highlight the cell or range on the worksheet. Names are global to the workbook. That is, a name assigned to a cell or cell range on one worksheet in a workbook can be used on other worksheets in the same workbook to reference the named cell or range. You can assign names to cells, ranges, formulas, and constants.

To assign names to selected cells, you can use the Define Name button (Formulas tab | Defined Names group). But worksheets often have column titles at the top of each column and row titles to the left of each row that describe the data within the worksheet, and you can use these titles to create names. If you make a mistake while creating a name, click the Name Manager button (Formulas tab | Defined Names group) to display the Name Manager dialog box. Select the range to edit or delete, and then click the appropriate button to edit or delete the selected range.

BTW
Cell References in Formulas
Are you tired of writing formulas that are difficult to decipher because of cell references? The Name Manager can help add clarity to your formulas by allowing you to assign names to cells. You then can use the names, such as Rate, rather than the cell reference, such as D2, in the formulas you create. To access the Name Manager, click the Name Manager button (Formulas tab | Defined Names group).

To Format Cells before Entering Values

While you usually format cells after you enter values, Excel also allows you to format cells before you enter the values. The following steps assign the currency style format with a floating dollar sign to the ranges D6:D8 and F6:F8 before the values are entered.

1. Select the range D6:D8 and, while holding down CTRL, select the nonadjacent range F6:F8.

2. Right-click one of the selected ranges to display a shortcut menu and then click Format Cells on the shortcut menu to display the Format Cells dialog box.

3. If necessary, click the Number tab (Format Cells dialog box) to display the Number sheet, select Currency in the Category list, and then select the fourth format, ($1,234.10) (red font color), in the Negative numbers list.

4. Click OK (Format Cells dialog box) to assign the currency style format with a floating dollar sign to the selected ranges, D6:D8 and F6:F8 in this case.

Q&A **What will happen when I enter values in these cells?**
As you enter numbers into these cells, Excel will display the numbers using the currency style format. You also could have selected the range C6:F8 rather than the nonadjacent ranges and assigned the currency style format to this range, which includes text. The currency style format has no impact on text in a cell.

BTW
When to Format
Excel lets you format cells (1) before you enter data; (2) when you enter data, through the use of format symbols; (3) incrementally after entering sections of data; and (4) after you enter all the data. Experienced users usually format a worksheet in increments as they build the worksheet, but occasions do exist when it makes sense to format cells before you enter any data.

To Enter the Loan Data

As shown in the Source of data section of the requirements document in Figure 4–2, five items make up the loan data in the worksheet: the item to be purchased, the price of the item, the down payment, the interest rate, and the term (number of years) over which the loan is paid back. The following steps enter the loan data.

1. Select cell D5. Type `House` and then click the Enter button in the formula bar to enter text in the selected cell.
2. With cell D5 still active, click the Align Right button (Home tab | Alignment group) to right-align the text in the selected cell.
3. Select cell D6 and then enter `519000` for the price of the house.
4. Select cell D7 and then enter `115000` for the down payment.
5. Select cell F4 and then enter `3.875%` for the interest rate.
6. Select cell F4, if necessary, and then click the Increase Decimal button (Home tab | Number group) once to increase the number of decimal places to three.

Q&A **How can I decrease the number of decimal places?**
You can click the Decrease Decimal button (Home tab | Number group) to decrease the number of decimal places.

7. Select cell F5 and then enter `15` for the number of years in the term (Figure 4–5).

Q&A **Why are the entered values already formatted?**
The values in cells D6 and D7 in Figure 4–5 are formatted using the currency style with two decimal places because you assigned this format to the cells prior to entering the values. Because you typed the percent sign (%) after typing 3.875 in cell F4, Excel formatted the interest rate using the percentage style with two decimal places (thus, the value originally appeared as 3.88). Using the Increase Decimal button increased the number of visible decimal places to three.

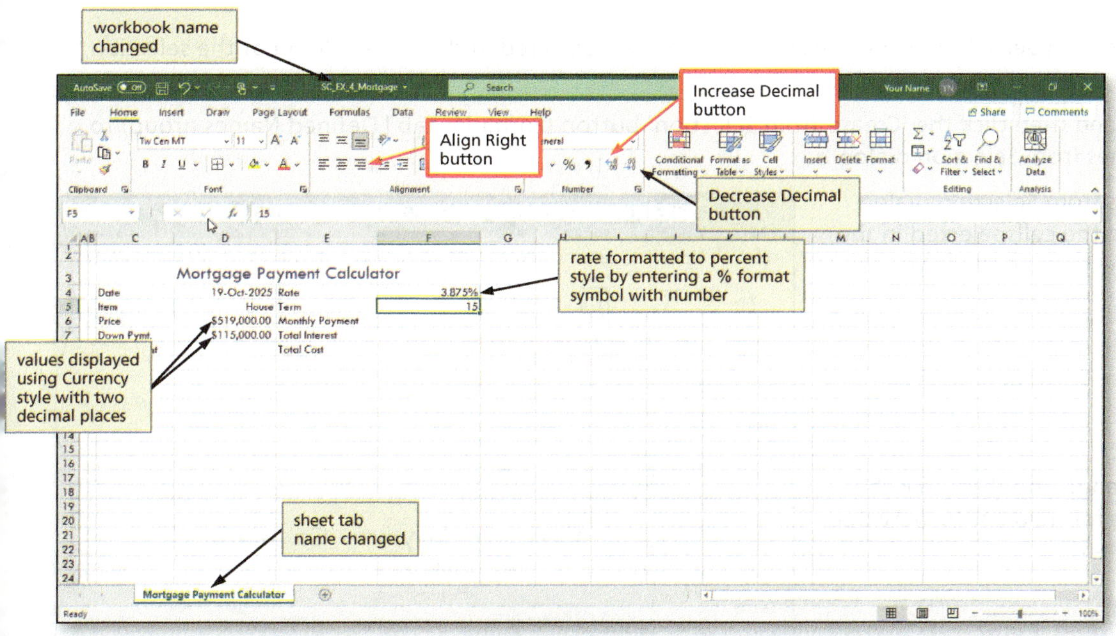

Figure 4–5

BTW
Entering Percentages
When you format a cell to display percentages, Excel assumes that whatever you enter into that cell in the future will be a percentage. Thus, if you enter the number .5, Excel translates the value as 50%. A potential problem arises, however, when you start to enter numbers greater than or equal to one. For instance, if you enter the number 25, do you mean 25% or 2500%? If you want Excel to treat the number 25 as 25% and Excel interprets the number 25 as 2500%, then click Options in Backstage view. When the Excel Options dialog box appears, click Advanced in the left pane, and make sure the 'Enable automatic percent entry' check box in the right pane is selected.

BTW
Entering Interest Rates
An alternative to requiring the user to enter an interest rate as a percentage, such as 3.875%, is to allow the user to enter the interest rate as a number without a percent sign (3.875) and then divide the interest rate by 1,200, rather than 12.

To Create Names Based on Row Titles

Why? Naming a cell that you plan to reference in a formula helps make the formula easier to read and remember. For example, the loan amount in cell D8 is equal to the price in cell D6 minus the down payment in cell D7. According to what you learned in earlier modules, you can enter the loan amount formula in cell D8 as =D6 – D7. By naming cells D6 and D7 using the corresponding row titles in cells C6 and C7, however, you can enter the loan amount formula as =Price – Down_Pymt., which is clearer and easier to understand than =D6 – D7. In addition to assigning a name to a single cell, you can follow the same steps to assign a name to a range of cells. The following steps assign the row titles in the range C6:C8 to their adjacent cell in column D and assign the row titles in the range E4:E8 to their adjacent cell in column F.

1

- Select the range C6:D8.
- Display the Formulas tab.
- Click the 'Create from Selection' button (Formulas tab | Defined Names group) to display the Create Names from Selection dialog box (Figure 4–6).

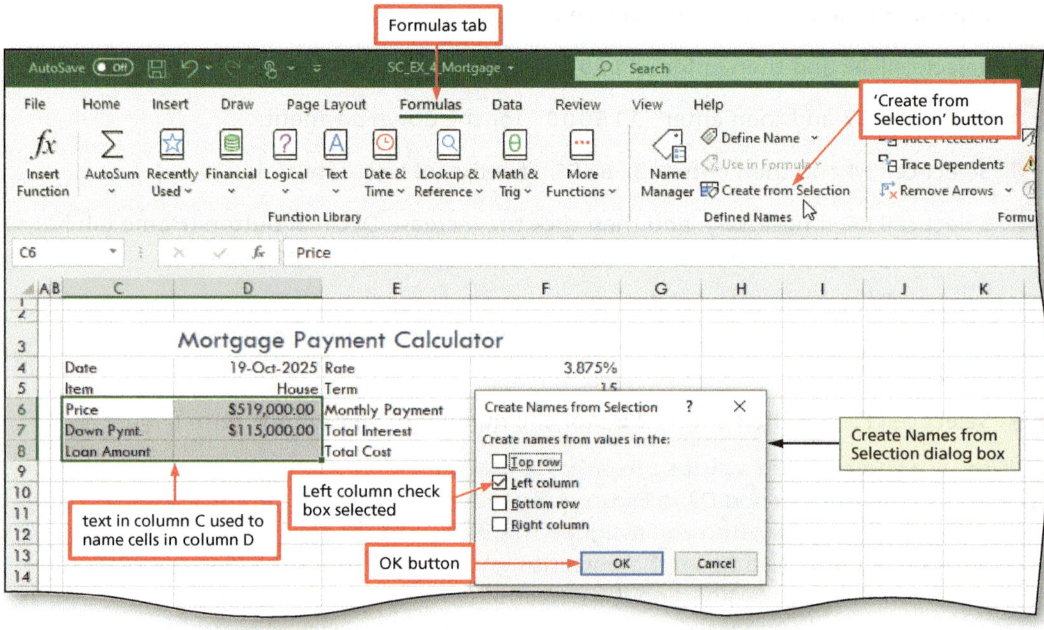

Figure 4–6

2

- Click OK (Create Names from Selection dialog box) to name the cells selected in the right column of the selection, D6:D8 in this case.
- Select the range E4:F8 and then click the 'Create from Selection' button (Formulas tab | Defined Names group) to display the Create Names from Selection dialog box.
- Click OK (Create Names from Selection dialog box) to assign names to the cells selected in the right column of the selection, F4:F8 in this case.

Q&A **Are names absolute or relative cell references?**
Names are absolute cell references. This is important to remember if you plan to copy formulas that contain names rather than cell references.

- Deselect the selected range and then click the Name box arrow in the formula bar to view the created names (Figure 4–7).

Q&A **Is a cell name valid when it contains a period, as with the Down_Pymt. cell name?**
Yes. Periods and underscore characters are allowed in cell names. A cell name may not begin with a period or an underscore, however.

Are there any limitations on cell names?
Names may not be longer than 255 characters.

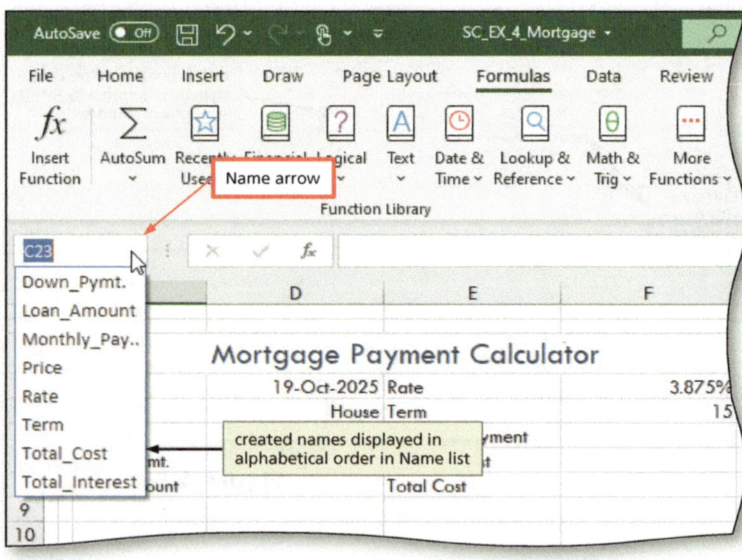

Figure 4–7

Other Ways

1. Select cell or range, type name in Name box, press ENTER
2. Select cell or range, click Define Name button (Formulas tab | Defined Names group), type name, click OK (New Name dialog box)
3. Select cell or range, click Name Manager button (Formulas tab | Defined Names group), click New (Name Manager dialog box), type name, click OK (New Name dialog box), click Close button (Name Manager dialog box)
4. Select range, press CTRL+SHIFT+F3

Consider This

What do you do if a cell you want to name does not have a text item in an adjacent cell?
If you want to assign a name that does not appear as a text item in an adjacent cell, use the Define Name button (Formulas tab | Defined Names group) or select the cell or range and then enter the name in the Name box in the formula bar.

Consider This

What do I need to consider when naming cells, and how can I use named cells?
You can use the assigned names in formulas to reference cells in the ranges D6:D8 or F4:F8. Excel is not case sensitive with respect to names of cells. You can enter the cell names in formulas in either uppercase or lowercase letters. To use a name that consists of two or more words in a formula, you should replace any space with the underscore character (_), as this is a commonly used standard for creating cell names. For example, the name, Down Pymt., can be written as down_pymt. or Down_Pymt. when you want to reference the adjacent cell D7. The Name Manager dialog box appears when you click the Name Manager button. The Name Manager dialog box allows you to create new names and edit or delete existing names.

To Enter the Loan Amount Formula Using Names

Why? Once you have created names, you can use them instead of cell references in formulas because they are easier to remember. To determine the loan amount, enter the formula =Price – Down_Pymt. in cell D8. Excel makes this easier by including any cell names you have assigned in the list of functions. The following steps enter the formula using names.

1

- Select cell D8.
- Type **=p** and then scroll down the Formula AutoComplete list until you see the Price entry (Figure 4–8).

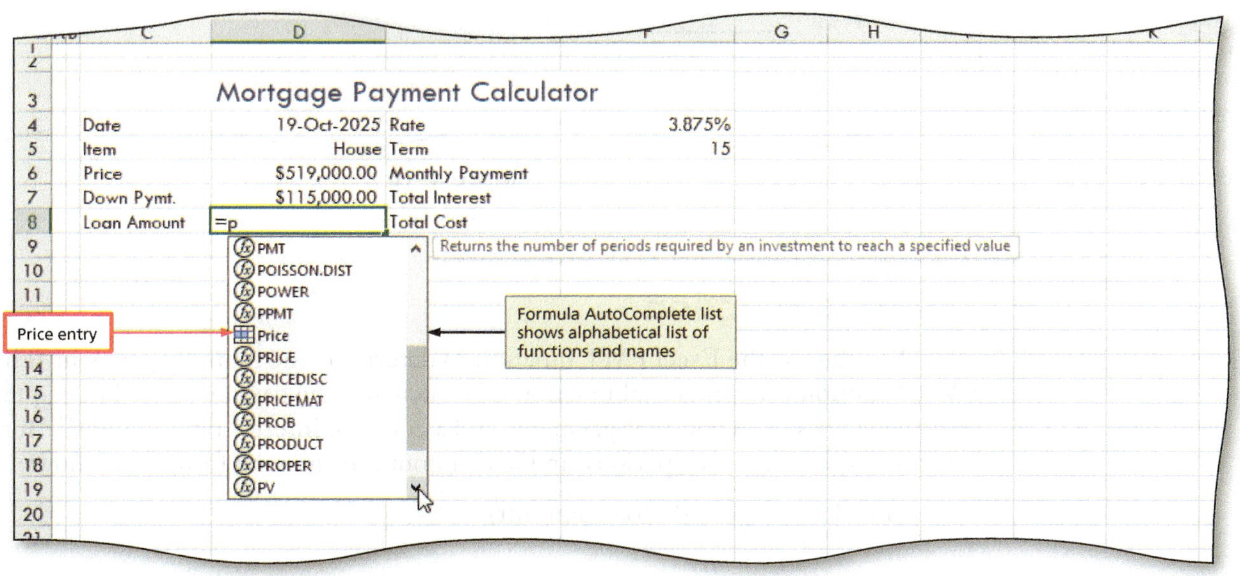

Figure 4–8

2

- Double-click Price to enter it in cell D8.
- Type **-d**.
- Scroll down to and double-click Down_Pymt. in the Formula AutoComplete list to select it and display the formula in both cell D8 and the formula bar using the cell names instead of the cell references (Figure 4–9).

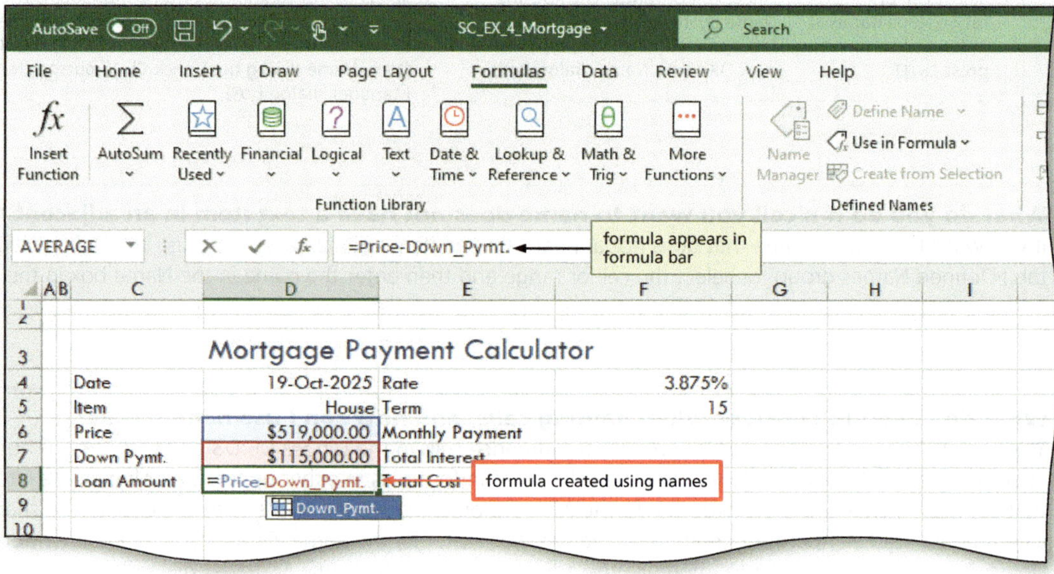

Figure 4–9

3

- Click the Enter button to assign the formula =Price – Down_Pymt. to the selected cell, D8 (Figure 4–10).

Q&A **What happens if I enter my formula using Point mode instead of using names?**
If you enter a formula using Point mode and click a cell that has an assigned name, Excel will insert the name of the cell rather than the cell reference.

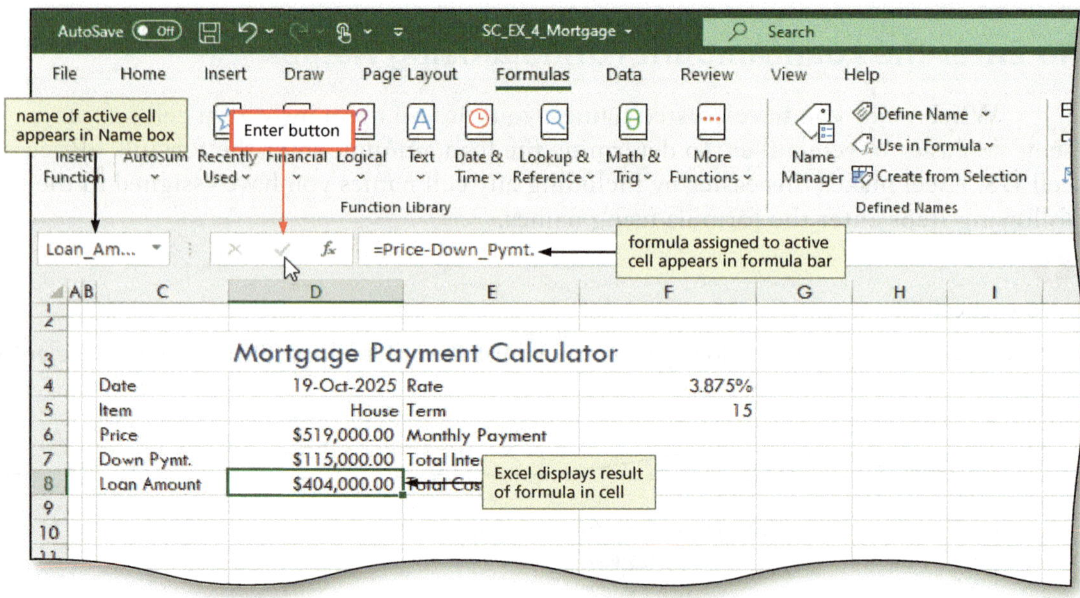

Figure 4–10

The PMT Function

You can use the Excel PMT function to determine the monthly payment. The **PMT function** is the financial function that calculates the payment schedule required to repay a loan based on constant payments and a constant interest rate. The PMT function has three arguments: rate, periods, and loan amount. Its general form is as follows:

=PMT (rate, periods, loan amount)

where rate is the interest rate per payment period, periods is the number of payments over the life of the loan, and loan amount is the amount of the loan.

In the worksheet shown in Figure 4–10, Excel displays the annual interest rate in cell F4. Financial institutions, however, usually calculate interest on a monthly basis. The rate value in the PMT function is, therefore, Rate / 12 (cell F4 divided by 12), rather than just Rate (cell F4). The periods (or number of payments) in the PMT function is 12 * Term (12 times cell F5) because each year includes 12 months, or 12 payments.

Excel considers the value returned by the PMT function to be a debit and, therefore, returns a negative number as the monthly payment. To display the monthly payment as a positive number, begin the function with a negative sign instead of an equal sign. The PMT function for cell F6 is:

–PMT(Rate/12, 12*Term, Loan_Amount)

monthly interest rate

number of payments

loan amount

To Enter the PMT Function

Why? The next step in building the mortgage payment calculator is to determine the monthly payment for the mortgage. The following steps use the keyboard, rather than Point mode or the Insert Function dialog box, to enter the PMT function to determine the monthly payment in cell F6.

1

- Select cell F6.
- Type the function `-pmt(Rate/12, 12*Term, Loan_Amount` in cell F6, which also displays in the formula bar (Figure 4–11).

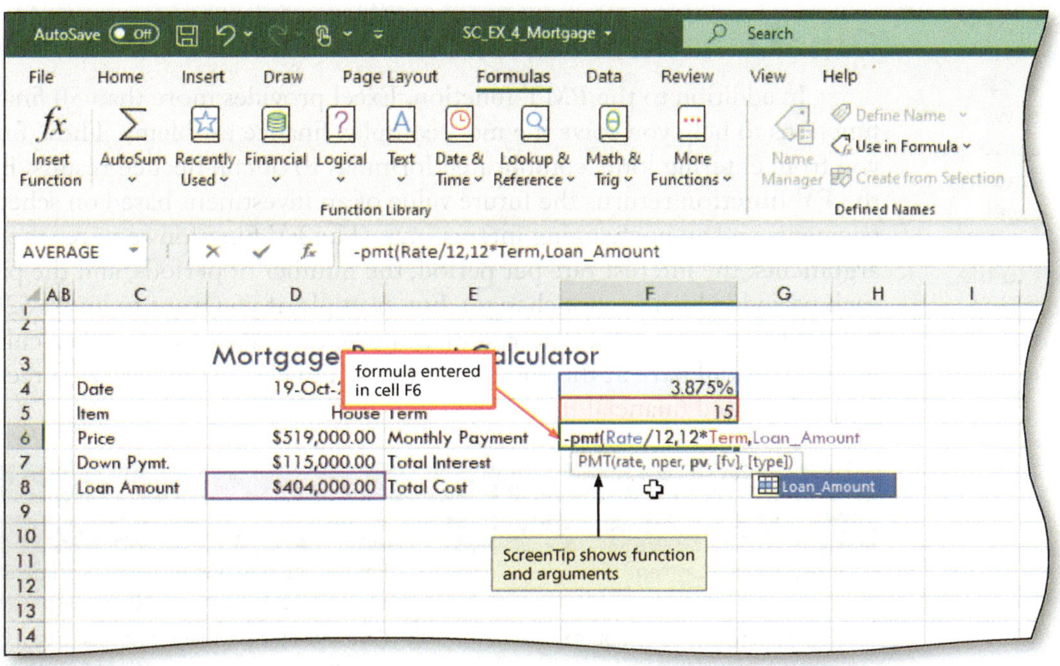

Figure 4–11

Q&A

What happens as I begin to enter the function?
The ScreenTip shows the general form of the PMT function (after you type the opening parenthesis). The arguments in brackets in the ScreenTip are optional and not required for the computation required in this project. The Formula AutoComplete list (Figure 4–8) shows functions and cell names that match the letters that you type on the keyboard. You can type the complete cell name, such as Loan_Amount, or double-click the cell name in the list. When you have completed entering the function and click the Enter button or press ENTER, Excel will add the closing parenthesis to the function. Excel also may scroll the worksheet to the right in order to accommodate the ScreenTip.

2

- Click the Enter button in the formula bar to complete the function (Figure 4–12).

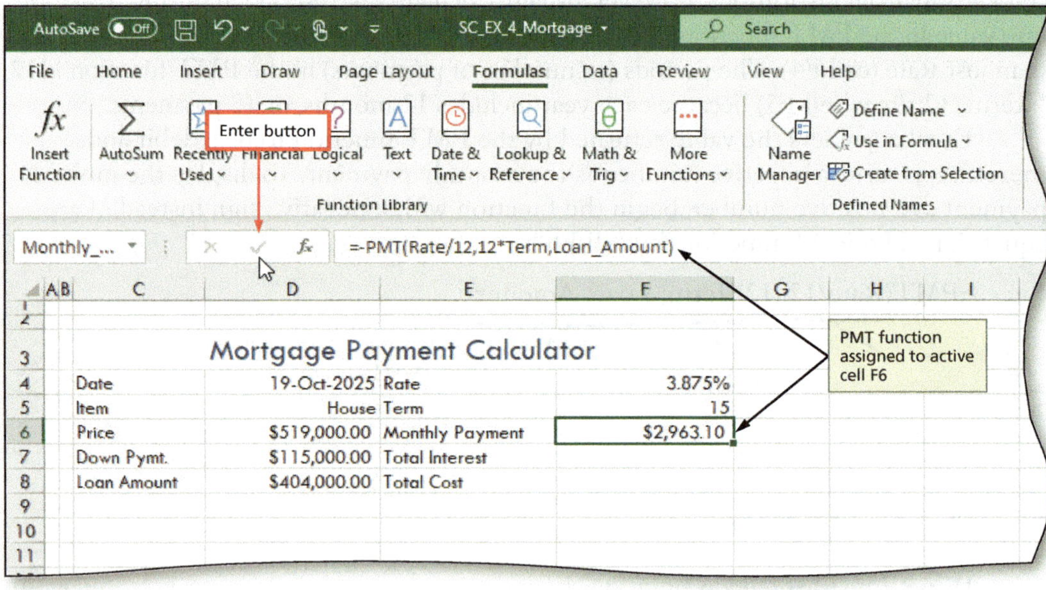

Figure 4–12

Other Ways

1. Click Financial button (Formulas tab | Function Library group), select PMT function, enter arguments, click OK
2. Click Insert Function button in formula bar, select Financial category, select PMT function, click OK, enter arguments, click OK (Function Arguments dialog box)

Other Financial Functions

In addition to the PMT function, Excel provides more than 50 financial functions to help you solve the most complex finance problems. These functions save you from entering long, complicated formulas to obtain needed results. For example, the **FV function** returns the future value of an investment based on scheduled payments and an unchanging interest rate. The FV function requires the following arguments: the interest rate per period, the number of periods, and the payment made each period (which cannot change). For example, if you want to invest $200 per month for five years at an annual interest rate of 6%, the FV function will calculate how much money you will have at the end of five years. Table 4–1 summarizes three of the more frequently used financial functions.

Table 4–1 Frequently Used Financial Functions

Function	Description
FV (rate, periods, payment)	Returns the future value of an investment based on periodic, constant payments and a constant interest rate.
PMT (rate, periods, loan amount)	Calculates the payment for a loan based on the loan amount, constant payments, and a constant interest rate.
PV (rate, periods, payment)	Returns the present value of an investment. The present value is the total amount that a series of future payments now is worth.

To Determine the Total Interest and Total Cost

The next step is to determine the total interest the borrower will pay on the loan (the lending institution's gross profit on the loan) and the total cost the borrower will pay for the item being purchased. The total interest (cell F7) is equal to the number of payments times the monthly payment, minus the loan amount:

=12*Term*Monthly_Payment–Loan_Amount

The total cost of the item to be purchased (cell F8) is equal to the price plus the total interest:

=Price+Total_Interest

The following steps enter formulas to determine the total interest and total cost using names.

1. Select cell F7, use the keyboard to enter the formula **=12 * term * monthly_ payment – loan_amount** to determine the total interest, and then click the Enter button.
2. Select cell F8 and then use the keyboard to enter the formula **=price + total_ interest** to determine the total cost.
3. Select an empty cell to deselect cell F8.
4. Save the workbook again on the same storage location with the same file name (Figure 4–13).

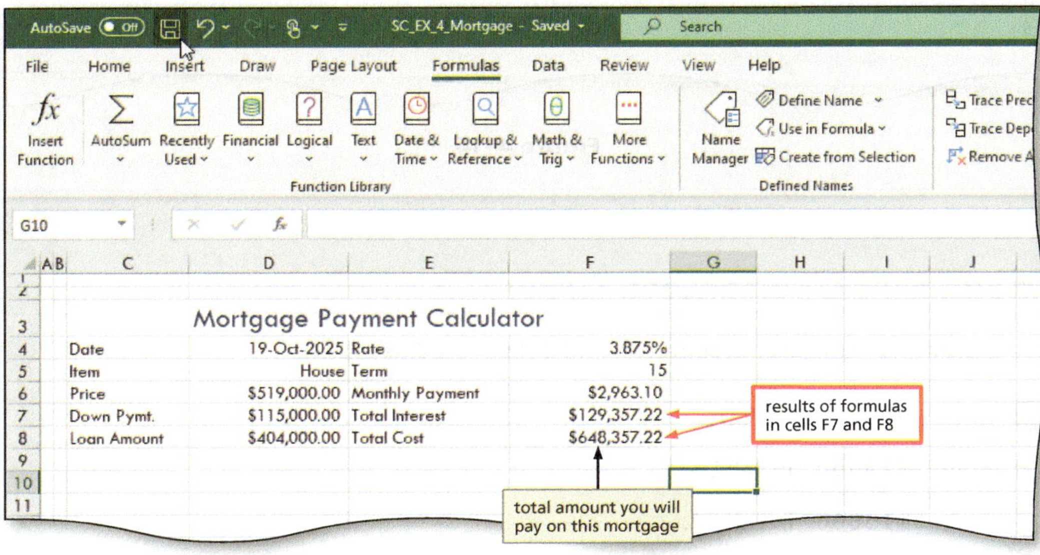

Figure 4–13

BTW

Range Finder

Remember to check all your formulas carefully. You can double-click a cell containing a formula and Excel will use Range Finder to highlight the cells that provide data for that formula. While Range Finder is active, you can drag the outlines from one cell to another to change the cells referenced in the formula, provided the cells have not been named.

BTW

Testing a Worksheet

It is good practice to test the formulas in a worksheet repeatedly until you are confident they are correct. Use data that tests the limits of the formulas. For example, you should enter negative numbers, zero, and large positive numbers when testing formulas.

To Enter New Loan Data

Assume you want to purchase a condominium for $200,000. You have $50,000 for a down payment and you want the loan for a term of 10 years. Cranford Credit Union currently is charging 4.125% interest for a 10-year loan. The following steps enter the new loan data.

1. Enter **Condominium** in cell D5.
2. Enter **200000** in cell D6.

3. Enter `50000` in cell D7.
4. Enter `4.125%` in cell F4.
5. Enter `10` in cell F5 and then select an empty cell to recalculate the loan information in cells D8, F6, F7, and F8 (Figure 4–14).

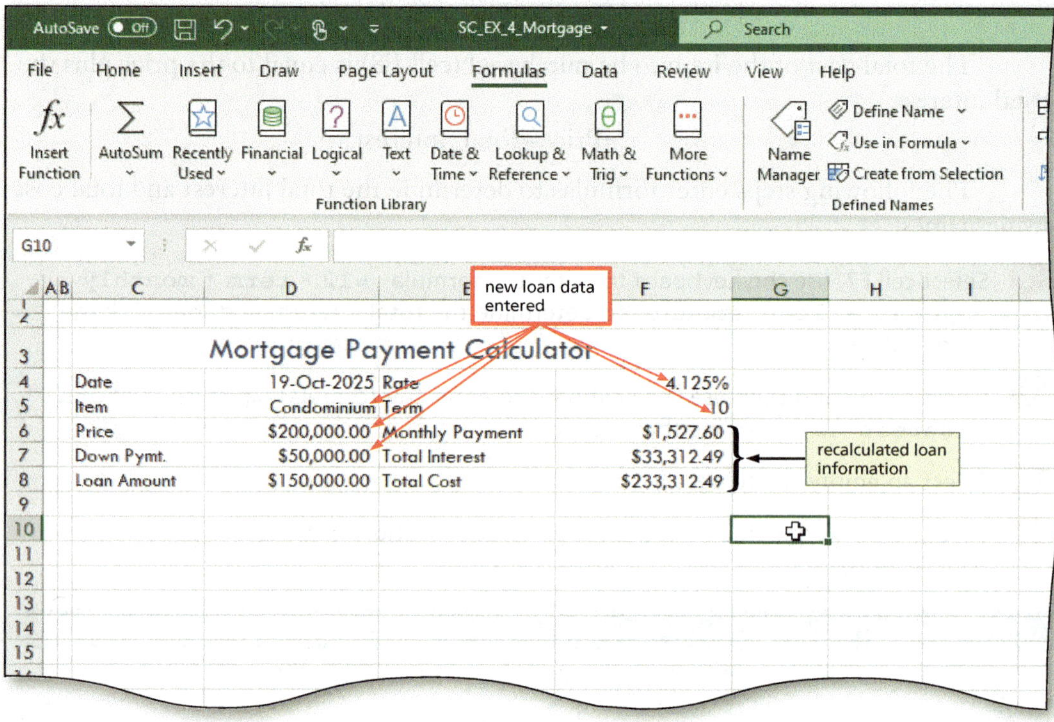

Figure 4–14

To Enter the Original Loan Data

The following steps reenter the original loan data.

1. Enter `House` in cell D5.
2. Enter `519000` in cell D6.
3. Enter `115000` in cell D7.
4. Enter `3.875` in cell F4.
5. Enter `15` in cell F5 and then select cell C10 to complete the entry of the original loan data.

Q&A

What is happening on the worksheet as I enter the original data?
Excel instantaneously recalculates all formulas in the worksheet each time you enter a value. Once you have re-entered all the initial data, Excel displays the original loan information, as shown in Figure 4–13.

Can the Undo button on the Quick Access Toolbar be used to change back to the original data?
Yes. The Undo button must be clicked five times, once for each data item. You also can click the Undo arrow and drag through the first five entries in the Undo list.

Using a Data Table to Analyze Worksheet Data

You already have seen that if you change a value in a cell, Excel immediately recalculates any formulas that reference the cell directly or indirectly. But what if you want to compare the results of the formula for several different values? Writing down or trying to remember all the answers to the what-if questions would be unwieldy. If you use a data table, however, Excel will organize the answers in the worksheet for you.

A data table is a range of cells that shows the resulting values when one or more input values are varied in a formula. Data tables have one purpose: to organize the answers to what-if questions. Data tables must be built in an unused area of the worksheet (in this case, the range C9:F22). Figure 4–15a illustrates the content needed for the Data Table command. A **one-input data table** (also called a **one-variable data table**) is a range of cells that shows resulting values when one input value in a formula is changed (in this worksheet, cell F4, the interest rate). Excel then calculates the results of one or more formulas and fills the data table with the results. Figure 4–15b shows the completed one-input data table.

The interest rates that will be used to analyze the loan formulas in this project range from 3.000% to 4.250%, increasing in increments of 0.125%. The one-input data table shown in Figure 4–15b illustrates the impact of varying the interest rate on three formulas: the monthly payment (cell F6), total interest paid (cell F7), and the total cost of the item to be purchased (cell F8). The series of interest rates in column C are called input values.

BTW

Expanding Data Tables

The data table created in this module is relatively small. You can continue the series of percentages to the bottom of the worksheet and insert additional formulas in columns to create as large a data table as you want.

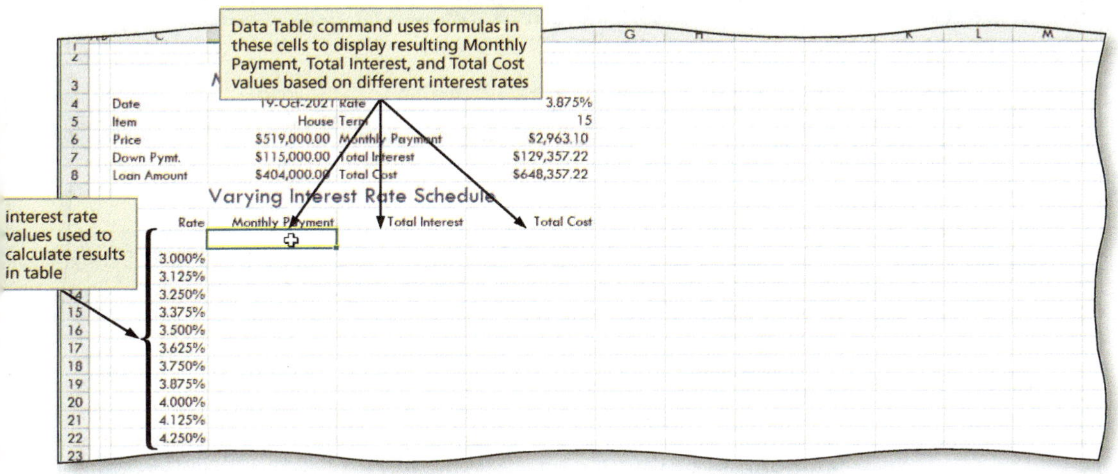

Figure 4–15 (a)

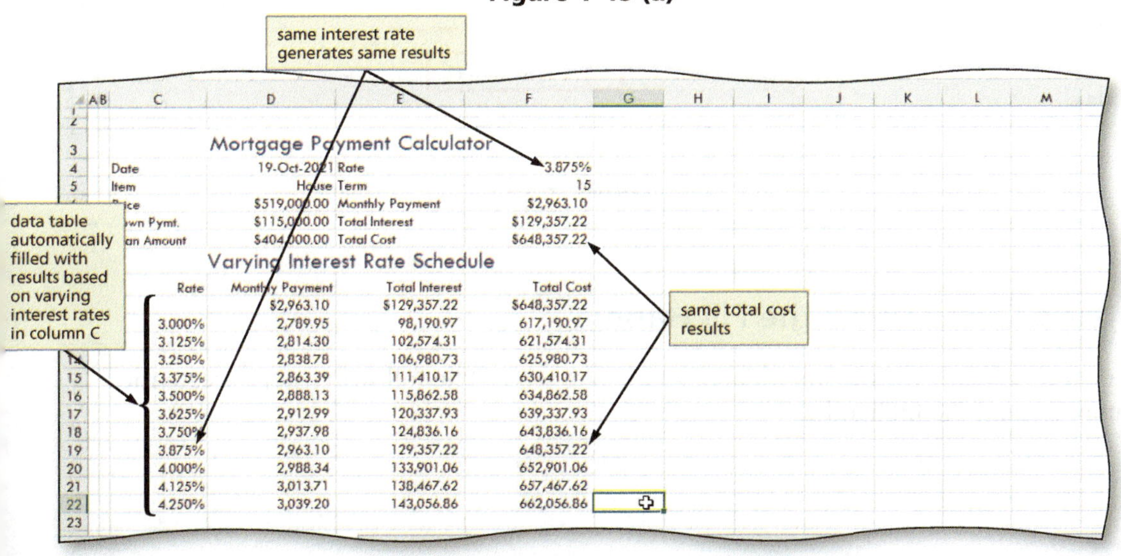

Figure 4–15 (b)

To Enter the Data Table Title and Column Titles

The first step in constructing the data table shown in Figure 4–15b is to enter the data table section title and column titles in the range C9:F10 and adjust the heights of rows 9 and 10.

1. Select cell C9 and then enter **`Varying Interest Rate Schedule`** as the data table section title.
2. Select cell C3 and then click the Format Painter button (Home tab | Clipboard group) to copy the format of the cell. Click cell C9 to apply the copied format to the cell.
3. Type **`Rate`** in cell C10, **`Monthly Payment`** in cell D10, **`Total Interest`** in cell E10, and **`Total Cost`** in cell F10 to create headers for the data table. Select the range C10:F10 and right-align the column titles.
4. Position the pointer on the bottom boundary of row heading 9 and then drag up until the ScreenTip indicates Height: 20.25 (27 pixels).
5. Position the pointer on the bottom boundary of row heading 10 and then drag down until the ScreenTip indicates Height: 17.25 (23 pixels).
6. Click cell C12 to deselect the range C10:F10 (Figure 4–16).

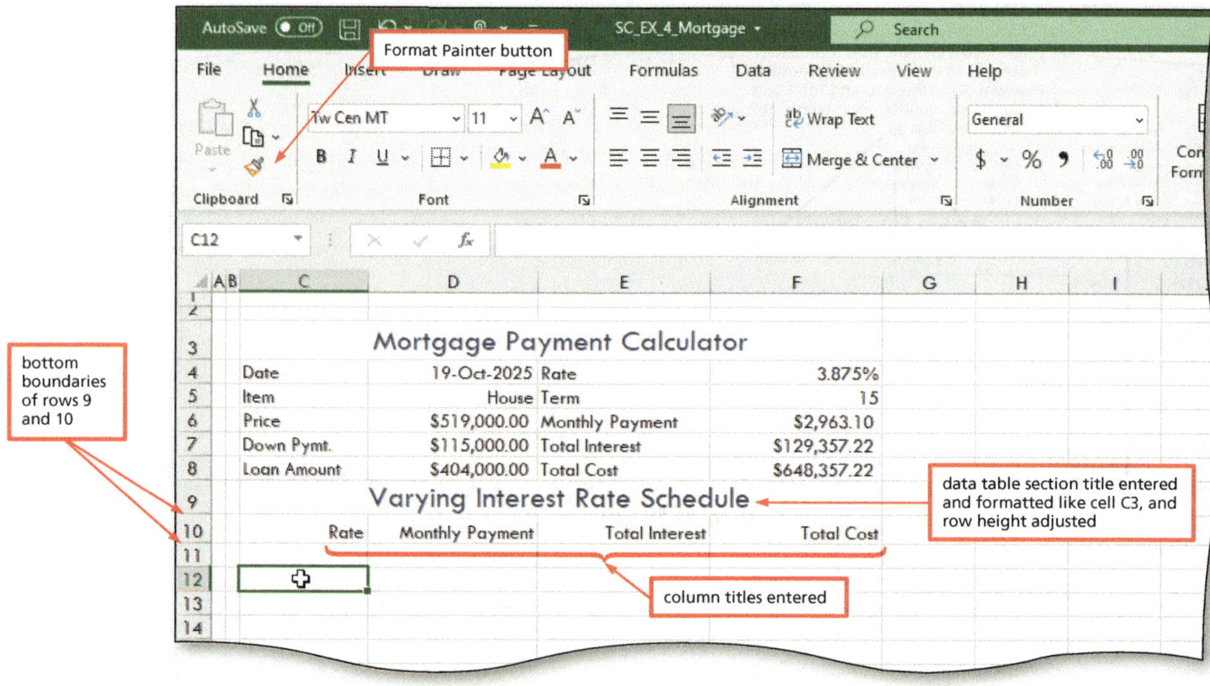

Figure 4–16

To Create a Percentage Series Using the Fill Handle

Why? These percentages will serve as the input data for the data table. The following steps create the percentage series in column C using the fill handle.

1

- With cell C12 selected, enter `3.0%` as the first number in the series.
- Select cell C13 and then enter `3.125%` as the second number in the series.
- Select the range C12:C13.
- Drag the fill handle through cell C22 to specify the fill area as indicated by the green border (Figure 4–17). Do not lift your finger or release the mouse button.

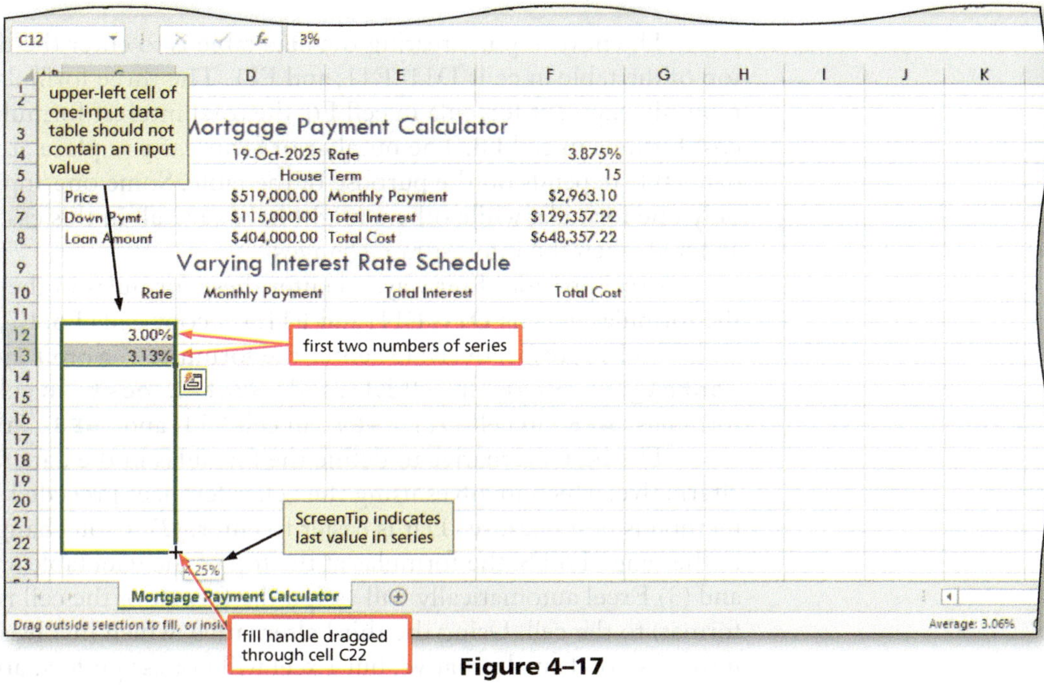

Figure 4–17

2

- Lift your finger or release the mouse button to generate the percentage series, in this case from 3.00% to 4.25%.
- Click the Increase Decimal button (Home tab | Number group) to increase the number of decimal places shown to 3.
- Click cell D11 to deselect the selected range, C12:C22 in this case (Figure 4–18).

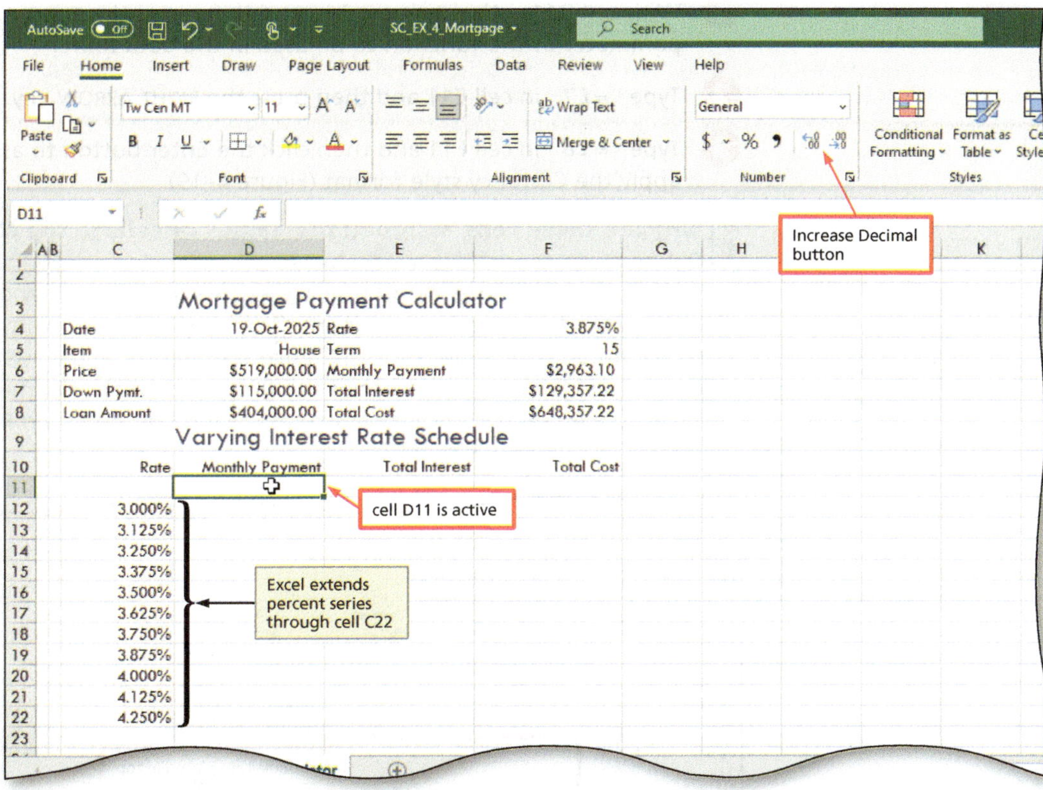

Figure 4–18

Q&A

What is the purpose of the percentages in column C?

The percentages in column C represent different annual interest rates, which will be used when calculating the data table. The series begins in cell C12, not cell C11, because the cell immediately to the upper left of the formulas in a one-input data table should not include an input value.

Other Ways

1. Right-drag fill handle in direction to fill, click Fill Series on shortcut menu

To Enter the Formulas in the Data Table

The next step in creating the data table is to enter the three formulas at the top of the table in cells D11, E11, and F11. The three formulas are the same as the monthly payment formula in cell F6, the total interest formula in cell F7, and the total cost formula in cell F8. The number of formulas you place at the top of a one-input data table depends on the purpose of the table. Some one-input data tables will have only one formula, while others might have several. In this case, three formulas are affected when the interest rate changes.

Excel provides four ways to enter these formulas in the data table: (1) retype the formulas in cells D11, E11, and F11; (2) copy cells F6, F7, and F8 to cells D11, E11, and F11, respectively; (3) enter the formulas **`=monthly_payment`** in cell D11, **`=total_interest`** in cell E11, and **`=total_cost`** in cell F11; or (4) enter the formulas **`=F6`** in cell D11, **`=F7`** in cell E11, and **`=F8`** in cell F11.

The best alternative to define the formulas in the data table is the fourth alternative, which involves using the cell references preceded by an equal sign. This method is best because (1) it is easier to enter; (2) if you change any of the formulas in the range F6:F8, the formulas at the top of the data table are immediately updated; and (3) Excel automatically will assign the format of the cell reference (currency style format) to the cell. Using the third alternative, which involves using cell names, is nearly as good an alternative, but Excel will not assign formatting to the cells when you use cell names. The following steps enter the formulas of the data table in row 11.

1. With cell D11 active, type **`=f6`** and then press the RIGHT ARROW key to enter the first parameter of the function to be used in the data table.
2. Type **`=f7`** in cell E11 and then press the RIGHT ARROW key.
3. Type **`=f8`** in cell F11 and then click the Enter button to assign the formulas and apply the Currency style format (Figure 4–19).

Q&A

Why are these cells assigned the values of cells in the Mortgage Payment Calculator area of the worksheet?

It is important to understand that the entries in the top row of the data table (row 11) refer to the formulas that the loan officer and customer want to evaluate using the series of percentages in column C. Furthermore, recall that when you assign a formula to a cell, Excel applies the format of the first cell reference in the formula to the cell. Thus, Excel applies the currency style format to cells D11, E11, and F11 because that is the format of cells F6, F7, and F8.

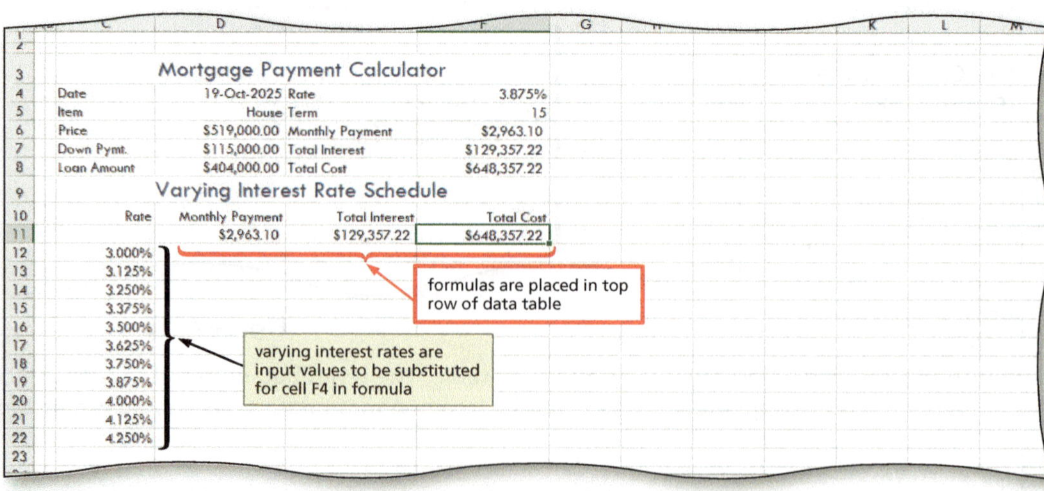

Figure 4–19

To Define a Range as a Data Table

After creating the interest rate series in column C and entering the formulas in row 11, the next step is to define the range C11:F22 as a data table. Cell F4 is the input cell for the data table, which means cell F4 is the cell in which values from column C in the data table are substituted in the formulas in row 11. **Why?** You want Excel to generate the monthly payment, monthly interest, and total cost for the various interest rates.

1

- Select the range C11:F22 as the range in which to create the data table.
- Display the Data tab and then click the 'What-If Analysis' button (Data tab | Forecast group) to display the What-If Analysis menu (Figure 4–20).

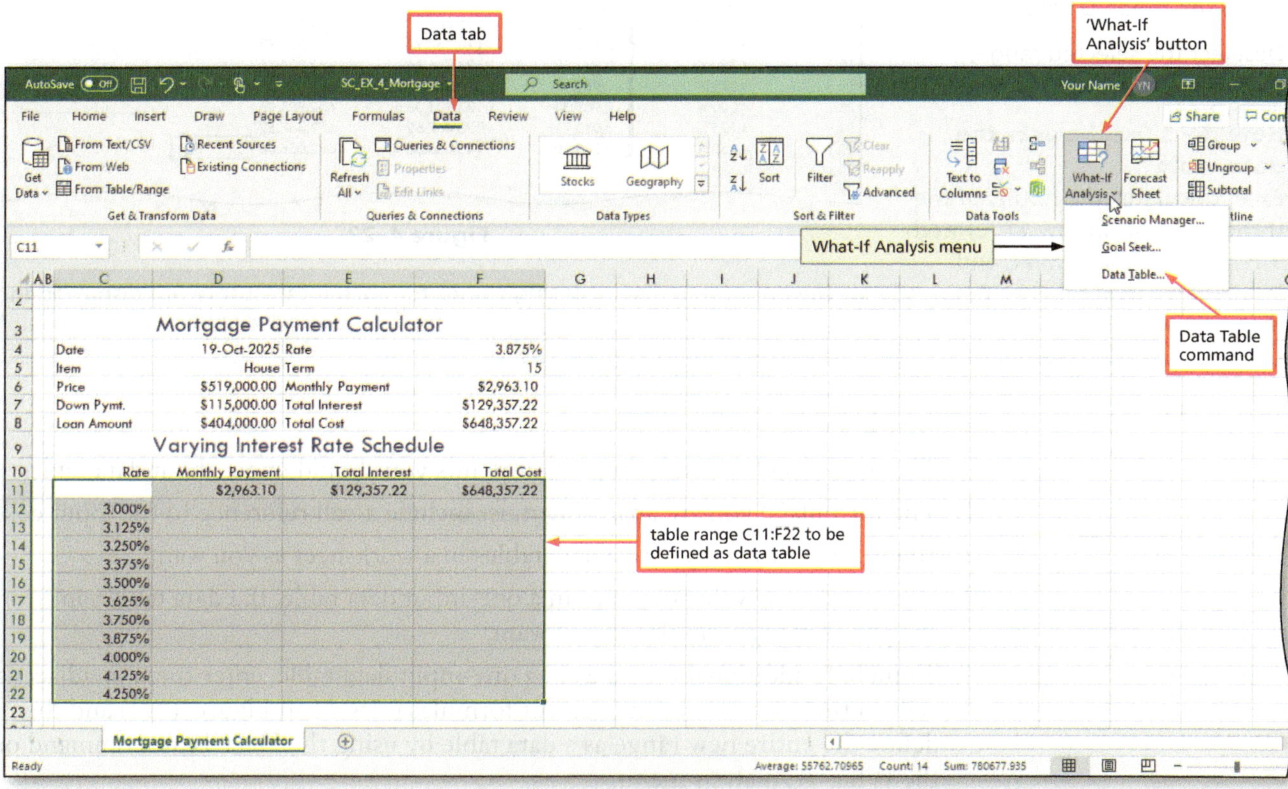

Figure 4–20

2

- Click Data Table on the What-If Analysis menu to display the Data Table dialog box.
- Click the 'Column input cell' box (Data Table dialog box) and then click cell F4 in the Mortgage Payment Calculator section of the spreadsheet to select the input cell for the data table (Figure 4–21).

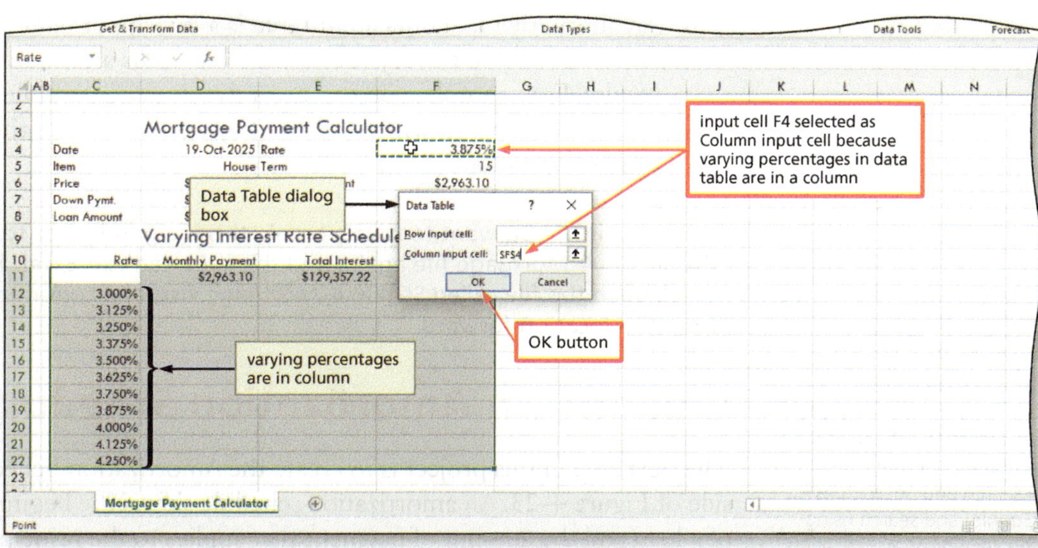

Figure 4–21

Q&A **What is the purpose of clicking cell F4?**
The purpose of clicking cell F4 is to select it for the Column input cell. A marquee surrounds the selected cell F4, indicating it will be the input cell in which values from column C in the data table are substituted in the formulas in row 11. $F$4 now appears in the 'Column input cell' box in the Data Table dialog box.

3

- Click OK (Data Table dialog box) to create the data table.
- Apply the currency style with no currency symbol and the fourth format in the Negative numbers list to the range D12:F22.
- Deselect the selected range, D12:F22 in this case (Figure 4–22).

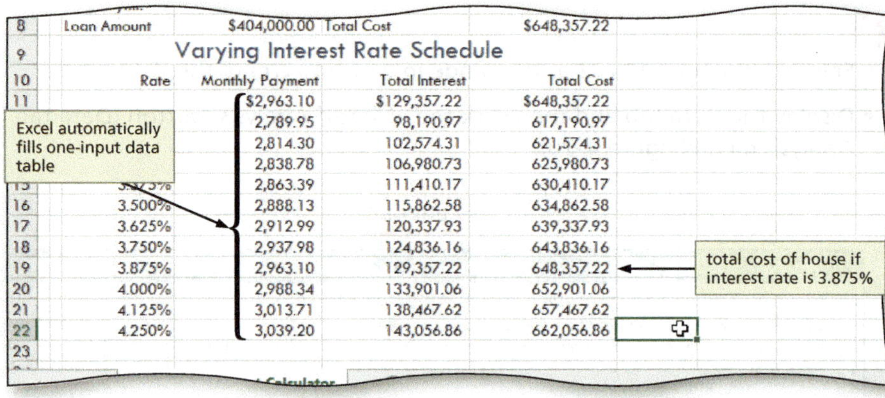

Figure 4–22

Q&A **How does Excel create the data table?**
Excel calculates the results of the three formulas in row 11 for each interest rate in column C and immediately fills columns D, E, and F of the data table. The resulting values for each interest rate are displayed in the corresponding rows.

More about Data Tables

The following list details important points you should know about data tables:

1. The formula(s) you are analyzing must include a cell reference to the input cell.
2. You can have as many active data tables in a worksheet as you want.
3. While only one value can vary in a one-input data table, the data table can analyze as many formulas as you want.
4. To include additional formulas in a one-input data table, enter them in adjacent cells in the same row as the current formulas (row 11 in Figure 4–22) and then define the entire new range as a data table by using the Data Table command on the What-If Analysis menu.
5. You delete a data table as you would delete any other item on a worksheet. That is, select the data table and then press DELETE.
6. An alternative to a one-input table is a two-input data table. A **two-input data table** allows you to vary the value in two cells and then see the recalculated results. For example, you can use a two-input data table to see how your monthly mortgage payment will be affected by changing both the interest rate and the term of the loan.

Break Point: If you want to take a break, this is a good place to do so. Be sure to save the SC_EX_4_Mortgage file again, and then you can exit Excel. To resume later, start Excel, open the file called SC_EX_4_Mortgage.xlsx, and continue following the steps from this location forward.

BTW
Amortization Schedules
Hundreds of websites offer amortization schedules. To find these websites, use a search engine, such as Google, and search using the keywords, amortization schedule.

Creating an Amortization Schedule

The next step in this project is to create the Amortization Schedule section on the right side of Figure 4–23. An amortization schedule shows the beginning and ending balances of a loan and the amount of payment that applies to the principal and interest for each year over the life of the loan. For example, if a customer wanted to pay off the loan after six years, the Amortization Schedule section would tell the loan officer what the payoff would be (cell J10 in Figure 4–23). The Amortization Schedule section shown in Figure 4–23 will work only for loans of up to 15 years; however, you could extend the table to any number of years. The Amortization Schedule section also contains summaries in rows 20, 21, and 22. These summaries should agree exactly with the corresponding amounts in the Mortgage Payment Calculator section in the range C3:F8.

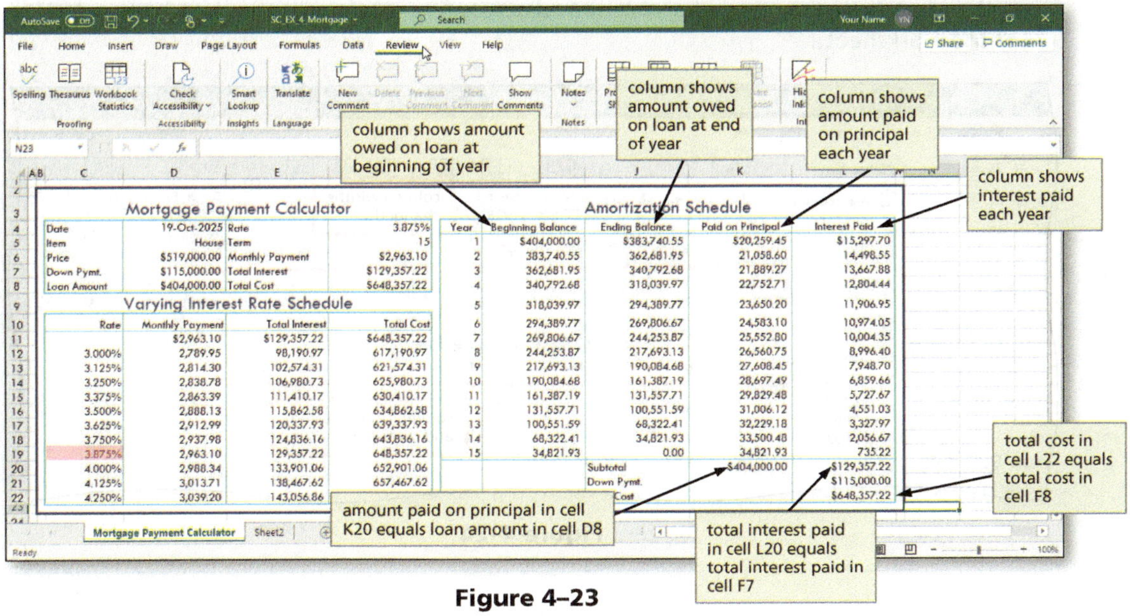

Figure 4–23

To Change Column Widths and Enter Titles

The first step in creating the Amortization Schedule section is to adjust the column widths and enter the section title and column titles. The following steps adjust column widths and enter column titles for the Amortization Schedule section.

1. Position the pointer on the right boundary of column heading G and then drag to the left until the ScreenTip shows Width: .85 (11 pixels) to change the column width.

2. Position the pointer on the right boundary of column heading H and then drag to the left until the ScreenTip shows Width: 6.00 (53 pixels) to change the column width.

3. Drag through column headings I through L to select them. Position the pointer on the right boundary of column heading L and then drag to the right until the ScreenTip shows Width: 16.00 (133 pixels) to change the column widths.

4. Select cell H3. Type `Amortization Schedule` and then press ENTER to enter the section title.

5. Select cell C3, click the Format Painter button (Home tab | Clipboard group) to activate the format painter, and then click cell H3 to copy the format of cell C3.

6. Click the 'Merge & Center' button (Home tab | Alignment group) to split the selected cell, cell H3 in this case. Select the range H3:L3 and then click the 'Merge & Center' button (Home tab | Alignment group) to merge and center the section title over the selected range.

7. Enter the following column headings in row 4: `Year` in cell H4, `Beginning Balance` in cell I4, `Ending Balance` in cell J4, `Paid on Principal` in cell K4, and `Interest Paid` in cell L4. Select the range H4:L4 and then click the Center button (Home tab | Alignment group) to center the column headings.

BTW

Column Borders

In this module, columns A and G are used as column borders to divide sections of the worksheet from one another, as well as from the row headings. A column border is an unused column with a significantly reduced width. You also can use row borders to separate sections of a worksheet.

8 Select cell H5 to display the centered section title and column headings (Figure 4–24).

Q&A **Why was cell H3 split, or unmerged, in Step 6?**
After using the format painter, Excel attempted to merge and center the text in cell H3 because the source of the format, cell C3, is merged and centered across four columns. The Amortization Schedule section, however, includes five columns. Splitting cell H3 changed cell H3 back to being one column instead of including four columns. Next, the section heading was merged and centered across five columns as required by the design of the worksheet.

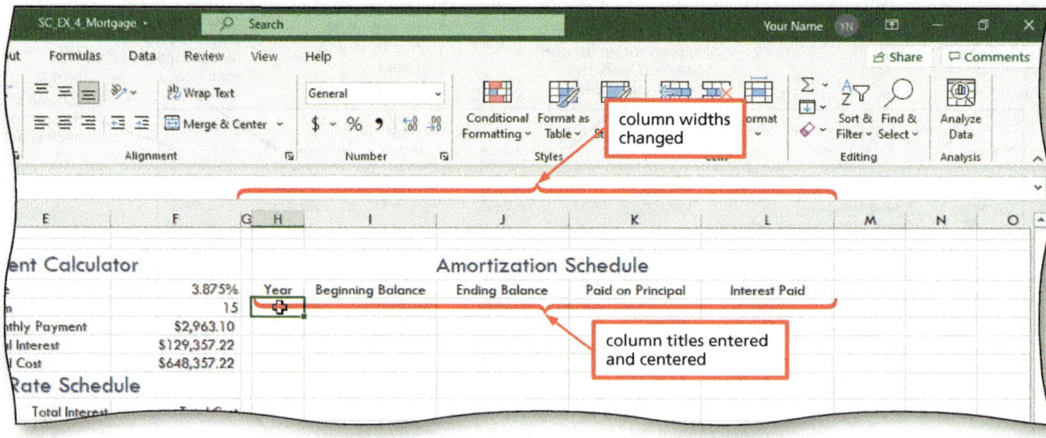

Figure 4–24

To Create a Series of Integers Using the Fill Handle

The next step is to use the fill handle to create a series of numbers that represent the years during the life of the loan. The series begins with 1 (year 1) and ends with 15 (year 15). The following steps create a series of years in the range H5:H19.

1 With cell H5 active, enter **1** as the initial year. Select cell H6 and then enter **2** to represent the next year.

2 Select the range H5:H6 and then drag the fill handle through cell H19 to complete the creation of a series of integers, 1 through 15 in the range H5:H19 in this case (Figure 4–25).

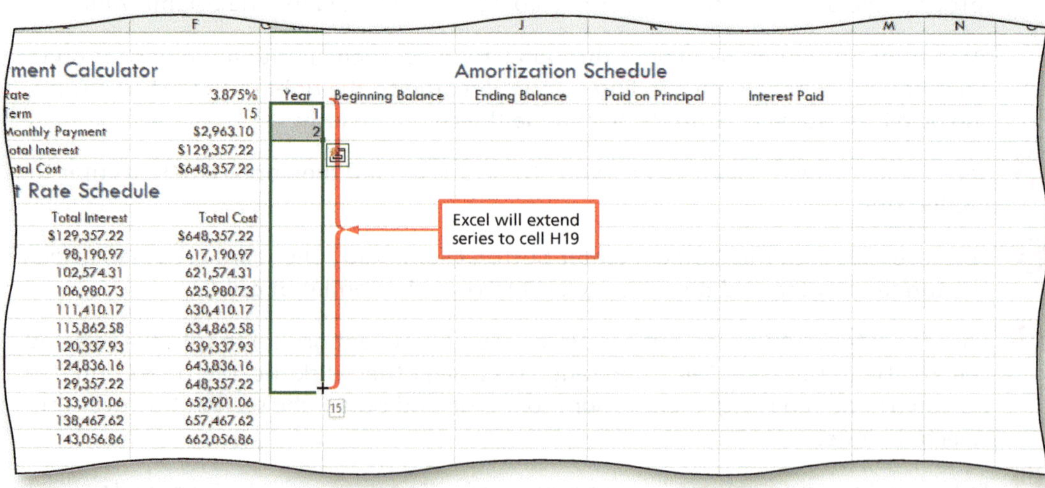

Figure 4–25

3 Release the mouse button.

Q&A **Why is year 5 of the amortization schedule larger than the other rows in the amortization schedule?**
The design of the worksheet called for a large font size for the varying interest rate schedule section of the worksheet, which is in row 9 of the worksheet. To accommodate the larger font size, the height of row 9 was increased. Year 5 of the worksheet is in the taller row 9 and, therefore, is taller than the other years in the amortization schedule.

Formulas in the Amortization Schedule

Four formulas form the basis of the amortization schedule. You will enter these formulas in row 5. Later, you will copy these formulas through row 19. The formulas are summarized in Table 4–2.

Table 4–2 Formulas for the Amortization Schedule

Cell	Column Heading	Formula	Example
I5	Beginning Balance	=D8	The beginning balance (the balance at the end of a year) is the initial loan amount in cell D8.
J5	Ending Balance	=IF(H5<=$F$5, PV($F$4/12, 12*($F$5–H5), –$F$6), 0)	The ending balance (the balance at the end of a year) is equal to the present value of the payments paid over the remaining life of the loan. (This formula is fully explained in the following text.)
K5	Paid on Principal	=I5–J5	The amount paid on the principal at the end of the year is equal to the beginning balance (cell I5) minus the ending balance (cell J5).
L5	Interest Paid	=IF(I5>0, 12*$F$6–K5, 0)	The interest paid during the year is equal to 12 times the monthly payment (cell F6) minus the amount paid on the principal (cell K5).

Of the four formulas in Table 4–2, perhaps the most difficult to understand is the PV function that will be assigned to cell J5. The **PV function** returns the present value of an annuity. An **annuity** is a series of fixed payments (such as the monthly payment in cell F6) made at the end of each of a fixed number of periods (months) at a fixed interest rate. You can use the PV function to determine the amount the borrower still owes on the loan at the end of each year. The PV function has three arguments: rate, number of periods, and payment amount per period. Its general form is as follows:

=PV(rate, period, payment)

where rate is the interest rate per payment period, period is the number of payments remaining in the life of the loan, and payment is the amount of the monthly payment.

The PV function is used to determine the ending balance after the first year (cell J5) by using a term equal to the number of months for which the borrower still must make payments. For example, if the loan is for 15 years (180 months), then the borrower still owes 168 payments after the first year (180 months–12 months). The number of payments outstanding can be determined from the formula 12*($F$5–H5) or 12*(15–1), which equals 168. Recall that column H contains integers that represent the years of the loan. After the second year, the number of payments remaining is 156 and so on.

If you assign the PV function as shown in Table 4–2 to cell J5 and then copy it to the range J6:J19, the ending balances for each year will be displayed properly. However, if the loan is for fewer than 15 years, any ending balances for the years beyond the term of the loan are invalid. For example, if a loan is taken out for 5 years, then the rows representing years 6 through 15 in the amortization schedule should be zero. The PV function, however, will display negative numbers for those years even though the loan already has been paid off.

To avoid displaying negative ending balances, the worksheet should include a formula that assigns the PV function to the range I5:I19 as long as the corresponding year in column H is less than or equal to the number of years in the term (cell F5). If the corresponding year in column H is greater than the number of years in cell F5, then the ending balance for that year and the remaining years should be zero. The following IF function causes either the value of the PV function or zero to be displayed in cell J5, depending on whether the corresponding value in column H is greater than—or less than or equal to—the number of years in cell F5. Recall that the dollar signs within the cell references indicate the cell references are absolute and, therefore, will not change as you copy the function downward.

=IF(H5<=$F$5, PV($F$4/12, 12*($F$5–H5), –$F$6), 0)

logical test: H5<=$F$5
value if true: PV($F$4/12, 12*($F$5–H5), –$F$6)
value if false: 0

In the preceding formula, the logical test determines if the year in column H is less than or equal to the term of the loan in cell F5. If the logical test is true, then the IF function assigns the PV function to the cell. If the logical test is false, then the IF function assigns zero (0) to the cell. You also could use two double-quote symbols (" ") to indicate to Excel to leave the cell blank if the logical test is false.

The PV function in the IF function includes absolute cell references (cell references with dollar signs) to ensure that the references to cells in column F do not change when the IF function later is copied down the column.

To Enter the Formulas in the Amortization Schedule

Why? Creating an amortization schedule allows you to see the costs of a mortgage and the balance still owed for any year in the term of the loan. This information can be very helpful when making financial decisions. The following steps enter the four formulas shown in Table 4–2 into row 5. Row 5 represents year 1 of the loan.

1

- Select cell I5 and then enter **=d8** as the beginning balance of the loan.
- Select cell J5 and then enter **=if(h5<=f5, pv(f4/12, 12* (f5-h5), -f6), 0)** as the entry (Figure 4–26).

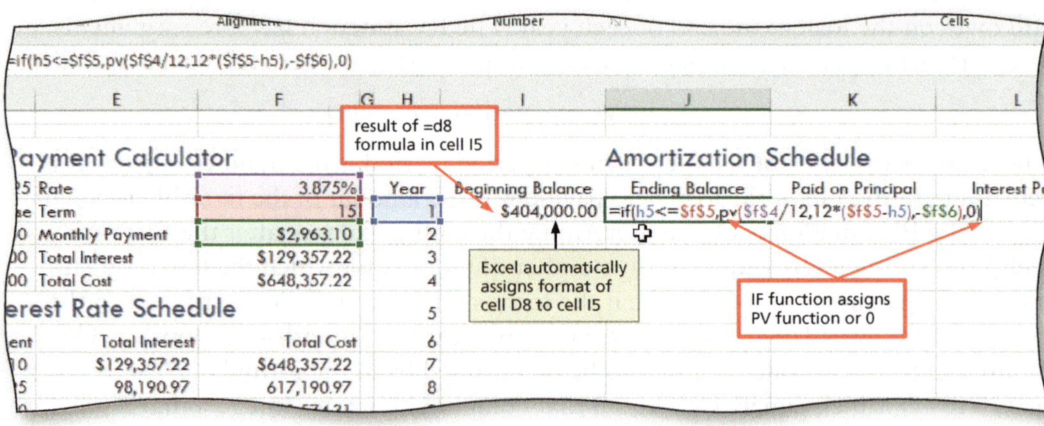

Figure 4–26

2

- Click the Enter button in the formula bar to insert the formula in the selected cell (Figure 4–27).

Q&A **What happens when the Enter button is clicked?**
Excel evaluates the IF function in cell J5 and displays the result of the PV function (383740.549), because the value in cell H5 (1) is less than the term of the loan in cell F5 (15). With cell J5 active, Excel also displays the formula in the formula bar. If the borrower wanted to pay off the loan after one year, the cost would be $383,740.55.

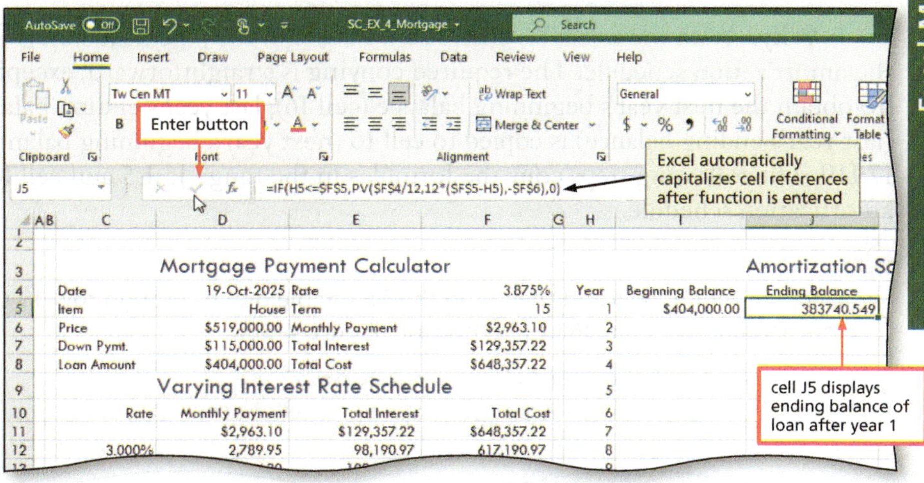

Figure 4–27

3

- Select cell K5. Enter the formula `=i5 - j5` and then press the RIGHT ARROW key to complete the entry and select cell L5.
- Type the formula `=if(i5 > 0, 12 * $f$6 - k5, 0)` in cell L5 (Figure 4–28).

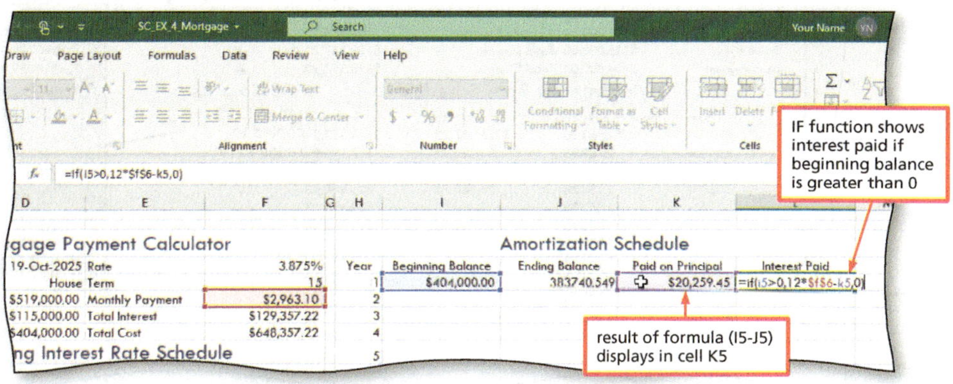

Figure 4–28

4

- Click the Enter button in the formula bar to complete the entry of the formula (Figure 4–29).

Q&A **Why are some of the cells in the range I5:L5 not formatted?**
When you enter a formula in a cell, Excel assigns the cell the same format as the first cell reference in the formula. For example, when you enter =d8 in cell I5, Excel assigns the format in cell D8 to cell I5. The same applies to cell K5. Although this method of formatting also works for most functions, it does not work for the IF function. Thus, the results of the IF functions in cells J5 and L5 are formatted using the general style format, which is the default format when you open a new workbook.

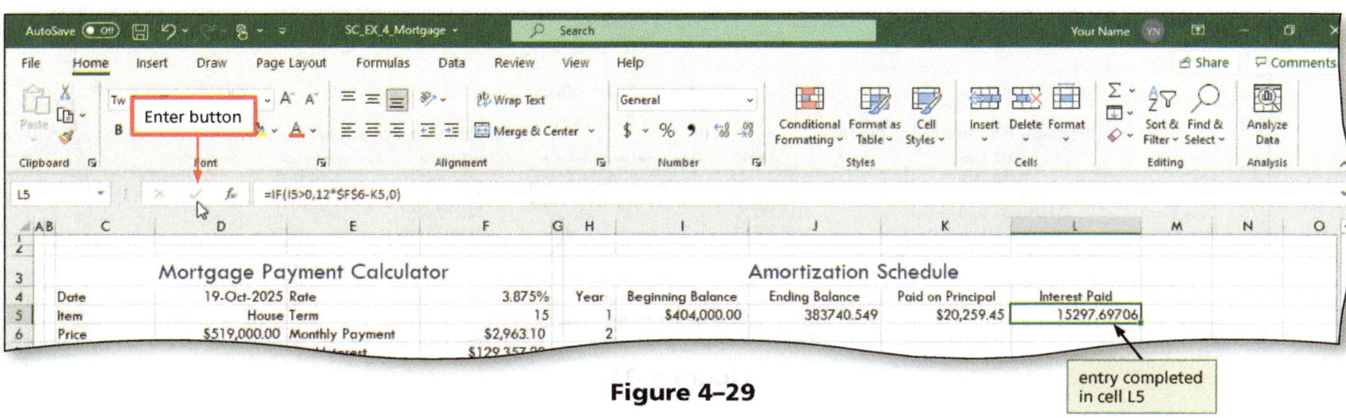

Figure 4–29

To Copy the Formulas to Fill the Amortization Schedule

Why? With the formulas entered into the first row, the next step is to copy them to the remaining rows in the amortization schedule. The required copying is straightforward, except for the beginning balance column. To obtain the next year's beginning balance (cell I6), last year's ending balance (cell J5) must be used. After cell J5 (last year's ending balance) is copied to cell I6 (next year's beginning balance), then I6 can be copied to the range I7:I19. The following steps copy the formulas in the range J5:L5 and cell I6 through to the remainder of the amortization schedule.

1

- Select the range J5:L5 and then drag the fill handle down through row 19 to copy the formulas through the amortization schedule, J6:L19 in this case (Figure 4–30).

Q&A **Why do some of the numbers seem incorrect?**
Many of the numbers are incorrect because the cells in column I, except for cell I5, do not yet contain values.

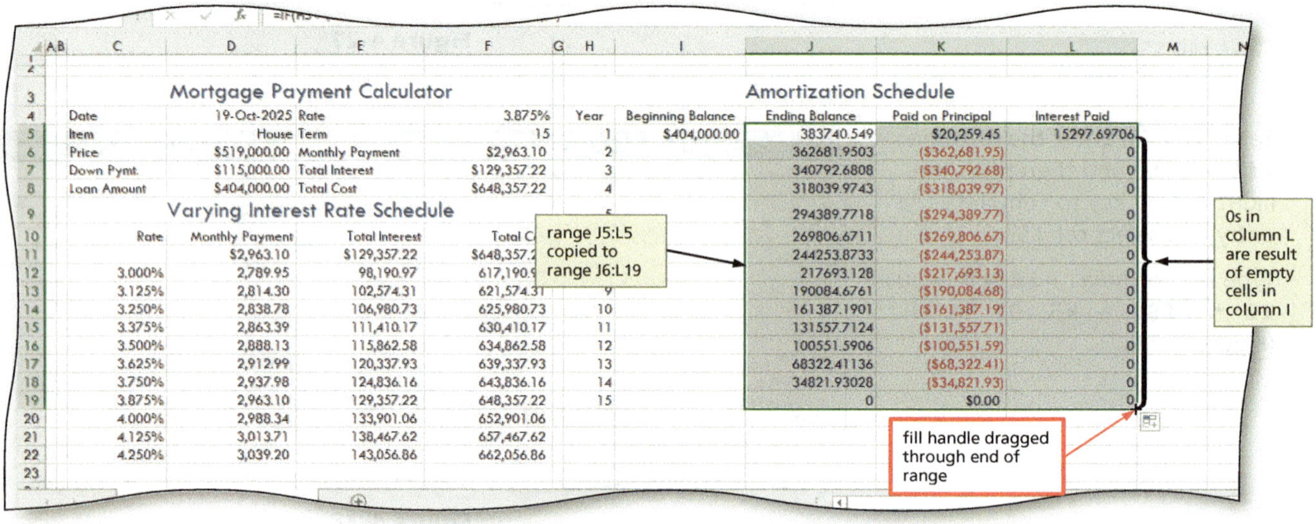

Figure 4–30

2

- Select cell I6, type `=j5` as the cell entry, and then click the Enter button in the formula bar to display the ending balance (383740.549) for year 1 as the beginning balance for year 2 (Figure 4–31).

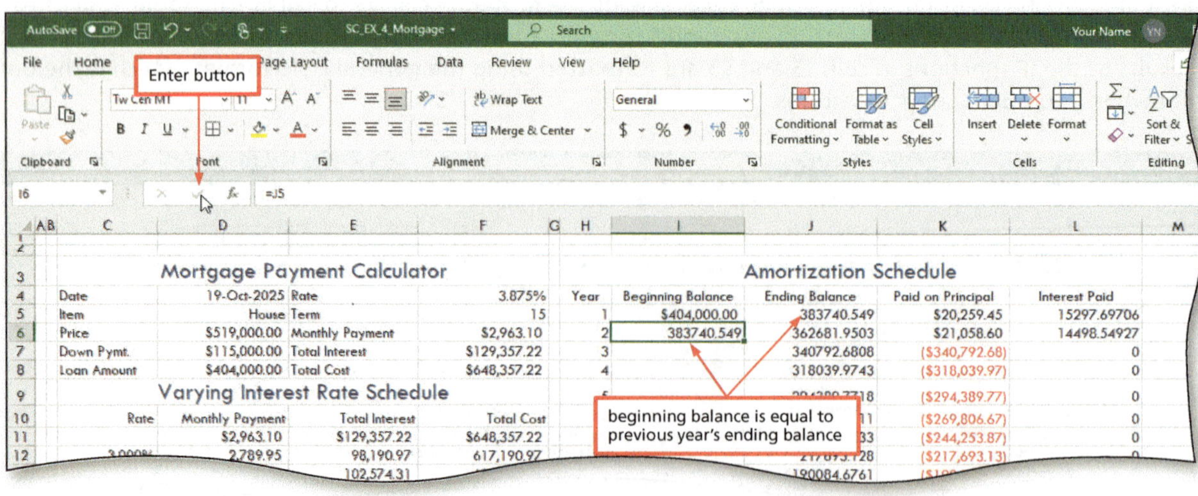

Figure 4–31

3

- With cell I6 active, drag the fill handle down through row 19 to copy the formula in cell I6 (=J5) to the range I7:I19 (Figure 4–32).

Q&A **What happens after the fill operation is complete?**
Because the cell reference J5 is relative, Excel adjusts the row portion of the cell reference as it is copied downward. Thus, each new beginning balance in column I is equal to the ending balance of the previous year.

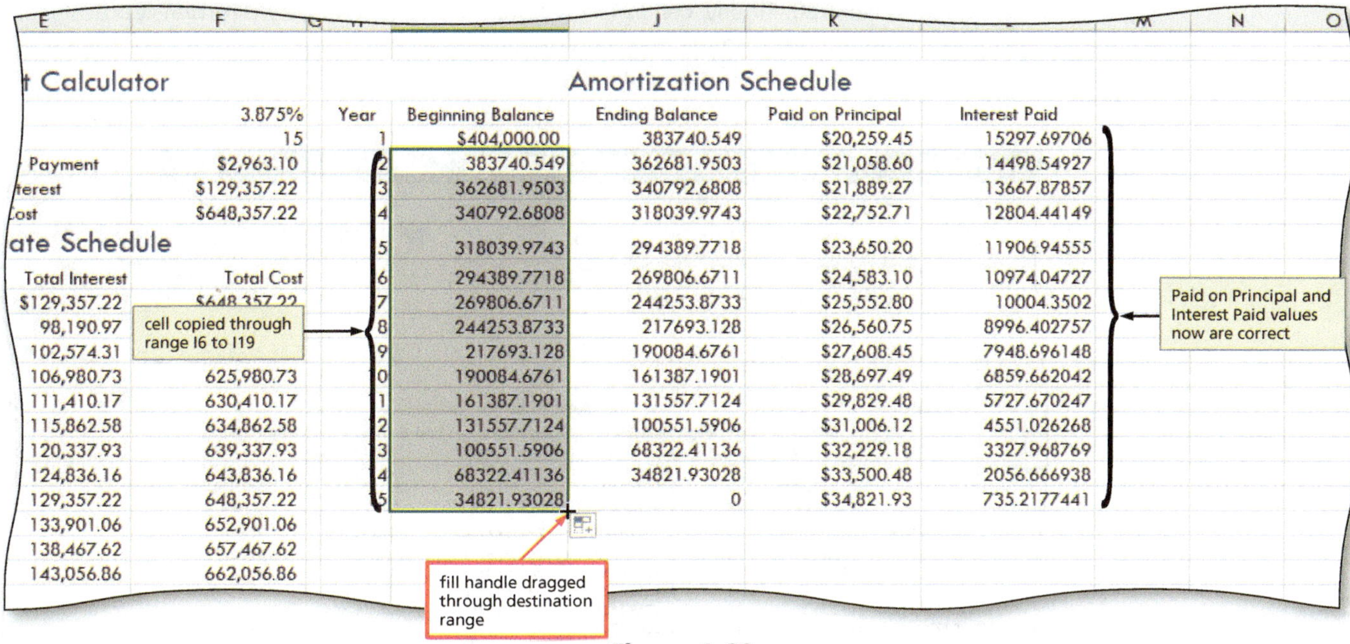

Figure 4–32

Other Ways

1. Select cells containing formulas to copy, click Copy (Home tab | Clipboard group), select destination cell or range, click Paste (Home tab | Clipboard group)

To Enter the Total Formulas in the Amortization Schedule

The next step is to determine the amortization schedule totals in rows 20 through 22. These totals should agree with the corresponding totals in the Mortgage Payment Calculator section (range F7:F8). The following steps enter the total formulas in the amortization schedule.

1. Select cell J20 and then enter `Subtotal` as the row title.
2. Select the range K20:L20 and then click the AutoSum button (Home tab | Editing group) to sum the selected range.
3. Select cell J21 and then enter `Down Pymt.` as the row title.
4. Select cell L21 and then enter `=d7` to copy the down payment to the selected cell.
5. Select cell J22 and then enter `Total Cost` as the row title.

6. Select cell L22, type `=K20 + L20 + L21` as the total cost, and then click the Enter button in the formula bar to complete the amortization schedule totals (Figure 4–33).

Q&A

What was accomplished in the previous steps?
The formula assigned to cell L22 (=K20+L20+L21) sums the total amount paid on the principal (cell K20), the total interest paid (cell L20), and the down payment (cell L21). Excel assigns cell K20 the same format as cell K5 because cell K5 is the first cell reference in =SUM(K5:K19). Furthermore, because cell K20 was selected first when the range K20:L20 was selected to determine the sum, Excel assigned cell L20 the same format it assigned to cell K20. Finally, cell L21 was assigned the currency style format, because cell L21 was assigned the formula =d7, and cell D7 has a currency style format. For the same reason, the value in cell L22 appears with the currency style format.

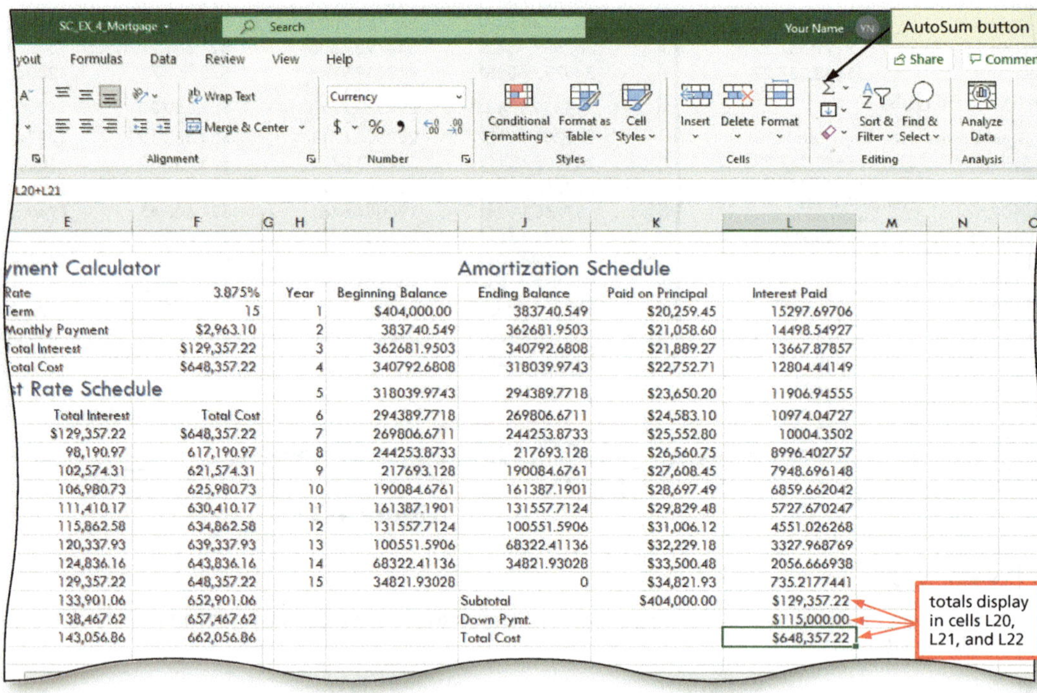

Figure 4–33

To Format the Numbers in the Amortization Schedule

The next step in creating the amortization schedule is to format it so that it is easier to read. When the beginning balance formula (=d8) was entered earlier into cell I5, Excel copied the currency style format along with the value from cell D8 to cell I5. The following steps copy the currency style format from cell I5 to the range J5:L5. The comma style format then will be assigned to the range I6:L19.

1. Select cell I5 and then click the Format Painter button (Home tab | Clipboard group) to turn on the format painter. Drag through the range J5:L5 to assign the currency style format to the cells.

2. Select the range I6:L19 and then right-click the selected range to display a shortcut menu. Click Format Cells on the shortcut menu to display the Format Cells dialog box and then, if necessary, click the Number tab (Format Cells dialog box) to display the Number sheet.

3. Select Currency in the Category list to select a currency format, select None in the Symbol list to choose no currency symbol if necessary, and then click the fourth format, (1,234.10), in the Negative numbers list to create a currency format.

4. Click OK (Format Cells dialog box) to apply the currency format to the selected range.

5. Deselect the range I6:L19 and display the numbers in the amortization schedule, as shown in Figure 4–34.

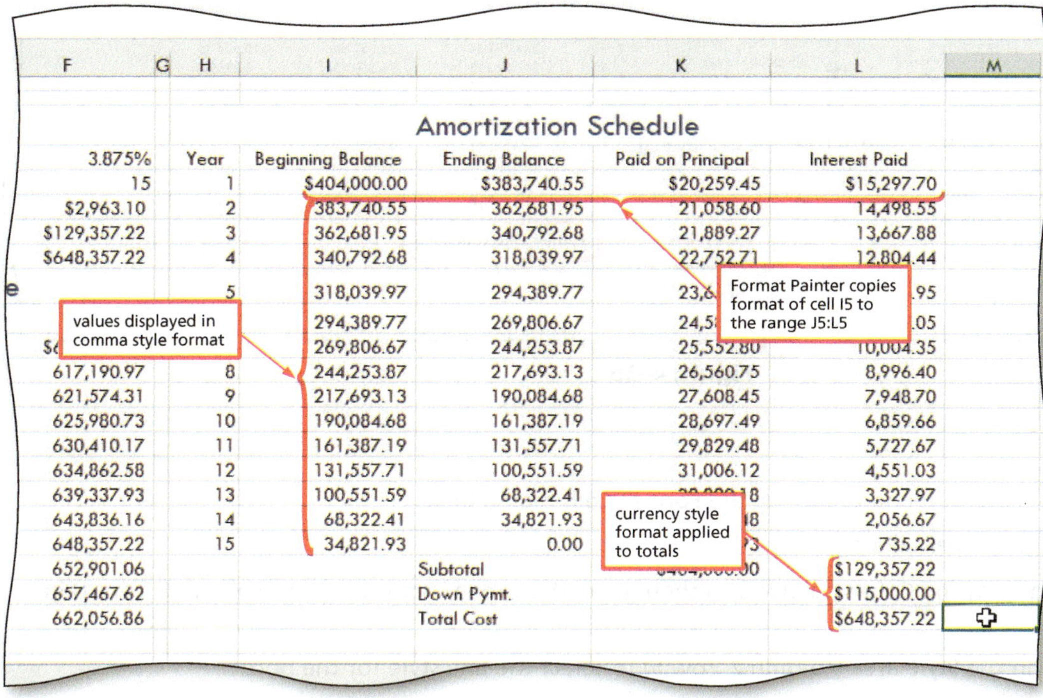

Figure 4–34

BTW

Round-Off Errors

If you manually add the numbers in column L (range L5:L19) and compare it to the sum in cell L20, you will notice that the total interest paid is $0.01 off. This round-off error is due to the fact that some of the numbers involved in the computations have additional decimal places that do not appear in the cells. You can use the ROUND function on the formula entered into cell L5 to ensure the total is exactly correct. For information on the ROUND function, click the Insert Function button in the formula bar, click 'Math & Trig' in the 'Or select a category' list, scroll down in the 'Select a function' list, and then click ROUND.

BTW

Undoing Formats

If you begin assigning formats to a range and then realize you made a mistake and want to start over, select the range, click the Cell Styles button (Home tab | Styles group), and then click Normal in the Cell Styles gallery.

Formatting the Worksheet

Previous modules introduced you to outlining a range using cell borders or cell background colors to differentiate portions of a worksheet. The Borders button (Home tab | Font group), however, offers only a limited selection of border thicknesses. To control the color and thickness, Excel requires that you use the Border sheet in the Format Cells dialog box.

To Add Custom Borders to a Range

Why? Borders can be used to distinguish the different functional parts of a worksheet. The following steps add a medium blue border to the Mortgage Payment Calculator section. To subdivide the row titles and numbers further, light borders also are added within the section, as shown in Figure 4–1.

1

- Select the range C4:F8 and then right-click to display a shortcut menu and mini toolbar (Figure 4–35).

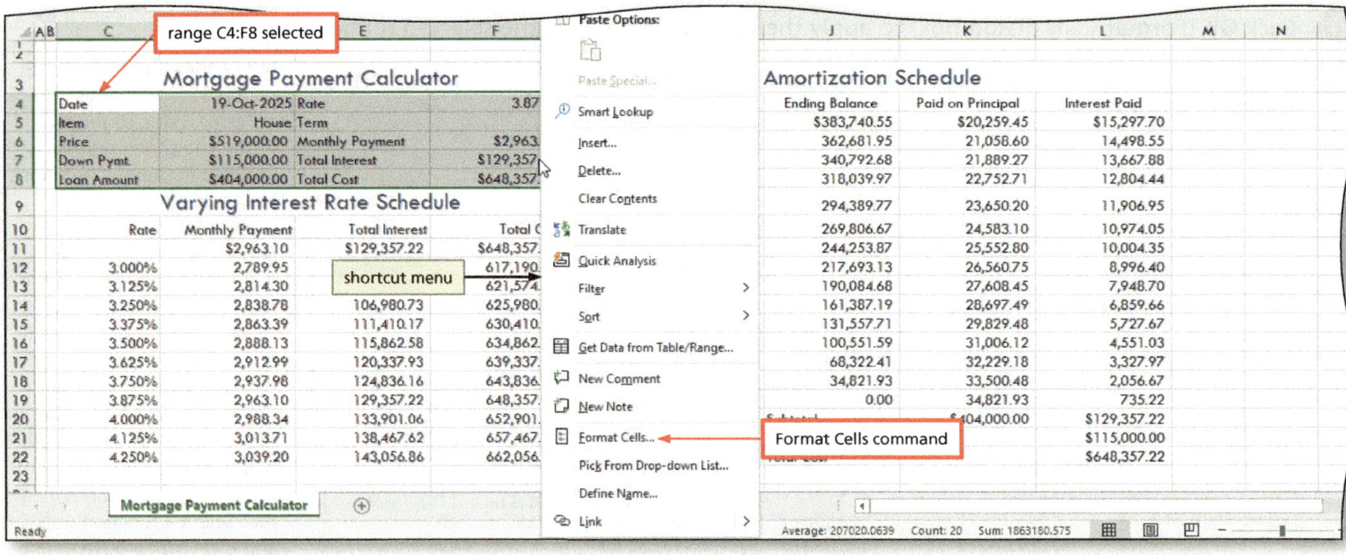

Figure 4–35

2

- Click Format Cells on the shortcut menu to display the Format Cells dialog box.
- Display the Border tab (Format Cells dialog box).
- Click the Color arrow to display the Colors palette and then select the Green, Accent 2 color (column 6, row 1) in the Theme Colors area.
- Click the medium border in the Style area (column 2, row 5) to select the line style for the border.
- Click the Outline button in the Presets area to preview the outline border in the Border area (Figure 4–36).

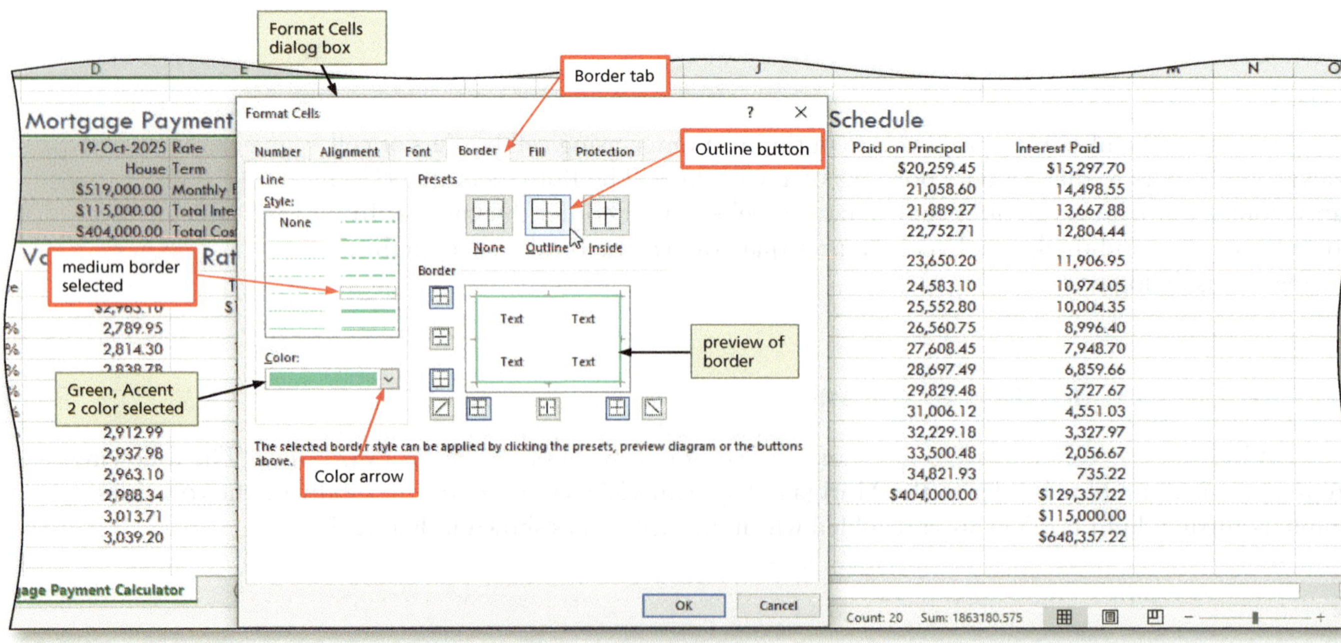

Figure 4–36

3

- Click the light border in the Style area (column 1, row 7) and then click the Vertical Line button in the Border area to preview the green vertical border in the Border area (Figure 4–37).

Q&A **How do I create a border?**
As shown in Figure 4–37, you can add a variety of borders with different colors to a cell or range of cells. It is important that you select border characteristics in the order specified in the steps, that is, (1) choose the border color, (2) choose the border line style, and then (3) choose the border type. This order first defines the border characteristics and then applies those characteristics. If you do these steps in any other order, you may not end up with the borders you intended.

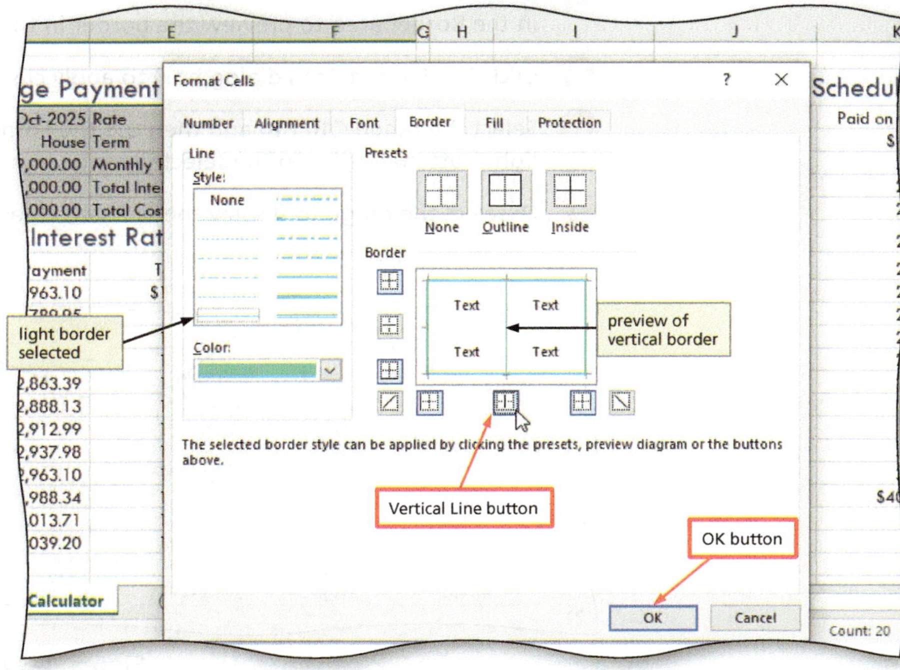

Figure 4–37

4

- Click OK to add a green outline with vertical borders to the right side of each column in the selected range, C4:F8 in this case. Click cell C10 to deselect the range (Figure 4–38).

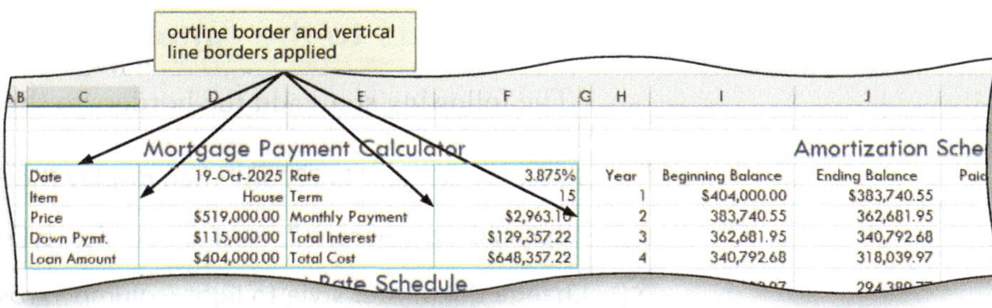

Figure 4–38

Q&A **How else can I add custom borders?**
If you want to specify exactly where borders should be drawn in your worksheet, you can draw the borders manually. To draw borders, click the Border button arrow (Home tab | Font group), click Draw Border, and then click the cell borders where you want to draw a border.

Other Ways

1. Click More Borders arrow (Home tab | Font group), click More Borders, select border options, click OK
2. Click Format button (Home tab | Cells group), click Format Cells, click Border tab, select border options, click OK

To Add Borders to the Varying Interest Rate Schedule

The following steps add the same borders you applied to the Mortgage Payment Calculator to the Varying Interest Rate Schedule.

1. Select the range C10:F22. Right-click the selected range to display a shortcut menu and then click Format Cells on the shortcut menu to display the Format Cells dialog box.
2. If necessary, click the Border tab (Format Cells dialog box) to display the Border sheet. Click the Color arrow to display the Colors palette and then click Green, Accent 2 (column 6, row 1) in the Theme Colors area to change the border color.
3. Click the medium border in the Style area (column 2, row 5). Click the Outline button in the Presets area to preview the border in the Border area.

4. Click the light border in the Style area (column 1, row 7). Click the Vertical Line button in the Border area to preview the border in the Border area.
5. Click OK (Format Cells dialog box) to apply custom borders to the selected range.
6. Select the range C10:F10 and then use the Format Cells dialog box to apply a green, light bottom border to the selected range.
7. Deselect the range to display the worksheet, as shown in Figure 4–39.

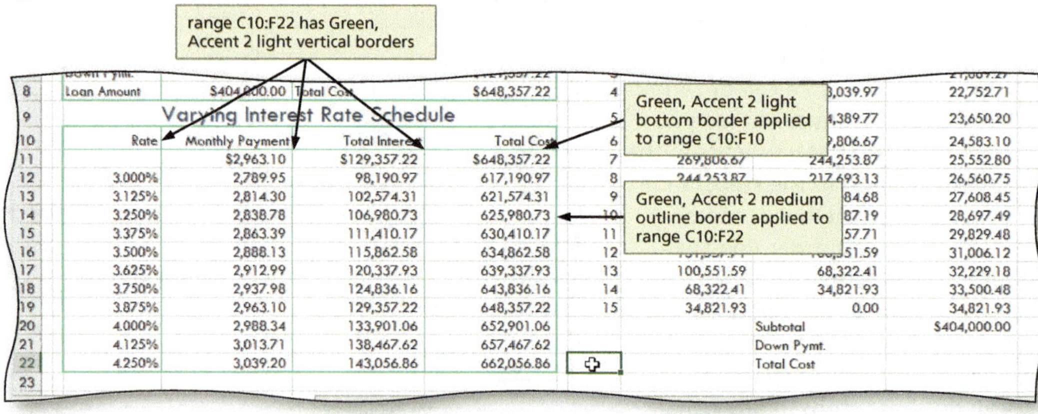

Figure 4–39

To Add Borders to the Amortization Schedule

The following steps add the borders to the Amortization Schedule.

1. Select the range H4:L22, and then display the Format Cells dialog box.
2. Apply a Green, Accent 2, medium border style using the Outline preset.
3. Change the border style to light (column 1, row 7) and then click the Vertical Line button in the Border area to preview the border in the Border area.
4. Click OK to apply custom borders to the selected range.
5. Select the range H5:L19 and then use the Format Cells dialog box to apply a green, light upper border and a green, light bottom border to the selected range.
6. Deselect the range to display the worksheet, as shown in Figure 4–40.

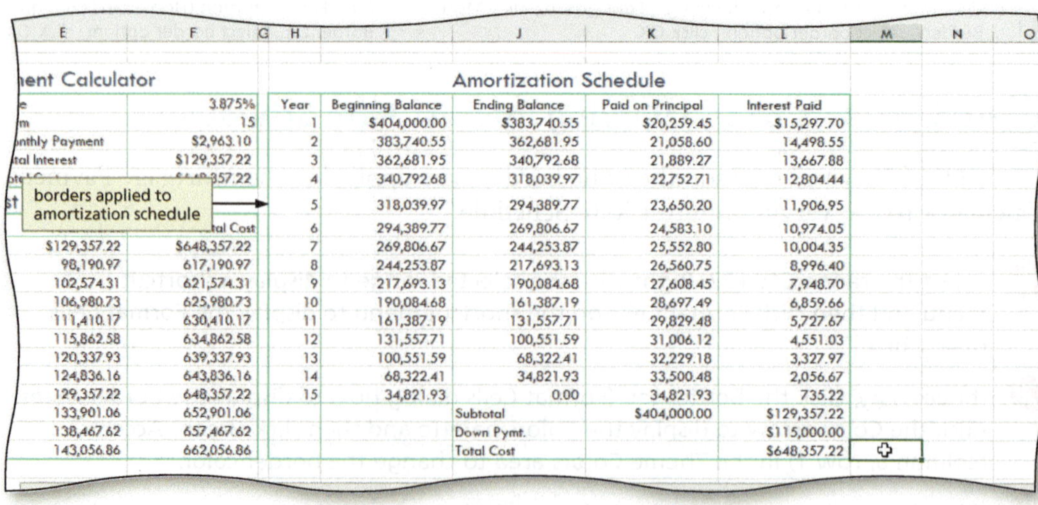

Figure 4–40

To Use Borders and Fill Color to Visually Define and Group the Financial Tools

The following steps add a border and fill color to the entire group of financial tools on the worksheet.

1. Change the height of row 23 to 8.25 (11 pixels).
2. Change the width of column M to 0.85 (11 pixels).
3. Select the range B2:M23.
4. Add a Blue-Gray, Text 2, (column 4, row 1) heavy style (column 2, row 6) Outline border to the selected range.
5. With the range B2:M23 still selected, click the Fill Color arrow (Home tab | Font group) and apply a fill color of White, Background 1 (column 1, row 1) to the selected range. Deselect the range (Figure 4–41).
6. Save the workbook again on the same storage location with the same file name.

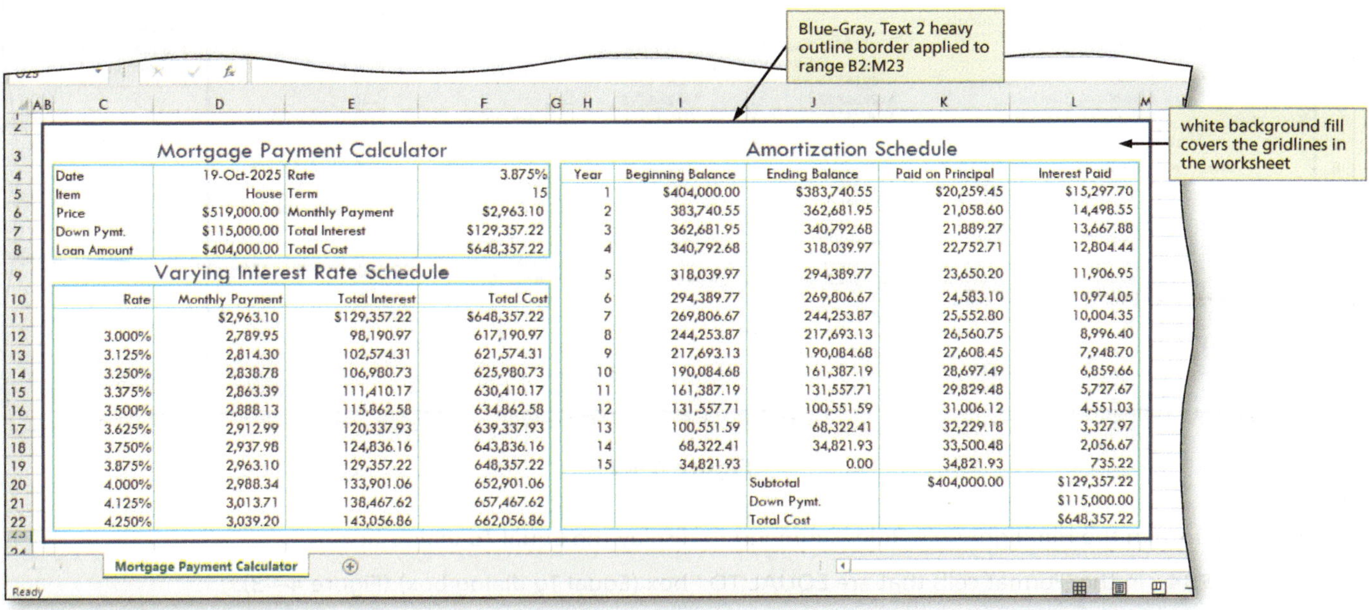

Figure 4–41

Highlighting Cells in the Data Table Using Conditional Formatting

If the interest rate in cell F4 is between 3.000% and 4.250% and its decimal portion is a multiple of 0.125 (such as 4.125%), then one of the rows in the data table agrees exactly with the monthly payment, interest paid, and total cost in the range F6:F8. For example, in Figure 4–41 row 19 (3.875%) in the data table agrees with the results in the range F6:F8, because the interest rate in cell C19 is the same as the interest rate in cell F4. Analysts often look for the row in the data table that agrees with the input cell results. You can use conditional formatting to highlight a row, or a single cell in the row.

BTW
Conditional Formatting
You can add as many conditional formats to a range as you like. After adding the first condition, click the Conditional Formatting button (Home tab | Styles group) and then click New Rule to add more conditions. If more than one condition is true for a cell, then Excel applies the formats of each condition, beginning with the first.

To Add a Pointer to the Data Table Using Conditional Formatting

Why? To make the row with the active interest rate stand out, you can add formatting that serves as a pointer to that row. To add a pointer, you can use conditional formatting to highlight the cell in column C that agrees with the input cell (cell F4). The following steps apply conditional formatting to column C in the data table.

1

- Select the range C12:C22 and then click the Conditional Formatting button (Home tab | Styles group) to display the Conditional Formatting gallery.
- Point to 'Highlight Cells Rules' to display the submenu (Figure 4–42).

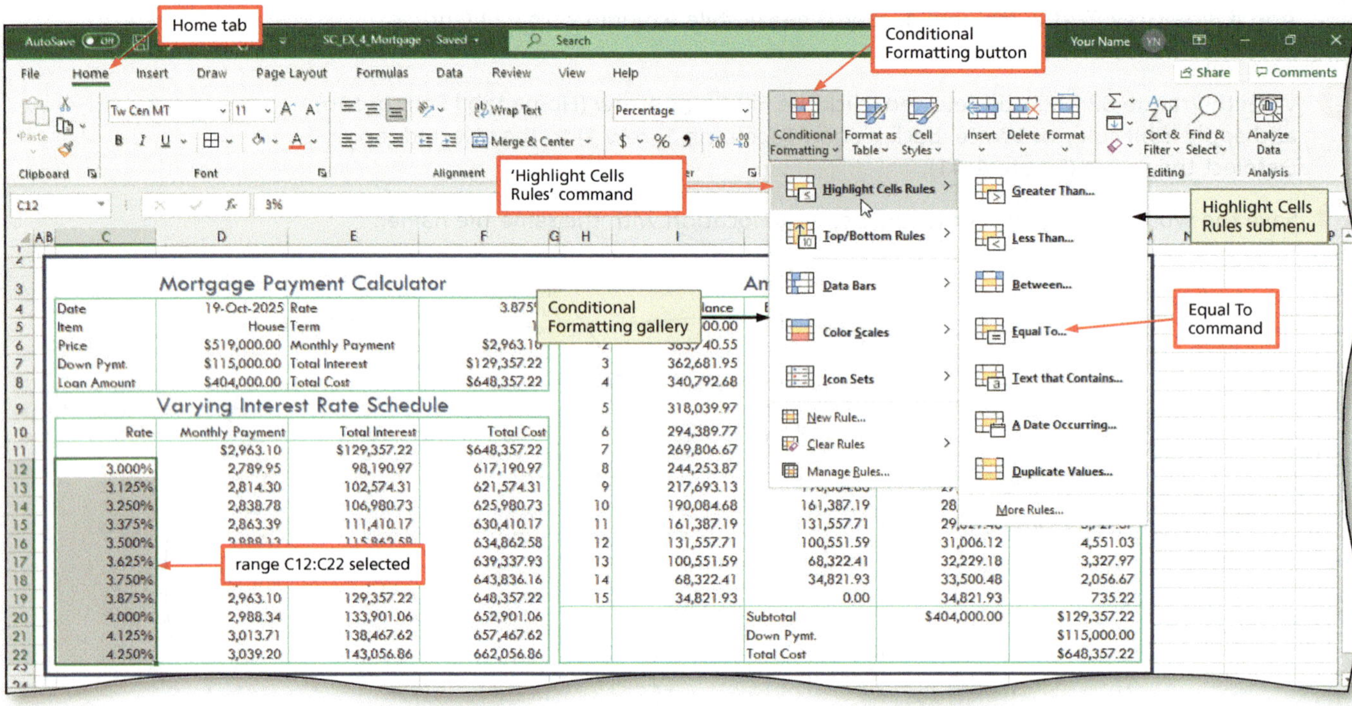

Figure 4–42

2

- Click Equal To on the Highlight Cells Rules submenu to display the Equal To dialog box.
- Type **=$F$4** in the 'Format cells that are EQUAL TO:' box (Equal To dialog box) (Figure 4–43).

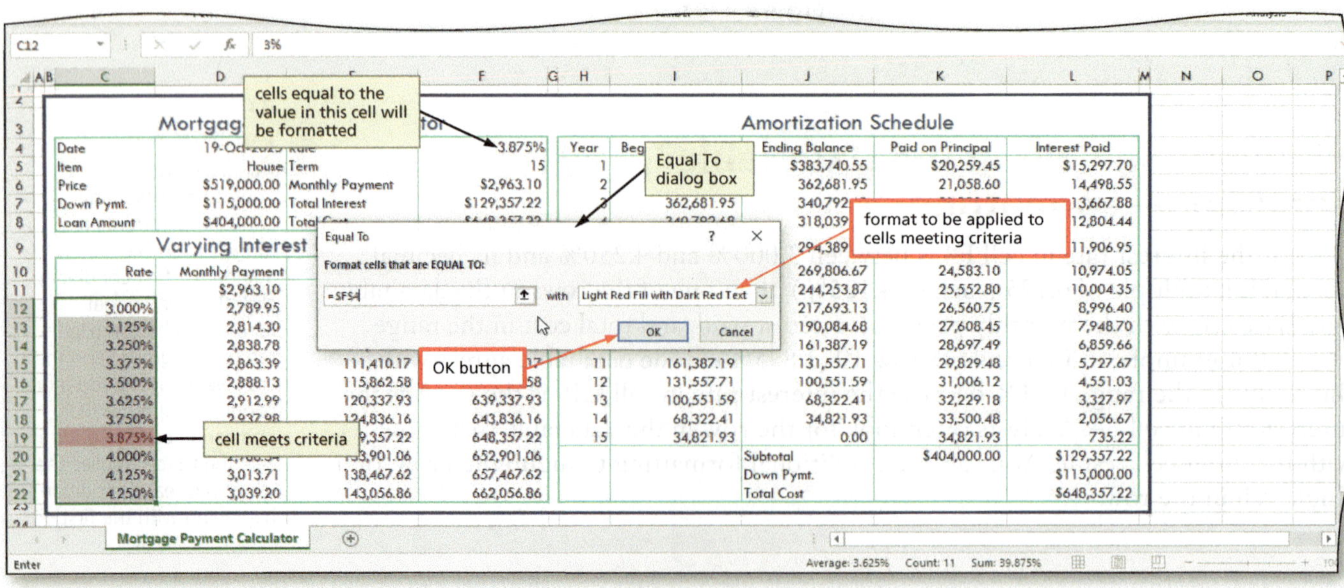

Figure 4–43

3

- Click OK to apply the conditional formatting rule.
- Deselect the range (Figure 4–44).

Q&A **How does Excel apply the conditional formatting?**
Cell C19 in the data table, which contains the value, 3.875%, appears with a red background and dark red text, because the value 3.875% is the same as the interest rate value in cell F4.

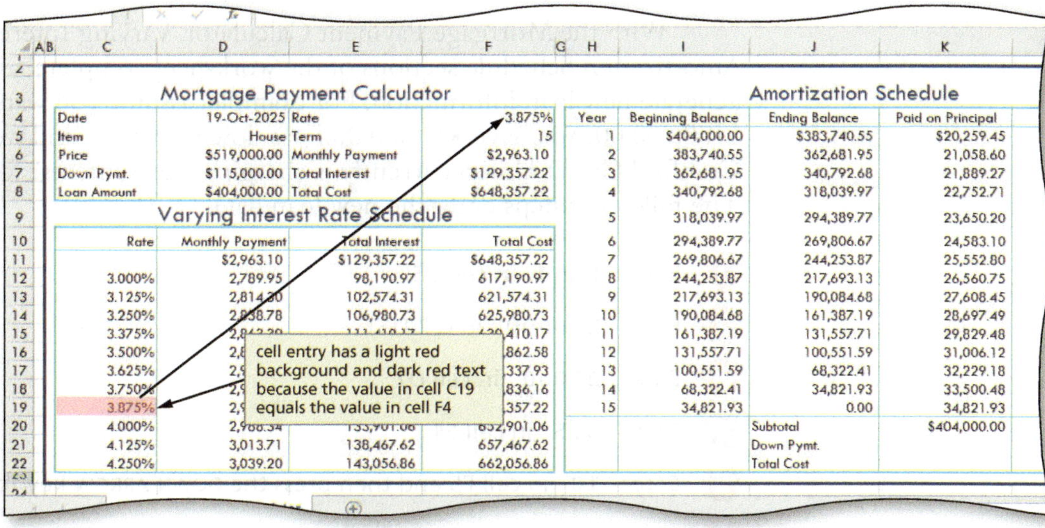

Figure 4–44

4

- Select cell F4 and then enter **4.125** as the interest rate (Figure 4–45).

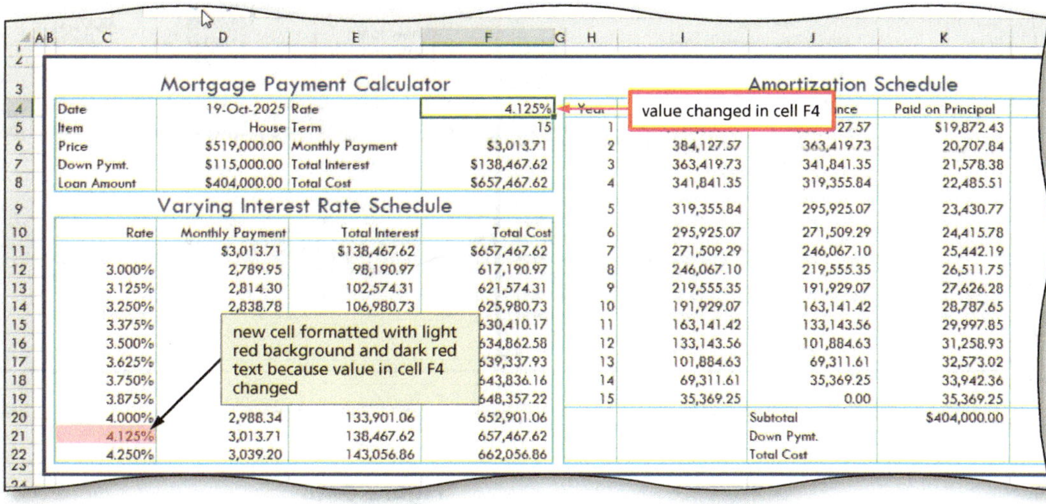

Figure 4–45

5

- Enter **3.875** in cell F4 to return the Mortgage Payment Calculator, Varying Interest Rate Schedule, and Amortization Schedule sections to their original states.

Q&A **What happened when I changed the interest rate from 3.875% to 4.125%?**
The cell containing the new rate received a red background and dark red text, while the original cell (cell C21) reverted to its original formatting (Figure 4–45). The red background and dark red text serve as a pointer in the data table to indicate which row agrees with the input cell (cell F4). When the loan officer using this worksheet enters a new percentage in cell F4, the pointer will move or disappear. The formatting will disappear if the interest rate in cell F4 falls outside the range of the data table or does not appear in the data table, for example, if the interest rate is 5.000% or 4.100%.

To Enter New Loan Data

With the Mortgage Payment Calculator, Varying Interest Rate Schedule, and Amortization Schedule sections of the worksheet complete, you can use them to generate new loan information. For example, assume you want to purchase land for $100,000.00. You have $25,000.00 for a down payment and want a ten-year loan. Cranford Credit Union currently is charging 3.5% interest for a ten-year loan on land. The following steps enter the new loan data.

1. Enter **Land** in cell D5.
2. Enter **100000** in cell D6.
3. Enter **25000** in cell D7.
4. Enter **3.5** in cell F4.
5. Enter **10** in cell F5 and then press the DOWN ARROW key to calculate the loan data.
6. Click on an empty cell to display the worksheet, as shown in Figure 4–46.

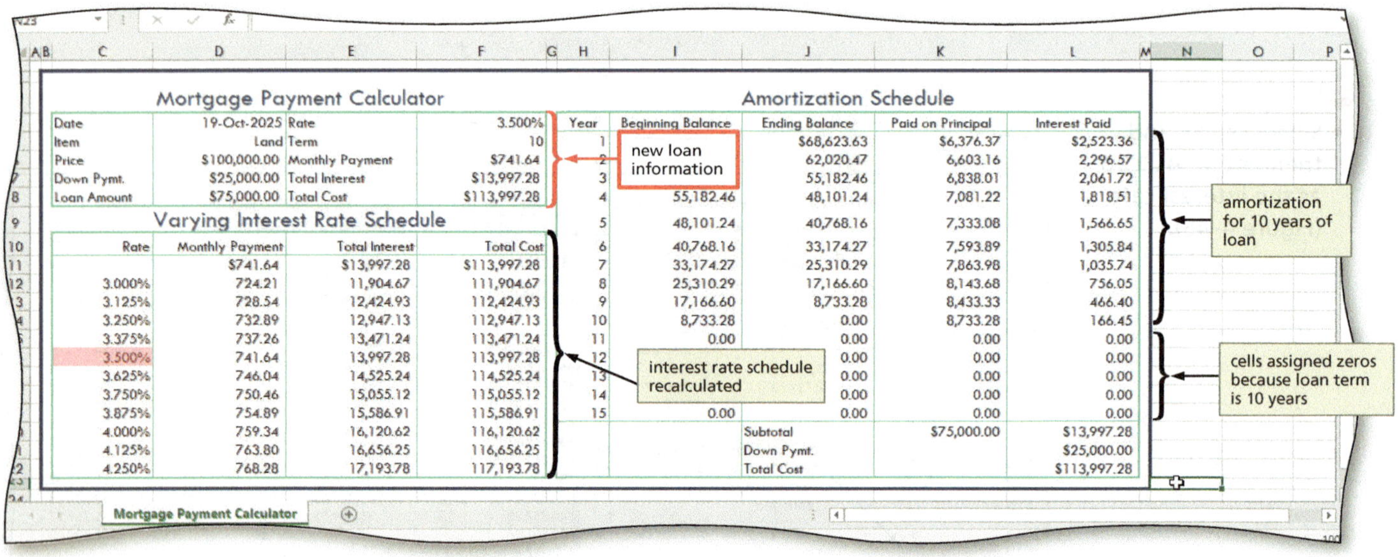

Figure 4–46

To Enter the Original Loan Data

The following steps reenter the original loan data.

1. Enter **House** in cell D5.
2. Enter **519000** in cell D6.
3. Enter **115000** in cell D7.
4. Enter **3.875** in cell F4.
5. Enter **15** in cell F5.

Printing Sections of the Worksheet

In Module 2, you learned how to print a section of a worksheet by first selecting it and then using the Selection option in the Print dialog box. If you find yourself continually selecting the same range in a worksheet to print, you can set a specific range to print each time you print the worksheet. When you set a range to print, Excel will continue to print only that range until you clear it.

To Set Up a Worksheet to Print

Why? Specifying print options allows you to conserve paper and toner and to customize the layout of your worksheet on the printed page. This section describes print options available in the Page and Sheet tabs in the Page Setup dialog box (Figure 4–47). These print options affect the way the worksheet will appear in the printed copy or when previewed. One important print option is the capability of printing in black and white, even when your printer is a color printer. Printing in black and white not only speeds up the printing process but also saves ink. The following steps ensure any printed copy fits on one page and prints in black and white.

1

- Display the Page Layout tab and then click the Page Setup Dialog Box Launcher to display the Page Setup dialog box.
- If necessary, click the Page tab (Page Setup dialog box) to display the Page sheet and then click Fit to in the Scaling area to set the worksheet to print on one page (Figure 4–47).

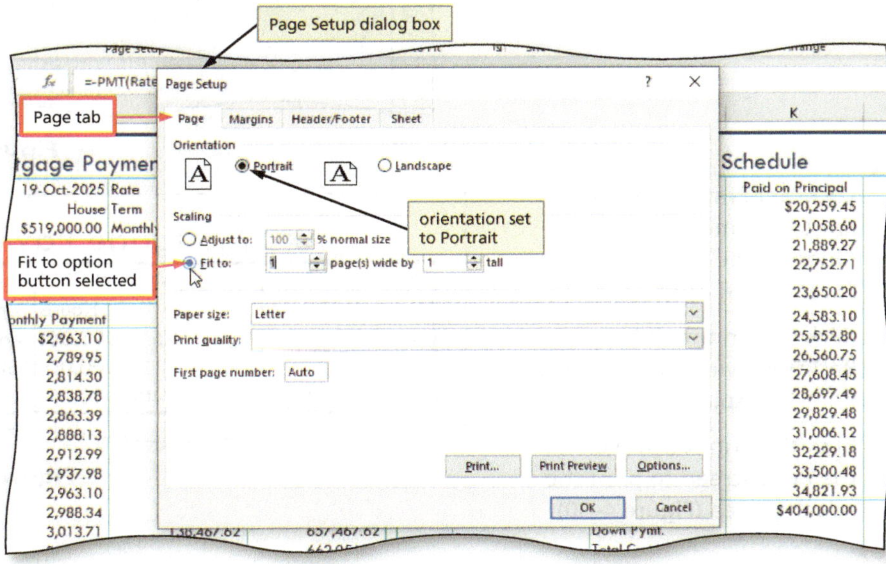

Figure 4–47

Q&A **How can I specify the printed height and width?**
Instead of using Backstage view, you can display the Page Layout tab and in the Scale to Fit group, use the Width and Height boxes to specify the number of pages for each direction.

2

- Click the Sheet tab (Page Setup dialog box) and then click 'Black and white' in the Print area to select the check box (Figure 4–48).

3

- Click OK (Page Setup dialog box) to close the dialog box.

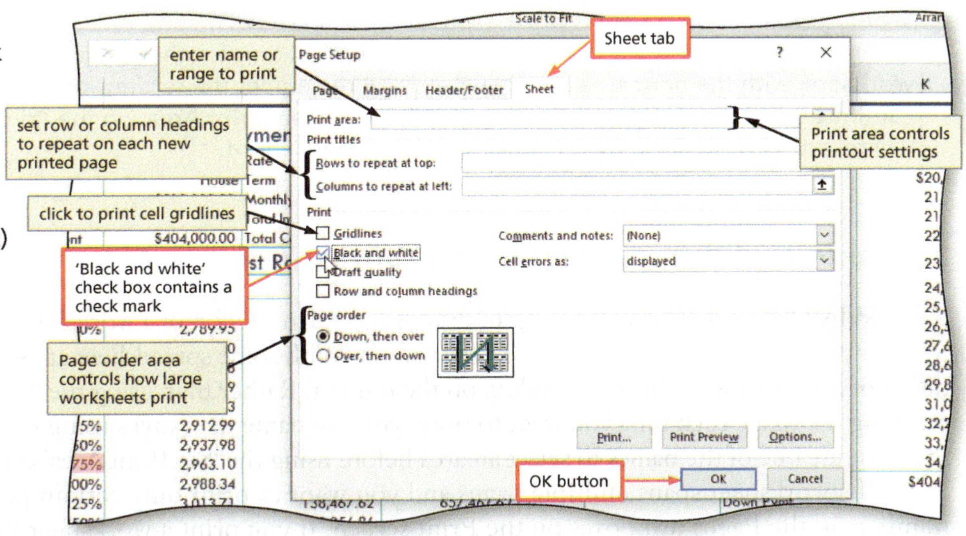

Figure 4–48

Other Ways

1. Click File tab, click Print tab, click Page Setup link, select options

To Set the Print Area

Why? If you do not need to print the entire worksheet, setting the print area allows you to easily specify the section you want to print. The following steps print only the Mortgage Payment Calculator section by setting the print area to the range C3:F8.

1

- Select the range C3:F8 and then click the Print Area button (Page Layout tab | Page Setup group) to display the Print Area menu (Figure 4–49).

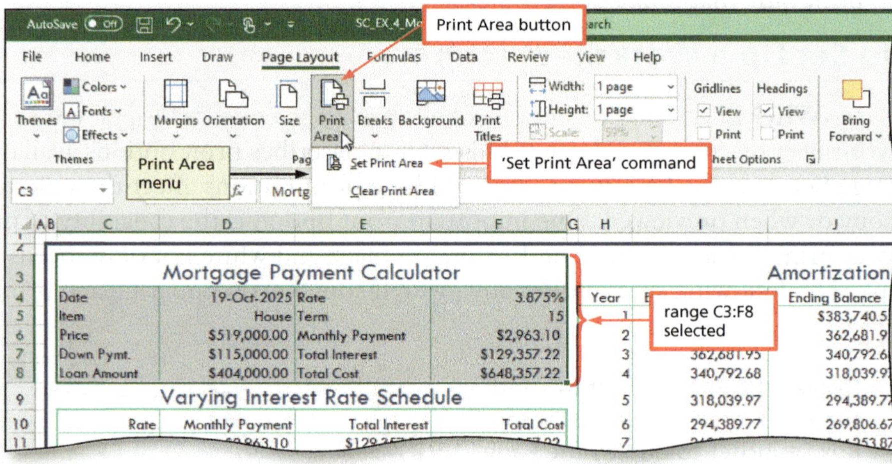

Figure 4–49

2

- Click 'Set Print Area' on the Print Area menu to set the range of the worksheet that Excel should print.
- Click File on the ribbon to open Backstage view and then click Print to display the Print screen.
- Click the Print button on the Print screen to print the selected area (Figure 4–50).

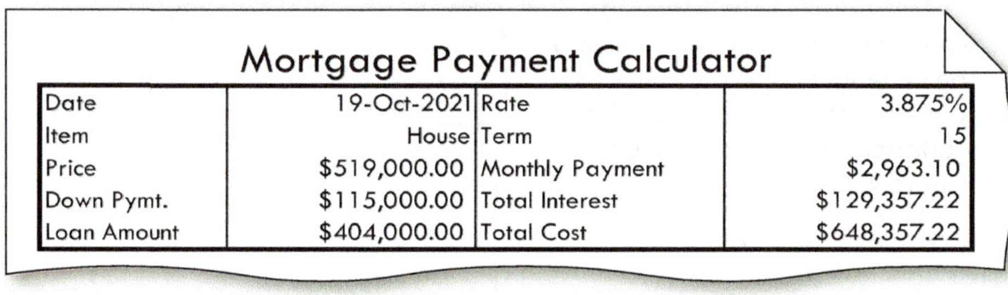

Mortgage Payment Calculator

Date	19-Oct-2021	Rate	3.875%
Item	House	Term	15
Price	$519,000.00	Monthly Payment	$2,963.10
Down Pymt.	$115,000.00	Total Interest	$129,357.22
Loan Amount	$404,000.00	Total Cost	$648,357.22

Figure 4–50

3

- Click the Print Area button (Page Layout tab | Page Setup group) to display the Print Area menu and then click the 'Clear Print Area' command to reset the print area to the entire worksheet.

Q&A **What happens when I set a print area?**
When you set a print area, Excel will print the specified range rather than the entire worksheet. If you save the workbook with the print area set, then Excel will remember the settings the next time you open the workbook and continue to print only the specified range. Clicking 'Clear Print Area' on the Print Area menu, as described in Step 3, will revert the settings so that the entire workbook will print.

To Name and Print Sections of a Worksheet

Why? If you regularly are going to print a particular section of a worksheet, naming the section allows you to specify that section whenever you need to print it. With some spreadsheet apps, you will want to print several different areas of a worksheet, depending on the request. Rather than using the 'Set Print Area' command or manually selecting the range each time you want to print, you can name the ranges using the Name box in the formula bar. You then can use one of the names to select an area before using the 'Set Print Area' command or Print Selection option.

If a worksheet spans multiple pages and you want to print only certain pages, you can enter the page numbers in the Pages text boxes on the Print screen. If you print a worksheet with multiple pages, you can specify print titles that will automatically repeat one or more rows or one or more columns on each page. To specify the rows or columns, click the Print Titles button (Page Layout tab | Page Setup group) and enter the desired row(s) and/or column(s) in the 'Rows to repeat at top' or 'Columns to repeat at left' text boxes. The following steps name the Mortgage Payment Calculator, the Varying Interest Rate Schedule, the Amortization Schedule sections, as well as the entire worksheet, and then print each section.

1

- Click the Page Setup Dialog Box Launcher to display the Page Setup dialog box, click the Sheet tab and then click 'Black and white' to remove the check mark and ensure that Excel prints in color on color printers.
- Click OK to close the Page Setup dialog box.
- If necessary, select the range C3:F8, click the Name box in the formula bar, and then enter `Mortgage_Payment` to name the range (Figure 4–51). *Hint:* Remember to include the underscore between Mortgage and Payment.

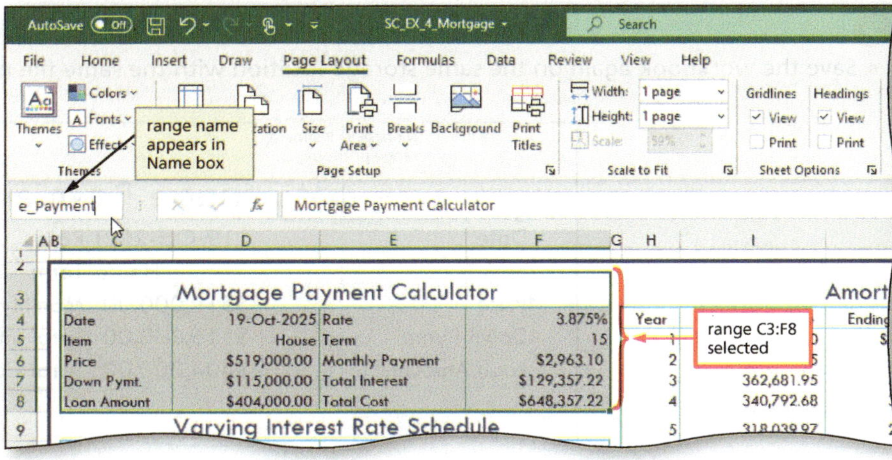

Figure 4–51

2

- Press ENTER to create the range name.
- Select the range C9:F22, click the Name box in the formula bar, type `Interest_Schedule` as the name of the range, and then press ENTER to create a range name.
- Select the range H3:L22, click the Name box in the formula bar, type `Amortization_Schedule` as the name of the range, and then press ENTER to create a range name.
- Select the range B2:M23, click the Name box in the formula bar, type `Financial_Tools` as the name of the range, and then press ENTER to create a range name.
- Select an empty cell and then click the Name box arrow in the formula bar to display the Name box list with the new range names (Figure 4–52).

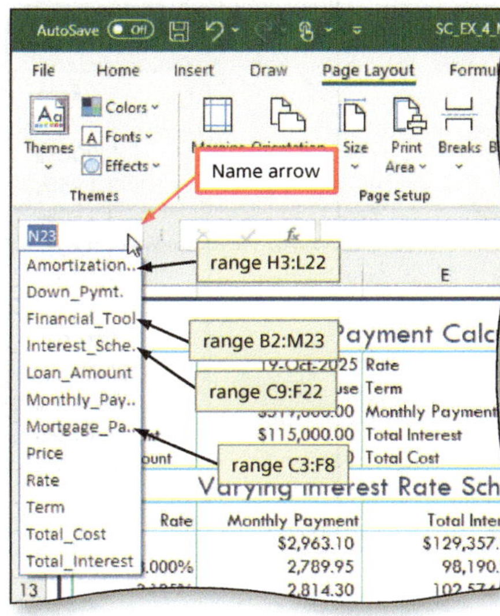

Figure 4–52

3

- Click Mortgage_Payment in the Name list to select the range associated with the name, C3:F8 in this case.
- Click File on the ribbon to open Backstage view and then click Print to display the Print screen.
- Click the 'Print Active Sheets' button in the Settings area and then click Print Selection to select the desired item to print (Figure 4–53).

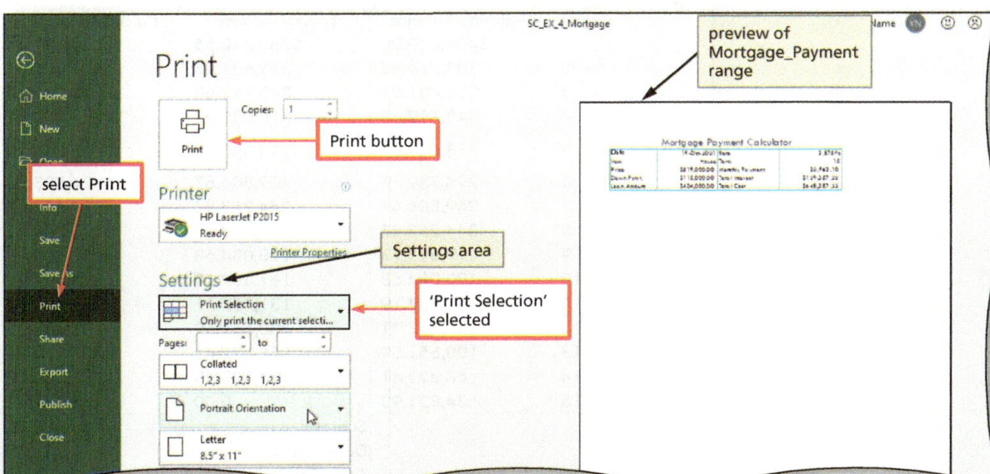

Figure 4–53

4

- Click the Print button in the Print gallery to print the selected named range, Mortgage_Payment in this case.
- One at a time, use the Name box to select the names Interest_Schedule, Amortization_Schedule, and Financial_Tools, and then print them following the instructions in Step 3 to print the remaining named ranges (Figure 4–54).

5

- Save the workbook again on the same storage location with the same file name.

Mortgage_Payment range printout

Mortgage Payment Calculator

Date	19-Oct-2021	Rate	3.875%
Item	House	Term	15
Price	$519,000.00	Monthly Payment	$2,963.10
Down Pymt.	$115,000.00	Total Interest	$129,357.22
Loan Amount	$404,000.00	Total Cost	$648,357.22

Figure 4–54(a)

Interest_Schedule range printout

Varying Interest Rate Schedule

Rate	Monthly Payment	Total Interest	Total Cost
	$2,963.10	$129,357.22	$648,357.22
3.000%	2,789.95	98,190.97	617,190.97
3.125%	2,814.30	102,574.31	621,574.31
3.250%	2,838.78	106,980.73	625,980.73
3.375%	2,863.39	111,410.17	630,410.17
3.500%	2,888.13	115,862.58	634,862.58
3.625%	2,912.99	120,337.93	639,337.93
3.750%	2,937.98	124,836.16	643,836.16
3.875%	2,963.10	129,357.22	648,357.22
4.000%	2,988.34	133,901.06	652,901.06
4.125%	3,013.71	138,467.62	657,467.62
4.250%	3,039.20	143,056.86	662,056.86

Figure 4–54(b)

Amortization_Schedule range printout

Amortization Schedule

Year	Beginning Balance	Ending Balance	Paid on Principal	Interest Paid
1	$404,000.00	$383,740.55	$20,259.45	$15,297.70
2	383,740.55	362,681.95	21,058.60	14,498.55
3	362,681.95	340,792.68	21,889.27	13,667.88
4	340,792.68	318,039.97	22,752.71	12,804.44
5	318,039.97	294,389.77	23,650.20	11,906.95
6	294,389.77	269,806.67	24,583.10	10,974.05
7	269,806.67	244,253.87	25,552.80	10,004.35
8	244,253.87	217,693.13	26,560.75	8,996.40
9	217,693.13	190,084.68	27,608.45	7,948.70
10	190,084.68	161,387.19	28,697.49	6,859.66
11	161,387.19	131,557.71	29,829.48	5,727.67
12	131,557.71	100,551.59	31,006.12	4,551.03
13	100,551.59	68,322.41	32,229.18	3,327.97
14	68,322.41	34,821.93	33,500.48	2,056.67
15	34,821.93	0.00	34,821.93	735.22
		Subtotal	$404,000.00	$129,357.22
		Down Pymt.		$115,000.00
		Total Cost		$648,357.22

Figure 4–54(c)

> **Q&A** **Why does the Financial_Tools range print on one page?** Recall that you selected the Fit to option earlier (Figure 4–47). This selection ensures that each of the printouts fits across the page in portrait orientation.

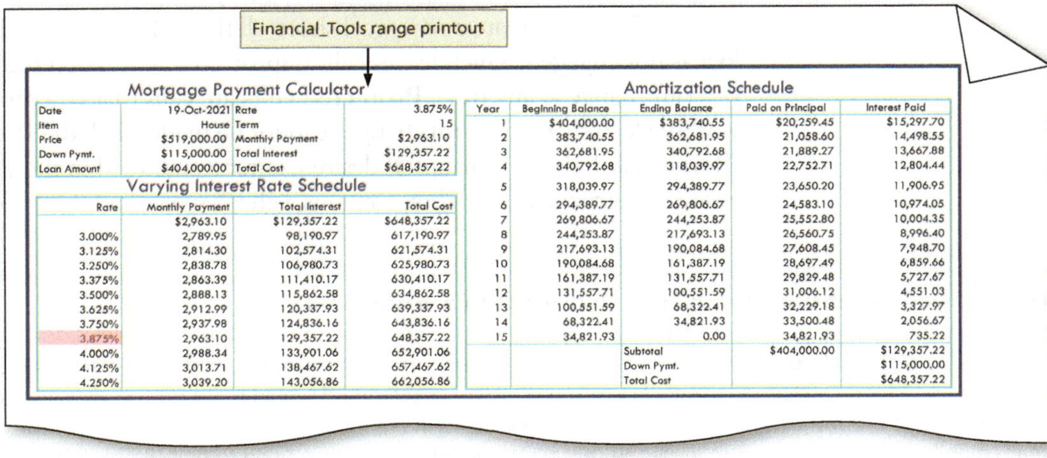

Mortgage Payment Calculator

Date	19-Oct-2021	Rate	3.875%
Item	House	Term	15
Price	$519,000.00	Monthly Payment	$2,963.10
Down Pymt.	$115,000.00	Total Interest	$129,357.22
Loan Amount	$404,000.00	Total Cost	$648,357.22

Varying Interest Rate Schedule

Rate	Monthly Payment	Total Interest	Total Cost
	$2,963.10	$129,357.22	$648,357.22
3.000%	2,789.95	98,190.97	617,190.97
3.125%	2,814.30	102,574.31	621,574.31
3.250%	2,838.78	106,980.73	625,980.73
3.375%	2,863.39	111,410.17	630,410.17
3.500%	2,888.13	115,862.58	634,862.58
3.625%	2,912.99	120,337.93	639,337.93
3.750%	2,937.98	124,836.16	643,836.16
3.875%	2,963.10	129,357.22	648,357.22
4.000%	2,988.34	133,901.06	652,901.06
4.125%	3,013.71	138,467.62	657,467.62
4.250%	3,039.20	143,056.86	662,056.86

Amortization Schedule

Year	Beginning Balance	Ending Balance	Paid on Principal	Interest Paid
1	$404,000.00	$383,740.55	$20,259.45	$15,297.70
2	383,740.55	362,681.95	21,058.60	14,498.55
3	362,681.95	340,792.68	21,889.27	13,667.88
4	340,792.68	318,039.97	22,752.71	12,804.44
5	318,039.97	294,389.77	23,650.20	11,906.95
6	294,389.77	269,806.67	24,583.10	10,974.05
7	269,806.67	244,253.87	25,552.80	10,004.35
8	244,253.87	217,693.13	26,560.75	8,996.40
9	217,693.13	190,084.68	27,608.45	7,948.70
10	190,084.68	161,387.19	28,697.49	6,859.66
11	161,387.19	131,557.71	29,829.48	5,727.67
12	131,557.71	100,551.59	31,006.12	4,551.03
13	100,551.59	68,322.41	32,229.18	3,327.97
14	68,322.41	34,821.93	33,500.48	2,056.67
15	34,821.93	0.00	34,821.93	735.22
		Subtotal	$404,000.00	$129,357.22
		Down Pymt.		$115,000.00
		Total Cost		$648,357.22

Figure 4–54(d)

Other Ways

1. Select cell or range, click Define Name button (Formulas tab | Defined Names group), type name, click OK (New Name dialog box)
2. Select cell or range, click Name Manager button (Formulas tab | Defined Names group), click New button, type name, click OK (New Name dialog box), click Close button (Name Manager dialog box)
3. Select cell or range, press CTRL+F3

Creating Formulas with Defined Names

Just as you can apply a name to a range of cells for printing, you can also use names to refer to ranges of cells in formulas. Naming a range of cells might make it easier for you to reference those cells as opposed to remembering the cell addresses corresponding to the range.

To Define a Name for a Range of Cells

1. Select the cell or range of cells to name.
2. Click the Define Name button (Formulas tab | Defined Names group).
3. Type the desired name in the Name text box.
4. Click OK.

Once you have defined a name for a cell or range of cells, you can use the name in one or more formulas. You can also use table names in formulas; you will learn more about table names in Module 6.

To Use a Defined Name in a Formula

1. Start typing the formula in the desired cell.
2. When you are ready to reference the cell or range of cells by its defined name, click the 'Use in Formula' button (Formulas tab | Defined Names group) to display a list of defined names.
3. Click the desired defined name to insert it into the formula.
4. Finish typing the formula.

Break Point: If you want to take a break, this is a good place to do so. You can exit Excel now. To resume later, start Excel, open the file called SC_EX_4_Mortgage, and continue following the steps from this location forward.

Protecting and Hiding Worksheets and Workbooks

When building a worksheet for novice users, you should protect the cells in the worksheet that you do not want changed, such as cells that contain text or formulas. Doing so prevents users from making changes to text and formulas in cells.

When you create a new worksheet, all the cells are assigned a locked status, but the lock is not engaged, which leaves cells unprotected. **Unprotected cells** are cells whose values you can change at any time. **Protected cells** are cells that you cannot change. To protect a workbook so that structural changes cannot be made, click the Protect Workbook button (Review tab | Protect group). If desired, enter a password in the Password (optional) text box, verify the Structure check box contains a check mark, and then click OK.

Consider This

How do you determine which cells to protect in a worksheet?

Deciding which cells to protect often depends upon the audience for your worksheet. In general, the highest level of security would be to protect all cells except those that require an entry by the user of the worksheet. This level of protection might be recommended for novice users, clients, or customers. A lesser safeguard would be to protect any cells containing formulas, so that users of the worksheet cannot modify the formulas. Finally, if you are creating a worksheet for your boss or a trusted team member, you might want to leave the cells unprotected, in case they need to edit the worksheet. In any case, you should protect cells only after the worksheet has been tested fully and the correct results appear. Protecting a worksheet is a two-step process:

1. Select the cells you want to leave unprotected and then change their cell protection settings to an unlocked status.
2. Protect the entire worksheet.

At first glance, these steps may appear to be backward. However, once you protect the entire worksheet, you cannot change anything, including the locked status of individual cells.

To Protect a Worksheet

Why? Protecting a worksheet allows you to determine which cells a user can modify. In the Mortgage Payment Calculator worksheet, the user should be able to make changes to only five cells: the item in cell D5, the price in cell D6, the down payment in cell D7, the interest rate in cell F4, and the term in cell F5 (Figure 4–55). These cells must remain unprotected so that the user can enter data. The remaining cells in the worksheet can be protected so that the user cannot change them. The following steps protect the Mortgage Payment Calculator worksheet.

1

- Select the range D5:D7 and then, while holding down CTRL, select the nonadjacent range F4:F5.
- Right-click one of the selected ranges to display a shortcut menu and mini toolbar (Figure 4–55).

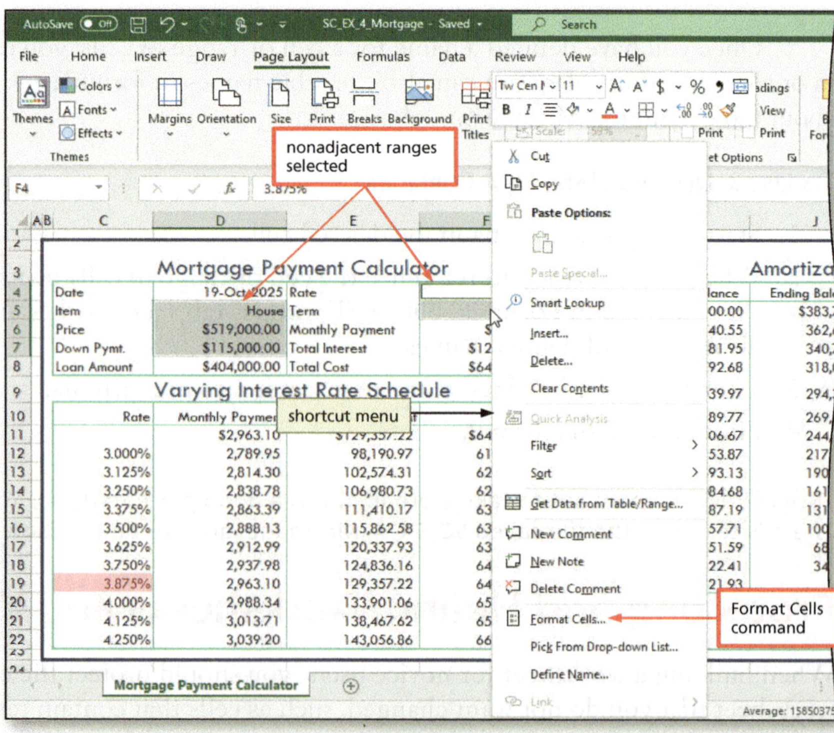

Figure 4–55

2

- Click Format Cells on the shortcut menu to display the Format Cells dialog box.
- Click the Protection tab (Format Cells dialog box) and then click Locked to remove the check mark (Figure 4–56).

Q&A

What happens when I remove the check mark from the Locked check box?
Removing the check mark from the Locked check box allows users to modify the selected cells (D5:D7 and F4:F5) after you use the Protect Sheet command.

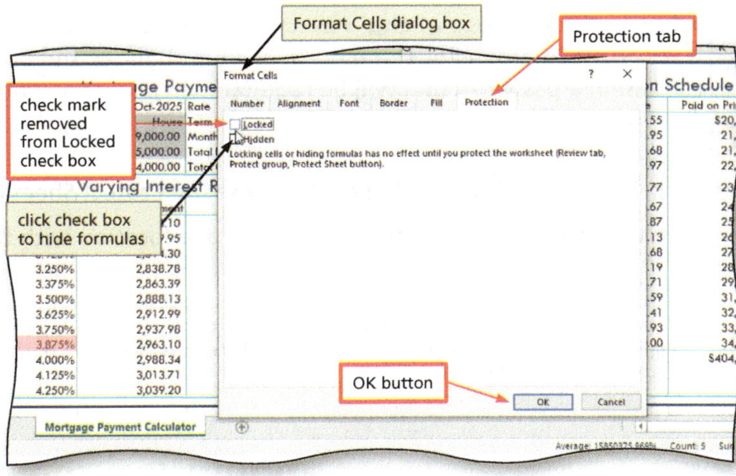

Figure 4–56

3

- Click OK to close the Format Cells dialog box.
- Deselect the ranges, and display the Review tab (Figure 4–57).

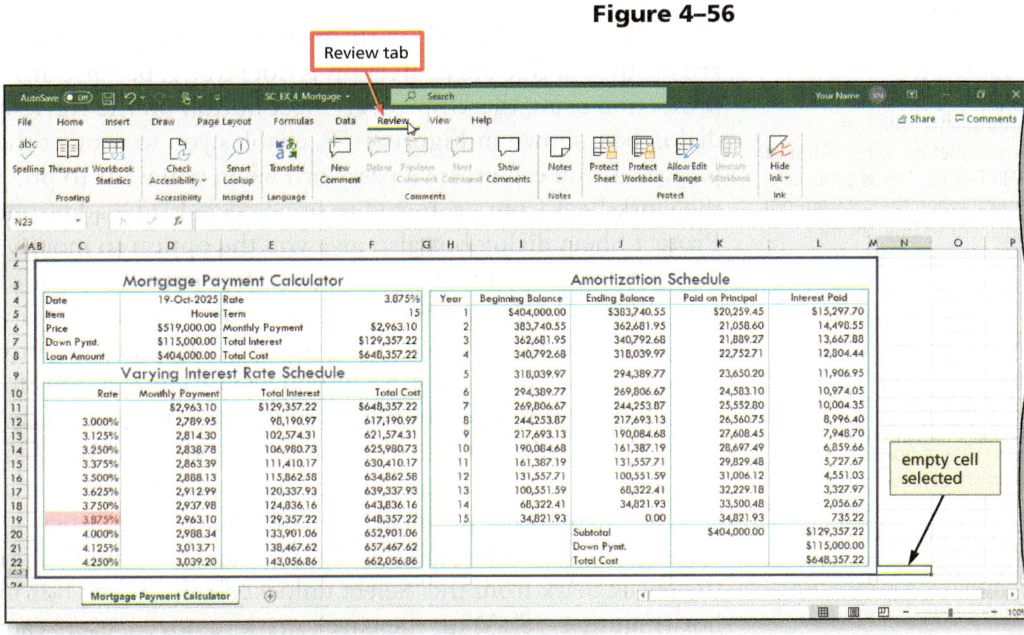

Figure 4–57

4

- Click the Protect Sheet button (Review tab | Changes group) to display the Protect Sheet dialog box.
- Verify that the 'Protect worksheet and contents of locked cells' check box (at the top of the Protect Sheet dialog box) and the first two check boxes in the list contain check marks so that the user of the worksheet can select both locked and unlocked cells (Figure 4–58).

Q&A

What do the three checked settings mean?
With all three check boxes selected, the worksheet (except for the cells left unlocked) is protected from modification. The two check boxes in the list allow users to select any cell on the worksheet, but they only can change unlocked cells.

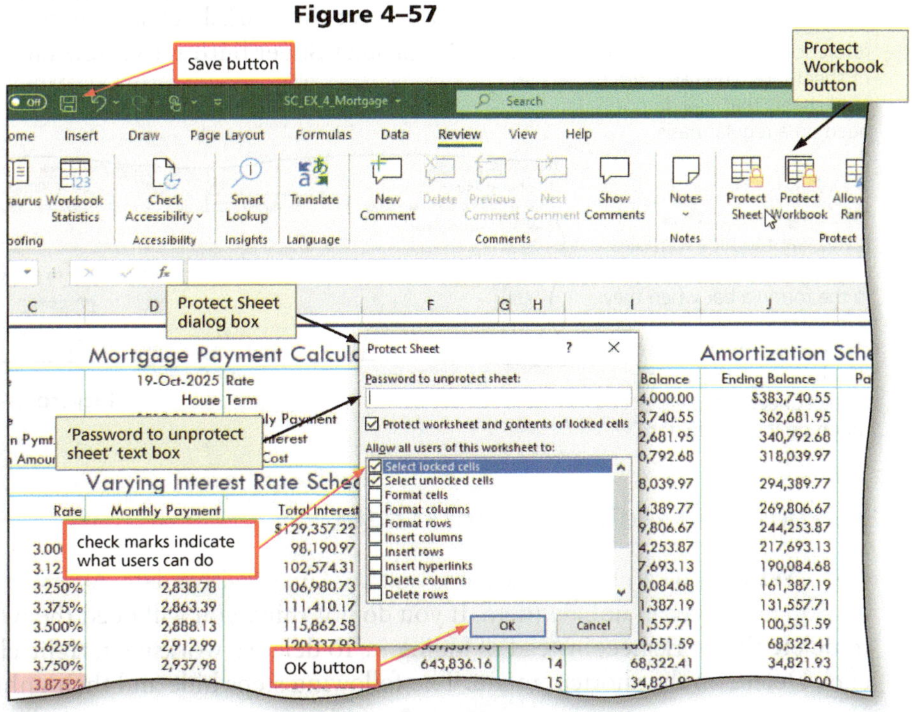

Figure 4–58

Q&A

What is the purpose of the 'Password to unprotect sheet' text box?
If you want to protect one or more cells from changes and do not want others to easily unprotect the sheet, you can assign a password that will be required when someone attempts to unprotect the sheet.

5

- Click OK (Protect Sheet dialog box) to close the Protect Sheet dialog box.
- Save the workbook again on the same storage location with the same file name.

Other Ways

1. Click Format Cells Dialog Box Launcher (Home tab | Font, Alignment, or Number group), click Protection tab, remove check mark from Locked check box, click OK
2. Click File tab, click Info tab, click Protect Workbook, click Protect Current Sheet, select options, click OK

BTW

Using Protected Worksheets

You can move from one unprotected cell to another unprotected cell in a worksheet by using TAB and SHIFT+TAB. This is especially useful when the cells are not adjacent to one another.

BTW

Hiding Worksheets

When sharing workbooks with others, you may not want them to see some of your worksheets. Hiding worksheets obscures the worksheets from casual inspection; however, it is not only for hiding worksheets from others' eyes. Sometimes, you have several worksheets that include data that you rarely require or that you use only as a reference. To clean up the list of sheet tabs, you can hide worksheets that you do not need on a regular basis.

BTW

Hiding Formulas

If you want to hide formulas so that users won't see them in the formula bar when they select a cell, select the Hidden check box in the Format Cells dialog box and then select Protect Sheet in the Protect group on the Review tab.

More about Worksheet Protection

Now all of the cells in the worksheet, except for the ranges D5:D7 and F4:F5, are protected. But the protection is not strong, because any user can remove the protection using the Unprotect Sheet button on the Review tab. The Protect Sheet dialog box, shown in Figure 4–58, enables you to protect the worksheet using a password. You can create a password when you want to prevent others from changing the worksheet from protected to unprotected. The additional settings in the list in the Protect Sheet dialog box also give you the option to modify the protection so that the user can make certain changes, such as formatting cells or inserting hyperlinks.

If you want to protect more than one worksheet in a workbook, either select each worksheet before you begin the protection process or click the Protect Workbook button, shown in Figure 4–58. If you want to unlock cells for specific users, you can use the 'Allow Edit Ranges' button (Review tab | Protect group).

When this protected worksheet is made available to users, they will be able to enter data in only the unprotected cells. If they try to change any protected cell, such as the monthly payment in cell F6, Excel will display a dialog box with an error message, as shown in Figure 4–59. You can eliminate this error message by removing the check mark from the 'Select unlocked cells' check box in the Protect Sheet dialog box (Figure 4–58). With the check mark removed, users cannot select a locked cell.

To unprotect the worksheet so that you can change all cells in the worksheet, click the Unprotect Sheet button (Review tab | Changes group).

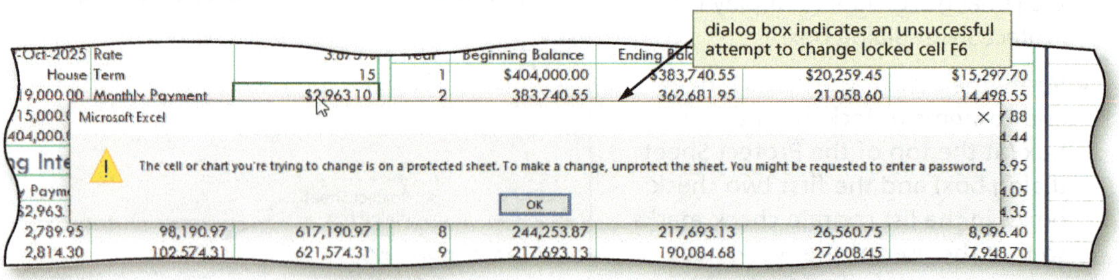

Figure 4–59

To Hide and Unhide a Worksheet

Why? You can hide worksheets that contain sensitive data. Afterwards, when you need to access these hidden worksheets, you can unhide them. If you do not think you will need the worksheet in the future, you may choose to delete the worksheet instead of hiding it. To delete a worksheet, right-click the desired worksheet tab and then click Delete on the shortcut menu. The following steps hide and then unhide a worksheet.

1

- Click the New sheet button to insert a new worksheet in the workbook.
- Right-click the Mortgage Payment Calculator sheet tab to display a shortcut menu (Figure 4–60).

Q&A

Why insert a new worksheet?
Workbooks must contain at least one visible worksheet. In order to hide the Mortgage Payment Calculator worksheet, there must be another visible worksheet in the workbook.

Why does the Unhide command on the shortcut menu appear dimmed?
The Unhide command appears dimmed when it is unavailable; because no worksheets are hidden, the command is unavailable.

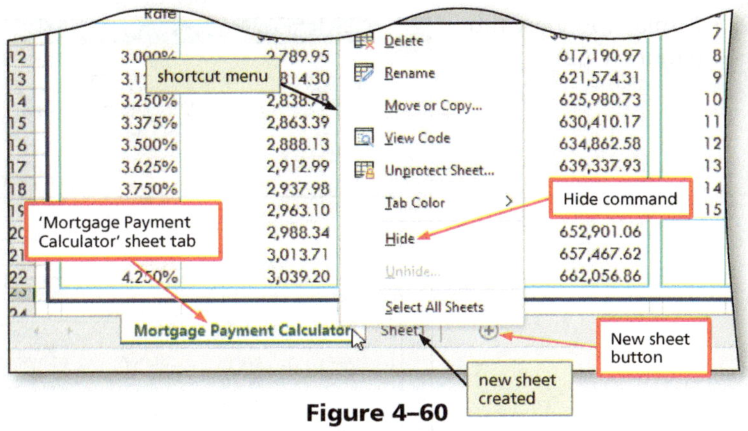

Figure 4–60

2

- Click Hide on the shortcut menu to hide the Mortgage Payment Calculator worksheet.
- Right-click any sheet tab to display a shortcut menu.
- Click Unhide on the shortcut menu to display the Unhide dialog box.
- If necessary, click Mortgage Payment Calculator in the Unhide sheet list (Unhide dialog box) to select the worksheet to unhide (Figure 4–61).

Q&A

Why should I hide a worksheet?
Hiding worksheets in a workbook is a common approach when working with complex workbooks that contain one worksheet with the results users need to see and one or more worksheets with essential data that, while important to the functionality of the workbook, is unimportant to users of the workbook. Thus, these data worksheets often are hidden from view. Although the worksheets are hidden, the data and formulas on the hidden worksheets remain available for use by other worksheets in the workbook.

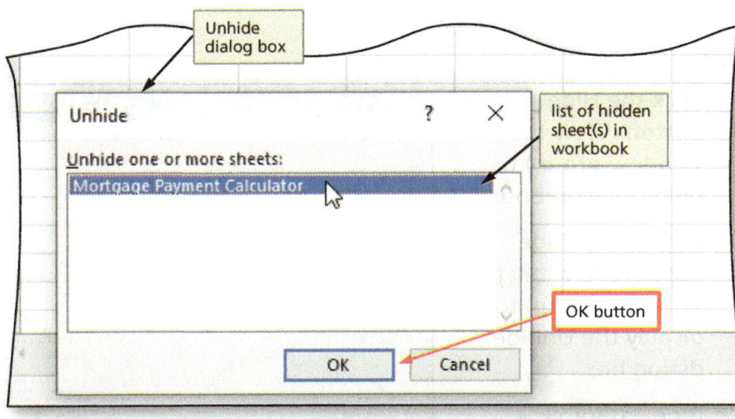

Figure 4–61

3

- Click OK (Unhide dialog box) to reveal the hidden worksheet.

To Hide and Unhide a Workbook

In addition to hiding worksheets, you also can hide an entire workbook. **Why?** This feature is useful when you have several workbooks open simultaneously and want the user to be able to view only one of them. Also, some users hide the entire workbook when the computer is unattended and they do not want others to be able to see the workbook. The following steps hide and unhide a workbook.

1

- Display the View tab (Figure 4–62).

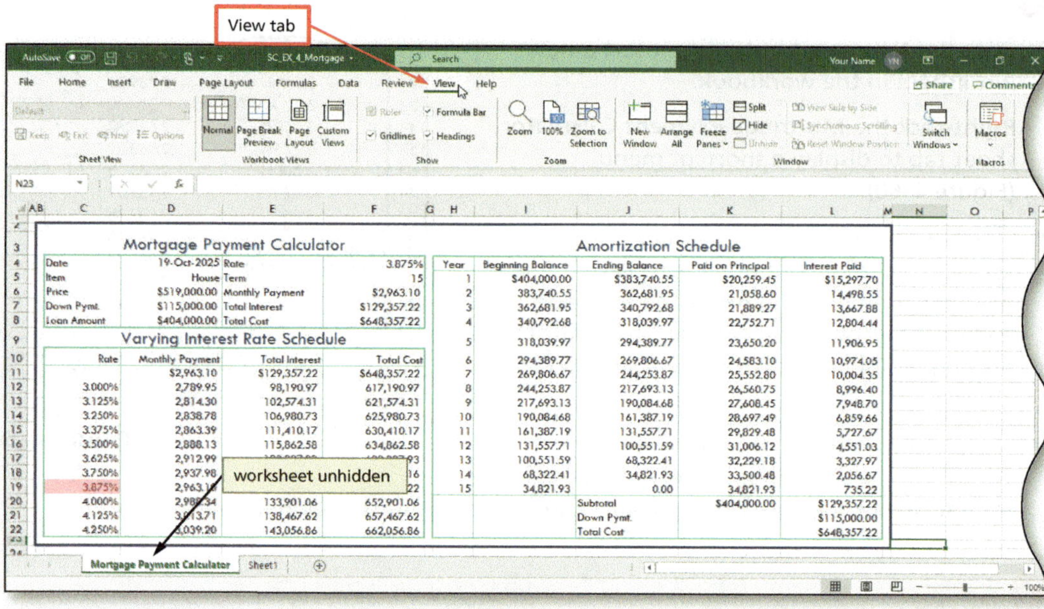

Figure 4–62

2

- Click the Hide button (View tab | Window group) to hide the workbook.
- Click the Unhide button (View tab | Window group) to display the Unhide dialog box.
- If necessary, click SC_EX_4_Mortgage in the Unhide workbook list (Unhide dialog box) to select a workbook to unhide (Figure 4–63).

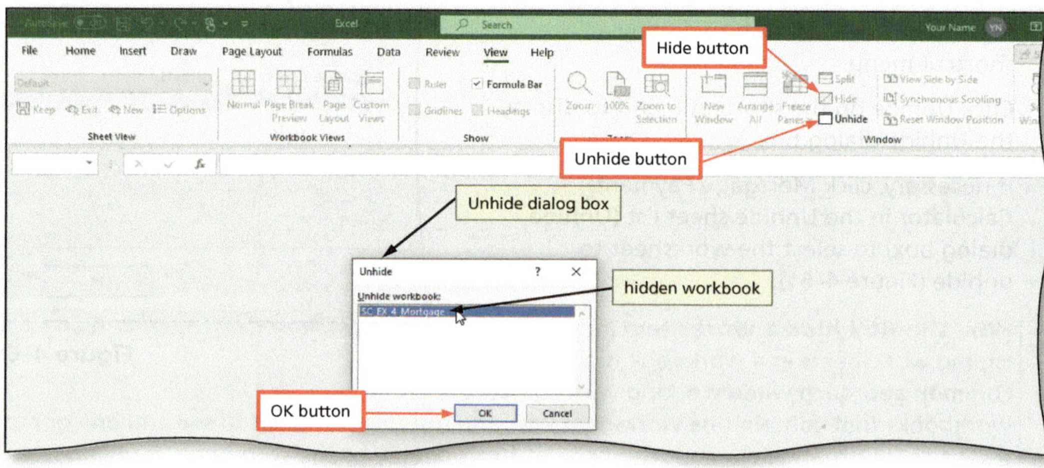

Figure 4–63

3

- Click OK (Unhide dialog box) to unhide the selected hidden workbook and display the workbook in the same state as it was in when it was hidden.

Formula Checking

Before you submit a workbook to a customer, client, or supervisor, you should check it for formula errors, just as you would check any document for spelling errors. Excel has a formula checker that checks all the formulas in a worksheet and alerts you to any problems. You start the formula checker by clicking the Error Checking button (Formulas tab | Formula Auditing group). Each time Excel encounters a cell containing a formula, it applies a series of rules and alerts you if a formula violates any of them. The formula checker displays a dialog box containing information about the formula and a suggestion about how to fix the error. You can view the error-checking rules, and choose the ones you want Excel to use, in the Formulas pane in the Excel Options dialog box, shown in Figure 4–64. Table 4–3 lists the Excel error-checking rules and briefly describes each one.

Table 4–3 Error-Checking Rules

Rule	Description
Cells containing formulas that result in an error	The cell contains a formula that does not use the expected syntax, arguments, or data types.
Inconsistent calculated column formula in tables	The cell contains formulas or values that are inconsistent with the column formula or tables.
Cells containing years represented as 2 digits	The cell contains a text date with a two-digit year that can be misinterpreted as the wrong century.
Numbers formatted as text or preceded by an apostrophe	The cell contains numbers stored as text.
Formulas inconsistent with other formulas in the region	The cell contains a formula that does not match the pattern of the formulas around it.
Formulas which omit cells in a region	The cell contains a formula that does not include a correct cell or range reference.
Unlocked cells containing formulas	The cell with a formula is unlocked in a protected worksheet.
Formulas referring to empty cells	The cells referenced in a formula are empty.
Data entered in a table is invalid	The cell has a data validation error.

To Enable Background Formula Checking

While you can run the formula checker at any time using the Formulas tab | Error Checking command, you may want Excel to automatically check your formulas and alert you to errors as you work. This is called working "in the background." Through the Excel Options dialog box, you can enable background formula checking. **Why?** You want Excel to continually review the workbook for errors in formulas as you create or manipulate data, formulas, and functions. The following steps enable background formula checking.

1

- Click File on the ribbon to open Backstage view and then click Options to display the Excel Options dialog box.
- Click Formulas in the left pane (Excel Options dialog box) to display options related to formula calculation, performance, and error handling in the right pane.
- Click any check box in the 'Error checking rules' area that does not contain a check mark so that all error checking rules are enabled (Figure 4–64). As you add check marks, click the 'Reset Ignored Errors' button in the Error Checking section to reset error checking.

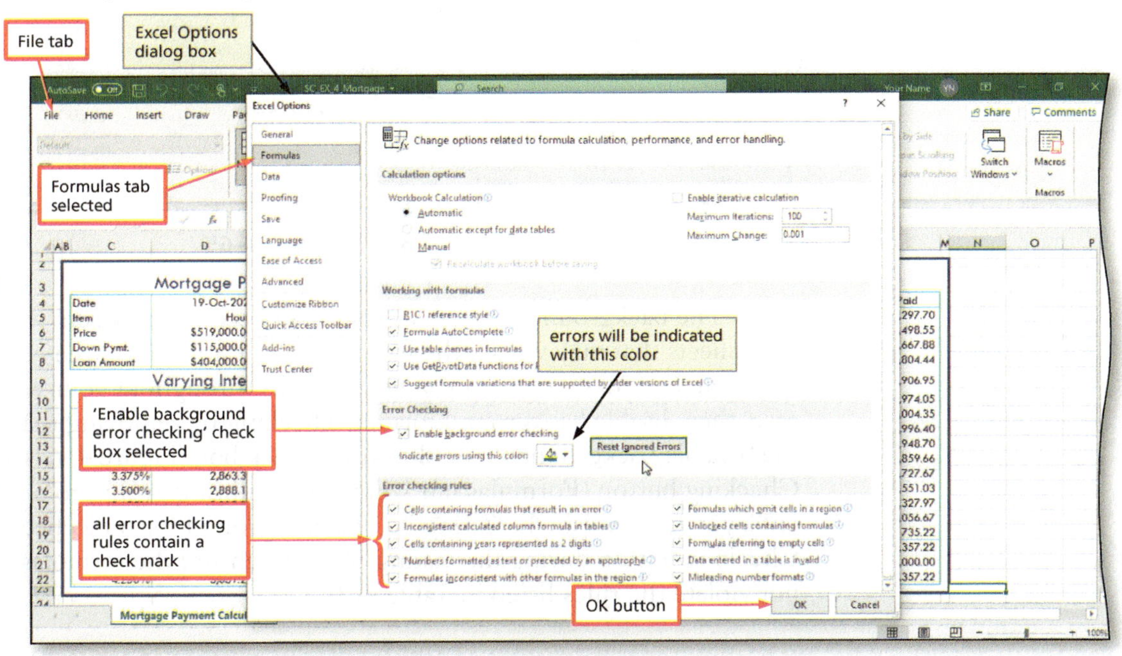

Figure 4–64

2

- Click OK (Excel Options dialog box) to close the Excel Options dialog box.
- If desired, sign out of your Microsoft account.
- Exit Excel.

BTW

Distributing a Workbook

Instead of printing and distributing a hard copy of a workbook, you can distribute the workbook electronically. Options include sending the workbook via email; posting it on cloud storage (such as OneDrive) and sharing the file with others; posting it on social media, a blog, or other website; and sharing a link associated with an online location of the workbook. You also can create and share a PDF or XPS image of the workbook, so that users can view the file in Acrobat Reader or XPS Viewer instead of in Excel.

More about Background Formula Checking

When background formula checking is enabled and a formula fails to pass one of the rules, Excel adds a small green triangle to the upper-left corner of the cell.

Assume, for example, that background formula checking is enabled and that cell F6, which contains the PMT function in the Mortgage Payment Calculator workbook, is unlocked. Because one of the error checking rules, shown in Table 4–3, stipulates that a cell containing a formula must be locked, Excel displays a green triangle in the upper-left corner of cell F6.

When you select the cell with the green triangle, a Trace Error button appears next to the cell. If you click the Trace Error button, Excel displays the Trace Error menu (Figure 4–65). The first item in the menu identifies the error (Unprotected Formula). The remainder of the menu lists commands from which you can choose. The first command locks the cell. Invoking the Lock Cell command fixes the problem so that the formula no longer violates the rule. Selecting the 'Error Checking Options' command displays the Excel Options dialog box with the Formulas tab active, as shown in Figure 4–64.

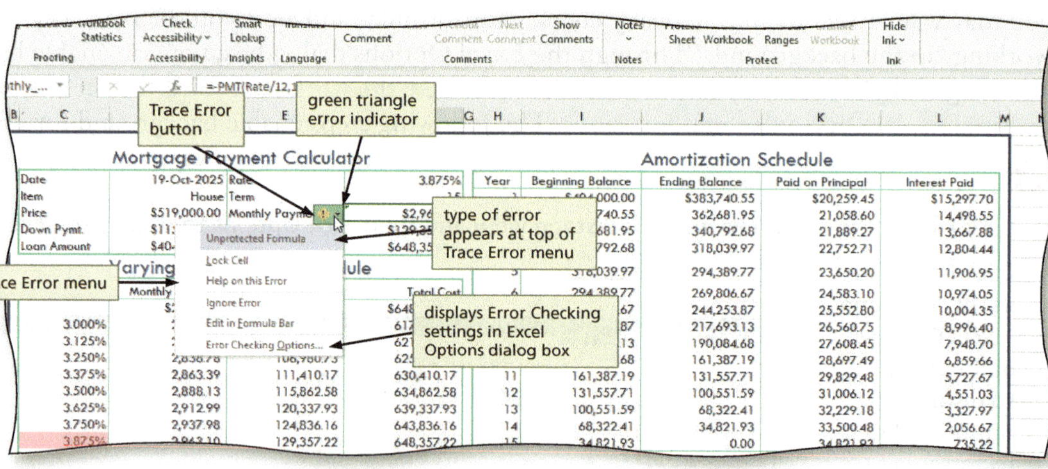

Figure 4–65

The background formula checker can become annoying when you are creating worksheets that may violate the formula rules until referenced cells contain data. You often can end up with green triangles in cells throughout your worksheet. If this is the case, then disable background formula checking by removing the check mark from the 'Enable background error checking' check box (Figure 4–64) and use the Error Checking button (Formulas tab | Formula Auditing group) to check your worksheet once you have finished creating it. Use background formula checking or the Error Checking button during the testing phase to ensure the formulas in your workbook do not violate the rules listed in Table 4–3.

Summary

In this module, you learned how to use names, rather than cell references, to enter formulas; use financial functions, such as the PMT and PV functions; analyze data by creating a data table and amortization schedule; set print options and print sections of a worksheet using names and the Set Print Area command; protect a worksheet or workbook; hide and unhide worksheets and workbooks; and check for errors.

Consider This: Plan Ahead

What decisions will you need to make when creating your next financial decision-making worksheet?

Use these guidelines as you complete the assignments in this module and create your own worksheets for evaluating financial scenarios.

1. Determine the worksheet structure.
   a) Determine the data you will need.
   b) Determine the layout of your data.
   c) Determine the layout of the financial calculator.
   d) Determine the layout of any data tables.
2. Create the worksheet.
   a) Enter titles, subtitles, and headings.
   b) Enter data, functions, and formulas.
   c) Assign names to cells and cell ranges.
   d) Create data tables.
3. Format the worksheet.
   a) Format the titles, subtitles, and headings.
   b) Format the numbers as necessary.
   c) Format the text.
4. Perform what-if analyses.
   a) Adjust values in the assumptions table to review scenarios of interest.
5. Secure the cell contents.
   a) Lock and unlock cells as necessary.
   b) Protect the worksheet.

Apply Your Knowledge

Reinforce the skills and apply the concepts you learned in this module.

Calculating Loan Payments

Note: To complete this assignment, you will be required to use the Data Files. Please contact your instructor for information about accessing the Data Files.

Instructions: Start Excel. Open the workbook called SC_EX_4-1.xlsx, which is located in the Data Files. The workbook you open contains loan information from which you will create a data table. You are to recreate the Loan Payment Calculator pictured in Figure 4–66. You will be instructed to print several times in this assignment. If requested or allowed by your instructor, consider saving paper by printing to a PDF file.

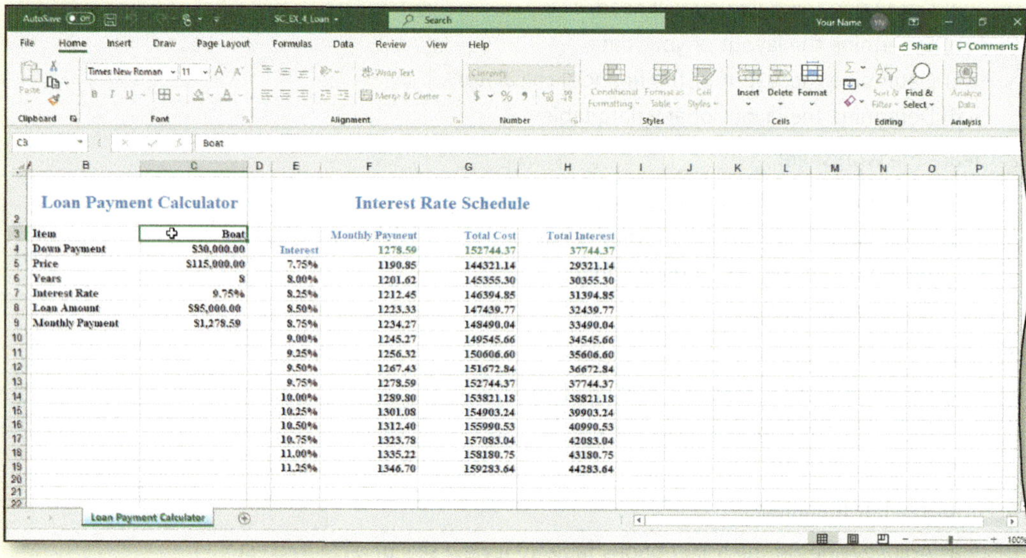

Figure 4–66

Perform the following tasks:

1. Select the range B4:C9. Use the 'Create from Selection' button (Formulas tab | Defined Names group) to create names for cells in the range C4:C9 using the row titles in the range B4:B9.
2. Enter the formulas shown in Table 4–4.

Table 4–4 Loan Payment Calculator and Interest Rate Schedule Formulas

Cell	Formula
C8	=Price–Down_Payment
C9	=-PMT(Interest_Rate/12, 12*Years, Loan_Amount)
F4	=Monthly_Payment
G4	=12*Monthly_Payment*Years+Down_Payment
H4	=G4–Price

3. Use the Data Table button in the What-If Analysis gallery (Data tab | Forecast group) to define the range E4:H19 as a one-input data table. Use the Interest Rate in the Loan Payment Calculator as the column input cell.
4. Use the Page Setup dialog box to select the Fit to and 'Black and white' options. Select the range B2:C9 and then use the 'Set Print Area' command to set a print area. Use the Print button on the Print screen in Backstage view to print the worksheet. Use the 'Clear Print Area' command to clear the print area.

5. Name the following ranges: B2:C9 – **`Calculator`**; E2:H19 – **`Rate_Schedule`**; and B2:H19 – **`All_Sections`**. Print each range by selecting the name in the Name box and using the Print Selection option on the Print screen in Backstage view.
6. Unlock the range C3:C7. Protect the worksheet so that the user can select only unlocked cells.
7. Press CTRL+` and then print the formulas version in landscape orientation. Press CTRL+` again to return to the values version.
8. Hide and then unhide the Loan Payment Calculator worksheet. Hide and then unhide the workbook. Delete the extra worksheet you made so that you could hide the Loan Payment Calculator worksheet. Unprotect the worksheet and then hide columns E through H. Select columns D and I and reveal the hidden columns. Hide rows 11 through 19. Print the worksheet. Select rows 10 and 20 and unhide rows 11 through 19. Protect the worksheet.
9. Determine the monthly payment and print the worksheet for each data set: (a) Item = **`Motorhome`**; Down Payment = **`$75,000.00`**; Price = **`$225,000.00`**; Years = **`7`**; Interest Rate = **`8.00%`**; (b) Item = **`Debt Consolidation Loan`**; Down Payment = **`$0.00`**; Price = **`$40,000.00`**; Years = **`5`**; Interest Rate = **`11.25%`**. Set the values in cells C3:C7 back to the Boat values after completing the above calculations.

   If requested by your instructor, add your initials to cell E3. You will need to unprotect the worksheet and unlock the cell to do so. Make sure to lock the cell and protect the worksheet after adding your initials.
10. Save the workbook with the file name, SC_EX_4_Loan, submit the revised workbook (as shown in Figure 4–66) in the format specified by your instructor, and exit Excel.
11. How would you revise the Interest Rate Schedule to be more informative to the user?

Extend Your Knowledge

Extend the skills you learned in this module and experiment with new skills. You may need to use Help to complete the assignment.

Planning Retirement

Note: To complete this assignment, you will be required to use the Data Files. Please contact your instructor for information about accessing the Data Files.

Instructions: Start Excel. Open the workbook SC_EX_4-2.xlsx, which is located in the Data Files. The workbook you open contains a financial calculator for a 403(b) retirement plan. You are to create a two-input data table that will help employees understand the impact that the amount they invest and the rate of return will have on their retirement earnings (Figure 4-67). Recall from the module that a two-input data table allows for two variables (amount invested and rate of return, in this case) in a formula.

Continued >

Extend Your Knowledge *continued*

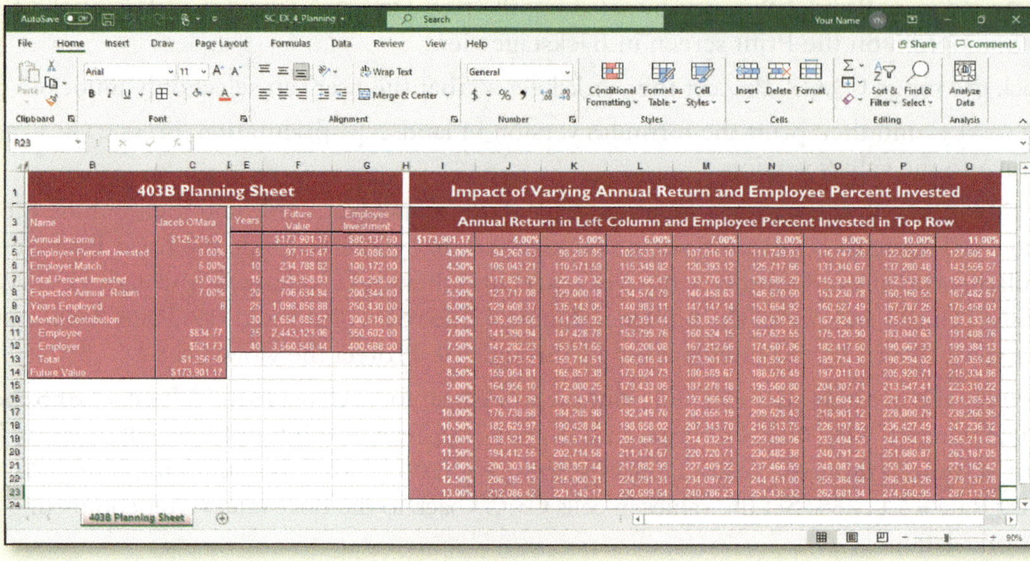

Figure 4–67

Perform the following tasks:

1. Enter **`Impact of Varying Annual Return and Employee Percent Invested`** in cell I1. Enter **`Annual Return in Left Column and Employee Percent Invested in Top Row`** in cell I3.
2. Save the workbook using the file name, SC_EX_4_Planning.
3. Change the width of column H to 0.92 (11 pixels). (Depending on your display settings, you may need to use the Column Width dialog box.) Merge and center the titles in cells I1 and I3 over columns I through Q. Format the titles using the Title cell style for both the title and subtitle, a font size of 18 for the title, and a font size of 16 for the subtitle. Change the column widths of columns I through Q to 13.14 (97 pixels). Format cells I1 and I3 to match the fill and font color in cell B1.
4. For a two-input data table, the formula you are analyzing must be assigned to the upper-left cell in the range of the data table. Because cell C14 contains the future value formula to be analyzed, enter **`=c14`** in cell I4.
5. Use the fill handle to create two lists of percentages: (a) 4.00% through 13.00% in increments of 0.50% in the range I5:I23 and (b) 4.00% through 11.00% in increments of 1.00% in the range J4:Q4.
6. Use the Data Table button in the What-If Analysis gallery (Data tab | Forecast group) to define the range I4:Q23 as a two-input data table. Enter **`C8`** in the 'Row input cell' box and **`C5`** in the 'Column input cell' box (Data Table dialog box). Click OK to populate the table.
7. Format the two-input data table using a White, Background 1 font color and the fill color used in cells B3:G12. Bold ranges I4:Q4 and I5:I23. Format cells J5:Q23 to match the number format used in cells F5:G12. Place a light style border around the range I3:Q23, light style borders between columns in that same range, and a light style bottom border on the range I4:Q4.
8. Protect the worksheet so that the user can select only unlocked cells (C3:C6 and C8:C9).
9. If necessary, change the print orientation to landscape. Print the worksheet using the Fit to option. Print the formulas version of the worksheet.

   If requested by your instructor, change the name in cell C3 to your name.
10. Save the file with the same filename and submit the revised workbook in the format specified by your instructor.
11. ❂ How could you improve the design of the worksheet to make the impact of various combinations of Employee Investment and Expected Annual Return more easily identified?

Expand Your World

Create a solution that uses cloud or web technologies by learning and investigating on your own from general guidance.

Down Payment Options for a Home

Note: To complete this assignment, you will be required to use the Data Files. Please contact your instructor for information about accessing the Data Files.

Instructions: You are planning to buy a home as soon as you can save enough to make a 15% down payment. Your task is to create a calculator that you can use to determine possible savings options, and to share this calculator with family using OneDrive. Start Excel. Open the workbook called SC_EX_4-3.xlsx, which is located in the Data Files. This workbook you open contains a basic structure to create a down payment calculator. You are to create a two-input data table to help determine the future value of savings.

Perform the following tasks:

1. Save the file using the file name SC_EX_4_Calculator.
2. Identify a home for sale in your local housing market that you would consider buying. Use the asking price for that home as the current value of the house, or use an online tool such as Zillow.com to find the current estimated value of the home. Enter this value in your Down Payment Calculator, and calculate the needed down payment.
3. Determine the amount you consider reasonable as a monthly savings toward a down payment, and enter this in your down payment calculator.
4. Use the Future Value function to calculate how much you could save, using the rate of return and years to save in the worksheet. Remember to use a minus sign before the function so that the calculation will appear positive.
5. Create a two-input data table that calculates the future value of savings. You can decide which two inputs you would like to use for your data table.
6. Format the worksheet using techniques you have learned to present the worksheet content in a visually appealing form (Figure 4–68).

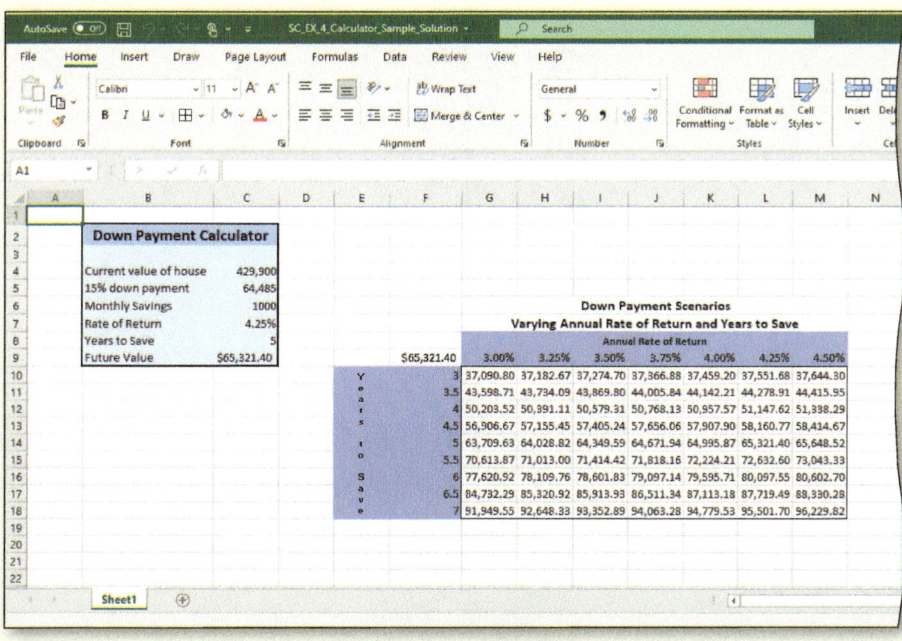

Figure 4–68

Continued >

Expand Your World *continued*

7. If requested by your instructor, save the file on OneDrive.
8. Submit the workbook as specified by your instructor.
9. Why did you select the two inputs used in your data table? How useful are they for evaluating down payment savings options?

In the Lab

Design and implement a solution using creative thinking and problem-solving skills.

Determining the Break-Even Point

Problem: You have been hired by Dominic Manero, owner of a small start-up company, to create a data table that analyzes the break-even point for a new product he is developing. He would like you to analyze the break-even point for prices ranging from $12.99 to $22.99 per unit, in $1.00 increments. You can calculate the number of units he must sell to break even (the break-even point) if you know the fixed expenses, the price per unit, and the expense (cost) per unit. The following formula determines the break-even point:

Break-Even Point = Fixed Expenses / (Price per Unit – Expense per Unit)

Assume Fixed Expenses = $8,000; Price per Unit = $14.99; and Expense per Unit = $8.00.

Perform the following tasks:

Part 1: Use the concepts and techniques presented in this module to determine the break-even point and then create the data table. Use the Price per Unit as the input cell and the break-even value as the result. Protect the worksheet so that only cells with data can be selected. Submit your assignment in the format specified by your instructor.

Part 2: You made several decisions while creating the worksheet for this assignment. How did you set up the worksheet? How did you decide how to create the data table? What was the rationale behind each of these decisions?

5 Working with Multiple Worksheets and Workbooks

Objectives

After completing this module, you will be able to:

- Format a consolidated worksheet
- Fill using a linear series
- Use date, time, and rounding functions
- Apply a custom format code
- Create a new cell style
- Copy a worksheet
- Drill to add data to multiple worksheets at the same time
- Select and deselect sheet combinations
- Enter formulas that use 3-D cell references
- Use the Paste gallery
- Format a 3-D pie chart with an exploded slice and leader lines
- Save individual worksheets as separate workbook files
- View and hide multiple workbooks
- Consolidate data by linking separate workbooks

Introduction

Typically, a business will need to store data unique to various areas, departments, locations, or regions. If you enter each location's data, for example, on a different worksheet in a single workbook, you can use the sheet tabs at the bottom of the Excel window to move from worksheet to worksheet or location to location. Note, however, that many business applications require data from several worksheets to be summarized on one worksheet. To facilitate this summarization, you can create a cumulative worksheet, entering formulas and functions that reference cells from the other worksheets. The process of combining data on multiple worksheets and displaying the result on another worksheet is called **consolidation**.

Another important concept presented in this module is the use of custom format codes and cell styles. Custom format codes allow you to specify, in detail, how a cell entry will appear. For example, you can create a custom format code to indicate how positive numbers, negative numbers, zeros, and text are displayed in a cell. Custom cell styles store specific font formatting for repeated use.

As you learn how to work with multiple worksheets and workbooks, you also will learn about the many Excel formatting features for pie charts, such as exploding slices and adding leader lines.

Project: Consolidated Expenses Worksheet

The project in the module follows proper design guidelines and uses Excel to create the worksheets shown in Figure 5–1. M&S Provisions manages three different food trucks that serve a variety of food and drinks. The management wants to project consolidated expenses for the next two years, along with separate worksheets for each food truck. The first worksheet shows the projected expenses for 2020, the projected percentage change, and the resulting expenses for 2021 and 2022. The 2020 expenses—consolidated from the three food trucks—will be highlighted in a 3-D pie chart.

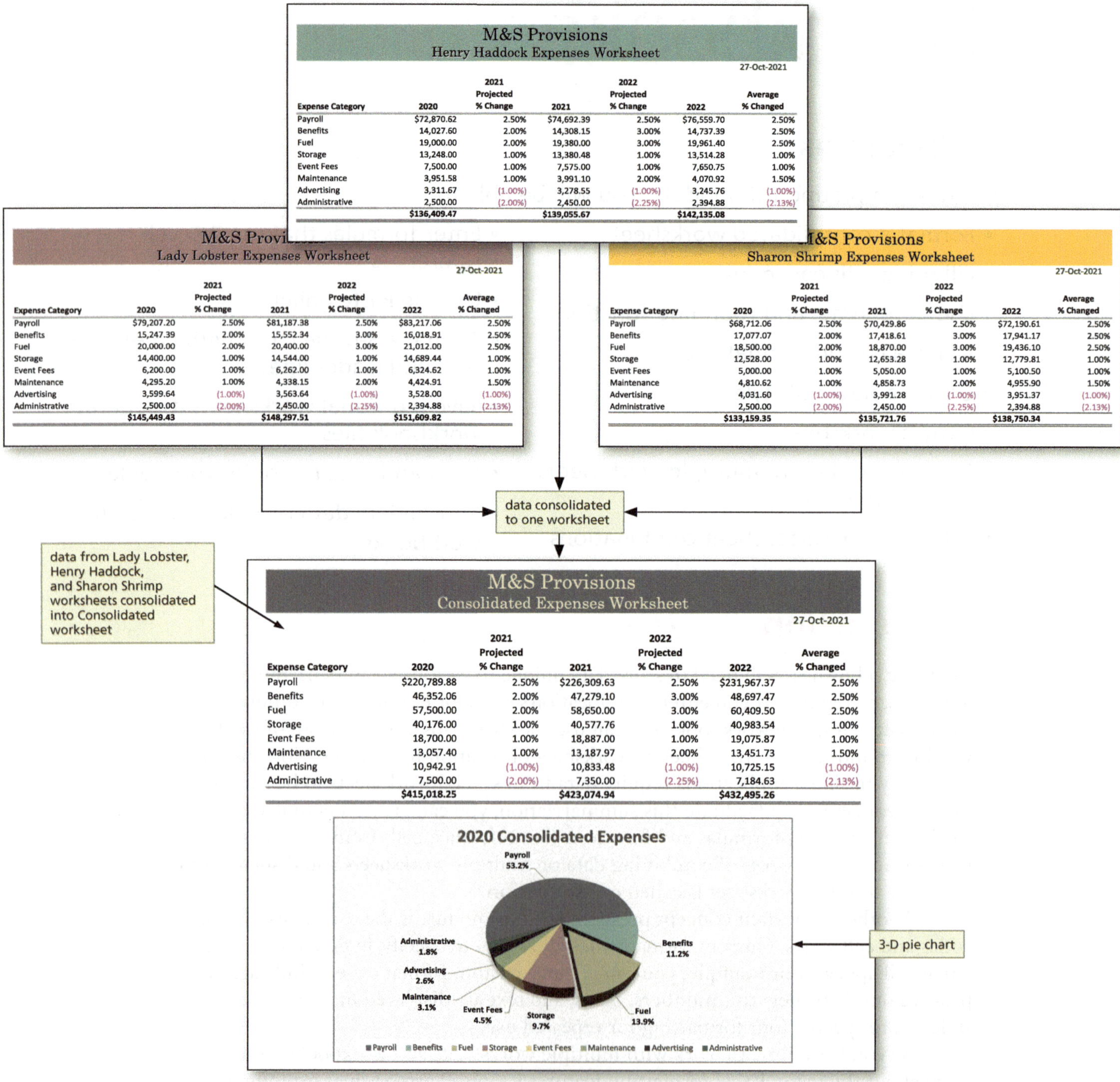

Expense Category	2020	2021 Projected % Change	2021	2022 Projected % Change	2022	Average % Changed
Payroll	$72,870.62	2.50%	$74,692.39	2.50%	$76,559.70	2.50%
Benefits	14,027.60	2.00%	14,308.15	3.00%	14,737.39	2.50%
Fuel	19,000.00	2.00%	19,380.00	3.00%	19,961.40	2.50%
Storage	13,248.00	1.00%	13,380.48	1.00%	13,514.28	1.00%
Event Fees	7,500.00	1.00%	7,575.00	1.00%	7,650.75	1.00%
Maintenance	3,951.58	1.00%	3,991.10	2.00%	4,070.92	1.50%
Advertising	3,311.67	(1.00%)	3,278.55	(1.00%)	3,245.76	(1.00%)
Administrative	2,500.00	(2.00%)	2,450.00	(2.25%)	2,394.88	(2.13%)
	$136,409.47		$139,055.67		$142,135.08	

Expense Category	2020	2021 Projected % Change	2021	2022 Projected % Change	2022	Average % Changed
Payroll	$79,207.20	2.50%	$81,187.38	2.50%	$83,217.06	2.50%
Benefits	15,247.39	2.00%	15,552.34	3.00%	16,018.91	2.50%
Fuel	20,000.00	2.00%	20,400.00	3.00%	21,012.00	2.50%
Storage	14,400.00	1.00%	14,544.00	1.00%	14,689.44	1.00%
Event Fees	6,200.00	1.00%	6,262.00	1.00%	6,324.62	1.00%
Maintenance	4,295.20	1.00%	4,338.15	2.00%	4,424.91	1.50%
Advertising	3,599.64	(1.00%)	3,563.64	(1.00%)	3,528.00	(1.00%)
Administrative	2,500.00	(2.00%)	2,450.00	(2.25%)	2,394.88	(2.13%)
	$145,449.43		$148,297.51		$151,609.82	

Expense Category	2020	2021 Projected % Change	2021	2022 Projected % Change	2022	Average % Changed
Payroll	$68,712.06	2.50%	$70,429.86	2.50%	$72,190.61	2.50%
Benefits	17,077.07	2.00%	17,418.61	3.00%	17,941.17	2.50%
Fuel	18,500.00	2.00%	18,870.00	3.00%	19,436.10	2.50%
Storage	12,528.00	1.00%	12,653.28	1.00%	12,779.81	1.00%
Event Fees	5,000.00	1.00%	5,050.00	1.00%	5,100.50	1.00%
Maintenance	4,810.62	1.00%	4,858.73	2.00%	4,955.90	1.50%
Advertising	4,031.60	(1.00%)	3,991.28	(1.00%)	3,951.37	(1.00%)
Administrative	2,500.00	(2.00%)	2,450.00	(2.25%)	2,394.88	(2.13%)
	$133,159.35		$135,721.76		$138,750.34	

Expense Category	2020	2021 Projected % Change	2021	2022 Projected % Change	2022	Average % Changed
Payroll	$220,789.88	2.50%	$226,309.63	2.50%	$231,967.37	2.50%
Benefits	46,352.06	2.00%	47,279.10	3.00%	48,697.47	2.50%
Fuel	57,500.00	2.00%	58,650.00	3.00%	60,409.50	2.50%
Storage	40,176.00	1.00%	40,577.76	1.00%	40,983.54	1.00%
Event Fees	18,700.00	1.00%	18,887.00	1.00%	19,075.87	1.00%
Maintenance	13,057.40	1.00%	13,187.97	2.00%	13,451.73	1.50%
Advertising	10,942.91	(1.00%)	10,833.48	(1.00%)	10,725.15	(1.00%)
Administrative	7,500.00	(2.00%)	7,350.00	(2.25%)	7,184.63	(2.13%)
	$415,018.25		$423,074.94		$432,495.26	

Figure 5–1

The requirements document for the M&S Provisions Consolidated Workbook is shown in Table 5–1. It includes the needs, source of data, summary of calculations, and other facts about its development.

Table 5–1 Requirements Document

Worksheet Title	M&S Provisions
Needs	The needs are as follows: 1. Create a workbook containing three worksheets (one for each of the three food trucks), one worksheet to consolidate the expenses, and a pie chart. 2. Each worksheet should be identical in structure and allow for display of the current expenses and projected expenses for the next two years. 3. The worksheets should print with a common header and footer. 4. The chart should show the 2020 consolidated expenses and draw attention to the largest expense after payroll.
Source of Data	M&S Provisions will provide the data for each of the three food trucks. Projection assumptions also will be provided by M&S Provisions.
Calculations	The following formulas should be included: a. 2021 Expenses = 2020 Expenses + (2020 Expenses * 2021 % Change) b. 2022 Expenses = 2021 Expenses + (2021 Expenses * 2022 % Change) c. Average % Change = (2021 % Change + 2022 % Change) / 2 d. Use the SUM function to determine totals Note: Use dummy data in the consolidated worksheet to verify the formulas. Round the percentages. Format other numbers using standard accounting rules, which require a dollar sign only on the first and last numbers in a currency column.
Other Tasks	Investigate a method the company can use to consolidate data from multiple workbooks into a new workbook.

In addition, using a sketch of the worksheet can help you visualize its design. The sketch of the consolidated worksheet (the first of the four worksheets in this workbook) consists of titles, column and row headings, the location of data values, and a general idea of the desired formatting, as shown in Figure 5–2.

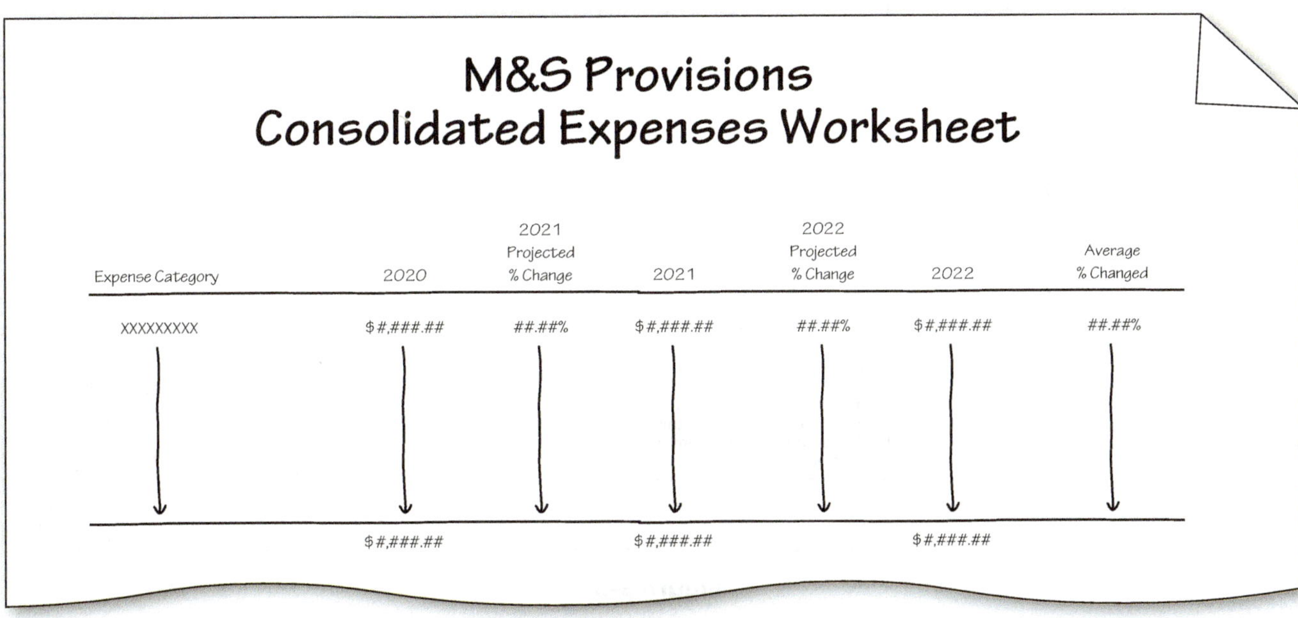

Figure 5–2

BTW
Ribbon and Screen Resolution
Excel may change how the groups and buttons within the groups appear on the ribbon, depending on the screen resolution of your computer. Thus, your ribbon may look different from the ones in this book if you are using a screen resolution other than 1366 × 768.

Creating the Consolidated Worksheet

The first step in creating the workbook is to create the consolidated expenses worksheet shown in Figure 5–1. This worksheet eventually will contain consolidated data with titles, column and row headings, formulas, and formatting. It also represents the format used on each of the individual locations, which will be copied to the three other worksheets. You will create sample data first, to verify formats and formulas.

To Start Excel and Open a File

The SC_EX_5-1 workbook is located in the Data Files. Please contact your instructor for information about accessing the Data Files. The file contains headings and formatting.

1. sam Start Excel and open the file named SC_EX_5-1 (Figure 5-3).
2. Click the Zoom In button the required number of times to zoom to approximately 120%.

Q&A
What is the best way to zoom?
You can use the Zoom In and Zoom Out buttons on the taskbar or drag the Zoom slider. Some users like using CTRL+WHEEL to zoom. The View tab also has some useful zoom tools.

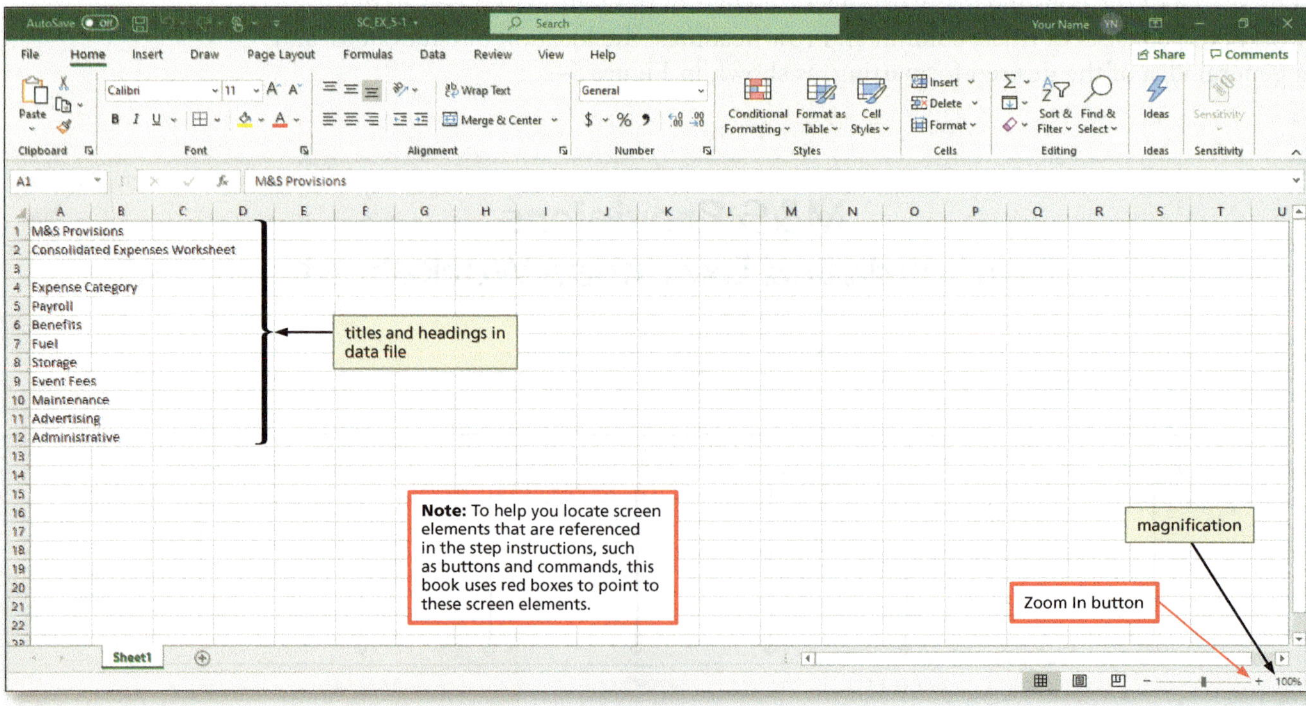

Figure 5–3

To Format the Worksheet

The following steps format the cells in the consolidated worksheet. The row heights and column widths need to be changed to accommodate the data in the worksheet.

1. Drag the bottom boundary of the row heading 4 down until the row height is 51.75 (69 pixels) to change the row height.
2. Drag the right boundary of column heading A to the right until the column width is 20.57 (149 pixels) to change the column width.
3. Click the heading for column B and then SHIFT+CLICK the heading for column G to select all the columns in the range.
4. Drag the right boundary of column heading G to 13.57 (100 pixels) to change the width of multiple columns.
5. Click cell A1 to deselect the columns (Figure 5–4).

BTW

Row Height and Column Width

If you are unable to select the exact row heights and column widths as instructed, it might be because of your display settings. In that case, choose a row height and column width as close as possible to the specified values.

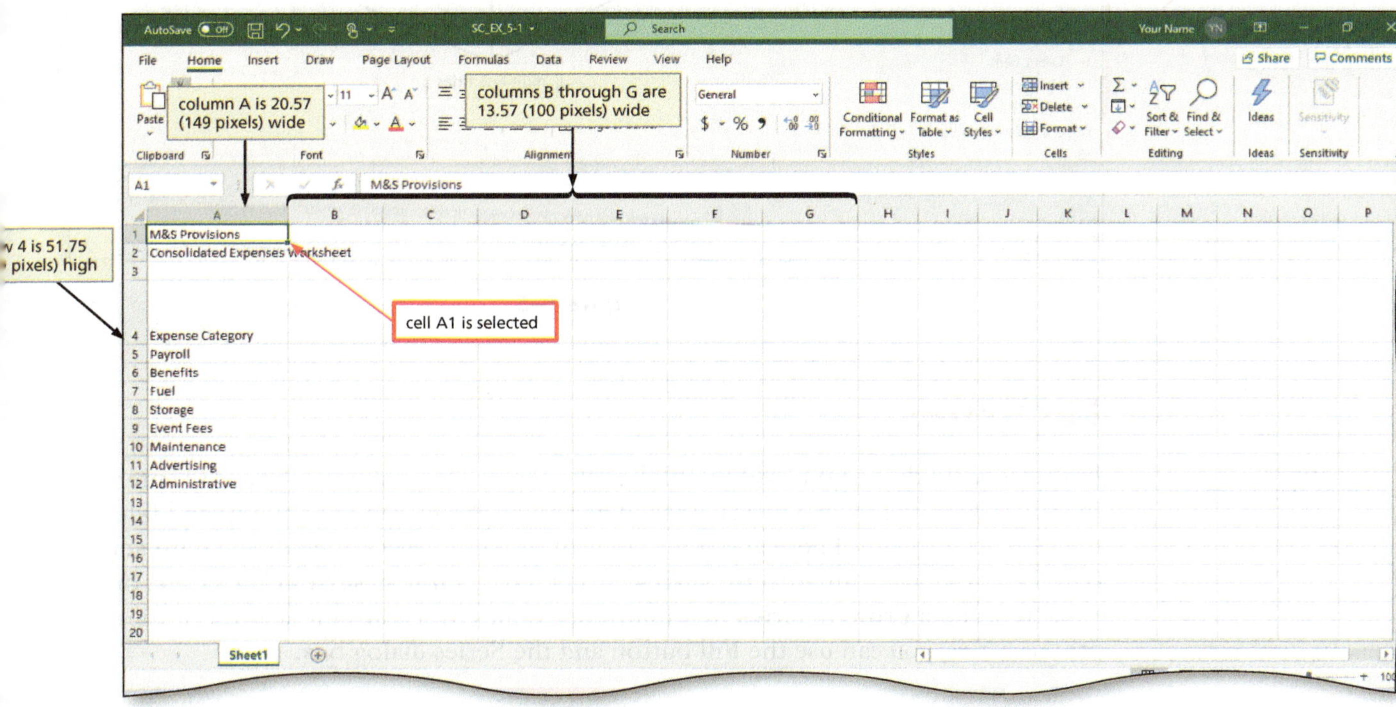

Figure 5–4

To Enter Column Titles

The following steps enter the column titles in row 4. Remember that multi-line titles are created by pressing ALT+ENTER to move to a new line within a cell.

1. Select cell B4. Type `2020` and then select cell C4 to enter the column heading.
2. Enter the following column titles beginning in row 4, as shown in Figure 5–5, pressing ALT+ENTER to move to a new line within a multi-line cell: **`2021 Projected % Change`**, **`2021`**, **`2022 Projected % Change`**, **`2022`**, and **`Average % Changed`**.

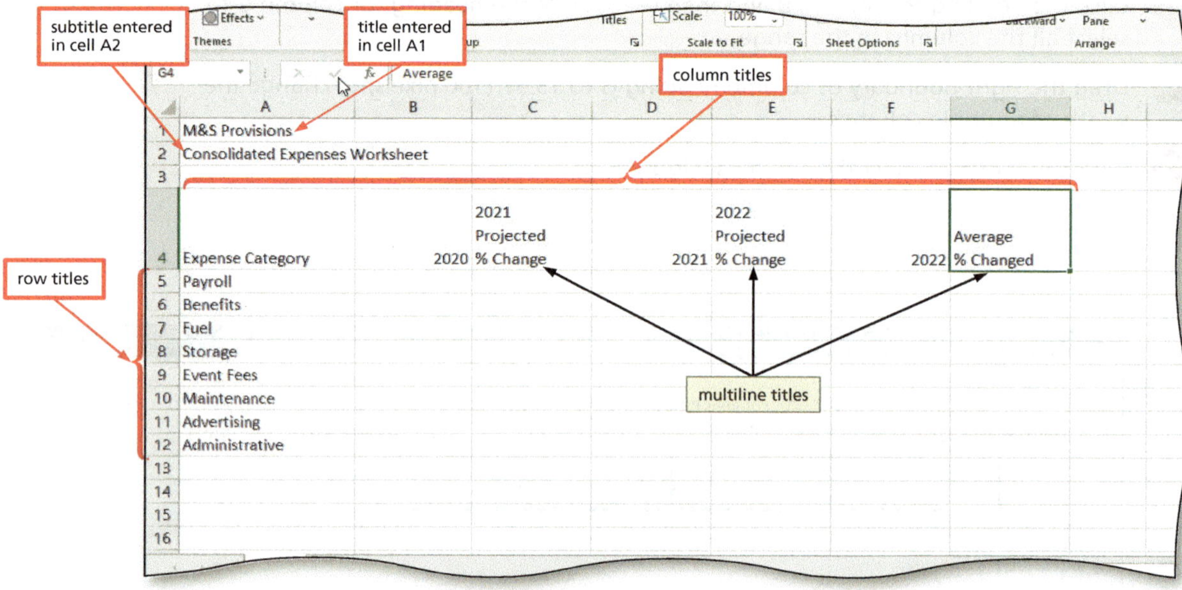

Figure 5–5

BTW
Touch Mode Differences
The Office and Windows interfaces may vary if you are using Touch Mode. For this reason, you might notice that the function or appearance of your touch screen differs slightly from this module's presentation.

Fill Series

In previous modules, you used the fill handle to create a numerical series. By entering the first two numbers in a series, Excel determined the increment amount and filled the cells accordingly. There are other kinds of series, however, including a **date series** (Jan, Feb, Mar, etc.), an **auto fill series** (1, 1, 1, etc.), a **linear series** (1, 2, 3, etc. or 2, 4, 6, etc.), and a **growth series** that multiplies values by a constant factor. For these precise series, you can use the Fill button and the Series dialog box.

To Create Linear Series

While creating the consolidated worksheet in this module, sample data is used for the 2020 expenditures, the 2021 projected % change, and the 2022 projected % change values. **Why?** Entering sample data creates placeholder content and assists in the layout of the consolidated worksheet.

You will use the fill handle to create a series of integers in column B. Normally you would enter the first two numbers in a series so that Excel can determine the increment amount; however, if your series is incremented by 1, you do not have to enter two numbers. You can CTRL+drag the fill handle to increment by 1 across cells.

If you want to increment by a different value, you can use the Series dialog box. In the Series dialog box, you can choose to increment by any step value, including positive and negative decimals, again by entering only a single value. The following steps create sample data in the consolidated worksheet.

1

- Select cell B5.
- Type `1` and then click the Enter button in the formula bar to enter the first value in the series.
- CTRL+drag the fill handle down through cell B12 to create a fill series incremented by 1 (Figure 5–6).

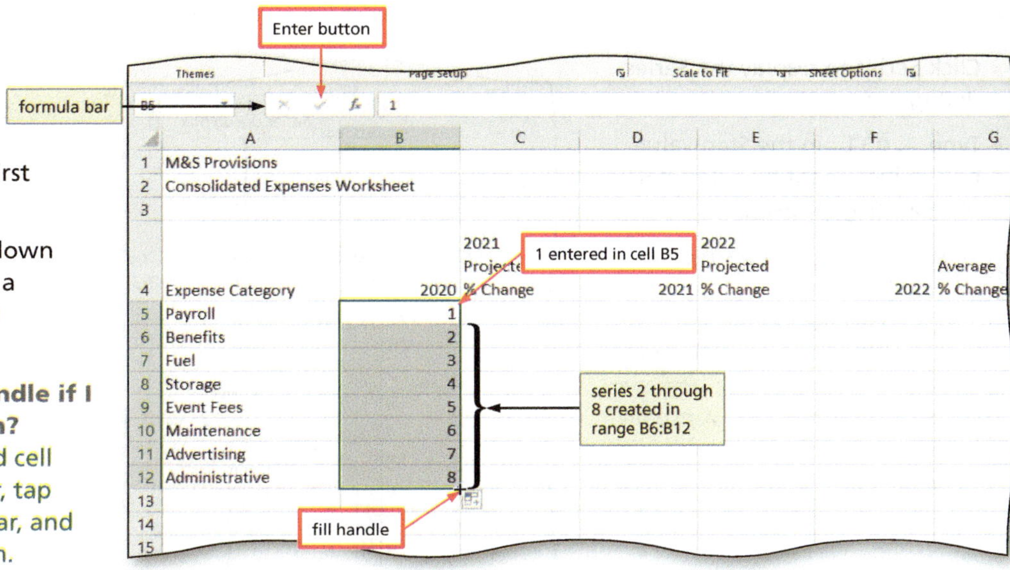

Figure 5–6

Q&A

How do I use the fill handle if I am using a touch screen?
Press and hold the selected cell to display the mini toolbar, tap AutoFill on the mini toolbar, and then drag the AutoFill icon.

What would happen if I did not use CTRL?
If you drag without CTRL, the cells would be filled with the number, 1.

2

- Select cell C5 and then type `3%` to enter a percentage in this column.
- Display the Home tab.
- Select the range C5:C12 and then click the Fill button (Home tab | Editing group) to display the Fill gallery (Figure 5–7).

Q&A

How are the directional commands in the Fill gallery used?
Those commands are alternatives to using the fill handle. Select an empty cell or cells adjacent to the cell that contains the data that you want to use. You then can fill the selection using the Fill button and the appropriate directional command.

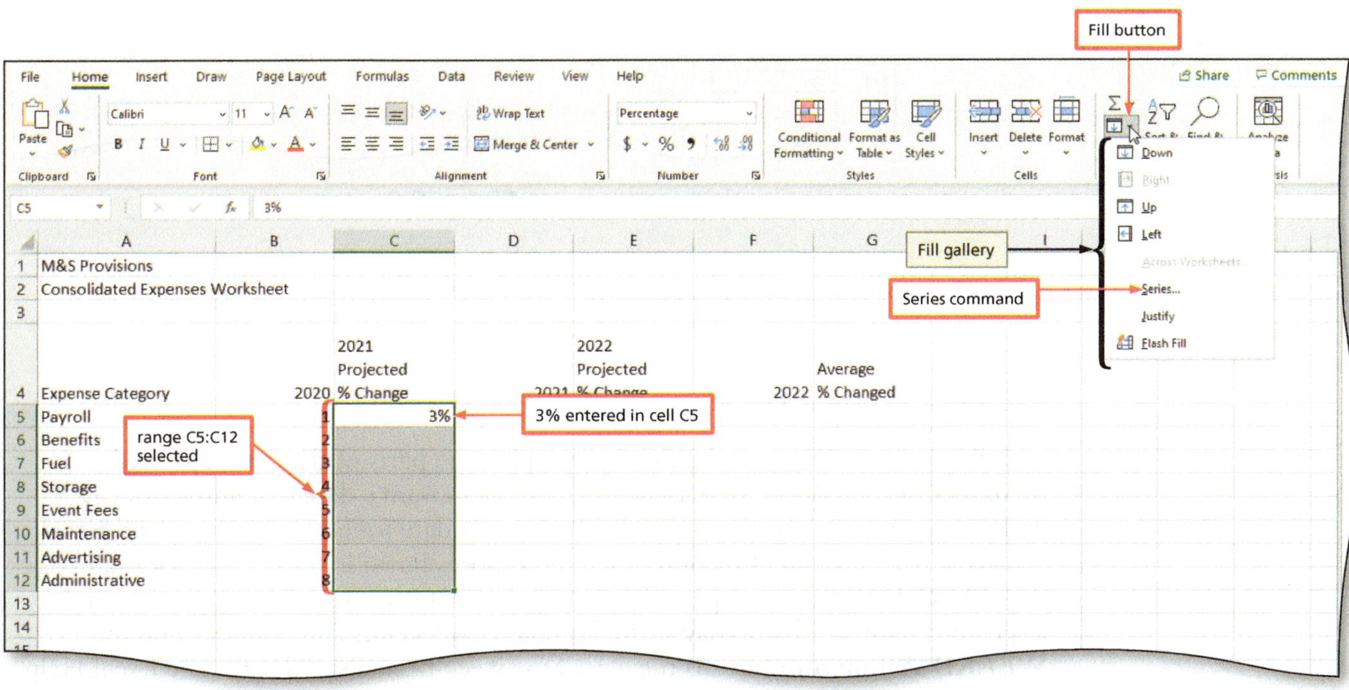

Figure 5–7

3

- Click Series to display the Series dialog box.
- Type `.031` in the Step value box to increment by a decimal number (Figure 5–8).

Q&A **Why am I using an increment of .031?**
You are generating random placeholder numbers. You can use any increment step; however, since this column will eventually be percentages, a decimal may be appropriate.

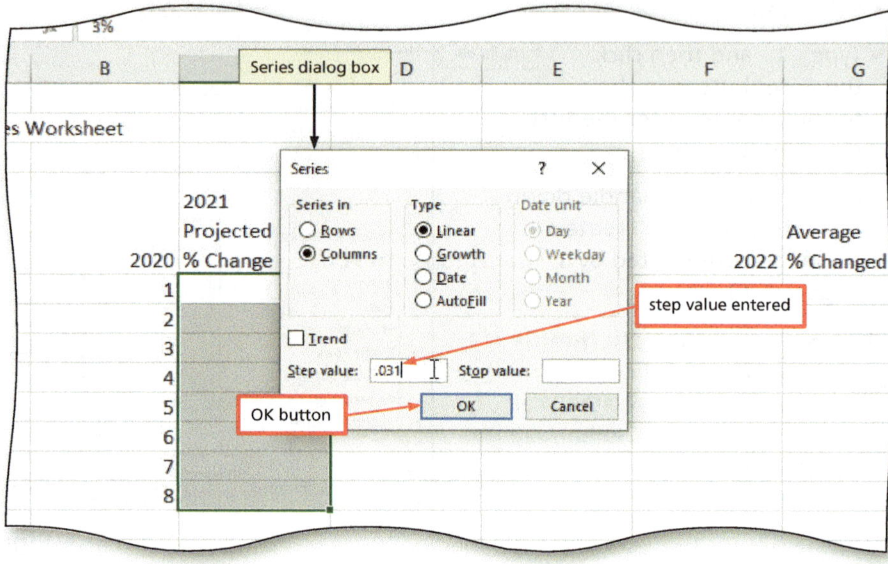

Figure 5–8

4

- Click OK (Series dialog box) to fill the series.
- Click the Increase Decimal button (Home tab | Number group) twice to display two decimal places.
- Repeat Steps 2, 3, and 4 to create a linear series beginning with `4%` and incrementing by `.02` in the range E5:E12.
- Click an empty cell to remove the selection (Figure 5–9).

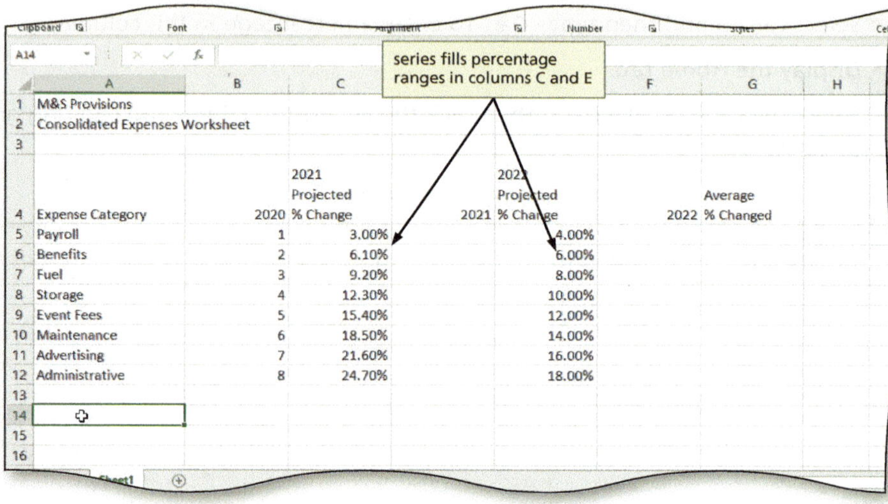

Figure 5–9

Other Ways

1. To increment by 1, enter first number; select original cell and blank adjacent cell, drag fill handle through range

Date, Time, and Round Functions

Entering dates in Excel can be as easy as typing the parts of the date separated by slashes, such as 6/14/2020. However, when you want a date that automatically updates, or you want to access part of the current date for a variety of reasons, Excel has many date and time functions, including those shown in Table 5–2. For example, the **WORKDAY function** provides an end date between a specified start date and a specified number of workdays, which excludes weekends and holidays, and the **WEEKDAY function** returns the day of the week from a serial date. Use Excel Help to search for more information about these and other date and time functions.

Table 5–2 Functions Related to Date and Time

	Function	Definition	Syntax	Example	Sample Result
Date Functions	DATE	Returns the formatted date based on the month, day, and year	DATE(year, month, day)	=DATE(120,6,14)	6/14/2020
	DATEVALUE	Converts a date that is stored as text to a serial number for calculations	DATEVALUE(date_text)	=DATEVALUE("6/14/2020")	43996
	DAY	Returns the day value from a serial date	DAY(serial_number)	=DAY(43996)	14
	MONTH	Returns the month value from a serial date	MONTH(serial_number)	=MONTH(43996)	6
	TODAY	Returns the current date	TODAY()	=TODAY()	6/14/2020
	WEEKDAY	Returns the day of the week from a serial date, with a second option for starting the week on Sunday (1) or Monday (2)	WEEKDAY(serial_ number,return_type)	=WEEKDAY(43996,1)	1 (Sunday)
	YEAR	Returns the year value from a serial date	YEAR(serial_number)	=YEAR(43996)	2020
	WORKDAY	Returns the end date after a start date and specified number of workdays, which excludes weekends and holidays. The results of this function should be formatted as a date.	WORKDAY(start_ date,days,holidays)	=WORKDAY(A1,100,A2:A4) (start date is formatted as a date in cell A1, and dates for holidays are formatted as dates in the range A2:A4)	4/21/2022
Time Functions	HOUR	Returns the hour value from a serial date	HOUR(serial_number)	=HOUR(0.33605324)	8
	MINUTE	Returns the minute value from a serial date	MINUTES(serial_number)	=MINUTE(0.33605324)	3
	SECOND	Returns the second value from a serial date	SECOND(serial_number)	=SECOND(0.33605324)	55
	TIME	Returns the formatted date based on the hour, minute, and second	TIME(hour, minute, second)	=TIME(8,3,55)	8:03 AM
	TIMEVALUE	Converts a time that is stored as text to a serial number for calculations	TIMEVALUE(time_text)	=TIMEVALUE("8:03:55 am")	0.336053241
Other Functions	NOW	Returns both date and time	NOW()	=NOW()	6/14/2020 8:03

Excel stores the date and time as a **serial number** representing the number of days since January 1900, followed by a fractional portion of a 24-hour day. For example, June 14, 2020, is stored internally as 43996. The time, for example 3:00 p.m., is stored internally as .625. Therefore the entire date and time would be stored as 43996.625. When you format a serial number, you can use the Short Date, Long Date, or Time formats (Format Cells dialog box). If, however, you have generated the serial number from a function such as MONTH, DAY, or YEAR, you must use the Number format because the return value is an integer; formatting it with a date or time format would produce an incorrect date.

If you are performing math with dates and times, your answer will result in a serial number. For example, if you wanted to calculate elapsed time from 9:00 a.m. to 3:30 p.m., subtraction would result in a serial number, 0.2708. You then would need to format the number with the TIME format (h:mm), which would result in 6:30 or 6 hours and 30 minutes (Figure 5–10).

BTW

Creating a Growth Series

You can create a growth series by doing the following: enter an initial value in the first cell, select the first cell and the range to fill, click the Fill button (Home tab | Editing group), click Series on the Fill menu, click Growth in the Type area (Series dialog box), and then enter a constant factor in the Step value box.

BTW
Updating the TODAY function
If the TODAY function does not update the date when you expect it to, you might need to change the settings that control when the worksheet recalculates. On the File tab, click Options, and then in the Formulas category under Calculation options, make sure that Automatic is selected.

BTW
Copying
To copy the contents of a cell to the cell directly below it, click in the target cell and press CTRL+D.

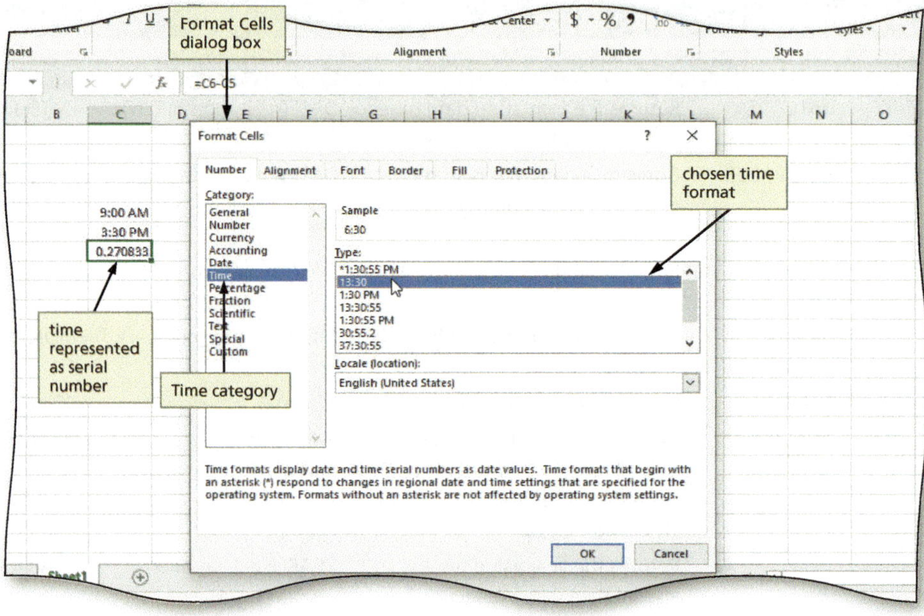

Figure 5–10

Another set of useful functions have to do with rounding. Rounding numbers off, especially for dollars and cents, prevents formulas from creating awkward answers with long decimal notations. Table 5–3 displays some of the more popular round functions.

Table 5–3 Rounding Functions

Function	Definition	Syntax	Example	Sample Result
ROUND	Rounds a number to a specified number of decimal places	ROUND(number,num_digits)	=ROUND(833.77,0)	834
ROUNDDOWN	Rounds a number down, toward zero	ROUNDDOWN(number, num_digits)	=ROUNDDOWN(833.77,0)	833
ROUNDUP	Rounds a number up, away from zero	ROUNDUP(number,num_digits)	=ROUNDUP(833.77,0)	834
MROUND	Returns a number rounded to the desired multiple	MROUND(number,multiple)	=MROUND(833.77,5)	835

CONSIDER THIS

When should you use the ROUND function?
When you multiply or divide decimal numbers, the answer may contain more decimal places than the format allows. If this happens, you run the risk of the column totals being off by a penny or so; resulting values of calculations could include fractions of a penny beyond the two decimal places that currency formats usually display.

To Use the TODAY Function

Recall that you have used the NOW function to access the system date and time. You also can use the **TODAY function**, which returns only the date. Both functions are designed to update each time the worksheet is opened. The function takes no arguments but accesses the internal clock on your computer and displays the current date. As with the NOW function, you can format the date in a variety of styles.

The TODAY function also is useful for calculating intervals. For example, if you want to calculate an age, you can subtract the birth year from the TODAY function to find that person's age as of this year's birthday. The following steps use the TODAY function to enter the system date into the worksheet. **Why?** The TODAY function will update each time the worksheet is opened.

1

- Select cell G3, type **=today()**, and then click the Enter button to enter the system date (Figure 5–11).

Q&A **Should I use lowercase or uppercase on functions?**
Either one will work. To delineate functions in the text passages of this book, they are displayed in all caps.

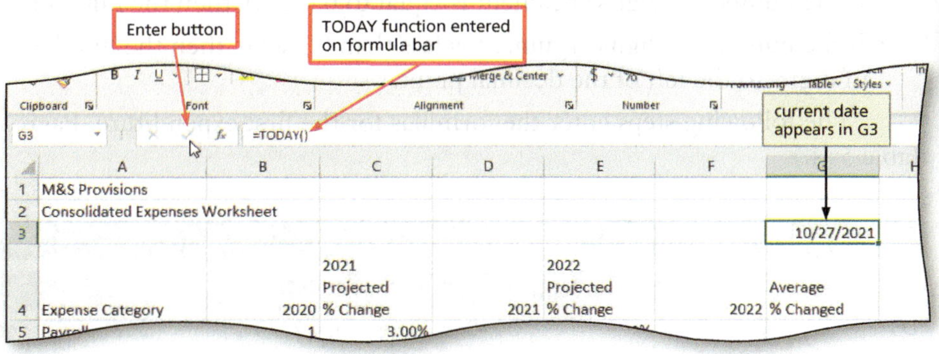

Figure 5–11

2

- Right-click cell G3 and then click Format Cells on the shortcut menu.
- If necessary, click the Number tab and then click Date in the Category list (Format Cells dialog box).
- Click 14-Mar-12 in the Type list to format the date (Figure 5–12).

Q&A **Why change the format of the date?**
The date might be displayed as a series of number signs if the date, as initially formatted by Excel, does not fit in the width of the cell.

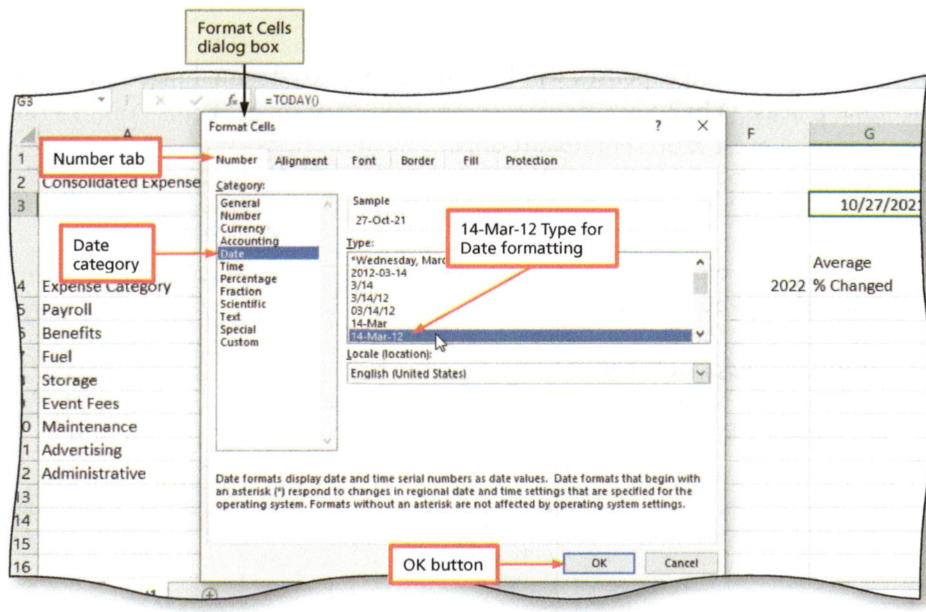

Figure 5–12

3

- Click OK (Format Cells dialog box) to close the dialog box.
- Click an empty cell to deselect the previous cell.

Other Ways

1. Select cell, click Date & Time button (Formulas tab | Function Library group), click TODAY, click OK (Function Arguments dialog box)

To Enter Formulas Using the ROUND Function

The **ROUND function** in Excel is used to round numbers to a specified number of decimal places. The general form of the ROUND function is

=ROUND(number, number of digits)

where the number argument can be a number, a cell reference that contains a number, or a formula that results in a number; and the number of digits argument can be any positive or negative number used to determine the number of places to which the number will be rounded. Positive numbers round to the right of the decimal point; for example, 18.257 formatted for 1 decimal place would display 18.3. Negative numbers round to the left of the decimal point; for example, 18.257 formatted for –1 decimal place would display 20.

The following is true about the ROUND function:

- If the number of digits argument is greater than 0 (zero), then the number is rounded to the specified number of digits to the right of the decimal point.
- If the number of digits argument is equal to 0 (zero), then the number is rounded to the nearest integer.
- If the number of digits argument is less than 0 (zero), then the number is rounded to the specified number of digits to the left of the decimal point.

The following steps enter the formulas for the first expenditure, Payroll, in cells D5, F5, and G5. (See Table 5–4.)

Table 5–4 Formulas for cells D5, F5, and G5

Cell	Description	Formula	Entry
D5	2021 Expense	ROUND(2020 Expense + 2020 Expense * 2021 % Change, 2)	=ROUND(B5 + B5 * C5, 2)
F5	2022 Expense	ROUND(2021 Expense + 2021 Expense * 2022 % Change, 2)	=ROUND(D5 + D5 * E5, 2)
G5	Average % Change	ROUND((2021 % Change + 2022 % Change) / 2, 4)	=ROUND((C5 + E5) / 2, 4)

The projected expenses will be rounded to two decimal places, while the average will be rounded to four decimal places. **Why?** Because the averages are very small at this point in the process, using four decimal digits provides the most representative results.

1

- Select cell D5, type **=round(b5+b5*c5,2)** and then click the Enter button in the formula bar to display the resulting value (Figure 5–13).

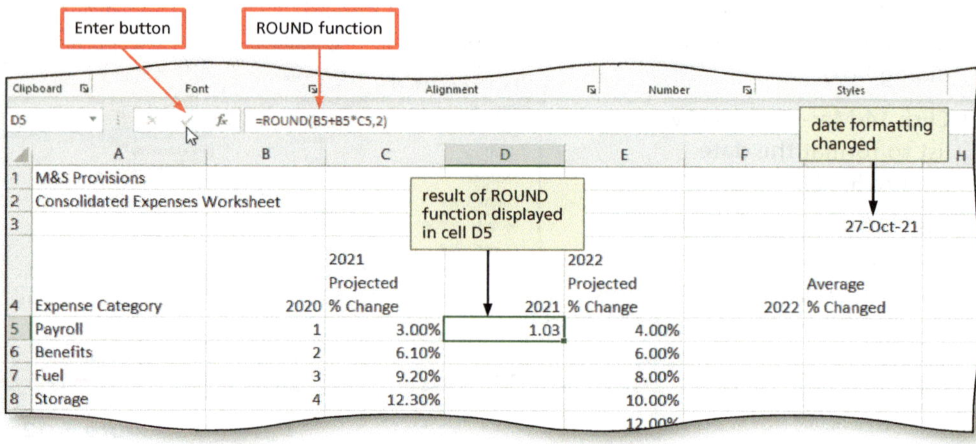

Figure 5–13

2

- Drag the fill handle on cell D5 down to copy the formula to cells D6:D12.
- Select cell F5, type **=round(d5+d5*e5,2)** and then click the Enter button to display the resulting value (Figure 5–14).

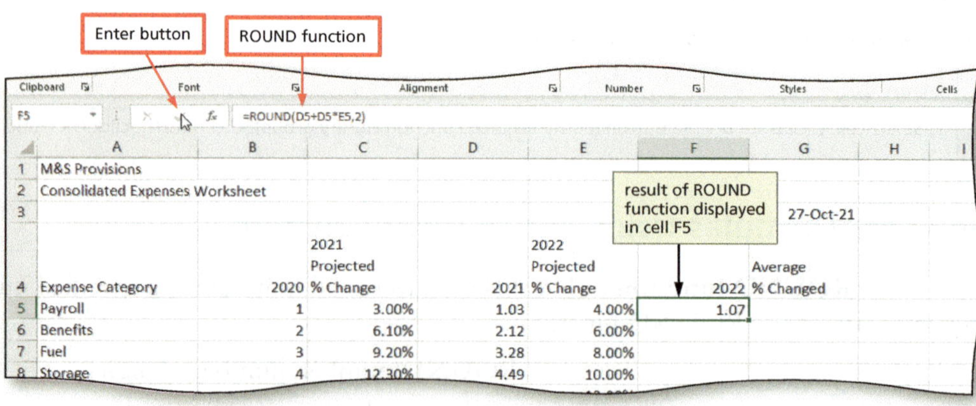

Figure 5–14

3

- Select cell G5, type **=round((c5+e5)/2,4)** and then click the Enter button to display the resulting value (Figure 5–15).

Q&A **Do I need to use two sets of parentheses in the function?**
Yes; the outer set of parentheses are for the function, and the inner set is to force Excel to add the two values before dividing to calculate the average. Recall that Excel follows the order of operations and performs multiplication and division before addition and subtraction, unless you use parentheses.

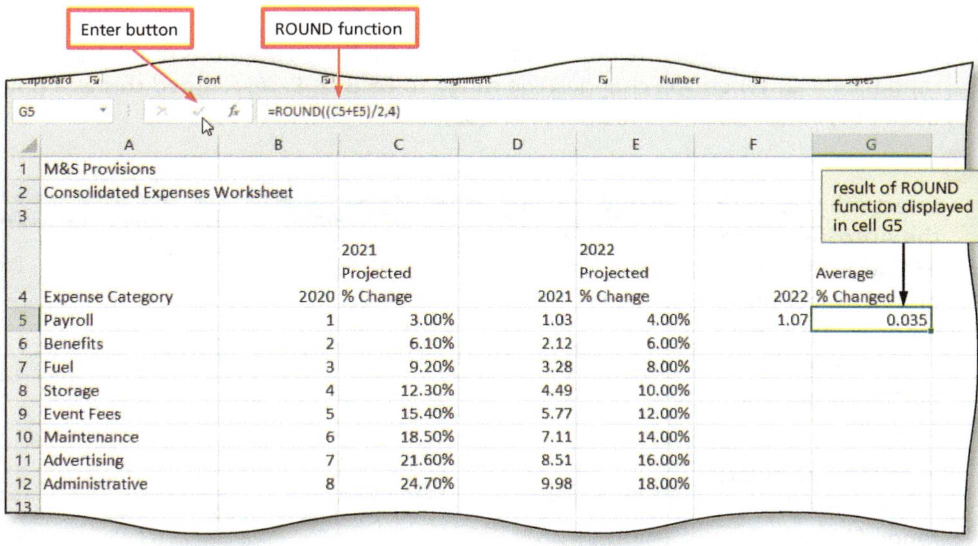

Figure 5–15

4

- Select cells F5:G5.
- Drag the fill handle down through cells F12:G12 to copy both formulas down to the selected range (Figure 5–16).

Q&A **Are the values in column G supposed to display all four decimal places?**
Yes, because you entered a 4 at the end of the function, Excel rounds to four decimal places; however, a default setting in Excel is to ignore zeroes at the end of decimal places, because they are not significant. You will change that default setting later in the module.

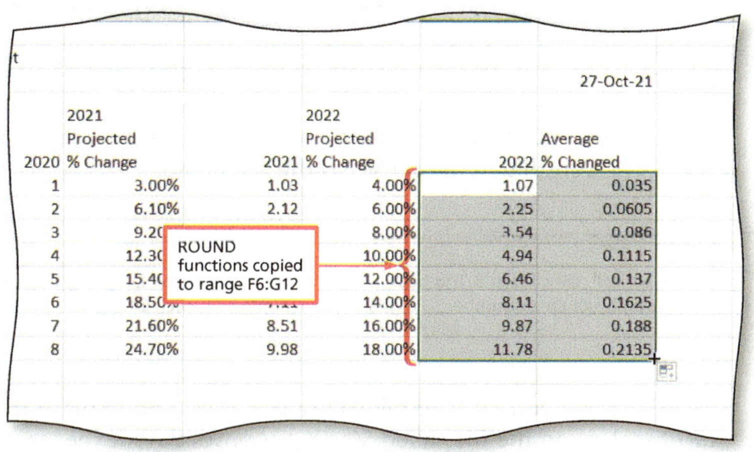

Figure 5–16

5

- Select cell B13.
- Click the AutoSum button (Home tab | Editing group), select the range B5:B12, and then click the Enter button to sum the column (Figure 5–17).
- If the Trace Error button is displayed, click it, and then click Ignore Error on the Trace Error menu to ignore an error that Excel mistakenly reported.

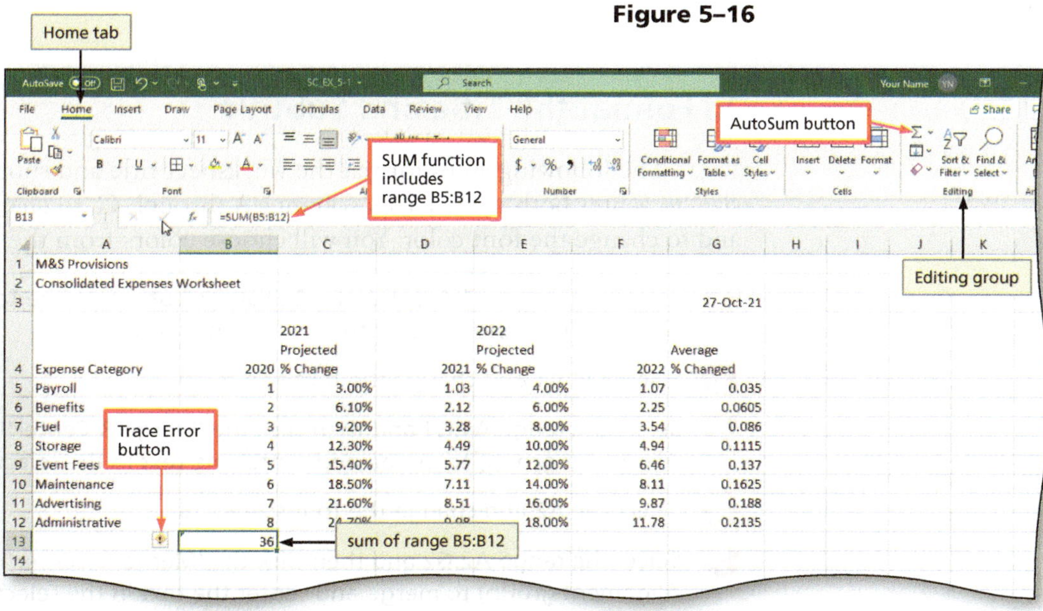

Figure 5–17

Q&A

Why did Excel report an error?

When you use the SUM function, Excel assumes that all contiguous numbers should be summed, in this case the range, B4:B12. When you changed the range to B5:B12, Excel flagged this as a potential error, due to the exclusion of cell B4, which also included a numeric value.

6

- Select cell D13, click the AutoSum button (Home tab | Editing group), select the range D5:D12, and then click the Enter button to sum the column.
- In cell F13, calculate the sum for the range F5:F12.
- Click an empty cell to deselect the previous cell (Figure 5–18).

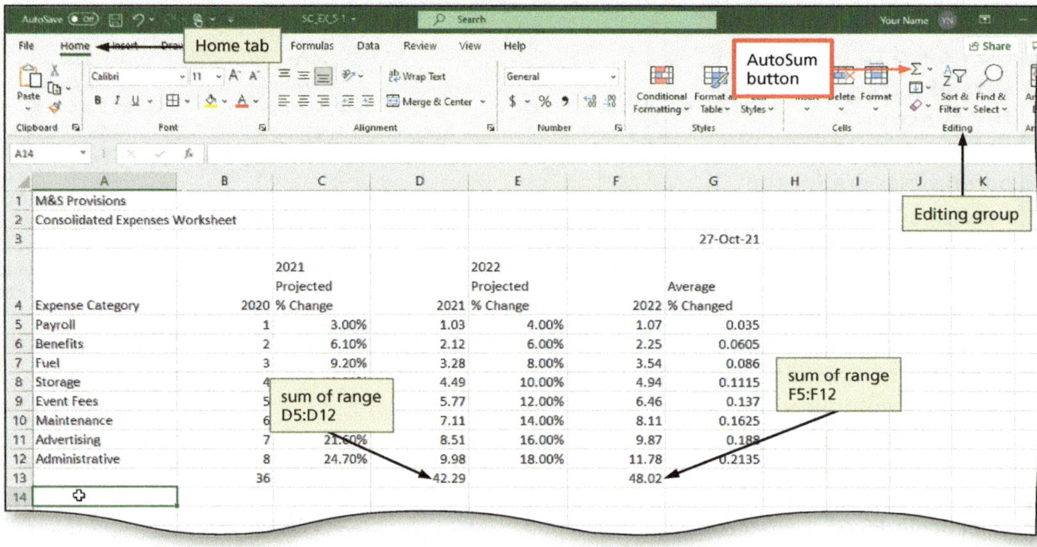

Figure 5–18

7

- Save the workbook on your hard drive, OneDrive, or location that is most appropriate to your situation using SC_EX_5_ConsolidatedExpenses as the file name.

Other Ways

1. Select cell, click Math & Trig button (Formulas tab | Function Library group), click ROUND, enter formula in Number box (Formula Arguments dialog box), enter number of digits in Num_digits box, click OK

Break Point: If you want to take a break, this is a good place to do so. You can exit Excel now. To resume later, start Excel, open the file called SC_EX_5_ConsolidatedExpenses, and continue following the steps from this location forward.

To Format the Title and Subtitle

The following steps format the worksheet title and subtitle to change the font size, to center both titles across columns A through G, to change the background color, and to change the font color. You will choose colors from the Feathered theme.

1. Select the range A1:A2, click the Cell Styles button (Home tab | Styles group), and then click the Title style to apply the style to the range.
2. Select cell A1 and change the font size to 20.
3. Select the range A1:G1 and then click the 'Merge & Center' button (Home tab | Alignment group) to merge and center the text in the selected range.
4. Select cell A2 and change the font size to 16.
5. Select the range A2:G2 and then click the 'Merge & Center' button (Home tab | Alignment group) to merge and center the text in the selected range.

6. Select the range A1:A2, click the Fill Color arrow (Home tab | Font group), and then click 'Blue-Gray, Accent 1' in the Fill Color gallery to change the fill color.

7. Click the Font Color arrow (Home tab | Font group) and then click 'Tan, Accent 5, Lighter 40%' (column 9, row 4) in the Font Color gallery to change the font color.

To Format the Column Titles and Total Row

The following steps center and underline the column titles and create borders on the total row.

1. Select the range B4:G4 and then click the Center button (Home tab | Alignment group) to center the text in the cells.

2. CTRL+click cell A4 to add it to the selected range, and then use the Cell Styles button (Home tab | Styles group) to apply the Heading 3 cell style.

3. Select the range A13:G13 and then assign the Total cell style to the range.

4. Click an empty cell to deselect the range (Figure 5–19).

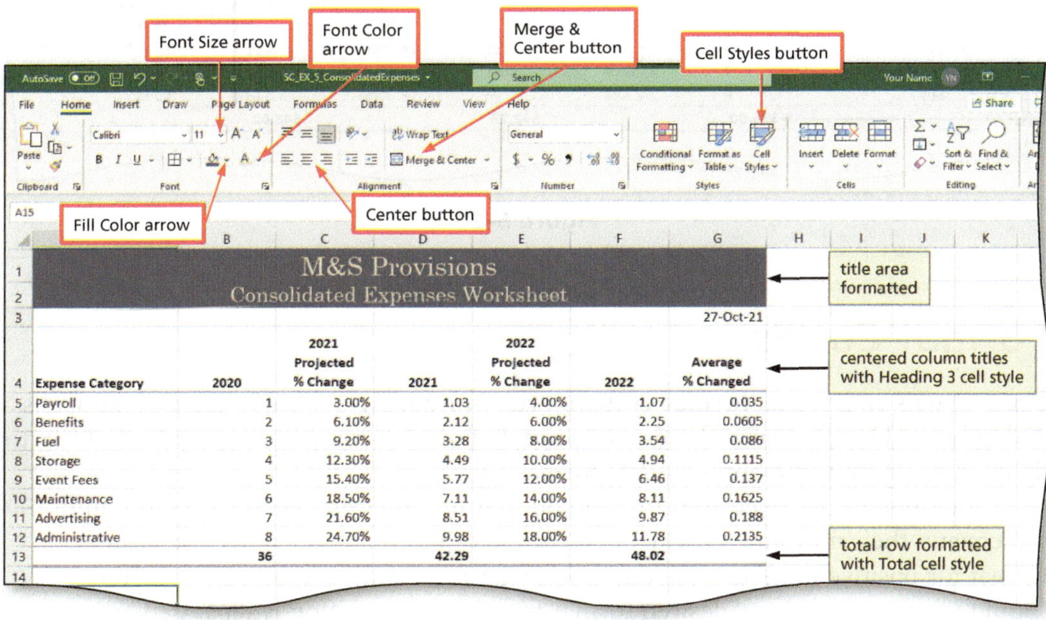

Figure 5–19

To Format with a Floating Dollar Sign

The consolidated worksheet for this module contains floating dollar signs in the first row of numbers and in the totals. The following steps use the Format Cells dialog box to assign a currency style with a floating dollar sign and two decimal places to the appropriate cells. Recall that a floating dollar sign always appears immediately to the left of the first significant digit in the cell, while the Accounting Number Format button (Home tab | Number group) creates a fixed dollar sign.

1. Select cell B5. While holding down CTRL, select the nonadjacent cells D5, F5, B13, D13, and F13. Right-click any selected cell to display the shortcut menu.

2. Click Format Cells on the shortcut menu to display the Format Cells dialog box. If necessary, click the Number tab (Format Cells dialog box) to display the Number sheet.

3. Click Currency in the Category list. If necessary, click the Symbol button and then click $ in the list.

4. Click the red ($1,234.10) in the Negative numbers list to select a currency format that displays negative numbers in red with parentheses and a floating dollar sign.

5. Click OK (Format Cells dialog box) to assign the Currency style.

6. Click an empty cell to deselect the previous cells (Figure 5–20).

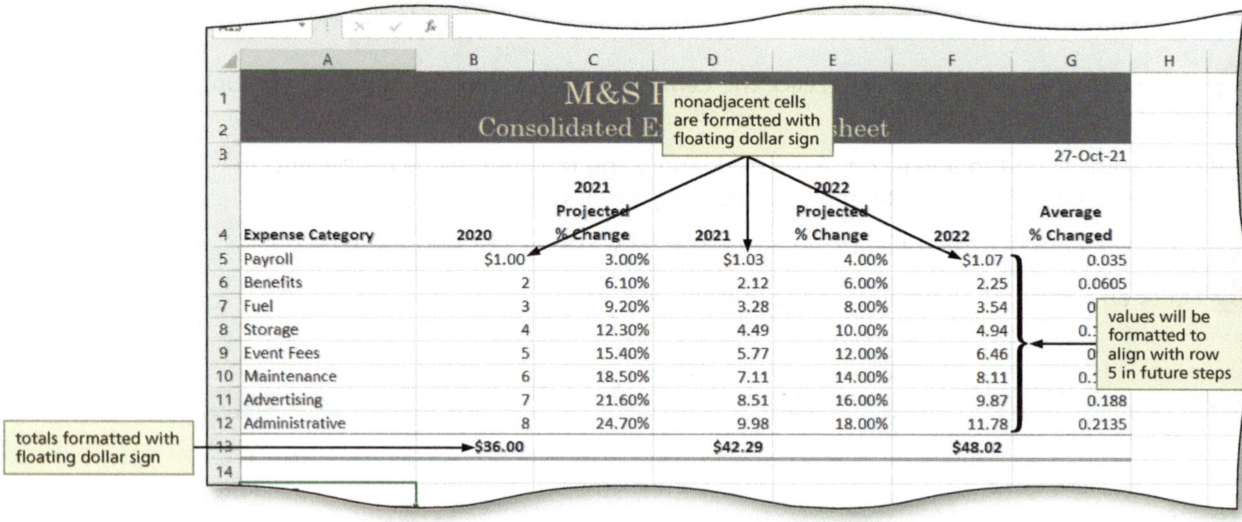

Figure 5–20

BTW

Selecting a Range of Cells

You can select any range of cells with entries surrounded by blank cells by clicking a cell in the range and pressing CTRL+SHIFT+* (asterisk).

BTW

Summing a Row or Column

You can reference an entire column or an entire row in a function argument by listing only the column or only the row. For example, = sum(a:a) sums all the values in all the cells in column A, and = sum(1:1) sums all the values in all the cells in row 1. You can verify this by entering **= sum(a:a)** in cell C1 of a blank worksheet and then begin entering numbers in a few of the cells in column A. Excel will respond by showing the sum of the numbers in cell C1.

Format Codes

Excel assigns an internal **format code** to every format style listed in the Format Cells dialog box. These format codes do not print, but act as a template, with placeholders to define how you want to apply unique formatting.

Before you create custom format codes or modify existing codes, you should understand their makeup. A format code can have up to four sections: the desired format for positive numbers, the desired format for negative numbers, how zeros should be treated, and any desired format for text. Each section is separated by a semicolon. For example, the following format code would produce results similar to the sample values shown.

$* #,##0.00;	[Magenta]$(#,##0.00);	* -??;	"The answer is "@
$ 15.75	$(1,238.99)	–	The answer is yes

A format code need not have all four sections. For most applications, a format code will have a positive section and possibly a negative section. If you omit the zero formatting section, zero values will use the positive number formatting.

Table 5–5 provides a list of some of the format code symbols and how they can be combined into a new format code. To view the entire list of format codes that are provided with Excel, select Custom in the Category list (Format Cells dialog box).

Table 5–5 Format Symbols in Format Codes

Format Symbol	Example of Symbol in Code	Description
# (number sign)	###.##	Serves as a digit placeholder. If the value in a cell has more digits to the right of the decimal point than number signs in the format, Excel rounds the number. All digits to the left of the decimal point are displayed.
0 (zero)	0.00	Works like a number sign (#), except that if the number is less than 1, Excel displays a 0 in the ones place.
. (period)	#0.00	Ensures Excel will display a decimal point in the number. The placement of zeros determines how many digits appear to the left and right of the decimal point.
% (percent)	0.00%	Displays numbers as percentages of 100. Excel multiplies the value of the cell by 100 and displays a percent sign after the number.
, (comma)	#,##0.00	Displays a comma as a thousands separator.
( )	#0.00;(#0.00)	Displays parentheses around negative numbers.
$, +, or –	$#,##0.00; ($#,##0.00)	Displays a floating sign ($, +, or –).
* (asterisk)	$*##0.00	Displays a fixed sign ($, +, or –) to the left, followed by spaces until the first significant digit.
[color]	#.##;[Red]#.##	Displays the characters in the cell in the designated color. In the example, positive numbers appear in the default color, and negative numbers appear in red.
" " (quotation marks)	$0.00 "Surplus"; $-0.00 "Shortage"	Displays text along with numbers entered in a cell.
_ (underscore)	#,##0.00_)	Adds a space. When followed by a parentheses, positive numbers will align correctly with parenthetical negative numbers.

BTW

Creating Customized Formats

Each format symbol within the format code has special meaning. Table 5–2 summarizes the more frequently used format symbols and their meanings.

BTW

Sample Data

As you develop more sophisticated workbooks, it will become increasingly important that you create good test data to ensure your workbooks are free of errors. The more you test a workbook, the more confident you will be in the results generated. Always take the time to select sample data that tests the limits of the formulas.

To Create a Custom Format Code

The following steps create and assign a custom format code to the ranges that contain percentages. **Why?** A workbook may call for a visual presentation of data that cannot be accomplished with the existing Excel format codes. The format code you set will display percentages with two decimal places to the right of the decimal point and also display negative percentages in magenta with parentheses.

1

- CTRL+drag to select the ranges C5:C12, E5:E12, and G5:G12, right-click any of the selected ranges to display the shortcut menu, and then click Format Cells to display the Format Cells dialog box.
- If necessary, click the Number tab (Format Cells dialog box) and then click Custom in the Category list.

- Delete the text in the Type box (Format Cells dialog box) and then type `0.00%;[Magenta](0.00%)` to enter a custom format code (Figure 5–21).

Q&A

What does the custom format mean?

The custom format has been modified to show percentages with two decimal places and to show negative percentages in magenta with parentheses. A zero value will display as 0.00%. In the Sample area, Excel displays a sample of the custom format assigned to the first number in the selected ranges.

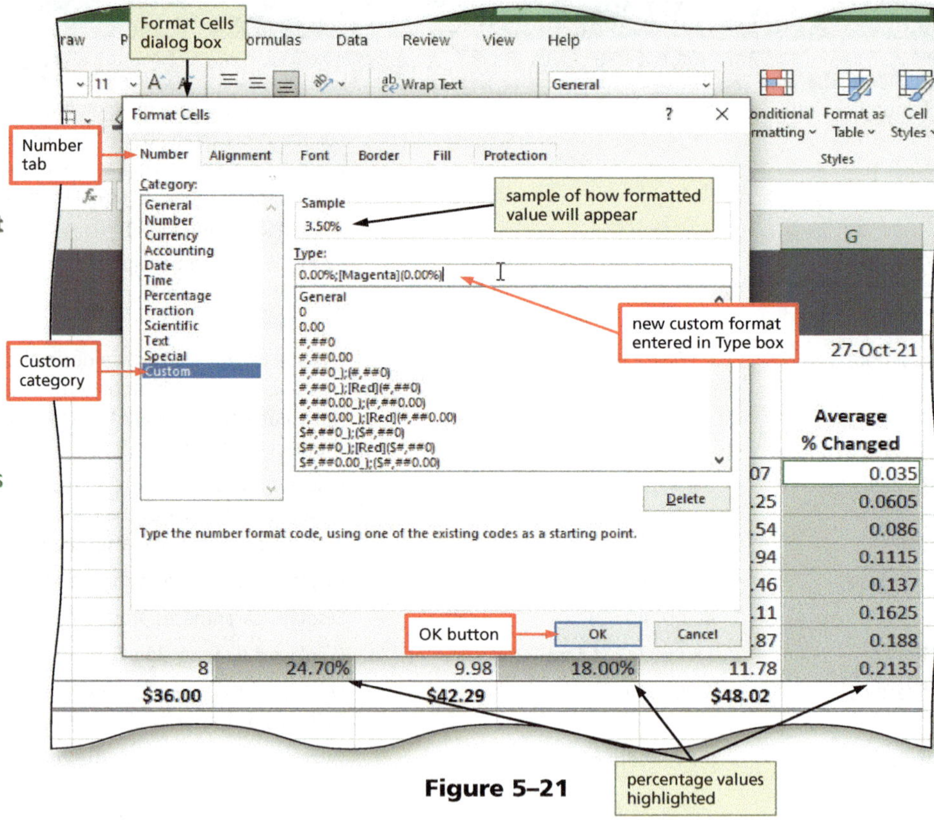

Figure 5–21

2

- Click OK (Format Cells dialog box) to display the numbers using the custom format code (Figure 5–22).

Q&A

Can I reuse the custom format code?

Yes. When you create a new custom format code, Excel adds it to the bottom of the Type list on the Number sheet (Format Cells dialog box) to make it available for future use.

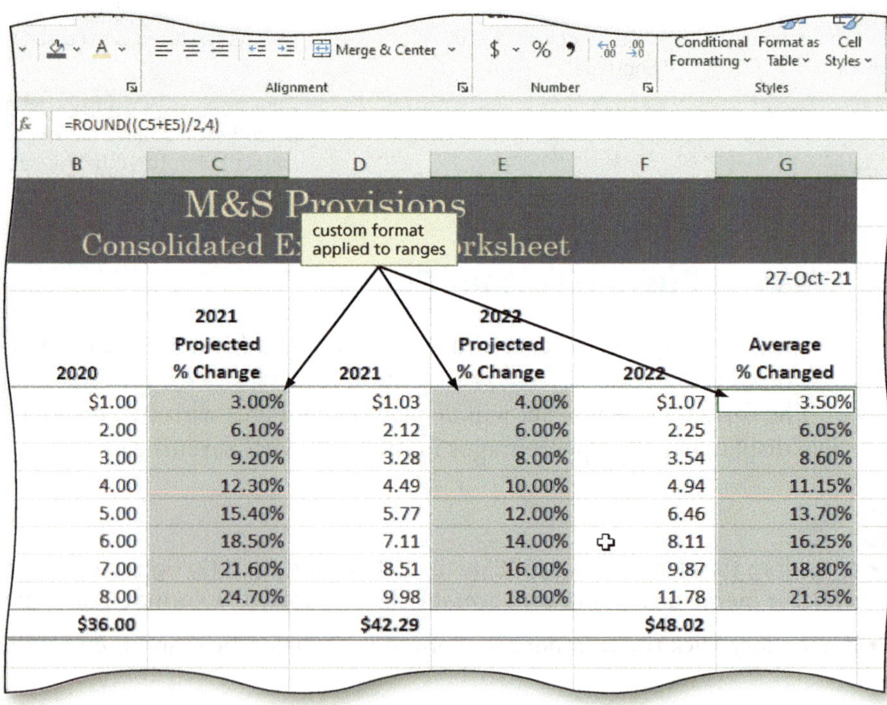

Figure 5–22

Other Ways

1. Select range or ranges, click the dialog box launcher in the Number group (Home tab | Number group), click Custom in Category list (Format Cells dialog box | Number tab), enter format code in Type box, click OK

To Format with the Comma Style

The following steps format the numbers other than the first row or totals with the comma style.

1. Select the ranges B6:B12, D6:D12, and F6:F12.
2. Click the Comma Style button (Home tab | Number group) to display the numbers in the selected ranges using the comma style.
3. Select an empty cell to deselect the range.

Q&A **Why is the comma style used for numbers that are not large enough to display commas?**
The comma style allows the values in the cells to align properly with the values in row 5, which are formatted with the currency style with floating dollar signs and parentheses for negative numbers.

Creating a Cell Style

Recall that a cell style is a group of built-in format specifications, such as font, font style, color, size, alignment, borders, and shading. A cell style also may contain information regarding nonvisual characteristics, such as cell protection. Earlier you used the Title cell style to format the worksheet headings. Now you will learn how to create a custom cell style.

CONSIDER THIS

Tips to remember when creating a new style

- When you are creating a cell style, pay close attention to the Style Includes area of the Style dialog box (Figure 5–24). A style affects the format of a cell or range of cells only if the corresponding check box is selected. For example, if the Font check box is not selected in the Style dialog box, then the cell maintains the font format it had before the style was assigned.
- If you assign two different styles to a cell or range of cells, Excel adds the second style to the first, rather than replacing it. If the two cell styles include different settings for an attribute, such as fill color, then Excel applies the setting for the second style.
- You can merge styles from another workbook into the active workbook by using the Merge Styles command in the Cell Styles gallery (Home tab | Styles group). Before you use the Merge Styles command, however, you must open the workbook that contains the desired styles.
- The six check boxes in the Style dialog box are identical to the six tabs in the Format Cells dialog box (Figure 5–24).

Once created, new cell styles appear at the top of the Cell Styles gallery and are saved for the current workbook. By right-clicking the style in the Cell Styles gallery, you can modify, duplicate, or delete the style. Create a new style in a workbook or merge styles when you plan to use a group of format specifications over and over.

It is easy to confuse cell styles and format codes. While they overlap slightly in some areas, cell styles have more to do with words, fonts, and borders, while format codes have more to do with values, decimal places, and special characters.

BTW
Normal Style
The Normal style is the format style that Excel initially assigns to all cells in a workbook. If you change the Normal style, Excel applies the new format specifications to all cells that are not assigned another style.

To Create a New Cell Style

The following steps create a new style called 4-Digit Year by modifying the existing Normal style. **Why?** Creating a new style allows you to group a number of cell formats together for ease, reuse, and consistency of application. The **Normal style** is the default style that is applied to all cells when you start Excel. The Normal style includes characteristics such as font, border, alignment, and other settings. You will create a new style to include a date and alignment format, along with other characteristics of the Normal style. The new style will use dark green text and be centered within the cell.

1

- Click the Cell Styles button (Home tab | Styles group) to display the Cell Styles gallery (Figure 5–23).

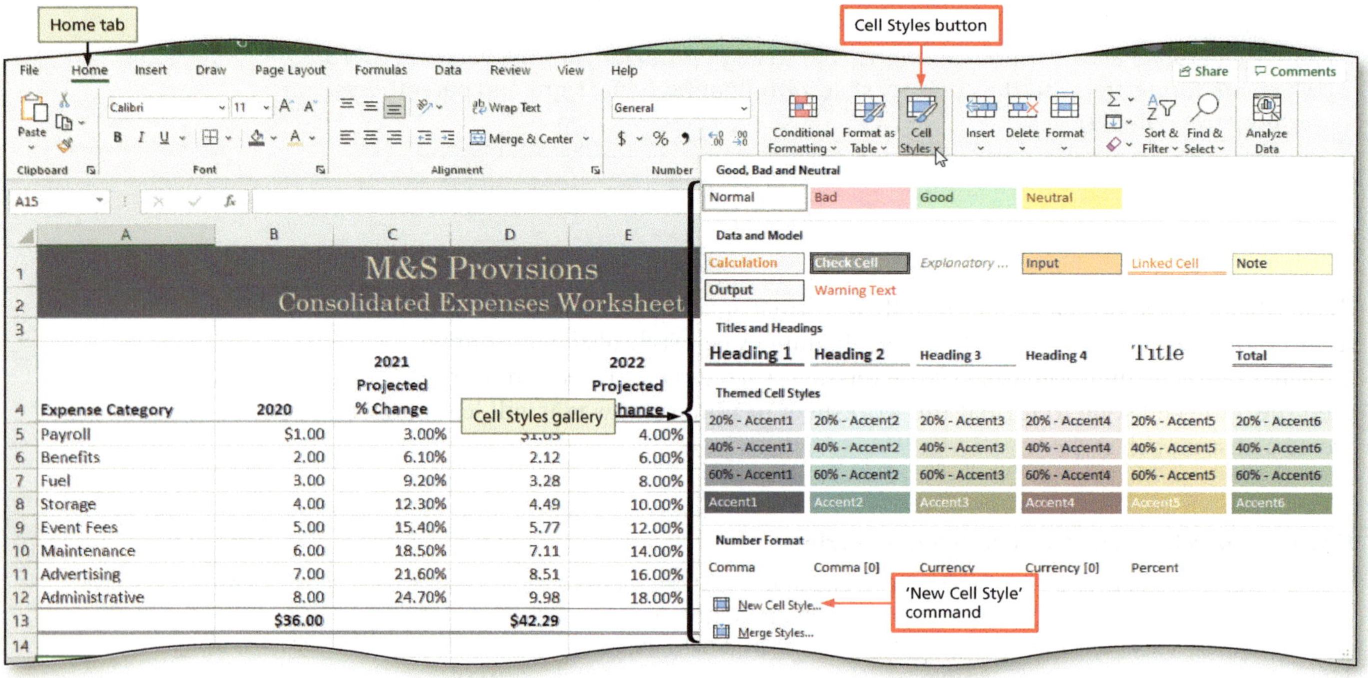

Figure 5–23

2

- Click 'New Cell Style' in the Cell Styles gallery to display the Style dialog box.
- In the Style name text box, type **`4-Digit Year`** to name the new style (Figure 5–24).

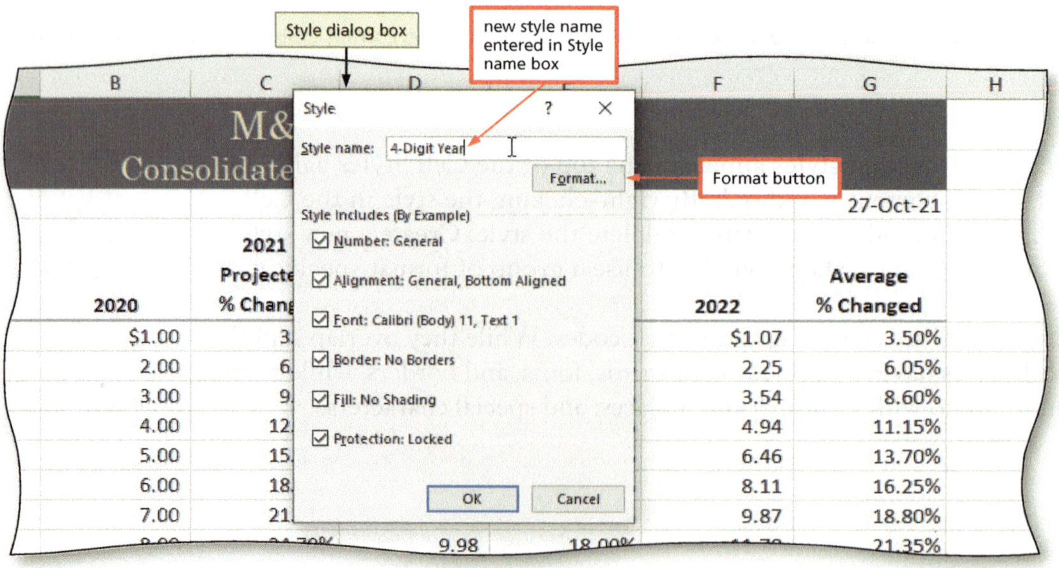

Figure 5–24

3

- Click the Format button (Style dialog box) to display the Format Cells dialog box.
- If necessary, click the Number tab (Format Cells dialog box), click Date in the Category list, and then click '14-Mar-2012' in the Type list to define the new style as a date style (Figure 5–25).

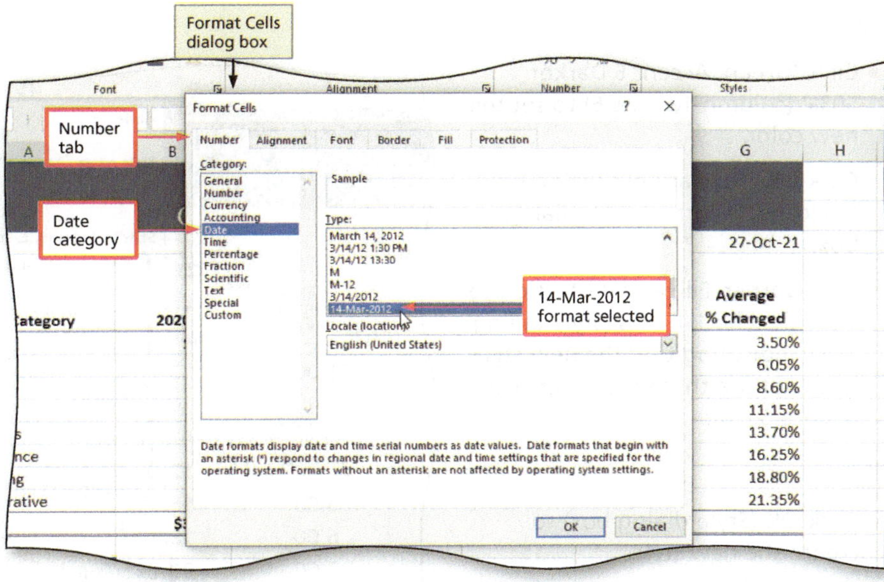

Figure 5–25

4

- Click the Alignment tab (Format Cells dialog box) to display the Alignment sheet. Click the Horizontal button, and then click Center to define the alignment of the new style (Figure 5–26).

Q&A **What is the difference between the text alignment options here and the ones on the Home tab?**
Many of them are the same; however, in this dialog box, you can make adjustments that are more precise. Keep in mind that you cannot use the buttons on the Home tab when you are creating a new style.

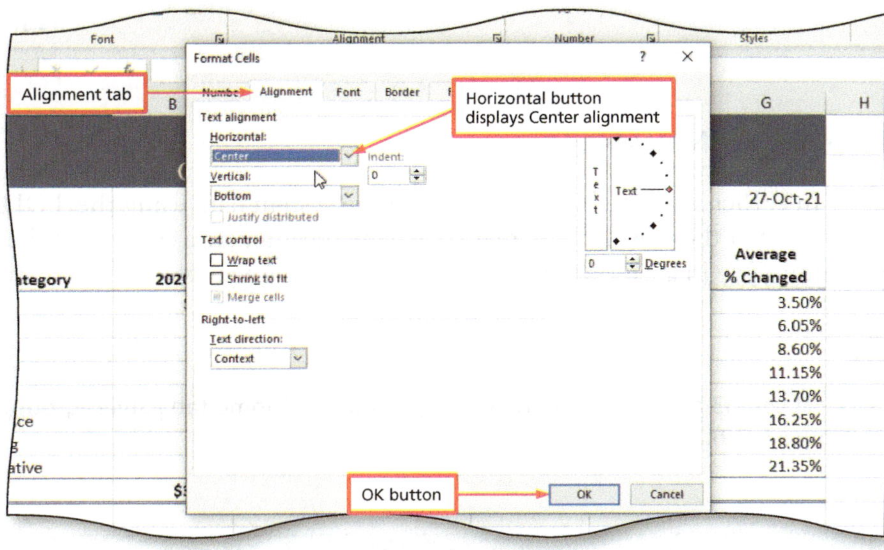

Figure 5–26

5

- Click the Font tab (Format Cells dialog box) and then click the Color button to display the Color gallery (Figure 5–27).

Q&A **What are superscript and subscript on the Font sheet?**
A **superscript** is a small number placed above the normal text line to indicate exponentiation. A **subscript** is a small number placed below the normal text line such as those used in scientific and chemical notations.

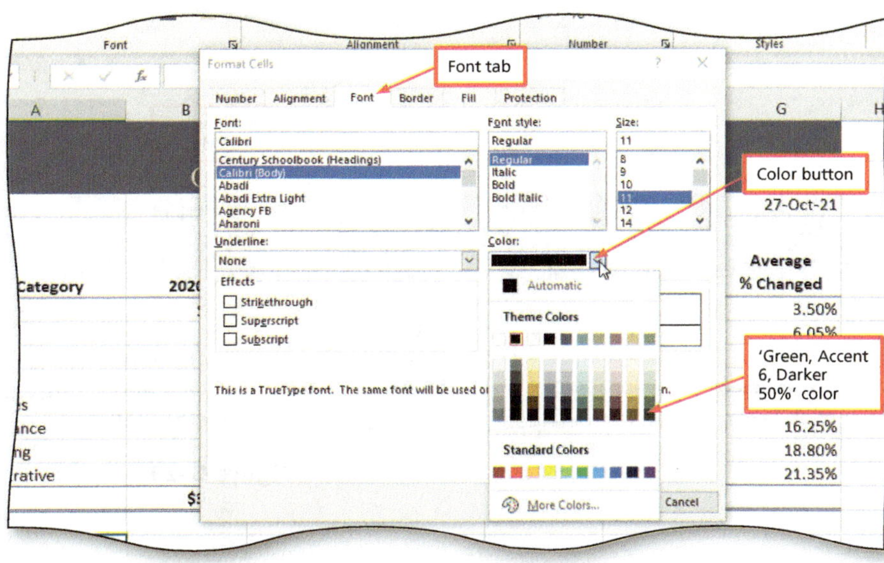

Figure 5–27

6

- Click 'Green, Accent 6 Darker 50%' (column 10, row 6) to set the new color.
- Click OK (Format Cells dialog box) to close the Format Cells dialog box.
- Click Border, Fill, and Protection to clear the check boxes (Style dialog box), indicating that the new style does not use these characteristics (Figure 5–28).

7

- Click OK (Style dialog box) to create the new style.

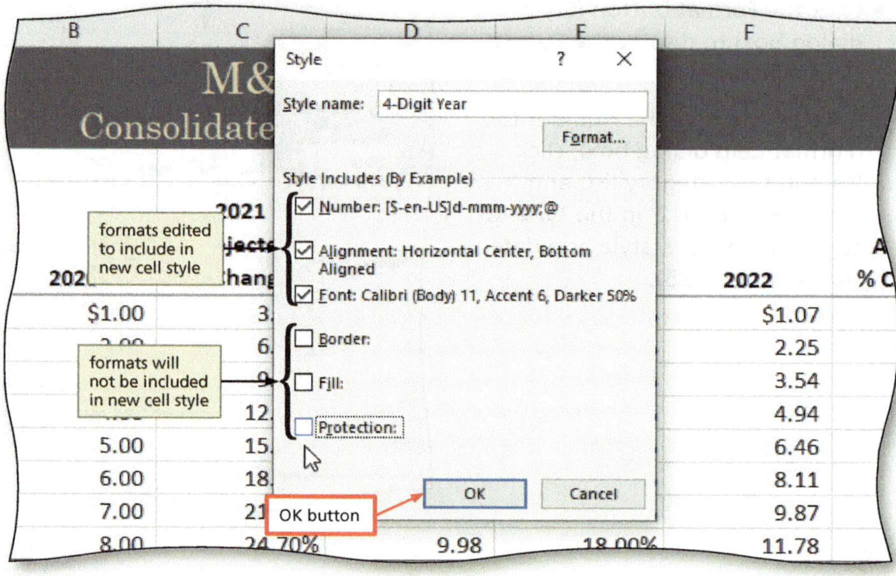

Figure 5–28

To Apply a New Style

In earlier steps, cell G3 was assigned the system date using the TODAY function. The following steps assign cell G3 the new 4-Digit Year style, which centers the content of the cell and assigns it the date format dd-mmm-yyyy in green. **Why?** Using a style ensures a consistent application of formatting instructions.

1

- Select cell G3 and then click the Cell Styles button (Home tab | Styles group) to display the Cell Styles gallery (Figure 5–29).

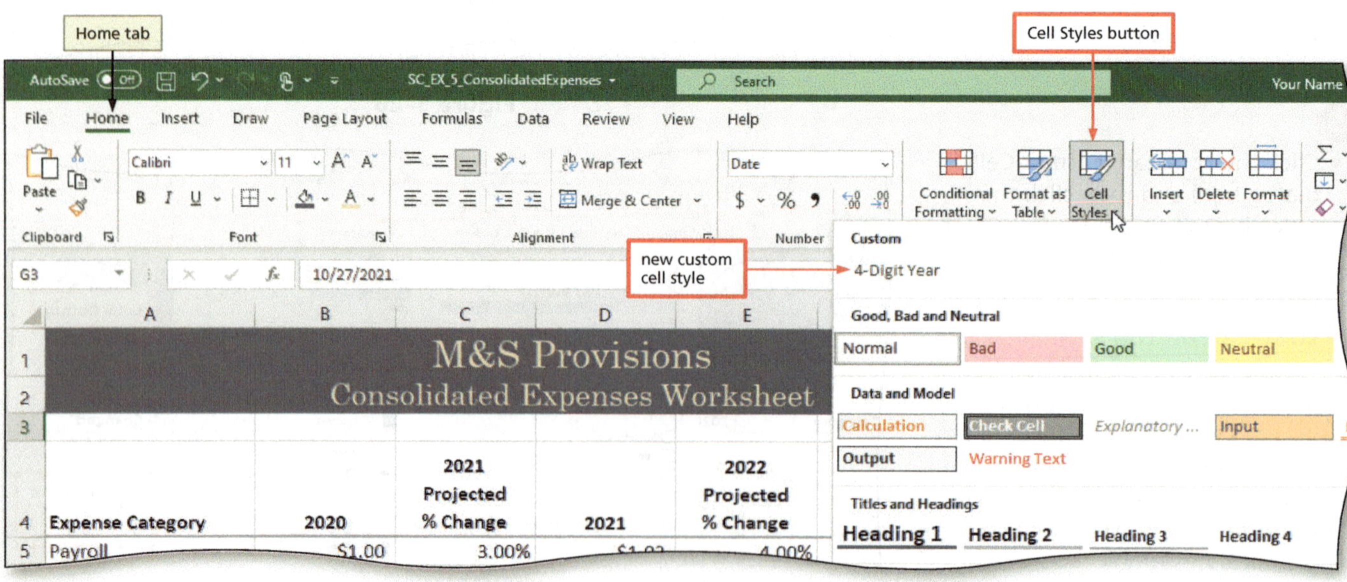

Figure 5–29

2

- Click the 4-Digit Year style to assign the new style to the selected cell (Figure 5–30).

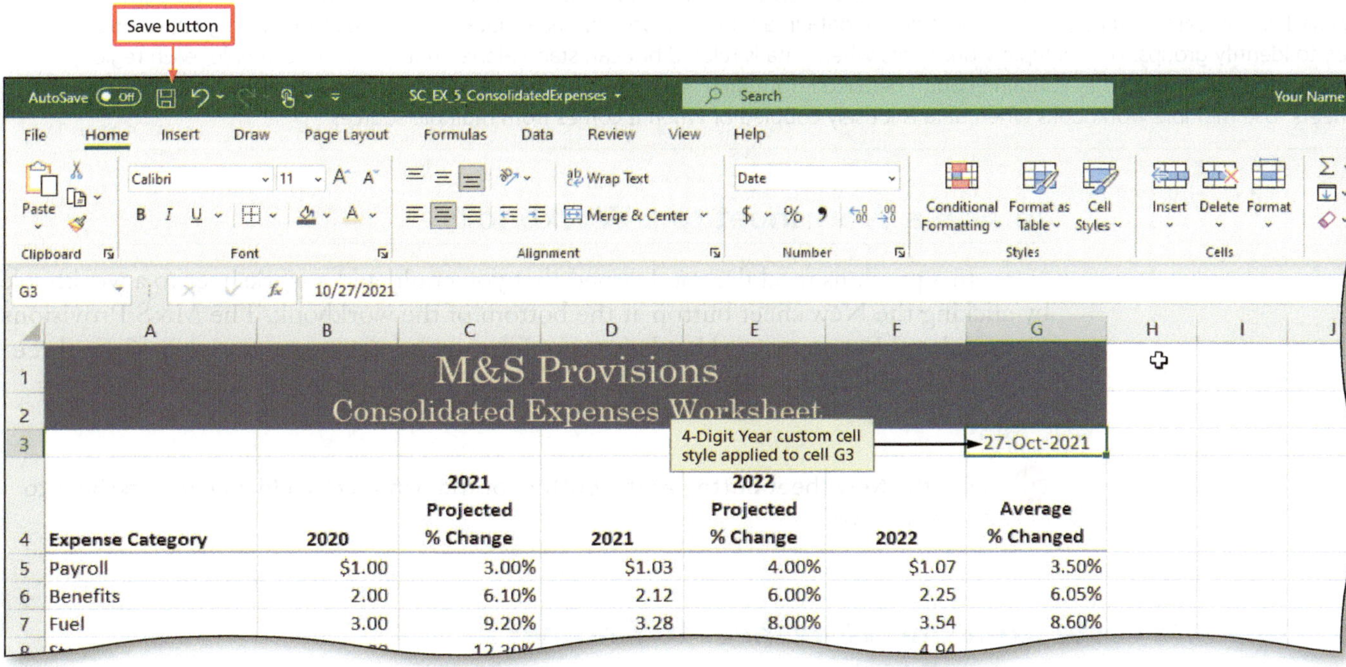

Figure 5–30

To Use the Spelling Checker

The formatting is complete. The following steps use the spelling checker to check the spelling in the worksheet, and then save the consolidated worksheet.

1. Select cell A1, click the Review tab, and then click the Spelling button (Review tab | Proofing group) to check the spelling in the workbook. Correct any misspelled words.
2. Click the Save button on the Quick Access Toolbar to save the workbook.

Break Point: If you want to take a break, this is a good place to do so. You can exit Excel now. To resume later, start Excel, open the file called SC_EX_5_ConsolidatedExpenses, and continue following the steps from this location forward.

Working with Multiple Worksheets

A workbook contains one worksheet by default. You can add more worksheets, limited only by the amount of memory in your computer. As workbooks begin to grow, you can search for text in the workbook by clicking the Find & Select button (Home tab | Editing group), clicking Find to display the Find and Replace dialog box, entering the text to find in the 'Find what text' box, and then clicking the Find Next or Find All button. When working with multiple worksheets, you should name and color the sheet tabs so that you can identify them easily. With the consolidated worksheet complete, the next steps are to insert and populate worksheets in the workbook by copying the data from the consolidated worksheet to the location worksheets, and adjusting the formatting and values. You will learn three different ways to copy data across worksheets.

BTW

Default Number of Worksheets

An alternative to adding worksheets is to change the default number of worksheets before you open a new workbook. To change the default number of worksheets in a blank workbook, click Options in the Backstage view and then change the number in the 'Include this many sheets' box in the 'When creating new workbooks' area (Excel Options dialog box).

CONSIDER THIS

How do I determine how many worksheets to add to a workbook?

Excel provides three basic choices when you consider how to organize data. Use a single worksheet when the data is tightly related. In this case, you may want to analyze the data in a table and use columnar data, such as department, region, or quarter, to identify groups. Use multiple worksheets when data is related but can stand alone on its own. For example, each region, department, or quarter may contain enough detailed information that you may want to analyze the data in separate worksheets. Use multiple workbooks when data is loosely coupled or when it comes from multiple sources.

To Add a Worksheet to a Workbook

In a previous module, you learned that you could add a worksheet to a workbook by clicking the New sheet button at the bottom of the workbook. The M&S Provisions Consolidated Expenses workbook requires four worksheets—one for each of the three venue sites and one for the consolidated totals. The following step adds the first new worksheet.

1 Click the New sheet button at the bottom of the window to add a new worksheet to the workbook.

To Copy and Paste from One Worksheet to Another

With two worksheets in the workbook, the next step is to copy the contents of Sheet1 to Sheet2. **Why?** When the desired content of the new worksheet mirrors or closely follows that of an existing worksheet, copying the existing content minimizes the chances of introducing errors. Sheet1 eventually will be used as the Consolidated worksheet with consolidated data. Sheet2 will be used for one of the three food truck worksheets.

In the process of copying, you must first select the populated cells. You can press CTRL+A to select the rectangular range that contains populated cells. You can press CTRL+A twice to select all of the rows and columns in the worksheet, you can drag around the cells to create a selection, or you can click the Select All button located just below the Name box at the intersection of the row and column headings. The manner in which you select all of the data depends on where you are in the worksheet and your personal preference of using the mouse versus the keyboard. The following steps copy the content of one worksheet to another using the Select All button.

1

- Click the Sheet1 sheet tab to display the worksheet.
- Click the Select All button to select the entire worksheet.
- Click the Copy button (Home tab | Clipboard group) to copy the contents of the worksheet (Figure 5–31).

Q&A **Can I use the shortcut keys, CTRL+C and CTRL+V, to copy and paste?**

Yes. In addition, you can use the shortcut menu to copy and paste.

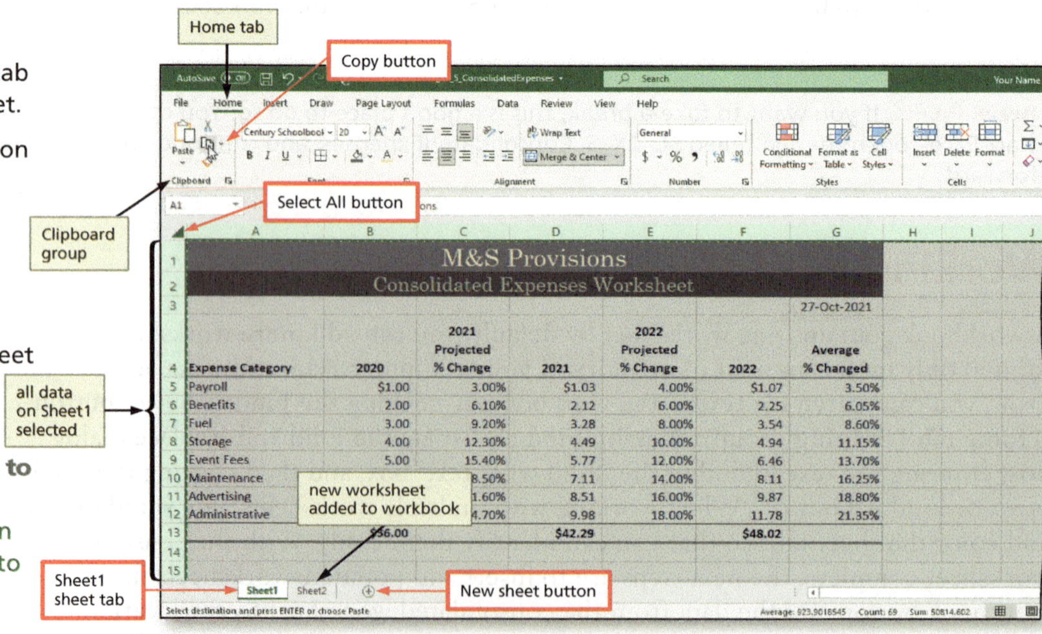

Figure 5–31

2

- Click the Sheet2 sheet tab at the bottom of the worksheet to display Sheet2.
- Press ENTER to copy the data from the Office Clipboard to the selected sheet.
- Zoom to approximately 120% (Figure 5–32).

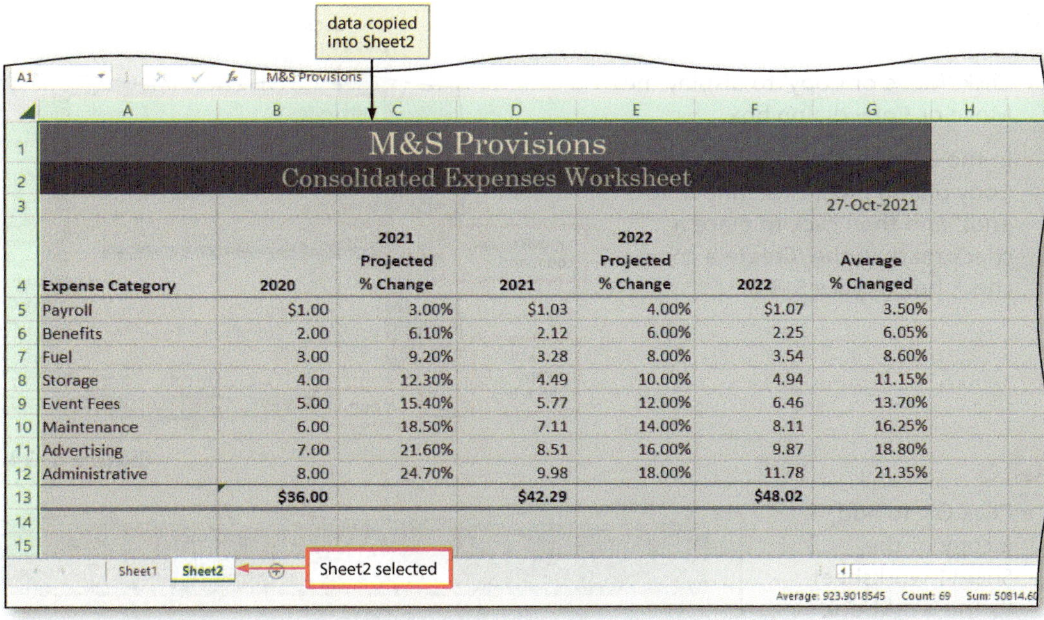

Figure 5–32

Q&A **Can I use the Paste button (Home tab | Clipboard group) to paste the data?** Yes. Recall that if you complete a paste operation using ENTER, however, the marquee disappears and the Office Clipboard is cleared, as it no longer contains the copied data following the action.

Other Ways

1. Select cells, press CTRL+C, select destination cell, press CTRL+V
2. Select cells, press CTRL+C, select destination cell, press ENTER
3. Right-click selected cells, click Copy, right-click destination cell, click appropriate Paste button

To Copy a Worksheet Using a Shortcut Menu

The following steps create a worksheet using the shortcut menu that appears when you right-click a sheet tab. **Why?** The shortcut menu and resulting dialog box allow you more flexibility in exactly where and how to move and copy.

1

- Right-click the Sheet1 sheet tab to display the shortcut menu (Figure 5–33).

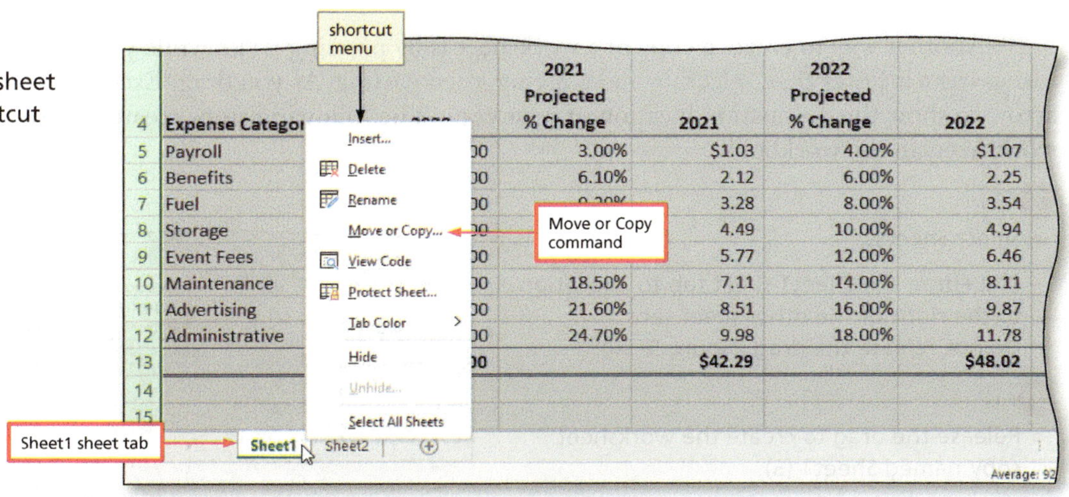

Figure 5–33

2

- Click 'Move or Copy' to display the Move or Copy dialog box.
- In the Before sheet list (Move or Copy dialog box), click '(move to end)' and then click to place a check mark in the 'Create a copy' check box (Figure 5–34).

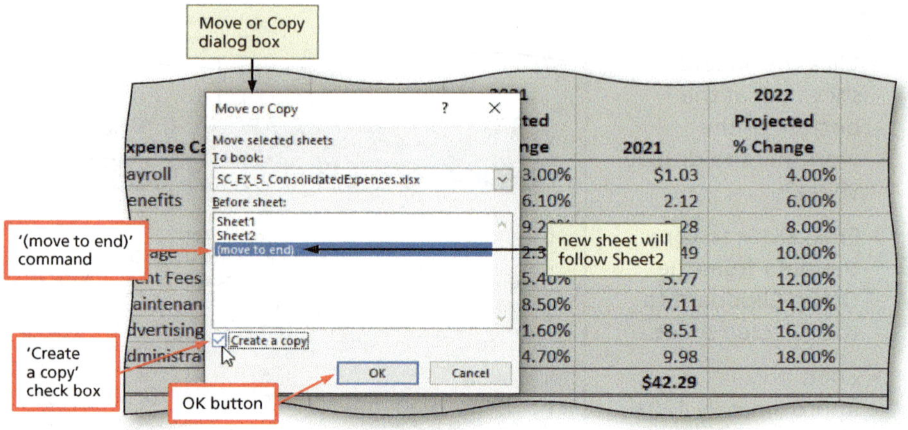

Figure 5–34

3

- Click OK to add a copy of the Sheet1 worksheet to the workbook (Figure 5–35).

Q&A **Why is it named Sheet1 (2) instead of Sheet3?**
Excel indicates that it is a copy by referring to the original sheet.

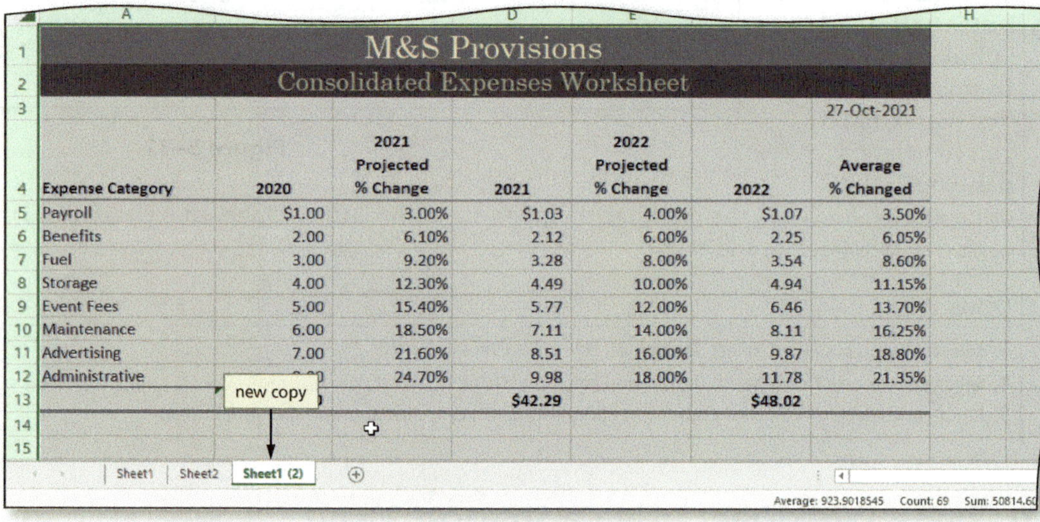

Figure 5–35

To Copy a Worksheet Using CTRL

Another way to create a copy of a worksheet is by pressing CTRL while you drag the sheet tab. **Why?** Using CTRL is faster than selecting and copying, then pasting. As you drag, Excel will display a small triangular arrow to show the destination location of your copy. The following steps create a third copy, for a total of four worksheets in the workbook.

1

- Select Sheet1.
- CTRL+drag the Sheet1 sheet tab to a location to the right of the other sheet tabs. Do not release the drag (Figure 5–36).

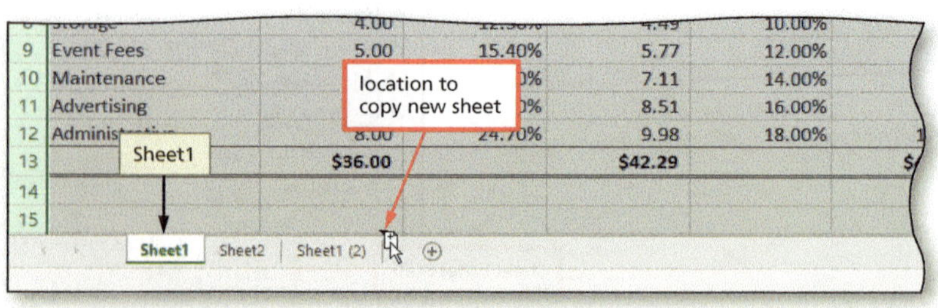

Figure 5–36

2

- Release the drag to create the worksheet copy named Sheet1 (3).

To Drill an Entry through Worksheets

The next step is to replace the sample numbers for the 2021 and 2022 projected percentage change. The percentage changes are identical on all four sheets. For example, the 2021 % change for payroll in cell C5 will be changed to 2.50% on all four sheets.

To speed data entry, Excel allows you to enter a number in the same cell through all selected worksheets. This technique is referred to as **drilling an entry. Why?** In cases where multiple worksheets have the same layout and the same calculations performed on data, drilling entries of data or formulas ensures consistency across the worksheets. When you drill, all affected sheets must be selected. Table 5–6 contains the new figures for cells C5:C12 and E5:E12.

Table 5–6 Projected % Change Values for 2021 and 2022

Category	Cell	2021 Projected % Change	Cell	2022 Projected % Change
Payroll	C5	2.5	E5	2.5
Benefits	C6	2	E6	3
Fuel	C7	2	E7	3
Storage	C8	1	E8	1
Event Fees	C9	1	E9	1
Maintenance	C10	1	E10	2
Advertising	C11	–1	E11	–1
Administrative	C12	–2	E12	–2.25

The following steps select all sheets, drill the 2021 and 2022 projected percentage change entries from Table 5–6 through all four worksheets, and then ungroup the selection.

1

- Right-click Sheet1 and then click 'Select All Sheets' on the shortcut menu to group the sheets.
- Select cell C5. Type `2.5` and then press the DOWN ARROW key to change sample data in the selected cell to the actual value.
- Enter the 15 remaining 2021 and 2022 Projected % Change values from Table 5–6 to the appropriate cells to display the actual percentages (Figure 5–37).

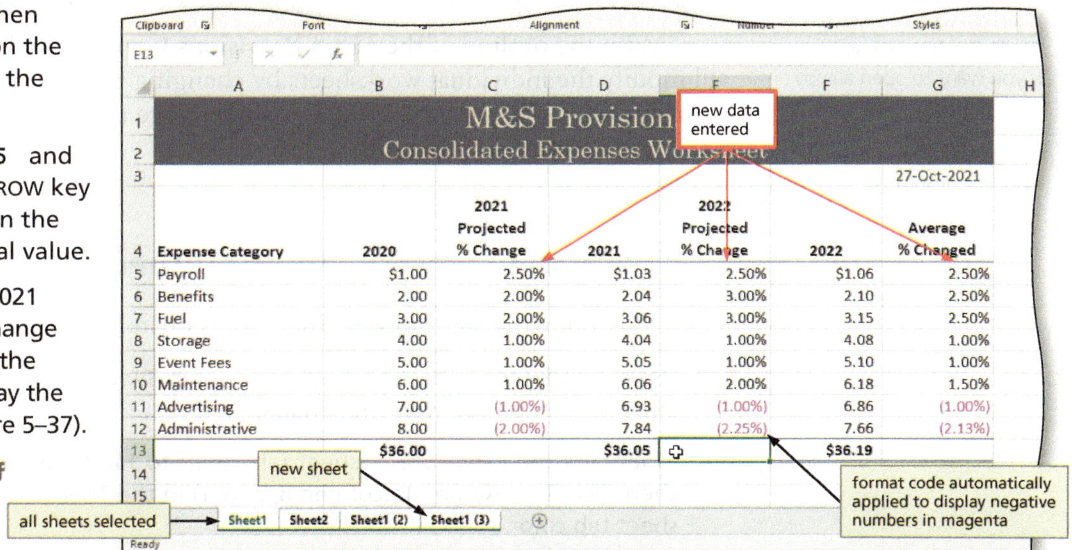

Figure 5–37

Q&A **What is the benefit of drilling data through worksheets?**
In these steps, 16 new numbers were entered on one worksheet. By drilling the entries through the other worksheets, 64 new numbers now appear, 16 on each of the worksheets. The Excel capability of drilling data through selected worksheets is an efficient way to enter data that is common among worksheets.

2

- Right-click Sheet1 and then click Ungroup Sheets on the shortcut menu.

Experiment

- One at a time, click the Sheet2 sheet tab, the Sheet1 (2) sheet tab, and the Sheet1 (3) sheet tab to verify that all four worksheets are identical.

BTW
Deleting Worksheets
Recall from Module 4 that you can delete a worksheet by right-clicking the sheet tab of the worksheet you want to delete, and then clicking Delete on the shortcut menu.

BTW
Selecting Multiple Worksheets
When multiple worksheets are selected, the Excel title bar reflects the selection by adding the notation, [Group]. All of the sheet tabs also are highlighted.

BTW
Opening Workbooks in New Windows
If you want to open a copy of the existing workbook in a new window, click the New Window button (View tab | Window group).

Selecting and Deselecting Sheets

Beginning Excel users sometimes have difficulty trying to select and deselect sheets. Table 5–7 summarizes how to select (group) and deselect (ungroup) multiple sheets using a mouse and keyboard.

Table 5–7 Summary of How to Select and Deselect Sheets

Task	How to Carry Out the Task
Select individual sheet	Click sheet tab.
Select all sheets	Right-click any sheet tab, click 'Select All Sheets' on shortcut menu.
Select adjacent sheets	Select the first sheet by clicking its tab, and then hold down SHIFT and click the sheet tab at the other end of the list of adjacent sheet tabs.
Select nonadjacent sheets	Select the first sheet by clicking its tab, then hold down CTRL and click the sheet tabs of the remaining sheets you want to select.
Deselect all sheets	Right-click any sheet tab, click Ungroup Sheets on shortcut menu or click the individual sheet tab that you wish to select.
Deselect one of many sheets	CTRL+click the sheet tab you want to deselect.

Customizing the Individual Worksheets

With the outline of the M&S Provisions Consolidated workbook created, you will modify the individual worksheets by changing the worksheet name, sheet tab color, and worksheet subtitle. You also will change the color of the title area and enter the 2020 Expenses in column B.

To Modify the Lady Lobster Worksheet

The following steps modify the Lady Lobster worksheet (Sheet2).

1. Double-click the Sheet2 sheet tab to select it. Type `Lady Lobster` and then press ENTER to change the worksheet name.
2. Right-click the Lady Lobster sheet tab, point to Tab Color on the shortcut menu, and then click 'Tan, Accent 4' (column 8, row 1) in the Theme Colors area to change the sheet tab color.
3. Double-click cell A2. Drag through the word, Consolidated, to select the text, and then type `Lady Lobster` to change the worksheet subtitle.
4. Select the range A1:A2. Click the Fill Color arrow (Home tab | Font group) and then click 'Tan, Accent 4' (column 8, row 1) in the Theme Colors area (Fill Color gallery) to change the fill color of the selected range.

5. Click the Font Color arrow (Home tab | Font group) and then click Automatic in the Font Color gallery to change the font color of the selected range.

6. Enter the following data in the indicated cells:

Cell	Data for Lady Lobster	Cell	Data for Lady Lobster
B5	79207.20	B9	6200.00
B6	15247.39	B10	4295.20
B7	20000.00	B11	3599.64
B8	14400.00	B12	2500.00

7. Click an empty cell to deselect the previous cell (Figure 5–38).

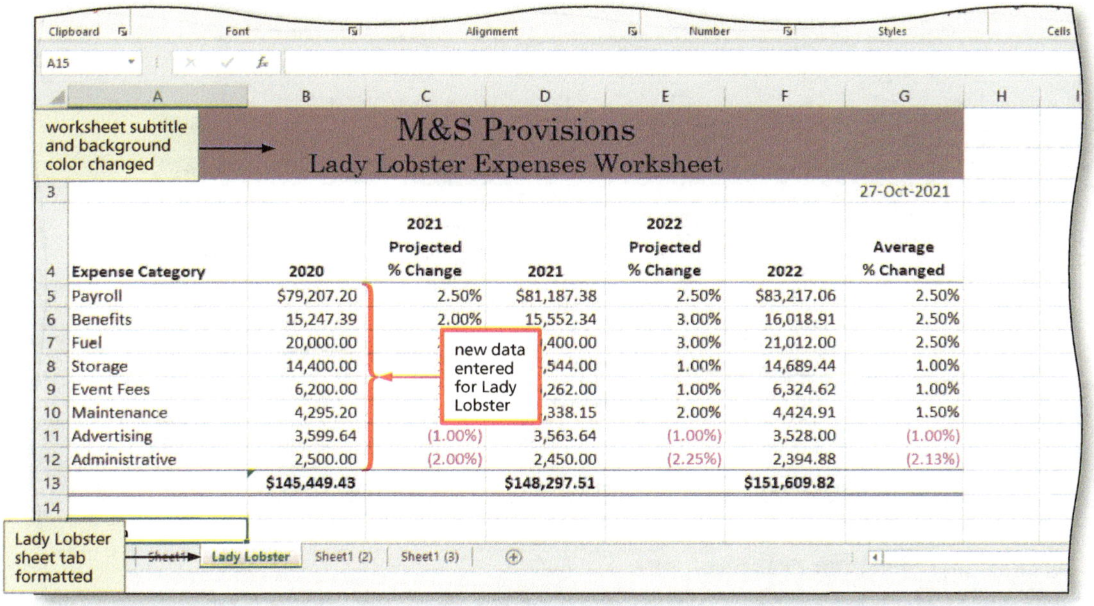

Figure 5–38

To Modify the Henry Haddock Sheet

The following steps modify the Henry Haddock worksheet Sheet1 (2).

1. Double-click the Sheet1 (2) sheet tab to select it. Type **Henry Haddock** and then press ENTER to change the worksheet name.

2. Right-click the Henry Haddock sheet tab, point to Tab Color on the shortcut menu, and then click 'Teal, Accent 2' (column 6, row 1) in the Theme Colors area to change the sheet tab color.

3. Double-click cell A2. Drag through the word, Consolidated, to select the text, and then type **Henry Haddock** to change the worksheet subtitle.

4. Select the range A1:A2. Click the Fill Color arrow (Home tab | Font group) and then click 'Teal, Accent 2' (column 6, row 1) in the Theme Colors area (Fill Color gallery) to change the fill color of the selected range.

5. Click the Font Color arrow (Home tab | Font group) and then click Automatic in the Font Color gallery to change the font color of the selected range.

6. Enter the following data in the indicated cells:

Cell	Data for Henry Haddock	Cell	Data for Henry Haddock
B5	72870.62	B9	7500.00
B6	14027.60	B10	3951.58
B7	19000.00	B11	3311.67
B8	13248.00	B12	2500.00

7. Click an empty cell to deselect the previous cell (Figure 5–39).

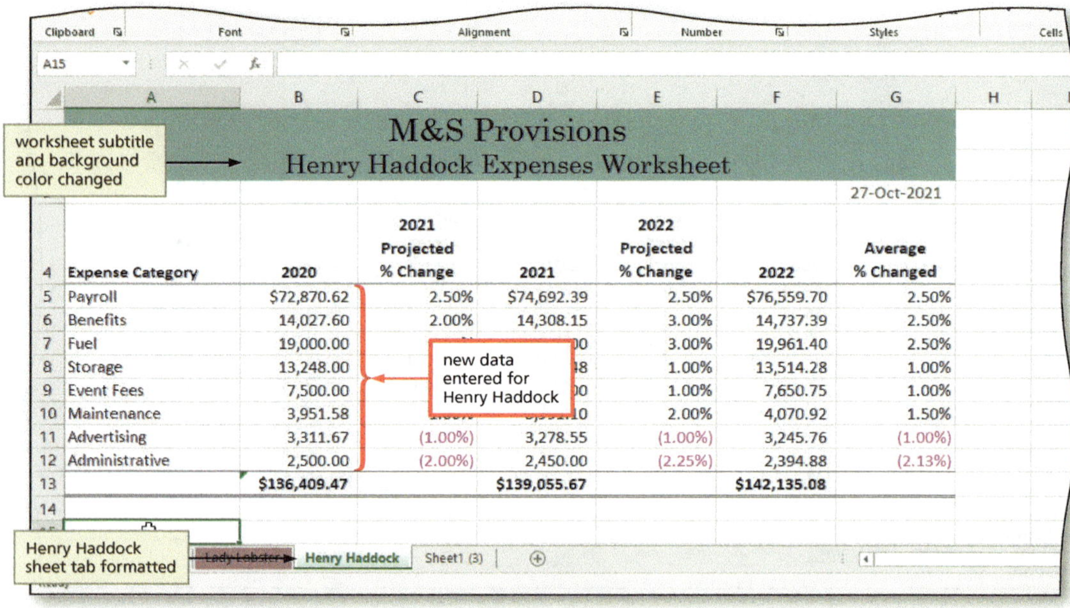

Figure 5–39

To Modify the Sharon Shrimp Worksheet

The following steps modify the Sharon Shrimp worksheet Sheet1 (3).

1. Double-click the Sheet1 (3) sheet tab to select it. Type `Sharon Shrimp` and then press ENTER to change the worksheet name.

2. Right-click the Sharon Shrimp sheet tab, point to Tab Color on the shortcut menu, and then click Orange in the Standard Colors area to change the sheet tab color.

3. Double-click cell A2. Drag through the word, Consolidated, to select the text, and then type `Sharon Shrimp` to change the worksheet subtitle.

4. Select the range A1:A2. Click the Fill Color arrow (Home tab | Font group) and then click Orange in the Standard Colors area (Fill Color gallery) to change the fill color of the selected range.

5. Click the Font Color arrow (Home tab | Font group) and then click Automatic in the Font Color gallery to change the font color of the selected range.

6. Enter the following data in the indicated cells:

Cell	Data for Sharon Shrimp	Cell	Data for Sharon Shrimp
B5	68712.06	B9	5000.00
B6	17077.07	B10	4810.62
B7	18500.00	B11	4031.60
B8	12528.00	B12	2500.00

7. Click an empty cell to deselect the previous cell (Figure 5–40).

8. Click the Save button on the Quick Access Toolbar.

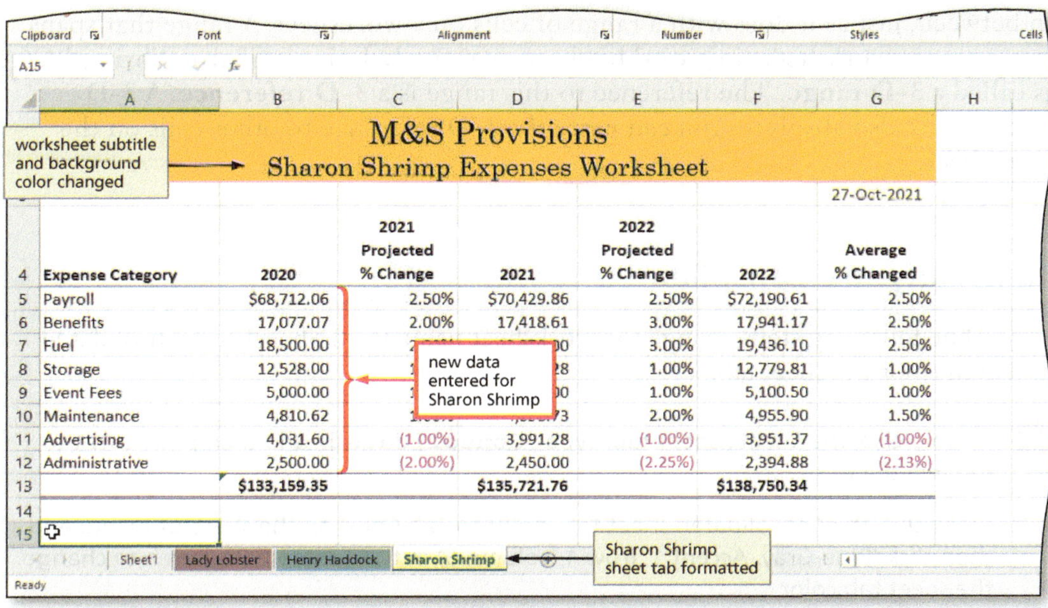

Figure 5–40

Referencing Cells Across Worksheets

With the three location worksheets complete, you now can consolidate the data. Because this consolidation worksheet contains totals of the data, you need to reference cell data from other worksheets.

BTW
Drilling an Entry
Besides drilling a number down through a workbook, you can drill a format, a function, or a formula down through a workbook.

BTW
Importing Data
Expenses, such as those entered into the range B5:B12, often are maintained in another workbook, file, or database. If the expenses are maintained elsewhere, ways exist to link to a workbook or to import data from a file or database into a workbook. Linking to a workbook is discussed later in this module. To see a list of typical sources of outside data, click the 'Get Data' button (Data tab | Get & Transform Data group).

BTW
3-D References
If you are summing numbers on noncontiguous sheets, hold down CTRL rather than SHIFT when selecting the sheets.

To reference cells in other worksheets within a single workbook, you use the worksheet name, which serves as the **worksheet reference**, combined with the cell reference. The worksheet reference must be enclosed within single quotation marks (') when the worksheet name contains a nonalphabetical character such as a space. Excel requires an exclamation point (!) as a delimiter between the worksheet reference and the cell reference. Therefore, the reference to cell B5 on the Lady Lobster worksheet would be entered as

= 'Lady Lobster'!B5

These worksheet and cell references can be used in formulas, such as

= 'Lady Lobster'!B5 + 'Henry Haddock'!B5 + 'Sharon Shrimp'!B5

A worksheet reference such as 'Lady Lobster' always is absolute, meaning that the worksheet reference remains constant if you were to copy the formula to other locations.

Worksheet references also can be used in functions and range references such as

= SUM('Lady Lobster:Sharon Shrimp'!B5)

The SUM argument ('Lady Lobster:Sharon Shrimp'!B5) instructs Excel to sum cell B5 on each of the three worksheets (Lady Lobster, Henry Haddock, and Sharon Shrimp). The colon (:) delimiter between the first worksheet name and the last worksheet name instructs Excel to include these worksheets and all worksheets in between, just as it does with a range of cells on a worksheet. A range that spans two or more worksheets in a workbook, such as 'Lady Lobster:Sharon Shrimp'!C6, is called a **3-D range**. The reference to this range is a **3-D reference**. A 3-D reference is also absolute. You can paste the 3-D reference to other cells on the worksheet.

To Modify the Consolidated Worksheet

The following steps change the worksheet name from Sheet1 to Consolidated and then color the sheet tab.

1. Double-click the Sheet1 sheet tab. Type `Consolidated` and then press ENTER to rename the tab.

2. Right-click the Consolidated sheet tab, point to Tab Color on the shortcut menu, and then click 'Blue-Gray, Accent 1' (row 1, column 5) in the Theme Colors area to change the sheet tab color.

To Enter a 3-D Reference

To consolidate the payroll expenses, the following steps create 3-D references in cells B5, D5, and F5 on the Consolidated worksheet. **Why?** Using 3-D references is the most efficient method of referencing cells that reside in the same location on different worksheets. You can enter a worksheet reference in a cell by typing the worksheet reference or by clicking the appropriate sheet tab while in Point mode. When you click the sheet tab, Excel activates the worksheet and automatically adds the worksheet name and an exclamation point after the insertion point in the formula bar. Then, click the desired cell or drag through the cells you want to reference on the sheet.

If the range of cells to be referenced is located on several worksheets (as when selecting a 3-D range), click the first sheet tab and then select the cell(s). Finally, SHIFT+click the last sheet tab you want to reference. Excel will include the cell(s) on the first worksheet, the last worksheet, and any worksheets in between.

1

- Select cell B5 and then click the AutoSum button (Home tab | Editing group) to display the SUM function (Figure 5–41).

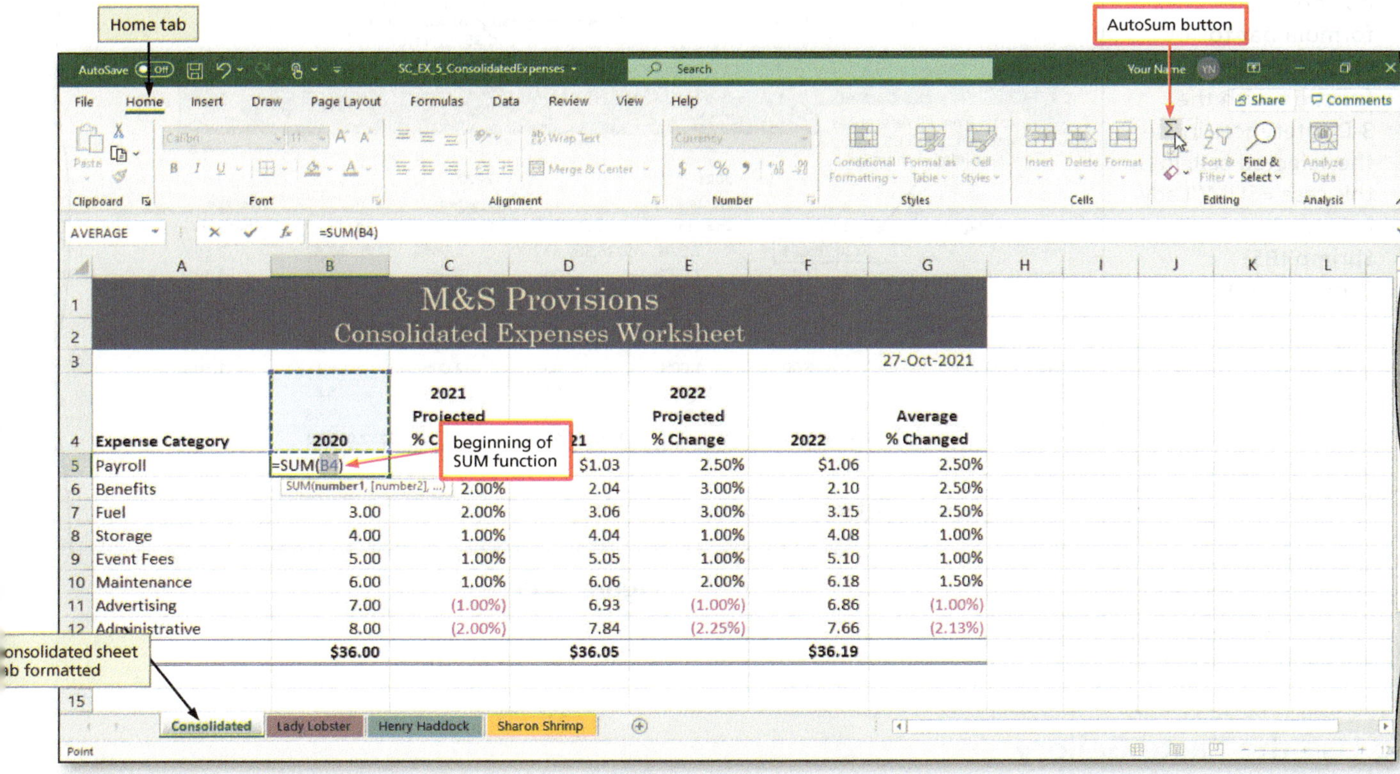

Figure 5–41

2

- Click the Lady Lobster tab and then click cell B5 to select the first portion of the argument for the SUM function.
- SHIFT+click the Sharon Shrimp tab to select the ending range of the argument for the SUM function (Figure 5–42).

Q&A **Could I just type the 3-D reference?** Yes, however the Point mode is used in this step, which prevents any errors in typing the reference.

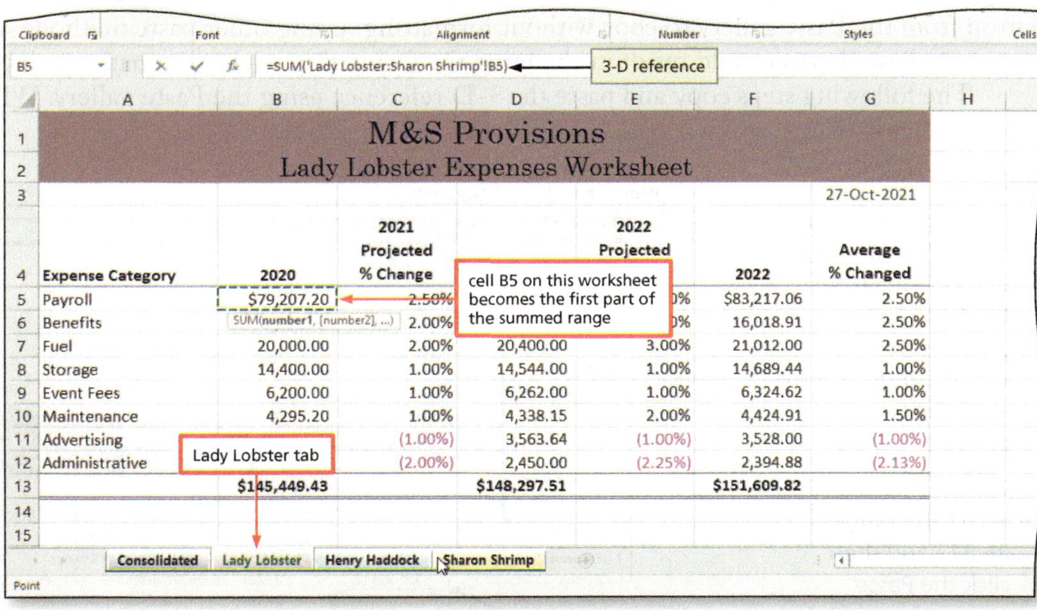

Figure 5–42

3

- Click the Enter button in the formula bar to enter the SUM function with the 3-D references in the selected cell, in this case =SUM('Lady Lobster:Sharon Shrimp'!B5) (Figure 5–43).

Q&A **Should each worksheet name in the function have individual sets of single quotes?**
No, in a 3-D reference that uses a range, Excel requires a single quote before the first worksheet name in the range and an ending single quote after the last worksheet name.

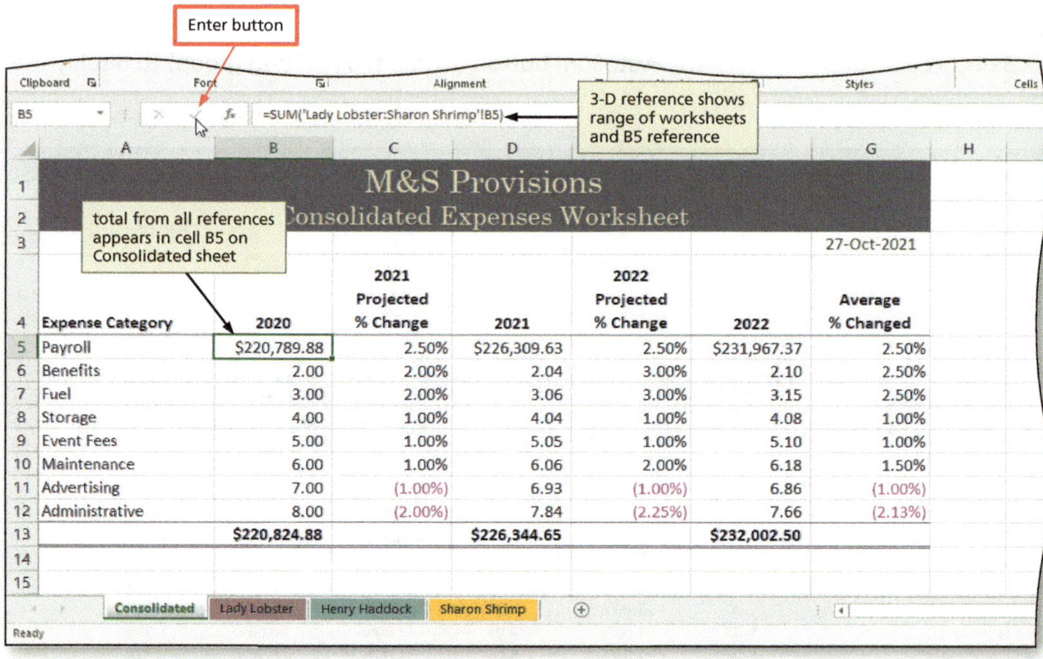

Figure 5–43

To Use the Paste Gallery

In earlier modules, you learned about the Paste Options button, which allows you to choose different ways to paste and copy formulas, values, and functions. The Paste gallery, which appears when you click the Paste arrow (Home tab | Clipboard group), offers many of the same choices, and depending on the type of pasting, many others. When copying a formula that includes a 3-D reference, it is advisable to choose the Formulas button from the Paste gallery to copy without formatting. Using other paste methods such as the fill handle, ENTER, or Paste button could result in changing the formatting of the destination cells.

The following steps copy and paste the 3-D reference using the Paste gallery. **Why?** Using the Paste gallery will not change the destination formatting.

1

- With cell B5 active on the Consolidated worksheet, click the Copy button (Home tab | Clipboard group) to copy the selected cell to the Office Clipboard.
- Select the range B6:B12 and then click the Paste arrow (Home tab | Clipboard group) to display the Paste gallery (Figure 5–44).

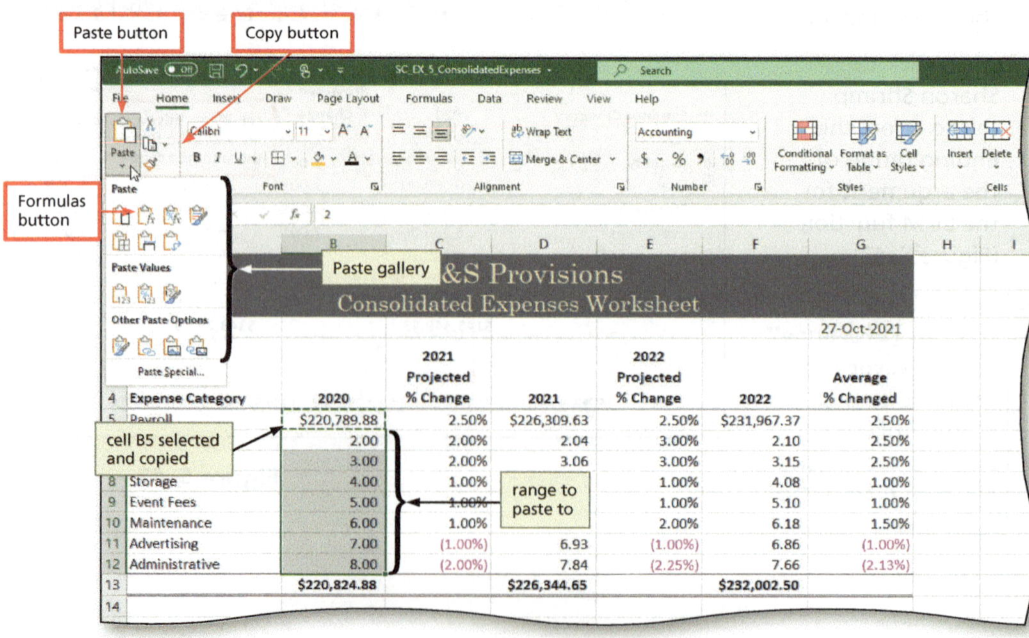

Figure 5–44

2

- Click the Formulas button (column 2, row 1) in the Paste gallery to copy the SUM function to the desired range, replicating the 3-D references.
- Press ESC to clear the marquee.
- Deselect the previous range (Figure 5–45).
- Click the Save button on the Quick Access Toolbar to save the workbook.

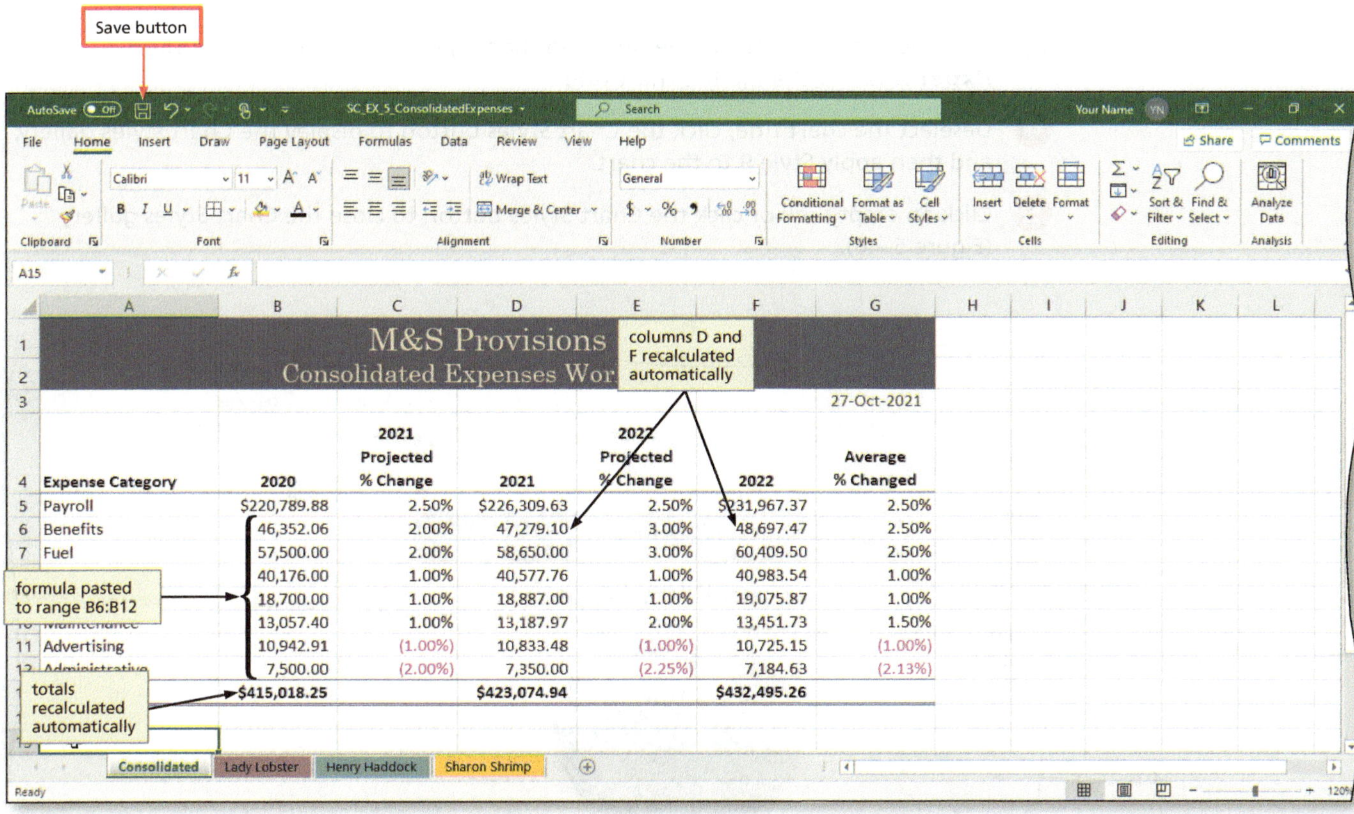

Figure 5–45

Other Ways

1. Right-click selected cell(s), click Copy, right-click destination cell(s), click appropriate Paste button

Break Point: If you want to take a break, this is a good place to do so. You can exit Excel now. To resume later, start Excel, open the file called SC_EX_5_ConsolidatedExpenses, and continue following the steps from this location forward.

Formatting Pie Charts

In Module 1, you created a pie chart. Pie charts show the contribution of each piece of data to the whole, or total, of the data. You can format a pie chart in many ways including resizing, moving, rotating, adding data labels and leader lines, adding a decorative background, and exploding a slice. In addition, if your chart displays numeric data labels, you can format the data by clicking a data label and then entering the desired formatting options and format code in the Number area of the Format Data Labels pane.

As outlined in the requirements document in Table 5–1, the worksheet should include a pie chart to represent graphically the 2020 expenses totals for all three food trucks. The pie chart resides at the bottom of the consolidated worksheet, so it will print on the same page.

BTW

Y-Rotation and Perspective

The Y-Rotation arrows tilt the chart toward the back or front, allowing you to control the elevation of the chart. You can tilt the chart toward or away from you in order to enhance the view of the chart. The Perspective value makes close slices appear larger and those further away appear smaller.

To Insert a 3-D Pie Chart on a Worksheet

The following steps insert the 3-D pie chart on the Consolidated worksheet.

1. Select the range A5:B12 to identify the category names and data for the pie chart.
2. Display the Insert tab, click the 'Insert Pie or Doughnut Chart' button (Insert tab | Charts group), and then click 3-D Pie in the Insert Pie or Doughnut Chart gallery to create the desired chart type.
3. Click the chart title, select the text, and then type `2020 Consolidated Expenses` to change the chart title.
4. Deselect the chart title, click the Chart Styles button to display the Chart styles gallery, and then apply Style 9 to the chart.
5. Click an empty cell or click the Chart Styles button to close the Chart Styles gallery (Figure 5–46).

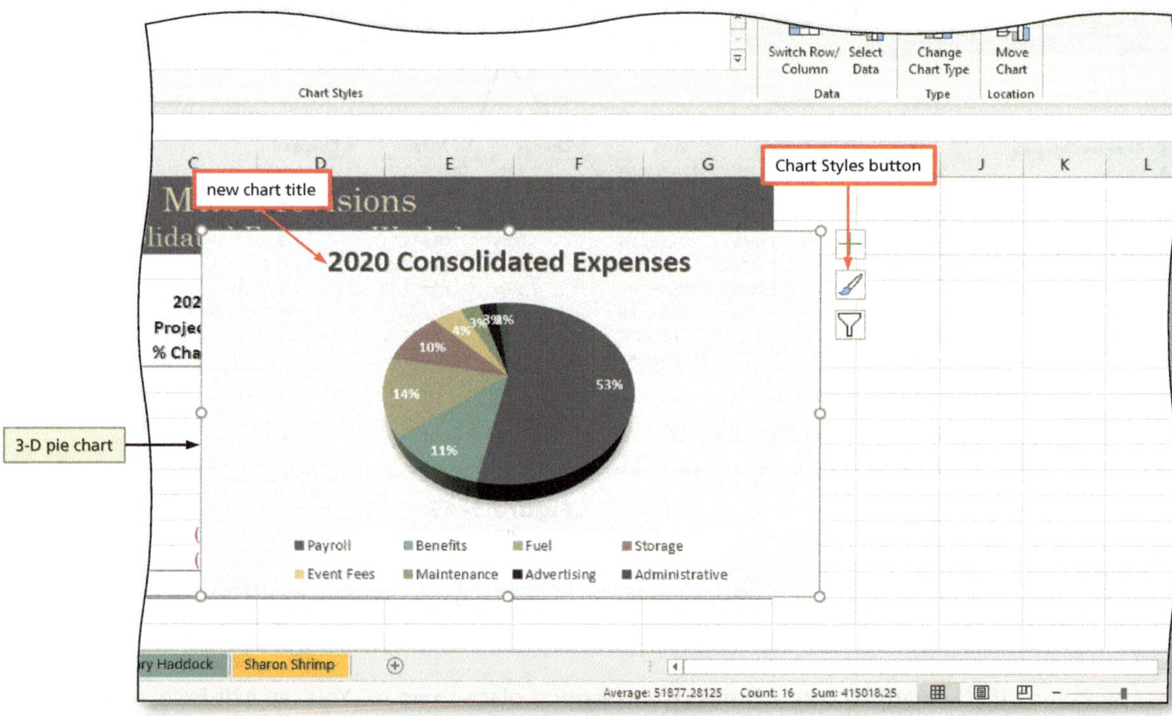

Figure 5–46

To Move a Chart on the Same Worksheet

As you learned in an earlier module, you can move a chart to a new worksheet or move a chart on the same worksheet. If you want move a chart to a different worksheet, select the chart and then select the Move Chart button (Chart Design tab | Location group). Then, select the New sheet radio button, type the name of the new sheet in the corresponding text box, and click OK. The following step moves the chart on the same worksheet to the space below the data that was used to create the chart. **Why?** By default, Excel places charts in the center of the worksheet. You need to move it in order to uncover the data on the worksheet.

1

- Point to the border of the chart. When the pointer changes to a four-headed arrow, drag the chart below the worksheet numbers to the desired location (in this case, approximately cell A15) (Figure 5–47).

Experiment

- Point to each of the styles in the Chart Styles group (Chart Design tab) and watch the chart change to reflect each style.

Q&A **Could I use the Move Chart button (Chart Design tab | Location group) to move the chart?**
No. That button moves the chart from sheet to sheet rather than to a new location on the same worksheet.

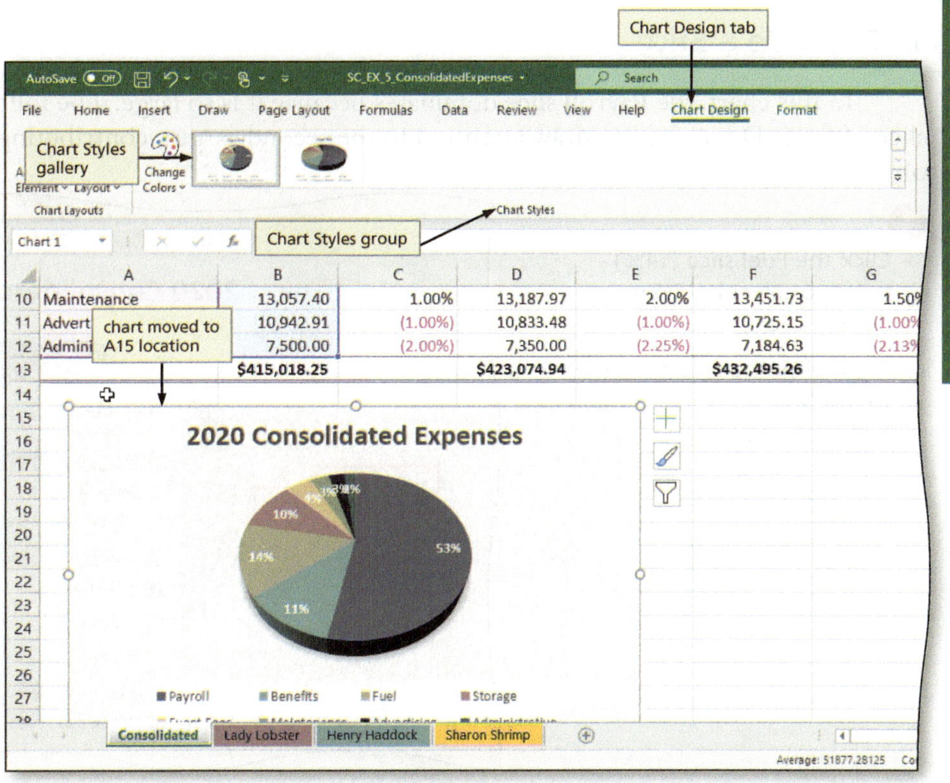

Figure 5–47

To Resize a Chart

If you want to resize a chart, you either can do so by dragging the sizing handles until the chart is the desired size, or you can resize the chart to exact dimensions. To resize a chart to exact dimensions, click to select the chart, click the Format tab on the Ribbon, and then enter the desired height and width in the Size group. The following step resizes the chart proportionally by dragging to make it larger and more legible. To resize a chart nonproportionally, do not hold SHIFT while dragging the resizing handles. **Why?** The chart as created by Excel may not be the optimal size for your worksheet needs.

1

- If necessary, scroll down until you can see both the bottom of the chart and row 32.
- SHIFT+drag the lower-right resizing handle of the chart until the chart is the desired size (in this case, approximately to cell F32).
- If necessary, zoom out until you can see the entire chart (Figure 5–48).

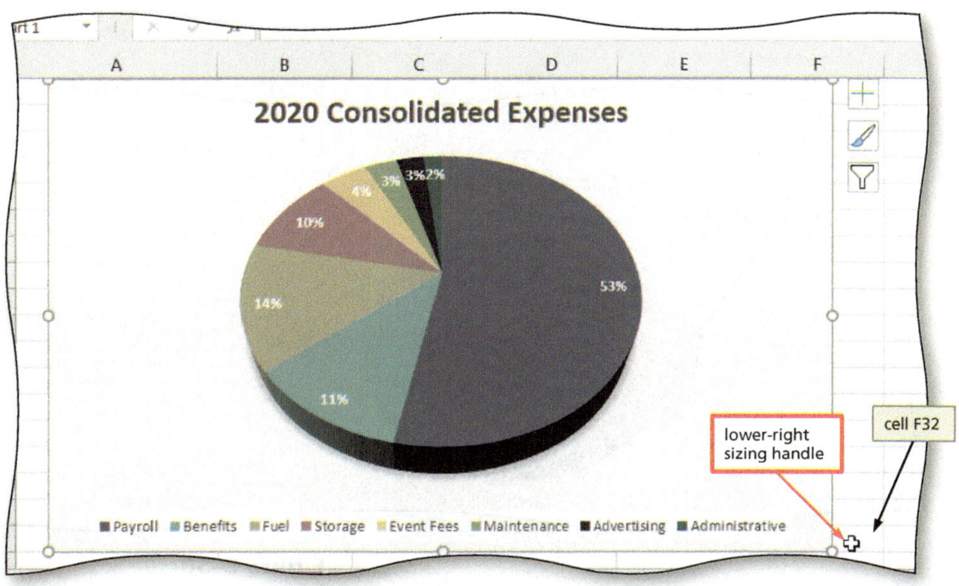

Figure 5–48

To Explode a Slice

In this chart, the Payroll slice dominates because it is so large. The following steps explode the next-largest slice of the 3-D pie chart to draw attention to the second-largest contributing expense. **Why?** Exploding, or offsetting, a slice in a chart emphasizes it.

1

- Click the Fuel slice (14%) twice to select it. (Do not double-click.)
- Right-click the selected slice to display the shortcut menu (Figure 5–49).

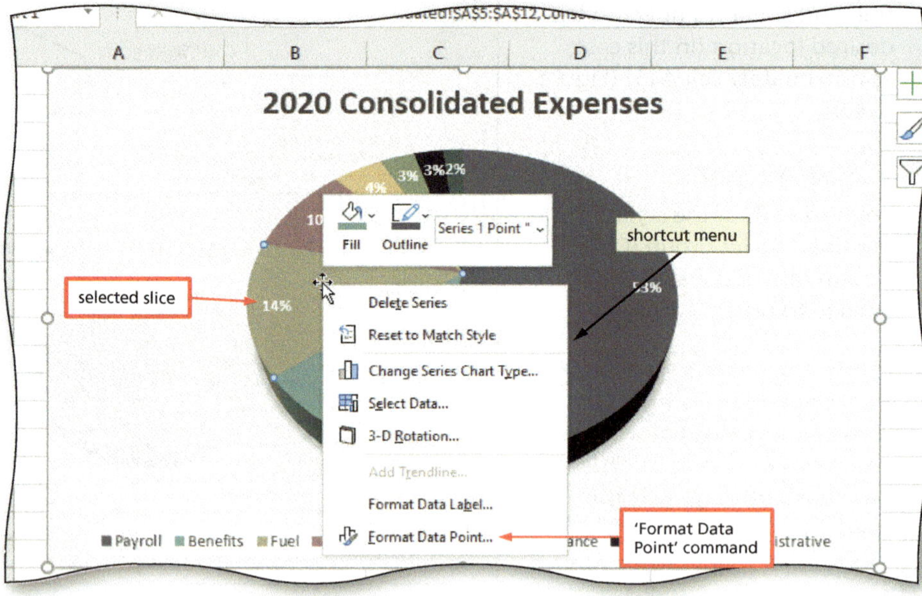

Figure 5–49

2

- Click 'Format Data Point' on the shortcut menu to open the Format Data Point pane.
- Drag the Point Explosion slider to the right until the Point Explosion box reads 15% to edit the offset distance for the slice (Figure 5–50).

Experiment

- Select different slices and use the Point Explosion slider to offset additional slices and note how the size of the chart changes as you offset additional slices. When done, reset the slices so that the Fuel slice is the only slice offset, set to 15%.

Q&A

Should I offset more slices?

You can offset as many slices as you want, but remember that the reason for offsetting a slice is to emphasize it. Offsetting multiple slices tends to reduce the impact on the reader and reduces the overall size of the pie chart.

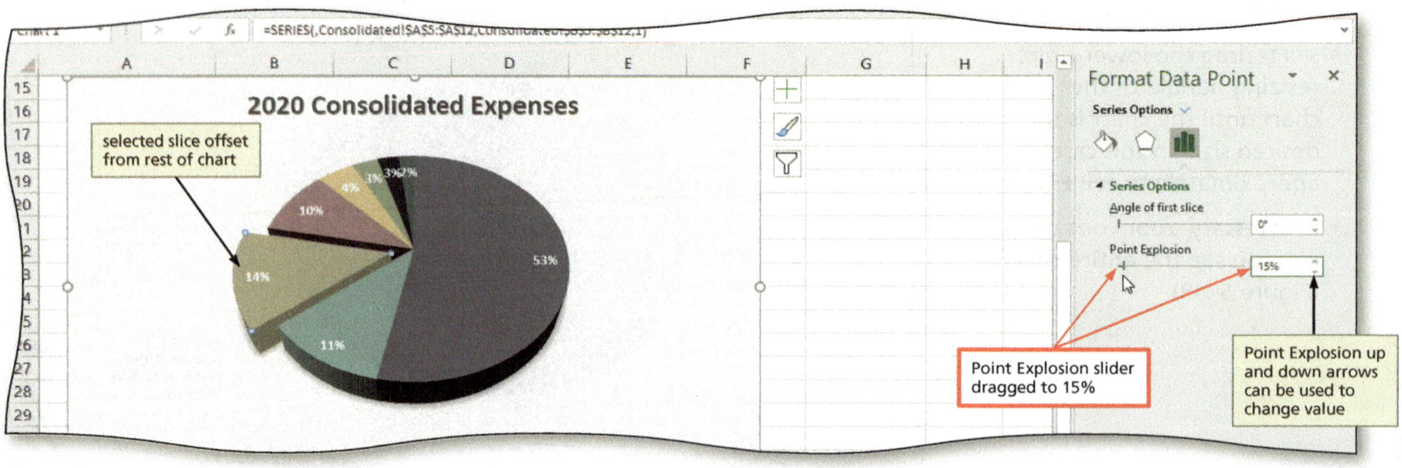

Figure 5–50

Other Ways

1. Click slice twice, drag away from other slices

To Rotate the 3-D Pie Chart

When Excel initially draws a pie chart, it always positions the chart so that one of the dividing lines between two slices is a straight line pointing to 12 o'clock (or 0°). As shown in Figure 5–50, that line currently divides the Administrative and Payroll slices. This line defines the rotation angle of the 3-D pie chart. Excel allows you to control the rotation angle, elevation, perspective, height, and angle of the axes. The following steps rotate the 3-D pie chart. **Why?** With a three-dimensional chart, you can change the view to better show the section of the chart you are trying to emphasize.

1

- Right-click the chart to display the shortcut menu, and then click '3-D Rotation' on the shortcut menu to open the Format Chart Area pane.
- In the X Rotation box (Format Chart Area pane), type **250** to rotate the chart (Figure 5–51).

Q&A

What happens if I click the X Rotation up arrow?
Excel will rotate the chart 10° in a clockwise direction each time you click the X Rotation up arrow.

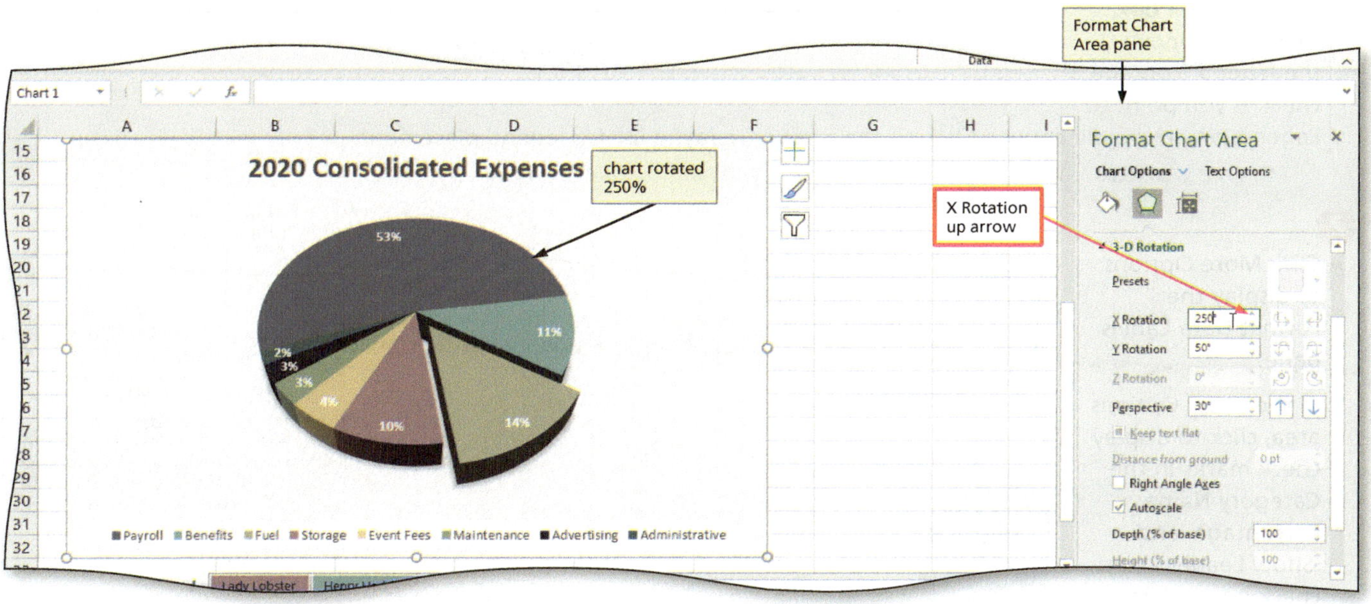

Figure 5–51

2

- Click the Close button (Format Chart Area pane) to close the pane.

To Format Data Labels

The following steps format the data labels using the Format Data Labels pane. You will choose the elements to include in the data label, set the position, choose number formatting, and create leader lines. **Why?** A **leader line** connects a data label with its data point helping you identify individual slices.

1

- Click the Chart Elements button to display the Chart Elements gallery. Point to Data Labels and then click the Data Labels arrow to display the Data Labels submenu (Figure 5–52).

Q&A **How does the Legend check box affect the pie chart?**

If you uncheck the Legend check box, Excel will remove the legend from the chart. If you point to Legend, an arrow will appear. Clicking the arrow displays a list for legend placement.

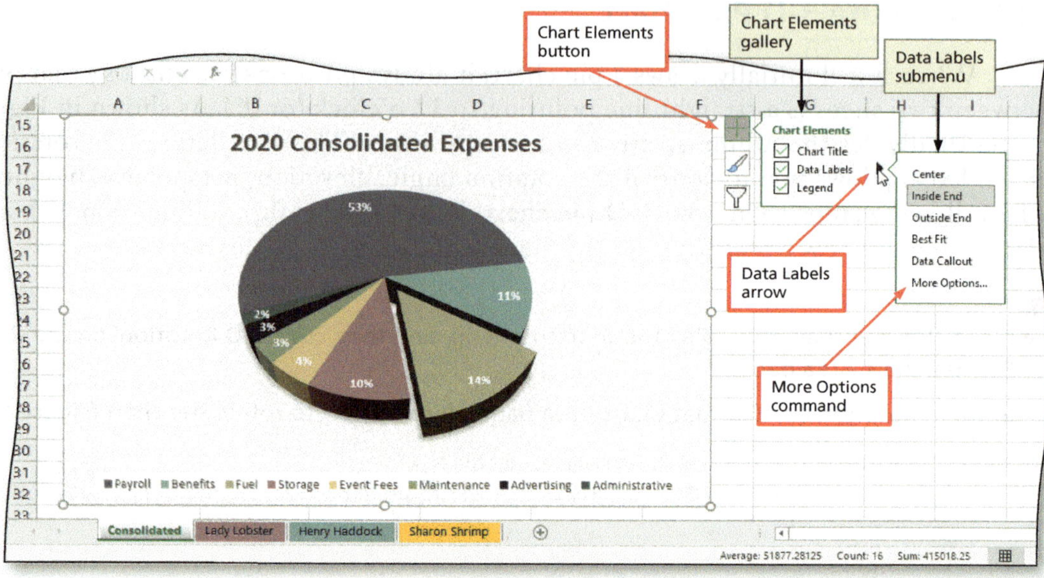

Figure 5–52

2

- Click More Options to display the Format Data Labels pane.
- In the Label Options area, click to display check marks in the Category Name, Percentage, and 'Show Leader Lines' check boxes. Click to remove check marks in any other check boxes, if necessary.
- In the Label Position area, click Outside End (Figure 5–53).

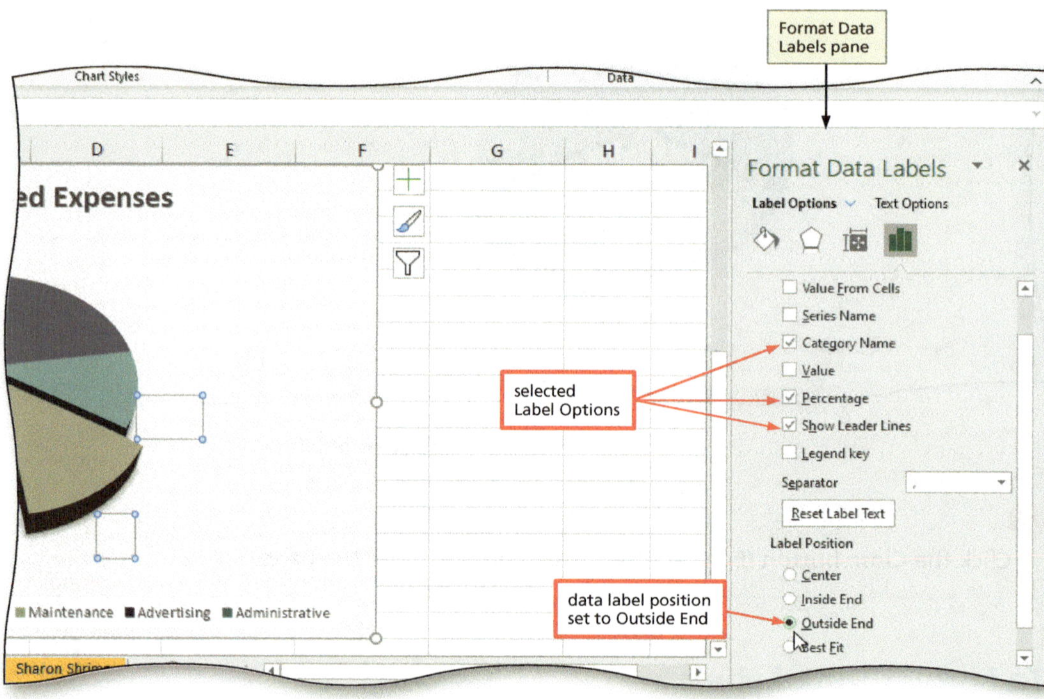

Figure 5–53

3

- Scroll down in the pane and click the Number arrow to display the Number settings.
- Scroll as necessary to click the Category button and then click Percentage to choose the number style.

- Select any text in the Decimal places text box and then type 1 to format the percentage with one decimal place (Figure 5–54).

Q&A **Why can I not see all the changes to the data labels in the chart?**
The data label content uses white text, so when you change the position to Outside End, the white text appears on a white background, making it invisible. You change the text color in the next step.

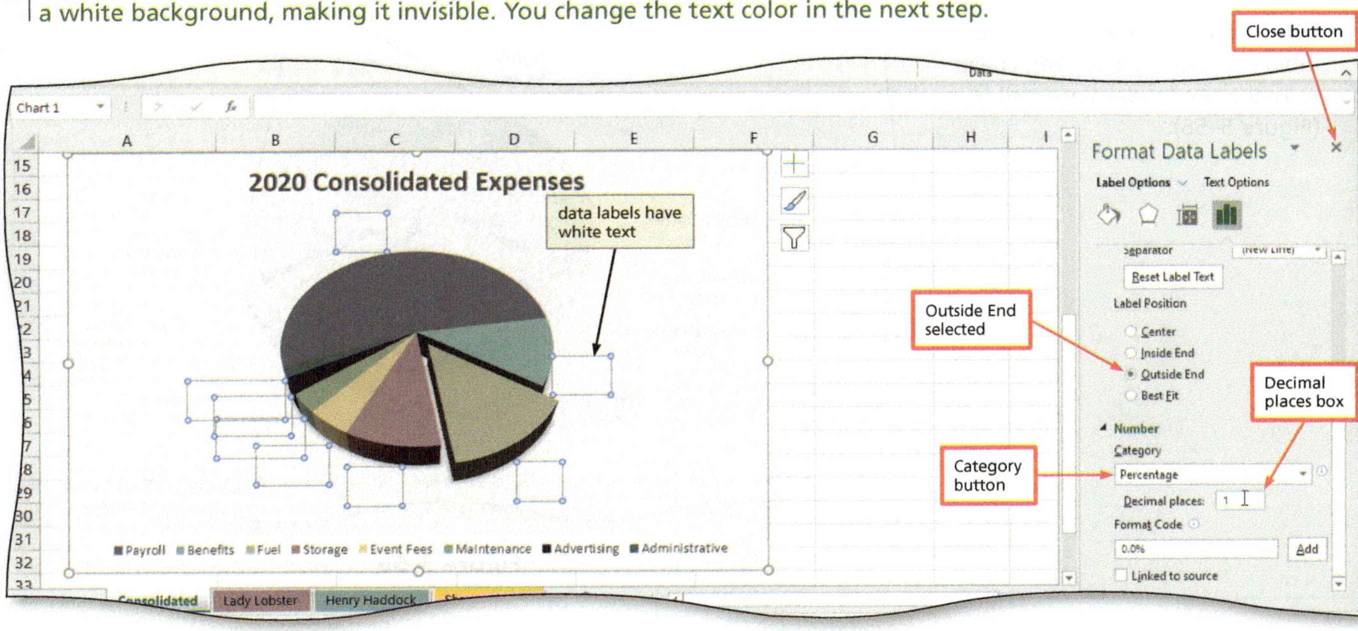

Figure 5–54

4

- Click Text Options in the Format Data Labels pane to display the text options.
- Click the Text Fill arrow to display the text fill options.
- If necessary, click the Solid fill option button.
- Click the Color button arrow to display the text color options, and then click Black, Text 1 (column 2, row 1) to change the color of the text (Figure 5–55).

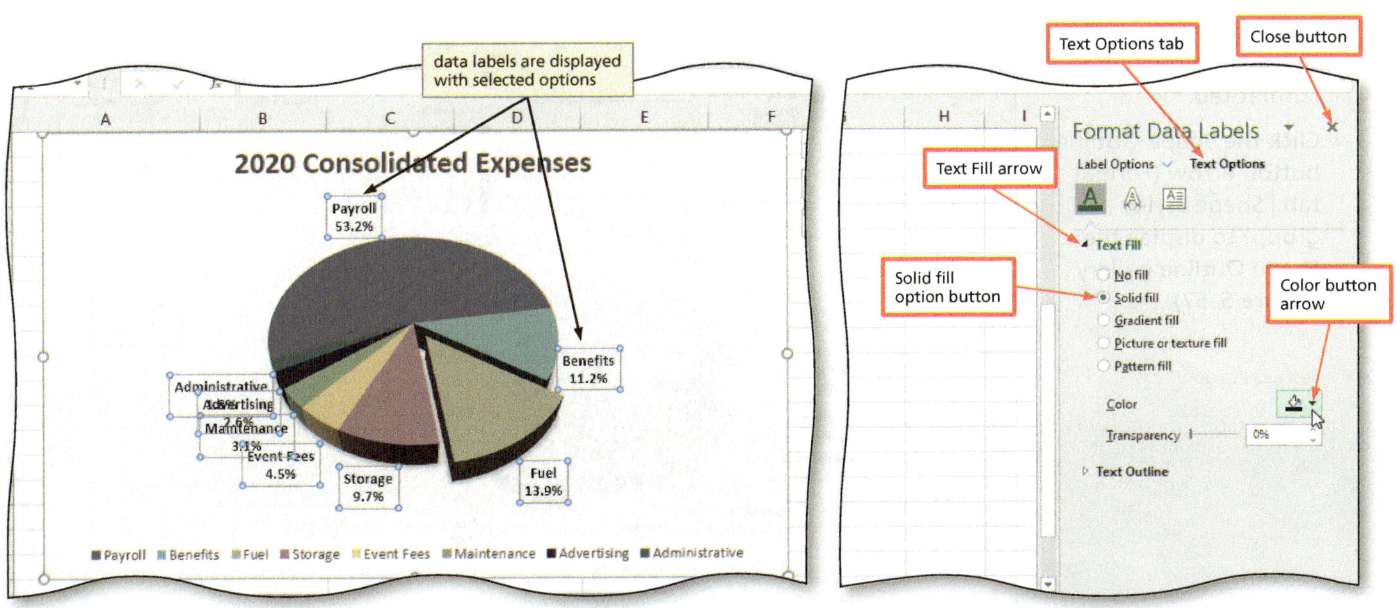

Figure 5–55

5

- Click the Close button on the Format Data Labels pane to close it.
- One at a time, drag each data label out slightly from the chart to make the leader lines visible (Figure 5–56).

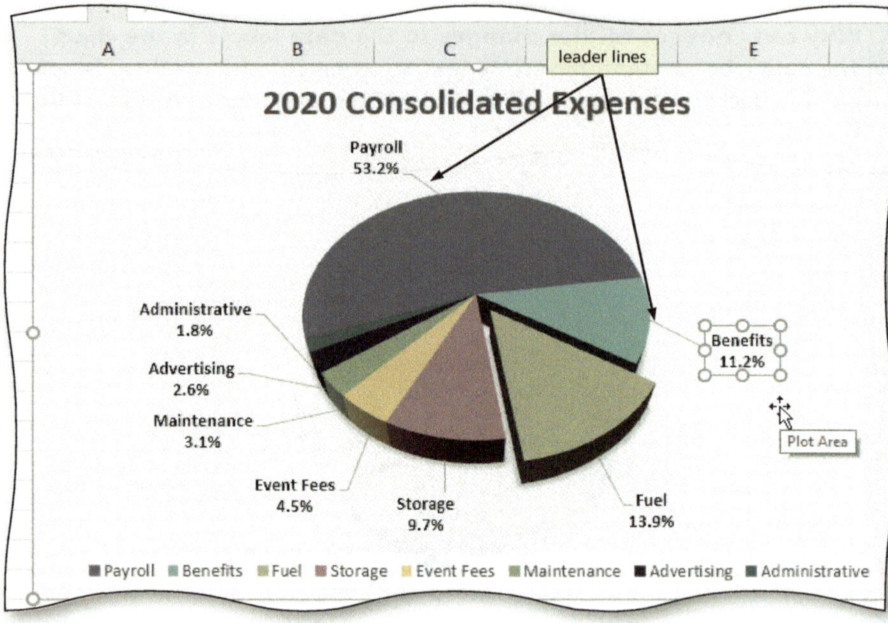

Figure 5–56

To Add a Chart Border

The following steps add a border to the 2020 Consolidated Expenses chart. In addition to adding a border to a chart, you can add a border to a chart element using these same steps. Instead of selecting the entire chart before adding the border, first select the element to which you want to add the border. **Why?** Adding a chart border helps to separate the chart from the other worksheet contents.

1

- If necessary, click to select the chart.
- Click Format on the ribbon to display the Format tab.
- Click the Shape Outline button arrow (Format tab | Shape Styles group) to display the Shape Outline gallery (Figure 5–57).

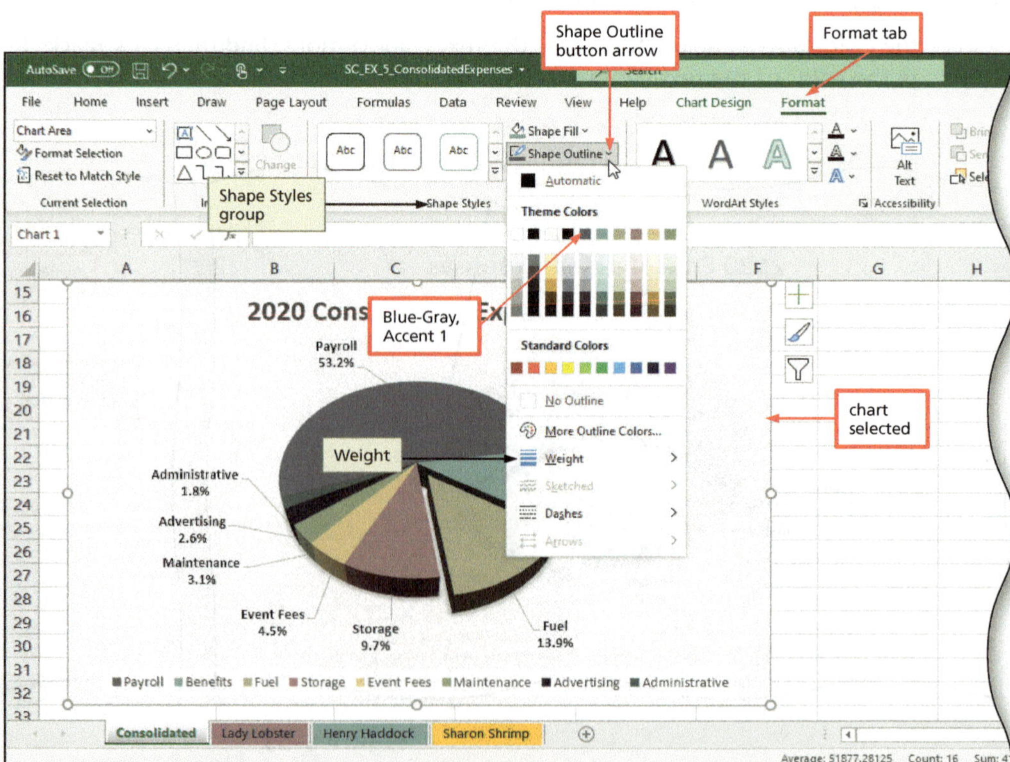

Figure 5–57

2

- Click Blue-Gray, Accent 1 (column 5, row 1) in the Theme Color area to apply a chart border.
- Click an empty cell on the worksheet to display the chart border (Figure 5–58).
- Click Save on the Quick Access Toolbar to save the workbook.

Q&A **What if I want to make the border thicker?**
In the Shape Options gallery, point to Weight (shown in Figure 5–57) and select the desired weight.

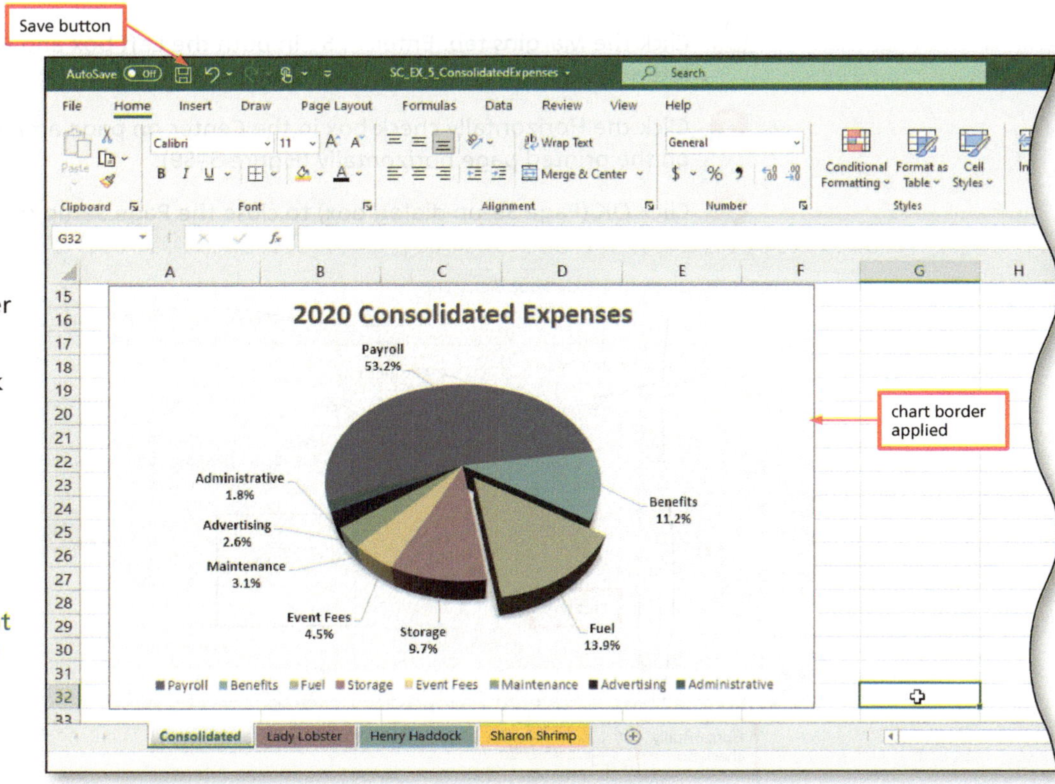

Figure 5–58

Printing Multiple Worksheets

Before printing a workbook with multiple worksheets, you should consider the page setup, which defines the appearance and format of a printed worksheet. You can add a header, which appears at the top of every printed page, and a footer, which appears at the bottom of every printed page. You also can change the margins to increase or decrease the white space surrounding the printed worksheet or chart. As you modify the page setup, remember that Excel does not copy page setup characteristics to other worksheets. Thus, even if you assigned page setup characteristics to the Consolidated worksheet before copying it to each location's worksheet, the page setup characteristics would not be copied to the new worksheet. If you want to change the page setup for all worksheets, you must select all worksheets first.

To Change Margins and Center the Printout Horizontally

The following steps select all of the worksheets and then use the Page Setup dialog box to change the margins and center the printout of each location's worksheet horizontally.

1. Right-click the Consolidated sheet tab and then click Select All Sheets on the shortcut menu.

2. Display the Page Layout tab and then click the Page Setup Dialog Box Launcher to display the Page Setup dialog box.

3. If necessary, click the Page tab (Page Setup dialog box) and then click Landscape to set the page orientation to landscape.

4. Click the Margins tab. Enter `.5` in both the Left box and Right box to change the left and right margins.

5. Click the Horizontally check box in the Center on page area to center the worksheet on the printed page horizontally (Figure 5–59).

6. Click OK (Page Setup dialog box) to close the Page Setup dialog box.

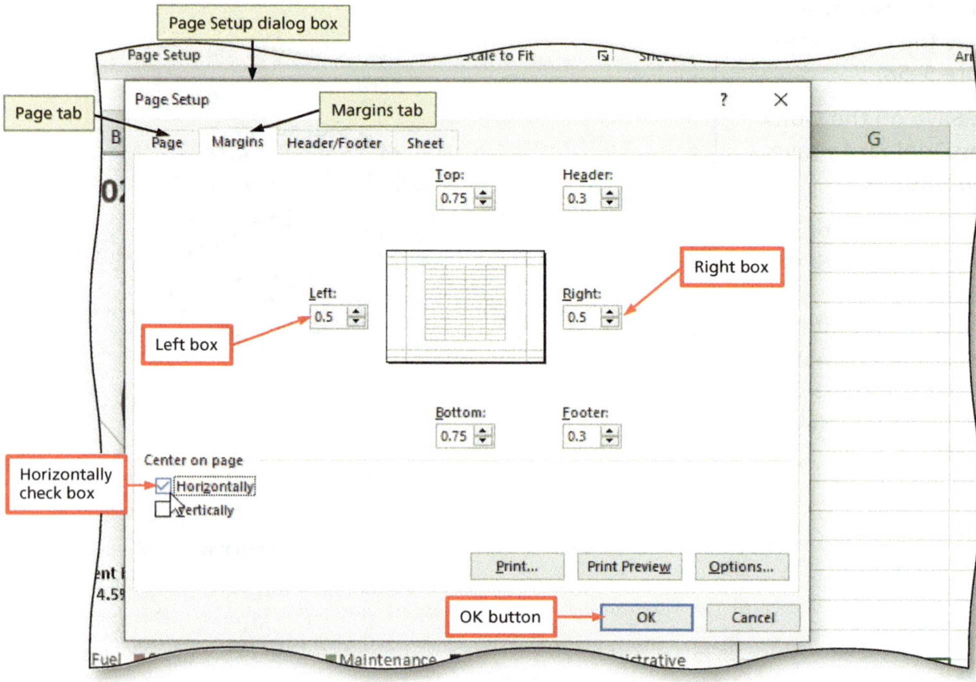

Figure 5–59

To Add a Header

The following steps use Page Layout view to change the headers on the worksheets.

BTW
Header and Footer Codes
When you click a button in the Header & Footer Elements group (Figure 5–61), Excel enters a code (similar to a format code) into the active header or footer section. A code such as &[Page] instructs Excel to insert the page number. When you click outside of the footer box that contains the code, the results of the code are visible.

1. With all of the worksheets still selected, click the Page Layout button on the status bar to display the first worksheet in Page Layout view.

2. If necessary, scroll the worksheet up until the Header area appears. Click the left header box and then type **`Shelly Cashman`** (or your name) to enter a page header in the left header box.

   If requested by your instructor, add your student ID number to the left header box, below the name entry.

3. Click the center header box and then type **`Expense Worksheet`** to enter the title.

4. Click the right header box and then click the Current Date button (Header & Footer tab | Header & Footer Elements group) to insert the current date (Figure 5–60).

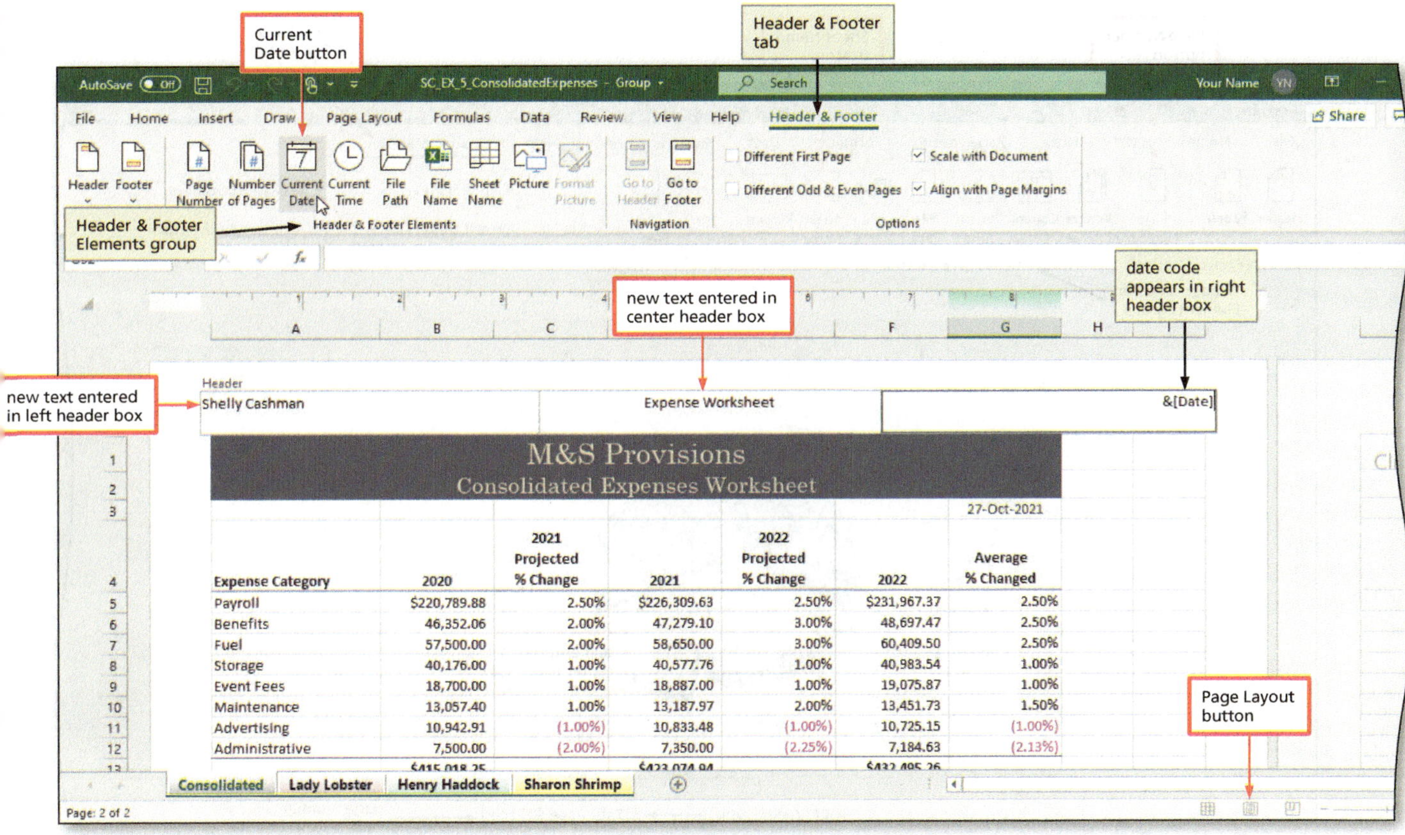

Figure 5–60

To Add a Footer

The following steps change the footers on the worksheets.

1. Scroll the workbook down to view the footer area.
2. Click the middle footer box to select it and then click the Sheet Name button (Header & Footer tab | Header & Footer Elements group) to insert the sheet name that appears on the sheet tab as part of the footer. Press SPACEBAR to add a space.
3. While in the same box, type **Page** as text in the footer. Press SPACEBAR and then click the Page Number button (Header & Footer tab | Header & Footer Elements group) to insert the page number in the footer (Figure 5–61).

Experiment

- Click the left footer box, and then click other buttons in the Header & Footer Elements group on the Header & Footer tab. When finished, delete the contents of the left footer box.

4. Click anywhere on the worksheet to deselect the page footer.
5. Click the Normal button on the status bar to return to Normal view.

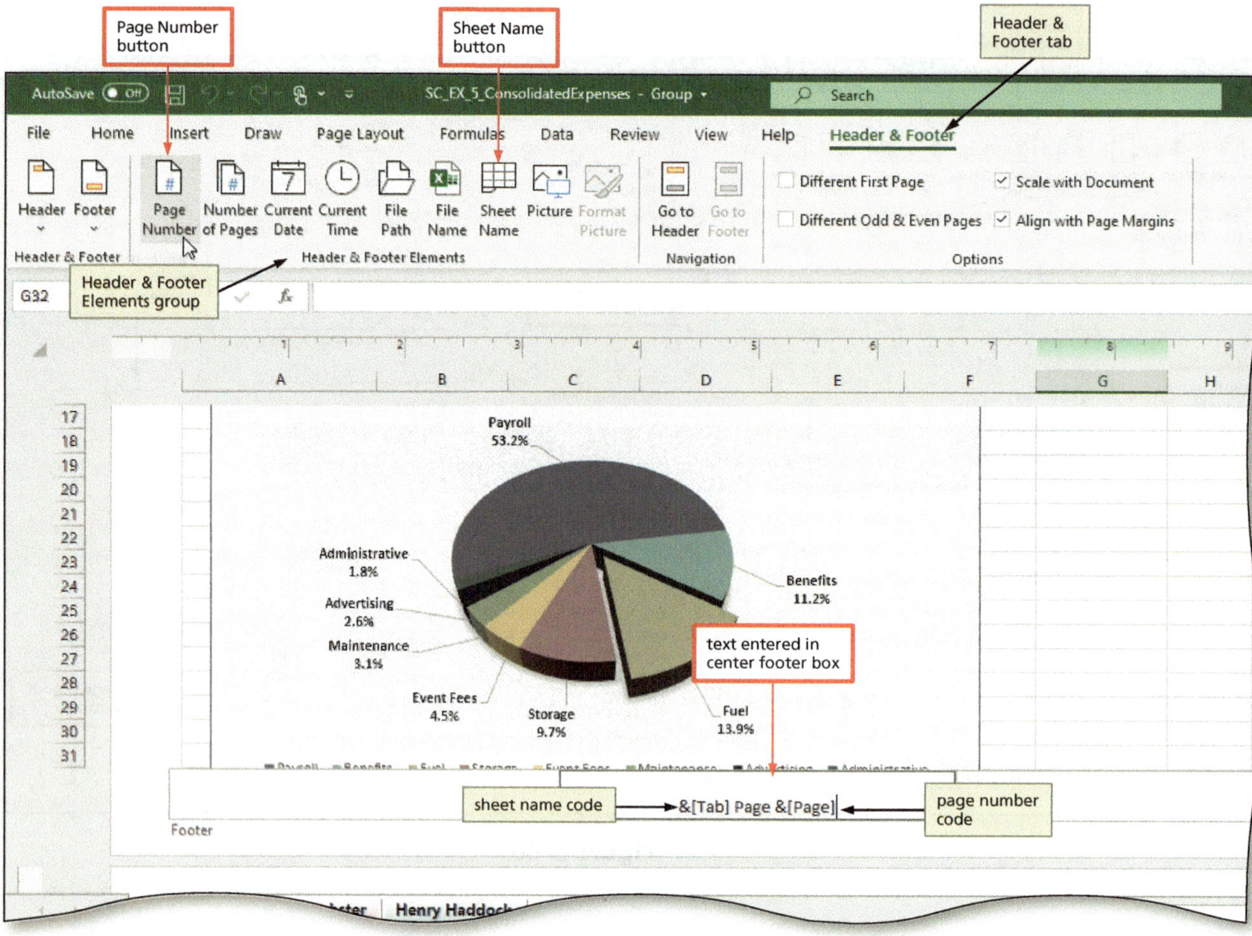

Figure 5–61

To Preview and Print All Worksheets in a Workbook

The following steps print all four worksheets in the workbook.

1. If necessary, right-click any sheet tab and then click Select All Sheets on the shortcut menu.
2. Ready the printer.
3. Click the File tab to open Backstage view. Click Print (Backstage view) to display the Print screen.
4. If necessary, click the No Scaling button and select 'Fit Sheet on One Page' so that each sheet prints only on one page.
5. Click the Next Page and Previous Page buttons below the preview to preview the other pages.
6. Click the Print button to print the workbook as shown in Figure 5–62.
7. Right-click the selected tabs and click Ungroup Sheets on the shortcut menu to deselect the four sheets.
8. Save the workbook.

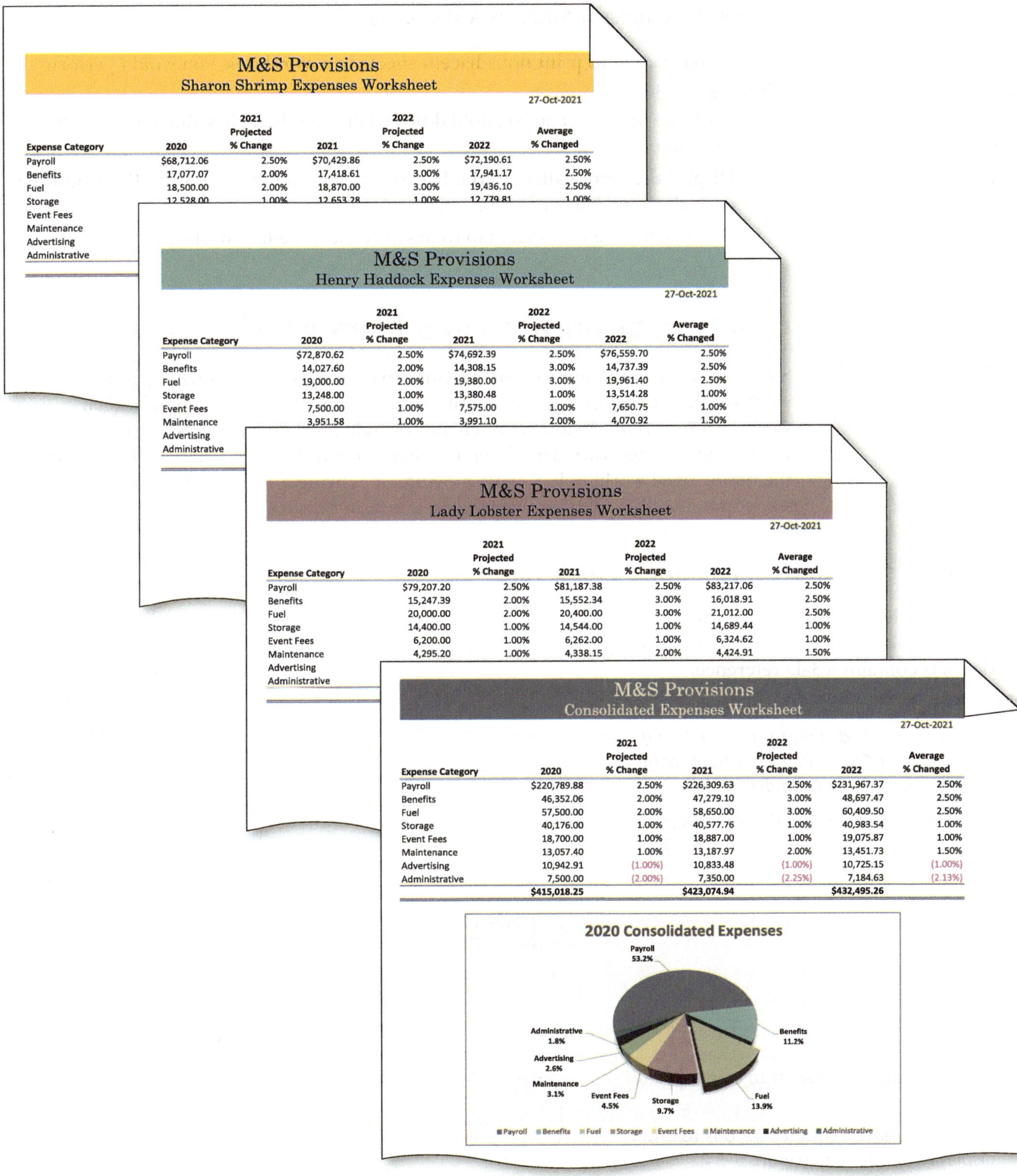

M&S Provisions
Sharon Shrimp Expenses Worksheet
27-Oct-2021

Expense Category	2020	2021 Projected % Change	2021	2022 Projected % Change	2022	Average % Changed
Payroll	$68,712.06	2.50%	$70,429.86	2.50%	$72,190.61	2.50%
Benefits	17,077.07	2.00%	17,418.61	3.00%	17,941.17	2.50%
Fuel	18,500.00	2.00%	18,870.00	3.00%	19,436.10	2.50%
Storage	12,528.00	1.00%	12,653.28	1.00%	12,779.81	1.00%
Event Fees						
Maintenance						
Advertising						
Administrative						

M&S Provisions
Henry Haddock Expenses Worksheet
27-Oct-2021

Expense Category	2020	2021 Projected % Change	2021	2022 Projected % Change	2022	Average % Changed
Payroll	$72,870.62	2.50%	$74,692.39	2.50%	$76,559.70	2.50%
Benefits	14,027.60	2.00%	14,308.15	3.00%	14,737.39	2.50%
Fuel	19,000.00	2.00%	19,380.00	3.00%	19,961.40	2.50%
Storage	13,248.00	1.00%	13,380.48	1.00%	13,514.28	1.00%
Event Fees	7,500.00	1.00%	7,575.00	1.00%	7,650.75	1.00%
Maintenance	3,951.58	1.00%	3,991.10	2.00%	4,070.92	1.50%
Advertising						
Administrative						

M&S Provisions
Lady Lobster Expenses Worksheet
27-Oct-2021

Expense Category	2020	2021 Projected % Change	2021	2022 Projected % Change	2022	Average % Changed
Payroll	$79,207.20	2.50%	$81,187.38	2.50%	$83,217.06	2.50%
Benefits	15,247.39	2.00%	15,552.34	3.00%	16,018.91	2.50%
Fuel	20,000.00	2.00%	20,400.00	3.00%	21,012.00	2.50%
Storage	14,400.00	1.00%	14,544.00	1.00%	14,689.44	1.00%
Event Fees	6,200.00	1.00%	6,262.00	1.00%	6,324.62	1.00%
Maintenance	4,295.20	1.00%	4,338.15	2.00%	4,424.91	1.50%
Advertising						
Administrative						

M&S Provisions
Consolidated Expenses Worksheet
27-Oct-2021

Expense Category	2020	2021 Projected % Change	2021	2022 Projected % Change	2022	Average % Changed
Payroll	$220,789.88	2.50%	$226,309.63	2.50%	$231,967.37	2.50%
Benefits	46,352.06	2.00%	47,279.10	3.00%	48,697.47	2.50%
Fuel	57,500.00	2.00%	58,650.00	3.00%	60,409.50	2.50%
Storage	40,176.00	1.00%	40,577.76	1.00%	40,983.54	1.00%
Event Fees	18,700.00	1.00%	18,887.00	1.00%	19,075.87	1.00%
Maintenance	13,057.40	1.00%	13,187.97	2.00%	13,451.73	1.50%
Advertising	10,942.91	(1.00%)	10,833.48	(1.00%)	10,725.15	(1.00%)
Administrative	7,500.00	(2.00%)	7,350.00	(2.25%)	7,184.63	(2.13%)
	$415,018.25		$423,074.94		$432,495.26	

Figure 5–62

To Print Nonadjacent Sheets in a Workbook

If you wanted to print nonadjacent sheets in a workbook, you would perform the following steps.

1. With the first sheet active, hold down CTRL, and then click the nonadjacent sheet tab.
2. Display the Print gallery in the Backstage view and then click the Print button to print the nonadjacent worksheets.
3. SHIFT+click the first sheet tab to deselect the nonadjacent sheet.

BTW
Distributing a Workbook
Instead of printing and distributing a hard copy of a workbook, you can distribute the workbook electronically. Options include sending the workbook via email; posting it on cloud storage (such as OneDrive) and sharing the file with others; posting it on social media, a blog, or other website; and sharing a link associated with an online location of the workbook. You also can create and share a PDF or XPS image of the workbook, so that users can view the file in Acrobat Reader or XPS Viewer instead of in Excel.

Creating Separate Files from Worksheets

Sometimes you may want to save individual worksheets as their own separate workbooks. For example, you may want to reveal only the data in an individual worksheet to certain customers or clients, or individual departments or franchises may want a copy of their own data. Keep in mind that any 3-D references will not work in the newly saved workbook. Saving, moving, or copying a worksheet to a new workbook sometimes is called splitting or breaking out the worksheets.

To Create a Separate File from a Worksheet

The following steps create a new workbook from each location worksheet. **Why?** Each individual food truck would like to receive a file with its own projections for the next two years. None of the three location worksheets contains a 3-D reference.

1

- Right-click the Lady Lobster sheet tab and then click 'Move or Copy' on the shortcut menu to display the Move or Copy dialog box.
- Click the To book button (Move or Copy dialog box) to display the choices (Figure 5–63).

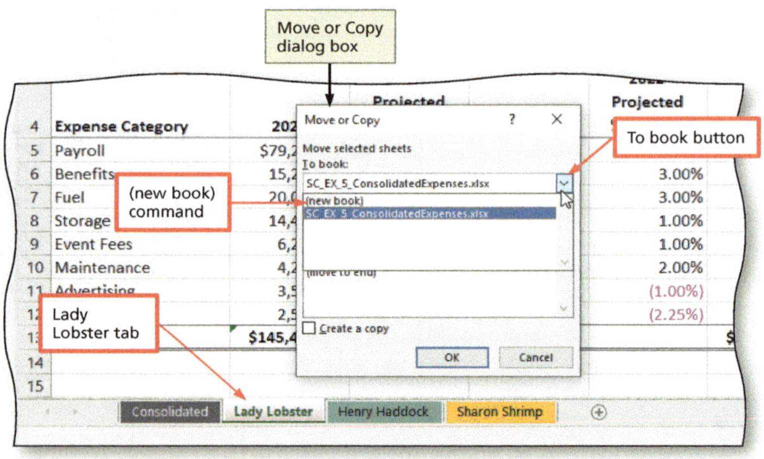

Figure 5–63

2

- Click (new book) in the list to create a new workbook.
- Click the 'Create a copy' check box to ensure it displays a check mark (Figure 5–64).

Q&A **What if I do not check the check box?**
In that case, Excel would remove the worksheet from the current workbook in a move function. The Consolidated sheet no longer would display values from the moved worksheet, breaking the 3-D reference.

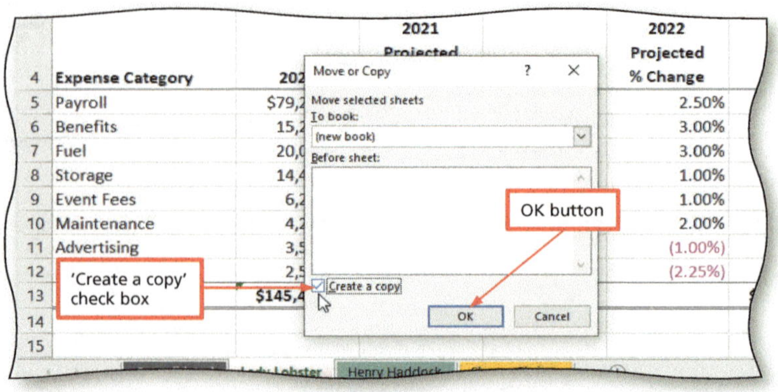

Figure 5–64

3

- Click OK to create the new workbook.
- Save the new file with the name SC_EX_5_LadyLobster in the same folder as the SC_EX_5_ConsolidatedExpenses file.

4

- Repeat Steps 1 through 3 to save the Henry Haddock and Sharon Shrimp worksheets as separate workbooks in the same location. Use the new file names, SC_EX_5_HenryHaddock and SC_EX_5_SharonShrimp.
- Close each workbook, including the SC_EX_5_ConsolidatedExpenses workbook.

Consolidating Data by Linking Separate Workbooks

Earlier in this module, the data from three worksheets was consolidated into a fourth worksheet in the same workbook using 3-D references; however, sometimes the data you need is not in the same workbook. In those cases, it is necessary to consolidate data from separate workbooks, which is also referred to as **linking**. A **link** is a reference to a cell, or range of cells, in another workbook. The consolidated main workbook that contains the links to the separate workbooks is called the **dependent workbook**. The separate, individual workbooks from which you need data are called the **source workbooks**.

You can create a link using the point mode if both the source workbook and dependent workbook(s) are open. If the source workbook is not open, you have to type the entire drive path, folder, worksheet name, and cell reference into the formula bar. This is known as an **absolute path**. You must include single quotes (') surrounding the drive, folder, workbook name, and worksheet name. You must surround the workbook name with brackets ([ ]). You must include an exclamation point (!) as a delimiter between the sheet name and cell reference. The exclamation point is called an **external reference indicator** and is used in a formula to indicate that a referenced cell is outside the active sheet. For example, you might type the following:

'C:\My Documents\[SC_EX_5_ConsolidatedExpenses.xlsx]LadyLobster'!D5

drive folder workbook name worksheet cell reference name

BTW
Consolidation
You also can consolidate data across different workbooks using the Consolidate button (Data tab | Data Tools group), rather than by entering formulas. For more information on the consolidate button, type `Consolidate data` in the Search box.

Moving Linked Workbooks

Special care should be taken when moving linked workbooks. You should move all of the workbooks together. If you move the dependent workbook without the source workbook(s), all links become absolute—even if you used the point mode to reference them. In addition, if you happen to move the dependent workbook to another computer, without the source workbook(s), the link is broken.

Excel may offer to update or enable your links when you open the dependent workbook independent of the source workbook(s). After moving workbooks, it is best to open the source workbooks first.

BTW
Circular References
A circular reference is a formula that depends on its own value. The most common type is a formula that contains a reference to the same cell in which the formula resides.

The remainder of this module demonstrates how to search for workbooks and how to link separate workbooks, creating a 2020 Consolidated Expenses Worksheet.

CONSIDER THIS

What happens if I update data in one or more of the linked workbooks?

If the source workbooks are open, Excel automatically reads the data in the source workbooks and recalculates formulas in the dependent workbook. Any value changes in the open source workbooks will update in the dependent workbook.

If the source workbooks are not open, then Excel displays a security warning in a pane below the ribbon. If you click the Enable Content button in the warning pane, Excel reads the data in the source workbooks and recalculates the formulas in the dependent workbook, but it does not open the source workbooks.

To Open a Data File and Save It to a New Location

The SC_EX_5-2 workbook is located in the Data Files. Please contact your instructor for information about accessing the Data Files. The file contains headings and formatting and is ready for linking. In the following steps, you will open the workbook and save it to the same location as the files created in the previous steps. If the Data Files are saved in the same location as your previously saved solution files, you can omit these steps.

1. Start Excel, if necessary, and open the file named SC_EX_5-2.
2. Go to Backstage view, click Save As, and then click Browse to open the Save As dialog box.
3. Navigate to the location of your previously saved files, and then click the Save button (Save As dialog box) to save the file in a new location.
4. Close the file without exiting Excel.

To Search for and Open Workbooks

Excel has a powerful search tool that you can use to locate workbooks (or any file) stored on the hard drive, using the Search box in the Open dialog box. **Why?** The search tool can be used when you cannot remember exactly the name of the file or its location. In this example, the search text will be used to locate the necessary workbooks. The following steps locate and open the four workbooks of interest.

1

- Go to Backstage view and then click Open to display the Open screen.
- Click Browse in the left pane and then navigate to the location of your previously saved solution files.
- Type `SC_EX_5` in the Search box as the search text and then click the arrow button to display the files associated with this module.
- One at a time, CTRL+click each of the workbooks that have the word SC_EX_5 in the title (Figure 5–65). The order and layout of your files may vary.

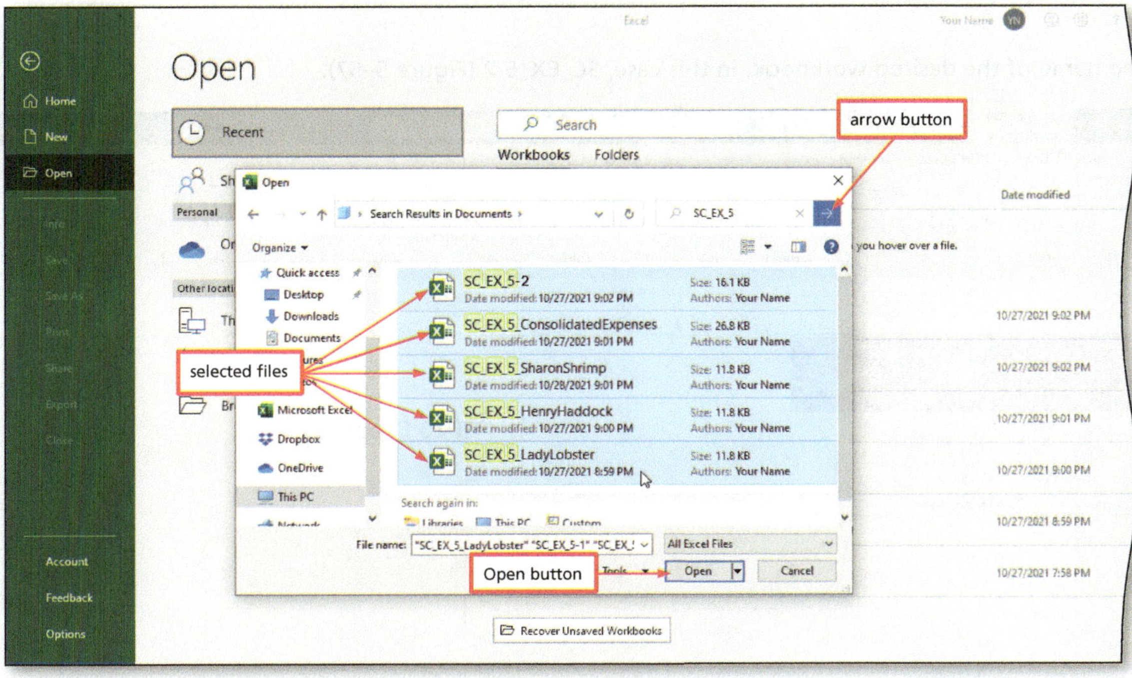

Figure 5–65

2

- Click the Open button (Open dialog box) to open the selected workbooks.

To Switch to a Different Open Workbook

The following steps switch to a different open workbook. **Why?** You may want to change quickly to another workbook to verify data.

1

- Display the View tab and then click the Switch Windows button (View tab | Window group) to display the names of the open workbooks (Figure 5–66). The order of your files may differ.

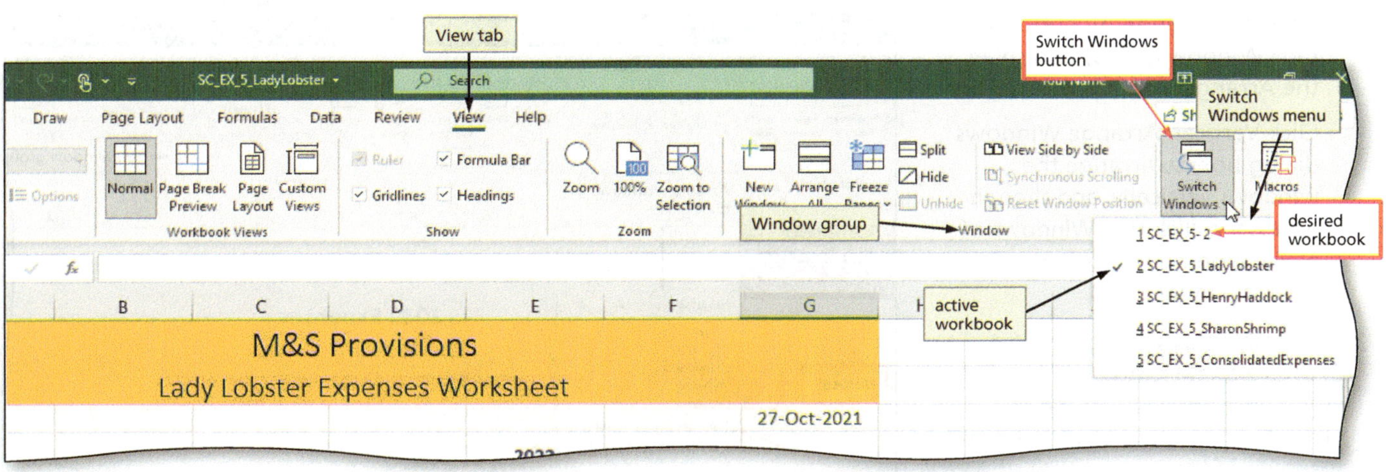

Figure 5–66

2

- Click the name of the desired workbook, in this case, SC_EX_5-2 (Figure 5–67).

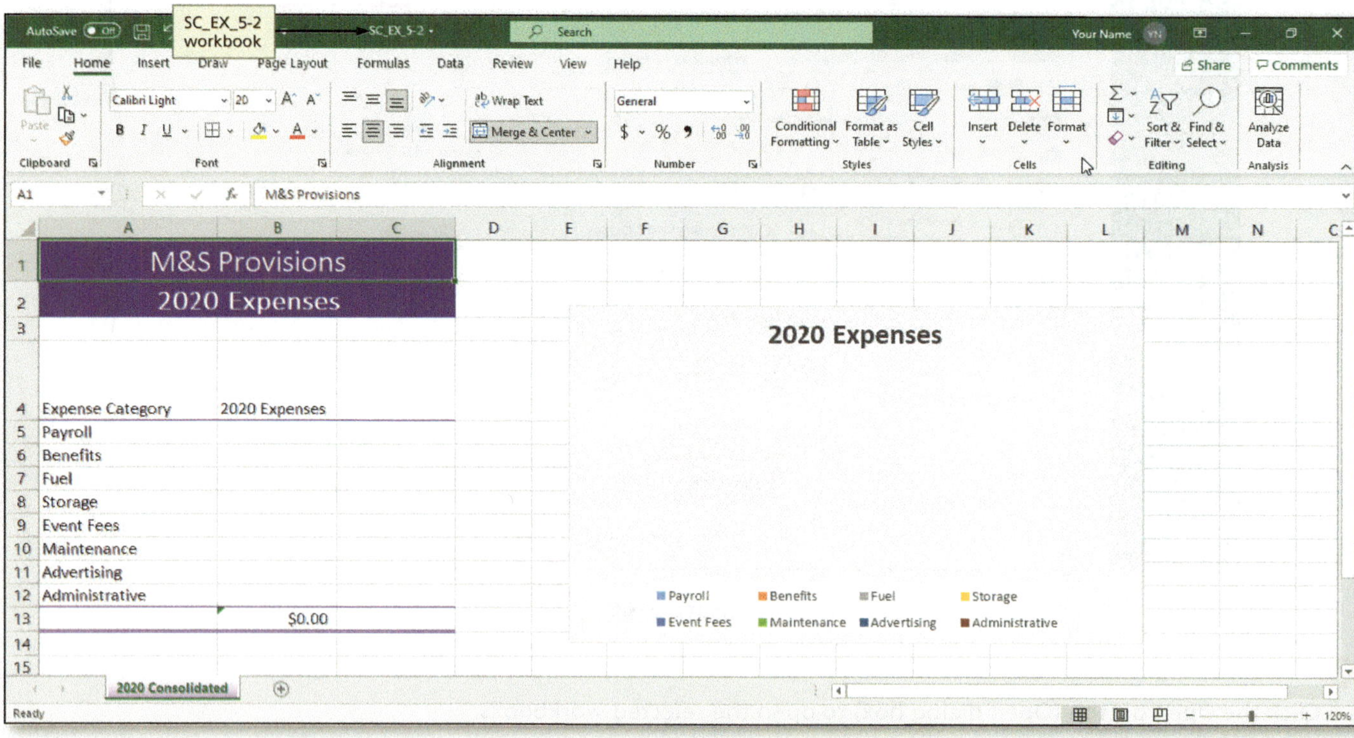

Figure 5–67

Other Ways

1. Point to Excel app button (Windows 10 taskbar), click desired live preview

To Arrange Multiple Workbooks

The following steps arrange the multiple open workbooks on the screen so that each one appears in its own window. **Why?** Viewing multiple workbooks gives you a chance to check for related data and verify formats.

1

- Click the Arrange All button (View tab | Window group) to display the Arrange Windows dialog box.
- Click Vertical (Arrange Windows dialog box) to arrange the windows vertically, and then, if necessary, click the 'Windows of active workbook' check box to clear it (Figure 5–68).

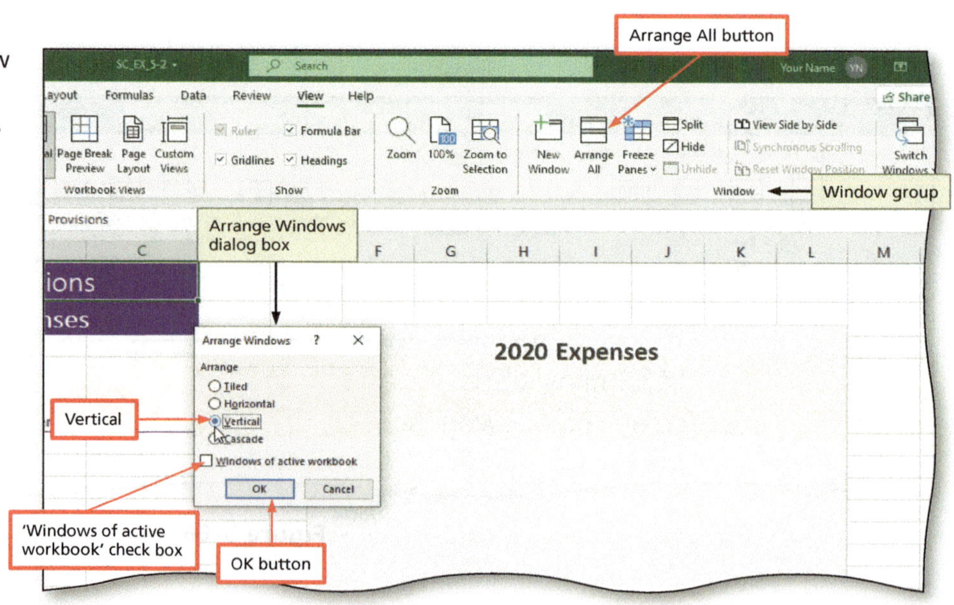

Figure 5–68

Q&A **How can I arrange workbooks in the Excel window?**
Multiple opened workbooks can be arranged in four ways as shown in the Arrange Windows dialog box. You can modify any of the arranged workbooks after first clicking within its window to activate it. To return to showing one workbook, double-click its title bar.

2

- Click OK (Arrange Windows dialog box) to display the opened workbooks arranged vertically (Figure 5–69). The order of your workbooks might vary.

Q&A **Why do the windows display horizontally across the screen, yet the screens were set to Vertical?**
The chosen effect determines the change on an individual window, not the group of windows. When you select Vertical, each individual window appears vertically as tall as possible. If you choose Horizontal, the windows appear as wide as possible.

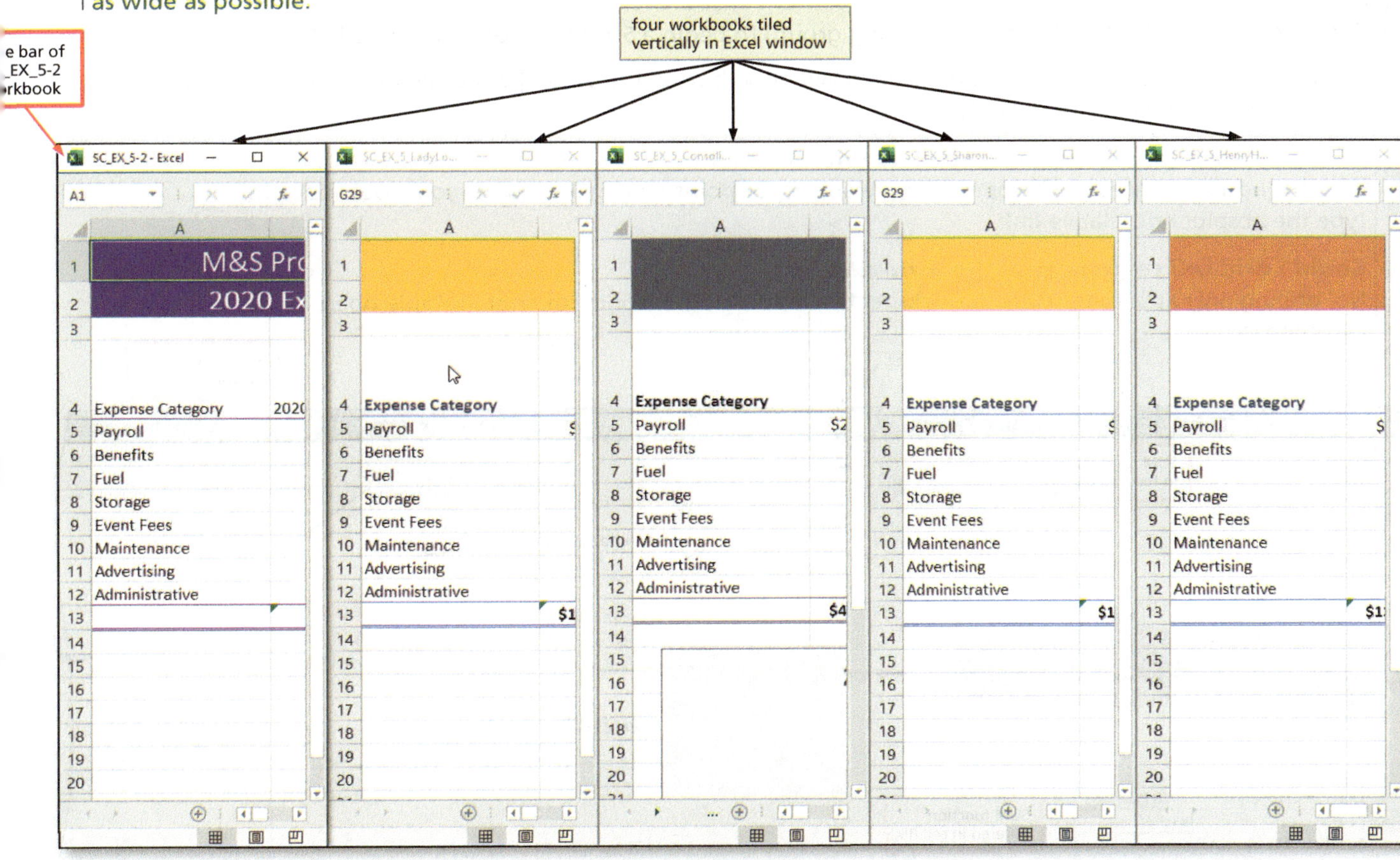

Figure 5–69

To Hide Workbooks

The following step hides all open workbooks except one. **Why?** Hiding is the best way to remove any tiling or arrangement.

1

- Double-click the title bar of the desired workbook to hide the other opened workbooks. In this case, double-click the SC_EX_5-2 title bar to maximize the window.
- Select cell B5 (Figure 5–70).

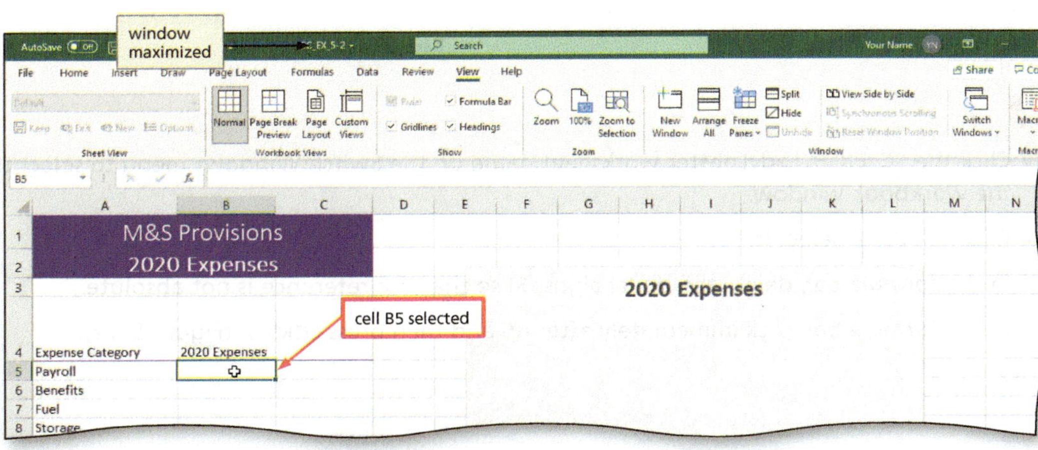

Figure 5–70

To Consolidate Data by Linking Workbooks

The following steps consolidate the data from the three location workbooks into the SC_EX_5-2 workbook. **Why?** When set up correctly, linking workbooks provides the user with a simple method of consolidating and updating linked data in the original workbook and any workbook with links to the updated data.

1

- Click the AutoSum button (Home tab | Editing group) to begin a SUM function entry in cell B5.
- Display the View tab and then click the Switch Windows button (View tab | Window group) to display the Switch Windows menu (Figure 5–71).

Q&A

Does the workbook have to be open to link to it?
Yes, the workbook needs to be open if you want to use point mode. Otherwise, you would have to type the absolute or relative link.

Could I drill cell references in the formula?
No, drilling only applies to selected worksheets within a single workbook, not multiple open workbooks.

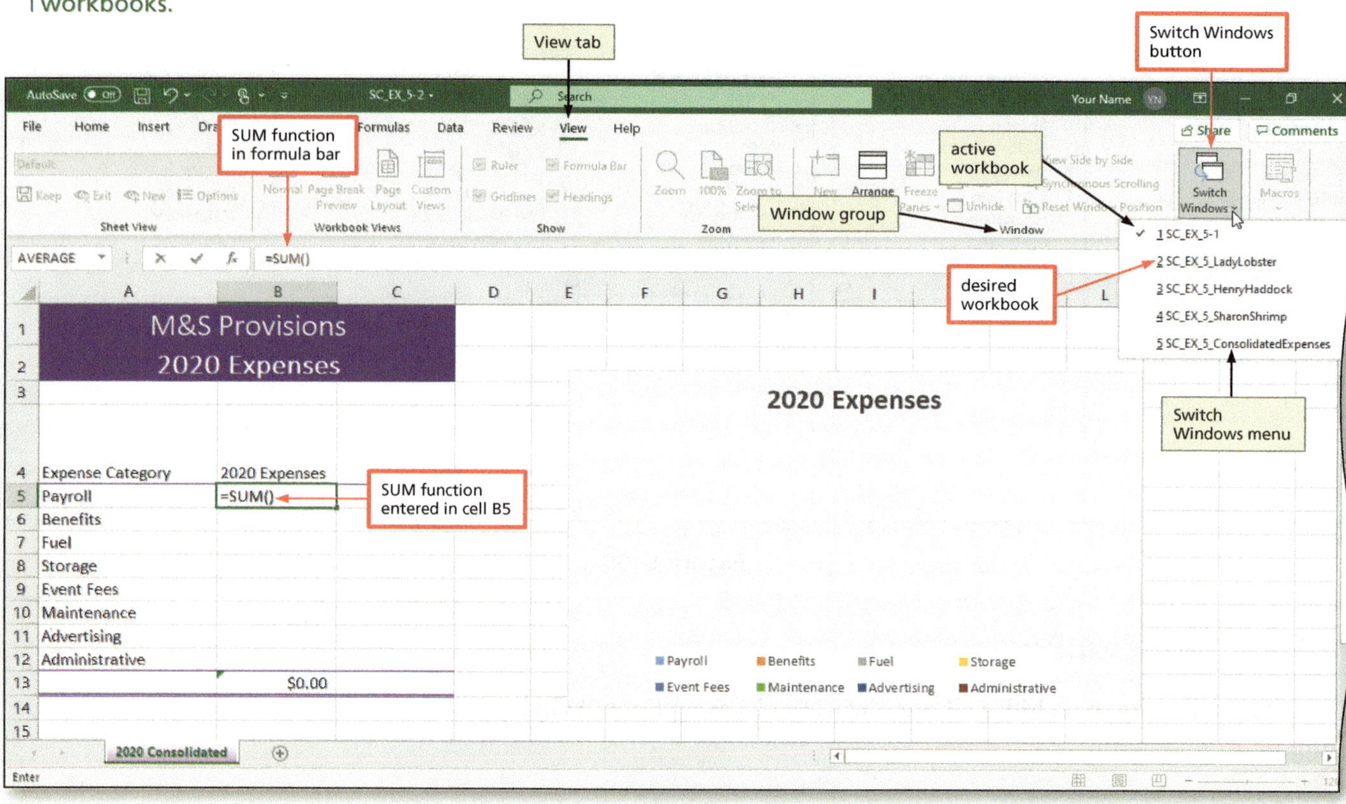

Figure 5–71

2

- Click the SC_EX_5_LadyLobster worksheet name on the Switch Windows menu to select the workbook. Maximize the workbook window.
- Click cell B5 to select it.
- In the formula bar, delete the dollar signs ($) so that the reference is not absolute.
- In the formula bar, click immediately after B5 and then press COMMA (Figure 5–72).

Q&A **Why do I have to remove the dollar signs ($)?**
Linked cell references are absolute ($B$5). You must edit the formula and change these to relative cell references because you plan to copy the SUM function in a later step. If the cell references were left as absolute, then the copied function always would refer to cell B5 in the three workbooks no matter where you copy the SUM function.

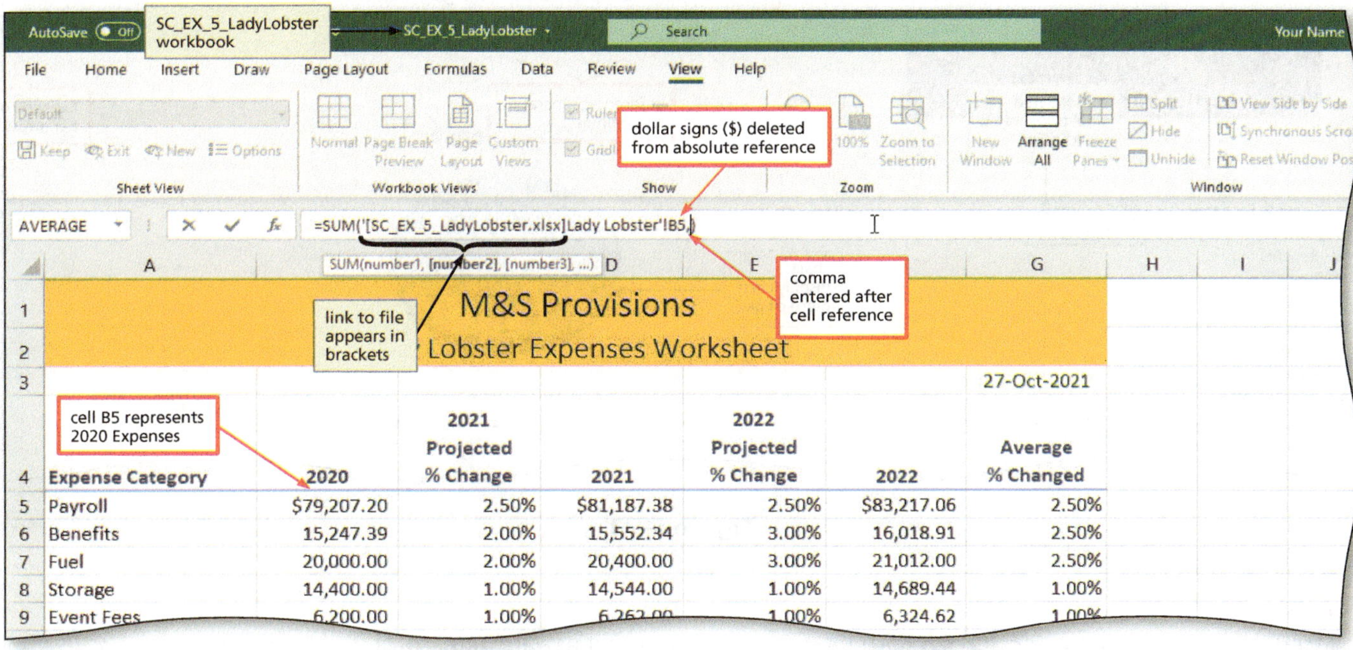

Figure 5–72

3

- Click the Switch Windows button (View tab | Window group) and then click the SC_EX_5_HenryHaddock workbook to display the workbook. Maximize the workbook window.
- Select cell B5 as the next argument in the SUM function.
- If necessary, click the Expand Formula Bar arrow (Formula bar) to display the entire formula. Delete the dollar signs ($) in the reference. Click immediately after B5 in the formula bar and then press COMMA.
- Click the Switch Windows button (View tab | Window group), and then click the SC_EX_5_SharonShrimp workbook. Maximize the workbook window.
- Select cell B5 as the final argument in the SUM function.
- In the formula bar, delete the dollar signs ($) in the reference.
- Click the Enter button in the formula bar to complete the SUM function and return to the SC_EX_5-2 workbook (Figure 5–73).

Q&A **What if I make a mistake while editing the formula?**
If you are still editing, click the Cancel button on the Formula bar, and start again. If you have entered the formula already, click the Undo button. Note that Excel formula error messages do not always indicate the exact location of the error.

Why did the pie chart start filling in?
Excel offers a live preview called **cell animation** that updates as you insert new data. The data file had the pie chart set up to reference the appropriate cells in column B.

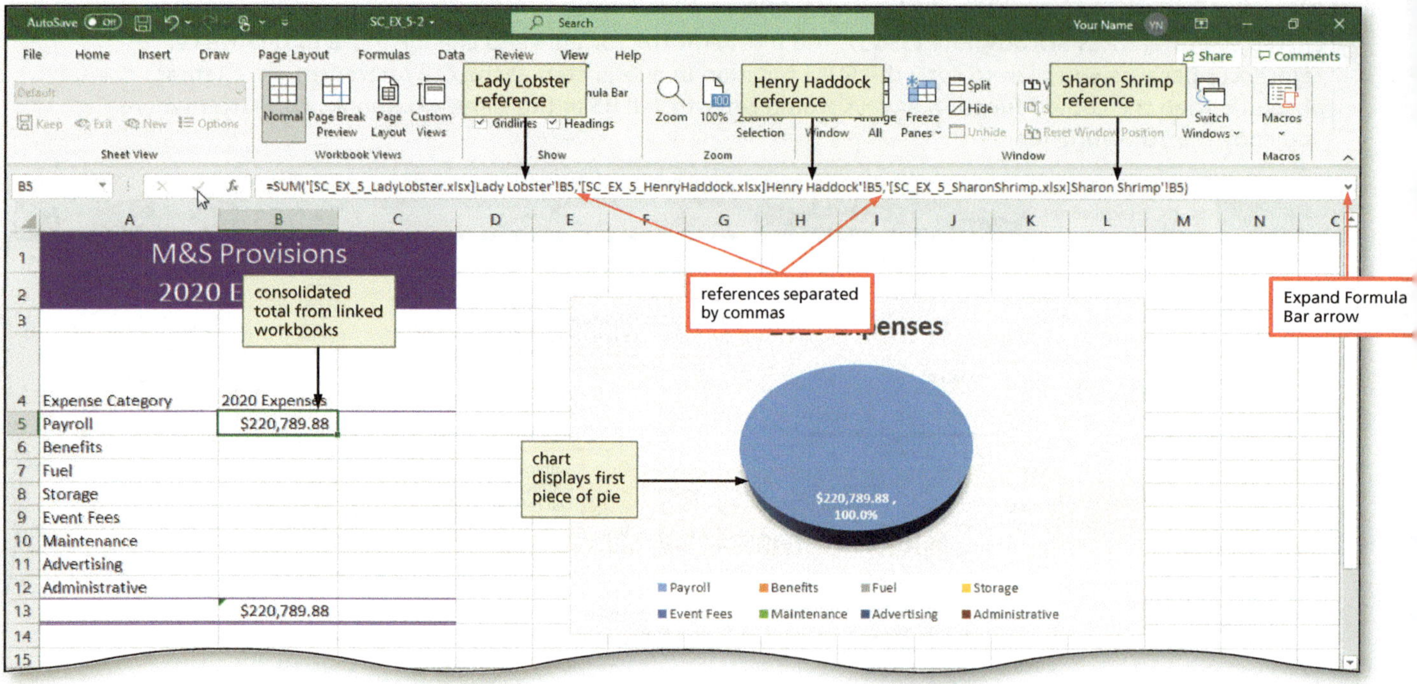

Figure 5–73

4

- With cell B5 active in the SC_EX_5-2 workbook, drag the cell's fill handle down through cell B12 to copy the formula to the range.
- Apply the comma format to cells B6:B12 to remove the floating dollar signs.
- Format the chart as necessary, exploding the Fuel slice, editing labels, and adding leader lines as shown in Figure 5–74.

Q&A

I cannot access the Chart Elements button. What should I do?

Click the Chart Elements arrow (Format tab | Current Selection group) and then choose the area you wish to format. Click the Format Selection button (Format tab | Current Selection group). The same dialog box or pane will open.

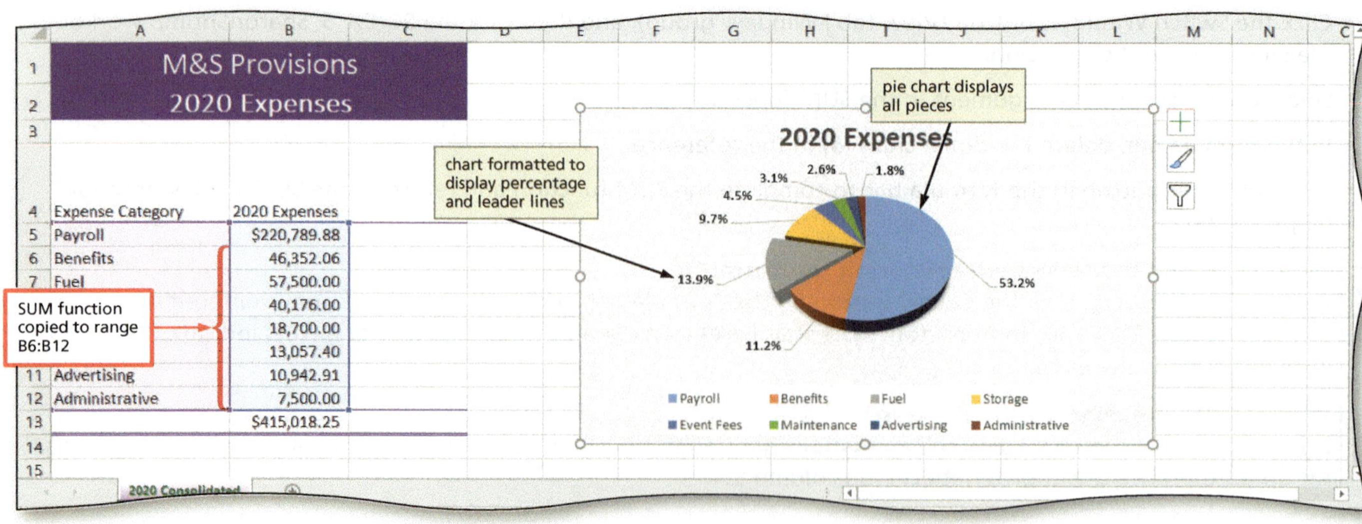

Figure 5–74

5

- Save the workbook with the name, SC_EX_5_2020ProjectedExpenses.
- If Excel displays a dialog box, click OK (Microsoft Excel dialog box) to save the workbook.

To Close All Workbooks at One Time

To close all four workbooks at one time and exit Excel, complete the following steps.

1. sam Right-click the Excel app button on the taskbar and then click 'Close all windows' on the shortcut menu to close all open workbooks and exit Excel.
2. If a dialog box appears, click the Save button to save any changes made to the files since the last save.

BTW

Recovering Unsaved Changes

If you have to recover an unsaved workbook in Excel, you may be able to do so by clicking File on the Ribbon, clicking Info, clicking Manage Workbook, and then clicking Recover Unsaved Workbooks.

Summary

In this module, you learned how to create and use a consolidated worksheet. After using the Fill button to create a series, you used the TODAY and ROUND functions to format data. You created a custom format code for a four-digit year and a custom cell style that used specialized percentage styles for both positive and negative numbers. You learned how to work with multiple worksheets including several ways to copy worksheet data to a new worksheet, and drill an entry through those new worksheets. As you created the consolidated worksheet, you entered a 3-D reference and used the Paste gallery to replicate that reference. You added a pie chart to the consolidated worksheet complete with an exploded slice and formatted data labels with leader lines. You printed the multiple worksheets. Finally, you learned how to break out or split the worksheets into separate workbooks and consolidate the data to a new workbook by linking. With multiple workbooks open, you switched to different worksheets, arranged them in the Excel window, and hid them.

CONSIDER THIS: PLAN AHEAD

What decisions will you need to make when creating your next workbook to evaluate and analyze data using consolidated worksheets?

Use these guidelines as you complete the assignments in this module and create your own worksheets for evaluating and analyzing data outside of this class.

1. Determine the workbook structure.
   a) Determine how many worksheets and/or workbooks you will need.
   b) Determine the data you will need for your worksheets.
   c) Determine the layout of your data on the consolidated worksheet.
2. Create and format the consolidated worksheet.
   a) Enter titles, subtitles, and headings.
   b) Enter placeholder data, functions, and formulas.
3. Format the worksheet.
   a) Format the titles, subtitles, and headings.
   b) Format the numbers as necessary.
   c) Create and use custom format codes and styles.
4. Create the additional worksheets.
   a) Determine the best method for adding additional worksheets, based on the data in the consolidated worksheet.
   b) Add the new worksheets to the workbook.

c) Add data and formatting to the new worksheets.

d) Create 3-D references where necessary to replace placeholders in the consolidated sheet with calculated values.

5. Create and use charts.

a) Select the data to chart.

b) Select a chart type for selected data.

c) Format the chart elements.

6. Consolidate workbooks.

a) Create separate workbooks from worksheets if necessary.

b) Link multiple workbooks to facilitate easy updating of data across workbooks.

Apply Your Knowledge

Reinforce the skills and apply the concepts you learned in this module.

Consolidating Payroll Worksheets

Note: To complete this assignment, you will be required to use the Data Files. Please contact your instructor for information about accessing the Data Files.

Instructions: Start Excel. Open the workbook SC_EX_5-3.xlsx, which is located in the Data Files. The workbook you open contains payroll information for four employees of a small company over the period of four quarters. You are to consolidate the payroll figures. At the conclusion of the instructions, the Annual Totals sheet should resemble the worksheet shown in Figure 5–75.

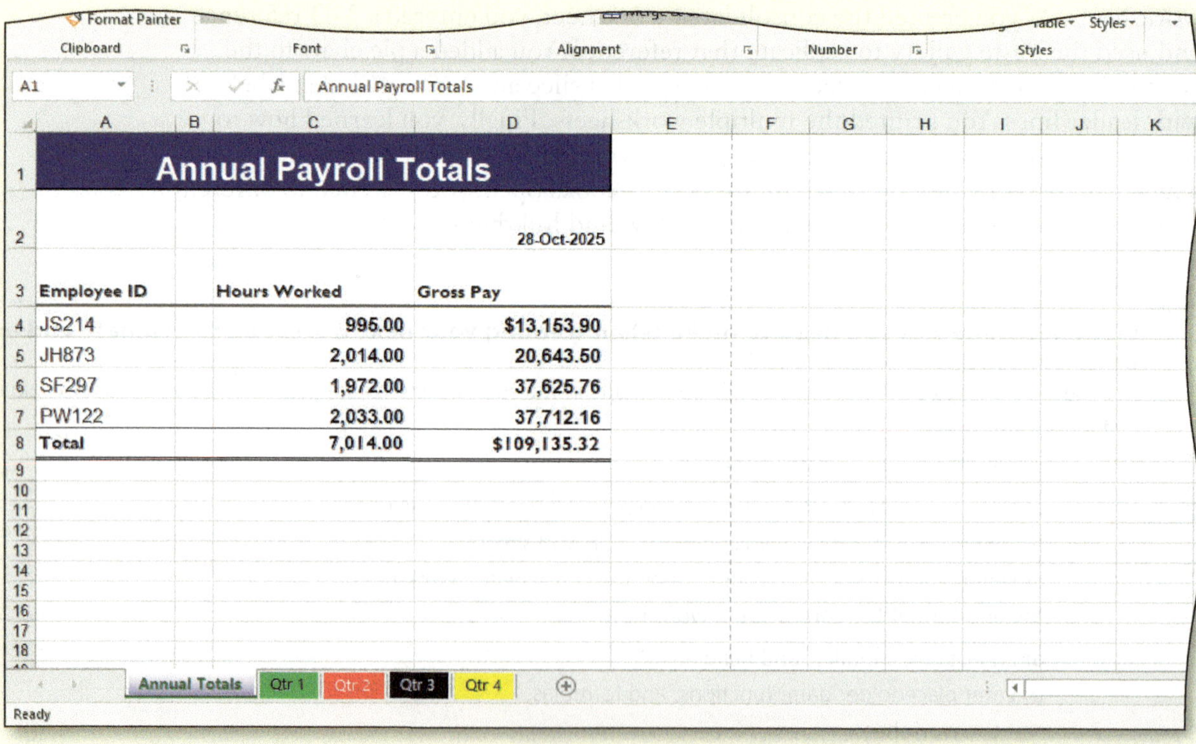

Figure 5–75

Perform the following tasks:

1. One by one, click each of the tabs and review the quarterly totals and formats. Change each tab color to match the background color of cell A1 on the corresponding worksheet.

2. Right-click the Annual Totals tab and then click Select All Sheets on the shortcut menu to group them. Perform the following steps.
   a. Insert the date in cell D2 using the TODAY function. Create the 4-Digit Year cell style created earlier in this module, but using the font color Black, Text 1 and right (indent) horizontal justification. Apply the cell style to cell D2.
   b. Format the column headings in the range A3:D3 using Heading 3 cell style. Format the range A8:D8 with the Total cell style.
   c. Use the SUM function to total columns C and D.
   d. Switch to Page Layout view. Add a worksheet header with the file name in the center of the header, and the current date in the right header. Add the sheet name, the word, Page, and page number to the center of the footer.
   e. If requested by your instructor, add your name to the left header.
   f. Click outside the header area. Click the 'Page Setup Dialog Box Launcher' to display the Page Setup dialog box. Center all worksheets horizontally on the page (Margins tab). Close the Page Setup dialog box. Return to Normal view.
3. Click the Qtr 1 sheet tab to select it. SHIFT+click the Qtr 4 sheet tab to select all four quarters without the Annual Totals worksheet. Perform the following steps:
   a. Select cell D4. Use the ROUND function with two decimal places to calculate the gross pay by multiplying B4 by C4.
   b. Use the fill handle to replicate the function to cells D5:D7.
   c. Select the range C4:C8 and format it with the comma style (Home tab | Number group).
   d. CTRL+click cells D4 and D8 to select them. Format the cells using the currency format (Format Cells dialog box), with a floating dollar sign and parentheses for negative numbers.
4. To consolidate the worksheets, click the Annual Totals sheet tab to select only the Annual Totals worksheet. To create a SUM function with a 3-D reference, select cell C4, and then click the AutoSum button (Home tab | Editing group). Click the Qtr 1 sheet tab to display the worksheet, and then click cell C4 to select the first portion of the argument for the SUM function. SHIFT+click the Qtr 4 sheet tab to select the ending range of the argument for the SUM function. Click the Enter button in the formula bar to enter the SUM function with the 3-D references in the selected cell.
5. On the Annual Totals sheet, copy the function in cell C4. Paste to the range C5:C7 using the Formulas button in the Paste gallery.
6. Repeat Steps 4 and 5 to create a 3-D reference in cell D4 and copy it to the range D5:D7.
7. On the Annual Totals sheet, format the range C4:D8 with the Comma style format. Next, CTRL+click cells D4 and D8 to select them. Format the cells using the currency format (Format Cells dialog box), with a floating dollar sign and parentheses for negative numbers.
8. Preview the five worksheets and print them if instructed to do so.
9. Click the Annual Totals sheet tab to select the sheet. Save the workbook as SC_EX_5_Payroll. Submit the workbook as requested by your instructor.
10. What would have been the effect if you had consolidated the workbook before rounding the gross pays for each quarter? If you then rounded all of the numbers, would the answers have been the same? Why or why not?

Extend Your Knowledge

Extend the skills you learned in this module and experiment with new skills. You may need to use Help to complete the assignment.

Creating and Editing Custom Format Codes

Note: To complete this assignment, you will be required to use the Data Files. Please contact your instructor for information about accessing the Data Files.

Instructions: Start Excel. Open the workbook called SC_EX_5-4.xlsx, which is located in the Data Files and shown in Figure 5–76a. This workbook you open contains data to format using custom format codes. For each of the entries in the Custom Formats sheet, you are to either create a new custom format code or edit the code already applied to the cell entry. When completed, the worksheet should appear as shown in Figure 5–76b. You should not change the entries in the cells, just the formatting code applied to the entries.

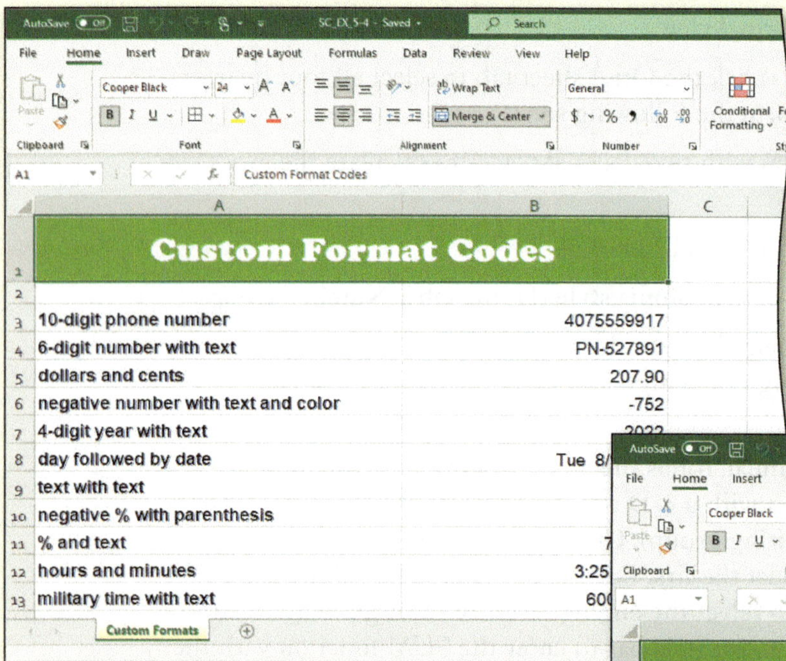

(a) Original Data

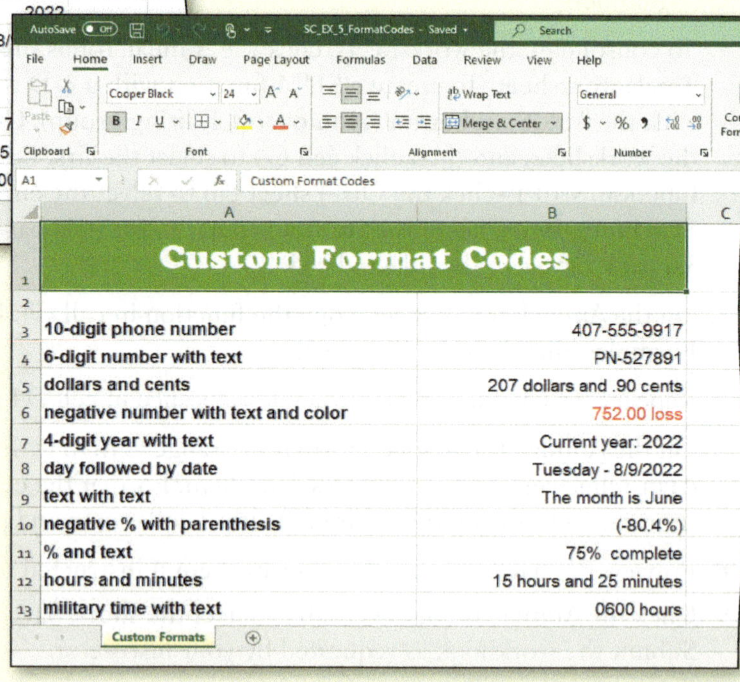

(b) Data with Custom Format Codes

Figure 5–76

Perform the following tasks:

1. Save the workbook as SC_EX_5_FormatCodes.
2. Select cell B3. Display the Format Cells dialog box, and note that the General format has been applied to this cell. Create a custom format code that will display the 10-digit number entered in cell B3 in the format shown in Figure 5–76b.
3. Select cell B4. Display the Format Cells dialog box, and note that a Custom Format code has been applied to this cell. Edit this custom format code to display the 6-digit number with text in cell B4 in the format shown in Figure 5–76b.
4. For each of the remaining cells in the range B5:B13, edit or create a custom format code to produce formatted cell contents that match Figure 5–76b.
5. Add a header to the worksheet that contains the file name (center) and page number (right).
6. If requested by your instructor, enter your phone number in cell B3 in place of the existing 10-digit number.
7. Save your changes to the workbook and submit the revised workbook as specified by your instructor.
8. For many of the entries, several custom formats can produce the result shown in Figure 5–76b. What criteria would you use to determine which custom format to use in instances where more than one format would produce the result in Figure 5–76b?

Expand Your World

Create a solution that uses cloud and web technologies by learning and investigating on your own from general guidance.

Consolidating and Charting Weather Data in a Workbook

Instructions: Start Excel. You are to gather and analyze weather data from four cities for a group environmental studies project. You decide to use Excel to create the charts and store the data.

Perform the following tasks:

1. Start Excel. Open a blank workbook, and save it with the file name, SC_EX_5_Weather.
2. Search online for average monthly weather statistics by city and state. Choose four different locations or use ones suggested by your instructor. Copy the weather statistics, such as precipitation and temperature, to your workbook. Create a separate worksheet for each city. Format the worksheets using techniques you have used in this module.
3. Create a master worksheet that consolidates all city data into a single table.
4. For each city, create a chart depicting the precipitation for each city. Use a type appropriate to your data. Use the city name as the title. Move all four charts to a single new worksheet (Figure 5–77).

Continued >

Expand Your World *continued*

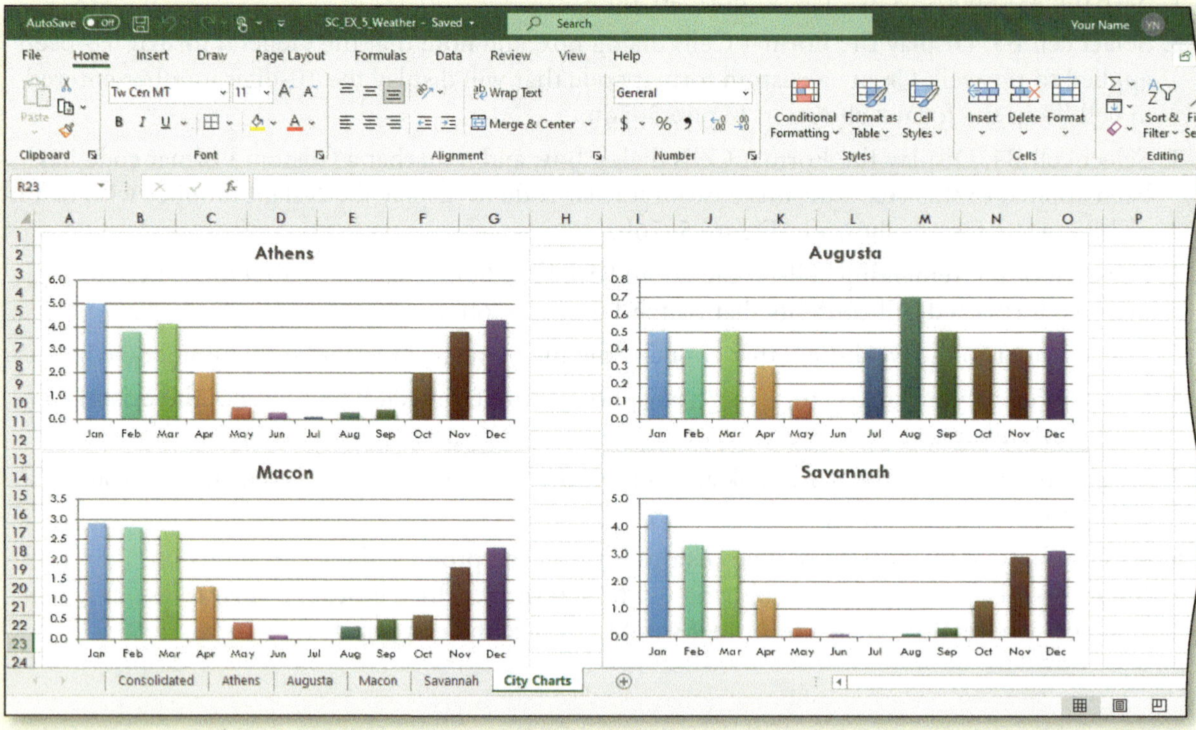

Figure 5–77

5. Save the workbook and submit it as specified by your instructor.
6. How did you choose your chart type? How could you make the charts more meaningful? Would you include data labels and leader lines? What kind of chart would you use for the consolidated worksheet?

In the Lab

Design and implement a solution using creative thinking and problem-solving skills.

Track Fitness Data

Problem: You have just started a new biking regimen. You decide to track your progress so that you can evaluate your bike rides. You decide to use Excel to track information about time, distance, and frequency of your rides. You plan to record the data for each ride and to consolidate data on a weekly basis so that you can see how you are progressing from week to week.

Perform the following tasks:

Part 1: Use the concepts and techniques presented in this module to create a workbook for tracking your biking data. You want to create a workbook that contains multiple worksheets to allow you to review daily data, as well as consolidated data. Use your knowledge of consolidation to design a workbook that will allow you to analyze your progress. You should have at least one computed field, such as average miles per ride in your worksheets. You should include at least one chart presenting fitness data. Submit your assignment in the format specified by the instructor.

Part 2: This exercise had you create a chart presenting fitness data. List two other ways you could chart the data in Excel. What are the strengths and weaknesses of each of the three chart types for the data you are presenting?

6 Creating, Sorting, and Querying a Table

Objectives

After completing this module, you will be able to:

- Create and manipulate a table
- Delete duplicate records
- Add calculated columns to a table with structured references
- Use the XLOOKUP function to look up a value in a table
- Use icon sets with conditional formatting
- Insert a total row
- Sort a table on one field or multiple fields
- Sort, query, and search a table using AutoFilter
- Remove filters
- Create criteria and extract ranges
- Apply database and statistical functions
- Use the MATCH and INDEX functions to find a value in a table
- Display automatic subtotals
- Use outline features to group, hide, and unhide data
- Create a treemap chart

Introduction

A **table**, also called a **database**, is an organized collection of rows and columns of similarly structured data on a worksheet. For example, a list of friends, a group of students registered for a class, an inventory list, a club membership roster, or an instructor's grade book—all can be arranged as tables on a worksheet. In these cases, the data related to each person or item is called a **record**, and the individual data items that make up a record are called **fields**. For example, in a table of clients, each client would have a separate record; each record might include several fields, such as name, address, phone number, current balance, billing rate, and status. A record also can include fields that contain references, formulas, and functions.

You can use a worksheet's row-and-column structure to organize and store a table. Each row of a worksheet can store a record, and each column can store one field for each record. Additionally, a row of column headings at the top of the worksheet can store field names that identify each field.

After you enter a table onto a worksheet, you can use Excel to (1) add and delete records, (2) change the values of fields in records, (3) sort the records so that Excel presents them in a different order, (4) determine subtotals for numeric fields, (5) display records that meet comparison criteria, and (6) analyze data using database functions. This module illustrates all six of these table capabilities.

Project: Rating Bank Account Managers

The project in this module follows proper design guidelines and uses Excel to create the worksheet shown in Figures 6–1a and 6–1b, and the chart (Figure 6–1c). A local bank with several branches collects funds for customer checking, savings, and investment accounts and makes loans to customers and businesses. Bank account managers meet with customers to discuss their banking needs, recommend appropriate accounts or loans, and perform all necessary tasks to open them. The account managers are paid a salary plus commission. Bank management produces a monthly workbook that lists the account managers, account or loan amounts, account types, and supervisor ratings, as well as commissions earned. The data in the workbook should be easy to summarize, sort, edit, and query.

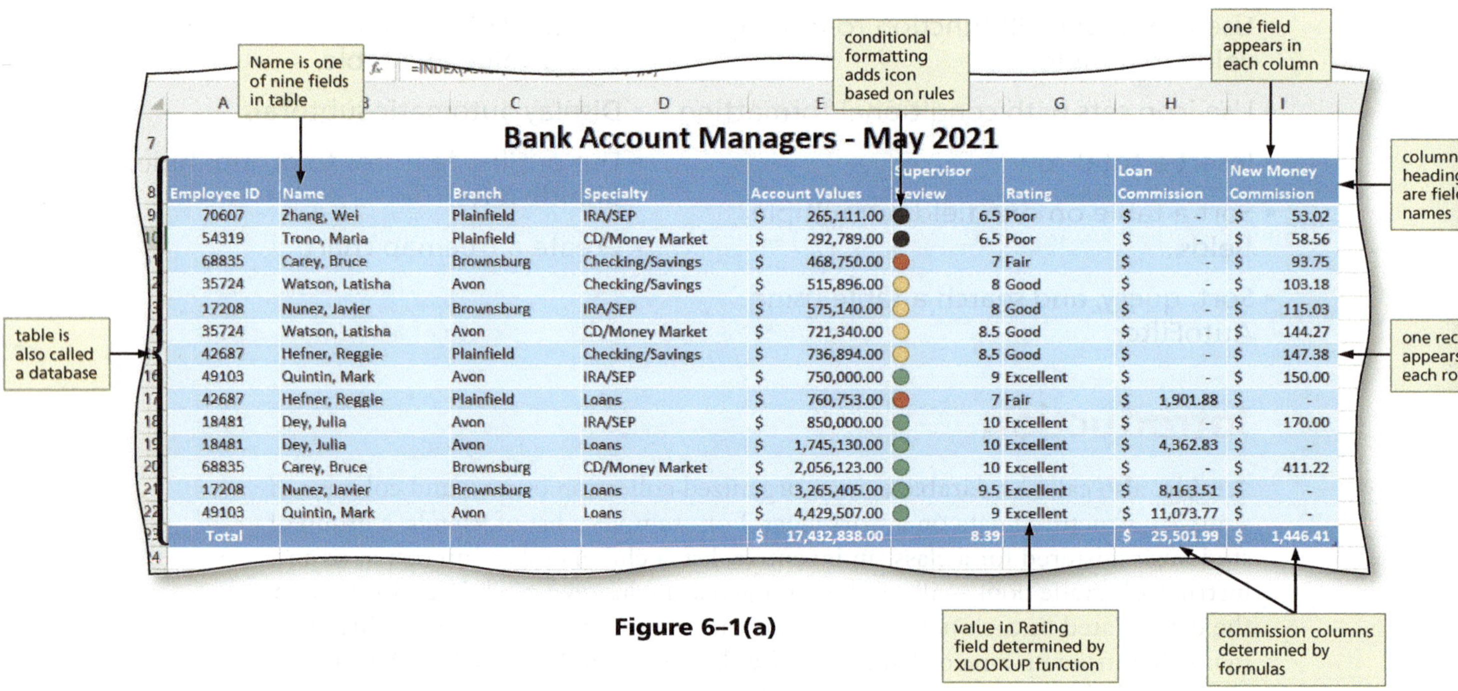

Employee ID	Name	Branch	Specialty	Account Values	Supervisor Review	Rating	Loan Commission	New Money Commission
70607	Zhang, Wei	Plainfield	IRA/SEP	$ 265,111.00	6.5	Poor	$ -	$ 53.02
54319	Trono, Maria	Plainfield	CD/Money Market	$ 292,789.00	6.5	Poor	$ -	$ 58.56
68835	Carey, Bruce	Brownsburg	Checking/Savings	$ 468,750.00	7	Fair	$ -	$ 93.75
35724	Watson, Latisha	Avon	Checking/Savings	$ 515,896.00	8	Good	$ -	$ 103.18
17208	Nunez, Javier	Brownsburg	IRA/SEP	$ 575,140.00	8	Good	$ -	$ 115.03
35724	Watson, Latisha	Avon	CD/Money Market	$ 721,340.00	8.5	Good	$ -	$ 144.27
42687	Hefner, Reggie	Plainfield	Checking/Savings	$ 736,894.00	8.5	Good	$ -	$ 147.38
49103	Quintin, Mark	Avon	IRA/SEP	$ 750,000.00	9	Excellent	$ -	$ 150.00
42687	Hefner, Reggie	Plainfield	Loans	$ 760,753.00	7	Fair	$ 1,901.88	$ -
18481	Dey, Julia	Avon	IRA/SEP	$ 850,000.00	10	Excellent	$ -	$ 170.00
18481	Dey, Julia	Avon	Loans	$ 1,745,130.00	10	Excellent	$ 4,362.83	$ -
68835	Carey, Bruce	Brownsburg	CD/Money Market	$ 2,056,123.00	10	Excellent	$ -	$ 411.22
17208	Nunez, Javier	Brownsburg	Loans	$ 3,265,405.00	9.5	Excellent	$ 8,163.51	$ -
49103	Quintin, Mark	Avon	Loans	$ 4,429,507.00	9	Excellent	$ 11,073.77	$ -
Total				$ 17,432,838.00	8.39		$ 25,501.99	$ 1,446.41

Figure 6–1(a)

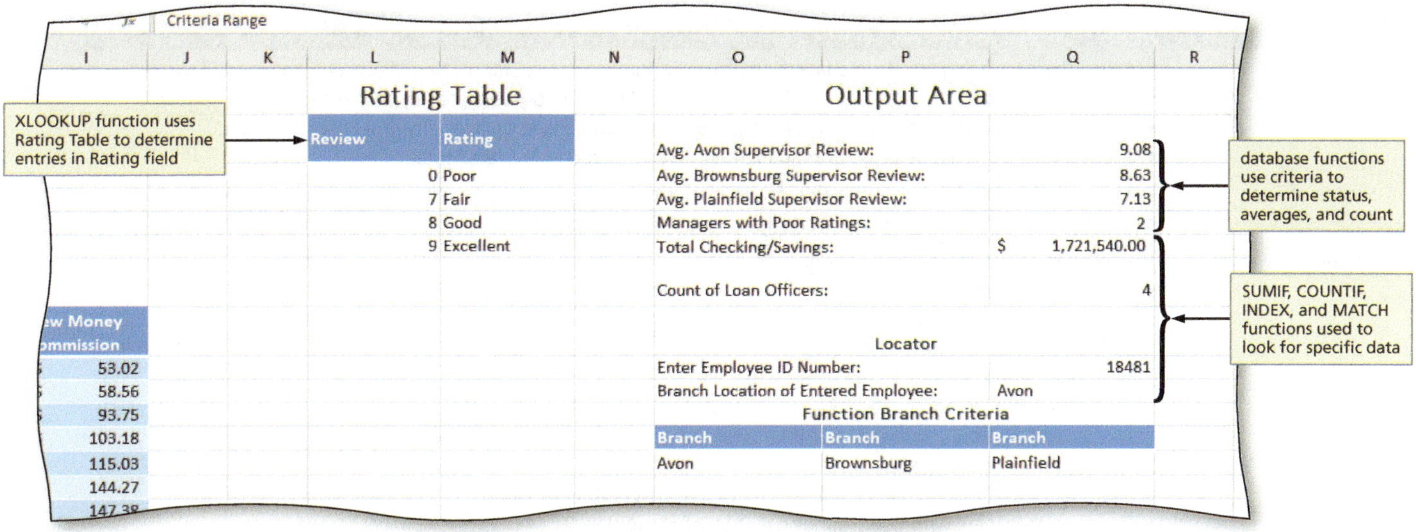

Figure 6–1(b)

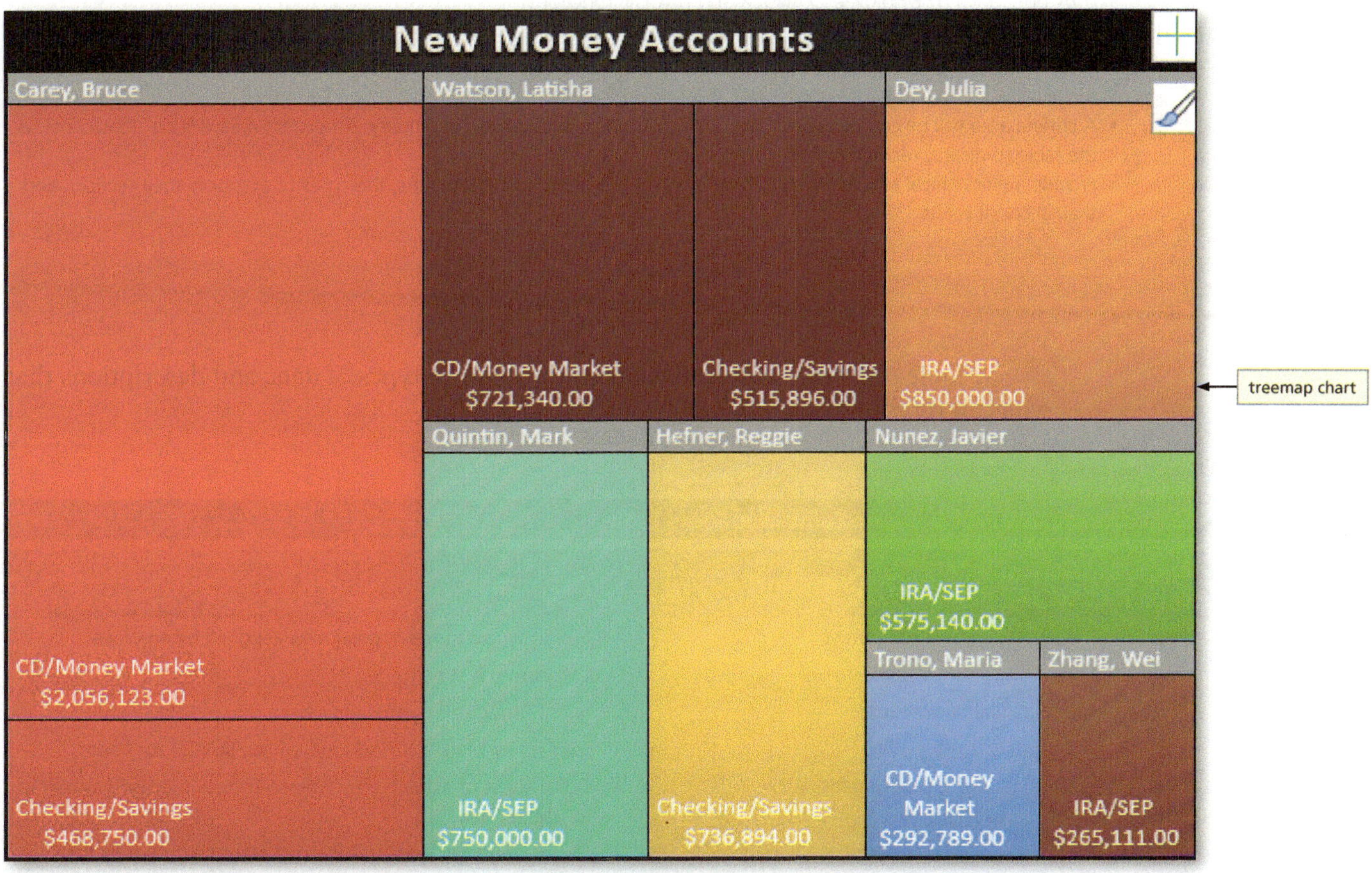

Figure 6–1(c)

Figure 6–2 shows a sample requirements document for the Bank Account Managers Table. It includes the needs, source of data, calculations, special requirements, and other facts about its development.

Worksheet Title	Bank Account Managers Table
Needs	• A worksheet table that lists the manager's employee ID number, name, branch, type of account, and monthly account values. • The worksheet also should assign an Excellent, Good, Fair, or Poor rating based on the supervisor's review. • The worksheet should calculate each manager's commission based on specialty and account values. • The worksheet should be easy for management to sort, search, filter, and total.
Source of Data	Data supplied by the bank includes the information listed in the first Needs bullet above and detailed in Table 6–1 below. Remaining numbers on the worksheet are based on calculations.
Calculations	The following calculations are needed: • Loan Commission = .0025 * Account Values only for Loans Specialty (IF function) • New Money Commission = .0002 * Account Values only for Specialty other than Loans (IF function) • Rating that is determined as follows: o Excellent = a high score of 9 to 10 o Good = an adequate score of 8 to 8.99 o Fair = a low score of 7 to 7.99 o Poor = a score below 7 • Average Supervisor Review score for each branch (DAVERAGE function) • Count of managers with Poor ratings (DCOUNT function) • Total Checking/Savings account values (SUMIF function) • Total count of loan officers (COUNTIF function) • Look up Branch by Employee ID (INDEX and MATCH functions)
Other Requirements	• Provide a way to search, sort, and select data based on certain criteria. • Provide an area to ascertain statistics about account managers, such as averages, counts, and totals based on specific factors. • A criteria area will be created above the table to store criteria for use in a query. An extract area will be created below the table to display records that meet the criteria. • Provide a hierarchical and visual chart to display all of the account managers, the types of accounts they service, and their account totals.

Figure 6–2

Table 6–1 describes the field names, columns, types of data, and descriptions that you can refer to when creating the table.

Table 6–1 Column Information for Bank Account Managers Table

Column Heading (Field Names)	Column in Worksheet	Type of Data	Description
Employee ID	A	Numeric	5-digit whole number, previously assigned by employer
Name	B	Text	Last name, first name
Branch	C	Text	Avon, Brownsburg, or Plainfield
Specialty	D	Text	CD/Money Market, Checking/Savings, IRA/SEP, or Loans
Account Values	E	Numeric	Dollar value of total money (loaned or new money) brought in for the month
Supervisor Review	F	Numeric	Decimal number with one decimal place, provided by the supervisor
Rating	G	Text calculation (XLOOKUP function)	Standing of Excellent, Good, Fair, or Poor rating based on the supervisor's review
Loan Commission	H	Percentage calculation (total loans made by account manager * .0025)	Dollar amount
New Money Commission	I	Percentage calculation (total new money brought in by account manager * .0002)	Dollar amount

Using a sketch of the worksheet can help you visualize its design. The sketch of the table consists of the title, column headings, location of data values, and an idea of the desired formatting (Figure 6–3a). (The sketch does not show the criteria area above the table or the extract area below the table.) The general layout of the table, output area, and required statistics and query are shown in Figure 6–3b.

Account Managers Table

Employee ID	Name	Branch	Specialty	Account Values	Supervisor Review	Rating	Loan Commission	New Money Commission
XXXXX	Last, First	XXXXX	XXXXXX	$9,999,999.99	99.99	XXXXXX	$99,999.99	$99,999.99
↓	↓	↓	↓	↓	↓	↓	↓	↓

(a) Data Table

Rating Table		Output Area	
Review	**Rating**	Avg. Avon Supervisor Review:	9.08
0	Poor	Avg. Brownsburg Supervisor Review:	8.63
7	Fair	Avg. Plainfield Supervisor Review:	7.13
8	Good	Managers with Poor Ratings:	2
9	Excellent	Total Checking/Savings:	$ 1,721,540.00
		Count of Loan Officers:	4
		Locator	
		Enter Employee ID Number:	18481
		Branch Location of Entered Employee:	Avon

Function Branch Criteria

Branch	**Branch**	**Branch**
Avon	Brownsburg	Plainfield

(b) Rating Table and Output Area

Figure 6–3

With a good understanding of the requirements document, a clear list of the necessary decisions, and a sketch of the worksheet, the next step is to use Excel to create the worksheet and chart. The raw data provided by the bank is provided in a Data File.

To Open and Save a File

The following steps open a file and save it with a new name. To complete these steps, you will be required to use the Data Files. Please contact your instructor for information about accessing the Data Files.

1. **sam** Start Excel and open the Data File named SC_EX_6-1.xlsx.
2. If the Excel window is not maximized, click the Maximize button on its title bar to maximize the window.
3. Save the workbook on your hard drive, OneDrive, or a location that is most appropriate to your situation, using SC_EX_6_BankAccountManagers as the file name.
4. If necessary, click cell A1 (Figure 6–4).

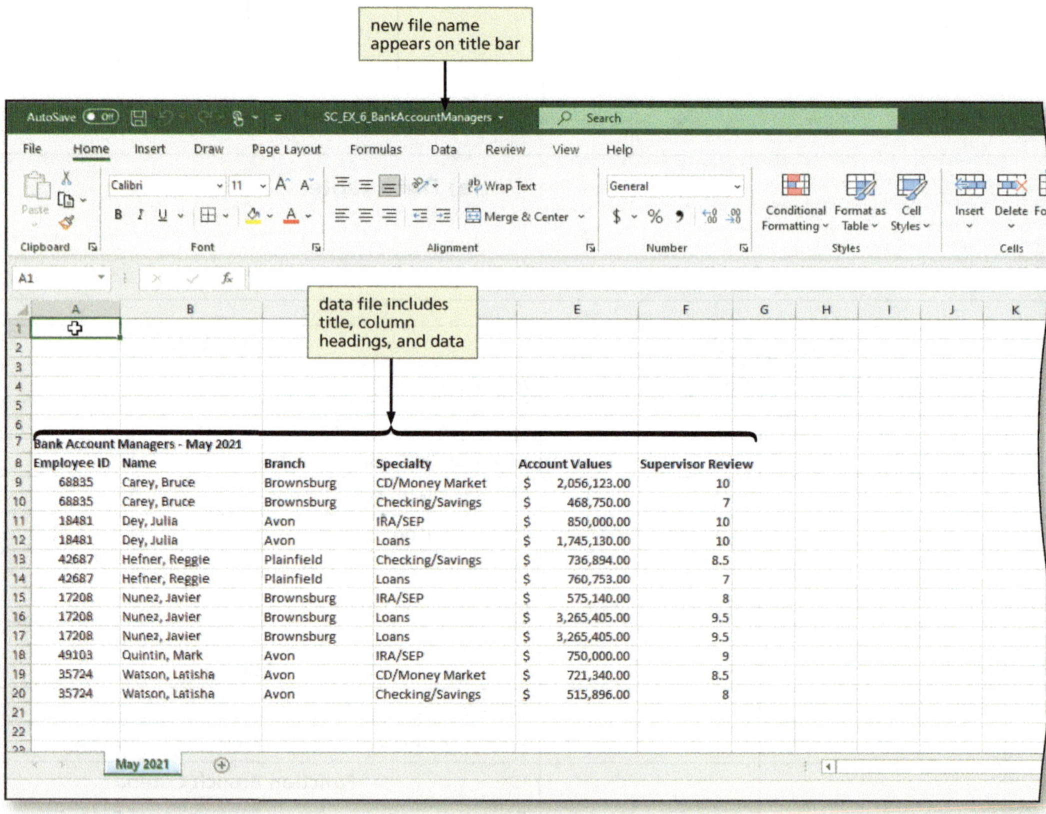

Figure 6–4

Table Guidelines

When you create a table in Excel, you should follow some basic guidelines, as listed in Table 6–2.

Table 6–2 Guidelines for Creating a Table in Excel

Table Size and Workbook Location
1. Do not enter more than one table per worksheet.
2. Maintain at least one blank row between a table and other worksheet entries.
3. A table can have a maximum of 16,384 fields and 1,048,576 records on a worksheet.
Column Headings (Field Names)
1. Place column headings (field names) in the first row of the table.
2. Do not use blank rows or rows with repeating characters, such as dashes or underscores, to separate the column headings from the data.
3. Apply a different format to the column headings than to the data. For example, bold the column headings and format the data below the column headings using a regular style. Most table styles follow these guidelines.
4. While column headings can be up to 32,767 characters in length, it is advisable to keep them short so more information can fit on the screen. The column headings should be meaningful.
Contents of Table
1. Each cell in any given column should have similar data. For example, Speciality entries should use the company standard wording for the types of accounts, such as IRA/SEP.
2. Format the data to improve readability, but do not vary the format of the data within the cells of a column.

BTW

Ribbon and Screen Resolution

Excel may change how the groups and buttons within the groups appear on the ribbon, depending on the screen resolution of your computer. Thus, your ribbon may look different from the ones in this book if you are using a screen resolution other than 1366 x 768.

Creating a Table

When you create a table in Excel, you can manage and analyze the data in that table independently from the rest of the data on the worksheet. The advantages of creating a table include:

- Automatic expansion of the table to accommodate data
- Header row remains visible while scrolling
- Automatic reformatting such as the recoloring of banded rows or columns
- Integrated filter and sort functionality
- Automatic fill and calculated fields
- Easy access to structured references
- Automatic adjustment of associated charts and ranges

BTW

Touch Mode Differences

The Office and Windows interfaces may vary if you are using Touch Mode. For this reason, you might notice that the function or appearance of your touch screen differs slightly from this module's presentation.

Consider This

How should you format a table?

Format a table so that the records are easy to distinguish from one another. The headings in the table should start several rows from the top in order to leave room for a criteria area. Using banded rows (background colors varying between rows) to format the table provides greater readability. Some columns require calculations that can be created by using the column headings or cell references within formulas. In some cases, calculated columns in tables require looking up values outside of the table. You can use special Excel lookup functions in such cases. Totals also can be added to the table for averages, sums, and other types of calculations.

To Format a Range as a Table

The easiest way to create a table is to apply a table style. **Why?** Table styles are a quick way to increase table readability and usability. Excel automatically creates the table when applying a table style to a range. You can create a table before or after entering column headings and data. Most automatically-applied styles contain banded rows. A **banded row** is a row that is highlighted or delineated in some way, usually applied to every other row in a table. The Table Design tab contains check boxes to turn banded rows or banded columns, on and off.

You also have the option of inserting a table. The Insert Table button (Insert tab | Tables group) will create a blank table in a specified range, using the default color scheme. The following steps format a range as a table.

1

- Zoom to 110% and then scroll down until cell A7 is at the top of the workspace.
- Select the range A8:F20, which includes the column headings.
- Click the 'Format as Table' button (Home tab | Styles group) to display the Format as Table gallery (Figure 6–5).

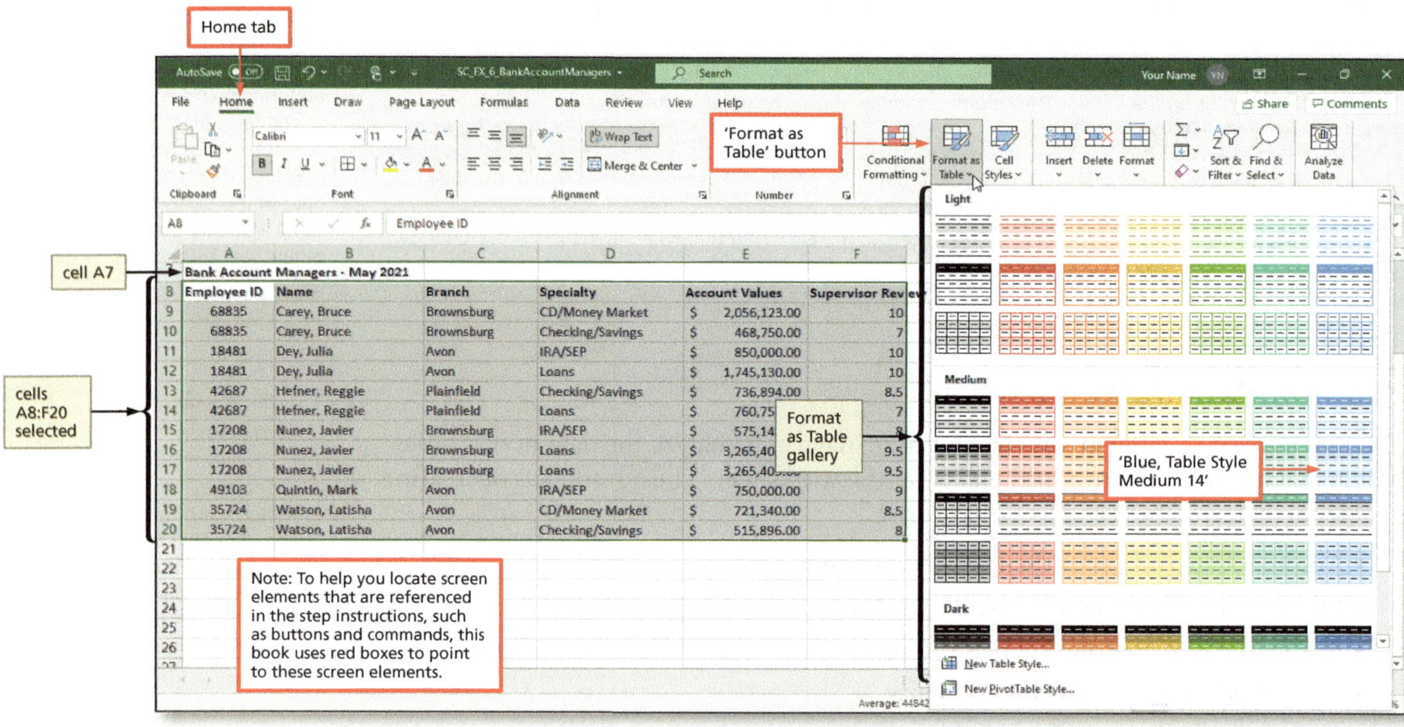

Figure 6–5

2

- Click 'Blue, Table Style Medium 14' in the Format as Table gallery to display the Format As Table dialog box.
- If necessary, click the 'My table has headers' check box to select the option to format the table with headers (Figure 6–6).

Q&A **What is a header?**
A table header is the column heading that appears above the data. In this case, you want to create the table and include the column headings.

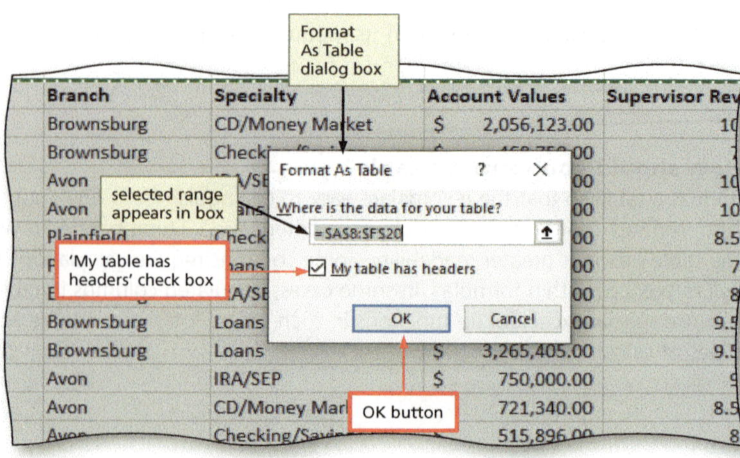

Figure 6–6

3

- Click OK (Format As Table dialog box) to create a table from the selected range.
- Click outside the table to deselect it (Figure 6–7).

Q&A **What are the buttons with the arrows beside the column headings?** The buttons are part of the AutoFilter that you will learn about later in the module.

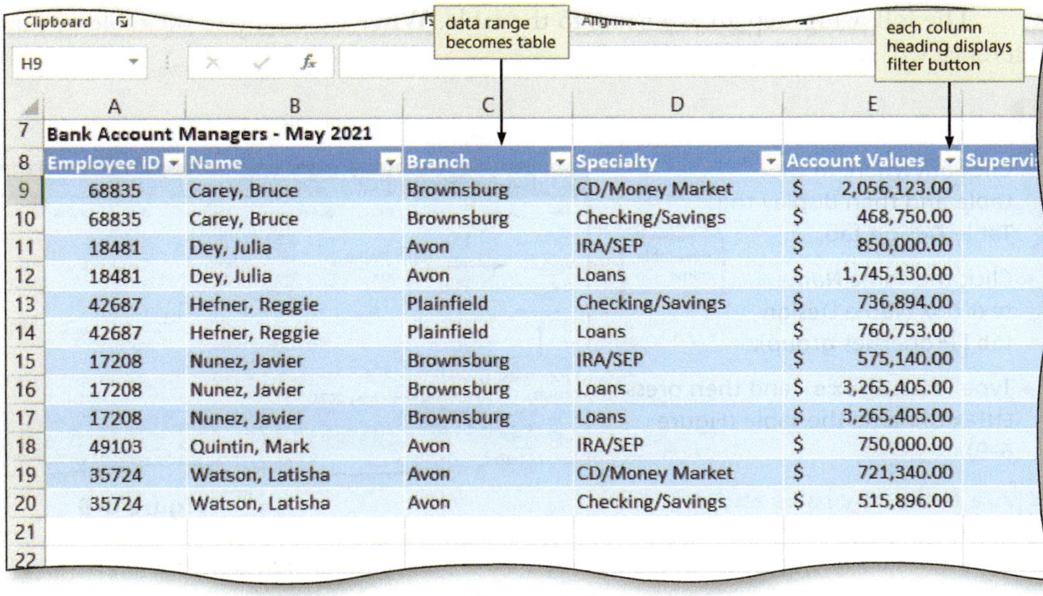

Figure 6–7

Other Ways

1. Select range, click Table button (Insert tab | Tables group), click OK, choose table style
2. Select range, press CTRL+T, click OK (Create Table dialog box), choose table style

To Wrap Text

The following steps wrap the text in cell F8 to make the heading easier to read.

1 Change the width of column F to 13. Change the height of row 8 to 30.

2 Select cell F8, and then click the Wrap Text button (Home tab | Alignment group) (Figure 6–8).

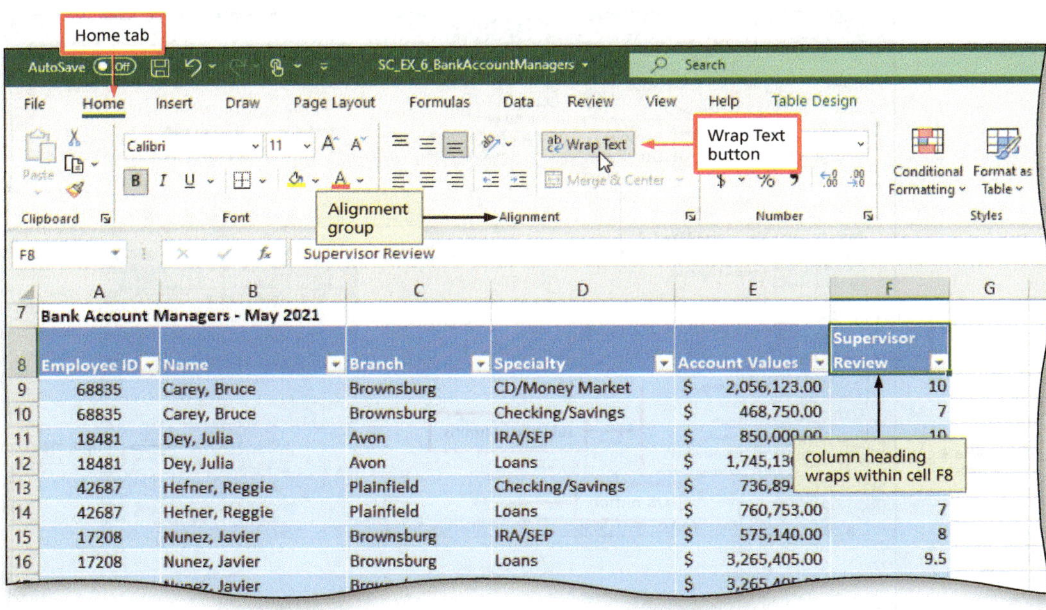

Figure 6–8

BTW

Ranges to Tables

If you select a range before clicking the 'Format as Table' button (Home tab | Styles group), Excel will fill in the range for you in the Format As Table dialog box.

To Name the Table

The following step gives a name to the table. **Why?** Referring to the table by name rather than by range reference will save time.

1

- Click anywhere in the table and then display the Table Design tab.
- Click the Table Name text box (Table Design tab | Properties group).
- Type **`Managers`** and then press ENTER to name the table (Figure 6–9).

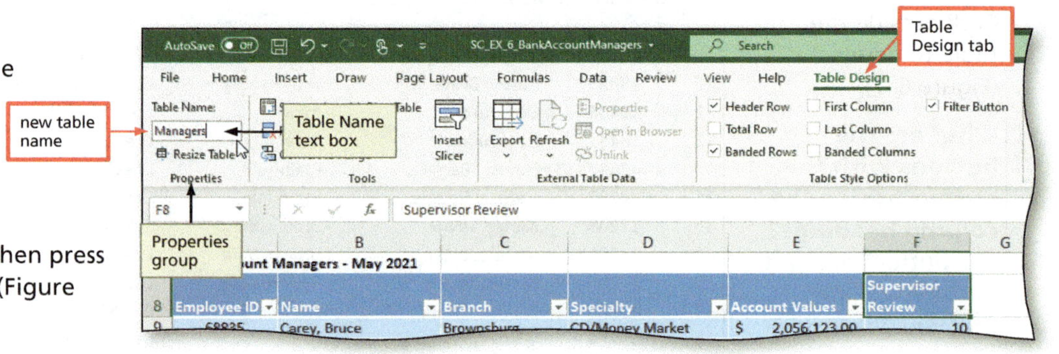

Figure 6–9

Q&A **Are there any rules about naming tables?**
Excel does not allow spaces in table names. Excel also requires that table names begin with a letter or underscore.

Other Ways

1. Select range, click Name Manager button (Formulas tab | Defined Names group), click New button (Name Manager dialog box), enter name (New Name dialog box), click OK, click Close

To Remove Duplicates

Duplicate entries may appear in tables. **Why?** Duplicates sometimes happen when data is entered incorrectly, by more than one person, or from more than one source. The following steps remove duplicate records in the table. In this particular table, the Loans total for Javier Nunez was entered twice by mistake. (Javier Nunez also has a record in the table for IRA/SEP accounts.)

1

- Click anywhere in the table.
- Click the Remove Duplicates button (Table Design tab | Tools group) to display the Remove Duplicates dialog box.
- If necessary, click the Select All button (Remove Duplicates dialog box) to select all columns (Figure 6–10).

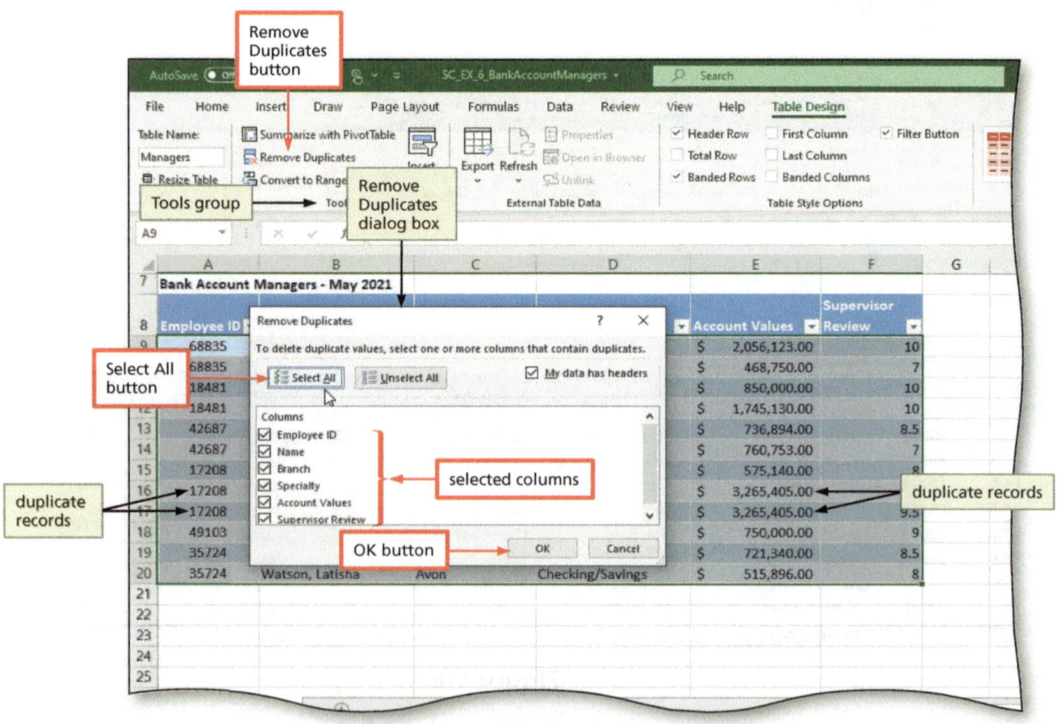

Figure 6–10

2

- Click OK (Remove Duplicates dialog box) to remove duplicate records from the table (Figure 6–11).

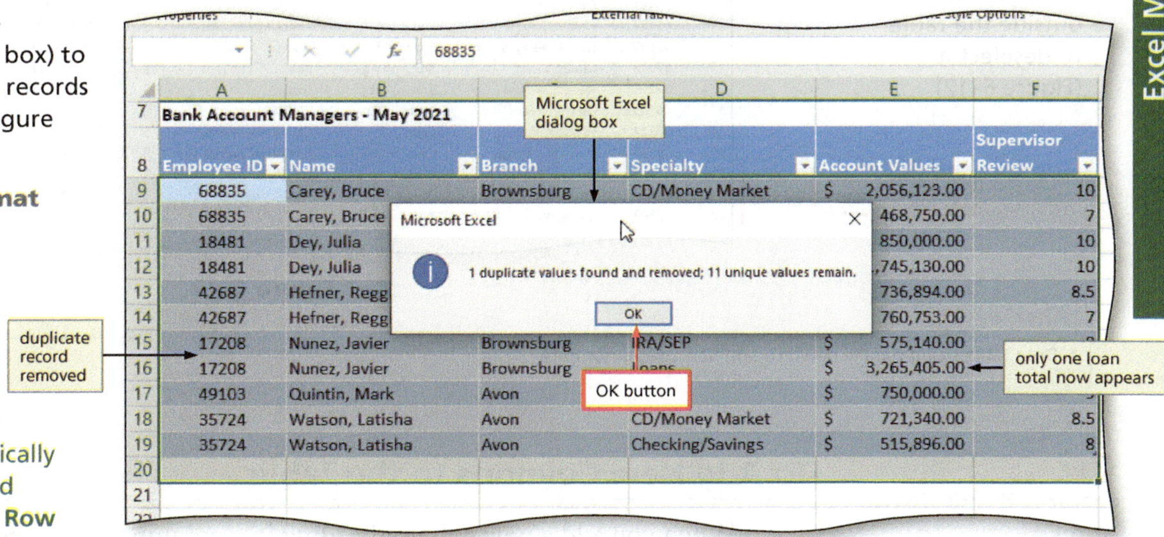

Figure 6–11

Q&A **Did Excel reformat the table?**
Yes. The Banded Rows check box (Table Design tab | Table Style Options group) is checked automatically when you selected the table format. **Row banding** causes adjacent rows to have different formatting, even if you delete a row; each row in the table is distinguishable from surrounding rows.

3

- Click OK (Microsoft Excel dialog box) to finish the process.

Experiment

- Examine the table to verify removal of the duplicate record for employee 17208 for Loans.

Other Ways

1. Select range, click Remove Duplicates button (Data tab | Data Tools group)

To Enter New Rows and Records into a Table

The following step enters new account mangers into the table. You will insert the information just below the table. **Why?** Data entered in rows or columns adjacent to the table becomes part of the table. Excel will format the new table data automatically.

1

- Select cell A20.
- Type the new entries below.

Experiment

- As you enter the data, notice that Excel tries to complete your fields based on previous common entries. You can press TAB to move between cells.

49103	Quintin, Mark	Avon	Loans	4,429,507.00	9
54319	Trono, Maria	Plainfield	CD/Money Market	292,789.00	6.5
70607	Zhang, Wei	Plainfield	IRA/SEP	265,111.00	6.5

- Click the Home tab. If necessary, click outside the table to deselect it (Figure 6–12).

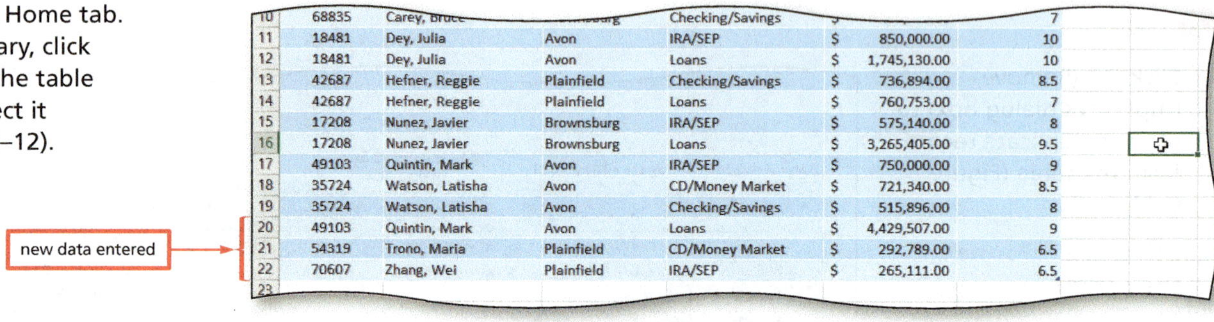

Figure 6–12

Other Ways

1. Drag table sizing handle down to add new row, enter data

BTW

Adding Blank Rows and Columns to Tables

If you want to add a blank row or column to a table, the easiest way is to right-click a cell within the table. Then, on the shortcut menu, click Insert. Excel displays options for columns and rows, above and below the selected cell.

To Add New Columns to the Table

When you add a new column heading in a column adjacent to the current column headings in the table, Excel automatically adds the adjacent column to the table's range and copies the format of the existing table heading to the new column heading. The following steps insert column headings for three new columns in the table.

1. Change the column width of column G to 13.00. Click cell G8. Type `Rating` and then click the Enter button to enter the heading.

2. Change the column width of column H to 13.00. Click cell H8. Type `Loan Commission` and then click the Enter button to enter the heading. If necessary, click the Wrap Text button Home tab | Alignment group) to wrap the text.

3. Change the column width of column I to 13.00. Click cell I8. Type `New Money Commission` and then click the Enter button to enter the heading. If necessary, wrap the text in the cell (Figure 6–13).

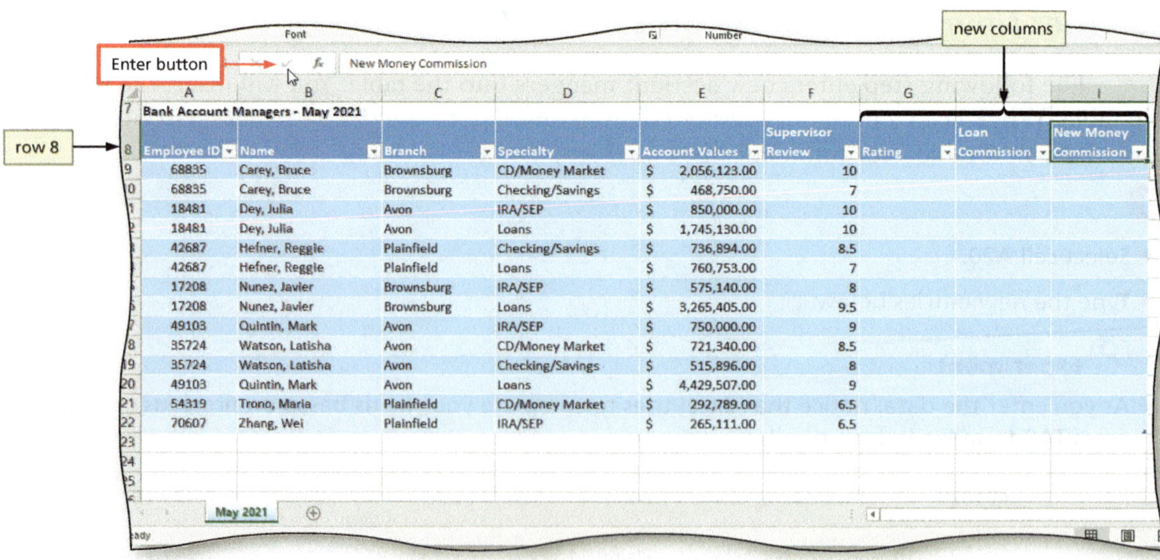

Figure 6–13

To Center Across Selection

The following steps center the title in cell A7 across a selection using the Format Cells dialog box. In earlier modules, recall you used the 'Merge & Center' button (Home tab | Alignment group) to center text across a range. **Why?** This earlier technique centered the title, but it removed access to individual cells, because the cells were merged. The Center Across Selection format centers text across multiple cells but does not merge the selected cell range into one cell.

1

- Select the range A7:I7. Right-click the selected range to display the shortcut menu (Figure 6–14).

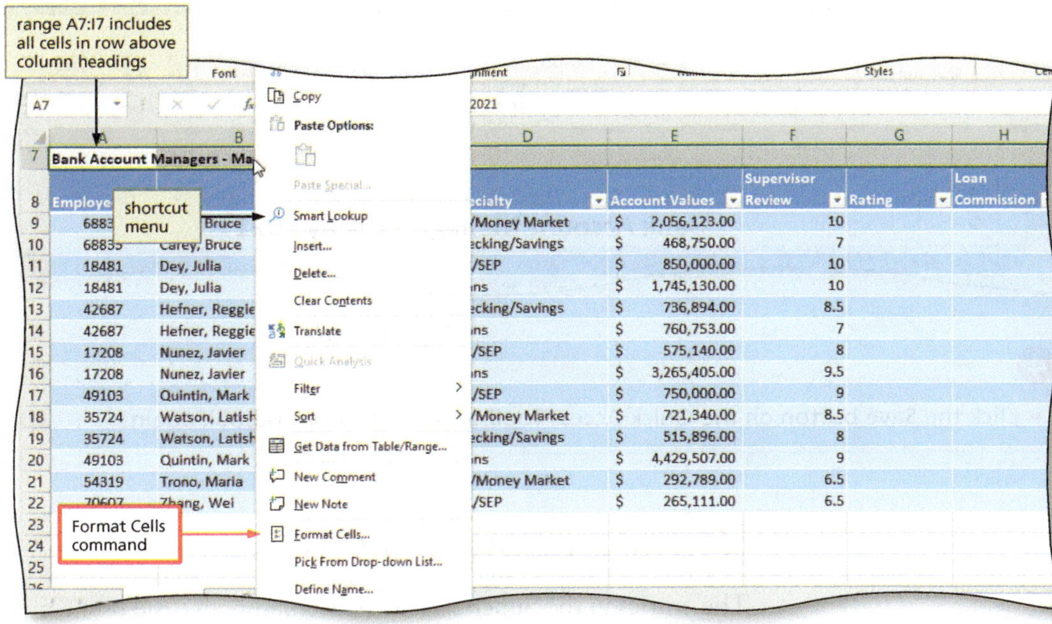

Figure 6–14

2

- Click Format Cells on the shortcut menu to display the Format Cells dialog box.
- Click the Alignment tab (Format Cells dialog box) and then click the Horizontal button in the Text alignment area to display a list of horizontal alignments (Figure 6–15).

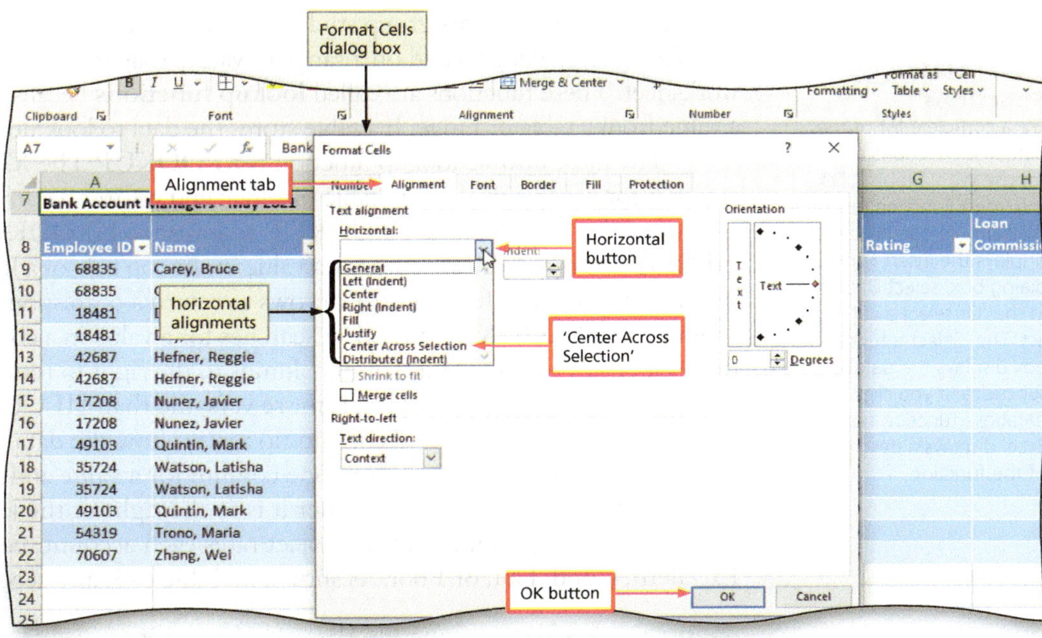

Figure 6–15

3

- Click 'Center Across Selection' in the Horizontal list (Format Cells dialog box) to select the option to center the title across the selection.
- Click OK (Format Cells dialog box) to apply the settings.
- Change the height of row 7 to 30. Change the font size of cell A7 to 22 (Figure 6–16).

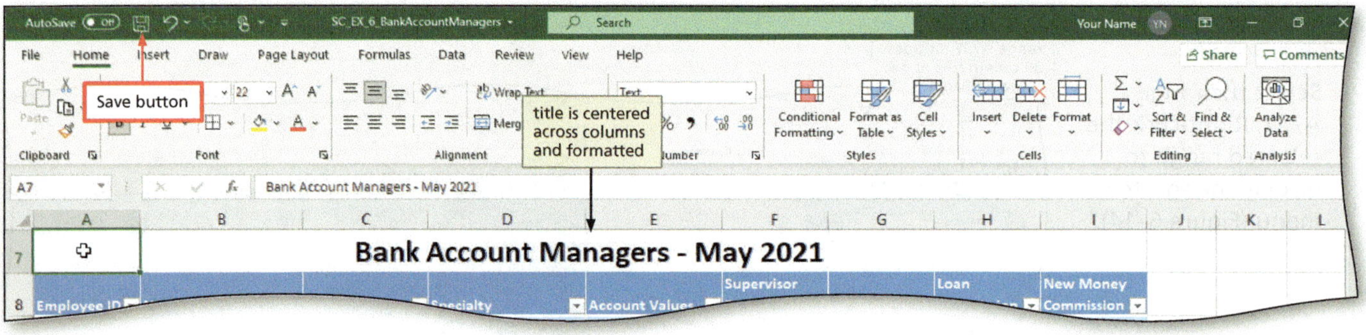

Figure 6–16

4

- Click the Save button on the Quick Access Toolbar to save the workbook again.

> **BTW**
> **Other Database Functions**
> For a complete list of the database functions available for use with a table, click the Insert Function button in the formula bar. When Excel displays the Insert Function dialog box, select Database in the 'Or select a category' list. The 'Select a function' box displays the database functions. If you click a database function name, Excel displays a description of the function.

Using a Lookup Table

The entries in the Supervisor Review column give the user a numerical evaluation of the rating for each account manager. Some people, however, prefer simple ratings or letter grades. Ranking the account managers groups them in the same way sports teams award their medals or instructors group student grades. Excel contains functions that allow you to assign such rankings based on a range of values that are stored in a separate area on the worksheet. These functions are called **lookup functions** because they look up and retrieve a value from a table or range. If a table stores the data to look up, it is called a **lookup table**.

The most flexible lookup function is XLOOKUP. The **XLOOKUP function** searches for a value in a lookup table or range and returns a corresponding value to the cell containing the function. XLOOKUP is similar to HLOOKUP and VLOOKUP. The **HLOOKUP function** searches for a value in the top row of a lookup table, and then searches down a specified number of rows to return a corresponding value in the same column. The **VLOOKUP function** searches for a value in a column of a lookup table, and then searches a specified number of columns to the right to return a value in the same row.

The XLOOKUP function is more versatile than HLOOKUP or VLOOKUP because it can search a row or column no matter how the data is organized. For example, you can use XLOOKUP to search one column for a value and return a result from the same row in another column, whether it is to the right or the left.

The Rating column in this project rates each account manager with a value of Excellent, Good, Fair, or Poor. As shown in Table 6–3, any account manager receiving a

Table 6–3 How the Ratings Are Determined

Supervisor Review	Rating
0 to 6.99	Poor
7 to 7.99	Fair
8 to 8.99	Good
9 and higher	Excellent

score of 9 or more receives an Excellent rating. An account manager with a score of 8 or more receives a Good rating. An account manager with a score of 7 or more receives a Fair rating. A score of less than 7 will display a Poor rating.

To facilitate the display of each account manager's rating, you will use the XLOOKUP function. The general form of the XLOOKUP function is

=XLOOKUP(lookup_value, lookup_array, return_array)

The three arguments of the XLOOKUP function represent the data that the function needs to do its job. The first argument is the **lookup value**, which is the data, or the location of the data, that you want to look up. In the case of the Managers table, that data is located in column F, the Supervisor Review. You only need to enter the first occurrence of the data, cell F9.

The second argument, lookup_array, is the location of the data to search. In this case, the lookup_array will be located away from the main table in the range L3:L6. In this project, the values to search are 0, 7, 8, and 9—the lowest value in each rating.

The third argument, return_array, is the location of the return values. The **return value** is the answer you want to appear as a result of the XLOOKUP function. In the Managers table, the return value will be Poor, Fair, Good, or Excellent. In this project, the return values will be located in the range M3:M6.

XLOOKUP has three optional arguments. The first, if_not_found, is text to return in case the lookup value is not found, such as "Rating not found." Use the second optional argument, match_mode, to specify the type of match you want, such as an exact match. Use the third optional argument, search_mode, to specify how to search, such as from bottom to top. In this project, you only need to specify a match_mode argument of -1 to look for an exact match in a range of values or return the next smaller number (the lowest value in each rating).

To Create an Area for Lookup and Return Arrays

Before using the XLOOKUP function, you must create the lookup and return arrays. The following steps create the arrays and headings in the range L1:M6.

1. Change the width of columns L and M to 14.
2. Click cell L1. Type `Rating Table` as the table array title and then click the Enter button in the formula bar.
3. Change the font size to 18 and apply bold formatting to cell L1.
4. Select the range L1:M1. Right-click the selection and then click Format Cells on the shortcut menu to display the Format Cells dialog box. On the Alignment tab (Format Cells dialog box), click the Horizontal button, and then click 'Center Across Selection'. Click OK to apply the settings.
5. In cell L2, type `Review` to enter the column heading.
6. In cell M2, type `Rating` to enter the column heading.
7. Select cell I8. Click the Format Painter button (Home tab | Clipboard group) and then drag through cells L2:M2 to copy the format of the selected cell to the column headings.

8 Enter the data shown below (Figure 6–17).

Cell	Data	Cell	Data
L3	0	M3	Poor
L4	7	M4	Fair
L5	8	M5	Good
L6	9	M6	Excellent

Q&A **Why does the lookup_array contain single digits instead of a range?**
You only have to enter the least value for each rating. Excel will evaluate all values in the range.

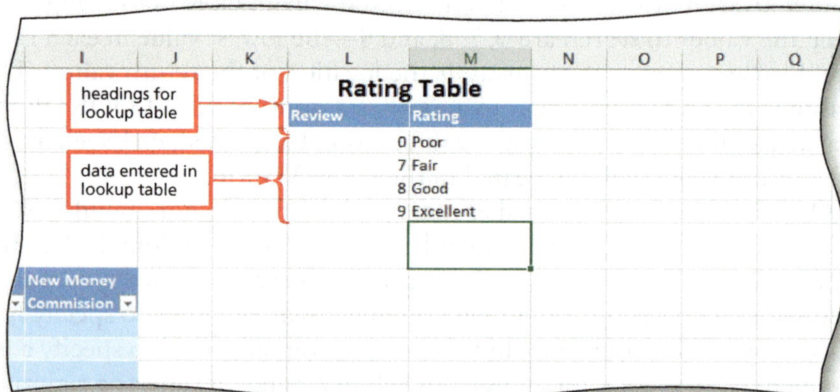

Figure 6–17

To Use the XLOOKUP Function

The following steps use the XLOOKUP function and the lookup and return arrays to determine the Rating for each account manager. **Why?** Using the XLOOKUP function with a table allows Excel to display the ratings, rather than the user typing them in individually.

1

- Click cell G9. Type `=xlookup(f9,$l$3:$l$6,$m$3:$m$6,,-1)` as the cell entry (Figure 6–18).

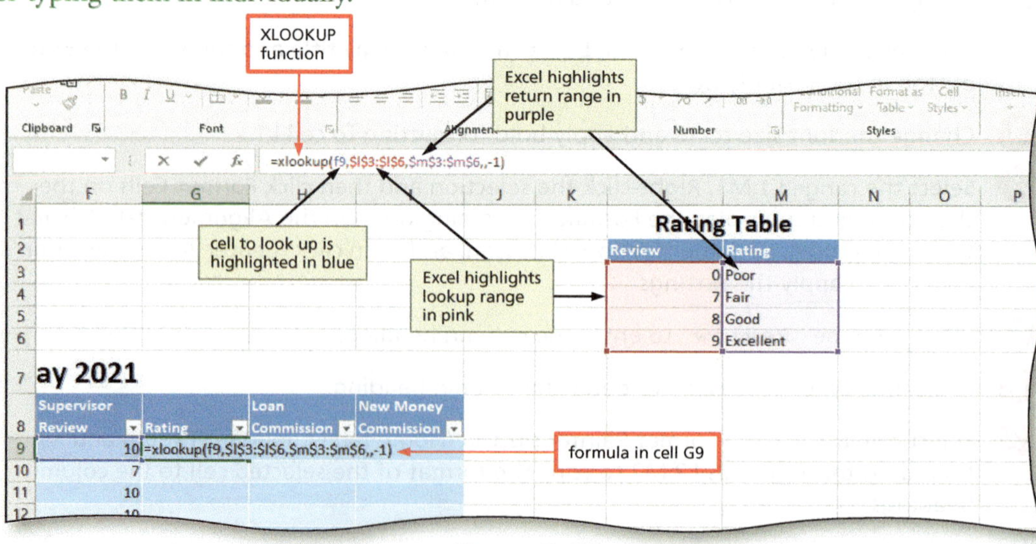

Figure 6–18

Q&A **Why should I use absolute cell references in the function?**
You need to use absolute cell references, indicated by the dollar signs, so that Excel will not adjust the table array location when it creates the calculated column in the next step. If Excel adjusted the cell references, you would see incorrect results in column G.

2

- Click the Enter button to create a calculated column for the selected field, the Rating field in this case.
- Scroll the worksheet to show the entire table with the completed column G (Figure 6–19).

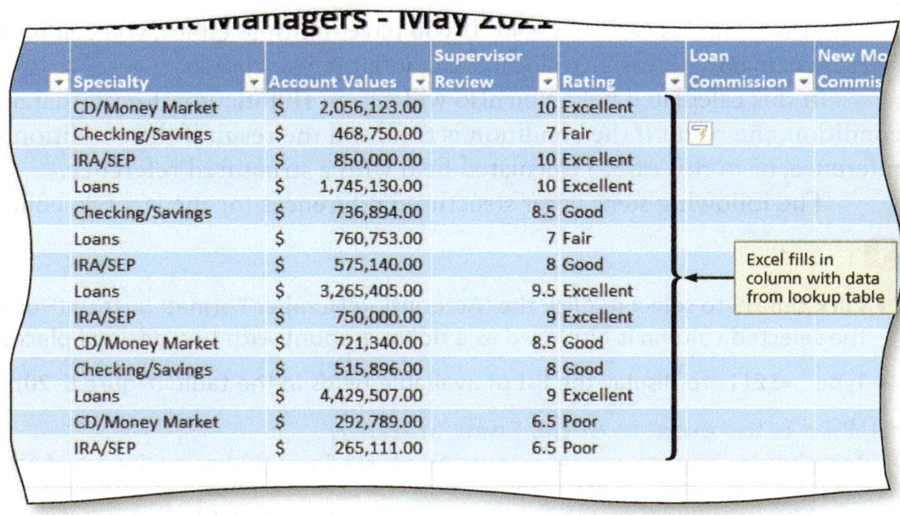

Figure 6–19

Q&A

What happens when you click the Enter button?
Because cell G9 is the first record in a table, Excel continues the calculated column by replicating the XLOOKUP function through row 22.

How does the XLOOKUP function determine the ratings?
The match_mode argument of -1 means the XLOOKUP function looks for an exact match; if it does not find one, it looks for the closest match less than the lookup value, and then returns the corresponding value from column M.

Other Ways

1. Click Insert Function box in formula bar, click 'Or select a category', click 'Lookup & Reference', click XLOOKUP in 'Select a function' list, click OK, enter arguments
2. Click 'Lookup & Reference' button (Formulas tab | Function Library group), click XLOOKUP, enter arguments

Adding Calculated Fields to the Table

A **calculated field** or **computational field** is a field (column) in a table that contains a formula, function, cell reference, structured reference, or condition. When you create a calculated field, Excel automatically fills in the column without the use of a fill or copy command; you do not have to use the fill handle to replicate formulas in a calculated field.

Table 6–4 describes the three calculated fields used in this project. You created the first one in the previous steps.

Table 6–4 Calculated Fields

Column Heading	Column	Calculated Field
Rating	G	Uses the XLOOKUP function to determine a rating based upon the Supervisor Review (column F).
Loan Commission	H	Uses the IF function to evaluate the Specialty column. If it is Loans, multiply the Account Values figure by .0025.
New Money Commission	I	Uses the IF function to evaluate the Specialty column. If it is not Loans, multiple the Account Values figure by .0002.

To Create Calculated Fields

When you type formulas in a calculated field, rather than using normal cell references, Excel allows you to type a structured reference. A **structured reference** is a reference that allows table formulas to refer to table columns by names that are automatically generated when the table is created. A structured reference uses some combination of the table name (such as Managers), the column heading (such as Account Values), or any named or special rows, rather than the usual column letter and row number references (such as E10). If you use a named row in a structured reference, you must use a # sign before the row name (such as #Totals). If a column heading used in a structured reference contains any spaces between words, its name must be enclosed in brackets (such as [Supervisor Review]).

Using structured references has several advantages. **Why?** Excel updates structured references automatically when any column heading changes or when you add new data to the table. Using this notation also makes formulas easier to read. If you have multiple tables, you can include the table name in the structured reference, making it easier to locate data in large workbooks.

In this calculated field, you also will use an IF function. Recall that an IF function has three parts: the condition, the result if the condition is true, and the result if the condition is false. The result can be a value, a reference, or in this case, a calculated field with a structured reference.

The following steps enter structured references for the last two columns of data in the table.

1

- Click cell H9 to select it. Click the 'Accounting Number Format' button (Home tab | Number group) so that data in the selected column is displayed as a dollar amount with two decimal places.
- Type `=if([` to display the list of available fields in the table (Figure 6–20).

Q&A **What is the purpose of the [(left bracket)?**
The [begins a structured reference and causes Excel to display the list of table fields (column headings).

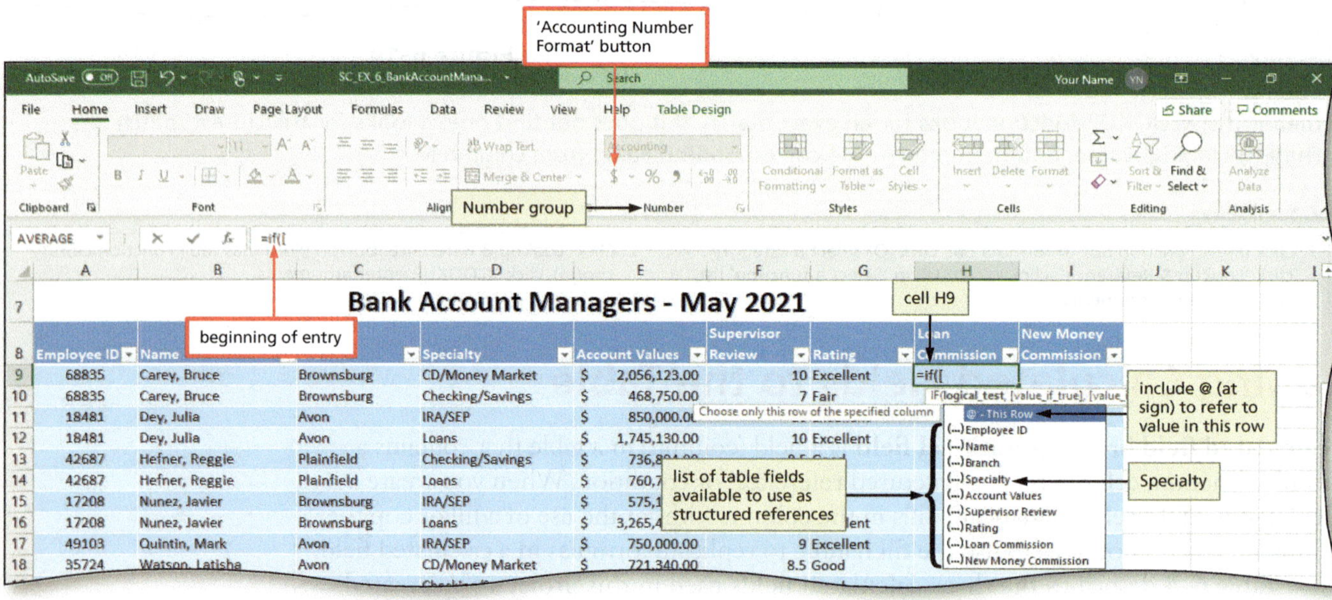

Figure 6–20

2

- Type @ to refer to the value in this row.
- Double-click Specialty to select the field to use for the IF function.
- Type `]="Loans", [@[Account Values]] *.0025,0)` to complete the structured reference and then click the Enter button to create the calculated column (Figure 6–21).

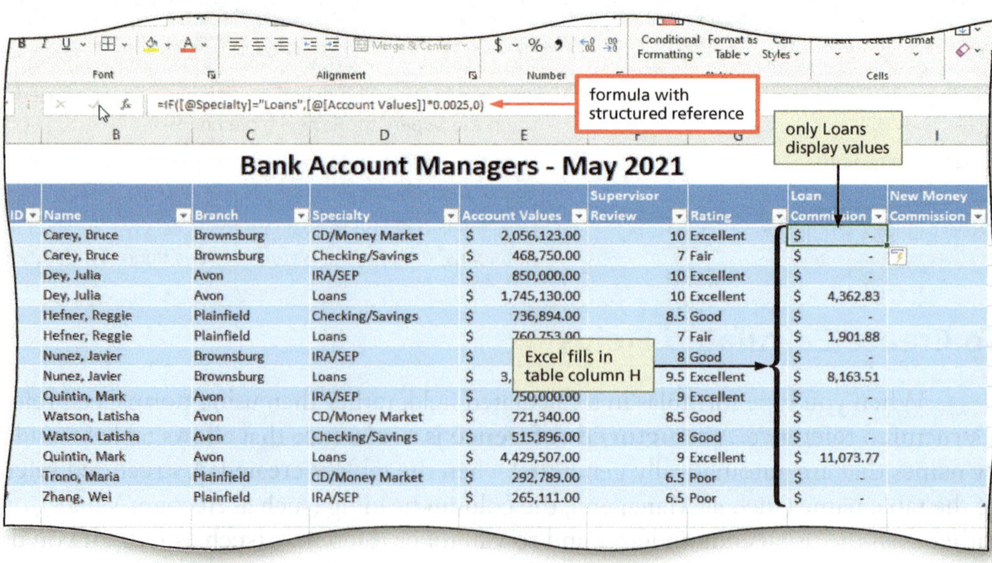

Figure 6–21

Q&A **Do I have to set the formatting before I enter the structured reference formula?**
No, you do not have to; however, applying formatting before entering the formula prompts Excel to generate the calculated column with your desired formatting. Otherwise, you would have to format the column manually after it generates.

Why am I multiplying by .0025?
The bank awards a commission of .25% to managers who negotiate loans.

Why does the structured reference to the Account Values field use a second set of brackets?
You insert an @ (at sign) and a field name within one set of brackets. If the field name includes a space, add brackets around the name, as in [@[Account Values]].

3

- Click cell I9 to select it.
- Click the 'Accounting Number Format' button (Home tab | Number group).
- Type `=if (` and click cell D9 to insert a field name, type `= "Loans", 0,` and click cell E9 to insert a field name, type `*.0002)` and then click the Enter button to create a calculated column (Figure 6–22).
- Click the Save button on the Quick Access Toolbar to save the workbook again.

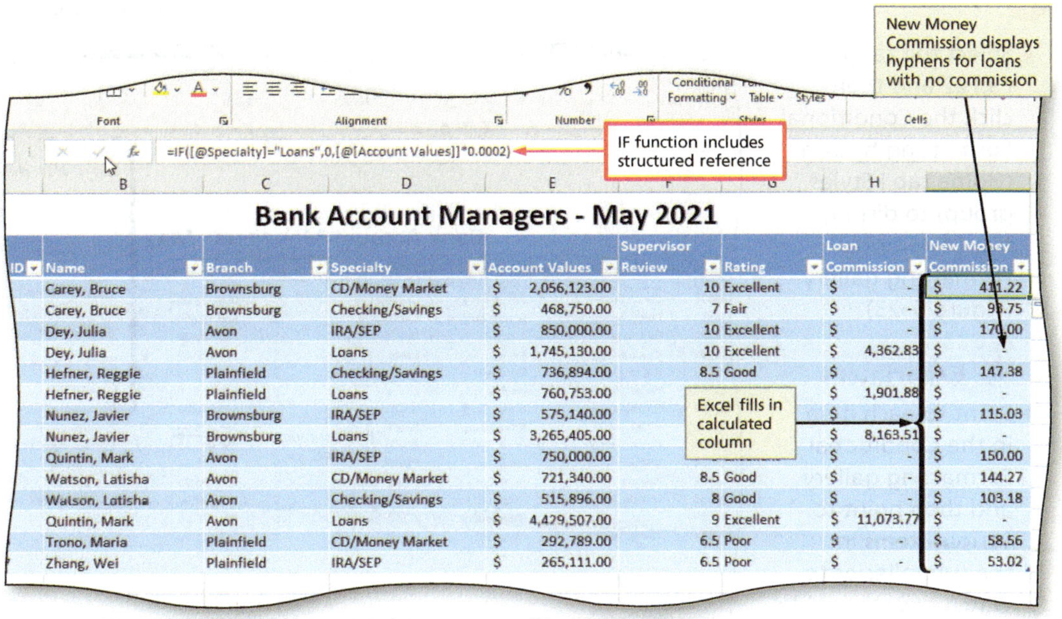

Figure 6–22

Q&A **How is this IF function different from the one in Step 2?**
In this entry, if the Specialty is Loans, then no amount will be entered—the "true" part of the function. The "false" part of the function will multiply all others by the commission rate of .0002.

Conditional Formatting

Conditional formatting allows you to create rules that change the formatting of a cell based on its value. For example, you might want negative values to appear highlighted in red. Excel includes five preset types of conditional formats: highlight, top and bottom rules, data bars, color scales, and icon sets, as well as the ability to create your own conditional formats. You can combine different types of formats on any cell or range. For example, based on a cell's value, you can format it to include both an icon and a specific background color.

The Conditional Formatting Rules Manager dialog box allows you to view all of the rules for the current selection or for an entire worksheet and change the order in which the rules are applied to a cell or range. In addition, you can stop applying subsequent rules after one rule is found to be true. For example, if the first rule specifies that a negative value should appear in red, then you may not want to apply any other conditional formats to the cell.

To Add a Conditional Formatting Rule with an Icon Set

In the Managers table, the Supervisor Review field provides succinct feedback to the user about performance of the account managers. Recall that you also created Rating words based on the XLOOKUP table. Another method to present the information visually is to display an icon next to the Supervisor Review number. Conditional formatting provides a variety of icons, including traffic signals, circles, flags, bars, and arrows. Icon sets include sets of three, four, or five icons. **Why?** You choose an icon set depending on how many ways you want to group your data. In the case of the ratings for the account managers, you will use four different icons. Once you choose an icon set, you define rules for each of the conditions. The following steps add a conditional format to the Supervisor Review field in the Managers table.

1

- Select the range F9:F22 and then click the Conditional Formatting button (Home tab | Styles group) to display the Conditional Formatting gallery (Figure 6–23).

Experiment

- Point to each item in the Conditional Formatting gallery and then point to various items in the subgalleries to watch how the table changes.

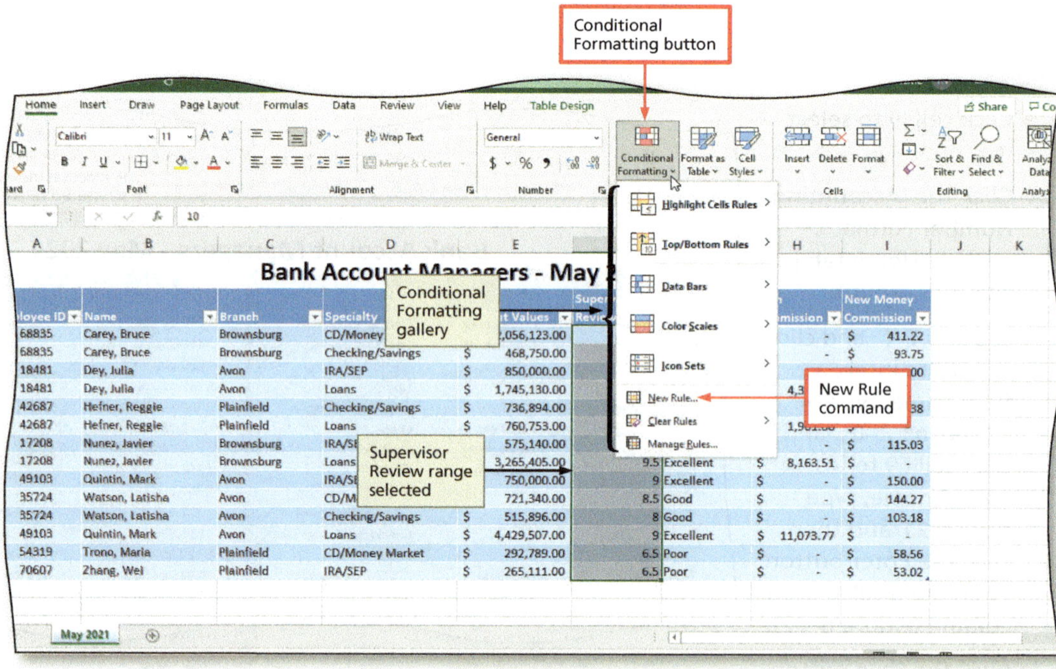

Figure 6–23

2

- Click New Rule in the Conditional Formatting gallery to display the New Formatting Rule dialog box.
- Click the Format Style button (New Formatting Rule dialog box) to display the Format Style list (Figure 6–24).

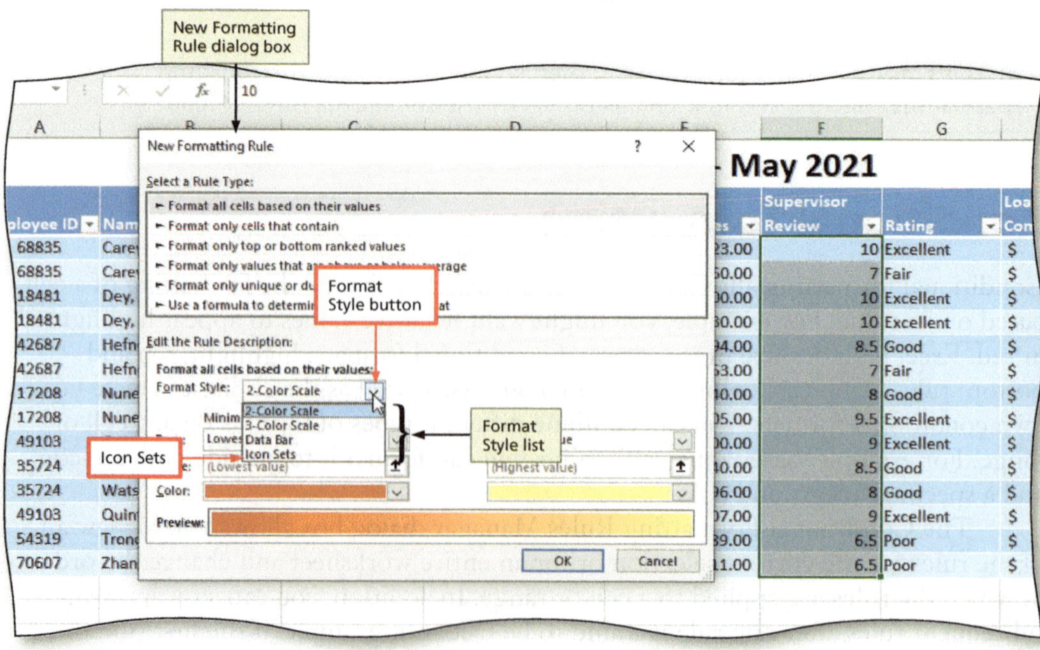

Figure 6–24

Q&A **What do the color scale formats do?** You can choose between two or three values and apply different color backgrounds. Excel graduates the shading from one value to the next.

3

- Click Icon Sets in the Format Style list (New Formatting Rule dialog box) to display the Icon Style area.
- Click the Icon Style arrow to display the Icon Style list and then scroll as necessary to display the '4 Traffic Lights' icon style in the list (Figure 6–25).

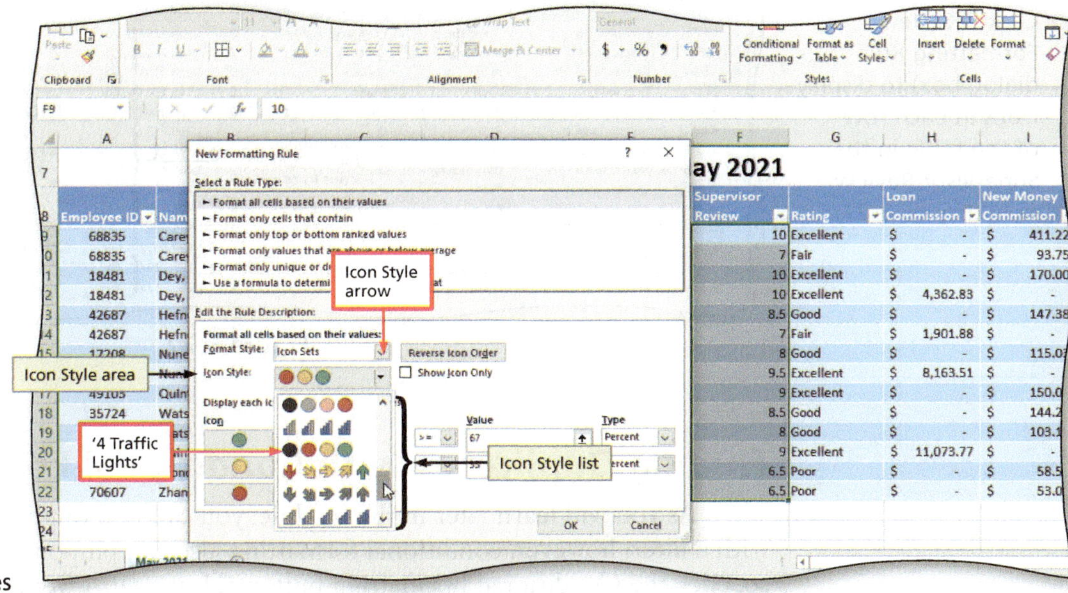

Figure 6–25

Experiment

- Click a variety of icon styles in the Icon Styles list to view the options for each style.

4

- Click the '4 Traffic Lights' icon style in the Icon Style list (New Formatting Rule dialog box) to select an icon style that includes four different circles.
- Click the first Type button and then click Number in the list to select a numeric value.
- Click the second Type button and then click Number in the list. Click the third Type button and then click Number in the list.
- Type 9 in the first Value box. Type 8 in the second Value box. Type 7 in the third Value box and then press TAB to complete the conditions (Figure 6–26).

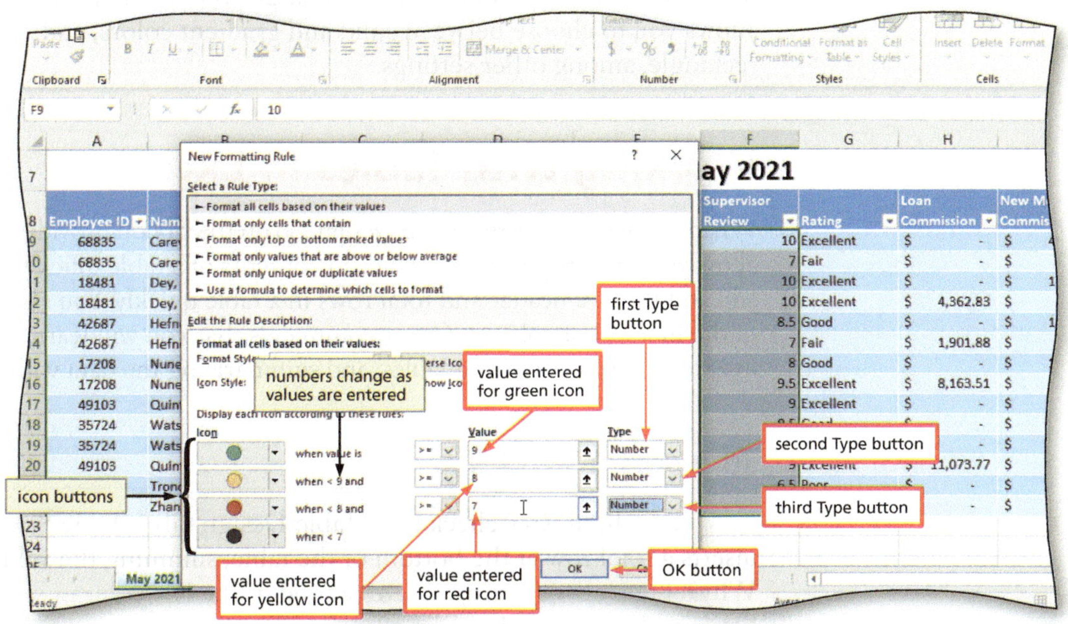

Figure 6–26

Q&A

Why do the numbers next to each icon change as I type?

Excel automatically updates this area as you change the conditions. Use this area as an easy-to-read status of the conditions that you are creating.

5

- Click OK (New Formatting Rule dialog box) to display icons in each row of the table in the Supervisor Review field (Figure 6–27).

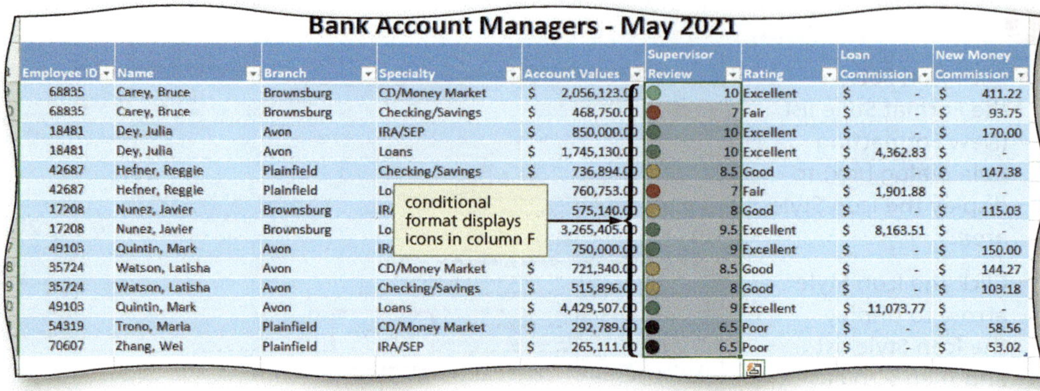

Figure 6–27

Finding Duplicates with Conditional Formatting

As you will learn later in the module, you can find duplicate values or records with a filter; however, conditional formatting also can pinpoint duplicates easily. To do so, click the Conditional Formatting button (Home tab | Styles group), and then click New Rule. When Excel displays the New Formatting Rule dialog box, click 'Format only unique or duplicate values' in the Select a Rule Type area (see Figure 6–26). You then can choose a highlight, style, or other format for duplicate values.

Data Bars

Another popular conditional formatting option is data bars. Chosen from the Conditional Formatting gallery (see Figure 6–23), **data bars** display as colored, horizontal rectangles in the cell. The larger the number, the wider the data bar. Excel allows you to choose between solid and gradient colors, and select the direction of the rectangle, among other settings.

Working with Tables in Excel

When a table is active, the Table Design tab on the ribbon provides powerful commands that allow you to alter the appearance and contents of a table quickly. For example, you can add and remove header and total rows in a table quickly. You also can change the style of the first or last column. Other commands that you will learn in later modules include inserting slicers, exporting tables, and summarizing the data with a PivotTable.

To Insert a Total Row

The Total Row check box (Table Design tab | Table Style Options group) inserts a total row at the bottom of the table, summing the values in the last column. **Why?** The default setting creates a total in the last column; however, total rows display a button beside each cell to create other totals and functions. If the values are nonnumeric, then Excel counts the number of records and puts that number in the total row. The following steps create a total row.

1

- Click anywhere in the table and then display the Table Design tab (Figure 6–28).

Experiment

- Select a variety of combinations of check boxes in the Table Style Options group on the Table Design tab to see their effect on the table. When finished, make sure that the check boxes are set as shown in Figure 6–28.

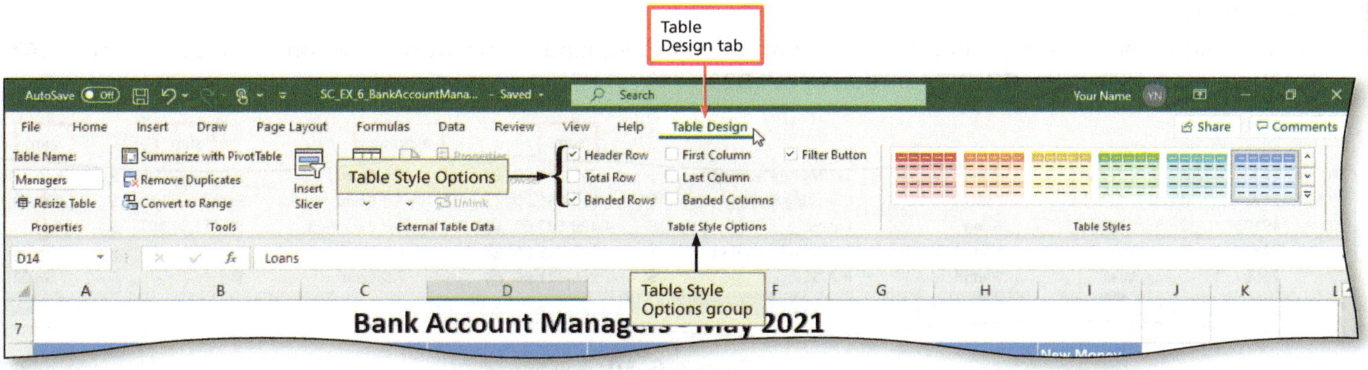

Figure 6–28

2

- Click the Total Row check box (Table Design tab | Table Style Options group) to display the total row and display the sum in the last column of the table, cell I23 in this case.
- Select cell E23 in the total row and then click the arrow on the right side of the cell to display a list of available functions (Figure 6–29).

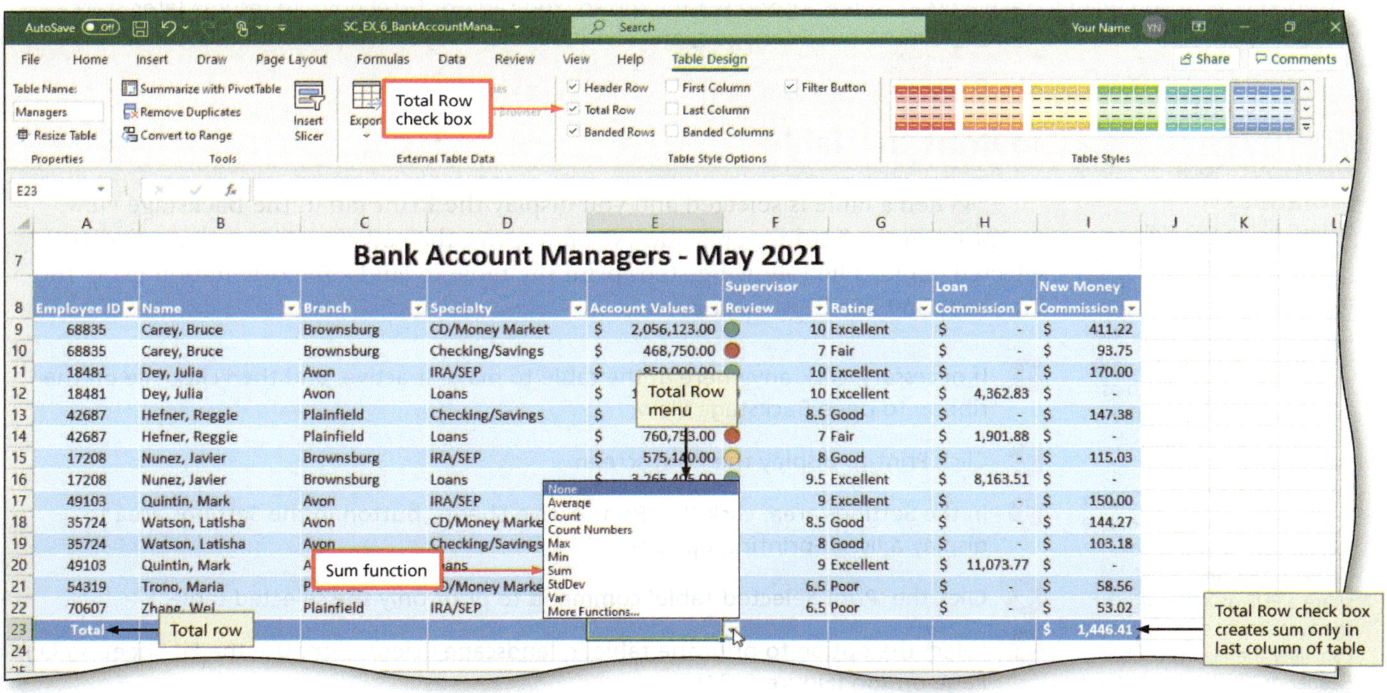

Figure 6–29

3

- Click Sum in the list to select the Sum function for the selected cell in the total row, thus totaling the account values.
- Repeat the process to create an average in cell F23 (Supervisor Review), thus averaging the supervisor reviews. Format the cell by decreasing the decimals to two decimal places. Repeat the process to create a sum in cell H23 (Loan Commission) (Figure 6–30).

Experiment

- Choose cells in the total row and experiment with the different kinds of statistical functions, such as using the MAX function in cell H23 or the COUNT function in cell D23.

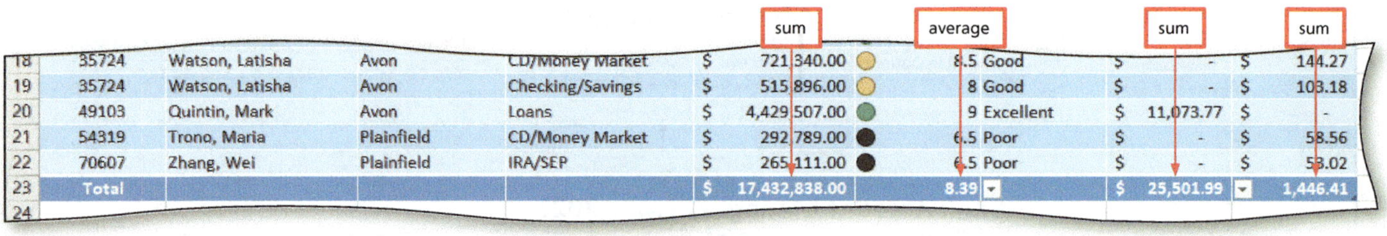

Figure 6–30

4

- Click the Save button on the Quick Access Toolbar to save the workbook again.

Other Ways

1. Right-click table, point to Table on shortcut menu, click Totals Row on submenu

Break Point: If you want to take a break, this is a good place to do so. You can exit Excel now. To resume later, start Excel, open the file called SC_EX_6_BankAccountManagers, and continue following the steps from this location forward.

BTW
Distributing a Workbook
Instead of printing and distributing a hard copy of a workbook, you can distribute the workbook electronically. Options include sending the workbook via email; posting it on cloud storage (such as OneDrive) and sharing the file with others; posting it on social media, a blog, or other website; and sharing a link associated with an online location of the workbook. You also can create and share a PDF or XPS image of the workbook, so that users can view the file in Acrobat Reader or XPS Viewer instead of in Excel.

To Print the Table

When a table is selected and you display the Print tab in the Backstage view, an option in the Settings area allows you to print the contents of just the active, or selected, table. The following steps print the table in landscape orientation using the Fit Sheet on One Page option.

1. If necessary, click anywhere in the table to make it active, and then click File on the ribbon to open Backstage view.
2. Click Print to display the Print screen.
3. In the Settings area, click the 'Print Active Sheets' button in the Settings area to display a list of printing options.
4. Click the 'Print Selected Table' command to print only the selected table.
5. Select the option to print the table in landscape orientation. Use the Fit Sheet on One Page option (Figure 6–31).
6. Click the Print button to print the table.

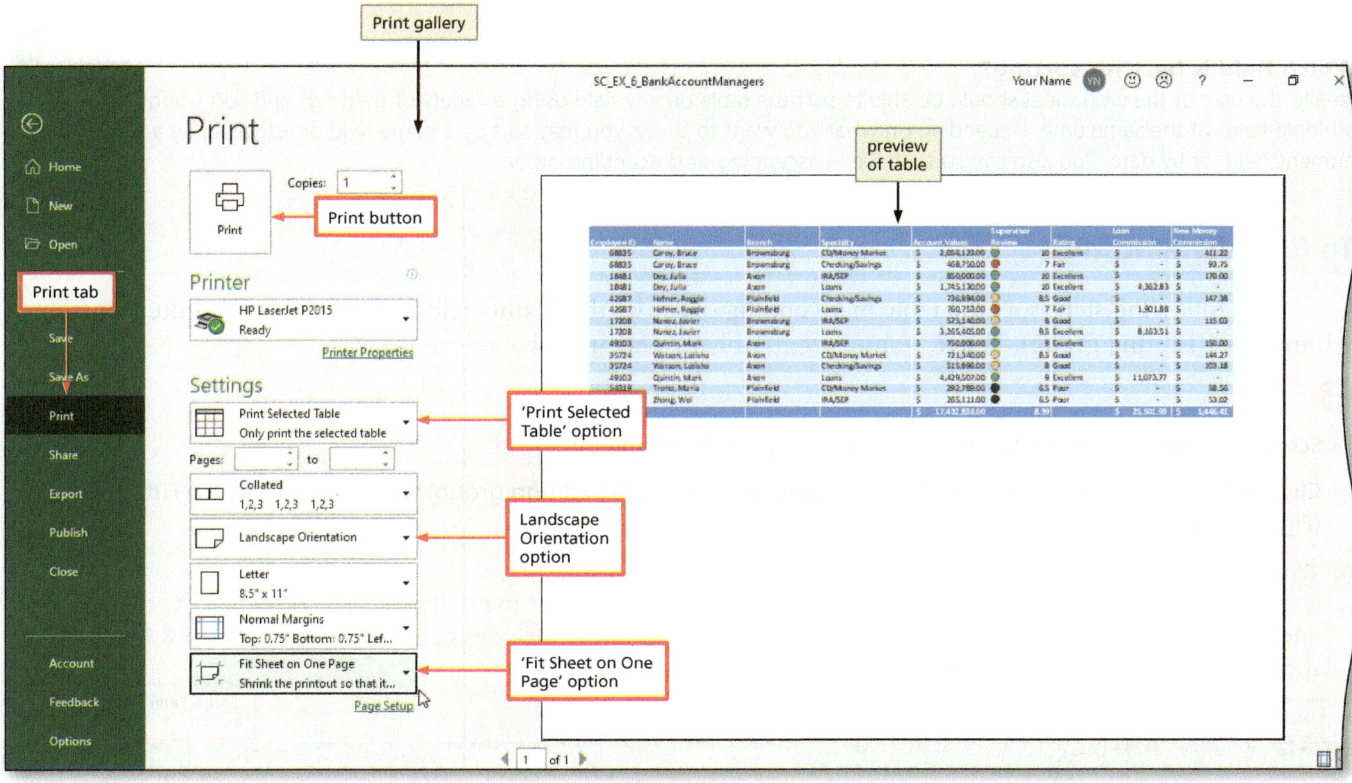

Figure 6–31

Sorting a Table

The data in a table is easier to work with and more meaningful if the records appear sequentially based on one or more fields. Arranging records in a specific sequence is called **sorting**. Data is in **ascending order** if it is sorted from lowest to highest, earliest to most recent, or alphabetically from A to Z. Data is in **descending order** if it is sorted from highest to lowest, most recent to earliest, or alphabetically from Z to A. The field or fields you select to sort are called **sort keys**. When you sort a table, all of the records in each row move together, so even if the selected cell is in the last name column, for example, the first name and all data in the row will be moved when the table is sorted by last name. It is always a good idea to save a copy of your worksheet before applying sorts.

You can sort data in a table by using one of the following techniques:

- Select a cell in the field on which to sort, click the 'Sort & Filter' button (Home tab | Editing group), and then click one of the sorting options on the Sort & Filter menu.
- With the table active, click the filter button in the column on which to sort and then click one of the sorting options on the menu.
- Use the Sort button (Data tab | Sort & Filter group).
- Use the 'Sort A to Z' or 'Sort Z to A' button (Data tab | Sort & Filter group).
- Right-click anywhere in a table and then point to Sort on the shortcut menu to display the Sort submenu.

BTW
Sorting Non-Table Data
If the data you wish to sort is not in a table, highlight the data first, then click the Sort & Filter button (Home tab | Editing group).

BTW
Sorting Dates
When you use AutoFilter to sort date fields, the filter menu will list commands such as 'Sort Newest to Oldest' and 'Sort Oldest to Newest.'

Consider This

Which field is best for sorting?

Ideally, the user of the worksheet should be able to sort the table on any field using a variety of methods and sort using multiple fields at the same time. Depending on what you want to show, you may sort by a name field or list value, by a numeric field, or by date. You also can sort a table in ascending or descending order.

To Sort Ascending

The following steps sort the table in ascending order by the Name field using the 'Sort & Filter' button (Home tab | Editing group). **Why?** Names commonly display in alphabetical order.

1

- Scroll to display the entire table. If necessary, display the Home tab.
- Click cell B9 and then click the 'Sort & Filter' button (Home tab | Editing group) to display the Sort & Filter menu (Figure 6–32).

Q&A **What if the column I choose includes numeric or date data?**
If the column you choose includes numeric data, then the Sort & Filter menu shows the 'Sort Smallest to Largest' and 'Sort Largest to Smallest' commands. If the column you choose includes date data, then the Sort & Filter menu shows the 'Sort Oldest to Newest' and 'Sort Newest to Oldest' commands.

Figure 6–32

2

- Click 'Sort A to Z' to sort the table in ascending order by the selected field, Name in this case (Figure 6–33).

Experiment

- Select other fields in the table and use the same procedure to sort on the fields you choose. When you are finished, remove any sorting, select cell A9, and repeat the two steps above.

Q&A **Can I undo the sort?**
Yes, you can click the Undo button (Quick Access Toolbar) or press CTRL+Z; however, if you close your file, the original order will be lost. If you want to undo a sort, it is a good practice to do so before continuing with other commands.

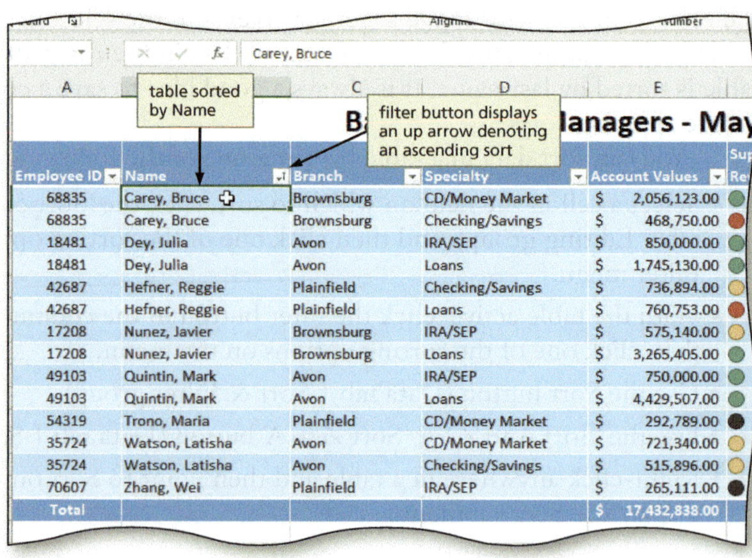

Figure 6–33

Other Ways

1. Select field in table, click 'Sort A to Z' button (Data tab | Sort & Filter group)
2. Click filter button of field on which to sort, click 'Sort A to Z'
3. Right-click column to sort, point to Sort on shortcut menu, click 'Sort A to Z'

To Sort Descending

The following step sorts the records in descending order by Account Values using the 'Sort Largest to Smallest' button on the Data tab. **Why?** Sometimes it is more convenient to use the Data tab and sort with a single click.

1

- Click cell E9 to position the sort in the Account Values column.
- Display the Data tab.
- Click the 'Sort Largest to Smallest' button (Data tab | Sort & Filter group) to sort the table in descending sequence by the selected field, Account Values, in this case (Figure 6–34).

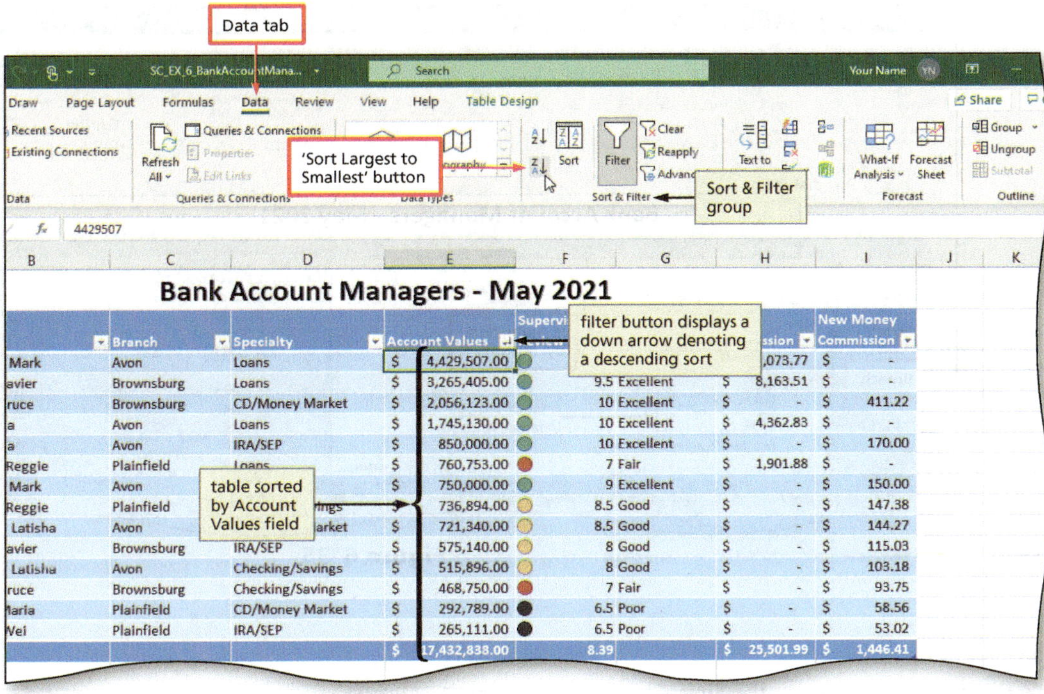

Figure 6–34

Other Ways

1. Select field in table, click 'Sort and Filter' button (Home tab | Editing group), click 'Sort Largest to Smallest'
2. Click filter button of field on which to sort, click 'Sort Largest to Smallest'
3. Right-click column to sort, point to Sort on shortcut menu, click 'Sort Largest to Smallest'

To Custom Sort a Table

While Excel allows you to sort on a maximum of 256 fields in a single sort operation, in these steps you will use the Custom Sort command to sort the Managers table using three fields. You will sort by Supervisor Review within Specialty within Branch. **Why?** That phrase means that the records within the table first are arranged by Branch (Avon, Brownsburg, or Plainfield). Then, within Branch, the records are arranged alphabetically by Specialty (CD/Money Market, Checking/Savings, IRA/SEP, Loans). Finally, within Specialty, the records are arranged from largest to smallest by the Supervisor Review number. In this case, Branch is the major sort key, Specialty is the intermediate sort key, and Supervisor Review is the minor sort key. You can sort any field in ascending or descending order, depending on how you want the data to look. The following steps sort the Managers table on multiple fields.

1

- Display the Home tab.
- With a cell in the table active, click the 'Sort & Filter' button (Home tab | Editing group) to display the Sort & Filter menu.
- Click Custom Sort on the Sort & Filter menu to display the Sort dialog box.
- Click the 'Column Sort by' button (Sort dialog box) to display the field names in the table (Figure 6–35).

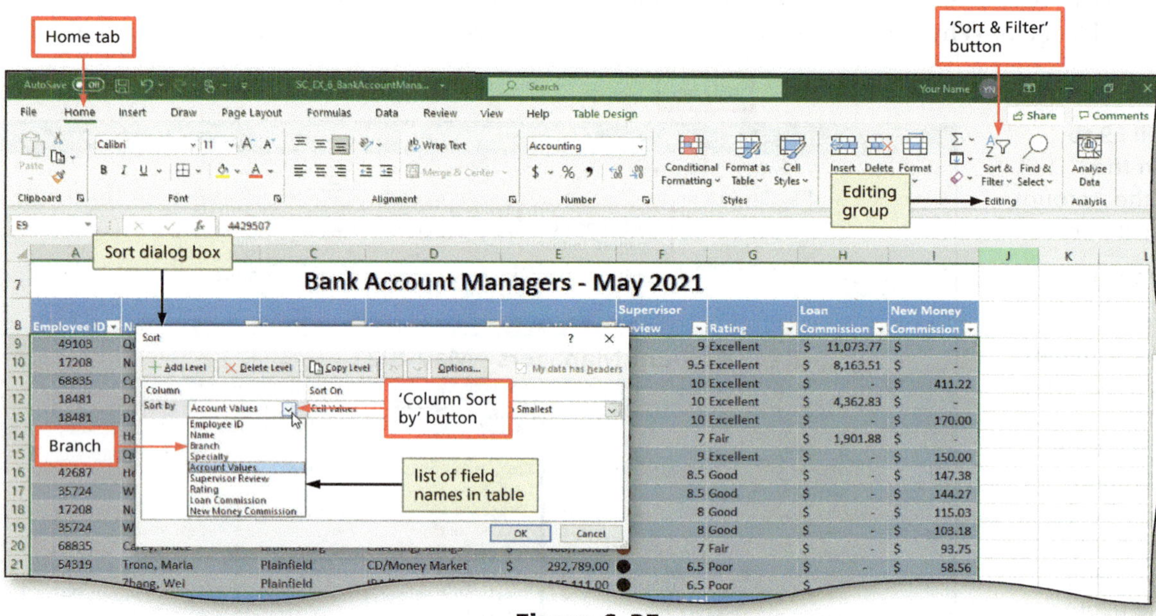

Figure 6–35

2

- Click Branch to select the first sort level, or major sort key.
- If necessary, click the Sort on button (Sort dialog box) and then click Cell Values in the Sort On list.
- If necessary, click the Order button and then click 'A to Z' to sort the field alphabetically (Figure 6–36).

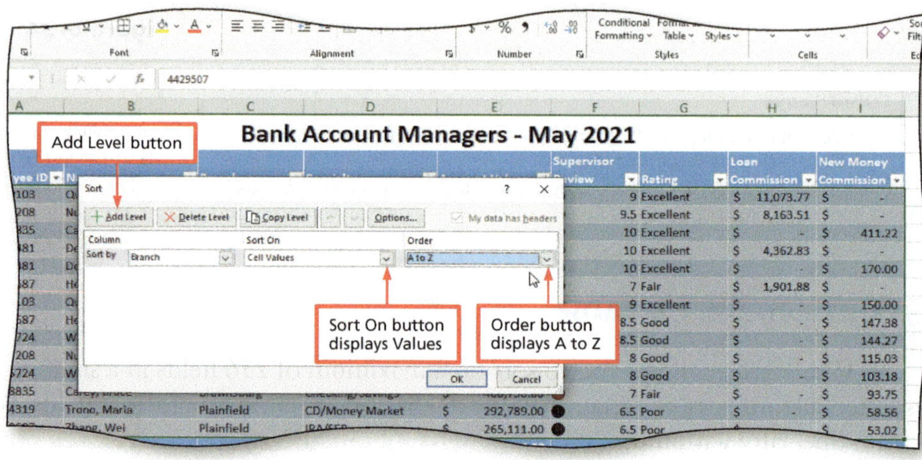

Figure 6–36

3

- Click the Add Level button (Sort dialog box) to add a second sort level.
- Click the Then by button and then click Specialty in the Then by list to select an intermediate sort key.

- If necessary, select Cell Values in the Sort On list.
- If necessary, select 'A to Z' in the Order list to sort the field alphabetically (Figure 6–37).

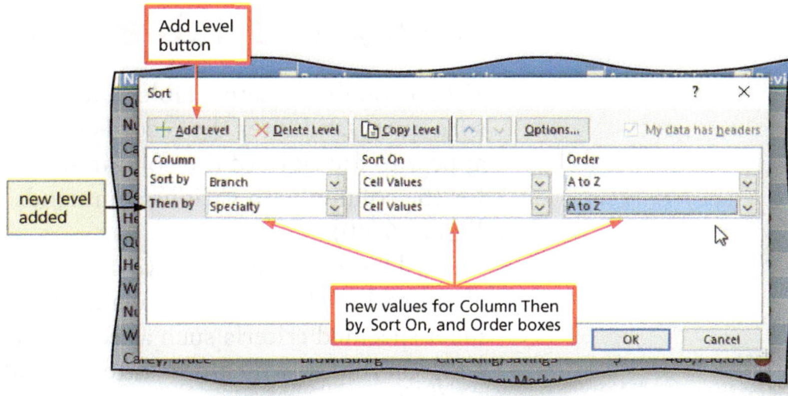

Figure 6–37

4

- Click the Add Level button to add a new sort level.
- Click the second Then by button and then click Supervisor Review to select a minor sort key.
- If necessary, select Cell Values in the Sort On list. Select 'Largest to Smallest' in the Order list to specify that the field should be sorted in reverse order (Figure 6–38).

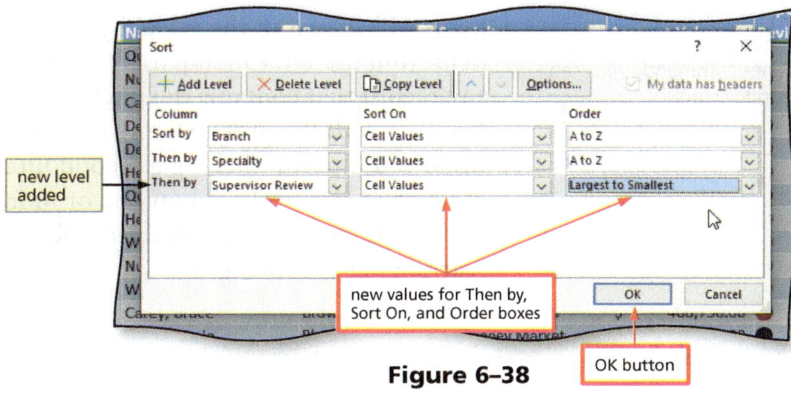

Figure 6–38

5

- Click OK to sort the table, in this case by Supervisor Review (descending) within Specialty (ascending) within Branch (ascending) (Figure 6–39).

Q&A

What should I do if I make a sorting error?
If you make a mistake in a sort operation, you can return the records to their previous order by clicking the Undo button on the Quick Access Toolbar or by pressing CTRL+Z. You can undo all steps back to when you originally opened the file—even if you have saved multiple times. Once you close the file however, you cannot undo a sorting error, and you would have to perform another sort.

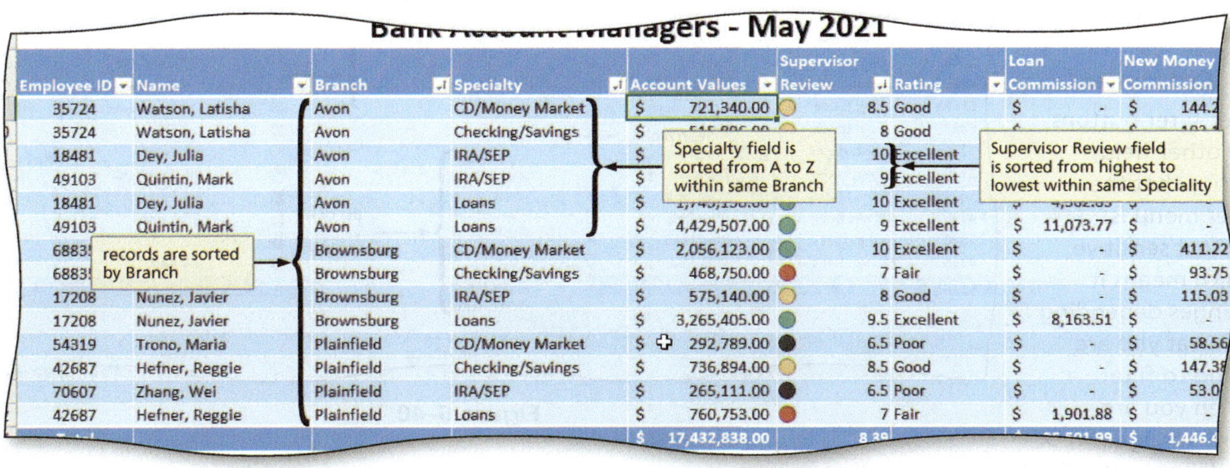

Figure 6–39

Querying a Table Using AutoFilter

When you first create a table, Excel automatically enables AutoFilter, a tool used to sort, query, and filter the records in a table. While using AutoFilter, the filter buttons appear to the right of the column headings. Clicking a button displays the filter menu for the column with various commands and a list of all items in the field (shown in Figure 6–40).

The sort commands work the same way as the sort buttons that you learned about earlier. The filter commands let you choose to display only those records that meet specified criteria such as color, number, or text. In this context, **criteria** means a logical rule by which data is tested and chosen. For example, you can filter the table to display a specific name or item by typing it in a Search box. The name you selected acts as the criterion for filtering the table, which results in Excel displaying only those records that match the criterion. Alternately, the selected check boxes indicate which items will appear in the table. By default, all of the items are selected. If you deselect an item from the filter menu, it is removed from the filter criterion. Excel will not display any record that contains the unchecked item.

As with the previous sort techniques, you can include more than one column when you filter by clicking a second filter button and making choices. The process of filtering records based on one or more filter criteria is called a **query**. After you filter data, you can copy, find, edit, format, chart, or print the filtered data without rearranging or moving it.

BTW

Scrolling Tables
When you scroll down in a table to display more rows, the column headings remain on the screen in a manner similar to using the Freeze Panes command (View tab | Window group).

To Sort a Table Using AutoFilter

The following steps sort the table by Account Values using the 'Sort Smallest to Largest' command on the filter menu. **Why?** Using the filter menu sometimes is easier than other sort methods; you do not have to leave the table area and move to the ribbon to perform the sort.

1

- Click the filter button in the Account Values column to display the filter menu (Figure 6–40).

Experiment

- Click filter buttons for other fields. Notice that the filter menu is context sensitive, which means it changes depending on what you are trying to filter. When you are finished, again click the Filter button in the Account Values column.

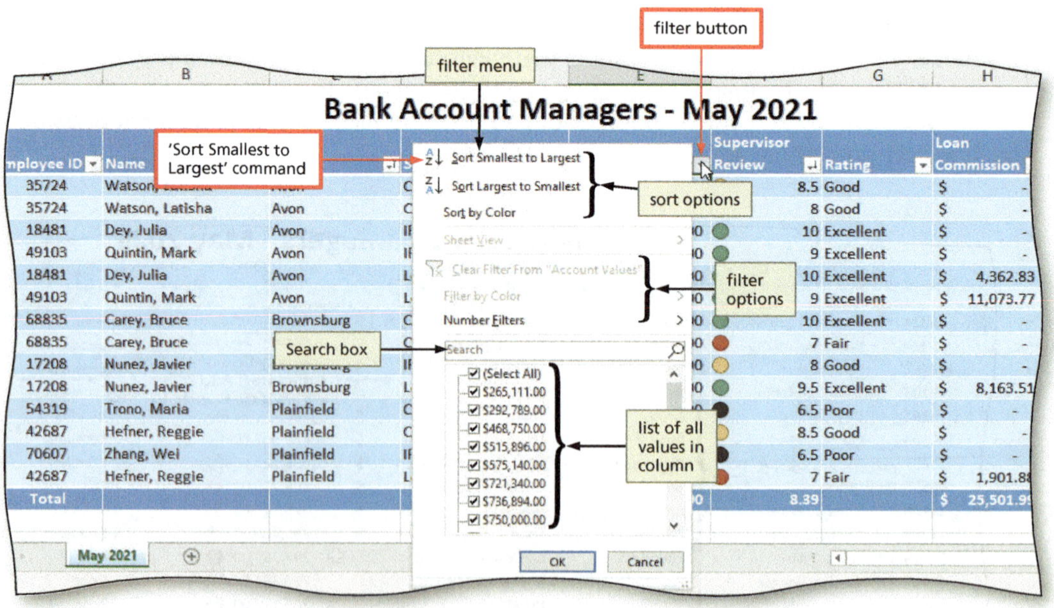

Figure 6–40

2

- Click 'Sort Smallest to Largest' on the filter menu to sort the table in ascending sequence by the selected field (Figure 6–41).

Q&A **Does performing a new sort overwrite the previous sort?**
Yes. A new sort undoes the previous sort, even if it is a custom sort or a sort based on multiple sort keys.

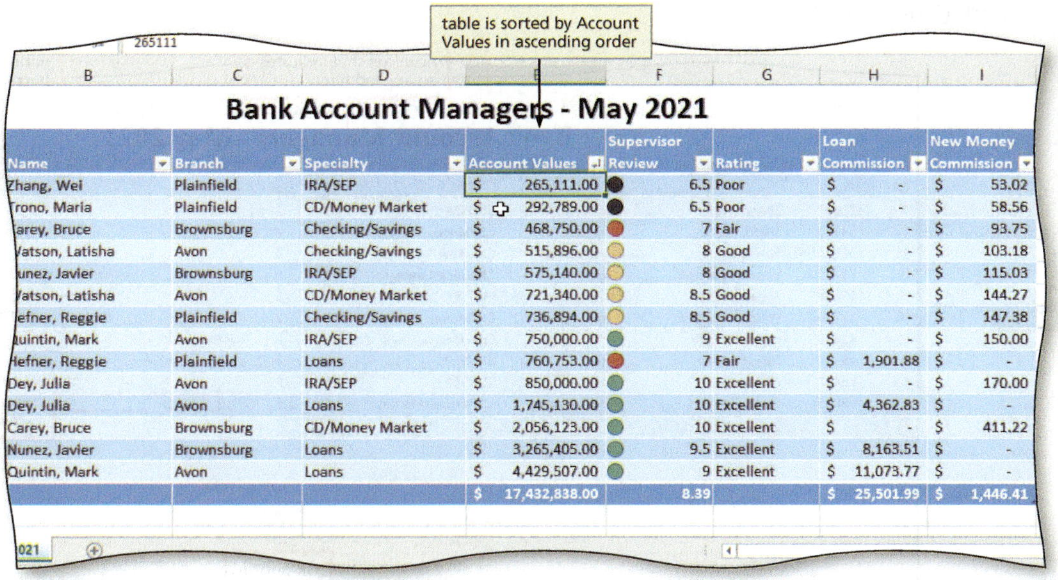

Figure 6–41

To Query a Table Using AutoFilter

The following steps query the Managers table using AutoFilter. **Why?** The AutoFilter will cause the table to display only specific records, which may be helpful in very large tables. In this case, using the check boxes on the filter menu, you will choose those records with a Specialty not equal to Loans and whose Rating is equal to Excellent.

1

- Click the filter button in cell D8 to display the filter menu for the Speciality column.
- Click Loans in the filter menu to remove the checkmark and cause Excel to hide rows for all managers who specialize in loans (Figure 6–42).

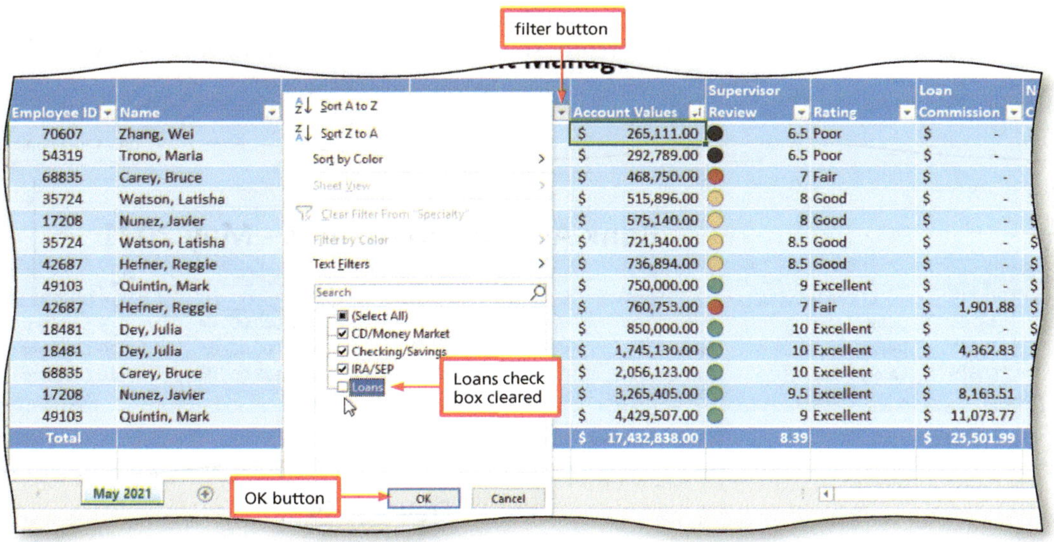

Figure 6–42

Q&A **What else appears on the filter menu?**
Below the Text Filters command is a list of all of the values that occur in the selected column. A check mark in the top item, (Select All), indicates that all values for this field are displayed in the table.

2

- Click OK to apply the AutoFilter criterion and display the records for all specialties except Loans.
- Click the filter button in cell G8 to display the filter menu for the Rating column.

- Click to remove the check marks beside Fair, Good, and Poor, so that only the Excellent check box contains a check mark (Figure 6–43).

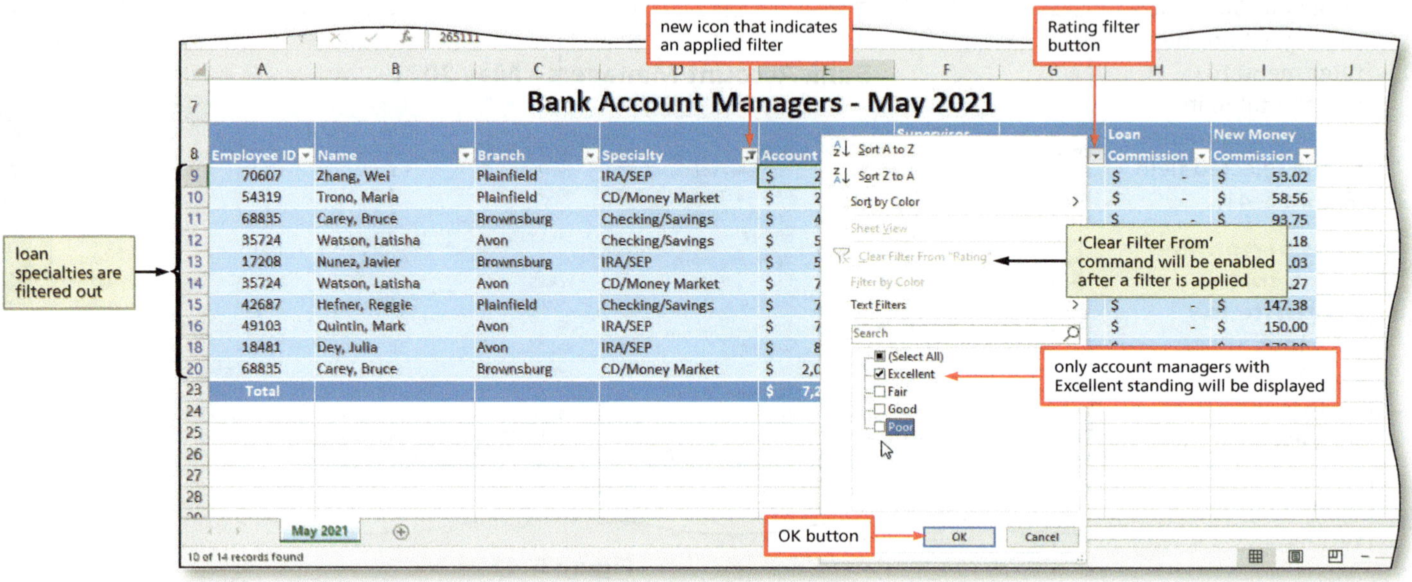

Figure 6–43

3

- Click OK to apply the AutoFilter criterion (Figure 6–44).

Q&A

Are both filters now applied to the table?
Yes. When you select a second filter criterion, Excel adds it to the first; hence, each record must pass two tests to appear as part of the final subset of the table.

Did the filter remove the previous sort?
No. Notice in Figure 6–44 that the records still are sorted in ascending order by Account Values.

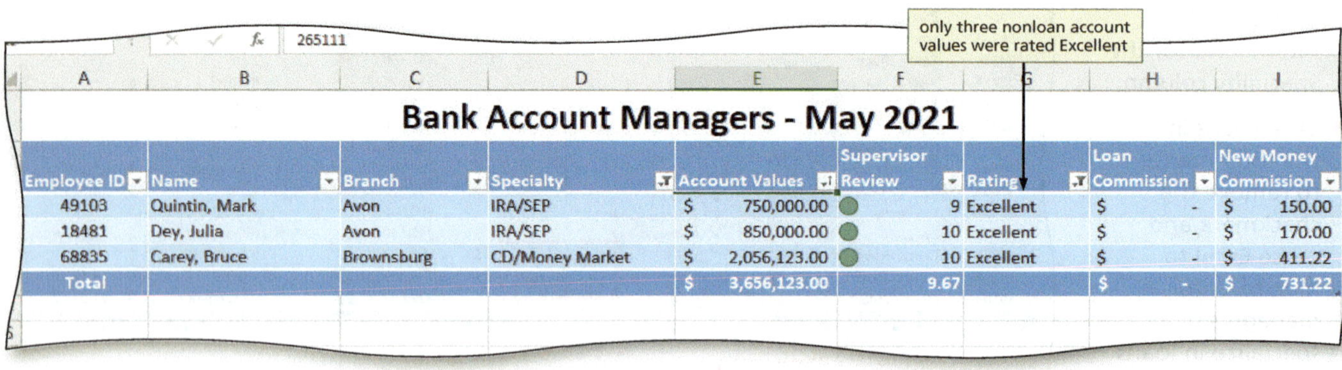

Figure 6–44

Other Ways

1. Click filter button, enter desired data in Search box (filter menu), click OK

To Remove Filters

You can remove a filter from a specific column or remove all of the filters in a table at once. Each filter menu has a 'Clear Filter From' command that removes the column filter (shown in Figure 6–43). The Clear button (Data tab | Sort & Filter group) removes all of the filters. The following step removes all filters at once to show all records in the table. **Why?** The filters, or query, hid some of the records in the previous steps.

1

- Click anywhere in the table and display the Data tab.
- Click the Clear button (Data tab | Sort & Filter group) to display all of the records in the table (Figure 6–45).

Figure 6–45

Other Ways

1. Click desired filter button, click (Select All) on filter menu
2. Right-click filtered column, point to Filter on shortcut menu, click 'Clear Filter From' command

To Search a Table Using AutoFilter

Using AutoFilter, you can search for specific records by entering data in the Search box. The sequence of data you enter is called the **search string**. For example, in a student table, you might want to search for a specific student ID number that might be difficult to locate in a large set of records. If an exact match exists, the value appears in the filter menu; then, if you click OK, the entire record appears in the table. Table searches are not case sensitive.

Alternately, you can search for similar or related data. In the Search box, you can type `?` (question mark) to represent any single character. For example in a quiz table, if you wanted to find answer1, answer2, and answer3, you could type `answer?` as the search string. Another way to search includes using an * (asterisk) to represent a series of characters. For example, in an inventory table, to find all of the items that relate to drive, you could type `*drive*` in the Search box. The filter would display results such as flash drives, CD-R drive, and drivers. The ? and * are called **wildcard characters**.

The following steps search for a specific record in a table using the filter menu. **Why?** When tables are large, searching for individual records using the filter menu is quick and easy.

1

- Click the filter button in the Name column to display the filter menu.
- Click the Search box, and then type `nunez` as the search string (Figure 6–46).

Q&A **Is this search the same as using the Find command?**
No. This command searches for data within the table only and then displays all records that match the search string. Two records matching the search appear in Figure 6–47. The Find command looks over the entire worksheet and highlights one cell.

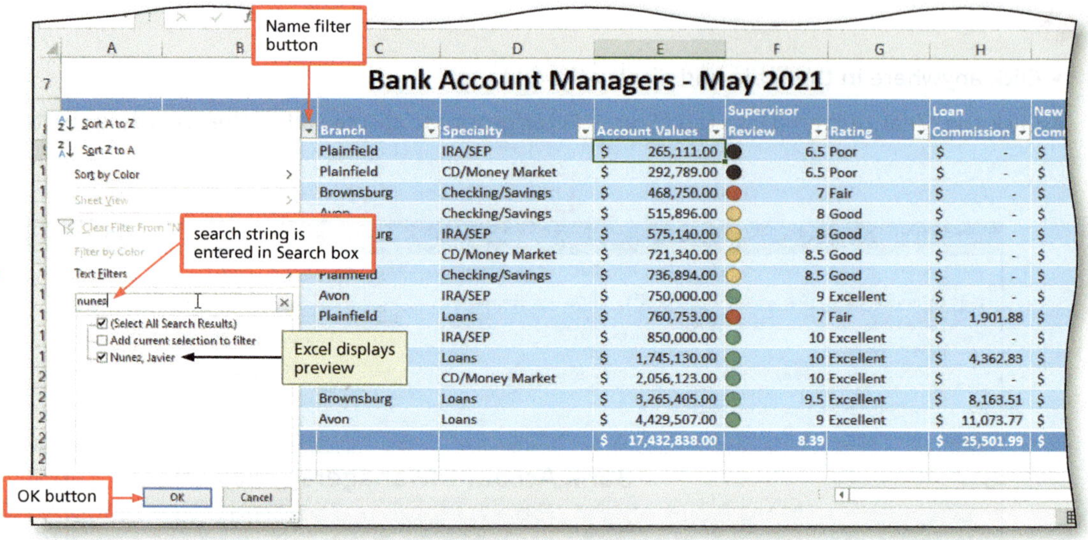

Figure 6–46

2

- Click OK to perform the search (Figure 6–47).

Experiment

- Search other columns for different kinds of data. Note that the total row reflects only the records displayed by the filter.

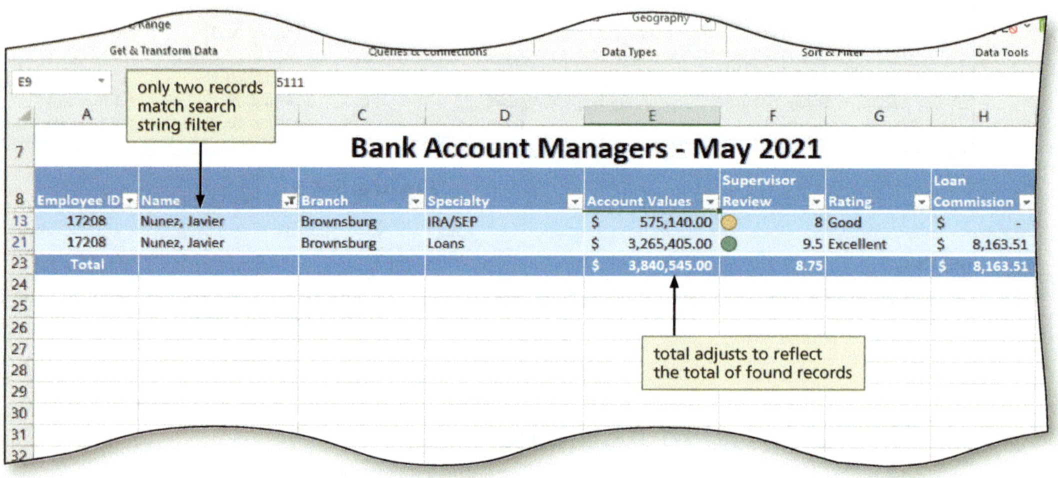

Figure 6–47

3

- Click the Clear button (Data tab | Sort & Filter group) to display all of the records in the table.

To Enter Custom Criteria Using AutoFilter

Another way to query a table is to use the Custom Filter command. The Custom Filter command allows you to enter custom criteria, such as multiple options or ranges of numbers. **Why?** Not all queries are exact numbers; many times a range of numbers is required. The following steps enter custom criteria to display records that represent managers whose Supervisor Review number is between 7 and 9, inclusive; that is, the number is greater than or equal to 7 and less than or equal to 9 (7 ≤ Supervisor Review ≤ 9).

1

- Click the filter button in cell F8 to display the filter menu for the Supervisor Review column.
- Point to Number Filters to display the Number Filters submenu (Figure 6–48).

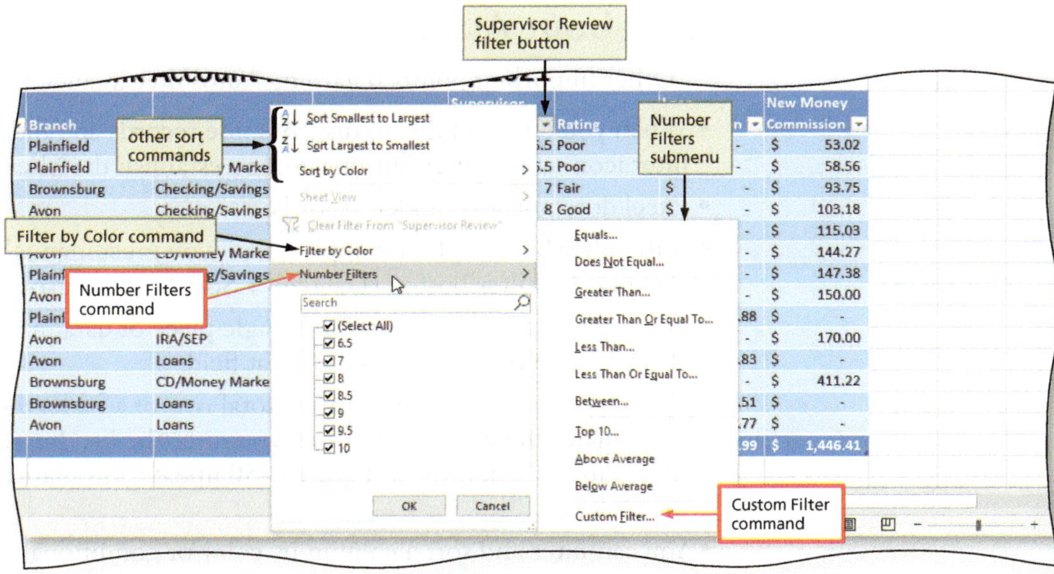

Figure 6–48

2

- Click Custom Filter on the Number Filters submenu to display the Custom AutoFilter dialog box.
- Click the first Supervisor Review button (Custom AutoFilter dialog box), click 'is greater than or equal to' in the list, and then type **7** in the first value box.
- Click the second Supervisor Review button. Scroll as necessary, and then click 'is less than or equal to' in the list. Type **9** in the second value box (Figure 6–49).

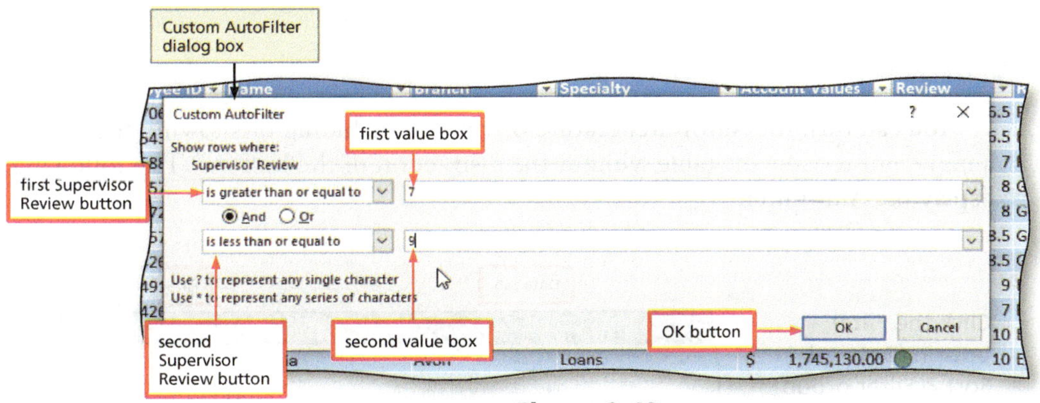

Figure 6–49

Q&A **How are the And and Or option buttons used?**
You can click option buttons to select the appropriate operator. The AND operator indicates that both parts of the criteria must be true; the OR operator indicates that only one of the two must be true.

3

- Click OK (Custom AutoFilter dialog box) to display records in the table that match the custom AutoFilter criteria, in this case, service calls in which the Supervisor Review number is between 7 and 9, inclusive (Figure 6–50).

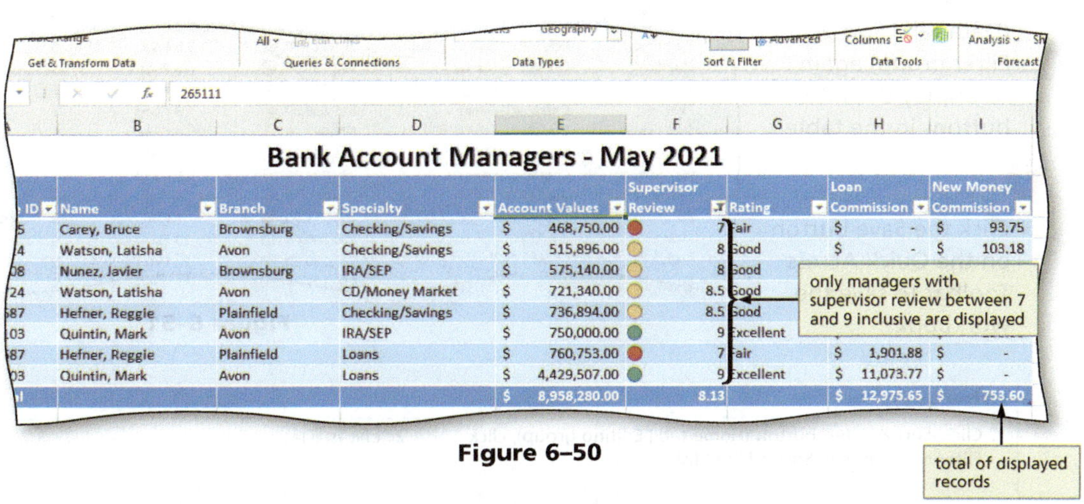

Figure 6–50

4

- Click the Clear button (Data tab | Sort & Filter group) to display all of the records in the table.

More about AutoFilters

Other important points regarding AutoFilter include the following:

- When you query a table to display some records and hide others, Excel displays a filter icon on the filter buttons used to establish the filter.
- Excel does not sort hidden records.
- If the filter buttons do not appear, then you must manually enable AutoFilter by clicking the Filter button (Data tab | Sort & Filter group).
- To remove a filter criterion for a single piece of data in a field, click the Select All check box on the filter menu for that field.
- When you create a formula in the total row of a table, the formula automatically recalculates the values even when you filter the list. For example, the results shown in the Total row in Figure 6–50 update automatically if you apply a filter to the table.
- You can filter and sort a column by color or conditional formatting using the 'Sort by Color' and 'Filter by Color' commands on the filter menu (shown in Figure 6–48).
- To reapply a filter or sort, click the Sort & Filter button (Home tab | Editing group), and then click Reapply.

To Turn Off AutoFilter

You can turn the AutoFilter feature off and on by hiding or showing the filter buttons. **Why?** Sometimes you may want to view the table without the distraction of the buttons. The following steps hide and then redisplay the AutoFilter.

1

- Click the Filter button (Data tab | Sort & Filter group) to hide the filter buttons in the table (Figure 6–51).

2

- Click the Filter button (Data tab | Sort & Filter group) again to display the filter buttons in the table.

3

- Click the Save button on the Quick Access Toolbar to save the workbook.

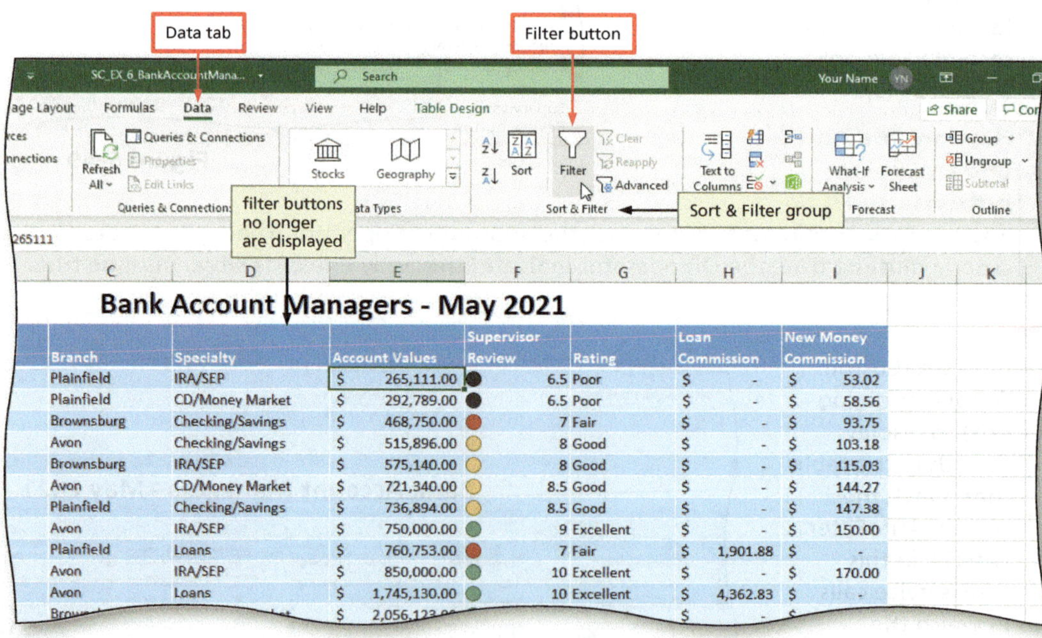

Figure 6–51

Other Ways

1. Click 'Sort & Filter' button (Home tab | Editing group), click Filter command in 'Sort & Filter' list
2. CTRL+SHIFT+L

Using Criteria and Extract Ranges

Another advanced filter technique called a criteria range manipulates records that pass comparison criteria. A **criteria range** is a location separate from the table used to list specific search specifications. Like a custom filter, a criteria range compares entered data with a list or table, based on column headings. Using a criteria range is sometimes faster than entering criteria through the AutoFilter system because once the range is established, you do not have to access any menus or dialog boxes to perform the query. You also can create an **extract range** in which Excel copies the records that meet the comparison criteria in the criteria range to another part of the worksheet.

Consider This

Does Excel provide another way to pull data out of a table?

Yes. You can create a criteria area and extract area on the worksheet. The criteria area can be used to enter rules regarding which records to extract, without having to change the AutoFilter settings. For example, the criteria area might ask for all full-time students with a grade of A from the table. The extract area can be used to store the records that meet the criteria. Extracting records allows you to pull data from a table so that you can analyze or manipulate the data further. For example, you may want to know which customers are delinquent on their payments. Extracting records that meet this criterion allows you then to use the records to create a mailing to such customers.

To Create a Criteria Range

When creating a criteria range, it is important to place it away from the table itself. Commonly, criteria ranges are located directly above the table. That way, if the table grows downward or to the right in the future, the criteria range will not interfere. Criteria ranges must include identical column headings to perform the search. It is a good practice to copy the necessary column headings rather than type them, to prevent errors. The following steps create a criteria range and copy the column headings.

1. Select the range A7:I8 and then press CTRL+C to copy the range.
2. Select cell A1 and then press ENTER to paste the Clipboard contents.
3. Change the title to `Criteria Range` in cell A1.
4. If necessary, use the format painter to copy the formatting from row 8 to row 2.
5. Select the range A2:I3, click the Name box, type `Criteria` as the range name, and then press ENTER (Figure 6–52).

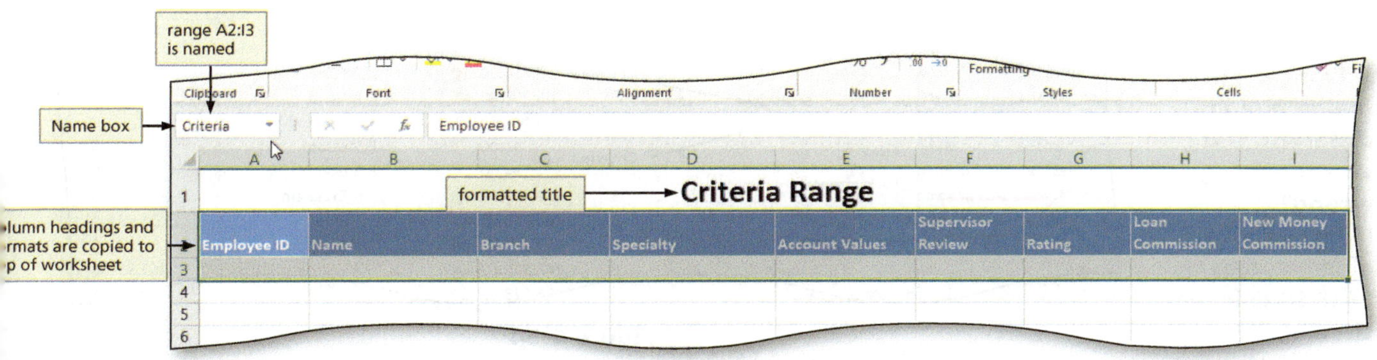

Figure 6–52

To Query Using a Criteria Range

The following steps use the criteria range and the Advanced Filter dialog box to query the table and display only the records that pass the test: Specialty = IRA/SEP AND Account Values > 300,000 AND Supervisor Review >= 8. The criteria data is entered directly below the criteria range headings. **Why?** Because the Advanced Filter dialog box searches for a match using column headings and adjacent rows.

1

- In cell D3, enter the criteria **IRA/SEP**, in cell E3 type **>300000**, and in cell F3 type **>=8** (Figure 6–53).
- If Excel turns off your filter buttons, click the Filter button (Data tab | Sort & Filter group).

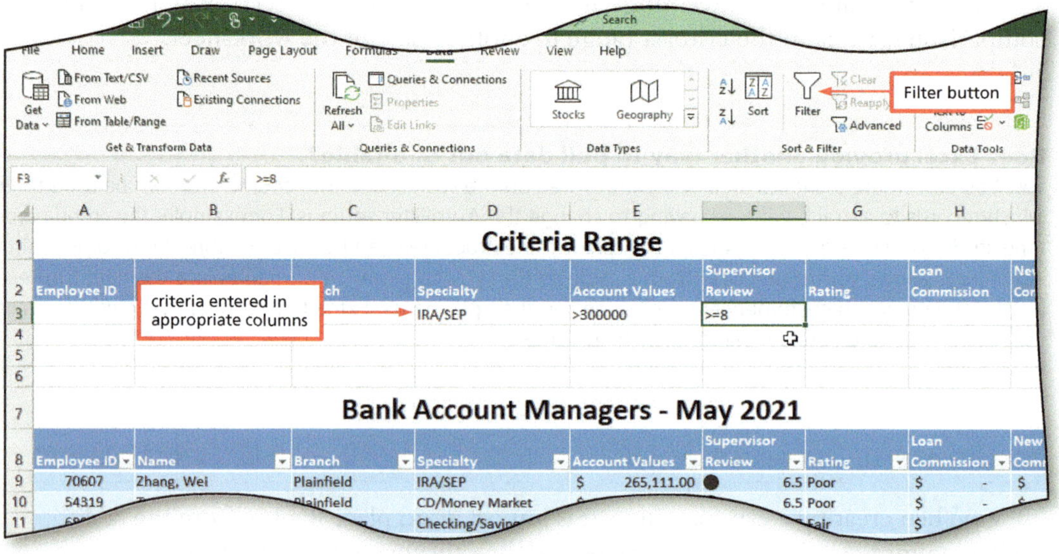

Figure 6–53

2

- Click the table to make it active.
- Click the Advanced button (Data tab | Sort & Filter group) to display the Advanced Filter dialog box (Figure 6–54).

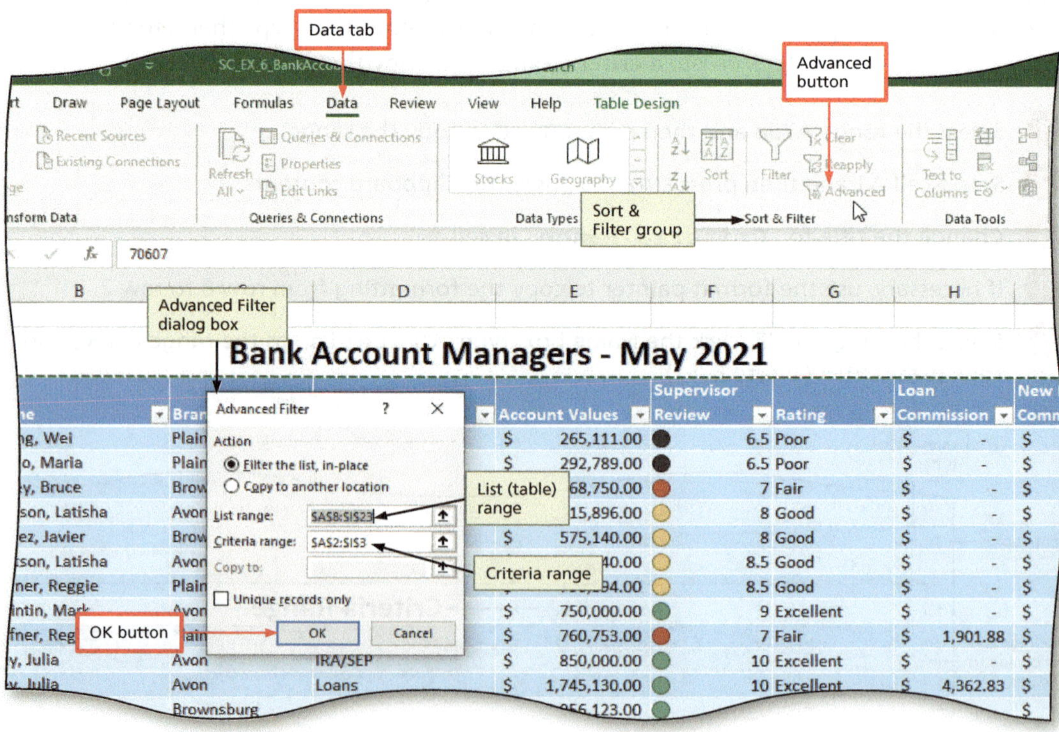

Figure 6–54

Q&A

My values in the Advanced Filter dialog box are different. Did I do something wrong?

If your values are different, type $A$8:$I$23 in the List range box. Excel selects the criteria range ($A$2:$I$3) in the Criteria range box, because you assigned the name Criteria to the range A2:I3 earlier.

3

- Click OK (Advanced Filter dialog box) to hide all records that do not meet the comparison criteria (Figure 6–55).

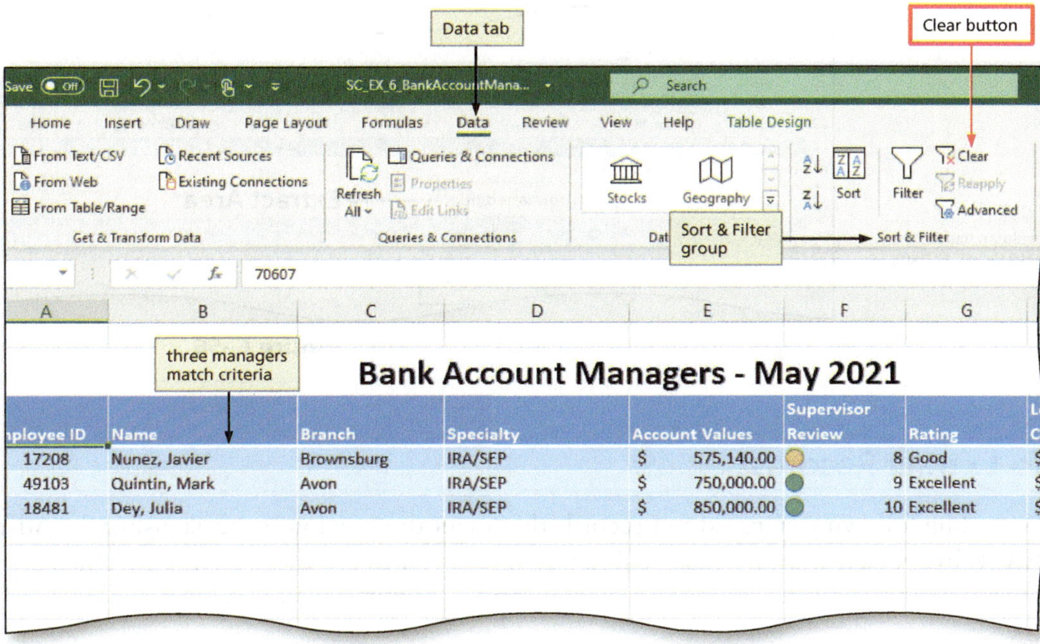

Figure 6–55

Q&A **What is the main difference between using the AutoFilter query technique and using the Advanced Filter dialog box with a criteria range?**
Like the AutoFilter query technique, the Advanced Filter command displays a subset of the table. The primary difference between the two is that the Advanced Filter command allows you to create more complex comparison criteria, because the criteria range can be as many rows long as necessary, allowing for many sets of comparison criteria.

4

- Click the Clear button (Data tab | Sort & Filter group) to show all records. If your banded rows no longer display correctly, click the 'Blue, Table Style Medium 14' button (Table Design tab | Table Styles group).

To Create an Extract Range

In the previous steps, you filtered data in place within the table itself; however, you can copy the records that meet the criteria to another part of the worksheet, rather than displaying them as a subset of the table. **Why?** Extracting the filtered data to another location leaves the table intact; and, it allows you to compare the data more easily. The following steps create an extract range below the table.

1. Select the range A7:I8 and then press CTRL+C to copy the range.
2. Select cell A25 and then press ENTER to paste the contents.
3. Change the title to `Extract Area` in cell A25.
4. Select the range A26:I45, click the Name box, type `Extract` as the range name, and then press ENTER.

Q&A **Why am I including so many rows in the extraction range?**
The table has many records; you want to make sure you have enough room for any search that the company might desire.

5. If necessary, use the format painter to copy the formatting and wrap column headings to match the table headings (Figure 6–56).

BTW
AND and OR Queries
If you want to create a query that includes searches on two fields, you enter the data across the same row in the criteria range. If you want to search for one piece of data OR another, enter the second piece of data on the next row.

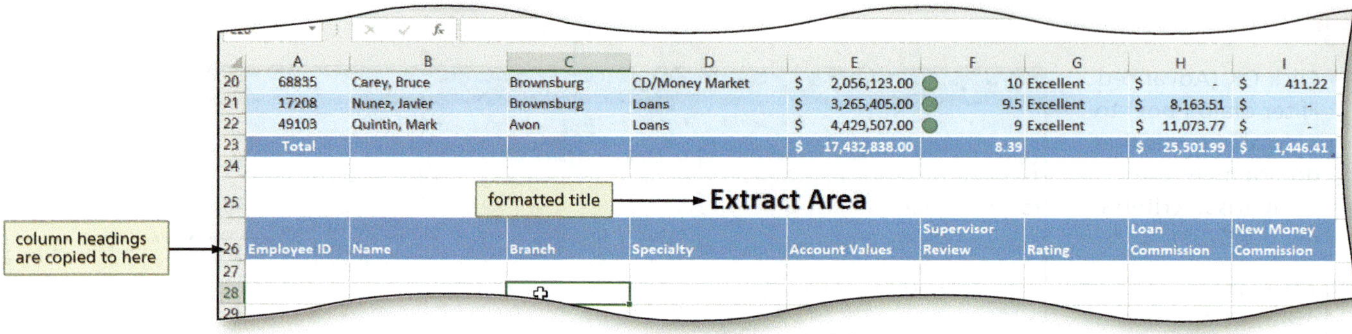

Figure 6–56

To Extract Records

The following steps extract records that meet the previous criteria, using the Advanced Filter dialog box. **Why?** The Advanced Filter dialog box allows you to use the complex criteria from a criteria range on the worksheet and send the results to a third location, leaving the table undisturbed.

1

- Click the table to make it active.
- Click the Advanced button (Data tab | Sort & Filter group) to display the Advanced Filter dialog box.
- Click the 'Copy to another location' option button in the Action area (Advanced Filter dialog box) to cause the records that meet the criteria to be copied to a different location on the worksheet (Figure 6–57).

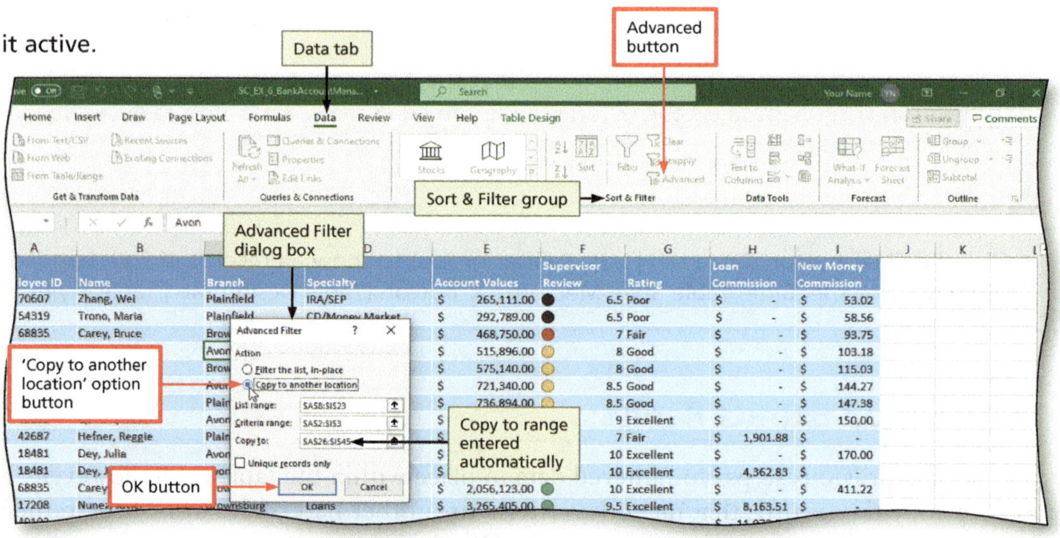

Figure 6–57

2

- Click OK to copy any records that meet the comparison criteria in the criteria range from the table to the extract range. Scroll to display the entire extraction area (Figure 6–58).

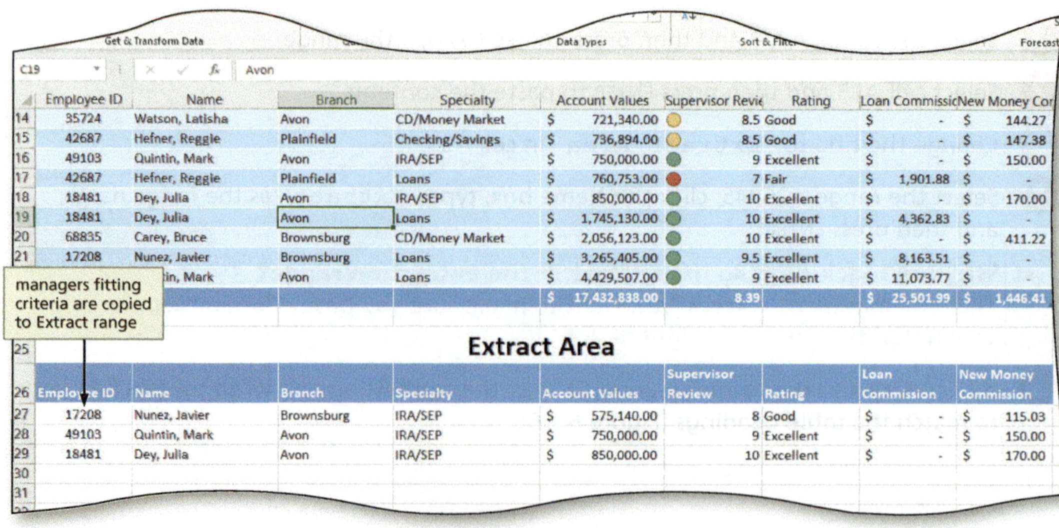

Figure 6–58

Q&A **What happens to the rows in the extract range if I perform another advanced filter operation?**
Each time you use the Advanced Filter dialog box with the 'Copy to another location' option, Excel clears cells below the field names in the extract range before it copies a new set of records that pass the new test.

3

- Click the Save button on the Quick Access Toolbar to save the workbook again.

Break Point: If you want to take a break, this is a good place to do so. You can exit Excel now. To resume later, start Excel, open the file called SC_EX_6_BankAccountManagers, and continue following the steps from this location forward.

More about the Criteria Range

The comparison criteria in the criteria range determine the records that will pass the test when the Advanced Filter dialog box is used. As you have seen, multiple entries in a single data row of the criteria range create an AND condition. The following examples describe different comparison criteria.

- If the criteria range contains a blank row, it means that no comparison criteria have been defined. Thus, all records in the table pass the test and will be displayed.
- If you want an OR operator in the same field, your criteria range must contain two (or more) data rows. Enter the criteria data on separate rows. Records that pass either (or any) comparison criterion will be displayed.
- If you want an AND operator in the same field name, you must add a column in the criteria range and duplicate the column heading.
- If you want an OR operator on two different fields, your criteria range must contain two (or more) data rows. Enter the criteria for each field on a separate row. Records will display that pass either (or any) comparison criterion.
- When the comparison criteria below different field names are in the same row, then records pass the test only if they pass all the comparison criteria, an AND condition. If the comparison criteria for the field names are in different rows, then the records must pass only one of the tests, an OR condition.

BTW
Keeping Data in Order
If you want to perform various sorts but need to have a way to return to the original order, you might consider adding a column that numbers the entries before sorting.

Using Database Functions

Excel includes 12 database functions that allow you to evaluate numeric data in a table. These functions each begin with the letter D for data table, to differentiate them from their worksheet counterparts. As the name implies, the **DAVERAGE function** calculates the average of numbers in a table field that pass a test. The general form of the DAVERAGE function is

=DAVERAGE(table range, “field name”, criteria range)

Another often-used table function is the DCOUNT function. The **DCOUNT function** counts the number of numeric entries in a table field that pass a test. The general form of the DCOUNT function is

=DCOUNT(table range, “field name”, criteria range)

In both functions, table range is the location of the table, field name is the name of the field in the table, and criteria range is the comparison criteria or test to pass. The criteria range must include a column heading with the data. Note that Excel requires that you surround field names with quotation marks unless you previously named the field.

Other database functions that are similar to the functions described in previous modules include the DMAX, DMIN, and DSUM functions. See Excel Help for a complete list of database functions.

BTW
The DGET Function
The DGET function extracts a single value from a column of a list or database that matches conditions that you specify. The three arguments include database, column number, and criteria.

BTW
Functions and Ranges
When using a function such as DAVERAGE or DCOUNT, Excel automatically adjusts the first argument if the table grows or shrinks. With functions such as SUMIF and COUNTIF, you have to correct the function argument to reflect the new range if the range grows or shrinks.

To Create an Output Area

In order to demonstrate the database functions and other functions, the following steps set up an output area in preparation for entering functions.

1. Change the width of columns O, P, and Q to 18.00.
2. Select cell O1 and then type `Output Area` to enter a criteria area title. Center the title across the selection O1:Q1.
3. Enter other labels as shown below. Bold the title cells O8 and O11, and center them across columns O through Q. Use the format painter to copy the formatting from cell L1 to cell O1, and then copy the formatting from cell L2 to cells O12:Q12. If necessary, ensure that cell O7 matches the formatting of cell O6 (Figure 6–59).

Cell	Text
O2	Avg. Avon Supervisor Review:
O3	Avg. Brownsburg Supervisor Review:
O4	Avg. Plainfield Supervisor Review:
O5	Managers with Poor Ratings:
O6	Total Checking/Savings:
O7	Count of Loan Officers:
O8	Locator
O9	Enter Employee ID Number:
O10	Branch Location of Entered Employee:
O11	Function Branch Criteria
O12	Branch
O13	Avon
P12	Branch
P13	Brownsburg
Q12	Branch
Q13	Plainfield

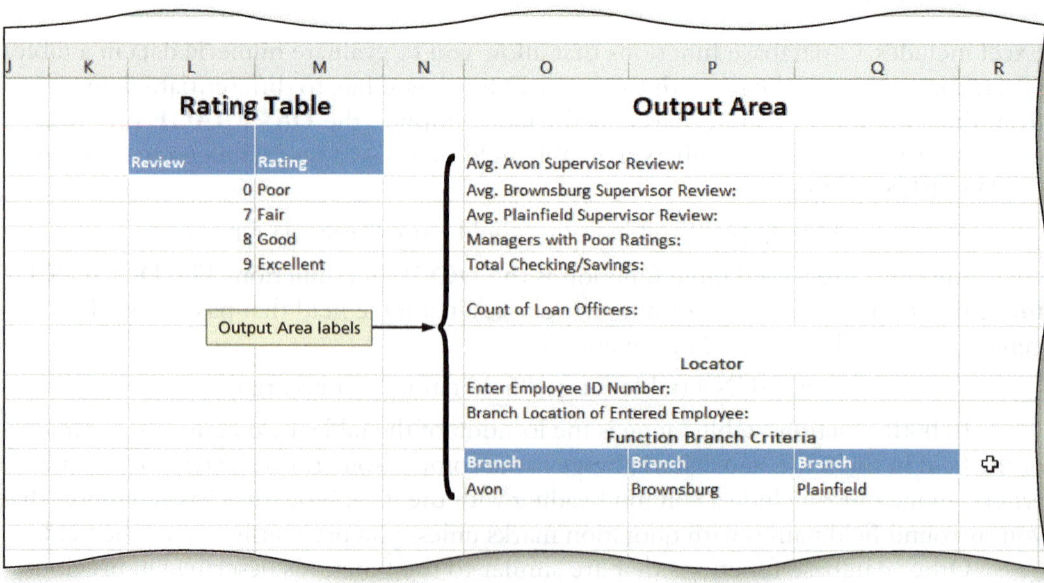

Figure 6–59

To Use the DAVERAGE and DCOUNT Database Functions

The following steps use the DAVERAGE function to find the average supervisor review at each branch. You will use the DCOUNT function to count the number of managers that have a Poor rating. **Why?** The DAVERAGE and DCOUNT functions allow you to enter a range to average, and criteria with which to filter the table. The DAVERAGE function requires a numeric field from the table range; therefore, you will use "Supervisor Review" as the second argument. Field names used as numeric arguments in these functions should be surrounded with quotation marks unless previously named.

1

- Select cell Q2 and then type **=DAVERAGE (a8:i22, "Supervisor Review",o12:o13)** to enter the database function (Figure 6–60).

Q&A **My function wraps. Did I do something wrong?**
No, it depends on how far to the right you are scrolled. If there is not enough room on the screen, Excel will wrap long cell entries.

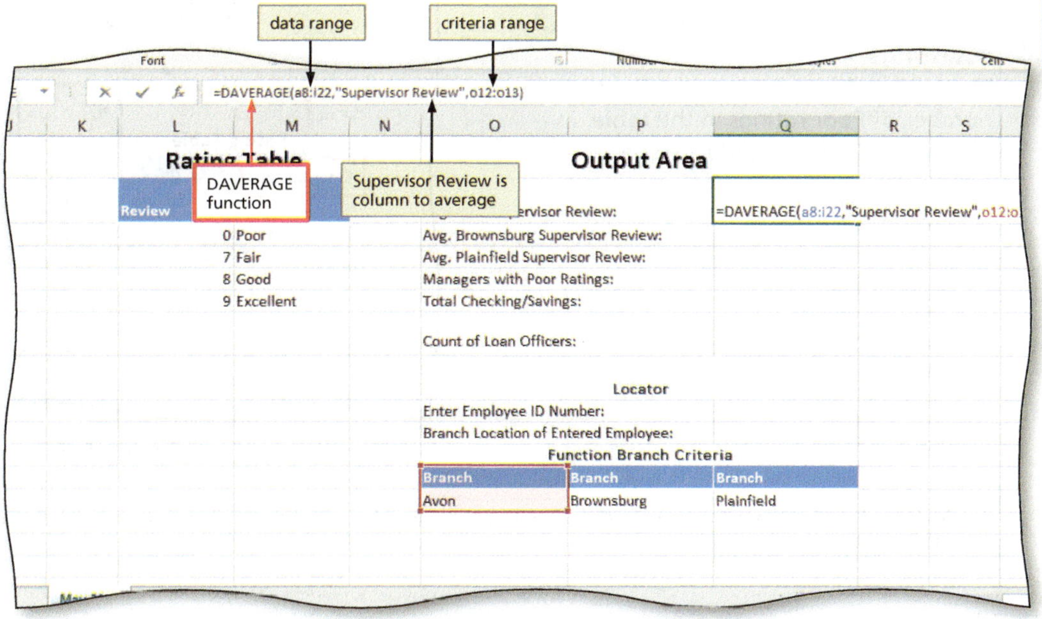

Figure 6–60

2

- Click the Enter button to finish the function and display the answer.
- Select cell Q3 and then type **=daverage (a8:i22, "Supervisor Review",p12:p13)**
- Select cell Q4 and then type **=daverage (a8:i22, "Supervisor Review",q12:q13)** (Figure 6–61).

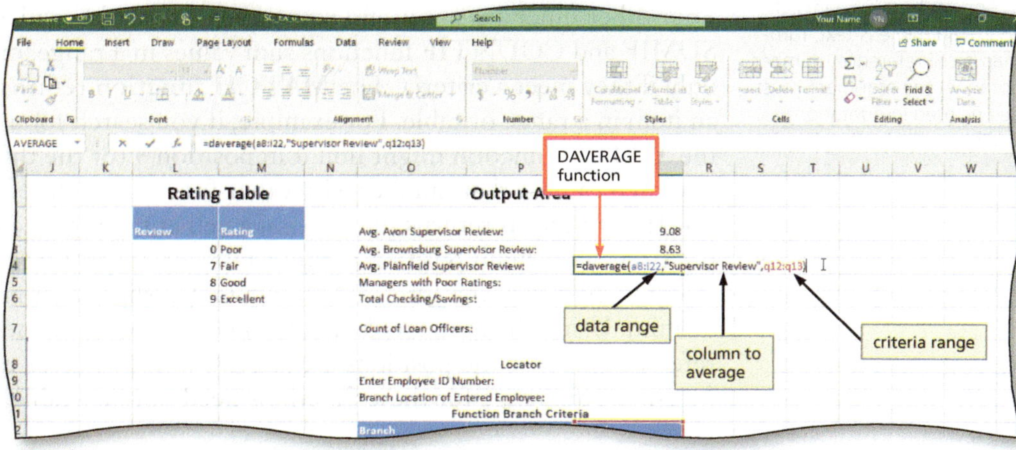

Figure 6–61

Q&A **Why do the three DAVERAGE functions, which use the Supervisor Review, generate different answers?**
The criteria range differentiates the entries. The range O12:O13 averages the Supervisor Review results for the Avon branch. The range P12:P13 averages Brownsburg managers. The range Q12:Q13 averages Plainfield managers.

Could I use the table name instead of the range, A8:I22, as the first argument in the function?
To use a table name, you would have to enter a structured reference such as Managers[#All] to reference the entire table.

3

- Click the Enter button to finish the function.
- If necessary, format cells Q2:Q4 with the number format and 2 decimal places.
- Select cell Q5 and then type `=dcount(a8:i22,"Supervisor Review",m2:m3)` to enter the database function.
- Click the Enter button to finish the function (Figure 6–62).

Q&A

What is the DCOUNT function actually counting?

The DCOUNT function is counting the number of Poor ratings in the table, as referenced by the M2:M3 criteria.

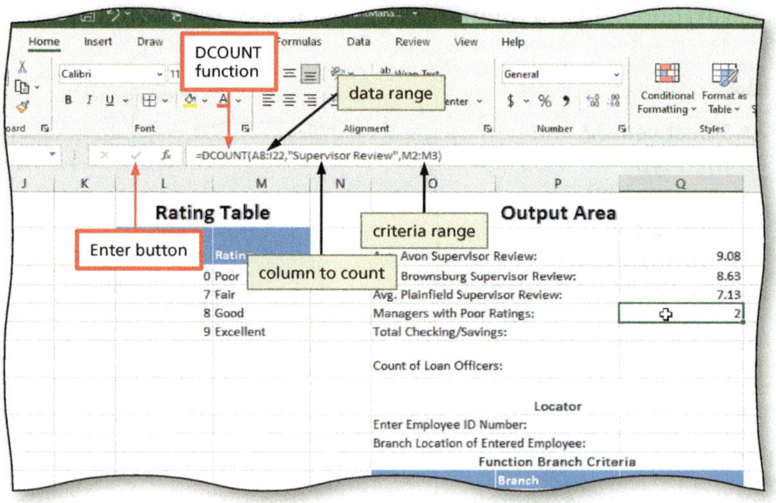

Figure 6–62

Other Ways

1. Click Insert Function box in formula bar, click 'Or select a category' button, click 'Database', double-click DAVERAGE or DCOUNT in 'Select a function' list, enter arguments

BTW

Using Quotation Marks

Many of the database functions require a field name as one of the arguments. If your field name is text, rather than a cell reference, number, or range, the argument must be enclosed in quotation marks.

Using the SUMIF, COUNTIF, MATCH, and INDEX Functions

Four other functions are useful when querying a table and analyzing its data. The SUMIF and COUNTIF functions sum values in a range, or count values in a range, only if they meet a criteria. The **MATCH function** returns the position number of an item in a range or table. For example, if you search for a specific student name, the MATCH function might find it in position 3 (or the third column in the table). You then can use that number with other functions, cell references, or searches. The **INDEX function** returns the value of a cell at the intersection of a particular row position and column position within a table or range. For example, you might want to know the age of the fifth student in a table, where ages are stored in the second column. Using the numbers 5 and 2 would eliminate the need to know the exact cell reference because the positions are relative to the table or range. Unlike the database functions, the range for these functions need not be a table.

To Use the SUMIF Function

The following step uses the SUMIF function to ascertain the sum of the account values for Checking/Savings accounts. **Why?** The SUMIF function allows you to sum a range based on criteria. The general format of the SUMIF function is

=SUMIF(criteria_range, data, sum_range)

The first argument is the criteria range, or the range you want to search. The second argument is the desired piece of data in that range; it must be enclosed in quotes if the data is alphanumeric. The third argument is the location of the values you want summed. In this case, you are searching column D (Specialty) for "Checking/Savings", and then summing column E (Account Values).

1

- Click cell Q6 and then type `=sumif (d9:d22, "Checking/ Savings",e9:e22)`.
- Press ENTER to enter the function.
- Apply the accounting number format style to cell Q6 (Figure 6–63).

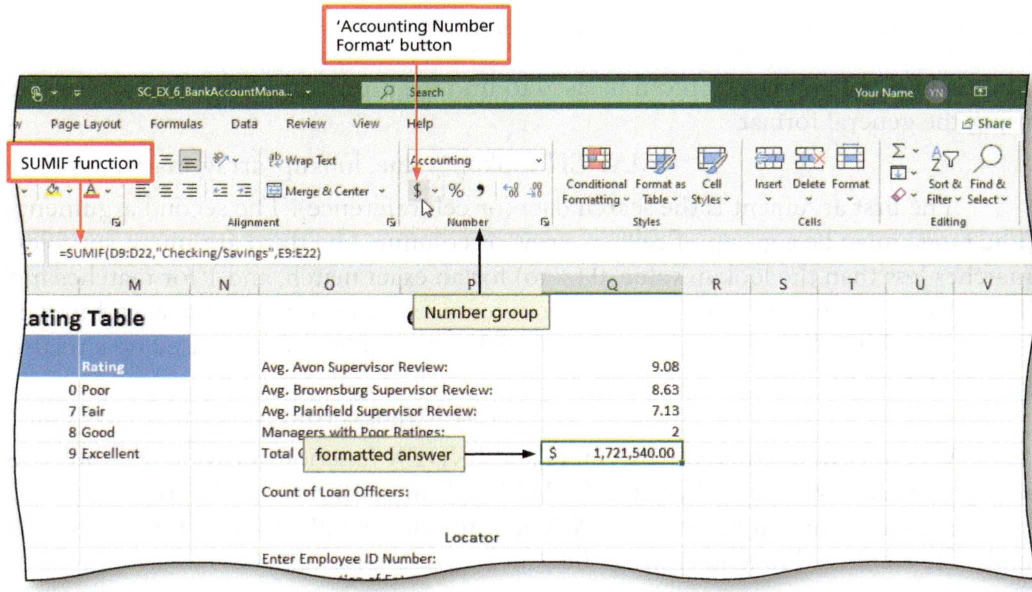

Figure 6–63

Other Ways

1. Click Insert Function box in formula bar, click 'Or select a category' button, click 'Math & Trig', double-click SUMIF in 'Select a function' list, enter arguments
2. Click 'Math & Trig' button (Formulas tab | Function Library group), click SUMIF, enter arguments

To Use the COUNTIF Functions

The following step uses the COUNTIF to ascertain the number of account managers who handle loans. **Why?** In large tables, counting the number of records that match certain conditions provides useful data for analysis. The general format of the COUNTIF function is

=COUNTIF(count_range, data)

The first argument is the range containing the cells with which to compare the data in the second argument. Again, if the data is text rather than numbers, the data must be enclosed in quotes. In this case, you are counting the number of "Loans" in Column D.

1

- In cell Q7, type `=countif (d9:d22, "Loans")` and then click the Enter button to enter the function (Figure 6–64).

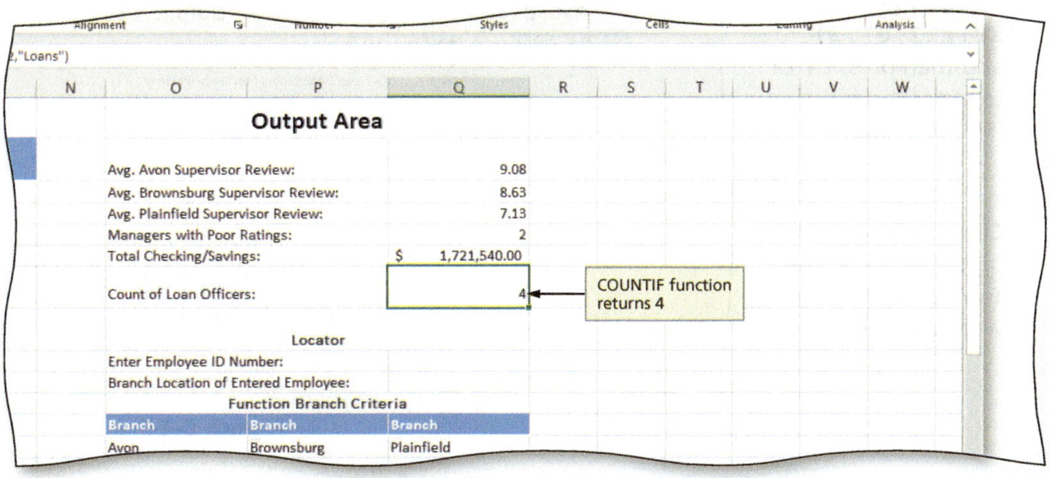

Figure 6–64

Other Ways

1. Click Insert Function box in formula bar, click 'Or select a category' button, click 'Statistical', double-click COUNTIF in 'Select a function' list, enter arguments
2. Click 'More Functions' button (Formulas tab | Function Library group), point to 'Statistical', click COUNTIF, enter arguments

To Use the MATCH and INDEX Functions

The MATCH function can be used to find the position number of a piece of data in a table or range, using the general format

=MATCH(lookup_value, lookup_array, match_type)

The first argument is the search data (or cell reference). The second argument is the range to search. The range must be a group of cells in a row or column. The third argument specifies the type of search: –1 for matches less than the lookup value, 0 (zero) for an exact match, and 1 for matches higher than the lookup value. The MATCH function returns a numeric reference to the column or row within the search area.

The INDEX function finds a specific value in a table or range based on a relative row and column. The general format is

=INDEX(range, row, column)

When used together, the MATCH and INDEX functions provide the ability to look up a particular value in a table based on criteria. Because the MATCH function returns the row location in this case, you can use it as the second argument in the INDEX function. For example, to find the Branch for a specific manager in the table, the combined functions would be

=INDEX(A9:I22, MATCH(Q9, A9:A22, 0), 3).

Within the INDEX function, A9:I22 is the table range; the MATCH function becomes the second argument and refers to the row; and the last argument, 3, refers to column C, the branch data. That final argument must be an integer rather than an alphabetic reference to the column. Within the MATCH function, Q9 is the location of the employee ID you wish to search for, followed by the range of IDs in A9:A22, followed by a designation of 0 for an exact match. Sometimes called nesting, the inner function is performed first.

The following steps assume you want to look up the Branch for any given manager by using the employee ID. **Why?** The table is not sorted by employee ID; this method makes it easier for the company to find the branch for a specific manager.

1

- Click cell Q9 and then type **18481** to enter a lookup value.
- In cell Q10, type **=index(a9:i22, match(q9, a9:a22,0),3)** and then press ENTER to enter the function (Figure 6–65).

2

- Click the Save button on the Quick Access Toolbar to save the workbook again.

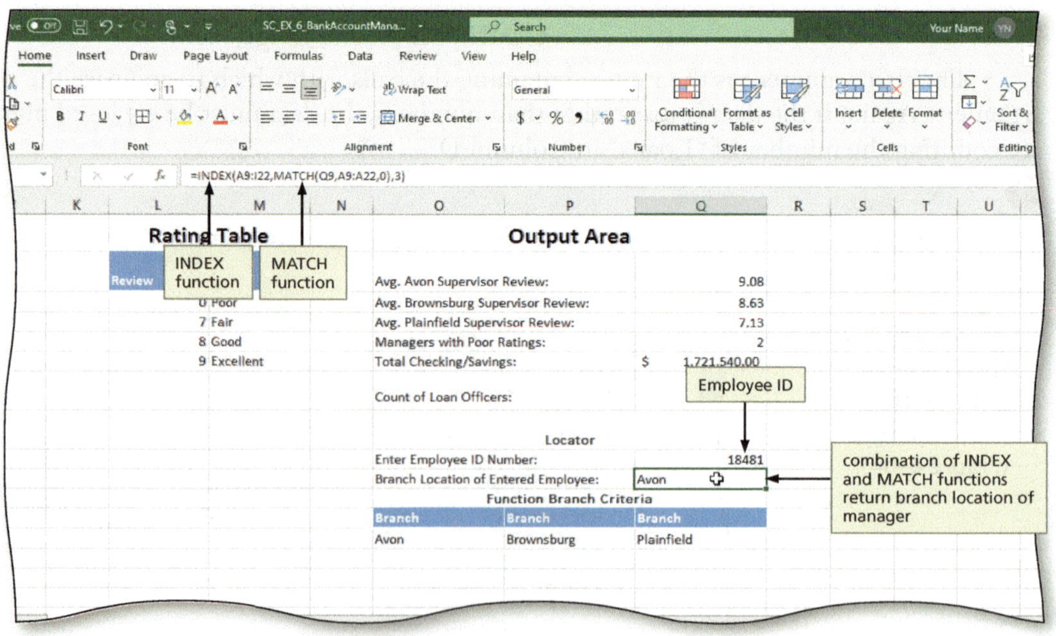

Figure 6–65

Other Ways

1. Click Insert Function box in formula bar, click 'Or select a category' button, click 'Lookup & Reference', double-click MATCH or INDEX in 'Select a function' list, enter arguments
2. Click 'Lookup & Reference' button (Formulas tab | Function Library group), click MATCH or INDEX, enter arguments

Other Functions

You have learned that logical operators help you compare cells and ranges. You used the IF function to evaluate a logical test containing a comparison operator. The IF function returns a value or reference if true and a different value or reference if false. Four logical functions are similar to their operator counterparts as they use function keywords with two or more logical comparisons as arguments. The **AND function** returns the word TRUE if the both arguments are true. The **OR function** returns TRUE if either part of the condition is true. A rarely used **XOR function** returns TRUE if either argument is true and returns FALSE if both are true or false. Finally, the **NOT function** uses a single argument and returns TRUE if the condition is false. Table 6–5 displays examples of the four logical functions.

Table 6–5 Examples of Logical Functions

Function	Description	Example	Explanation
AND	Returns TRUE if all of the arguments are TRUE	=AND(A1="Yes", B2<5)	Returns TRUE if cell A1 is equal to "Yes" and B2 is less than 5. Otherwise, it returns FALSE.
OR	Returns TRUE if either argument is TRUE	=OR(A1="Yes", B2<5)	Returns TRUE if either cell A1 is equal to "Yes" or B2 is less than 5. If neither of the conditions is met, it returns FALSE.
XOR	Returns a logical Exclusive Or of all arguments	=XOR(A1="Yes", B2<5)	Returns TRUE if either cell A1 is equal to "Yes" or B2 is less than 5. If neither of the conditions is met or both conditions are met, it returns FALSE.
NOT	Returns the reversed logical value of its argument; if the argument is FALSE, then it returns TRUE, and vice versa	=NOT(A1="Yes")	Returns TRUE if cell A1 is anything other than "Yes."

In a previous module, you learned about the Transpose paste option, which return a vertical range of cells as a horizontal range, or vice versa. The **TRANSPOSE function** works in a similar manner. For example, if you have the values 100, 200, and 300 in a column running down (cells A1, A2, and A3), you could change them to display in a row running across. To do so, select the first cell in the destination location and then type

=TRANSPOSE(A1:A3).

The **AVERAGEIF function** returns the average of values within a range that meet a given criteria. The function takes two arguments: range and criteria. For example, you could find the average A-level test score in a named range using

=AVERAGEIF(scores, >=90).

An optional third argument allows the criteria to be measured against the first range, while averaging a different range.

Summarizing Data

Another way to summarize data is by using subtotals. A subtotal is the sum of a subset of data while a grand total sums all of the data in a row or column. You can create subtotals automatically, as long as the data is sorted. For subtotals, the field on which you sort is called the **control field**. For example, if you choose the Branch field as your control field, all of the Avon, Brownsburg, and Plainfield entries will be grouped together within the data range. You then might request subtotals for the Account Values and Customer Bill field. Excel calculates and displays the subtotal each time the Branch field changes. A grand total displays at the bottom of the range. The most common subtotal uses the SUM function, although you can use other functions. If you change the control field, Excel updates the subtotal automatically. Note that the subtotal feature cannot be used with the table feature, only with normal ranges of data.

The Subtotal command displays outline symbols beside the rows or above the columns of the data you wish to group. The **outline symbols** include plus and minus signs for showing and hiding grouped portions of the worksheet, as well as brackets identifying the groups. For example, you might want to minimize the display of account managers who have a Poor rating and show only those with Fair, Good, and Excellent ratings. Outlining is extremely useful for making large tables more manageable in size and appearance.

To Sort the Data

Subtotals can only be performed on sorted data. The following step sorts the table by Branch.

1. Scroll to display the table. Click any cell within the table. If necessary, click the Filter button (Data tab | Sort & Filter group) to display the filter arrows. Click the filter button in cell C8 and then click the 'Sort A to Z' command to sort the Branch data.

To Convert a Table to a Range

In preparation for creating subtotals, the following steps convert the table back to a range. **Why?** The Subtotal command is not available for tables.

1

- Right-click anywhere in the table and then point to Table on the shortcut menu to display the Table submenu (Figure 6–66).

2

- Click 'Convert to Range' (Table submenu) to display a Microsoft Excel dialog box.
- Click Yes (Microsoft Excel dialog box) to convert the table to a range.

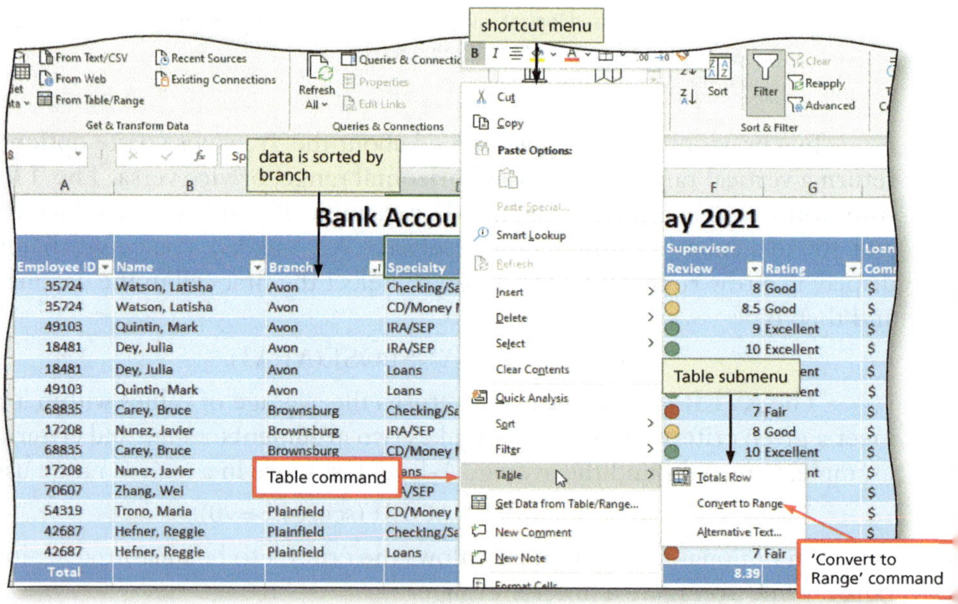

Figure 6–66

Other Ways

1. Click 'Convert to Range' button (Table Design tab | Tools group), click Yes (Microsoft Excel dialog box)

To Display Subtotals

The following steps display subtotals for the Account Values based on Branch. **Why?** Subtotals are useful pieces of data for comparisons and analysis.

1

- Click in one of the numeric fields you wish to subtotal (in this case, column E).
- Click the Subtotal button (Data tab | Outline group) to display the Subtotal dialog box.
- Click the 'At each change in' button (Subtotal dialog box) and then click Branch to select the control field.

- If necessary, click the Use function button and then select Sum in the Use function list.
- In the 'Add subtotal to' list (Subtotal dialog box), click Account Values to select values to subtotal. Clear any other check boxes (you may need to scroll to see all check boxes) (Figure 6–67).

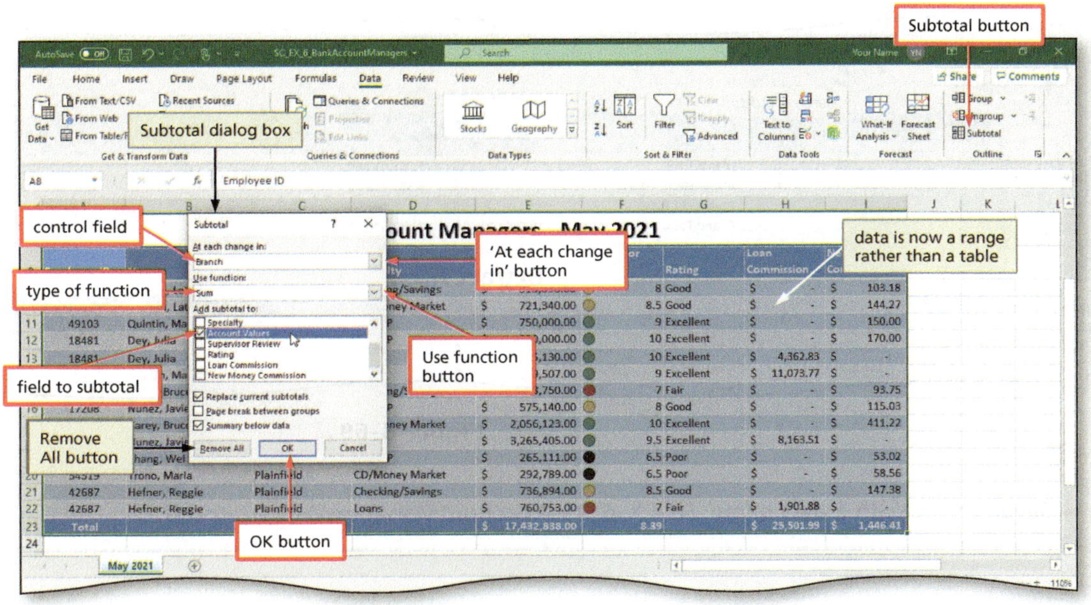

Figure 6–67

2

- Click OK (Subtotal dialog box) to add subtotals to the range. Deselect the range, if necessary.
- Zoom to 100% magnification.
- Scroll as necessary so that you can see the entire subtotal and outline area (Figure 6–68).

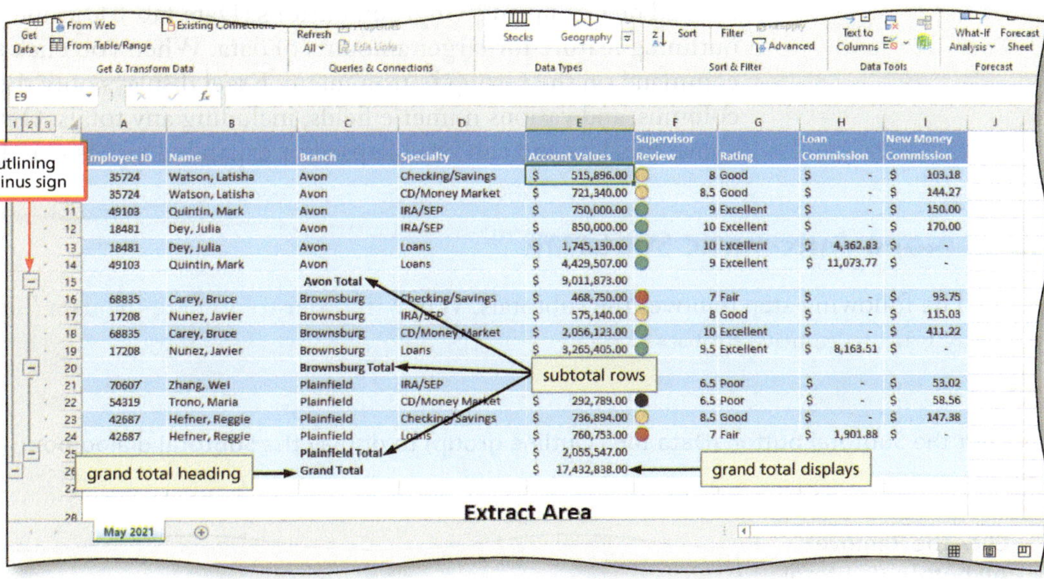

Figure 6–68

Q&A **What changes does Excel make to the worksheet?**
Excel adds three subtotal rows—one subtotal for each different Branch—and one grand total row for the entire table. The names for each subtotal row come from the sorted control field and appear in bold. Thus, the text, Avon Total, in cell C15 identifies the row that contains the subtotal for Account Values for the Avon branch. Excel also displays the outlining feature to the left of the row numbers.

To Use the Outline Feature

Excel turns on the outline feature automatically when you create subtotals. The following steps use the outline feature of Excel. **Why?** The outline feature allows you to hide and show data and totals.

1

- Click the second outlining column header to collapse the outline and hide the data (Figure 6–69).

Experiment

- One at a time, click each of the plus signs (+) in column two on the left side of the window to display detail records for each Branch.

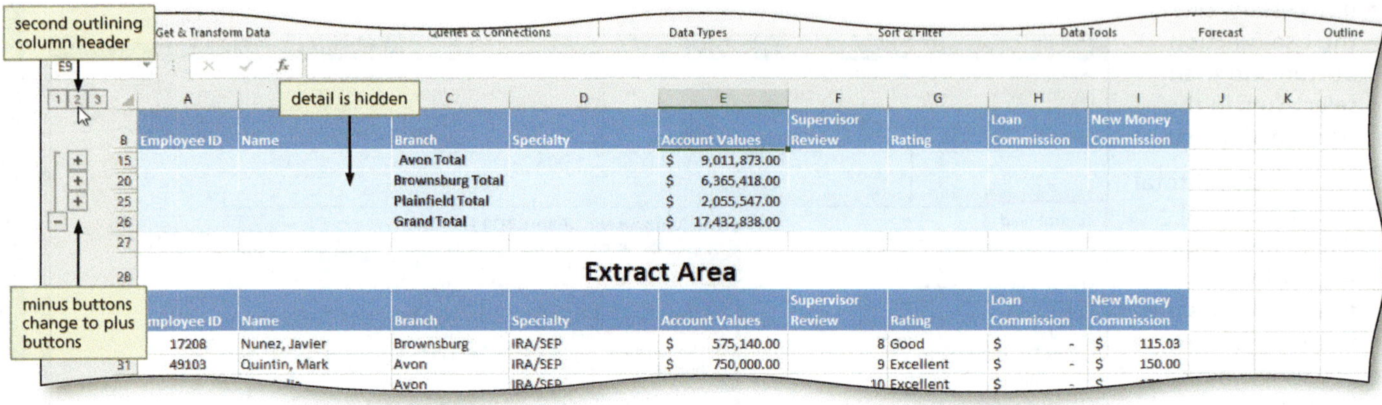

Figure 6–69

2

- Save the file with a new name, SC_EX_6_BankAccountManagersWithSubtotals.

Auto Outline

The Group and Ungroup buttons (Data tab | Outline group) provide another outlining feature for larger amounts of data. When you click the Auto Outline command on the Group button menu, Excel displays only the header column or columns, and various numeric fields, including any totals. Outlining headers display above the data and can be collapsed or expanded just as you did with the subtotals.

To Remove Automatic Subtotals

The following step removes the subtotals. **Why?** In order to prepare the data for other subtotals or sorts, you may want to remove subtotals.

1

- Click the Subtotal button (Data tab | Outline group) to display the Subtotal dialog box.

2

- Click the Remove All button (Subtotal dialog box) to remove all subtotals (Figure 6–70).

3

- Close the file without quitting Excel. If you are prompted to save the file, click the Don't Save button (Microsoft Excel dialog box).

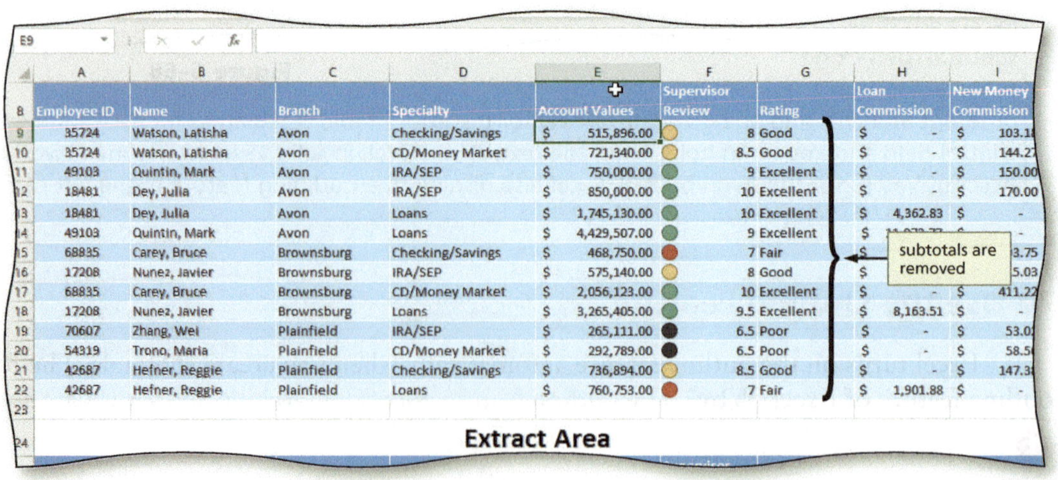

Figure 6–70

Treemap Charts

A **treemap chart** provides a hierarchical, visual view of data, making it easy to spot patterns and trends. Instead of hierarchical levels, treemap charts use rectangles to represent each branch and subbranch (or data category) by size, enabling users to display categories by color and proximity, and to compare proportions. One of the fields in a treemap chart must be numeric, in order to generate the size of each rectangle. The data series, or selected range of data, must be contiguous—you cannot chart multiple data series with a treemap chart. As with other types of charts, you can format fonts, colors, shape, and text effects, as well as add data fields and adjust data labels. Treemap charts compare values and proportions among large amounts of data that might be difficult to show with other types of charts.

To Create a Treemap Chart

The following steps create a treemap chart to compare account managers who have brought in new money (money other than loans). **Why?** The company would like to see the general proportion of money related to various account types using the manager's name as the tree branch and the Specialty as the subbranch. The Account Values will be reflected by the size of the rectangles.

1

- Open the file named SC_EX_6_BankAccountManagers. Scroll as necessary to display the table.
- Click any cell in the table. If necessary, click the Filter button (Data tab | Sort & Filter group) to display the filter buttons. Sort the data in ascending order by Name. Click the Filter button in cell D8, click Loans to remove the check mark, and click OK.
- Drag to select cells B8:E22.
- Display the Insert tab and then click the 'Insert Hierarchy Chart' button (Insert tab | Charts group) to display the gallery (Figure 6–71).

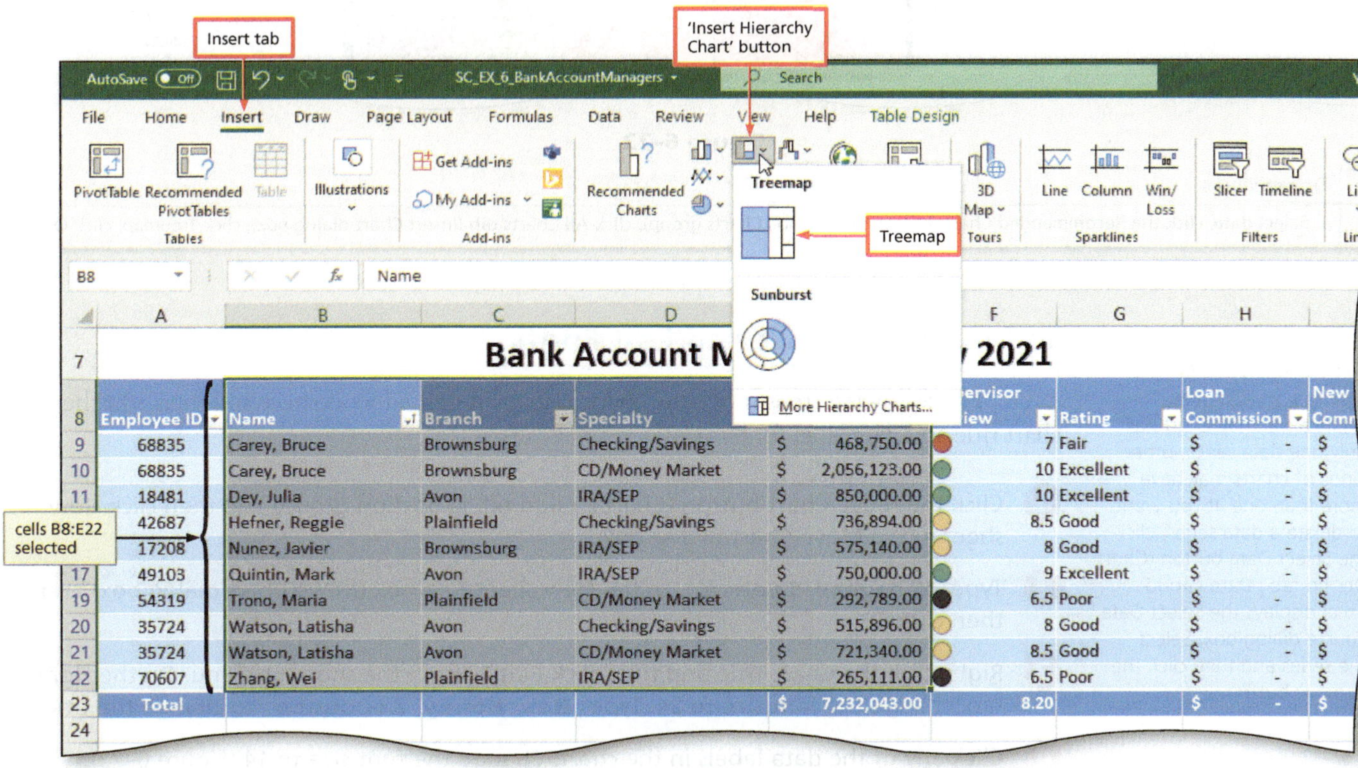

Figure 6–71

Q&A **Do I have to use the table file rather than the file with subtotals?**
Recall that you removed the table formatting in the file with subtotals. It is easier to start with the data stored as a table.

2

- Click Treemap (Insert Hierarchy Chart gallery) to insert the chart.
- Click Style 6 (Chart Design tab | Chart Styles group) to select the style.
- Click the Chart Elements button located to the right of the chart and then click the Legend check box to remove the check mark (Figure 6–72).

Experiment

- Point to each rectangle in the chart to see a ScreenTip showing from which data points the rectangle was created.

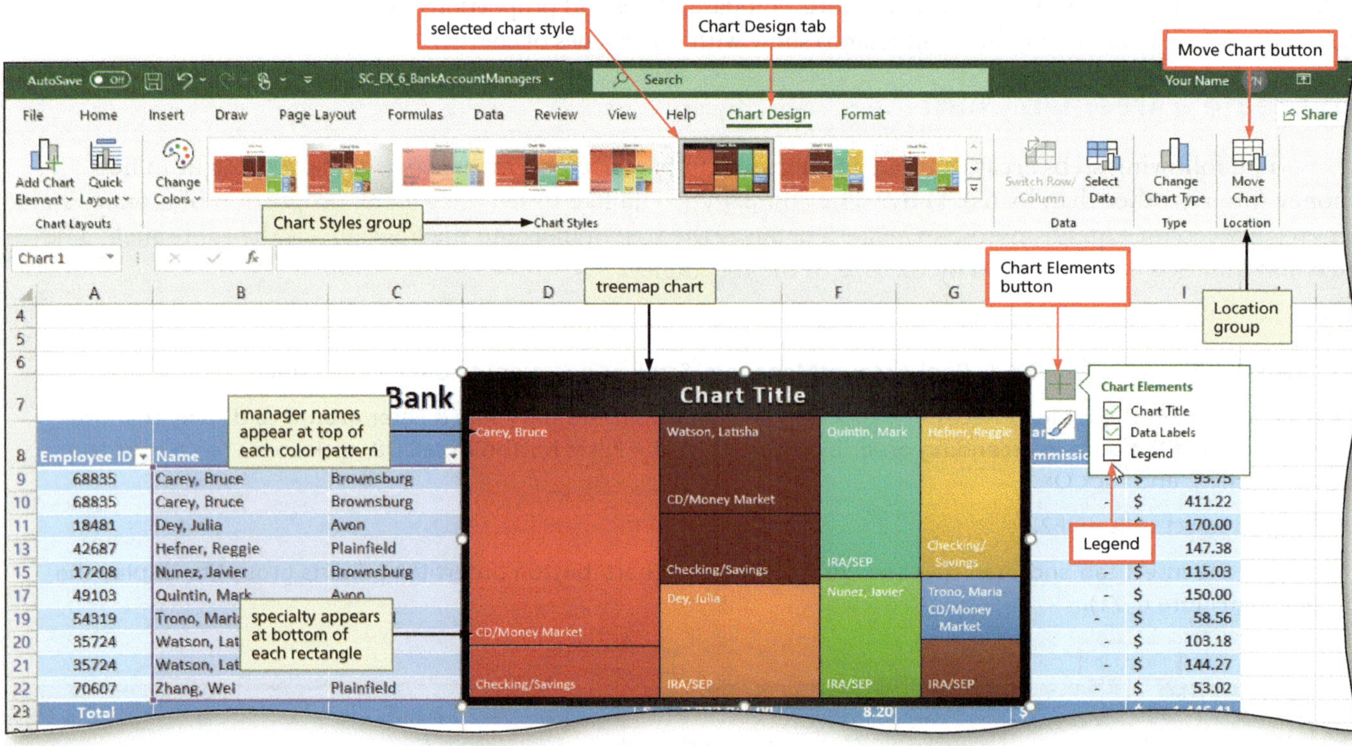

Figure 6–72

Other Ways

1. Select data, click the Recommended Charts button (Insert tab | Charts group), click All Charts tab (Insert Chart dialog box), click Treemap, click OK

BTW

Removing Data Series in Charts

While a treemap chart has only one data series, other kinds of charts may have more than one. If you want to delete a data series, click the Select Data button (Chart Design tab | Data Group). Excel displays the Select Data Source dialog box. Select the series and then click the Remove button.

To Move the Chart and Edit Fonts

The following steps move the chart to its own named worksheet and then edit the chart title and data label fonts.

1. Click the Move Chart button (Chart Design tab | Location group) and then click New sheet in the Move Chart dialog box.
2. Type **Managers Treemap** in the New sheet text box (Move Chart dialog box) and then click OK.
3. Right-click the Chart Title and then click Edit Text on the shortcut menu. On the Home tab, change the font size to 24. Type **New Money Accounts** to change the title.
4. Click any of the data labels in the chart. Change the font size to 14 (Figure 6–73).

Q&A

How is the data presented in this chart?

The treemap allows you to compare each manager with other managers: how much money they handled (size of color block) and specialties (number of subdivisions within each color block).

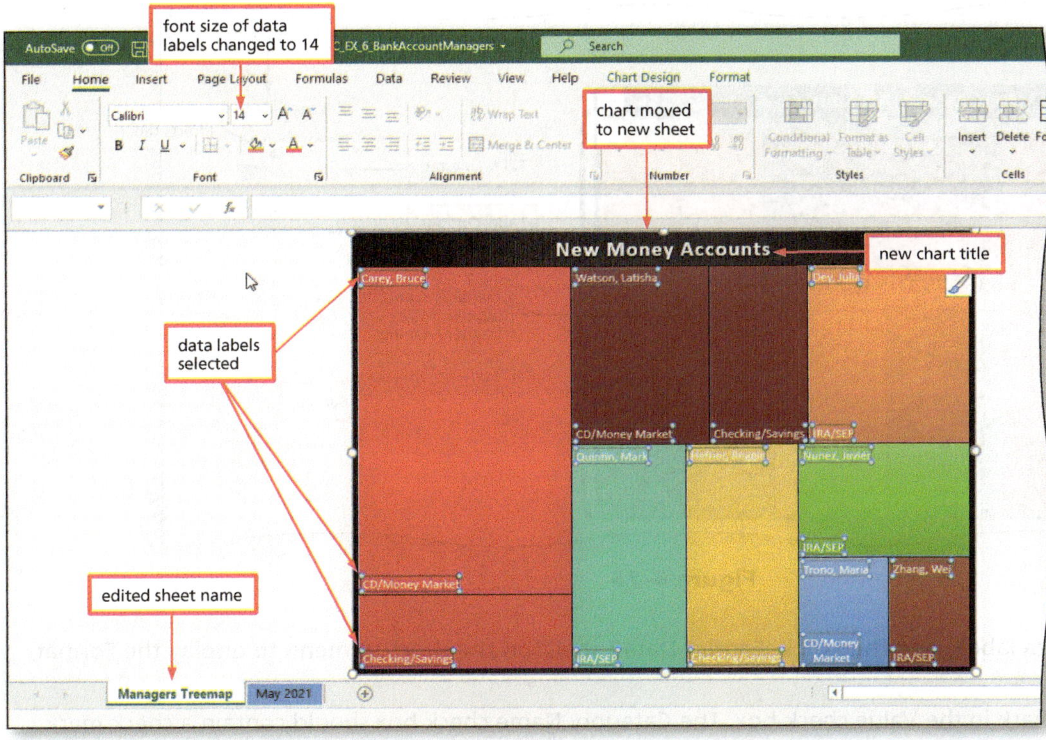

Figure 6–73

To Edit Treemap Settings

The following steps format the chart with settings that are unique to treemaps. **Why?** Changing some of the settings will make the branches stand out and make the chart more user-friendly.

1

- Right-click any of the rectangles to display the shortcut menu. Do not right-click a data label (Figure 6–74).

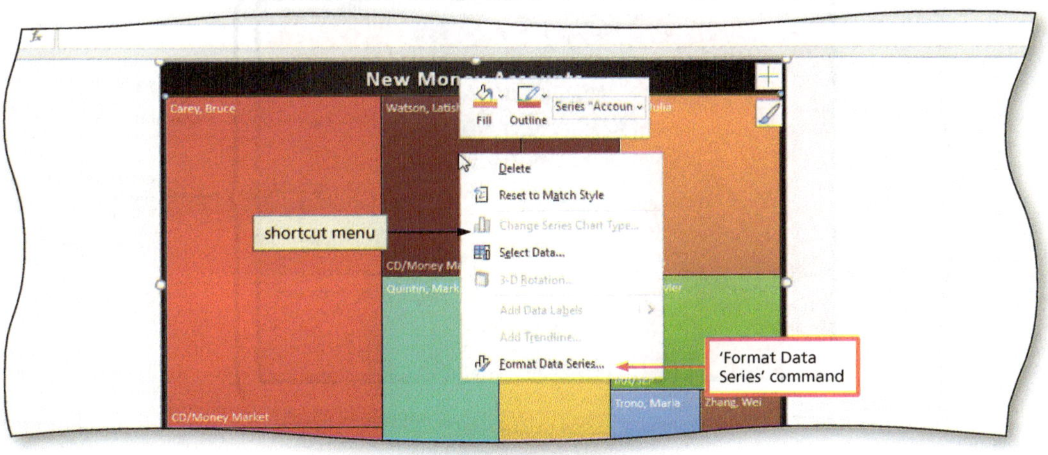

Figure 6–74

2

- Click 'Format Data Series' on the shortcut menu to display the Format Data Series pane.
- Click Banner in the Label Options area (Figure 6–75).

Experiment

- Click each of the label options and watch the chart change. When you are finished experimenting, click Banner.

Q&A **What other choices can I make in the Format Data Series pane?**
In the Effects section, you can add shadows, a glow, or other special effects. In the Fill & Line section, you can change the color of the fill and the borders for each rectangle.

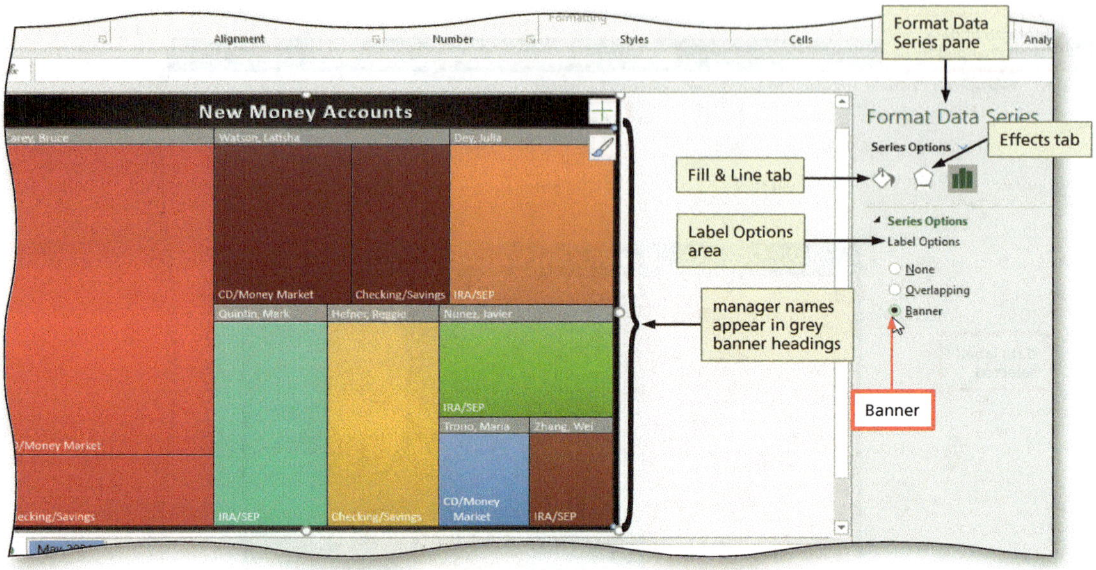

Figure 6–75

3

- Right-click any of the data labels, and then click 'Format Data Labels' on the shortcut menu to display the Format Data Labels pane.
- Click to display a check mark in the Value check box. The Category Name check box should contain a check mark already.
- Click the Separator arrow and then click (New Line) in the list to display each value on a new line under its category name (Figure 6–76).

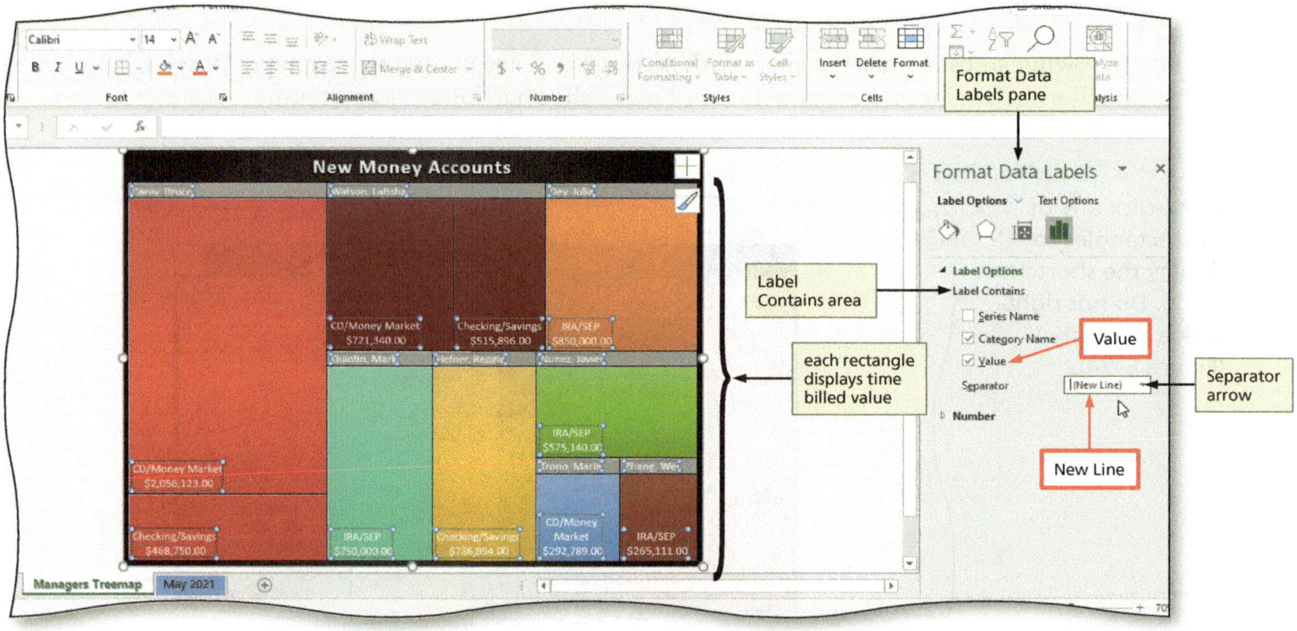

Figure 6–76

Experiment

- Click various combinations of the check marks and watch the chart change. When you are finished experimenting, select only Category Name and Value.

4 sam Save the file with SC_EX_6_BankAccountManagersWithTreemap as the file name.

5 Click the Close button on the right side of the title bar to close the file and close Excel.

6 If the Microsoft Office Excel dialog box is displayed, click the Don't Save button.

More about Data Series

While a treemap chart has only one data series, other kinds of charts may have more than one. If you want to delete a data series, click the Select Data button (Chart Design tab | Data Group). Excel displays the Select Data Source dialog box. Select the series and then click the Remove button.

If you want to change the color of a an individual data series or category, select the series on the chart, click the Shape Fill button (Format tab | Shape Styles group) and then click the desired style.

BTW

Large Labels in a Treemap

When you have large numbers and labels in small boxes, you sometimes will have to get creative. Your options include reducing the font size, removing the decimal places or dollar signs, limiting the data further, or editing the longer labels in the data table itself.

Summary

In this module, you learned how to use Excel to create, sort, format, and filter a table (also called a database) of managers. Topics covered included calculated fields using structured references, looking up values with the XLOOKUP function, conditional formatting using icon sets, querying a table using AutoFilters with customized criteria, creating criteria and extracting ranges to an output area using SUMIF, COUNTIF, MATCH, and INDEX database functions, summarizing data with subtotals and outlines, as well as creating a treemap chart.

Consider This

What decisions will you need to make when creating your next worksheet with a table to create, sort, and query?

Use these guidelines as you complete the assignments in this module and create your own worksheets for evaluating and analyzing data outside of this class.

1. Enter data for the table.
    a) Use columns for fields of data.
    b) Put each record on a separate row.
    c) Create user-friendly column headings.
    d) Format the range as a table.
    e) Format individual columns as necessary.
2. Create other fields.
    a) Use calculated fields with structured references.
    b) To apply rankings or settings, use a lookup table.
    c) To apply conditional formatting, consider icon sets or color groupings.
    d) Use total rows.
3. Sort the table.
    a) Sort ascending, descending, or combinations using tools on the Home tab and the Data tab.
4. Employ table AutoFilters for quick searches and sorts.
5. Create criteria and extract ranges to simplify queries.
6. Use functions.
    a) Use DAVERAGE and DCOUNT for database functions analyzing table data.
    b) Use SUMIF, COUNTIF, MATCH, and INDEX to find answers based on conditions.
7. Summarize data with subtotals and use outlining.
8. Create a treemap chart.

Apply Your Knowledge

Reinforce the skills and apply the concepts you learned in this module.

Creating a Table with Conditional Formatting

Note: To complete this assignment, you will be required to use the Data Files. Please contact your instructor for information about accessing the Data Files.

Instructions: Start Excel. Open the workbook called SC_EX_6-2.xlsx, which is located in the Data Files. The spreadsheet you open contains a list from Sport Physical Therapy, including billing codes, times, and therapists. You are to create a table to include the name of the therapists based on a lookup table as shown in Figure 6–77. The conditional formatting is based on the unit of time billed to insurance.

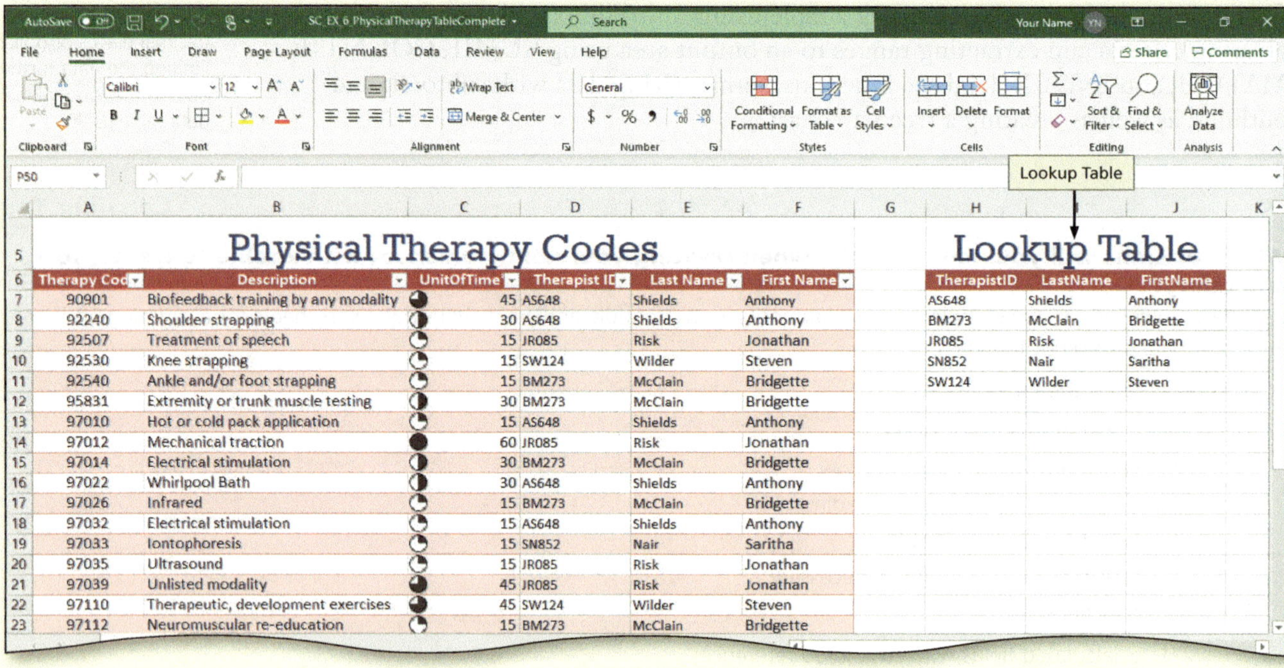

Figure 6–77

Perform the following tasks:

1. Save the file with the name, SC_EX_6_PhysicalTherapyTableComplete.
2. Select the range, A6:D36. Click the 'Format as Table' button (Home tab | Styles group) and then click 'Red, Table Style Medium 3' in the Format as Table gallery. When Excel displays the Format As Table dialog box, if necessary, click the 'My table has headers' check box to select the option to format the table with headers.
3. Name the table, Therapies, by using the Table Name text box (Table Design tab | Properties group).
4. Remove duplicates in the table by clicking the Remove Duplicates button (Table Design tab | Tools group). When Excel displays the Remove Duplicates dialog box, click the Select All button and then click OK.
5. Insert a new column in the table (column E), with the column heading, Last Name.
6. Insert a new column in the table (column F), with the column heading, First Name. Change both column widths to 14.5.

7. Change the row height of row 5 to 39. Click cell A5. Apply the Title cell style, the Rockwell font, and a font size of 28. Center the title across the selection, A5:F5, using the Format Cells dialog box and the 'Center Across Selection' command.
8. To create the lookup table, enter the data from Table 6–6, beginning with Lookup Table in cell H5. Use the format painter to copy the format from cell A5 to cell H5. Copy the headings from cells D6:F6 to cells H6:J6.

Table 6–6 Therapist Table

Lookup Table		
Therapist ID	**Last Name**	**First Name**
AS648	Shields	Anthony
BM273	McClain	Bridgette
JR085	Risk	Jonathan
SN852	Nair	Saritha
SW124	Wilder	Steven

9. Change the column width of columns H, I, and J to 13. Center the heading, Lookup Table, across cells H6:J6.
10. In cell E7, type `=xlookup(d7,$h$7:$h$11,$i$7:$i$11)` to enter the Last Name column in the main table. Repeat the process to enter a function for the First Name in cell F7. (Hint: The return_array argument of the function will be absolute references to the values in the range J7:J11.)
11. To apply conditional formatting:
    a. Select the range C7:C35, click the Conditional Formatting button (Home tab | Styles group), and then click New Rule to display the New Formatting Rule dialog box.
    b. Click the Format Style button (New Formatting Rule dialog box) to display the Format Style list.
    c. Click Icon Sets in the Format Style list (New Formatting Rule dialog box) to display the Icon area.
    d. Click the Icon Style arrow and then click 5 Quarters in the Icon Style list (New Formatting Rule dialog box) to select an icon style that includes five different black and white circles.
    e. Click the first Type button and then click Number in the list to select a numeric value. Repeat the process for the other three Type buttons.
    f. Type `60` in the first Value box, type `45` in the second Value box, type `30` in the third Value box, and type `15` in the fourth Value box. Press TAB to complete the conditions.
    g. Click OK (New Formatting Rule dialog box) to display icons in each row of the table.
12. Save the file again.
13. Use the Sort Ascending button on the Data tab to sort the table in ascending order by description.
14. Use the 'Sort & Filter' button on the Home tab to sort in descending order by unit of time.
15. Use the Sort button on the Data tab to create a custom sort by Therapist ID in ascending order, and then within Therapist ID by Therapy Code in ascending order.
16. Change the name of the sheet tab to Therapies.
17. Save the file, and then submit the workbook in the format specified by your instructor, and exit Excel.
18. What other kind of criteria, filter, or output might be helpful if the table were larger? When might you use some of the database and statistical functions on this kind of data? Why?

Extend Your Knowledge

Extend the skills you learned in this module and experiment with new skills. You may need to use Help to complete the assignment.

Using Functions

Note: To complete this assignment, you will be required to use the Data Files. Please contact your instructor for information about accessing the Data Files.

Instructions: Start Excel. Open the workbook called SC_EX_6-3, which is located in the Data Files. The workbook you open contains a list of IT employees along with their gender, age, years on the job, and knowledge of programming languages. You are to summarize the data in a variety of ways as shown in Figure 6–78.

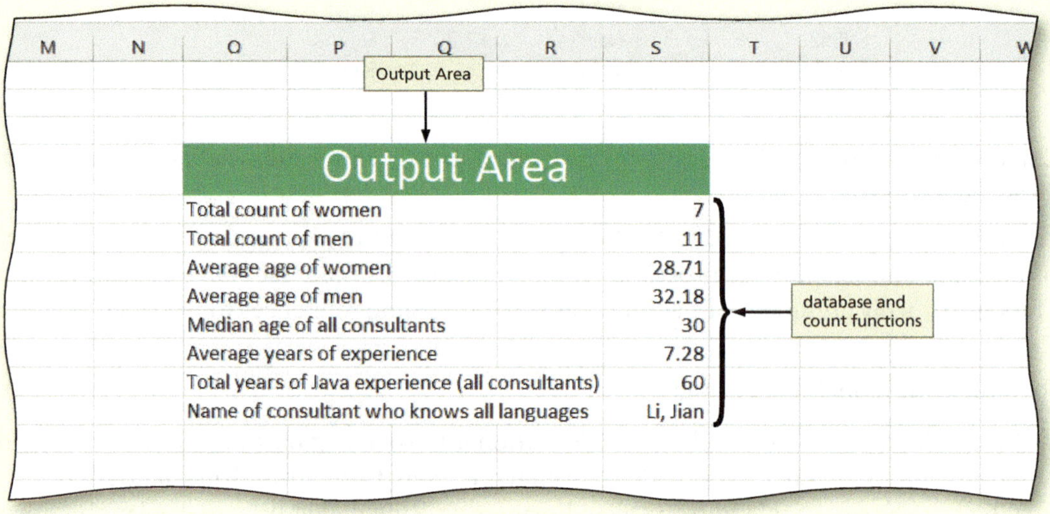

Figure 6–78

Perform the following tasks:

1. Save the workbook using the file name, SC_EX_6_ConsultantTableComplete.
2. Create a new column called Count in column L. Use the COUNTIF function in cell L11 to count all of the Y entries in the row—indicating the number of languages in which the consultant is proficient.
3. Select cells A9:L9. Merge and center the heading.
4. Name the table, Consultants.
5. Beside the table, create summary title and row headings as shown in Figure 6–78, and adjust the height of row 10 (the table column headings) to 15.75.
6. Use the COUNTIF function to obtain a total count for women and men. Use the AVERAGEIF function for the average ages. (Hint: Use Help to learn about the AVERAGEIF function.) Round off the averages to two decimal places.
7. Use the MEDIAN function to find the median age of all consultants. (Hint: If necessary, use Help to learn about the MEDIAN function.)
8. Use the AVERAGE function to average the years of experience.
9. Use the SUMIF function to find the total years of Java experience in the company.
10. Use the MATCH function wrapped inside the INDEX function, as you did in the module, to find the one consultant who is proficient in all seven languages. Right-align the cell contents.

11. Round off the averages to two decimal places, if necessary.
12. Save the file again and submit the assignment as requested by your instructor.
13. Which functions used structured references? Why?

Expand Your World

Create a solution that uses cloud and web technologies by learning and investigating on your own from general guidance.

Converting Files

You would like to place your Excel table on the web in a user-friendly format. You decide to investigate a Web 2.0 tool that will help you convert your table to HTML.

Instructions: Start Excel. Open any completed exercise from this module.

Perform the following tasks:

1. Drag through the table and column headings to select them. Press CTRL+C to copy the table cells.
2. Start a browser and navigate to https://tableizer.journalistopia.com/ (Figure 6–79).

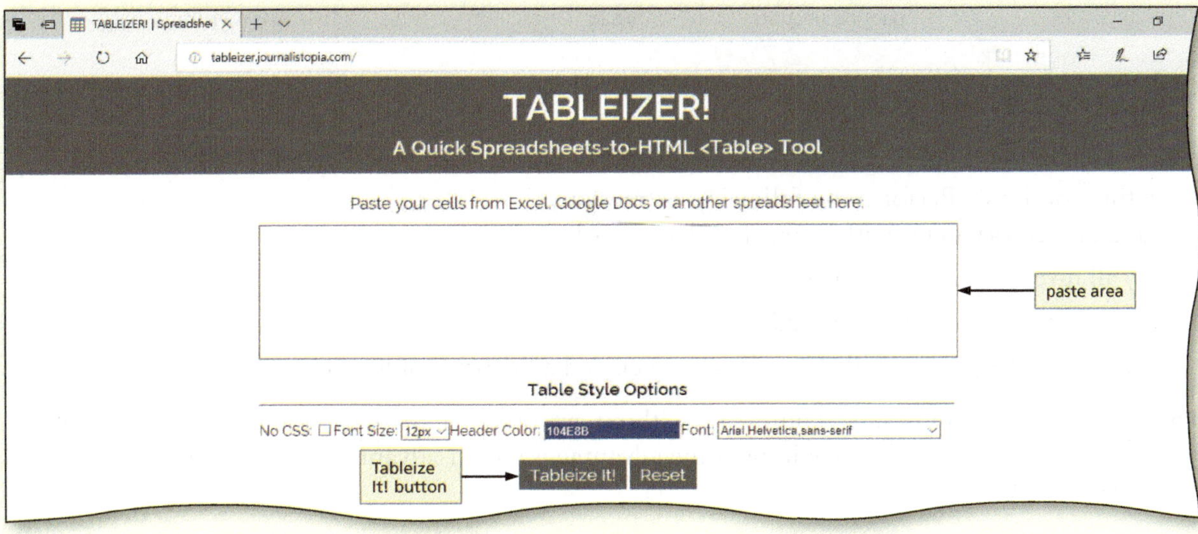

Figure 6–79

3. Click inside the gray paste area, and then press CTRL+V to paste the cells.
4. Click the Tableize It! button and wait a few seconds.
5. If you want to create an HTML page, copy the HTML code generated by Tableizer into a text editor such as Notepad. Save the Notepad file with the file name, SC_EX_6_MyTable.html. Display the file in a browser.
6. Many websites use tables to compare products, services, and pricing plans. Research HTML tables and web accessibility. What kinds of issues do screen readers have with HTML tables? Is it the best way to present information on the web?

In the Lab

Design and implement a solution using creative thinking and problem-solving skills.

Create and Query an Inventory

Problem: A local company would like to be able to search their shipping supplies inventory in an easy manner. They have given you sample data shown in Table 6–7.

Table 6–7 Inventory Data

Inventory Number	Description	Unit	Quantity in Stock	List Price
CX1D1	mailing labels	carton	25	$12.86
ED7XL	bubble wrap	roll	4	$27.59
T562W	packing tubes	single	14	$ 1.75
VP45L	corrugated boxes	bundle	17	$26.80
DC30W	packing tape	case	11	$65.00
LX550	poly mailers	carton	9	$ 8.99
SR123	packing peanuts	bag	5	$21.00

Perform the following tasks:

Part 1: Create the criteria range, the table, and the extract range with formatted headings and data. Save the workbook. Perform the following extractions.

a) all inventory items with more than 10 in stock

b) all inventory items in cartons

c) all inventory items under $25

d) all inventory items with 10 or less in stock and a list price of less than $10

Part 2: Do you think small companies without extensive database experience might use tables such as this every day? What would be some advantages and disadvantages? What calculated fields might you add to this table?

7 Creating Templates, Importing Data, and Working with SmartArt, Images, and Screenshots

Objectives

After completing this module, you will be able to:

- Create and use a template
- Import data from a text file, an Access database, a webpage, and a Word document
- Use text functions
- Paste values and paste text
- Transpose data while pasting it
- Convert text to columns
- Replicate formulas
- Use the Quick Analysis gallery
- Find and replace data
- Insert and format a bar chart
- Insert and modify a SmartArt graphic
- Add pictures to a SmartArt Graphic
- Apply text effects
- Include a hyperlinked screenshot
- Use ALT text
- Differentiate ways to link and embed

Introduction

In today's business environment, you often find that you need to create multiple worksheets or workbooks that follow the same basic format. A **template** is a special-purpose workbook you can create and use as a pattern for new, similar workbooks or worksheets. A template usually consists of a general format (worksheet title, column and row titles, and numeric formatting) and formulas that are common to all the worksheets. Templates can be saved to a common storage location so that everyone in a company can use them to create standardized documents.

Another important concept to understand is the Excel capability to use and analyze data from a wide variety of sources. In this module, you will learn how to **import**, or bring in, data from various external sources into an Excel worksheet and then analyze that data. Excel allows you to import data from a number of types of sources, including text files, webpages, database tables, data stored in Word documents, and XML files.

Finally, a chart, graphic, image, icon, or screenshot often conveys information or an idea better than words or numbers. You can insert and modify graphics, images, and screenshots to enhance the visual appeal of an Excel workbook and illustrate its contents. Many of the skills you learn when working with graphics in Excel will be similar when working in other Office programs, such as Word, Publisher, or PowerPoint.

Project: Meyor Insurance

Meyor Insurance (MI) is a retail and online outlet for individual insurance policies. The company owner has requested that the in-office and online sales results for the last two years be compared among its four branch offices. One of the branches provides the requested data in a plain text format (Figure 7–1a) rather than in an Excel workbook. To make use of that data in Excel, the data must be imported before it can be formatted and manipulated. The same is true of formats in which the other locations store data, such as Microsoft Access tables (Figure 7–1b), webpages (Figure 7–1c), or Microsoft Word documents (Figure 7–1d). Excel provides the tools necessary to import and manipulate the data from these sources into a single worksheet (Figure 7–1e). Using the data from the worksheet, you will create a bar chart to summarize total sales by category (Figure 7–1f). Finally, you will add SmartArt graphics that include images (Figure 7–1g) and a hyperlinked screenshot to support your work (Figure 7–1h).

Figure 7–2 illustrates the requirements document for the MI Sales Analysis workbook. It includes the needs, sources of data, calculations, charts, and other facts about the workbook's development.

In addition, using a sketch of the main worksheet can help you visualize its design. The sketch of the worksheet consists of titles, column and cell headings, the location of data values, and a general idea of the desired formatting in the worksheet. The data will include 2020 and 2021 data, with a summary on the right (Figure 7–3a). Figure 7–3b displays a basic sketch of the requested graph, a bar chart, showing the 2021 totals by category.

With a good understanding of the requirements document, an understanding of the necessary decisions, and a sketch of the worksheet and graph, the next step is to use Excel to create the workbook.

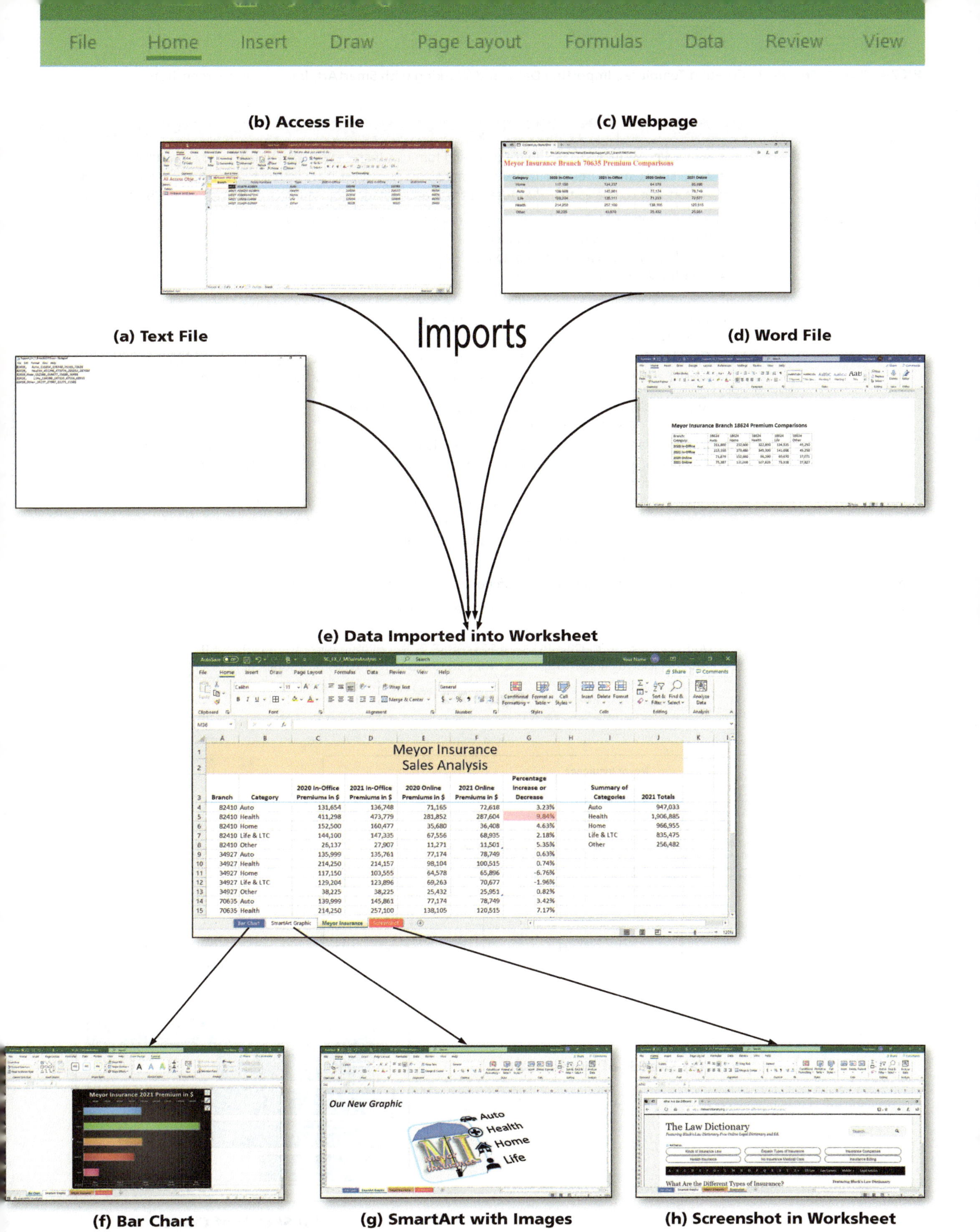
File
Home
Insert
Draw
Page Layout
Formulas
Data
Review
View
(b) Access File
(c) Webpage
Meyor Insurance Branch 70635 Premium Comparisons
(a) Text File
Imports
(d) Word File
Meyor Insurance Branch 18624 Premium Comparisons
(e) Data Imported into Worksheet
Meyor Insurance
Sales Analysis
Meyor Insurance 2021 Premium in $
Our New Graphic
Auto
Health
Home
Life
The Law Dictionary
What Are the Different Types of Insurance?
(f) Bar Chart
(g) SmartArt with Images
(h) Screenshot in Worksheet

Figure 7–1

Worksheet Title	Meyor Insurance Sales Analysis
Needs	• A template with headings, sample data, and formulas than can be used to create similar worksheets • A workbook, made from the template, containing a worksheet that combines sales data from the four branches • A chart that compares the 2021 total sales for each category of insurance products that the branch sells
Source of Data	The four agents will submit data from their respective branches as follows: • Branch 82410 saves data in a text file. • Branch 34927 uses an Access database. • Branch 70635 maintains web data. • Branch 18624 uses Word to store data in a table.
Calculations	Include the following formula in the template for each line item: • =((D4+F4)/(C4+E4))-1 This formula takes the total of 2021 in-office and online sales divided by the total of 2020 in-office and online sales to arrive at a percentage, and then subtracts 1 to arrive at just the increase or decrease. Include the following two functions to help summarize the data: • IF(COUNTIF($B$4:B4,B4)=1,B4,"") This formula finds the unique categories in column B. It includes the COUNTIF function that will return true if there is only one occurrence; the IF function will then display that occurrence. If no match is made, the IF function will display a blank. • =SUMIF($B$4:$B$100,I4,$D$4:$D$100)+SUMIF($B$4:$B$100,I4,$F$4:$F$100) This function will add the 2021 in-office and online sales on a category basis. It adds the value in column D plus the value in column F, if cell I4 matches the value from column B. The function will look through row 100 as the maximum number of records.
Chart Requirements	Create a bar chart to compare the categories for sales in 2021. Include the chart on a separate worksheet.
Other Requirements	• Design a SmartArt graphic to include the picture and icon given to you by the company, to be placed on a separate worksheet. • On a separate worksheet, include a screenshot of the website they recommend for questions about insurance (https://thelawdictionary.org/article/what-are-the-different-types-of-insurance).

Figure 7–2

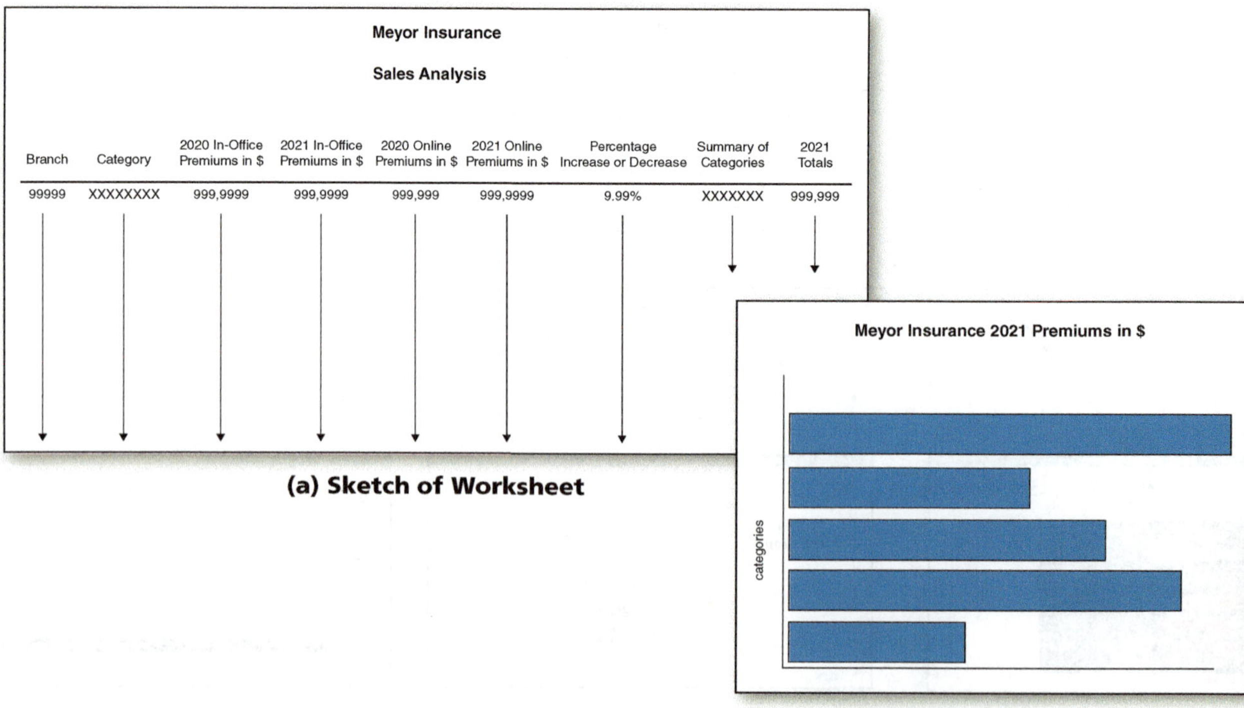

(a) Sketch of Worksheet

(b) Sketch of Chart

Figure 7–3

Creating Templates

The first step in building the project in this module is to create and save a template that contains the titles, column and row headings, formulas, and formats. After the template is saved, it can be used every time a similar workbook is developed. Because templates help speed and simplify their work, many Excel users create a template for each project on which they work. Templates can be simple—possibly using a special font or worksheet title; or they can be more complex—perhaps using specific formulas and format styles, such as the template for the MI Sales Analysis workbook.

Consider This

What factors should you keep in mind when building a template?

A template usually contains data and formatting that will appear in every workbook created from that template. Because the template will be used to create a number of other worksheets, make sure you consider the layout, cell formatting, and contents of the workbook as you design the template. Set row heights and column widths. Use placeholders for data when possible and use dummy data to verify formulas. Format the cells in the template.

Creating a template, such as the one shown in Figure 7–4, follows the same basic steps used to create a workbook. The main difference between developing a workbook and a template is the file type used when saving the template.

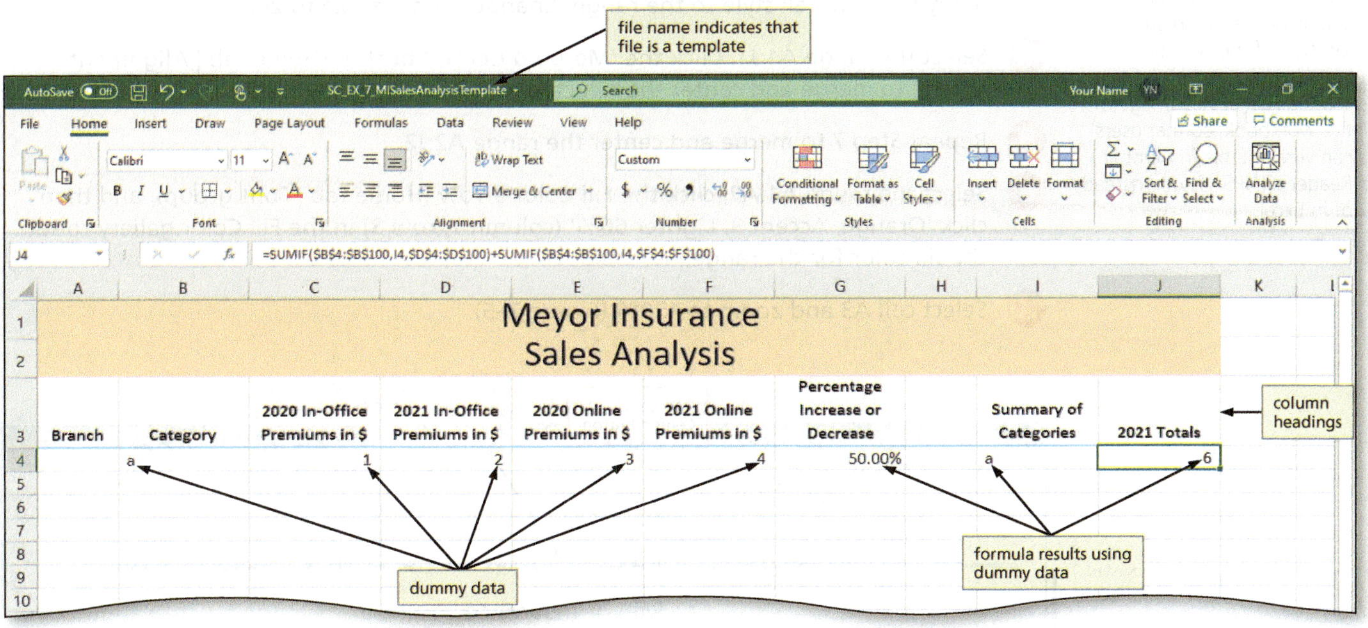

Figure 7–4

To Open a Blank Workbook and Format the Rows and Columns

The following steps open a blank workbook and set the row height and column widths.

1. **sam** Start Excel.
2. Click the Blank workbook thumbnail on the Excel start screen to create a blank workbook and display it in the Excel window.

BTW
Ribbon and Screen Resolution
Excel may change how the groups and buttons within the groups appear on the ribbon, depending on the screen resolution of your computer. Thus, your ribbon may look different from the ones in this book if you are using a screen resolution other than 1366 × 768.

3. If the Excel window is not maximized, click the Maximize button on its title bar to maximize the window.

4. Change the row height of rows 1 and 2 to 25. Change the height of row 3 to 45.

BTW
Touch Mode Differences
The Office and Windows interfaces may vary if you are using Touch Mode. For this reason, you might notice that the function or appearance of your touch screen differs slightly from this module's presentation.

To Enter Titles in the Template

The following steps enter and format the titles in cells A1 and A2.

1. In cell A1, enter `Meyor Insurance` as the worksheet title.
2. In cell A2, enter `Sales Analysis` as the worksheet subtitle.
3. Display the Page Layout tab. Click the Themes button (Page Layout tab | Themes group) and then click Parallax in the gallery to apply the Parallax theme to the worksheet.
4. Click the Fonts button (Page Layout tab | Themes group) and then click Calibri in the Fonts gallery to apply the Calibri font to the worksheet.
5. Set the column widths as follows: A = 9.00, B through G = 15.00, H = 8.00, I and J = 14.00.
6. Select the range A1:A2. Click the Cell Styles button (Home tab | Styles group) and then apply the Title cell style to the range. Change the font size to 24.
7. Select the range A1:J1. Click the 'Merge & Center' button (Home tab | Alignment group) to merge and center the selected cells.
8. Repeat Step 7 to merge and center the range A2:J2.
9. Select the range A1:A2, click the Fill Color arrow (Home tab | Font group), and then click 'Orange, Accent 3, Lighter 60%' (column 7, row 3) in the Fill Color gallery to set the fill color for the range.
10. Select cell A3 and zoom to 120% (Figure 7–5).

BTW
Distributing a Document
Instead of printing and distributing a hard copy of a workbook, you can distribute the workbook electronically. Options include sending the workbook via email; posting it on cloud storage (such as OneDrive) and sharing the file with others; posting it on social media, a blog, or other website; and sharing a link associated with an online location of the workbook. You also can create and share a PDF or XPS image of the workbook, so that users can view the file in Acrobat Reader or XPS Viewer instead of in Excel.

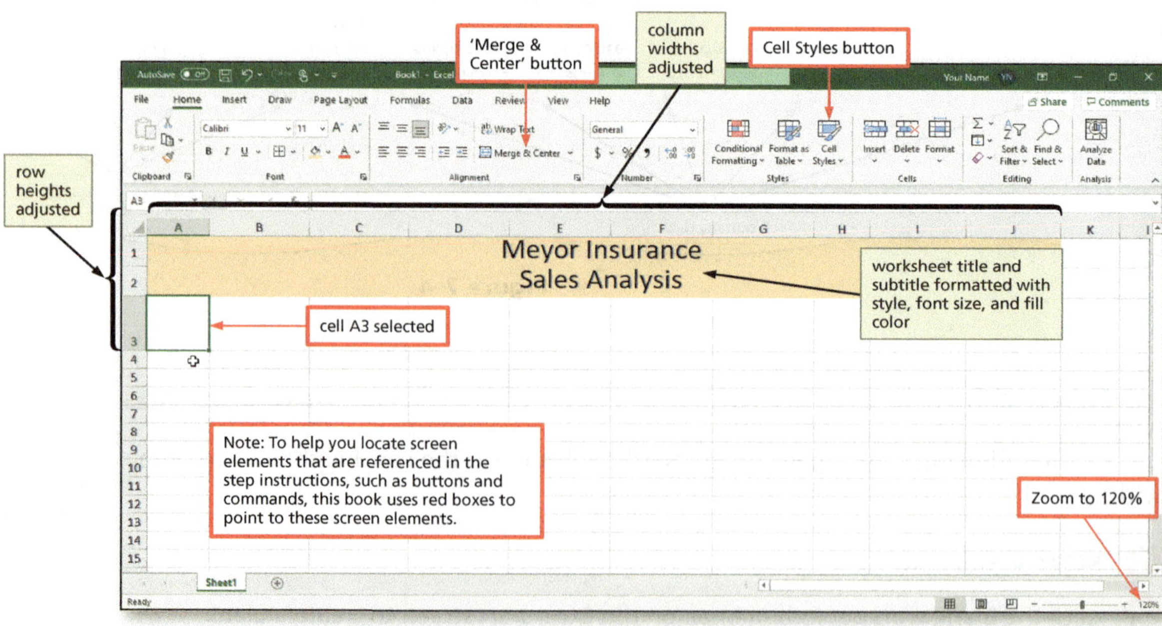

Figure 7–5

To Enter Column Titles in the Template

The following steps enter and format the column titles in row 3.

1. Select cells A3:J3 and then click the Wrap Text button (Home tab | Alignment group) to apply the formatting. Click the Center button (Home tab | Alignment group) and then apply the Heading 3 cell style to the range.
2. Type the following column titles into the appropriate cells (Figure 7–6).

A3	Branch
B3	Category
C3	2020 In-Office Premiums in $
D3	2021 In-Office Premiums in $
E3	2020 Online Premiums in $
F3	2021 Online Premiums in $
G3	Percentage Increase or Decrease
H3	<blank>
I3	Summary of Categories
J3	2021 Totals

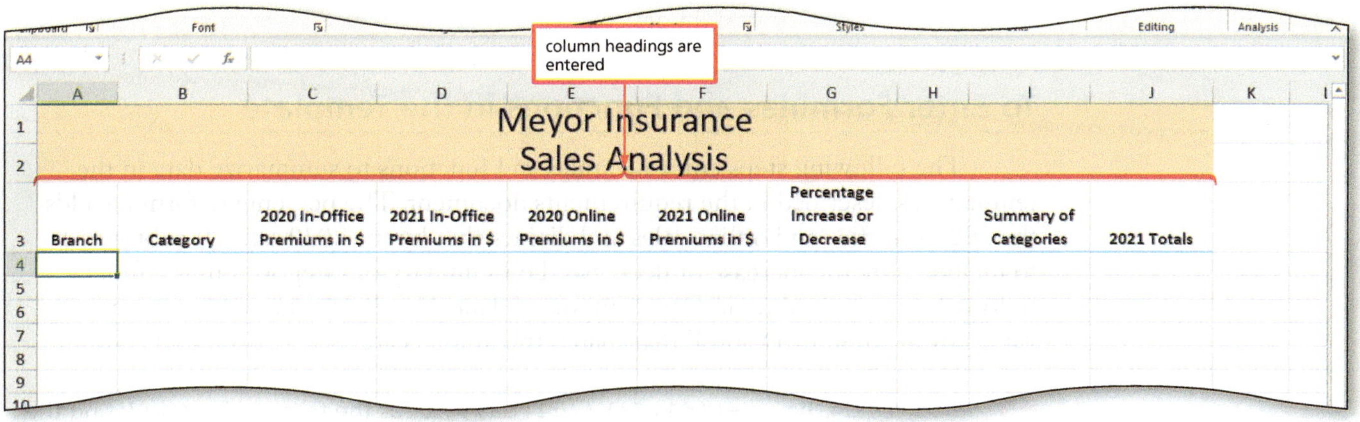

Figure 7–6

To Enter Sample Data in the Template

When you create a template, it is good practice to use sample data or dummy data in place of actual data to verify the formulas in the template. Entering simple text, such as a, b, or c, and numbers, such as 1, 2, or 3, allows you to check quickly to see if the formulas are generating the proper results. In templates with more complex formulas, you may want to use numbers that test the extreme boundaries of valid data, such as the lowest or highest possible number, or a maximum number of records.

In preparation for entering formulas, the following steps enter sample data in the template.

1. Select cell B4. Type **a** to enter the first piece of sample data.
2. Select cell C4. Type **1** to enter the first number in the series.

3. Enter the other dummy data as shown in Figure 7–7.

4. Select the range C4:F4. Apply the comma style with no decimal places to the selected range.

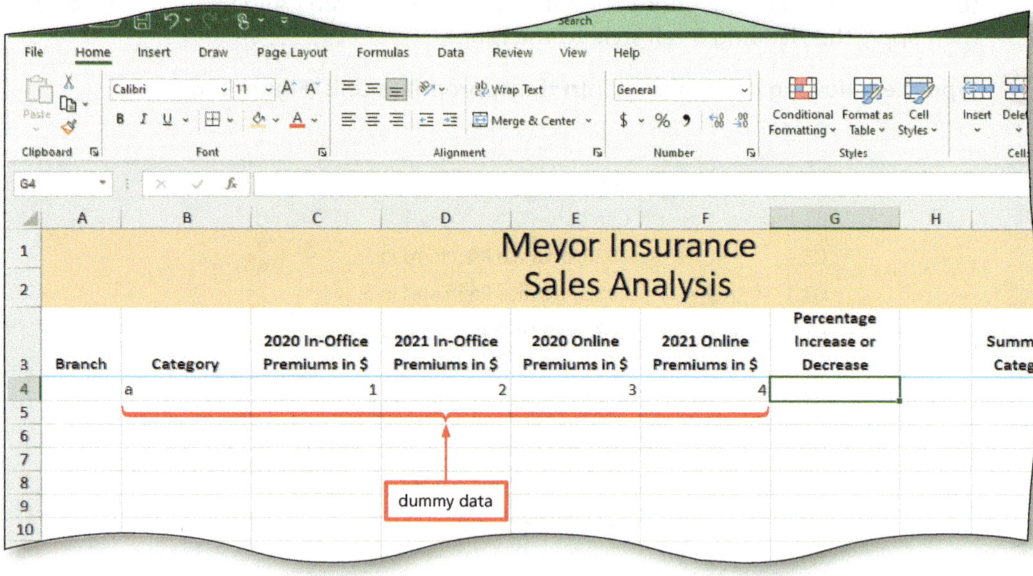

Figure 7–7

To Enter Formulas and Functions in the Template

The following steps enter formulas and functions to summarize data in the template, as described in the requirements document. The percentage formula adds the 2021 in-office and online sales and divides that by the 2020 sales. It subtracts 1 to include only the increase or decrease. The summary of categories uses a function to look for unique values in future imported data. The 2021 totals add any imported values from columns D and F that match the unique category identified in column I.

1. Select cell G4. Type `=((d4+f4)/(c4+e4))-1` as the formula for calculating the percentage increase or decrease from 2020 to 2021 and then click the Enter button.

2. Format cell G4 with a percent sign and two decimal places.

3. Select cell I4. Type `=if(countif($b$4:b4,b4)=1,b4,"")` to enter a function that displays a value from the Category list if it is unique. Click the Enter button.

4. Select cell J4. Type `=sumif($b$4:$b$100,i4,$d$4:$d$100)+sumif($b$4:$b$100,i4,$f$4:$f$100)` to enter a function that adds columns d and f, if the value returned in cell I4 matches the data in the Category list in column B. The function will look through row 100 as the maximum number of records. Click the Enter button.

5. Format cell J4 with a comma and no decimal places.

6. Change the sheet tab name to Meyor Insurance to provide a descriptive name for the worksheet.

7. Change the sheet tab color to Orange, Accent 3 to format the tab (Figure 7–8).

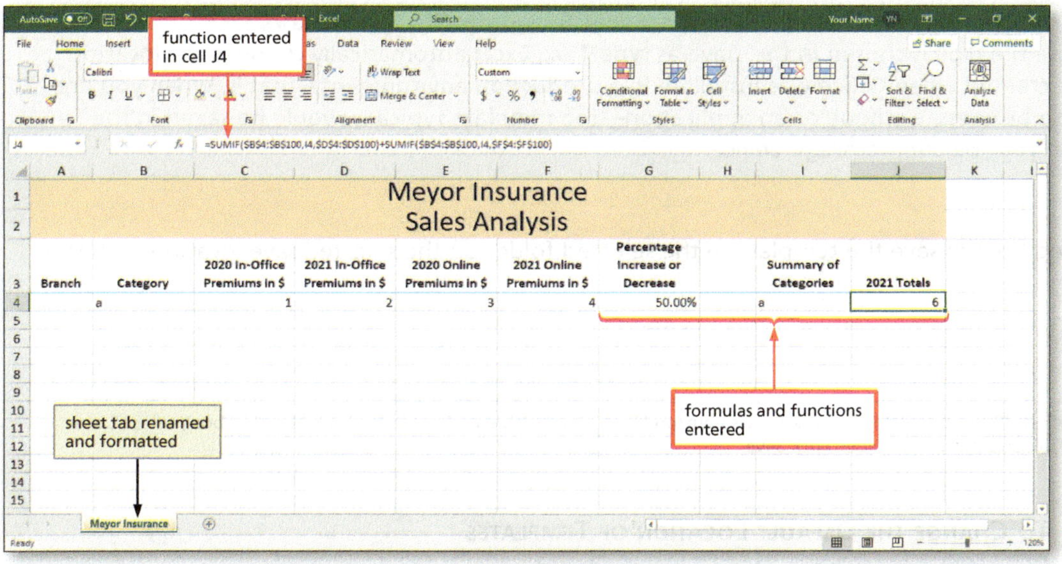

Figure 7–8

To Save the Template

Saving a template is similar to saving a workbook, except that the file type, Excel Template, is selected in the 'Save as type' box (Save As dialog box). Excel saves the file with the extension, .xltx, to denote its template status. Saving in that format prevents users from accidentally saving over the template file, and causes Excel to open new workbooks based on the template with the proper format. In business situations, it is a good idea to save the template in the default Templates folder location. **Why?** Company templates saved in the Templates folder appear with other templates when users need to find them. In lab situations, however, you should save templates on your personal storage device. The following steps save the template using the file name, SC_EX_7_MISalesAnalysisTemplate.xltx, on your storage device.

1

- Click cell A4 to position the current cell.
- Click the File tab and click Save As to display the Save As screen and then click the Browse button to display the Save As dialog box.
- Type **SC_EX_7_MISalesAnalysisTemplate** in the File name box to enter a name for the file.
- Click the 'Save as type' arrow and then click Excel Template (or Excel Template (*.xltx)) in the list to specify that this workbook should be saved as a template.
- Navigate to your storage device and desired folder, if any (Figure 7–9).

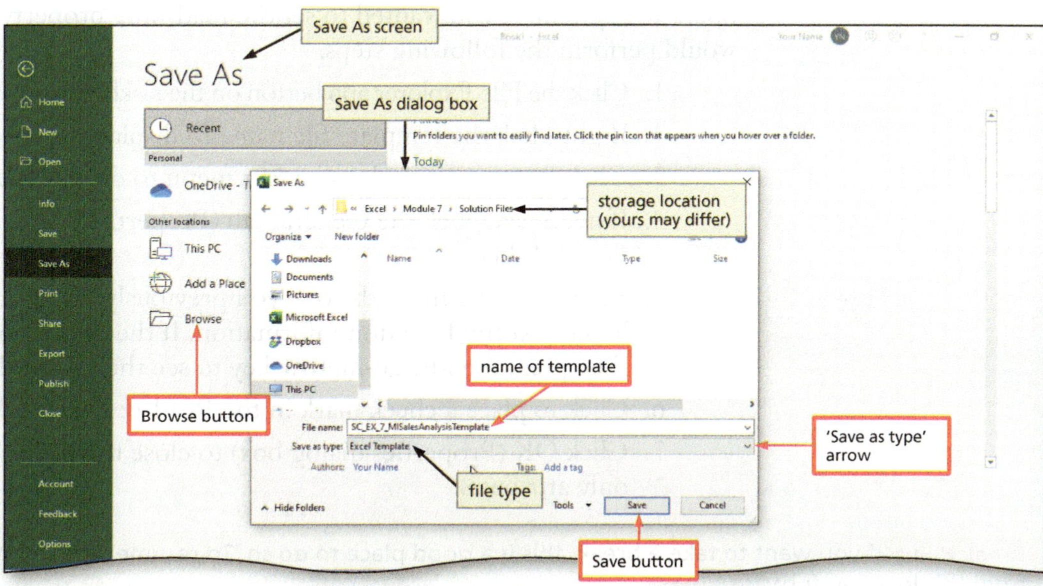

Figure 7–9

Q&A

Why does Excel change the folder location when the Excel Template file type is chosen?

When the Excel Template file type is chosen in the 'Save as type' box, Excel automatically changes the location to the Templates folder created when Office was installed. In a production environment—that is, when you are creating a template for a business, a school, or an application—the template typically would be saved in the Templates folder, not on your personal storage device.

2

- Click Save (Save As dialog box) to save the template in the selected folder on the selected save location with the entered file name.
- Exit Excel.

Other Ways

1. Press CTRL+S, click More options ('Save this file' box), click Browse button (Save As screen), type file name (Save As dialog box), select Excel Template in 'Save as type' box, select drive or folder, click Save

To Change the Default Location of Templates

If you wanted to change the default location where templates are stored, you would perform the following steps.

1. Click File on the ribbon to open Backstage view.
2. Click Options to display the Excel Options dialog box.
3. Click Save in the left pane (Excel Options dialog box) and then in the Save workbooks area, enter the desired path in the 'Default personal templates location' box.
4. Click OK (Excel Options dialog box).

To Set the Read-Only Attribute

Once a template is created, you may want to change the file's attribute, or classification, to read-only. With a **read-only file**, you can open and access the file normally, but you cannot make permanent changes to it. That way, users will be forced to save changes to the template with a new file name, keeping the original template intact and unchanged for the next user.

While you can view system properties in Excel, you cannot change the read-only attribute from within Excel. Setting the read-only attribute is a function of the operating system. If you wanted to set the read-only property of the template, you would perform the following steps.

1. Click the File Explorer app button on the taskbar. Navigate to your storage location.
2. Right-click the template file name to display the shortcut menu.
3. Click Properties on the shortcut menu to display the Properties dialog box.
4. If necessary, click the General tab (Properties dialog box) to display the General sheet.
5. Verify that the file is the one you previously saved on your storage device by looking at the Location information. If the path is long, click in the path and then press the RIGHT-ARROW key to see the rest of the path.
6. Click to place a check mark in the Read-only check box in the Attributes area.
7. Click OK (Properties dialog box) to close the dialog box and apply the read-only attribute.

Break Point: If you want to take a break, this is a good place to do so. To resume later, continue following the steps from this location forward.

To Open a Template-Based File and Save It as a Workbook

As with other Office apps, you can open an Excel template in one of several ways:

- If you use the Open gallery in Backstage view, you will open the template file itself for editing.
- If you have stored the template in the default template storage location, you can click the New tab in Backstage view and then click Personal. Clicking the template file in the Personal gallery will open a new file based on the template.
- If you stored the template in another location, you must double-click the file in the File Explorer window to create a new file based on the template.

When you open a file based on a template, Excel names the new workbook using the template name with an appended digit 1 (e.g., Monthly Budget Template1). **Why?** Adding a 1 to the file name delineates it from the template; it is similar to what Excel does when you first run Excel and it assigns the name Book1 to the new workbook. You can save the file with a new file name if you want.

The following steps open a file based on the template. You then will save it in the .xlsx format with a new file name in order to proceed with data entry.

1

- Click the File Explorer button on the taskbar to start the File Explorer app.
- Navigate to your Data File storage location (Figure 7–10).

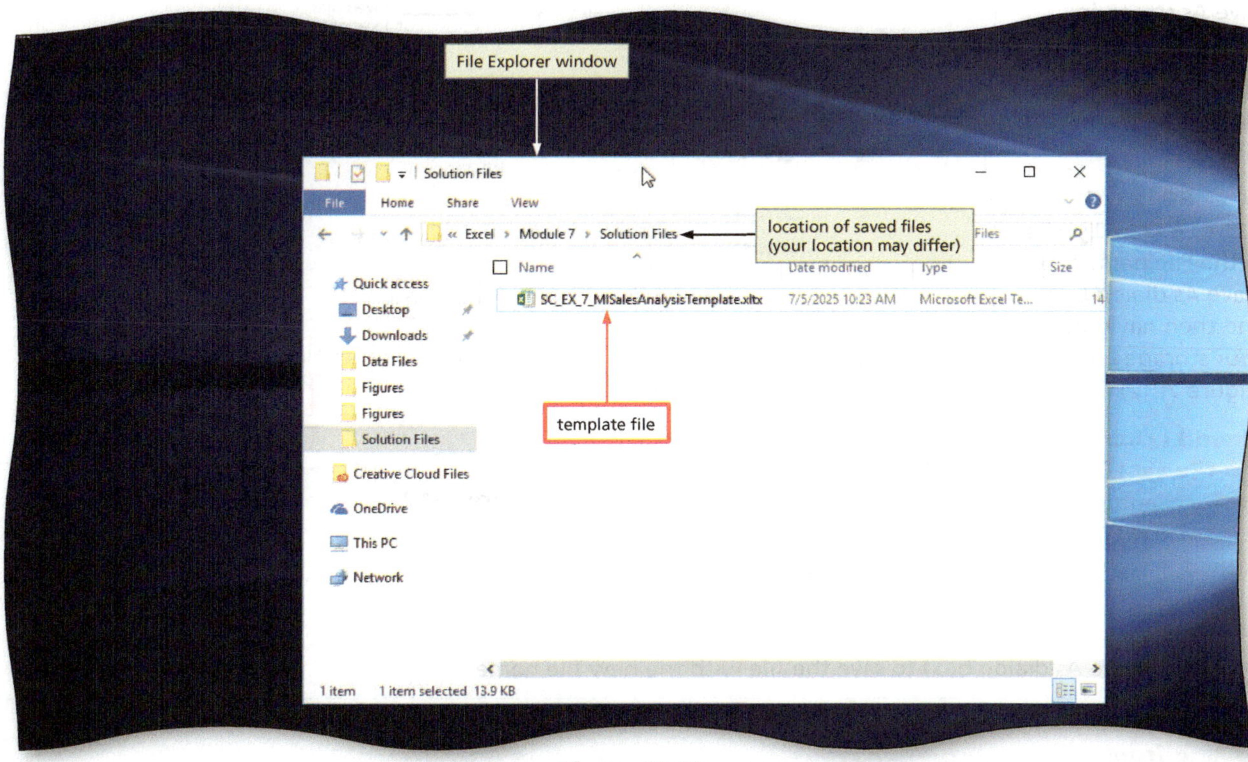

Figure 7–10

2

- Double-click the file named SC_EX_7_MISalesAnalysisTemplate.xltx to open a new file based on the template (Figure 7–11).

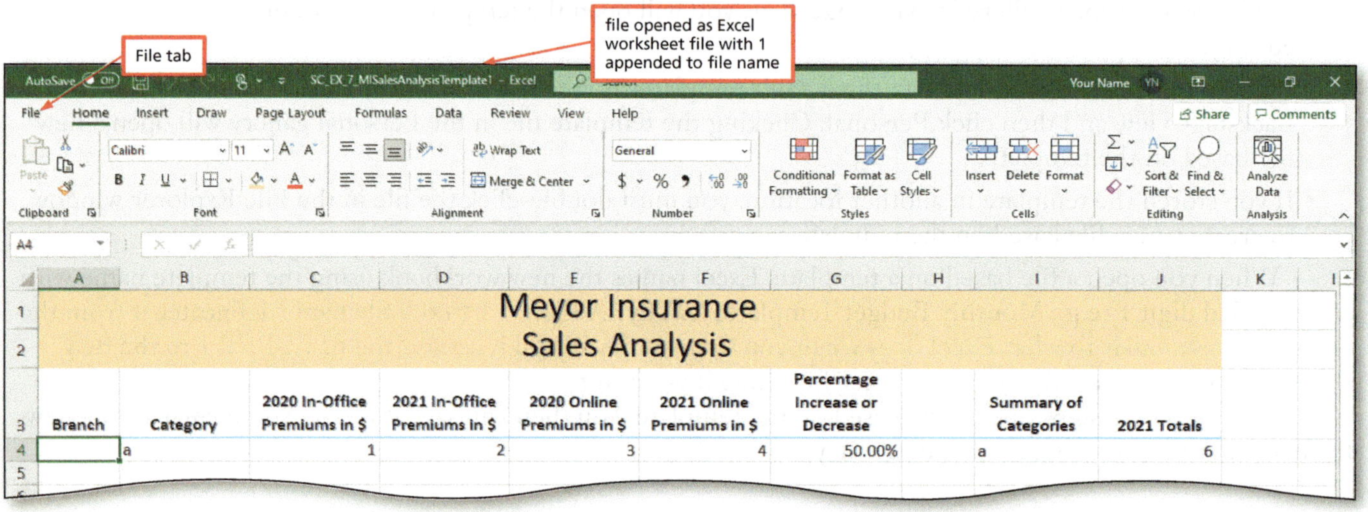

Figure 7–11

3

- Click the File tab and then click Save As to display the Save As screen in Backstage view.
- Click Browse to display the Save As dialog box.
- Type **SC_EX_7_MISalesAnalysis** in the File name box (Save As dialog box) and then navigate to your storage location (Figure 7–12).

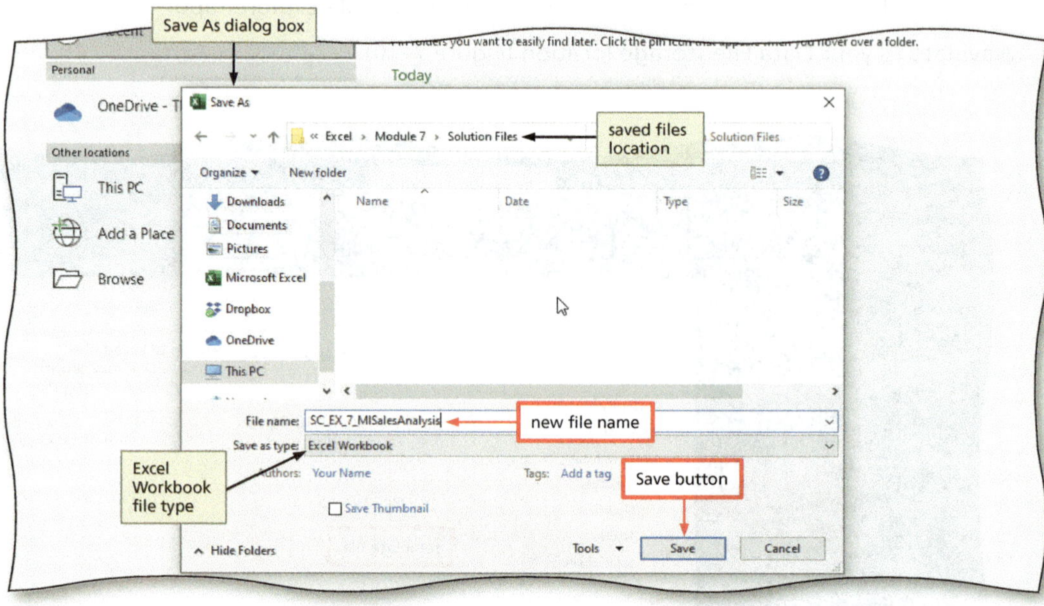

Figure 7–12

Q&A **Should I change the file type?**
No. Excel automatically selects Excel Workbook as the file type when you attempt to save a file based on a template.

4

- Click Save (Save As dialog box) to save the file with the new file name.

BTW
Importing from Databases
Excel can import data from a wide variety of sources including databases stored in XML files and those stored on SQL servers. You also can use Microsoft Query to retrieve data from corporate databases. The Get Data button (Data tab | Get & Transform Data group) presents an extensive list with submenus.

Importing Data

Data may come from a variety of sources and in a range of formats. Even though many users keep data in databases, such as Microsoft Access, it is common to receive text files with fields of data separated by commas. More and more companies are creating HTML files and posting data on the web. Word documents, especially those including tables of data, often are used in business as a source of data for workbooks. **XML (Extensible**

Markup Language), a popular format for data exchange, is a set of encoding rules that formats data to be readable by both humans and devices.

Excel uses query tools to assist you in importing data. You can load the data directly to your worksheet, or first shape that data in ways that meet your needs. For example, you can remove a column or row, change a data type, or merge data before moving it into your worksheet. Excel keeps track of your changes in a special pane.

Excel has an extensive selection of file formats. You can import data from databases such as Oracle, MySQL, and Sybase; from online services such as Salesforce and Sharepoint; and from **Azure**, the Microsoft cloud service, which allows you to build, manage, and deploy applications. A special From Folder command even imports data about the files in a folder to which you are connected. These and many more forms of data are listed when you click the Get Data button (Data tab | Get & Transform Data group). Importing data into Excel can create a link that can be used to update data whenever the original file changes.

BTW

Importing Azure Data

While the Windows Azure Marketplace is no longer available, some of the specific kinds of data are available with Power Query. Click the Get Data button (Data tab | Get & Transform Data group) and then click From Azure to see a complete list.

BTW

Data Connection Wizard

If you import some kinds of data that require authentication, such as Analysis Services or OData Data Feeds, Excel will present a series of dialog boxes called the Data Connection Wizard, as it tries to help you enter server names, database names, passwords, etc.

Consider This

How should you plan for importing data?

Before importing data, become familiar with the layout of the data, so that you can anticipate how each data element will be arranged in the worksheet. In some cases, the data will need to be transposed, meaning that the rows and columns need to be switched. You also might need to format the data, move it, or convert it from or to a table.

In the following sections, you will import data from four different insurance branches and in four different popular formats, including a text file, an Access file, web data, and a Word document. Using a variety of import techniques, you will look for data inconsistencies, format the data as necessary, and replicate the formulas to create the consolidated worksheet shown as a printout in Figure 7–13.

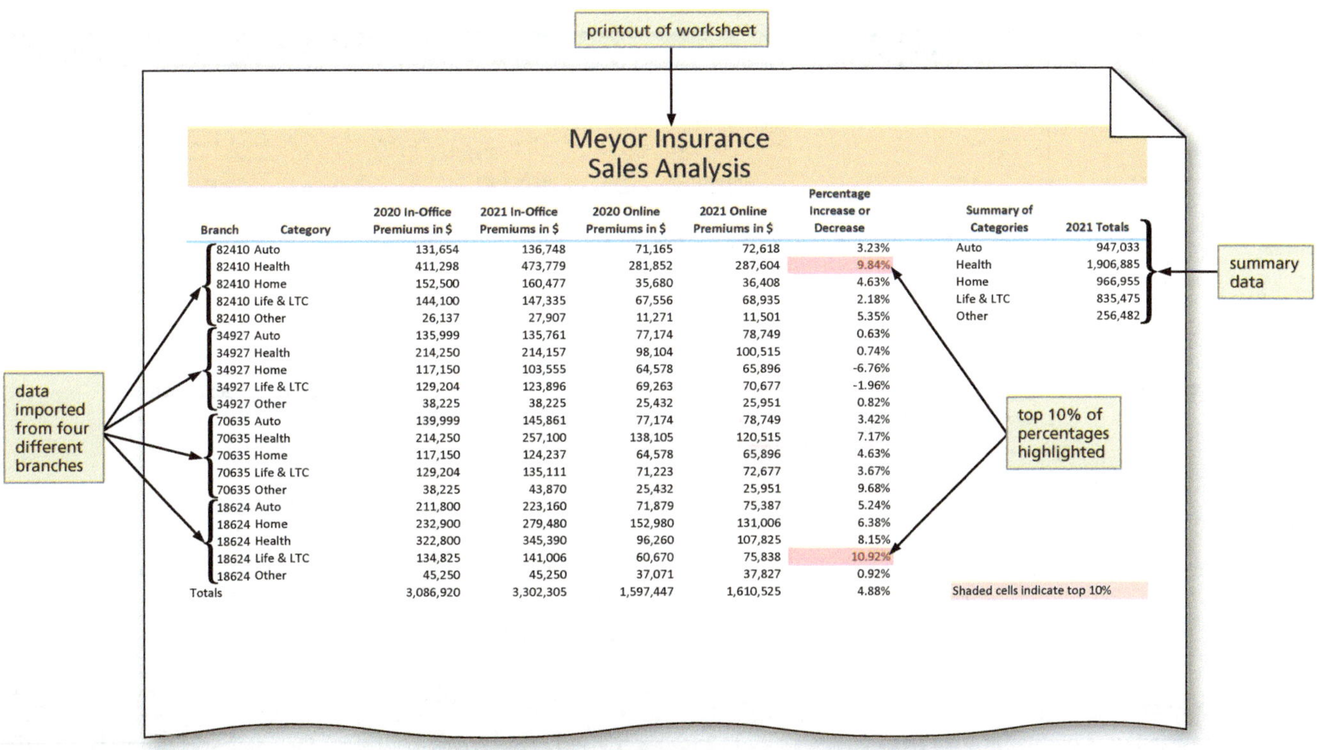

Meyor Insurance
Sales Analysis

Branch	Category	2020 In-Office Premiums in $	2021 In-Office Premiums in $	2020 Online Premiums in $	2021 Online Premiums in $	Percentage Increase or Decrease	Summary of Categories	2021 Totals
82410	Auto	131,654	136,748	71,165	72,618	3.23%	Auto	947,033
82410	Health	411,298	473,779	281,852	287,604	9.84%	Health	1,906,885
82410	Home	152,500	160,477	35,680	36,408	4.63%	Home	966,955
82410	Life & LTC	144,100	147,335	67,556	68,935	2.18%	Life & LTC	835,475
82410	Other	26,137	27,907	11,271	11,501	5.35%	Other	256,482
34927	Auto	135,999	135,761	77,174	78,749	0.63%		
34927	Health	214,250	214,157	98,104	100,515	0.74%		
34927	Home	117,150	103,555	64,578	65,896	-6.76%		
34927	Life & LTC	129,204	123,896	69,263	70,677	-1.96%		
34927	Other	38,225	38,225	25,432	25,951	0.82%		
70635	Auto	139,999	145,861	77,174	78,749	3.42%		
70635	Health	214,250	257,100	138,105	120,515	7.17%		
70635	Home	117,150	124,237	64,578	65,896	4.63%		
70635	Life & LTC	129,204	135,111	71,223	72,677	3.67%		
70635	Other	38,225	43,870	25,432	25,951	9.68%		
18624	Auto	211,800	223,160	71,879	75,387	5.24%		
18624	Home	232,900	279,480	152,980	131,006	6.38%		
18624	Health	322,800	345,390	96,260	107,825	8.15%		
18624	Life & LTC	134,825	141,006	60,670	75,838	10.92%		
18624	Other	45,250	45,250	37,071	37,827	0.92%		
Totals		3,086,920	3,302,305	1,597,447	1,610,525	4.88%	Shaded cells indicate top 10%	

Figure 7–13

Text Files

A **text file** contains data with little or no formatting. Many programs, including Excel, offer an option to import data from a text file. Text files may have a file extension such as .txt, .csv, .asc, or .cdl, among others. Companies sometimes generate these text files from input fields via proprietary business applications.

In text files, commas, tabs, or other characters often separate the fields. Alternately, the text file may have fields of equal length in columnar format. Each record usually exists on a separate line. A **delimited file** is a file in which each record is on a separate line and the fields are separated by a special character, called a **delimiter**. A delimited file in which the data is separated by commas is called a **comma-delimited text file**. A **fixed-width file** contains data fields of equal length with spaces between the fields. In the case of a fixed-width file, a special character need not separate the data fields. During the import process, Excel provides a preview to help identify the type of text file being imported.

To Import Data from a Text File

The following steps import a comma-delimited text file into the MI Sales Analysis workbook using the Load To command. **Why?** The Load To command imports data as a table, directly into the current worksheet. Alternately, the Load command imports data into a new sheet within the workbook. The text file contains data about sales for Branch #82410 (shown in Figure 7–1a). To complete these steps, you will be required to use the Data Files. Please contact your instructor for information about accessing the Data Files.

1

- With the Meyor Insurance worksheet active, select cell A5.
- Click Data on the ribbon to display the Data tab.
- Click the 'From Text/CSV' button (Data tab | Get & Transform Data group) to display the Import Data dialog box.
- If necessary, navigate to the location of the Data Files to display the files (Figure 7–14).

Q&A **Should I import data to cell A4?**
No. The import process will not overwrite current data, as in cell B4. You will delete the dummy data later in the module.

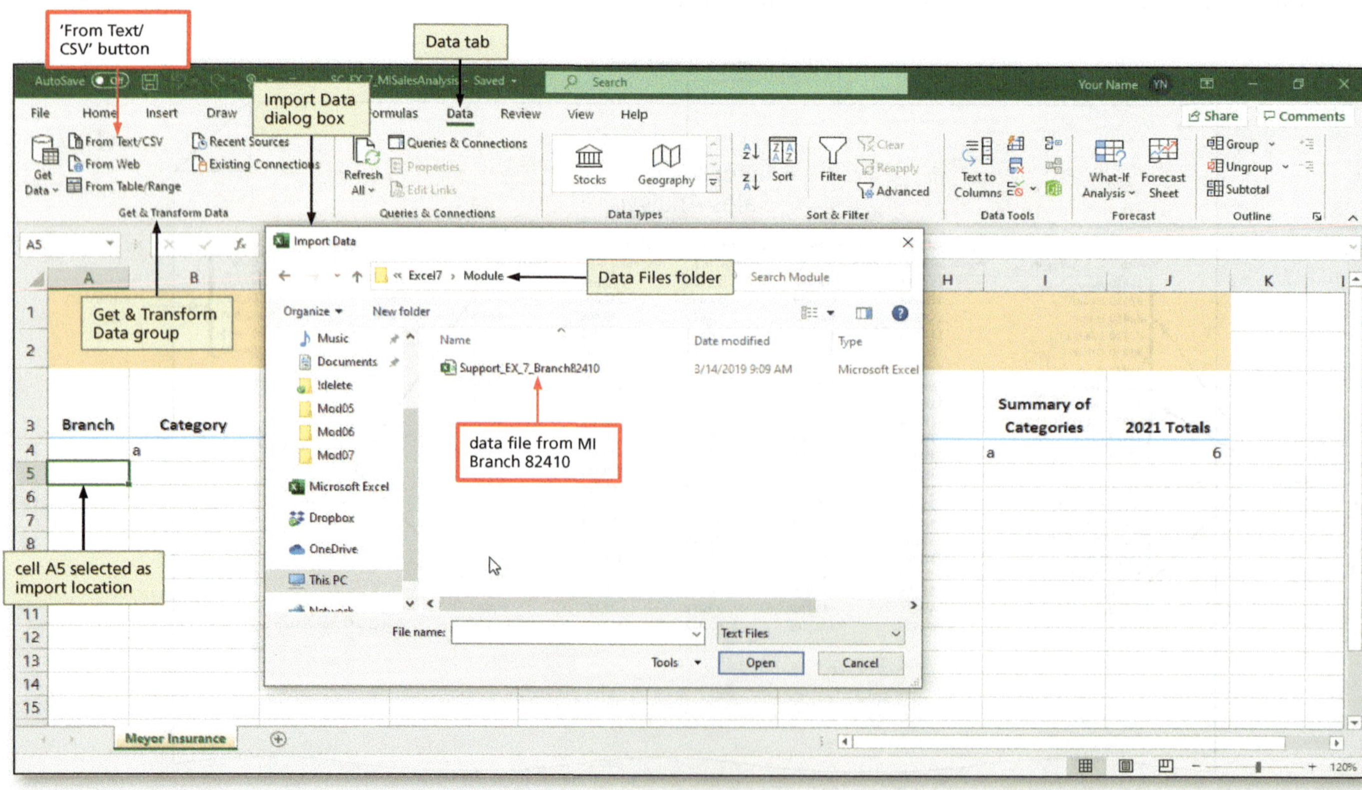

Figure 7–14

2

- Double-click the file name 'Support_EX_7_Branch82410.csv' to display the preview window.
- Click the Load arrow (Figure 7–15).

Q&A **What happened to the Text Import Wizard?**
The Text Import Wizard has been replaced by the query functions. If you want to use the wizard, click File, click Options, and then click Data (Excel Options dialog box). Click to display a check mark in the 'From Text (Legacy)' check box. Click the OK button. A Legacy Wizards option will be added to the Get Data list.

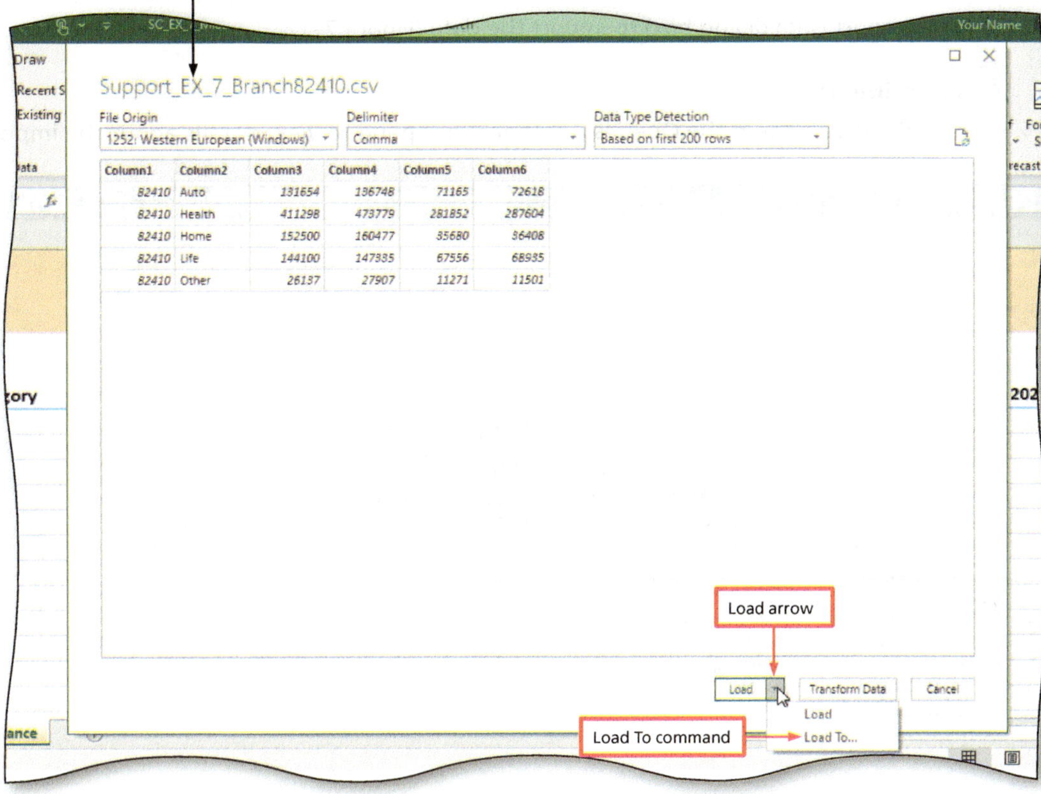

Figure 7–15

3

- Click Load To to display the Import Data dialog box.
- Click the Existing worksheet option button to place the data in the current worksheet rather than on a new sheet (Figure 7–16).

Q&A **What is shown in the Import Data dialog box when importing from a text file?**
The Import Data dialog box allows you to choose whether to import the data into a table, a PivotTable Report, a PivotChart, or only create a connection to the data. You also can choose to import the data to an existing worksheet or a new worksheet.

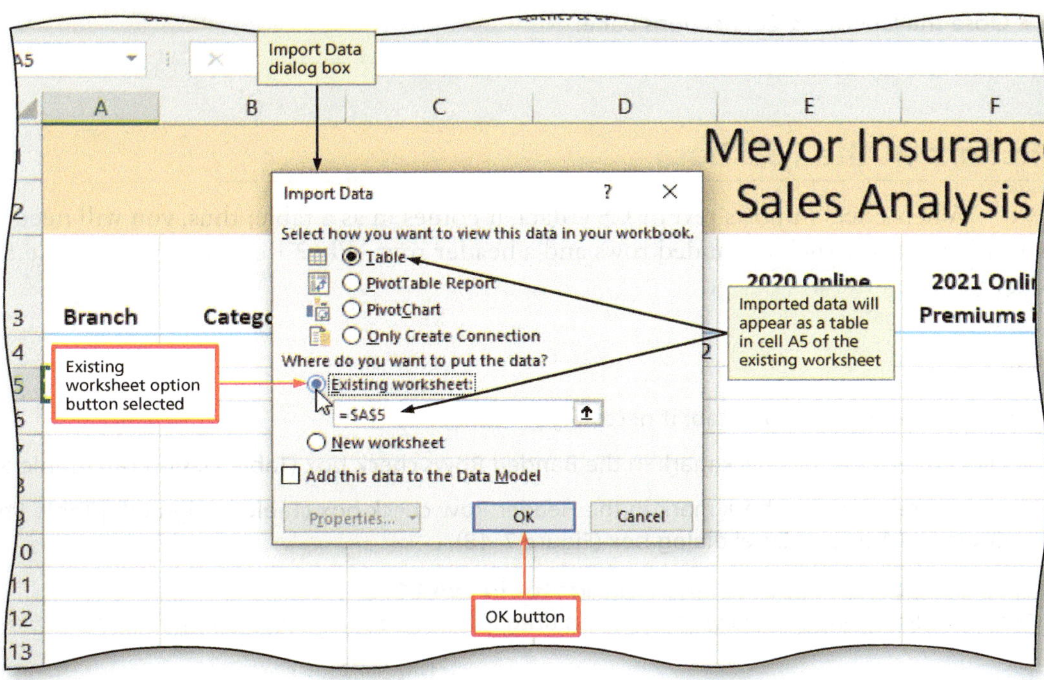

Figure 7–16

4

- Click OK (Import Data dialog box) to import the data (Figure 7–17).

Experiment

- Point to the green bar in the Queries & Connections pane to view details about the imported data.

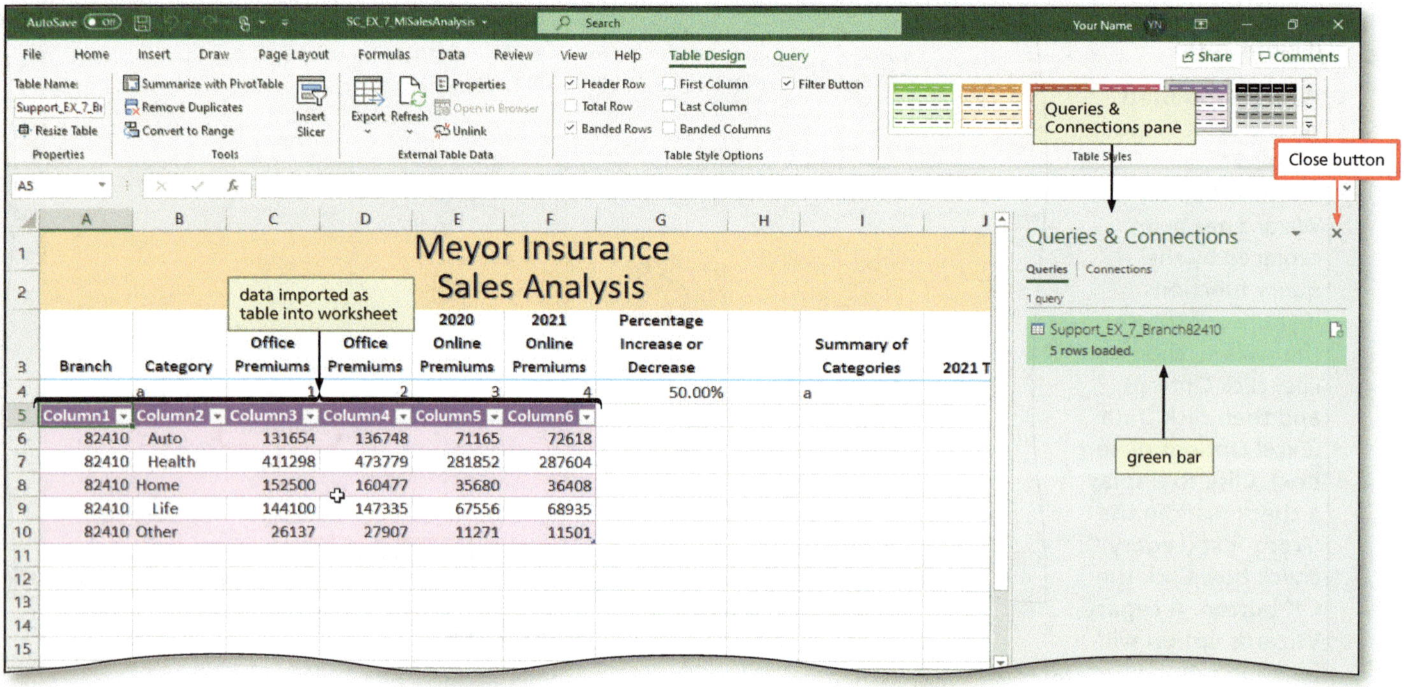

Figure 7–17

5

- Close the Queries & Connections pane.

To Format the CSV Data

When Excel imports text or CSV data, it comes in as a table; thus, you will need to remove features specific to tables, such as banded rows and a header row. **Why?** Removing those table features will format the data to match the worksheet.

1

- Display the Table Design tab, if necessary.
- Click to remove the check mark in the Banded Rows check box (Table Design tab | Table Style Options group).
- Click to remove the check mark in the Header Row check box (Table Design tab | Table Style Options group) to display a Microsoft Excel dialog box (Figure 7–18).

Q&A **What is the small, blue corner indicator in cell F10?**
That indicator is a table corner. You can drag it to add more row or columns to the table, if adjacent cells are empty.

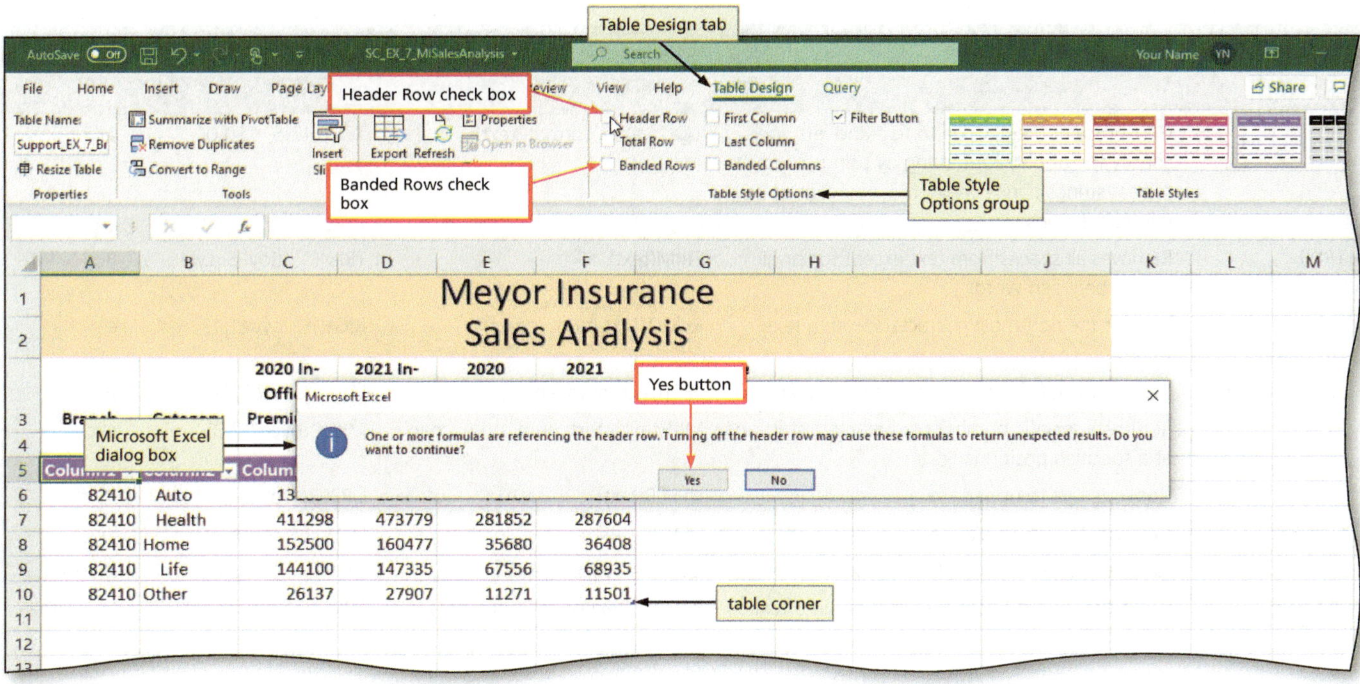

Figure 7–18

2

- Click the Yes button to remove the header row.
- Delete row 5.
- Because the import changed the column widths, select columns B:G and change the column width back to 15.

Text Formatting

Sometimes imported data will have some input inconsistencies and will need to be reformatted. It is important to check imported data closely and make corrections as necessary, without changing any values. Excel has a series of text functions to help you convert numbers to text, correct inconsistencies in capitalization, and trim off excess spaces, as well as functions to retain only parts of a cell's contents or join pieces of text together.

For example, the **CONCAT function** (which stands for "concatenate," or join) joins two or more text data items into a single expression. The **LEFT function** displays a specified number of characters from the beginning of a specified text string, and the **RIGHT function** displays a specified number of characters from the end of a specified text string The **PROPER function** converts the first letter of each word in a text string to uppercase, similar to title case in word processing.

Table 7–1 displays some of the available text functions.

Table 7–1 Text Functions

Function	Purpose	Syntax	Example	Result
TEXT	Converts a numeric value to text and lets you specify the display formatting by using special format strings (Once converted, you cannot use it in calculations.)	TEXT(value, format_text)	TEXT(42.5, "$0.00")	$42.50
TRIM	Removes all spaces from text except for single spaces between words	TRIM(text)	TRIM(" Roy S. Lyle ")	Roy S. Lyle
RIGHT	Returns the rightmost characters from a text value	RIGHT(text,[num_chars])	RIGHT("Joyce",1)	e
LEFT	Returns the leftmost characters from a text value	LEFT(text,[num_chars])	LEFT ("Joyce",2)	Jo
MID	Returns a specific number of characters starting at a specified position	MID(text, start_num, num_chars)	MID("Joyce",2,3)	oyc
UPPER	Converts text to uppercase	UPPER(text)	UPPER("Joyce")	JOYCE
LOWER	Converts text to lowercase	LOWER(text)	LOWER("Joyce")	joyce
CONCAT	Joins several text items into one text item	CONCAT(text1, [text2], ...)	CONCAT ("Mari","lyn")	Marilyn
PROPER	Converts the first letter of each word in a text string to uppercase	PROPER(text or cell reference)	PROPER("my name")	My Name

To Use the Trim Function

The following steps trim extra spaces from the category data you imported. **Why?** You notice that the data was stored with extra spaces, making it impossible to align the words in the column. In a separate part of the workspace, you will use the TRIM function to remove all spaces from text except for single spaces between words. You then will paste the trimmed values to replace the originals.

1

- Select cell B11, type **=trim(b5)** and then click the Enter button to trim the spaces from the data in cell B5 and display it in cell B11 (Figure 7–19).

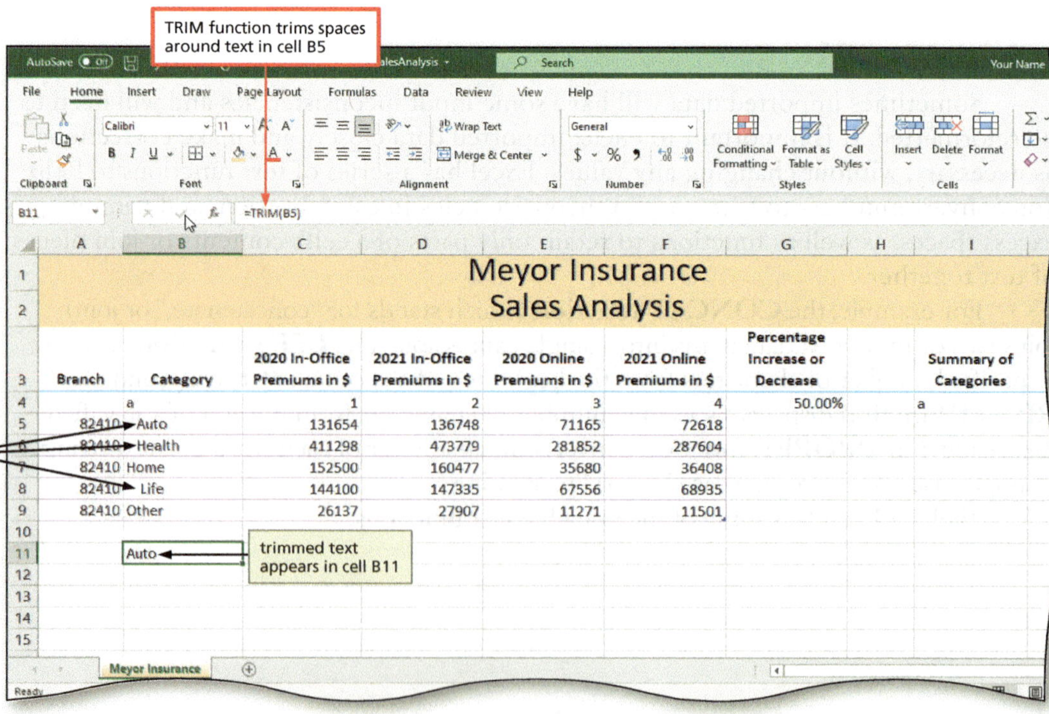

Figure 7–19

2

- Drag the fill handle of cell B11 down through cell B15 to display the trimmed data for all categories.
- Do not deselect the data (Figure 7–20).

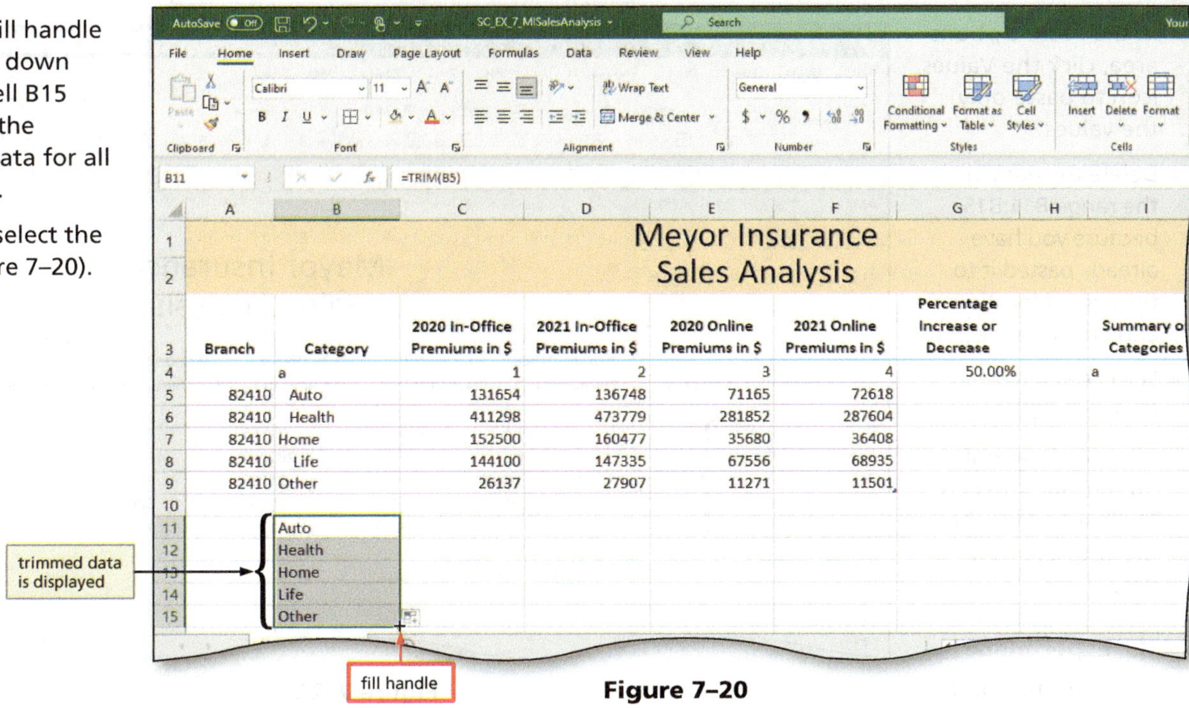

Figure 7–20

To Paste Values Only

The following steps cut the data from cells B11 through B15 and paste only the trimmed values back to cells B5 through B9. **Why?** If you simply paste the contents of the clipboard using CTRL+V, you will retain the trim function notation. You want only the trimmed values. To paste values, you will use Paste Options.

1

- With the range B11:B15 still selected, press CTRL+C to copy the data.
- Right-click cell B5 to display the shortcut menu (Figure 7–21).

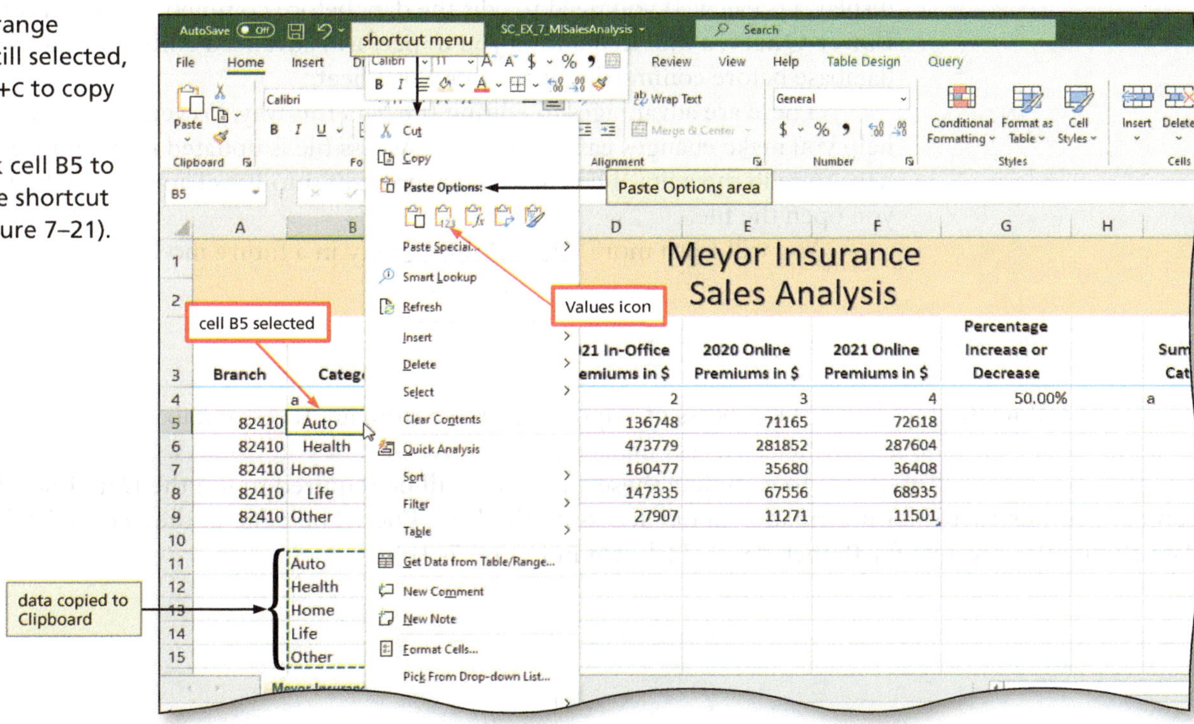

Figure 7–21

2

- In the Paste Options area, click the Values icon to paste only the values.
- Delete the data in the range B11:B15 because you have already pasted it to the correct location and no longer need it.
- Select cell A10 (Figure 7–22).
- Click the Save button on the Quick Access Toolbar to save the file with the new data.

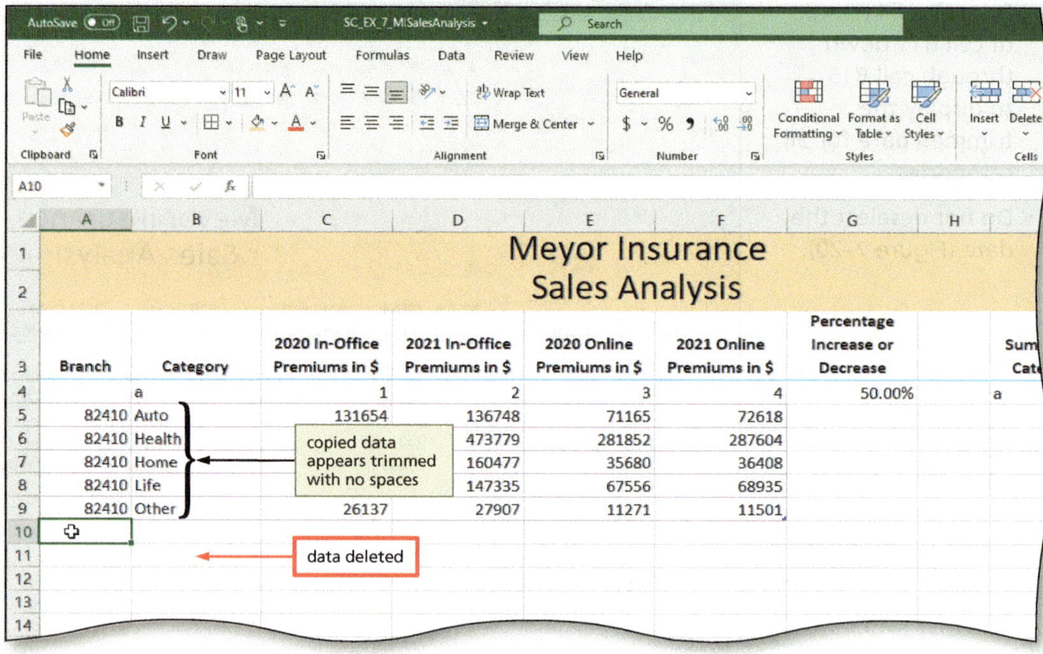

Figure 7–22

Experiment

- Click various cells in the range B5:B9 to verify that the values were pasted, rather than the TRIM function.

Access Files

Data from Microsoft Access files are stored in tabular format. Each row is a record; columns represent fields. When you import Access files, you usually import an entire table, which includes column headings and sometimes extra data. Excel will display a preview. If you need to edit the data before completing the import, Excel uses **Power Query**, a tool that allows you to perform advanced editing or querying of the database before committing it to your worksheet.

There are advantages to editing the data this way. Power Query has many tools to help you make changes easily, and if the Access file is updated in the future, you will not have to redo the edits. The changes are brought into Excel automatically the next time you open the file.

You will learn more about Power Query in a future module.

To Import Data from an Access Table

The following steps begin the process of importing a table from an Access database. **Why?** Access is used by many businesses, and importing an Access file is representative of how you would work with many other different kinds of database files. To complete these steps, you will be required to use the Data Files. Please contact your instructor for information about accessing the Data Files. The table in the Access database contains data about sales revenue for Branch #34927 (shown in Figure 7–1b).

1

- Verify that cell A10 is selected so that the Access table is imported starting in cell A10.
- Click the Get Data button (Data tab | Get & Transform Data group) to display the Get Data menu.
- Point to the From Database command to display the submenu (Figure 7–23).

Experiment

- Point to other commands on the Get Data menu, noting the wide variety of sources that Excel will accept. When you are finished, point to the From Database command again.

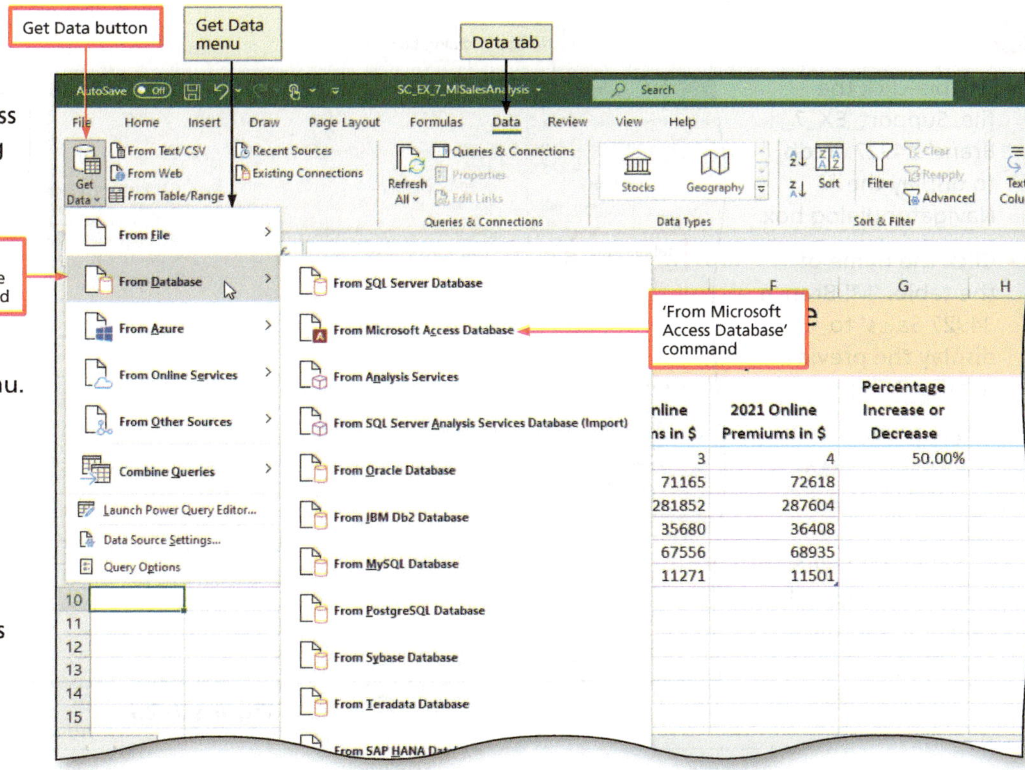

Figure 7–23

2

- Click 'From Microsoft Access Database' to display the Import Data dialog box.
- If necessary, navigate to the location of the Data Files (Figure 7–24).

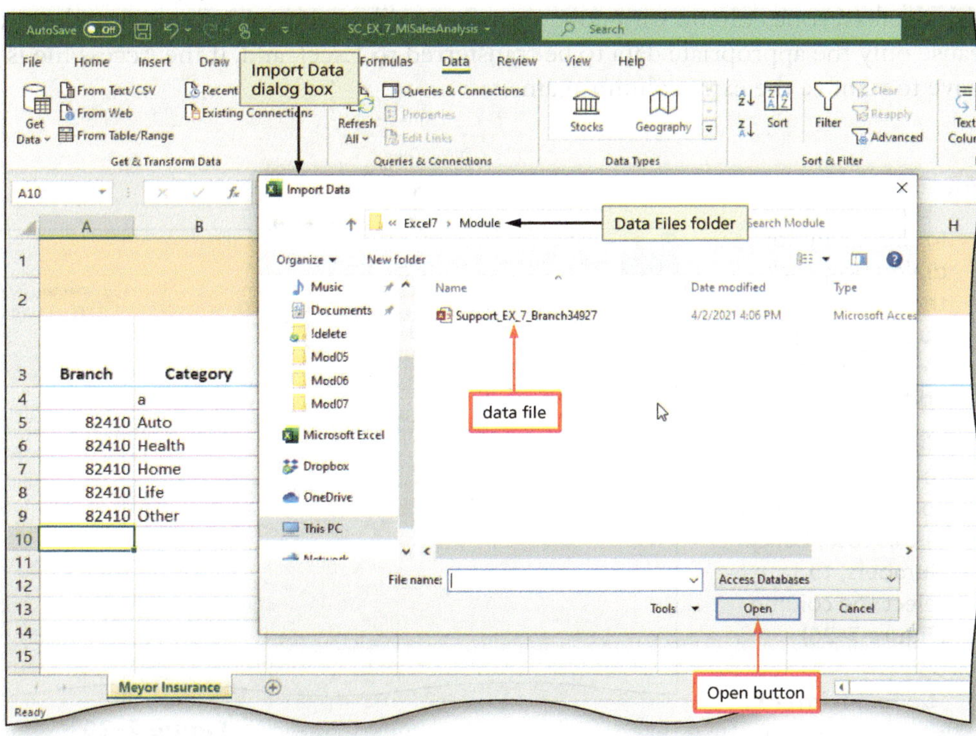

Figure 7–24

3

- Double-click the file, Support_EX_7_Branch34927.accdb, to display the Navigator dialog box.
- Click the name of the table, 'MI Branch 34927 Sales' to display the preview (Figure 7–25).

Q&A

What if the database contains more than one table?

The Navigator dialog box will display all available tables. You can import only one table at a time.

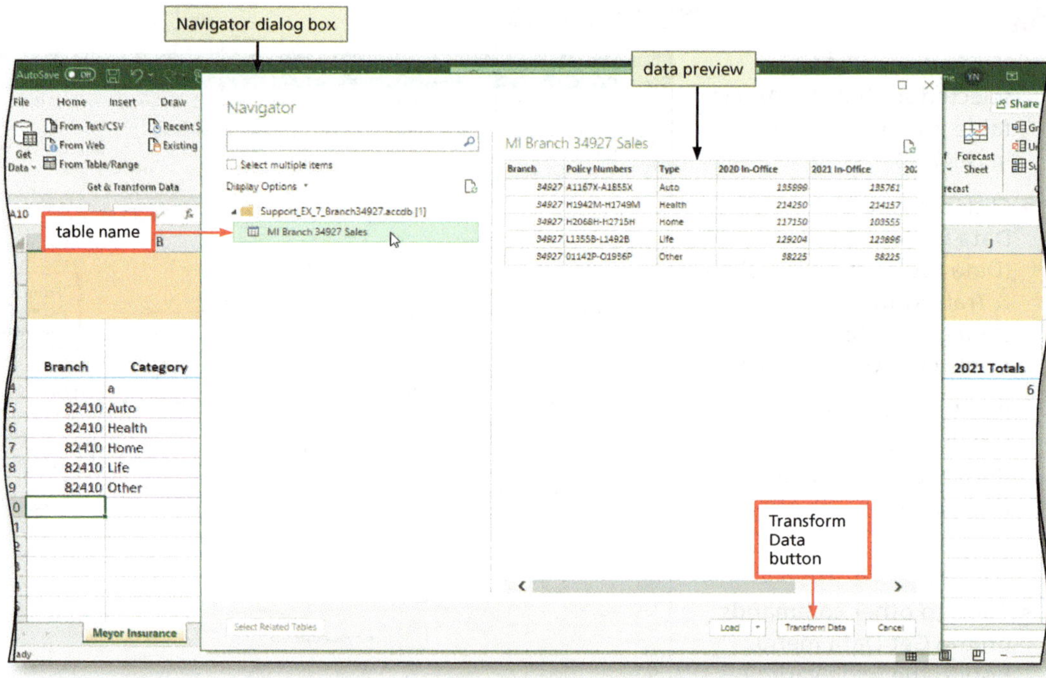

Figure 7–25

To Delete a Column Using Power Query

Sometimes imported files contain data that is not needed, such as total rows, extra columns, or undesired records. The Excel Power Query opens in a new window, allowing you to edit many kinds of imported data. In this database, one column with policy numbers will not be used. Removing the column before importing will cause only the appropriate data to be transferred to Excel, and, if the Access file is updated later, you will not have to remove the extra column again.

1

- In the Navigator dialog box, click the Transform Data button to display the Power Query Editor window.
- Click the desired column heading you wish to delete, in this case, Policy Numbers, to select the column (Figure 7–26).

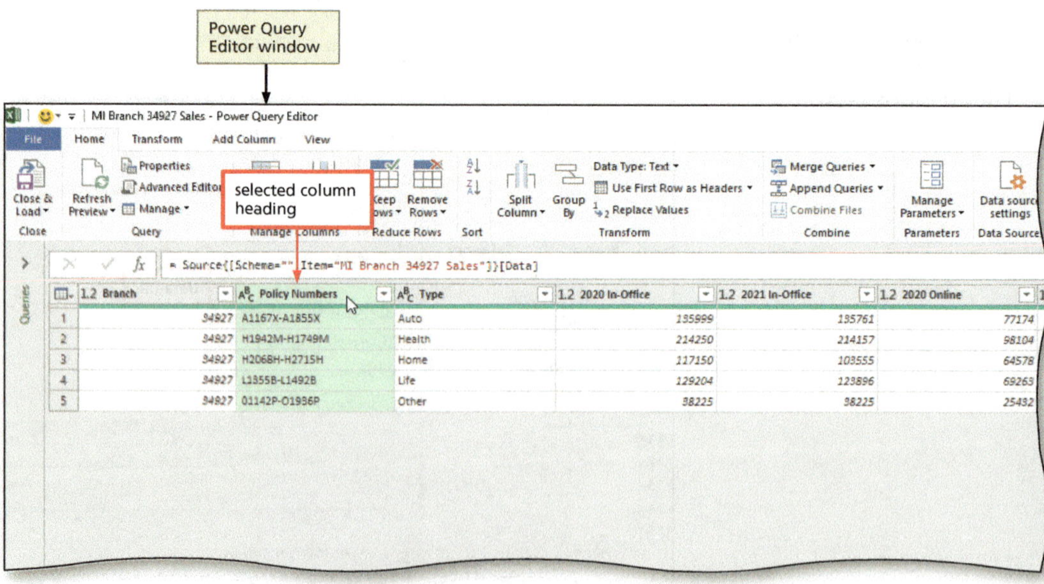

Figure 7–26

Experiment

- Examine all of the editing choices in the Power Query Editor window.

2

- Click the Remove Columns button (Power Query Editor Home tab | Manage Columns group) to remove the column from the import.
- Click the 'Close & Load' arrow (Power Query Editor Home tab | Close group) to display the 'Close & Load' menu (Figure 7–27).

Q&A | **What is the purpose of the APPLIED STEPS area?**
The APPLIED STEPS area allows you to track edits to the data and undo them if necessary.

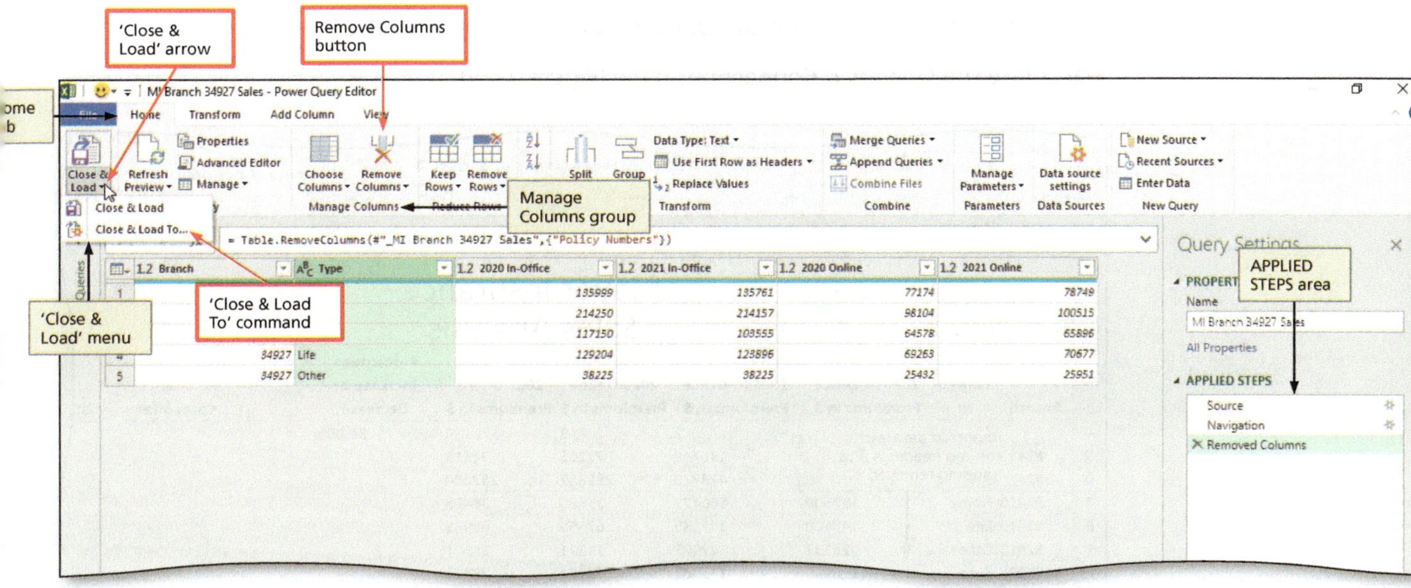

Figure 7–27

3

- Click the 'Close & Load To' command to close the Power Query Editor Window and to display the Import Data dialog box.
- If necessary, click the Existing worksheet option button to place the data in the current worksheet rather than on a new sheet (Figure 7–28).
- Click OK (Import Data dialog box) to import the data.

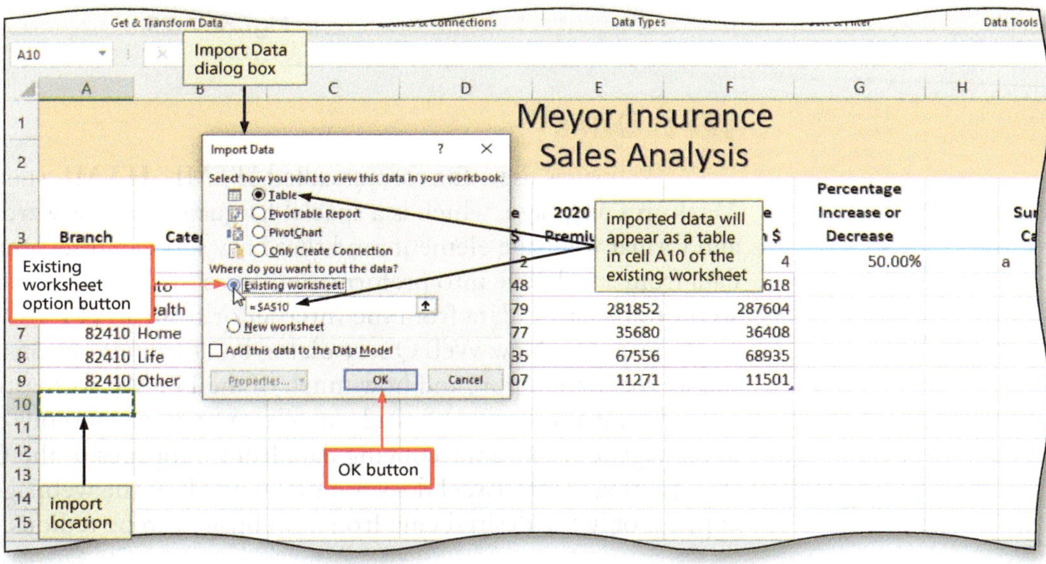

Figure 7–28

To Format the Access Data

The following steps format the Access data.

1. With cell A10 selected, click the Banded Rows check box (Table Design tab | Table Style options) to remove its check mark.
2. Click the Header Row check box (Table Design tab | Table Style options) to remove its check mark. When Excel displays a dialog box, click the Yes button.
3. Delete row 10 to move the data up.
4. Click the Save button on the Quick Access Toolbar to save the file
5. Close the Queries & Connections pane (Figure 7–29).

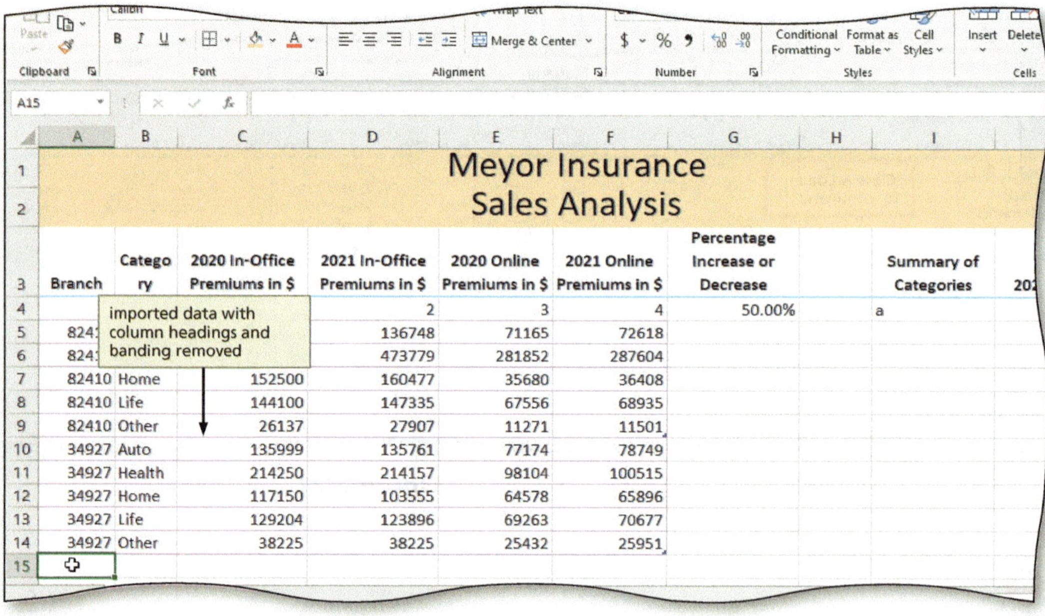

Figure 7–29

Web Data

Webpages use a file format called HTML. **HTML** stands for **Hypertext Markup Language**, which is a special language that software developers use to create and format webpage elements and that browsers can interpret. Excel can import data from a webpage into preformatted areas of the worksheet using a web query. A **web query** selects data from the Internet or from an HTML file to add to the Excel worksheet. The New Web Query dialog box includes options to specify which parts of the webpage to import and how much of the HTML formatting to keep.

Using a web query has advantages over other methods of importing data from a webpage. For example, copying data from webpages to the Office Clipboard and then pasting it into Excel does not maintain all of the webpage formatting. In addition, copying only the desired data from a webpage can be tedious.

To Import Data from a Webpage

The following steps create a new web query and then import data from a webpage into the worksheet. To complete these steps, you will be required to use the Data Files. Please contact your instructor for information about accessing the Data Files. Performing these steps does not require being connected to the Internet. **Why?** In this case, the webpage (shown in Figure 7–1c) is stored with the Data Files; normally you would have to be connected to the Internet.

1

- Select cell A15 to specify the destination location and then display the Data tab.
- Click the From Web button (Data tab | Get & Transform Data group) to display the From Web dialog box.
- In the URL box, type the web address, in this case the location of the data file: Type the drive letter followed by a COLON (:), the path location of the Data Files, followed by the name of the desired file, in this case, Support_EX_7_Branch70635.html. Separate the name of each folder with a BACKSLASH (\). For example, type `c:\users\username\documents\cis 101\data files\Support_EX_7_Branch70635.html` to insert the file name. Your file path will differ (Figure 7–30).

Q&A **Could I navigate to the file and double-click?** No, double-clicking the file would open it in a browser, rather than creating a query. You must type in the location, just as you would for a URL. Contact your instructor for the exact path and location.

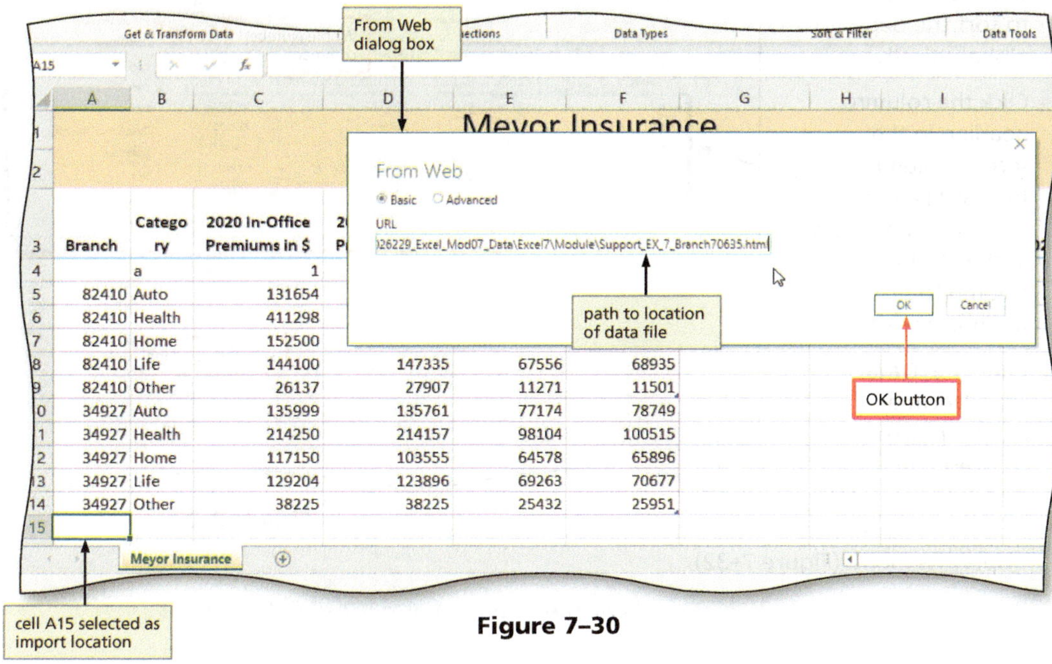

Figure 7–30

2

- Click OK (From Web dialog box) to display the Navigator dialog box.
- If necessary, click the table name, then click the Web View tab to look at the data (Figure 7–31).

Q&A **Can I accept the data as is?** No. Notice the data categories are not in the same order as in your worksheet. The data is not right-aligned, and the first column is Category, not the branch number.

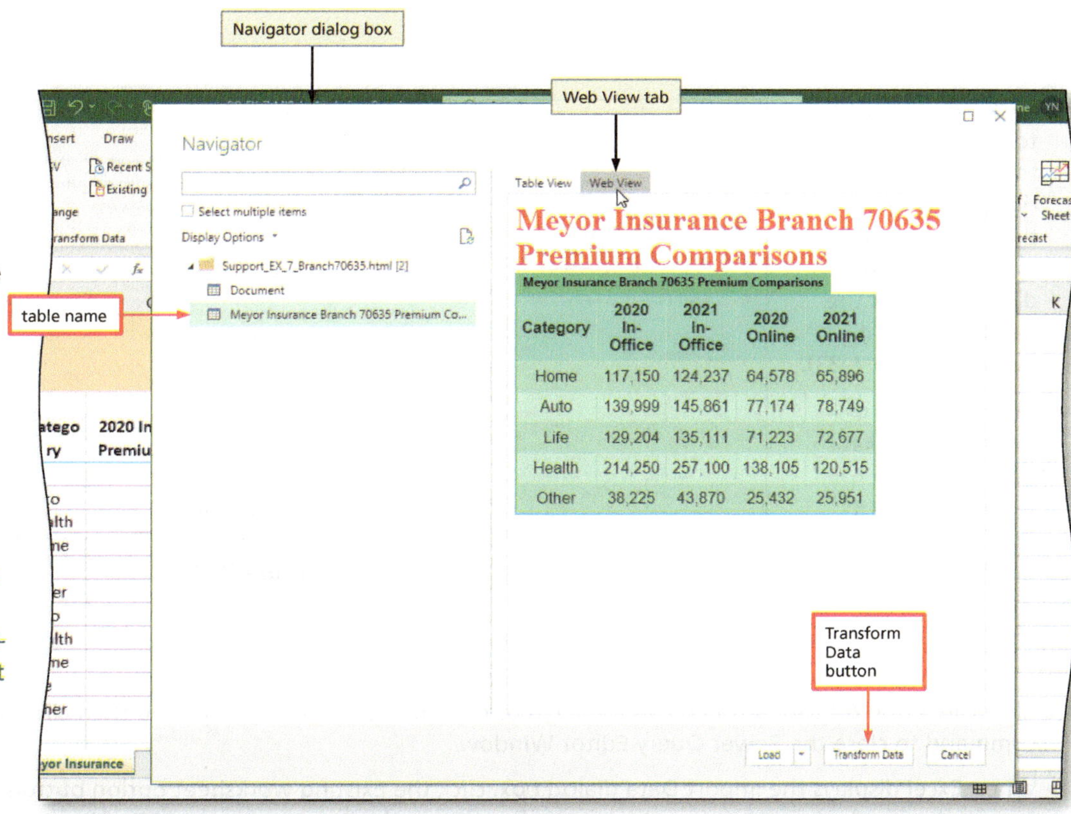

Figure 7–31

3

- Click the Transform Data button to display the Power Query Editor window.
- With the first column selected, click the Sort Ascending button (Power Query Editor Home tab | Sort group) to sort the data alphabetically.
- Click the column heading in the second column, then SHIFT+click the column heading in the 2021 Online column to select all of the numeric data.
- Click the 'Data Type:Decimal Number' arrow (PowerQuery Editor Home tab | Transform group) to display its menu (Figure 7–32).

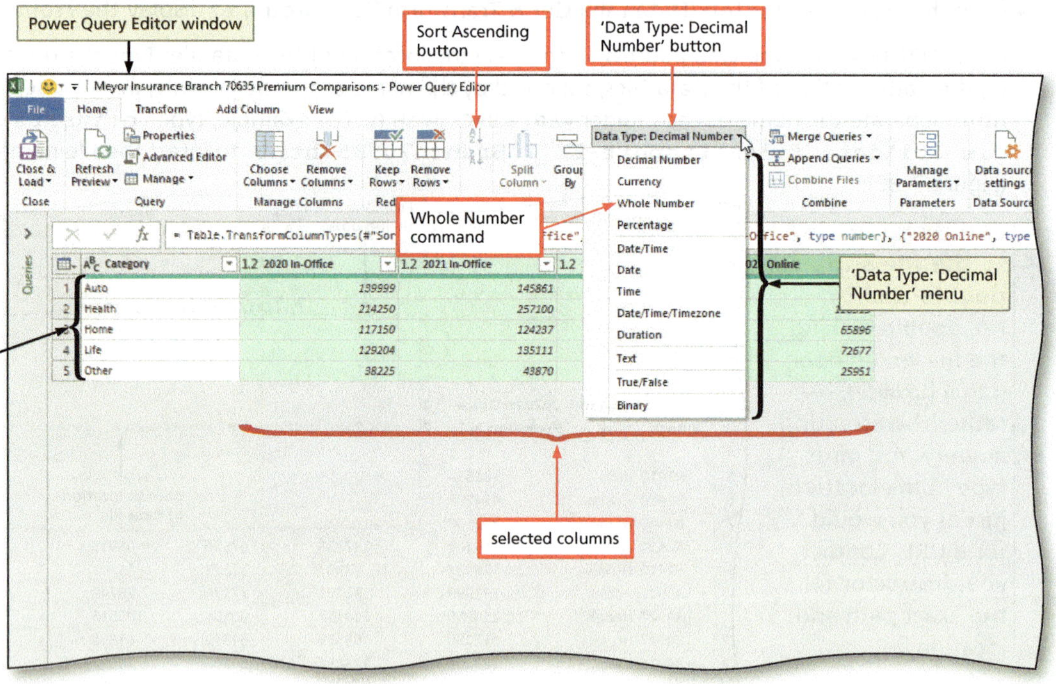

Figure 7–32

Q&A **What should I do if my button is named 'Data Type: Whole Number"?**
You can click the button and then perform Step 4 without affecting the data.

4

- Click Whole Number to convert the data to numbers and right-align them. If the Change Column Type dialog box is displayed, click the Replace Current button (Figure 7–33).

Q&A **Should I try to insert the missing Branch column?**
No. You can add that directly to the worksheet.

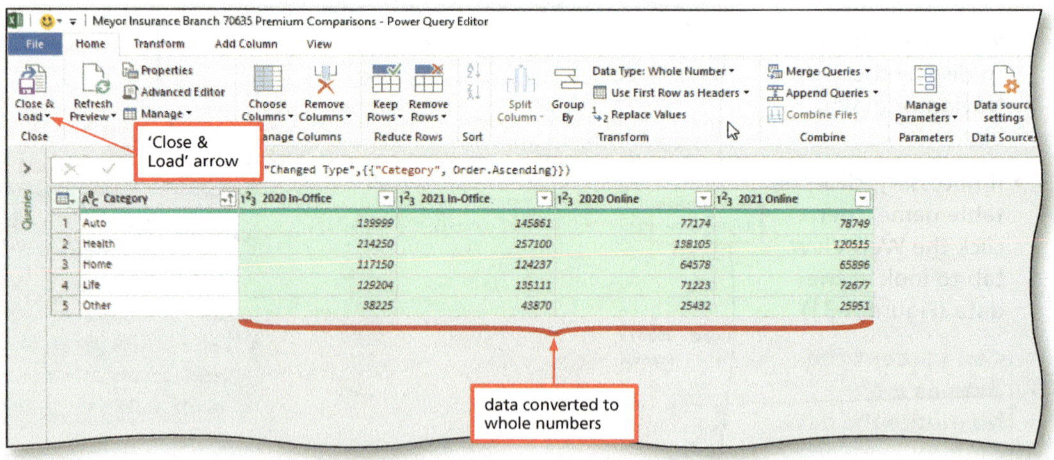

Figure 7–33

5

- Click the 'Close & Load' arrow (Power Query Editor Home tab | Close group) and then click the 'Close & Load To' command to close the Power Query Editor Window.
- When Excel displays the Import Data dialog box, click the Existing worksheet option button. Because there is no Branch data in the imported file, change the location of the import to **=$B$15** (Figure 7–34).
- Click the OK button (Import Data dialog box) to import the data.

Q&A

Why should I use a web query instead of copying and pasting from a webpage?
Using a web query has advantages over other methods of importing data from a webpage. For example, copying data from webpages to the Office Clipboard and then pasting it into Excel does not maintain all of the webpage formatting. In addition, copying only the desired data from a webpage can be tedious. Finally, copying and pasting does not create a link to the webpage for future updating.

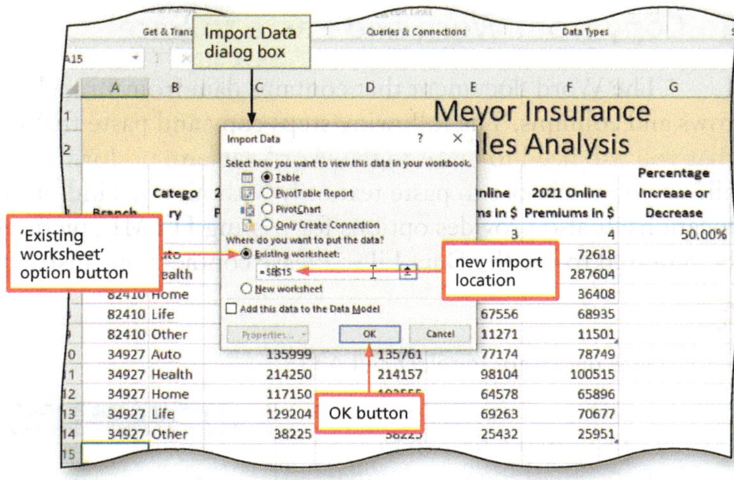

Figure 7–34

6

- Select cell B15, and then click the Banded Rows check box (Table Design tab | Table Style options) to remove its check mark.
- Click the Header Row check box (Table Design tab | Table Style options) to remove its check mark. When Excel displays a dialog box, click the Yes button.
- Delete Row 15 to move the data up.
- In cell A15, enter **70635**. Drag the fill handle down through A19.
- Close the 'Queries & Connections' pane (Figure 7–35).

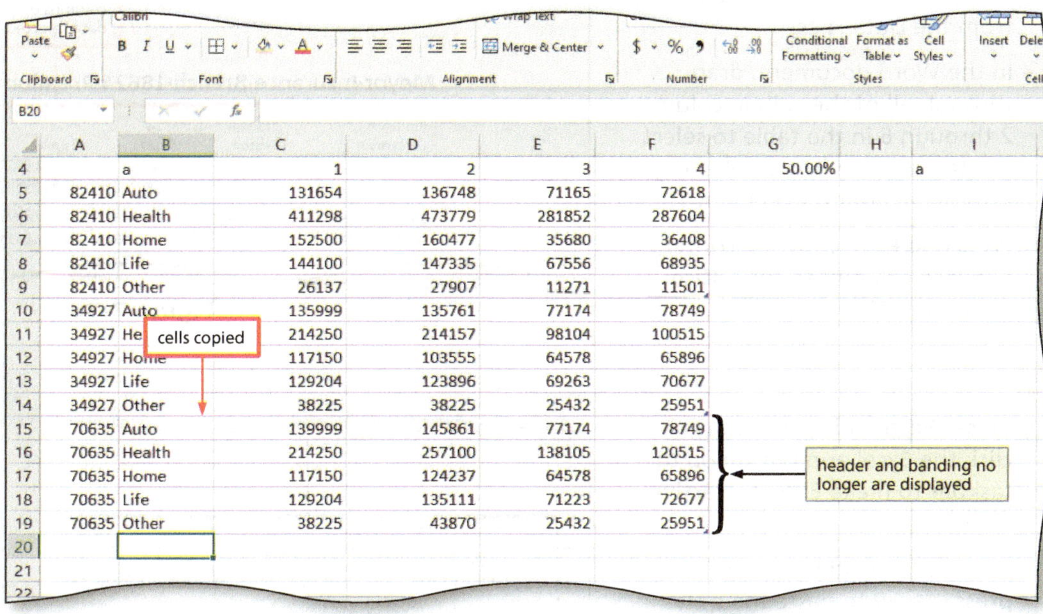

Figure 7–35

7

- Click the Save button on the Quick Access Toolbar to save the file.

Using Word Data

A Word document often contains data stored in a table. While you could save your Word data in a text format such as .txt and import it as you did earlier, you can copy and paste directly from Word to Excel. A few things should be taken into consideration, however. On some occasions, Word data requires some manipulation once you paste it into Excel. For example, the Word data may be easier to work with if the rows and columns were switched, and, thus, you will need to transpose the data. In other situations, you may find that Excel did not paste the data into separate columns, and, thus, you will need to split the data or convert the text into columns. Finally, some text-to-column conversions need extra space or columns when the data is split, requiring you to move other data out of the way. An example of each will occur in the following sections, as you copy, paste, transpose, move, and split data from Word to Excel.

To Copy from Word and Paste to Excel

The Word document that contains data from Branch #18624 (Figure 7–1d) includes a Word table with rows and columns. The following steps copy and paste that data from Word into Excel. **Why?** The manipulations that you will need to make to the Word data are performed more easily in Excel. The Paste Special command allows you to choose to paste text only without any kind of formatting from the source or the destination locations; it also provides options for pasting HTML, pictures, and hyperlinks. To complete these steps, you will be required to use the Data Files. Please contact your instructor for information about accessing the Data Files.

1

- Scroll as necessary to select cell A30.

Q&A **Why did I select cell A30 in Excel?** You will paste the data to that location, out of the way, in order to manipulate it.

- Start Word and then open the Word document named, Support_EX_7_Branch18624.docx, from the Data Files.
- In the Word document, drag through all of the cells in columns 2 through 6 in the table to select the table cells without selecting the row headings in column 1.
- Press CTRL+C to copy the contents of those columns to the Office Clipboard (Figure 7–36).

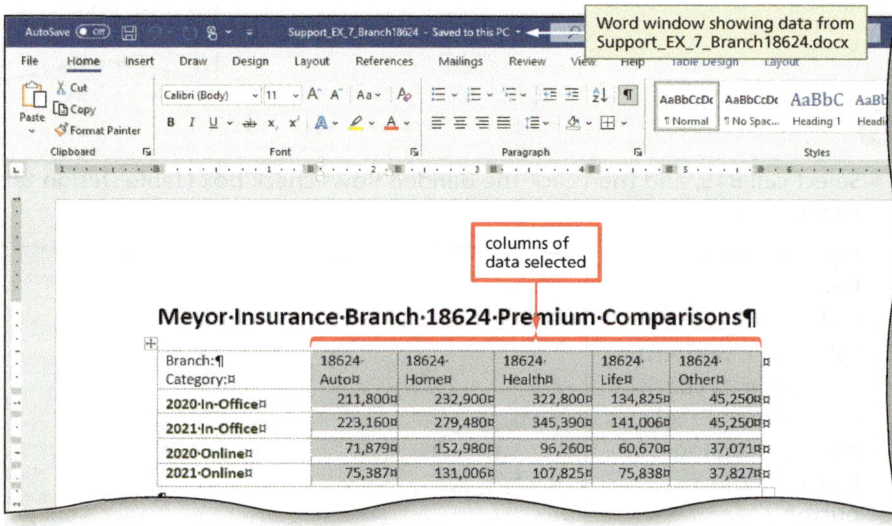

Figure 7–36

2

- Close Word and, if necessary, click the Excel app button on the taskbar to make Excel the active window.
- With cell A30 still selected, press CTRL+V to paste the data.
- Scroll as necessary to display the data, but do not select any other cells (Figure 7–37).

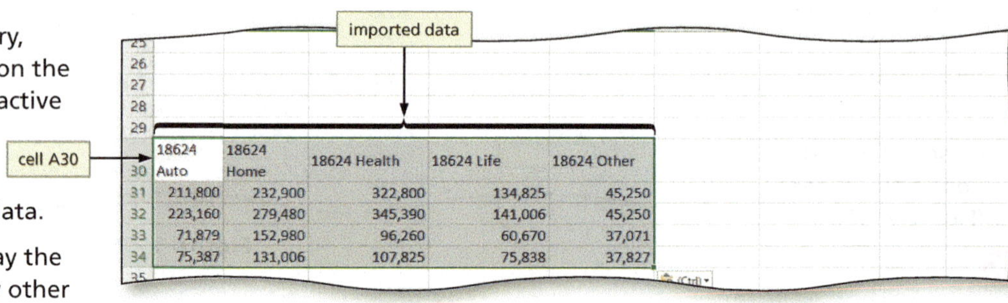

Figure 7–37

To Transpose Columns and Rows

Recall that the Paste gallery may display many different kinds of paste options, depending upon the data on the Office Clipboard and the paste location. When you copy and paste within Excel (rather than across apps), the Paste gallery displays many more options for pasting, such as pasting only the formulas, pasting only the values, pasting as a picture, and pasting transposed data, among others. The Transpose option in the Paste gallery automatically flips the rows and columns during the paste. In other words, the row headings become column headings or vice versa. All pasted data is switched as well. The following steps copy the data and paste it, transposed. **Why?** The original Word data had category titles across the top; the spreadsheet template expects titles down the left side.

1

- With the range A30:E34 still selected, press CTRL+C to copy the selection to the Office Clipboard.
- Scroll as necessary, and then select cell A20 to prepare for pasting the data to that location.
- Click the Paste arrow (Home tab | Clipboard group) to display the Paste gallery (Figure 7–38).

Experiment

- Using live preview, point to each of the paste options in the Paste gallery to see how the pasted format changes.

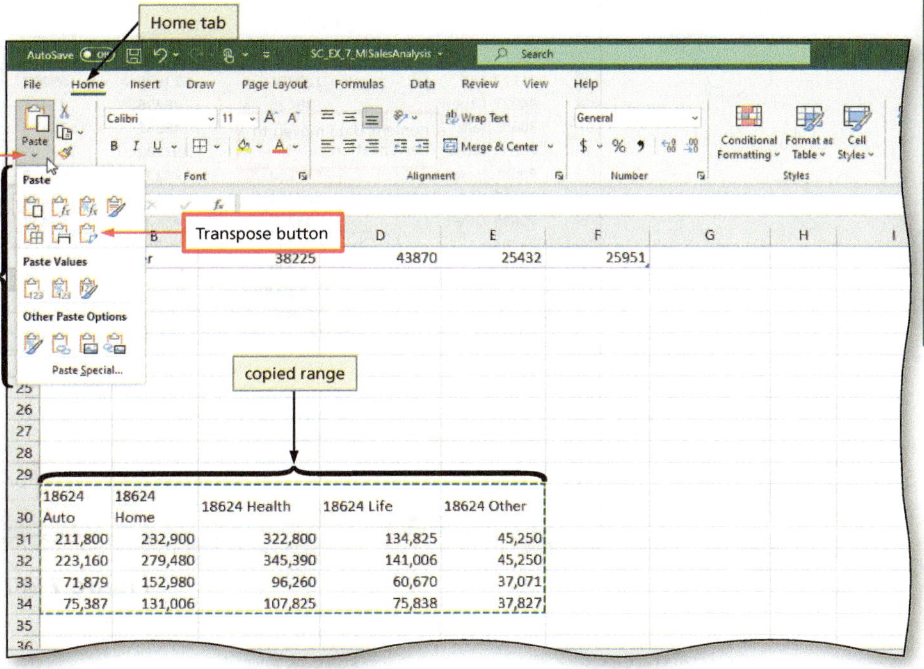

Figure 7–38

Q&A **Why do I have to copy the data to the clipboard again?**
The Transpose paste command is available only when Excel recognizes the cell format. You cannot transpose directly from copied Word tables.

2

- Click the Transpose button in the Paste gallery to transpose and paste the copied cells to the range beginning with cell A20.
- If necessary, select cells A20:A24, and then click the Wrap Text button (Home tab | Alignment group) to turn off text wrapping (Figure 7–39).

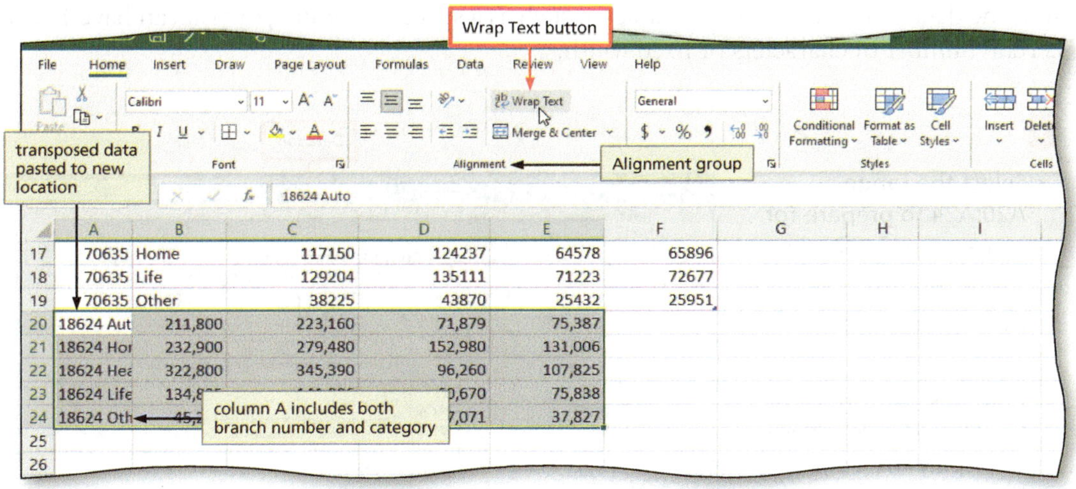

Figure 7–39

To Delete, Cut, and Paste Data

The following steps delete the original Word data from range A30:E34 because you no longer need it. The steps also move some of the transposed data to make room for splitting column A into two columns. You will format the data later in this module.

1. Delete the data in the range A30:E34.
2. To move the dollar values to the correct columns, select the range B20:E24 and then press CTRL+X to cut the data.
3. Select cell C20 and then press CTRL+V to paste the data (Figure 7–40).

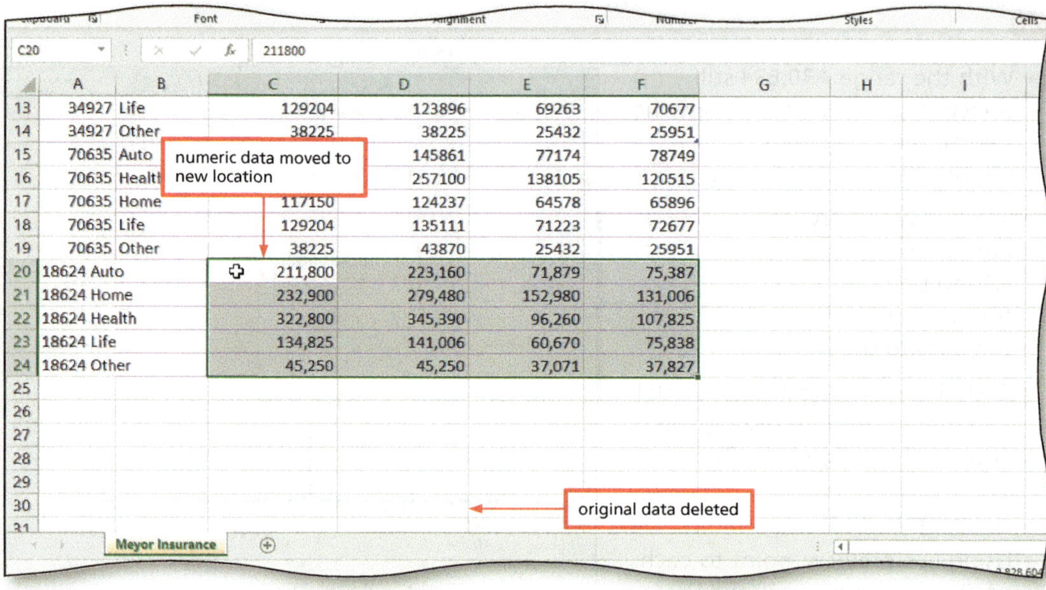

Figure 7–40

To Convert Text to Columns

Column A of the imported data from Branch #18624 includes both the branch and category in the same cell. The following steps split the data. **Why?** The data must be separated using the Excel 'Text to Columns' command so that the category information is in column B. You have two choices when splitting the column. You can have Excel split the data based on a specific character, such as a space or comma, or you can have Excel split the data based on a certain number of characters or fixed width.

1

- Select the range A20:A24 to prepare for converting the text to columns.
- Display the Data tab.
- Click the 'Text to Columns' button (Data tab | Data Tools group) to display the Convert Text to Columns Wizard - Step 1 of 3 dialog box.
- Click the Fixed width option button (Figure 7–41).

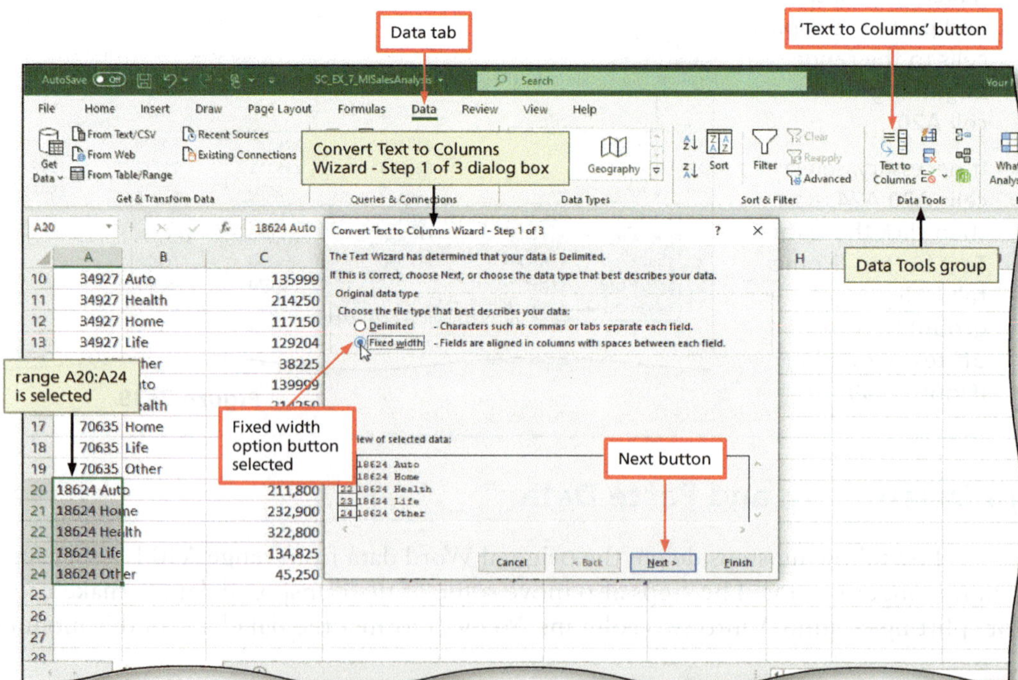

Figure 7–41

Q&A **What other tasks can be accomplished using the Convert Text to Columns Wizard?**
With the Delimited option, you can split the data into separate columns by specifying a break at a specific character.

2

- Click the Next button (Convert Text to Columns Wizard - Step 1 of 3 dialog box) to accept a fixed width column and to display the Convert Text to Columns Wizard - Step 2 of 3 dialog box (Figure 7–42).

Experiment

- Click the Next button to view options related to formatting or skipping parts of the data before splitting it. Do not make any changes.

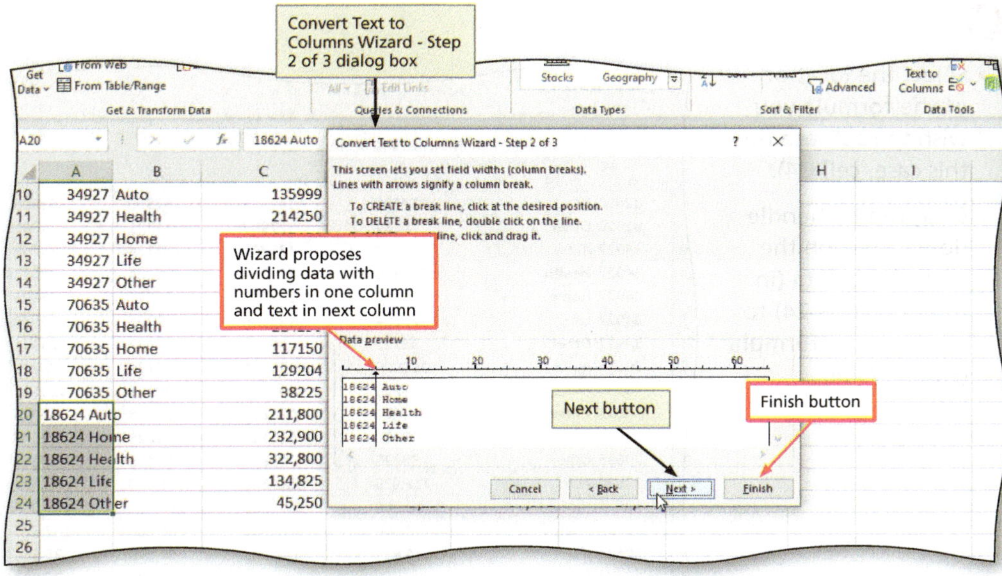

Figure 7–42

3

- Click the Finish button (Convert Text to Columns Wizard - Step 2 of 3 dialog box) to close the dialog box. If Excel displays a dialog box, click the Yes button to separate the data in column A into two columns (Figure 7–43).
- If necessary, adjust column widths to match those shown in the figure.

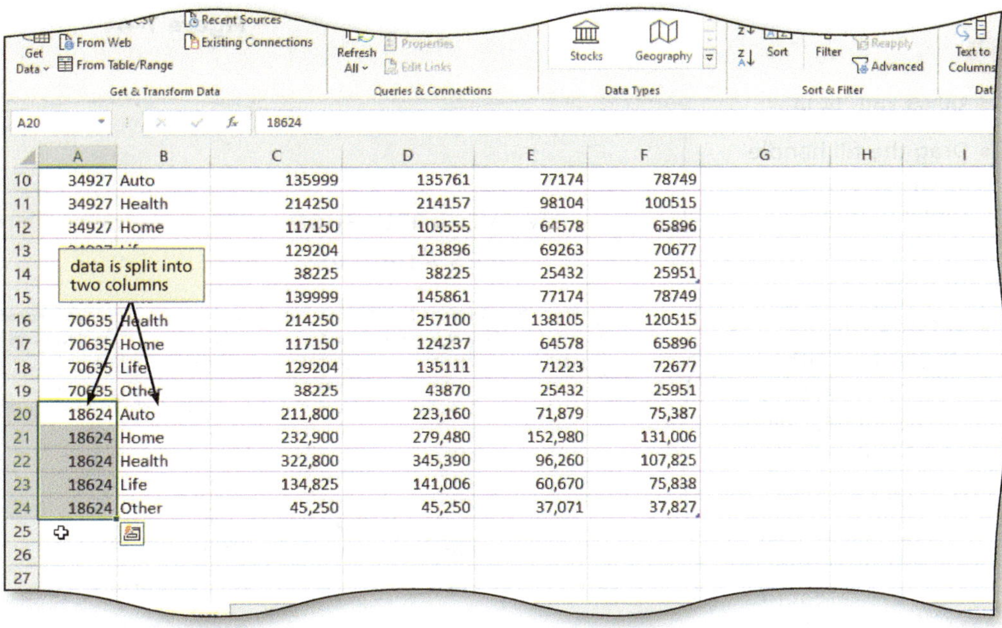

Figure 7–43

To Replicate Formulas

When you opened the workbook derived from the template, it contained a worksheet title, headings for each column, and a formula to calculate the percentage increase or decrease from 2020 to 2021. The formula and functions in cells G4, I4, and J4 must be copied or filled to complete the calculations. Some spreadsheet specialists refer to copying formulas as **replication**. You often replicate formulas after completing an import. **Why?** Usually, the total number of records to be imported is unknown when you first begin a workbook. The following steps use the fill handle to replicate the formulas. You also will perform some final formatting edits.

1

- Select the location of the formula you wish to replicate (in this case, cell G4).
- Drag the fill handle down through the end of the data (in this case, row 24) to replicate the formula (Figure 7–44).

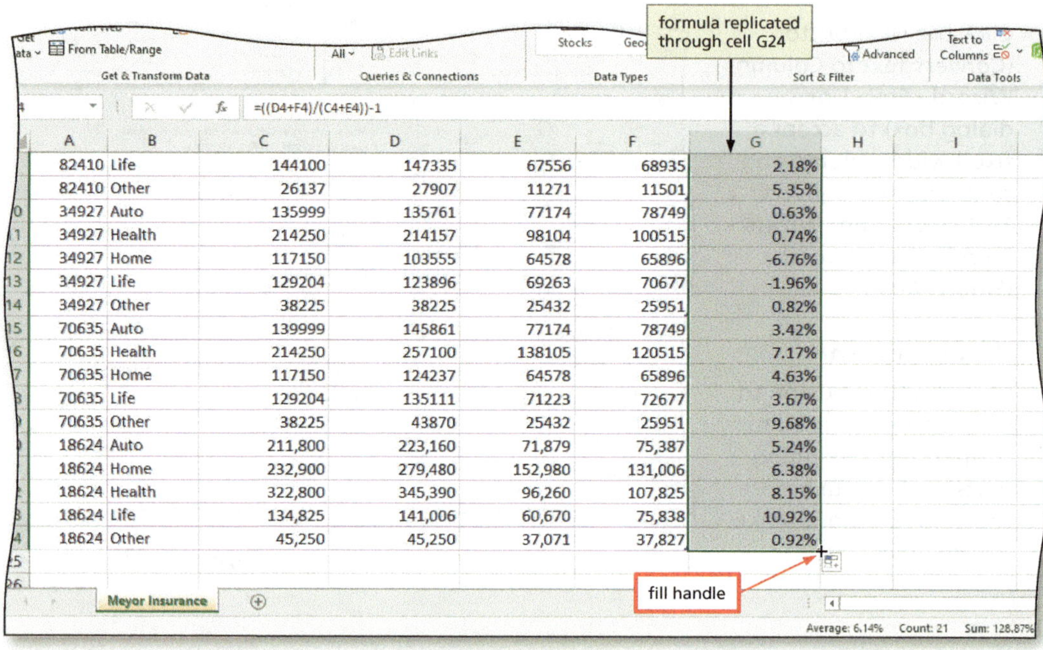

Figure 7–44

2

- Select cells I4:J4.
- Drag the fill handle down through row 9 to replicate the formulas and functions.
- Because you no longer need the dummy data from the template, delete row 4 (Figure 7–45).

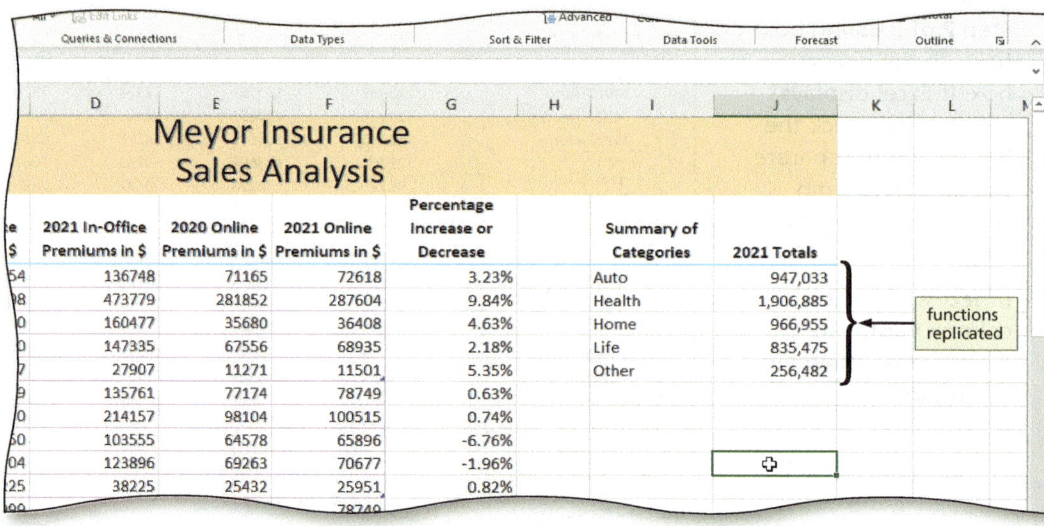

Figure 7–45

Q&A **Why did I stop the replication of the summary at row 10?** Only five categories are used for the branches; however, you can replicate further if more categories are added.

3

- Click the Save button (Quick Access Toolbar) to save the workbook with the same name in the same location.

Break Point: If you want to take a break, this is a good place to do so. You can exit Excel now. To resume later, start Excel, open the file called SC_EX_7_MISalesAnalysis, and continue following the steps from this location forward.

Using the Quick Analysis Gallery

Recall that in a previous module you used the status bar to see a basic analysis of selected data. Another tool for analyzing data quickly is the Quick Analysis gallery. Quick Analysis first appears as a button below and to the right of selected data. When you click the button, Excel displays the Quick Analysis gallery (Figure 7–46).

Each tab at the top of the gallery displays its own set of buttons to help you complete a task easily. For example, notice in Figure 7–46 that the Formatting tab displays conditional formatting options. The tabs always apply to the selected area of the worksheet. In addition, the Quick Analysis gallery uses live preview—in other words, you can preview how the feature will affect your data by pointing to the button in the gallery.

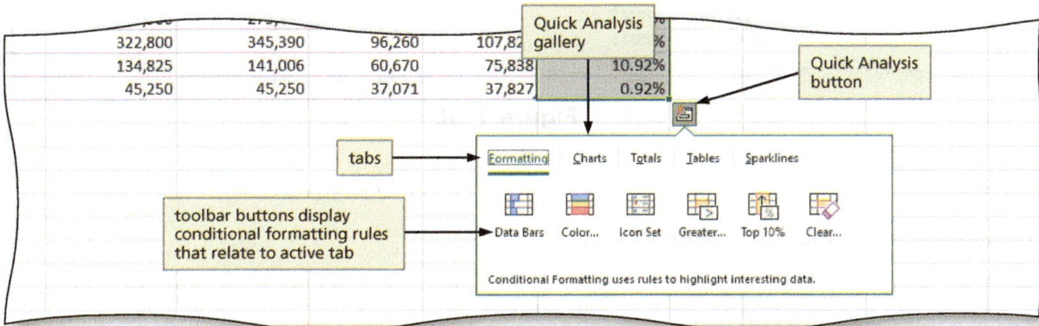

Figure 7–46

The Totals tab in the Quick Analysis toolbar can be used to create totals quickly, as long as none of the data is in tables. When you click Totals, Excel displays a variety of formulas and functions as thumbnails, including SUM, AVERAGE, and COUNT. Pointing to any thumbnail gives you a live preview of the answer. Clicking the thumbnail inserts the formula into the worksheet.

To Format Using the Quick Analysis Gallery

The following steps use the Quick Analysis gallery to format the top 10% of column G, the percentage increase or decrease in sales. **Why?** The company executives want to see the branches and categories with the highest increase in sales. Formatting using the Quick Analysis gallery is much faster than using the ribbon to apply conditional formatting.

1

- Select the range you want to analyze, in this case G4:G23.
- Click the Quick Analysis button to display the Quick Analysis gallery.
- If necessary, click the Formatting tab to display the Quick Analysis gallery formatting options (Figure 7–47).

Experiment

- Point to each of the buttons on the Quick Analysis gallery to display a live preview.

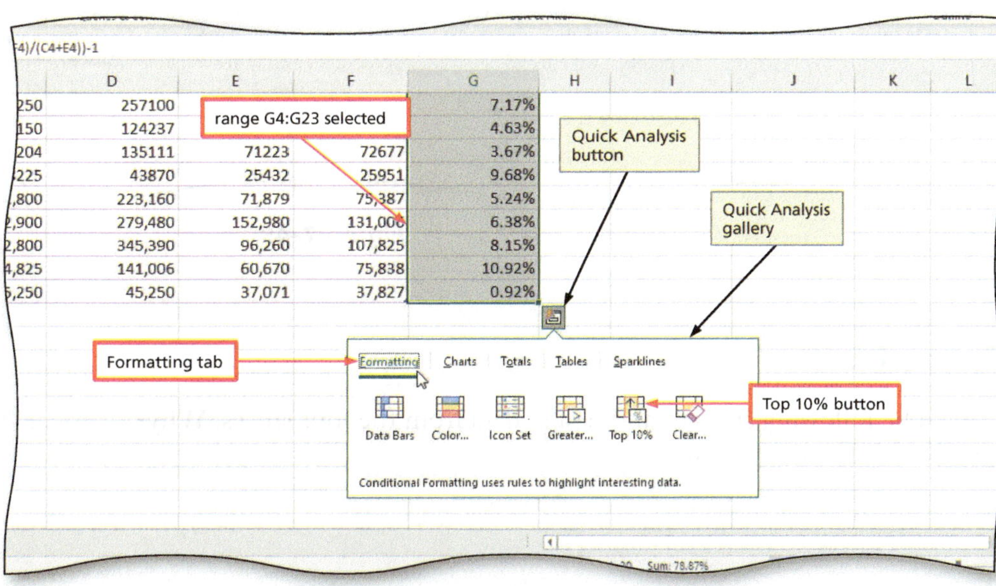

Figure 7–47

2

- Click the Top 10% button (Quick Analysis gallery).
- Click outside the selection and scroll as necessary to display the cells highlighted by the conditional formatting (Figure 7–48).

Q&A **Why did Excel highlight the numbers in light red?** The default value for conditional formatting is light red.

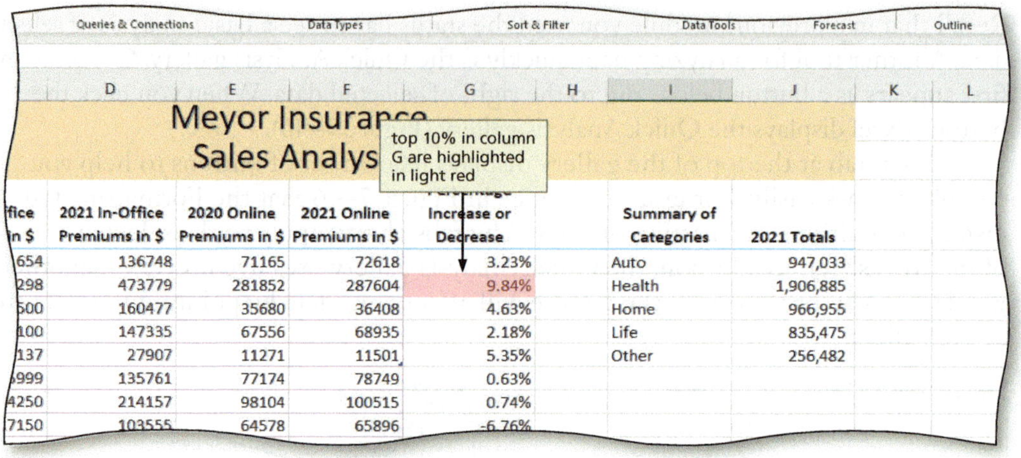

Figure 7–48

Experiment

- Scroll through the list to display see other top 10% highlighting.

3

- Click cell I24. Type `Shaded cells indicate top 10%` and then press ENTER to create a legend for the formatting.
- Drag through cells I24:J24 and display the Home tab.
- Click the Fill Color arrow (Home tab | Font Group) and then click Red, Accent 4, Lighter, 80% (second row, eighth column).
- Click outside the selection to view the formatting (Figure 7–49).

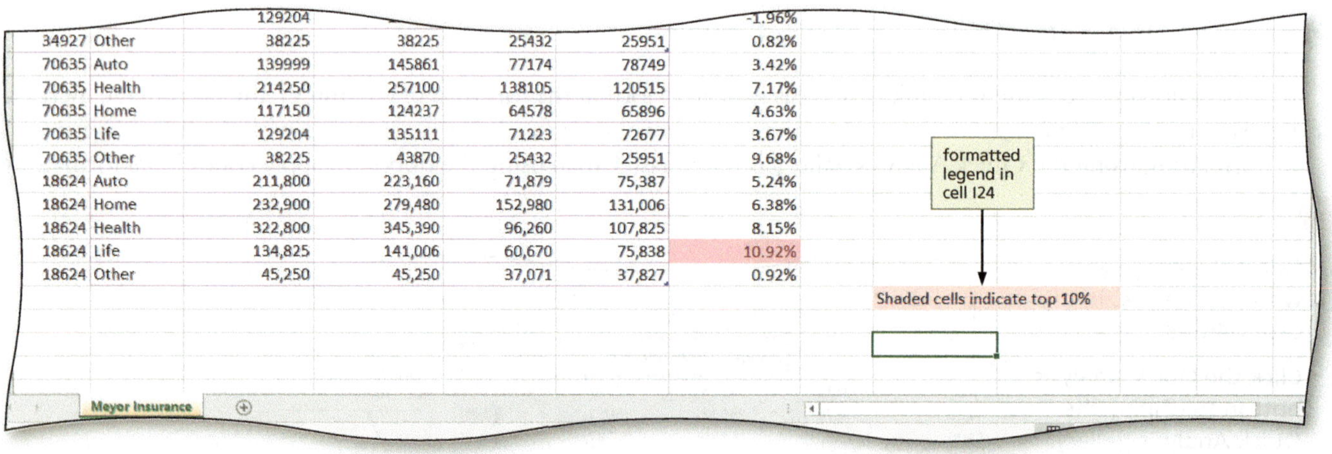

Figure 7–49

To Total Data

The following steps total the sales data from the four stores. **Why?** Companies routinely want to examine grand totals for all branches.

1

- Click cell C24. Type `=sum(c4:c23)` and then click the ENTER button.
- Drag the fill handle to the right, to replicate the totals for columns D through F (Figure 7–50).

Q&A **Could I use the Quick Analysis Gallery to create the totals?**
No. The Quick Analysis button will not appear because the data crosses multiple table imports.

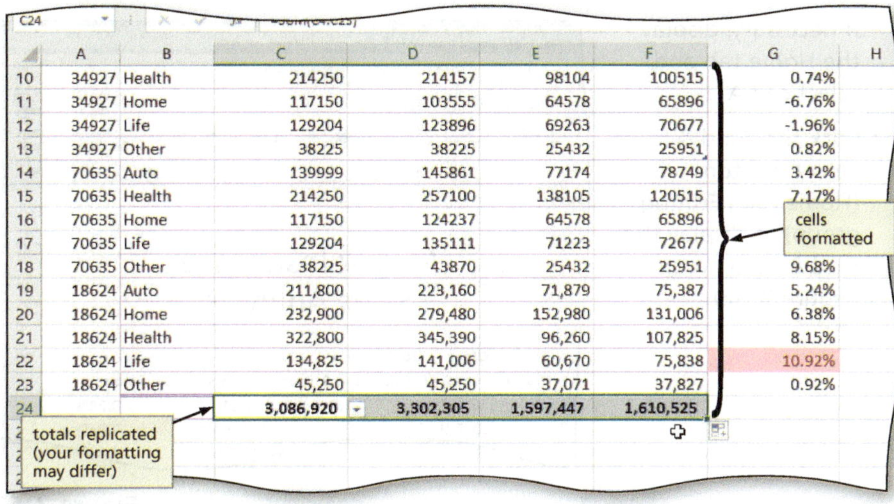

Figure 7–50

2

- Select cell A24 and then type `Totals` to enter a row heading.
- Replicate cell G23 down to G24 to indicate the total percentage increase or decrease (Figure 7–51).

3

- Add the Comma Style formatting with no decimal places to the premium figures in columns C:F.

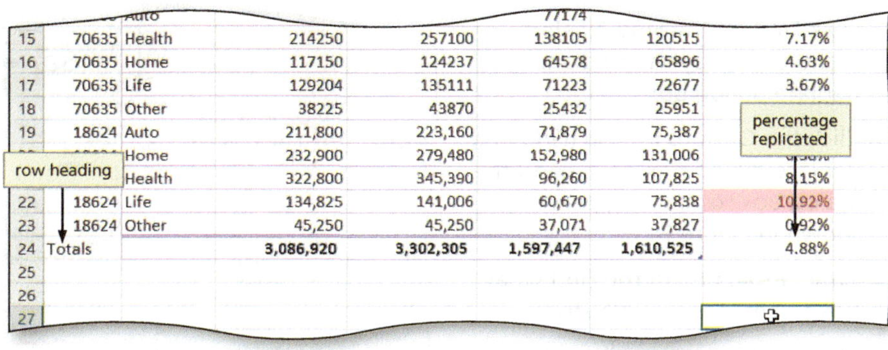

Figure 7–51

Q&A **What if the pasted Word values don't align exactly with the other worksheet values?**
You can clear the formatting from the pasted Word values using the Clear Formats button (Home tab | Editing group | Clear arrow) and reapply the Comma Style.

Using the Find and Replace Commands

To locate a specific piece of data in a worksheet, you can use the Find command on the Find & Select menu. The data you search for sometimes is called the **search string**. To locate and replace the data, you can use the Replace command on the Find & Select menu. If you have a cell range selected, the Find and Replace commands search only the range; otherwise, the Find and Replace commands begin at cell A1, regardless of the location of the active cell. The Find and Replace commands are not available for charts.

Selecting either the Find or Replace command displays the Find and Replace dialog box. The Find and Replace dialog box has two variations. One version displays minimal options, while the other version displays all of the available options. When you select the Find or Replace command, Excel displays the dialog box variation that was used the last time either command was selected.

To Find Data

The following steps show how to locate the search string, Health. The Find and Replace dialog box that displays all the options will be used to customize the search by using the Match case and 'Match entire cell contents' options. **Why?** Match case means that the search is case sensitive and the cell contents must match the data exactly the way it is typed. 'Match entire cell contents' means that the data cannot be part of another word or phrase and must be unique in the cell.

1

- If necessary, display the Home tab and select cell A1.
- Click the 'Find & Select' button (Home tab | Editing group) to display the Find & Select menu (Figure 7–52).

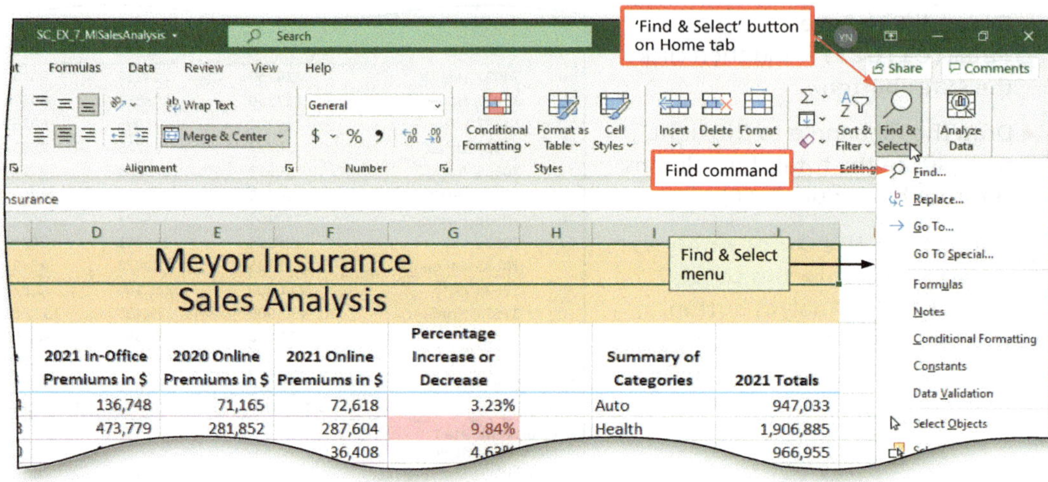

Figure 7–52

2

- Click Find on the Find & Select menu to display the Find and Replace dialog box.
- Click the Options button (Find and Replace dialog box) to expand the dialog box so that it appears as shown in Figure 7–53.
- Type **Health** in the Find what box to enter the search string.
- Click Match case and then click 'Match entire cell contents' to place check marks in those check boxes (Figure 7–53).

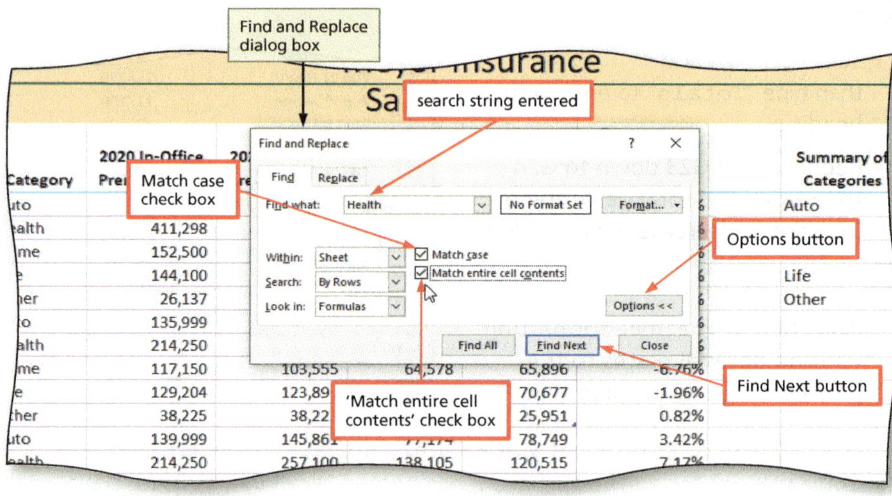

Figure 7–53

Q&A **Why does the appearance of the Options button change?**
The two arrows pointing to the left on the Options button indicate that the more comprehensive Find and Replace dialog box is active.

3

- Click the Find Next button (Find and Replace dialog box) to cause Excel to begin the search and locate an occurrence of the search string (Figure 7–54).

Q&A **What if Excel does not find any occurrences of the search string?**
If the Find command does not find the string for which you are searching, Excel displays a dialog box indicating it searched the selected worksheets and cannot find the search string.

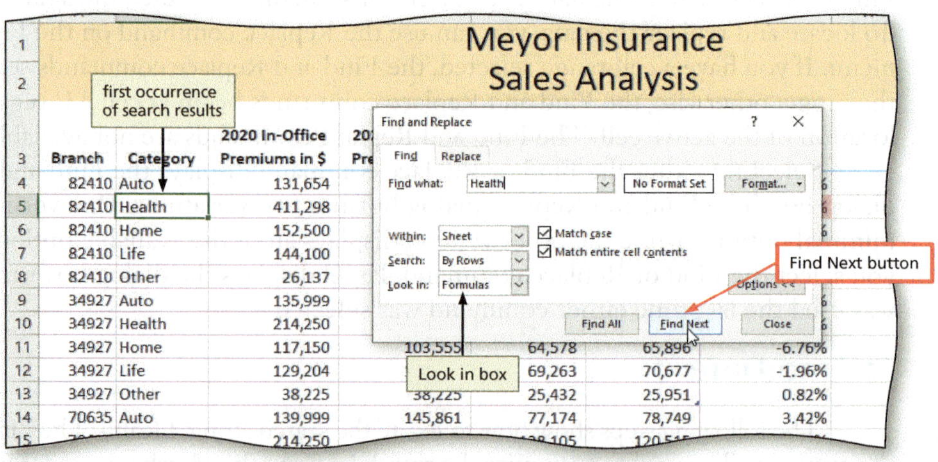

Figure 7–54

4

- Continue clicking the Find Next button (Find and Replace dialog box) to find the string, Health, in three other cells on the worksheet.
- Click the Close button (Find and Replace dialog box) to stop searching and close the Find and Replace dialog box.

Q&A

What happens if you continue clicking the Find Next button?
Excel will cycle through the cells again. You have to watch the row and column references to determine if you have found them all.

What happens when you click the Find All button (Find and Replace dialog box)?
Excel further expands the Find and Replace dialog box to list all occurrences and their locations in a table format below the buttons.

Why did Excel not find the word Health in cell I5?
The default value in the Look in box (shown in Figure 7–55) was to search for formulas, which includes cells with entered text but does not include the result of functions such as the one from the template, replicated in cell I5.

Other Ways

1. Press CTRL+F, enter search string, click Find Next button (Find and Replace dialog box)

Working with the Find and Replace Dialog Box

The Format button in the Find and Replace dialog box allows you to fine-tune the search by adding formats, such as bold, font style, and font size, to the search string. The Within box options include Sheet and Workbook. The Search box indicates whether Excel will search vertically through rows or horizontally across columns. The Look in box allows you to select Formulas, Values, or Comments. If you select Formulas, Excel will look in all cells except those containing functions or comments. If you select Values, Excel will look for the search string in cells that do not contain formulas, such as text or functions. If you select Comments, Excel will look only in comments.

If you select the Match case check box, Excel will locate only cells in which the string is in the same case. For example, when matching the case, accessories is not the same as Accessories. If you select the 'Match entire cell contents' check box, Excel will locate only the cells that contain the search string and no other characters. For example, Excel will find a cell entry of Other, but not Others.

To Find and Replace

The Replace command replaces the found search string with new data. You can use it to find and replace one occurrence at a time, or you can use the Replace All button to replace the data in all locations at once. The following steps show how to use the Replace All button. **Why?** You want to replace the string, Life, with the string, Life & LTC, to indicate that long-term-care policies are included with the life premiums. You also can change cell formatting using the Format button in the Find and Replace dialog box.

1

- Click the Find & Select button (Home tab | Editing group) to display the Find & Select menu.
- Click Replace on the Find & Select menu to display the Find and Replace dialog box.
- Type `Life` in the Find what box and then type `Life & LTC` in the Replace with box to specify the text to find and to replace.

- If necessary, click Match case and then click 'Match entire cell contents' to place check marks in those check boxes (Figure 7–55).

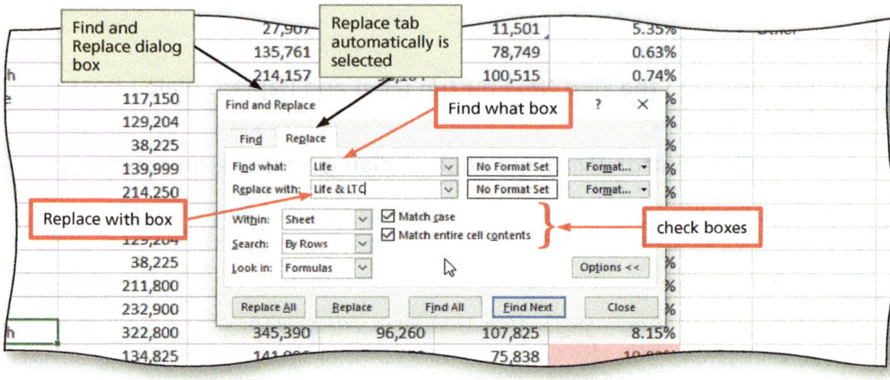

Figure 7–55

2

- Click the Replace All button (Find and Replace dialog box) to replace the string (Figure 7–56).

Q&A **What happens when Excel replaces the string?**
Excel replaces the string, Life, with the replacement string, Life & LTC, throughout the entire worksheet. If other worksheets contain matching cells, Excel replaces those cells as well. Excel displays the Microsoft Excel dialog box indicating four replacements were made.

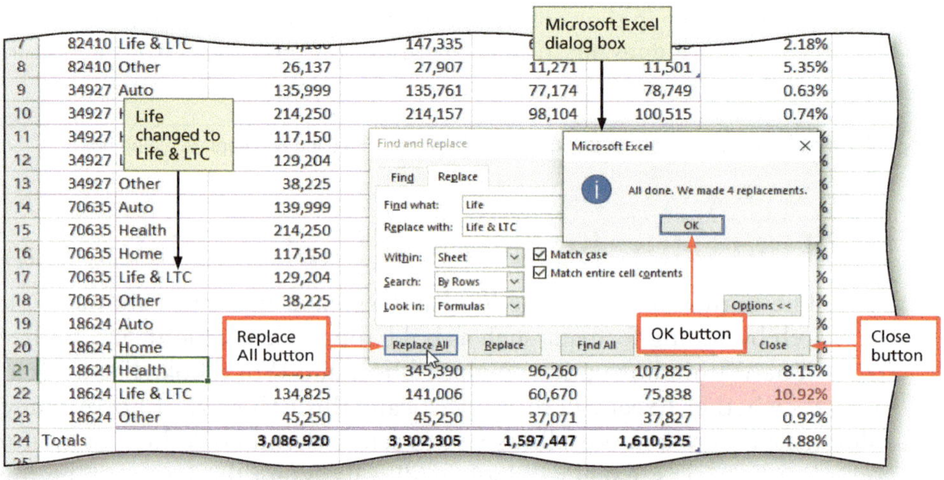

Figure 7–56

3

- Click OK (Microsoft Excel dialog box).
- Click Close (Find and Replace dialog box).
- Click the Save button (Quick Access Toolbar) to save the file again.

Q&A **Why did Excel change the function value in cell I7?**
Cell I7 is a function and therefore would not be changed because of the Formula designation in the Find and Replace dialog box; however, cell I7 searches column B. So, when Excel changed column B, the function itself changed cell I7.

Other Ways

1. Press CTRL+H, enter search string, enter replace string, click Replace All button (Find and Replace dialog box)

To Format Styles and Borders

The following steps remove the table styles from cells A4:F23 and remove the borders from cells G5:J23 so all the cells in the range display the same style. G4:J4 will retain the top border for the title cells directly above them.

1. Drag to select cells A4:F23.
2. Display the Table Design tab.
3. Click the More button (Table Design tab | Table Styles group).
4. When Excel displays the Table Styles gallery, click the None style in the Light area.

5 Select cells G5:J23.

6 Right-click the selection and then click Format Cells on the shortcut menu.

7 Click the Border tab (Format Cells dialog box) and then click None in the Presets area.

8 Click OK to close the dialog box.

9 Click the Save button (Quick Access Toolbar) to save the file.

Inserting a Bar Chart

The requirements document shown in Figure 7–2 specifies that the workbook should include a bar chart, sometimes called a bar graph. A bar chart uses parallel, horizontal bars of varying lengths to measure and compare categories of data or amounts, such as sales, counts, or rates. The bars can be all one color, or each bar may be a different color.

Consider This

When should you use a bar chart?

You should use a bar graph when you want to compare different groups of data. Because bar charts plot numerical data in rectangular blocks against a scale, viewers can visualize the categories by distinguishing the relative lengths of the bars. You also can use a bar graph to display numerical data when you want to present distributions of data. Bar charts tend to be better than column charts for positive numbers, larger numbers of categories, and longer data labels.

If you are comparing more than one piece of data per category, the chart becomes a clustered bar chart. The only differences between a bar chart and a column chart are in orientation and the amount of room for data labels. Longer data labels display better using bar charts. If you have any negative values, the bars appear pointing left; columns would appear pointing down. You will create the bar chart shown in Figure 7–57 by using the Quick Analysis gallery and formatting the data, axes, and title.

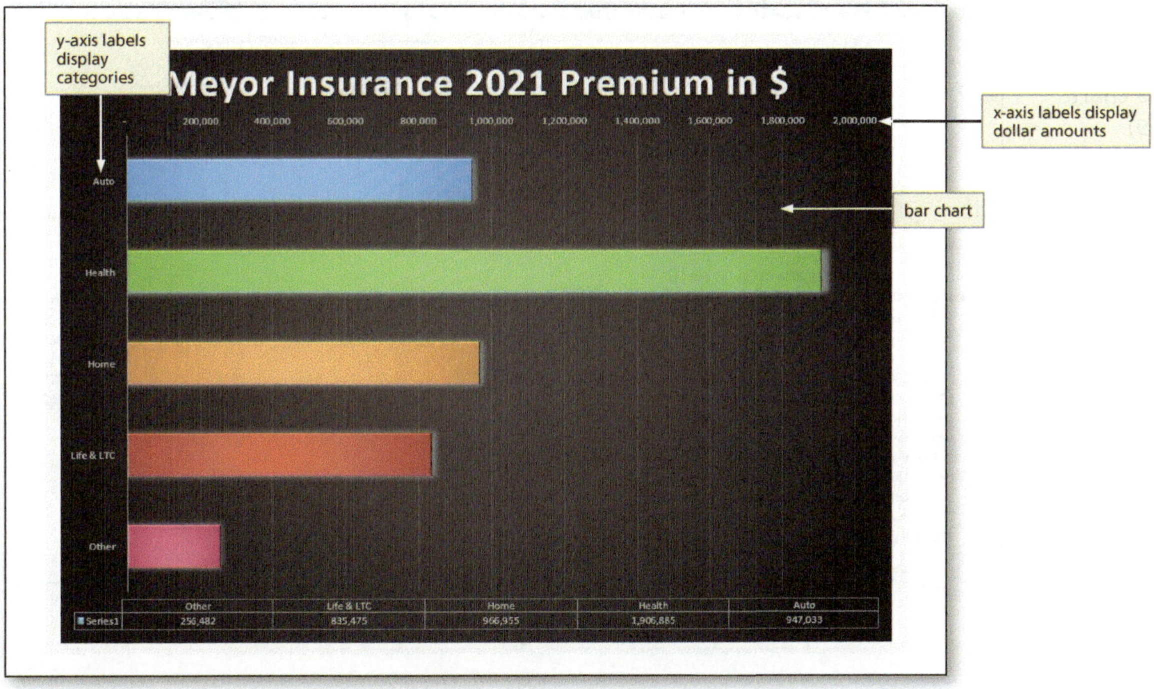

Figure 7–57

To Insert a Chart Using the Quick Analysis Gallery

The following steps insert a chart using the Quick Analysis gallery. **Why?** The Quick Analysis gallery is near the data and provides an easy way to access charts. The Quick Analysis gallery recommends charts that match the data.

1

- Select the range I4:J8 to select the data to include in the chart.
- Click the Quick Analysis button to display the Quick Analysis gallery.
- Click the Charts tab to display the buttons related to working with charts in the gallery (Figure 7–58).

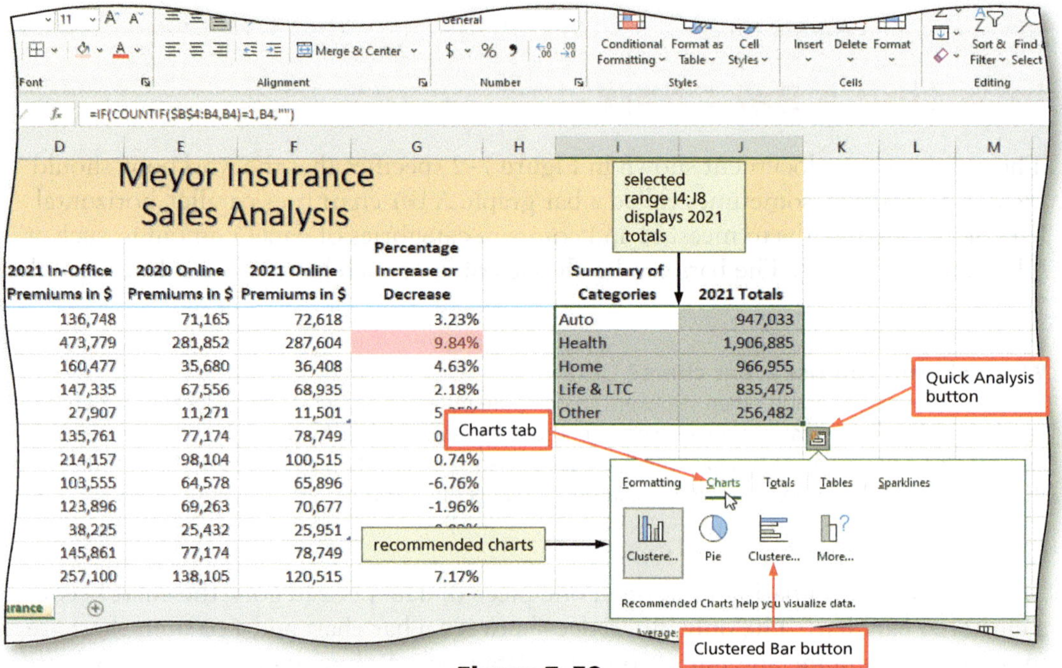

Figure 7–58

2

- Click the Clustered Bar button (Quick Analysis gallery) to insert the chart (Figure 7–59).

Q&A **Why are only three charts displayed?**
Excel lists the charts that it recommends for your data. You can click the More Charts button (Quick Analysis gallery) to open the Insert Chart dialog box and choose another chart style.

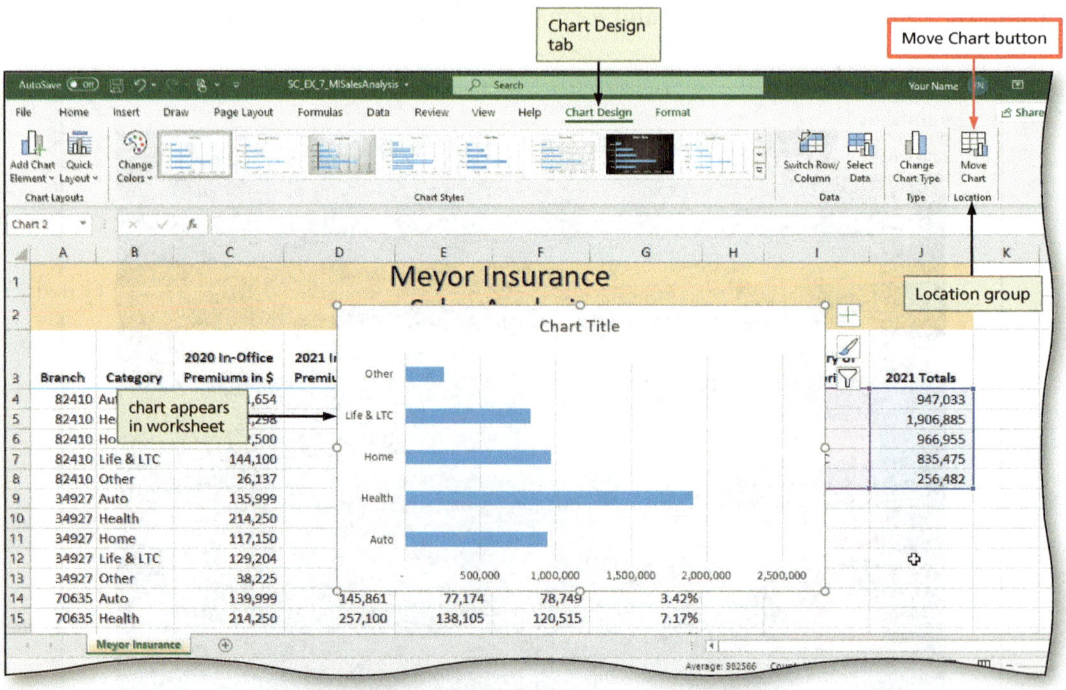

Figure 7–59

3

- Click the Move Chart button (Chart Design tab | Location group) to display the Move Chart dialog box.
- Click the New sheet option button and then type `Bar Chart` as the sheet name in the New sheet box (Figure 7–60).

4

- Click OK (Move Chart dialog box) to move the chart to the new sheet.

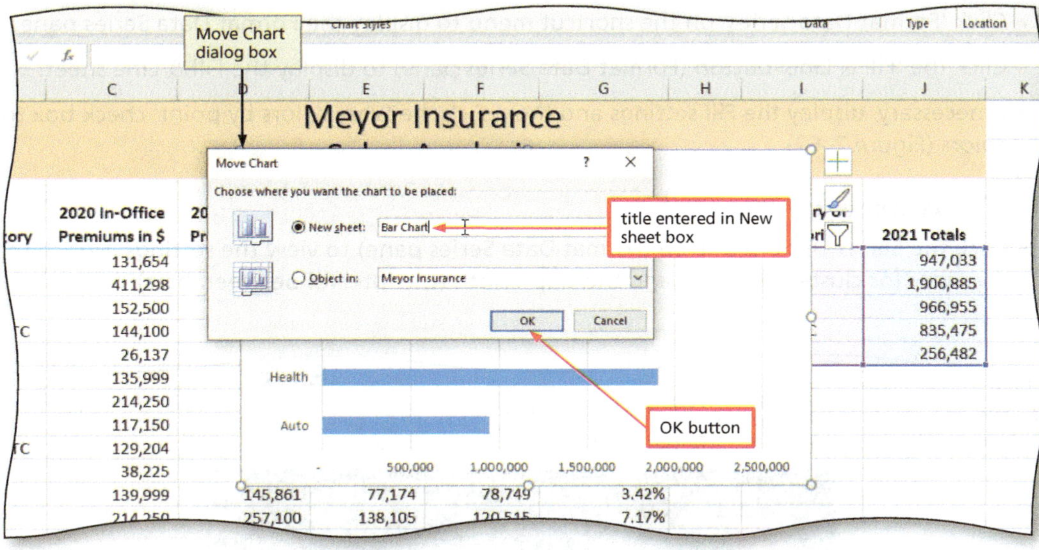

Figure 7–60

- Change the sheet tab color to Blue (Standard Colors area).

To Format the Chart

The Chart Design tab contains many buttons and tools to format a chart, including legends, styles, outlines, and the data bars. You can switch rows and columns using the Switch Row/Column button in the Data group, which changes the bars from horizontal to vertical or vice versa. You can also change the fill of any chart element (such as its background, a data series element, or a title) using the Shape Fill button in the Shape Styles group. The fill can be a color or a picture. The following steps change the style of the chart, as well as the color, bevel, and shadow of all the category bars, using the Format Data Series command on the shortcut menu. **Why?** You always should customize the chart with formatting that applies to the data and the concept you are trying to portray.

1

- If necessary, click the chart to select it. Click the Style 7 button (Chart Design tab | Chart Styles group) to change the style of the chart.
- Right-click any of the data bars on the chart to display the shortcut menu (Figure 7–61).

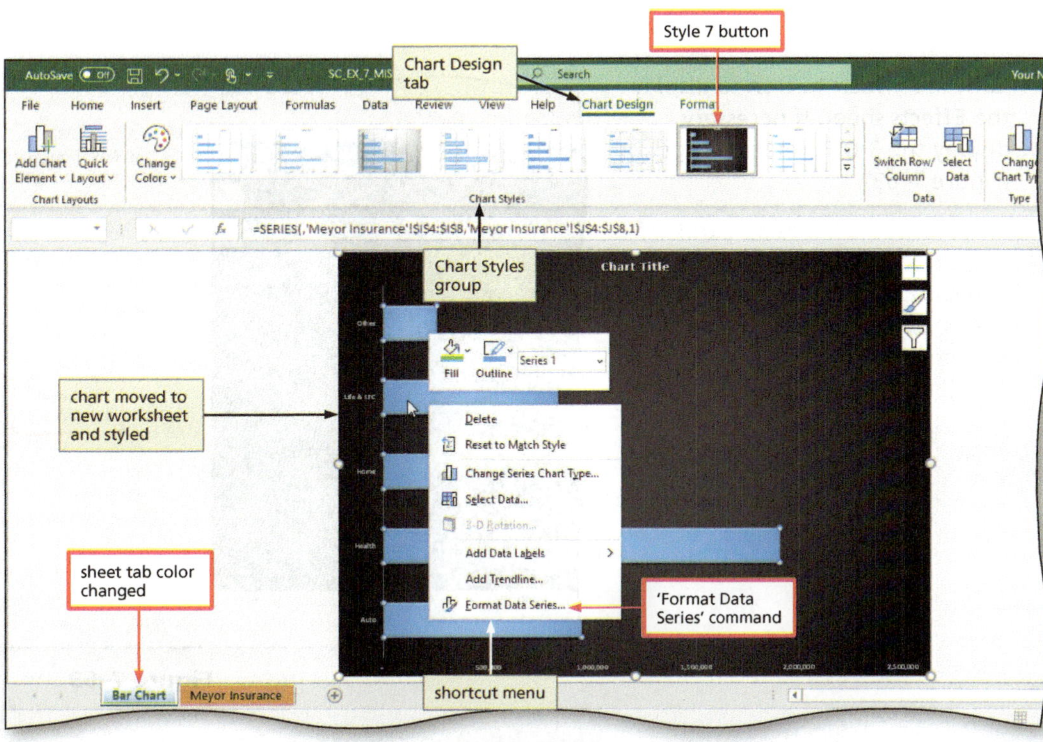

Figure 7–61

2

- Click 'Format Data Series' on the shortcut menu to display the Format Data Series pane.
- Click the 'Fill & Line' button (Format Data Series pane) to display the Fill & Line sheet.
- If necessary, display the Fill settings and then click the 'Vary colors by point' check box to display the bars in various colors (Figure 7–62).

Experiment

- Click the Series Options button (Format Data Series pane) to view the settings. Notice that you can set the Series Overlap (for clustered charts) and the Gap Width (the interval between bars).

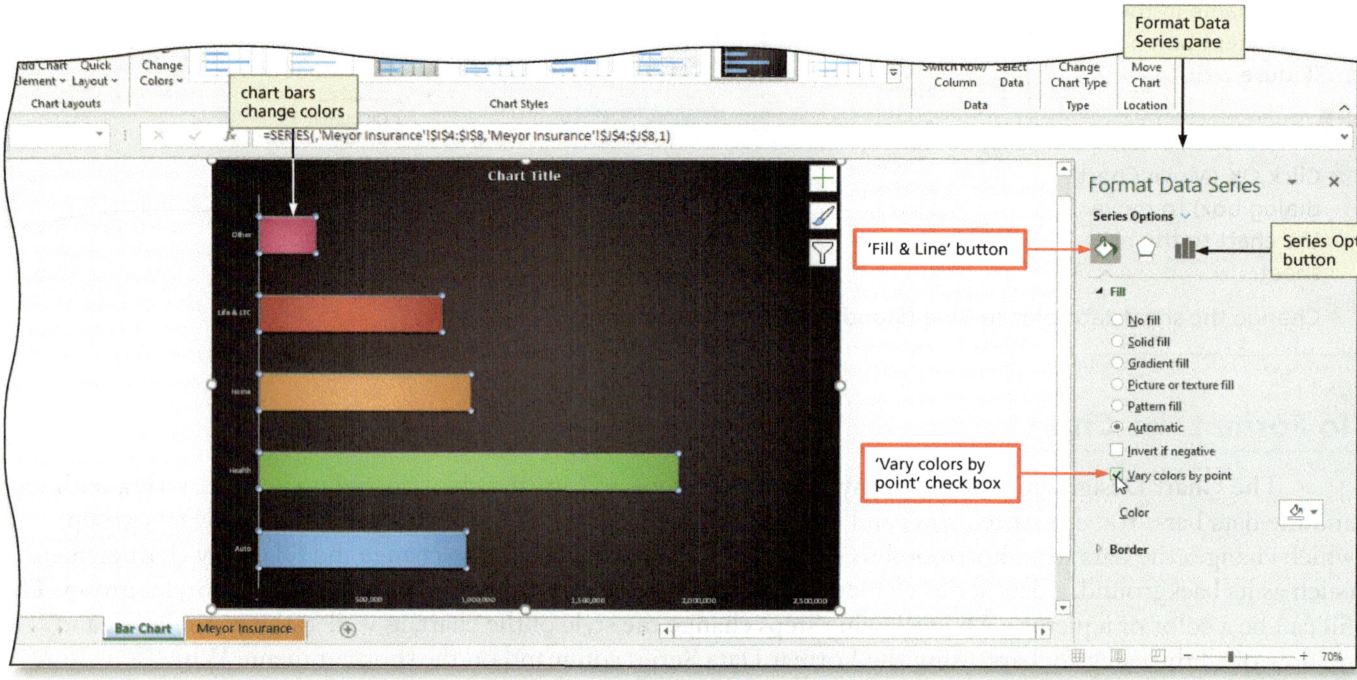

Figure 7–62

3

- Click the Effects button to display the Effects sheet. If necessary, display the 3-D Format settings (Figure 7–63).

Q&A **What kinds of effects can I change on the Effects sheet?**
You can change the shadow, glow, edges, bevel, and 3-D format of the bars.

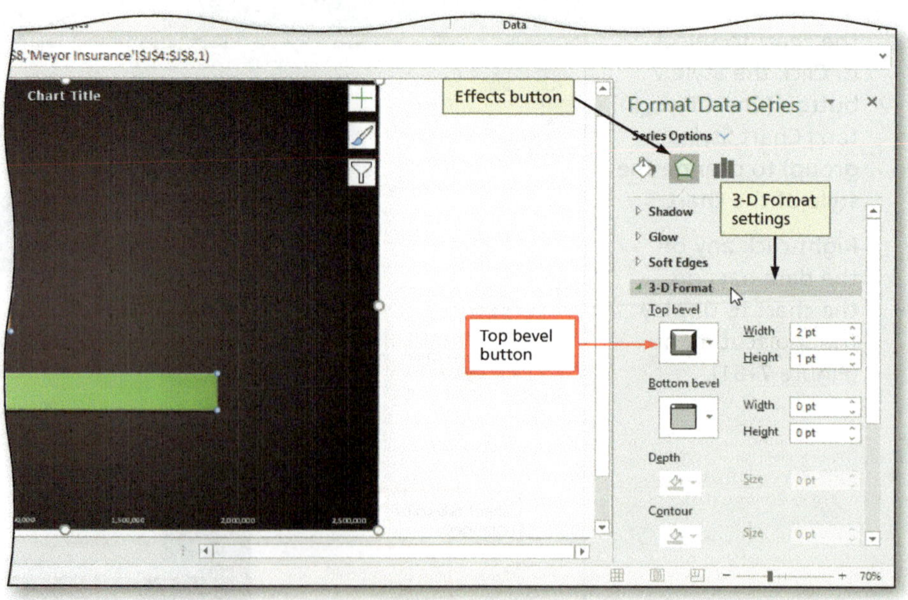

Figure 7–63

4

- Click the Top bevel button to display the Top bevel gallery (Figure 7–64).

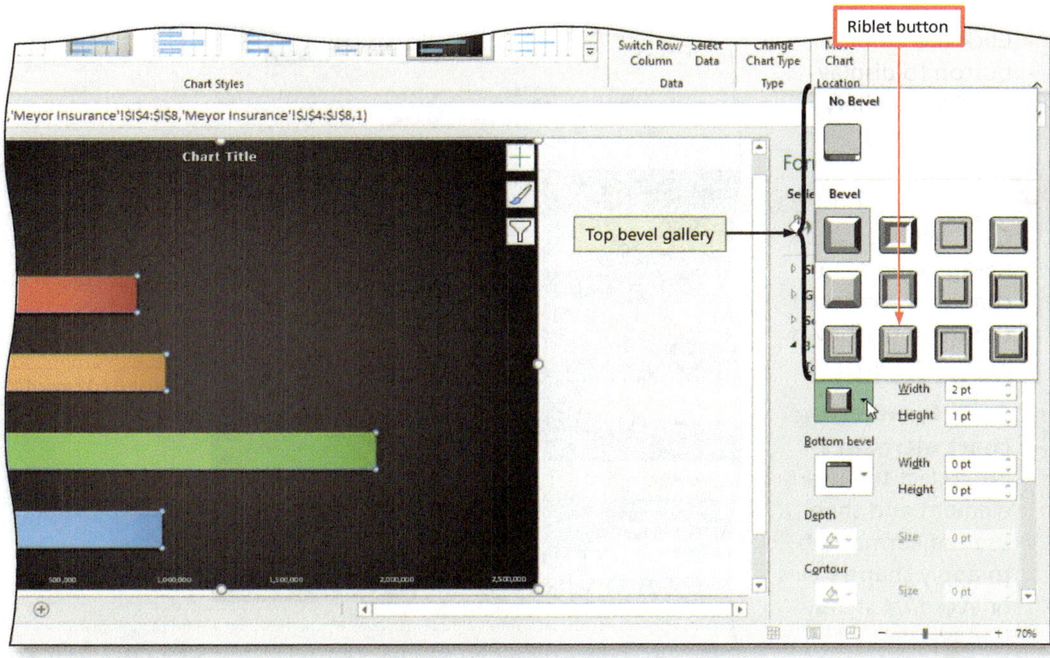

Figure 7–64

5

- Click the Riblet button (Top bevel gallery) to apply a Riblet bevel to the bars in the chart.
- Click Shadow in the Format Data Series pane, and then click the Presets button to display the Shadow gallery (Figure 7–65).
- In the Outer area, click the Offset: Center thumbnail to select a placement for the shadow.

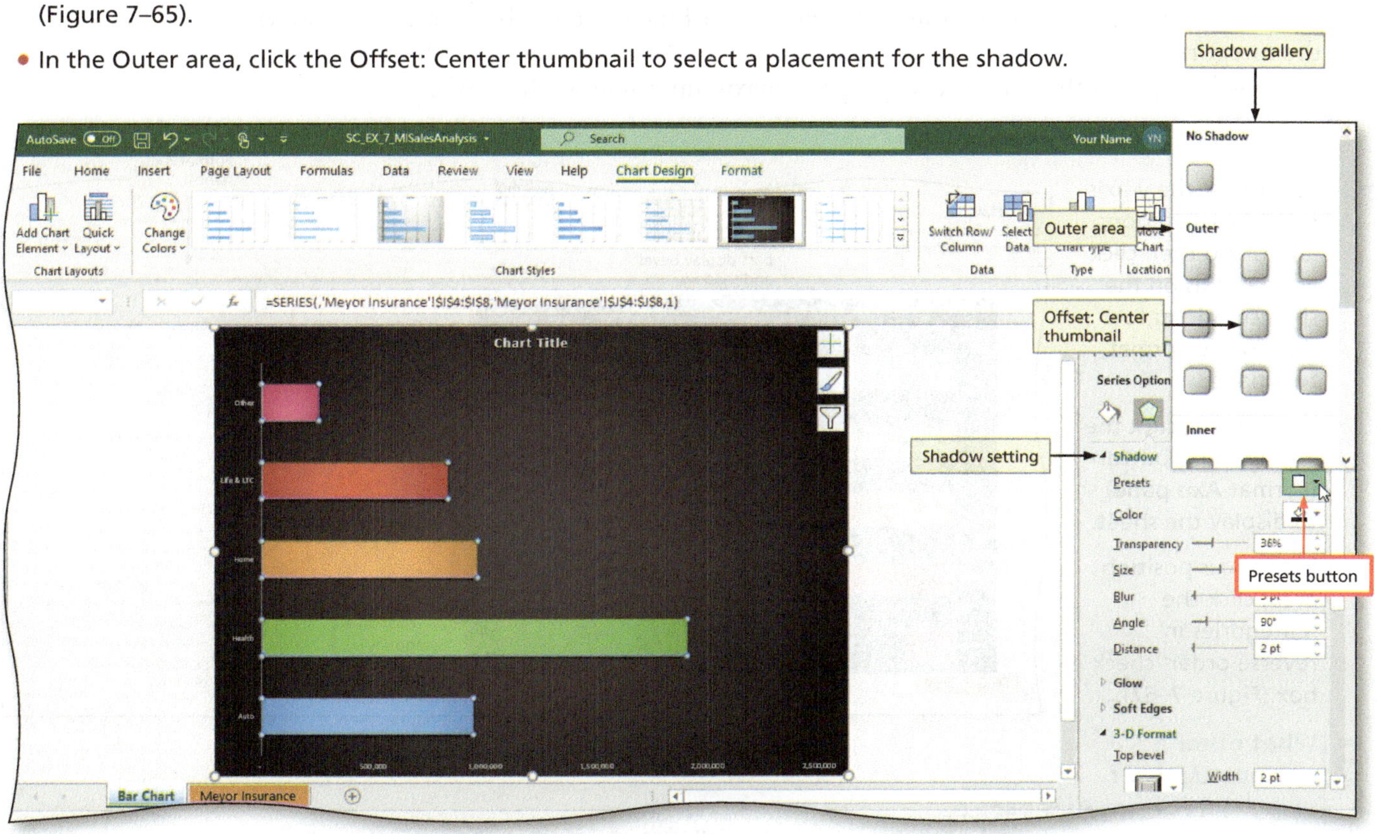

Figure 7–65

6

- Click the Color button to display the Color gallery (Figure 7–66).

7

- Click 'White, Background 1' to change the color of the shadow (shown in Figure 7–67).

Q&A **Can I format other chart elements?**
Yes, select the chart element and then use the Format tab to apply shape styles or WordArt styles.

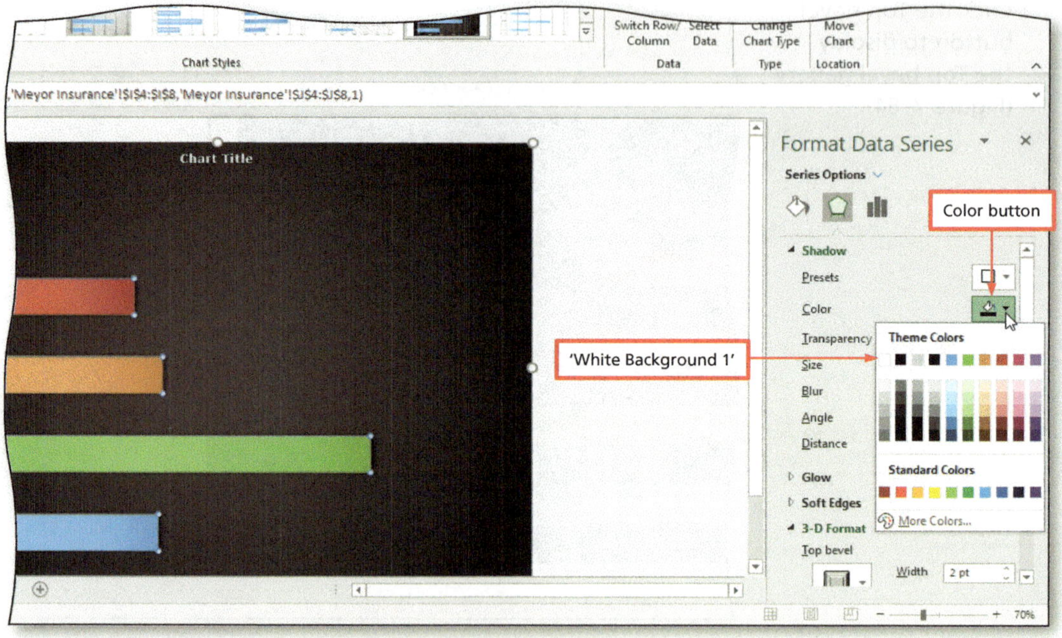

Figure 7–66

To Format Axis Options

The following steps format the y axis and x axis of the clustered bar chart. You also will change the order of the categories. **Why?** Changing the order will put the minor category of Other at the bottom of the chart. You also will lengthen the bars by changing the maximum value on the x axis.

1

- Right-click the y-axis or vertical category labels and then click Format Axis on the shortcut menu to display the Format Axis pane.
- If necessary, click the Axis Options button (Format Axis pane) to display the sheet.
- In the Axis position area, click the 'Categories in reverse order' check box (Figure 7–67).

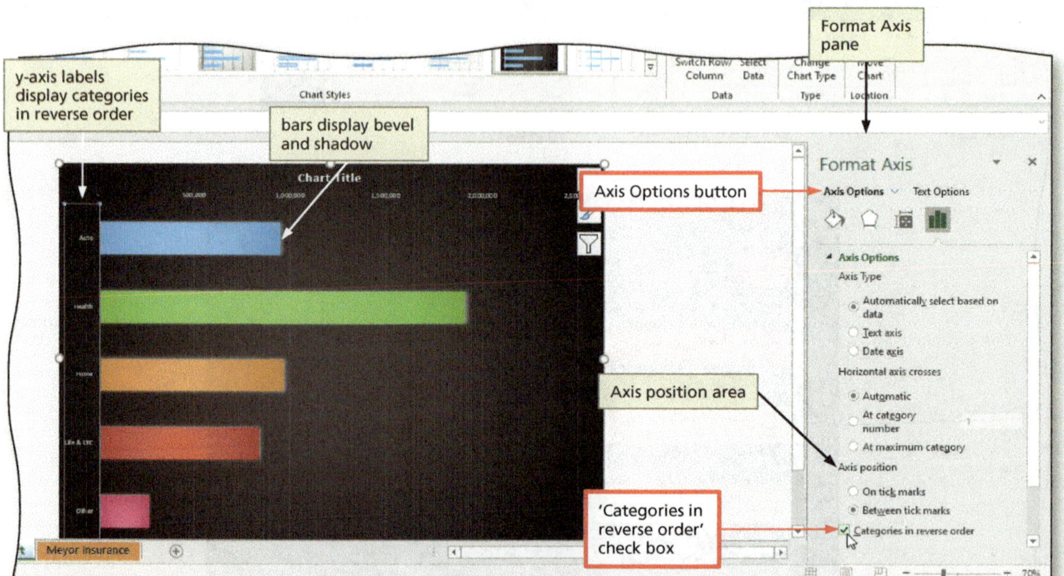

Figure 7–67

Q&A **What other options can I set using the Format Axis pane?**
You can change how tick marks, labels, and numbers display. On the Size & Properties tab, you can set the alignment, text direction, and margins of the axes. The Fill & Line tab and the Effects tab are similar to the Format Data Series pane that you used earlier.

2

- Right-click the x-axis or horizontal labels across the top of the chart and then click Format Axis on the shortcut menu to display the Format Axis pane.
- If necessary, click the Axis Options tab (Format Axis pane) to display the Bounds area.
- In the Maximum box, type **2.0E6** and then press ENTER to indicate that two million will be the maximum value (Figure 7–68).

Q&A **What is the meaning of 2.0E6?**
The entry 2.0E6 is the scientific notation for two million.

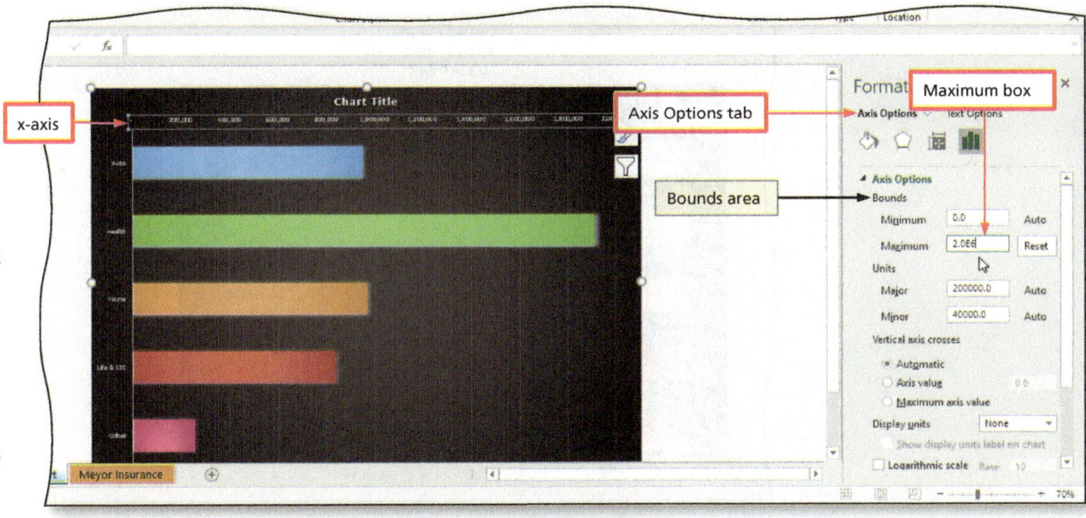

Figure 7–68

To Add Data Labels

The following steps add data labels to the bars. **Why?** Data labels will show viewers the exact value for each category, rather than having them estimate based on the x axis.

1

- Click the Chart Elements button, which displays as a plus sign when you point to the upper-right corner of the chart, to display the Chart Elements list.
- Click Data Labels, and then click the Data Labels arrow to display the Data Labels submenu (Figure 7–69).

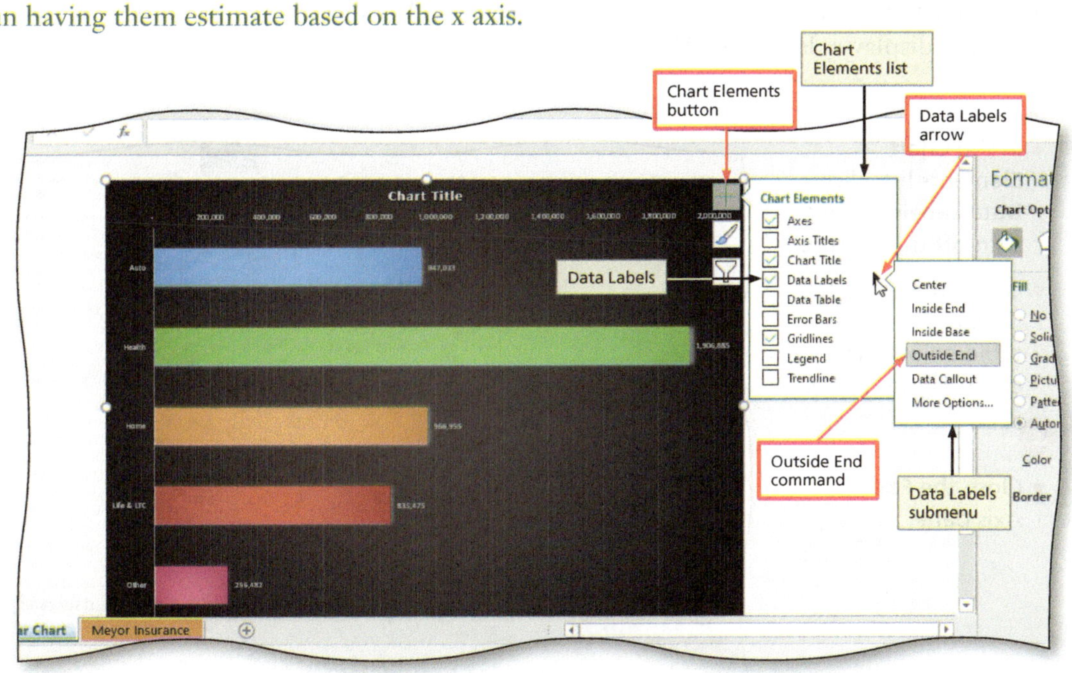

Figure 7–69

2

- Click Outside End (Figure 7–70).

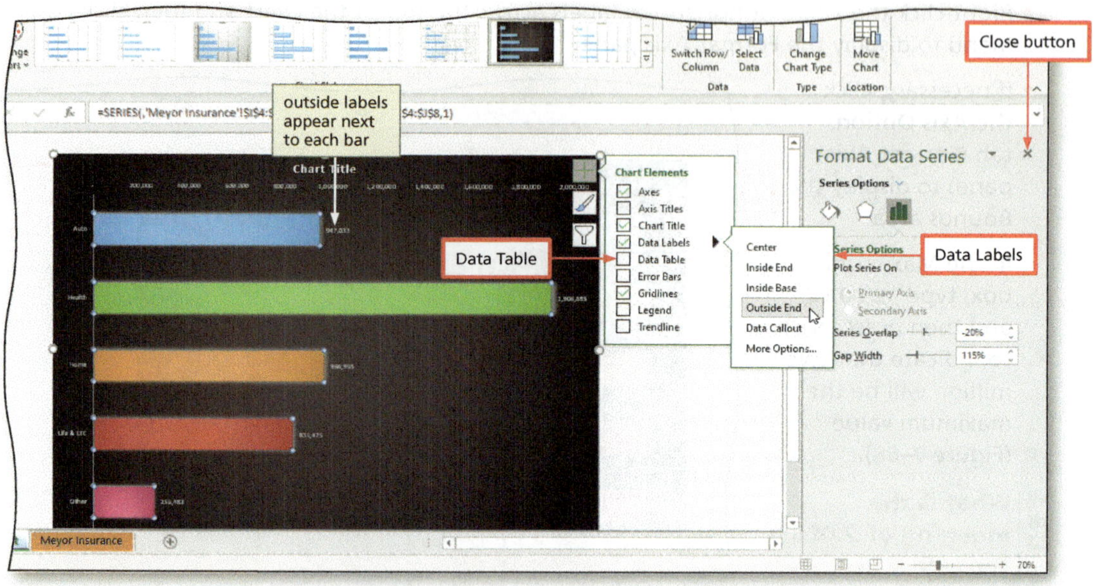

Figure 7–70

To Display a Data Table

In Excel, you can add a data table to a chart. A **data table** is a chart element that displays the data as a grid below the chart itself. Data tables are available for line charts, area charts, column charts, or bar charts. You can format a data table using fills, borders, legends, and other text effects. In the following step, you will turn off data labels and display a data table. **Why?** Displaying the data both ways is probably unnecessary.

1

- In the Chart Elements list, click Data Labels again to turn off the feature.
- Click Data Table to display the data table below the chart (Figure 7–71).

2

- Close the Format Axis pane.

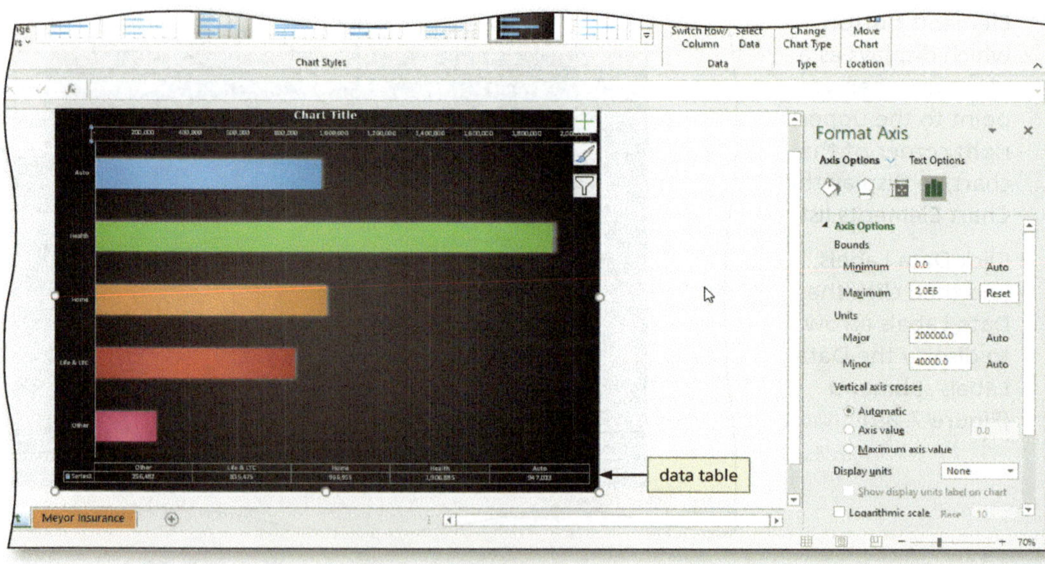

Figure 7–71

To Format the Chart Title

The following steps format the chart title by changing the font size, editing the text, and applying a chart text outline.

1. Click the chart title and select all of the text.
2. Display the Home tab and change the font size to 32.
3. Type **`Meyor Insurance 2021 Premiums in $`** to change the title (Figure 7–72).
4. Click the Save button (Quick Access Toolbar).

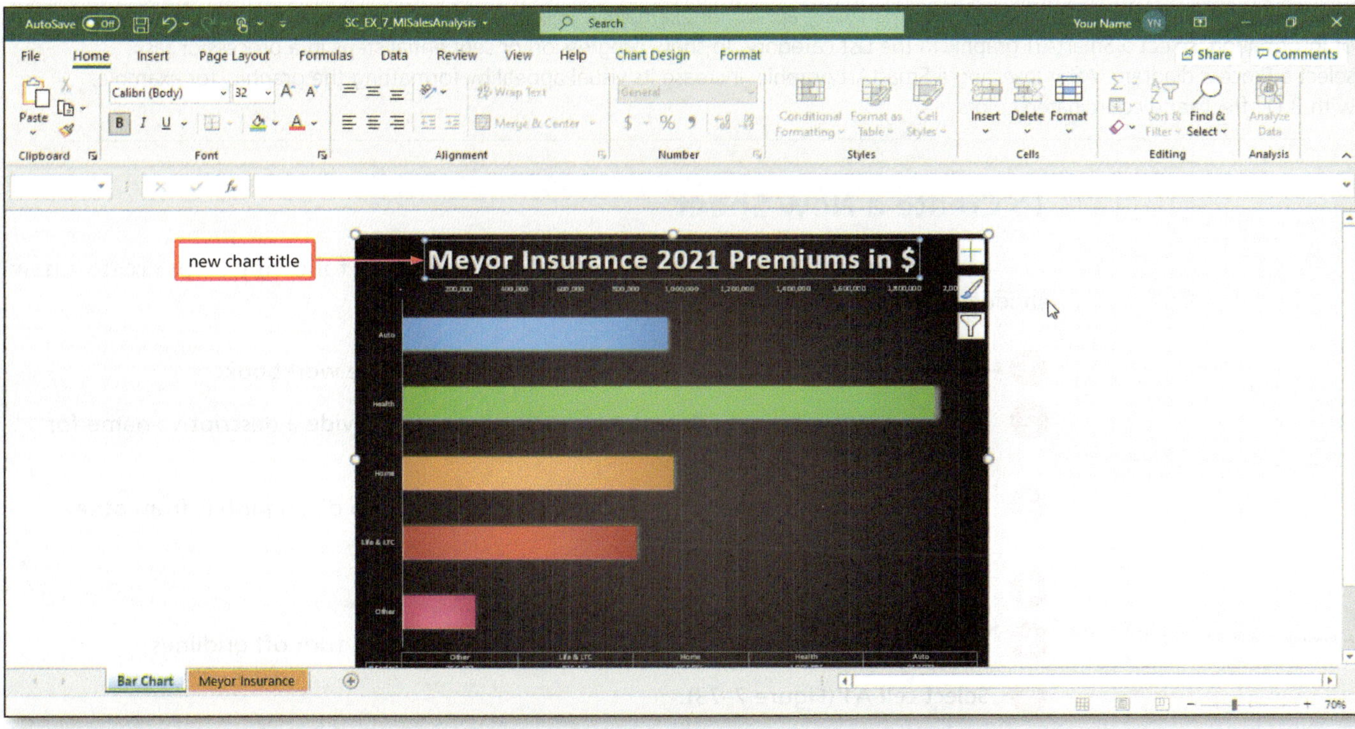

Figure 7–72

To Change the Chart Text Outline

If you wanted to outline the text in the chart, you would perform the following steps.

1. Select the text on the chart.
2. Right-click the text and then, depending on the location of the text, click either Format Axis, Format Legend, or Format Chart on the shortcut menu.
3. When Excel displays the appropriate Format pane, click the Text Options tab.
4. In the Text Outline area, click the Solid Line option button, and set the desired color, width, and other formatting.

Break Point: If you want to take a break, this is a good place to do so. You can exit Excel now. To resume later, start Excel, open the file called SC_EX_7_MISalesAnalysis, and continue following the steps from this location forward.

Working with SmartArt Graphics

A **SmartArt graphic** is a customizable diagram that you use to pictorially present lists, processes, and relationships. For example, you can use a SmartArt graphic to illustrate the manufacturing process to produce an item. Excel includes nine types of SmartArt graphics: List, Process, Cycle, Hierarchy, Relationship, Matrix, Pyramid, Picture, and

Office.com. Each type of graphic includes several layouts, or templates, from which to choose. After selecting a SmartArt graphic type and layout, you customize the graphic to meet your needs and present your information and ideas in a compelling manner.

In the following sections, you will create a SmartArt graphic with shapes, pictures, and text. You then will add a style to the SmartArt graphic.

Consider This

How do you choose the type of SmartArt graphics to add?

Consider what you want to illustrate in the SmartArt graphic. For example, if you are showing nonsequential or grouped blocks of information, select a SmartArt graphic in the List category. To show progression or sequential steps in a process or task, select a Process diagram. After inserting a SmartArt graphic, increase its visual appeal by formatting the graphic, for example, with 3-D effects and coordinated colors.

To Create a New Sheet

In preparation for inserting a SmartArt graphic, the following steps create a new sheet and hide gridlines.

1. Click the New sheet button to create a third sheet in the workbook.
2. Rename the worksheet `SmartArt Graphic` to provide a descriptive name for the worksheet.
3. Change the color of the tab to 'White, Background 1' to distinguish it from other sheets.
4. Click View on the ribbon to display the View tab.
5. Click the Gridlines check box (View tab | Show group) to turn off gridlines.
6. Select cell A1 (Figure 7–73).

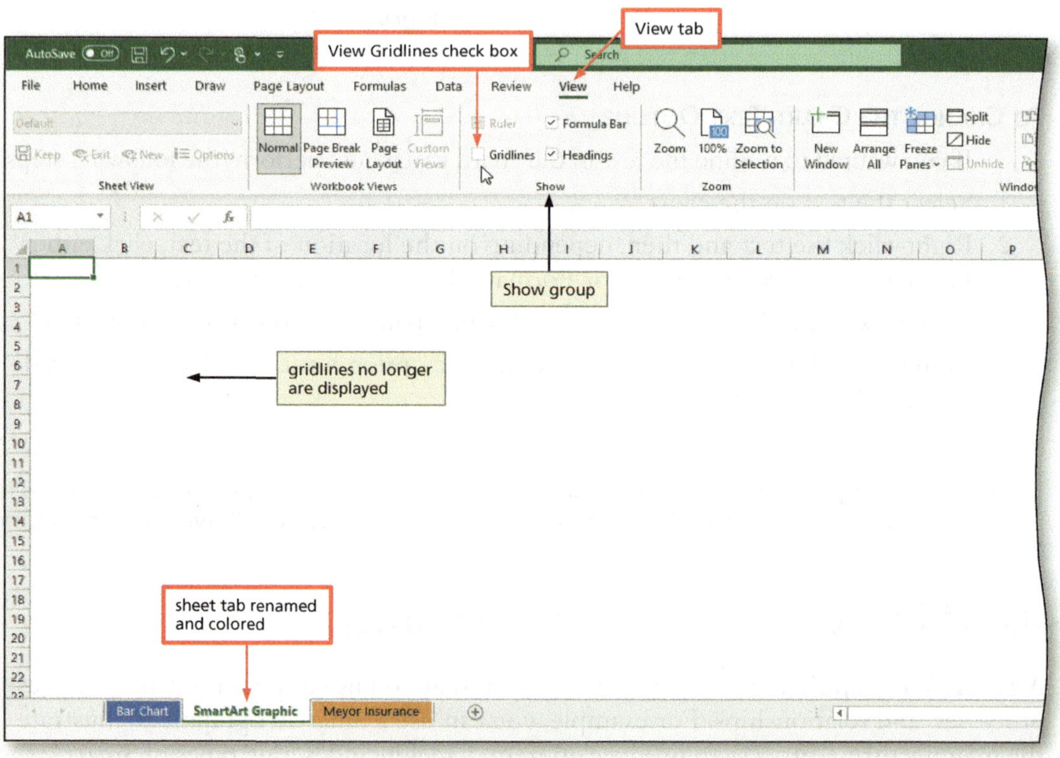

Figure 7–73

To Insert a SmartArt Graphic

To illustrate the categories of policies sold by MI, you decide to use a SmartArt graphic. **Why?** A SmartArt graphic with pictures can be used in marketing and promotional material for the company. The following steps insert a SmartArt graphic named Accented Picture.

1

- Display the Insert tab.
- Click the Illustrations button (Insert tab | Illustrations group), and then click the SmartArt button to display the Choose a SmartArt Graphic dialog box.
- Click the desired type of SmartArt in the left pane; in this case, click Picture to display the available SmartArt layouts in the middle pane (Choose a SmartArt Graphic dialog box).
- Click the desired layout, in this case, the Accented Picture layout, to see a preview of the chart in the preview area (Figure 7–74).

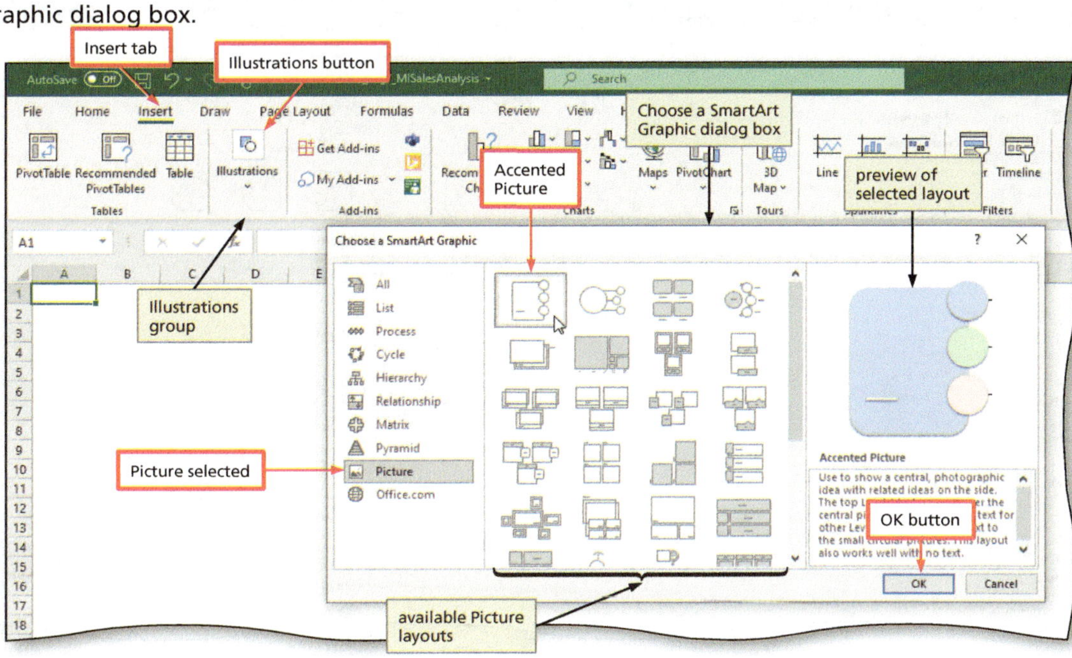

Figure 7–74

Q&A **What do the middle and right panes of the dialog box display?**
The middle pane of the dialog box (the layout gallery) displays available types of picture charts, and the right pane (the preview area) displays a preview of the selected SmartArt graphic.

Experiment

- Click the various SmartArt graphics to see a preview of each in the preview area. When you are finished, click Accented Picture in the middle pane.

2

- Click OK (Choose a SmartArt Graphic dialog box) to insert an Accented Picture SmartArt graphic in the worksheet (Figure 7–75).

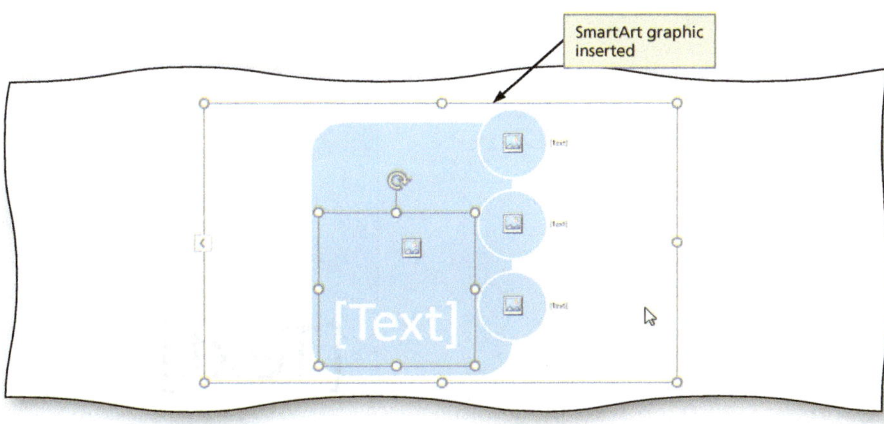

Figure 7–75

To Color and Resize the SmartArt Graphic

The following steps change the color of the SmartArt graphic and then resize it. **Why?** You want the graphic to appear visually pleasing and as large as possible in the given space.

1

- Click the Change Colors button (SmartArt Design tab | SmartArt Styles group) to display the Change Colors gallery (Figure 7–76).

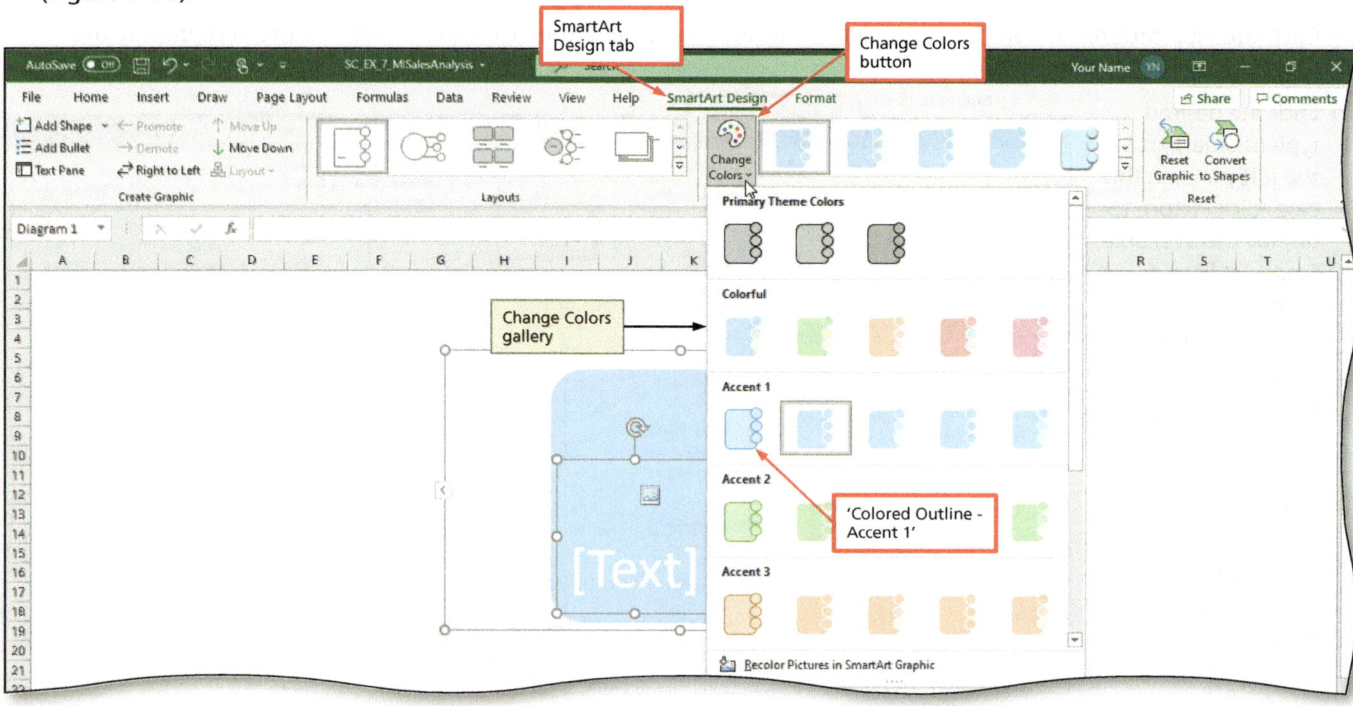

Figure 7–76

2

- Click 'Colored Outline - Accent 1' in the gallery to change the color.
- Drag the sizing handles to resize the SmartArt graphic to fill the range F1:Q23 (Figure 7–77).

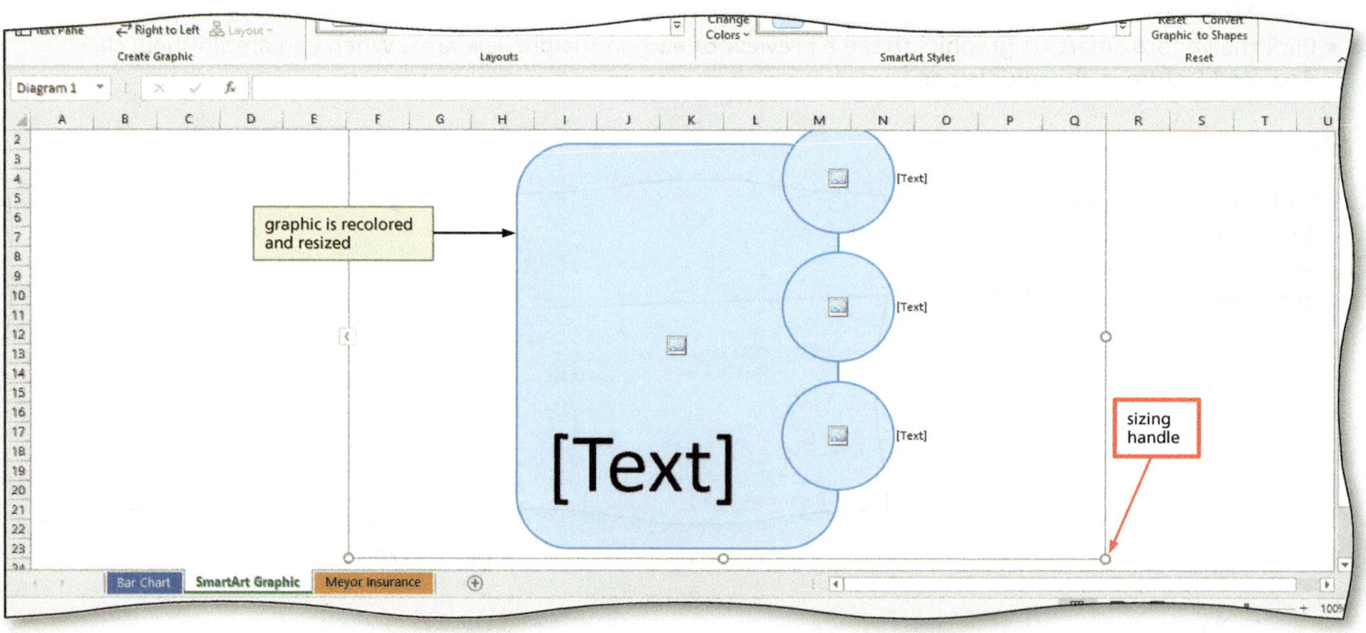

Figure 7–77

Experiment

- Click the Format tab and look at the various groups, buttons, and galleries available to format SmartArt graphics.

To Add a Shape to a SmartArt Graphic

Many SmartArt graphics include more than one shape, such as a picture, text box, or combinations, grouped in levels. Level 1 is considered the largest object or main level. Level 2 is a sublevel and may display one to three shapes when first created. You can add a shape or text box to each level. You also can **demote** or **promote** a shape, which means you can move the shape to a lower level or an upper level, respectively.

The default Accented Picture SmartArt graphic layout includes a large shape for level 1 and three smaller shapes at level 2. The following step adds a new shape to level 2 in the SmartArt graphic. **Why?** You decide to show four categories in the SmartArt graphic.

1

- Click the Add Shape button (SmartArt Design tab | Create Graphic group) to add another level 2 shape (Figure 7–78).

Q&A **Can I add a style to the shape?**
Yes. To do so, select the shape, and then click the More button (Format tab | Shape Styles group). Excel displays a gallery with many Theme Styles and Presets.

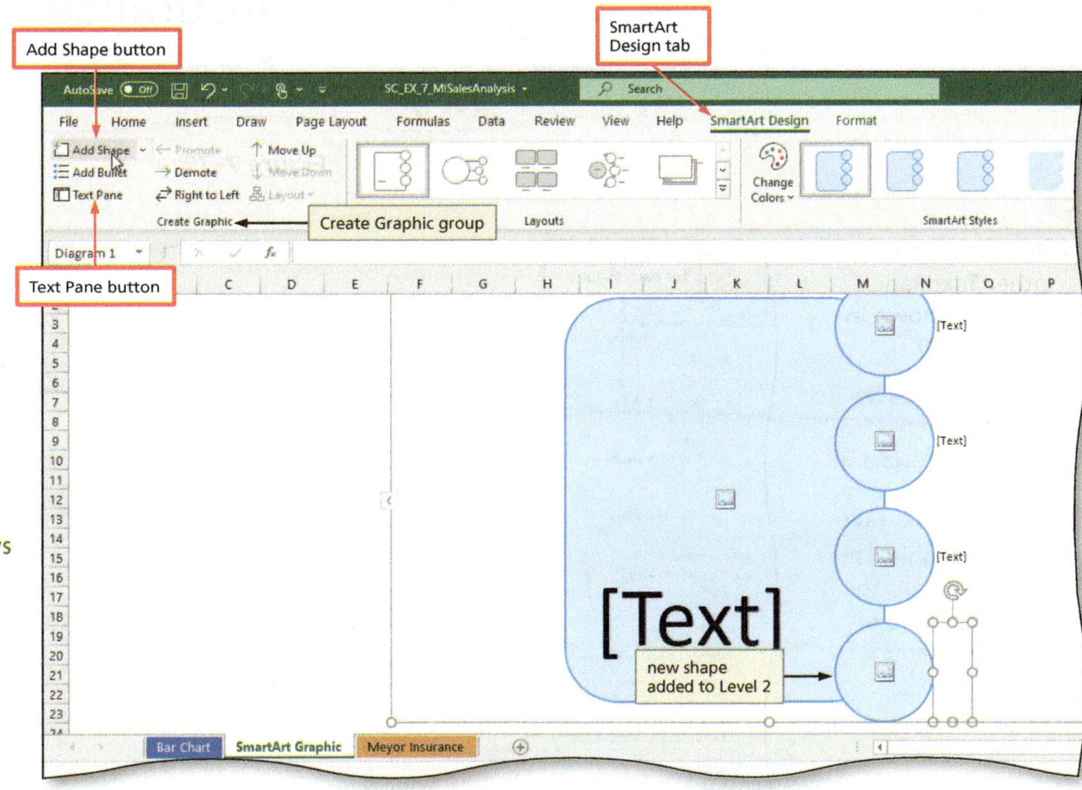

Figure 7–78

Other Ways

1. Right-click SmartArt graphic, point to Add Shape on shortcut menu, click 'Add Shape After' or 'Add Shape Before' on Add Shape submenu

To Add Text to a SmartArt Graphic

The following steps add text to the SmartArt graphic. You can type text directly in the text boxes of the SmartArt graphic, or you can display a Text Pane and add text to the shape through the Text Pane. The Text Pane displays a bulleted outline corresponding to each of the shapes in the SmartArt graphic. **Why?** You may find it easier to enter text in the Text Pane because you do not have to select any object to replace the default text.

1

- If the Text Pane does not appear, click the Text Pane button (SmartArt Design tab | Create Graphic group) to display the Text Pane.
- Click the first bulleted item in the Text Pane and then type `Meyor Insurance` to replace the default text (Figure 7–79).

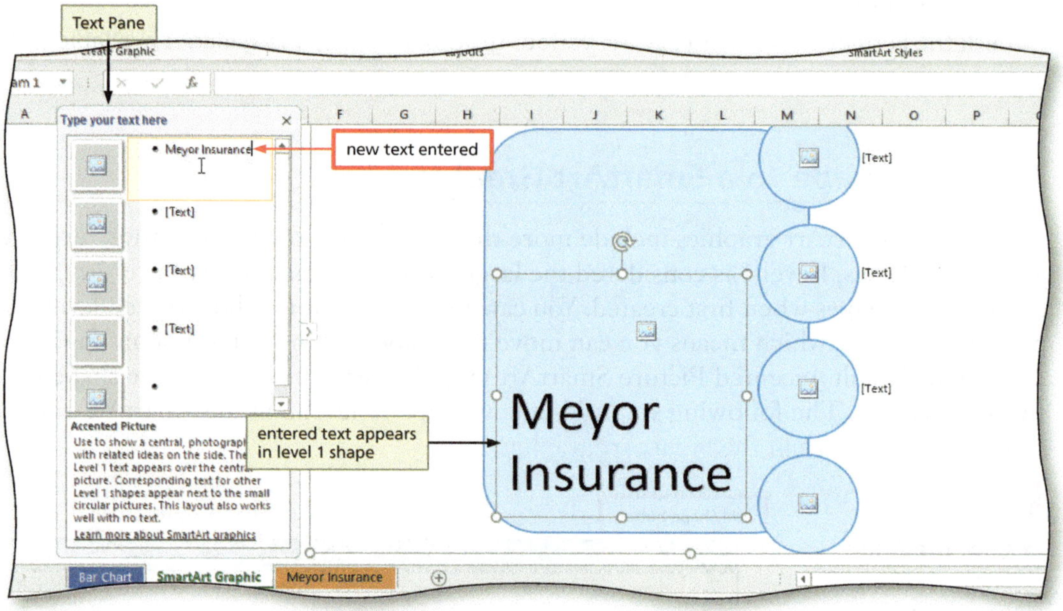

Figure 7–79

2

- Enter text in the other Text Pane boxes as shown in Figure 7–80.

Q&A **Did Excel resize my font?**
Yes. Excel resizes all of the level 2 fonts to autofit the text in the graphic. Thus, it is important to resize the graphic before adding text.

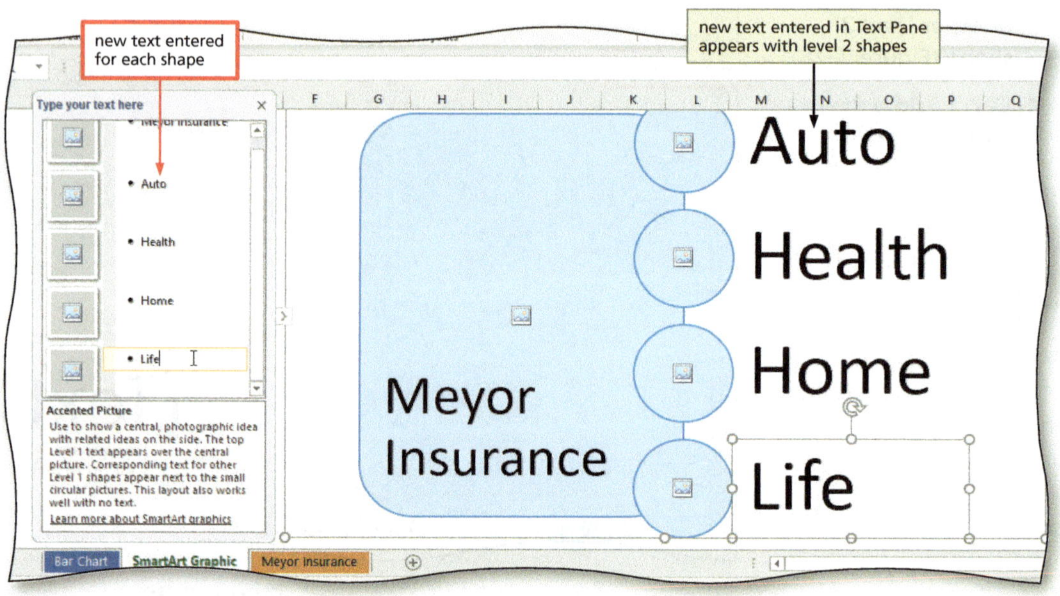

Figure 7–80

Other Ways

1. Click left arrow on edge of SmartArt graphic border to open Text Pane, type text
2. Click individual text box in SmartArt graphic, type text

To Add a Style to a SmartArt Graphic

Excel allows you to change the style of your SmartArt graphic. **Why?** The SmartArt styles create different special effects for added emphasis or flair. The following steps change the style of the SmartArt graphic.

1

- If necessary, display the SmartArt Design tab.
- Click the More button (SmartArt Design tab | SmartArt Styles group) to display the SmartArt Styles gallery (Figure 7–81).

Experiment

- Point to each of the SmartArt styles in the gallery to see a live preview of the effect on the worksheet.

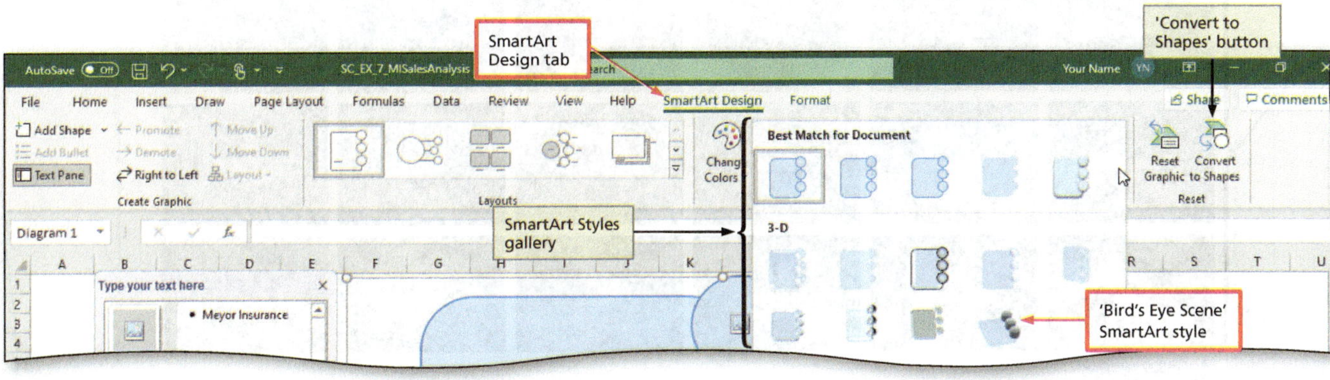

Figure 7–81

2

- Click the 'Bird's Eye Scene' style to apply it to the SmartArt graphic (Figure 7–82).

Q&A

What does the 'Convert to Shapes' button do?

Clicking the 'Convert to Shapes' button (SmartArt Design tab | Reset group) converts the SmartArt graphic to individual shapes that can be resized, moved, or deleted independently of the others.

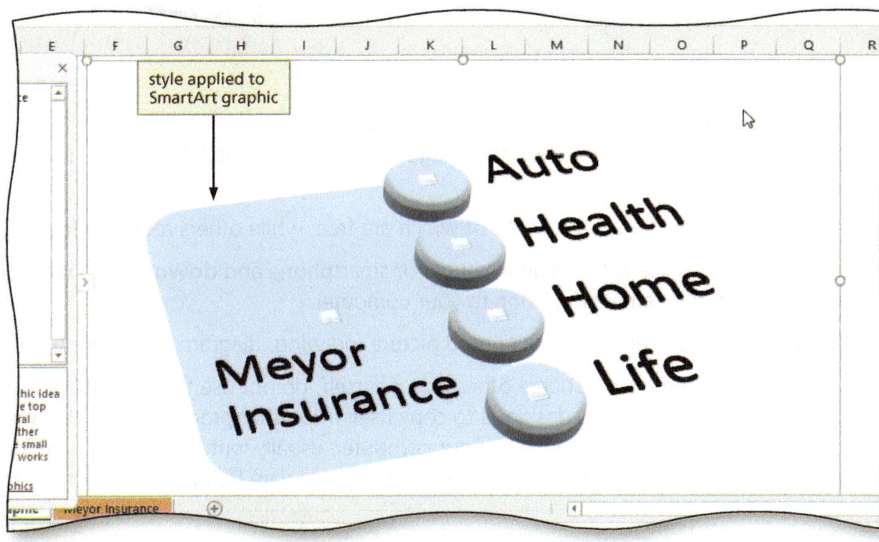

Figure 7–82

Pictures and Icons

The next step is to add pictures and icons to the SmartArt Graphic. Excel offers three different choices when inserting a picture. The 'From a File' command allows you to choose a digital picture of almost any file type that is stored on an accessible storage device. If you choose Online Pictures, Excel opens a Bing search with various categories (Figure 7–83). You can search one of the categories or enter a keyword. The third command, From Icons, lets you choose an icon from an online collection. An **icon** is usually a graphic representation of a picture, idea, or process. Excel includes a large number of icons, which can be formatted once they are added to the worksheet.

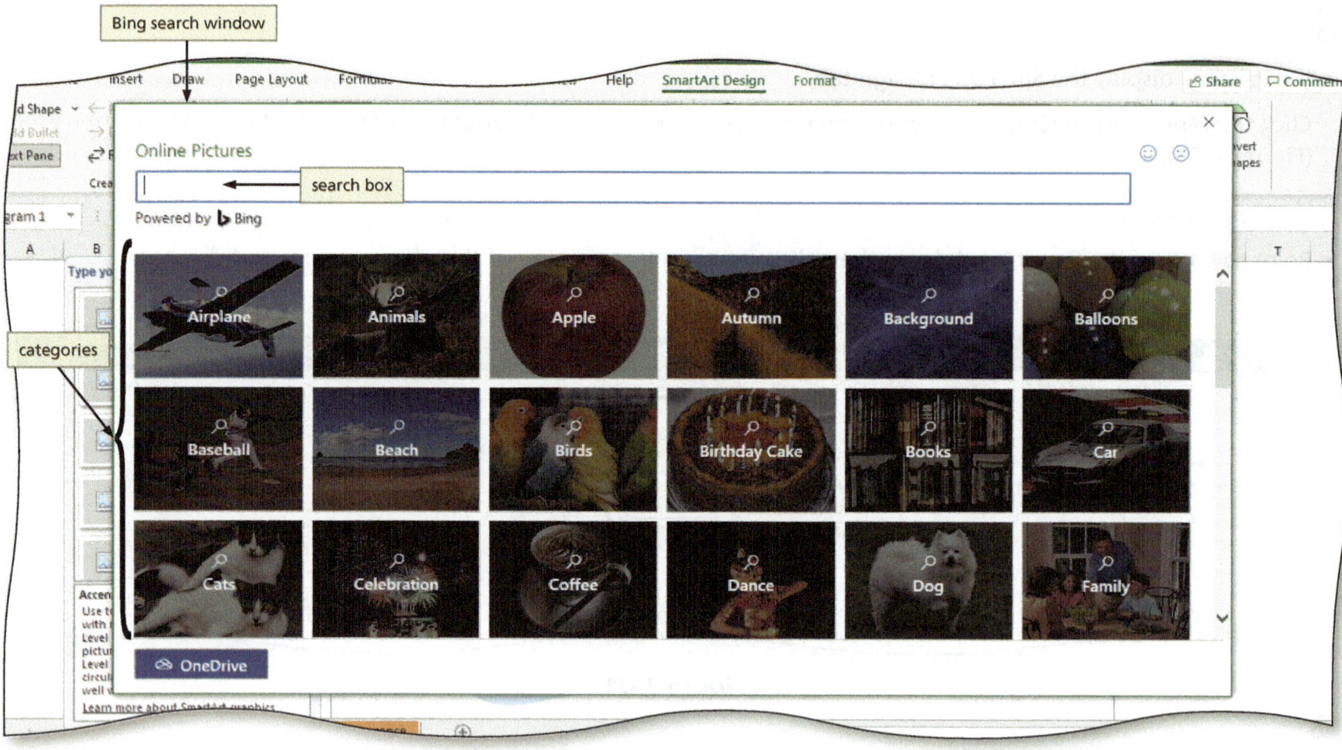

Figure 7–83

Consider This

How do I locate a picture to use in a worksheet?

To use a picture in a Excel worksheet, the image must be stored digitally in a file. Files containing pictures are available from a variety of sources:

- The web has pictures available, some of which are free, while others require a fee.
- You can take a picture with a digital camera or smartphone and **download** it, which is the process of copying the picture (or other file) from the camera or phone to your computer.
- With a scanner, you can convert a printed picture, drawing, diagram, or other object to a digital file.

If you receive a picture from a source other than yourself, do not use the file until you are certain it does not contain a virus. A **virus** is a computer program designed to copy itself into other programs with the intention of causing mischief, harm, or damage to files, programs, and apps on your computer, usually without your knowledge or permission. Use an **antivirus program** or app to locate and destroy viruses or other malware before they infect a device.

In the following sections, you will insert a picture from a file for the Level 1 part of the SmartArt graphic. The Level 2 graphics will be icons.

To Add a Picture to a SmartArt Graphic

The following steps add a picture to the SmartArt graphic. **Why?** The CEO wants to highlight the concept of protection by using an umbrella graphic. Other times, you may want to locate stock images categorized by image type, or images or clip art from the web, also called online pictures. Excel uses a Bing Image Search to help you locate images licensed under Creative Commons. **Creative Commons** is a nonprofit organization that makes it easy for content creators to license and share their work by supplying easy-to-understand copyright licenses; the creator chooses the conditions under which the work can be used. The resulting images may or may not be royalty and copyright free. You must read the specific license for any image you plan to use, even for educational purposes. In this module, you will add pictures from the Data Files. Please contact your instructor for information about accessing the Data Files.

1

- In the Text Pane, click the first Insert Picture icon (next to Meyor Insurance) to display the Insert Pictures dialog box (Figure 7–84).

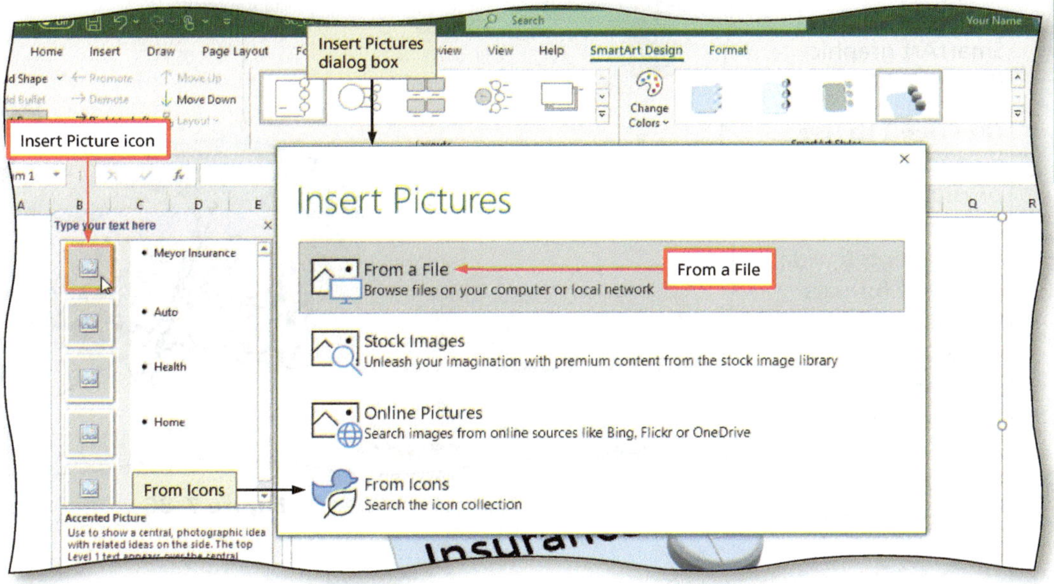

Figure 7–84

2

- Click the From a File button to display the Insert Picture dialog box and then browse to the Data Files (Figure 7–85).

Q&A **Why do the files in my dialog box appear differently?**
Your system may display a different view. If you want to match the display in Figure 7–85, click the 'Change your view' arrow, and then click Large icons.

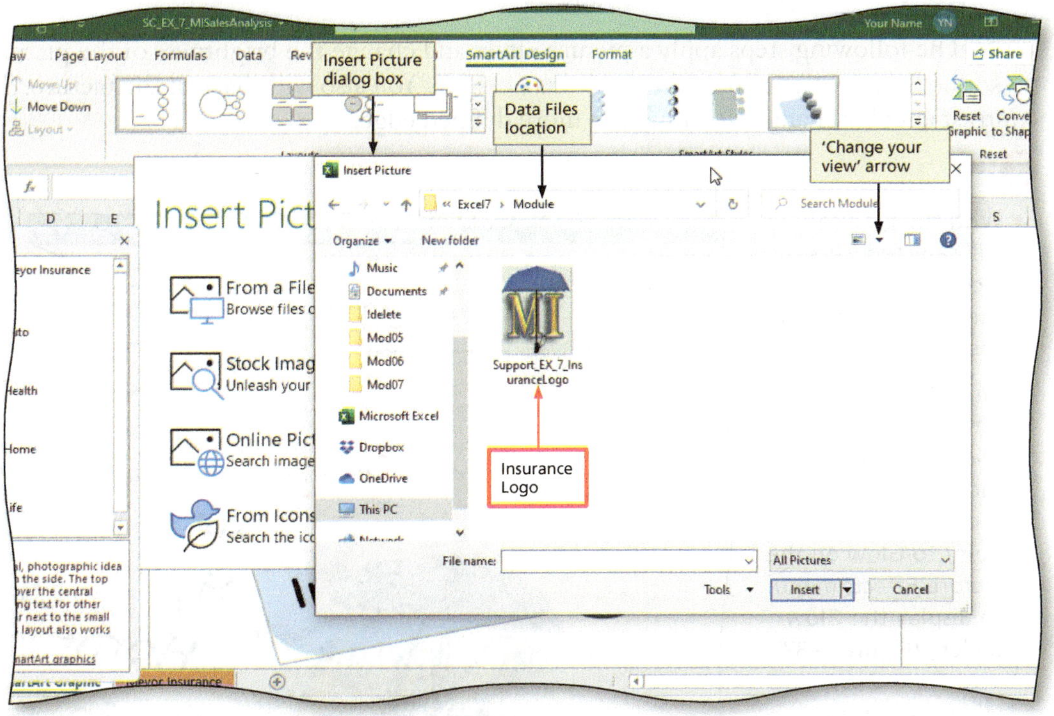

Figure 7–85

3

- Double-click the file named Support_EX_7_InsuranceLogo.gif Insurance Logo to place it in the SmartArt graphic (Figure 7–86).

Q&A

Do I need to use a special type of picture file or format?
Excel accepts a wide variety of formats including .png, .gif, .bmp, .jpg, and .tif, among others. Excel will resize the graphic as necessary to fit the space in the SmartArt graphic.

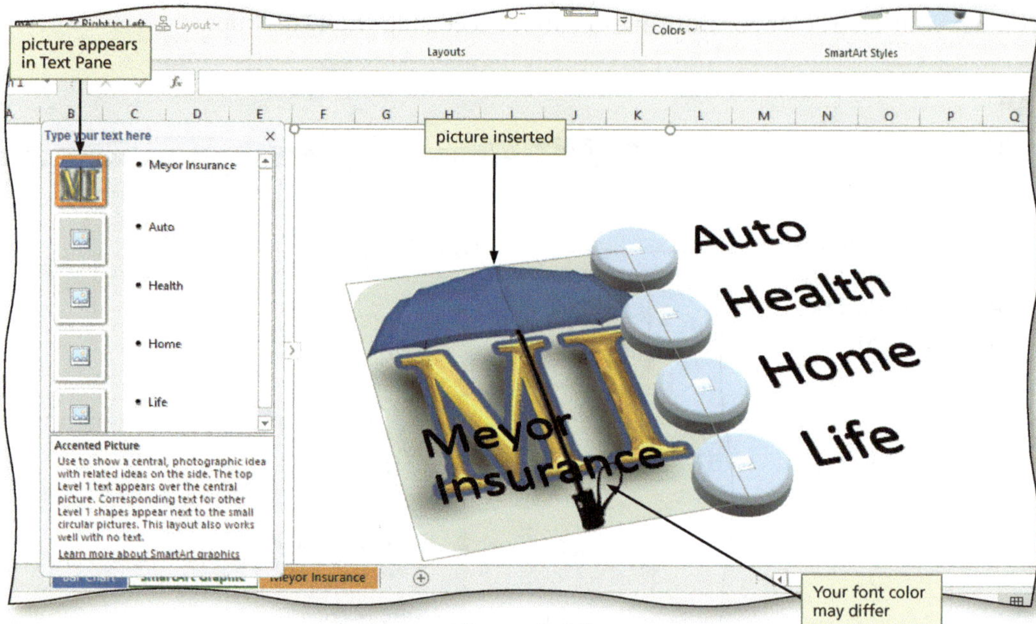

Figure 7–86

Other Ways

1. Click Insert Picture icon in SmartArt graphic, select location (Insert Pictures dialog box), double-click picture

To Apply Picture Effects

The following steps apply a picture effect and change the brightness of the picture. **Why?** You want to make the SmartArt graphic as attractive as possible. You also will sharpen the picture. **Sharpening** increases the contrast at color changes to emulate a more defined edge.

1

- With the picture still selected, click Picture Format on the ribbon to display the tab.
- Click the Picture Effects button (Picture Format tab | Picture Styles group), and then point to Glow on the Picture Effects menu to display the Glow gallery (Figure 7–87).

Experiment

- Point to each item on the Picture Effects menu to view the galleries. When you are finished, point to Glow again.

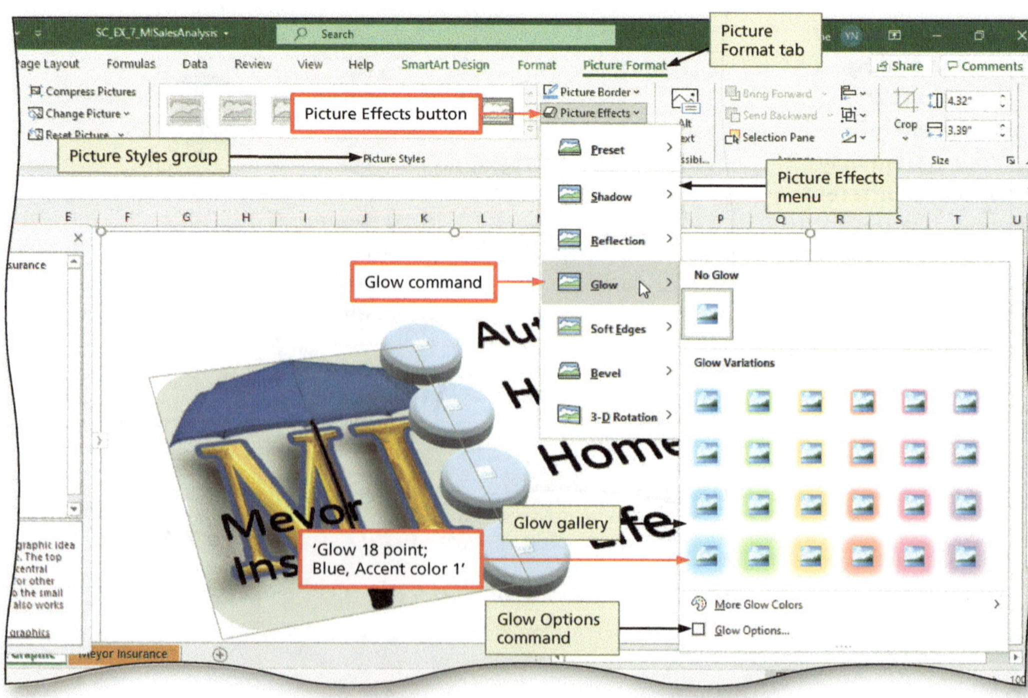

Figure 7–87

Q&A **What does the Glow Options command do?**
Each of the Picture Effects menu's Options commands opens the Format Picture pane. The Glow Options include controls to manipulate the color, size, and transparency.

2

- In the Glow Variations area (Glow gallery), click 'Glow 18 point; Blue, Accent color 1' to select a blue glow that complements the umbrella in the picture.
- Click the Corrections button (Picture Format tab | Adjust group) to display the Corrections gallery (Figure 7–88).

Experiment

- Point to each preview in the Corrections gallery to preview its effect on the picture.

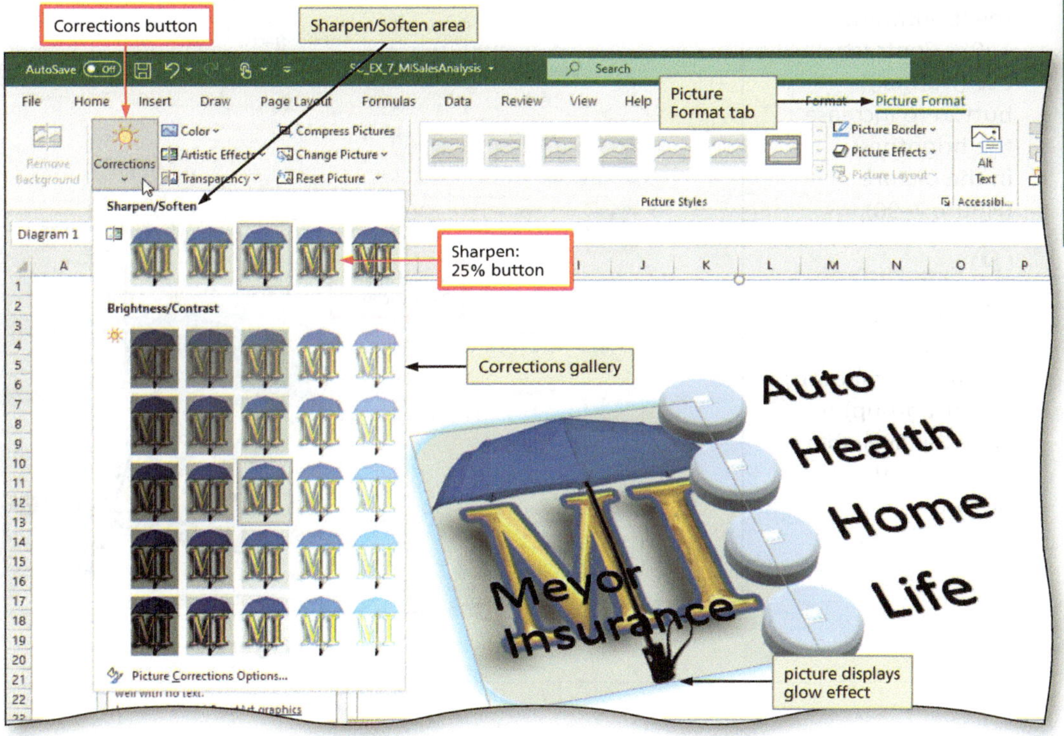

Figure 7–88

3

- In the Sharpen/Soften area, click the Sharpen: 25% button to sharpen the picture.
- Click the Corrections button (Picture Format tab | Adjust group) again to display the Corrections gallery (Figure 7–89).

Q&A **What does the Compress Pictures command do?**
The Compress Pictures command reduces the size of the pictures by deleting any cropped areas and flattening any grouped objects.

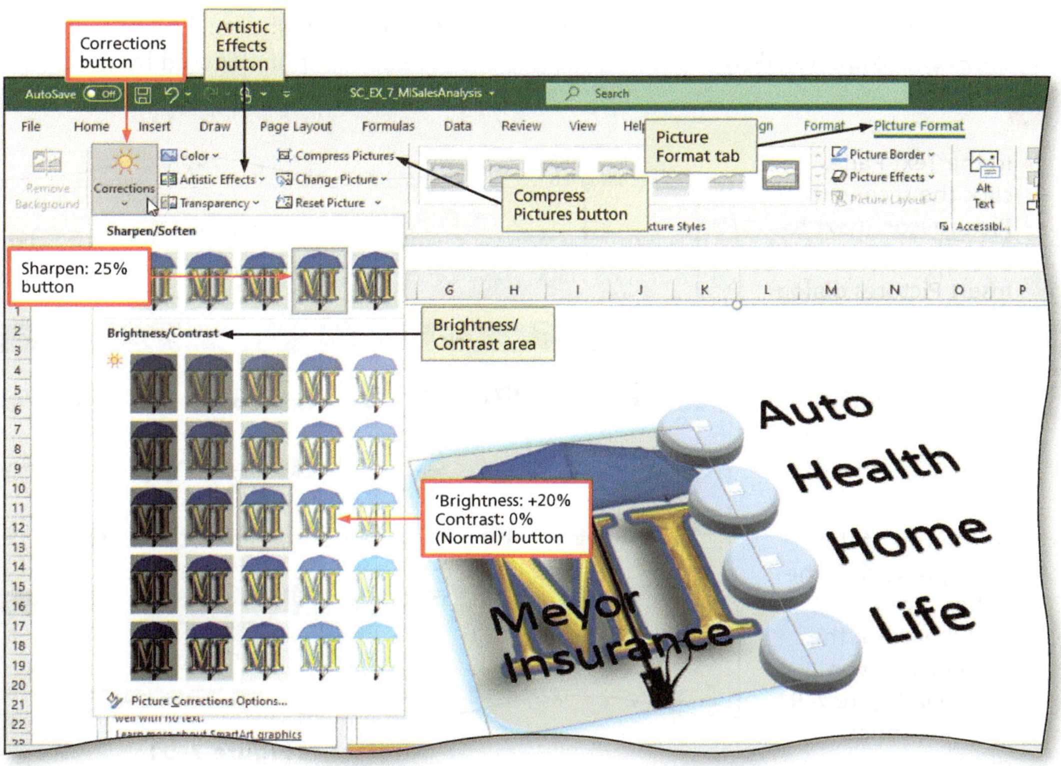

Figure 7–89

4

- In the Brightness/ Contrast area, click the 'Brightness: +20% Contrast: 0% (Normal)' button to increase the brightness in the picture (Figure 7–90).

Experiment

- Click the Artistic Effects button (Picture Format tab | Adjust group) to view the available effects for the picture.

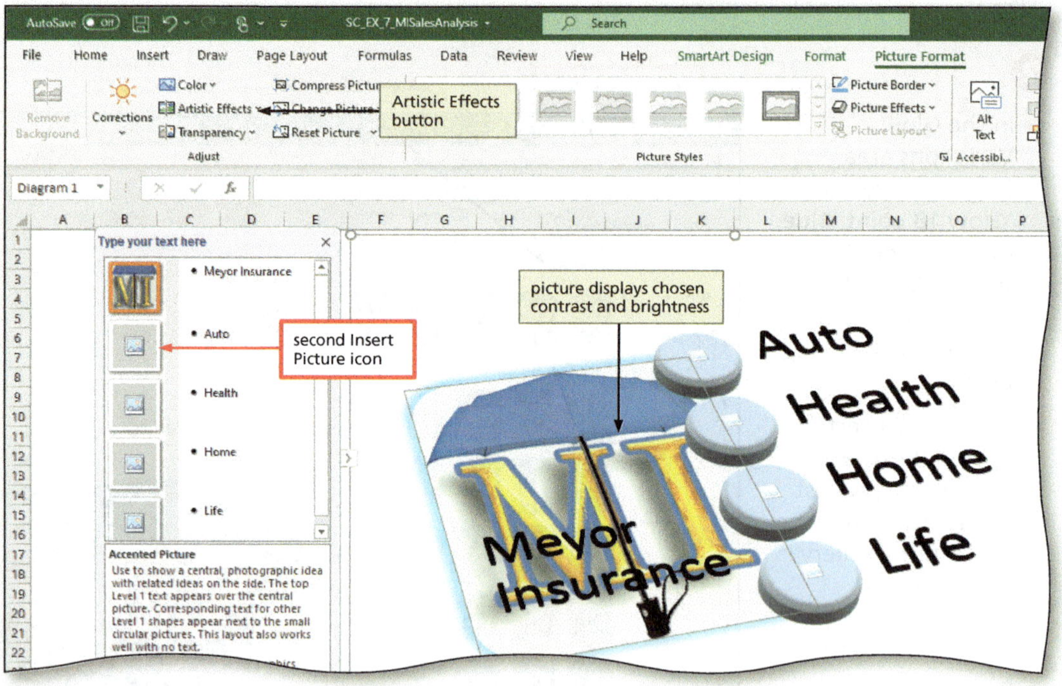

Figure 7–90

To Insert Icons

Excel includes a library of icons you can use in your worksheets. The following steps insert icons for the four Level 2 graphics. **Why?** Icons will represent the kinds of policies sold by the insurance company.

1

- In the Text Pane, click the second Insert Picture icon (next to Auto) to display the Insert Pictures dialog box.
- Click From Icons (shown in Figure 7–84) to display the Insert Icons dialog box.
- At the top of the dialog box, click the Vehicles category, and then click the automobile icon shown in Figure 7–91. The categories displaying on your screen may differ.

Figure 7–91

Experiment

- Scroll through the Insert Icons dialog box to see the categories and varieties of icons.

2

- Click Insert (1) (Insert Icons dialog box) to insert the icon.
- Click the Graphics Format tab on the ribbon to display the tab.
- Click the Graphics Fill button (Graphics Format tab | Graphics Styles group) to display the Graphics Fill gallery (Figure 7–92).

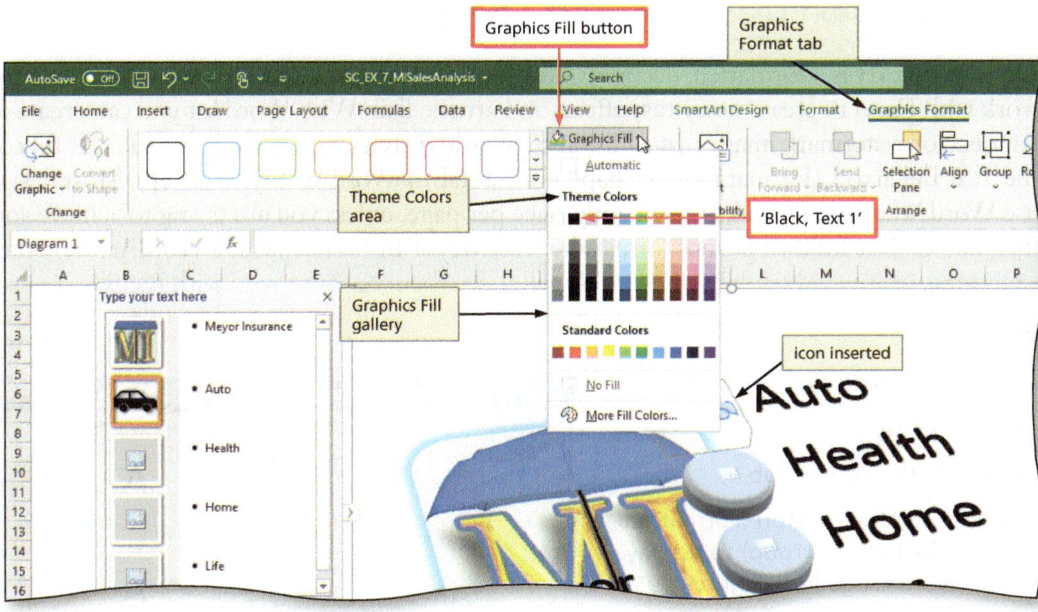

Figure 7–92

Q&A **Why did Excel change the color when the icon was inserted?**
Excel matched the color to the chosen color scheme of the SmartArt graphic.

3

- Click 'Black, Text 1' in the Theme Colors area (Graphics Fill gallery) to recolor the icon.
- With the icon still selected, click the Graphics Outline button in the Graphics Styles group, and then select the Blue, Accent 1 theme color (Figure 7–93).

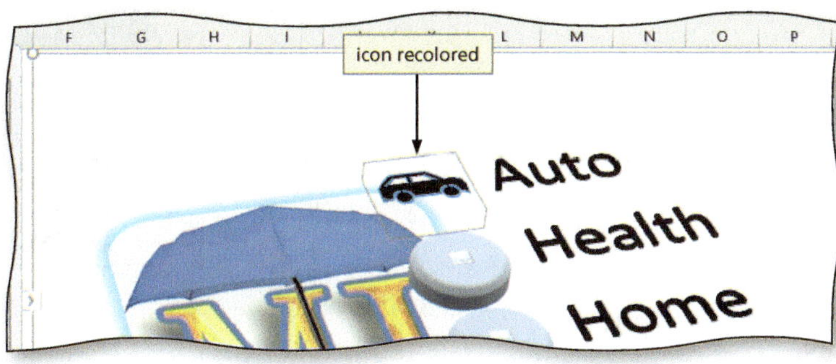

Figure 7–93

4

- Repeat Steps 1 through 3 to insert and recolor icons for Health, Home, and Life as shown in Figure 7–94.

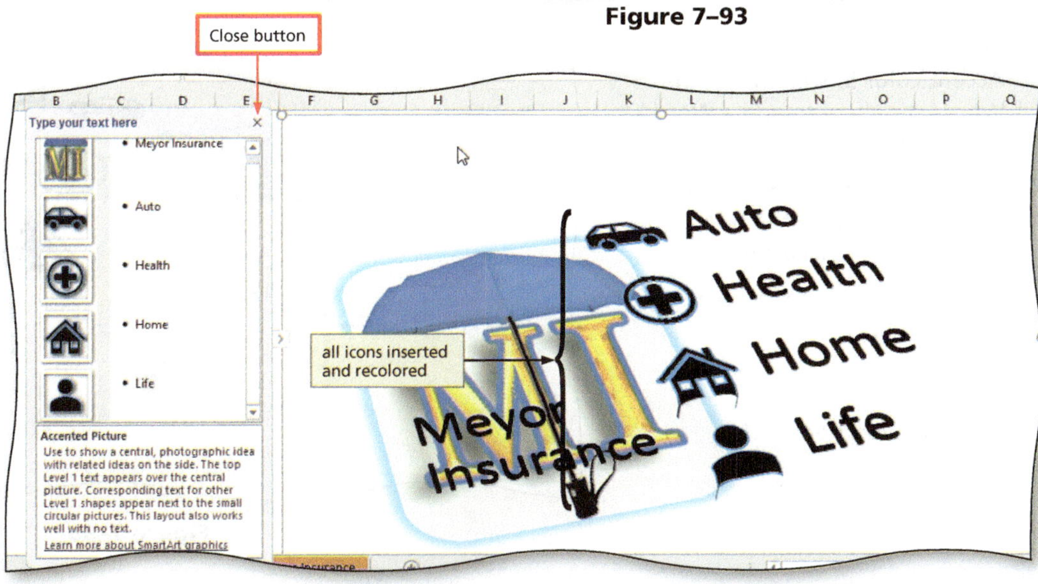

Figure 7–94

Q&A **What if I cannot find the correct icon to insert?**
If you want to search for an icon, enter the search text in the Search box (shown in Figure 7–91) to display search results matching the text you entered.

- Close the Text Pane.
- Click the Save button (Quick Access Toolbar) to save the file.

To Format Text Using WordArt Styles

WordArt is a formatted, decorative text in a text box. In Excel, WordArt displays a gallery of text styles that work with Excel to create fancy text effects and artistic flair. With WordArt you can create eye-catching headlines, banners, or watermark images. In addition to WordArt styles, you can change the text fill color of WordArt by clicking the Text Fill arrow (Format tab (or Shape Format tab) | WordArt Styles group). Most designers agree that you should use WordArt sparingly and, at most, only once per page, unless you are trying to achieve some kind of special effect or illustration. The following steps format the text, Meyor Insurance, with a WordArt style that creates an outline. **Why?** Outlining, also called stroking the letters, will make them easier to read with the picture background.

1

- Select the text, Meyor Insurance.
- Bold the text.
- Display the Format tab.
- Click the More button (Format tab | WordArt Styles group) to display the WordArt gallery (Figure 7–95).

Figure 7–95

2

- Click 'Fill: White; Outline: Pink, Accent color 5; Shadow' in the WordArt gallery to add a WordArt style to the text.
- Click outside of the SmartArt graphic to remove the selection and view the formatting.
- Close the Text Pane, if necessary (Figure 7–96).

3

- Save the workbook.

Figure 7–96

To Insert an Individual Image into a Workbook

If you wanted to insert an individual image into your workbook, you would perform the following steps.

1. Select the cell at which you wish the image to display.
2. Display the Insert tab.
3. Click the Illustrations button (Insert tab | Illustrations group), click Pictures, and then click This Device to display the Insert Picture dialog box.
4. Navigate to the location of the picture to insert and then double-click the file to insert the picture in the worksheet.
5. Resize the picture as necessary.
6. To format the picture, display the Picture Format tab.
7. Click the Picture Styles More button (Picture Format tab | Picture Styles group) to display the Picture Styles gallery.
8. Click the desired picture style to apply the style to the image.

Break Point: If you want to take a break, this is a good place to do so. You can exit Excel. To resume later, start Excel, open the file called SC_EX_7_MISalesAnalysis, and continue following the steps from this location forward.

Text Boxes

To add text to a workbook that is separate from the text in cells, chart titles, or labels, you can insert a text box. You then can enter the text that you want. Text boxes can be static, presenting read-only information, or they can be bound or linked to a cell by typing an equal sign (=) in the formula bar and then a cell reference, formula, or function. The text inside the box is easily formatted. You can edit the shape of the text box by using the Edit Shapes button (Shape Format tab | Insert Shapes group).

To Draw a Text Box

The following steps draw a text box to create a decorative heading for the SmartArt graphic. **Why use text boxes in Excel?** The advantage to using a text box is that you can move the text box and resize it; it floats freely in the worksheet and is independent of row and column boundaries, preserving the layout of the data on the worksheet.

1

- Select cell A1 on the SmartArt Graphic sheet and display the Insert tab.
- Click the Text button (Insert tab | Text group) to display a gallery with additional buttons related to inserting text objects (Figure 7–97).

Figure 7–97

2

- Click the Text Box button and then move the pointer into the worksheet.
- Drag to create a text box in the upper-left corner of the worksheet, approximately 6 columns wide and 7 rows tall.
- Type `Our New Graphic` to enter the text (Figure 7–98).

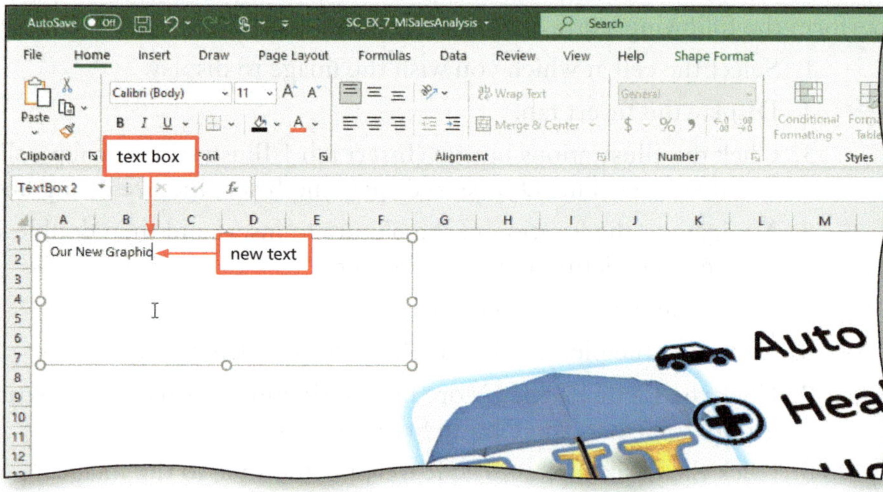

Figure 7–98

3

- Select the text and then change the font size to 36. Bold and italicize the text.
- Click the Shape Outline button (Shape Format tab | Shape Styles group) and then click No Outline to remove the border of the text box.
- Click away from the text box to view it without selection (Figure 7–99).

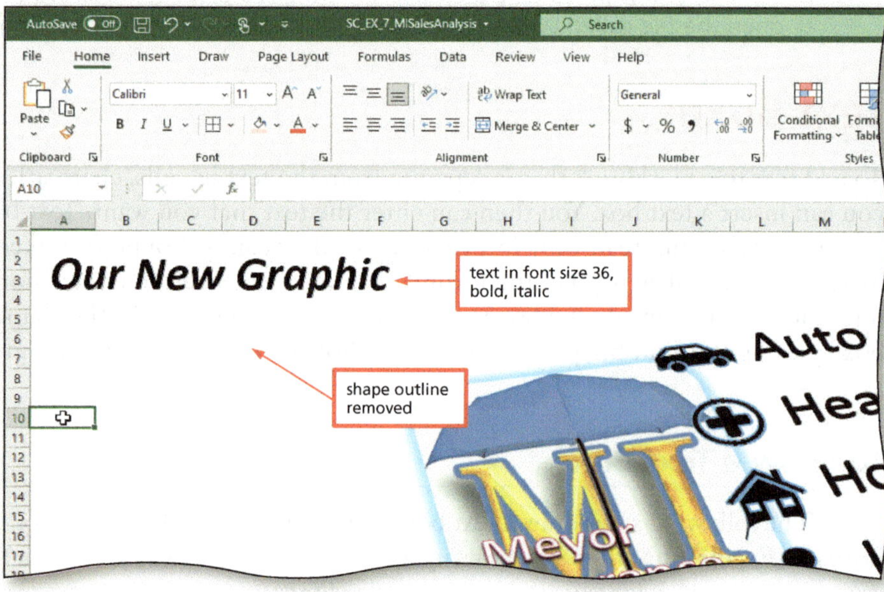

Figure 7–99

Alternative Text

A special consideration when using graphics is accessibility. Screen readers that read worksheets and webpages for people with disabilities can provide feedback about pictures, but only if the picture has alternative text. **Alternative text**, also called **ALT text** or an **ALT tag**, is descriptive text that appears as an alternative to a graphic image. Screen readers read the alternative text aloud. Graphics without alternative text are not usable by screen readers, so people with disabilities will not hear picture descriptions. Browsers may display alternative text while graphics are loading or when graphics are missing.

To Add ALT Text

The following steps insert alternative text for the SmartArt graphic. **Why?** You want the worksheet to be accessible by everyone, including those who use screen readers.

1

- Right-click the border of the SmartArt graphic to display the shortcut menu (Figure 7–100).

Q&A **Are there rules about appropriate alternative text?**
Sources vary on appropriate alternative text; however, most users agree that alternative text should not be redundant of other text, and should convey the meaning or purpose.

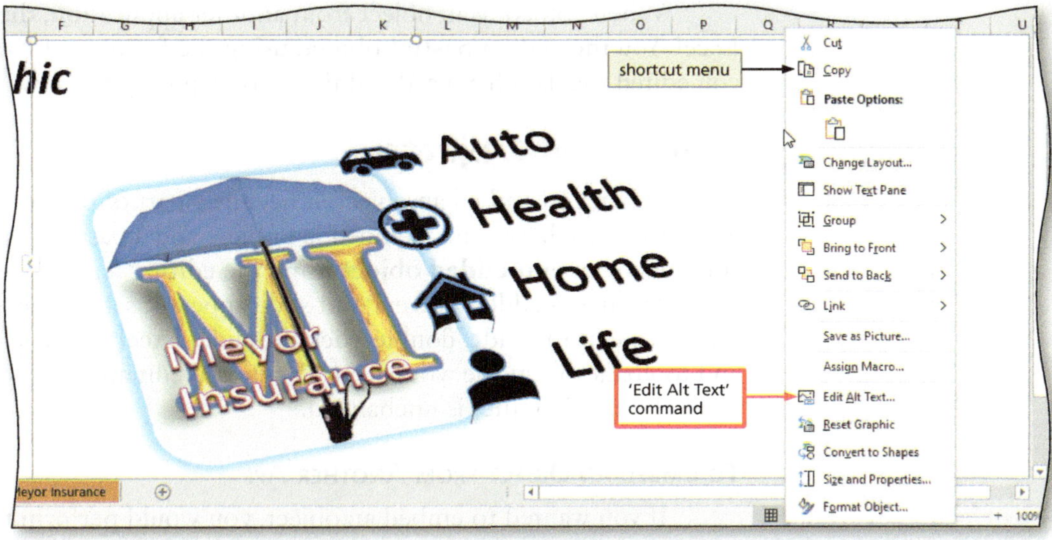

Figure 7–100

2

- Click 'Edit Alt Text' to display the Alt Text pane and click in its text box
- In the text box (Alt Text pane), type `Meyor Insurance SmartArt graphic representing the types of available policies` to enter an appropriate alternative text (Figure 7–101).

Q&A **Some of my text has a red underline. Is that a problem?**
Make sure your words are spelled correctly. A red underline indicates a misspelled word, or a word that is not in the Excel dictionary. Many names are not in the dictionary.

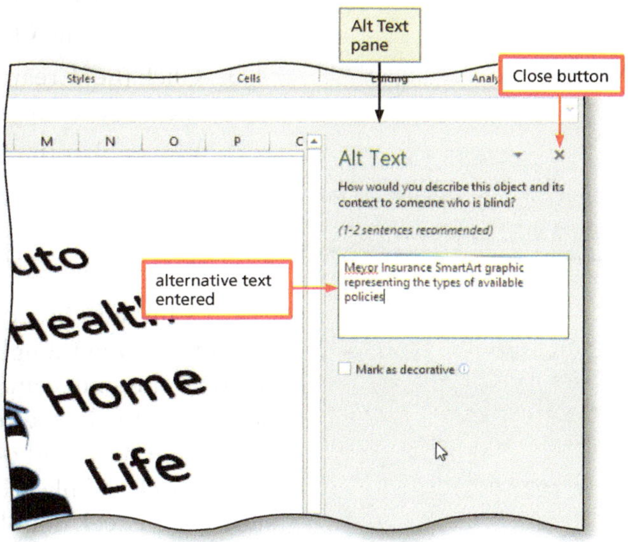

Figure 7–101

3

- Close the Alt Text pane.
- Save the workbook.

Object Linking and Embedding

In this module, you inserted a chart, a SmartArt graphic, and a SmartArt shape. With Office 365, you also can insert an **object** which is an independent element on a worksheet (such as a document, chart, or graphic)—even if that object were created in another app. For example, you could insert a PowerPoint slide into an Excel worksheet. In this case, the PowerPoint slide (the object) is called the **source document** (the document from which items are being copied) and the Excel worksheet is called the **destination document** (the document to which items are being pasted). You can use one of three techniques to insert objects from one app to another: copy and paste, embed, or link. The combining of objects and data from two or more applications using linking or embedding is known as **integration**.

Copy and Paste

When you copy an object from another application, the source object appears in Excel. You then edit a **pasted object**, using the features of Excel. For example, earlier you edited the data from a Word file by transposing the rows and columns in Excel.

Embedded Objects

When you embed an object, it becomes part of the destination document. The difference between an embedded object and a pasted object is that you edit the contents of an **embedded object** using the editing features of the source app. For example, an embedded PowerPoint slide appears as a PowerPoint document within Excel. To edit the slide, double-click the slide. Excel will display PowerPoint menus and toolbars within the worksheet. When you edit an embedded object, the original PowerPoint slide (file) is unchanged.

To Embed an Object from Another App

If you wanted to embed an object, you would perform the following steps.

1. Start Excel.
2. Click the Text button (Insert tab | Text group), and then click the Object button to display the Object dialog box.
3. Click the 'Create from File' tab and then click the Browse button. Navigate to the location of your object and double-click the file.
4. Ensure that the Link checkbox does not display a check mark.
5. Click the OK button (Object dialog box) to embed the object.

Linked Objects

A **linked object**, by contrast, does not become a part of the destination document, even though it appears to be a part of it. Rather, a connection is established between the source and destination documents so that when you open the destination document, the linked object displays as part of it. When you edit a linked object, the source app starts and opens the source document that contains the linked object. For example, a linked PowerPoint slide remains as a PowerPoint slide. To edit the slide from Excel, double-click the slide to start PowerPoint and display the slide in a PowerPoint window. Unlike an embedded object, if you edit the PowerPoint slide by opening it from PowerPoint, the linked object will be updated in the Excel worksheet.

You would use linking when the contents of an object are likely to change and when you want to ensure that the most current version of the object appears in the source document. Another reason to link an object is if the object is large, such as a video clip or a sound clip.

To Link an Object from Another App

If you wanted to link an object, you would perform the following steps.

1. Start Excel.
2. Click the Text button (Insert tab | Text group), and then click the Object button to display the Object dialog box.
3. Click the 'Create from File' tab and then click the Browse button. Navigate to the location of your object and double-click the file.
4. Click the Link to file checkbox so that it displays a check mark.
5. Click the OK button (Object dialog box) to link the object.

If you wanted to link or embed Excel data into another app, you would perform the same techniques, but starting in the other app. For example, to link worksheet data to a Word document, you would open Word, click the Object button (Insert tab | Text group) and proceed to link the worksheet.

To Edit the Link to a File

To edit the link to a file, you would perform the following steps.

1. Start Excel and open the file with the link.
2. Click File to open Backstage View. On the Info screen, click the 'Edit Links to Files' button to display the Edit Links dialog box.
3. Click the Change Source button (Edit Links dialog box).
4. Edit the location in the Change Links dialog box.
5. Click OK (Change Links dialog box).
6. Click Close (Edit Links dialog box).

To Create a New Object

Integration tools also let you create a new object in Excel based on another app. For example, you can create a WordPad document to include further text information or create a PowerPoint slide to illustrate an example. The command opens the app associated with the new object. Once created, the new object is embedded, and can be edited as described above. To create a new object, perform the following steps.

1. Start Excel.
2. Click the Text button (Insert tab | Text group), and then click the Object button to display the Object dialog box.
3. Click the 'Create New' tab.
4. In the Browse box, scroll as necessary to choose the type of embedded object you wish to create.
5. Click OK (Object dialog box) to embed the object.
6. While the tools of the source app are visible, insert content or formatting as necessary.
7. Click outside the object to redisplay the tools of the destination app.

To Break an External Link

Sometimes you may want to break an external link between Excel and another app, so that the destination object will no longer update when the source object is modified. To do so, perform the following steps. When Excel breaks the link, the object becomes an Excel picture or shape, depending on the source app.

1. Click the Edit Links button (Data tab | 'Queries & Connections' group) to display the Edit Links dialog box.
2. In the Source area, select the desired file.
3. Click the Break Link button (Edit Links dialog box).
4. When Excel displays a dialog box, click the Break Links button.
5. Click Close (Edit Links dialog box).

To Update a Linked Object from Another App

When you open an Excel file that contains linked objects (as opposed to embedded objects), Excel checks for changes and offers you the chance to update the linked object. To update a linked object from another app, you would perform the following steps.

1. Start the app that created the linked object (e.g., Word).
2. Edit the file as necessary, save, and then close the app.

3. Start Excel.
4. When Excel displays the Microsoft Excel dialog box, click Update.
5. If Excel displays a dialog box about trusting the file, click OK.

Using Screenshots on a Worksheet

Excel allows you to take a screenshot of any open window and add it to a workbook. Using the screenshot feature, you can capture whole windows or only part of a window. For example, if your company has a webpage, you can take a screenshot of the page and insert it into a workbook before presenting the workbook at a meeting. In addition, you can capture a screen clipping to include in your Excel workbook. A **screen clipping** is a portion of the screen, usually of one object or a section of a window. You first will create a new worksheet in the workbook to hold the screenshot and then insert a screenshot of a webpage.

To Create Another New Sheet

In preparation for inserting the screenshot, the following steps create another new sheet.

1. Click the New sheet button to create a fourth sheet in the workbook. If necessary, drag the sheet tab to the right of the other tabs.
2. Rename the worksheet `Screenshot` to provide a descriptive name for the worksheet.
3. Change the color of the tab to Red (Standard Colors area) and hide the gridlines on the worksheet.
4. If necessary, click cell A1 to make it the active cell (Figure 7–102).

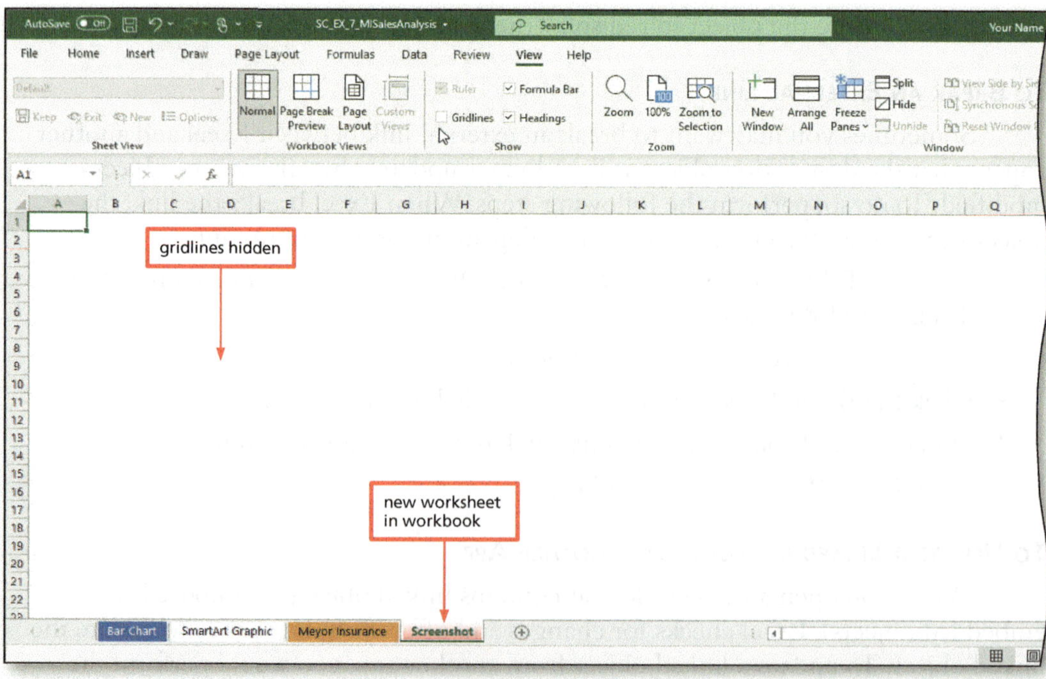

Figure 7–102

To Insert a Screenshot on a Worksheet

The staff at Meyor Insurance often shares helpful insurance websites with customers. The following steps add a screenshot to a worksheet. **Why?** In anticipation of an upcoming meeting where the sales analysis will be reviewed, the CEO requests a screenshot of a popular website that answers typical insurance questions.

1

- Start Microsoft Edge or a similar browser.
- Type **https://www.iii.org/article/what-covered-standard-homeowners-policy** in the address bar and then press ENTER to display the webpage (Figure 7–103).

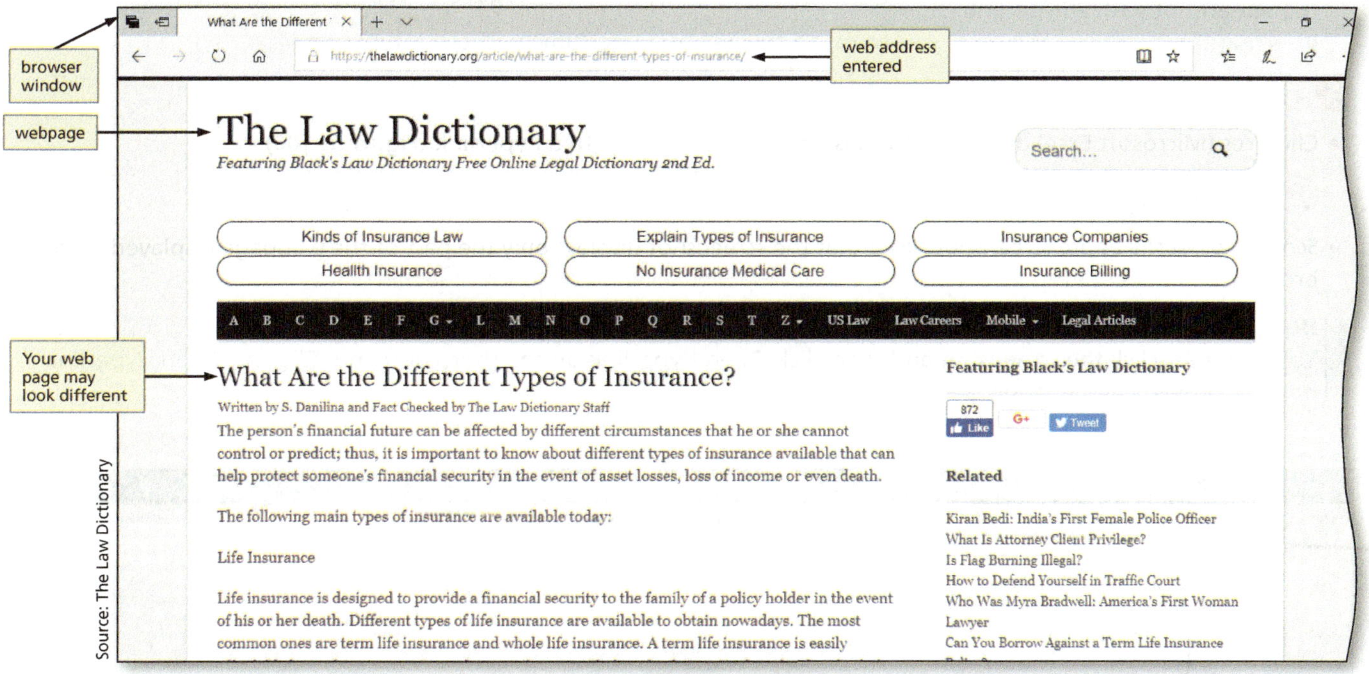

Figure 7–103

2

- Click the Excel app button on the taskbar to return to Excel.
- Display the Insert tab.
- Click the Illustrations button (Insert tab | Illustrations group), and then click the Screenshot button to display the Screenshot gallery (Figure 7–104).

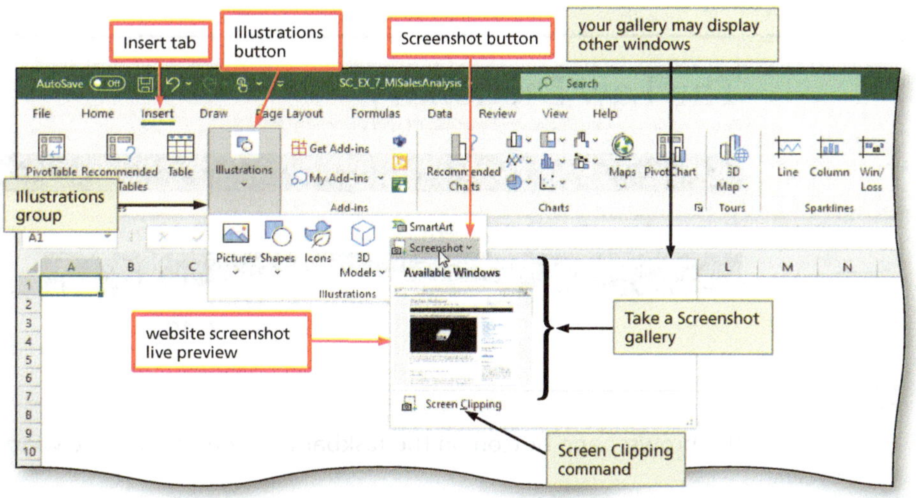

Figure 7–104

Q&A

My browser window is not displayed in the gallery. Did I do something wrong?

If Excel cannot link to your browser, you may have to insert a screen clipping instead of a screenshot. To do so, click Screen Clipping (Take a Screenshot gallery), navigate to the desired window, and then draw a rectangle over the portion of the screen you want to insert into the Excel workbook. Note that this process inserts a picture rather than a hyperlinked screenshot and displays the Picture Format tab.

3

- Click the live preview of the Law Dictionary web page to start the process of inserting a screenshot (Figure 7–105).

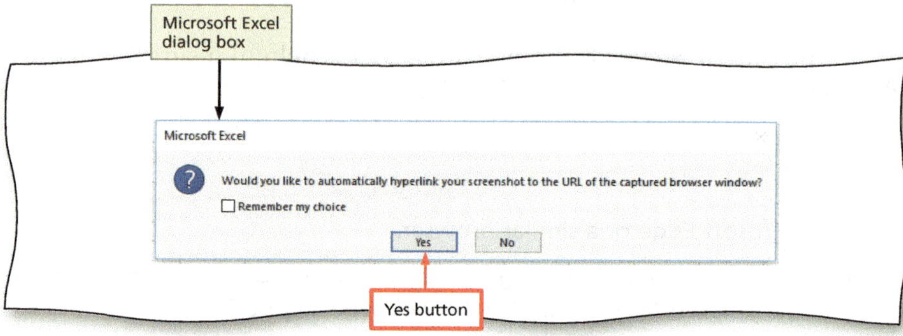

Figure 7–105

Q&A **Should I include the hyperlink?** If you plan to present your workbook to an audience and wish to view the updated website in a browser, you should insert the screenshot with a hyperlink. Inserting the hyperlink also gives you access to the link at a later time without retyping it.

4

- Click Yes (Microsoft Excel dialog box) to insert the screenshot with a hyperlink (Figure 7–106).

Experiment

- Scroll to view the entire screenshot. Note that the screenshot displays only the part of the webpage displayed in the browser.

Q&A **How do you use the hyperlink?** You can right-click the screenshot and then click Open Hyperlink on the shortcut menu. Clicking Open Hyperlink opens a browser and displays the website.

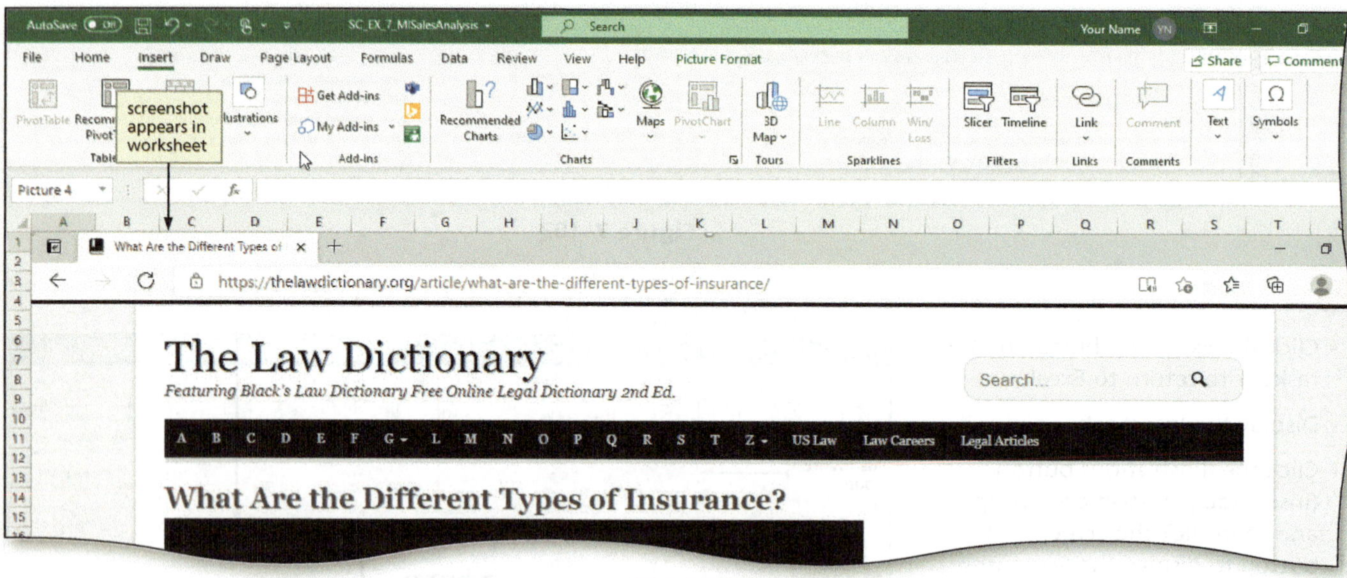

Figure 7–106

5

- Right-click the browser app button on the taskbar and then click Close window on the shortcut menu to exit the browser.

To Move an Object

The following steps move the screenshot. **Why?** You need to make room for some new shapes later in the module.

1

- Right-drag the screenshot to a location near cell D3 (Figure 7–107).

Q&A **Can you drag the screenshot to a new location without holding down the right mouse button?**
No. Because the screenshot is a hyperlink, clicking it opens the linked website. If you do not have the ability to right-drag, you would have to click the Selection Pane button (Page Layout tab | Arrange group) and then select the screenshot in the Selection pane. Once selected, you could move it in the normal way.

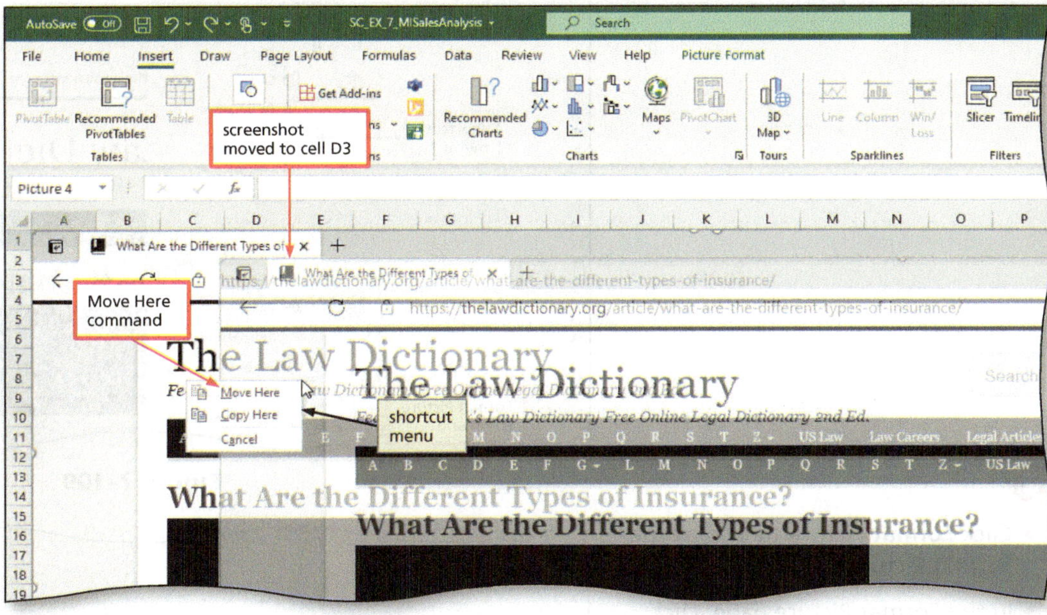

Figure 7–107

2

- When Excel displays the shortcut menu, click Move Here to move the screen shot (Figure 7–108).

Q&A **Is right-dragging the best way to move a picture?**
If the picture is a hyperlink, yes. If the picture is not a hyperlink, you can simply drag it to a new location on the same worksheet. If you need to move the picture to a different worksheet, you should cut and paste.

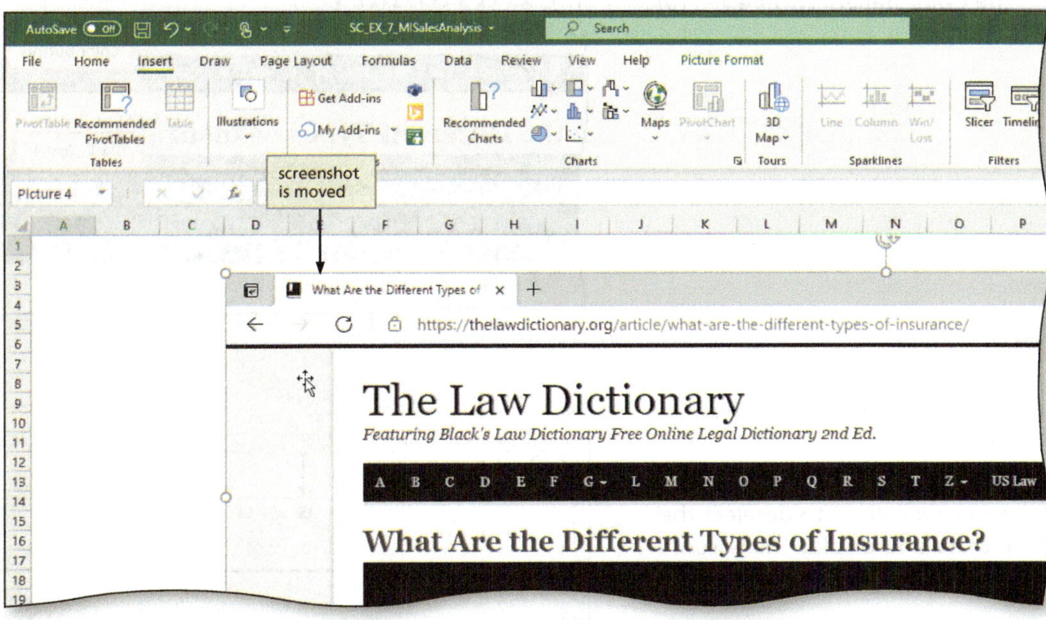

Figure 7–108

To Add a Picture Border

The following steps add a border to the screenshot. **Why?** A border helps to delineate the edges of the screenshot from the worksheet itself.

1

- Right-click the screenshot to display the shortcut menu (Figure 7–109).

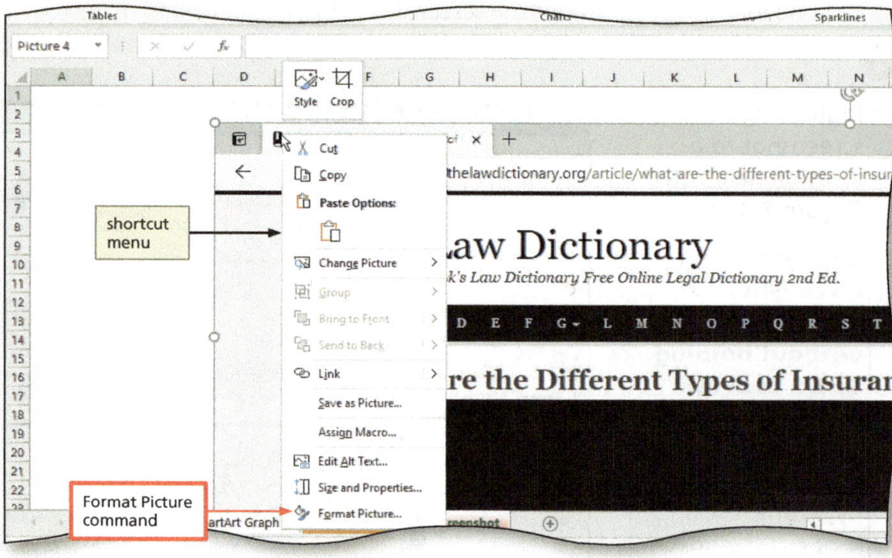

Figure 7–109

2

- Click Format Picture to display the Format Picture pane.
- In the Format Picture pane, click the 'Fill & Line' button, click Line to display the options, then click the Solid Line option button.
- Click the Color button to display the Color gallery (Figure 7–110).

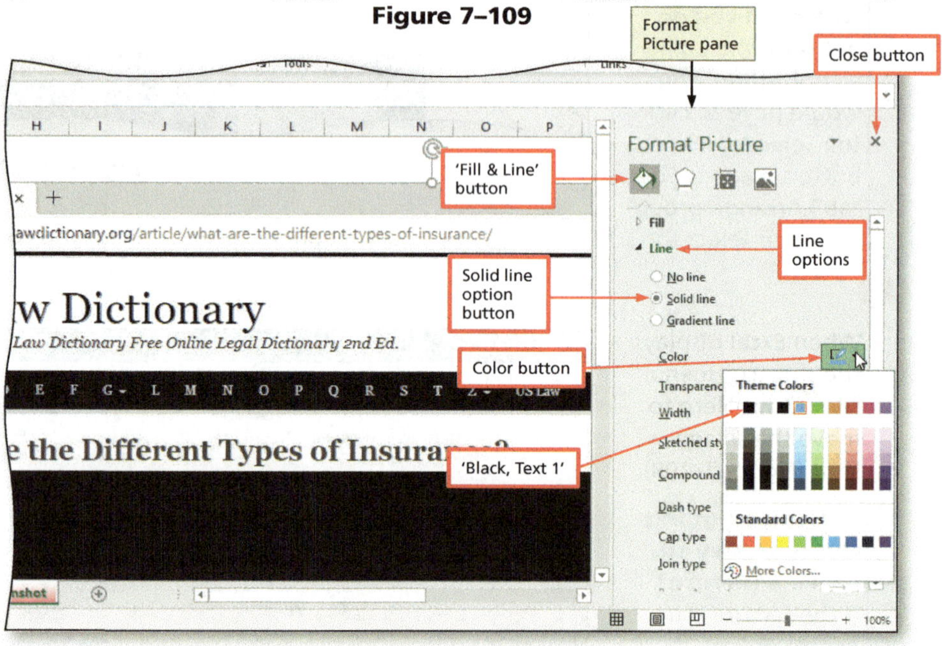

Figure 7–110

3

- Click 'Black Text 1' to apply a border.
- Close the Format Picture pane and click cell A1 to deselect the picture and display the border (Figure 7–111).

Q&A **Is there a different method to apply borders to pictures than on screenshots?**
No, you apply borders the same way.

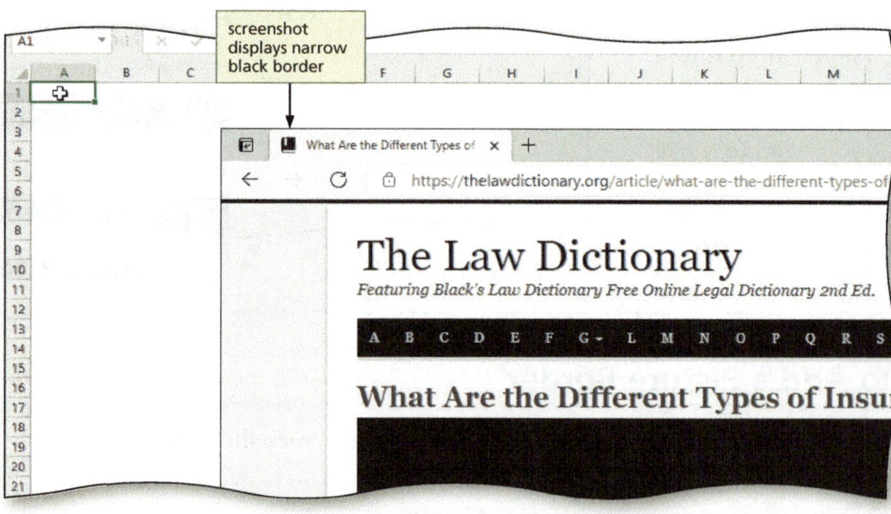

Figure 7–111

Other Ways

1. Click Picture Border button (Picture Format tab | Picture Styles group), choose color, choose format

Shapes

Excel has more than 150 shapes that you can use to create, graphics, banners, illustrations, logos and other ornamental objects. A **shape** is a drawing object, such as a rectangle, oval, triangle, line, block arrow, or other shape. You can change the color and weight of shape outlines, and can apply fill effects, shadows, reflections, glows, pictures, and other special effects to shapes. Adding text, bullets, or numbering to shapes increases the graphic possibilities. You even can edit points, which creates sizing handles along the edge to convert your shape into something new and unique.

To Create a Shape and Copy It

Earlier in the module you added a new shape to the SmartArt graphic. Now you will create a shape using the Shapes gallery **Why?** A shape can improve and upgrade the look of your worksheet. Shapes also can be used as buttons or hyperlinks. Text within shapes can be dynamic when linked to a formula.

The following steps create a block arrow to point out the source of the screenshot.

1

- Click the Illustrations button (Insert tab | Illustrations group), and then click the Shapes button to display the Shapes gallery (Figure 7–112).

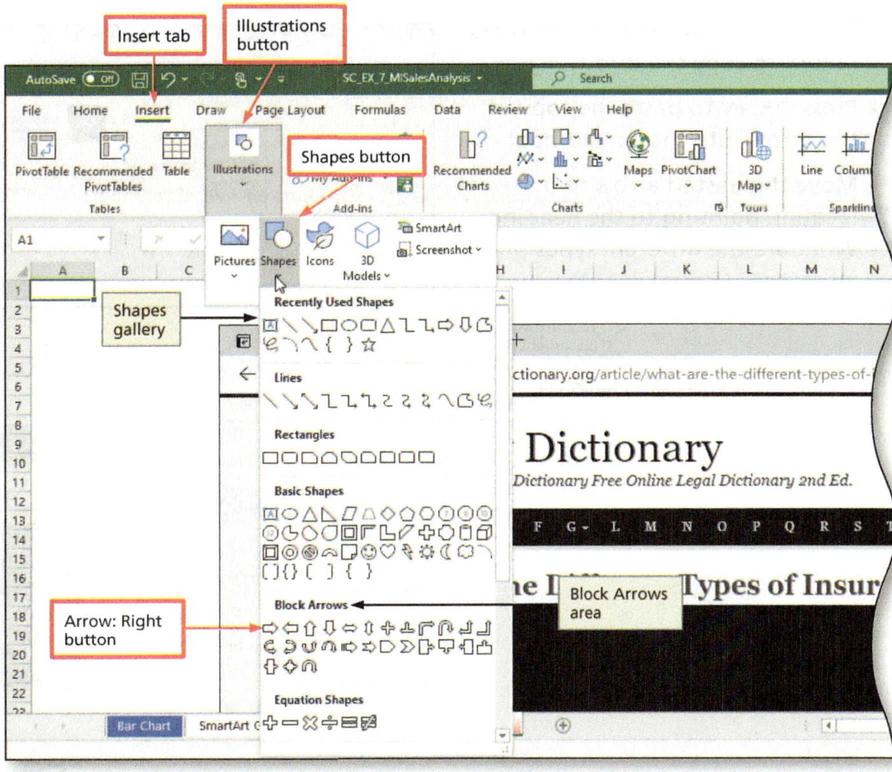

Figure 7–112

2

- In the Block Arrows area, click the Arrow: Right button.
- Move the pointer into the worksheet, to the left of the screenshot.

- Drag right to create an arrow, approximately four columns wide, that points to the words, The Law Dictionary. Do not deselect the arrow (Figure 7–113).

Q&A

How do I add text to a shape?
Once you draw the shape, right-click it, and then click Edit Text on the shortcut menu.

Why is the arrow filled in with blue?
The default fill color in the Parallax theme is blue. You can change the color using the Shape Fill button (Shape Format tab | Shape Styles group).

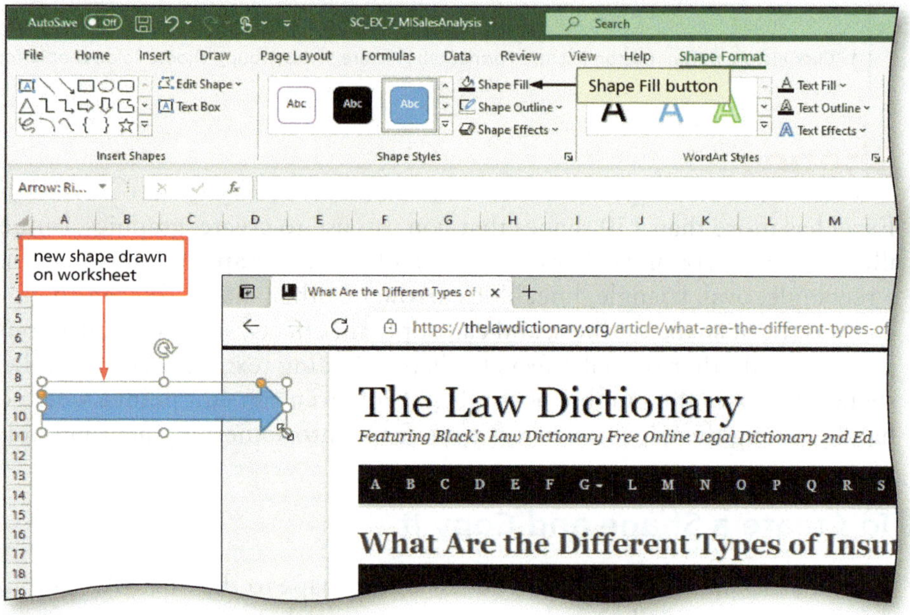

Figure 7–113

3

- With the arrow still selected, press CTRL+C to copy the arrow.
- Press CTRL+V to paste the copy of the arrow into the spreadsheet.
- Move the pasted arrow to a location pointing to the heading, What are the different types of insurance? (Figure 7–114).

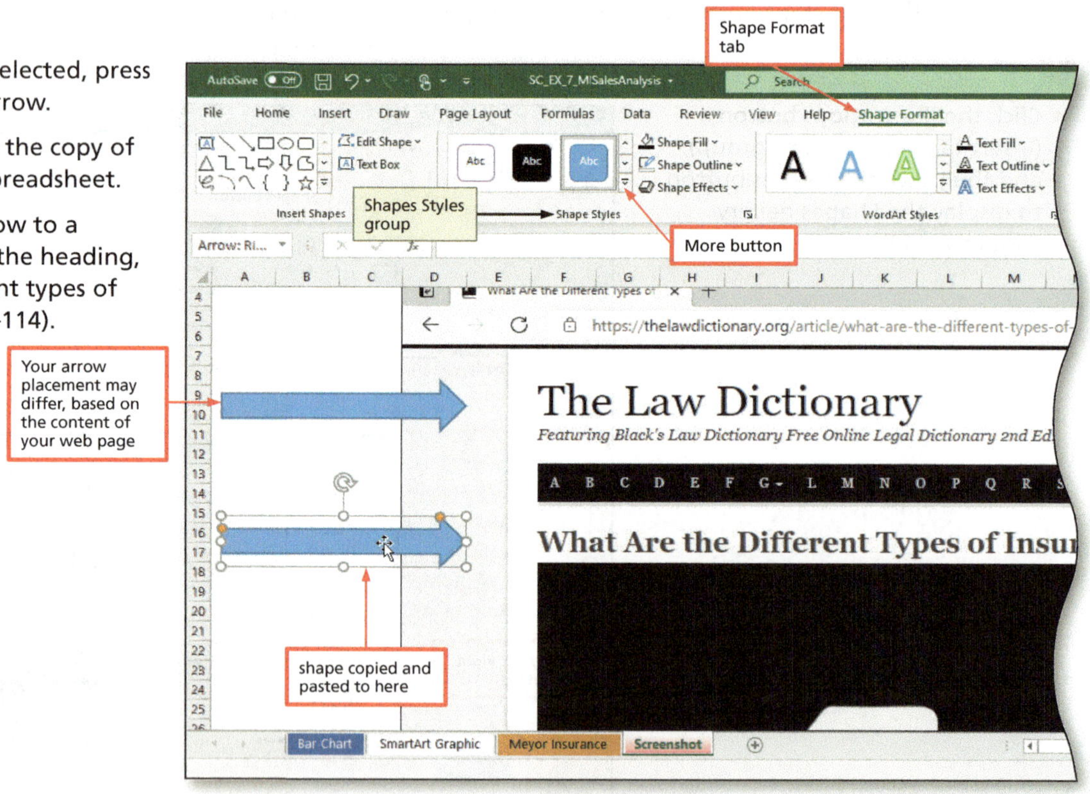

Figure 7–114

To Add a Shape Style and Shape Effect

In the following steps, you will add a shape style and a shape effect. **Why?** A shape style can help to add contrast between the shape and the background. Adding an effect to a shape can make it appear as though it is floating above the page.

1

- With the pasted arrow still selected, click the More button (Shape Format tab | Shape Styles group) to display the Shape Styles gallery (Figure 7–115).

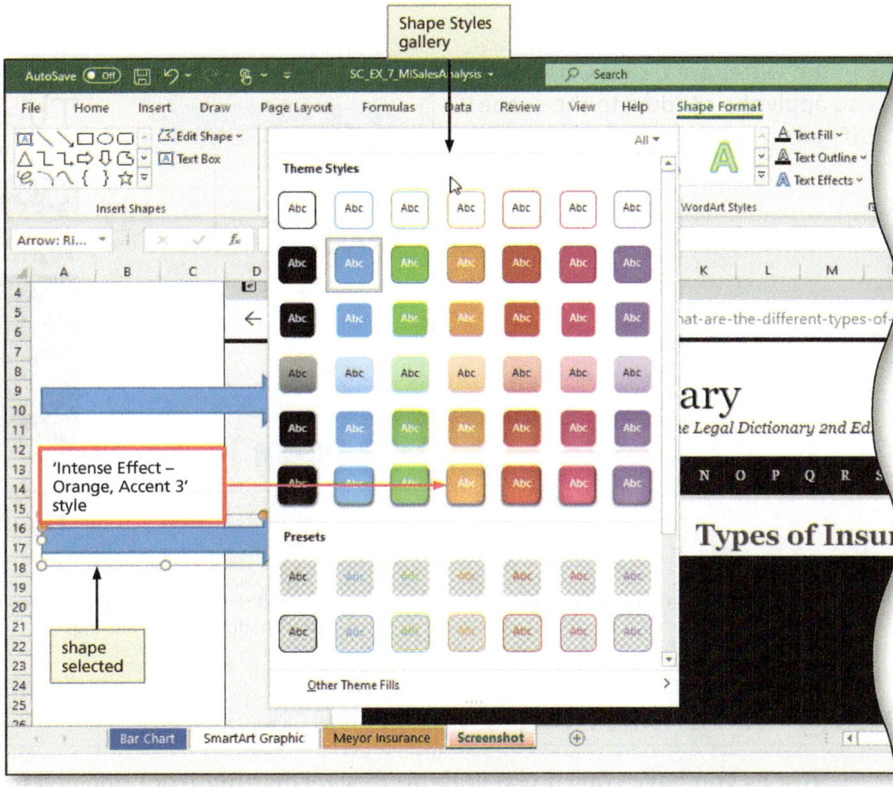

Figure 7–115

2

- Click 'Intense Effect – Orange, Accent 3' to choose the style.
- Click the Shape Effects button (Shape Format tab | Shape Styles group) and point to Shadow to display the Shadow gallery (Figure 7–116).

Experiment

- Point to different thumbnails in the Shadow gallery and watch the live preview change the selected shape.

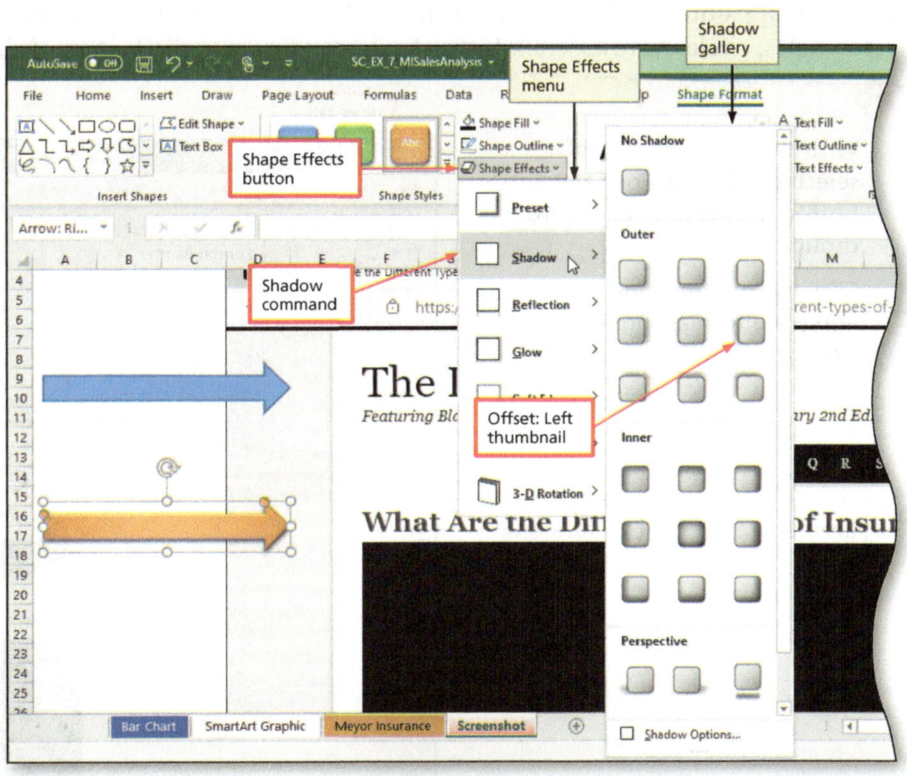

Figure 7–116

3

- In the Outer area, click Offset: Left to apply the shadow to the shape (Figure 7–117).

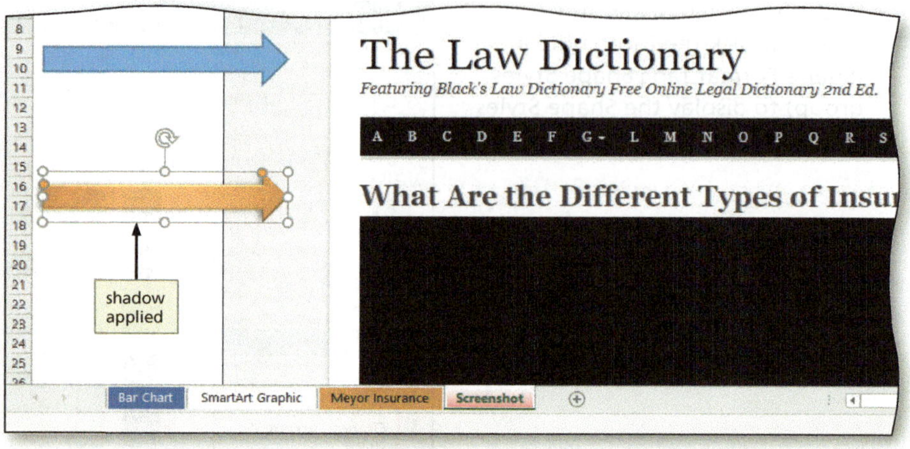

Figure 7–117

Other Ways

1. Click Style button (Mini toolbar), choose settings
2. Right-click shape, click Format Shape, click Effects button (Format Shape pane), click Shadow, choose settings

Using the Format Painter with Objects

Just as you have copied text and number formatting from one cell to another with the Format Painter, you can use it to copy all of the formatting from one object and apply it to another one. In the case of shapes, the Format painter applies formats such as color, style, special effects, and borders—even to different shapes (rectangles, circles, arrows, etc.). If the shape contains text, the format of the text also is copied.

1

- With the lower arrow still selected, click the Format Painter button (Home tab | Clipboard group).
- Click the original blue arrow to apply the formatting. Do not deselect (Figure 7–118).

Q&A **Can I edit the form of the shape?**
Yes. Click the Edit Shape button (Shape Format tab | Insert Shapes group) to change to a different shape or to edit points or edges of the current shape.

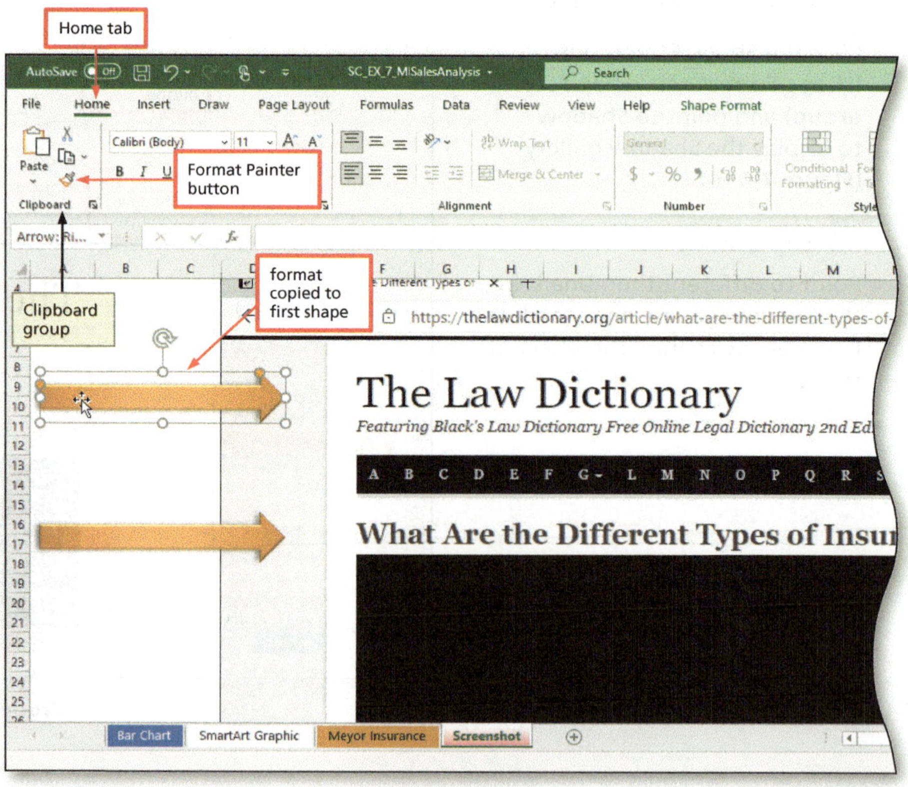

Figure 7–118

Other Ways

1. Select source object, press CTRL+SHIFT+C, select destination object, press CTRL+SHIFT+V

To Align Shapes

In the following steps, you will align the two arrows. **Why?** Aligning shapes makes the worksheet look more professional.

1

- SHIFT+click the second arrow so that both arrows are selected.
- Click the Align button (Shape Format tab | Arrange group) to display the Align menu (Figure 7–119).

Q&A **What do the Snap commands do?**
When you click a Snap command, Excel turns on the ability to **snap** or align objects to the nearest grid intersection or snap to other shapes and objects. The snapping takes place as you draw, resize, or move a shape or other object in Excel.

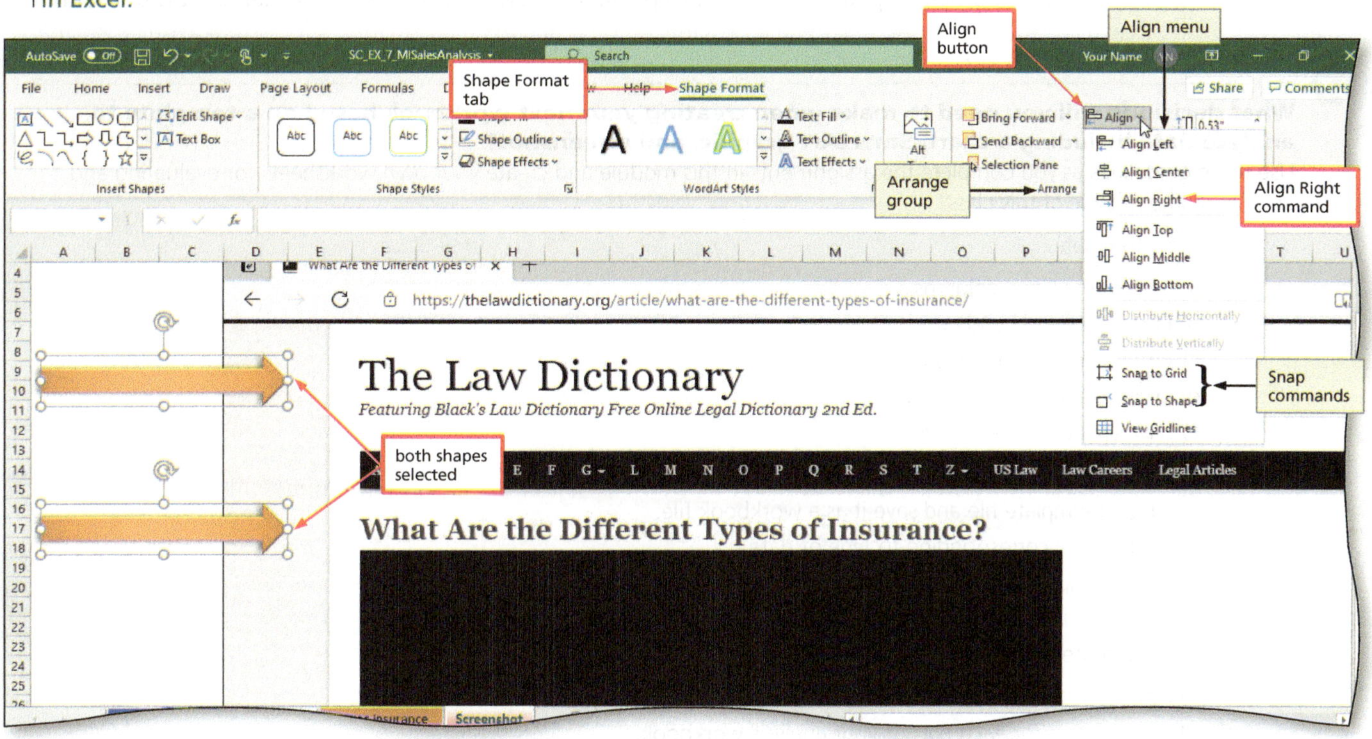

Figure 7–119

2

- Click Align Right in the Align gallery to align the right margin of the shapes (Figure 7–120).

Q&A **Why are the distribute commands unavailable?**
The **distribute** commands apply even spacing between more than two shapes or objects.

3

- In Excel, click the Save button on the Quick Access Toolbar.
- **sam** Click the Close button in the upper-right corner of the title bar to exit Excel.

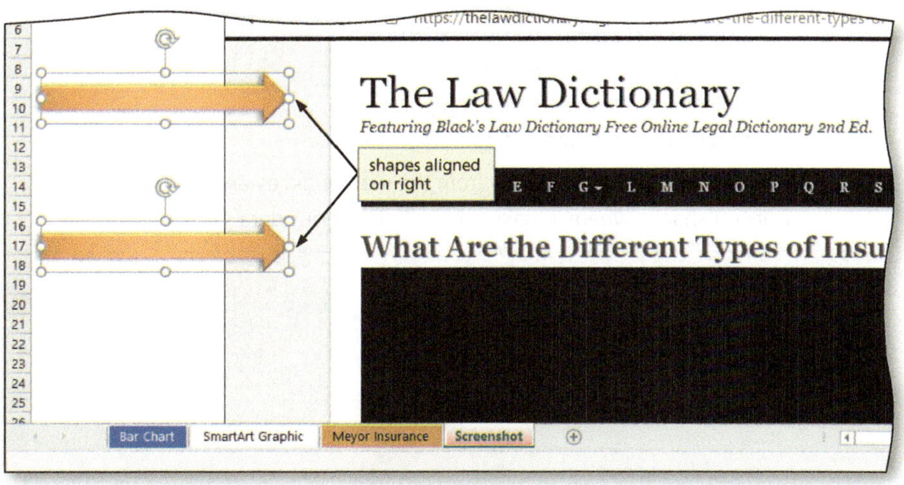

Figure 7–120

Summary

In this module, you learned how to create a template that can be used every time a similar workbook is developed. Starting from the template, you gathered external data by importing a text file, an Access database, a Word document, and a website. You formatted the data and transposed it when necessary. You replicated the formulas and functions, and then used Quick Analysis to display specific formatting. Then, you created a bar chart, formatting the bars with a style, color, and bevel. After reversing the order of the categories, you edited the number format of the horizontal labels. While creating a SmartArt graphic, you inserted pictures relevant to the spreadsheet and formatted the SmartArt with text, styles, and ALT text. You learned about object linking and embedding and inserted a hyperlinked screenshot as well as shapes in the workbook.

Consider This: Plan Ahead

What decisions will you need to make when creating your next workbook based on a template to analyze data including a chart, SmartArt graphic, and screenshot?

Use these guidelines as you complete the assignments in this module and create your own worksheets for evaluating and analyzing data outside of this class.

1. Create a template.
   a) Format rows and columns.
   b) Enter titles and headings.
   c) Enter sample or dummy data.
   d) Enter formulas and functions.
   e) Save as a template file type.
2. Create a new workbook based on the template and import data.
   a) Open a template file and save it as a workbook file.
   b) Import data corresponding to type of data.
   c) Format imported data.
   d) Paste special and transpose data when necessary.
3. Format using the Quick Analysis gallery.
   a) Apply formatting or totals using the Quick Analysis gallery.
4. Create new sheets for each part of your analysis workbook.
5. Use SmartArt graphics to illustrate data.
   a) Gather appropriate pictures.
   b) Use text effects to enhance text.
   c) Insert icons and alt text.
   d) Add effects to enhance graphics.
6. Use screenshots to aid in presenting analysis.
   a) Hyperlink screenshots from the web, if necessary.
7. Insert shapes where it makes sense to point out data.

Apply Your Knowledge

Reinforce the skills and apply the concepts you learned in this module.

Using a Template to Create a Consolidated Workbook

Note: To complete this assignment, you will be required to use the Data Files. Please contact your instructor for information about accessing the Data Files.

Instructions: You are to create the consolidated workbook and SmartArt graphic for Vegas Tourism shown in Figure 7–121.

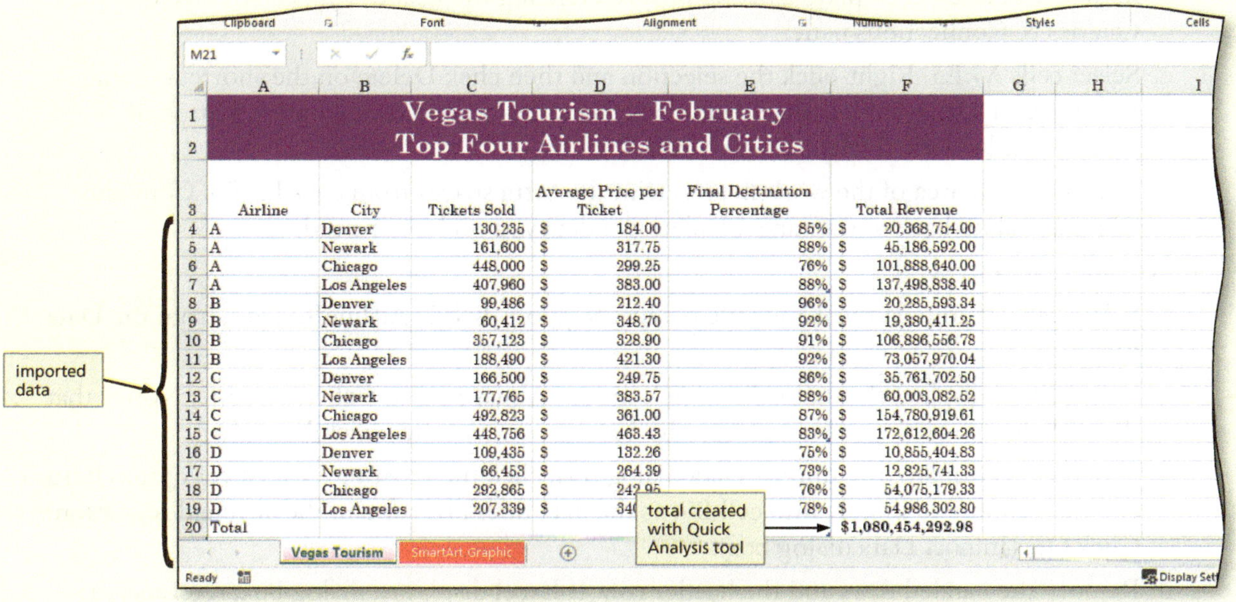

	A	B	C	D	E	F
1	Vegas Tourism – February					
2	Top Four Airlines and Cities					
3	Airline	City	Tickets Sold	Average Price per Ticket	Final Destination Percentage	Total Revenue
4	A	Denver	130,235	$ 184.00	85%	$ 20,368,754.00
5	A	Newark	161,600	$ 317.75	88%	$ 45,186,592.00
6	A	Chicago	448,000	$ 299.25	76%	$ 101,888,640.00
7	A	Los Angeles	407,960	$ 383.00	88%	$ 137,498,838.40
8	B	Denver	99,486	$ 212.40	96%	$ 20,285,593.34
9	B	Newark	60,412	$ 348.70	92%	$ 19,380,411.25
10	B	Chicago	357,123	$ 328.90	91%	$ 106,886,556.78
11	B	Los Angeles	188,490	$ 421.30	92%	$ 73,057,970.04
12	C	Denver	166,500	$ 249.75	86%	$ 35,761,702.50
13	C	Newark	177,765	$ 383.57	88%	$ 60,003,082.52
14	C	Chicago	492,823	$ 361.00	87%	$ 154,780,919.61
15	C	Los Angeles	448,756	$ 463.43	83%	$ 172,612,604.26
16	D	Denver	109,435	$ 132.26	75%	$ 10,855,404.83
17	D	Newark	66,453	$ 264.39	73%	$ 12,825,741.33
18	D	Chicago	292,865	$ 242.95	76%	$ 54,075,179.33
19	D	Los Angeles	207,339	$ 34[illegible]	78%	$ 54,986,302.80
20	Total					$1,080,454,292.98

(a) Imported Data in Worksheet

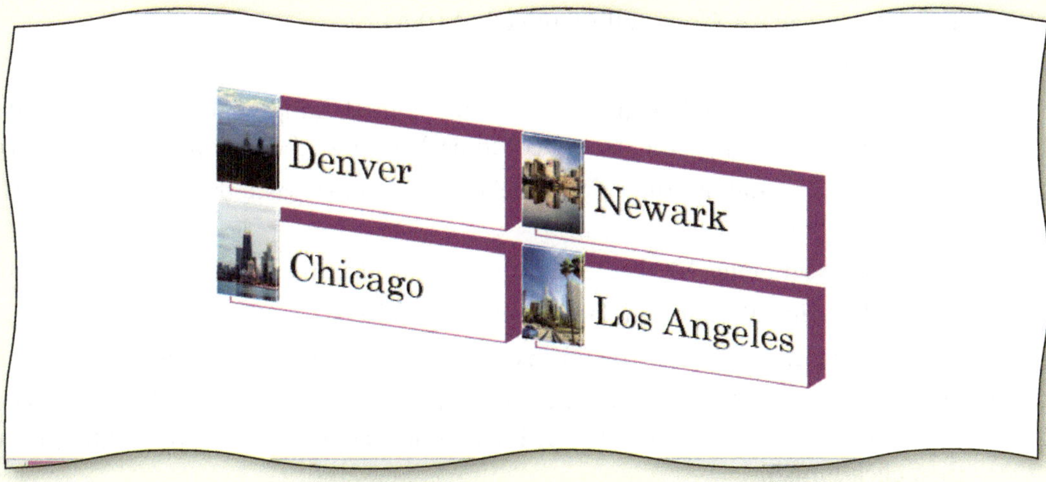

Jeff Zehnder/Shutterstock.com; Sean Pavone/Shutterstock.com; AndriuH/Shutterstock.com; f11photo/shutterstock.com

(b) SmartArt Graphic

Figure 7–121

Perform the following tasks:

1. Open a File Explorer window and double-click the file named SC_EX_7-6.xlsx from the Data Files.
2. Add a second sheet to the workbook, named SmartArt Graphic. Color the tab red.

Continued >

Apply Your Knowledge *continued*

3. To import a text file:
   a. Make the Vegas Tourism worksheet active, and then select cell A5. Use the Data tab to import the text file named, Support_EX_7_AirlineA.csv, from the Data Files.
   b. When Excel displays the dialog box, click the Load arrow and then click Load To.
   c. When Excel displays the Import Data dialog box, click the Existing Worksheet option button to select it. Click OK (Import Data dialog box).
   d. Click the new table and then use the Table Design tab to remove the banded rows and the header row. If Excel displays a dialog box, referencing the header row, click Yes. Close the Queries & Connections pane.
   e. Select cells A5:E5. Right-click the selection and then click Delete on the shortcut menu. When Excel displays the Delete dialog box, click the 'Shift cells up' option button, if necessary. Click OK (Delete dialog box).
   f. Use a separate area of the worksheet to trim the extra spaces from cells B5:B8. Copy the trimmed values back to the range. Delete the data you no longer need.
4. To import an Access table:
   a. Select cell A9. Import the Access file named, Support_EX_7_AirlineB.accdb, from the Data Files.
   b. When Excel displays the dialog box, click the Las Vegas Flights February table. Notice that the table has no airline column. Click the Load arrow and then click Load To.
   c. When Excel displays the Import Data dialog box, click the Existing Worksheet option button and then choose to import into cell B9, as the data does not contain the airline designation. Click OK (Import Data dialog box).
   d. Remove the banded rows and the header row. If Excel displays a dialog box, referencing the header row, click Yes. Close the Queries & Connections pane. Delete the resulting empty row.
   e. Type **B** in cell A9. Copy cell A9 to cells A10:A12.
5. To paste data from Word:
   a. Select cell A20. Start Word and open the file named, Support_EX_7_AirlineC.docx. In the Word table, select all of the data in columns 2 through 5 and copy it. Close Word.
   b. Return to Excel and use the Paste Special command to paste the data as Text (Paste Special dialog box) in cell A20.
   c. Copy the Excel range A20:D23. Click cell A13 and transpose the data while pasting it.
   d. Delete the original imported data in cells A20:D23.
   e. Cut the data in cells B13:D16 and paste it to cell C13 to move it one column to the right.
   f. Select cells A13:A16. Click the 'Text to Columns' button (Data tab | Data Tools group). In the Convert Text to Columns Wizard dialog box, choose the Fixed Width option button, and then click Finish.
6. To import Web data:
   a. Select cell A17. Click the From Web button (Data tab | Get & Transform Data group). In the URL box, enter the location of the HTML data file, such as c:\users\username\documents\cis 101\data files\Support_EX_7_AirlineD.html, and then press ENTER.
   b. When Excel displays the Navigator dialog box, click the name of the table, February Flights to Vegas – Top Four Cities, and click the Web View tab. Click the Transform Data button (Navigator dialog box) to open the Power Query Editor window.

c. Remove the Airport column. Click the 'Close & Load' arrow (Power Query Editor Home tab | Close group) and then click the 'Close & Load To' command to close the Power Query Editor Window.

d. When Excel displays the Import Data dialog box, if necessary, click the Existing worksheet option button, and then click OK.

e. Remove the banded rows and the header row. If Excel displays a dialog box, referencing the header row, click Yes.

f. Delete the blank row. Close the Queries & Connections pane.

7. Use the fill handle to replicate cell F4 to F5:F20.
8. Copy the formatting from C4:F4 to C5:F20.
9. Delete row 4.
10. Select cells F4:F19. Click the Quick Analysis button and create a total in cell F20. In cell A20, type the word, `Total`.
11. Adjust column widths as necessary.

If directed by your instructor, insert your name and course number in cell A21.

12. Go to the SmartArt Graphic sheet. Click the Gridlines check box (View tab | Show group) to turn off gridlines.
13. Click the Illustrations button (Insert tab | Illustrations group) and then click the SmartArt button. Click List in the left pane (Choose a SmartArt Graphic dialog box) and then click Picture Strips in the middle pane. Click the OK button to insert the graphic.
14. Click the Add Shape button (SmartArt Design tab | Create Graphic group).
15. One at a time, using the Text Pane, replace the word, Text, with the words, Denver, Newark, Chicago, and Los Angeles, respectively.
16. Change the SmartArt style to Brick Scene.
17. One at a time, click the picture icon in each part of the graphic, and search the web for a graphic related to the city. Make sure you review the license to ensure you can comply with any copyright restrictions.
18. Resize the graphic to fill the area D1:L24.
19. Save the file with the file name, SC_EX_7_VegasTourismAnalysis, and submit the revised workbook in the format specified by your instructor.
20. In what format do you think most companies submit data? Why? If the data changes, how do consolidated workbooks adjust? Do all the formats lend themselves to recalculating? Why or why not?

Extend Your Knowledge

Extend the skills you learned in this module and experiment with new skills. You may need to use Help to complete the assignment.

Inserting a SmartArt Organization Chart and Image on a Worksheet

Note: To complete this assignment, you will be required to use the Data Files. Please contact your instructor for information about accessing the Data Files.

Instructions: Start Excel. Open the workbook SC_EX_7-7, which is located in the Data Files. You are to add a SmartArt graphic and an image to the workbook and then format both graphics.

Continued >

Extend Your Knowledge *continued*

Perform the following tasks:

1. Insert a SmartArt graphic on the Billing Department sheet using the Hierarchy type and the Hierarchy layout.
2. Select the last shape on the right in the third row of the SmartArt graphic and then add a shape.
3. Display the Text Pane and drag its border to the right side of the chart. Use copying and pasting techniques to insert the names from column A into the SmartArt, as shown in Figure 7–122. Insert your name in place of one of the employees.

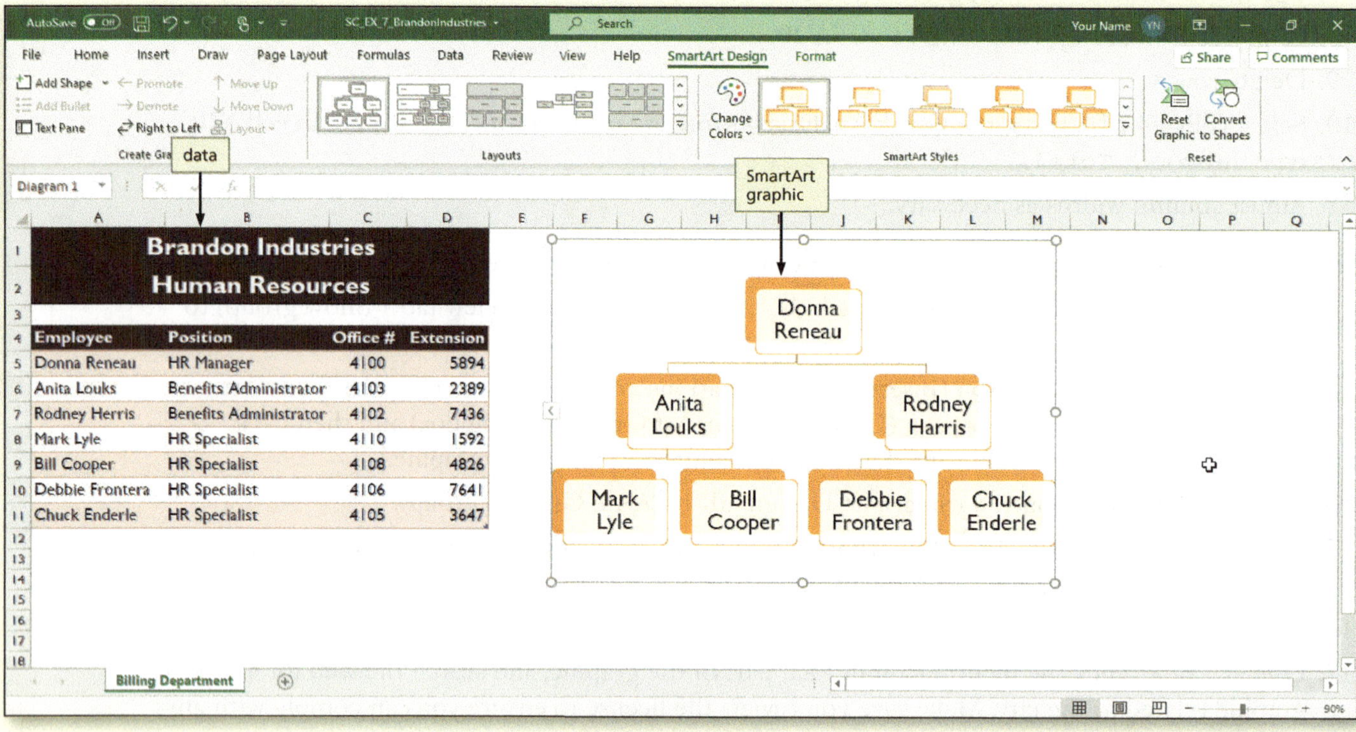

Figure 7–122

4. Change the color scheme of the hierarchy chart to 'Dark 2 Fill' in the Change Colors gallery.
5. Use the SmartArt Styles gallery to change the style to Cartoon.
6. Move the SmartArt Graphic to the right of the data.
7. Use Help to read about formatting pictures. Insert an online picture related to the search term, business meeting. Format the picture using the Metal Rounded Rectangle picture style (Picture Format tab | Picture Styles group).
8. Change the picture border to 'Orange, Accent 6, Lighter 60%'.
9. Add a Picture Effect (Picture Format tab | Picture Styles group) using the 3-D Rotation named 'Perspective: Contrasting Left'.
10. Add ALT text that says `This is a picture of the HR team at Brandon Industries.`
11. Move and resize the picture so that it fits beside the SmartArt graphic.
12. Add your name and course number to the worksheet.
13. Save the file with the file name SC_EX_7_BrandonIndustries, and submit the revised workbook in the format specified by your instructor.
14. When do you think a company would use a spreadsheet like this? What formatting and changes might make it even more useful?

Expand Your World

Create a solution that uses cloud and web technologies by learning and investigating on your own from general guidance.

Using Web Data

Problem: You would like to import some web statistics about your state. You decide to retrieve U.S. census data from the web (Figure 7–123).

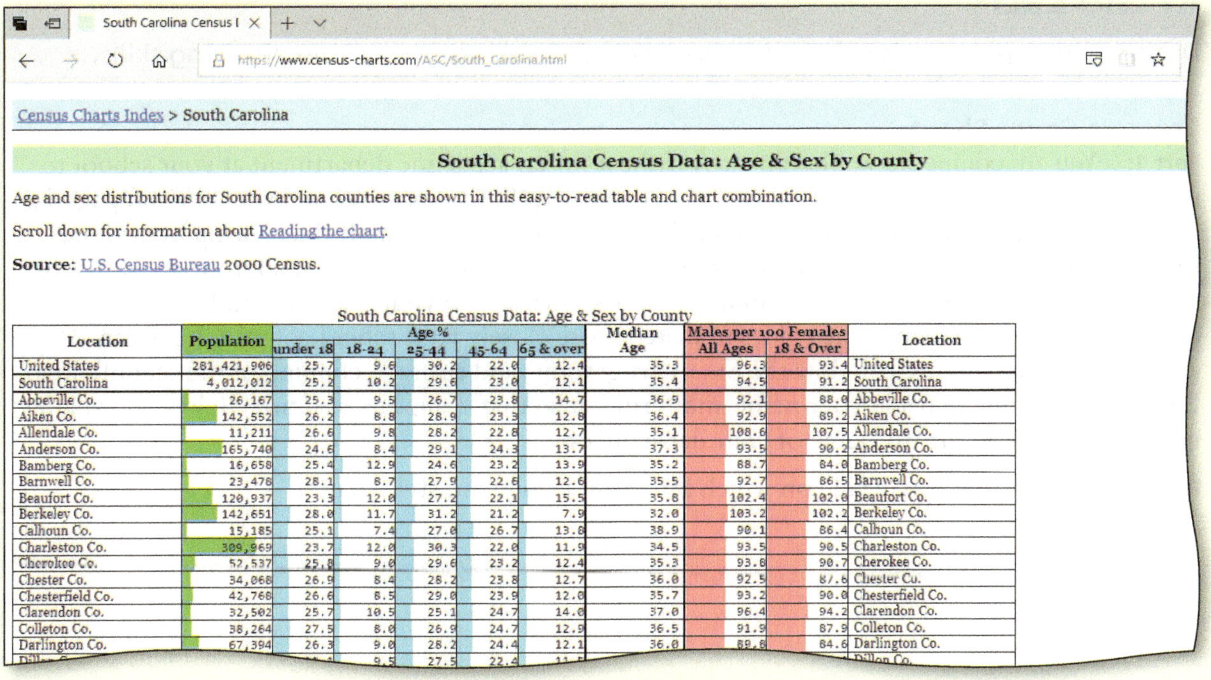

Location	Population	Age %					Median Age	Males per 100 Females		Location
		under 18	18-24	25-44	45-64	65 & over		All Ages	18 & Over	
United States	281,421,906	25.7	9.6	30.2	22.0	12.4	35.3	96.3	93.4	United States
South Carolina	4,012,012	25.2	10.2	29.6	23.0	12.1	35.4	94.5	91.2	South Carolina
Abbeville Co.	26,167	25.3	9.5	26.7	23.8	14.7	36.9	92.1	88.0	Abbeville Co.
Aiken Co.	142,552	26.2	8.8	28.9	23.3	12.8	36.4	92.9	89.2	Aiken Co.
Allendale Co.	11,211	26.6	9.8	28.2	22.8	12.7	35.1	108.6	107.5	Allendale Co.
Anderson Co.	165,740	24.6	8.4	29.1	24.3	13.7	37.3	93.5	90.2	Anderson Co.
Bamberg Co.	16,658	25.4	12.9	24.6	23.2	13.9	35.2	88.7	84.0	Bamberg Co.
Barnwell Co.	23,478	28.1	8.7	27.9	22.6	12.6	35.5	92.7	86.5	Barnwell Co.
Beaufort Co.	120,937	23.3	12.0	27.2	22.1	15.5	35.8	102.4	102.0	Beaufort Co.
Berkeley Co.	142,651	28.0	11.7	31.2	21.2	7.9	32.0	103.2	102.2	Berkeley Co.
Calhoun Co.	15,185	25.1	7.4	27.0	26.7	13.8	38.9	90.1	86.4	Calhoun Co.
Charleston Co.	309,969	23.7	12.0	30.3	22.0	11.9	34.5	93.5	90.5	Charleston Co.
Cherokee Co.	52,537	25.8	9.0	29.6	23.2	12.4	35.3	93.8	90.7	Cherokee Co.
Chester Co.	34,068	26.9	8.4	28.2	23.8	12.7	36.0	92.5	87.6	Chester Co.
Chesterfield Co.	42,768	26.6	8.5	29.0	23.9	12.0	35.7	93.2	90.0	Chesterfield Co.
Clarendon Co.	32,502	25.7	10.5	25.1	24.7	14.0	37.0	96.4	94.2	Clarendon Co.
Colleton Co.	38,264	27.5	8.0	26.9	24.7	12.9	36.5	91.9	87.9	Colleton Co.
Darlington Co.	67,394	26.3	9.0	28.2	24.4	12.1	36.0	89.8	84.6	Darlington Co.
[illegible]	[illegible]	[illegible]	9.5	27.5	22.4	[illegible]	[illegible]	[illegible]	[illegible]	Dillon Co.

Figure 7–123

Instructions:

1. Start a browser and navigate to https://www.census-charts.com/.
2. In the Data by State and County area, click 'Age and Sex' and then click your state.
3. When the website presents the data, copy the URL address.
4. Start Excel and open a blank workbook.
5. Hide the gridlines and rename the sheet, Screenshot. Use the Screenshot button (Insert tab | Illustrations group) to insert a screenshot of your data, or if necessary, use screen clipping. Close the browser.
6. Add a new sheet to the workbook, named Web Data.
7. Select cell B2. Click the 'From Web' button (Data tab | Get & Transform Data group). Paste the URL into the address text box in the From Web dialog box. Click the OK button (From Web dialog box).
8. If Excel displays the Access Web content dialog box, click the Connect button.
9. When Excel displays the Navigator dialog box, click the state table and then click the Transform Data button.
10. When Excel displays the Power Query Editor window, delete the last four columns and the first two rows. Use the 'Close and Load To' command to load the data to the existing worksheet.

Continued >

Expand Your World *continued*

11. When Excel displays the data, add and format a title, format the column headings, and adjust column widths, if necessary. Save the file with the file name, SC_EX_7_WebData, and submit the revised workbook in the format specified by your instructor.
12. What kinds of analysis could you perform in Excel on the data you downloaded from the census website? What would make the data more meaningful and useful? Why?

In the Lab

Design and implement a solution using creative thinking and problem-solving skills.

Create a Cover Sheet

Part 1: You are competing to design a cover sheet for an academic department at your school to include in their workbooks when they send out statistics. Start a browser and view the webpage for your chosen department at your school. Create a workbook and turn off the viewing of gridlines for the first sheet. Insert a screenshot of the department webpage and size it appropriately. Insert a SmartArt list to highlight three or four of the best qualities of your department. Use text effects to enhance the text. Change the colors to match more closely your school colors. Choose an appropriate SmartArt style. Below the SmartArt graphic, add a screen clipping of the school's logo. Finally, next to the logo add your name and format it so that it appears as a title. Below your name, in a smaller font, insert the name of your department.

Part 2: How did you decide on which SmartArt layout and style to use?

8 Working with Trendlines, PivotTables, PivotCharts, and Slicers

Objectives

After completing this module, you will be able to:

- Analyze worksheet data using a trendline
- Create a PivotTable report
- Format a PivotTable report
- Apply filters to a PivotTable report
- Create a PivotChart report
- Format a PivotChart report
- Apply filters to a PivotChart report
- Analyze worksheet data using PivotTable and PivotChart reports
- Create calculated fields
- Create slicers to filter PivotTable and PivotChart reports
- Format slicers
- Examine other statistical and process charts
- Create a Box and Whisker Chart

Introduction

In both academic and business environments, people are presented with large amounts of data that need to be analyzed and interpreted. Data are increasingly available from a wide variety of sources and gathered with ease. Analysis of data and interpretation of the results are important skills to acquire. Learning how to ask questions that identify patterns in data is a skill that can provide businesses and individuals with information that can be used to make decisions about business situations.

Project: Bell & Rodgers Accounting

Bell & Rodgers Accounting is a firm that began six years ago with 50 employees who perform a wide variety of accounting and tax services. They keep records on clients, employees, billable hours, and revenue, among other things. Over the six years, they have hired several more accountants at their two locations in Durante and Jamison.

The owners at Bell & Rodgers are interested in reviewing billable hours for the past six years. They also have requested a comparison of the last two years of revenue figures for the different service types. In this module, you will learn how to use the trendline charting feature in Excel to examine data for trends. You also will analyze revenue data for Bell & Rodgers Accounting using PivotTable and PivotChart reports. The results of this analysis are shown in Figure 8–1.

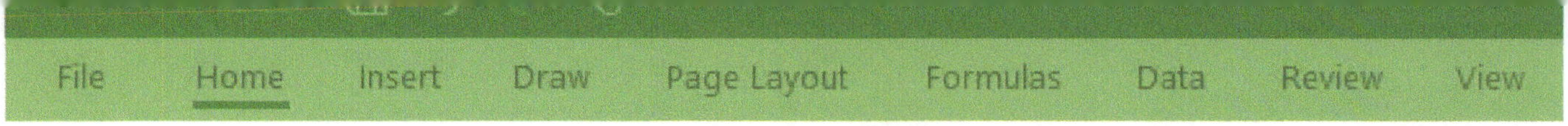

(a) Trendline

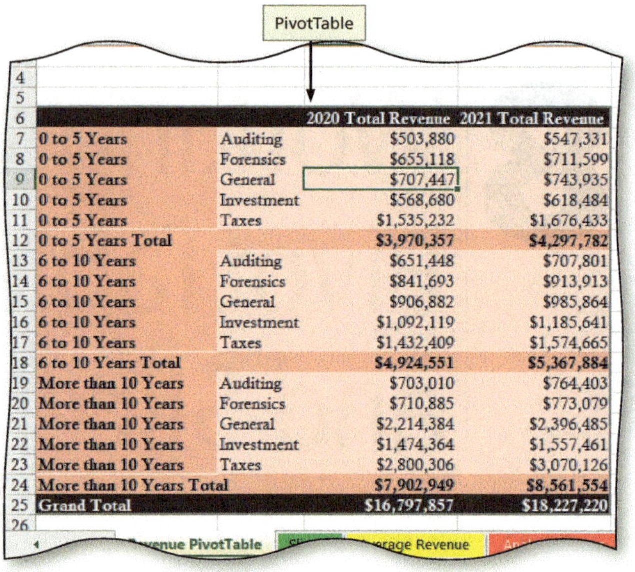

(b) PivotTable Report

(c) PivotChart Report

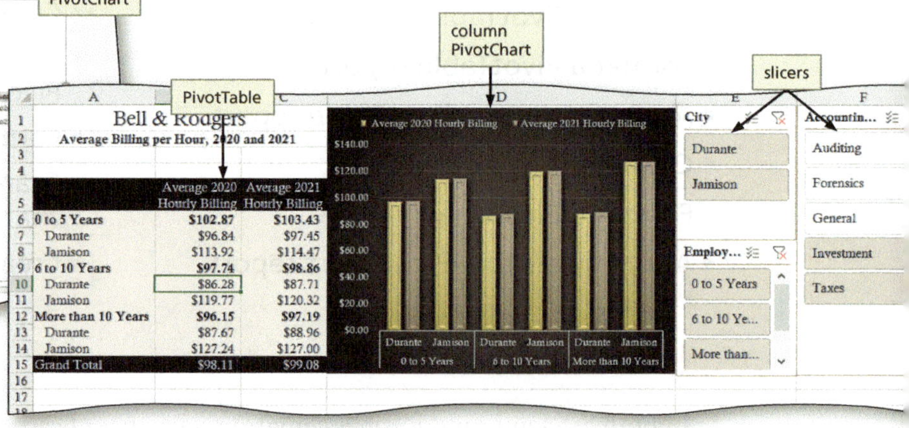

(d) Slicers

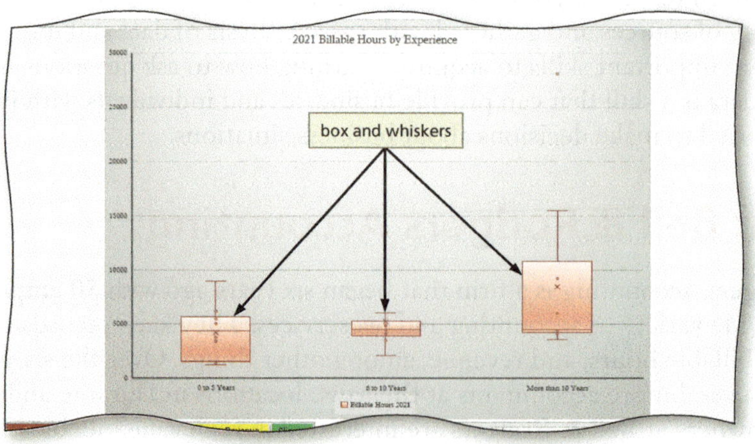

(e) Box and Whisker Chart

Figure 8–1

A **trendline** (Figure 8–1a) is a line that represents the general direction in a series of data. Trendlines often are used to represent changes in one set of data over time. Excel can overlay a trendline on certain types of charts, allowing you to compare changes in one set of data with overall trends.

In addition to trendlines, PivotTable reports and PivotChart reports provide methods to manipulate and visualize data. A **PivotTable report** (Figure 8–1b) is a workbook table designed to create meaningful data summaries that analyze worksheets containing large amounts of data. As an interactive view of worksheet data, a PivotTable report lets users summarize data by selecting and grouping categories. When using a PivotTable report, you can change, or pivot, selected categories quickly without needing to manipulate the worksheet itself. You can examine and analyze several complex arrangements of the data and may spot relationships you might not otherwise see. For example, you can look at years of experience for each employee, broken down by type of accounting service, and then look at the yearly revenue for certain subgroupings without having to reorganize your worksheet.

A **PivotChart report** (Figure 8–1c) is an Excel feature that lets you summarize worksheet data in the form of a chart, and rearrange parts of the chart structure to explore new data relationships. Also called simply PivotCharts, these reports are visual representations of PivotTables. For example, if Bell & Rodgers wanted to view a pie chart showing percentages of total revenue for each service type, a PivotChart could show that percentage categorized by city without having to rebuild the chart from scratch for each view. When you create a PivotChart report, Excel creates and associates a PivotTable with that PivotChart.

Slicers (Figure 8–1d) are graphic objects that you click to filter the data in PivotTables and PivotCharts. Each slicer button clearly identifies its purpose (the applied filter), making it easy to interpret the data displayed in the PivotTable report.

Figure 8–1e displays a box and whisker chart. You will create that chart later in this module as you learn about various kinds of statistical and process charts.

Using trendlines, PivotTables, PivotCharts, slicers, and other charts, a user with little knowledge of formulas, functions, and ranges can perform powerful what-if analyses on a set of data.

Figure 8–2 illustrates the requirements document for the Bell & Rodgers accounting analysis. It includes the needs, source of data, calculations, and other facts about the worksheet's development.

Worksheet Title	Bell & Rodgers Accounting Analysis
Needs	Evaluate different sets of data: 1. Total billable hours for 2016–2021. Provide a visual representation of billing over the past six years and a forecast for the next two years based on the current trend. 2. Revenue data for 2020 and 2021 for both locations, with details identifying years of employee experience, accounting type, billable hours, and revenue. For this data, use PivotTables and PivotCharts to look for patterns and anomalies in the data, based on different arrangements of data to discover relationships. Some specific items of interest include Total Revenue and Average Revenue for Employee Experience and Accounting Type by City. 3. Set up slicers to facilitate easy examination of various subgroupings for users with little or no Excel experience. 4. Create a box and whisker chart to look at the distribution of numerical data, including the highs and lows for 2021 billable hours by experience.
Calculations	In addition to total revenue for the various groupings, calculations will include product comparisons of average revenue for groupings. Create calculations of the average revenue for various combinations.
Source of Data	The owners will supply the data in the workbook SC_EX_8-1.xlsx.

Figure 8–2

To Start Excel and Open a Workbook

The following steps start Excel and open a workbook named SC_EX_8-1.xlsx. The workbook currently has two worksheets, one showing detailed billing and revenue, named Analysis Figures, and one summarizing the data, named 6-Year Billable Hours.

To complete these steps, you will be required to use the Data Files. Please contact your instructor for information about accessing the Data Files.

BTW
Touch Mode Differences
The Office and Windows interfaces may vary if you are using Touch Mode. For this reason, you might notice that the function or appearance of your touch screen differs slightly from this module's presentation.

1. sam Start Excel.
2. Open the file named SC_EX_8-1.xlsx from the Data Files.
3. If the Excel window is not maximized, click the Maximize button on its title bar to maximize the window. If necessary, change the magnification to 120%.
4. Save the file on your storage device with the name, SC_EX_8_Bell&RodgersAccountingAnalysis.

Line Charts and Trendlines

BTW
Ribbon and Screen Resolution
Excel may change how the groups and buttons within the groups appear on the ribbon, depending on the screen resolution of your computer. Thus, your ribbon may look different from the ones in this book if you are using a screen resolution other than 1366 × 768.

A **line chart** is a chart that displays data as lines across categories. A line chart illustrates the amount of change in data over a period of time, or it may compare multiple items. Some line charts contain data points that usually are plotted in evenly spaced intervals to emphasize the relationships between the points. A 2-D line chart has two axes but can contain multiple lines of data, such as two data series over the same period of time. A 3-D line chart may include a third axis, illustrated by depth, to represent the second data series or even a new category.

Using a trendline on certain Excel charts allows you to illustrate the behavior of a set of data to determine if there is a pattern. Trends most often are thought about in terms of how a value changes over time, but trends also can describe the relationship between two variables, such as height and weight. In Excel, you can add a trendline to most types of charts, such as unstacked 2-D area, bar, column, line, inventory, scatter (X, Y), and bubble charts, among others. Chart types that do not examine the relationship between two variables, such as pie and doughnut charts that examine the contribution of different parts to a whole, cannot include trendlines.

Consider This

How do you determine which trends to analyze?

Before you add a trendline to a chart, you need to determine which data series to analyze. If the chart displays only one data series, Excel uses it automatically. If the chart involves more than one data series, you select the one you want to use as a trendline. Then you can analyze current or future trends.

To analyze a current trend, make sure you have enough data available for the period you want to analyze. For example, two years of annual sales totals might not provide enough data to analyze sales performance. Five years of annual sales totals or two years of monthly sales totals are more likely to present a trend.

To analyze a future trend, you use a trendline to project data beyond the values or scope of the data set in a process called forecasting. **Forecasting** is an analysis tool that helps predict data values that are outside of a data set. For example, if a data set is for a 10-year period and the data show a trend in that 10-year period, Excel can predict values beyond that period or estimate what the values may have been before that period.

When you add a trendline to a chart, you can set the number of periods to forecast forward or backward in time. For example, if you have six years of sales data, you can forecast two periods forward to show the trend for eight years: six years of current data and two years of projected data. You also can display information about the trendline on the chart itself to help guide your analysis. For example, you can display the equation used to calculate the trend and show the **R-squared value**, which is a number from 0 to 1 that measures the strength of the trend. An R-squared value of 1 means the estimated values in the trendline correspond exactly to the actual data.

To Create a 2-D Line Chart

Why? Line charts are suited to charting a variable, in this case billable hours, over a number of time periods. The following steps create a 2-D line chart of the Bell & Rodgers billing data. You will add a trendline to the chart later in the module.

1

- If necessary, click the '6-Year Billable Hours' sheet tab.
- Select cells A4:G5 to select the range to be charted (Figure 8–3).

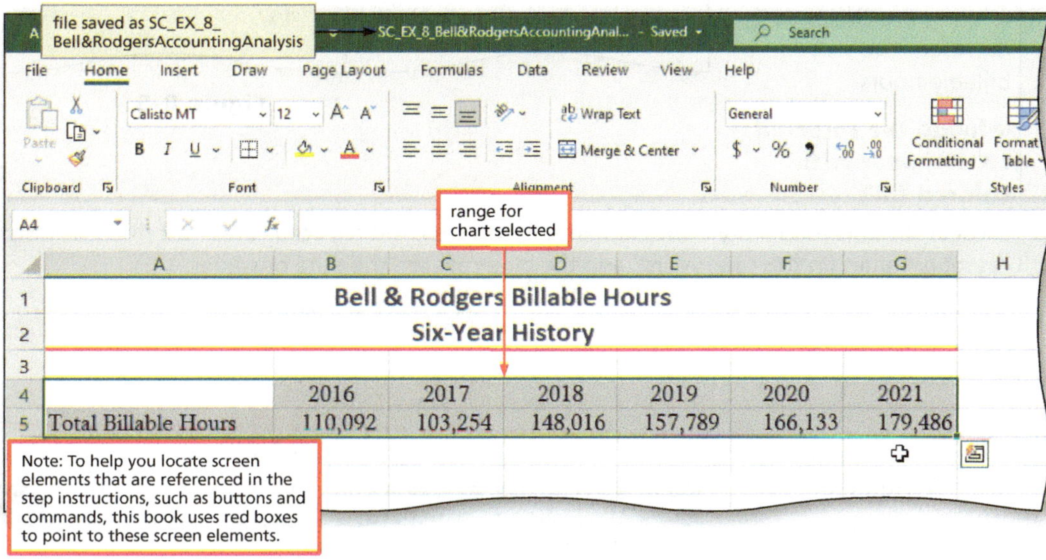

Figure 8–3

2

- Click Insert on the ribbon to display the Insert tab.
- Click the 'Insert Line or Area Chart' button (Insert tab | Charts group) to display the Insert Line and Area Chart gallery (Figure 8–4).

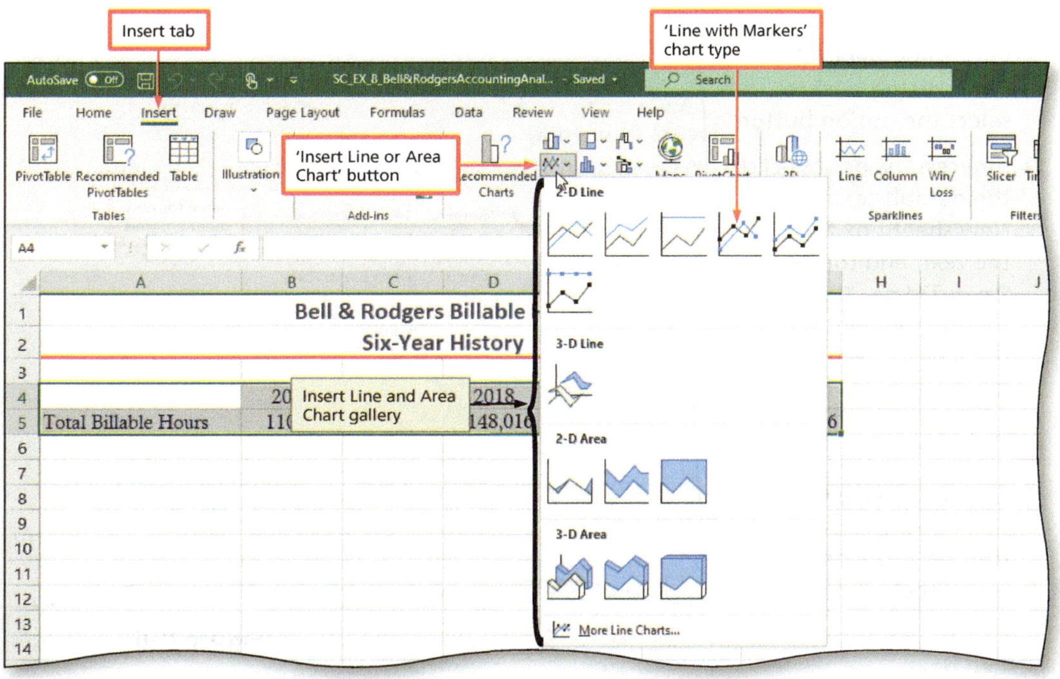

Figure 8–4

3

- Click 'Line with Markers' in the 2-D Line area to insert a 2-D line chart with data markers (Figure 8–5).

Q&A

What are data markers?

A data marker is the symbol in a chart that represents a single value from a worksheet cell. In this case, the data markers are circles that represent the six years of billable hours.

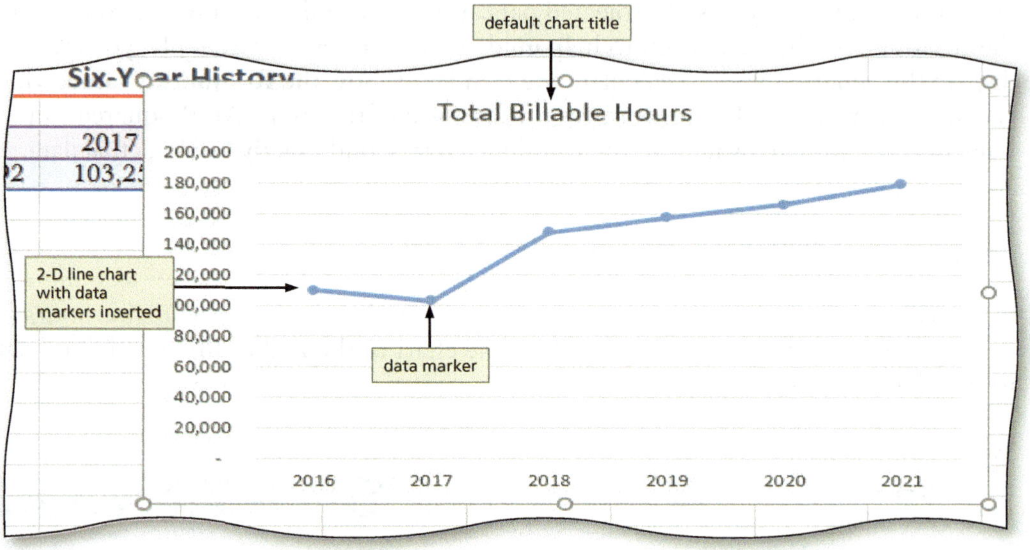

Figure 8–5

Why do the selected cells appear with colored fill?

Excel uses colors to identify chart elements. In this case, the red cell is the chart title, the purple cells are the x-axis or category values (in this case, years), and the blue cells are the data or values.

4

- If necessary, display the Chart Design tab.
- Click the Move Chart button (Chart Design tab | Location group) to display the Move Chart dialog box.
- Click New sheet (Move Chart dialog box) to select the option button.
- If necessary, double-click the default text in the New sheet box to select the text, and then type `Trendline Chart` to enter a name for the new worksheet (Figure 8–6).

5

- Click OK (Move Chart dialog box) to move the chart to a new worksheet.

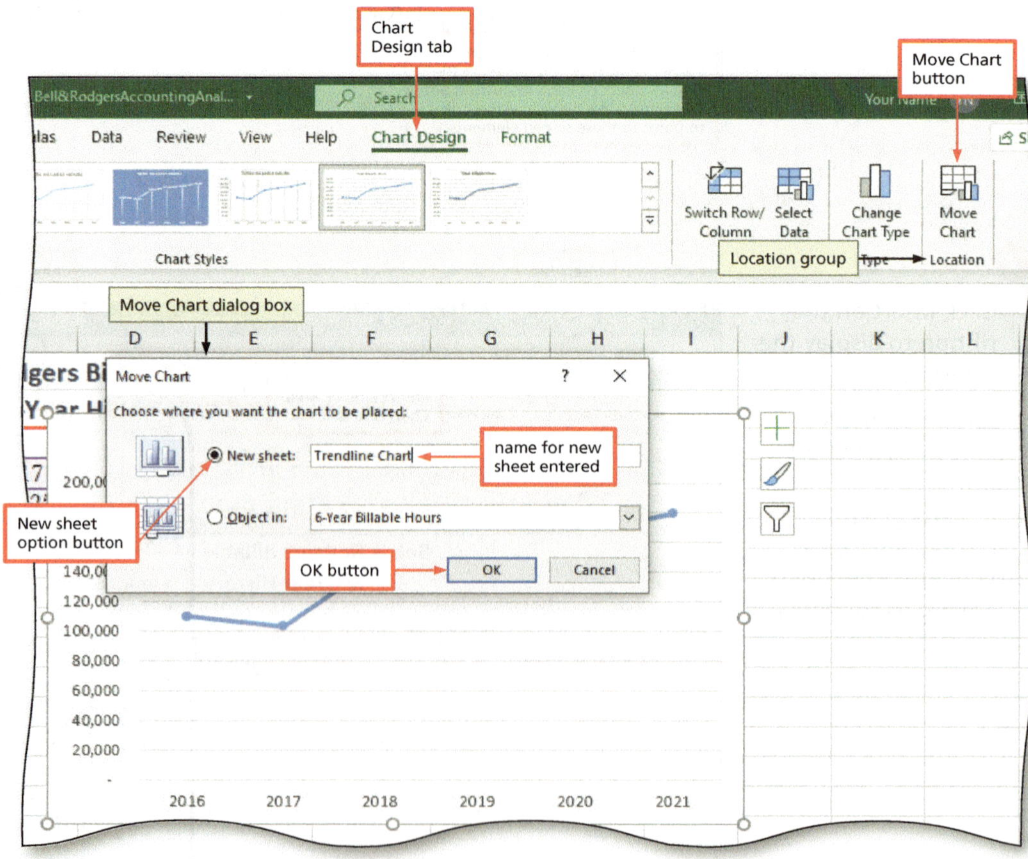

Figure 8–6

Other Ways

1. Click Quick Analysis button, click Charts tab, click Line button

To Format a 2-D Line Chart

You can format 2-D line charts by editing various chart elements, changing the style or color of the chart, or formatting the data series. In the following steps you will edit the title, format the y-axis, and change the chart style. **Why?** Customizing the chart will make the data easier to read. You also will change the **bounds** of the chart axis, which are the beginning or ending values on an axis.

1

- Click the chart title.
- Edit the title to read `Total Billable Hours 2016 - 2021` to enter the new chart title.
- Bold the text (Figure 8–7).

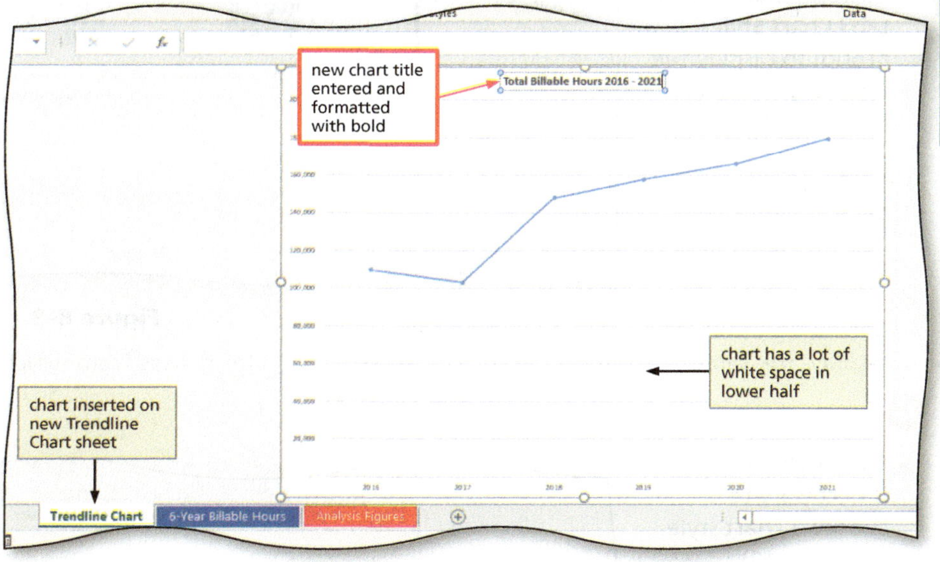

Figure 8–7

2

- Double-click the y-axis to display the Format Axis pane.
- If necessary, click the Axis Options tab.
- In the Minimum box (Axis Options area), type `100000` and then press ENTER to set a lower value for the y-axis (Figure 8–8).

Q&A

Why should I change the minimum value?
If you adjust the minimum value to a position slightly below the lowest data point, you will have less white space in your chart, making it more legible. Be aware, however, that trends represented in line charts may appear exaggerated when the lowest data point is not zero. Do not change the value if you are confident your data will change.

What is the purpose of the Reset button?
When you click the Reset button, Excel automatically adjusts the lower bounds to back to zero.

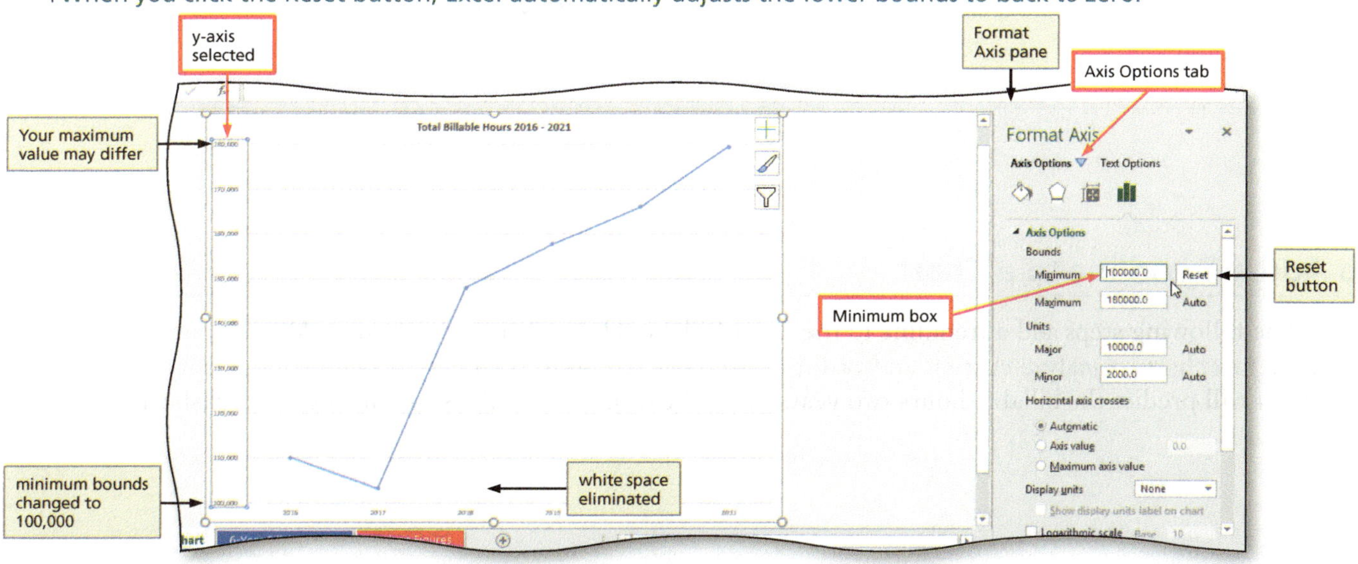

Figure 8–8

3

- Display the Chart Design tab if necessary.
- Click the More button (Chart Design tab | Chart Styles group) to display the Chart Styles Gallery (Figure 8–9).

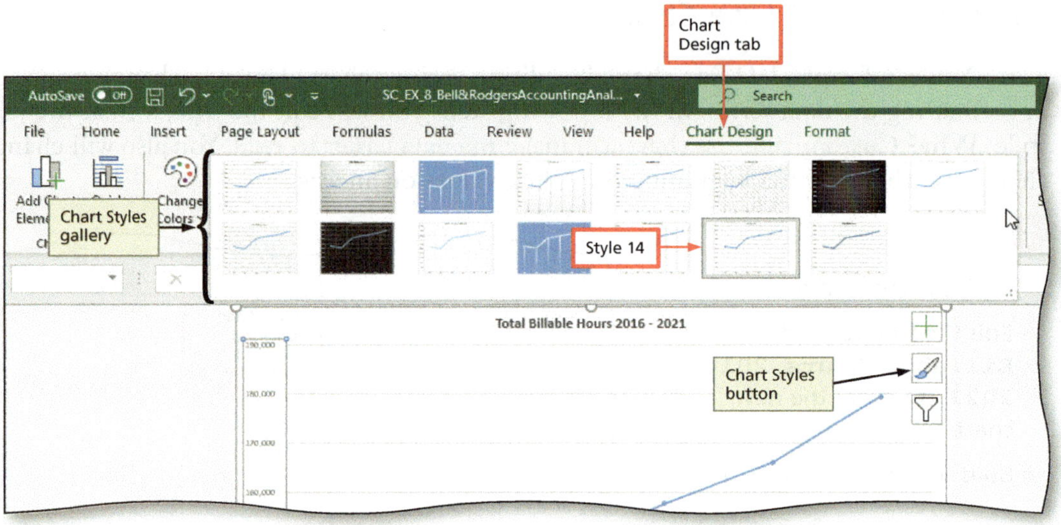

Figure 8–9

Q&A **What is the purpose of the Chart Styles button on the chart?**
The Chart Styles button on the chart displays the same styles as on the ribbon, as well as a Color gallery from which you may choose.

4

- Click Style 14 if necessary to choose a chart style (Figure 8–10).

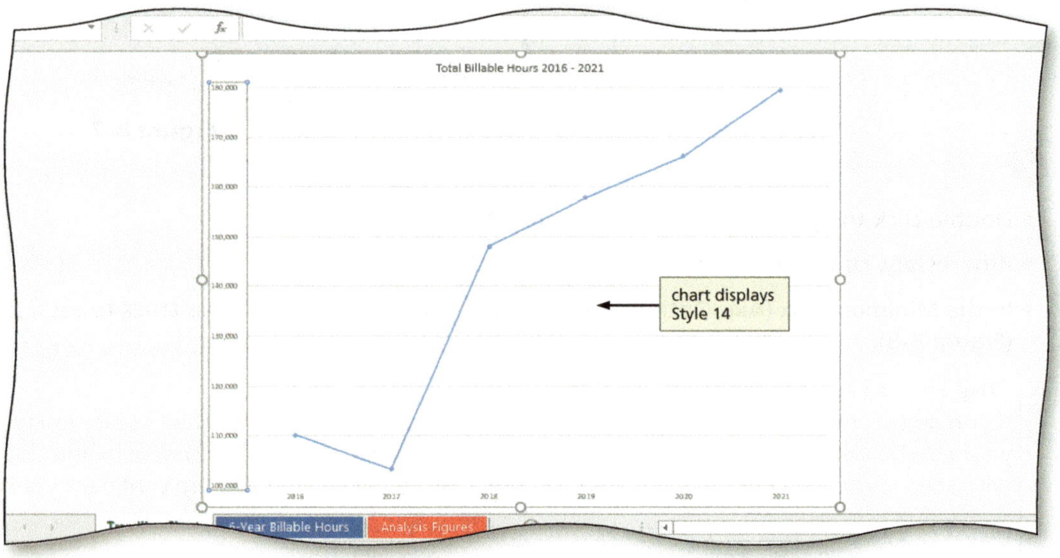

Figure 8–10

Q&A **What is the difference between a theme and a style?**
Both formatting options change the color, fonts, effects, and overall look and feel. A theme changes your entire workbook. A style only affects a specific element in a worksheet; for example, a chart style might change the graph lines from horizontal to vertical.

To Add a Trendline to a Chart

The following steps add a trendline to the Total Billable Hours 2016 – 2021 chart. **Why?** You add a trendline to a chart to analyze current and/or future trends. A trendline can only be added to an existing chart. The chart will predict the billable hours two years beyond the data set in the six-year figures worksheet.

1

- Click the 'Add Chart Element' button (Chart Design tab | Chart Layouts group) to display the Add Chart Element menu.
- Point to Trendline to display the Trendline gallery (Figure 8–11).

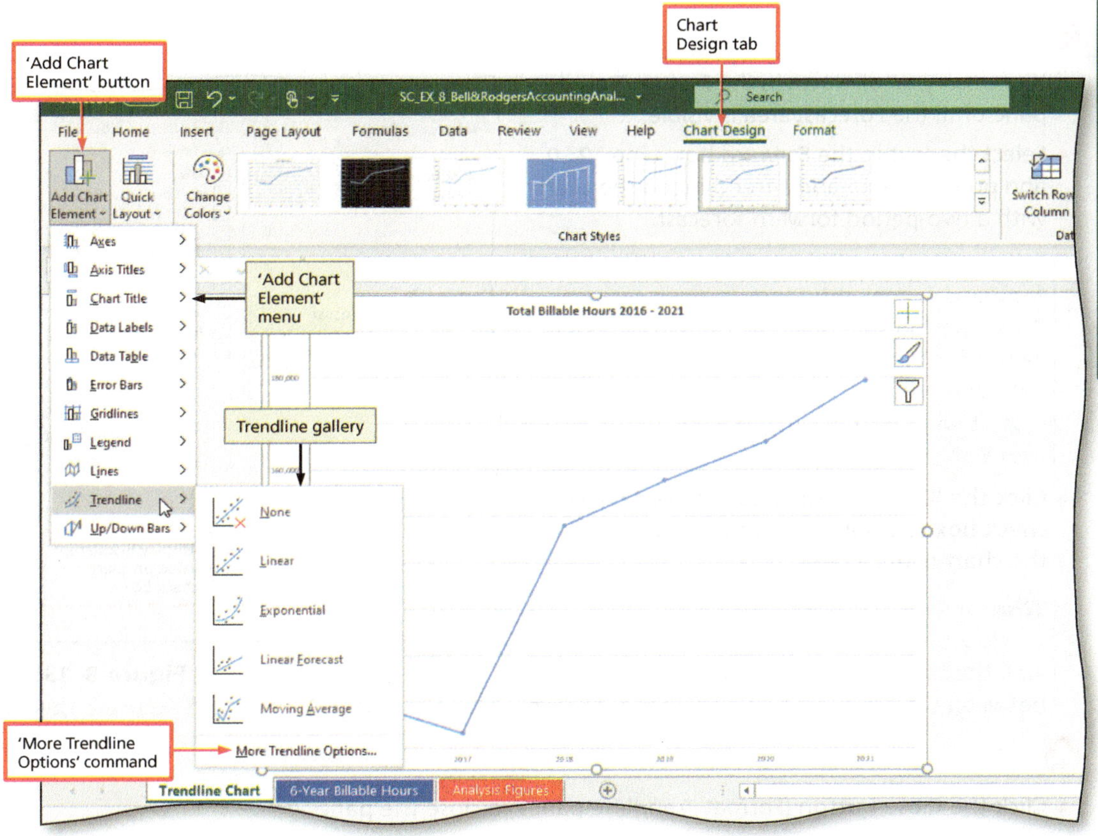

Figure 8–11

2

- Click 'More Trendline Options' (Trendline gallery) to display the Format Trendline pane.
- If necessary, click the Trendline Options button.
- If necessary, click Linear in the Trendline Options area to select a linear trendline type (Figure 8–12).

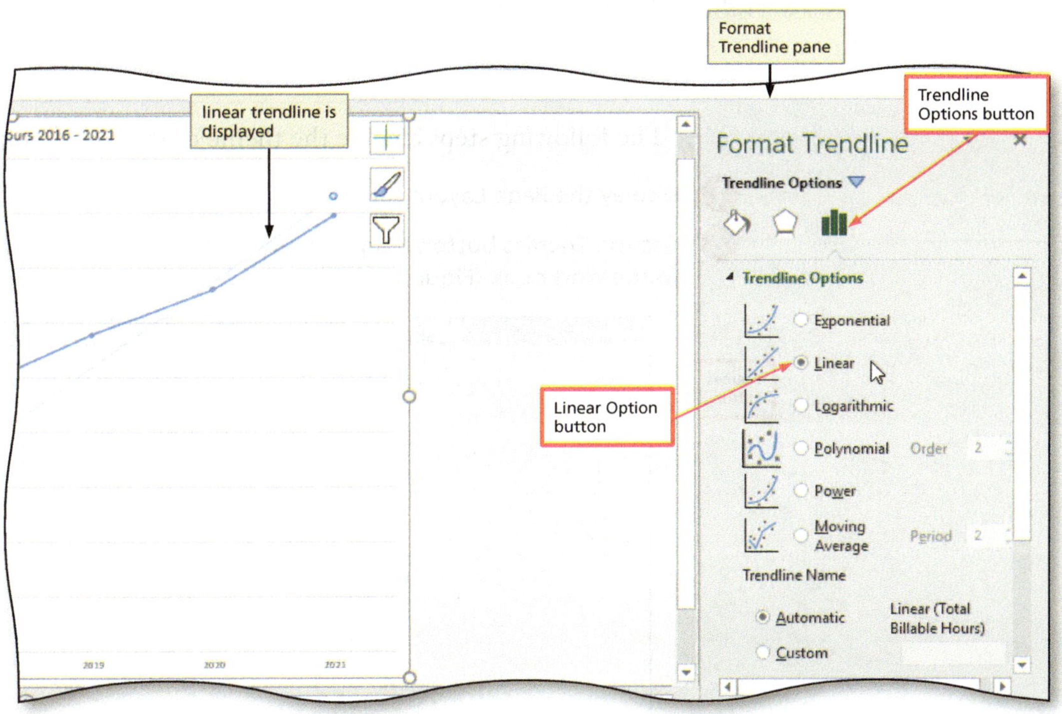

Figure 8–12

Q&A

Why should I select the Linear option button in this case?
The 2-D line chart you created is a basic line chart, so it is appropriate to apply a linear trendline, which shows values that are increasing or decreasing at a steady rate.

My trendline runs off the chart. Did I do something wrong?
It may be that your chart did not adjust the bounds automatically. Right-click the vertical axis, click Format Axis on the shortcut menu, and then click the upper bounds Reset button.

3

- If necessary, scroll down in the Format Trendline pane until the Forecast area is visible.
- Select the text in the Forward box, type **2.0**, and press ENTER to add a trendline to the chart with a two-period forward forecast.

Q&A **What does it mean to enter a two-period forward forecast?**
A two-period forward forecast estimates the values for the two time periods that follow the data you used to create the line chart. In this case, it will estimate total billable hours for the next two years.

- Click the 'Display R-squared value on chart' check box to display the R-squared value on the chart (Figure 8–13).

Q&A **What is the R-squared value?**
The R-squared value is a measure of how well the trendline describes the relationship between total billable hours and time. The closer the value is to 1, the more accurate the trendline.

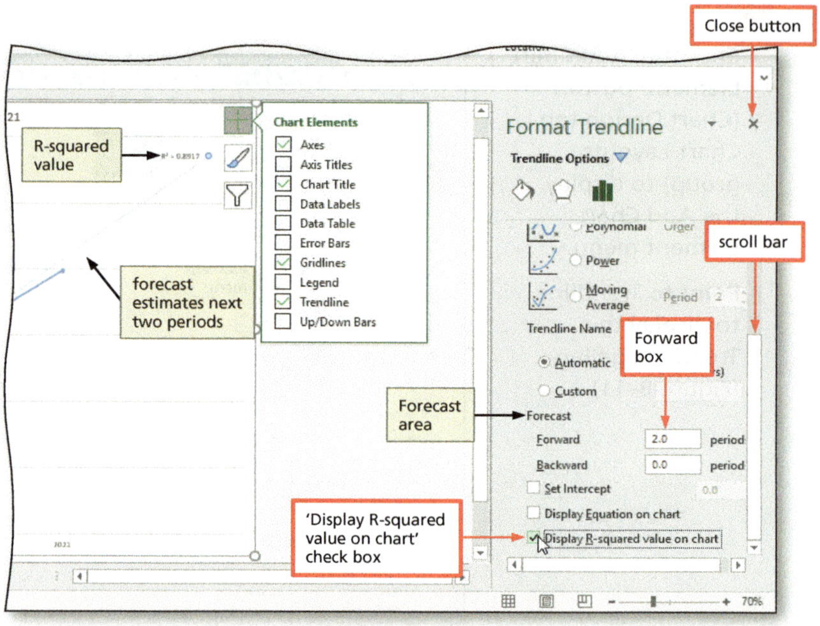

Figure 8–13

4

- Click the Close button (Format Trendline pane) to close the pane.

Other Ways

1. Right-click graphed line, click Add Trendline on shortcut menu

To Change the Theme

The following steps change the theme of the workbook.

1 Display the Page Layout tab.

2 Use the Themes button (Page Layout tab | Themes group) and apply the Slate theme to the workbook (Figure 8–14).

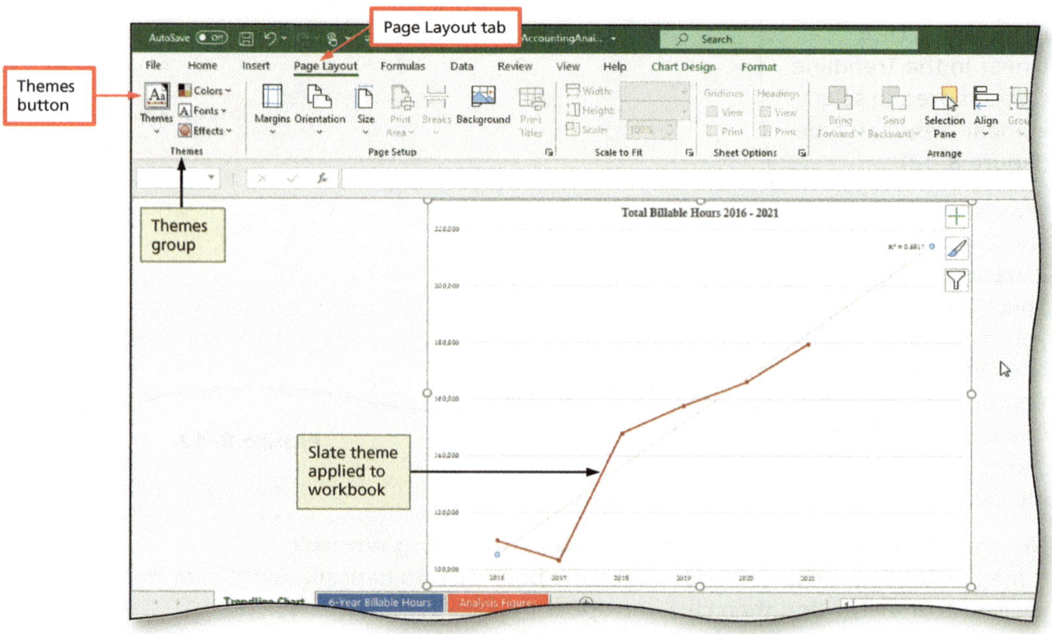

Figure 8–14

More about Trendlines

It is important to take note of the axes when looking at trendlines. Charts with trendlines are often reformatted to start the vertical axis at a number other than zero, particularly when the values on the vertical axis are high. When interpreting a trendline, you should look at the vertical axis to see if it starts at zero. If it does not, be aware that trends represented by the trendline may appear exaggerated. Figure 8–15 shows a chart with a trendline that uses the same data as the chart in Figure 8–14. The difference between the two charts is in the vertical axis, which starts at zero in Figure 8–15 and at 100,000 in Figure 8–14. The difference between the projected values for 2020 and 2021 appears much larger in Figure 8–14 where the axis starts at 100,000. When looking at charts, always check the axes to be sure that the differences shown in the chart are not being overstated visually.

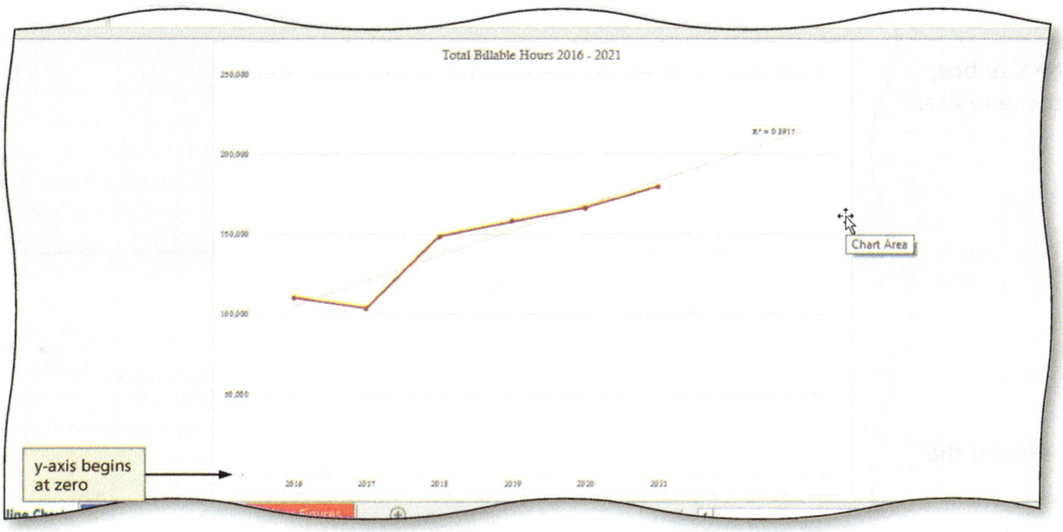

Figure 8–15

To Change the Format of a Data Point

The following steps change the format of the 2018 data point. **Why?** When graphing data, you may want to call visual attention to a particular data point or points.

1

- Slowly click the 2018 data point twice to select the single point. Do not double-click.
- Right-click the selected data point to display the shortcut menu (Figure 8–16).

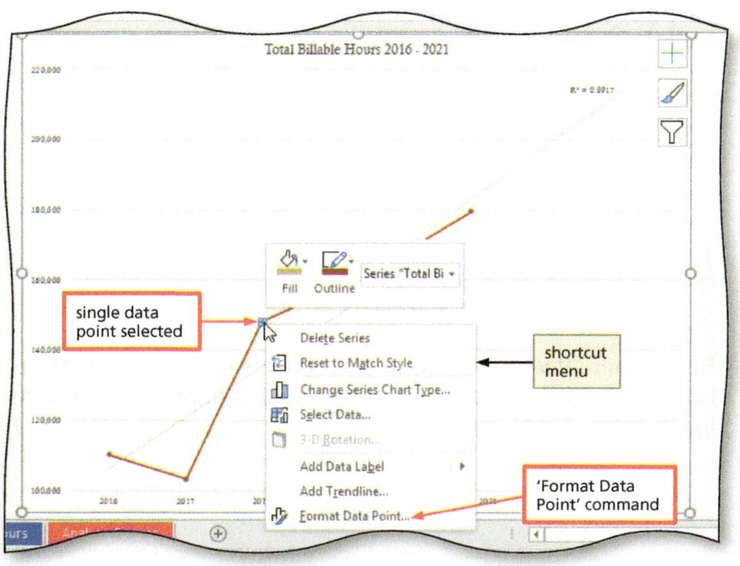

Figure 8–16

2

- Click 'Format Data Point' on the shortcut menu to display the Format Data Point pane.
- Click the 'Fill & Line' button (Format Data Point pane) to display the Fill & Line options.
- Click Marker, and then if necessary, click Marker Options to expand the section.
- Click the Built-in option button to enable changes to the data point (Figure 8–17).
- Select the contents of the Size box, and then type `12` as the new size.

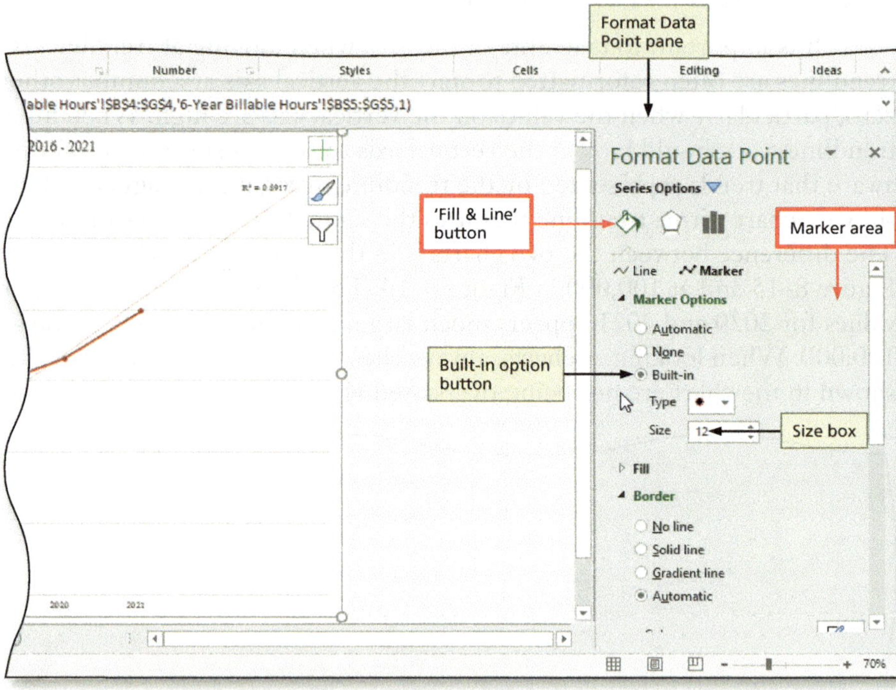

Figure 8–17

3

- If necessary, click Fill to expand the Fill section.
- Click the Color button and then click 'Black, Text 1' in the Theme Colors area to change the color of the data point to black.
- Click away from the data point to view the change (Figure 8–18).
- Close the Format Data Point pane and click the Save button (Quick Access Toolbar) to save the workbook with the same name in the same location.

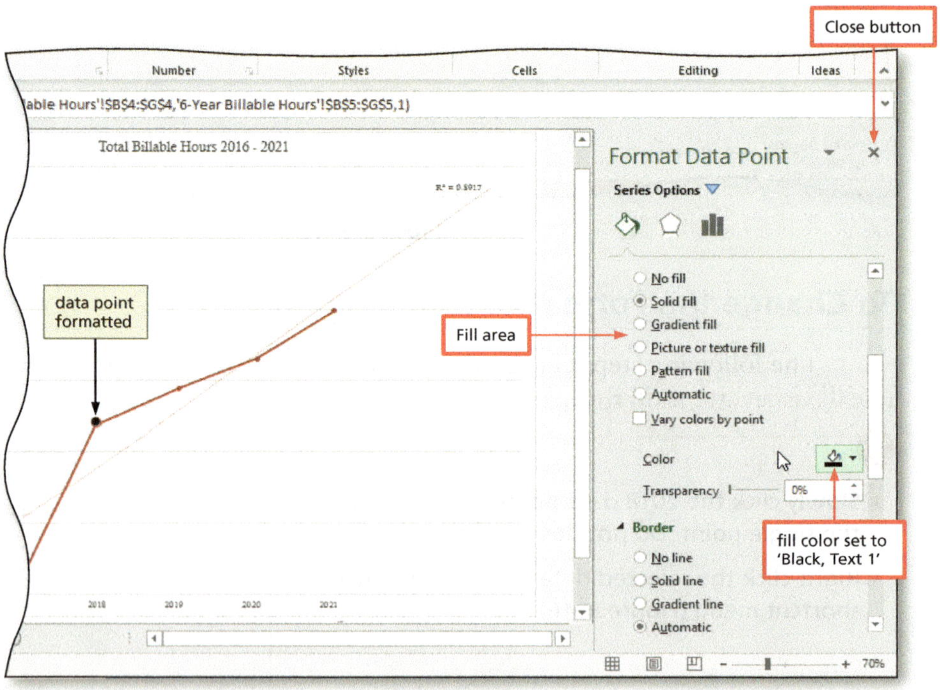

Figure 8–18

Break Point: If you want to take a break, this is a good place to do so. You can exit Excel now. To resume later, start Excel, open the file called SC_EX_8_Bell&RodgersAccountingAnalysis.xlxs, and continue following the steps from this location forward.

Creating and Formatting PivotTable Reports

A PivotTable report, also called a PivotTable, is an interactive tool that summarizes worksheet data. It uses filter buttons in the cells and a pane to change the way the data is presented without changing any of the original data. Normally, when working with data tables or lists of data, each different reorganization of the data requires a new table or list. In contrast, you can reorganize data and examine summaries in a PivotTable report with a few clicks. PivotTable reports allow you to view different summaries of the data quickly and easily, using just a single table.

When creating a PivotTable report, you can use categories in the data to summarize different groups or totals. PivotTables use two types of fields: data fields, which contain values that the PivotTable will summarize, and category fields, which describe the data by categorizing it. Category fields typically correspond to columns in the original data, and data fields correspond to summary values across categories. You can change row and column groupings quickly to summarize the data in different ways or to ask new questions. Reorganizing the table reveals different levels of detail and allows you to analyze specific subgroups.

One PivotTable created in this project is shown in Figure 8–19. It summarizes the Bell & Rodgers data to show the total revenue and average revenue in 2020 and 2021 for each level of experience by accounting type (Auditing, Forensics, General, Investment, and Taxes). The filter button in cell A4 filters the results by experience, and the filter button in cell B4 filters the results by accounting type. Columns C and D show the values for the total revenue in 2020 and 2021, and columns E and F show the values for the average revenue in 2020 and 2021.

BTW

Selecting PivotTable Ranges

When creating PivotTables, you can click anywhere in the range that contains the data. You do not have to select the range.

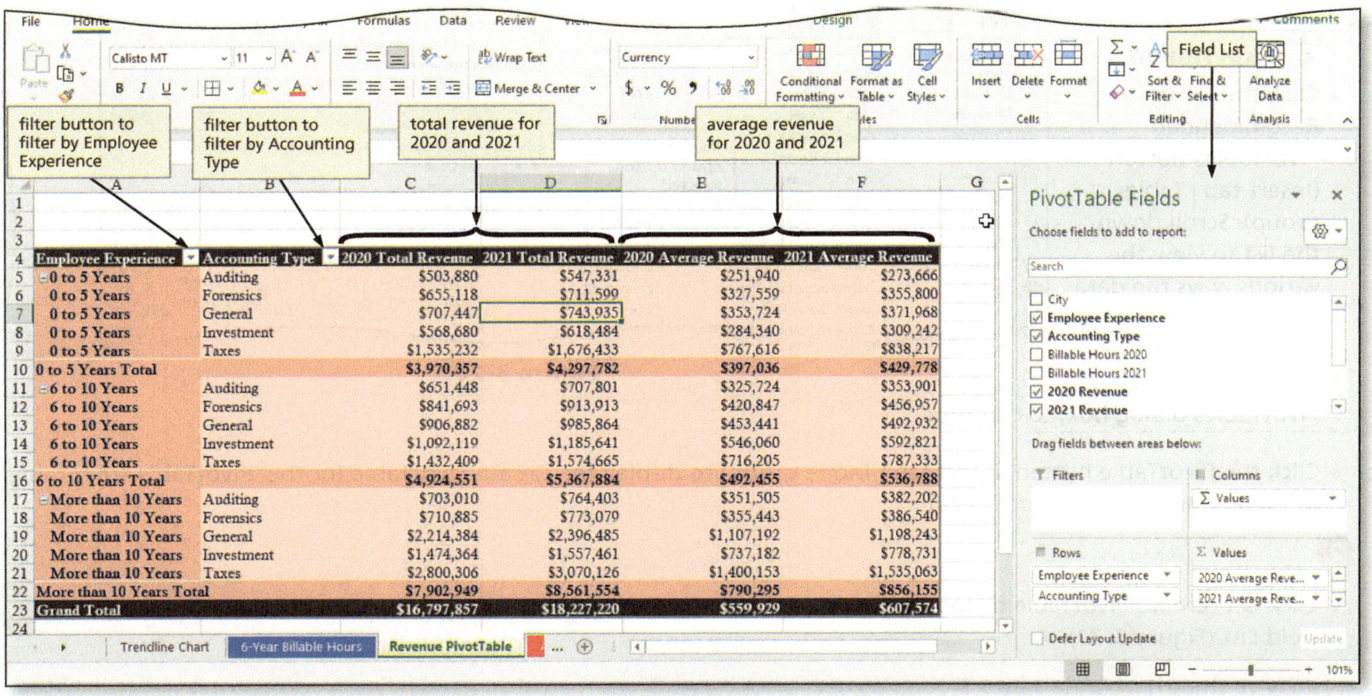

Figure 8–19

Consider This

How do you determine which fields to use in a PivotTable?

You can create PivotTable and PivotChart reports in almost any configuration of your existing data. To use this powerful tool effectively, you need to create these reports with various questions in mind. Look at the categories you can use to describe your data and think about how the various categories can interact. Common questions relate to how the data changes over time and how the data varies in geographical locations, such as states or regions, different functional groups within an organization, different product groupings, and demographic groupings, such as age.

To Create a Blank PivotTable

The following steps create a blank PivotTable report using the ribbon. **Why?** Creating a blank PivotTable allows you to create a framework within which to analyze the available data. When you create a PivotTable, each column heading from your original data will represent a field accessible via the Field List (formerly called the PivotTable Fields task pane).

1

- Click the Analysis Figures sheet tab to make the worksheet active.
- Click cell B3 to select a cell containing data for the PivotTable.
- Display the Insert tab.

Experiment

- Click the Recommended PivotTables button (Insert tab | Tables group). Scroll down the list to view the various ways the data might be represented as a PivotTable. Click Cancel (Recommend PivotTables dialog box) to continue.

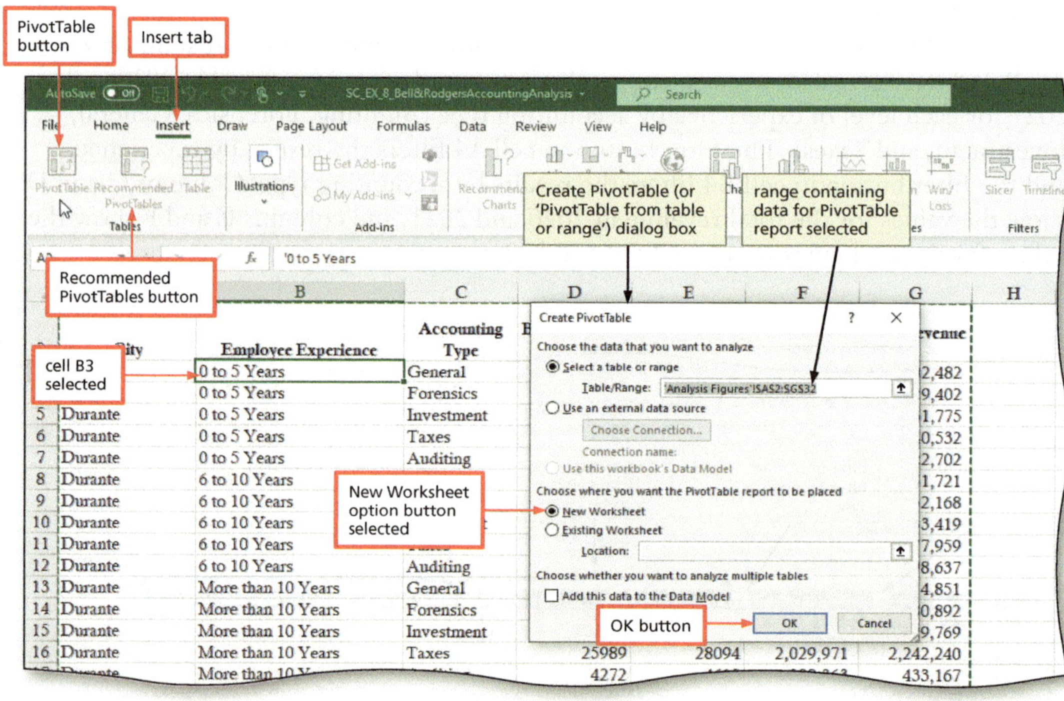

Figure 8–20

- Click the PivotTable button (Insert tab | Tables group) to display the Create PivotTable (or the 'PivotTable from table or range') dialog box (Figure 8–20).

2

- Click OK (Create PivotTable dialog box) to create a blank PivotTable report on a new worksheet and display the Field List (Figure 8–21).

Q&A

Why is the PivotTable blank?

When you create a PivotTable, you first create the structure. The resulting PivotTable is blank until you add fields to it, which you will do in the next set of steps.

My Field List just disappeared. What happened?

If you click outside of the PivotTable, the pane no longer will appear. To redisplay the pane, click in the PivotTable.

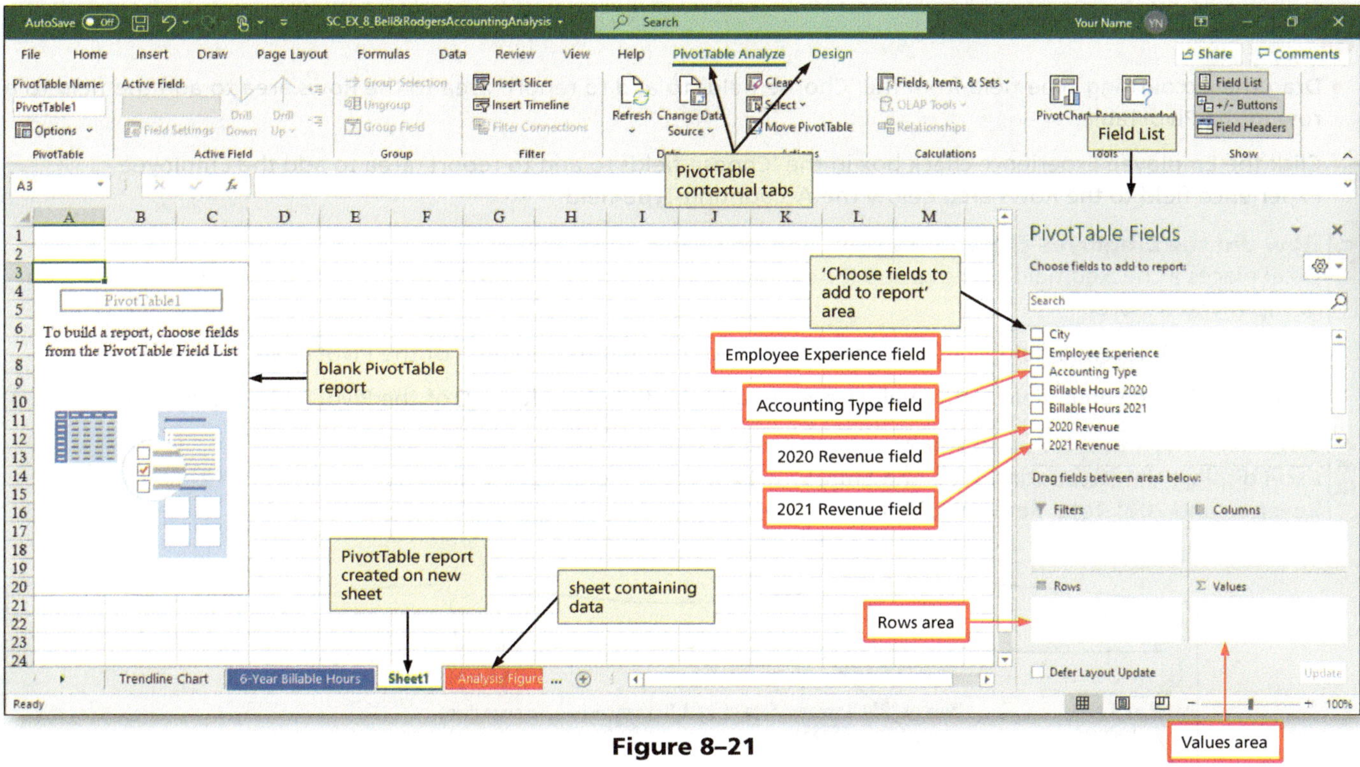

Figure 8–21

Other Ways

1. Click cell in range, click Recommended PivotTables (Insert tab | Tables group), click Blank PivotTable button (Recommended PivotTables dialog box), click OK

To Add Data to the PivotTable

Why? Once the blank PivotTable is created, it needs to be populated using any or all of the fields in the Field List. You can add data by selecting check boxes in the Field List or by dragging fields from the Choose fields area to the one of the four boxed areas in the lower part of the pane. Once you add a field, it becomes a button in the pane, with its own button menu. Table 8–1 describes the four areas in the Field List and their common usage.

Table 8–1 Field Areas in the PivotTable Fields Pane

Areas	Use
Filters	Fields added to the Filters area create a report filter and filter button in the PivotTable, representing a subset that meets a selection criterion.
Columns	Normally, Excel creates a field in the Columns area when multiple fields are dragged to the Values area. Fields directly added to the Columns area should contain summary numeric data.
Rows	Fields added to the Rows area become rows in the PivotTable. Subsequent fields added to the Rows area become subsets of the first field.
Values	Fields added to the Values area must contain numeric data from the source data.

The following step adds data to the PivotTable. The rows will show the accounting type and, within that, the years of employee experience. As you add the 2020 Total Revenue and 2021 Total Revenue fields to the Values area, Excel will create columns.

1

- Drag the Accounting Type field from the 'Choose fields to add to report' area to the Rows area to add the field to a row in the PivotTable.
- Click the Employee Experience check box in the 'Choose fields to add to report' area to add the Employee Experience field to the Rows area below the Accounting Type field.

Q&A **How did the Employee Experience field end up in the Rows area?**
Excel places a checked field in the group it determines is correct for that field. You can drag the field to a different group if you choose.

- Drag the 2020 Revenue field to the Values area to add the field to column B of the PivotTable.
- Drag the 2021 Revenue field to the Values area to add the field to column C of the PivotTable (Figure 8–22).

Q&A **What is shown in the PivotTable?**
Excel displays the Accounting Type and Employee Experience fields as rows in the PivotTable. The 2020 Total Revenue and 2021 Total Revenue display as columns.

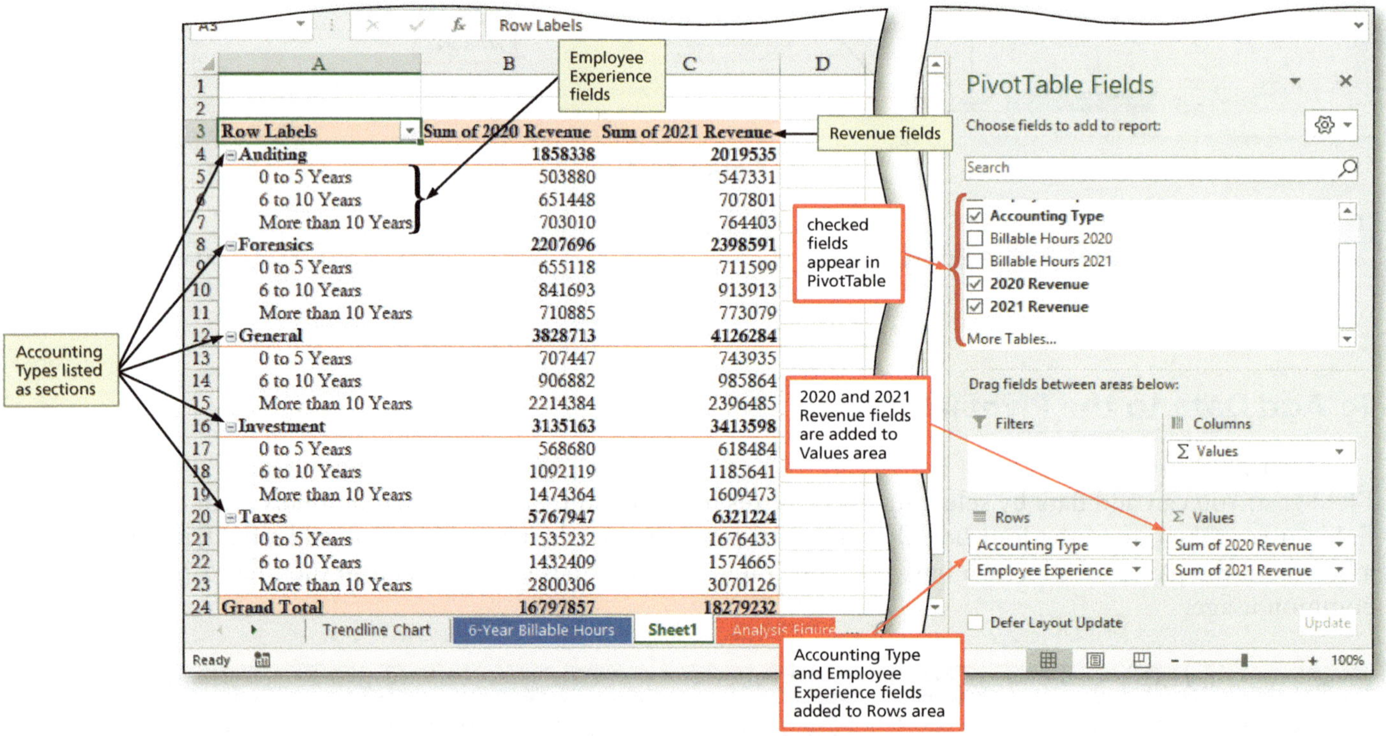

Figure 8–22

Other Ways

1. Click check box for each field name (Field List)

To Change the Layout of a PivotTable

You can display a PivotTable in one of three layouts; however, sometimes you may want to change the layout. **Why?** When using multiple row labels, a different layout can make identifying the groups and subgroups easier for the reader. By default, PivotTable reports are presented in a compact layout. The following steps change the layout of the PivotTable report to the tabular layout and then add item labels to all rows. The tabular layout will display totals below each accounting type.

1

- If necessary, display the Design tab.
- Click the Report Layout button (Design tab | Layout group) to display the Report Layout menu (Figure 8–23).

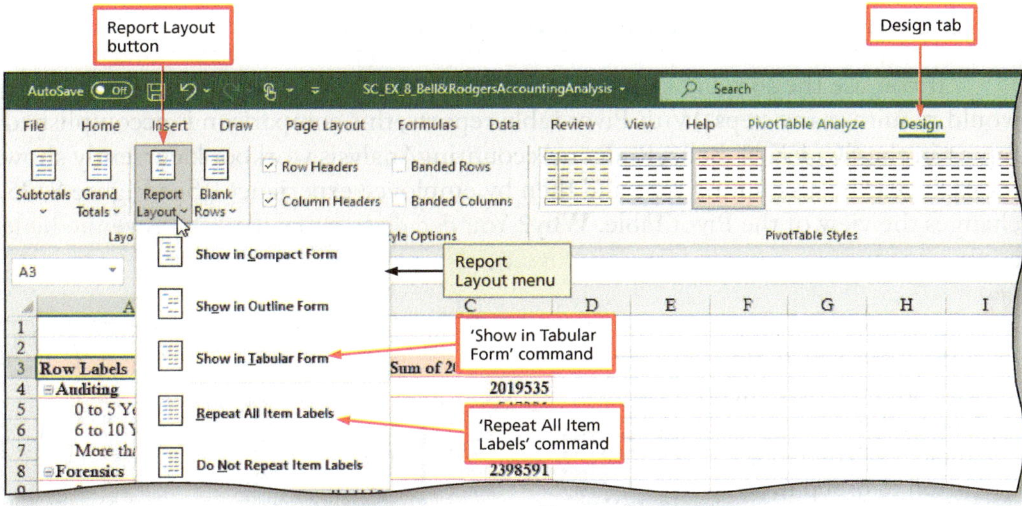

Figure 8–23

2

- Click 'Show in Tabular Form' to display the PivotTable report in a tabular format (Figure 8–24).

Experiment

- Click all the layout options to review the differences in the layout. When done, click 'Show in Tabular Form' once again.

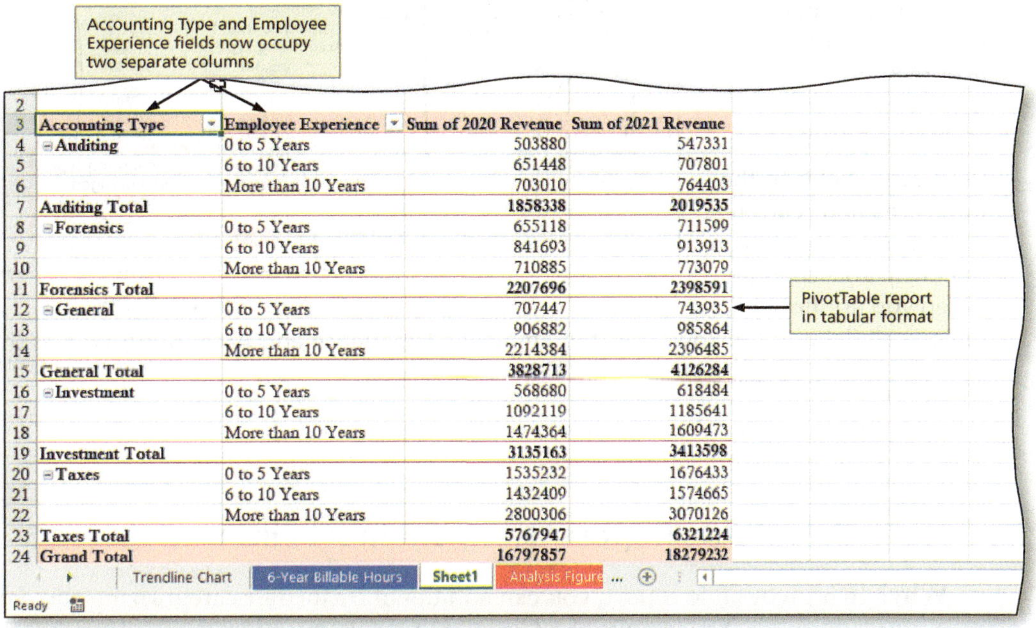

Figure 8–24

3

- Click the Report Layout button (Design tab | Layout group) again, and then click 'Repeat All Item Labels' to display Accounting Type labels for all Employee Experience entries (Figure 8–25).

Experiment

- Point to any cell in column C or D to see the ScreenTip that displays information about the value.

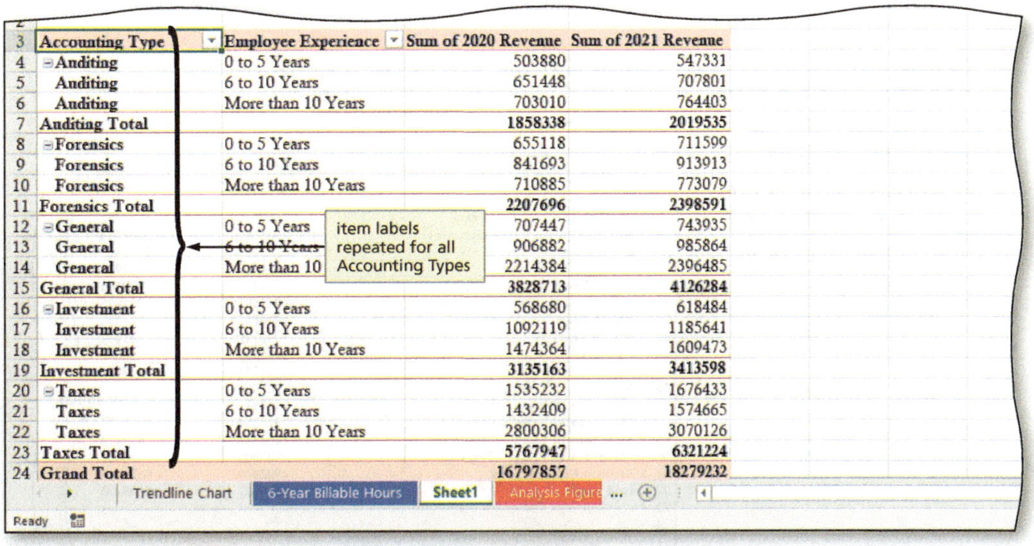

Figure 8–25

To Change the View of a PivotTable Report

If you use the sort and summary features in Excel, comparing the revenue for each service type and region would require many steps. With PivotTable reports, this comparison is accomplished quickly. The PivotTable report in the SC_EX_8_Bell&RodgersAccountingAnalysis workbook currently shows the sum of the revenue for each year by accounting type and then by employee experience. (See Figure 8–25.) The following step changes the view of the PivotTable. **Why?** You decide to show the total revenue by level of experience for each accounting type.

1

- In the Rows area (Field List), drag the Accounting Type button below the Employee Experience button to group total sales by Employee Experience (rather than by Accounting Type) (Figure 8–26).

Experiment

- Drag other fields to the Rows area and rearrange it to see how the data in the PivotTable changes. When you are finished, remove all fields in the Rows area but Employee Experience and Accounting Type as shown in Figure 8–26.

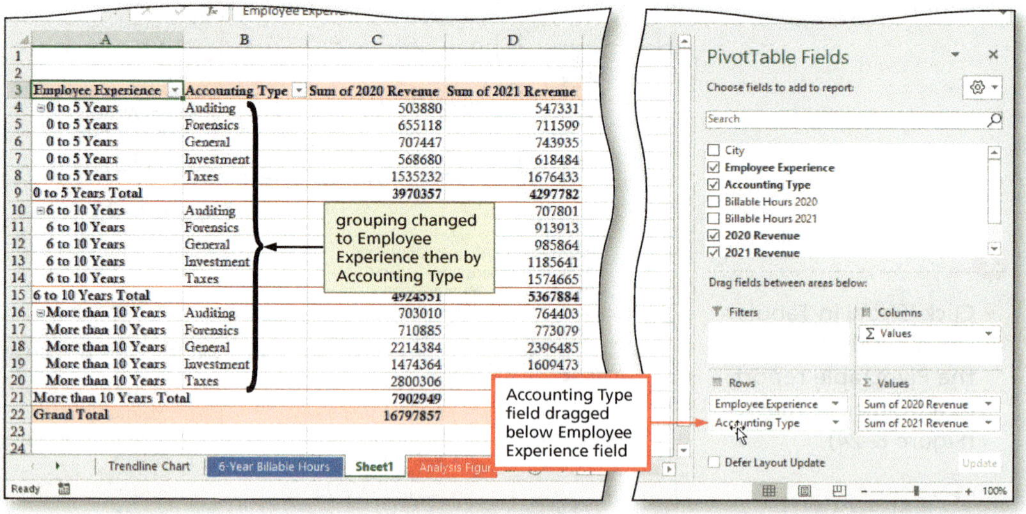

Figure 8–26

Other Ways

1. In the Rows area, click Accounting Type arrow, click Move Down on menu

To Filter a PivotTable Report Using a Report Filter

Why? In a PivotTable report, you can add detail by further categorizing the data to focus on a particular subgroup or subgroups. You can use the City field to view sales in a particular venue by service type and region. Viewing a PivotTable report for a subset of data that meets a selection criterion is known as filtering. The following steps add a report filter to change the view of the PivotTable and then filter the PivotTable by City.

1

- Drag the City field from the 'Choose fields to add to report' area (Field List) to the Filters area to create a report filter in the PivotTable (Figure 8–27).

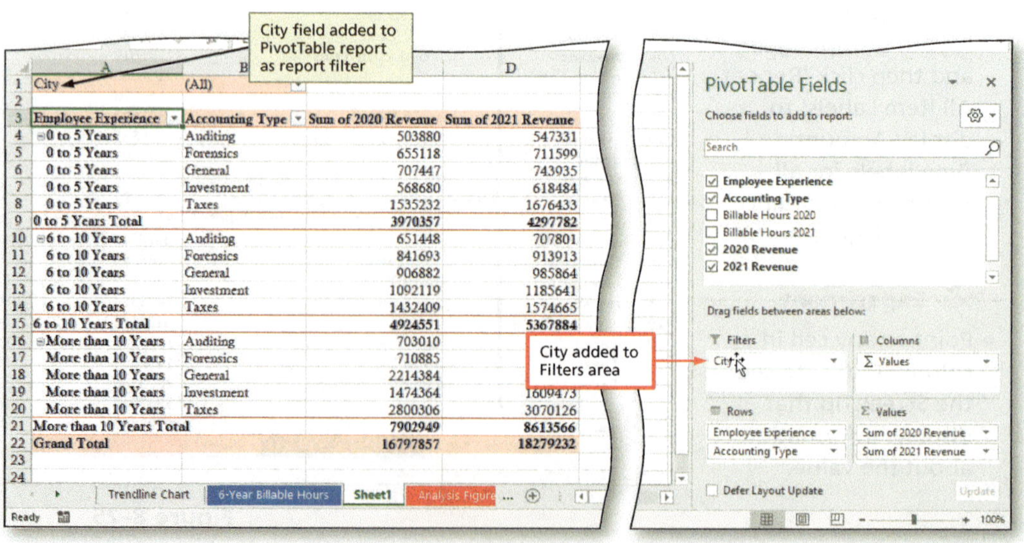

Figure 8–27

2

- Click the filter button in cell B1 to display the filter menu for column B, City in this case.
- Click Durante on the filter menu to select the Durante criterion (Figure 8–28).

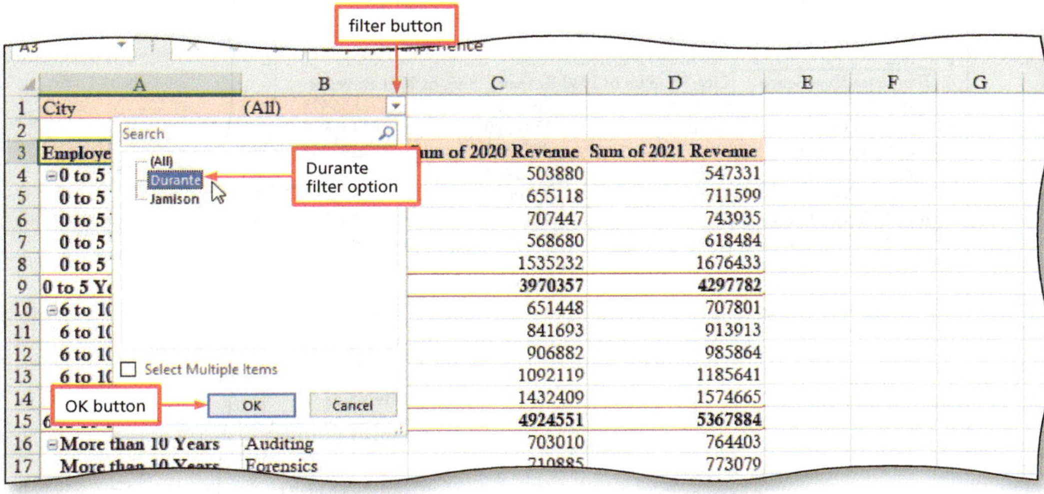

Figure 8–28

3

- Click OK to display totals for Durante only (Figure 8–29).

Q&A **What is shown now in the PivotTable report?**
Now the PivotTable shows total revenue for each level of experience and accounting type for Durante only.

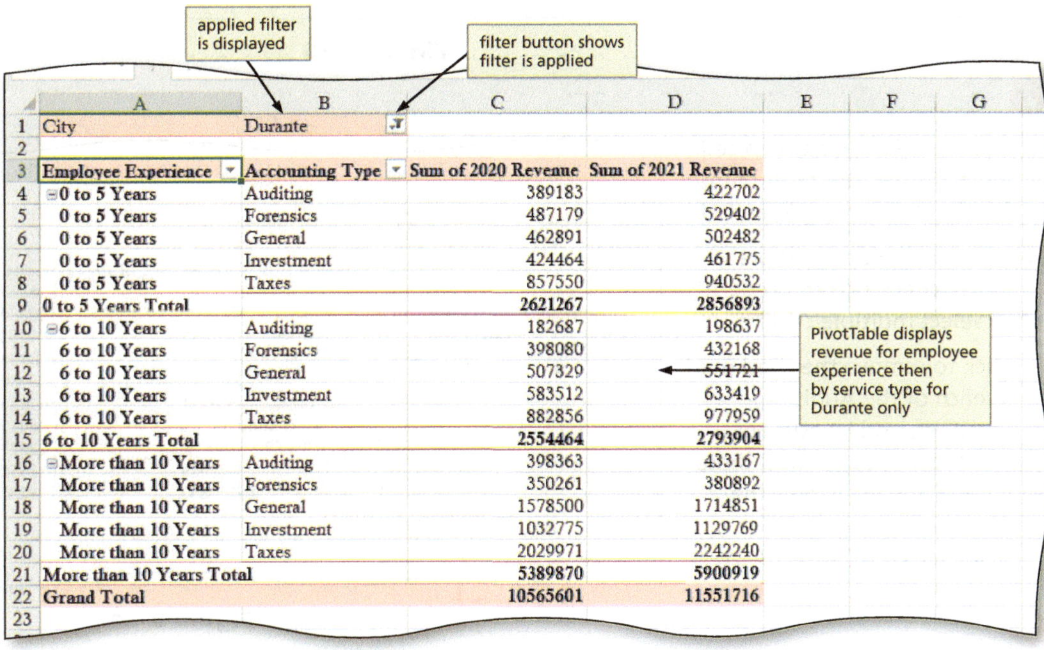

Figure 8–29

To Filter a PivotTable Report Using Multiple Selection Criteria

Why? You may need to identify a subset that is defined by more than one filter criterion. The following steps change the filter field and select multiple criteria on which to filter.

1

- Drag the Accounting Type button from the Rows area to the Filters area.
- Drag the City button from the Filters area to the Rows area below Employee Experience (Figure 8–30).

Q&A **What does the PivotTable now show?**
Excel now filters the entire report by Accounting type and does not show that as a detail line within the report.

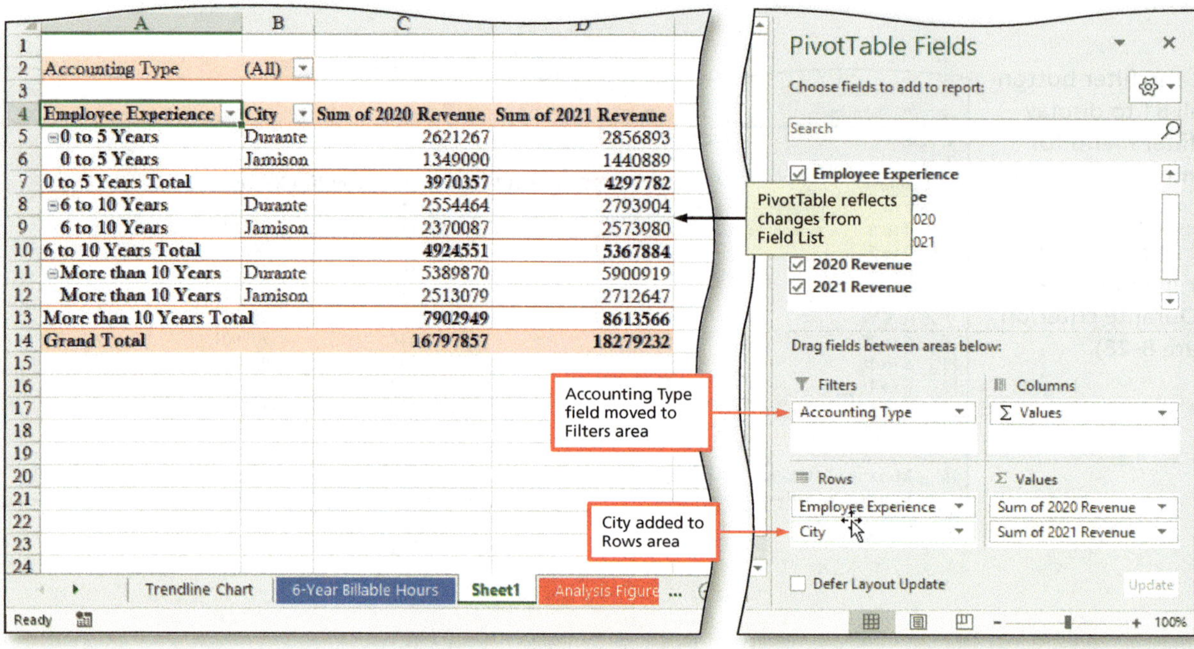

Figure 8–30

2

- Click the filter button in cell B2 to display the filter menu for the Accounting Type field.
- Click the 'Select Multiple Items' check box to prepare to select multiple criteria.
- Click to remove the checkmark in each of the Auditing, Forensics, and Investment check boxes to deselect these criteria and leave only the General and Taxes service plans selected (Figure 8–31).

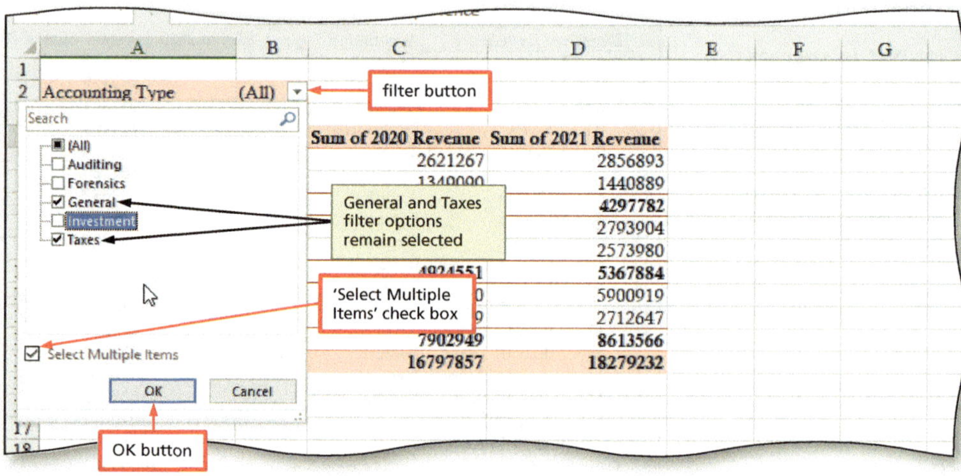

Figure 8–31

3

- Click OK to display revenue totals for General and Taxes accounting types in the cities of Durante and Jamison (Figure 8–32).

Q&A **How do I know which criteria have been selected?**
With a multiple item filter, you need to click the filter button to see which criteria have been selected.

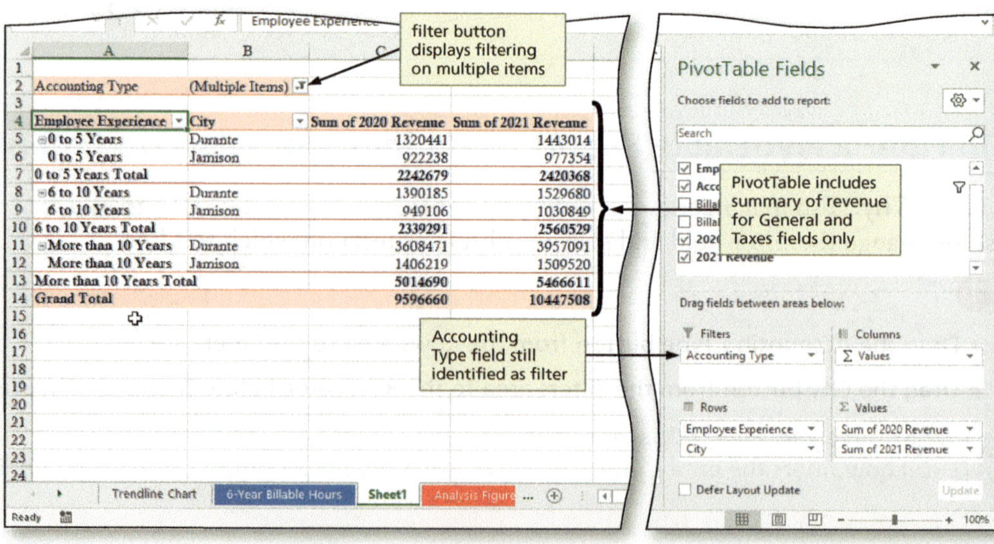

Figure 8–32

To Remove a Report Filter from a PivotTable Report

Why? When you no longer need to display filtered data in a PivotTable, you can remove the filter easily. The following step removes the Accounting Type report filter from the PivotTable report.

1

- Click the filter button in cell B2 and then click the (All) check box to include all service type criteria in the PivotTable report.
- Click OK.
- Drag the Accounting Type button out of the Filters area (Field List) to remove the field from the PivotTable report (Figure 8–33).

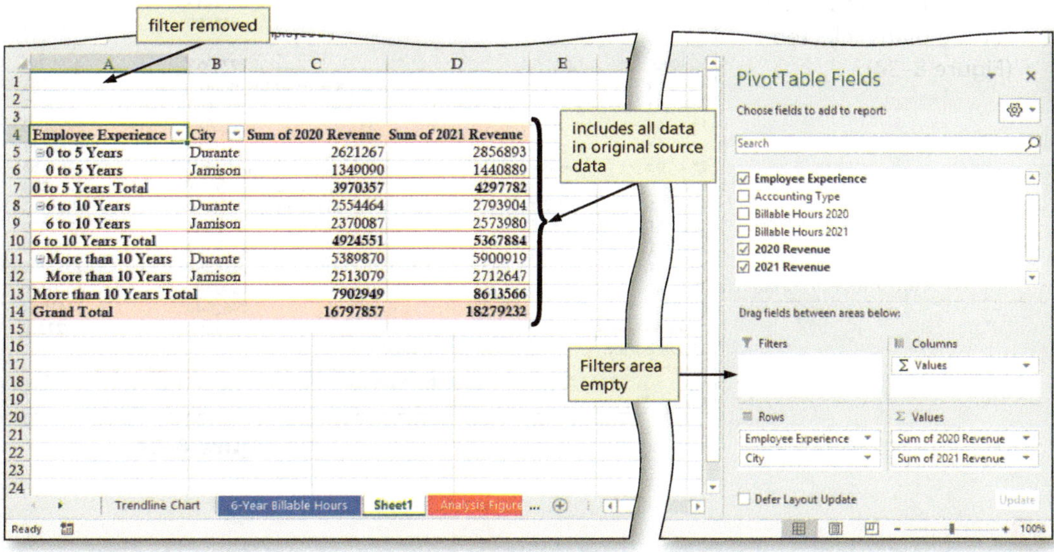

Figure 8–33

Q&A **Should I drag it to a specific location?**
No. You can drag it out of the box to any blank area on the worksheet.

To Remove and Add Data to the PivotTable Report

The following steps remove the City field from the Rows area and add the Accounting Type field.

1. In the Field List, drag the City button out of the Rows area to remove the field from the report.
2. Click the Accounting Type check box in the 'Choose fields to add to report' area to add the Accounting Type field to the Rows area below the Employee Experience field.

To Filter a PivotTable Report Using the Row Label Filter

Report filters are added to the PivotTable report by adding a field to the Filters area of the Field List. **Why?** In a PivotTable report, you may want to look at a subset of data based on fields that are already in use. When the field of interest is already part of the PivotTable and included in the Rows area of the Field List, you can use row label filters to view a subset of the data. Like other filter buttons, row label filters display within the column heading. When you click the filter button, Excel displays a menu of available fields. The following steps use a row label filter for Accounting Type to restrict data in the PivotTable to the General and Taxes accounting types.

1

- Click the filter button in cell B4 to display the filter menu for the Accounting Type field.

Q&A **I do not have a filter button in cell B4. How do I access the filter?**
The filter buttons may be hidden. Click the Field Headers button (PivotTable Analyze tab | Show group) to turn on the field headers and make the filter buttons visible.

Why does cell B4 not appear selected when I use the filter button?
Filtering happens independently of cell selection. You do not need to select the cell in which the filter button is located in order to use the filter.

- Click the Auditing, Forensics, and Investment check boxes on the filter menu to leave only the General and Taxes service plans selected (Figure 8–34).

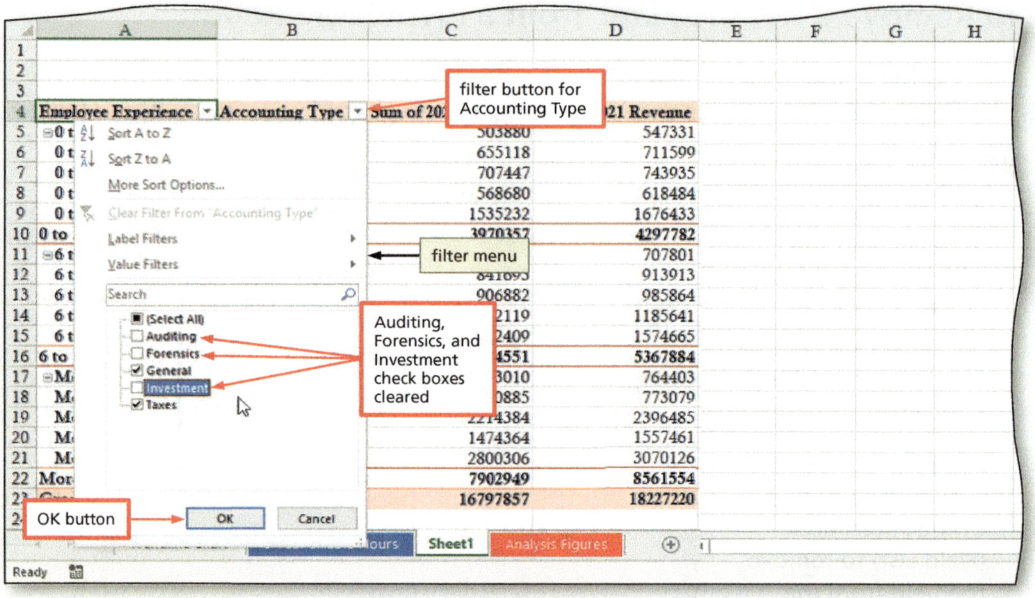

Figure 8–34

2

- Click OK to display totals for General and Taxes only, categorized by experience (Figure 8–35).

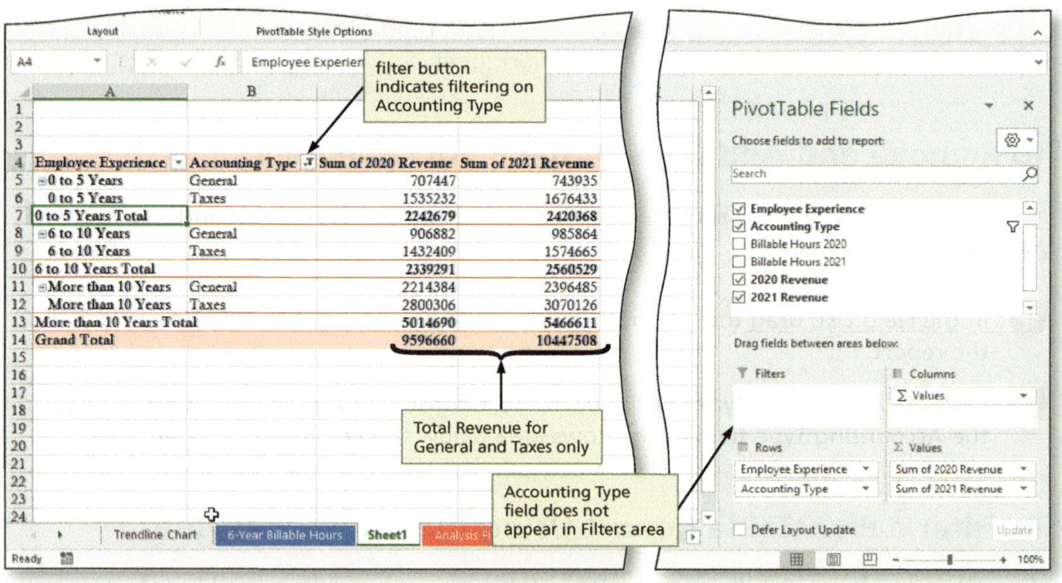

Figure 8–35

To Clear the Filter

Why? Once you have reviewed the subset of data, you may want to remove the criteria using the Row Label filter to display all records. The following steps clear the filter in order to display all records.

1

- Click the filter button in cell B4 again to display the filter menu for the Accounting Type field (Figure 8–36).

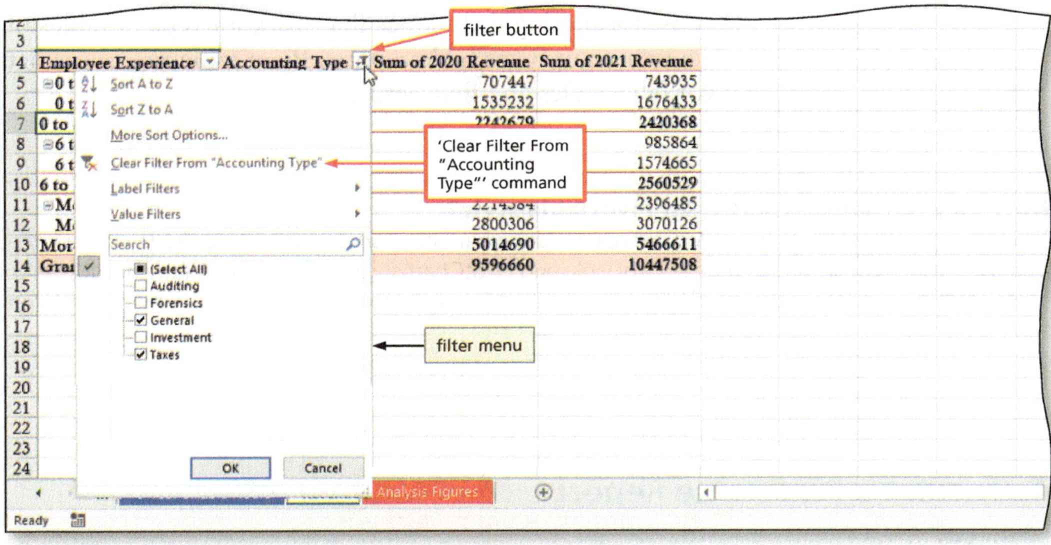

Figure 8–36

2

- Click 'Clear Filter From "Accounting Type"' on the filter menu to display totals for all service types in all regions (Figure 8–37).

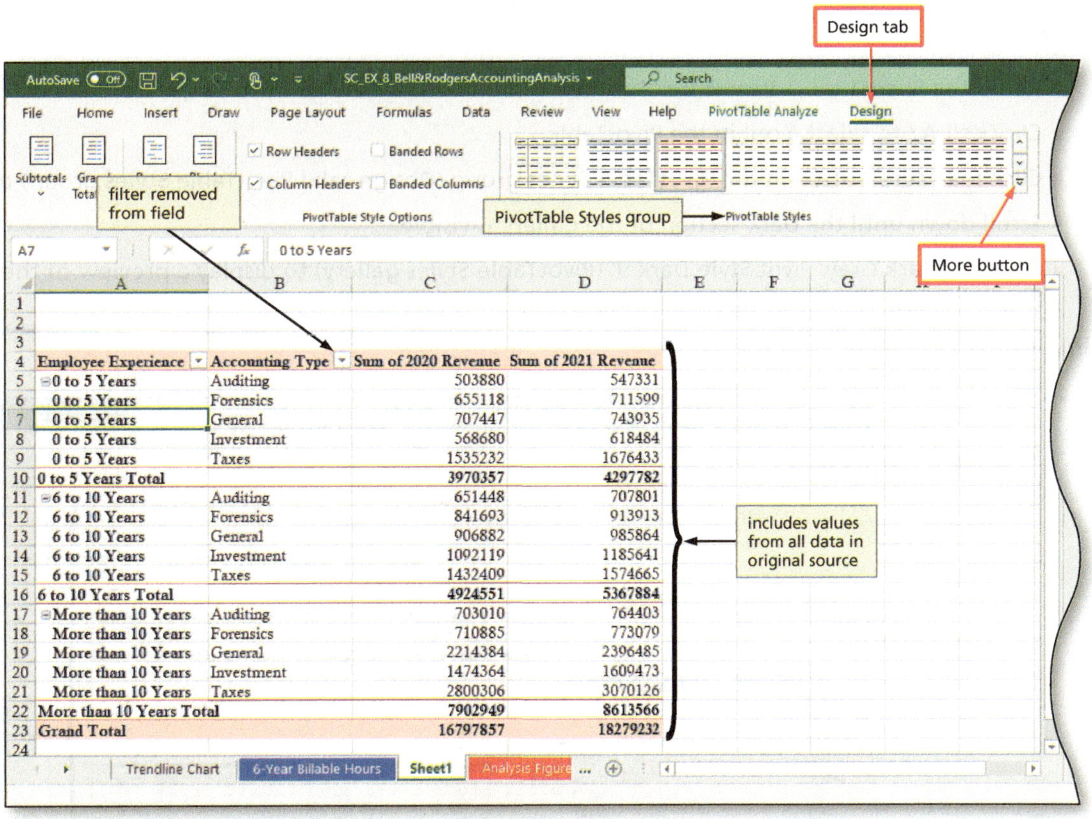

Figure 8–37

Other Ways

1. Click filter button, click (Select All) check box on filter menu, click OK

Formatting PivotTable Reports

You can use several formatting options to enhance the appearance of PivotTable reports and make the content easier to read. Excel includes a number of preset PivotTable report styles to simplify this task. These styles function in a similar fashion to the Excel table styles. Take care when formatting PivotTable reports, however, because formatting techniques that work for regular tables of data do not behave in the same fashion in PivotTable reports. PivotTable report formatting requires the use of PivotTable styles and field settings.

Consider This

How do you choose a particular PivotTable style?

When you plan PivotTables and PivotCharts, consider what information you want to display in each report. As you are developing a report, review the galleries of PivotTable and PivotChart styles to find the best one to display your data. For example, some PivotTable styles include banded rows and columns, which can make it easier to scan and interpret the report.

To Format a PivotTable Report

Why? PivotTable reports benefit from formatting to enhance their readability. The following steps format a PivotTable report by applying a PivotTable style and specifying number formats for the fields.

1

- Name the Sheet1 tab, **`Revenue PivotTable`**, and set the color to Tan, Accent 2.
- Click cell A7 to select a cell in the PivotTable.
- Click the More button in the PivotTable Styles group (Design tab | PivotTable Styles group) to expand the gallery.
- Scroll down until the Dark section of the gallery is visible.
- Point to 'Dark Gray, Pivot Style Dark 9' (PivotTable Styles gallery) to display a preview of the style in the PivotTable (Figure 8–38).

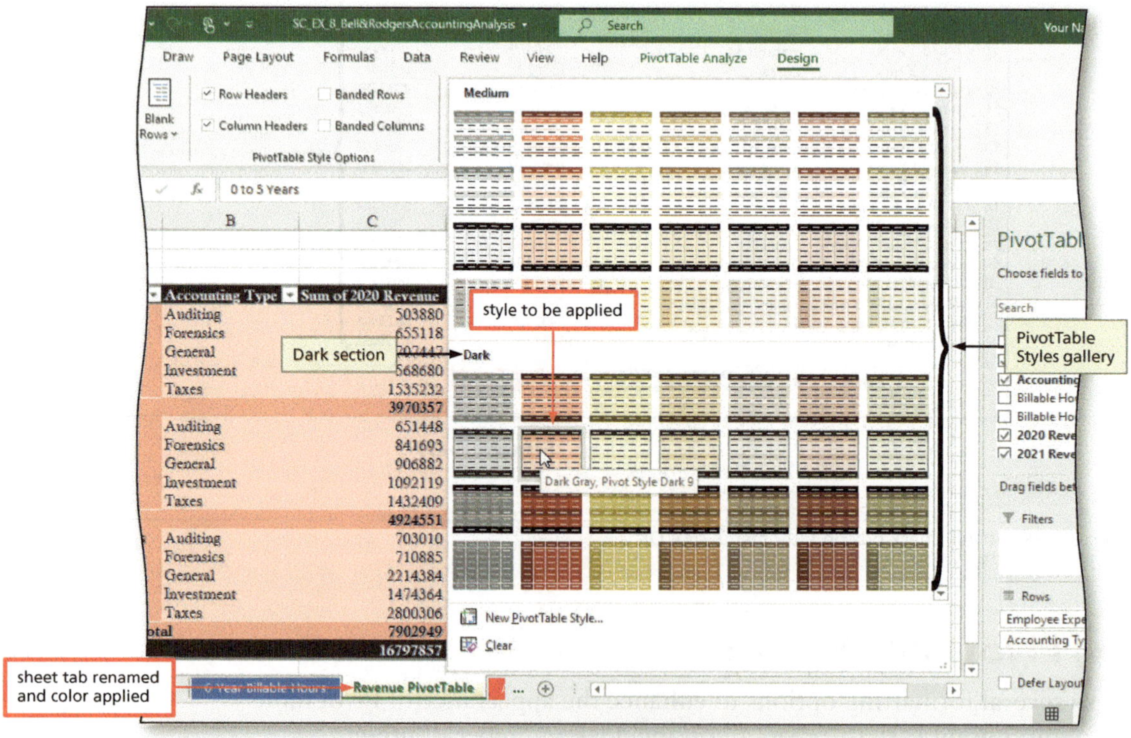

Figure 8–38

2

- Click 'Dark Gray, Pivot Style Dark 9' in the PivotTable Styles gallery to apply the style to the PivotTable report.
- Right-click cell C6 and then click Number Format on the shortcut menu to display the Format Cells dialog box.
- Click Currency in the Category list (Format Cells dialog box) to select the Currency number format.
- Type 0 in the Decimal places box to specify no decimal places (Figure 8–39).

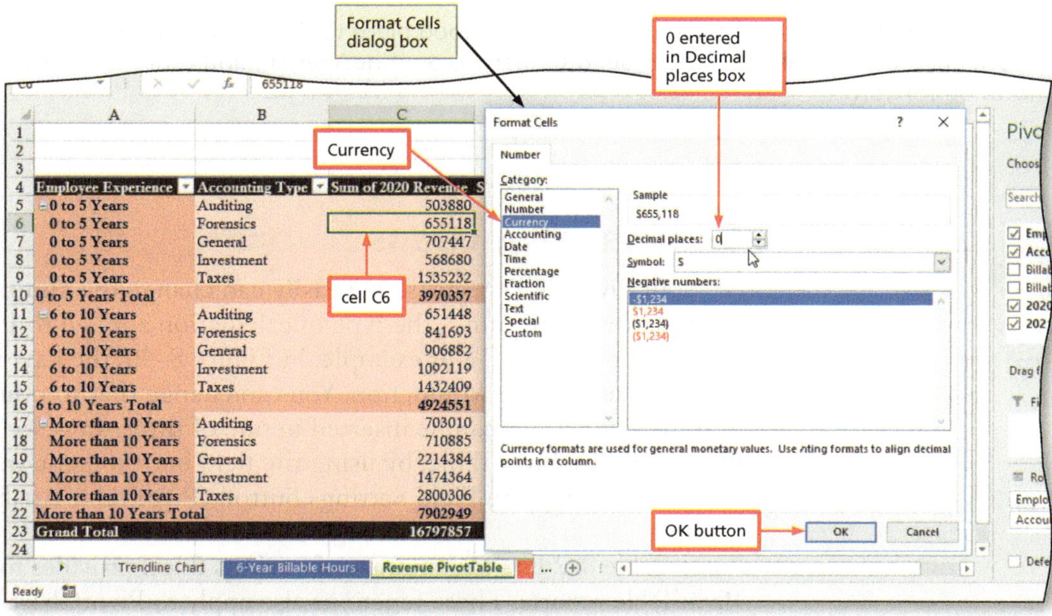

Figure 8–39

Q&A **Can I use the formatting options on the Home tab?**
Yes, but you would have to highlight all of the cells first and then apply the formatting. The Number Format command is easier.

3

- Click OK to apply the Currency style with no decimal places to all 2020 revenue values in the PivotTable report.

Q&A **Why does the number format change apply to all Revenue values?**
In a PivotTable, when you format a single cell using Number Format, that formatting is applied to the entire set of values to which that single cell belongs.

4

- Right-click cell D6 and then apply the Currency number format with zero decimal places to all 2021 revenue values.
- Click cell E24 to deselect the PivotTable report.
- Click the Save button on the Quick Access Toolbar to save the workbook (Figure 8–40).

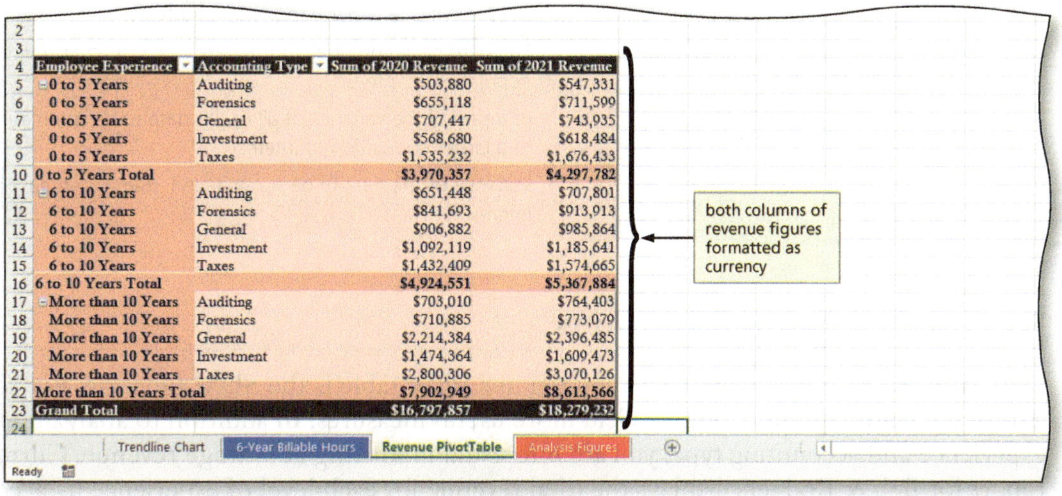

Figure 8–40

Break Point: If you want to take a break, this is a good place to do so. You can exit Excel now. To resume later, start Excel, open the file called SC_EX_8_Bell&RodgersAccountingAnalysis, and continue following the steps from this location forward.

Summary Functions

In PivotTable reports, you easily can change the **summary function**, the function that determines the type of calculation applied to PivotTable data, such as SUM or COUNT. For example, in Figure 8–40, the data is totaled for 2020 and 2021 using a SUM function. You can change that to other summary functions. Summary functions can be inserted in one of three ways: by using the shortcut menu of a cell in the PivotTable, by using the field button menu in the Values area (Field List), or by using the Field Settings button (PivotTable Analyze tab | Active Field group).

Table 8–2 lists the summary functions Excel provides for analysis of data in PivotTable reports. These functions also apply to PivotChart Reports.

Table 8–2 Summary Functions for PivotTable Report and PivotChart Report Data Analysis

Summary Function	Description
Sum	Sum of the values (default function for numeric source data)
Count	Number of data values
Average	Average of the values
Max	Largest value
Min	Smallest value
Product	Product of the values
Count Numbers	Number of data values that contain numeric data
StdDev.s	Estimate of the standard deviation of all of the data to be summarized, used when data is a sample of a larger population of interest
StdDev.p	Standard deviation of all of the data to be summarized, used when data is the entire population of interest
Var.s	Estimate of the variance of all of the data to be summarized, used when data is a sample of a larger population of interest
Var.p	Variance of the data to be summarized, used when data is the entire population of interest

To Switch Summary Functions

Why? The default summary function in a PivotTable is the SUM function. For some comparisons, using a different summary function will yield more useful measures. In addition to analyzing the total revenue by experience and accounting type, you are interested in looking at average revenue. Currently, the PivotTable report for Bell & Rodgers displays the total revenue for each level of experience by accounting type. Average revenue by accounting type and then by experience might be a better measure for comparing the revenue. The following steps switch summary functions in a PivotTable using the shortcut menu.

1

- Right-click cell C5 to display the shortcut menu and then point to 'Summarize Values By' to display the Summarize Values By submenu (Figure 8–41).

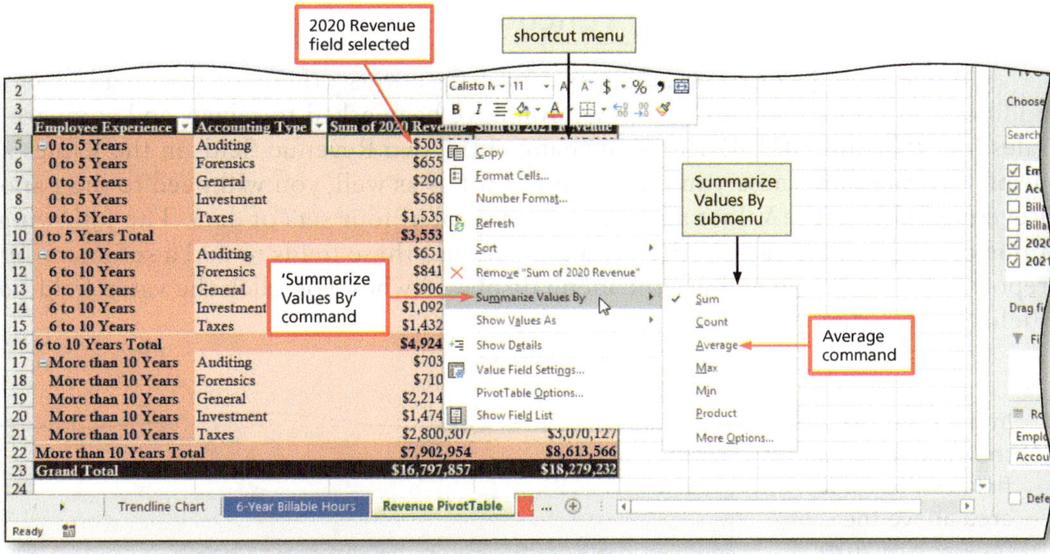

Figure 8–41

2

- Click Average on the Summarize Values By submenu to change the summary function from Sum to Average (Figure 8–42).

Q&A **Why did the column title in cell C4 change?**
When you change a summary function, the column heading automatically updates to reflect the new summary function chosen.

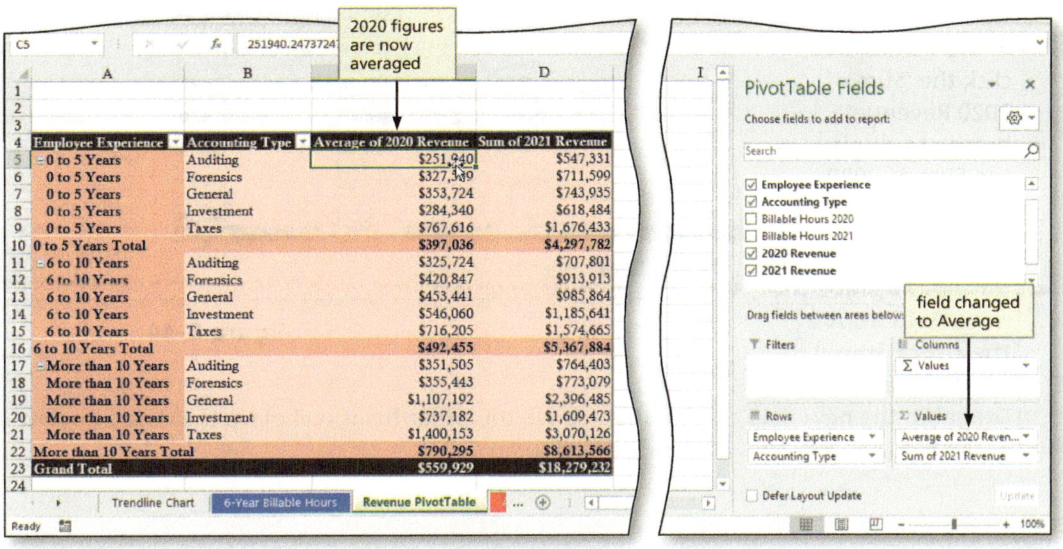

Figure 8–42

3

- Repeat Steps 1 and 2 to change the summary function used in column D from Sum to Average (Figure 8–43).

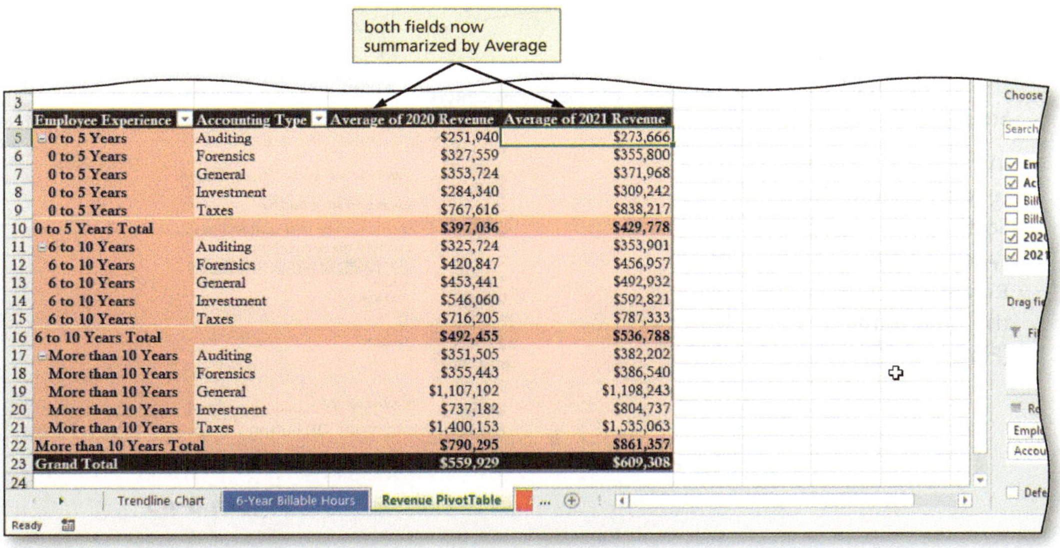

Figure 8–43

To Insert a New Summary Function

Why? In addition to changing summary functions, you may need to add new fields to analyze additional or more complex questions. You have been asked to review and compare both total and average sales for 2020 and 2021. Earlier you changed the two Revenue fields in the Values area (Field List) to display averages. Because you now want the totals as well, you will need to drag another copy of the two Revenue fields to the Values area, creating a total of four sets of data. The following steps add a second value calculation for each of the two years and use these fields to add a summary function in the PivotTable report. This time, you will use the menu displayed when you click the value field button to access the Value Field Settings dialog box.

1

- In the Field List, drag the 2020 Revenue field to the Values area above the 'Average of 2020 Revenue' button to add a third field to the PivotTable.
- In the Values area, click the 'Sum of 2020 Revenue' button to display the Sum of 2020 Revenue menu (Figure 8–44).

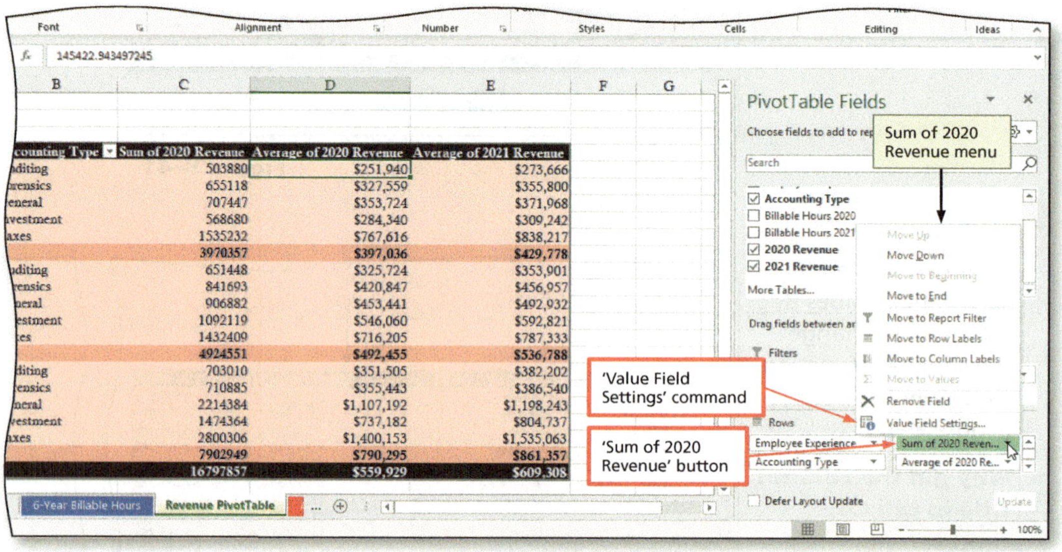

Figure 8–44

Q&A **Why did I place the new field above the other items in the Values area?**
Dragging the new field to a location above the other fields will place the data in a new column before the others in the PivotTable report, in this case in column C.

2

- Click 'Value Field Settings' to display the Value Field Settings dialog box.
- In the Custom Name text box (Value Field Settings dialog box), type **`2020 Total Revenue`** to change the field name (Figure 8–45).

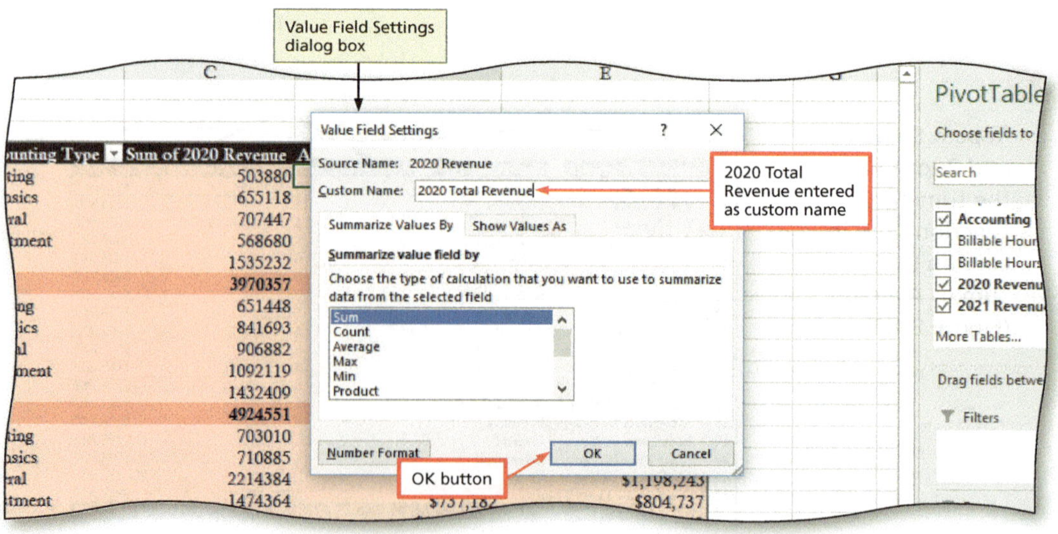

Figure 8–45

3

- Click OK (Value Field Settings dialog box) to apply the custom name.
- In the Field List, drag the 2021 Revenue field to the Values area to add a fourth field. Place it between the '2020 Total Revenue' button and the 'Average of 2020 Revenue' button.
- In the Values area, click the 'Sum of 2021 Revenue' button to display its menu, and then click 'Value Field Settings' to display the Value Field Settings dialog box.
- In the Custom Name text box, type **`2021 Total Revenue`** and then click OK (Value Field Settings dialog box) to rename the field.
- Using the buttons in the Values area, rename the other two fields to customize the column headings in cells E4 and F4 as shown in Figure 8–46.
- Using the shortcut menu, if necessary, format the values in columns C and then D to the Currency category, 0 decimal places, and the $ symbol (Figure 8–46).

Q&A

How many items should I have in the Values area now?
You can use the scroll buttons in the Values area to see the four fields: 2020 Total Revenue, 2021 Total Revenue, 2020 Average Revenue, and 2021 Average Revenue.

My format change did not change all of the cells. What did I do wrong?
You may have formatted a single cell using the ribbon. To format all numbers in the column, use the Number Format command on the shortcut menu.

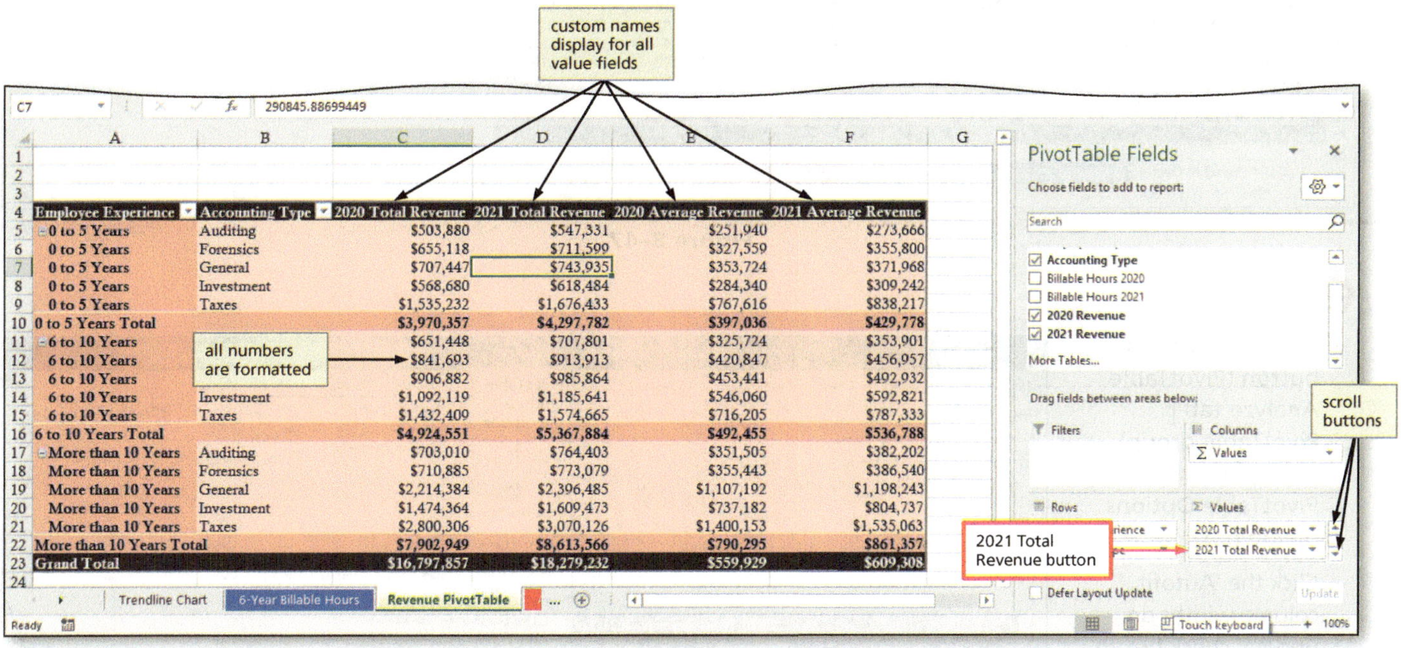

Figure 8–46

To Customize the Field Headers and Field List

The following steps hide the Field List, hide the field headers, and then turn off column autofitting. **Why?** Customizing the display of the field headers and the field list can provide a less cluttered worksheet.

1

- Display the PivotTable Analyze tab.
- Click the Field List button (PivotTable Analyze tab | Show group) to hide the Field List.
- Click the Field Headers button (PivotTable Analyze tab | Show group) to hide the field headers.

- If necessary, click the '+/– Buttons' button to display the expand and collapse buttons in the PivotTable (Figure 8–47).

Q&A **How can I display the Field List and field headers after hiding them?**
The Field List and Field Headers buttons (PivotTable Analyze tab | Show group) are toggle buttons—clicking them again turns the display back on.

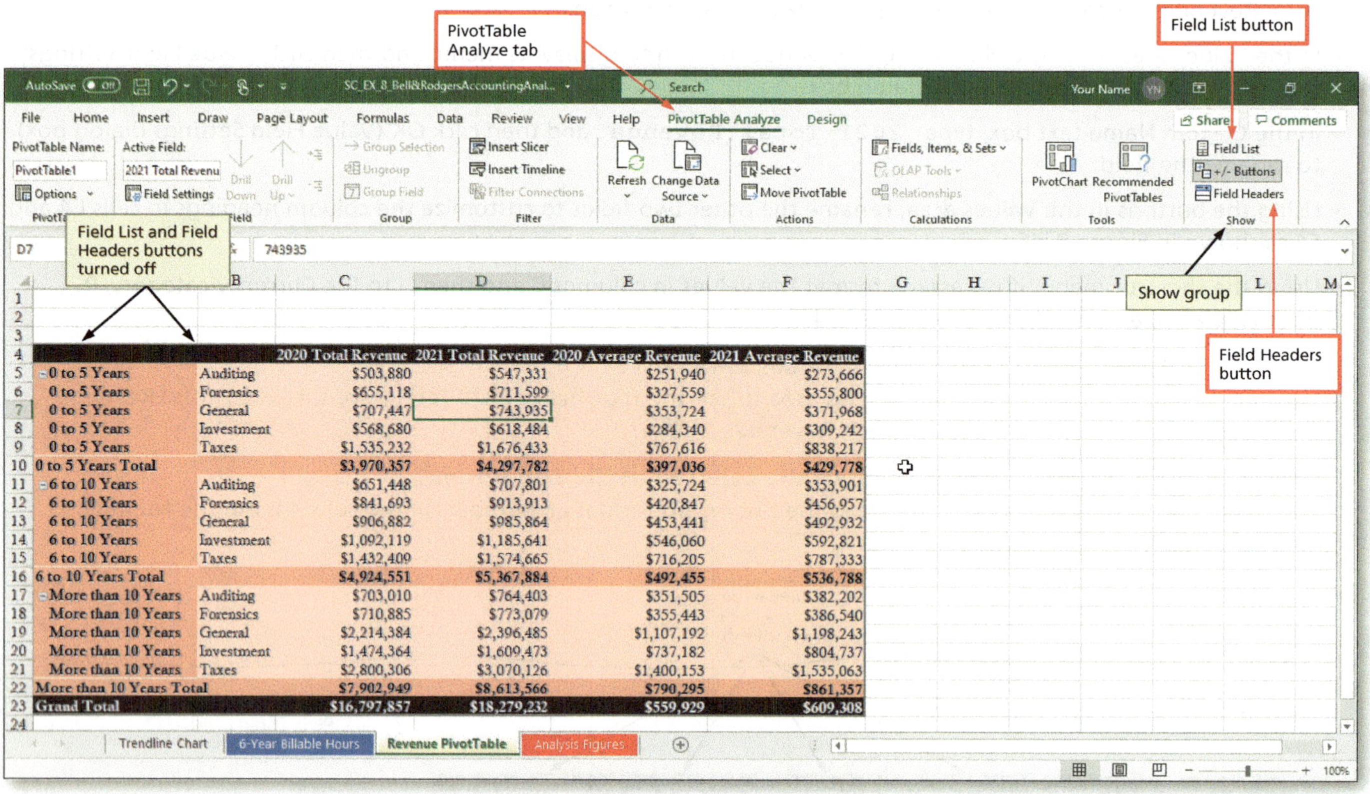

Figure 8–47

2

- Click the Options button (PivotTable Analyze tab | PivotTable group) to display the PivotTable Options dialog box.
- Click the 'Autofit column widths on update' check box to remove the checkmark (Figure 8–48).

3

- Click OK (PivotTable Options dialog box) to turn off the autofitting of column widths if updates should take place.

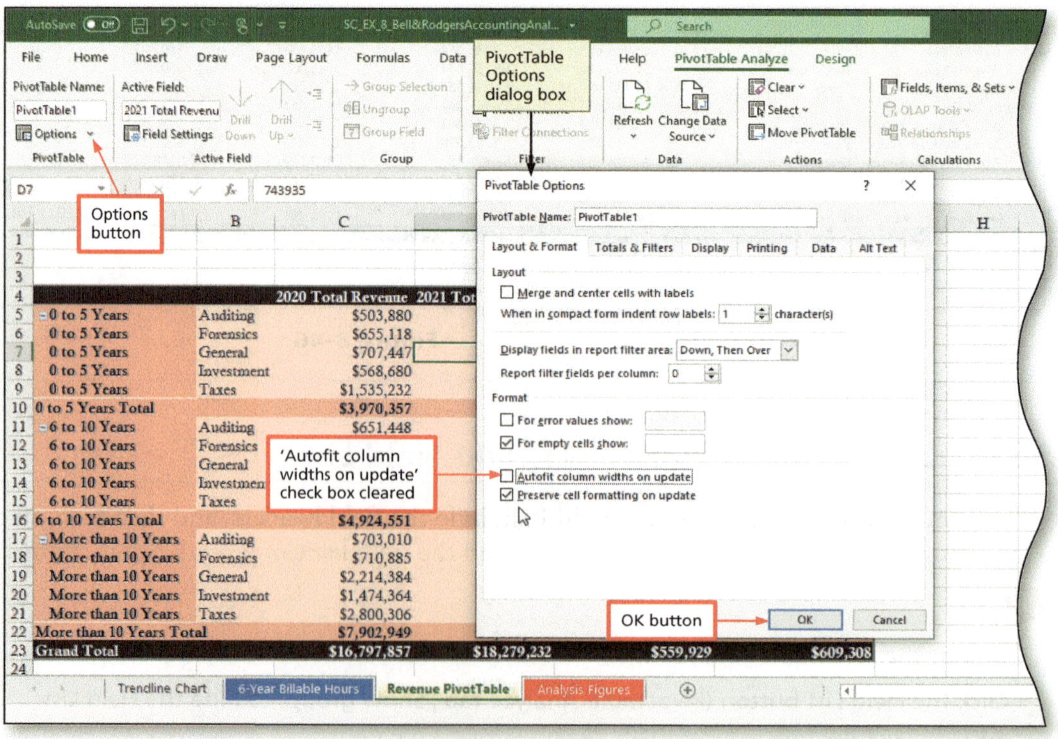

Figure 8–48

To Expand and Collapse Categories

The Expand and Collapse buttons expand and collapse across categories, reducing the amount of detail visible in the report without removing the field from the report. The following steps expand and collapse categories using the buttons and shortcut menus, and then suppress the display of the Expand and Collapse buttons in the report. **Why?** In some instances, the report may be more visually appealing without the Expand or Collapse buttons in the report.

1

- Click the Collapse button in cell A5 to collapse the '0 to 5 Years' of experience information (Figure 8–49).

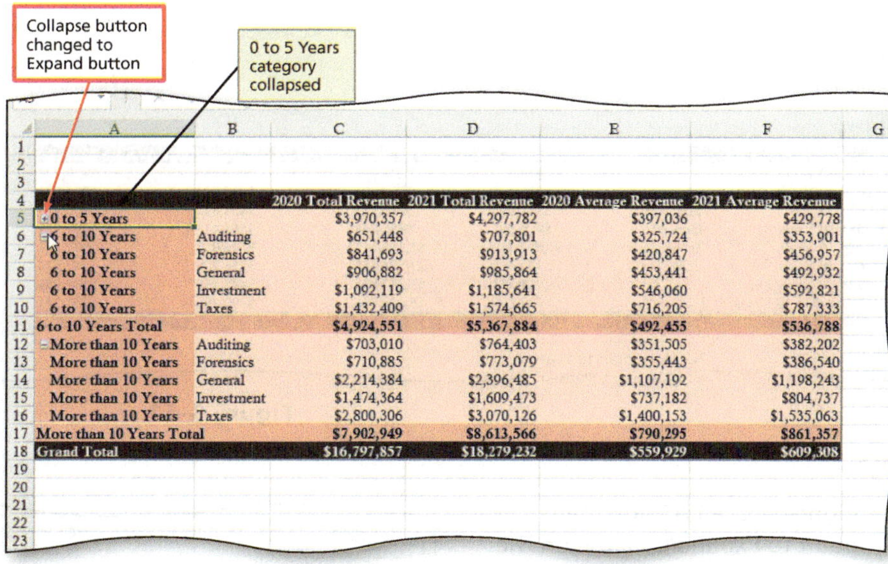

Figure 8–49

2

- Right-click cell A12 to display the shortcut menu and then point to Expand/Collapse to display the Expand/Collapse submenu (Figure 8–50).

Q&A **Which method should I use to expand and collapse?**
Either way is fine. Sometimes the Collapse button is not visible, in which case you would have to use the shortcut menu.

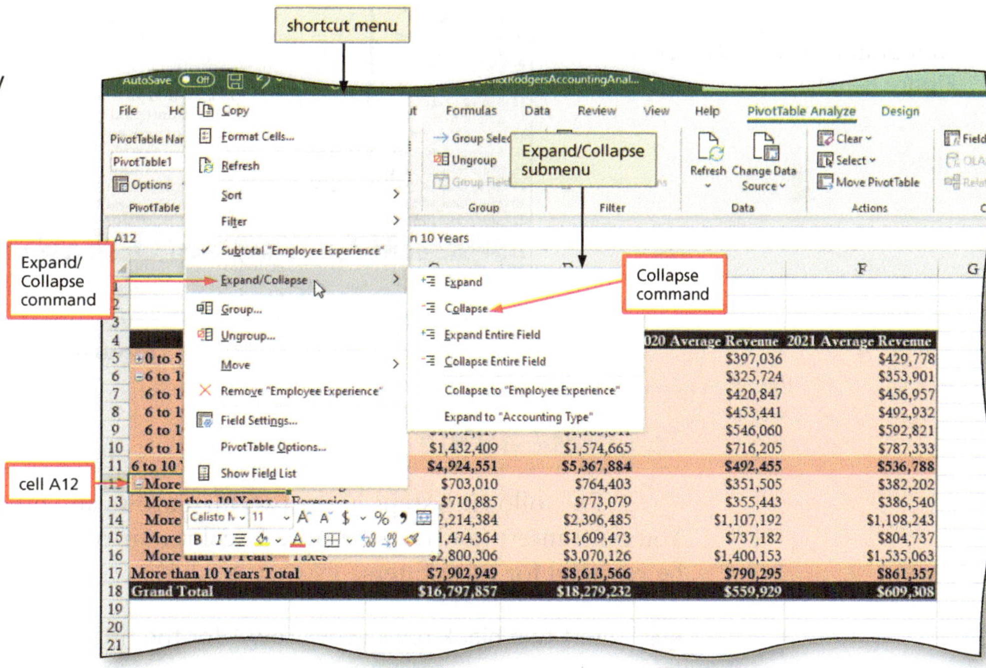

Figure 8–50

3

- Click Collapse on the Expand/Collapse submenu to collapse the 'More than 10 Years' data.
- Click the '+/– Buttons' button (PivotTable Analyze tab | Show group) to hide the Expand and Collapse buttons in the PivotTable (Figure 8–51).

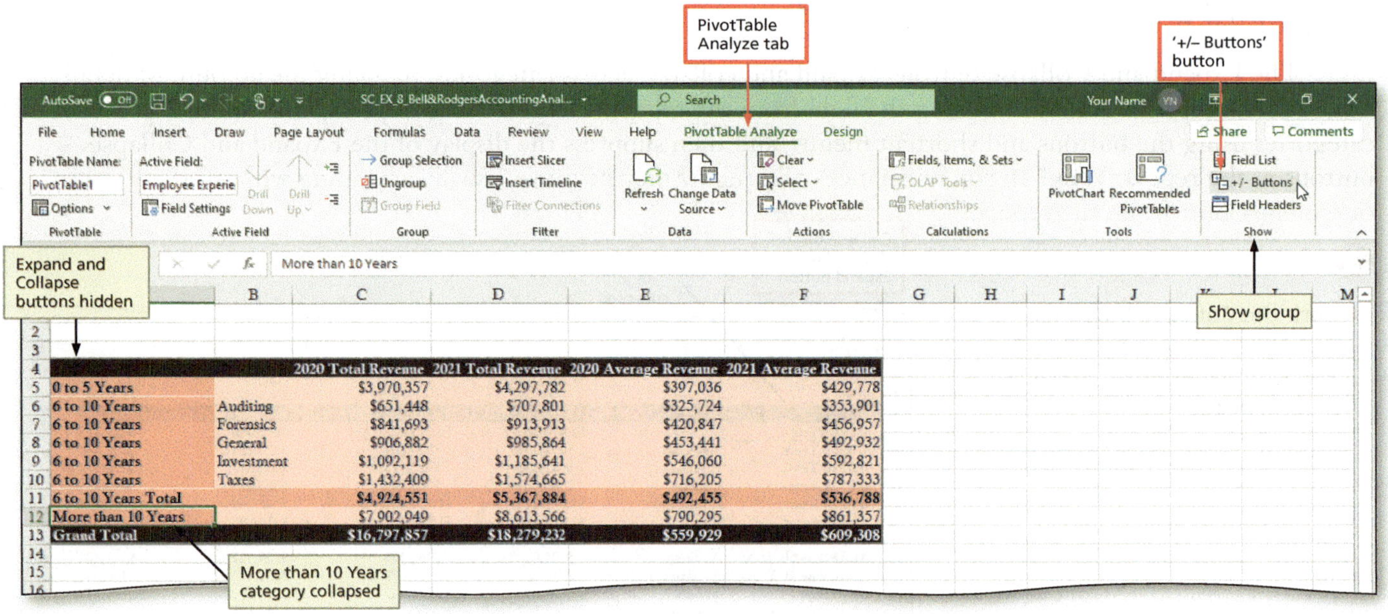

Figure 8–51

4

- Right-click cell A5 and then point to Expand/Collapse on the shortcut menu to display the Expand/Collapse submenu.
- Click 'Expand Entire Field' on the Expand/Collapse submenu to redisplay all data (shown in Figure 8–52).

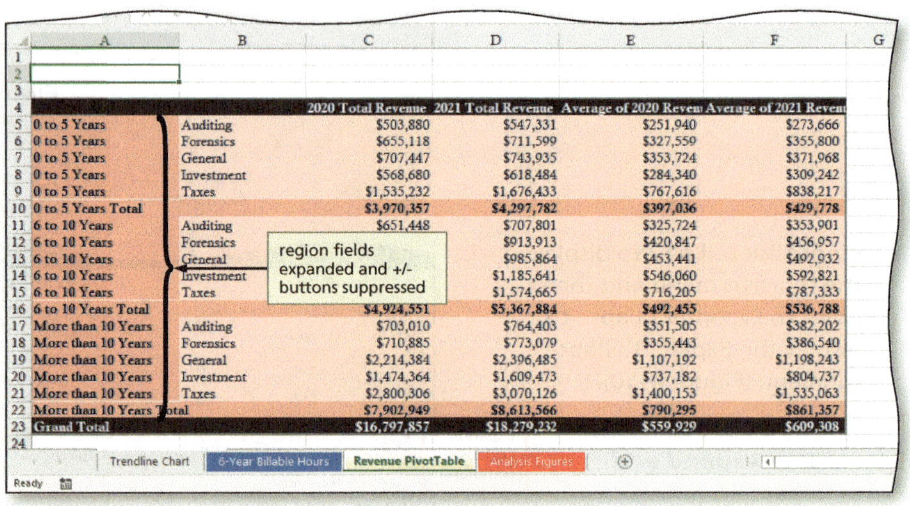

Figure 8–52

To Create a Title

The following steps insert two blank rows and create a title for the PivotTable. You must insert new rows because Excel requires the two rows above the PivotTable to be reserved for extra filters.

1. Insert two blank rows above row 1 for the title and subtitle.
2. In cell A1, enter the title `Bell & Rodgers Accounting Report` and then enter the subtitle `2020 and 2021` in cell A2.
3. Merge and center the text in cell A1 across A1:F1.
4. Merge and center the text in cell A2 across A2:F2.
5. Apply the Title style to cell A1 and bold the cell.
6. Apply the Heading 4 style to cell A2.

To Update a PivotTable

When you update cell contents in Excel, you also update related tables, formula calculations, and charts; however, this does not work for PivotTables. **Why?** PivotTables do not update automatically when you change the underlying data for the PivotTable report. You must update the PivotTable manually to recalculate summary data in the PivotTable report. Two figures in the original data worksheet are incorrect: the 2021 Billable Hours and Total Revenue at the Durante location for accountants with more than 10 years' experience working with investments. The following steps correct the typographical errors in the underlying worksheet, and then update the PivotTable report.

1

- Click the Analysis Figures sheet tab to make it the active worksheet.
- Click cell E15 and then type `9225` as the new value.
- Click cell G15, type `1077757`, and then press ENTER to change the contents of the cell (Figure 8–53).

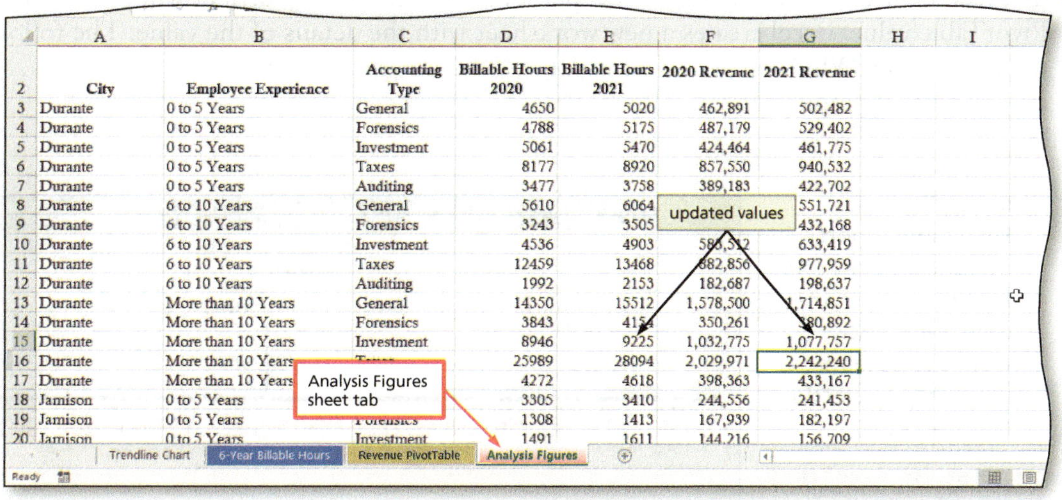

Figure 8–53

Q&A **What data will this change in the PivotTable?**
Upon updating the PivotTable, the 2021 total revenue and the 2021 average revenue will change, reflected in cells D22 and F22.

2

- Click the Revenue PivotTable sheet tab to make it the active worksheet.
- If necessary, click inside the PivotTable report to make it active.
- Display the PivotTable Analyze tab on the ribbon.
- Click the Refresh button (PivotTable Analyze tab | Data group) to update the PivotTable report to reflect the change to the underlying data (Figure 8–54).

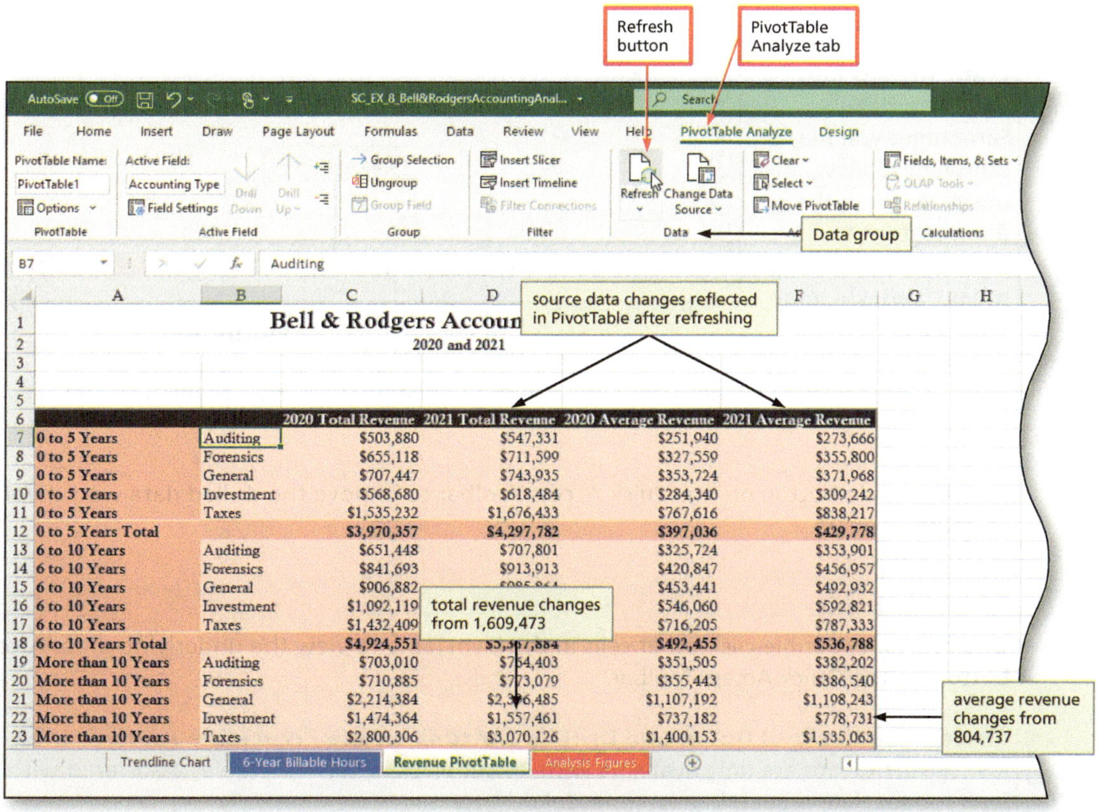

Figure 8–54

Q&A

Do I always have to refresh the data?

Yes. The contents of a PivotTable are not refreshed when the data from which they are created changes. This means you must refresh the PivotTable manually when underlying data changes.

If I add rows or columns to the data, will refreshing update the PivotTable?

If your data is in a data table, yes. Otherwise, you will have to create a new PivotTable.

To Drill Down into PivotTable

An easy way to view the underlying data associated with a PivotTable value is to drill down, a visualization that lets the user drill into, or go to deeper levels in, the data. To drill down, you simply double-click a PivotTable value. Excel creates a new worksheet with the details of the value. The following steps drill down into the PivotTable. **Why?** You want to see detailed information about a value, in this case, all of the 2021 investment accounting for employees with 6 to 10 years of experience.

1

- In the Revenue PivotTable report, double-click cell D16 to drill down in the data. Click away from the data to remove the selection (Figure 8–55).

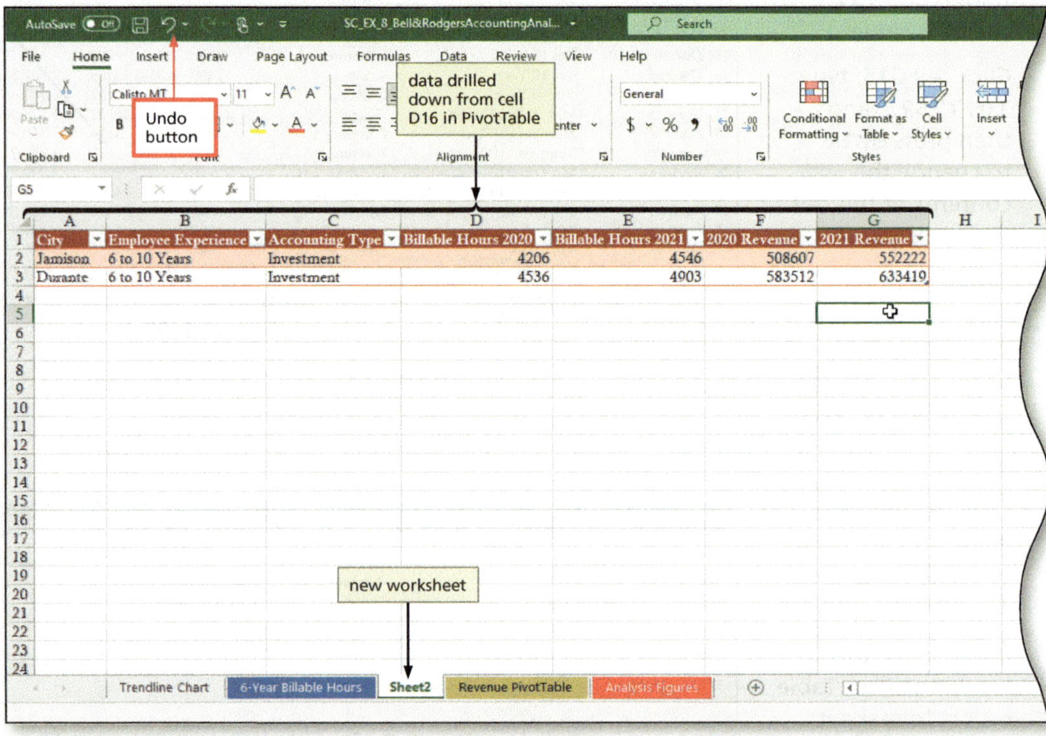

Figure 8–55

Q&A

What did Excel do?

Excel found all of the data related to the value in D16 and displayed it in a new worksheet.

What should I do with the data?

Sometimes you may just want to view the data or use the filter buttons to drill down further; other times, you may want to print it. If it important to have a permanent record of the data behind a value, rename the new worksheet and save it with the workbook.

2

- Click the Undo button on the Quick Access Toolbar to remove the drilled data worksheet and return to the PivotTable report.

Experiment

- One at a time, double-click other cells in the PivotTable to view the underlying data. After each, click the Undo button on the Quick Access Toolbar.

Q&A

Could I use the Drill Down and Drill Up buttons on the PivotTable Analyze tab?

No. Those buttons are only available with Power Pivot or for PivotTables associated with a data model. You will learn about data models in a later module.

3

- Click the Save button on the Quick Access Toolbar to save the workbook.

Break Point: If you want to take a break, this is a good place to do so. You can exit Excel now. To resume later, start Excel, open the file called SC_EX_8_Bell&RodgersAccountingAnalysis, and continue following the steps from this location forward.

Creating and Formatting PivotChart Reports

A PivotChart report, also called a PivotChart, is an interactive chart that allows users to change, with just a few clicks, the groupings that graphically present the data in chart form. As a visual representation of PivotTables, each PivotChart Report must be associated or connected with a PivotTable report. Most users create a PivotChart from an existing PivotTable; however, you can create a new PivotTable and PivotChart at the same time. If you create the PivotChart first, Excel will create the PivotTable automatically.

To Create a PivotChart Report from an Existing PivotTable Report

If you already have created a PivotTable report, you can create a PivotChart report for that PivotTable using the PivotChart button (PivotTable Analyze tab | Tools group). The following steps create a 3-D clustered column PivotChart report from the existing PivotTable report. **Why?** The PivotChart will show the two-year data for each accounting type side by side.

1

- If necessary, click cell A7 to select it in the PivotTable report.
- Click the Field List button (PivotTable Analyze tab | Show group) to display the Field List.
- Click the PivotChart button (PivotTable Analyze tab | Tools group) to display the Insert Chart dialog box.
- Click '3-D Clustered Column' in the Column Chart gallery to select the chart type (Figure 8–56).

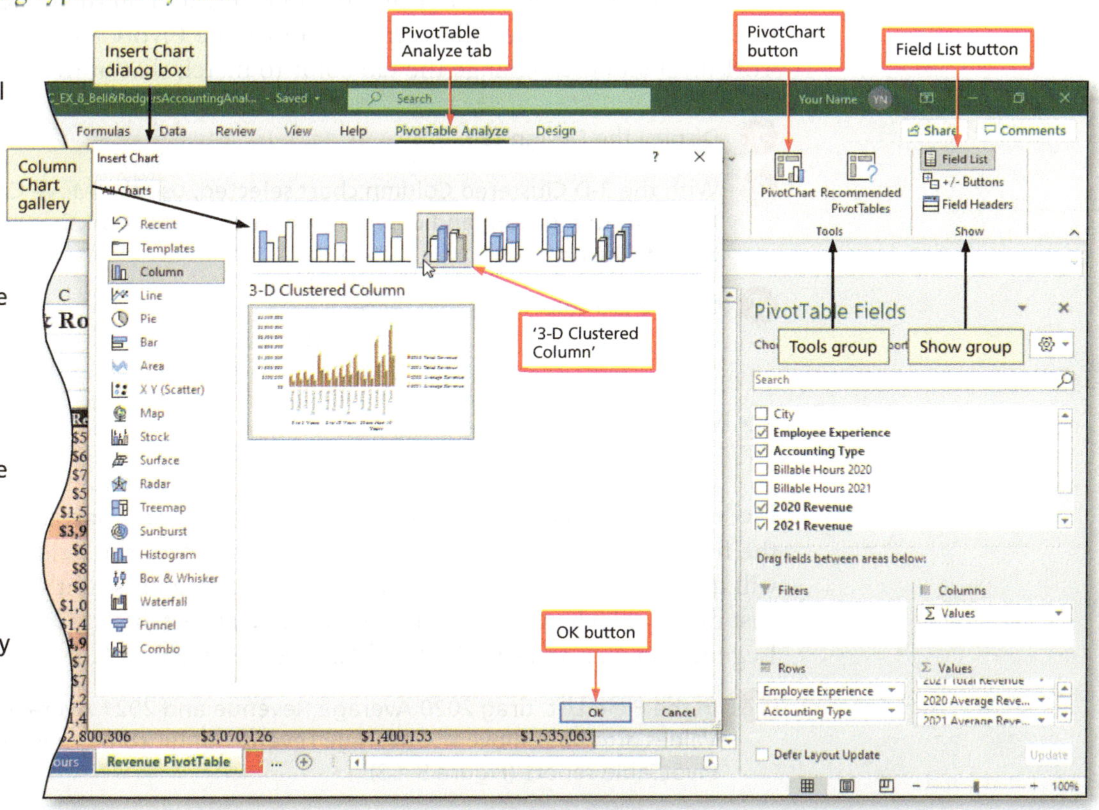

Figure 8–56

2

- Click OK (Insert Chart dialog box) to add the chart to the Revenue PivotTable worksheet (Figure 8–57).

Q&A

My chart does not display field buttons across the top. Did I do something wrong?

No. It may be that they are turned off. Click the Field Buttons button (PivotChart Analyze tab | Show/Hide Group) to turn them on.

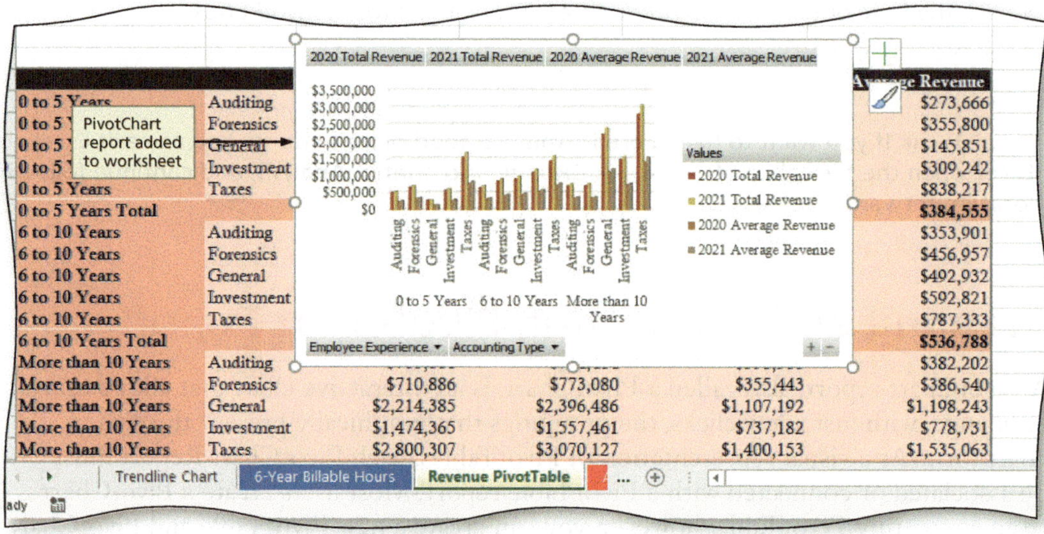

Figure 8–57

Other Ways

1. Click Insert PivotChart button (Insert tab | Charts group), select chart type (Insert Chart dialog box), click OK
2. Select data for PivotChart, press F11 to create default chart

To Move the PivotChart Report

By default, a PivotChart report will be created on the same page as the associated PivotTable report. The following steps move the PivotChart report to a separate worksheet and then change the tab color to match that of the PivotTable report tab.

1. Display the Design tab.
2. With the 3-D Clustered Column chart selected, use the Move Chart button (Design tab | Location group) and move the chart to a new worksheet named **`Revenue PivotChart`**.
3. Set the tab color to Brown, Accent 1.

To Remove Fields

The following step deletes the average revenue data from the PivotTable and PivotChart reports. Because the PivotTable and PivotChart are connected, removing the fields from one worksheet automatically removes the fields from the other. You will use the Field List related to PivotCharts, which is slightly different from the Field List displayed when using a PivotTable. The areas labeled Columns and Rows become Legend and Axis areas in the Field List, respectively.

1. In the Field List, drag 2020 Average Revenue and 2021 Average Revenue out of the Values area to remove the average revenue data from the PivotChart report and PivotTable report (Figure 8–58).

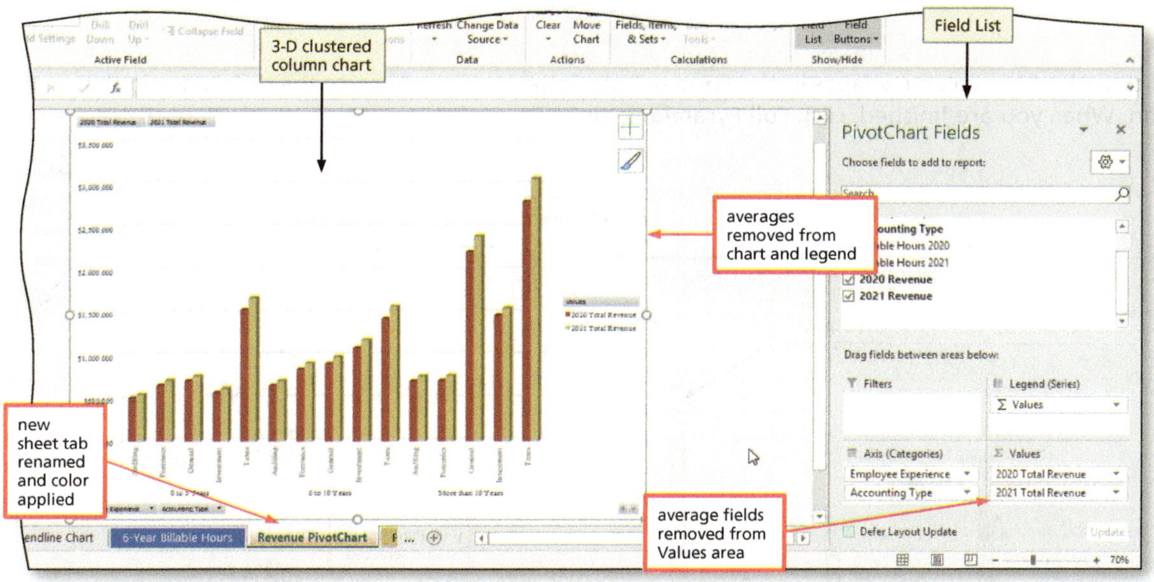

Figure 8–58

To Change the PivotChart Type and Reset Chart Elements

Why? Selecting a chart type instead of using the default type provides variety for the reader. The default chart type for a PivotChart is a clustered column chart. However, PivotCharts can support most chart types, except scatter (X, Y), stock, and bubble. The following steps change the PivotChart type to Full Pyramid, add a title to the PivotChart report, and apply formatting options to the chart.

1

- Click one of the reddish-brown '2020 Total Revenue' columns to select the data series.
- Right-click to display the shortcut menu (Figure 8–59).

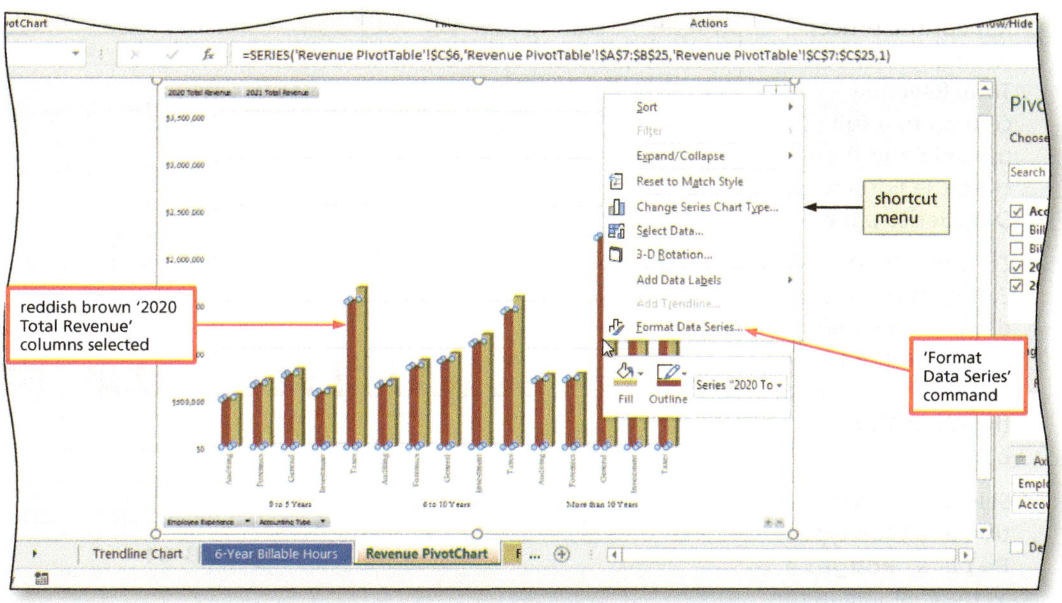

Figure 8–59

2

- Click 'Format Data Series' on the shortcut menu to open the Format Data Series pane.
- If necessary, click the Series Options button.
- In the Column shape section (Series Options area), click Full Pyramid (Figure 8–60).

Experiment

- One at a time, click each of the column shapes in the Format Data Series pane and notice the difference in the PivotChart column. When you are finished, click Full Pyramid again.

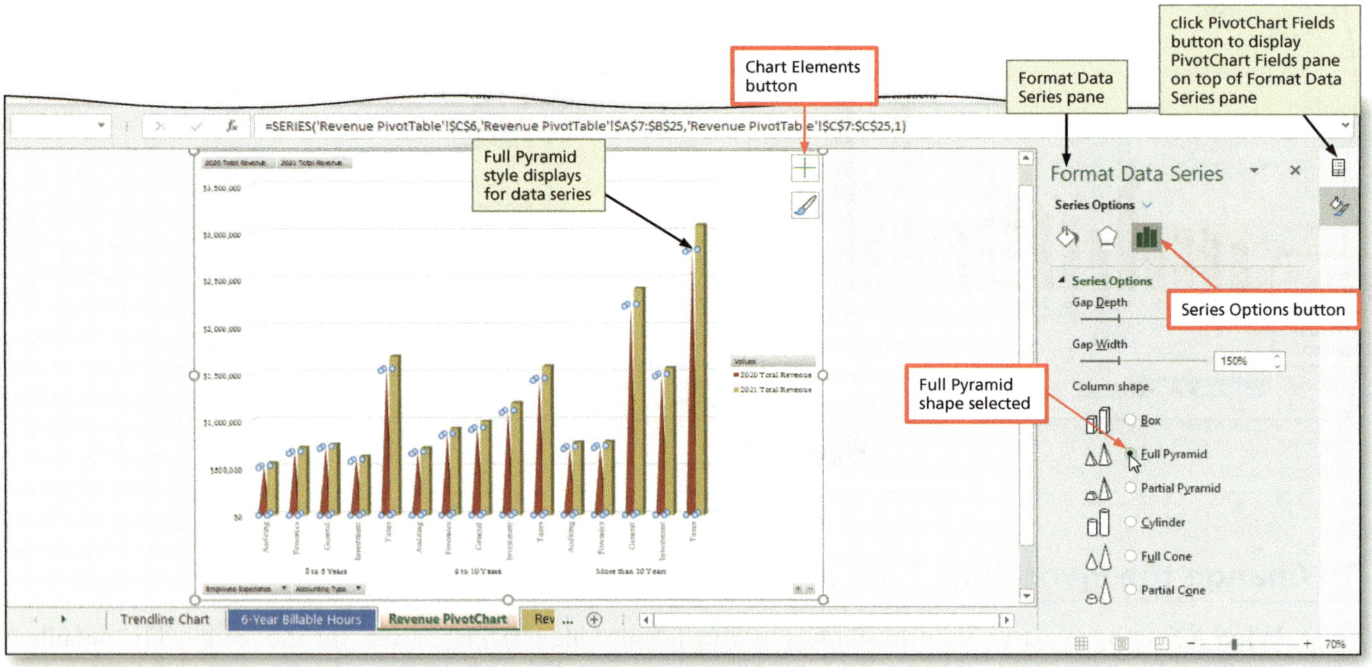

Figure 8–60

3

- Repeat the process to change the 2021 Total Revenue column to a full pyramid and then close the Format Data Series pane.
- Click the Chart Elements button to display the menu and then click to place a checkmark in the Chart Title check box.
- Select the chart title and then type **Bell & Rodgers** as the first line in the chart title. Press ENTER to move to a new line.

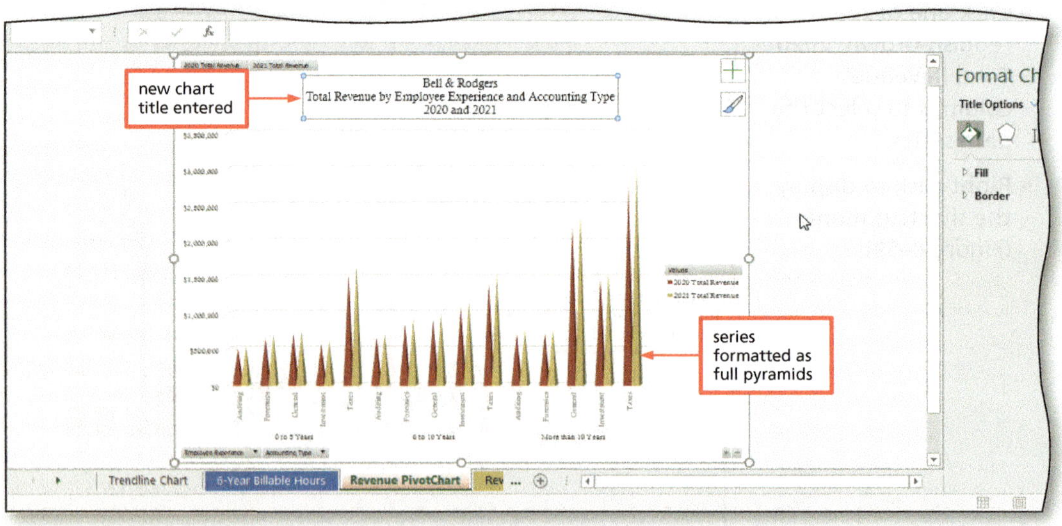

Figure 8–61

- Type **Total Revenue by Employee Experience and Accounting Type** as the second line in the chart title and then press ENTER to move to a new line.
- Type **2020 and 2021** as the third line in the chart title.
- Select all of the text in the title and change the font color to 'Black, Text 1' (Figure 8–61).

4

- Display the Format tab.
- Click the Chart Elements arrow (Format tab | Current Selection group) to display the Chart Elements menu (Figure 8–62).

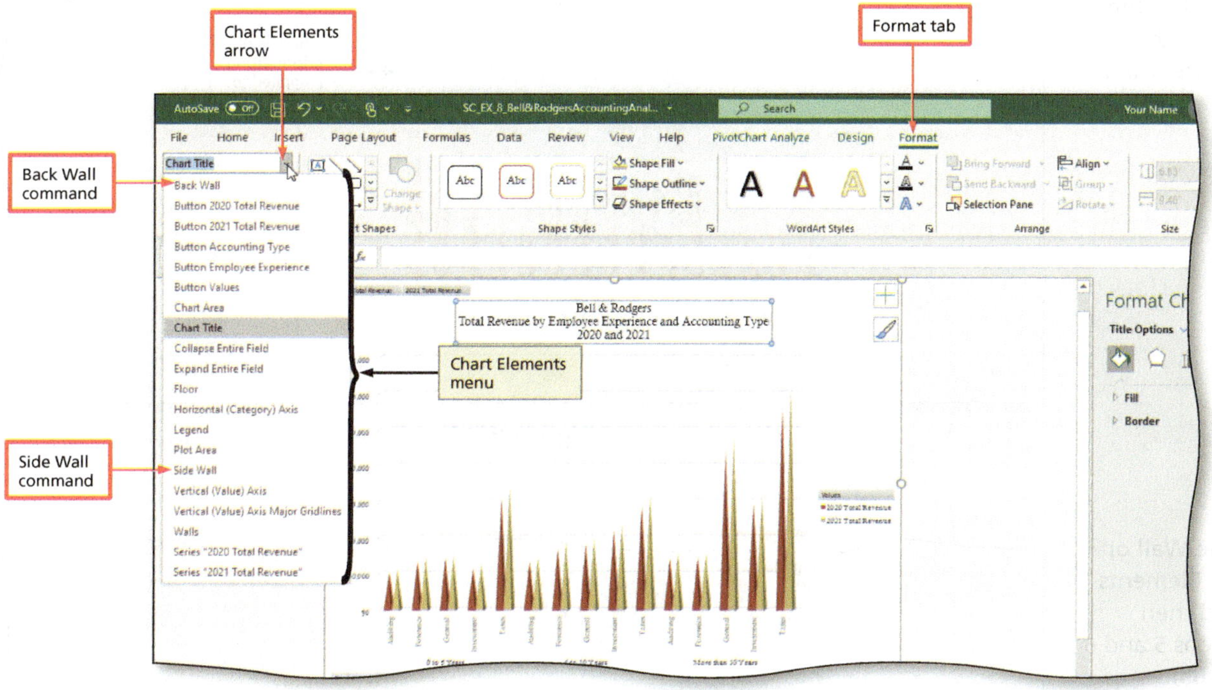

Figure 8–62

5

- Click Back Wall on the Chart Elements menu to select the back wall of the chart.
- Click the Shape Fill button (Format tab | Shape Styles group) to display the Shape Fill gallery and then click Light Blue in the Standard Colors.
- Click the Shape Fill arrow again and then point to Gradient in the Shape Fill gallery to display the Gradient submenu (Figure 8–63).

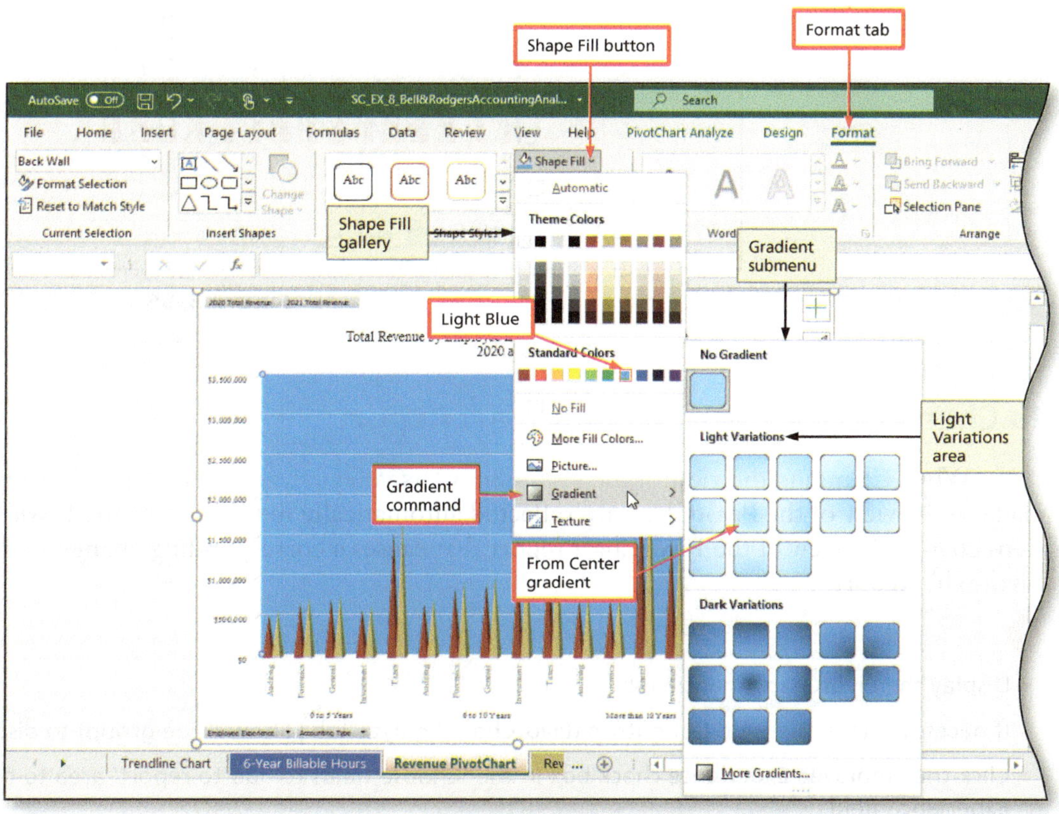

Figure 8–63

6

- Click From Center in the Light Variations area to apply a gradient fill to the back wall of the chart (Figure 8–64).

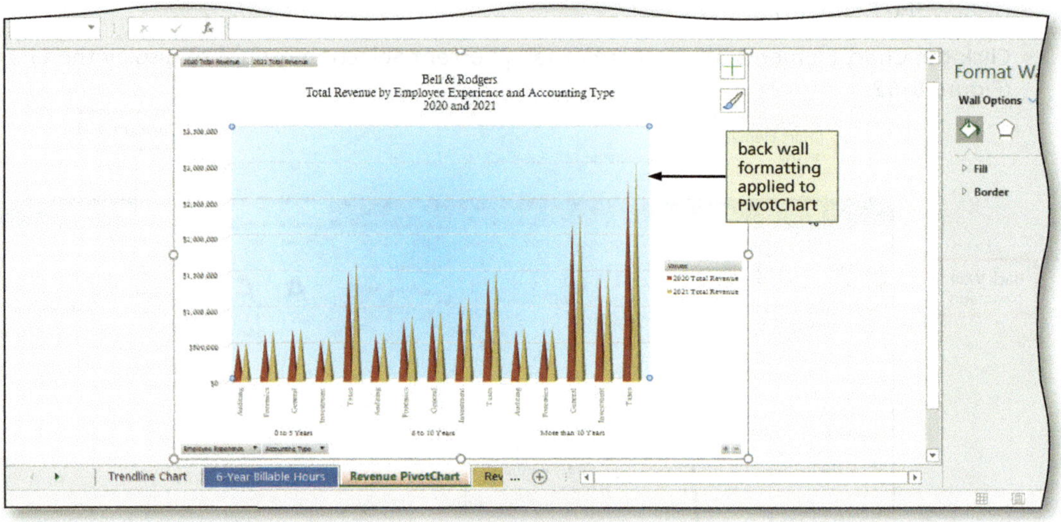

Figure 8–64

7

- Select Side Wall on the Chart Elements menu and then repeat Steps 5 and 6 (Figure 8-65).
- If necessary, close the Format Wall pane.

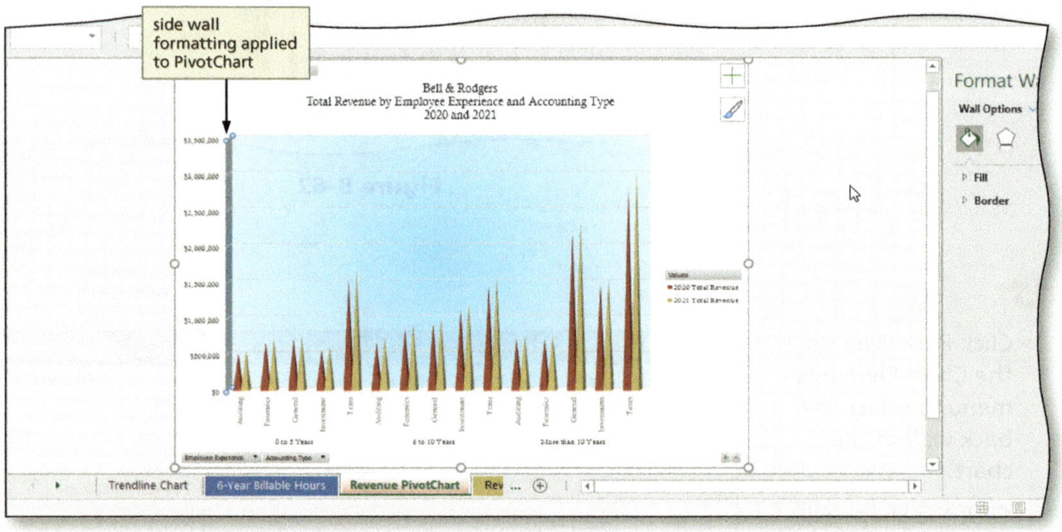

Figure 8–65

To Change the View of a PivotChart Report

Why? Changing the view of the PivotChart lets you analyze different relationships graphically. Changes made to the view of the PivotChart are reflected automatically in the view of the PivotTable. The following steps change the view of the PivotChart report that causes a corresponding change in the view of its associated PivotTable report.

1

- Display the PivotChart Analyze tab.
- If necessary, click the Field List button (PivotChart Analyze tab | Show /Hide group) to display the Field List.
- Click the Employee Experience check box in the 'Choose fields to add to report' area to deselect the Employee Experience field.
- Place a checkmark in the City check box to select the field and add it to the Axis area (Figure 8–66).

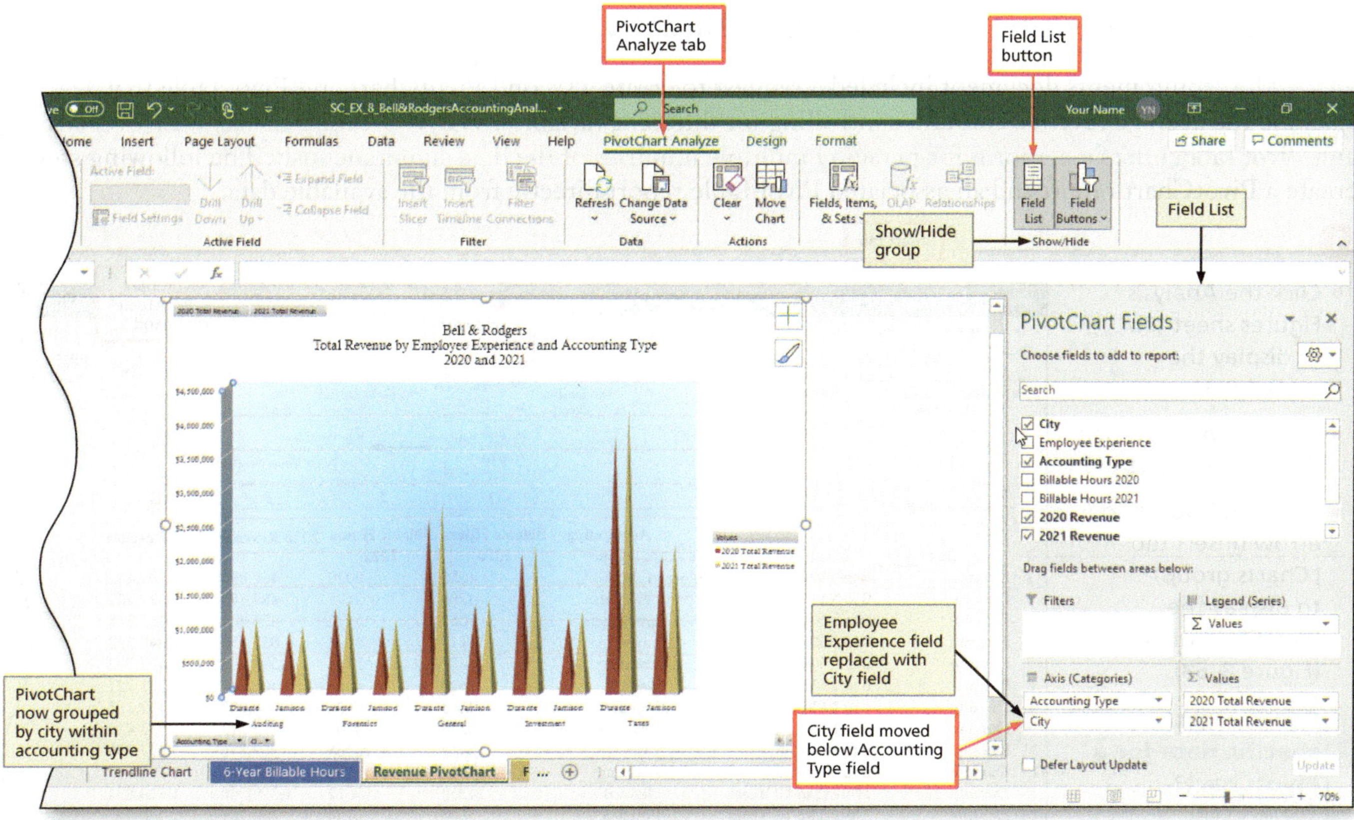

Figure 8–66

2

- Click the Revenue PivotTable sheet tab to view the changes in the corresponding PivotTable report (Figure 8–67).

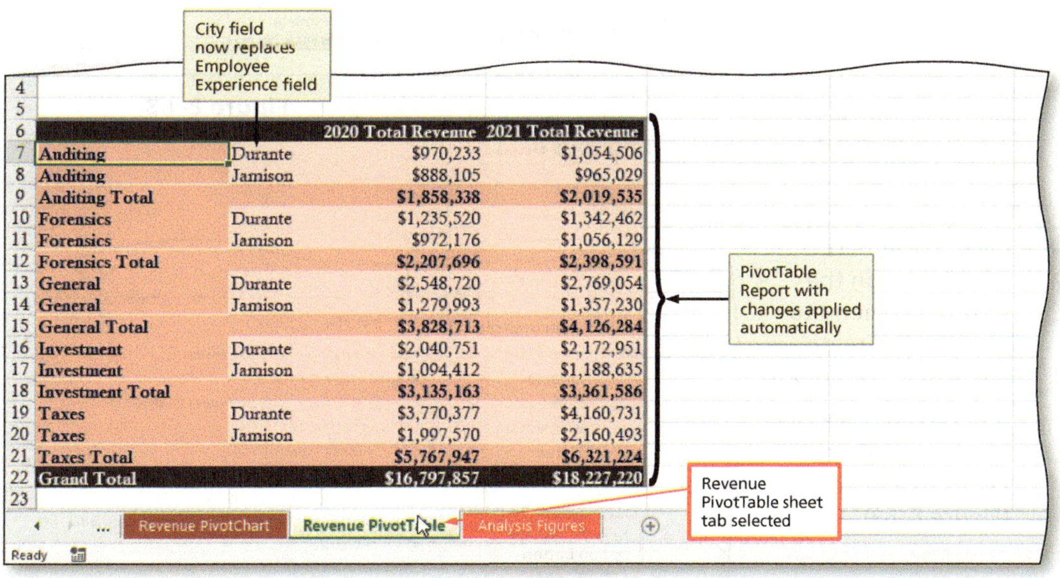

		2020 Total Revenue	2021 Total Revenue
Auditing	Durante	$970,233	$1,054,506
Auditing	Jamison	$888,105	$965,029
Auditing Total		$1,858,338	$2,019,535
Forensics	Durante	$1,235,520	$1,342,462
Forensics	Jamison	$972,176	$1,056,129
Forensics Total		$2,207,696	$2,398,591
General	Durante	$2,548,720	$2,769,054
General	Jamison	$1,279,993	$1,357,230
General Total		$3,828,713	$4,126,284
Investment	Durante	$2,040,751	$2,172,951
Investment	Jamison	$1,094,412	$1,188,635
Investment Total		$3,135,163	$3,361,586
Taxes	Durante	$3,770,377	$4,160,731
Taxes	Jamison	$1,997,570	$2,160,493
Taxes Total		$5,767,947	$6,321,224
Grand Total		$16,797,857	$18,227,220

Figure 8–67

Q&A **What usually happens when the view of the PivotChart report changes?**
Changes to the PivotChart are reflected automatically in the PivotTable. Changes to category (x-axis) fields, such as City, are made to row fields in the PivotTable. Changes to series (y-axis) fields appear as changes to column fields in the PivotTable.

3

- Click the Save button on the Quick Access Toolbar to save the workbook.

To Create a PivotChart and PivotTable Directly from Data

The requirements document included a request to create a second PivotChart and PivotTable that examine the average revenue amount, controlling for different variables. **Why?** Creating a second PivotChart and PivotTable offers a platform for pursuing multiple inquiries of the data simultaneously. The following steps create a PivotChart report and an associated PivotTable report directly from the available data.

1

- Click the Analysis Figures sheet tab to display the worksheet.
- Click cell A3 and then display the Insert tab.
- Click the PivotChart arrow (Insert tab | Charts group) to display the PivotChart menu (Figure 8–68).

Q&A **Can I select specific data for a PivotChart?**
Yes, you can highlight the cells before creating the PivotChart. By default, Excel includes the table around the chosen cell; or, if the data is not a table, Excel assumes all contiguous data.

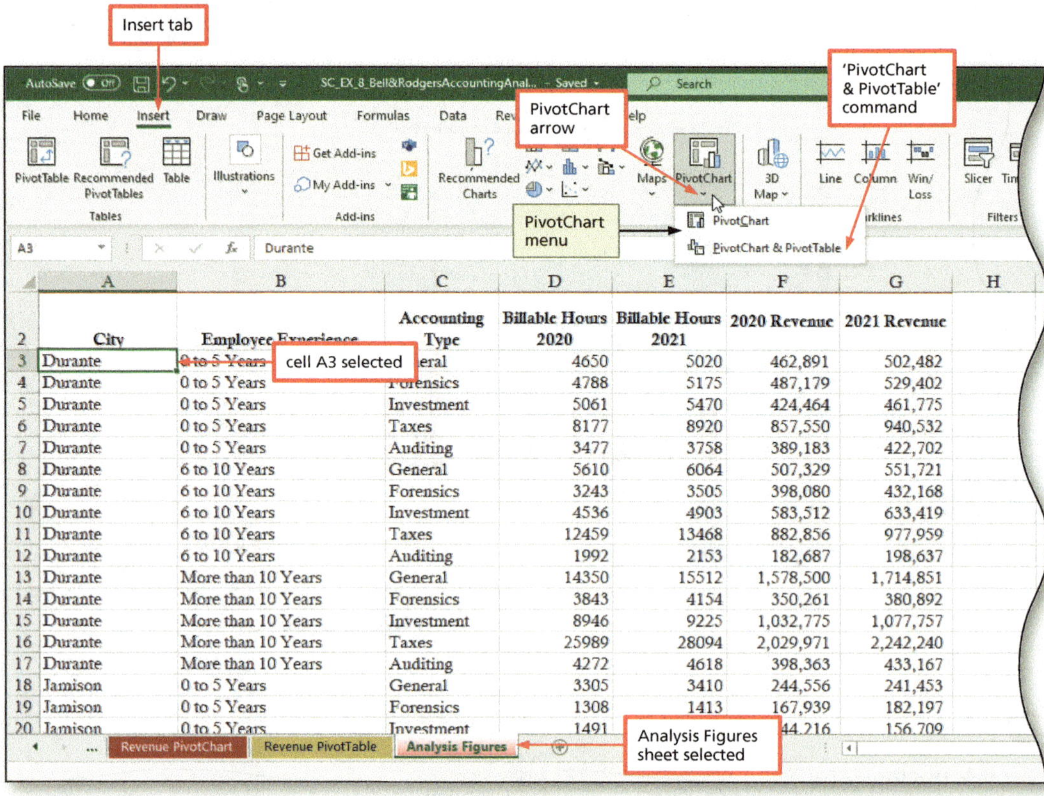

Figure 8–68

2

- Click 'PivotChart & PivotTable' on the PivotChart menu to display the Create PivotTable dialog box.
- If necessary, click New Worksheet (Create PivotTable dialog box) (Figure 8–69).

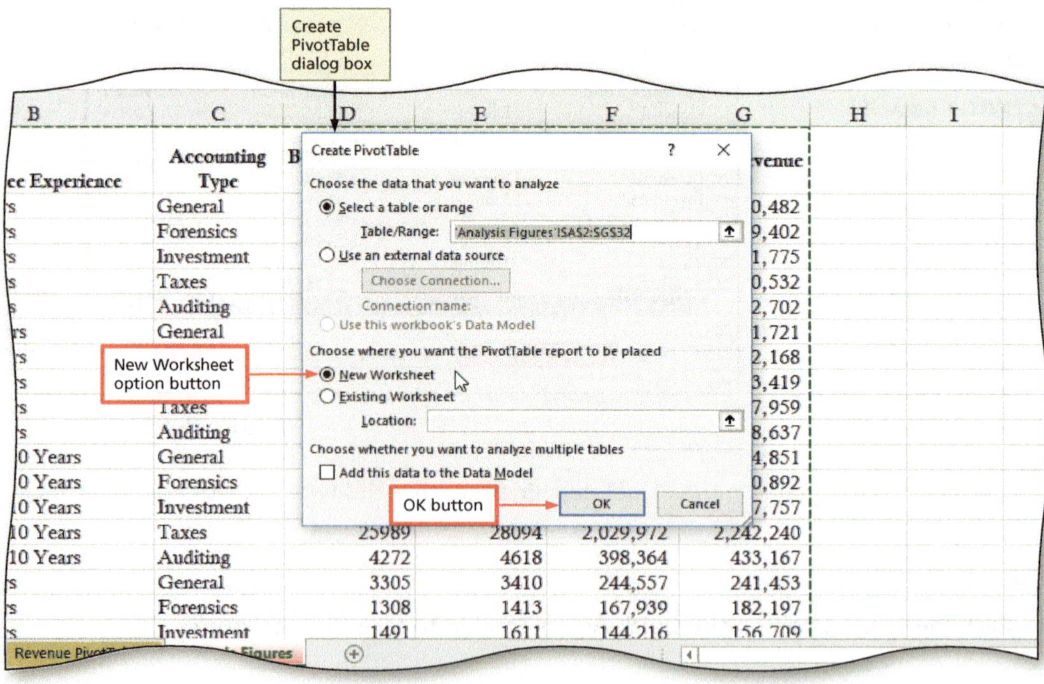

Figure 8–69

3

- Click OK to add a new worksheet containing a blank PivotTable and blank PivotChart (Figure 8–70).

Q&A **What does the Field List display when creating a blank PivotChart?** Based on the location of your selected cell when you started the process, the Field List displays the available fields for you to place in the Filters and Axis areas.

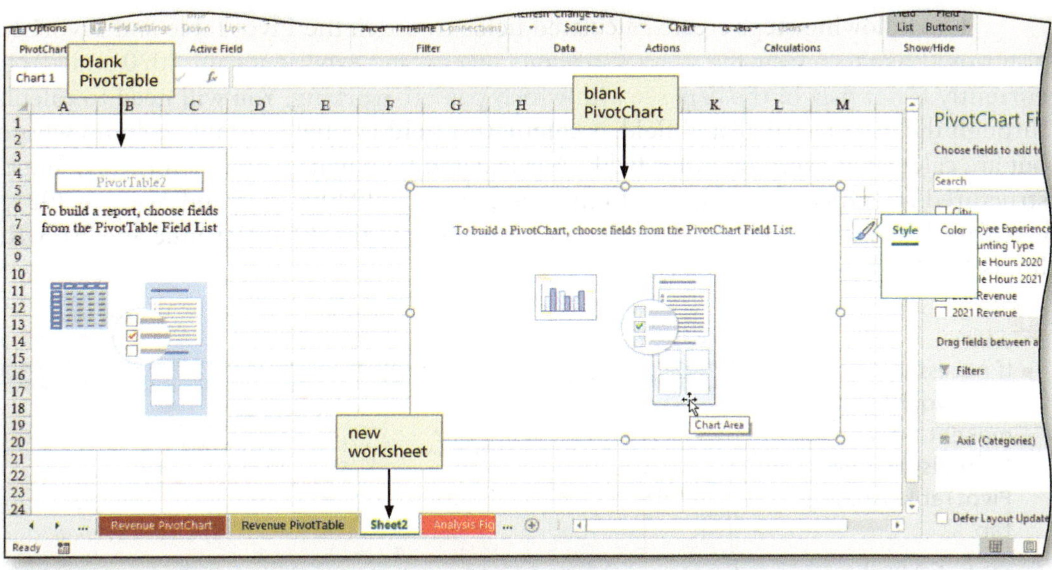

Figure 8–70

4

- Use the Field List to add the Employee Experience and City fields to the Axis area.
- Add the 2020 Revenue and 2021 Revenue fields to the Values area in the Field List (Figure 8–71).

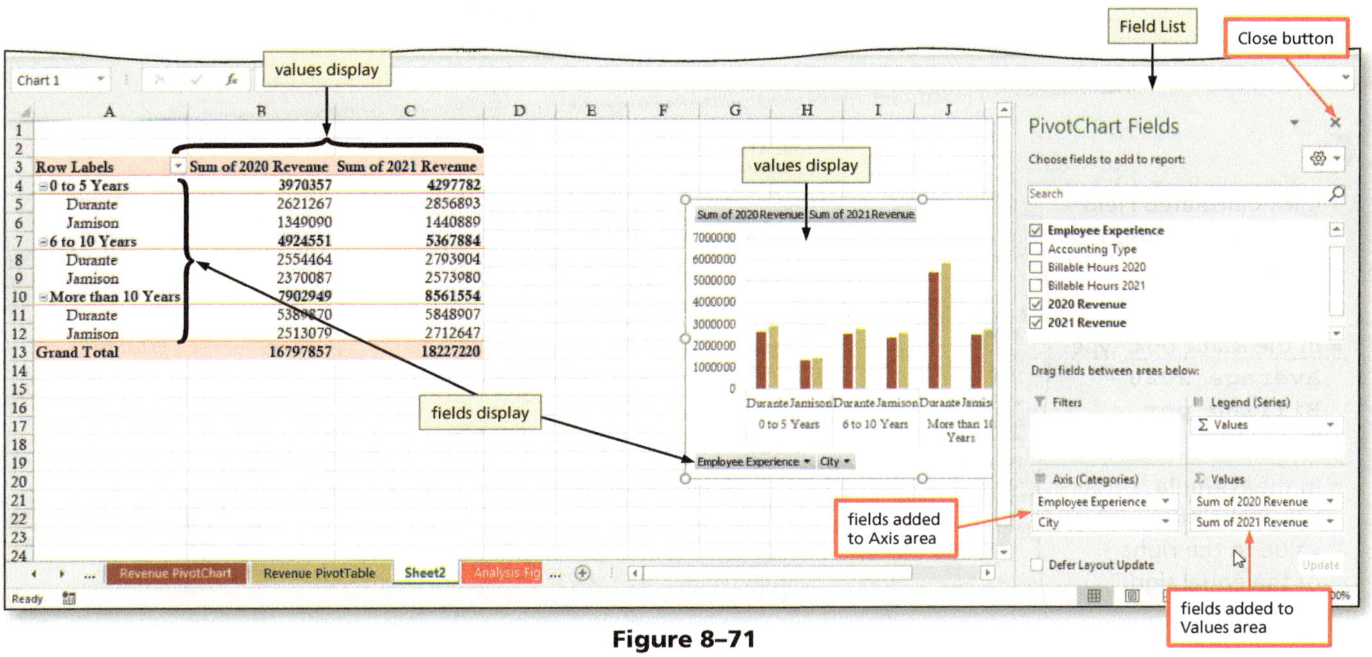

Figure 8–71

5

- Close the Field List.
- Rename the new worksheet, `Average Revenue`, in preparation for creating averages in the next steps, and choose the Yellow tab color in the Standard Colors area.

To Create a Calculated Field to a PivotTable Report

The following steps create calculated fields to use in the PivotTable and PivotChart reports. **Why?** You would like to review the average revenue by city and experience for 2020 and 2021, but this information currently is not part of the data set with which you are working. You will need to calculate the values you need through the use of a calculated field. A **calculated field** is a field or table column whose values are not entered but are calculated based on other fields. A calculated field may contain a formula, function, cell reference, structured reference, or condition. In this case, Average 2020 Billing and Average 2021 Billing will be new calculated fields, based on dividing the existing values of the 2020 Revenue and 2021 Revenue by the billable hours for 2020 and 2021, respectively.

1

- If necessary, click the PivotTable to make it active and then display the PivotTable Analyze tab.
- Click the 'Fields, Items, & Sets' button (PivotTable Analyze tab | Calculations group) to display the Fields, Items, & Sets menu (Figure 8–72).

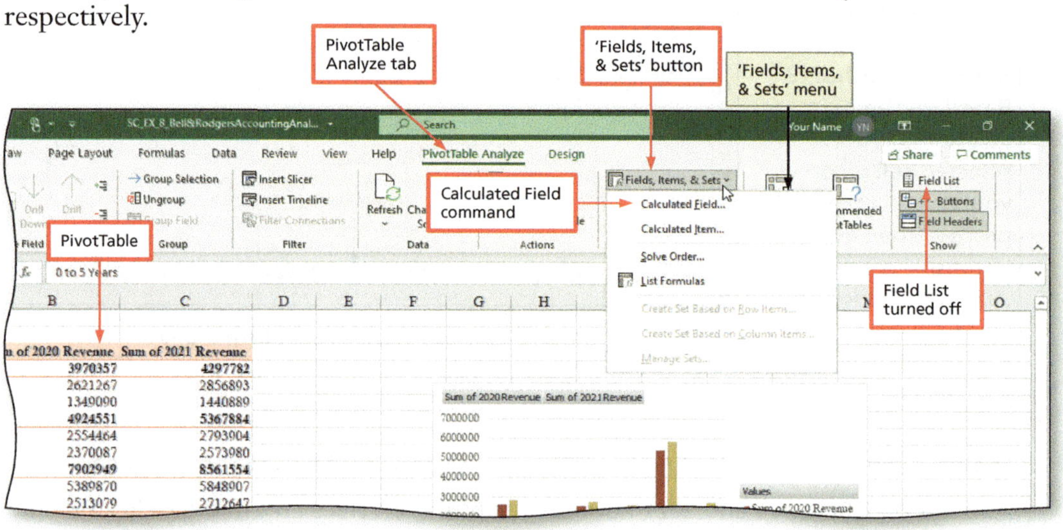

Figure 8–72

2

- Click Calculated Field to display the Insert Calculated Field dialog box.
- In the Name box, type **`Average 2020 Billing per Hour`**.
- In the Formula box, delete the value to the right of the equal sign, in this case, 0.
- In the Fields list, double-click the 2020 Revenue field to insert it in the Formula text box.

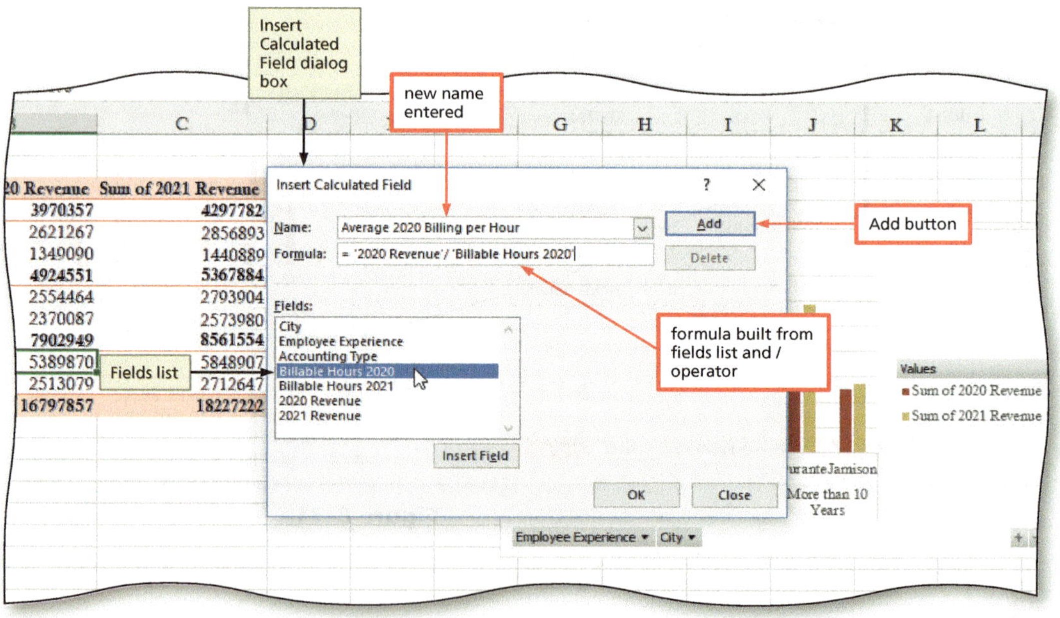

Figure 8–73

- Type / (slash) and then double-click the 'Billable Hours 2020' field to complete the formula, which should read = '2020 Revenue' / 'Billable Hours 2020' (Figure 8–73).

3

- Click the Add button (Insert Calculated Field dialog box) to add the calculated field to the Fields list.
- Repeat Step 2 to create a calculated field named Average 2021 Billing per Hour, calculated using 2021 Revenue divided by Billable Hours 2021 (Figure 8–74).

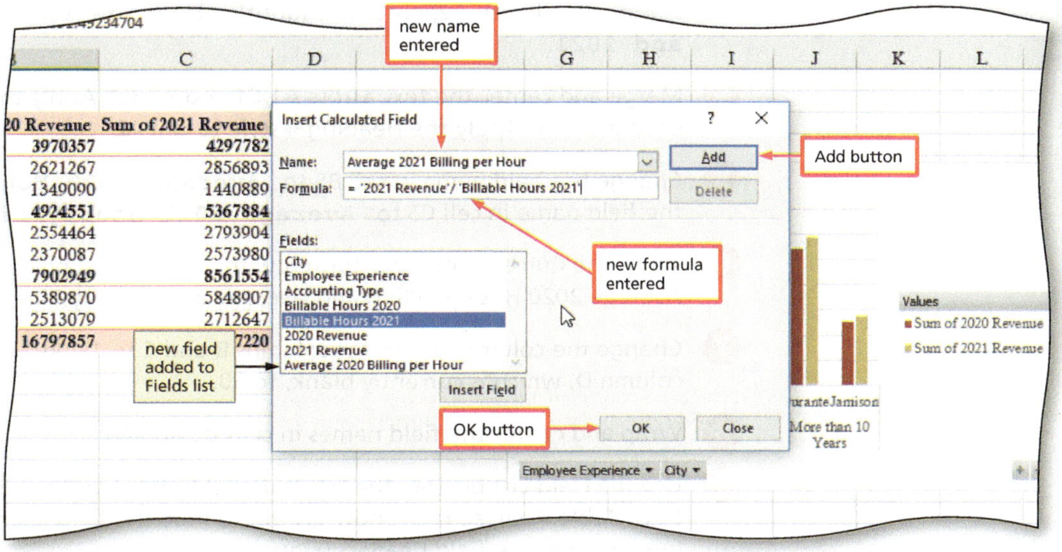

Figure 8–74

4

- Click the Add button (Insert Calculated Field dialog box) and then click OK to close the dialog box.
- If necessary, drag the PivotChart to the right so it does not cover the PivotTable (Figure 8–75).

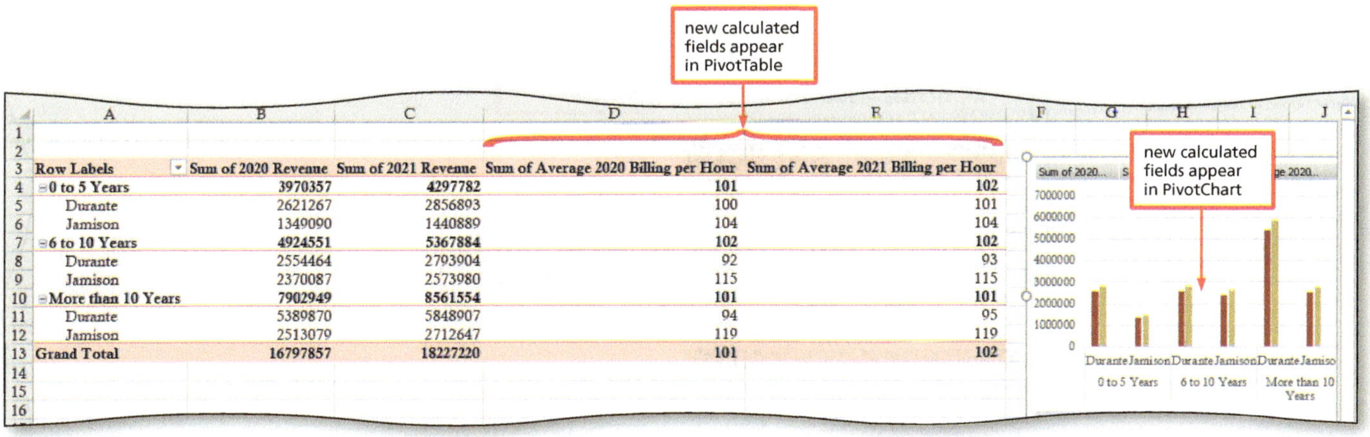

Figure 8–75

To Format the PivotTable

Now that you have added a calculated field, you can format the PivotTable and PivotChart so they look professional and are easy to interpret. The following steps format the PivotTable report.

1 If necessary, click the Field List button (PivotTable Analyze tab | Show/Hide group) to display the Field List and then click to remove the checkmark in the 2020 Revenue check box and the 2021 Revenue check box to remove these fields from the PivotTable and PivotChart.

2 If necessary, click cell A3 to select it. Display the Design tab and then apply the 'Tan, Pivot Style Medium 19' style to the PivotTable.

3. Insert two blank rows above the PivotTable. In cell A1, enter the title **`Bell & Rodgers`**. In cell A2, enter the subtitle **`Average Billing per Hour, 2020 and 2021`**.

4. Merge and center the text across A1:C1 and A2:C2. Apply the Title style to cell A1 and bold the text. Apply the Heading 4 style to cell A2.

5. Change the field name in cell B5 to **`Average 2020 Hourly Billing`**. Change the field name in cell C5 to **`Average 2021 Hourly Billing`**.

6. Apply the Currency number format with two decimal places and the $ symbol to the Average 2020 Hourly Billing and Average 2021 Hourly Billing fields.

7. Change the column widths for columns B and C to 12.00, and change the width for column D, which is currently blank, to 50.

8. Wrap and center the field names in cells B5 and C5.

9. Use the Field List button, the '+/– Buttons' button, and the Field Headers button (PivotTable Analyze tab | Show group) to hide the field list, the Expand/Collapse buttons, and the field headers (Figure 8–76).

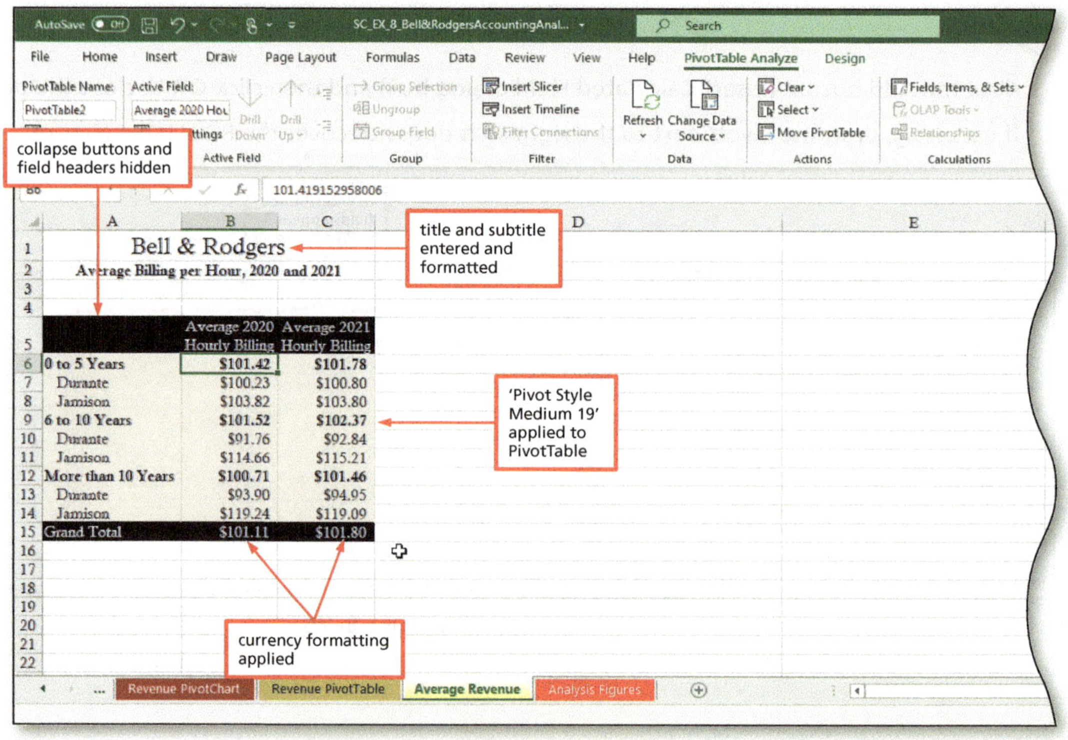

Figure 8–76

To Format the PivotChart

The following steps format the PivotChart report.

1. If necessary, click in the PivotChart report to select it.

2. Move and resize the PivotChart report so that it fills the range D1:D15.

3. Apply Style 12 in the Chart Styles gallery (Design tab | Chart Styles group).

4. Use the 'Change Colors' button (Design tab | Chart Styles group) to change the colors to 'Colorful Palette 3' in the Colorful area.
5. If necessary, position the legend at the top of the PivotChart report.
6. Click the Field Buttons button (PivotChart Analyze tab | Show/Hide group) to hide the field buttons.
7. Increase the magnification to 120%.
8. Save the workbook (Figure 8–77).

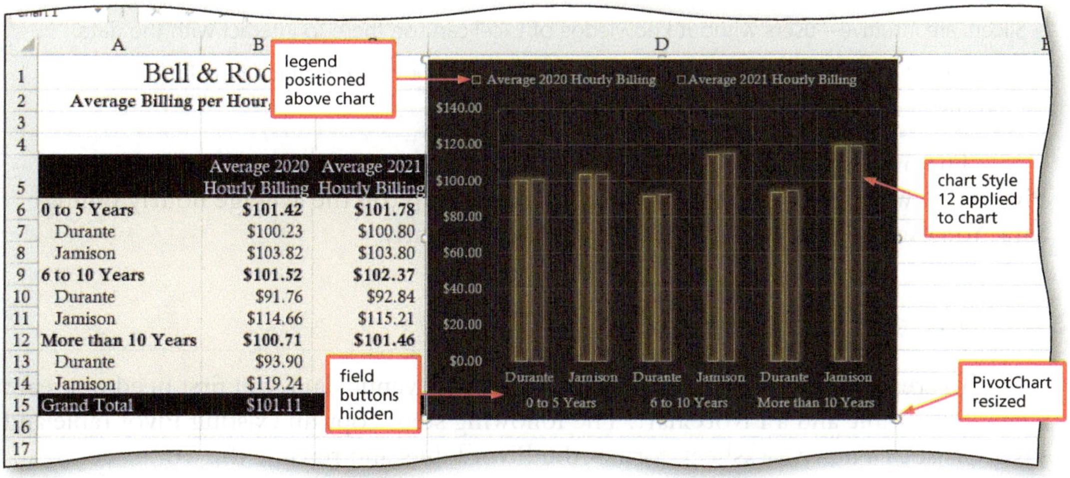

Figure 8–77

More About PivotCharts

If you need to make a change to the underlying data for a PivotChart, you can click the Change Data Source button (PivotChart Analyze tab | Data group). You also can refresh PivotChart data after the change by clicking the Refresh button (PivotChart Analyze tab | Data group).

As you have seen, Excel automatically creates a legend when you create a PivotChart. The legend is from the fields in the Values area of the Field List. To move the legend in a PivotChart, right-click the legend and then click Format Legend on the shortcut menu. The Format Legend pane will display options for placing the legend at various locations in the chart area.

As with tables and PivotTables, you can filter the data in a Pivot Chart. Any fields in the Axis (Categories) area of the Field List, display as filter buttons in the lower-left corner of the chart area. To filter a PivotChart, click one of the buttons; the resulting menu will allow you to sort, search, and select.

Working with Slicers

One of the strengths of PivotTables is that you can ask questions of the data by using filters. Being able to identify and examine subgroups is a useful analytical tool; however, when using filters and autofilters, the user cannot always tell which subgroups have the filters and autofilters selected without clicking filter buttons. Slicers are easy-to-see buttons that you can click to filter the data in PivotTables and PivotCharts, making the data easier to interpret. With slicers, the subgroups are immediately identifiable and can be changed with a click of a button or buttons.

BTW
Distributing a Workbook
Instead of printing and distributing a hard copy of a workbook, you can distribute the workbook electronically. Options include sending the workbook via email; posting it on cloud storage (such as OneDrive) and sharing the file with others; posting it on social media, a blog, or other website; and sharing a link associated with an online location of the workbook. You also can create and share a PDF or XPS image of the workbook so that users can view the file in Acrobat Reader or XPS Viewer instead of in Excel.

BTW

Printing

If you want to improve the quality of Excel printouts that contain graphical elements, such as images, charts, and tables, you can instruct Excel to print high-quality graphics in workbooks by clicking File on the ribbon to open Backstage view, clicking the Options tab in Backstage view to display the Excel Options dialog box, clicking Advanced in the left pane (Excel Options dialog box), scrolling to the Print area in the right pane, placing a checkmark in the 'High quality mode for graphics' check box, and then clicking OK. Then use Backstage view to print the workbook as usual.

Consider This

Why would you use slicers rather than row, column, or report filters?

One effective way to analyze PivotTable data is to use slicers to filter the data in more than one field. They offer the following advantages over filtering directly in a PivotTable:

- In a PivotTable, you use the filter button to specify how to filter the data, which involves a few steps. After you create a slicer, you can perform this same filtering task in one step.
- You can filter only one PivotTable at a time, whereas you can connect slicers to more than one PivotTable to filter data.
- Excel treats slicers as graphic objects, which means you can move, resize, and format them as you can any other graphic object. As graphic objects, they invite interaction.
- Slicers are intuitive—users without knowledge of Excel can use them to interact with the data.
- Slicers make it easy for users to understand exactly what is shown in a filtered PivotTable or PivotChart.

The owner of Bell & Rodgers has asked you to set up a PivotChart and PivotTable with a user-friendly way for anyone to explore the average hourly billing data. You can use slicers to complete this task efficiently.

To Copy a PivotTable and PivotChart

To create a canvas for exploratory analysis of revenue data, you first need to create a new PivotTable and a PivotChart. The following steps copy an existing PivotTable and PivotChart to a new worksheet, format the PivotTable, and rename the worksheet.

1. Create a copy of the Average Revenue worksheet and then move the copy so that it precedes the Average Revenue worksheet.
2. Rename the new worksheet, `Slicers`, and apply the Green tab color from the Standard Colors area.
3. Apply chart Style 8 to the PivotChart.
4. Set the column width of column E to 18 and column F to 19.00.
5. If necessary, turn off the display of field headers and +/– buttons for the PivotTable (Figure 8–78).

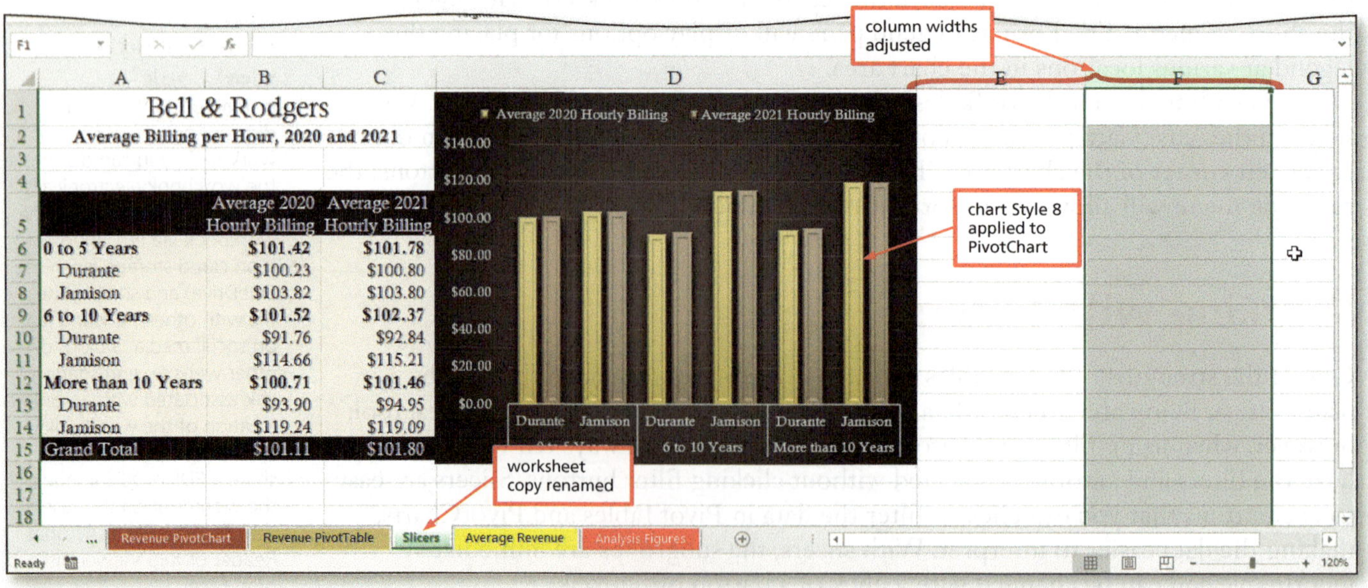

Figure 8–78

To Add Slicers to the Worksheet

The following steps add slicers that provide an easier way to filter the new PivotTable and PivotChart. **Why?** To analyze sales data for specific subgroups, you can use slicers instead of PivotTable filters.

1

- If necessary, click to make the PivotChart active and then display the PivotChart Analyze tab.
- Click the Insert Slicer button (PivotChart Analyze tab | Filter group) to display the Insert Slicers dialog box.
- Click to place checkmarks in the City, Employee Experience, and Accounting Type check boxes (Figure 8–79).

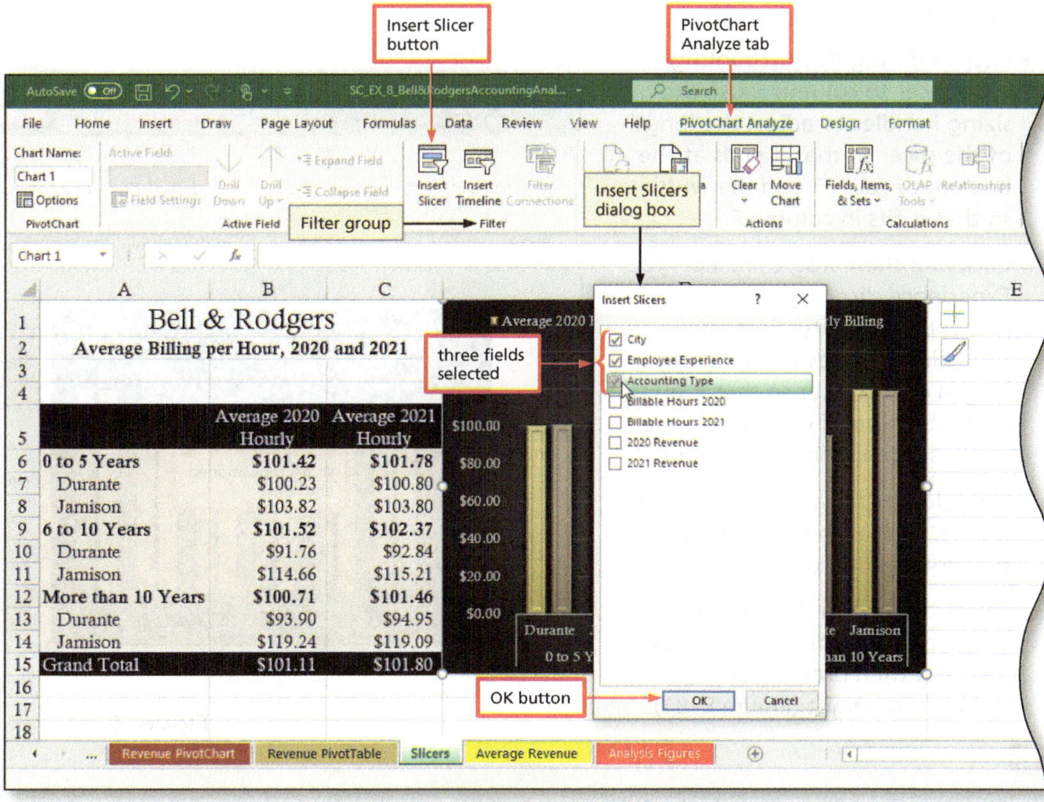

Figure 8–79

2

- Click OK (Insert Slicers dialog box) to display the selected slicers on the worksheet (Figure 8–80).

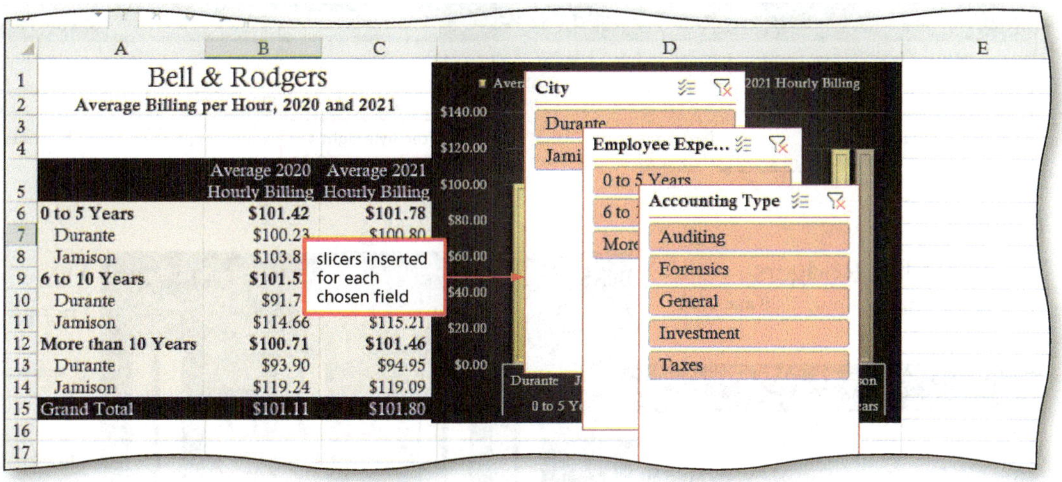

Figure 8–80

To Format Slicers

You can format slicers in a variety of ways. Using the Slicer tab, you can customize slicer settings, resize slicer buttons to exact dimensions, change the number of columns in a slicer, or connect a slicer to a different PivotChart using the Report Connections button (Slicer tab | Slicer group). The following steps move the slicers to the right of the PivotChart and then format them. **Why?** The slicers need to be moved and formatted so that they do not obscure the PivotTable or PivotChart, and are easy to read and use.

1

- Click the title bar of the City slicer and then drag the slicer to column E. Use the sizing handles to adjust the length of the slicer so that it ends at the bottom of row 6 and fits the width of the slicer so that it ends at the right edge of column E.
- Click and drag the Accounting Type slicer to column F. Use the sizing handles to adjust the length of the slicer so that it ends at the bottom of row 15 and the width so that it fits in column F.
- Click and then drag the Employee Experience slicer to column E, just below the City slicer. Use the sizing handles to change the length of the slicer so that it ends at the bottom of row 15 and the width so that it fits in column E.
- Hold down CTRL and then, one at a time, click each of the slicer title bars to select all three.
- Select the text in the Height box (Slicer tab | Buttons group), type **.4** and then press ENTER to set the button height (Figure 8–81).

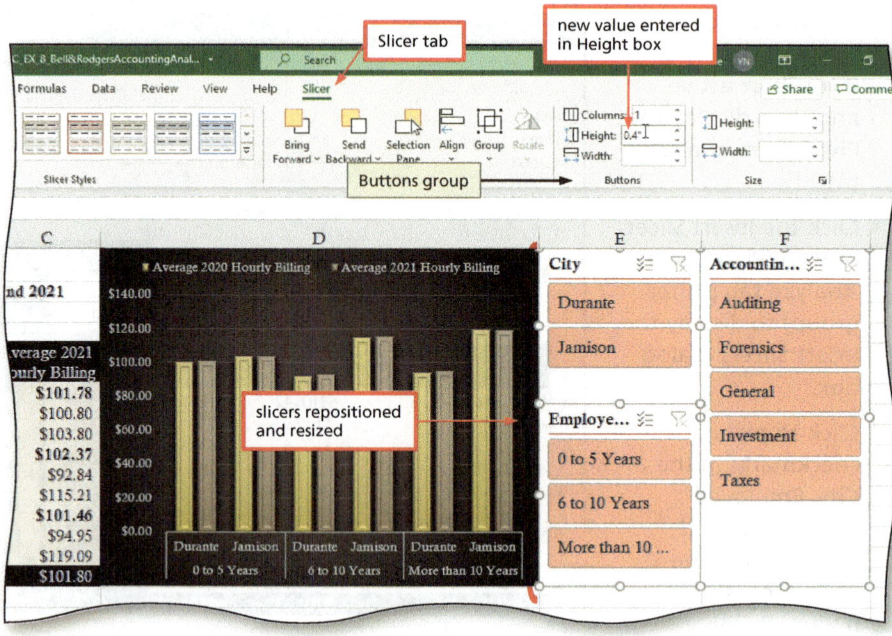

Figure 8–81

2

- Click the 'Tan, Slicer Style Light 4' Slicer style (Slicer tab | Slicer Styles group) to apply it to the slicers (Figure 8–82).

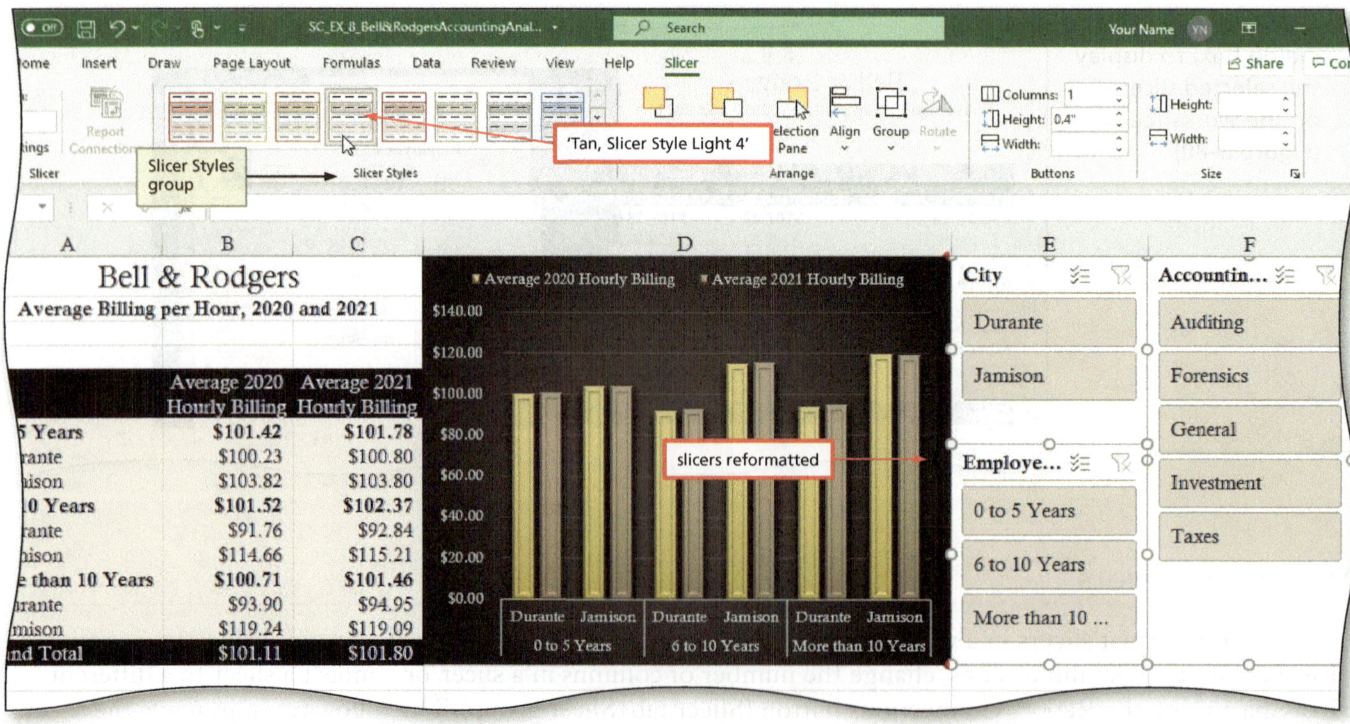

Figure 8–82

3

- Click any cell to deselect the slicers.

Q&A
How do you resize slicers and slicer buttons to exact dimensions?
Use the Height and Width boxes (Slicer tab | Size group and Buttons group) to change the size of a slicer or of slicer buttons.

To Use the Slicers

Why? Slicers provide you with a visual means of filtering data by simply clicking subgroups of interest to change the data displayed in the PivotTable and PivotChart. Slicers based on row label fields provide the same results as filters in a PivotTable. They narrow the table down to a visible subgroup or subgroups. Clicking a slicer button displays only the data that corresponds to the variable name on the slicer. You can select multiple fields by using the Multi-Select button in the slicer title bar or by using CTRL+click to add a button (in the same slicer) to the display. Note that slicers filter data in both the PivotTable and the PivotChart.

The following steps use slicers to review average sales for different combinations of Employee Experience and City.

1

- Click Durante in the City slicer to display only the data for Durante in the PivotTable and PivotChart calculations.
- Hold down CTRL and then click '0 to 5 Years' in the Employee Experience slicer. Release CTRL to remove that data and show the 6 to 10 Years and More than 10 Years data only (Figure 8–83).

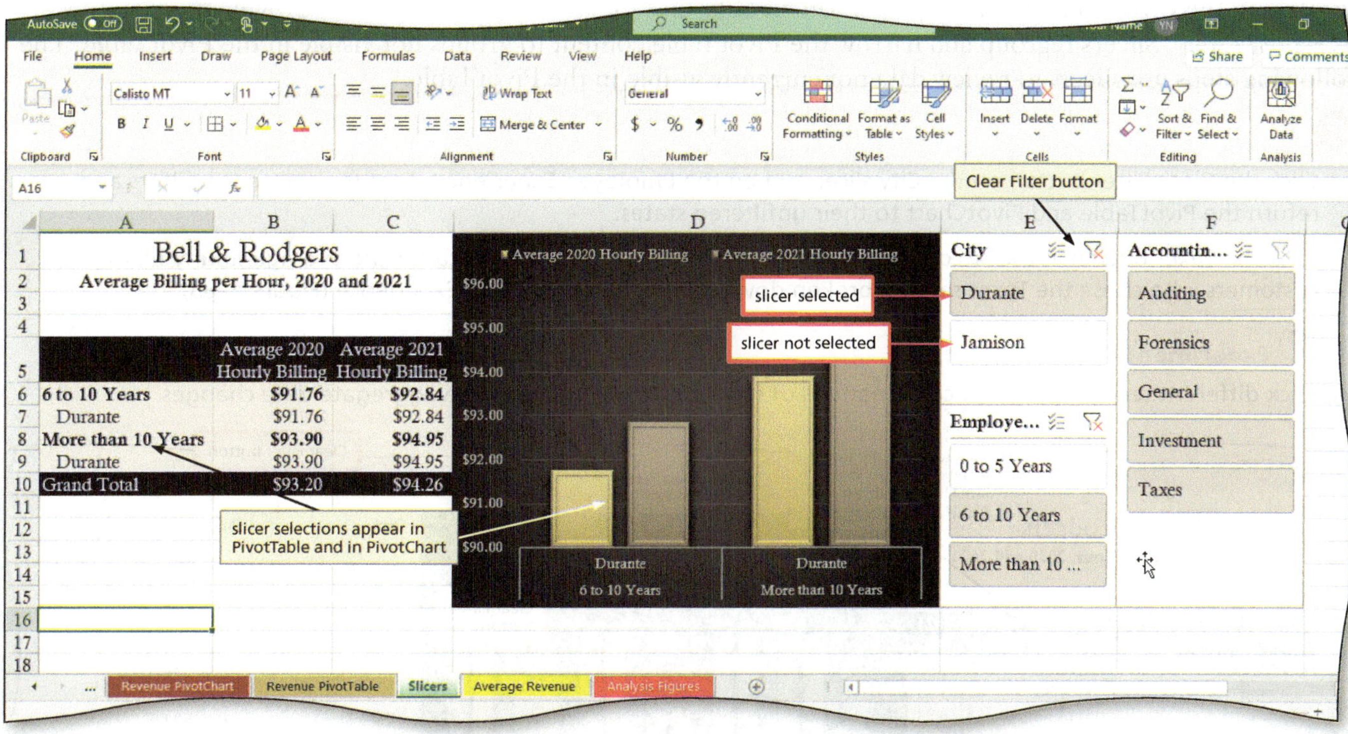

Figure 8–83

2

- Click Jamison in the City slicer to see the data for Jamison from the 6 to 10 Years and More than 10 Years data only (Figure 8–84).

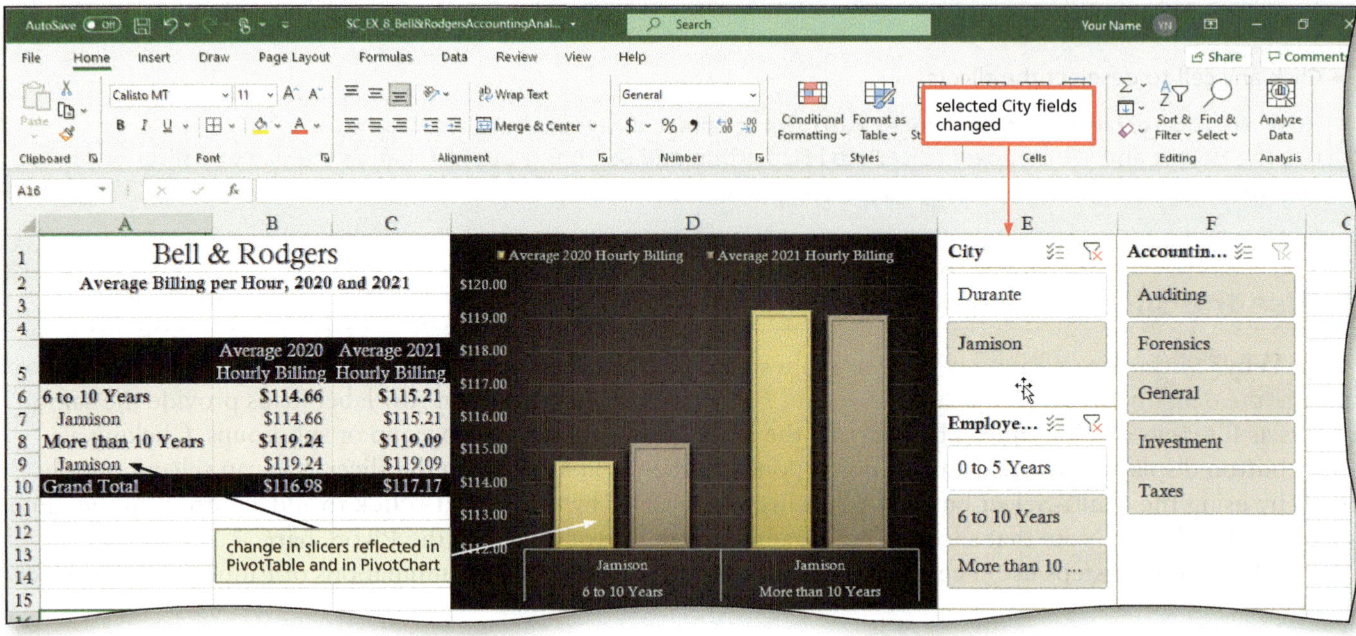

Figure 8–84

To Use Slicers to Review Data Not in a PivotTable

You can look for possible explanations of patterns by using slicers to analyze data other than that which displays in the PivotTable. **Why?** Slicers based on fields not included in the PivotTable provide the same results as report filters. Slicers regroup and narrow the PivotTable content to groups not visible in the PivotTable. The following steps use slicers to review data not currently visible in the PivotTable.

1

- Click the Clear Filter button on the City slicer and on the Employee Experience slicer to remove the filters and return the PivotTable and PivotChart to their unfiltered states.
- Click the Taxes button in the Accounting Type slicer to see the aggregate data for the average hourly billing for customers who chose the Taxes service, broken down by City and Employee Experience (Figure 8–85).

Experiment

- Click different service types and combinations of service types to see how the aggregate data changes.

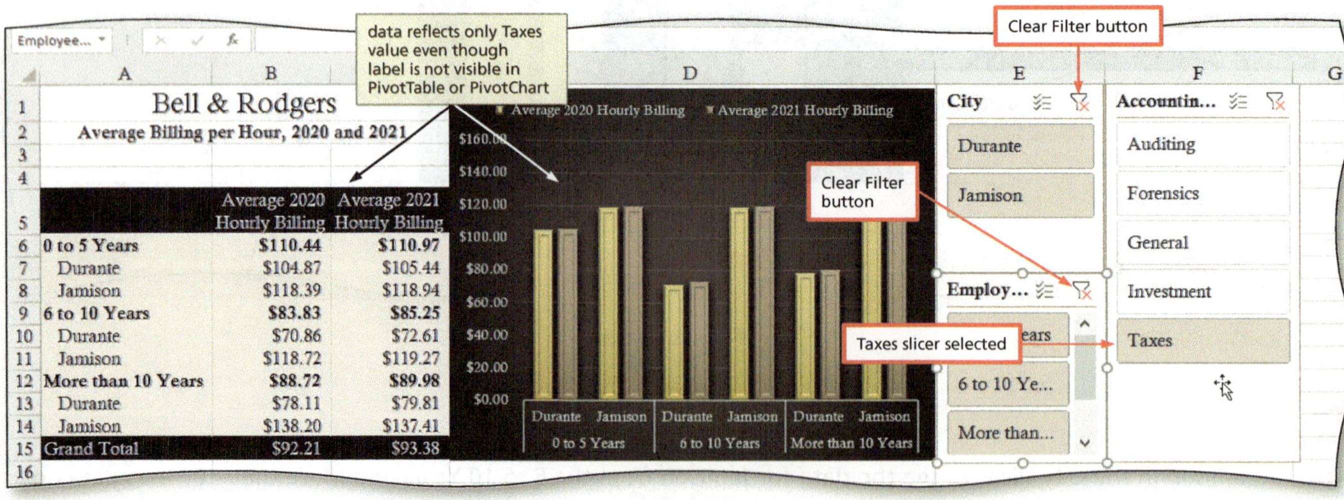

Figure 8–85

2

- With the Taxes button selected, if necessary, click the Multi-Select button in the slicer header, and then click the Investment button in the Accounting Type slicer to view the aggregate data for both Taxes and Investments, broken down by City and Employee Experience (Figure 8–86).

Q&A **How can I save a particular PivotTable setup?**
PivotTables are dynamic by nature. To save a particular configuration, make a copy of the worksheet, and use the Protect Sheet command (Review tab | Protect group) to keep changes from being made to the worksheet copy. You can continue to use the PivotTable on the original worksheet to analyze the data.

3

- Save the workbook.

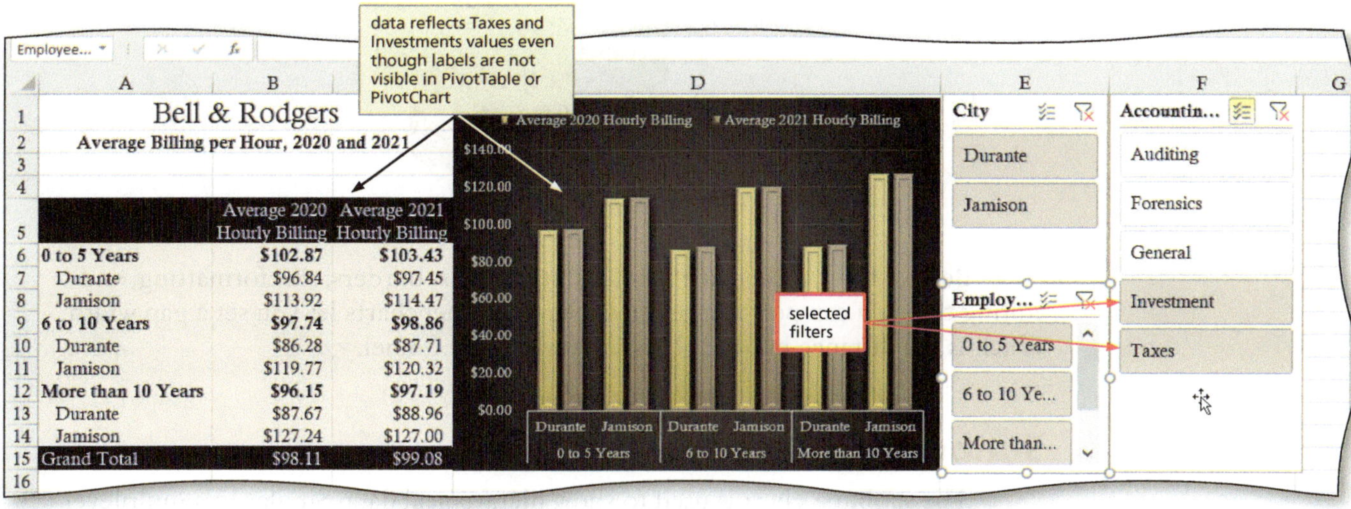

Figure 8–86

Other Excel Charts

Large amounts of data, while sometimes crucial for data management, can be cumbersome and hard to read, especially when you are trying to see data trends and relationships. Earlier in this module you created PivotCharts from a PivotTable report and from the data itself, also called raw data. Excel provides many additional chart types to help you create easy-to-read, intuitive overviews of your data. Deciding which kind of chart to use depends on what data you want the chart to portray, how the data is grouped, the relationship of the data to totals, and sometimes personal preference. You also can set alternative text to charts, which is descriptive text for screen readers.

Recall that most charts have two buttons near the upper-right corner to specify chart elements and chart styles. Advanced formatting usually involves the use of the Format pane or the Format tab on the ribbon.

Funnel Charts

Funnel charts show values across various stages in a process as progressively smaller horizontal bars creating a funnel-like effect. Types of data used for funnel charts might include the process of narrowing down a pool of job applicants to hired employees, a sales pipeline, or an order fulfillment process. Figure 8-87 uses data from an ecommerce software website to show how website hits drill down into licensed users.

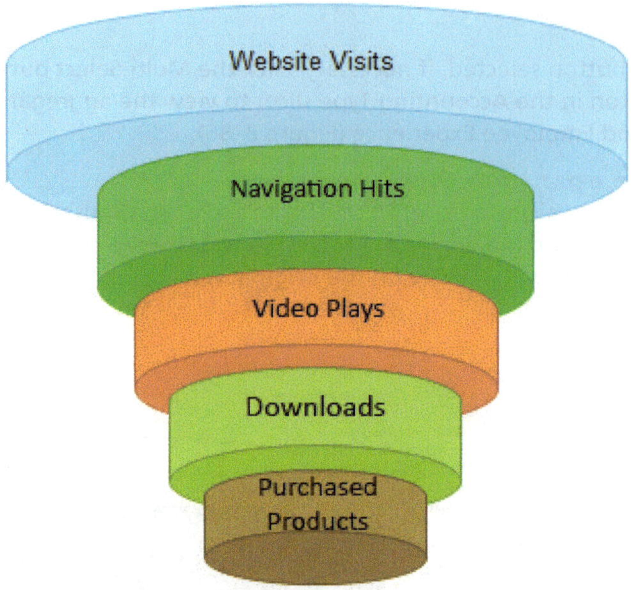

Figure 8–87

Besides the typical color schemes, styles, fills, borders, axis formatting, and editing that you can perform on most charts, funnel charts let you set a gap width, which is the distance between bars or levels in the funnel.

Sunburst Charts

The sunburst chart is used to show hierarchical data. Similar to a multilevel pie or donut chart, each level of the hierarchy is represented by a ring or circle. The innermost circle is the top of the hierarchy; relationships are shown via the outer rings. Types of data used for sunburst charts might include the reporting relationships in an organization, taxonomies, or sales or events shown by time (month-weeks-days) or locations (country-state-city). Figure 8–88 uses a sunburst chart to demonstrate online learning component relationships, and the focus on interactivity.

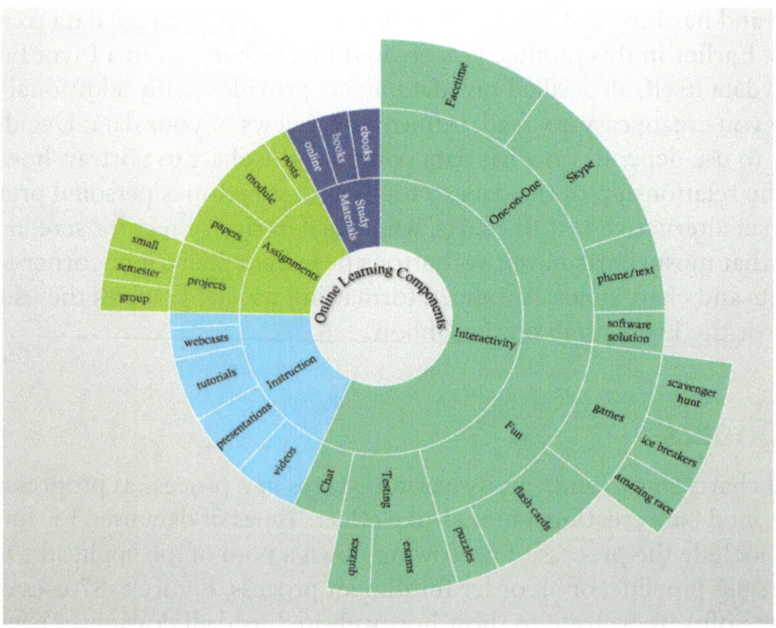

Figure 8–88

Colors in a sunburst chart are based on the theme and color style of the worksheet. Interesting effects can be created by adjusting the size of shadows, soft edges, and glows. With numeric data, you can add values to the sunburst chart in the same manner you do with a treemap.

Waterfall Charts

A waterfall chart shows how an initial value is affected by a series of positive and negative changes. The initial and the final value columns often start on the horizontal axis, while the intermediate values are floating columns. A waterfall chart shows how one data point grew or declined over a period of time, allowing users to see which categories within the data point improved and which ones declined. Typically, columns are color-coded so you quickly can tell positive numbers from negative ones. Waterfall charts can be used for company growth, profit/loss, or inventory. Figure 8–89 uses a waterfall chart to show changes in regional sales over a six-month period. Data labels appear as percentages on the floating columns.

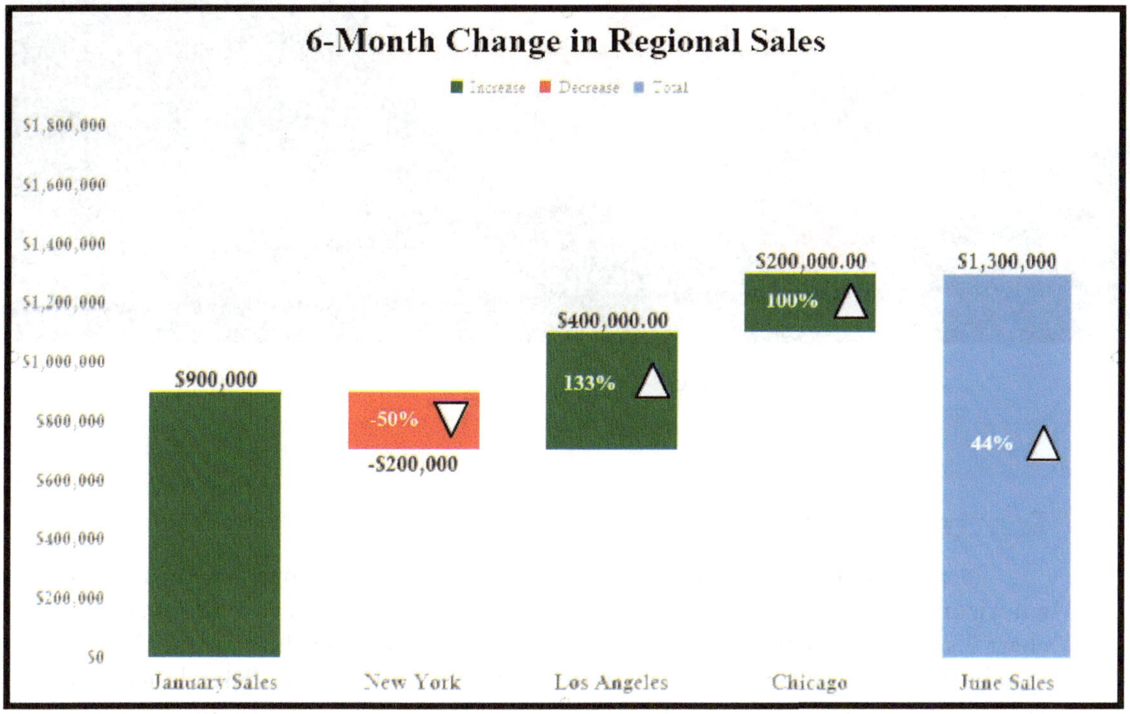

Figure 8–89

Map Charts

If your data has geographical regions or postal codes, you can create a map chart to compare values and show categories across those regions. To do so, highlight the list of locations and the matching data such as populations, land masses, or other statistical information. Then, when you choose to insert a map chart, Excel executes a Bing search to create a map. Figure 8–90 displays a map of the United States with statistical data about heart-related deaths.

Formatting options include cartographic projections (including flat, spherical, and others), area (displays of data, regions, world), and labels (names of countries, states, etc.). You even can format individual locations by clicking them and then making changes in the Format pane. The chart in Figure 8–90 displays a solid color chart area (background) and a gradient legend.

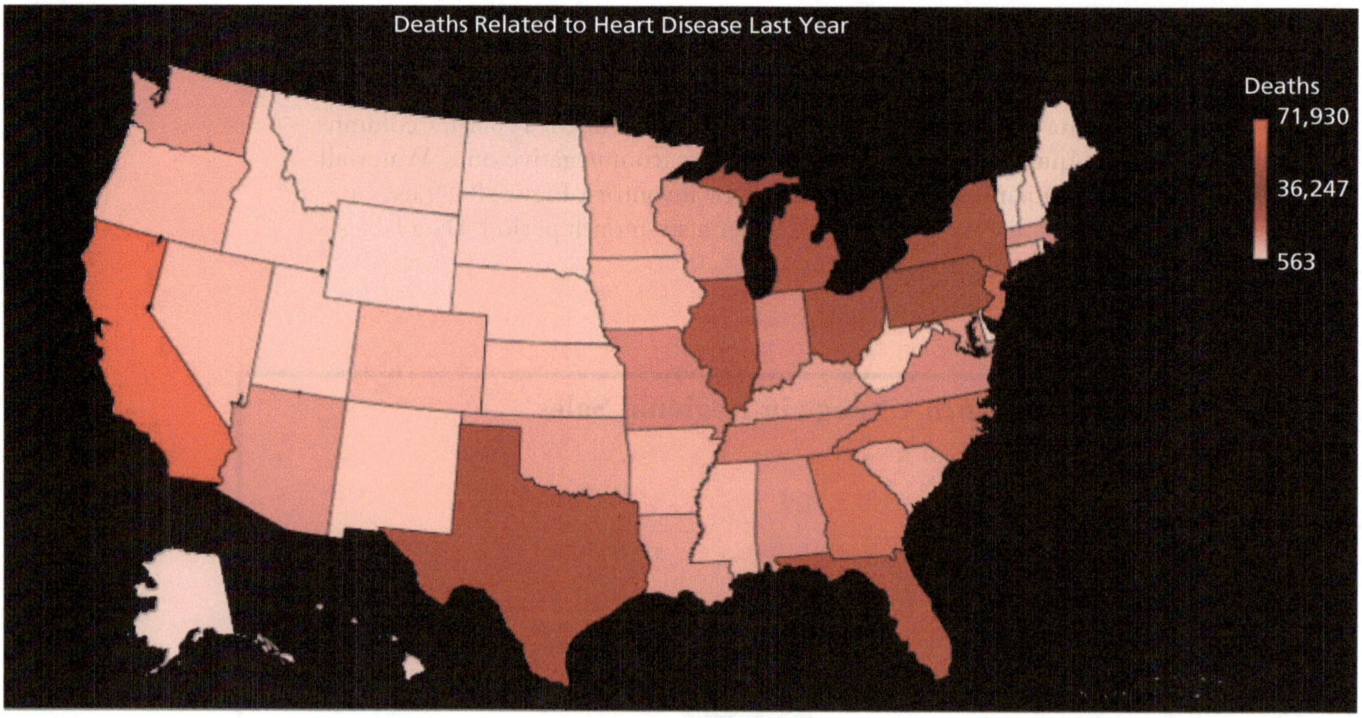

Figure 8–90

Scatter Charts

Scatter charts displays two value axes to show one set of numerical data along a horizontal (x) axis and another set of numerical values along a vertical (y) axis. The chart displays points at the intersection of x and y numerical values. These data points may be distributed evenly or unevenly across the horizontal axis, depending on the data. Scatter charts, also called X-Y scatter charts or scatter plots, should be used when there are many different data points and you want to highlight the similarities or see the distribution of your data.

Figure 8–91 shows sales data—the days of the month along the horizontal axis at the bottom, and the amount of sales on the vertical axis on the side. The plot area (area inside the chart) displays an Excel built-in texture.

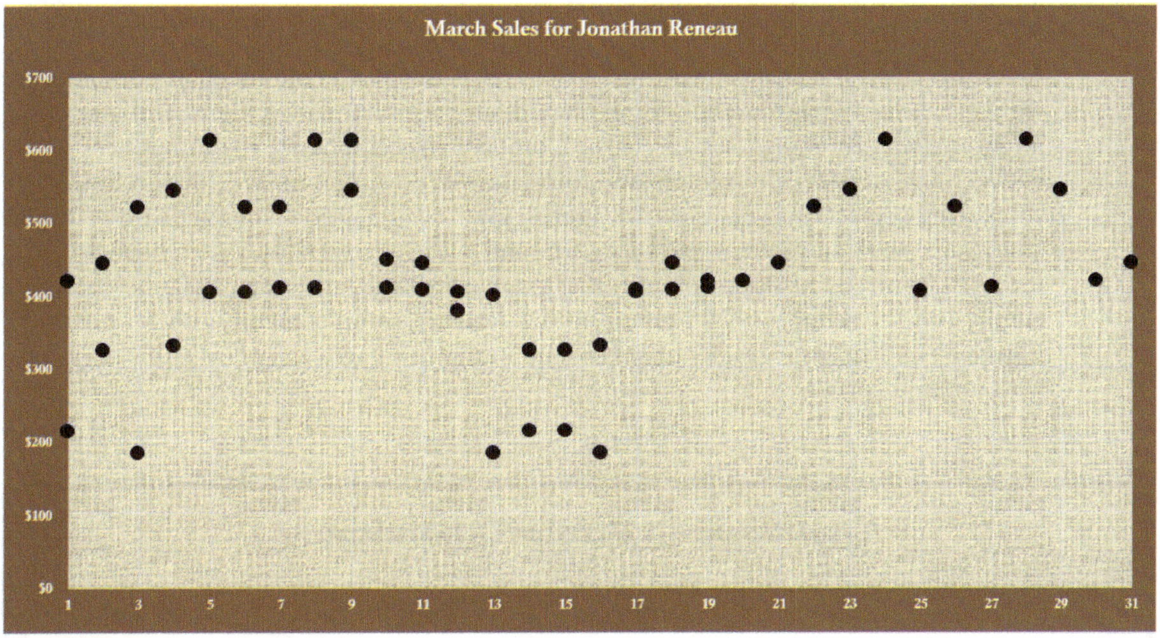

Figure 8–91

Histogram Chart

A histogram is a type of column chart that shows the frequency of data. It consists of rectangles whose height is proportional to the frequency of a variable. The x-axis across the bottom contains ranges of data values called bins. The y-axis is the frequency. Figure 8–92 displays the average winter temperature in Los Angeles and displays a picture chart area (background). You can set a gap width between columns.

Figure 8–92

Combo Charts

A **combo chart** is a chart consisting of two charts, such as a column chart combined with a line chart, that together graph related but dissimilar data. Other combinations might include bar charts or area charts. Combo charts emphasize the differences between sets of data; for example, in-store sales are down but online sales are up, or comparing projections versus actual figures. Figure 8–93 uses a column chart to display attendance at an amusement park for 2019 and a line chart to display attendance for 2020. While a clustered column chart could show the same data, a combo chart emphasizes the difference by presenting the data in a completely different way. Figure 8–93 displays a gradient background in the chart area as well as a thick border with mitered corners.

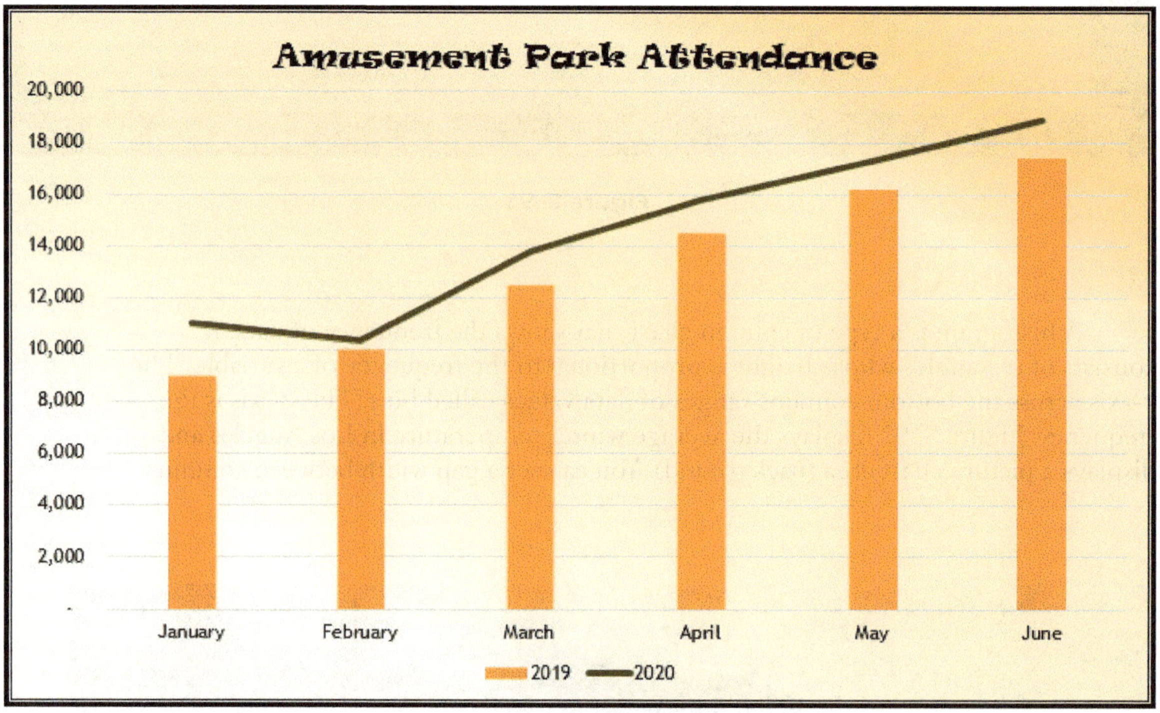

Figure 8–93

Box and Whisker Charts

A box and whisker chart (Figure 8–94) is a statistical graph that shows distribution of numerical data into quartiles. A **quartile** is a way to divide ordered data into equal groups based on finding the median. Simply put, the box part of the chart shows the median and the two groups around the median with equal sets of numbers. The high and low values in the ordered data are displayed by lines extending vertically, called whiskers. Any value that is 1.5 times below or above the box is called an outlier and is represented by a dot in the box and whisker chart.

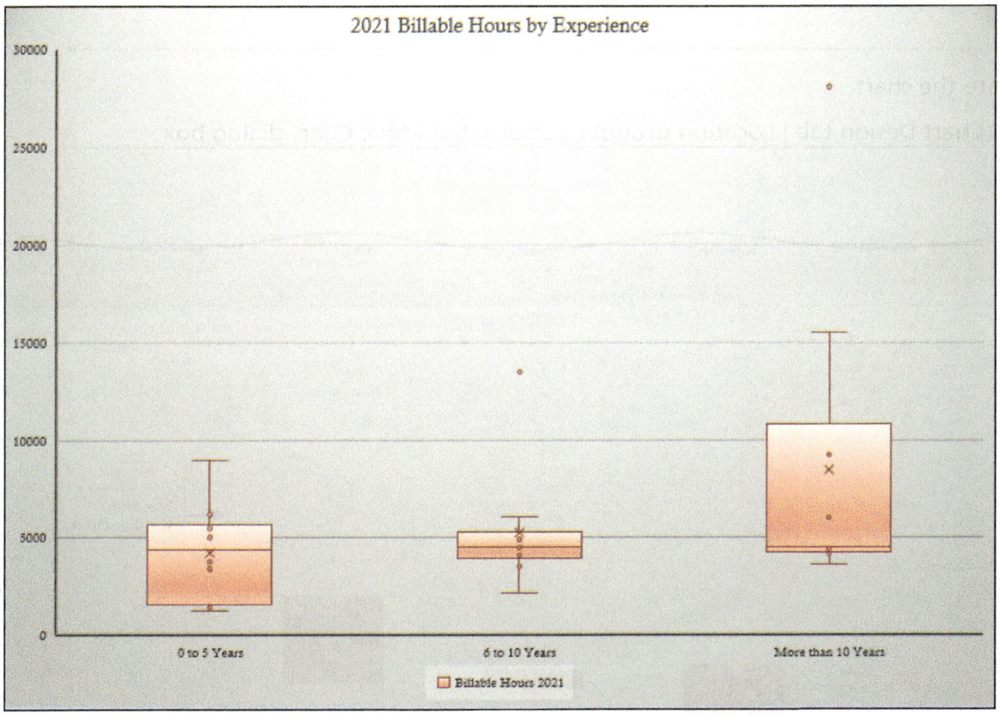

Figure 8–94

To Create a Box and Whisker Chart

The Bell & Rodgers company would like to compare the billable hours in 2021 by using the years of employee experience: 0 to 5 years, 6 to 10 years, and more than 10 years. In each category, the company would like to see the box and whisker notation. **Why?** The company is looking for the median billable hours by experience and any billable hours that are extremely high or low in each category. The following steps create a box and whisker chart.

1

- Click the Analysis Figures tab to display the Analysis Figures sheet.
- Select cells B2:B32. CTRL+drag cells E2:E32 to add the range to the selection.
- Click the 'Insert Statistic Chart' button to display its gallery (Insert tab | Charts group (Figure 8–95).

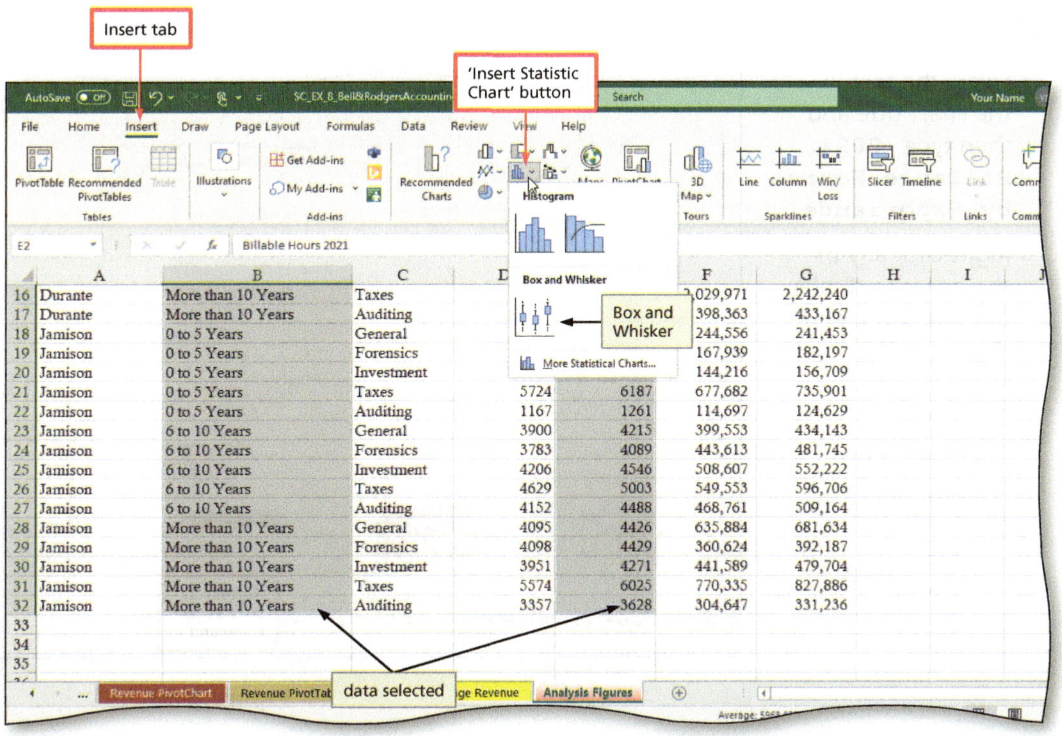

Figure 8–95

2

- Click Box and Whisker to create the chart.
- Click the Move Chart button (Chart Design tab | Location group) to display the Move Chart dialog box.
- Click New sheet (Move Chart dialog box) to select the option button.
- If necessary, double-click the default text in the New sheet box to select the text, and then type `Box and Whisker Chart` to enter a name for the new worksheet.
- Click OK (Move Chart dialog box) to move the chart to a new worksheet.
- Color the worksheet tab Light Blue in the Standard Colors area (Figure 8–96).

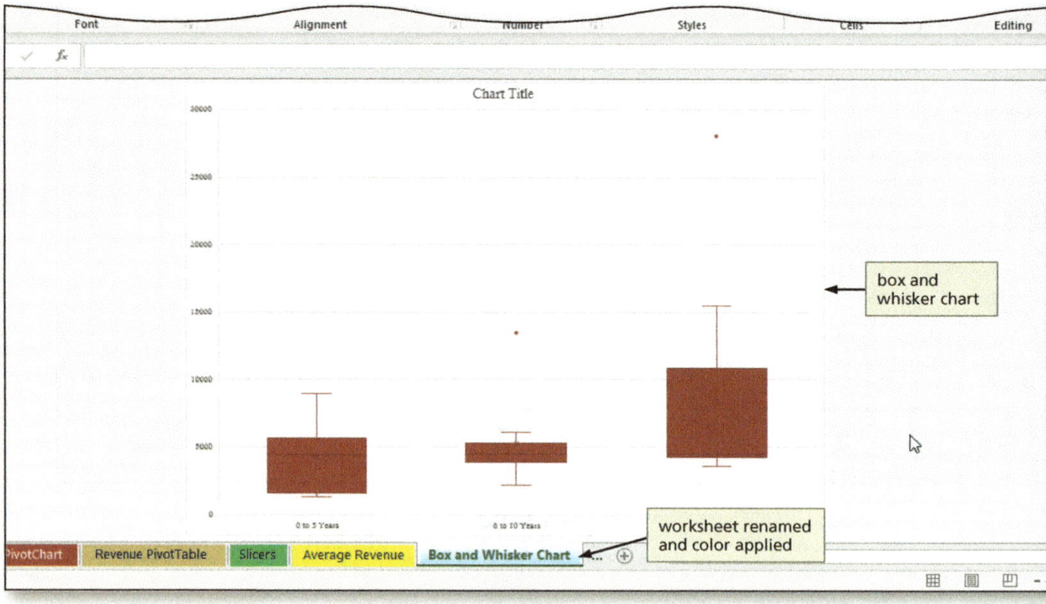

Figure 8–96

To Format a Box and Whisker Chart

The following steps edit the chart title, apply a chart style, and format the box and whisker data series.

1

- Select the text in the chart title and then type `2021 Billable Hours by Experience`.
- Right-click any of the boxes to display the shortcut menu (Figure 8–97).

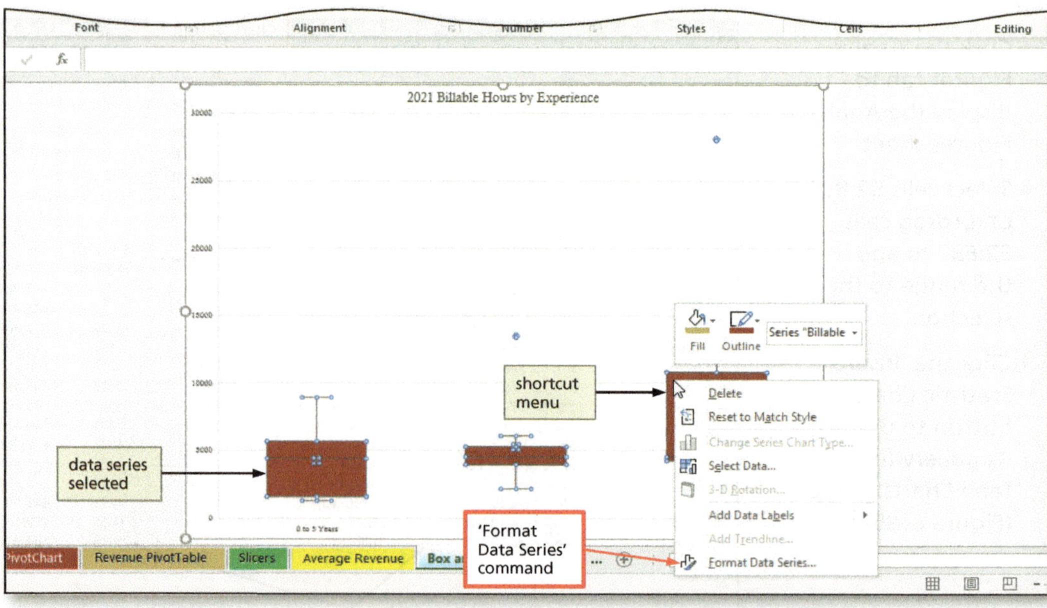

Figure 8–97

2

- Click 'Format Data Series' to display the Format Data Series pane.
- If necessary, click the Series Options button to display the Series Options sheet.
- Click the 'Show Inner Points' check box to display the various data values as dots on the chart (Figure 8–98).

Experiment

- Click other combinations of check boxes to see how the chart changes. When you are finished, click the check boxes shown in Figure 8–98.

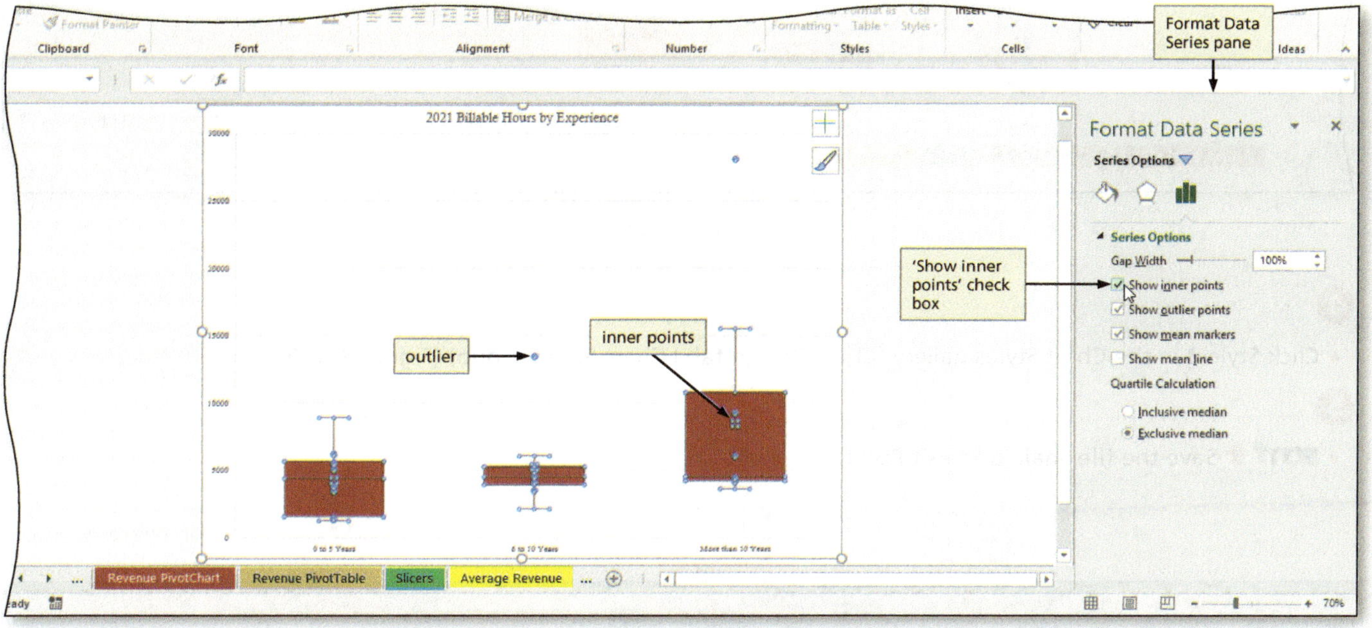

Figure 8–98

3

- In the Format Data Series pane, click the 'Fill & Line' button to display the Fill & Line sheet.
- Click Fill if necessary to display the choices for filling the boxes in the chart.
- Click the Gradient fill option button (Figure 8–99).

Experiment

- One at a time, click each of the other option buttons to see how the chart changes. When you are finished, click the Gradient option button.

Q&A **What are the other gradient settings?**
You can choose from various preset gradients and types. The Gradient stops bar lets you customize the amount of color from darkest to lightest. As you click each stop, you can set its color, position, amount of transparency, and brightness.

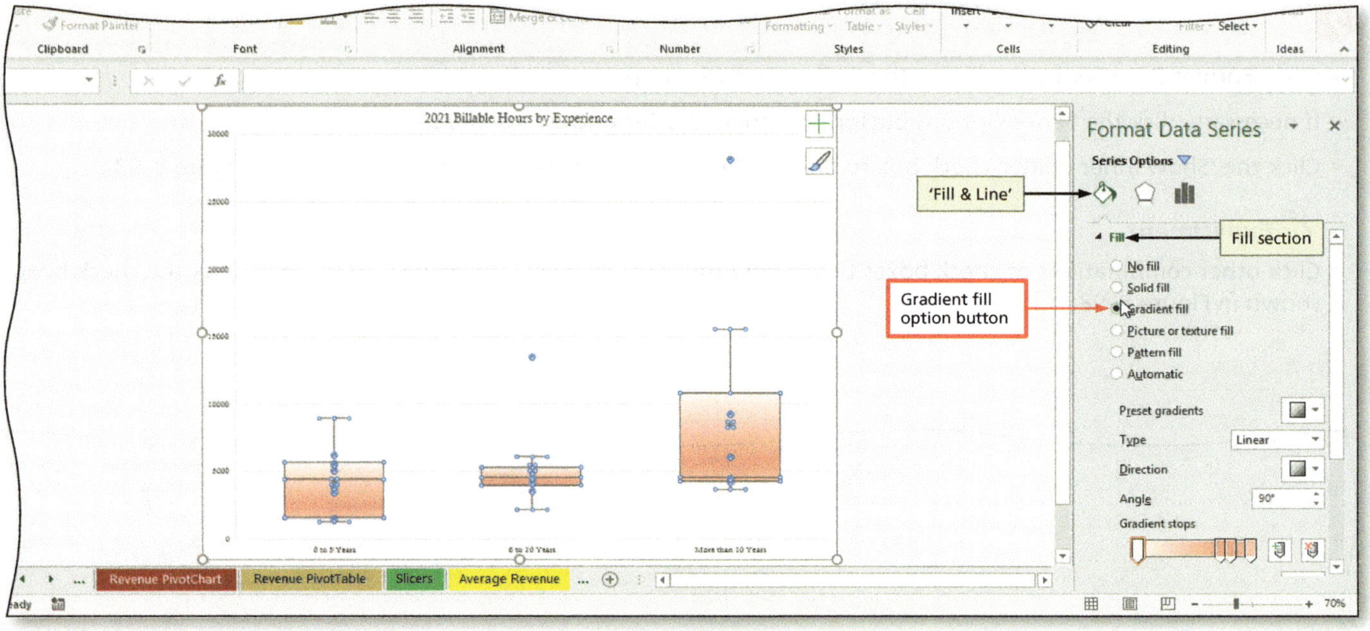

Figure 8–99

4

- Click Style 3 in the Chart Styles gallery (Chart Design tab | Chart Styles group) (Figure 8–100).

5

- **sam** Save the file again and exit Excel.

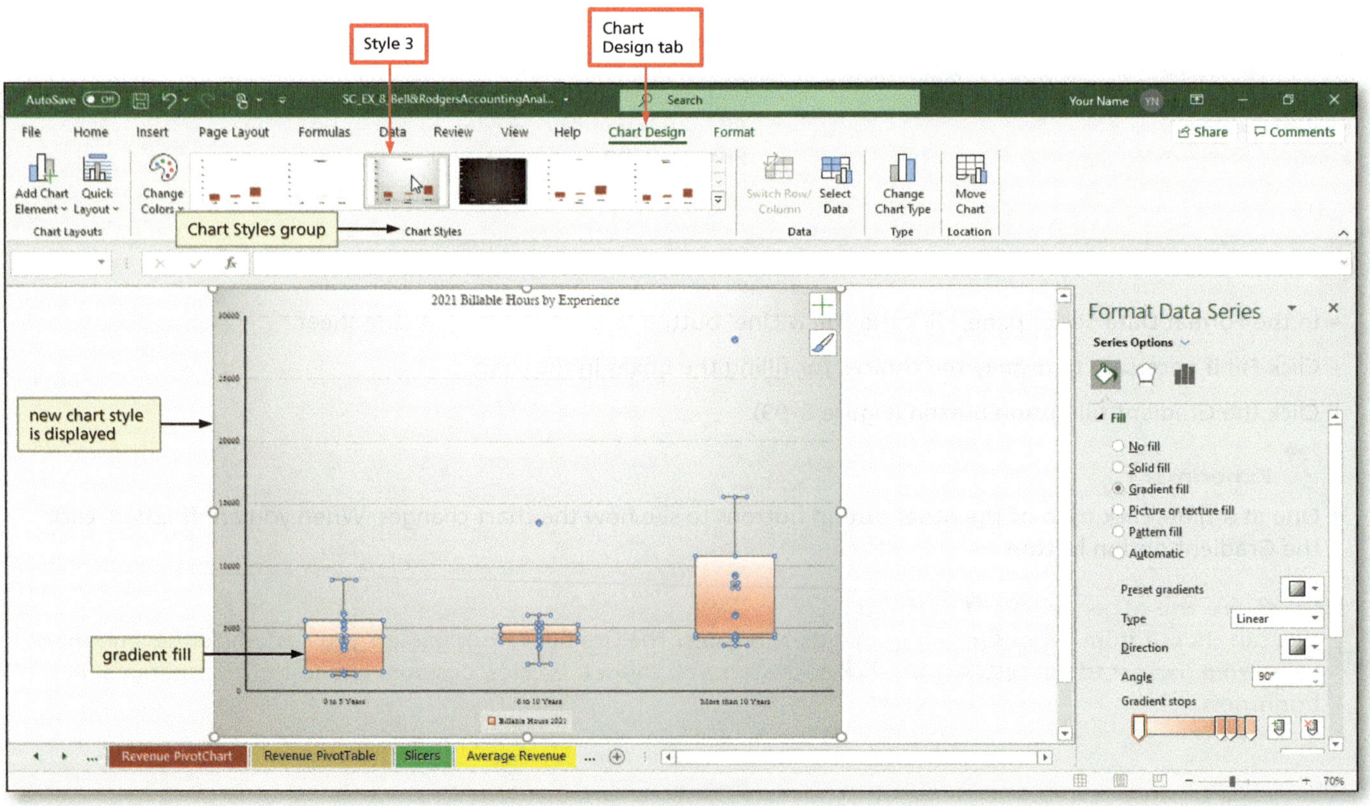

Figure 8–100

Summary

In this module, you learned how to create a 2-D line chart and add a trendline to extend the trend to two more time periods. You added an R-squared (R^2) value to the trendline to measure the strength of the trend and formatted a data point. You created and formatted a PivotTable report based on raw data. Using the Field List, you added row fields and columns to the PivotTable. You created calculated fields in the PivotTable using summary functions. To see the power of the PivotTable, you inserted, deleted, and organized fields to view the data in different ways. You created and formatted a PivotChart Report from a PivotTable, filtering and analyzing data. You then created both a PivotTable and PivotChart from scratch and added a calculated field. Finally, you created slicers to make manipulating PivotTables and PivotCharts easier and added a box and whisker chart.

Consider This: Plan Ahead

What decisions will you need to make when creating your next worksheet to analyze data using trendlines, PivotCharts, and PivotTables?

Use these guidelines as you complete the assignments in this module and create your own worksheets for evaluating and analyzing data outside of this class.

1. Identify trend(s) to analyze with a trendline.
    a. Determine data to use.
    b. Determine time period to use.
    c. Determine type and format of trendline.
2. Identify questions to ask of your data.
    a. Determine which variables to combine in a PivotTable or PivotChart.
3. Create and format PivotTables and PivotCharts.
    a. Add all fields to the field list.
    b. Use formatting features for PivotTables and PivotCharts.
4. Manipulate PivotTables and PivotCharts to analyze data.
    a. Select fields to include in PivotTables and PivotCharts.
    b. Use filters to review subsets of data.
    c. Use calculated fields and summary statistics to look at different measures of data.
    d. Create and use slicers to look at subsets of data.

Apply Your Knowledge

Reinforce the skills and apply the concepts you learned in this module.

Creating a PivotTable and PivotChart

Note: To complete these steps, you will be required to use the Data Files. Please contact your instructor for information about accessing the Data Files.

Instructions: Start Excel. Open the workbook SC_EX_8-2.xlsx, which is located in the Data Files. The workbook you open contains an order entry sheet for a restaurant supply company. You are to create a PivotTable and PivotChart from the Order Database. Figure 8–101 shows the completed Inventory worksheet.

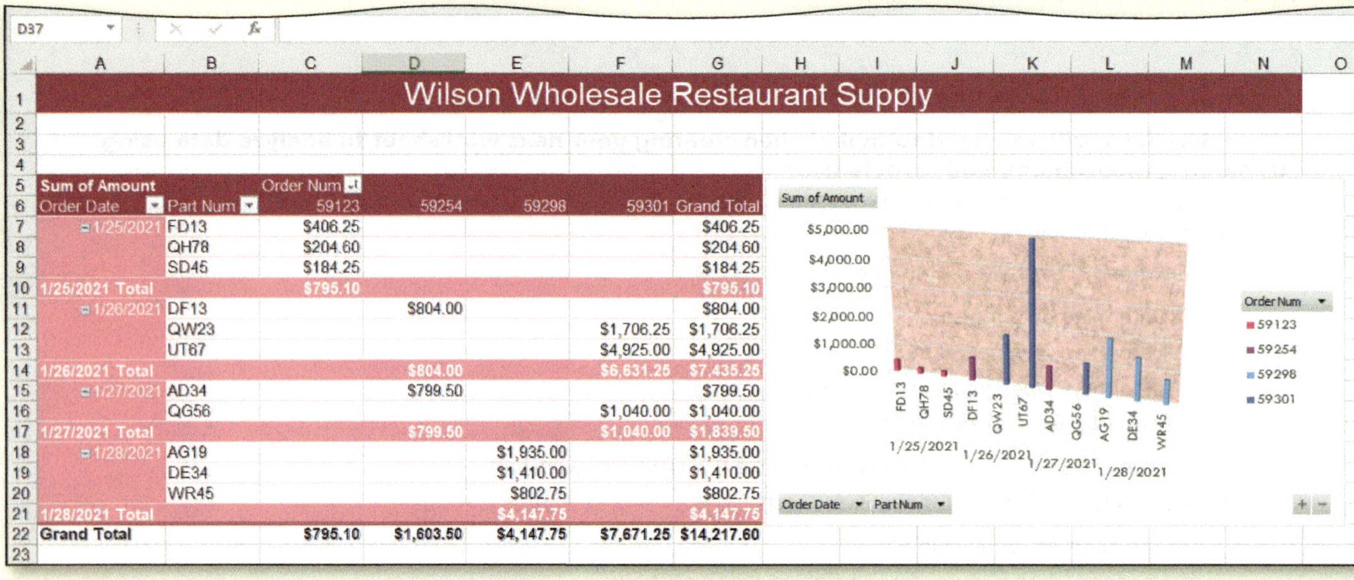

Figure 8–101

Perform the following tasks:

1. Save the workbook as SC_EX_8_RestaurantSupplyComplete. Select cell A3 and then click the PivotTable button (Insert tab | Tables group) to display the Create PivotTable (or 'PivotTable from table or range') dialog box. Make sure New Worksheet is selected and then click OK.
2. Drag the Order Num and Description fields from the 'Choose fields to add to report' area to the Rows area to add the fields to the PivotTable.
3. Drag the Amount field from the 'Choose fields to add to report' area to the Values area to add the sum of the Amount field to the PivotTable.
4. Drag the Order Date field from the 'Choose fields to add to report' area to the Filters area.
5. Click the More button (Design tab | PivotTable Styles group) and choose the 'Rose, Pivot Style Medium 7' style.
6. Format the Total data as currency with dollar signs and two decimal places. If necessary, widen columns so all data and headings display correctly.
7. Click the Report Layout button (Design tab | Layout group) to display the Report Layout menu. Change the PivotTable report layout to tabular.
8. Click the filter button in cell B1 to display the filter menu. Click the 'Select Multiple Items' check box to select it. Select only orders from January 25 and January 26.

9. Click the filter button again and select all dates.
10. Move the Order Num field to the Columns Area. Remove the Description field from the Rows area. Move the Order Date and add the Part Num fields to the Rows area.
11. If necessary, format any remaining dollar amounts as currency.
12. Click the PivotChart button (PivotTable Analyze tab | Tools group) and select the 3-D Clustered Column.
13. Move the PivotChart to a location beside the PivotTable and resize it as shown in Figure 8–101. In the PivotChart, click the OrderNum filter button and then click 'Sort Smallest to Largest' on the menu.
14. Insert two more blank lines at the top of the worksheet. Type `Wilson Wholesale Restaurant Supply` as the title. Merge and center it across both the PivotTable and PivotChart. Change the font color and fill color to match the PivotTable headers. Change the font size to 20.
15. Click the PivotChart. Click the Chart Elements arrow (Format tab | Current Selection group) and choose Back Wall. Click the Shape Fill button (Format tab | Shape Styles group), click Texture, and then click 'Pink tissue paper' in the Texture gallery. Click the Shape Effects button (Format tab | Shape Styles group), click 3-D Rotation, and then, in the Perspective area, click 'Perspective: Contrasting Left'.
16. Right-click the vertical axis labels, and then click Format Axis on the shortcut menu. In the Axis Options area, change the Major Units to 1000.

    If requested by your instructor, in cell L2, type `Data Analyzed by,` followed by your name.
17. Name the worksheet Inventory and change the tab color to Pink, Accent 1. Save the workbook again, and then close the workbook.
18. Submit the revised workbook in the format specified by your instructor and exit Excel.
19. List two changes you would make to the PivotTable report to make it more easily interpreted by the user and explain why you would make these changes. These changes could be to the formatting, layout, or both.

Extend Your Knowledge

Extend the skills you learned in this module and experiment with new skills. You may need to use Help to complete the assignment.

Grouping Content in PivotTables

Note: To complete this assignment, you will be required to use the Data Files. Please contact your instructor for information about accessing the Data Files.

Instructions: Start Excel. Open the workbook SC_EX_8-3.xlsx from the Data Files. The workbook you open contains data about the number of books sold via an ecommerce website for each day of the year. You are to create a PivotTable and PivotChart for Sophie's Online Books that analyzes books sold in 2020.

Perform the following tasks:

1. Save the workbook using the file name, SC_EX_8_OnlineBooksComplete.
2. Use Help to learn to group or ungroup data in a PivotTable.

Continued >

Extend Your Knowledge *continued*

3. Select the data in the Sales Data worksheet (cells A3:B257). Create a PivotTable on a new worksheet. Use Date as the Rows field and use Books Sold as the Values field. Note that Excel breaks the date field down into months and quarters.
4. Name the new worksheet `Books Sold PivotTable`. Color the sheet tab green. Change the PivotTable style to 'Light Green, Pivot Style Medium 21'.
5. In cell A1, type `Sophie's Online Books` to create a title. In cell A2, type `Books Sold 2020` to create a subtitle. Merge and center the titles across columns A and B. Format cell A1 using the Title cell style and A2 using the 'Light Green, 20% - Accent6' cell style. Change the font color in both cells to black, if necessary.
6. Format the Books Sold data values to be Number with commas, but no decimal places. Remove the Field Header for column A.
7. Click cell A4 and use the Group Field command (PivotTable Analyze tab | Group group) to group the daily figures by months and quarters.
8. Change the width of columns A and B to 17 (Figure 8–102).
9. Create a PivotChart and locate it on the same worksheet as the PivotTable. Use the 3-D Clustered Column chart type and set up the chart to have no legend.
10. Right-click the chart area, and then choose '3-D Rotation' on the shortcut menu. In the Format Chart Area pane, set the X rotation to 100° and Y rotation to 50°.
11. Edit the chart title text to match the PivotTable title and subtitle. Format the data series in the chart to use a solid fill, light green fill color. Resize the chart to fill the area between cell D2 and K20.

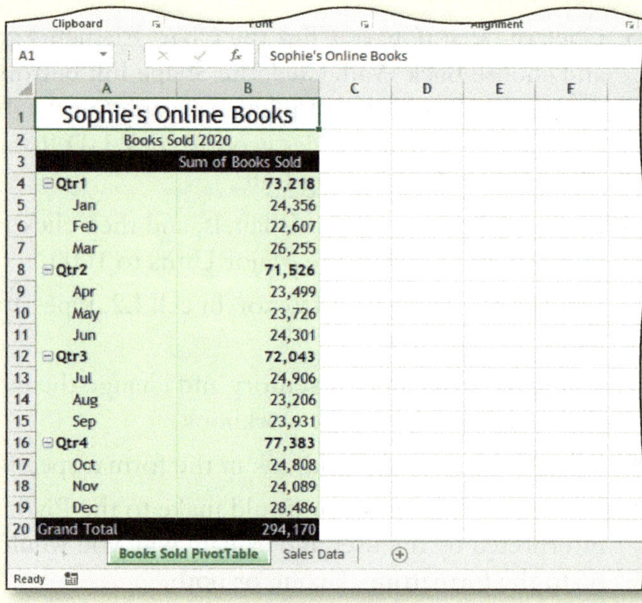

Figure 8–102

If requested by your instructor, add a worksheet header with your name and course number.

12. Because Excel changes the column width of the PivotTable as you change the grouping, double-check that the column widths of A and B are still 17.
13. Preview and then print the PivotTable worksheet in landscape orientation.
14. Save the workbook.
15. Submit the revised document in the format specified by your instructor.
16. What other chart type would you use to present this data for the user? Why would you choose that particular chart type?

Expand Your World

Create a solution that uses cloud and web technologies by learning and investigating on your own from general guidance.

Creating PivotTable Reports and PivotCharts with Web Data

Instructions: Start Excel. You are to create a PivotTable, PivotChart, and map chart from data you obtain from the web.

Perform the following tasks:

1. Open a browser and navigate to https://www.data.gov/, a searchable, open database of files stored by the U.S. government.
2. In the search box, type **`Leading Causes of Death United States`** and then press ENTER.
3. In the search results, navigate to the link, '**`NCHS - Leading Causes of Death: United States`**', and then click the CSV (Comma Separated Values) button. Save the file on your storage device.
4. Start Excel and open a blank workbook. Import the CSV file. *Hint:* Use the 'From Text/CSV' button (Data tab | Get & Transform Data group). Load the data into the existing worksheet.
5. Save the workbook using the file name, SC_EX_8_CausesOfDeath.
6. Delete the column named 113 Cause Name, leaving the columns for Year, Cause Name, State, Deaths, and Age-adjusted Death Rate. If necessary, close the Queries & Connections pane.
7. Use the Cause Name filter button to hide the All Causes records from the list. Use the State filter button to remove the United States field from the list.
8. Click any cell in the data and insert a PivotTable on a separate worksheet and perform the following analysis:
   a. Using the Field list, drag the State field to the Columns area, the Cause Name field to the rows area, and Deaths to the Values area. Filter the data to show deaths from Heart disease, Stroke, and Diabetes.
   b. Format the numbers with the comma separator and no decimal places.
   c. Apply a PivotTable Style.
   d. Experiment by dragging fields to various PivotTable areas to show different views of the data.
9. Create a Line PivotChart from the PivotTable and do the following:
   a. Move the chart to a new worksheet.
   b. If necessary, use the filter button on the Line Chart to edit out the United States numbers, so you are seeing just the 50 states and the District of Columbia.
   c. Format the PivotChart with a title, style, and an appropriate legend.
   d. Filter the PivotChart to show only data for your state and the states that border it, or a region of the United States.

Continued >

Expand Your World *continued*

e. Give each worksheet a descriptive name and color (Figure 8–103).

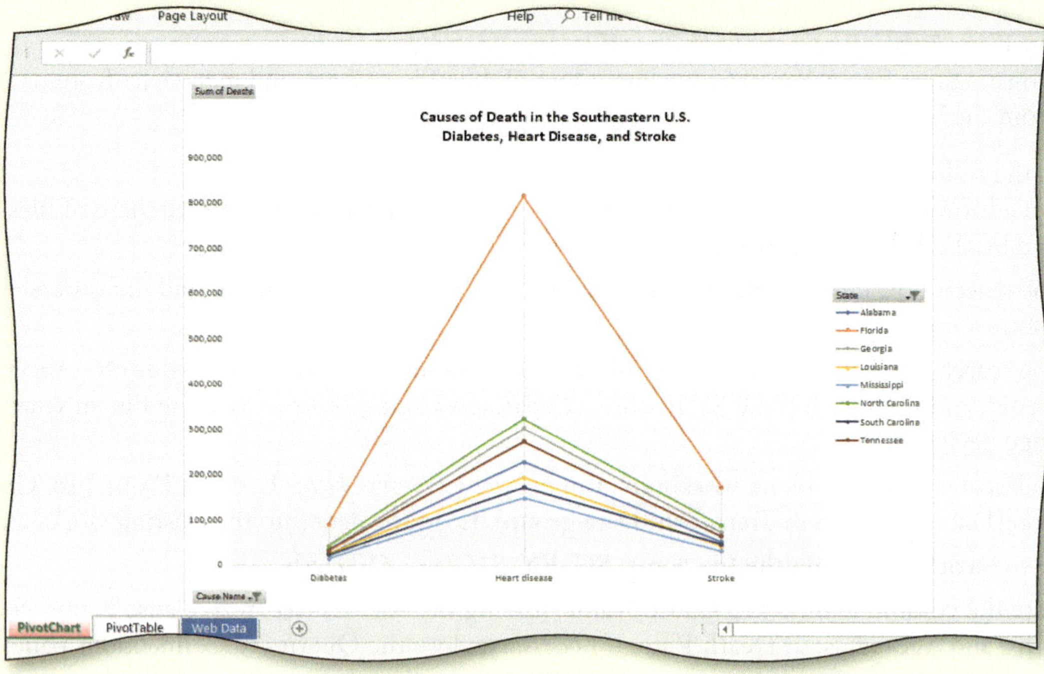

Figure 8–103

f. Experiment by clicking the Cause Name filter button to choose other diseases.

g. Return to the PivotTable and experiment with drilling down into the data.

10. Go back to the original web data. Use the Year filter button to select only the most recent year. Filter the Cause Name for Heart disease only. Filter the State column with the region you chose in Step 9.

11. Select the resulting State and Deaths data. Create a map chart similar to Figure 8–90 from the filtered data. *Hint:* Click the Maps button (Insert tab | Charts group).

    a. If Bing prompts you to allow its search, click the I Accept button.

    b. Move the map to a new worksheet. Name the worksheet, Regional Map.

    c. Display the Format Data Series Pane and the Series Options sheet. Click the Map Area button and then click 'Only Regions with Data'.

    d. Edit the title, color, and series name. *Hint:* To change the series name, right-click the legend, click Select Data, and click the Edit button.

    e. Format the data labels to display both Category Name and Value. If the entire state name will not display, reduce the font size of the label. Change the font color as necessary to ensure readability.

12. Save the workbook again.

13. Submit the revised workbook as specified by your instructor.

14. In this data, you dealt with 50 states and 10 diseases. With large amounts of data, what are the advantages to using PivotTables? What are the problems with PivotCharts?

In the Lab

Design and implement a solution using creative thinking and problem-solving skills.

Create Charts

Note: To complete this assignment, you will be required to use the Data Files. Please contact your instructor for information about accessing the Data Files.

Problem: The Saint Luke School District would like summary results from the latest round of statewide student testing in 4th, 7th, 10th, and 12th grade. Data has been compiled for the three testing areas, Math, Science, and English, for each of the 10 schools in the district.

Perform the following tasks:

Part 1: Open the workbook SC_EX_8-4.xlsx from the Data Files and then save the workbook using the file name, SC_EX_8_ SaintLukeSchoolDistrictComplete. The data includes both the average score for each grade and school combination and the test goals. Create a PivotTable with slicers and instructions for use. The PivotTable should show averages and goals organized by school and grade. Format the columns headings as necessary. Submit your assignment in the format specified by your instructor.

Part 2: How did the data from the Saint Luke School District pose a special challenge when creating the PivotTable? How might you address that challenge? What slicers did you decide to use? Why?

9 Formula Auditing, Data Validation, and Complex Problem Solving

Objectives

After completing this module, you will be able to:

- Use formula auditing techniques to analyze a worksheet
- Trace precedents and dependents
- Use error checking to identify and correct errors
- Add data validation rules to cells
- Use trial and error to solve a problem on a worksheet
- Use goal seeking to solve a problem
- Circle invalid data on a worksheet
- Enable the Solver add-in
- Use Solver to solve a complex problem
- Use the Scenario Manager to record and save sets of what-if assumptions
- Create a Scenario Summary report
- Create a Scenario Summary PivotTable
- Draw with inking techniques

Introduction

Excel offers many tools that can be used to solve complex problems. In previous modules, simple what-if analyses have shown the effect of changing one value on another value of interest. This module introduces you to auditing the formulas in a worksheet, validating data, and solving complex problems. **Formula auditing** allows you to examine formulas to determine which cells are referenced by those formulas and examine cells to determine which formulas are built upon those cells. Auditing the formulas in a worksheet can give insight into how a worksheet is structured and how cells are related to each other. Formula auditing is especially helpful when you are working with a workbook created by someone else.

Data validation allows you to set cells so that the values they accept are restricted in terms of type and range of data. This feature can be set up to display prompts and error messages when users select a cell or enter invalid data. You also can use data validation to circle cells containing data that does not meet the criteria you specified.

When trying to solve some problems, you can make an educated guess if you are familiar with the data and the structure of the workbook. **Trial and error** is a way to perform what-if analysis by changing one or more of the input values to see how they affect the other cells in the workbook. For simpler problems, you may find a solution using this process. For more complex problems, you might need to use the error and validation techniques in Excel to find a satisfactory solution.

One of the tools that Excel provides to solve complex problems is **Solver**, which allows you to specify up to 200 cells that can be adjusted to find a solution to a problem. Solver also lets you place limits or constraints on allowable values for some or all of those cells. A **constraint** is a limitation on the possible values that a cell can contain. Solver will try many possible solutions to find one that solves the problem subject to the constraints placed on the data.

Project: Instrument Logistics Analysis

BTW
Ribbon and Screen Resolution
Excel may change how the groups and buttons within the groups appear on the ribbon, depending on the screen resolution of your computer. Thus, your ribbon may look different from the ones in this book if you are using a screen resolution other than 1366 × 768.

In this module, you will learn how to use the Instrument Logistics Analysis workbook shown in Figure 9–1. Instrument Logistics is a small company that receives shipments of musical instruments from manufacturers, which it then distributes to wholesalers around the country. To ship its goods, the company purchases extra space on trucks from trucking firms. This week they are wanting to ship three types of instruments currently in stock: guitars, drum sets, and keyboards. Typically, the company deals with the instruments' physical volume in cubic feet, the weight in pounds, the profit per instrument, and the number of instruments in stock. The company will need to enter the number of each instrument to ship, making sure it is one or more, and less than, the number in stock. The objective is to maximize the profit while filling up as much of the truck as possible.

The Weekly Shipment worksheet, shown in Figure 9–1a, was created to determine the most cost-effective way of scheduling trucks to meet existing needs. The worksheet includes the details of the requirements for the three instruments, taking into account the truck capacities as well as the weight and volume of the instruments.

The details of the first solution determined by Solver are shown in Figure 9–1b. Solver was given the goal of maximizing the total profits (cell E13) while also accommodating the following constraints: the number of instruments assigned to each truck (range B9:D9) cannot be negative or fractional. The total volume and weight must not exceed the truck constraints shown in cells B16:B17. The company wants to ship at least one of each instrument per truck. Applying these constraints, Solver calculated the optimal instruments to ship shown in the range B9:D9 to achieve the goal of maximizing total profit and filling the truck. Solver modified the shipping quantities for each instrument (B9:D9) that resulted in changes in the total volume and weight per truck (E11:E12). If you applied a different set of constraints, Solver would determine a new solution.

BTW
Touch Mode Differences
The Office and Windows interfaces may vary if you are using Touch Mode. For this reason, you might notice that the function or appearance of your touch screen differs slightly from this module's presentation.

When Solver finishes solving a problem, you can create an Answer Report. An Answer Report (Figure 9–1c) summarizes the answer found by Solver, identifying which constraints were in place and which values in the worksheet were manipulated in order to solve the problem within the constraints.

The Excel **Scenario Manager** is a what-if analysis tool that allows you to record and save different sets, or scenarios, of what-if assumptions for the same worksheet. In this case, you will use Scenario Manager to manage the two sets of Solver data for the Weekly Shipment Worksheet. The Scenario Manager also allows you to create reports that summarize the scenarios on your worksheet. Both the Scenario Summary report (Figure 9–1d) and the Scenario PivotTable (Figure 9–1e) concisely present the differences among different shipping scenarios. Like any PivotTable, the Scenario PivotTable allows you to interact with the data easily.

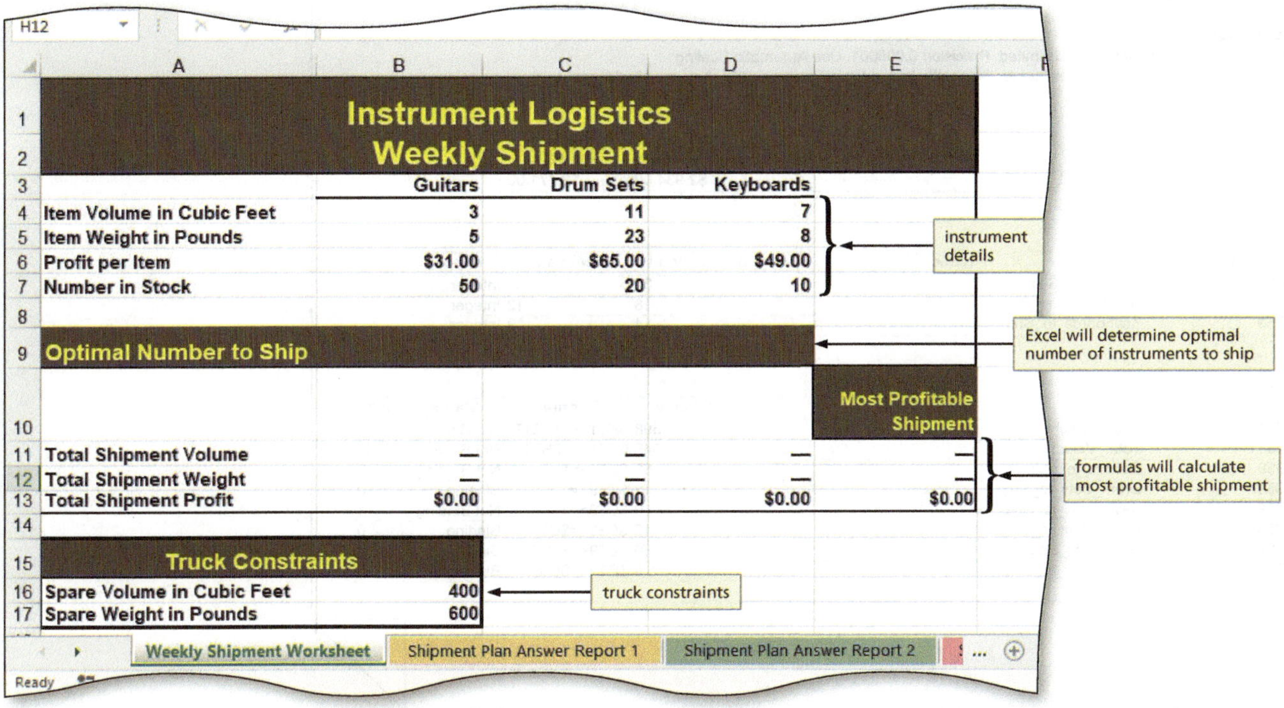

(a) Scheduling Plan Worksheet

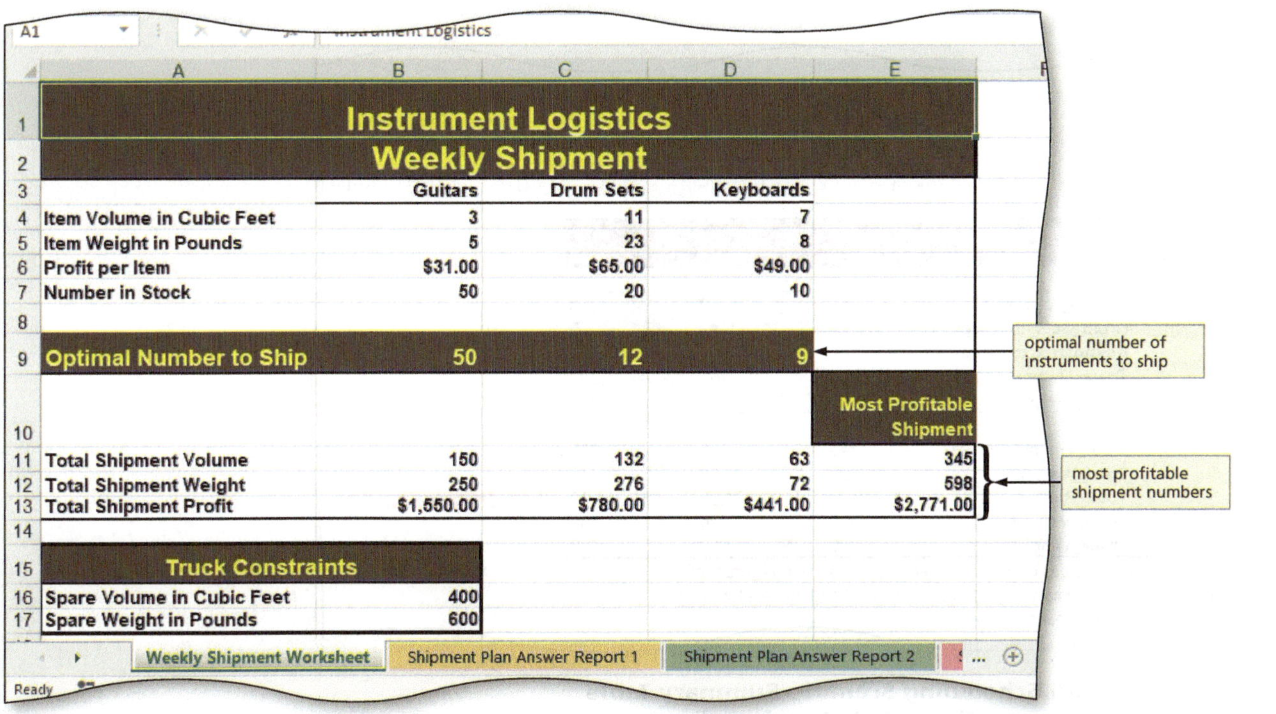

(b) Solver Solution
Figure 9–1 (Continued)

Microsoft Excel 16.0 Answer Report
Worksheet: [SC_EX_9_Instrument_Logistics_Analysis.xlsx]Weekly Shipment Worksheet
Report Created: 10/9/2025 1:22:33 PM
Result: Solver found a solution. All Constraints and optimality conditions are satisfied.
Solver Engine
Engine: Simplex LP
Solution Time: 0.031 Seconds.
Iterations: 2 Subproblems: 8
Solver Options
Max Time Unlimited, Iterations Unlimited, Precision 0.000001, Use Automatic Scaling
Max Subproblems Unlimited, Max Integer Sols Unlimited, Integer Tolerance 0%, Assume NonNegative

Objective Cell (Max)

Cell	Name	Original Value	Final Value
$E$13	Total_Profit	$2,934.00	$2,771.00

Variable Cells

Cell	Name	Original Value	Final Value	Integer
$B$9	Guitars_to_Ship	35	50	Integer
$C$9	Drum_Sets_to_Ship	18	12	Integer
$D$9	Keyboards_to_Ship	14	9	Integer

Constraints

Cell	Name	Cell Value	Formula	Status	Slack
$E$12	Total_Weight	598	$E$12<=$B$17	Not Binding	2
$E$11	Total_Volume	345	$E$11<=$B$16	Not Binding	55
$B$9	Guitars_to_Ship	50	$B$9>=1	Not Binding	2
$C$9	Drum_Sets_to_Ship	12	$C$9>=1	Binding	0
$D$9	Keyboards_to_Ship	9	$D$9>=1	Not Binding	1
$C$9	Drum_Sets_to_Ship	12	$C$9<=$C$7	Binding	0
$B$9	Guitars_to_Ship	50	$B$9<=$B$7	Binding	0
$D$9	Keyboards_to_Ship	9	$D$9<=$D$7	Binding	0
$B$9:$D$9=Integer					

(c) Scheduling Plan Answer Report

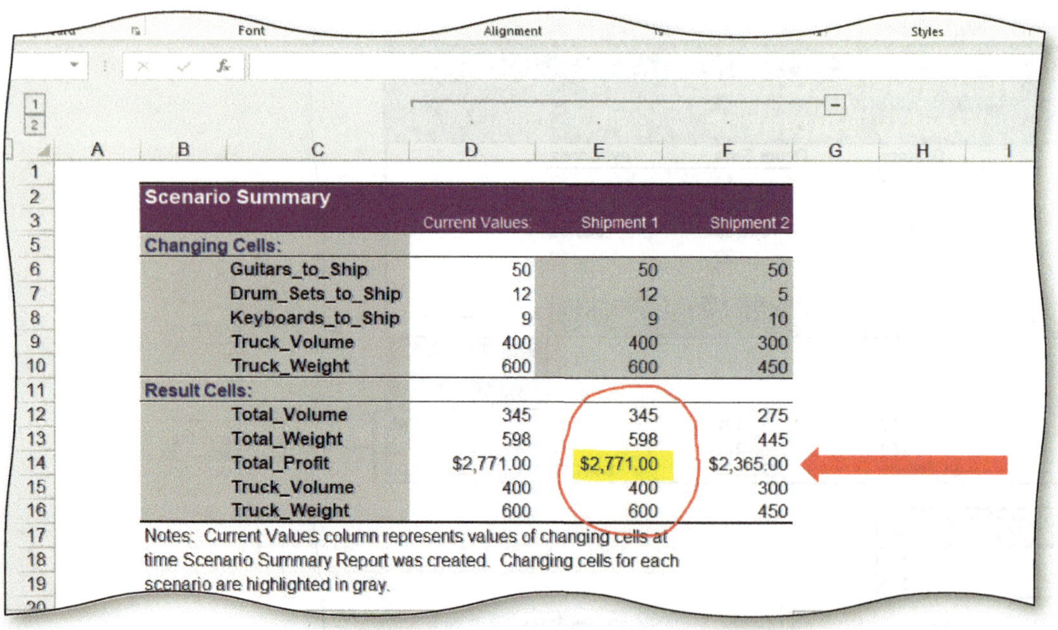

	Current Values	Shipment 1	Shipment 2
Scenario Summary			
Changing Cells:			
Guitars_to_Ship	50	50	50
Drum_Sets_to_Ship	12	12	5
Keyboards_to_Ship	9	9	10
Truck_Volume	400	400	300
Truck_Weight	600	600	450
Result Cells:			
Total_Volume	345	345	275
Total_Weight	598	598	445
Total_Profit	$2,771.00	$2,771.00	$2,365.00
Truck_Volume	400	400	300
Truck_Weight	600	600	450

Notes: Current Values column represents values of changing cells at time Scenario Summary Report was created. Changing cells for each scenario are highlighted in gray.

(d) Scheduling Scenario Summary Table
Figure 9–1 (Continued)

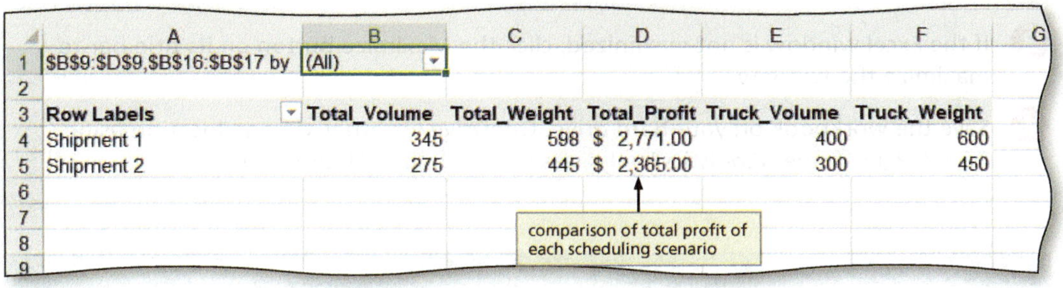

	A	B	C	D	E	F	G
1	$B$9:$D$9,$B$16:$B$17 by	(All)					
2							
3	Row Labels	Total_Volume	Total_Weight	Total_Profit	Truck_Volume	Truck_Weight	
4	Shipment 1	345	598	$ 2,771.00	400	600	
5	Shipment 2	275	445	$ 2,365.00	300	450	

(e) Scenario PivotTable
Figure 9–1

Figure 9–2 illustrates the requirements document for the Instrument Logistics Analysis workbook. It includes the needs, source of data, and other facts about its development.

Worksheet Title	Instrument Logistics Analysis
Needs	Evaluate three different sets of instrument data to determine the optimal scheduling distribution to minimize total cost and maximize profits.
Data	• Three types of instruments: guitars, drum sets, and keyboards. • Data related to each instrument include volume, weight, profit, and number in stock.
Constraints	• Constraints related to the truck include spare volume in cubic feet and spare weight in pounds. • Each shipment must include at least one of each instrument. • Instrument numbers cannot be fractional or negative.
Source of Data	All instrument information is available in the SC_EX_9-1.xlsx workbook on the Weekly Shipment Worksheet.
Calculations	All formulas are set up in the workbook with some errors. The worksheets in the workbook should be reviewed to familiarize yourself with the following calculations. • Total Shipment Volume is volume times number of instruments to ship. • Total Weight Volume is weight times number of instruments to ship. • Total Profit is profit per item times number of instruments to ship.
Other Requirements	Create a Shipment Scenario Summary. Create a Shipment Scenario Pivot Table. Create two Shipment Plan Answer Reports.

Figure 9–2

With a good understanding of the requirements document and an understanding of the necessary decisions, the next step is to use Excel to create the workbook. In this module, you will learn how to create the Instrument Logistics Analysis workbook shown in Figure 9–1.

To Start Excel and Open a Workbook

The following steps start Excel and open a workbook named SC_EX_9-1. The Weekly Shipment Worksheet tab shows the overall shipping plan and constraints for the instruments and trucks. To complete these steps, you will be required to use the Data Files. Please contact your instructor for information about accessing the Data Files.

1. sam Start Excel.
2. Open the file named SC_EX_9-1.xlsx from the Data Files.

3. If the Excel window is not maximized, click the Maximize button on its title bar to maximize the window.

4. Save the workbook on your hard drive, OneDrive, or other storage location using SC_EX_9_InstrumentLogisticsAnalysis as the file name (Figure 9–3).

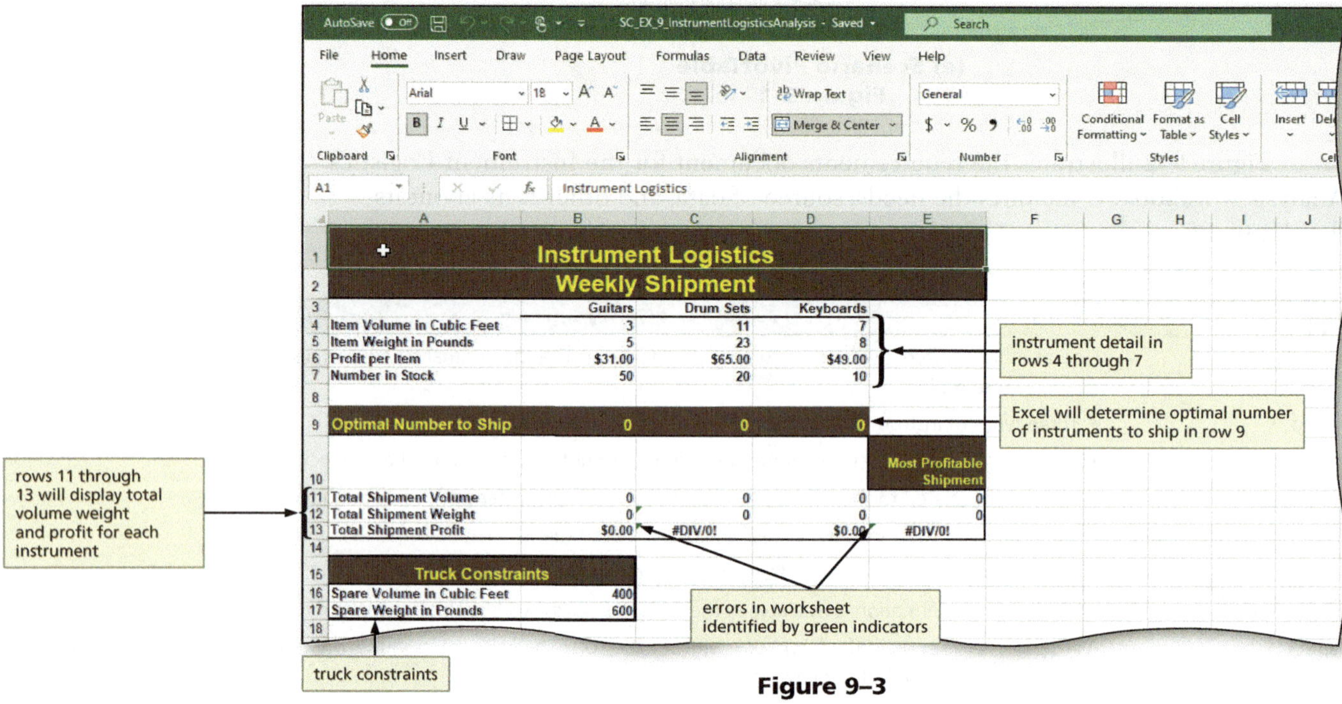

Figure 9–3

About the Weekly Shipment Worksheet

The Weekly Shipment Worksheet shown in Figure 9–3 provides information about three instruments and four types of data: volume, weight, stock levels, and profits. Rows 4 and 5 contain the volume and weight for each of the three instruments. Row 6 contains the profit per item; row 7 shows the number in stock. The range B9:D9 will show the optimal number of instruments to ship that maximizes the total profit to Instrument Logistics, which is the problem that needs to be solved in this module. The total volume, weight, and profits for each instrument (rows 11 to 13) are based on the number of instruments to ship—shown in the range B9:D9—multiplied by the corresponding values in rows 4 through 6. As the number of instruments changes, the values in the range B11:D13 are updated.

Your goal is to determine the optimal number of instruments to ship in each category without exceeding the maximum volume and weight per truck, 400 and 600, respectively (cells B16:B17), while maximizing total profits for the company (cell E13).

As outlined in the requirements document in Figure 9–2, a second set of constraints also must be analyzed. Thus, the information in the range B16:B17 will be modified to reflect the constraints associated with the different scenario, with a volume of 300 and a weight of 450.

The worksheet also contains some errors which will be addressed in the following sections.

BTW

Getting Familiar with a Worksheet
When working with a new worksheet, you should try to become familiar with formulas, functions, and errors. You also should click the Name Manager button (Formulas tab | Defined Names group) to see what ranges or cells may have useful predefined names.

To View Named Cells

In workbooks prepared by others, it is always a good idea to double-check for named cells and ranges. The Weekly Shipment Worksheet contains several named cells. Named cells help identify concepts in the worksheet and can be used in formulas, for data validation, and as bookmarks. Later in the module, you will see that named cells are used by Excel to make constraints and answer reports easier to read. The following steps view named cells.

1. Click the Name Manager button (Formulas tab | Defined Names Group) to display the Name Manager dialog box.
2. To see the full name of each named cell, widen the first column by pointing to the border between the column headings until the pointer changes to a double-headed arrow, then double-click.
3. Review the named cells and their location (Figure 9–4).
4. Close the Name Manager dialog box.

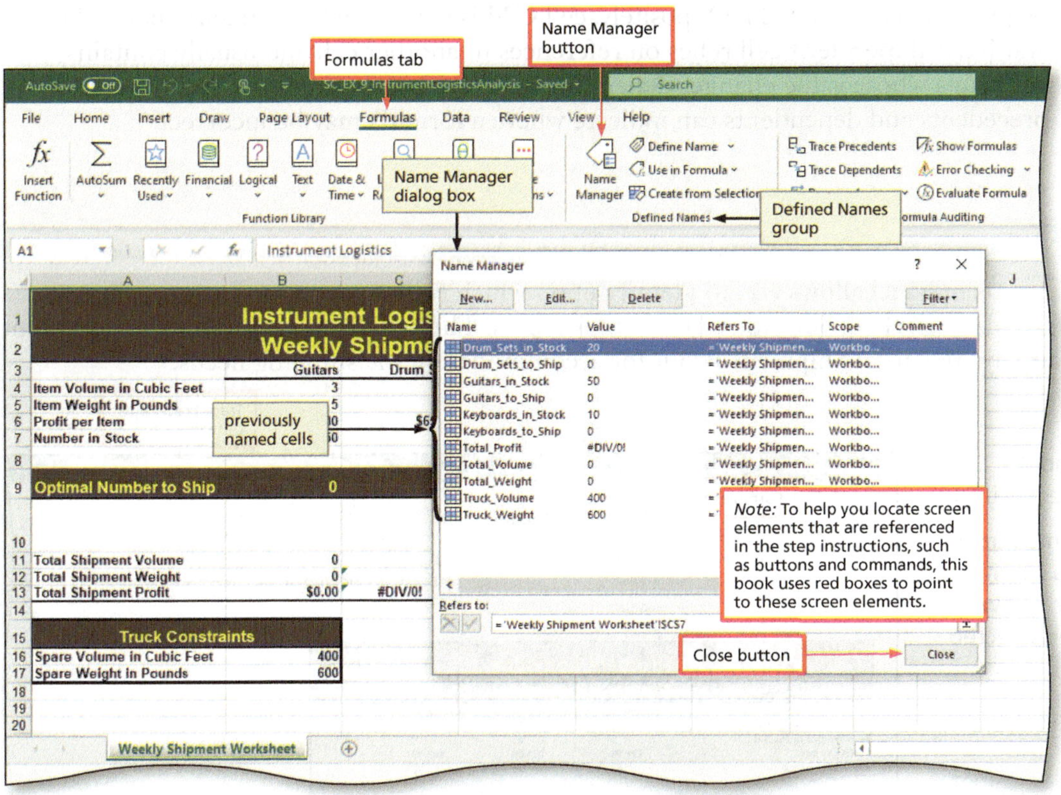

Figure 9–4

Formula Auditing

Formula auditing is the process of tracking errors, checking worksheet logic, and reviewing formulas for errors. Errors may be obvious, with results that indicate that a formula is incorrect. For example, in Figure 9–3, cells C12, C13, and E13 display error codes. These errors are flagged by the error indicator, a green triangle, in the upper-left corner of those cells, and two of the three errors display an error code, #DIV/0!.

BTW

Naming Cell Ranges

Naming ranges for use with input variables is helpful when dealing with multiple input variables. Assign names to all the input variables before creating your first scenario. Named ranges will make scenario reports easier to understand and interpret.

BTW
Tracing Precedents and Dependents
When all levels of precedents or dependents have been identified, Excel will sound a beep if you try to trace another level.

Errors also may be less obvious, introduced through formulas that, while technically correct, result in unintended results in the worksheet or formulas that are inconsistent with other similar formulas. Error indicators with no accompanying error code, such as that found in cell C12, should be examined for these less-obvious errors. A complex worksheet should be reviewed to correct obvious errors and to correct formulas that do not produce error indicators but still do not produce the intended results.

Excel provides formula auditing tools, found in the Formula Auditing group on the Formulas tab, that can be used to review the formulas in a worksheet. Some tools, such as the Error Checking command, deal with identified errors. Other auditing tools provide visual cues to identify how cells in a worksheet are related to each other. **Tracer arrows** are blue, worksheet auditing arrows that point from cells that might have caused an error to the active cell containing an error. Tracer arrows identify cells that are related to other cells through their use in a formula. Red tracer arrows indicate that one of the referenced cells contains an error.

BTW
Tracer Arrow Lines
If a tracer arrow line appears as a black dashed line connected to a small worksheet icon, it indicates that precedent cells exist on another worksheet. You can double-click a dashed tracer line to move to the connected worksheet.

A formula that references other cells is said to have precedents. A **precedent** is a cell referenced in a formula that references other cells. For example, cell C24 might contain the formula, = C23/$B$1. Cells C23 and B1 are precedents of cell C24. Cells C23 and B1 may contain their own precedents, and these cells also would be precedents of cell C24. Oppositely, cell C24 is considered dependent upon C23 and B1. A **dependent** cell relies on references to another cell and usually contains a formula whose value changes depending on the values in the input cells. Tracing precedents and dependents can indicate where a formula may be incorrect.

To Trace Precedents

Why? Tracing precedents in Excel allows you to identify upon which cells a particular formula is based, not only directly by the formula in the cell, but indirectly via precedents. The following steps trace the precedent cells for cell E13, which displays the Total Shipment Profit for accommodating the shipping needs.

1

- Display the Formulas tab if necessary, and then select cell E13.
- Click the Trace Precedents button (Formulas tab | Formula Auditing group) to draw a tracer arrow across precedents of the selected cell (Figure 9–5).

Q&A **How do I interpret the precedent arrows?**
The arrow in Figure 9–5 terminates with an arrowhead on the traced cell, in this case cell E13. The arrow that runs through the range of cells B13:D13 indicates that all cells in the range are precedents of the traced cell.

Is it always red?
No. If a referenced cell contains a formula and that formula also contains an error, then a red line is drawn between the formula cells; otherwise the arrow is blue.

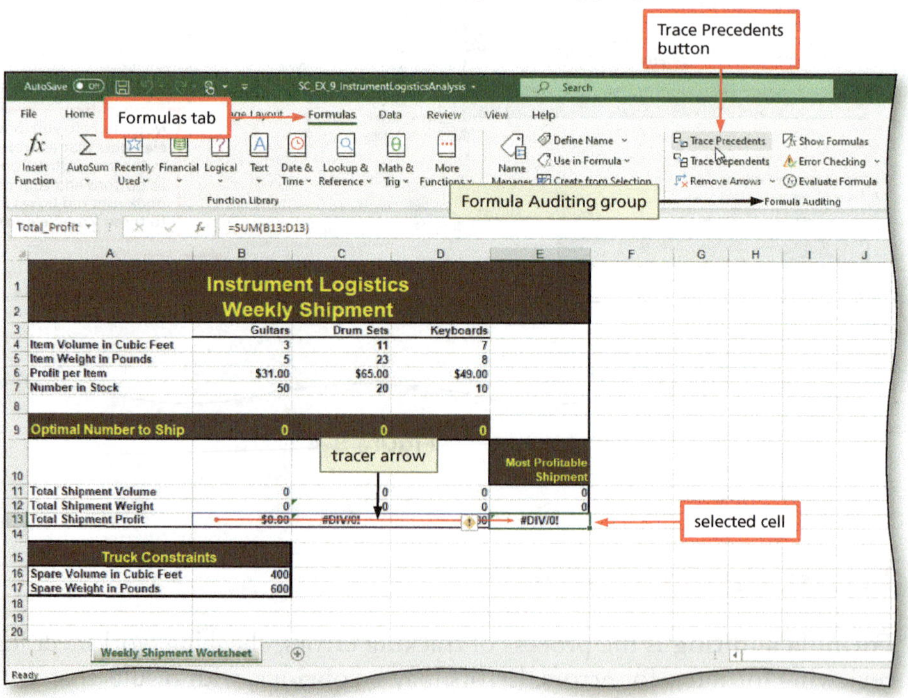

Figure 9–5

2

- Click the Trace Precedents button (Formulas tab | Formula Auditing group) again to draw arrows indicating precedents of cells B13:D13 (Figure 9–6).

Q&A

How do I interpret the new precedent arrows?
The new arrows in Figure 9–6 have arrowheads on traced cells and dots on cells that are direct precedents of the cells with arrowheads. For instance, cell B13 has a tracer arrow pointing to it with a blue line appearing in the range B6:B12 and dots in cell B6 and B9. This indicates that the cells containing dots are precedents of cell B12, while the other cells, without dots, are not.

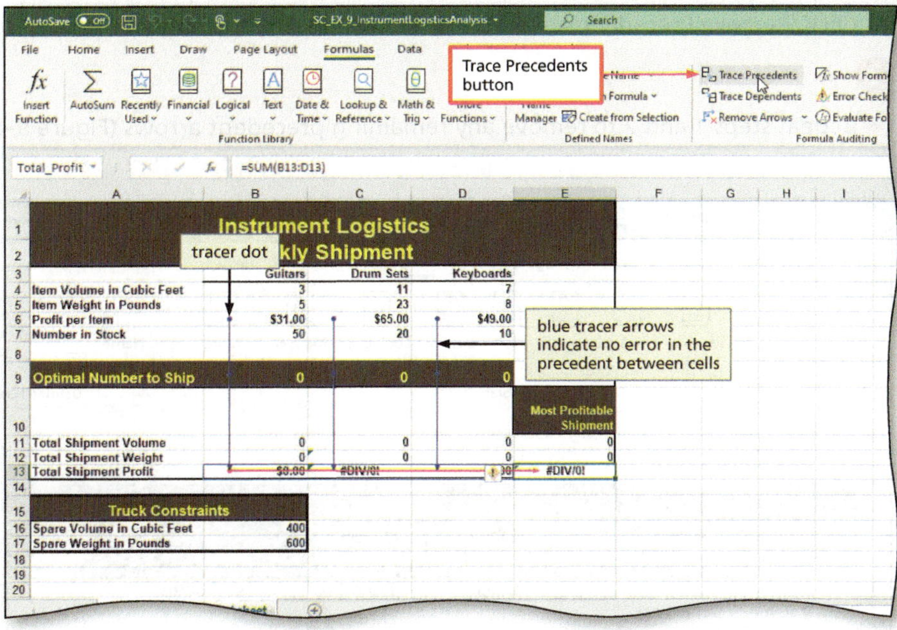

Figure 9–6

To Remove the Precedent Arrows

Why? Reducing visual clutter makes the worksheet easier to edit. The following steps remove the precedent arrows level by level and then correct the formula in cell C12.

1

- Click the 'Remove Arrows' arrow (Formulas tab | Formula Auditing group) to display the 'Remove Arrows' menu (Figure 9–7).

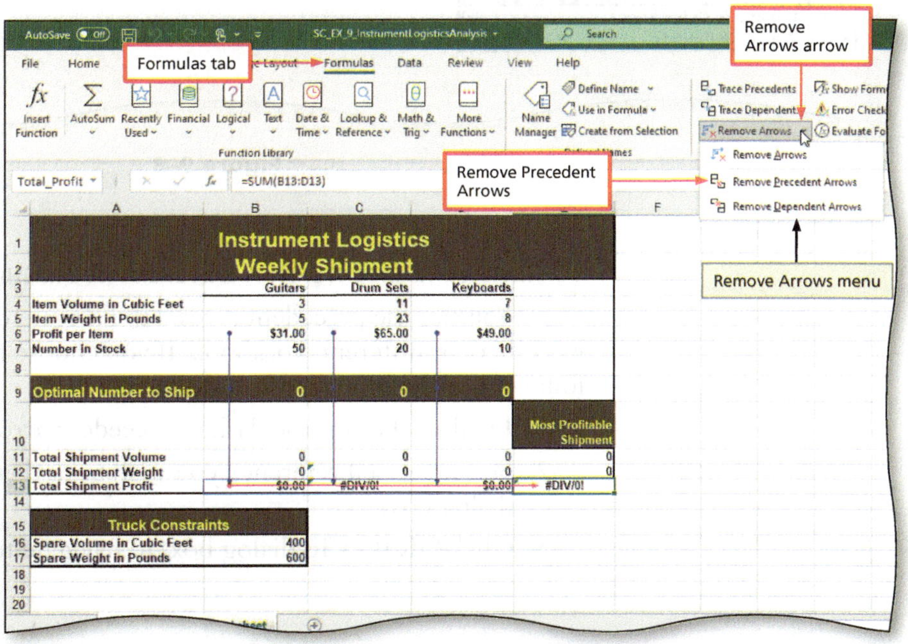

Figure 9–7

2

- Click 'Remove Precedent Arrows' on the Remove Arrows menu to remove precedent arrows.

3

- Repeat steps 1 and 2 to remove any remaining precedent arrows (Figure 9–8).

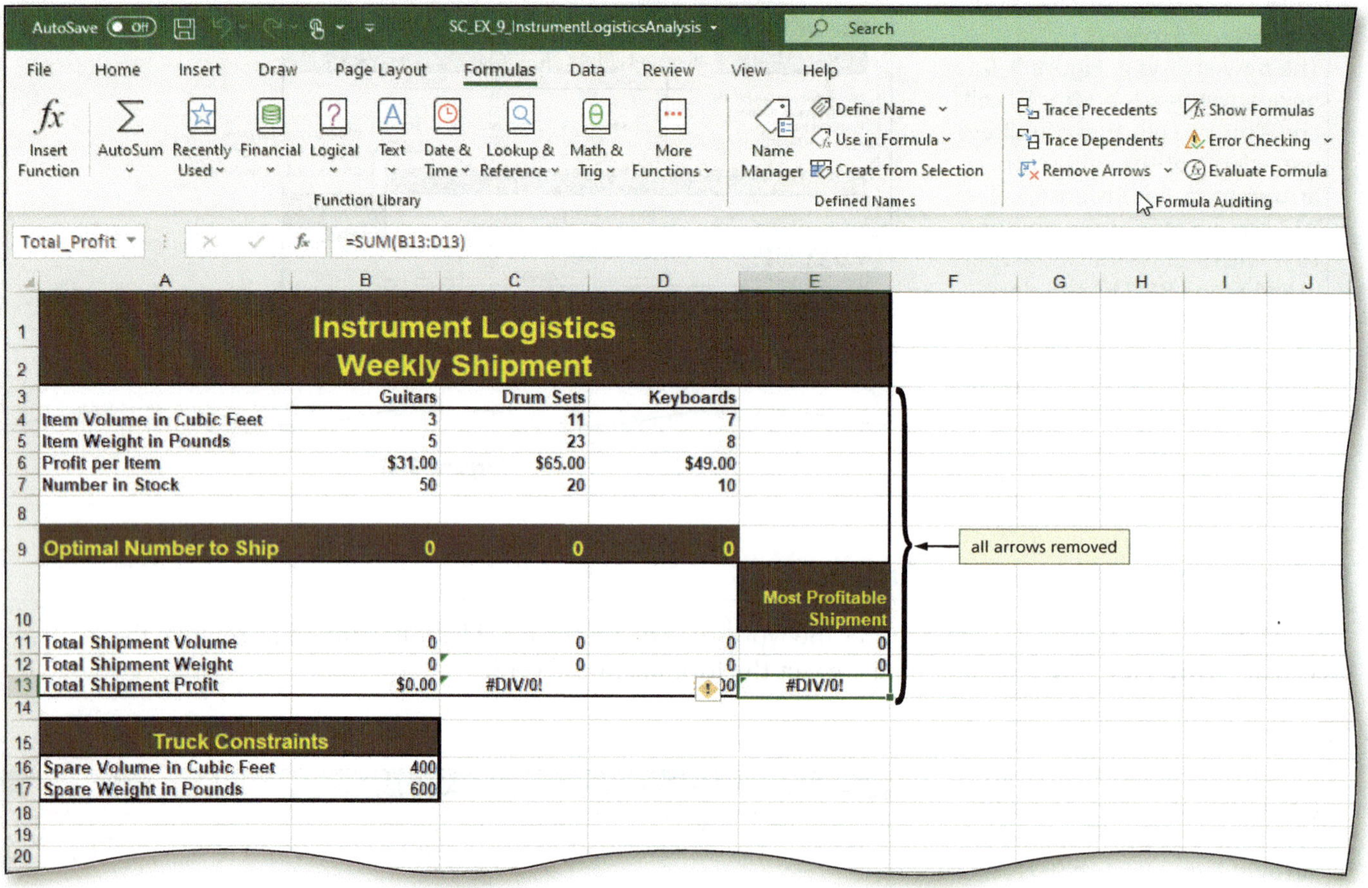

Figure 9–8

To Review Precedents on a Different Worksheet Using the Go To Command

You can use precedent arrows to navigate directly to precedents on a different worksheet or different workbook. If you choose to use this feature, you would use the following steps:

1. Double-click on the dashed precedent arrow to display the Go To dialog box.
2. Select the cell reference you wish to navigate to, from the Go To list (Go To dialog box).
3. Click OK (Go To dialog box) to navigate to the selected cell reference.

To Trace Dependents

Why? Identifying dependents highlights where changes will occur in the worksheet as a result of changing the value in the referenced cell. The following steps trace the dependents of cell C9, which will display the optimal number of drum sets to ship.

1

- Select cell C9.
- Click the Trace Dependents button (Formulas tab | Formula Auditing group) to draw arrows to dependent cells (Figure 9–9).

Q&A

What is the meaning of the dependent arrows?
As shown in Figure 9–9, the arrowheads indicate which cells directly depend on the selected cell. In this case, cell C9 is explicitly referenced in formulas located in cells C11, C12, and C13, indicated by the arrow tips.

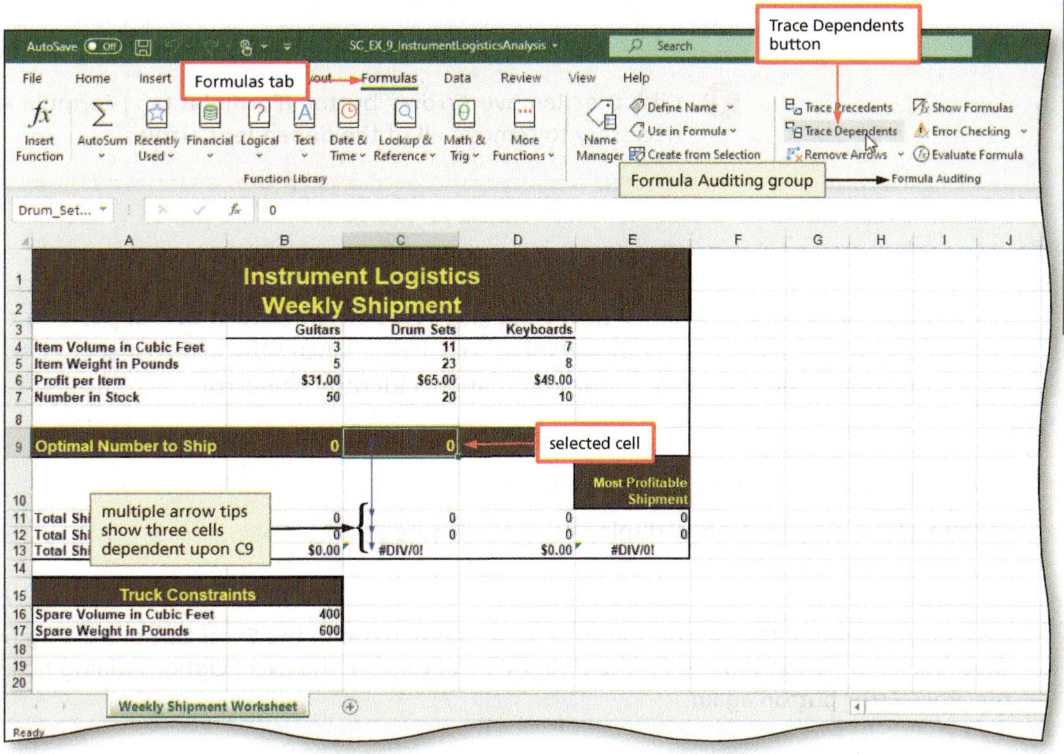

Figure 9–9

2

- Click the Trace Dependents button again to draw arrows indicating the indirectly dependent cells—cells that depend directly or indirectly on the selected cell (Figure 9–10).

Q&A

How do I know when I have identified all remaining dependents?
You can click the Trace Dependents button again. If no additional dependents are present, Excel does not draw additional arrows but plays an error tone.

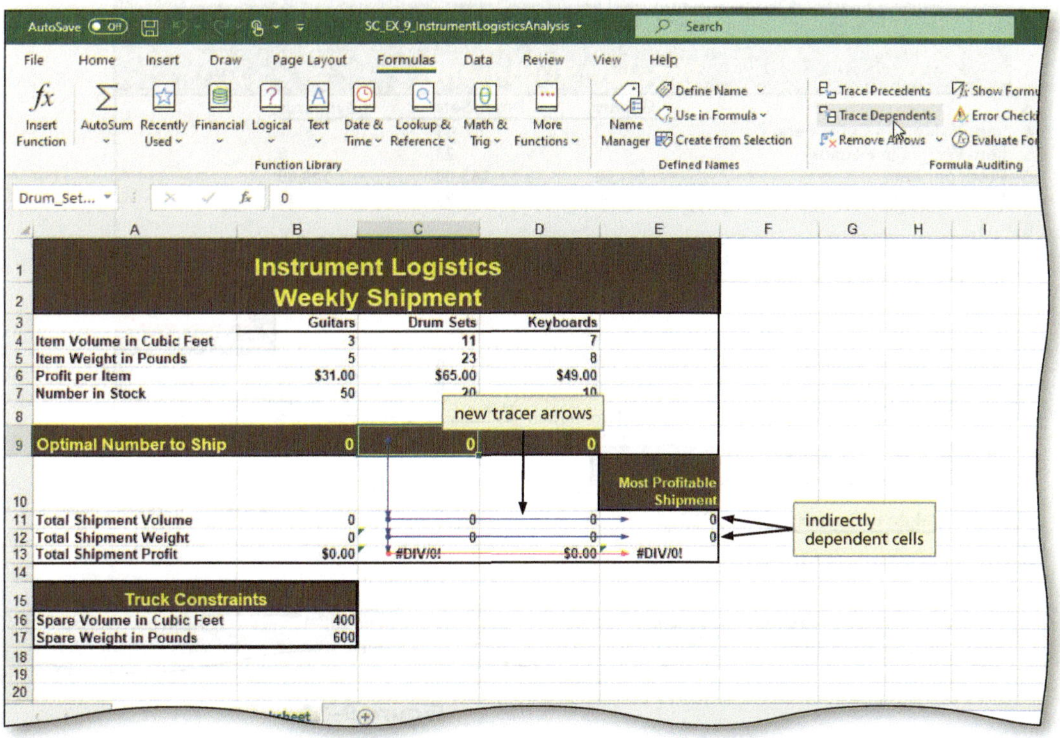

Figure 9–10

How can I tell the difference between dependents and precedents?
The tracer arrows always point in the direction of the data flow.

To Remove the Dependent Arrows

The following step clears the dependent arrows from the worksheet.

1 Click the 'Remove Arrows' button (Formulas tab | Formula Auditing group) as necessary to remove all of the dependent arrows.

To Use the Trace Error Button

Another way to trace errors is to the use the Trace Error button that appears in the worksheet itself. **Why?** The Trace Error button offers commands that may help identify the error further. The following steps use the Trace Error button and the Trace Error command to identify the error.

1

- Select cell E13 to display the Trace Error button.
- Click the Trace Error button to display its menu (Figure 9–11).

Experiment

- Click Error Checking Options on the Trace Error menu to open the Excel Options dialog box. Read the Error checking rules. When you are finished, click Cancel to close the Excel Options dialog box without any changes. Click the Trace Error button again.

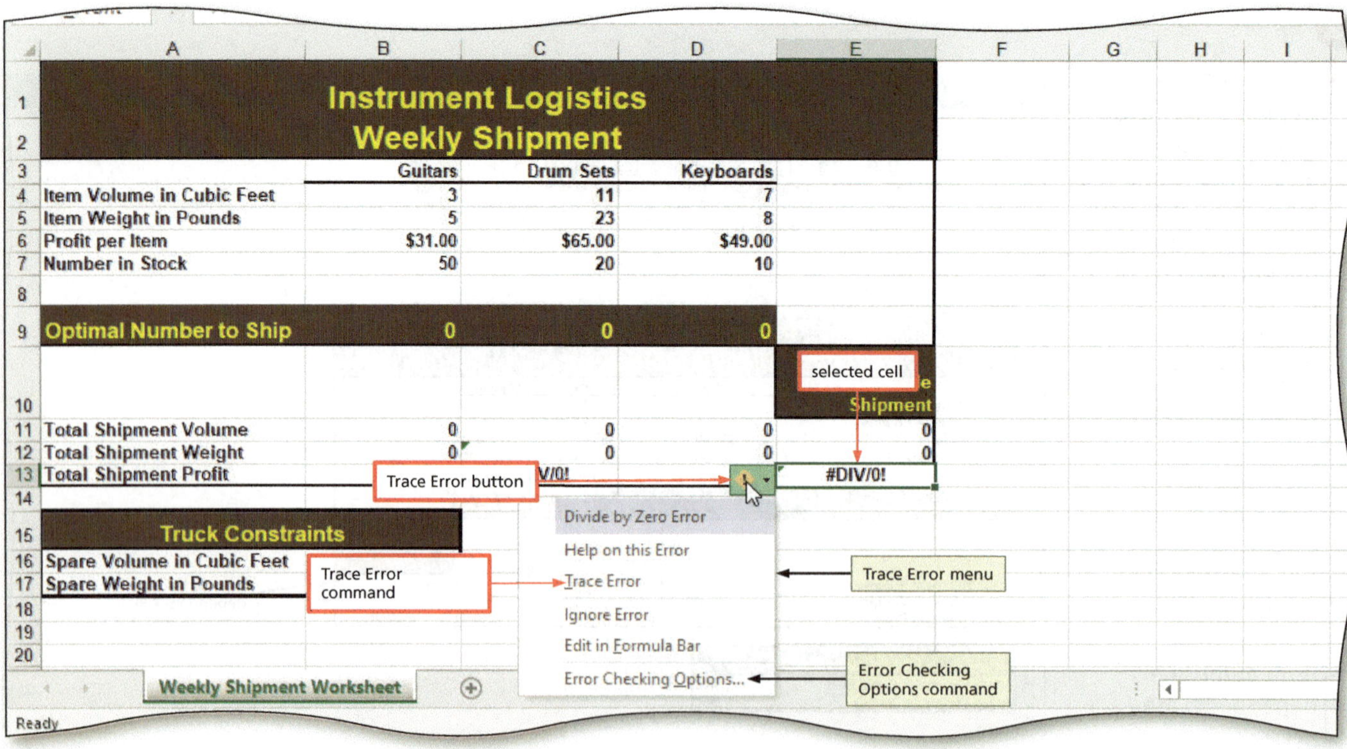

Figure 9–11

2

- Click Trace Error on the menu to display precedent arrows directly involved in the error (Figure 9–12).

Q&A **How is tracing the error different from tracing precedents?**
The Trace Error command displays only the precedent arrows involved in the error. Depending on the kind of error, the Trace Error command also moves the selection to the probable erroneous cell.

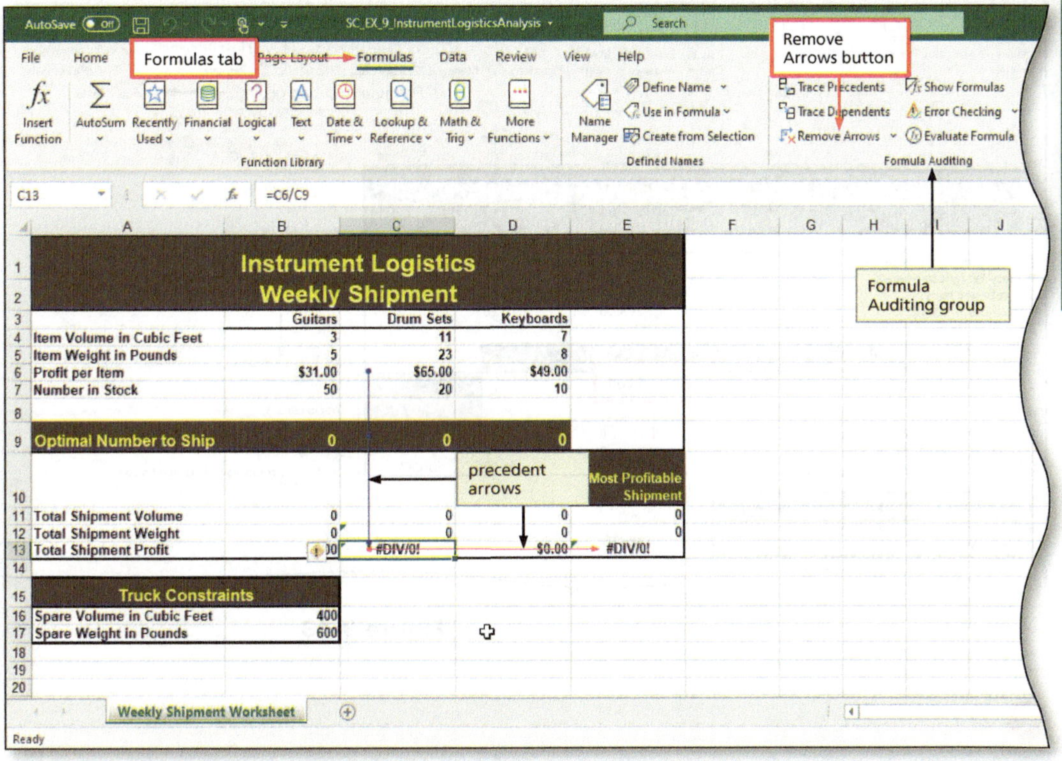

Figure 9–12

3

- Click the Remove Arrows button (Formulas tab | Formula Auditing group) to remove all of the arrows.

Other Ways

1. Click Error Checking arrow (Formulas tab | Formula Auditing Group), click Trace Error on menu

To Use Error Checking to Correct Errors

After tracing the precedents and dependents, and using the Trace Error command, you decide to correct the #DIV/0! in cell C13 first. **Why?** All the arrows indicate that C13 may be causing the error shown in E13.

The following steps use error checking features to find the source of these errors and correct them.

1

- Select cell C13.
- Click the Error Checking button (Formulas tab | Formula Auditing group) to display the Error Checking dialog box. If necessary, drag the dialog box away from the figures on the worksheet so the figures are visible.
- Read the message in the Error Checking dialog box that identifies that the formula is dividing by zero or empty cells (Figure 9–13).

Q&A **What is the purpose of the Next button?**
Excel will move to the next cell in which it finds an error code or an error indicator. Excel moves forward or backward through the workbook, row by row, when you click the Next or Previous button. Clicking the Next button does not move to a precedent or dependent cell.

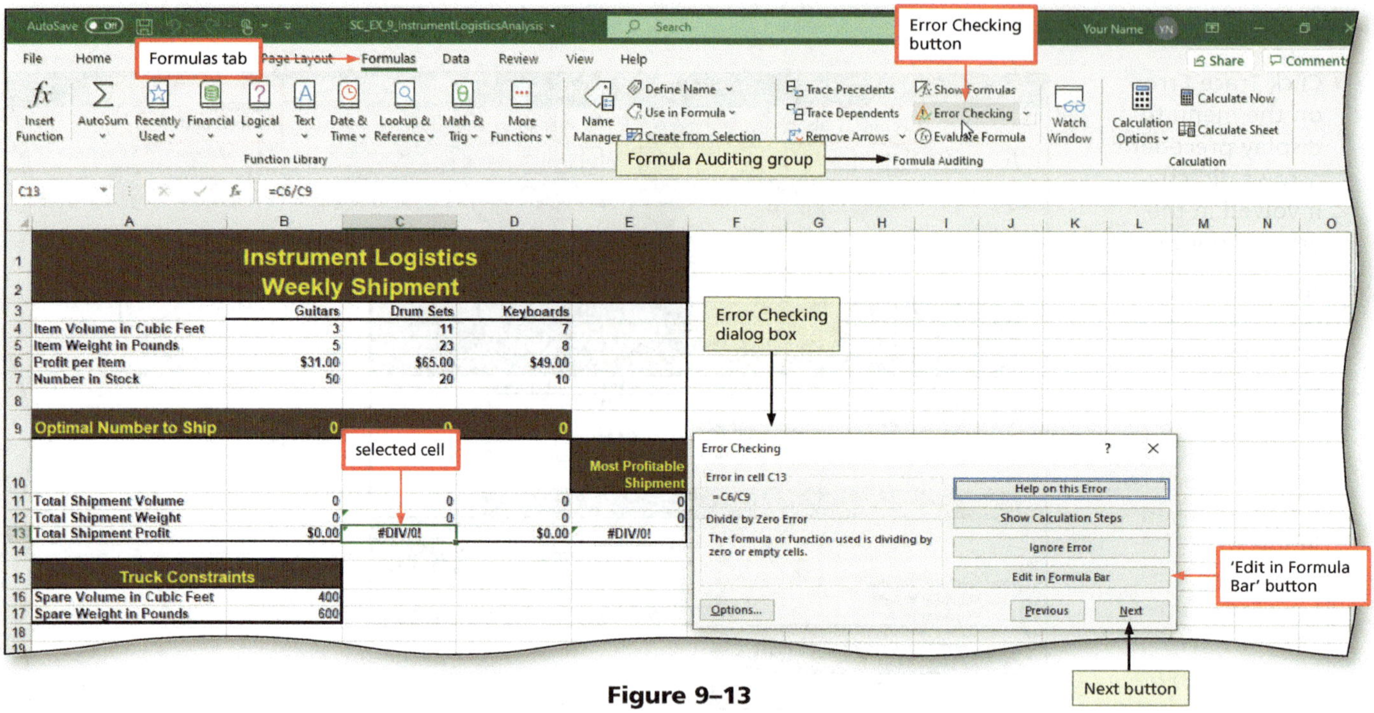

Figure 9–13

2

- Look at the formula in cell C13. Rather than dividing, it should multiply C6 by C9, which is the 'Profit per Item' by the 'Optimal Number to Ship'.
- Click the 'Edit in Formula Bar' button (Error Checking dialog box) and edit cell C13 to read **=C6*C9** (Figure 9–14).

Q&A **Why are some cells highlighted in different colors?**
Excel highlights the cells involved in the current formula. The cell highlighted in red indicates a possible error.

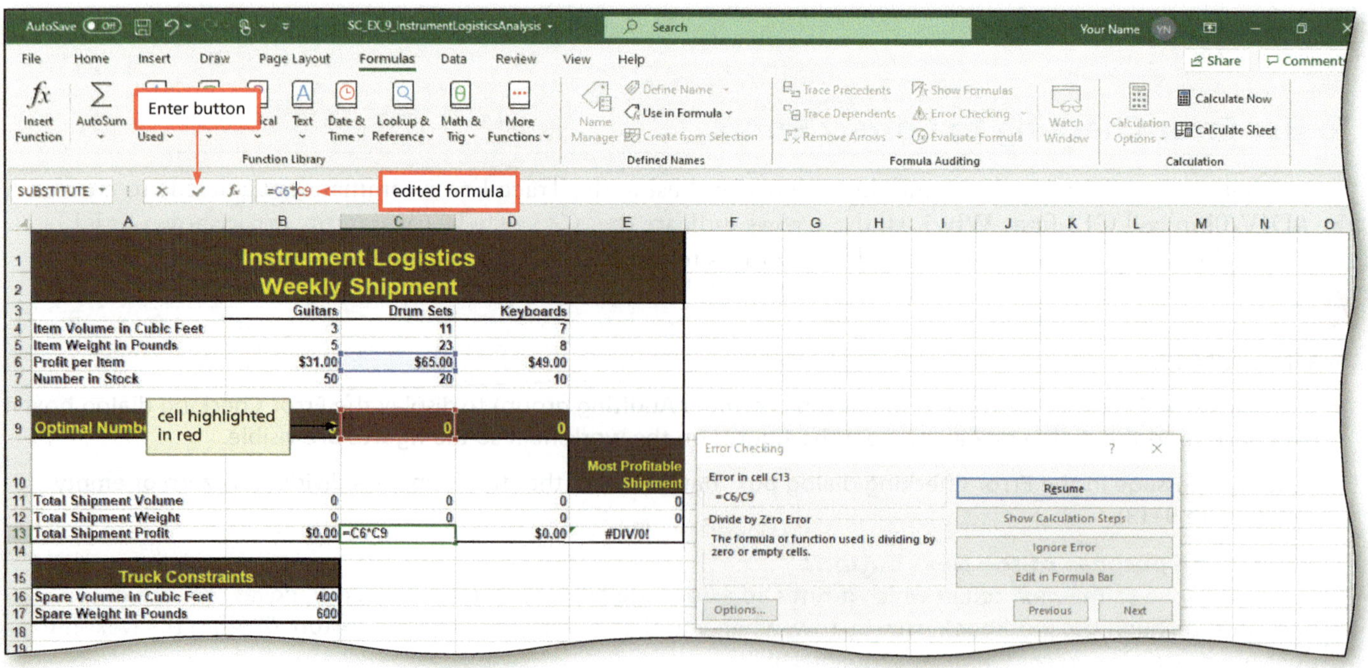

Figure 9–14

3

- Click the Enter button in the formula bar to complete the edit of the cell and to correct the error in cell C13 and the dependent error in cell E13 (Figure 9–15).

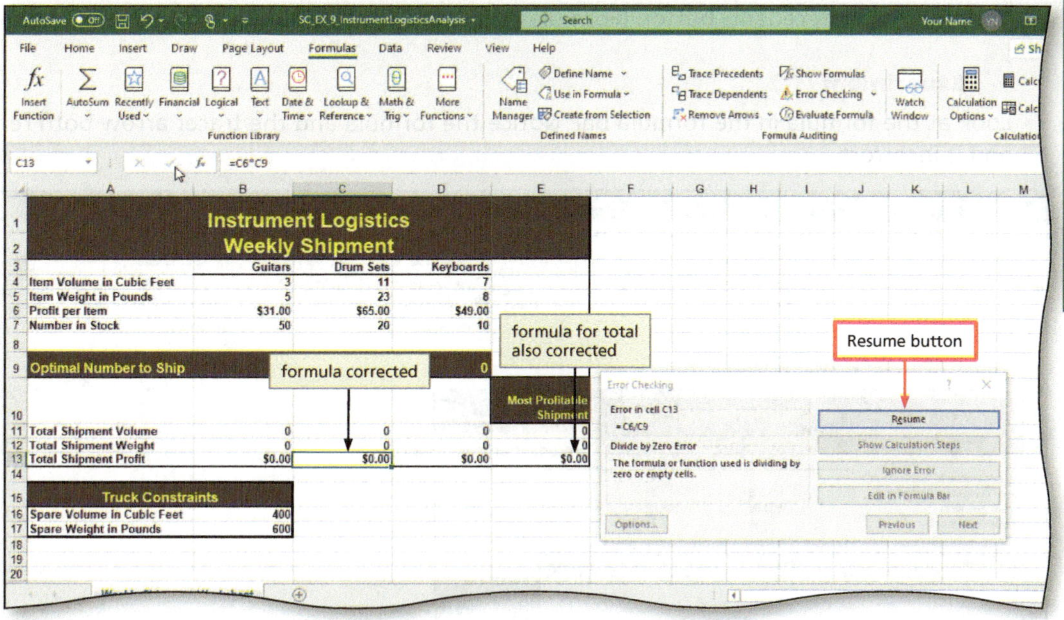

Figure 9–15

Q&A **Why did correcting one error in cell C13 correct the other #DIV/0! error in the worksheet?**
The other cell containing a #DIV/0! error was directly or indirectly dependent on the value in cell C13; thus correcting the error in cell C13 provided a valid value for use in the other formulas.

4

- Click the Resume button (Error Checking dialog box) to continue checking errors. Excel will move to the error in cell C12 (Figure 9–16).

Experiment

- Click the 'Help on this Error' button (Error Checking dialog box) and read about the error in the browser window that Excel opens. When you are finished, close the browser window.

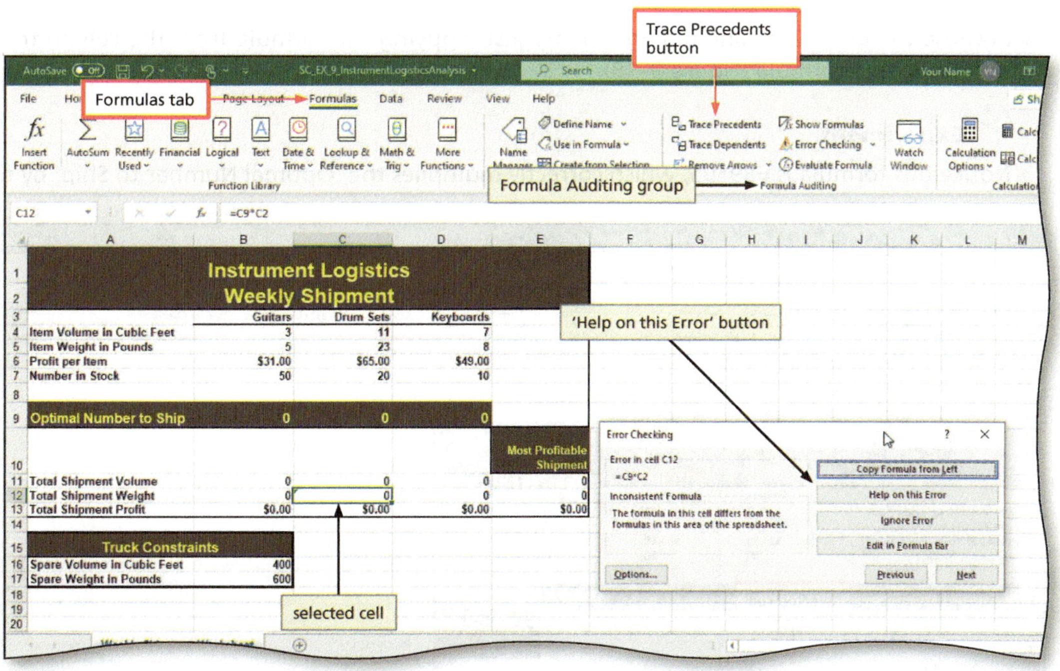

Figure 9–16

5

- Click the Trace Precedents button (Formulas tab | Formula Auditing group) to display the tracer arrow (Figure 9–17).

Experiment

- Look at the formula in the formula bar. Notice the formula and the tracer arrow both reference C2, which is text and is incorrect.

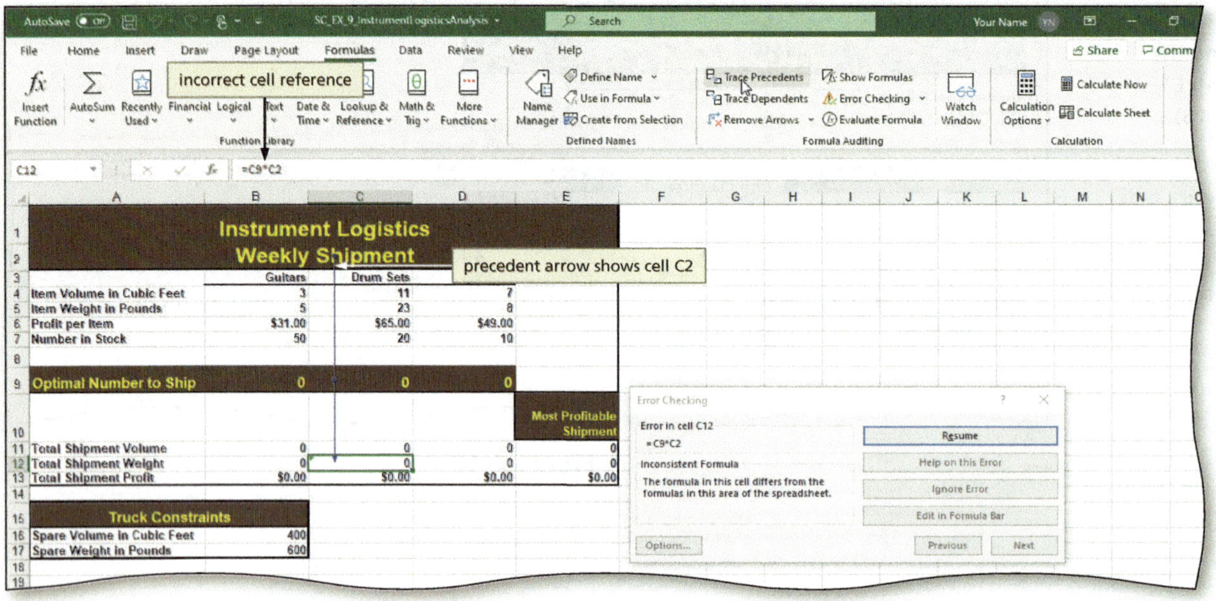

Figure 9–17

6

- Because the Error Checking dialog box suggests copying the formula from the cell on the left, click cell B12 to view the suggested formula (Figure 9–18).

Experiment

- Notice this formula is =B9*B5, which correctly multiplies the 'Optimal Number to Ship' by the 'Item Weight in Pounds'.

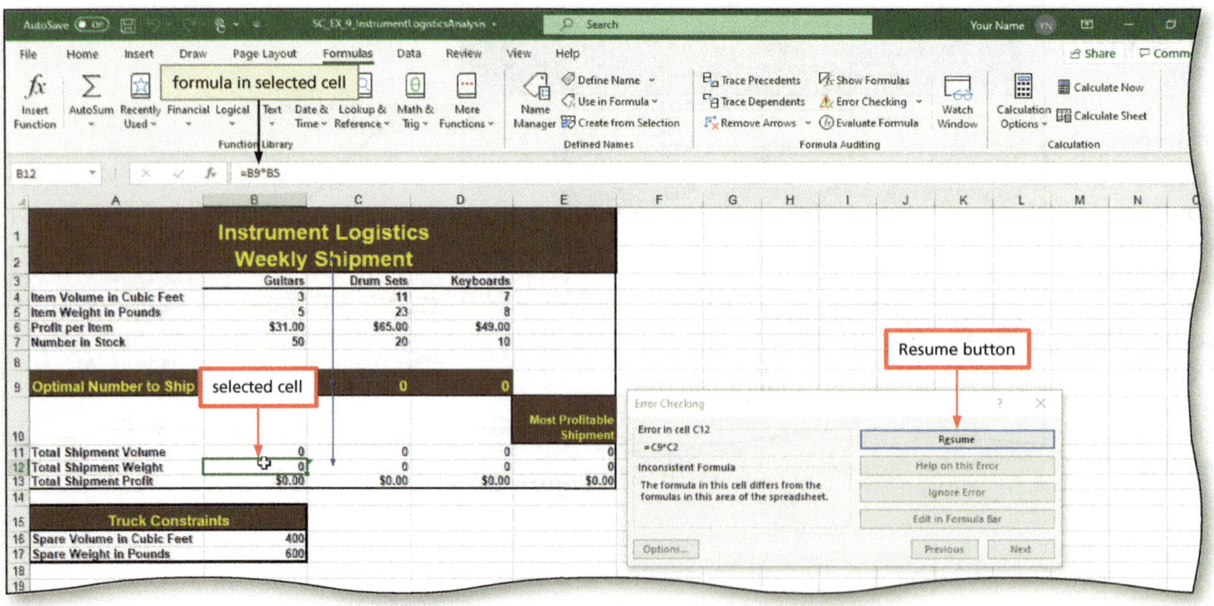

Figure 9–18

7

- Click the Resume button (Error Checking dialog box) to move to the error in cell C12 (Figure 9–19).

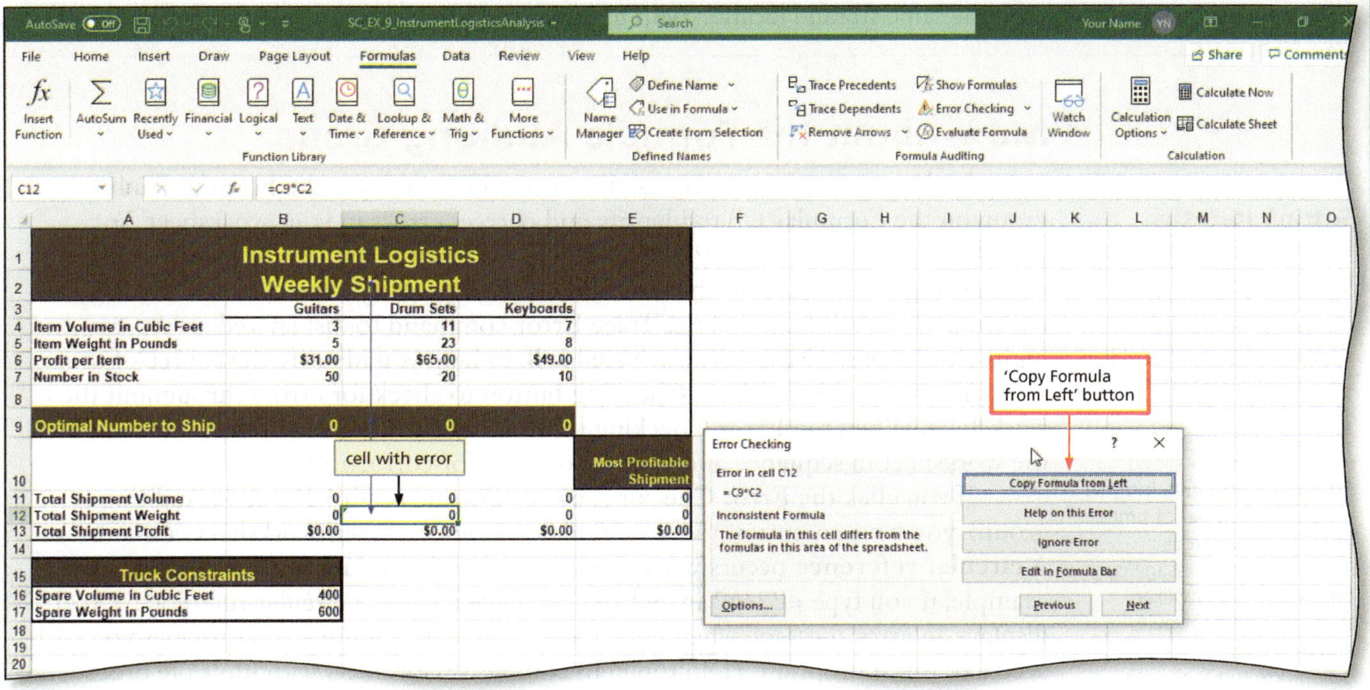

Figure 9–19

8

- Click the 'Copy Formula from Left' button (Error Checking dialog box) to fix the error (Figure 9–20).

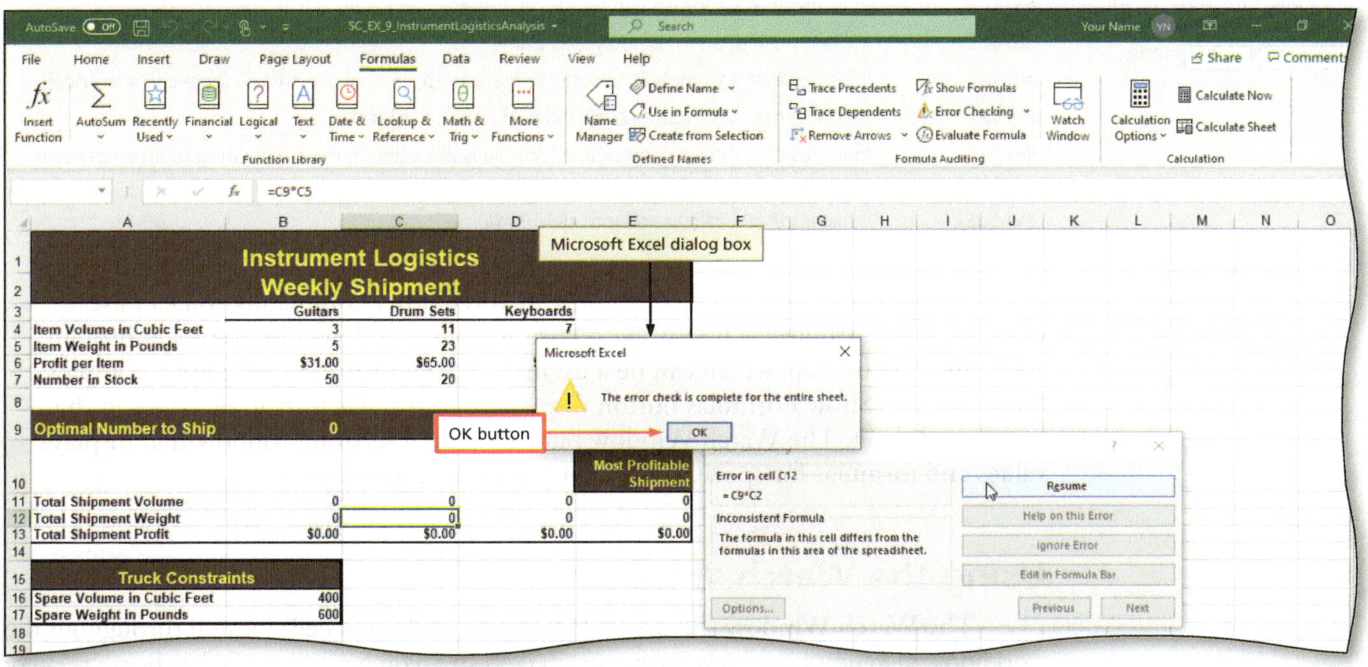

Figure 9–20

9

- Click OK (Microsoft Excel dialog box) as the error correction is complete.
- Save the workbook again on the same storage location with the same file name.

More about the Formula Auditing Group

BTW
Setting Iterative Calculation Options
In certain situations, you will want Excel to recalculate a formula that contains a circular reference, to enable Excel to converge upon an acceptable solution. Changing the iterative calculation option allows Excel to recalculate a formula a specified number of times after the initial circular reference error message is dismissed. To allow Excel to recalculate a formula, display the Excel Options dialog box and then click the Formulas tab. In the Calculation options area, click to select the 'Enable iterative calculation' check box. You can specify the maximum number of iterations and maximum amount of change between iterations. Be aware that turning on this option will slow down the worksheet due to the additional computations.

In the previous steps, you used some of the buttons in the Formula Auditing group on the Formulas tab to identify and correct errors in your worksheet. You already have used the Trace Precedents, Trace Dependents, and 'Remove All Arrows' buttons to gain insight into the structure of the worksheet. You used the Trace Error button in the worksheet and the Trace Error command to display red arrows to highlight the precedents of the selected cell, to help you identify the source of the error. You also used the Error Checking button to check for errors throughout the worksheet. When the Error Checking button is clicked, Excel highlights each error in the worksheet in sequence and displays options for correcting the error.

If you click the Error Checking arrow (Formulas tab | Formula Auditing group), you have an option to fix a circular reference, if your worksheet contains one. A **circular reference** occurs when one of the defining values in a cell is itself. For example, if you type =B2/A2 in cell B2, you have created a circular reference. Excel displays an error message when you create a circular reference and provides you with access to the appropriate Help topic. In complex worksheets with multiple precedent levels, these errors are not uncommon.

Table 9–1 lists other common error codes identified in Excel.

Table 9–1 Common Excel Error Codes

Error Code	Description
#DIV/0!	Indicates that a formula divides a number by zero
#N/A!	Indicates that a formula cannot locate a referenced value
#NAME?	Indicates use of an invalid function name
#NULL!	Indicates that a formula incorrectly contains a space between two or more cell references
#NUM!	Indicates that a formula contains invalid numeric values
#REF!	Indicates that a cell reference in a formula is not valid; it may be pointing to an empty cell, for instance
#VALUE!	Indicates that a calculation includes nonnumeric data

The Formula Auditing group contains three other commands you can use when auditing formulas. The Evaluate Formula button allows you to move through a formula step by step, which can be a useful tool when working with long, complex formulas. The Show Formulas button displays the formulas instead of values in the active worksheet. The Watch Window button opens a separate window that displays values and formulas for specific cells that you choose to monitor.

Using the Watch Window

The **Watch Window** (Figure 9–21a) displays values of cells located throughout the workbook and allows you to keep an eye on cells that you have identified as being related; this allows you to observe changes to the cells even when viewing a different worksheet or workbook. For example, if you were watching cell E13, which displays 'Total Shipment Profit' for the most profitable shipment, and you changed the value in cell B13, the

Watch Window would display the updated value of cell E13 on the Weekly Shipment Worksheet. You add cells to the Watch Window using the Add Watch button and the Add Watch dialog box (Figure 9–21b). The Watch Window continues to show the values of watched cells even as you navigate the worksheet and the cells no longer are in view. Similarly, if you change the view to another worksheet or workbook, the Watch Window allows you to continue to monitor the cell values.

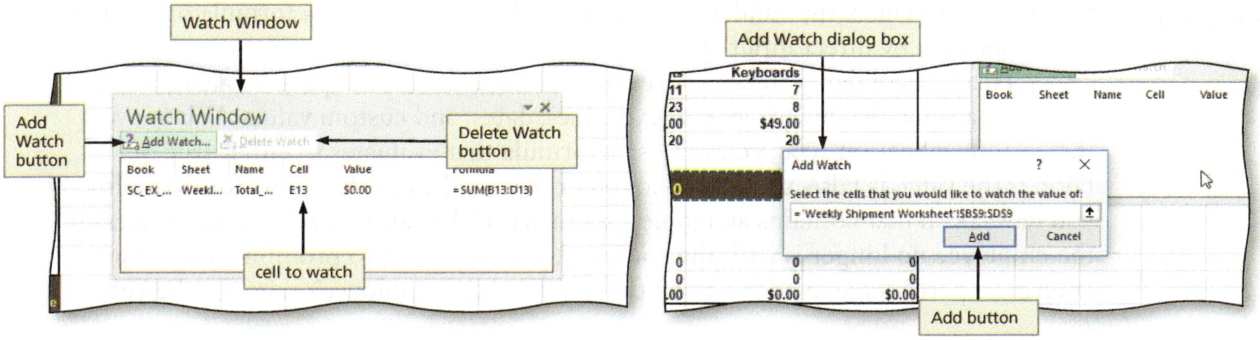

(a) Watch Window **(b) Add Watch dialog box**

Figure 9–21

To Open the Watch Window

If you wanted to open the Watch Window, you would perform the following steps:

1. If necessary, display the Formulas tab.
2. Click the Watch Window button (Formulas tab | Formula Auditing group) to open the Watch Window (Figure 9–21a).
3. If necessary, move the Watch Window to a location where it does not obscure cells you want to edit.

To Add Cells to the Watch Window

If you wanted to add cells to the Watch Window, you would perform the following steps:

1. Click the Add Watch button on the Watch Window toolbar to display the Add Watch dialog box (Figure 9–21b).
2. Select the cell or cells to be watched.
3. Click the Add button (Add Watch dialog box) to add the selected cells to the Watch Window.

To Delete Cells from the Watch Window

If you wanted to delete cells from the Watch Window, you would perform the following steps:

1. In the Watch Window dialog box, select the cell you want to stop watching.
2. Click the Delete Watch button in the Watch Window to delete the selected cell from the Watch Window (Figure 9-21a).

Data Validation

When creating advanced worksheets, some user-entered values my need to fall within certain ranges or contain specific types of data. For example, cells B9:D9 in the Weekly Shipment Worksheet display the optimal number of instruments to ship. Recall from the requirements that shipment amounts must be whole numbers and at least one of

BTW

Errors and Data

Excel cannot identify cells that contain formulas that are mathematically correct but logically incorrect without the use of data validation rules. It is up to the user to create validation rules that restrict solutions to logical values.

each type of instrument must be included in each shipment but no more than are in stock of each type of instrument. Excel provides you with tools to restrict the values that can be placed in cells to valid values. You can place restrictions on values, provide a message to the user when a cell with restrictions is selected, and create an error message that is displayed when an invalid value is entered.

Excel data validation rules apply only when you enter data into the cell manually. Excel does not check the validation rules if a cell is calculated by a formula or set in a way other than by direct input by the user.

The types of data validation criteria you can use include specific values, whole numbers, a value in a list (such as a text value), dates, and custom values. When using the custom validation type, you can use a formula that evaluates to either true or false. If the value is false, users may not enter data in the cell. Suppose, for example, you have a cell that contains an employee's salary. If the salary is zero, which indicates the employee no longer is with the company, you may want to prohibit a user from entering a percentage in another cell that contains the employee's raise for the year.

To Add Data Validation to Cells

Why? In the Weekly Shipment Worksheet, the numbers of each type of instrument to ship must be nonnegative whole numbers. The cells that need to be restricted are cells B9:D9. You can use data validation to apply these conditions and restrictions to the cells. The following steps add data validation to cells in the range B9:D9.

1

- Display the Data tab and then select cells B9:D9.
- Click the Data Validation button (Data tab | Data Tools group) to display the Data Validation dialog box.
- Click the Allow arrow (Data Validation dialog box | Settings tab) to view the list of allowed restrictions on the input data (Figure 9–22).

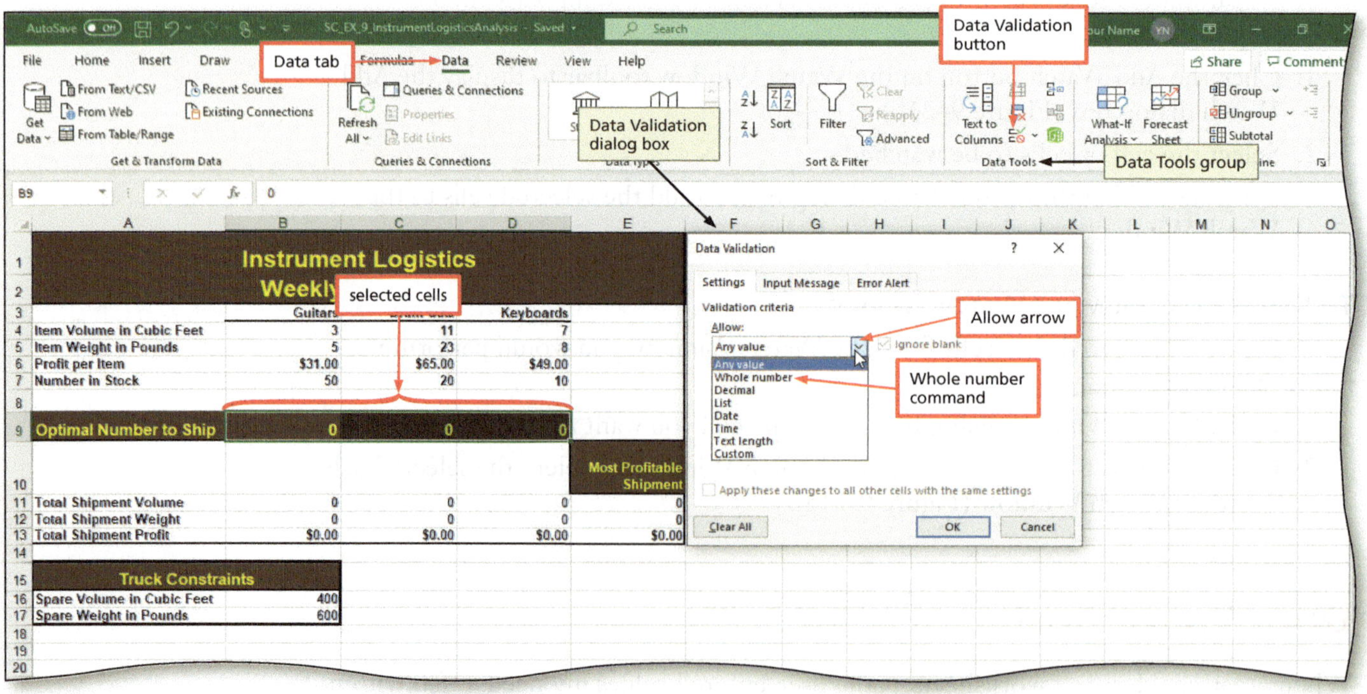

Figure 9–22

Q&A **What are the allowed restrictions?**
The Any value selection allows you to enter any value but still allows you to specify an input message for the cell. The Whole number, Decimal, Date, and Time selections permit only values of those types to be entered in the cell. The List selection allows you to specify a range that contains a list of valid values for the cell. The Text length selection allows only a certain length of text string to be entered in the cell. The Custom selection allows you to specify a formula that validates the data entered by the user. Each selection displays its own set of options.

2

- Click Whole number in the Allow list to display options for whole numbers.
- Click the Data arrow to view its list (Figure 9–23).

Q&A **What is in the Data list?**
The Data list includes the standard logical operators for numeric, date, and time data. The list is not available for other data types.

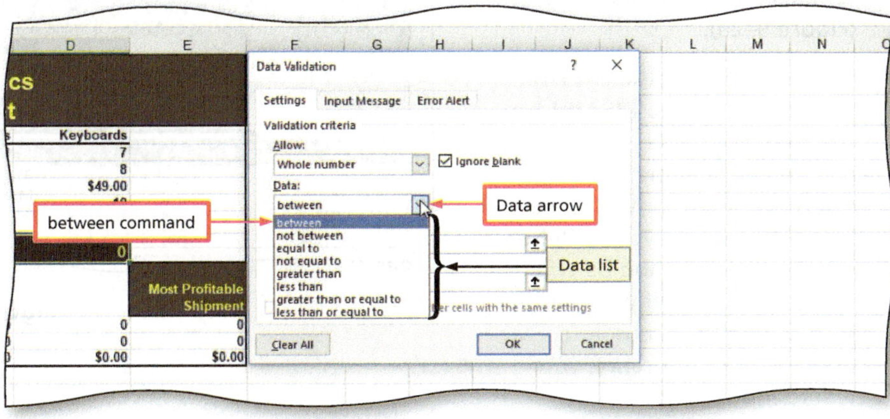

Figure 9–23

3

- Click between in the Data list to select it.
- Type 1 in the Minimum box to specify that the values in the selected cells must be whole numbers greater than or equal to one (Figure 9–24).

Q&A **What am I entering 1?**
Recall that the requirements document specifies that at least one of each instrument should be shipped.

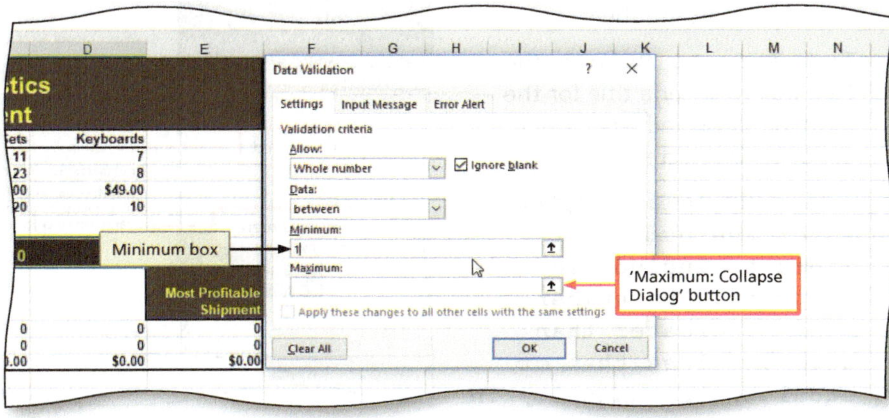

Figure 9–24

4

- Click the 'Maximum: Collapse Dialog' button to collapse the dialog box and go to the worksheet (Figure 9–25).

Q&A **Why is the dialog box collapsed?**
When you click a Collapse Dialog button associated with any input box, you are telling Excel that you want to choose the value from the worksheet rather than type it in yourself. Excel collapses the dialog box to get it out of the way.

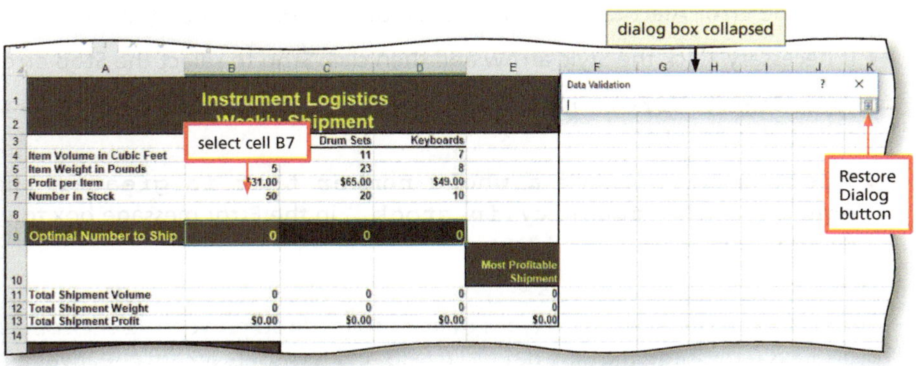

Figure 9–25

5

- In the worksheet, click cell B7 to choose the cell for the Maximum value.
- Click the Restore Dialog button (Data Validation dialog box) to maximize the dialog box (Figure 9–26).

Q&A **Will all three values in the validation range (B9:D9) be compared to B7?**
No. Excel will apply a relative reference; in other words, B9 will be compared to B7, C9 will be compared to C7, and D9 will be compared to D7. If you wanted to compare to an absolute, nonchanging reference, you would input =$B$7.

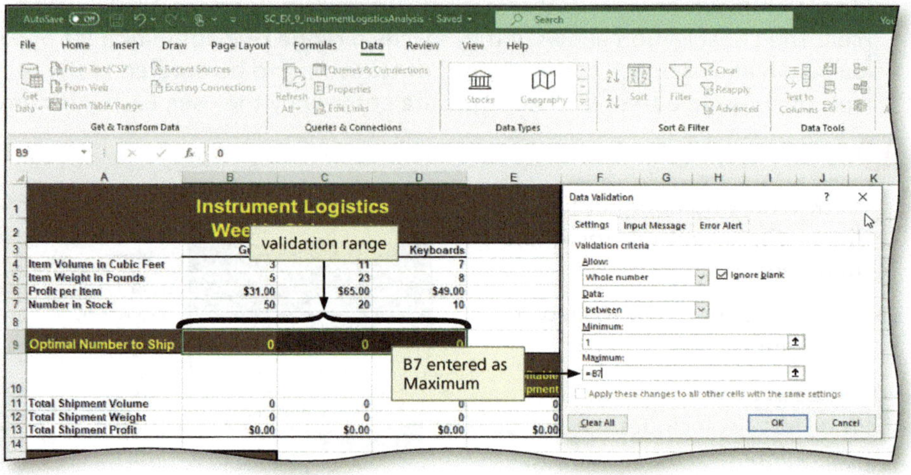

Figure 9–26

6

- Click the Input Message tab (Data Validation dialog box) to display the Input Message sheet.
- Type `Item to Ship` in the Title box to enter a title for the message displayed when cell B9, C9, or D9 is selected.
- In the Input message box, type `Enter the number of items to include in this shipment. The number must be greater than zero and less than or equal to the quantity in stock.` to enter the text for the message (Figure 9–27).

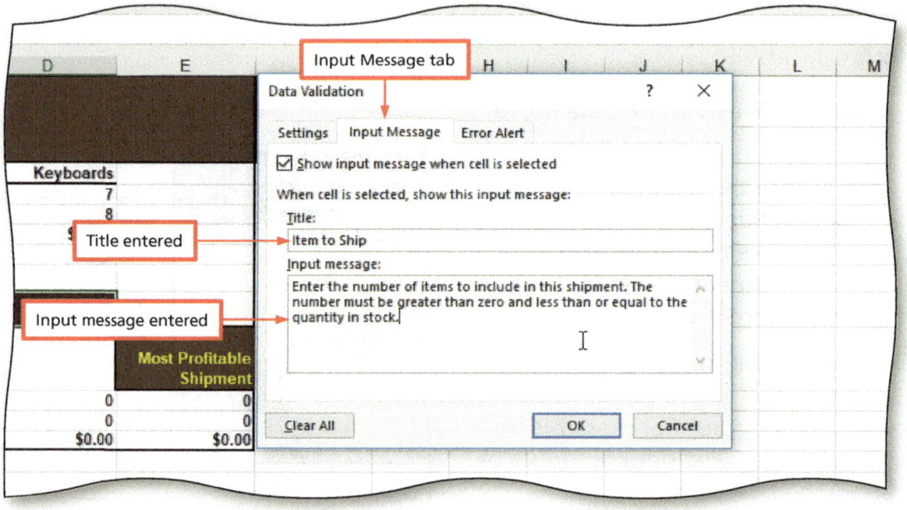

Figure 9–27

7

- Click the Error Alert tab (Data Validation dialog box) to display the Error Alert sheet.
- If necessary, Click the Style arrow and then click Stop to select the Stop error style.
- Type `Input Error` in the Title box to enter a title for the error message displayed if invalid data is entered in cell B9, C9, or D9.
- Type `You must enter a whole number that is greater than zero and less than or equal to the quantity in stock.` in the Error message box to enter the for the error message (Figure 9–28).

Q&A **What is a Stop error style?**
You can select one of three types of error styles. Stop prevents users from entering invalid data in a cell. Warning displays a message that the data is invalid and lets users accept the invalid entry, edit it, or remove it. Information displays a message that the data is invalid but still allows users to enter it.

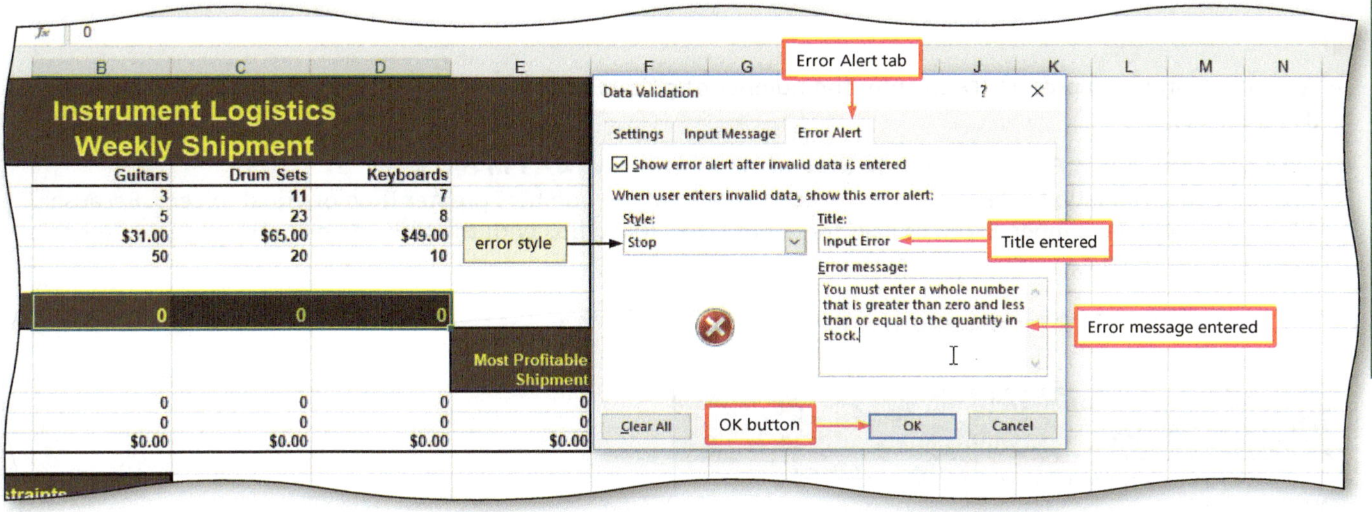

Figure 9–28

8

- Click OK (Data Validation dialog box) to accept the data validation settings for cells B9:D9.
- Click outside the data range to remove the selection.

To Test the Validation

The following steps test the validation rules. **Why?** It is always a good idea to test validation rules to make sure they work as you expect them to.

1

- Click cell B9 to make it the active cell and display the 'Items to Ship' input message (Figure 9–29).

Experiment

- Click cells C9 and D9 to make sure the same input message appears. Click cell B9.

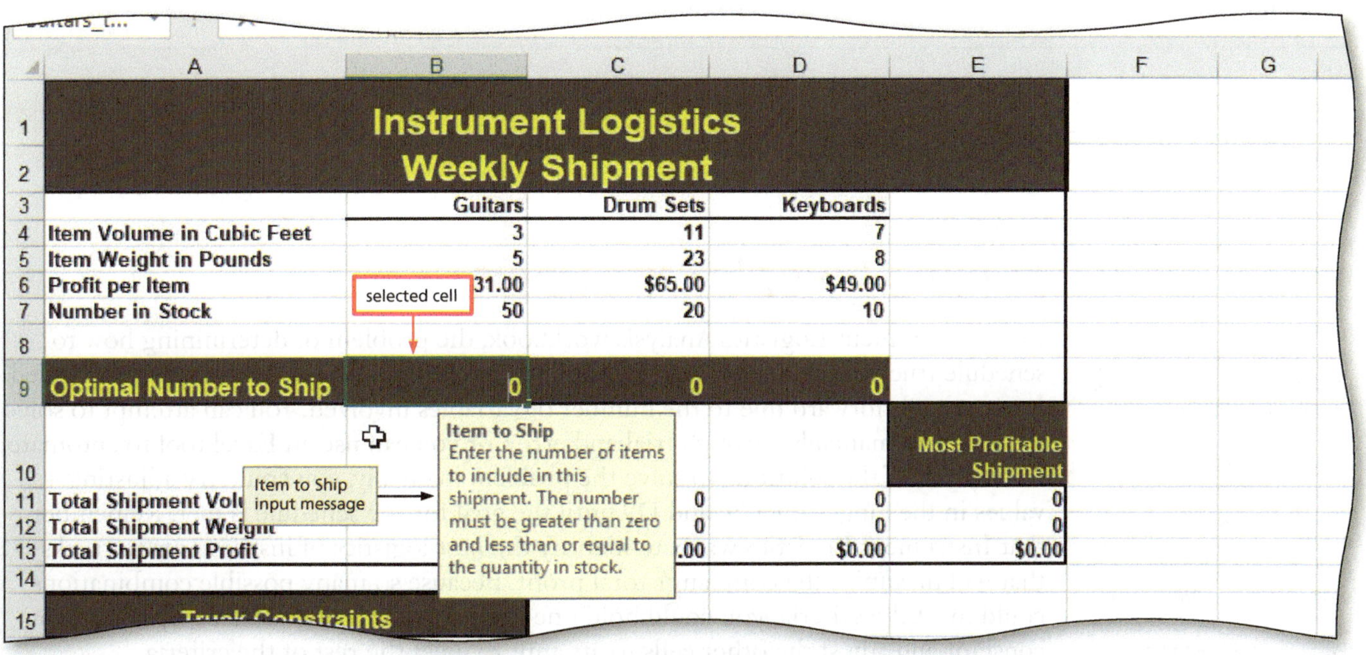

Figure 9–29

2

- Type **47.5** and then press ENTER to enter the number of guitars to ship and to display the Input Error dialog box (Figure 9–30).

Q&A **Why does the Input Error dialog box appear after entering 47.5 in cell B9?**
You set a data validation rule in cell B9 that accepts only whole numbers greater than or equal to zero. Because 47.5 is not a whole number, Excel displays the Input Error dialog box with the title and error message you specified when you set the data validation rule.

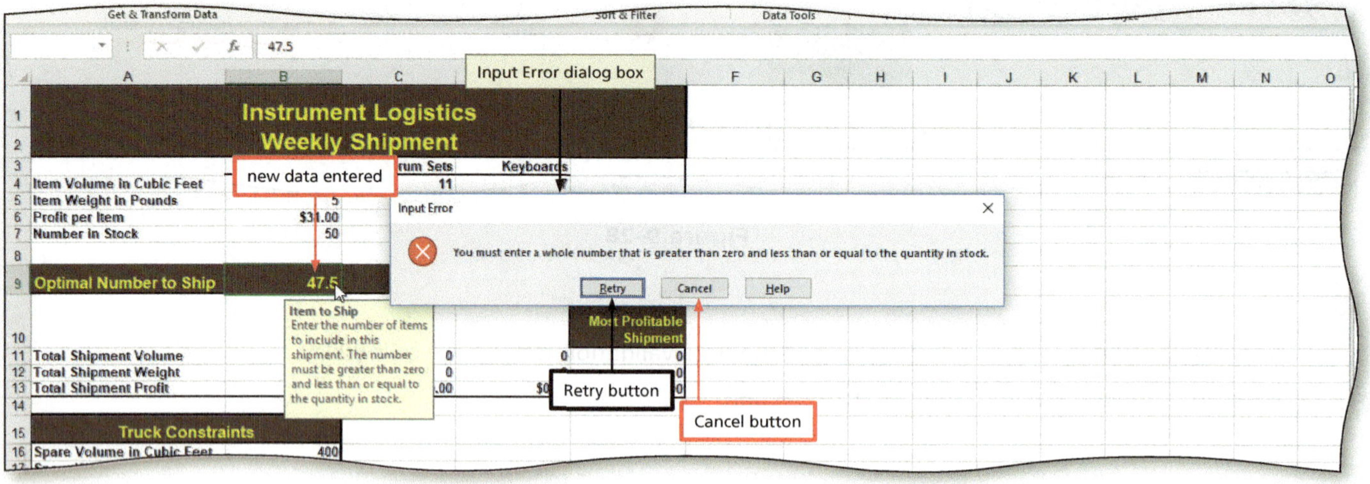

Figure 9–30

3

- Click Cancel (Input Error dialog box) to return to cell B9.

Experiment

- Repeat Step 1 using values that are negative and values that are more than the number in stock. When you are finished, click Cancel (Input Error dialog box).
- Save the workbook again on the same storage location with the same file name. If Excel displays an Input Error dialog box, click Cancel.

Break Point: If you want to take a break, this is a good place to do so. You can exit Excel now. To resume later, start Excel, open the file called SC_EX_9_InstrumentLogisticsAnalysis.xlsx, and continue following the steps from this location forward.

BTW
Copying Validation Rules
You can copy validation rules from one cell to other cells using the Paste Special command. Select the cell that contains the validation rules you want to copy and then click Copy. Select the cell or cells to which you want to apply the validation rules, click the Paste button arrow, and then click Paste Special. Click Validation in the Paste area and then click the OK button (Paste Special dialog box).

Solving Complex Problems

In the Instrument Logistics Analysis workbook, the problem of determining how to schedule trucks to maximize weight, volume, and profit within the constraints provided is not straightforward due to the number of variables involved. You can attempt to solve the problem manually through trial and error, or you can use an Excel tool to automate some or all of the solution. To solve the problem manually, you could try adjusting values in the ranges B9, C9, and D9 until the goal for the schedule is met. Remember that Instrument Logistics wants to identify the best logistics of instruments to trucks that will maximize the company's total profit. Because so many possible combinations could meet the criteria, you could hold one or more of the cells affected by constraints constant and adjust the other cells to attempt to meet the rest of the criteria.

Consider This

How should you approach solving a complex problem?

When considering an approach to a complex problem in Excel, start with the least complex method of attempting to solve the problem. In general, the following methods can be useful in the order shown:

1. **Use trial and error** to modify the values in the worksheet. Use a commonsense approach, and keep in mind the range of acceptable answers to your problem. For example, the number of instruments should not be a negative number.
2. **Use the Excel Goal Seek feature** to have Excel automatically modify a cell's value in a worksheet in an attempt to reach a certain goal in a dependent cell.
3. **Use the Excel Solver feature** to provide Excel with all of the known rules, or constraints, of your problem as well as the goal you are seeking. Allow Solver to attempt as many different solutions to your problem as possible.

To Use Trial and Error to Attempt to Solve a Complex Problem

Trial and error is not making blind guesses; rather, it is a process of making incremental changes in order to observe the impact on the desired result. **Why?** With an understanding of how the worksheet is set up and how the various values interact, you can make informed changes, or trials, based on how each decision affects the worksheet. In the first trial for the Instrument Logistics workbook, you will enter valid data for each of the instruments; then you will compare the total weight and volume to that allowed on the truck. The following steps use trial and error to attempt to solve a complex problem. In this case, you are trying to maximize the profit while filling the truck without going over.

1

- Enter **47** in cell B9 as the number of guitars to ship, and then press TAB.
- Enter **18** in cell C9 as the number of drum sets to ship, and then press TAB.
- Enter **9** in cell D9 as the number of keyboards to ship, and then press ENTER (Figure 9–31).

Q&A **Do the values entered in Step 1 solve the scheduling problem?**
No. Both the Volume and Weight in cells E11:E12 exceed the truck constraints shown in cells B16:B17.

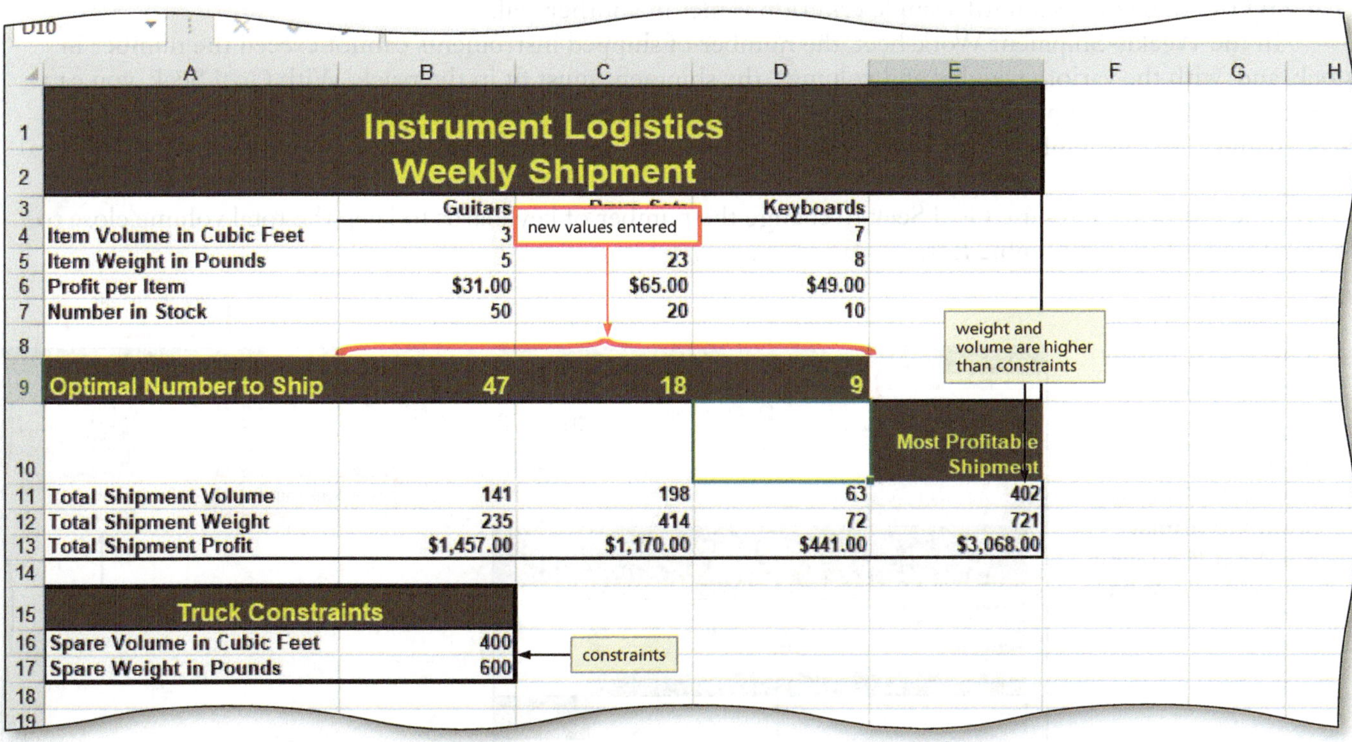

Figure 9–31

2

- Click cell B9 to make it the active cell.
- Enter 35 and then press ENTER to reduce the number of guitars to ship (Figure 9–32).

Q&A

Does the value entered in Step 2 solve the scheduling problem?
No. The weight is still too heavy. Compare cells E12 and B17.

What are some problems with using trial and error?
While trial and error can be used on simple problems, it has many limitations when used to solve complex problems. Endless combinations of values could be entered in cells B7, C7, D7, C9, B9, and D9 to try to come up with a solution. Using trial and error, it is difficult to determine if a solution you reach satisfies the goal of maximizing the total profit.

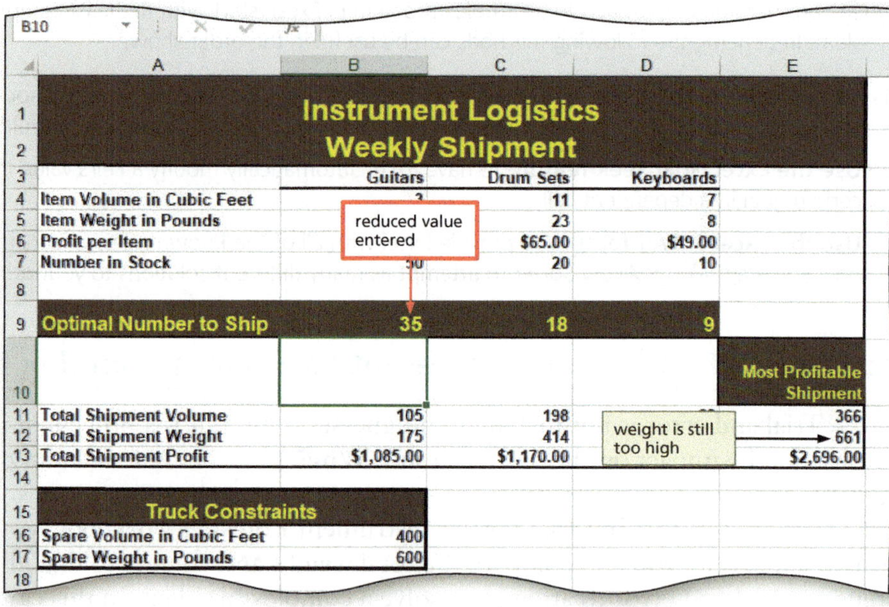

Figure 9–32

To Use Goal Seek to Attempt to Solve a Complex Problem

If you know the result you want a formula to produce, recall that you can use **Goal Seek** to determine the value of a cell on which a formula depends. Goal seeking takes trial and error one step further by automatically changing the value of a cell until a single criterion is met in another cell.

In the Weekly Shipment Worksheet, the number of shipped instruments cannot exceed the number in stock, and, with the various weights and volumes, the shipment must fit in the truck. With Goal Seek, you can manipulate one of these precedent cells to find a solution that meets the constraints. You decide to have Goal Seek manipulate the number of keyboards. **Why?** You want to try to achieve the goal of 400 cubic feet, the total volume for the shipment.

The following steps use Goal Seek to change the number of keyboards to keep the total volume close to but under or equal to 400 cubic feet.

1

- If necessary, display the Data tab.
- Click the 'What-If Analysis' button (Data tab | Forecast group) to display the What-If Analysis menu (Figure 9–33).

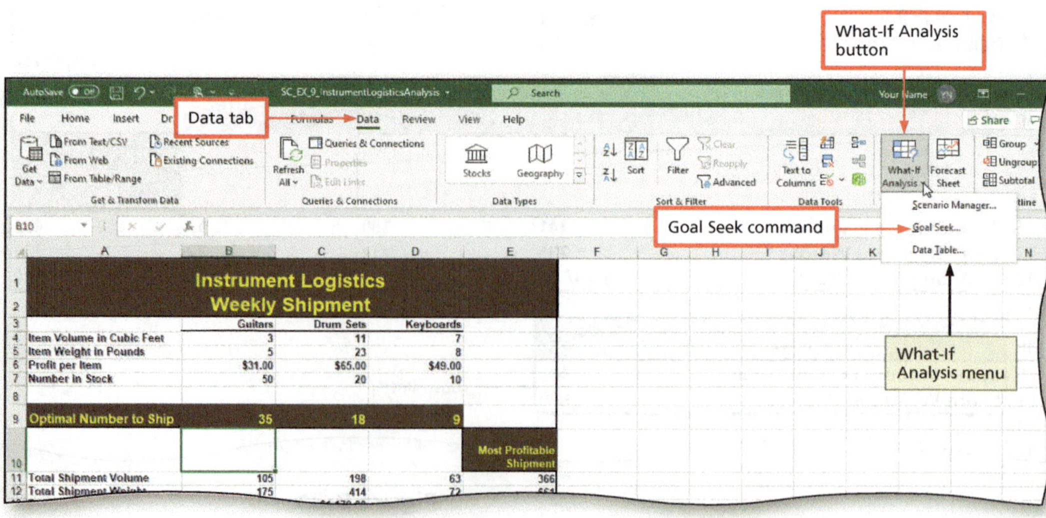

Figure 9–33

2

- Click Goal Seek on the What-If Analysis menu to display the Goal Seek dialog box. Drag the dialog box so that it does not cover the data on the worksheet.
- Type **$E$11** in the Set cell box (Goal Seek dialog box) to specify which cell should contain the goal value.
- Type **400** in the To value box as the goal value.
- Type **$D$9** in the 'By changing cell' box (Figure 9–34).

Q&A **Could I have clicked those cells in the worksheet instead of typing them?**
Yes, just be sure that Excel applies the absolute reference $ before both the row and column so no replications are made.

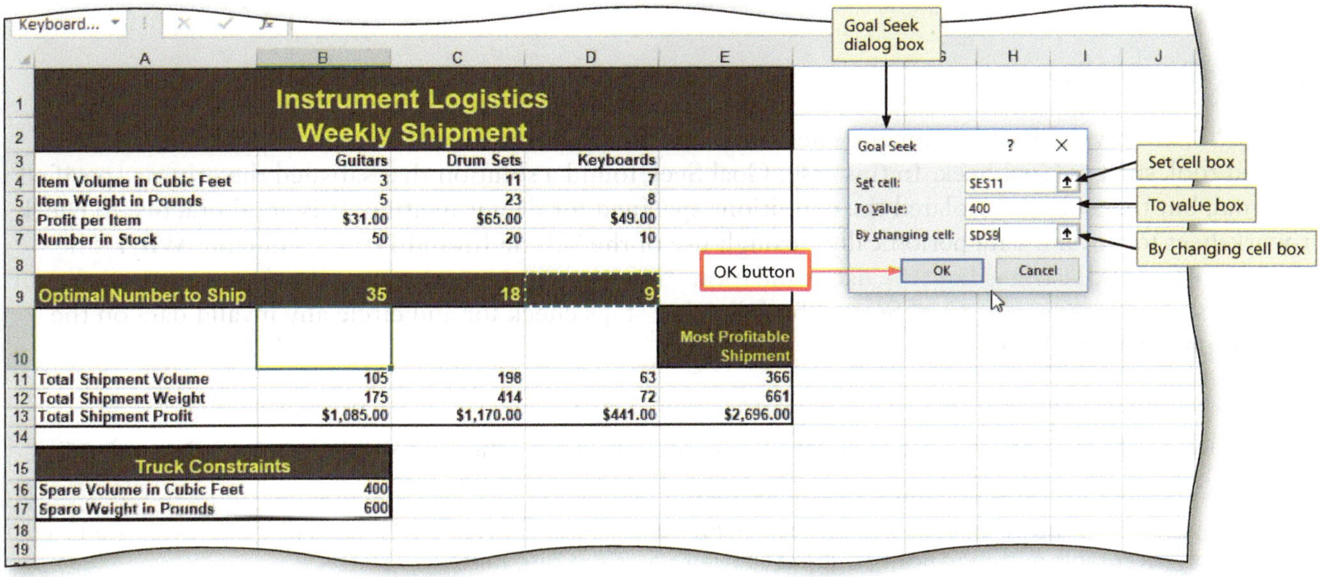

Figure 9–34

3

- Click OK (Goal Seek dialog box) to seek the goal of 400 cubic feet in cell E11 and display the Goal Seek Status dialog box (Figure 9–35).

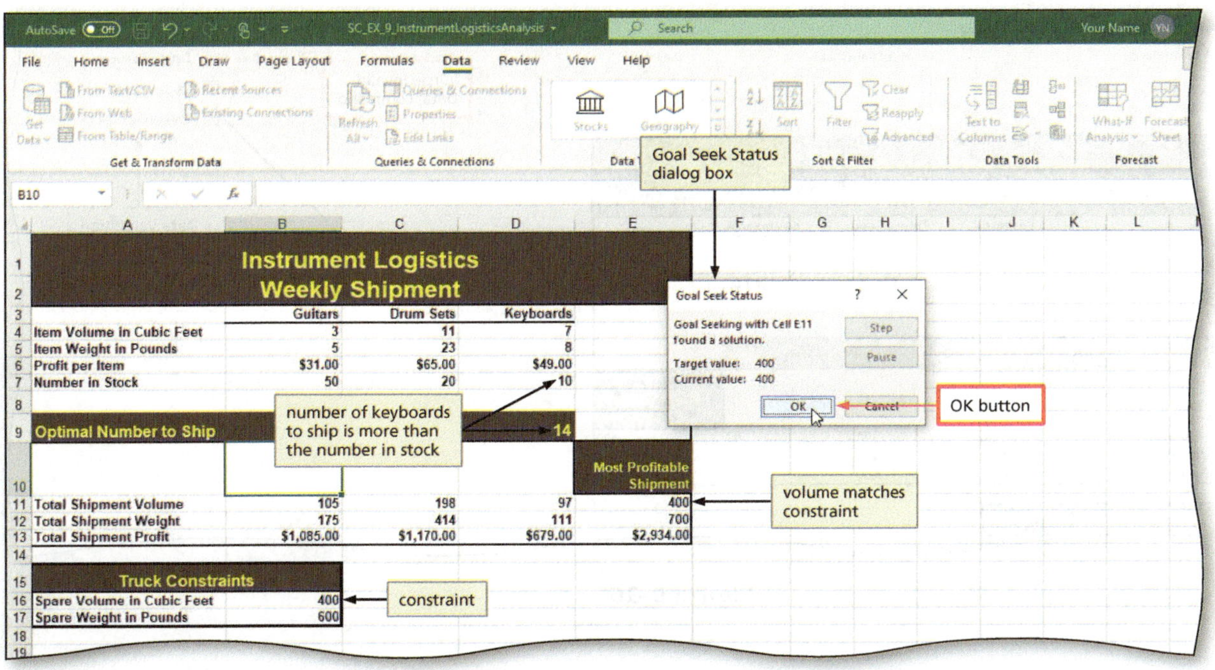

Figure 9–35

Experiment

- Watch Excel create iterations in trying to come close to 400.

Q&A **How can the number of keyboards to ship (D9) be more than the number is stock (D7) when the data validation rule disallowed numbers greater than the number in stock?**
Data validation rules are applied only to data that is entered into a cell. Entries that are the result of calculations and goal seeking will not produce a data validation error.

4

- Click OK (Goal Seek Status dialog box) to close the dialog box and display the updated worksheet.

To Circle Invalid Data

The 'Circle Invalid Data' command checks for invalid data entered as the result of a formula or automated tool, such as Goal Seek. In this case, Goal Seek found a solution that satisfied the criteria specified for the goal, but that solution violated the conditions specified for data validation. It is good practice to check your worksheet for invalid data periodically through use of the 'Circle Invalid Data' command. **Why?** The previous set of steps illustrates how the data validation rules apply only to data directly entered into a cell, not to the results of actions such as Goal Seek. The following steps check for and circle any invalid data on the Weekly Shipment Worksheet.

1

- Click the Data Validation arrow (Data tab | Data Tools group) to display the Data Validation menu (Figure 9–36).

Q&A **What are some limitations of using goal seeking?**
Goal seeking allows you to manipulate only one cell in order to reach a goal. In this example, Goal Seek produced a result that is acceptable mathematically, but not logically, as is the case here.

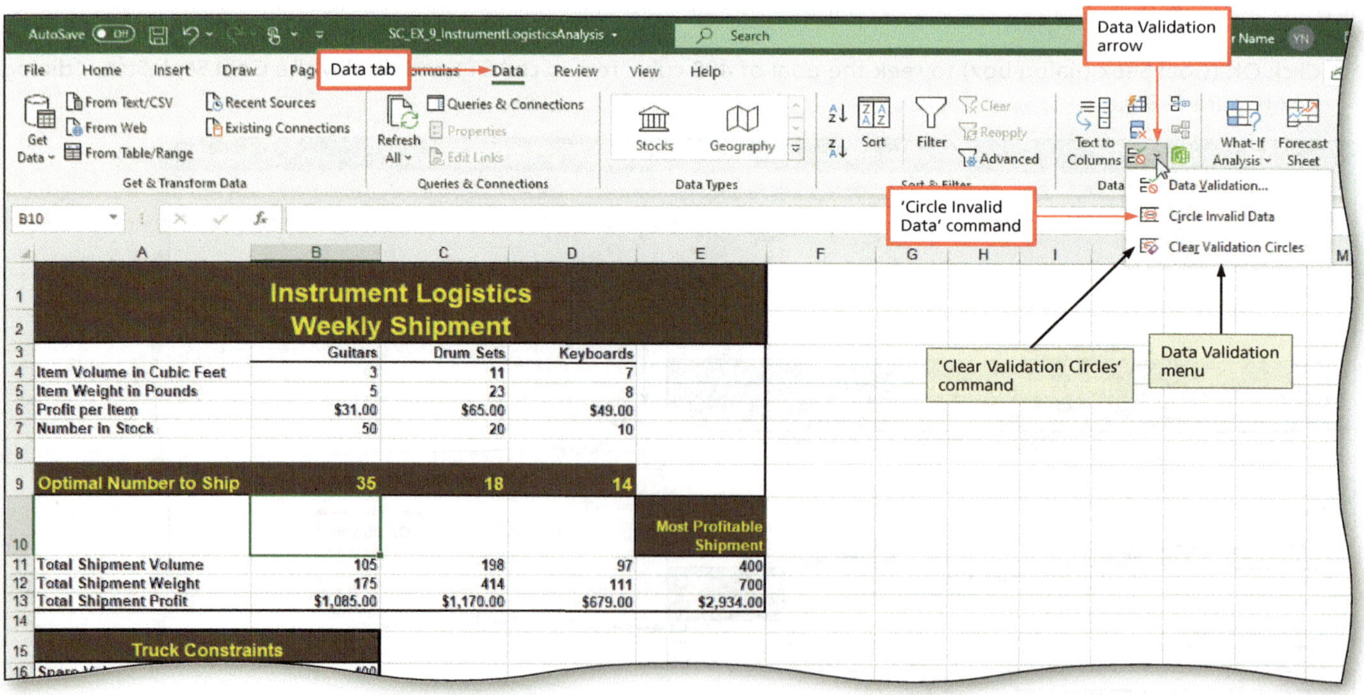

Figure 9–36

2

- Click 'Circle Invalid Data' on the Data Validation menu to place a red validation circle around any invalid data, in this case cell D9 (Figure 9–37).

Q&A **How does Excel determine invalid data?**
Excel only can identify data you have specified in the data validation process earlier in the module. In this case, the optimal number to ship is greater than the quantity in stock.

Now that I have identified invalid data, what do I do with that information?
Once you identify invalid data in a worksheet, you should determine how to correct the data.

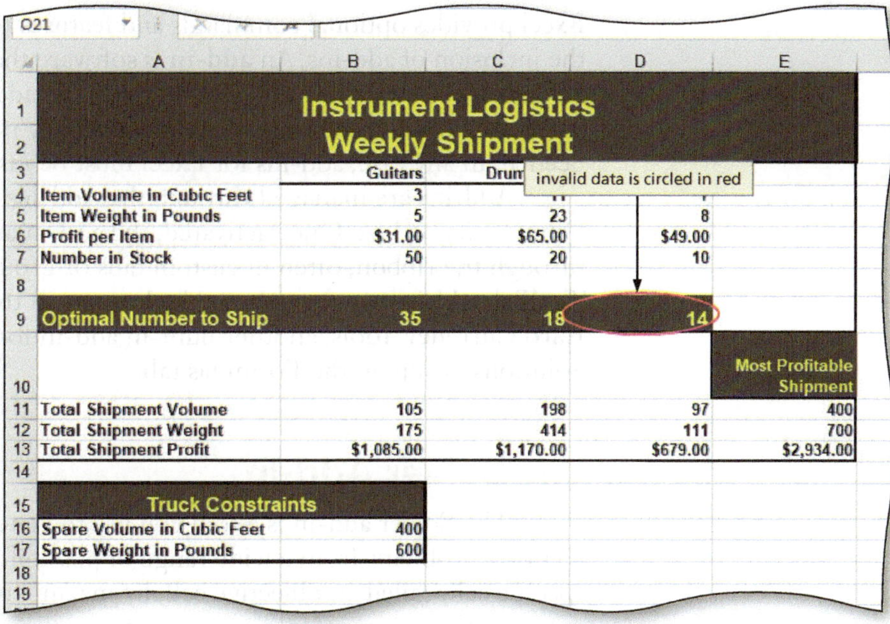

Figure 9–37

To Clear Validation Circles

Why? Once the invalid data has been identified, it is easier to work when the worksheet is clear of extraneous marks. The following step clears the validation circles.

1

- Click the Data Validation arrow (Data tab | Data Tools group) to display the Data Validation menu (shown in Figure 9-36).
- Click 'Clear Validation Circles' on the Data Validation menu to remove the red validation circle (Figure 9–38).

Q&A **Has the scheduling problem been solved?**
No. As noted previously, the number of keyboards is more than the number in stock. Also, the weight is significantly over the truck constraint.

2

- Save the workbook again on the same storage location with the same file name.

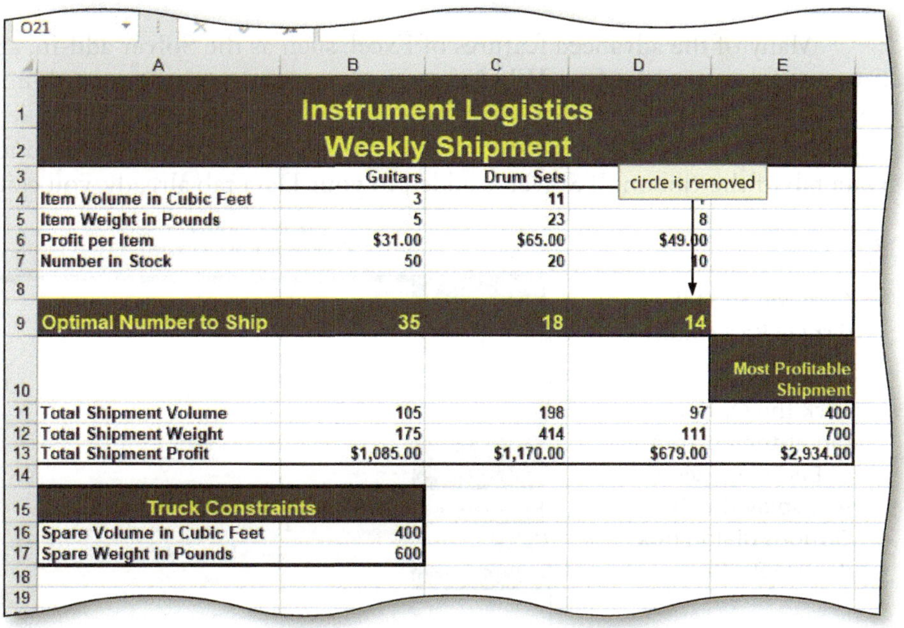

Figure 9–38

Customizing Excel Add-Ins

Excel provides optional commands and features to solve complex problems through the inclusion of add-ins. An **add-in** is software that adds commands and features to Microsoft Office applications. Although some add-ins are built into Excel, including the Solver add-in used in this module, you may need to download and install others as needed. In any case, add-ins for Excel must be installed before they are available for use.

Add-ins are managed through the Add-ins tab accessible through the Excel Options dialog box. Once activated, the add-in and related commands are accessible through the ribbon, often in custom tabs or groups. If installed, the Solver and Analysis ToolPak add-ins are represented by buttons in the Analyze group on the Data tab. Euro Currency Tools, another built-in add-in for Excel, appears as commands in the Solutions group on the Formulas tab.

The Solver Add-In

The Solver add-in is a tool you use to generate the best possible solution for complex problems from a wide range of possibilities. Solver works to optimize a specific cell, called an objective cell, by maximizing, minimizing, or setting it to a specific value. For example, you want to maximize the total profit (cell E13). Because of the number of precedents, it can be difficult to determine which values should change. When you decrease the number of items to ship for one instrument, you have to increase the number assigned to another instrument to ensure that all trucks are full. This change has an impact on costs and resulting profit. Solver considers all of the various constraints when determining the best solution. The countless options make it difficult to identify the best solution to the problem using other methods of what-if analysis such as trial and error or Goal Seek.

To Enable the Solver Add-In

Many of the advanced features of Excel, such as the Solver add-in, are hidden until the user adds the feature to the user interface. **Why?** Excel is a powerful application with many features that the average user does not need to access on a regular basis. These features are hidden to keep the interface from becoming too overwhelming. The following steps will add the Solver add-in to Excel and verify the additional features on the Data tab of the ribbon. If Solver is added to your Data tab already, you can skip these steps.

1

- Click the File tab to display Backstage view.
- Click the Options tab at the bottom of Backstage view to display the Excel Options dialog box (Figure 9–39).

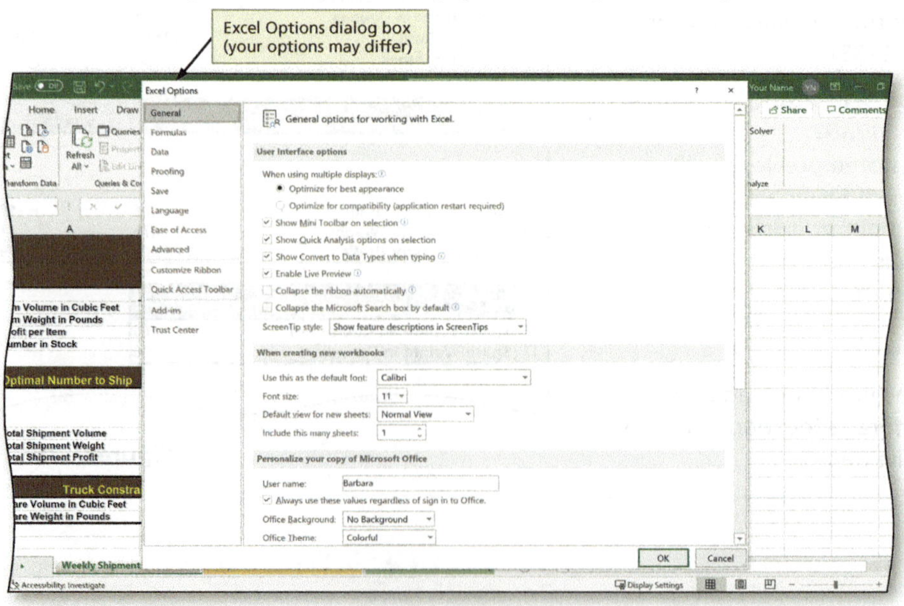

Figure 9–39

2

- Click the Add-ins tab to display the 'View and manage Microsoft Office Add-ins' screen (Figure 9–40).

Q&A **Why is my list of add-ins different?**
Depending on the applications installed and enabled for use in Excel, the list of active, inactive, and available add-ins may be different.

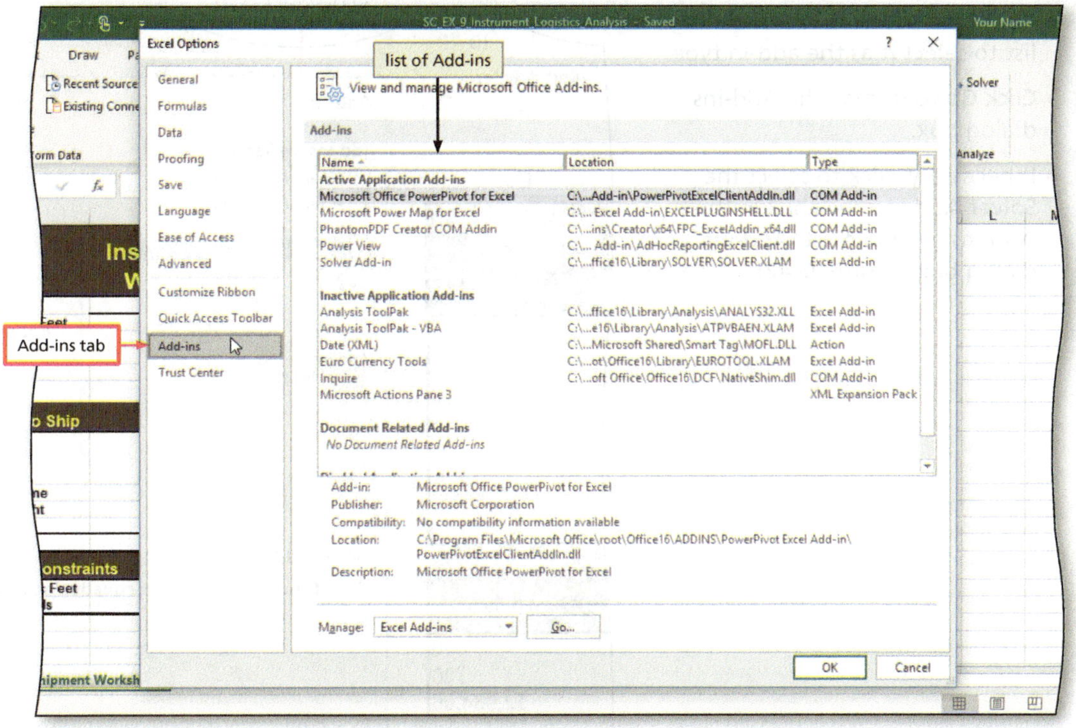

Figure 9–40

3

- Click the Manage button to display the list of add-in types (Figure 9–41).

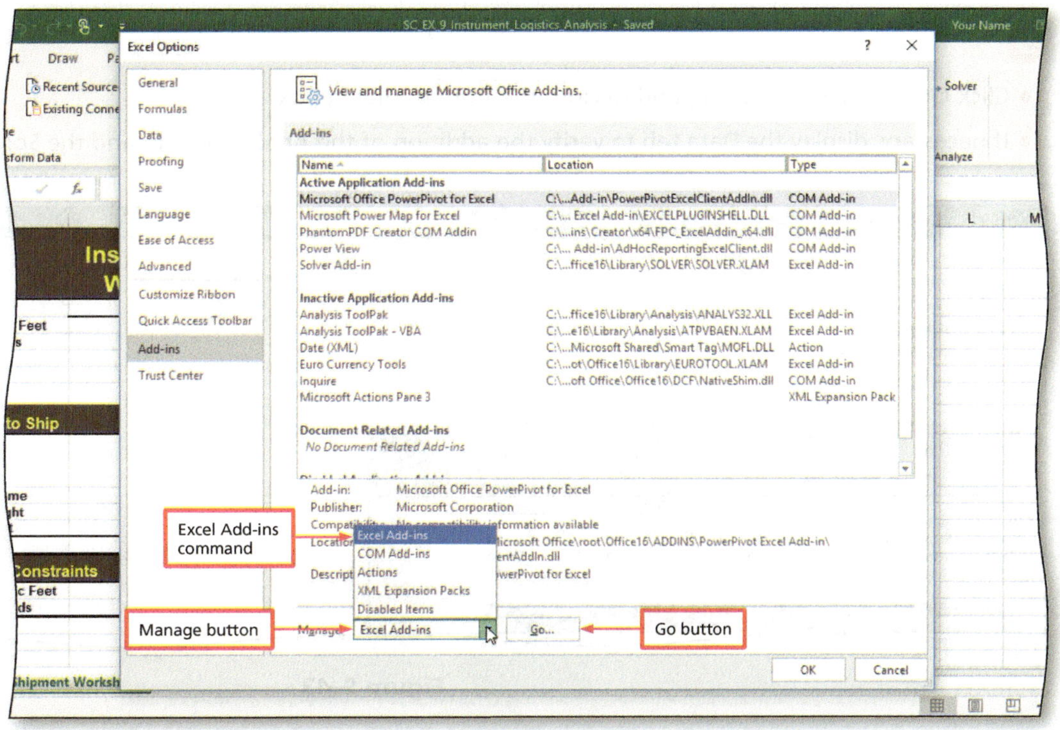

Figure 9–41

4

- Click Excel Add-ins in the Manage list to select it as the add-in type.
- Click Go to display the Add-ins dialog box.
- If necessary, click to select the Solver Add-in check box in the Add-ins available list (Add-ins dialog box) (Figure 9–42).

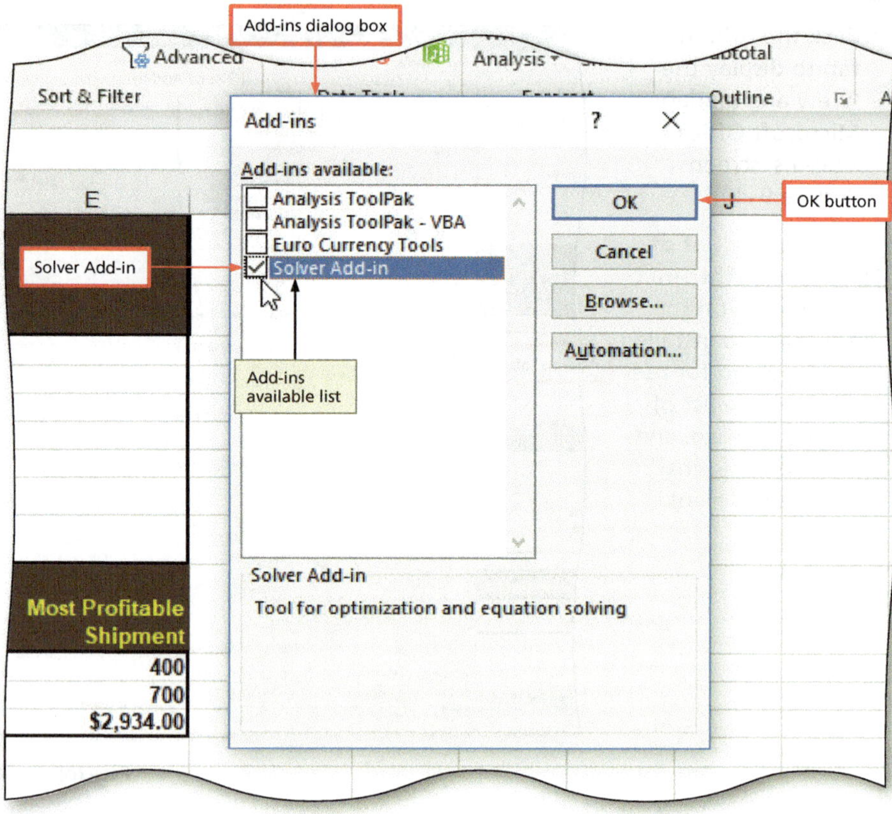

Figure 9–42

5

- Click OK to apply the setting and to close the Add-ins dialog box.
- If necessary, display the Data tab to verify the addition of the Analyze group and the Solver button (Figure 9–43).

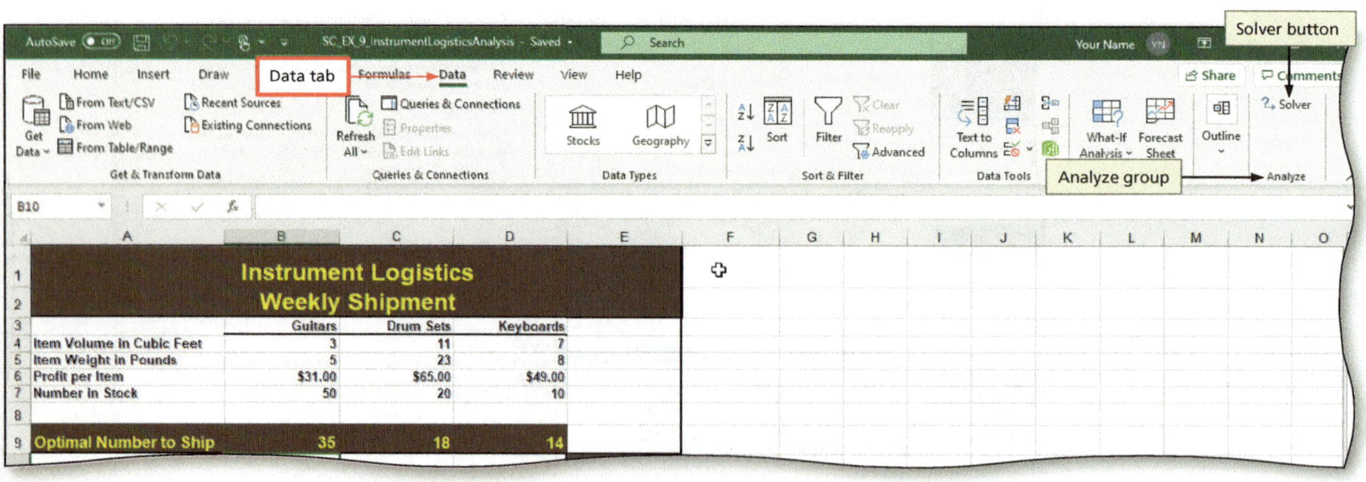

Figure 9–43

Solver Requirements

Regardless of the technique Solver uses to solve a problem, it requires three different types of inputs from the user: the objective, or the result you need for the target cell; variable cells, the values that can change; and constraints, the conditions that the solution has to meet.

The technique Solver uses to solve a problem depends on the model that the user selects as best representing the data. For the current scheduling problem, you will use LP Simplex, a technique in Solver associated with linear programming. **Linear programming** is a complex mathematical process used to solve problems that include multiple variables and the minimizing or maximizing of result values. Solver essentially tries as many possible combinations of solutions as it can. On each attempt to solve the problem, Solver checks to see if it has found a solution. The other two techniques are beyond the scope of this book.

In order for Solver to solve the scheduling problem, Solver must modify data until an optimum value is reached for the selected cell. The cells modified by Solver are called **decision variable cells**, also known as changing cells or adjustable cells. In this case, these are cells in the ranges B9:D9. The cell that Solver is working to optimize, either by finding its maximum or its minimum value, is known as the **objective cell**, or target cell. In this case, Solver is trying to maximize the total profit of the shipment, which makes cell E13 the objective cell. Solver will attempt to maximize the value of cell E13 by varying the values in the decision variable cells within the constraints set by Instrument Logistics.

Recall that constraints have been placed on certain values in the problem and are listed in the requirements document. For example, one constraint in the Weekly Shipment Worksheet is that each truck must contain at least one of each instrument. Other constraints include the truck volume and weight limits as well as the number of instruments in stock. The constraints are summarized in Table 9–2. In the table, the word, int, applies an integer constraint which means Solver must use a positive whole number.

BTW
Using Solver to Solve Complex Problems
Solver allows you to solve complex problems where a number of variables can be changed in a worksheet in order to meet a goal in a particular cell. Unlike Goal Seek, Solver is not restricted to changing one cell at a time and can efficiently evaluate many combinations for a solution.

Table 9–2 Constraints for Solver

Cell or Range or Named Cell	Operator	Constraint
$B$9:$D$9	>=	1
$B$9:$D$9	int	integer
Guitars_to_Ship	<=	Guitars_in_Stock
Drum_Sets_to_Ship	<=	Drum_Sets_in_Stock
Keyboards_to_Ship	<=	Keyboards_in_Stock
$E$11	<=	$B$16
$E$12	<=	$B$17

When Solver reaches a solution to a problem, it generates an Answer Report. An **Answer Report** is a Solver report summarizing the results of a successful solution. It shows the answer for the objective cell, the values used in the changing cells to arrive at that answer, and the constraints that were applied to the calculation. By creating an Answer Report, you satisfy the requirement to document the results of the scheduling calculation.

To Enter Constraints with Solver

To solve the shipping problem for Instrument Logistics, you give Solver the goal of maximizing the total profit of the shipment, shown in cell E13, within the constraints set in the requirements document. To accomplish this goal, Solver can modify the number of instruments of each type (represented by the ranges B9, C9, and D9). **Why use Solver?** Solver allows Excel to evaluate multiple combinations of values and constraints for changing variables to find an optimal solution to a complex problem.

The following steps use Solver to find the optimal solution to the scheduling problem in the Weekly Shipment Worksheet within the given constraints.

1

- Click the Solver button (Data tab | Analyze group) to display the Solver Parameters dialog box. Drag the title bar to move the dialog box so you can see the figures in the worksheet.
- If necessary, click the Set Objective box (Solver Parameters dialog box) and then, in the worksheet, click cell E13 to set the objective cell, in this case the total profit (Figure 9–44).

Q&A **Are there any restrictions on which cell can be the objective?**
The value in the Set Objective box must be a single cell reference or name, and the cell must contain a formula.

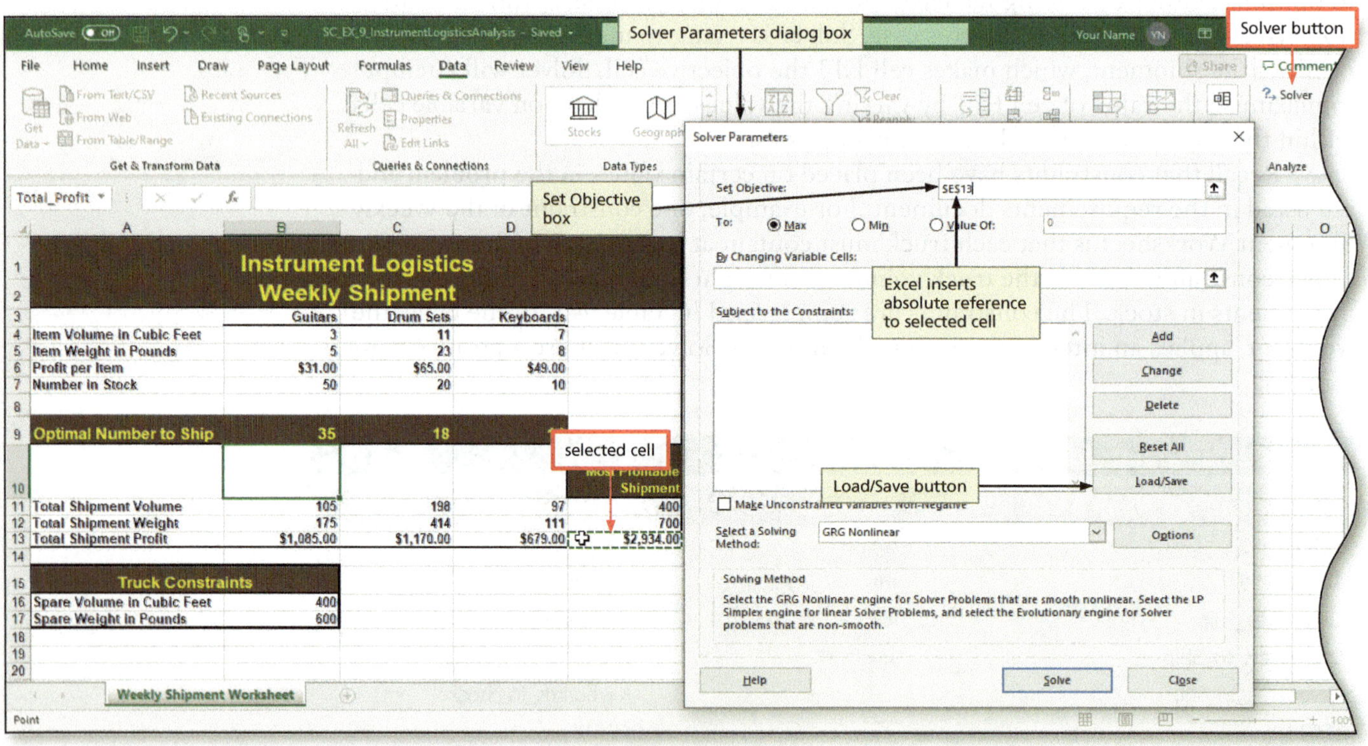

Figure 9–44

2

- Click the Max option button in the To area (Solver Parameters dialog box) if necessary to specify that the value of the target cell should be as large as possible, maximizing the total profit.
- Click the 'By Changing Variable Cells' box and then, in the worksheet, select the range B9:D9 to set the cells that you want Solver to manipulate (Figure 9–45).

Q&A **Can you save the constraints you add to the Solver?**
Yes. You can click the Load/Save button (Solver parameters dialog box) to load constraints you have saved previous or to save a new one, called a Solver model. Models are saved to an empty part of the worksheet, but do not print or display.

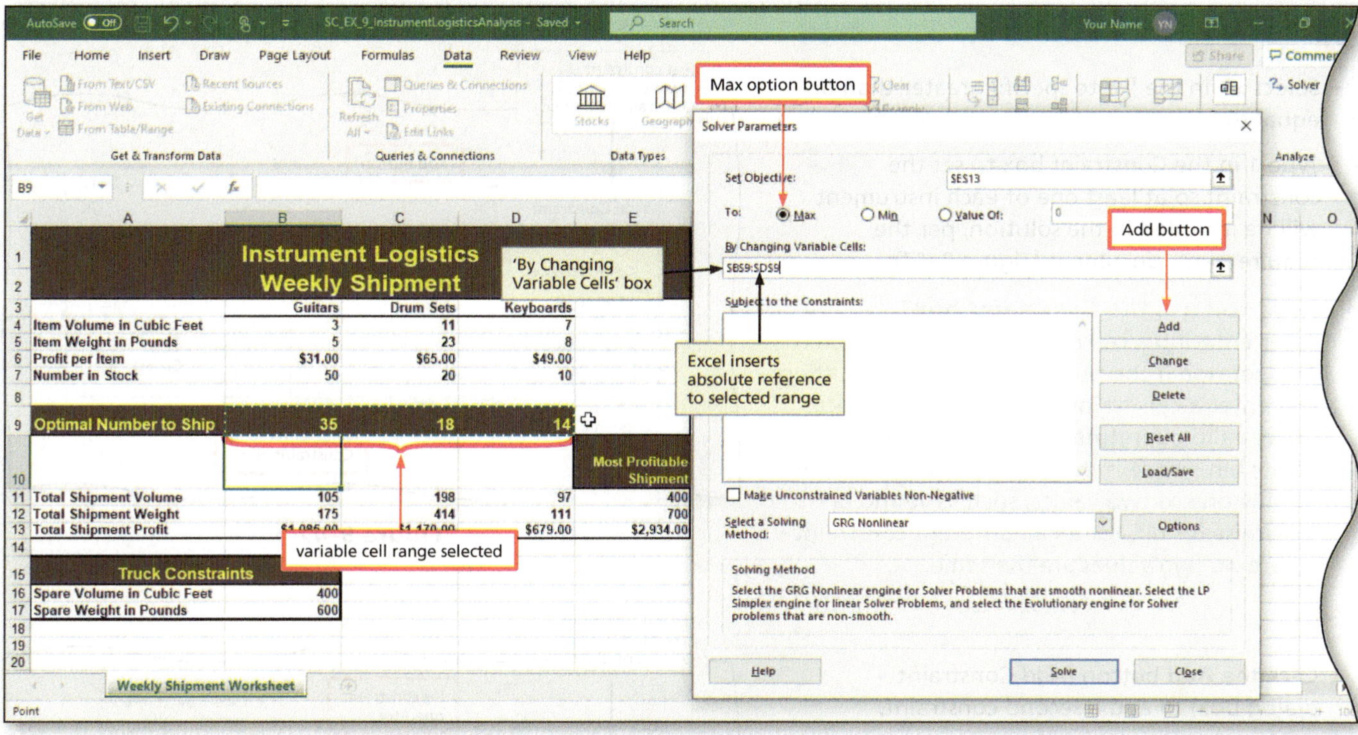

Figure 9–45

3

- Click the Add button (Solver Parameters dialog box) to display the Add Constraint dialog box.
- If necessary, click the 'Cell Reference: Collapse Dialog' button. Select the range B9:D9 to set the value of the Cell Reference box. Click the Expand Dialog button, if necessary.
- Click the middle arrow to display the list of constraint operators (Figure 9–46).

Q&A

What does the Add Constraint dialog box do?
It is a way to set limitations on the possible values that a cell or range can contain.

What happened to the dialog box while I selected the range?
Excel collapsed the dialog box to give you more room to select cells.

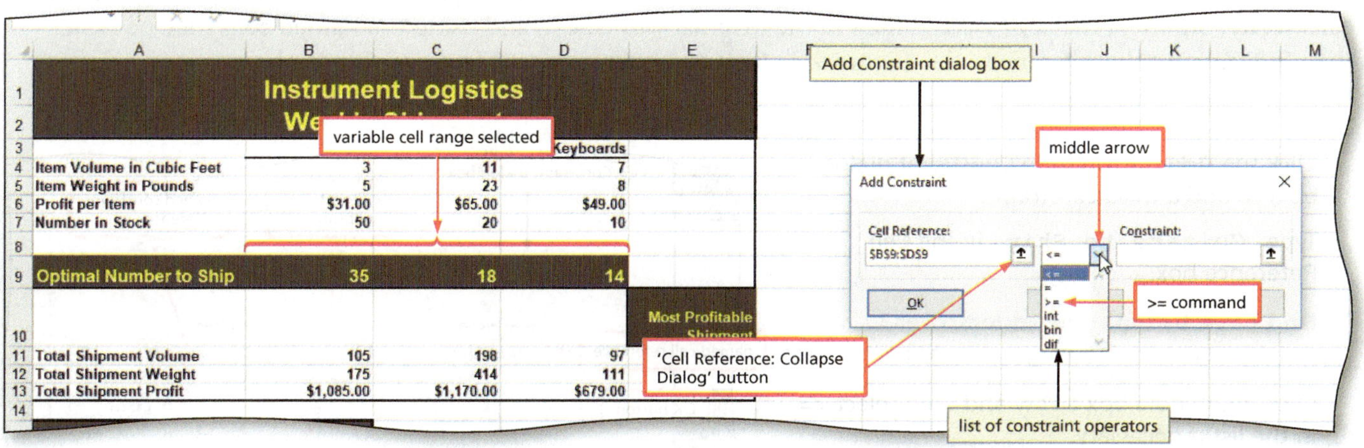

Figure 9–46

4

- Select >= in the list to specify greater than or equal to.
- Type 1 in the Constraint box to set the constraint so at least one of each instrument will be included in the solution, per the requirements document (Figure 9–47).

Q&A **How do I use the Constraint box?**
After entering a cell reference, you must select an operator. If the operator is <=, >=, or =, then you enter a constraint value or cell reference. Other valid operators are int, for an integer value; bin, for cells that contain a binary value of only one of two values, such as yes/no or true/false; or dif, for an all different constraint where no two values are the same.

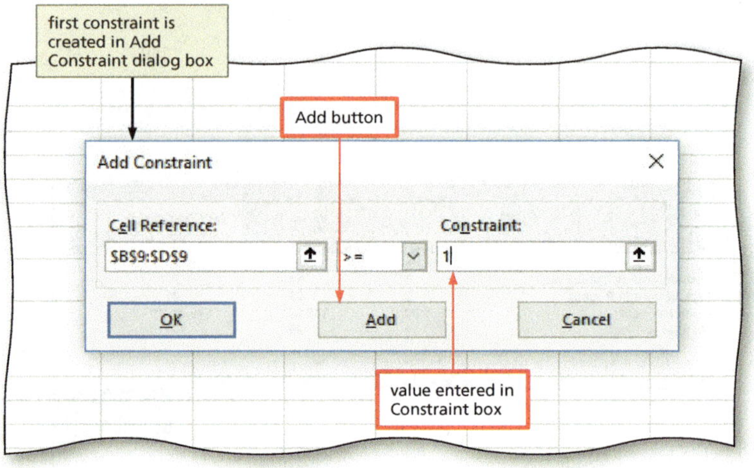

Figure 9–47

5

- Click the Add button (Add Constraint dialog box) to add a second constraint.
- Select the range B9:D9 to set the value of the Cell Reference box.
- Click the middle box arrow and then select int in the list to set a constraint on the cells in the range B9:D9 to be assigned only integer values.
- Do not close the Add Constraint dialog box (Figure 9–48).

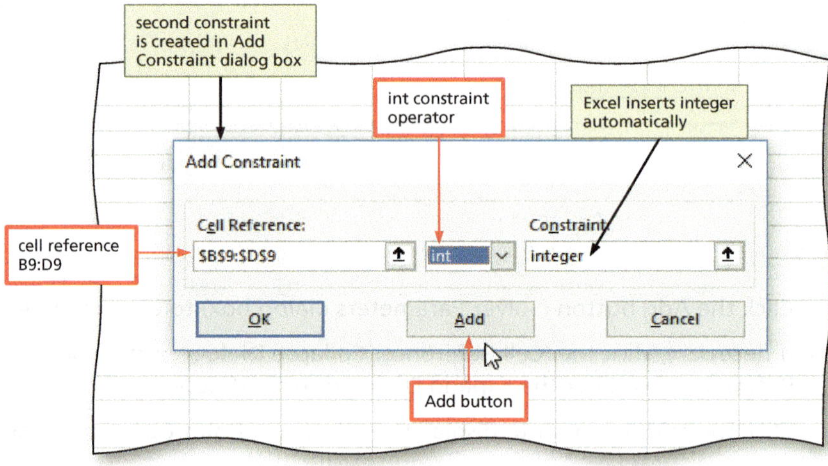

Figure 9–48

To Enter Constraints with Named Cells

You also can use cell and range names with Solver. The following steps create a constraint using named cells. **Why?** Many of the cells were named in the original worksheet, and using the named cells may be easier than figuring out the references. See Figure 9–4. Cell and range names carry over into Solver.

1

- Click the Add button (Add Constraint dialog box) to add a third constraint.
- Type **`Guitars_to_Ship`** in the Cell Reference box.

Q&A **Do I have to type the underscores?**
Yes. Named cells and ranges cannot have spaces.

- Click the middle box arrow and then select <= in the list if necessary.
- Click the Constraint box, and then type **`Guitars_in_Stock`** to specify that the number to ship should be less than or equal to the number in stock (Figure 9–49).

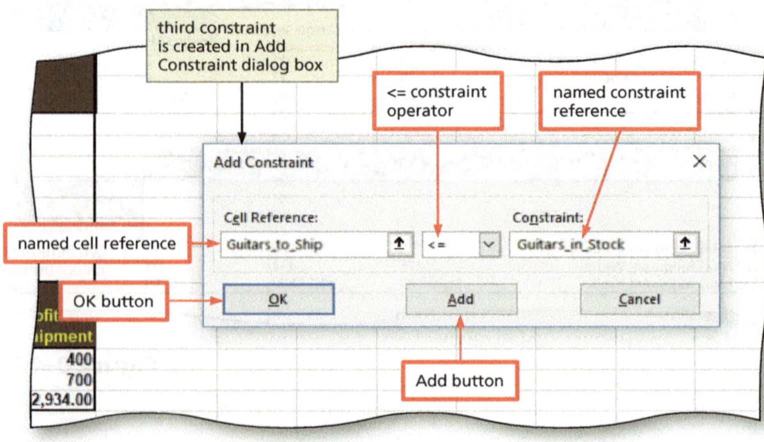

Figure 9–49

2

- Click the Add button (Add Constraint dialog box) to add the next constraint.

Q&A **Nothing happened when I clicked the Add button. Did I do something wrong?**
No. The constraint is added behind the scenes and will display in the Solve Parameters dialog box after you add the last constraint.

- Enter the remaining constraints as shown in Table 9–2, beginning with the constraint for Drum_Sets_to_Ship.
- After entering the last constraint, click OK (Add Constraint dialog box) to close the dialog box and display the Solver Parameters dialog box.
- Do not close the Solver Parameters dialog box. (Figure 9–50).

Q&A **What should I do if a constraint does not match the ones shown in Figure 9–49?**
Your order may differ, but the constraints should be the same. If they are not, select the constraint in error, click the Change button (Solver Parameters dialog box), and then enter the constraint as shown in Table 9–2. To delete a constraint, select the constraint you want to delete, and then click the Delete button.

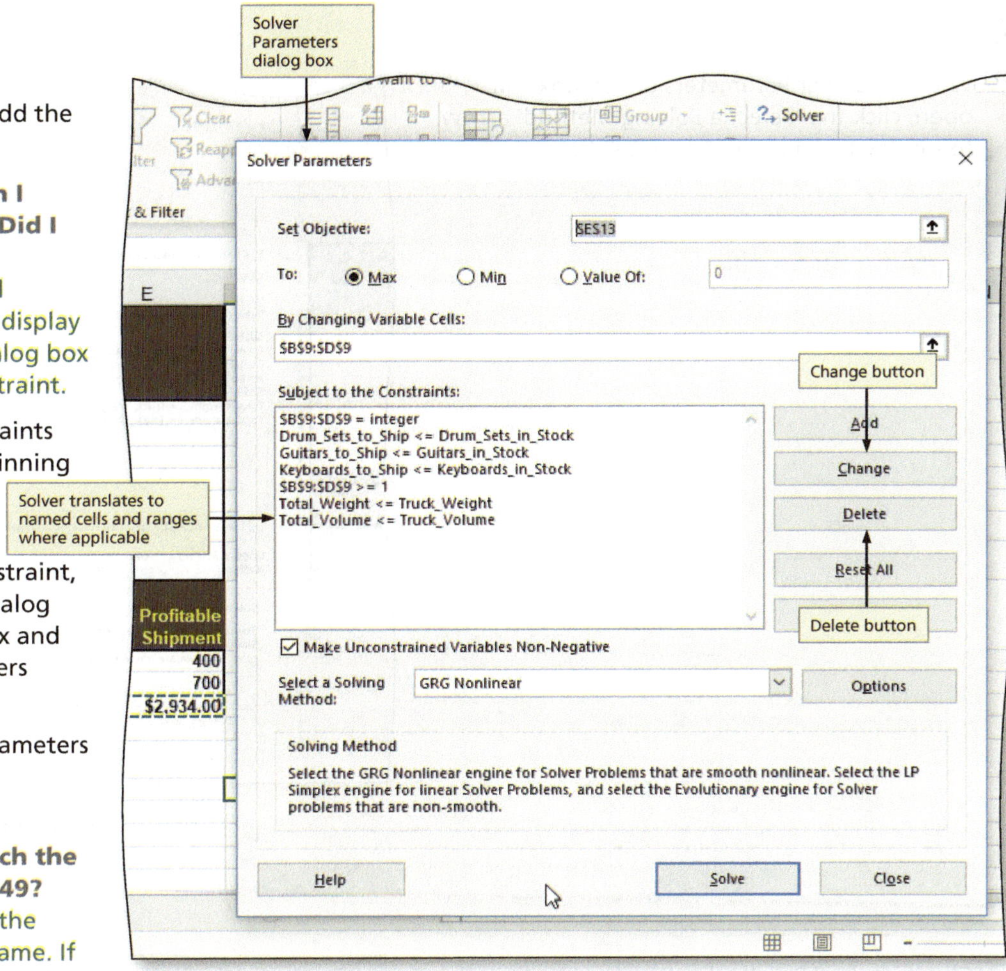

Figure 9–50

To Set Solver Options

Now that you have entered all of the constraints for the problem, the following steps set options in order to obtain the optimal solution. You will choose the Simplex LP solving method. LP stands for linear progression, and Simplex refers to the basic problem-solving method used to solve linear problems. Linear problems are ones in which a "straight-line" approach of cause and effect can seek to determine a goal value by modifying values that impact the goal. For example, a decrease in costs results in an increase in profits.

To ensure that Solver finds the true optimal solution—possibly at the expense of more solution time—you will set the Integer Optimality % tolerance to zero. **Why?** Setting the value to zero will help Solver to find an optimal solution when one of the constraints says that a value must be an integer.

1

- With the Solver Parameters dialog box still open, click the 'Select a Solving Method' arrow to display the choices (Figure 9–51).

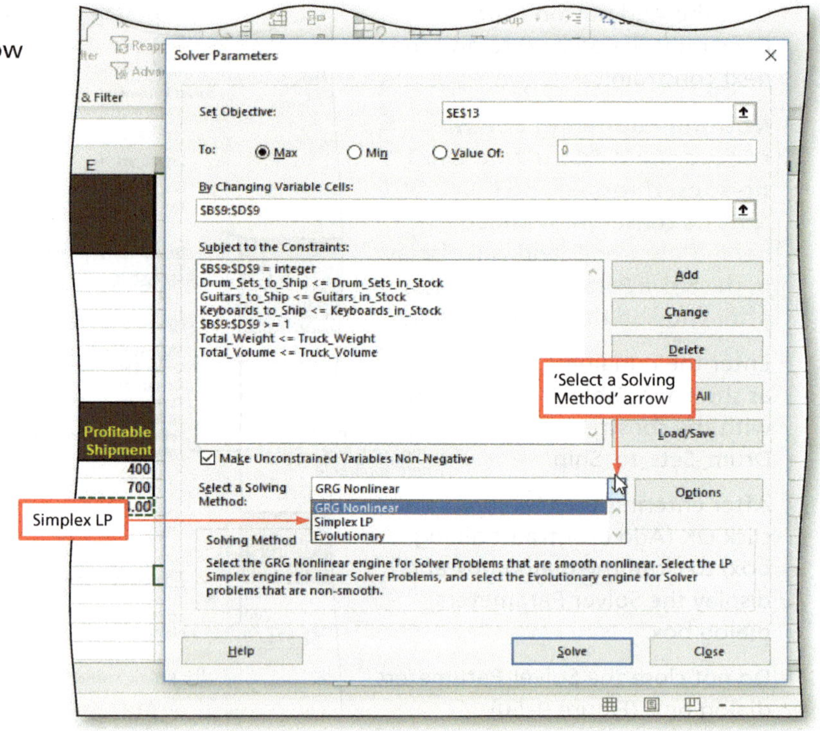

Figure 9–51

- Click Simplex LP in the list to select the linear progression method (Figure 9–52).

Q&A **What are the other choices?**
GRG Nonlinear is the Generalized Reduced Gradient optimizing algorithm in which the change of the objective cell is not proportional to the change of the dependent cells. The Evolutionary method finds a better solution, but because it does not rely on derivative or gradient information, it usually requires running Solver several times as you search for the best one.

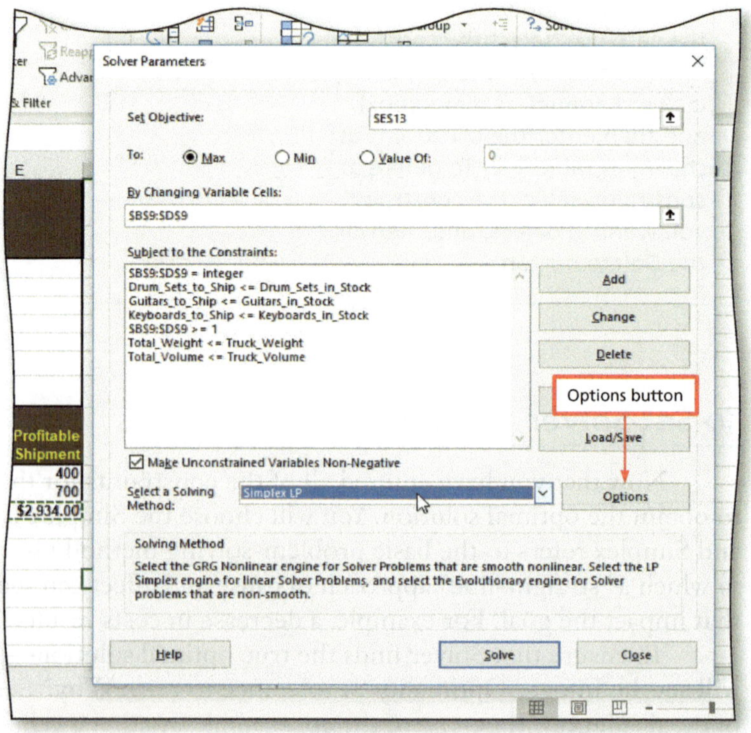

Figure 9–52

2

- Click the Options button (Solver parameters dialog box) to display the Options dialog box.
- If necessary, click the 'Use Automatic Scaling' check box to select it.
- Set the 'Integer Optimality (%)' to 0 to extend the amount of time that Solver takes to find an optimal solution.
- Verify that all other dialog box settings match those in Figure 9–53.
- In particular, ensure that only the Use Automatic Scaling option is selected.

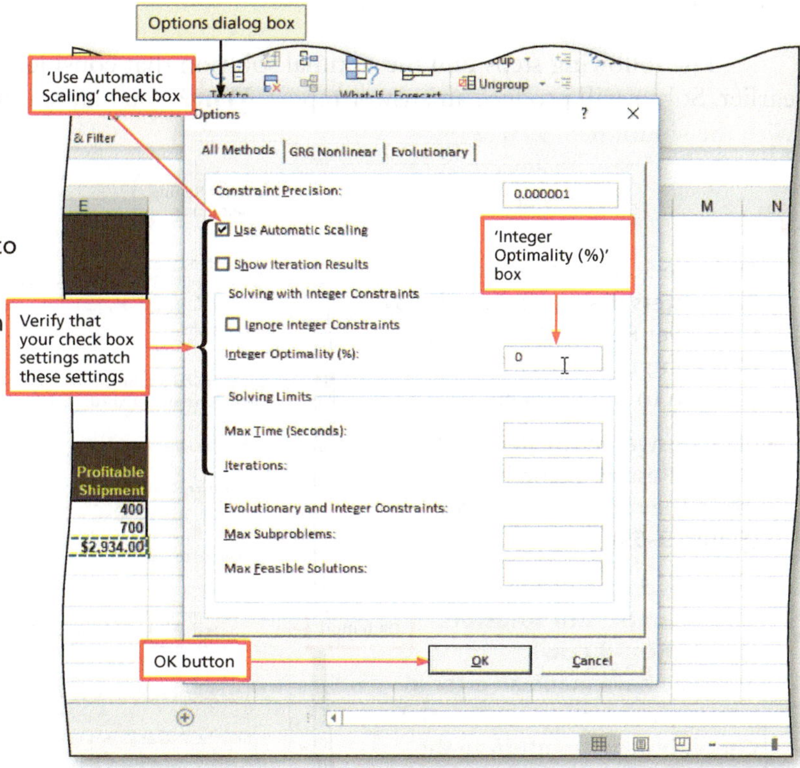

Figure 9–53

3

- Click OK (Options dialog box) to return to the Solver Parameters dialog box (Figure 9–54).

Experiment

- Click the Help button (Solver Parameters dialog box) to open Help related to Solver in a browser window. Read the general explanation and click on various links to read specific instruction. When you are finished, close the browser window and return to Excel.

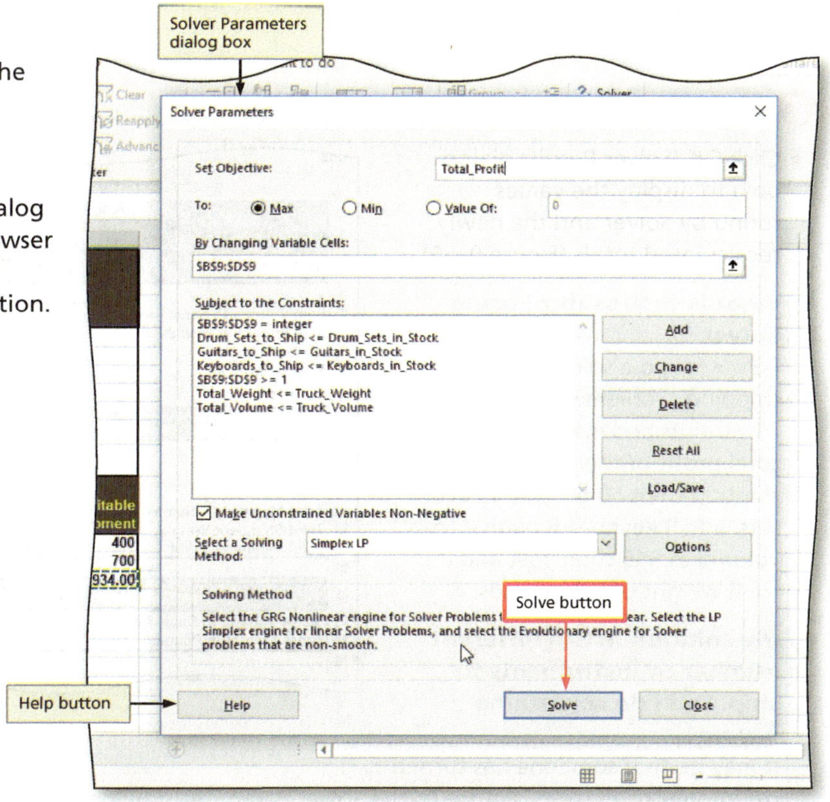

Figure 9–54

To Find the Optimal Solution

The following steps find the optimal solution that considers the constraints and options that you entered earlier. Solver will produce an answer report. **Why?** You may want to view a summary of how Solver came up with the solution.

1

- Click the Solve button (Solver Parameters dialog box) to display the Solver Results dialog box, indicating that Solver found a solution to the problem.
- Click Answer in the Reports list (Solver Results dialog box) to select the report to generate (Figure 9–55).

Q&A **I received an error message or a nonoptimal solution. What should I do?**
You may have made an error in one of the constraints. Click the Cancel button to return to the worksheet. Click the Solver button (Data tab | Analyze group) and look closely at the constraints. They should match Figure 9–51. Edit them as necessary.

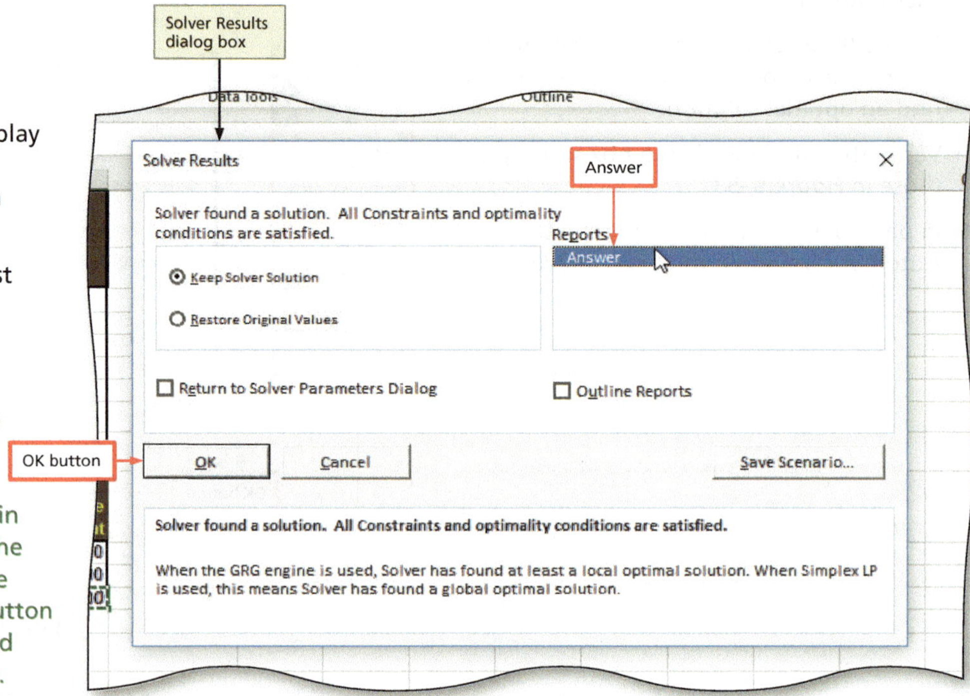

Figure 9–55

2

- Click OK (Solver Results dialog box) to display the values found by Solver and the newly recalculated totals (Figure 9–56).

Q&A **What is the result of using Solver?**
Solver found a solution to the shipping problem that meets the constraints and maximizes the total profit of the shipment. The solution ships 50 guitars, 12 drum sets, and 9 keyboards, with a total volume of 345 cubic feet and a total weight of 598 pounds.

My solution lists a different number of instruments to ship. Did I do something wrong?
It may be that someone has turned off integer constraints. Return to the Solver Parameters dialog box, click the Options button, and then click the All Methods tab. Remove the checkmark for 'Ignore Integer Constraints'. The 'Use Automatic Scaling' check box should be checked. Click OK and then solve again.

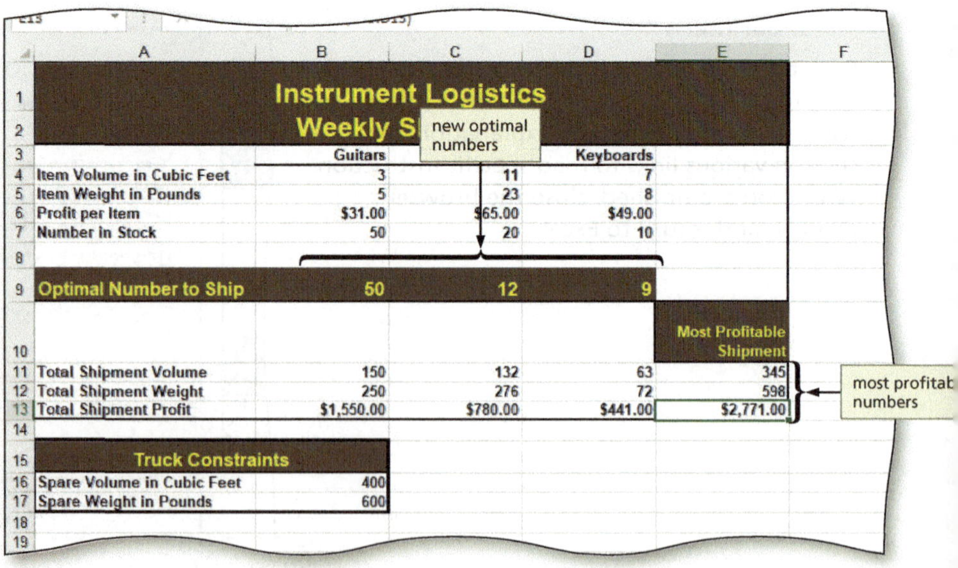

Figure 9–56

To View the Solver Answer Report

Solver generates the requested Answer Report on a separate worksheet after it finds a solution. The Answer Report summarizes the problem that you have presented to Solver. It shows the original and final values of the objective cell along with the original and final values of the changing cells that Solver modified to find the answer. Additionally, it lists all of the constraints that you entered.

Why? The Answer Report documents that a particular problem has been solved correctly. Because it lists all of the relevant information in a concise format, you can use the Answer Report to make certain that you have entered all of the constraints and allowed Solver to modify all the necessary values to solve the problem. You also can use the report to reconstruct the Solver model in the future.

The following steps view the Solver Answer Report.

1

- Click the Answer Report 1 sheet tab to display the Solver Answer Report (Figure 9–57).

Q&A **What is shown in the Answer Report?**
The Answer Report shows additional information about the constraints and how they were used to solve the problem. The Status column, beginning in cell F28, indicates whether a constraint was binding. A constraint that is **binding** is one that limits the final solution in some way and must be included in the Solver model. A constraint that is not binding is one that is not a limiting factor in the solution that Solver provides.

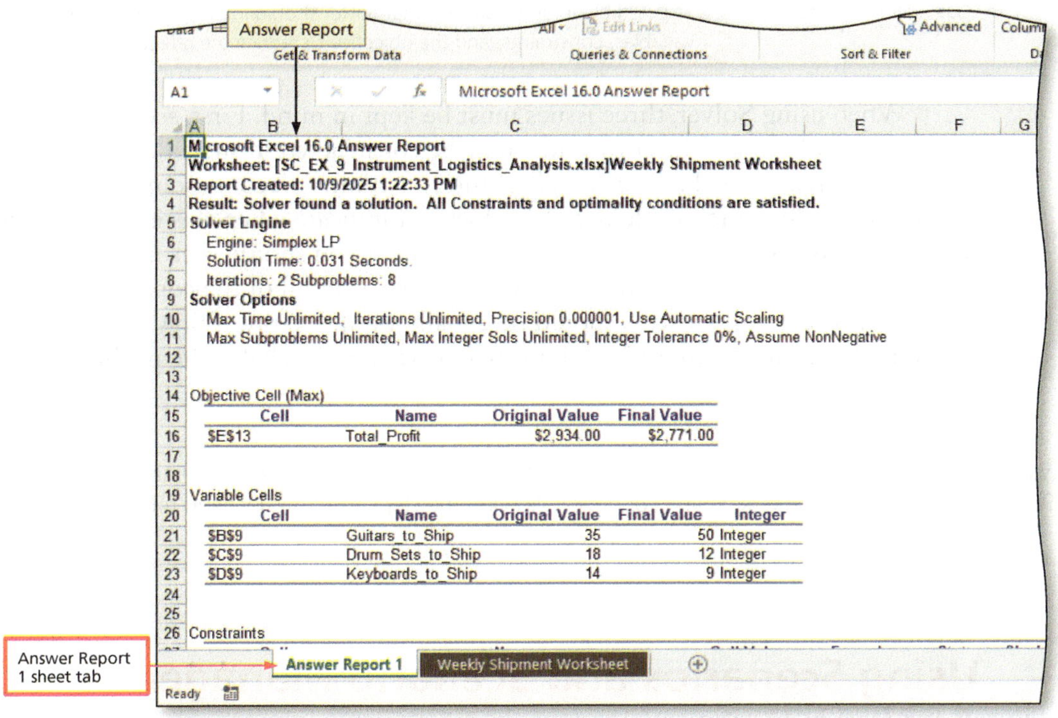

Figure 9–57

2

- Drag the Answer Report 1 sheet tab to the right of the Weekly Shipment Worksheet tab to move the worksheet in the workbook.
- Double-click the Answer Report 1 sheet tab to select the name.
- Type `Shipment Plan Answer Report 1` and then press ENTER to rename the worksheet.
- Change the color of the sheet tab to 'Gold, Accent 2'.

3

- Save the workbook again on the same storage location with the same file name.

More about Solver Options

BTW
Viewing Other Solutions
If you want to view solutions other than the one Solver identifies as optimal, select the Show Iteration Results check box in the Options dialog box. After each iteration, the Show Trial Solution dialog box will be displayed, and you will have the option of saving that scenario and then stopping Solver or continuing on to the next solution.

When you selected the Simplex LP method of solving the production problem in the Solver Parameters dialog box, you selected a linear programming method that assumes the problem follows a cause and effect relationship. Changes to one value have a direct impact on another value. After choosing the Solver method, you can select various options to further configure the inner workings of Solver. Note that Excel saves the most recently used Solver parameters and options. Table 9–3 presents some of the more commonly used Solver options.

Table 9–3 Commonly Used Solver Parameters

Parameter	Meaning
Max Time	The total time that Solver should spend trying different solutions, expressed in seconds
Iterations	The number of possible answer combinations that Solver should try
Constraint Precision	Instructs Solver in how close it must come to the target value in order to consider the problem to be solved. For example, if the target value is 100 and you set tolerance to 5%, then generating a solution with a target value of 95 is acceptable.
Use Automatic Scaling	Selected by default, specifies that Solver should internally rescale values of variables, constraints, and the objective to reduce the effect of outlying values

When using Solver, three issues must be kept in mind. First, some problems do not have solutions. The constraints may be constructed in such a way that Solver cannot find an answer that satisfies all of the constraints. Second, sometimes multiple answers solve the same problem. Solver does not indicate when this is the case, and you will have to use your own judgment to determine if you should seek another solution. As long as you are confident that you have given Solver all of the constraints for a problem, however, all answers should be equally valid. Finally, if Solver fails to find a solution, more time or more iterations may be required to solve the problem.

Break Point: If you want to take a break, this is a good place to do so. You can exit Excel now. To resume later, start Excel, open the file called SC_EX_9_InstrumentLogisticsAnalysis.xlsx, and continue following the steps from this location forward.

Using Scenarios and Scenario Manager to Analyze Data

BTW
Baseline Scenarios
For each model, it is helpful to define a baseline scenario that represents the starting assumptions. Even if the results of the baseline scenario do not figure prominently in the final analysis, they represent the starting point and should be saved.

A **scenario** is a named set of values you use in a what-if analysis; the Excel Scenario Manager lets you store and manage different scenarios. In this project, you will create different shipping plans—scenarios—based on different assumptions. For example, you have created a shipping plan that required finding the optimal number of instruments to ship based on several constraints, one of which was the free space on the truck. Changing the truck volume or weight would create a new scenario. Each set of values in these examples represents a what-if assumption. You use the Scenario Manager to keep track of various scenarios and produce a report detailing the what-if assumptions and results for each scenario.

The primary uses of the Scenario Manager are to:

1. Create different scenarios with multiple sets of changing cells.
2. Build summary worksheets that contain the different scenarios.
3. View the results of each scenario on your worksheet.

You will use the Scenario Manager for each of these three applications. After you create the scenarios, you will instruct Excel to build the summary worksheets, including a Scenario Summary worksheet and a Scenario PivotTable worksheet.

To Save the Current Data as a Scenario

Why? The current data on the Weekly Shipment Worksheet consists of constraints and values that correctly solve the shipping problem. These values can be saved as a scenario that can be accessed later or compared with other scenarios. The following steps save the current data using the Scenario Manager dialog box.

1

- Make the Weekly Shipment Worksheet the active sheet.
- Click the 'What-If Analysis' button (Data tab | Forecast group) to display the What-If Analysis menu (Figure 9–58).

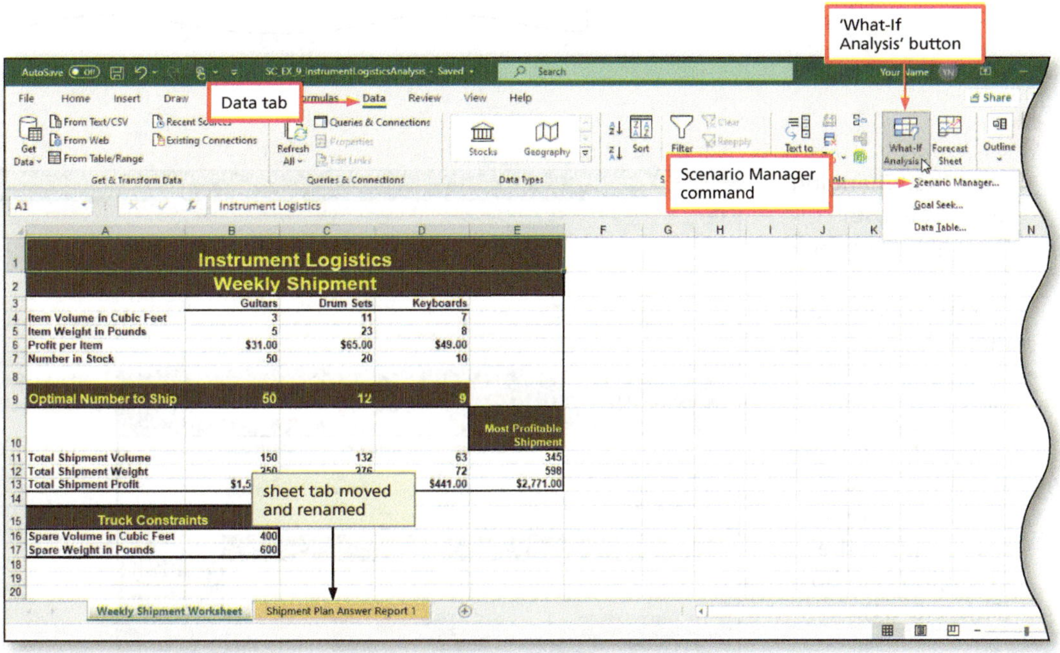

Figure 9–58

2

- Click Scenario Manager on the What-If Analysis menu to display the Scenario Manager dialog box, which indicates that no scenarios are defined (Figure 9–59).

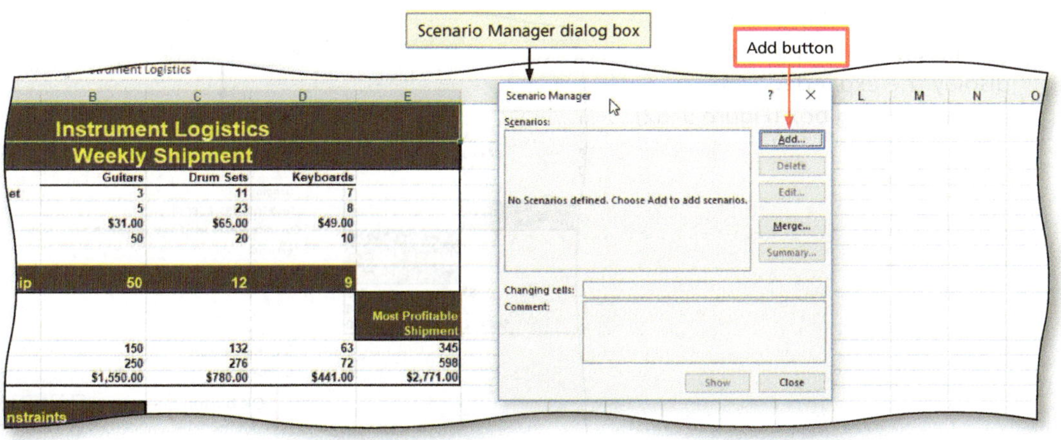

Figure 9–59

3

- Click the Add button (Scenario Manager dialog box) to open the Add Scenario dialog box.
- Type `Shipment 1` in the Scenario name box (Add Scenario dialog box) to provide a name for the scenario (Figure 9–60).

Q&A **I have information in the Comment box. Is that OK?**
Yes. Excel may add information about your user name and the date in the Comment box.

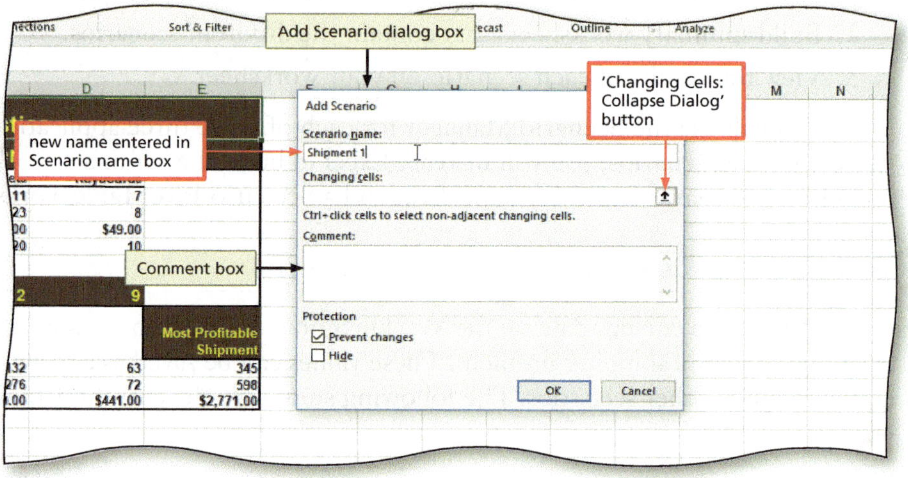

Figure 9–60

4

- Click the 'Changing Cells: Collapse Dialog' button (Add Scenario dialog box) to collapse the dialog box.
- Select the range B9:D9, type , (comma), and then select the range B16:B17 to enter the ranges in the Changing cells box (Figure 9–61).

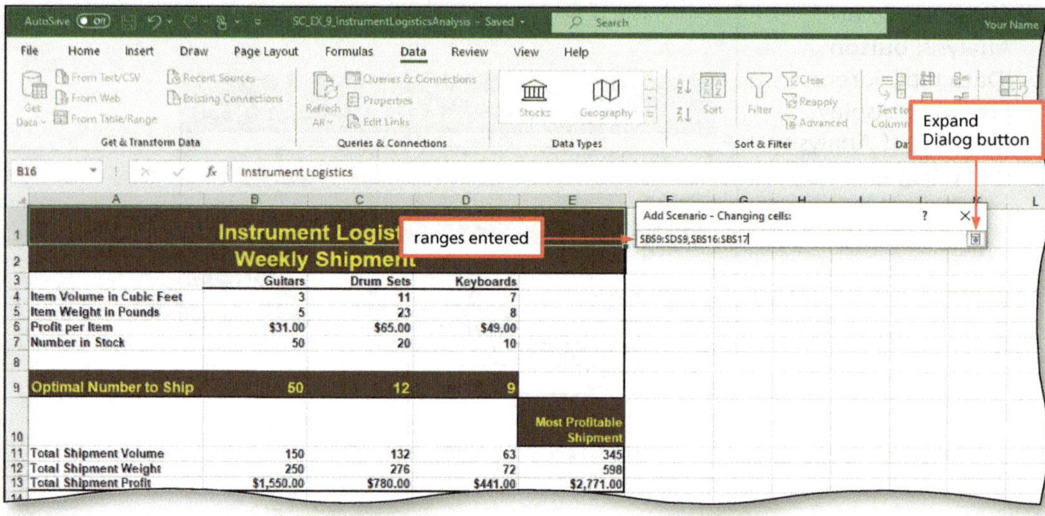

Figure 9–61

5

- Click the Expand Dialog button (Add Scenario dialog box) to display the expanded Edit Scenario dialog box (Figure 9–62).

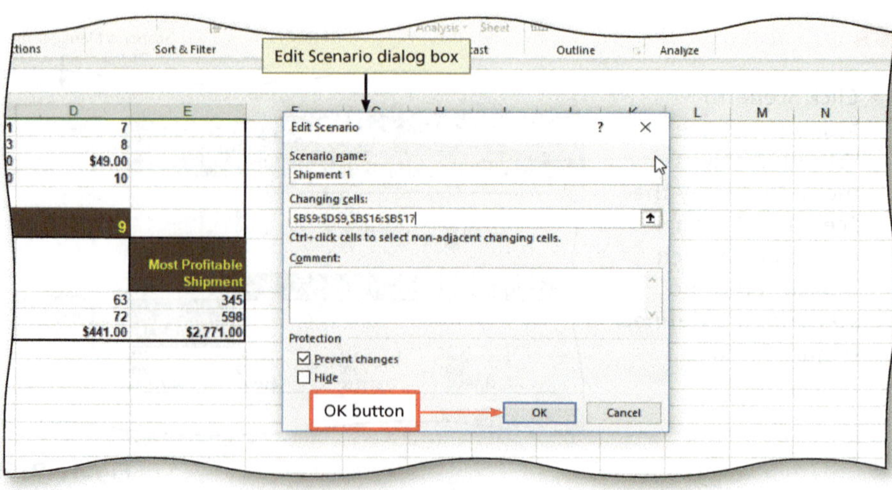

Figure 9–62

6

- Click OK (Edit Scenario dialog box) to accept the settings and display the Scenario Values dialog box.
- Click OK (Scenario Values dialog box) to display the Scenario Manager dialog box with the Shipment 1 scenario selected in the Scenarios list (Figure 9–63).

Q&A **What can I do with the scenario?**
After the scenario has been saved, you can recall it at any time using the Scenario Manager or create a Scenario Summary, as you will do later in this module.

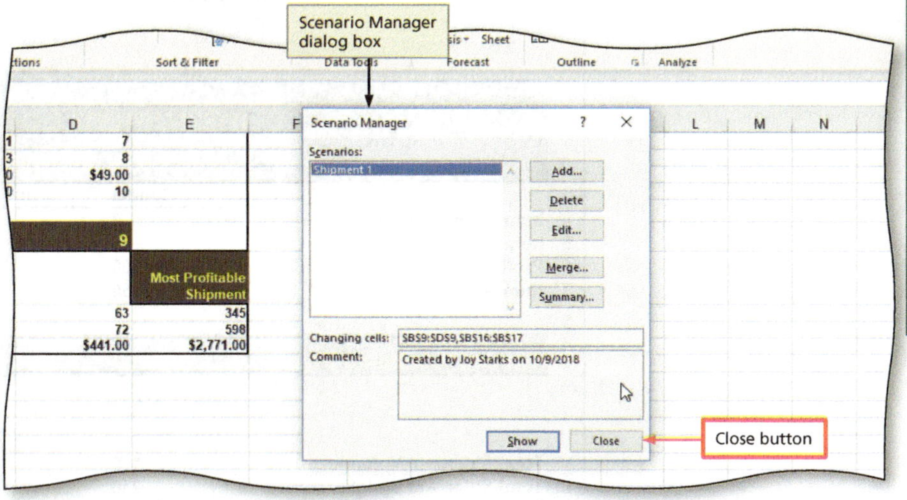

Figure 9–63

7

- Click Close (Scenario Manager dialog box) to save the Shipment 1 scenario in the workbook.

Other Ways

1. When running Solver, click Save Scenario (Solver Results dialog box), enter scenario name, click OK (Save Scenario dialog box), click OK (Solver Results dialog box)

Creating a New Scenario

After saving the Shipment 1 scenario, you will enter new data for the Shipment 2 scenario directly in the worksheet and then use Solver to solve the problem in the same way that you solved the Shipment scenario. Because both scenarios are based on the same model, you do not need to reenter the constraints into the Scenario Manager. A second Answer Report will solve the needs of the requirements document.

To Add the Data for a New Scenario

A truck with less room has become available. The shipping manager would like to see the difference in profit should the company fill this smaller load. The constraints for the Shipment 2 scenario therefore require a change in available truck volume and weight. These values must be entered into the appropriate cells before you can use Solver. The following steps add the data for a new scenario.

1. Click cell B16 and then type `300` as the truck volume.
2. Click cell B17 and then type `450` as the truck weight.
3. Click cell C17 to deselect cell B17 (Figure 9–64).

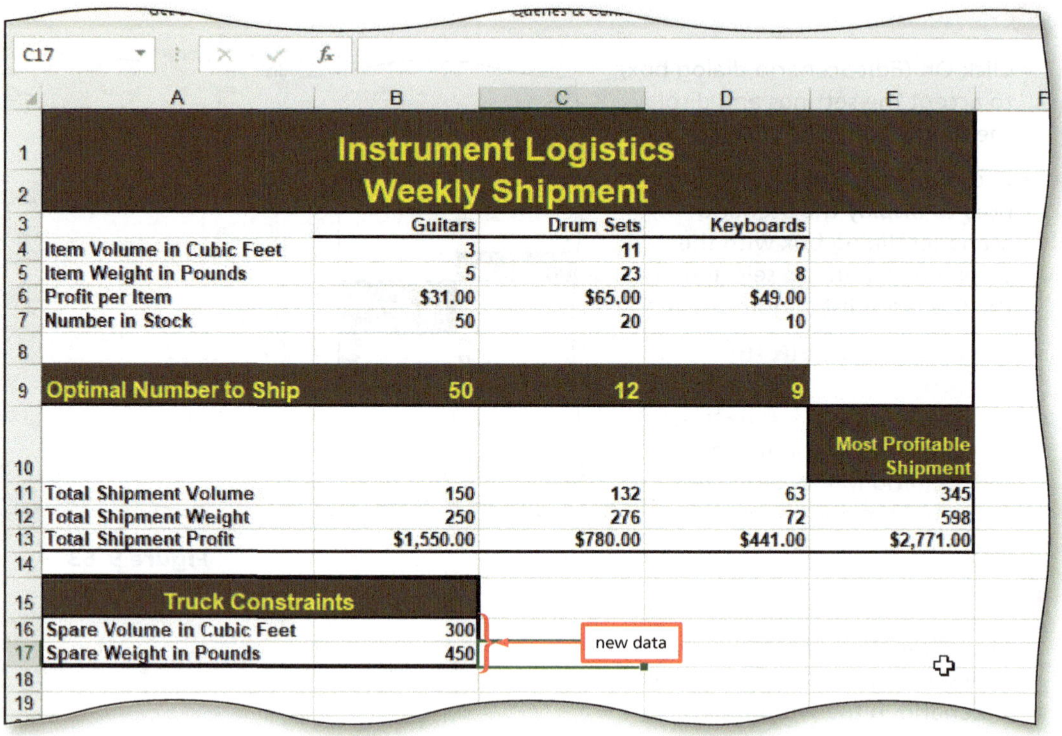

Figure 9–64

To Use Solver to Find a New Solution

Why? After entering the new values, the total volume and weight shown in the range B16:B17 no longer satisfy the shipping constraints for the new scenario. You now must use Solver again to determine if a solution exists for the constraints of Shipment 2. The following steps use Solver to seek a solution.

1

- Click the Solver button (Data tab | Analyze group) to display the Solver Parameters dialog box with the objective cell, changing cells, and constraints used with the previous scenario (Figure 9–65).

Q&A

Why am I not updating the constraints?

When you set up the constraints in Solver for Shipment 1, you used cell references and named cells rather than actual values for the number of each type of instrument. Entering the new values in cells B16:B17 automatically updated the constraints.

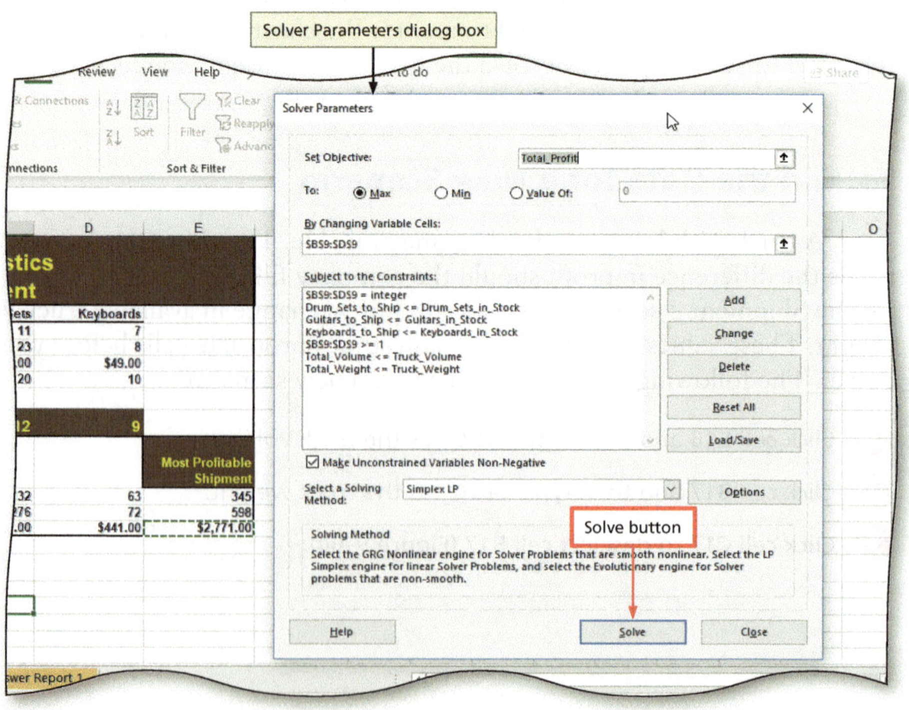

Figure 9–65

2

- Click the Solve button (Solver Parameters dialog box) to solve the problem and display the Solver Results dialog box.
- Click Answer in the Reports list to select a report type (Figure 9–66).

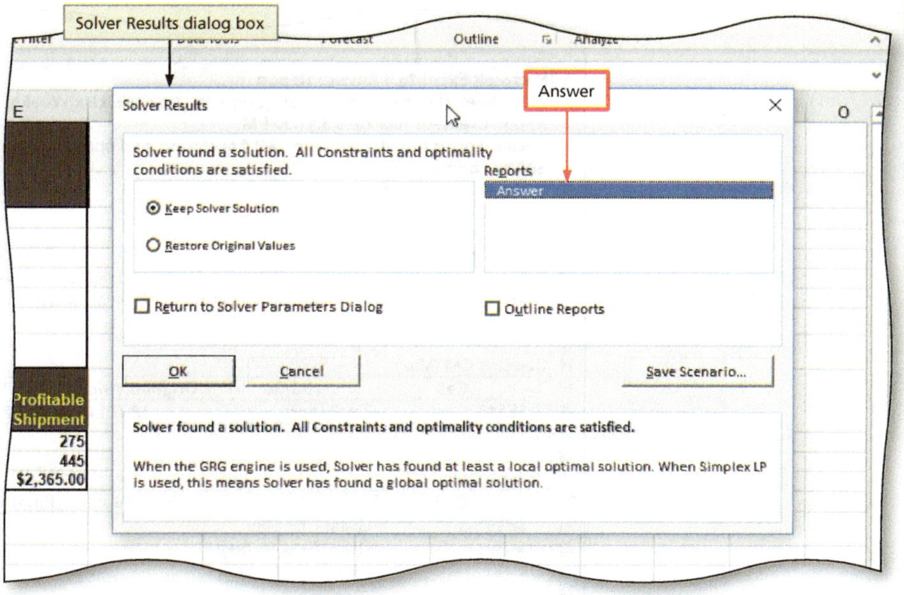

Figure 9–66

3

- Click OK (Solver Results dialog box) to display the solution found by Solver (Figure 9–67).

Q&A **What did Solver accomplish?**
Solver found a solution that satisfies all of the constraints and maximizes the total profit. In this new scenario, total profit will be $2,365.00.

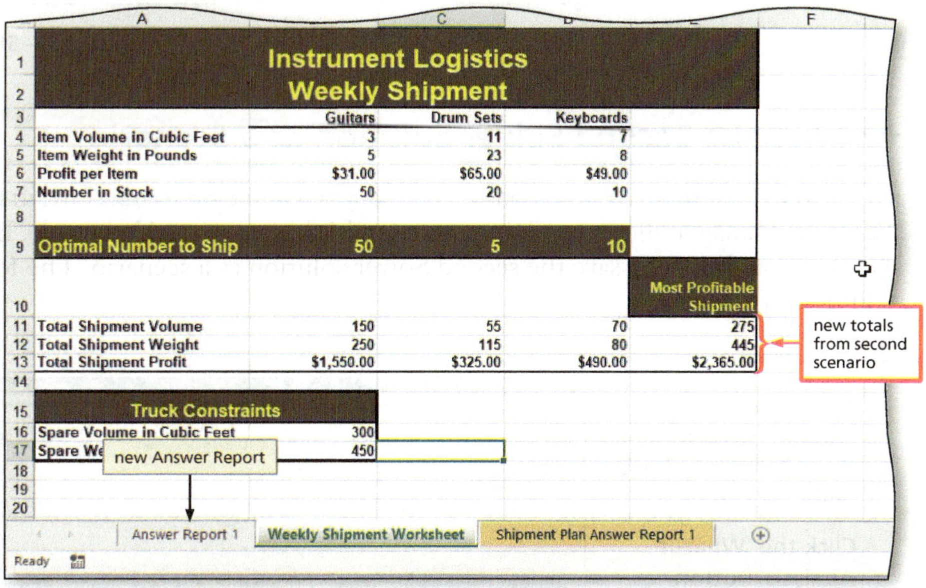

Figure 9–67

To View the Solver Answer Report for the Shipment 2 Solution

The next step views the Answer Report for the Shipment 2 solution.

1. Drag the new Answer Report 1 sheet tab to the right of the Shipment Plan Answer Report 1 sheet tab to move the worksheet.
2. Rename the Answer Report 1 worksheet as `Shipment Plan Answer Report 2`.
3. Change the sheet tab color to 'Green, Accent 4' (Figure 9–68).

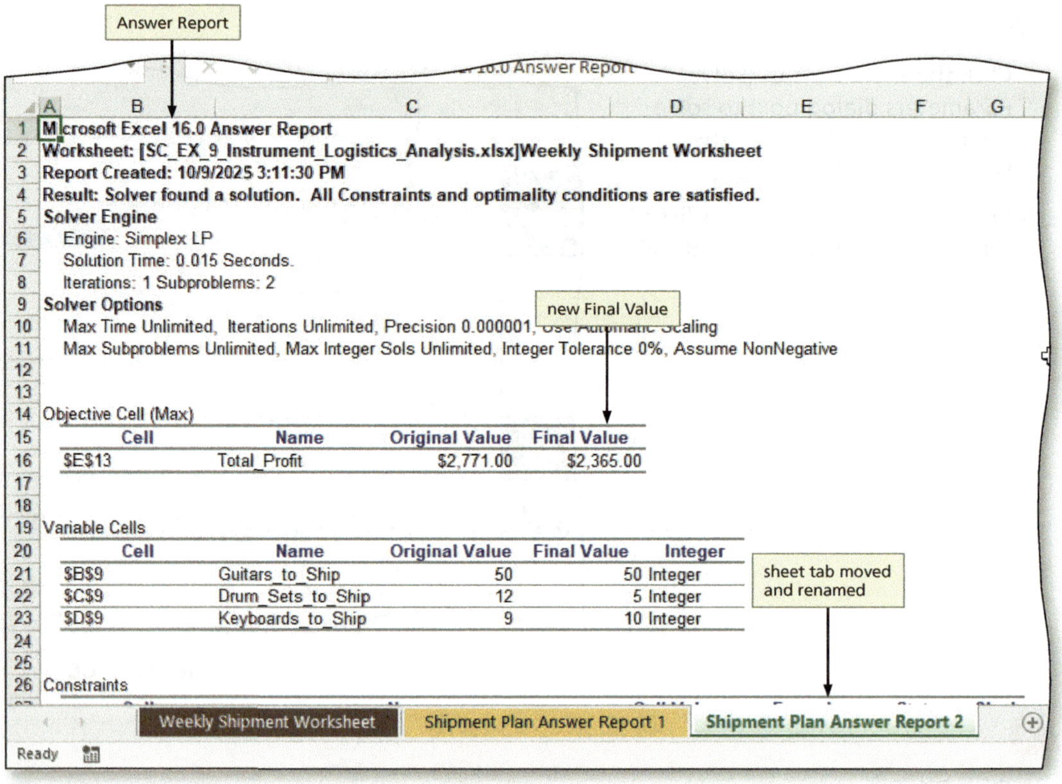

Figure 9–68

To Save the Second Solver Solution as a Scenario

Why? With a second scenario created, you can begin to take advantage of the Scenario Manager. The Scenario Manager allows you to compare multiple scenarios side by side. In order to use the Scenario Manager for this, you first must save the second Solver solution as a scenario. The following steps save the second Solver solution as a scenario.

1

- Make the Weekly Shipment Worksheet the active worksheet and click cell A1.
- Click the 'What-If Analysis' button (Data tab | Forecast group) and then click Scenario Manager on the What-If Analysis menu to display the Scenario Manager dialog box (Figure 9–69).

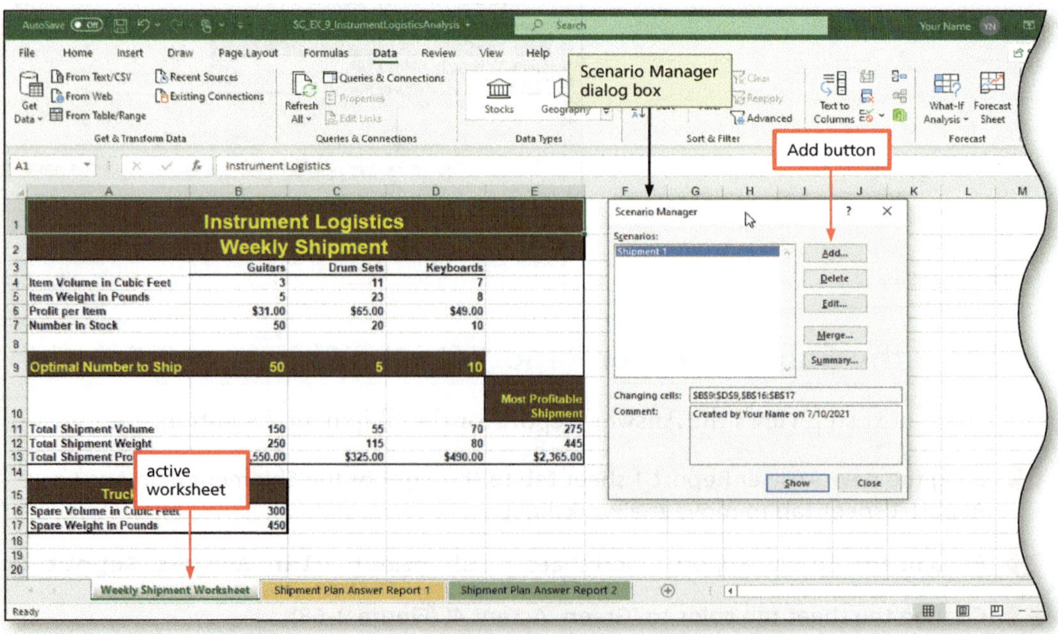

Figure 9–69

2

- Click the Add button (Scenario Manager dialog box) to display the Add Scenario dialog box.
- Type `Shipment 2` in the Scenario name box to name the new scenario (Figure 9–70).

Q&A **Do I have to make any other changes?**
No. The new figures will be saved automatically with the scenario.

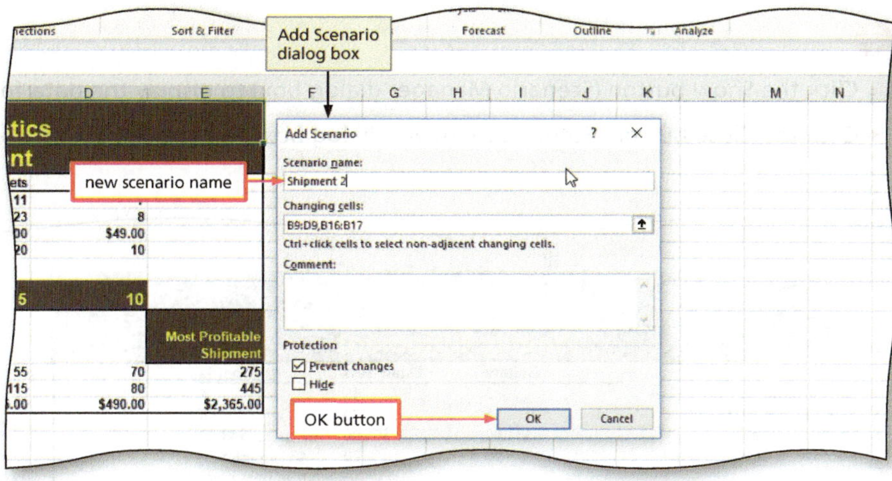

Figure 9–70

3

- Click OK (Add Scenario dialog box) to display the Scenario Values dialog box with the current values.
- Click OK (Scenario Values dialog box) to display the updated Scenarios list in the Scenario Manager dialog box.
- Click the Close button (Scenario Manager dialog box) to save the Shipment 2 scenario and close the dialog box.

To Show a Saved Scenario

Why? You can display and review any scenario in the workbook by using the Show button in the Scenario Manager dialog box. The following steps display the Shipment 1 scenario created earlier.

1

- Click the 'What-If Analysis' button (Data tab | Forecast group) to display the What-If Analysis menu.
- Click Scenario Manager on the What-If Analysis menu to display the Scenario Manager dialog box.
- Click the scenario of interest, Shipment 1 in this case, to select it (Figure 9–71).

Q&A **Can I edit a scenario?**
Yes. Select the scenario (Scenario Manager dialog box) and then click the Edit button. Excel will display the Edit Scenario dialog box, allowing you to change the scenario name, edit the cells, or add a comment.

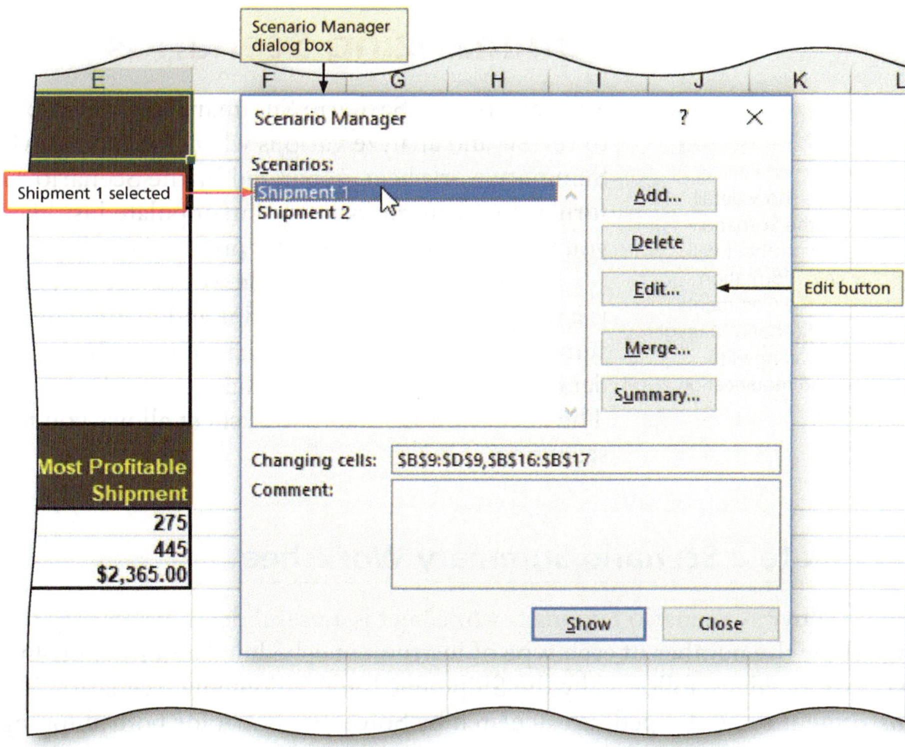

Figure 9–71

2

- Click the Show button (Scenario Manager dialog box) to display the data for the selected scenario in the worksheet.
- Click the Close button (Scenario Manager dialog box) to close the dialog box (Figure 9–72).

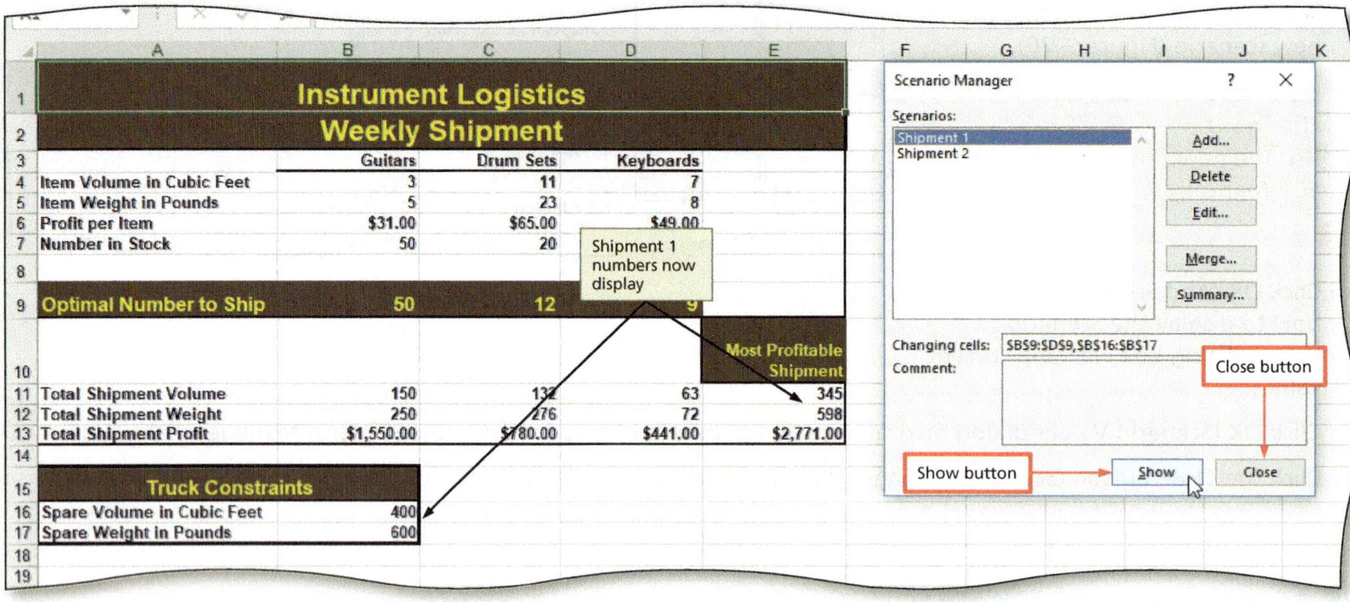

Figure 9–72

Summarizing Scenarios

BTW
Scenario Summary Details
Clicking the show detail button on the Scenario Summary worksheet will display any information entered in the Comments box of the Scenario Manager dialog box, along with creation and modification information.

You can create a Scenario Summary worksheet or a Scenario PivotTable worksheet to review and analyze various what-if scenarios when making decisions. A Scenario Summary worksheet, generated by the Scenario Manager, is a worksheet in outline format that you can print and manipulate just like any other worksheet. Recall that you worked with outlines in a previous module.

The Scenario PivotTable worksheet generated by the Scenario Manager also is a worksheet that you can print and manipulate like other worksheets. PivotTables summarize large amounts of data and can be rearranged and regrouped to show the data in various forms. Recall that you worked with PivotTables in a previous module. The Scenario PivotTable worksheet allows you to compare the results of multiple scenarios.

To Create a Scenario Summary Worksheet

Why? A Scenario Summary worksheet is a useful decision-making tool. The Scenario Summary worksheet will show the number of each type of instrument scheduled and total profit of the shipment for the current worksheet values, followed by the Shipment 1 and Shipment 2 scenarios. The optimal number of each type of instrument to be shipped, as calculated by Solver, is shown for both shipping plans. The following steps create a Scenario Summary worksheet.

1

- Click the 'What-If Analysis' button (Data tab | Forecast group) to display the What-If Analysis menu.
- Click Scenario Manager on the What-If Analysis menu to display the Scenario Manager dialog box (Figure 9–73).

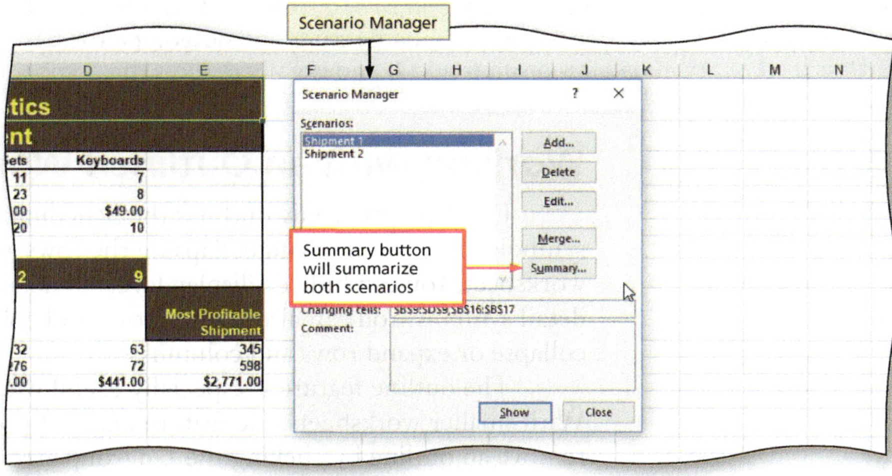

Figure 9–73

2

- Click the Summary button (Scenario Manager dialog box) to display the Scenario Summary dialog box.
- If necessary, click the Scenario summary option button in the Report type area (Scenario Summary dialog box).
- Click the 'Result cells: Collapse Dialog' button (Scenario Summary dialog box) and then use CTRL+click to select the cells E11:E13, B16, and B17.
- Click the Expand Dialog button to return to the Scenario Summary dialog box (Figure 9–74).

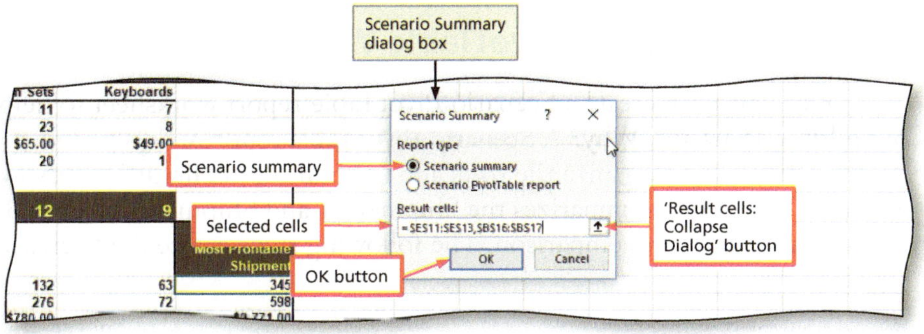

Figure 9–74

3

- Click OK (Scenario Summary dialog box) to generate a Scenario Summary report.
- Rename the Scenario Summary sheet tab as `Shipment Scenario Summary` to provide a descriptive name for the sheet.
- Change the sheet tab color to 'Rose, Accent 6'.
- Drag the Shipment Scenario Summary sheet tab to the right of the Shipment Plan Answer Report 2 sheet tab to reposition the worksheet in the workbook (Figure 9–75).

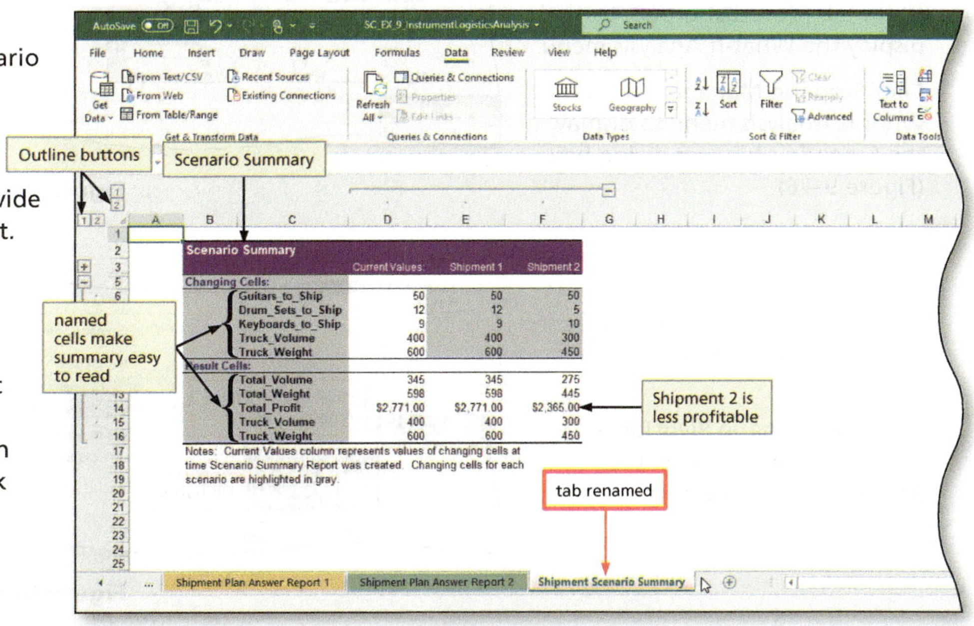

Figure 9–75

Q&A

What is shown in the Scheduling Scenario Summary worksheet?
The current values are shown in column D, and scenarios Shipment 1 and Shipment 2 are shown side by side (in columns E and F), allowing you to compare results and determine the best available option. As you might expect, less truck space equals less profit (row 14) and greatly reduces the number of drum sets to ship (row 7).

Working with an Outlined Worksheet

Excel automatically outlines the Scheduling Scenario Summary worksheet. The symbols for expanding and collapsing the rows appear above and to the left of the worksheet. You can hide or display levels of detail by using the hide detail and show detail symbols. You can also use the row- and column-level show detail buttons to collapse or expand rows and columns.

The outline feature is especially useful when working with very large worksheets. With smaller worksheets, the feature may not provide any real benefits. You can remove an outline by clicking the Ungroup arrow (Data tab | Outline group) and then clicking Clear Outline on the Ungroup menu.

To Create a Scenario PivotTable Worksheet

Excel also can create a Scenario PivotTable report worksheet to help analyze and compare the results of multiple scenarios. **Why?** A Scenario PivotTable report worksheet gives you the ability to summarize the scenario data and reorganize the rows and columns to obtain different views of the summarized data. The Scenario PivotTable summarizes the Shipment 1 and Shipment 2 scenarios and displays the result cells for the two scenarios for easy comparison. The following steps create the Scenario PivotTable worksheet.

1

- Click the Weekly Shipment Worksheet tab to make it active. You may have to scroll through the sheet tabs to locate the worksheet.
- Click the 'What-If Analysis' button (Data tab | Forecast group) to display the What-If Analysis menu.
- Click Scenario Manager on the What-If Analysis menu to display the Scenario Manager dialog box (Figure 9–76).

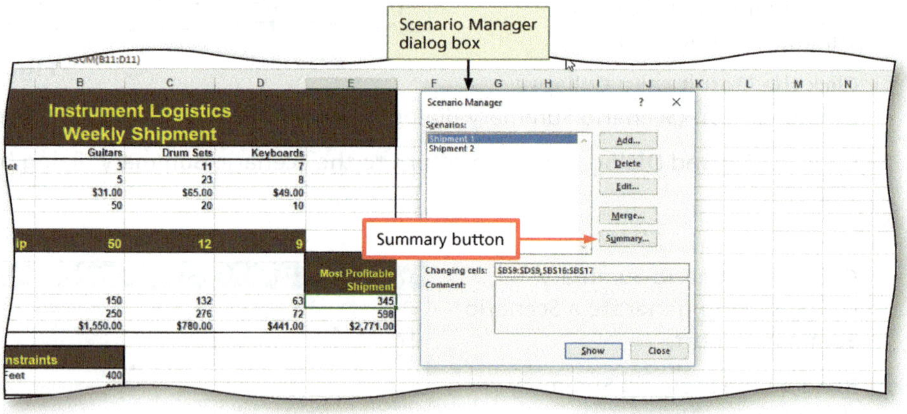

Figure 9–76

2

- Click the Summary button (Scenario Manager dialog box) to display the Scenario Summary dialog box.
- Click the 'Scenario PivotTable report' option button in the Report type area (Scenario Summary dialog box) (Figure 9–77).

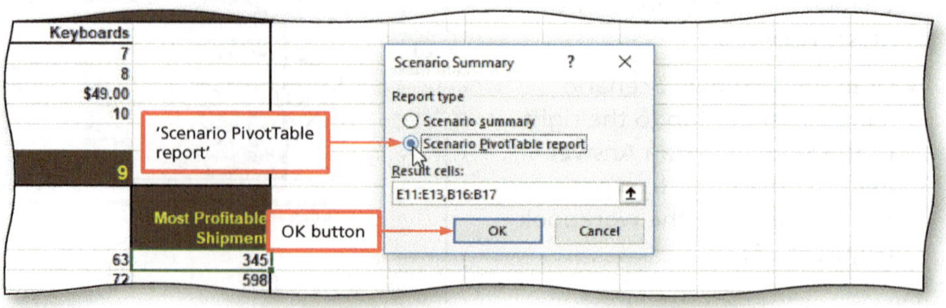

Figure 9–77

3

- Click OK (Scenario Summary dailog box) to create the Scenario PivotTable (Figure 9–78).

Experiment

- Examine the various boxes, sections, and settings in the Field List.

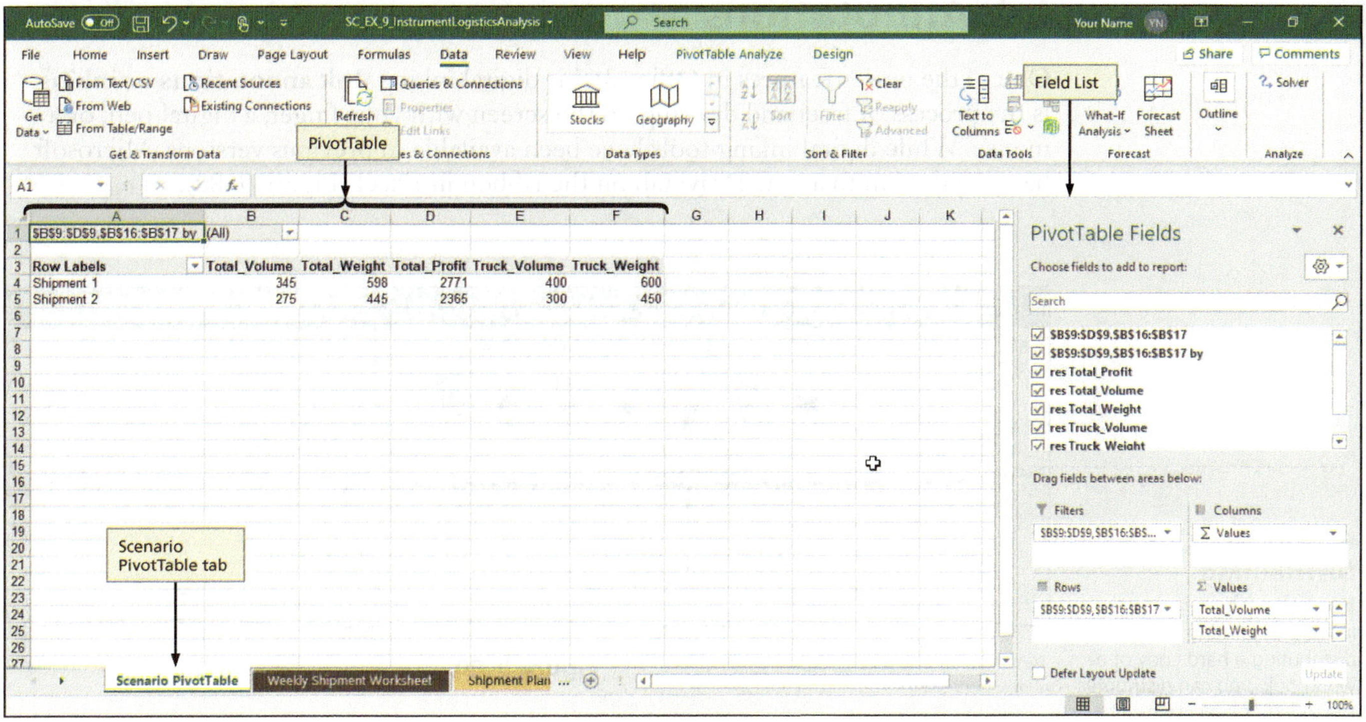

Figure 9–78

4

- Rename the Scenario PivotTable worksheet as **`Shipment Scenario PivotTable`** to provide a descriptive name for the worksheet.
- Change the sheet tab color for the Shipment Scenario PivotTable worksheet to 'Aqua, Accent 5'.
- Drag the Shipment Scenario PivotTable sheet tab to the right of the Shipment Scenario Summary sheet tab to reposition the worksheet in the workbook.
- Format cells D4:D5 using the Accounting number format.
- Click cell A2 to deselect any other cell (Figure 9–79).

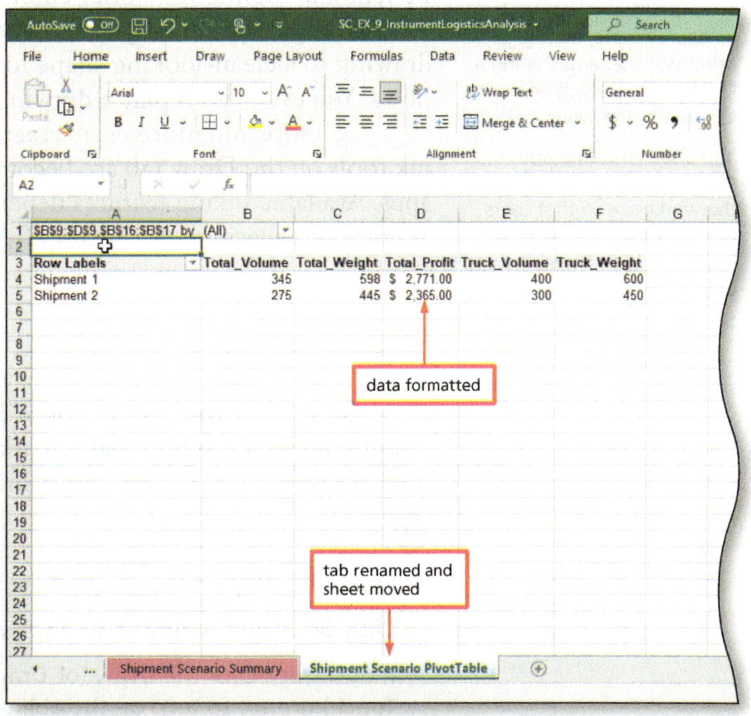

Figure 9–79

Q&A

How can I use the PivotTable?

After creating the PivotTable, you can treat it like any other worksheet. Thus, you can print or chart a PivotTable. If you update the data in one of the scenarios, click the Refresh All button (Data tab | Queries & Connections group) to update the PivotTable. Note that if you merely change values on a scenario worksheet, it is not the same as changing the scenario. If you want to change the data in a scenario, you must enter the new data using the Scenario Manager.

5

- Save the workbook again on the same storage location with the same file name.

Ink Annotations

One of the newer features in Office 365 is digital inking. **Ink annotations** or **inking** is the process of freehand drawing on the screen with your finger, a digital pen, or a mouse. While digital inking tools have been available in previous versions, Microsoft has added them to a new Draw tab on the ribbon in Excel (Figure 9–80).

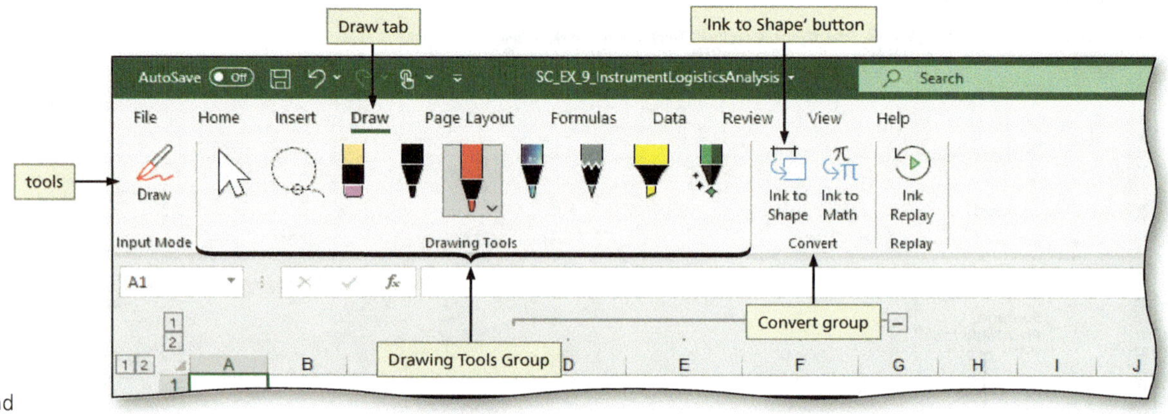

Figure 9–80

BTW
Distributing Workbooks
Instead of printing and distributing a hard copy of a workbook, you can distribute the workbook electronically. Options include sending the workbook via email; posting it on cloud storage (such as OneDrive) and sharing the file with others; posting it on social media, a blog, or other website; and sharing a link associated with an online location of the workbook.

You also can create and share a PDF or XPS image of the workbook so that users can view the file in Acrobat Reader or XPS Viewer instead of in Excel

The Pens gallery includes pens, pencils, and highlighters. When you click a pen, Excel displays five thickness settings as well as 16 solid colors and eight special effects. Pencils and highlighters offer color choices only. An 'Ink to Shape' button (Draw tab | Convert group) allows you to draw shapes roughly; Excel then will change your drawing to a clean-looking shape for creating things such as diagrams and process flows. You even can replay a drawing.

As more and more users create worksheets on mobile devices, the pen and ink tools on the Draw tab are becoming primary input mechanisms across the apps. Available inking features depend on the type of device you are using. Use ink annotations sparingly for better effects.

To Draw with a Pen

In the following steps, you will use the Draw tab to circle Shipment 1 on the 'Shipment Scenario Summary' worksheet. **Why?** You will mark which Shipment you want to use by circling the shipment that has a larger profit.

1

- Make the 'Shipment Scenario Summary' worksheet active.
- Click Draw on the ribbon to display the Draw tab.
- If necessary, click the Draw (or Draw with Touch) button (Draw tab | Input Mode (or Touch) group) to turn on the ability to draw.

Experiment

- One at a time, point to each drawing implement to display its ScreenTip.
- Click the second pen, 'Pen: Red, 0.5 mm', in the gallery to select it. If your pen ScreenTip is different, click the pen, and then click the pen arrow to display its gallery and then click. 0.5 mm and Red.
- In the worksheet, draw a rough circle around the Shipment 1 results (Figure 9–81).

Q&A **What if I make a mistake or want to redo my circle?**
Press CTRL+Z and try again. Or, you can click the Eraser button (Draw tab | Drawing Tools group) and then click the drawing.

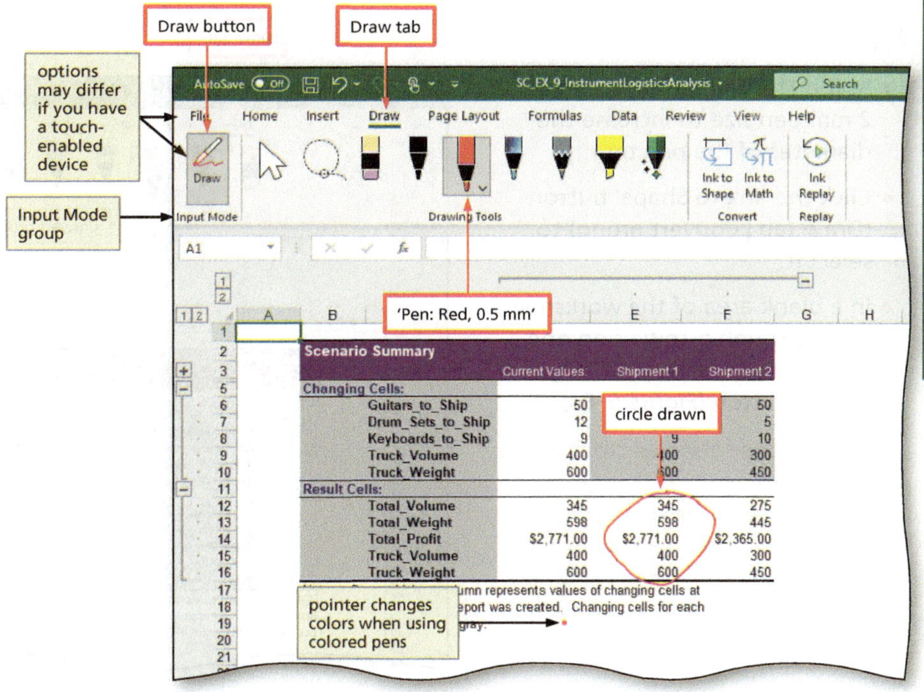

Figure 9–81

To Use the 'Ink to Shape' Tool

In the following steps, you will use the Draw tab to draw a rough arrow. **Why?** You want to point out the profit line on the summary. Excel then will convert the rough drawing to a distinctive arrow shape.

1

- If necessary, click the second pen, labelled 'Pen: Red, 0.5 mm', to display its arrow.
- Click the pen arrow to display the pen gallery (Figure 9–82).

Experiment

- Point to various items in the pen gallery to view the ScreenTips.

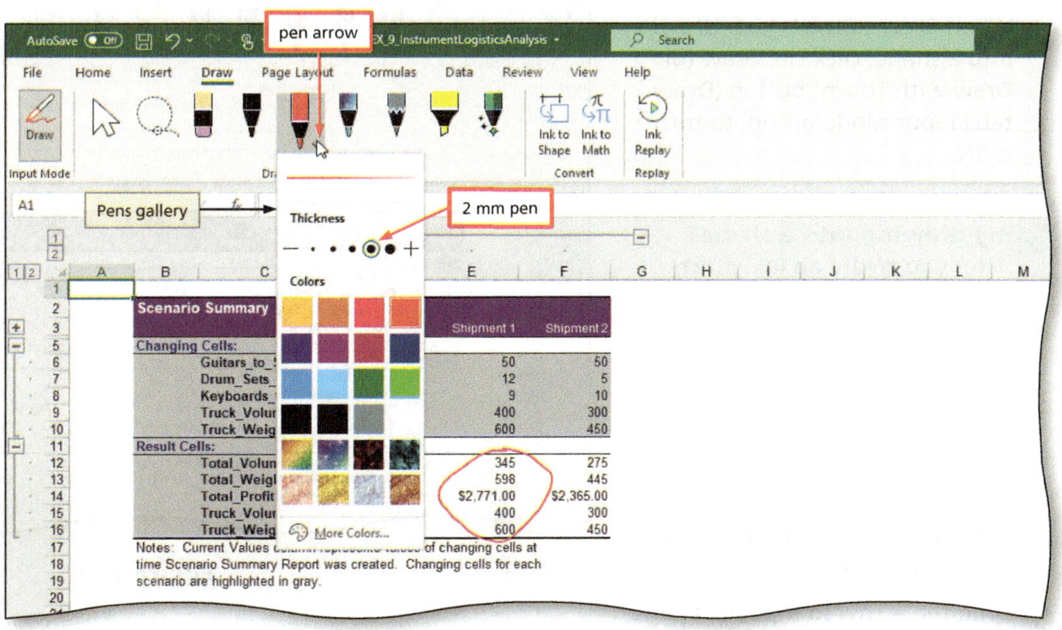

Figure 9–82

2

- In the Thickness area, click the 2 mm pen size to increase the diameter of the pen tip.
- Click the 'Ink to Shape' button (Draw tab | Convert group) to select it.
- In a blank area of the worksheet, draw a rough arrow using one motion. Do not lift your finger or mouse button (Figure 9–83).

Q&A **What other shapes can I draw and convert?**
You can draw squares, rectangles, diamonds, pentagons, ellipses, connectors, and others. Look up 'Convert ink to shapes' in Excel Help for a complete listing.

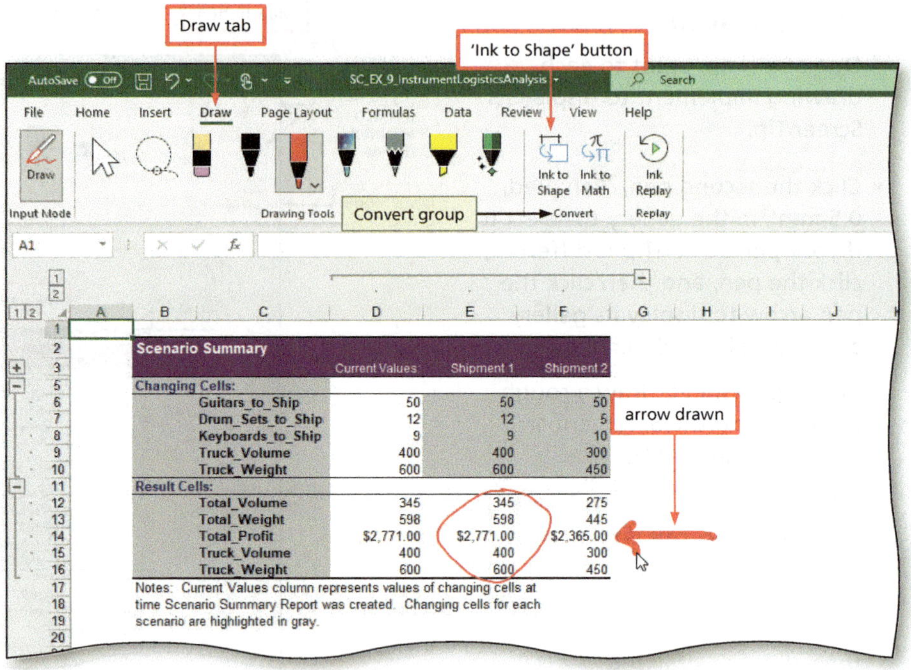

Figure 9–83

3

- Lift your finger or release the mouse button.
- When Excel converts your drawing into a shape, click the Draw (or Draw with Touch) button (Draw tab | Input Mode group) to turn it off.

Q&A **What if Excel does not convert my drawing into a shape?**
After you create an ink effect, you can use the Lasso Select tool (Draw tab | Drawing Tools group) to draw around all, or part, of the drawing. Excel will convert the lassoed area to an object with sizing handles and the ability to move, delete, or copy the object.

- Use the sizing handles to resize the arrow as necessary.
- Drag the arrow so it points at line 14 (Figure 9–84).

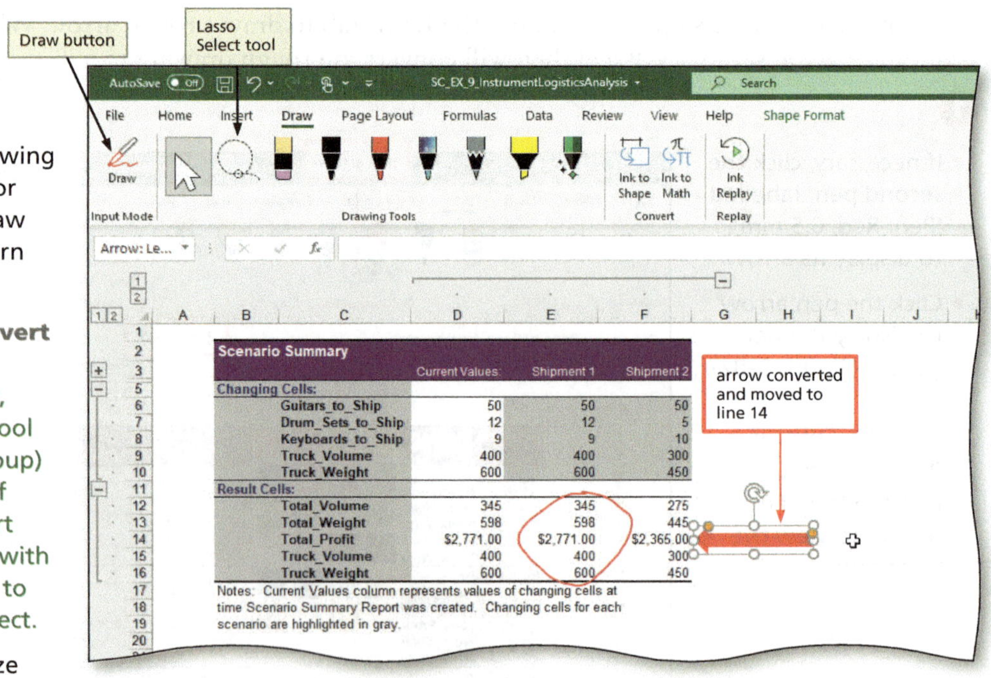

Figure 9–84

To Highlight with Ink

In the following steps, you will use the Draw tab to highlight an area on the worksheet. **Why?** Highlighting the bigger profit will draw attention to your choice even further.

1

- In the Drawing Tools group, click 'Highlighter: Yellow 6 mm'.
- Drag through the profit for Shipment 1 to highlight the figure (Figure 9–85).

Experiment

- Click the Ink Replay button (Draw tab | Replay group) to watch Excel replay your inking annotations.

2

- sam Because the project is now complete, you can save the file again and exit Excel.

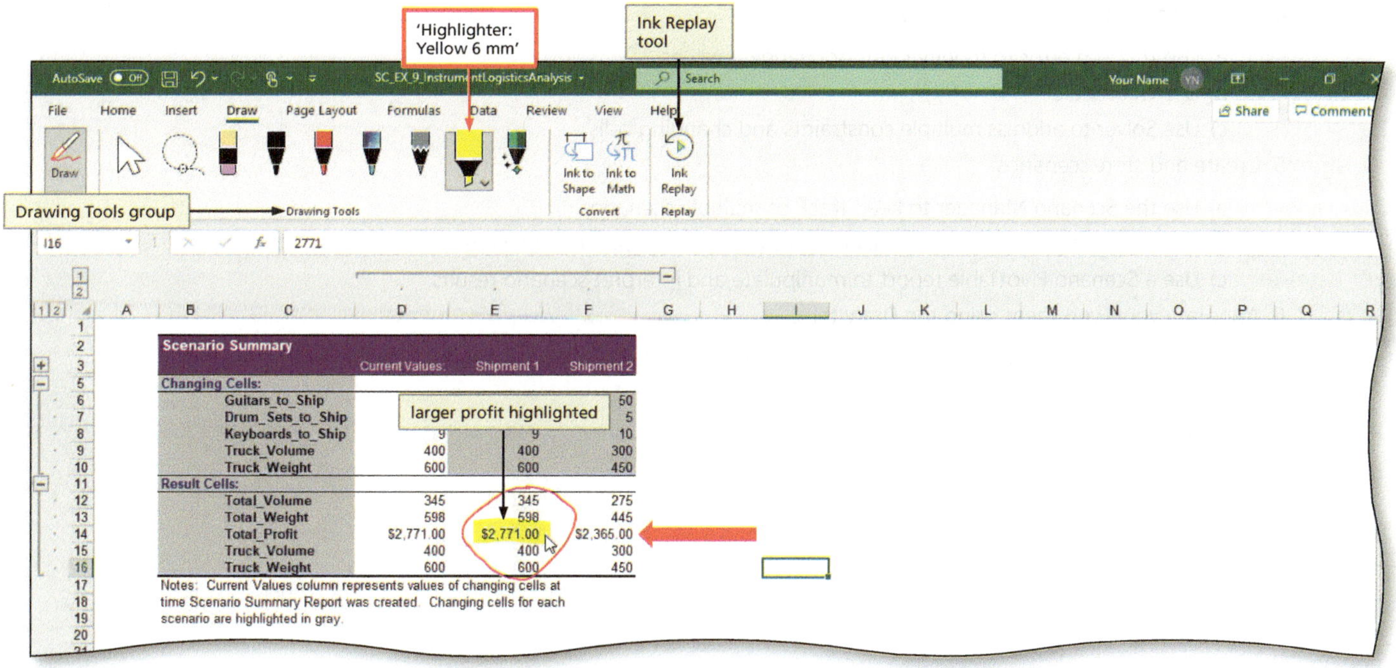

Figure 9–85

Summary

In this module, you learned how to analyze a worksheet using formula auditing techniques and tracer arrows. You used error checking features to determine how to fix errors in the worksheet. You established data validation rules and informed users with input messages about the validation rules. You solved a complex problem with Excel, using trial and error, Goal Seek, and Solver. You used the Scenario Manager to manage different problems on the same worksheet and then summarized the results of the scenarios with a Scenario Summary worksheet and a Scenario PivotTable worksheet. Finally, you added ink annotations to the worksheet using the new Draw tab.

Consider This: Plan Ahead

What decisions will you need to make when creating your next worksheet to solve a complex problem?

Use these guidelines as you complete the assignments in this module and create your own worksheets for evaluating and analyzing data outside of this class.

1. Review and analyze workbook structure and organization.
   a) Review all formulas.
   b) Use precedent and dependent tracing to determine dependencies.
   c) Use formula auditing tools to correct formula errors.
2. Establish data validation rules.
   a) Identify changing cells.
   b) Determine data restrictions to address using data validation.
3. Configure useful add-ins.
   a) Identify missing add-ins.
   b) Use Excel Options to enable necessary add-ins.
   c) Verify inclusion on the ribbon.
4. Determine strategies for problem solving.
   a) Use trial and error to modify input or changing values.
   b) Use Goal Seek.
   c) Use Solver to address multiple constraints and changing cells.
5. Create and store scenarios.
   a) Use the Scenario Manager to keep track of multiple scenarios.
   b) Use a Scenario Summary worksheet to present and compare multiple scenarios.
   c) Use a Scenario PivotTable report to manipulate and interpret scenario results.
6. Annotate your worksheet using the Draw tab.
   a) Use the pen, pencil, and highlighter sparingly for better effects.
   b) When you need a quick shape, use the 'Ink to Shape' tool.

Apply Your Knowledge

Reinforce the skills and apply the concepts you learned in this module.

Using Solver to Plan Festival Advertising

Note: To complete this assignment, you will be required to use the Data Files. Please contact your instructor for information about accessing the Data Files.

Instructions: Start Excel. Open the workbook called SC_EX_9-2.xlsx, which is located in the Data Files. The workbook you open contains information about your town's two annual festivals, one in June and one in October. You are to determine how best to promote the festivals, making the most of the town's advertising budget. Figure 9–86a shows the completed Answer Report. Figure 9–86b shows the completed Scenario Summary.

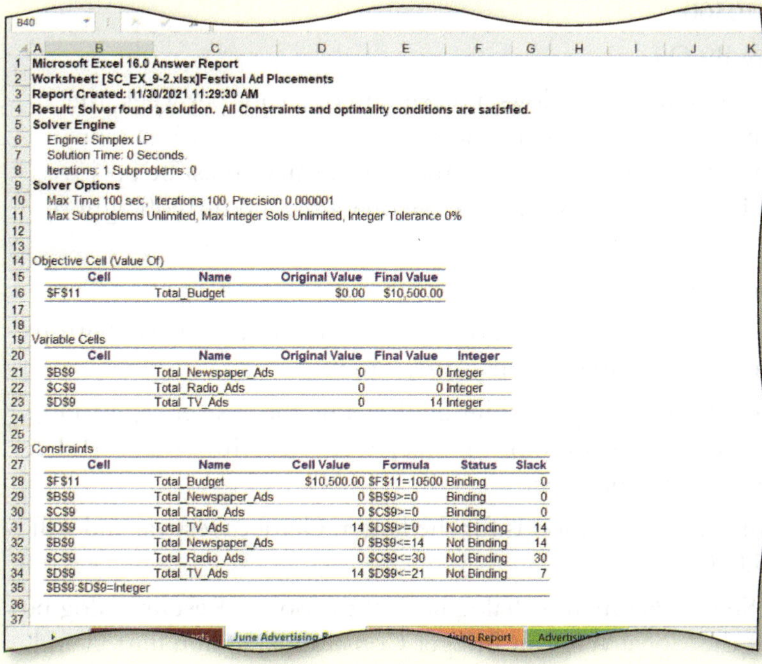

(a) Answer Report

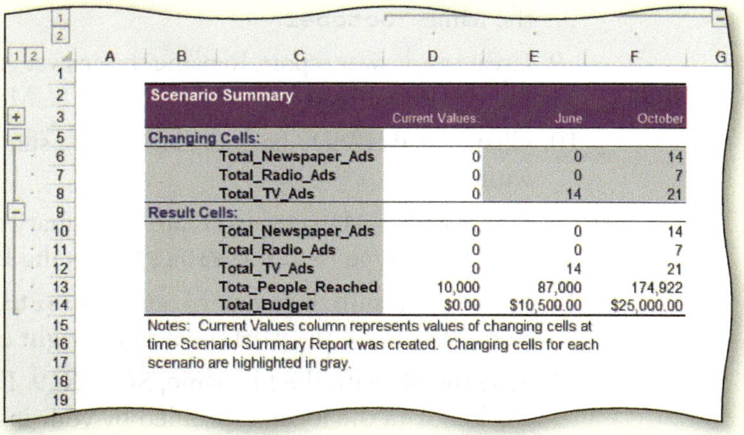

(b) Scenario Summary

Figure 9–86

Continued >

Apply Your Knowledge *continued*

Perform the following tasks:

1. Trace precedents and dependents on the two cells with errors: F9 and E7.
2. Use Error Checking to evaluate the error in cell F9. Use the solution suggested by Error Checking.
3. Trace the error in cell E7. Because the Social Media cost of zero is valid, the division error appears. In cell E7, type `=E5` because all people might be reached by Social Media with no cost.
4. Use Solver to determine the best mix of advertising for the advertising dollars. The costs for the month of June are already in the worksheet (B6:D6).
    a. The objective is an advertising budget of $10,500 (the Value Of parameter), which will display in cell F11.
    b. Set the Value Of parameter to 10500.
    c. The changing variables cells are B9:D9.
    d. The constraints are as follows: the newspaper allows a maximum of 14 ads per week, the radio station allows a maximum of 30 advertisement spots per week, and the TV station allows a maximum of 21 advertisements per week. The Ads Placed values must be positive whole numbers (Hint: Use the int operator as well as the >= operator, and turn off 'ignore integer constraints.')
    e. Use the Simplex LP solving method.
5. After you click the Solve button (Solver Parameters dialog box), use the Save Scenario button (Solver Results dialog box) to save the scenario with the name, `June`.
6. Instruct Solver to create the Answer Report for your solution. Rename the answer report tab, `June Advertising Report`. Change the tab color to 'Blue, Accent 1'. Move the worksheet to the right of the 'Festival Ad Placement' worksheet.
7. Create a second solution using Solver. This solution is for the larger, October festival and will have an advertising budget of $25,000.
8. After you click the Solve button (Solver Parameters dialog box), if the Solver Results dialog box says it cannot find a solution, click the 'Solve Without Integer Constraints' option button and solve again. Use the Save Scenario button (Solver Results dialog box) to save the scenario with the name, `October`.
9. Create an answer report. Rename the answer report tab, `October Advertising Report`. Change the tab color to 'Orange, Accent 2'. Move the worksheet to the right of the other worksheets.
10. Change cells B9:D9 back to zero, so the summary report you create in the next step will begin with zeroes.
11. Use Scenario Manager to create a summary report. When Excel displays the Scenario Summary dialog box, type `B9:D9,F10:F11` as the Result cells box.
12. Name the resulting summary tab, `Advertising Summary`. Change the tab color to 'Green, Accent 6'. Move the worksheet to the right of the other worksheets.
13. Save the file with the file name, SC_EX_9_FestivalAdvertising, and submit the revised workbook in the format specified by your instructor.
14. Exit Excel.
15. How would you determine which scenario makes the best use of the advertising dollars? If the budget was a secondary concern, what cell might you use as an objective? Would it be a max, min, or value?

Extend Your Knowledge

Extend the skills you learned in this module and experiment with new skills. You may need to use Help to complete the assignment.

Validating Car Loan Calculator Data

Note: To complete this assignment, you will be required to use the Data Files. Please contact your instructor for information about accessing the Data Files.

Instructions: Start Excel. Open the workbook SC_EX_9-3.xlsx, which is located in the Data Files. The workbook you open contains a template that calculates the monthly payment for a car loan. The workbook has some errors. You are to correct these errors and create data validation rules. Figure 9–87 shows the worksheet with the errors fixed and an input message for the price of the car.

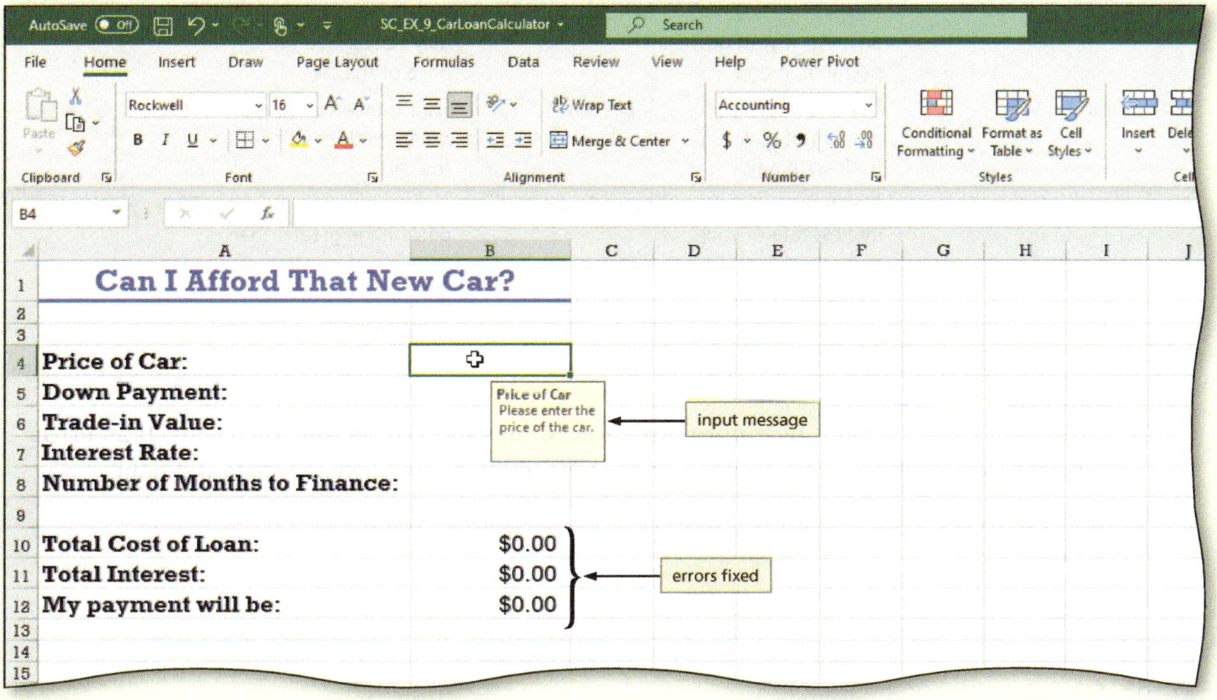

Figure 9–87

Perform the following tasks:

1. To validate the data in cells B10:B12, first do the following:
   a. Examine the formula in cell B10. Trace the error. Check for both precedent and dependent cells. Remove the tracer arrows.
   b. Examine the formula in cell B11. Trace the error. Check for both precedent and dependent cells. Remove the tracer arrows.
   c. Examine the formula in cell B12. Trace the error. Check for both precedent and dependent cells. Remove the tracer arrows.
2. Use Help to review the IF() function. In cells B10 and B11, use the IF( ) function to execute the formula only when the dependent value is greater than 0. (*Note:* Cell B10 may still show a #NUM error until you fix other errors.)

Continued >

Extend Your Knowledge *continued*

3. Use Help to review the IFERROR() function, and then use it in cell B12 to display zero if any other errors occur. (Hint: Use the current PMT() function as the first argument in the IFERROR() function and use 0 as the second argument.)
4. Create data validation constraints and messages for each of the cells in Table 9–4. (Hint: B4:B6 should be formatted in Accounting style with two decimal places.) Use the Error message column to help you determine the constraint.

Table 9–4 Data Constraints and Messages

Cell	Input Message Title	Input Message	Error Alert Title	Error Message	Error Alert Style
B4	Price of Car	Please enter the price of the car.	Input Error	The price of the car must be greater than zero.	Stop
B5	Down Payment	Please enter the amount of your down payment, if any.	Input Error	Your down payment may not exceed the price of the car.	Stop
B6	Trade-in Value	Please enter the amount of your trade-in, if any.	Input Error	Your trade-in value may not exceed the price of the car.	Stop
B7	Interest Rate	Please enter the interest rate of your loan.	Input Error	Please enter a percentage greater than zero.	Stop
B8	Number of Months	Please enter the number of months you wish to finance.	Input Error	Please enter a whole number between 1 and 72.	Stop

5. Test the data validation rules by entering the following values in the specified cells. If an error message appears, click the Retry button or the Cancel button and then enter valid data.

   B4: 25000

   B5: 1000

   B6: 1250

   B7: 5

   B8: 60
6. Apply appropriate number formatting to the cells in the range B4:B8.
7. Save the file with the file name, SC_EX_9_CarLoanCalculator, and submit the revised workbook in the format specified by your instructor.
8. In step 3, why did you need to use the IFERROR() function, rather than the IF function? Was there another way you could have solved the errors other than using those functions? What effect would locking the cells with the formulas have on the rest of the spreadsheet?

Expand Your World

Create a solution that uses cloud and web technologies by learning and investigating on your own from general guidance.

Add-Ins for Excel Online

You use Excel Online through your OneDrive account and understand that there are limitations to the online versions of the Office apps compared to the desktop applications. You are interested in discovering add-ins that can improve your overall productivity with Excel Online.

Instructions:

1. Sign into OneDrive and create a new workbook using Excel Online.
2. Explore the Office Add-ins collection available from the Insert tab of the ribbon in the new workbook.
3. Browse options in the Education and Productivity categories of the Store as well as those in another category of your choice.
4. Create a document that summarizes the features of an add-in from each of the three categories.
5. Save the file with the file name, SC_EX_9_ExcelAddIns, and submit the revised workbook in the format specified by your instructor.
6. Compare the add-ins available in Excel to those available for Excel Online. Choose two add-ins and evaluate the strengths and weaknesses of each. Which would you recommend, and why?

In the Lab

Design and implement a solution using creative thinking and problem-solving skills.

Do You Want to Be a Millionaire?

Note: To complete this assignment, you will be required to use the Data Files. Please contact your instructor for information about accessing the Data Files.

Problem: You decide to use a financial calculator to see how much you might have to save each year to retire a millionaire!

Perform the following tasks:

Part 1: Start Excel and open the file named SC_EX_9-4.xlsx. Examine the Retirement Schedule worksheet and examine the various calculations. The worksheet, shown in Figure 9–88, makes the following assumptions:

a. The starting balance deposited in the retirement account is stored in cell B3.
b. The first annual contribution is in cell C3. The calculator assumes a $200 increase in contributions each year.
c. The rate of return (column D) is based on a fairly aggressive investment strategy, 8 percent, until the age of 60. It then reduces to a moderate investment strategy of 5 percent.

Use Goal Seek to set the final ending balance (E38) to $1,000,000 by changing cell B3, the initial starting balance. Write down the new B3 value on a piece of paper. Click Cancel to undo the changes and return to the original values.

Use Goal Seek again by changing cell C3, the annual contribution. Write down the new value in cell C3. Click Cancel to undo the changes.

Use Solver to set the objective in cell E38 to `1000000` by changing the values in cells B3:D3. Set constraints for cells B3 and C3 to be greater than or equal to one. Set a constraint for cell D3 to be less than or equal to .08 (8 percent) and greater than or equal to zero. Select the GRG Nonlinear solving method (because you are dealing with a percentage rate of return). When Excel displays the Solver Results dialog box, choose to produce an answer report. Move the new worksheet to the right of the original one, and change the tab color to 'Brown, Accent 2'.

Experiment with other constraints. For example, suppose the most you can start the account with is $25,000. Perhaps you can only add a maximum of $500 a year. Will Solver find a solution with those constraints? Write down your answers; do not save the file.

Continued >

In the Lab *continued*

Montgomery Financial Consultants
Retirement Calculator

Age	Starting Balance	Annual Contribution	Return	Ending Balance
30	$ 25,000.00	$ 500.00	8%	$ 27,540.00
31	27,540.00	700.00	8%	$ 30,499.20
32	30,499.20	900.00	8%	$ 33,911.14
33	33,911.14	1,100.00	8%	$ 37,812.03
34	37,812.03	1,300.00	8%	$ 42,240.99
35	42,240.99	1,500.00	8%	$ 47,240.27
36	47,240.27	1,700.00	8%	$ 52,855.49
37	52,855.49	1,900.00	8%	$ 59,135.93
38	59,135.93	2,100.00	8%	$ 66,134.80
39	66,134.80	2,300.00	8%	$ 73,909.59
40	73,909.59	2,500.00	8%	$ 82,522.35
41	82,522.35	2,700.00	8%	$ 92,040.14
42	92,040.14	2,900.00	8%	$ 102,535.35
43	102,535.35	3,100.00	8%	$ 114,086.18
44	114,086.18	3,300.00	8%	$ 126,777.08
45	126,777.08	3,500.00	8%	$ 140,699.24
46	140,699.24	3,700.00	8%	$ 155,951.18
47	155,951.18	3,900.00	8%	$ 172,639.28
48	172,639.28	4,100.00	8%	$ 190,878.42
49	190,878.42	4,300.00	8%	$ 210,792.69
50	210,792.69	4,500.00	8%	$ 232,516.11
51	232,516.11	4,700.00	8%	$ 256,193.40
52	256,193.40	4,900.00	8%	$ 281,980.87
53	281,980.87	5,100.00	8%	$ 310,047.34
54	310,047.34	5,300.00	8%	$ 340,575.13
55	340,575.13	5,500.00	8%	$ 373,761.14
56	373,761.14	5,700.00	8%	$ 409,818.03
57	409,818.03	5,900.00	8%	$ 448,975.47
58	448,975.47	6,100.00	8%	$ 491,481.51
59	491,481.51	6,300.00	8%	$ 537,604.03
60	537,604.03	6,500.00	5%	$ 571,309.23
61	571,309.23	6,700.00	5%	$ 606,909.69
62	606,909.69	6,900.00	5%	$ 644,500.17
63	644,500.17	7,100.00	5%	$ 684,180.18
64	684,180.18	7,300.00	5%	$ 726,054.19
65	726,054.19	7,500.00	5%	$ 770,231.90

Retirement Schedule

Figure 9–88

Save the file with the file name, SC_EX_9_RetirementCalculator. Submit the revised workbook and answers to the Part 2 critical thinking questions in the format specified by your instructor.

Part 2: You made several decisions while creating the worksheet in this assignment: initial starting balance, annual contribution, and constraints. What was the rationale behind each of these decisions? Which of the solutions seemed the most feasible to you? Why?

10 Data Analysis with Power Tools and Creating Macros

Objectives

After completing this module, you will be able to:

- Explain the Excel power tools
- Customize the ribbon and enable data analysis
- Use the Get & Transform data commands
- Create a query using Power Query Editor
- Build a PivotTable using Power Pivot
- Explain data modeling
- Create a measure
- View cube functions
- Use Power BI
- Create a report in Power BI
- Use 3D Maps
- Save a tour as an animation
- Create hyperlinks
- Use the macro recorder to create a macro
- Execute a macro

Introduction

Excel has a wide range of interlinked power tools for data analysis—Get & Transform, Power Pivot, Power BI (Business Intelligence), and 3D Maps—whether you need to export data for business intelligence, pivot or manipulate data to find trends, create data models, or show data more visually.

Table 10–1 describes the power tools available to analyze Excel data. In this module, you will only touch on each of the power tools. The topic is vast and would require a lot of time and data modeling experience to explore all of the features associated with each tool. Power BI is a separate program available as a free download and is designed to analyze Excel data. Power Pivot may not be available in all versions of Excel. While you may have limited access to these tools, you will be able to work through the majority of the steps in this module.

Table 10–1 Power Tools

Tool	Purpose
Get & Transform (formerly called Power Query)	The Get & Transform commands enable you to extract, connect, refine, and transform large amounts of data into an accessible Excel file. You can use Get & Transform to exert greater control over columns, formulas, and filtering tools, and also to modify data types and extract PivotTables.
Power Pivot	Power Pivot enables you to import and compare large amounts of data from multiple sources to analyze relationships between tables of data. You can use Power Pivot to create and model data tables, feed data to other Power Tools, and use data analysis expressions. Power Pivot is not available with all versions of Excel.
Power BI	Power BI, or Power Business Intelligence, is a collection of tools that enables you to understand and communicate large amounts of data in the form of visualizations. Power BI includes a range of tools for report generation, data modeling, sharing and collaboration, including a free desktop app and an online service.
3D Maps (formerly called Power Map)	3D Maps let you plot and visualize geographic or temporal data on a three-dimensional map. With filtering, you can compare how different factors affect your data. You can use a 3D Map to build custom regions, capture screenshots, and build cinematic time tours or animations through your data.

In addition to using Excel power tools, you will create hyperlinks to move quickly to other parts of the workbook, animations, and external websites. You also will record a macro to automate a task.

Project: Business Decisions Demographics

The project in this module follows proper design guidelines and uses Excel and Power BI to create the workbook and Power BI report shown in Figures 10–1 and 10–2. The Rural Hospital Advancement Commission (RHAC) of the state health department in Missouri wants to address the needs of rural counties by building a new hospital. They are hiring a business analytics firm to find the best location based mainly on population. The business analytics firm specializes in examining raw data, looking for patterns, correlations, and other associations to help companies and organizations make better business decisions. Using data from the U.S. Census Bureau, the firm plans to present several forms of visual data to its client using Excel power tools.

Figure 10–1a shows the opening worksheet that includes a screen capture, a symbol, and hyperlinks to the other pages. Figure 10–1b queries the external data to display the 10 least populous counties. Figure 10–1c lists all counties, along with the number of housing units and total area from a different data table.

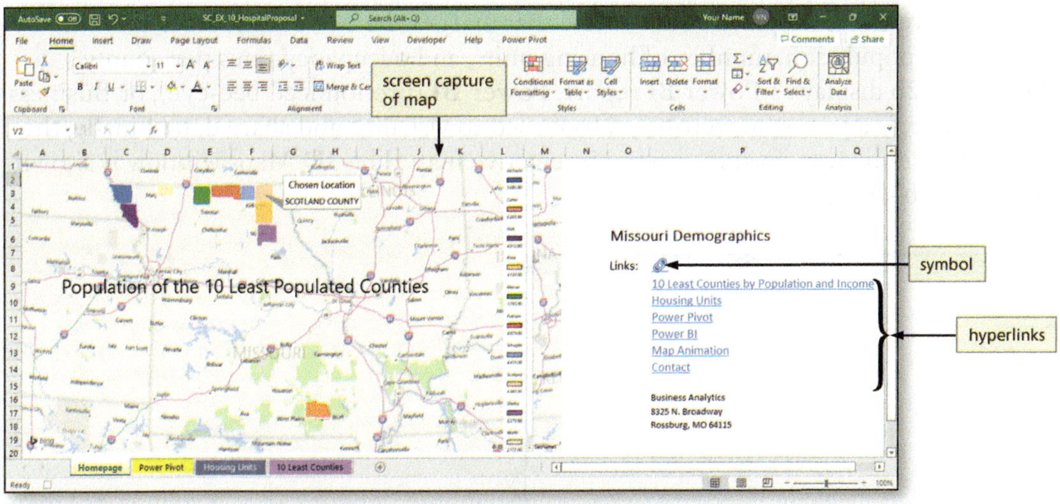

(a) Homepage with Hyperlinks

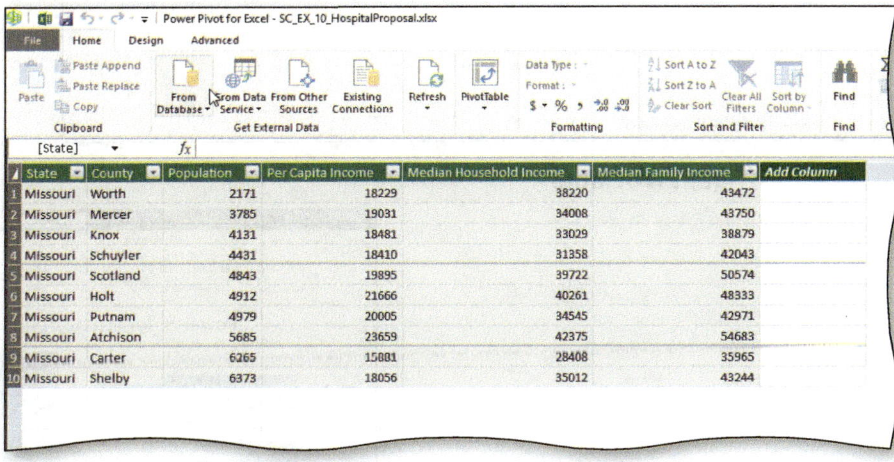

(b) 10 Least Populous Counties

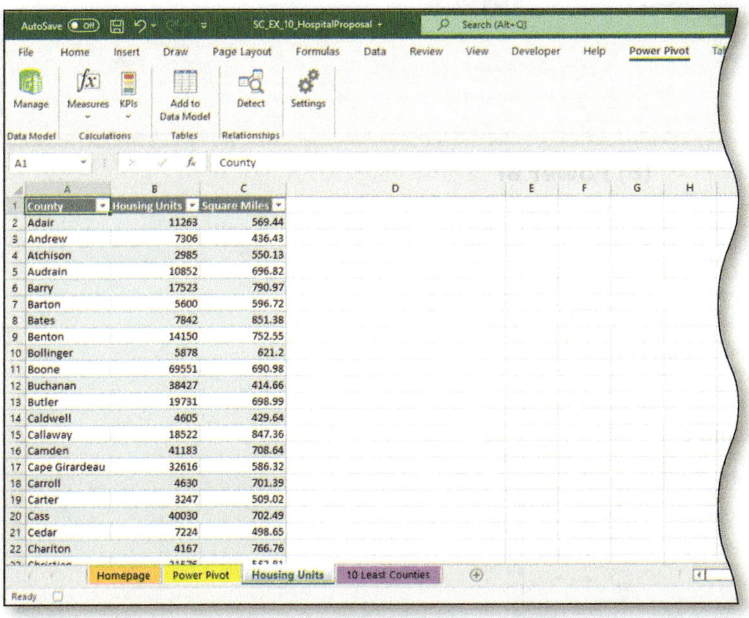

(c) Housing Units by County

Figure 10–1

Figure 10–2a displays a PivotTable that merges the two data sources to display the population, number of housing units, and occupancy rates per county. Figure 10–2b displays a Power BI report. **Power BI** (pronounced bee-eye), or Business Intelligence, is a powerful web-based tool used to visualize and share data. Finally, the data then will be transformed into an interactive map. The 3D Maps window is shown in Figure 10–2c.

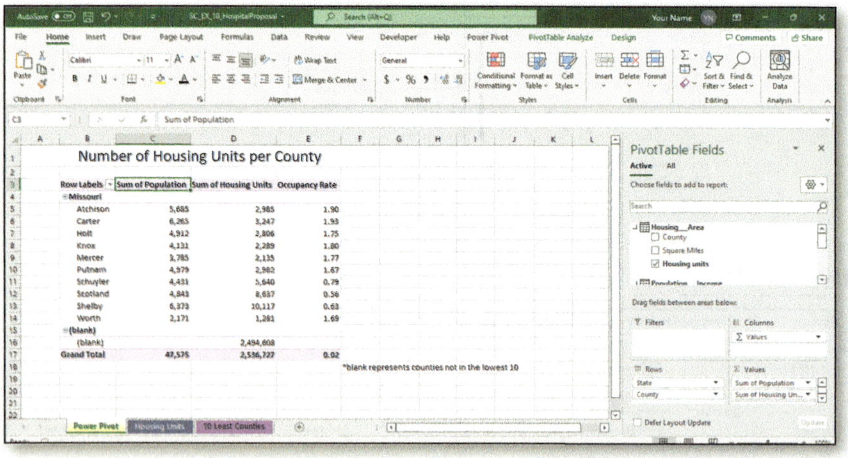

(a) PivotTable

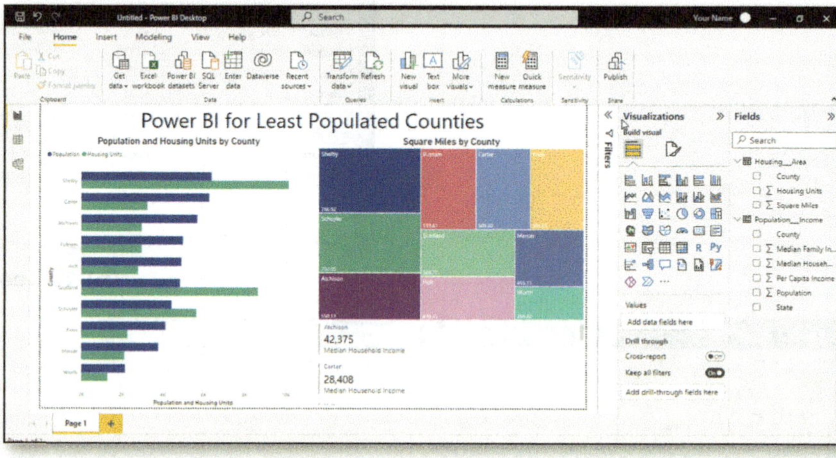

(b) Power BI

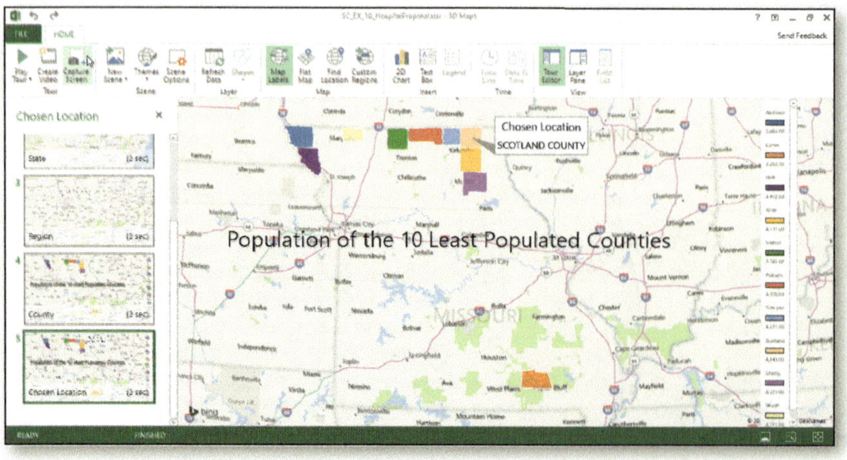

(c) 3D Maps

Figure 10–2

Figure 10–3 illustrates the requirements document for the Hospital Proposal workbook. It includes the needs, source of data, and other facts about its development.

Worksheet Title	Demographic Analysis for Proposed Rural Hospital
Needs	The business analytics firm would like to present a variety of data visualizations to the client, including: 1. The 10 least populous counties in order from least to most, and income for each. 2. A list of all of the counties in the state, along with the number of housing units in each, and the total area represented in square miles. 3. A Power Pivot report combining the data sources to show the relationship between county, population, and housing units. 4. A Power BI report showing the population, housing units, square miles, and median household income for each county. 5. An animated map showing the counties with the least population. 6. An attractive opening worksheet with hyperlinks to each of the above items, 1 through 5, a hyperlink to the Power BI website, and a symbol.
Source of Data	Data is available in two external sources, downloaded from the U.S. Census Bureau: Support_EX_10_MOHousingSqMiles.xlsx and Support_EX_10_MOPopulationIncomeByCounty.xlsx.
Calculations	Average occupancy rate for each county, which is calculated by taking the population of the county divided by the number of housing units. This calculation will appear in the Power Pivot report.

Figure 10–3

Workflow

Recall that in previous modules you imported data from a variety of sources including an Access database, a Word table, a comma-delimited text file, and a table from the web. The workflow to create connections for use with the power tools is similar:

- **Connect to the data:** Make connections to data in the cloud, in a service, or from local sources. You can work with the connected data by creating a permanent connection from your workbook to that data source, ensuring that the data you work with is always up to date.
- **Transform the data:** Shape the data locally to meet your needs; the original source remains unchanged.
- **Combine data from various sources:** Create a data model from multiple data sources and get a unique view into the data.
- **Share the data:** Save, share, or use transformed data for reports and presentations.

With a good understanding of the requirements and an understanding of the necessary decisions, the next step is to use Excel to create the workbook. In this module, you will learn how to create the workbook and Power BI report shown in Figures 10–1 and 10–2.

BTW

The Ribbon and Screen Resolution

Excel may change how the groups and buttons within the groups appear on the ribbon, depending on the computer's screen resolution. Thus, your ribbon may look different from the ones in this book if you are using a screen resolution other than 1366 x 768.

To Create a Workbook

The following steps start Excel and open a blank workbook. Then, after changing the color scheme, you will use the Save As dialog box to save the workbook on your storage device.

1. sam Start Excel.
2. Click the Blank workbook from the template gallery in Backstage view.

3. If necessary, maximize the Excel window.
4. Set the color scheme to Violet.
5. Display Backstage view, click Save As, and then click Browse to open the Save As dialog box.
6. Browse to your storage device.
7. In the File name box, type SC_EX_10_HospitalProposal as the file name.
8. Click Save (Save As dialog box) to save the file.

To Copy Data Files

Sometimes data sources move to different locations. You probably have noticed while surfing the web that some webpages no longer exist or have been redirected. On your computer, you may have links that no longer work after moving a file to a different folder. Therefore, if you are using local data—that is, the data stored on your computer—it is a good idea to store the workbook and any connected data sources in the same folder location.

The following steps copy two files from the Data Files to your storage location. See your instructor for more information about this process. If you already have downloaded the Data Files to the same storage location that you are using to create and save files in this module, you can skip these steps.

To complete these steps, you will be required to use the Data Files. Please contact your instructor for information about accessing the Data Files.

1. Click the File Explorer button on the Windows taskbar to open a File Explorer window.
2. Navigate to the location of the Data Files for this module.
3. Select both the Support_EX_10_MOHousingSqMiles.xlsx file and the Support_EX_10_MOPopulationIncomeByCounty.xlsx file, and then copy and paste the files into your storage location folder.
4. Close the File Explorer window.

To Enable Data Analysis

The following steps verify that Data Analysis has been enabled in the version of Excel that you are running. **Why?** Data analysis commands are required in order to use the power tools and they are not enabled by default in a standard Excel installation.

1

- Display Backstage view and then click Options to open the Excel Options dialog box.
- In the left pane of the dialog box, click Data to display the Data options area.
- If necessary, click to display a check mark in the 'Enable Data Analysis add-ins: Power Pivot, Power View and 3D Maps' check box (Figure 10–4).

Q&A

I do not see the Enable option. What should I do?

You may have a version of Excel that does not support data analysis and the power tools. Continue with the steps and contact your instructor or IT administrator.

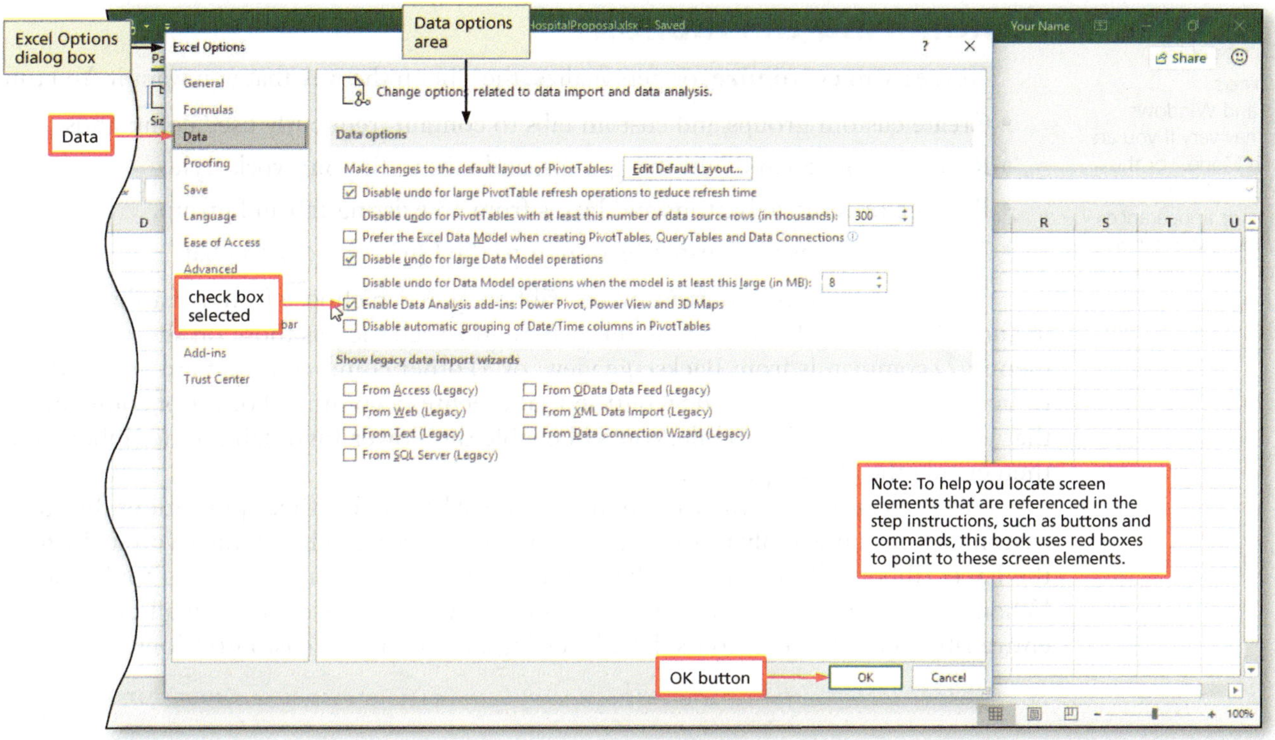

Figure 10–4

2

- Click OK (Excel Options dialog box) to close the dialog box and enable the data analysis tools.

Q&A **Should I see a change in Excel?**
No. Changing the setting ensures that you will not see an error message when you try to use the power tools later in the module.

To Add in Power Map

If you could not enable data analysis in the previous steps, you may need to add Power Map to your version of Excel in order to run 3D Maps. Recall from a previous module that you used the Add-ins option to add Solver to Excel. The following steps add in Power Map.

1. Display Backstage view and then click Options to open the Excel Options dialog box.
2. In the left pane of the dialog box, click Add-ins to display the Add-ins options.
3. Near the bottom of the dialog box, click the Manage arrow and then click COM Add-ins.
4. Click the Go button to open the COM Add-ins dialog box.
5. Click to display a check mark in the 'Microsoft Power Map for Excel' check box. If you have a check box for Power Pivot, select that as well.
6. Click OK (COM Add-ins dialog box).

BTW
Touch Screen Differences
The Office and Windows interfaces may vary if you are using Touch Mode. For this reason, you might notice that the function or appearance of your touch screen differs slightly from this module's presentation.

Customizing the Ribbon

It is easy to **customize**, or personalize, the ribbon the way that you want it. You can

- Create custom groups and custom tabs to contain frequently used commands.
- Rearrange or rename buttons, groups, and tabs to fit your work style.
- Rename or remove buttons and boxes from an existing tab and group.
- Add new buttons to a custom group or to the Quick Access Toolbar.

When you add new buttons to the ribbon, you can choose from a list that includes 1) commands that you use elsewhere in Excel, such as those on shortcut menus; 2) commands from Backstage view; or 3) other commands that are not on the ribbon. Or, you can create a new button that executes a command or set of commands that you record. In this module, you will enable the Power Pivot tab on the ribbon and then enable the Developer tab.

You can customize the ribbon in all of the Microsoft Office applications, but the customizations only apply to the application you are using. The changes you make to the Excel ribbon will not change the ribbon in any other Microsoft Office application. When you no longer need the customization, it can be removed individually, or the entire ribbon can be reset to its default settings, removing all customizations.

Consider This

What should I keep in mind when customizing the ribbon?

- Customize the ribbon when you need to access new features of Excel, or when you regularly need to access commands that are not part of the ribbon already.
- If the new command will be used at various times, with different tabs, consider adding the command or button to the Quick Access Toolbar.
- If you need to add a single command to the ribbon, choose a tab with plenty of room to hold the new command and its new group.
- If you need to add several commands, consider creating a new tab on the ribbon.
- If you are using a computer in a lab situation, you may not have permission to change the ribbon. Check with your instructor or IT administrator.
- If you are using a computer in a lab situation, reset the ribbon when you are done.

To Customize the Ribbon

The following steps customize the ribbon. **Why?** Due to space constraints on the ribbon and the advanced nature of the power tools, some of the commands do not appear automatically. You will enable the Power Pivot tab on the ribbon and then enable the Developer tab that you will use later in the module.

The Power Pivot tool is not available in all versions of Excel. If you do not see the Power Pivot tab in the following steps, contact your instructor or IT administrator to see if your version of Excel can run Power Pivot; you may have to use an Add-in process.

1

- Right-click a blank area of the ribbon to display the shortcut menu (Figure 10–5).

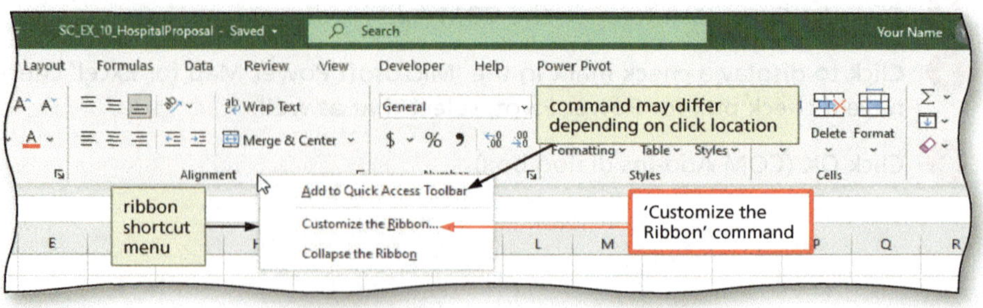

Figure 10–5

2

- Click the 'Customize the Ribbon' command on the shortcut menu to display the Customize Ribbon area of the Excel Options dialog box.
- In the Main Tabs area, scroll as necessary, and then click to display a check mark in both the Developer and the Power Pivot check boxes, if necessary (Figure 10–6).

Q&A **I do not see Power Pivot. What should I do?**
Contact your instructor or IT administrator to see if your version of Excel can run Power Pivot. If not, you can still continue with these steps and use the Developer ribbon.

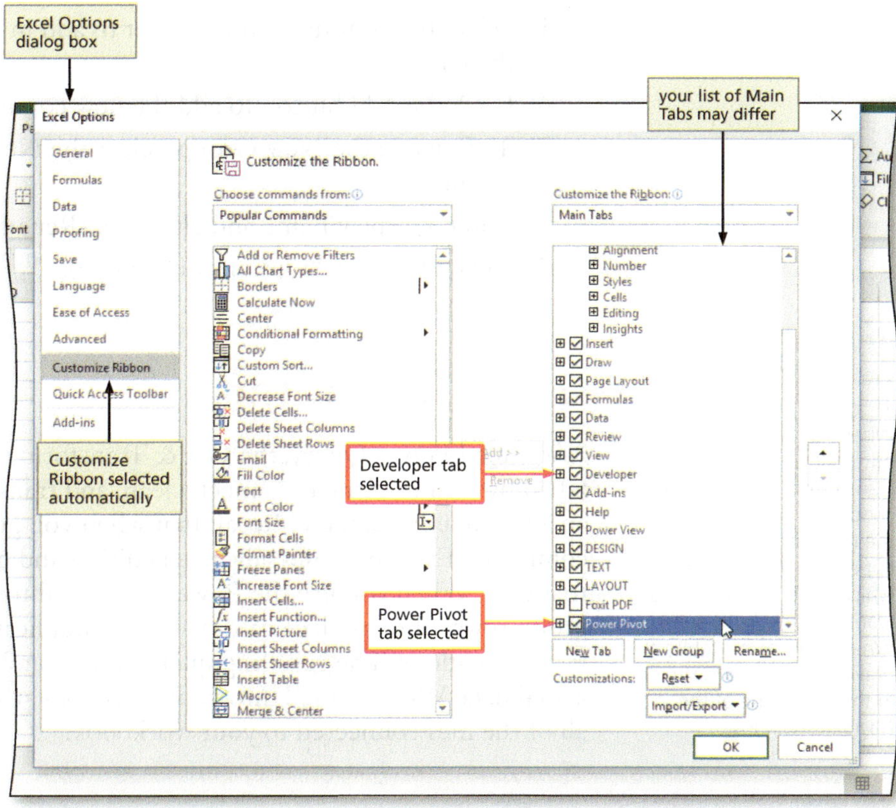

Figure 10–6

3

- Click OK (Excel Options dialog box) to display the customization on the ribbon (Figure 10–7).

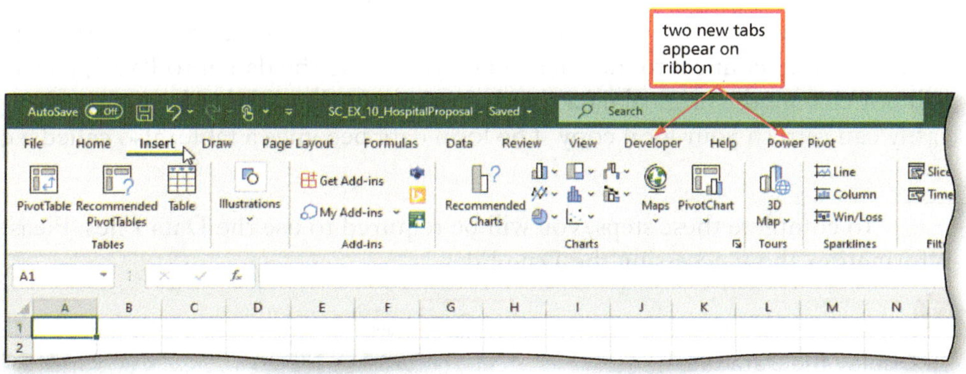

Figure 10–7

Other Ways

1. Display Backstage view, click Options, click Customize Ribbon (Excel Options dialog box), click appropriate check box in Main Tabs list, click OK

To Add a New Group

If you wanted to add a new group to customize the ribbon, you would perform the following steps.

1. Right-click a blank area of the ribbon to display the shortcut menu.
2. Click the 'Customize the Ribbon' command on the shortcut menu to display the Excel Options dialog box.
3. In the Main Tabs area, navigate to and then select the tab where you want the New Group to be added.
4. Click the New Group button to insert a New Group in the selected tab.

5. Select the command(s) you want to add in the new group from the column on the left.
6. Click the Add button to add the new command(s) to the New Group.
7. To Rename the New Group, select the New Group and click the Rename button.
8. Enter a display name and click OK (Rename dialog box).
9. Click OK (Excel Options dialog box).

BTW

Getting Data from Access Databases

When you click the Get Data button (Data Tab | Get & Transform Data group) and choose an Access database, the Navigator window appears so you can select which table (or tables) you want to use in your query. When you select a table, a preview of its data is shown in the right pane of the Navigator window.

Get & Transform

Also called Power Query, the Get & Transform commands located on the Data tab allow you to extract, connect, clean, and transform large amounts of data into an accessible Excel table. Recall that when you get data using a Get & Transform command, Excel provides advanced editing and querying techniques to use with that data. When you use the Power Query Editor, you are provided with tools to group rows, filter, replace values, remove duplicates, and edit columns to facilitate transformations. The resulting query table then becomes a displayed subset of the actual data. When loaded into your workbook, the Queries & Connections pane shows all of the files connected to your workbook.

To Get Data

The following steps connect to a table with data provided by the U.S. Census Bureau for the state of Missouri. The table is located in the Data Files. **Why?** Connecting with the U.S. Census Bureau website is somewhat cumbersome and requires many steps. You will use the Get Data button (Data tab | Get & Transform Data group) to connect to the data. When you bring the data into Excel, you are working with a local copy; you will not change the original data source in any way. Should the data source be updated externally, however, you easily can refresh your local copy. The local data becomes a table, also called a query.

To complete these steps, you will be required to use the Data Files. Please contact your instructor for information about accessing the Data Files.

1

- Display the Data tab.
- Click the Get Data button (Data tab | Get & Transform Data group) to display the Get Data menu.
- Point to the From File command to display the From File submenu (Figure 10–8).

Experiment

- Point to the other commands on the Get Data menu and look at the various sources from which you can get data. When you are done, point to From File again.

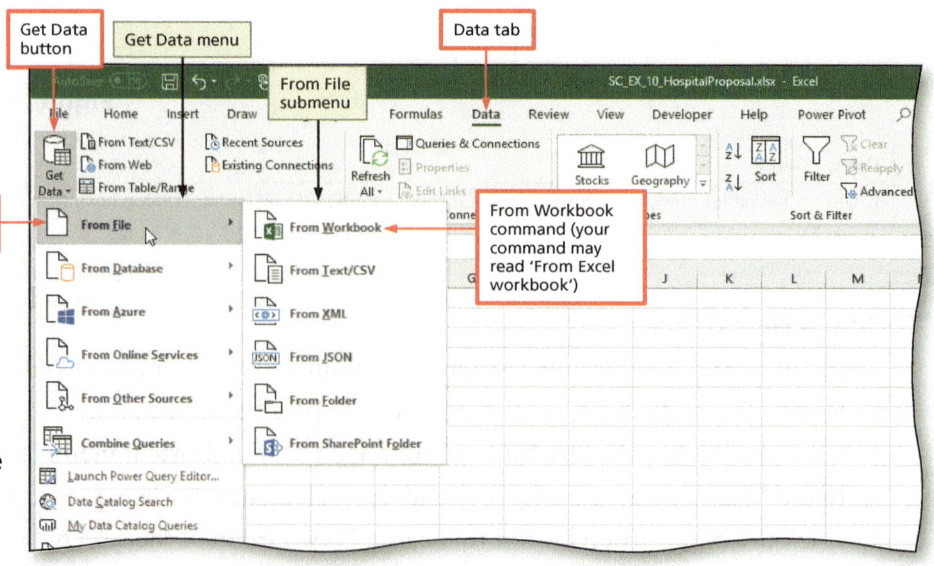

Figure 10–8

2

- Click From Workbook (or' From Excel Workbook') on the From File submenu to display the Import Data dialog box.
- If necessary, navigate to your storage location to display the files (Figure 10–9).

Q&A

Could I have clicked From Web and navigated to the Census data?
Yes; however, you would have had to perform many additional steps to drill down to the desired data for this project.

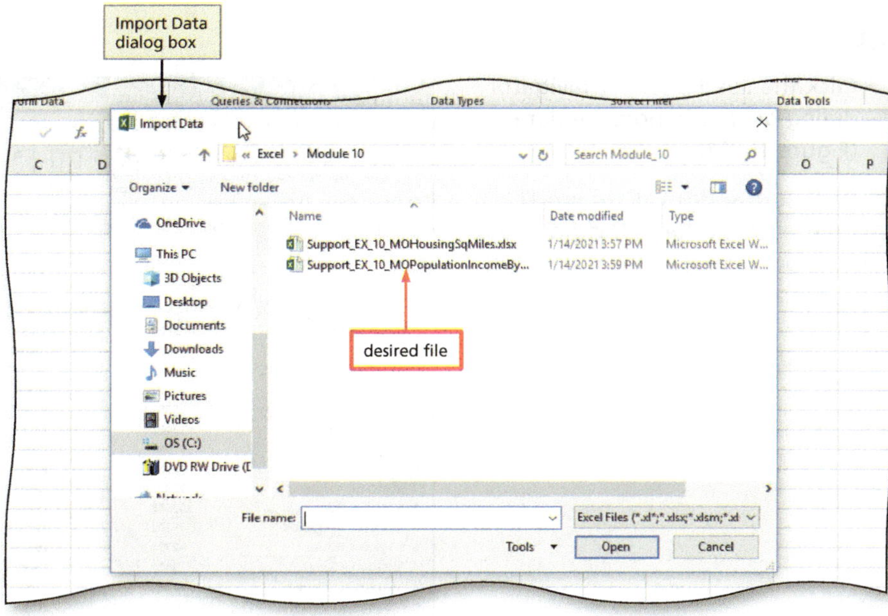

Figure 10–9

3

- Double-click the file named Support_EX_10_MOPopulationIncomeByCounty.xlsx to display the Navigator dialog box.
- Click the table named Population & Income to preview the data (Figure 10–10).

Q&A

What does the Transform Data button do?
If you know that you want to edit the data before creating the query, you can click the Transform Data button to display the Power Query Editor window.

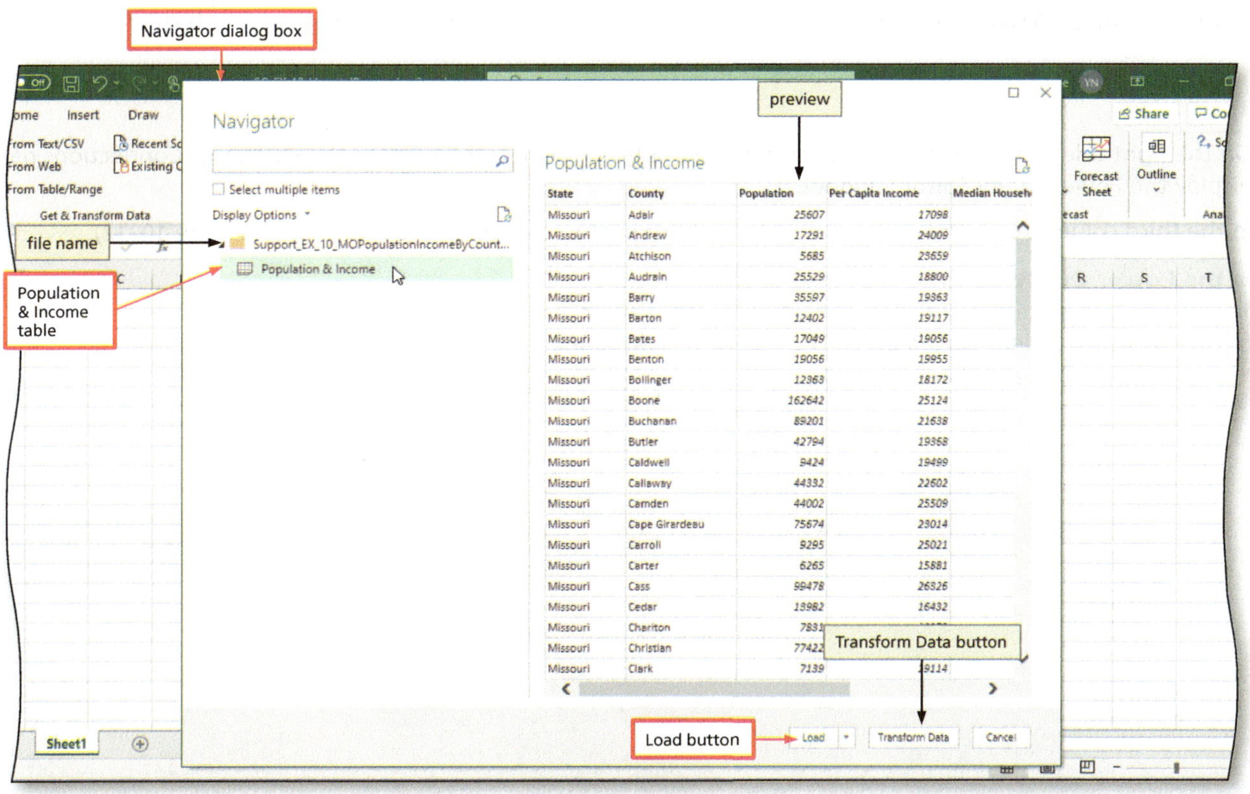

Figure 10–10

4

- Click the Load button (Navigator dialog box) to import the data (Figure 10–11).

Q&A **How is the data displayed?**
Excel shows column headings and 117 rows of data for the counties in Missouri in a table format, using colors from the chosen color scheme.

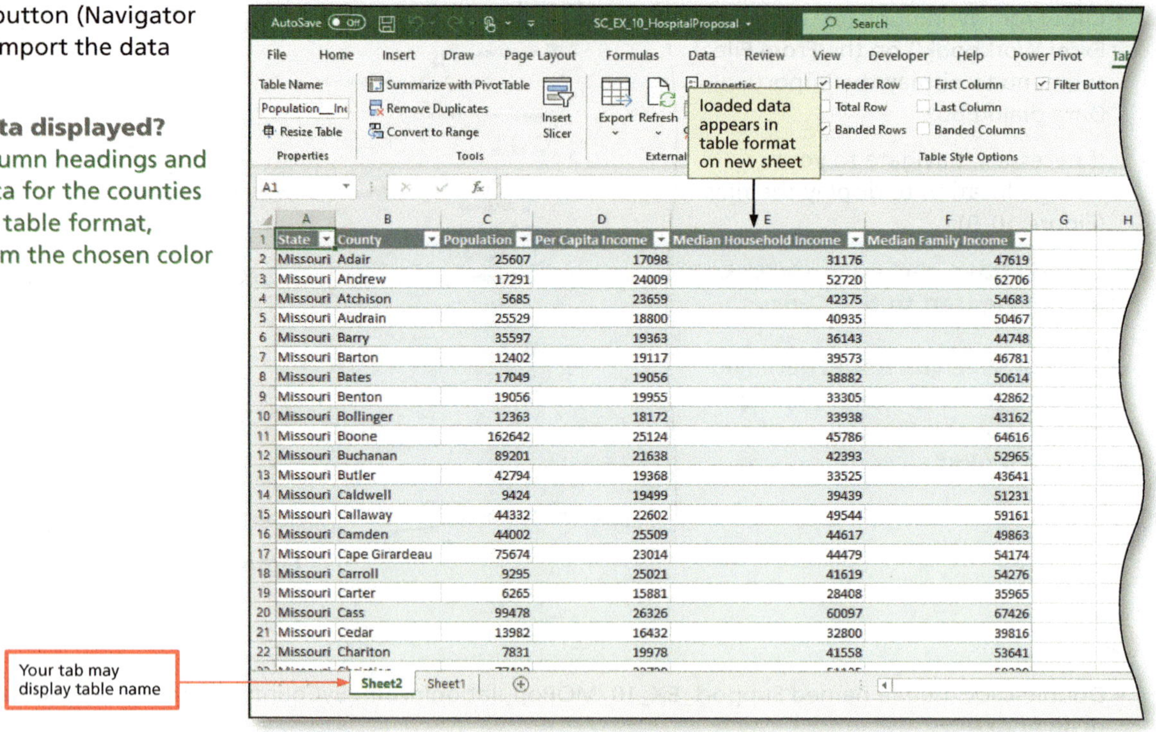

Figure 10–11

To Edit Data Using the Power Query Editor

In the following steps you will use the Power Query Editor to sort the data and only display the 10 least populous counties. **Why?** The RHAC wants to narrow down the counties to the places with the fewest people.

1

- On the right side of the screen, double-click the 'Population & Income' query in the Queries & Connections pane to display the Power Query Editor window.
- In the third column, click the Population column filter button to display the filter menu (Figure 10–12).

Q&A **Is the Power Query Editor a separate app?**
The Power Query Editor window is like an app within an app; it has its own ribbon, tabs, and groups and is navigated independently from Excel. The Query Settings pane on the right allows you to make changes to the data and keeps track of each change in order.

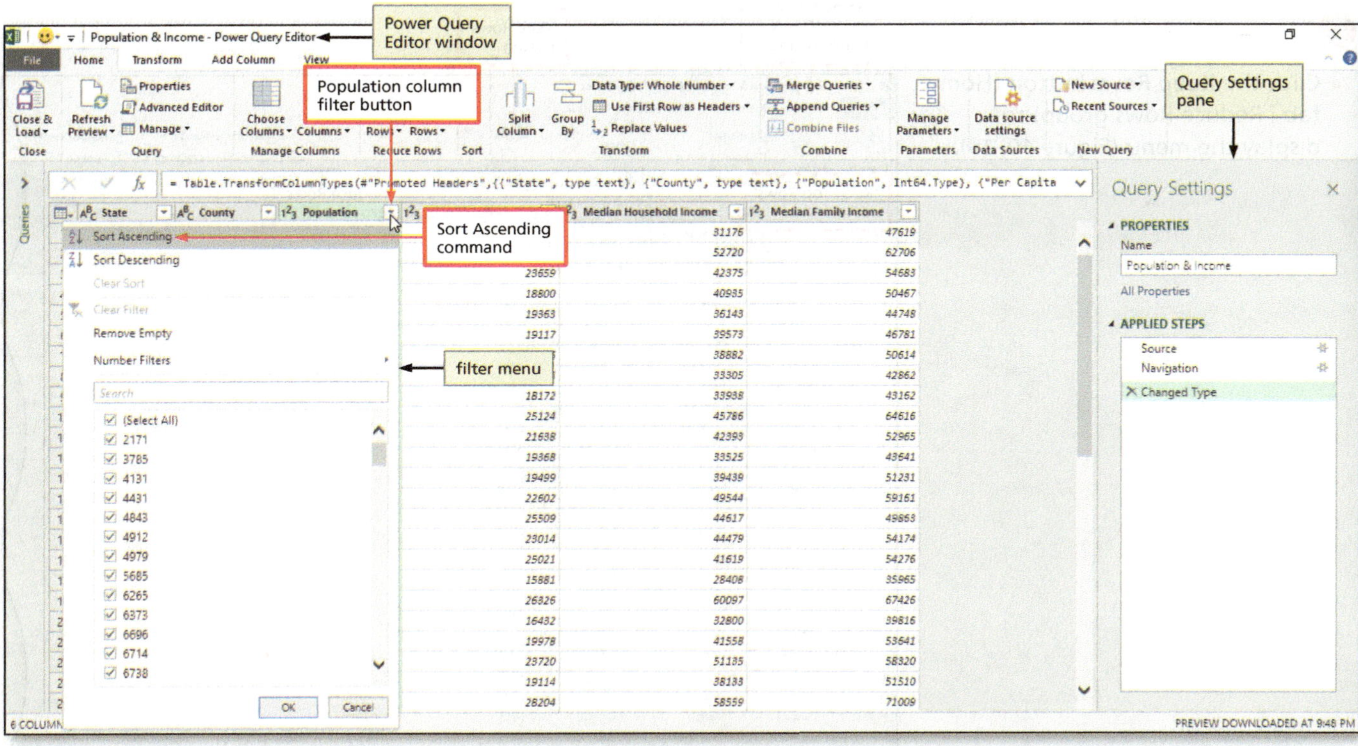

Figure 10–12

2

- On the filter menu, click Sort Ascending to sort the data in order by population with the least populous county first (Figure 10–13).

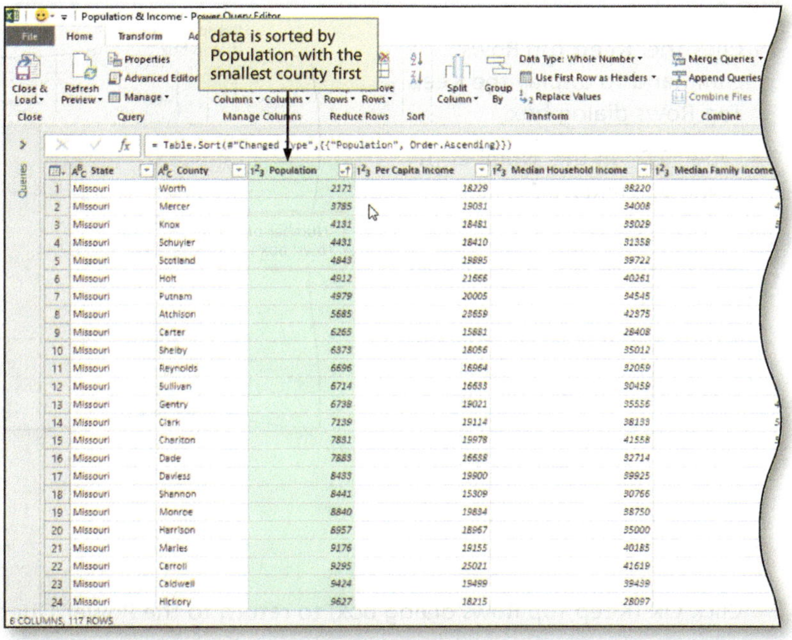

Figure 10–13

3

- Click the Keep Rows button (Home tab | Reduce Rows group) to display the menu (Figure 10–14).

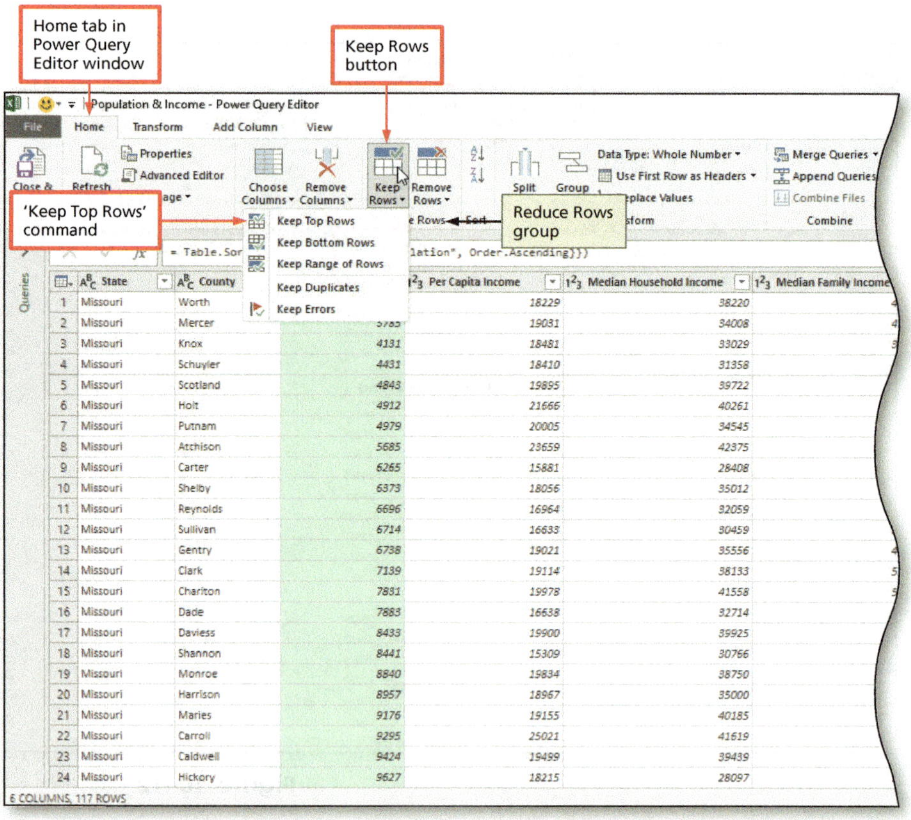

Figure 10–14

4

- Click the 'Keep Top Rows' command to display the Keep Top Rows dialog box.
- Type `10` in the 'Number of rows' box (Figure 10–15).

Q&A **Could I have just deleted the rows in the main Excel window?**
You could have; however, that would permanently delete the local copy of the data. Using the Power Query Editor, you can restore the data if you need it later.

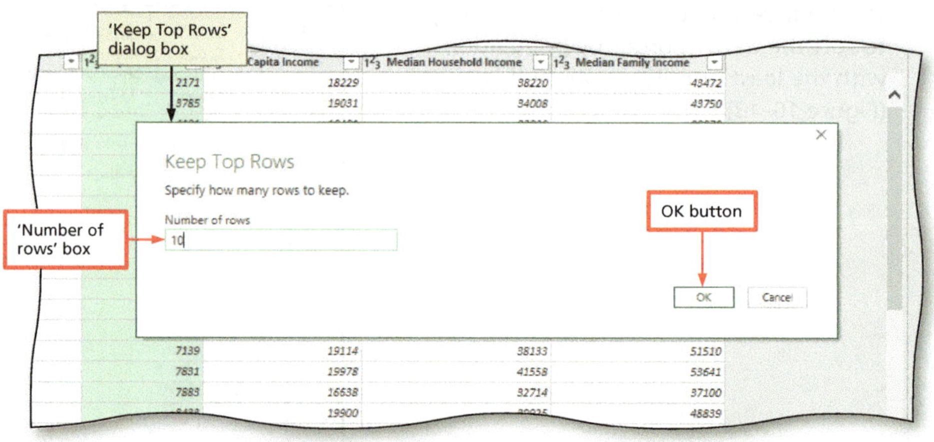

Figure 10–15

5

- Click OK (Keep Top Rows dialog box) to return to the Power Query Editor window (Figure 10–16).

Q&A **What happens if my source data moves?**
If you suspect that your source data has moved, display the Power Query Editor window and then click the Refresh Preview button (Power Query Editor window | Home tab | Query group). If an error message appears, click the 'Go To Error' button, click the Edit Details button, and then navigate to the new location of the file. When your table appears, click the final step in the Applied Steps area. You may have to click the Expand Data filter button in the Data column and remove extraneous columns.

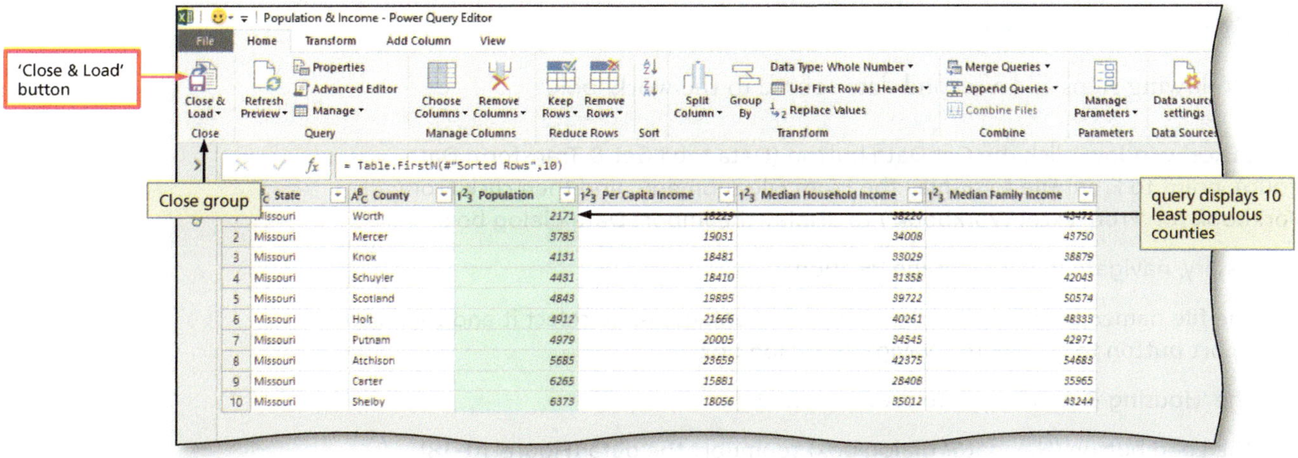

Figure 10–16

6

- Click the 'Close & Load' button (Home tab | Close group) to load the transformed data into the worksheet in the Excel window.
- Rename the sheet tab with the name `10 Least Counties`.
- Recolor the sheet tab with the color Lavender, Accent 1 (Figure 10–17).

Experiment

- Point to the file on the Queries & Connections pane to see the preview window.

Q&A

What is the new tab on the ribbon?

It is the Query tab (shown in Figure 10–17), which allows you to make additional queries easily. The tab appears when you click anywhere in the data itself.

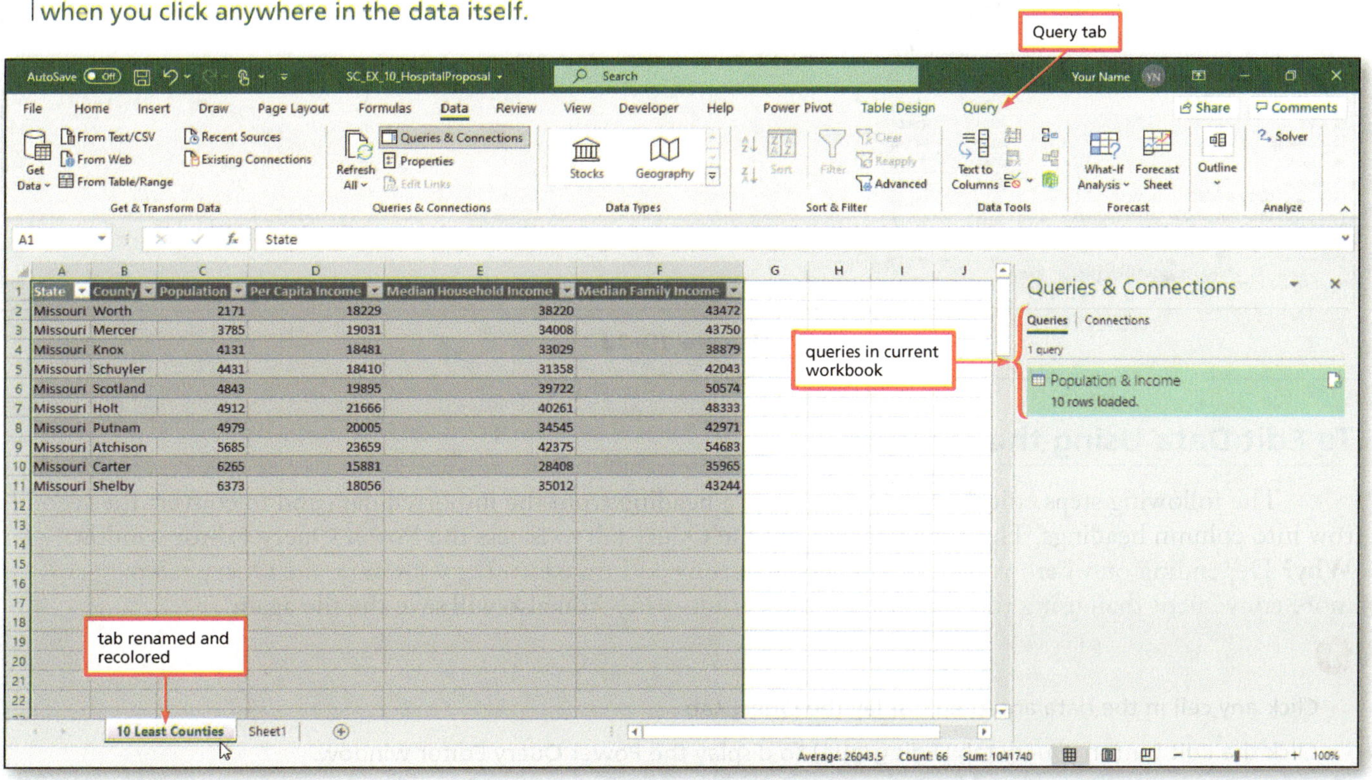

Figure 10–17

Other Ways

1. Click Edit button (Query tab | Edit group), filter data, edit columns and rows, click 'Close & Load' button
2. Right-click table in Queries & Connections pane, click Edit (shortcut menu), filter data, edit columns and rows, click 'Close & Load' button

To Get Another Data Source

The following steps add a second data source to the workbook.

1. In the Excel window, click the Get Data button (Data tab | Get & Transform Data group), point to From File to display the From File submenu, and then click From Workbook (or 'From Excel Workbook') to display the Import Data dialog box.
2. If necessary, navigate to your storage location.
3. Click the file named Support_EX_10_MOHousingSqMiles.xlsx to select it and then click the Import button to display the Navigator dialog box.
4. Click the 'Housing & Area' table to preview the data.
5. Click the Load button (Navigator dialog box) to import the data (Figure 10–18).

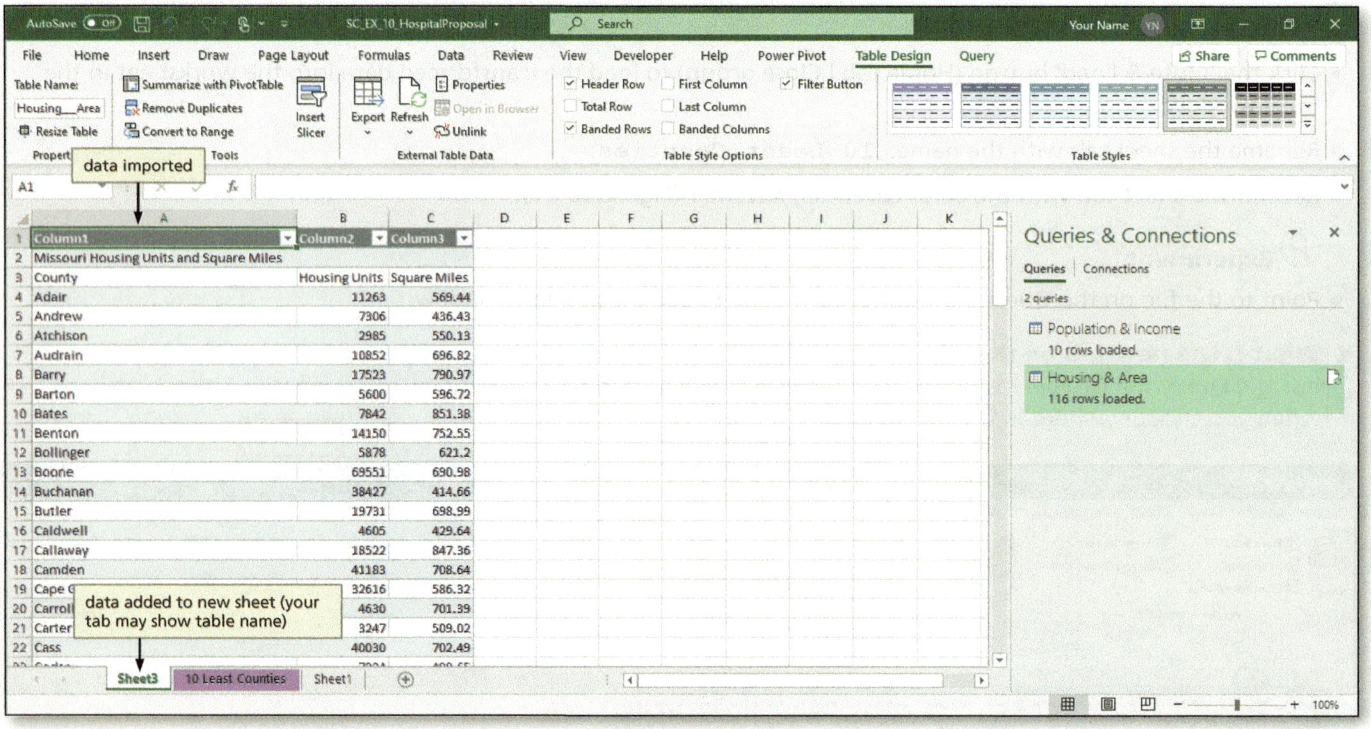

Figure 10–18

To Edit Data Using the Query Tab

The following steps edit the query to remove a heading from the imported data and to convert the second row into column headings. This time you will use the Query tab to access the Power Query Editor window. **Why?** Depending on where you in the process of getting and transforming your data, the Query tab may be more convenient than using the Queries & Connections pane. You also will save the file again.

1.
- Click any cell in the data and then display the Query tab.
- Click the Edit button (Query tab | Edit group) to display the Power Query Editor window.
- In the Power Query Editor window, click the Remove Rows button (Power Query Editor Home tab | Reduce Rows group) to display the Remove Rows menu (Figure 10–19).

Q&A

How can I delete columns using the Power Query Editor?

You can delete columns using the Remove Columns button (Power Query Editor Home tab | Manage Columns group).

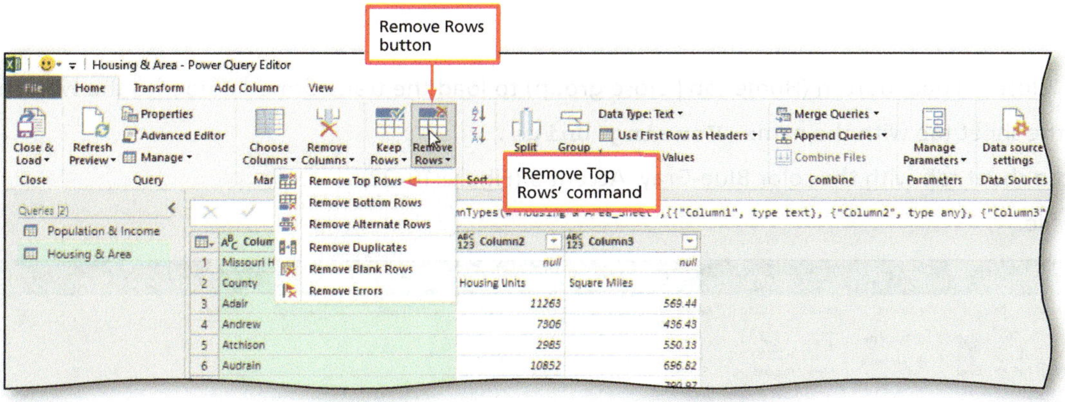

Figure 10–19

2

- Click the 'Remove Top Rows' command to display the Remove Top Rows dialog box.
- Type 1 in the Number of rows box (Figure 10–20).

Q&A **Why am I removing the first row?**
The first row is the title of the imported worksheet; it is not part of the data itself.

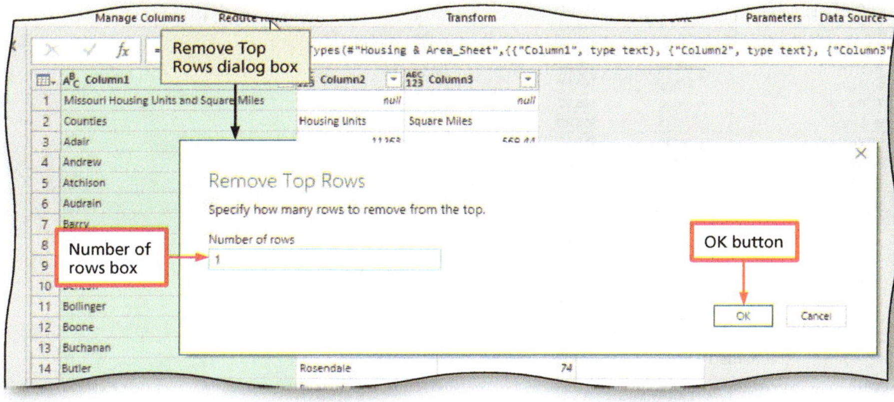

Figure 10–20

3

- Click OK (Remove Top Rows dialog box) to remove the first row.
- Click the 'Use First Row as Headers' button (Home tab | Transform group) to use the imported table's column headings (Figure 10–21).

Q&A **What is the Applied Steps area in the Query Settings pane?**
The Applied Steps area displays each manipulation that you performed on the data, in order. You can click a step to return to that view of the data or delete the step. Your list of steps may vary.

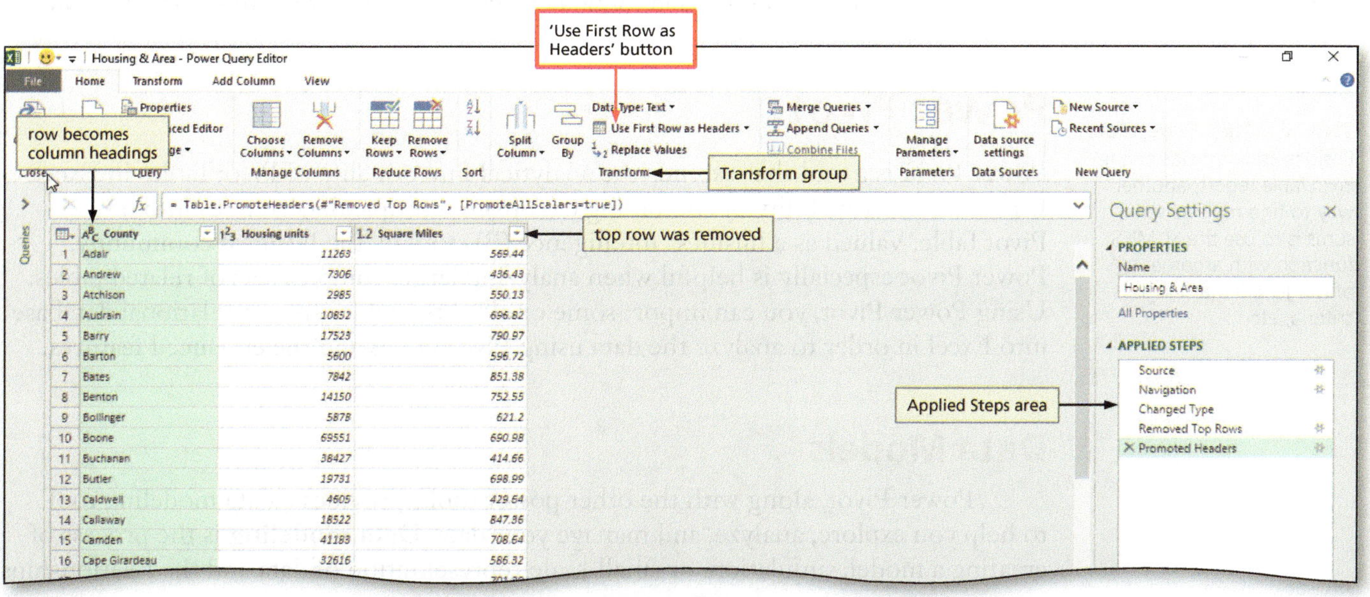

Figure 10–21

4

- Click the 'Close & Load' button (Home tab | Close group) to load the transformed data into the worksheet.
- Rename the sheet tab with the name **`Housing Units`.**
- Recolor the sheet tab with the color Blue-Gray, Accent 3 (Figure 10–22).
- Save the file.

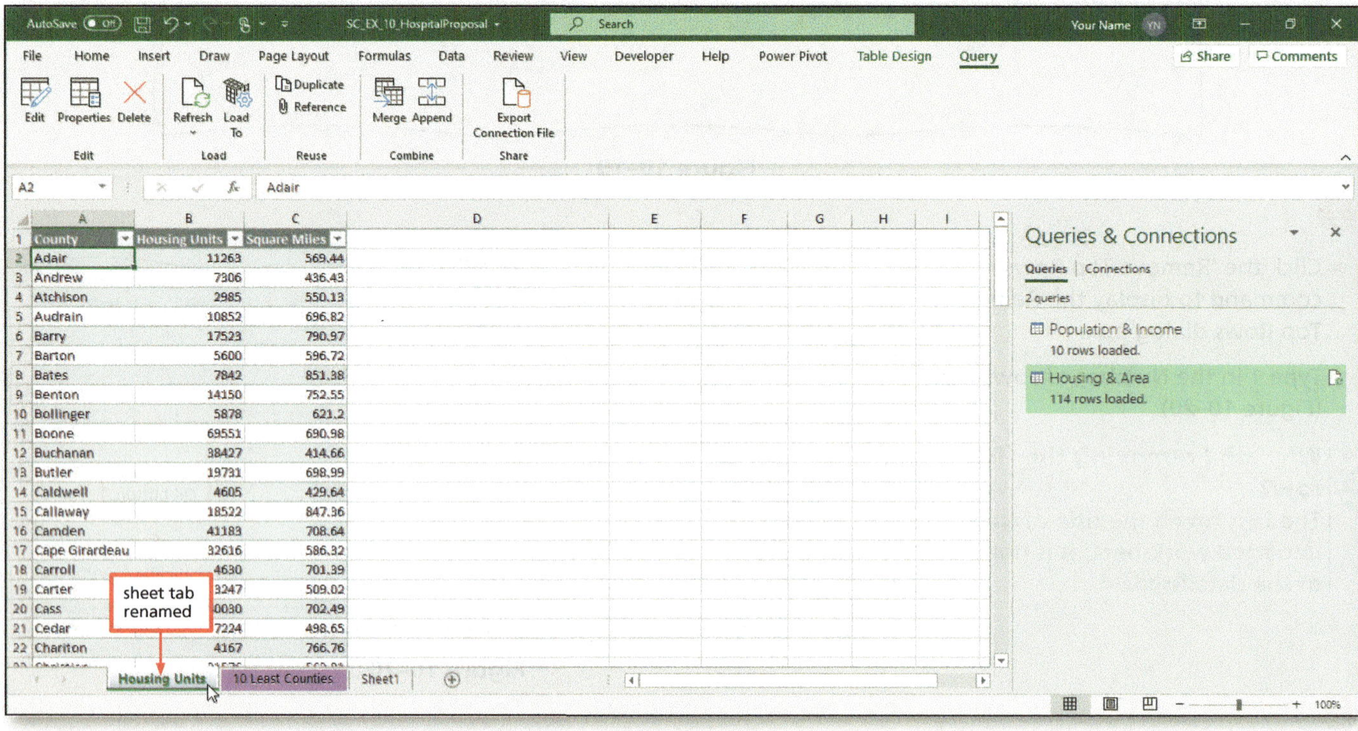

Figure 10–22

Other Ways

1. Double-click 'Housing & Area' query (Queries & Connections pane), filter data, edit columns and rows, click 'Close & Load' button
2. Right-click table in Queries & Connections pane, click Edit (shortcut menu), filter data, edit columns and rows, click 'Close & Load' button

Break Point: If you want to take a break, this is a good place to do so. You can exit Excel now. To resume later, start Excel, open the file called SC_EX_10_HospitalProposal.xlsx, and continue following the steps from this location forward.

BTW

The SUMIFS Function

Besides adding fields to the PivotTable report, another way to find multi-criteria sums is to use the SUMIFS function with arguments of range, criteria, range, criteria, etc.

Power Pivot

Power Pivot is a tool that extends the analytical functionality of PivotTables in Excel. It includes the capability of combining data from multiple data sources into one PivotTable. Valued as a business intelligence (BI) tool by the business community, Power Pivot especially is helpful when analyzing large, complex sets of related tables. Using Power Pivot, you can import some or all of the tables from a relational database into Excel in order to analyze the data using PivotTables and the enhanced features.

Data Models

Power Pivot, along with the other power tools, provides a data modeling tool to help you explore, analyze, and manage your data. **Data modeling** is the process of creating a model, simulation, or small-scale representation of data and the relationships among pieces of data. Data modeling often includes multiple ways to view the same data and ensure that all data and processes are identified. A **data model** documents the processes and events to capture and translate complex data into easy-to-understand information. It is an approach for integrating data from multiple tables, effectively building a relational database inside Excel. A **relational database** consists of a collection of tables that can be joined through a common field and that can be accessed or reassembled without having to reorganize the tables.

Consider This

Are data models unique to Power Pivot?

No. You used the concept of a data model when you created PivotTable and PivotChart reports; a field list is a visual representation of a data model. The difference between Power Pivot and a PivotTable is that you can create a more sophisticated data model using Power Pivot. When importing relational data, the creation of a data model occurs automatically when you select multiple tables. However, if the tables are from different sources, they may have to be added to the data model manually.

To Add a Query to a Data Model

Recall that a query is a request for information from a data source. The following steps add a query to the data model. **Why?** You cannot create the Power Pivot PivotTable unless queries are added to the data model. You will use the 'Add to Data Model' command. If you do not have Power Pivot, simply read these steps.

1

- If necessary, display the Housing Units worksheet and then click in the table to make it active.
- Click Power Pivot on the ribbon to display the Power Pivot tab (Figure 10–23).

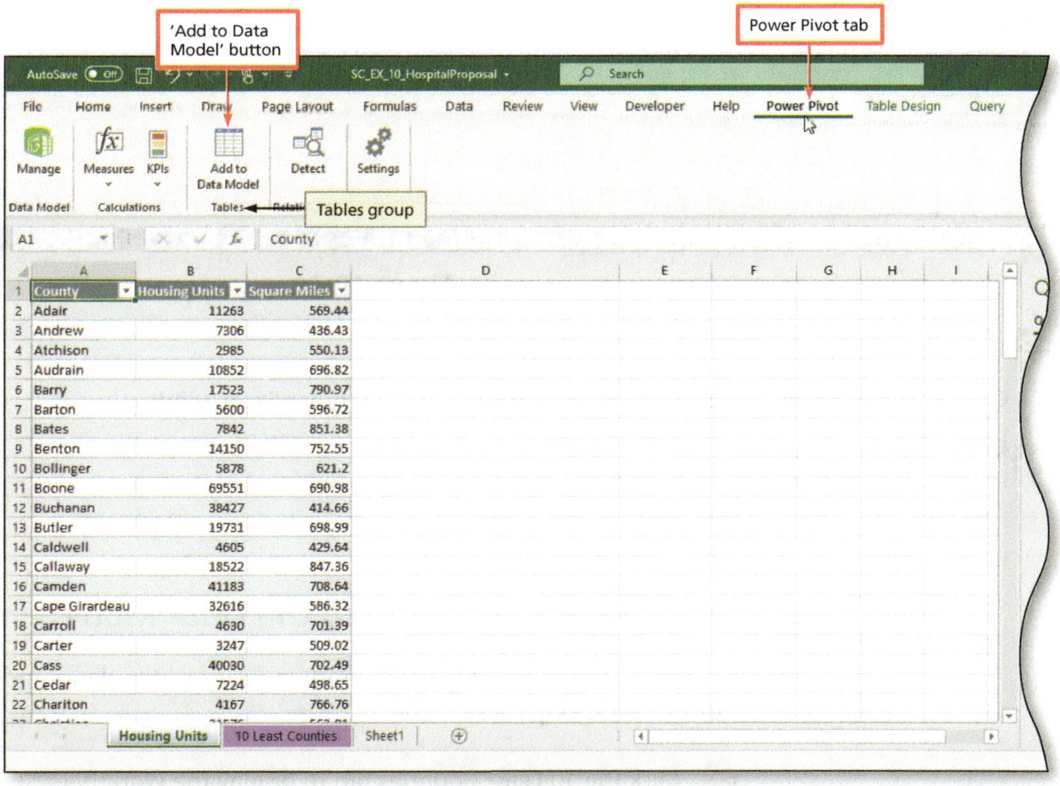

Figure 10–23

2

- Click the 'Add to Data Model' button (Power Pivot tab | Tables group) to add the data on the current worksheet to the data model and to display the Power Pivot for Excel window. Maximize the window, if necessary (Figure 10–24).

Q&A

What window is displayed?
Excel displays the maximized Power Pivot for Excel window that contains tabs and groups used when working with multiple tables from multiple sources.

My column headings do not display the entire name. Is that a problem?
No. You can widen the column, however, by dragging the column heading border to the right.

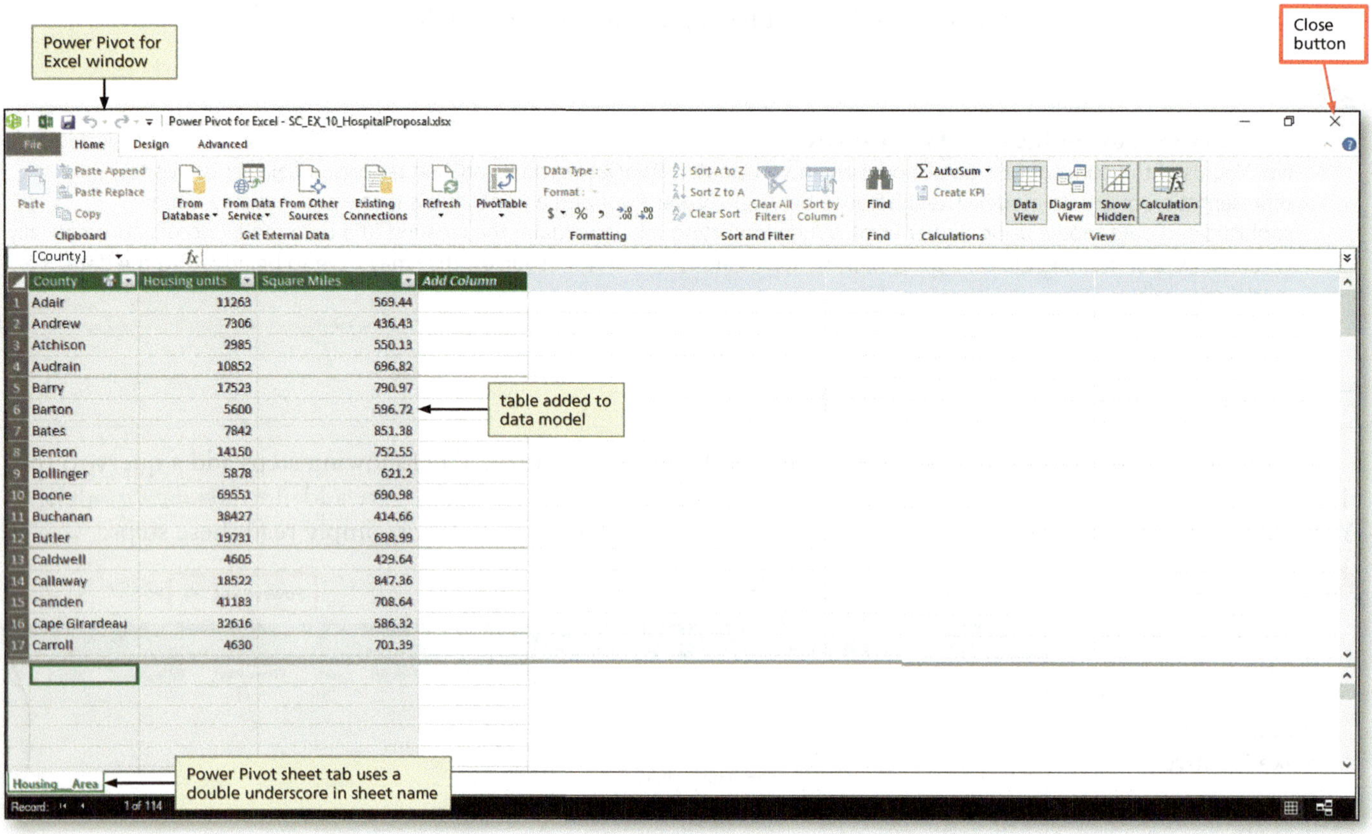

Figure 10–24

3

- Close the Power Pivot for Excel window to return to the regular Excel window.

Q&A

Did anything change on the screen?
No, but behind the scenes Excel added the file to the data model.

To Add Another Query to the Data Model

The following steps add another query to the data model. If you do not have Power Pivot, skip these steps.

1. Click the 10 Least Counties tab to display the worksheet.
2. Click any cell in the data.
3. Click the 'Add to Data Model' button (Power Pivot tab | Tables group) to add a second query to the data model. Do not close the Power Pivot for Excel window (Figure 10–25).

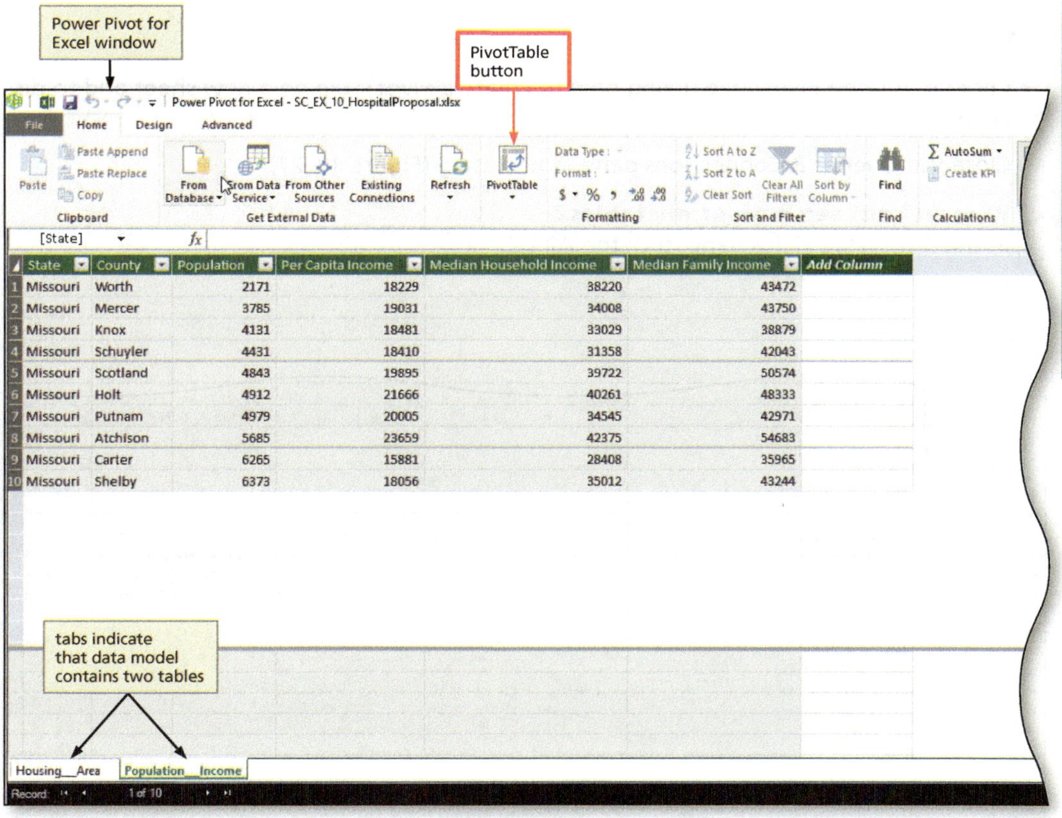

Figure 10–25

To Build a PivotTable Using Power Pivot

The following steps create a PivotTable using Power Pivot, based on the two queries. **Why?** Using Power Pivot provides you with the most flexibility and functionality when building a PivotTable. Once created, you can update a Power Pivot PivotTable in the same way you update regular PivotTables. Simply click the Refresh button (Power PivotTable Analyze tab | Data group). If you do not have access to Power Pivot, you can create a regular PivotTable report.

1

- With the Power Pivot for Excel window still open and any table cell selected, click the PivotTable button (Power Pivot for Excel | PivotTable group) to display the Create PivotTable dialog box.
- If necessary, click the New Worksheet option button to select it (Figure 10–26).

Q&A **Can I make a PivotTable without Power Pivot?**
Yes. Click the PivotTable button (Insert tab | Tables group). In the Create PivotTable dialog box, click to display a check mark in the 'Add this data to the Data Model' check box.

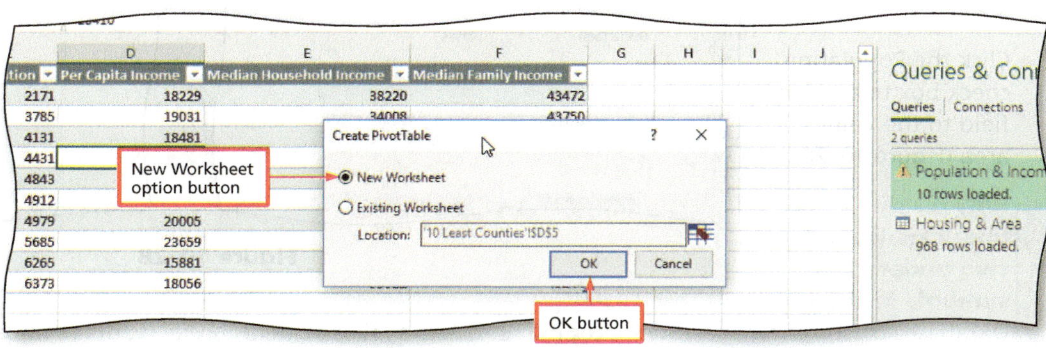

Figure 10–26

2

- Click OK (Create PivotTable dialog box) to create a PivotTable on a new sheet and to display the PivotTable Fields pane.
- Close the Queries & Connections pane, if necessary (Figure 10–27).

Q&A **Why do I not see both of my tables?**
In the PivotTable Fields pane, click the All tab.

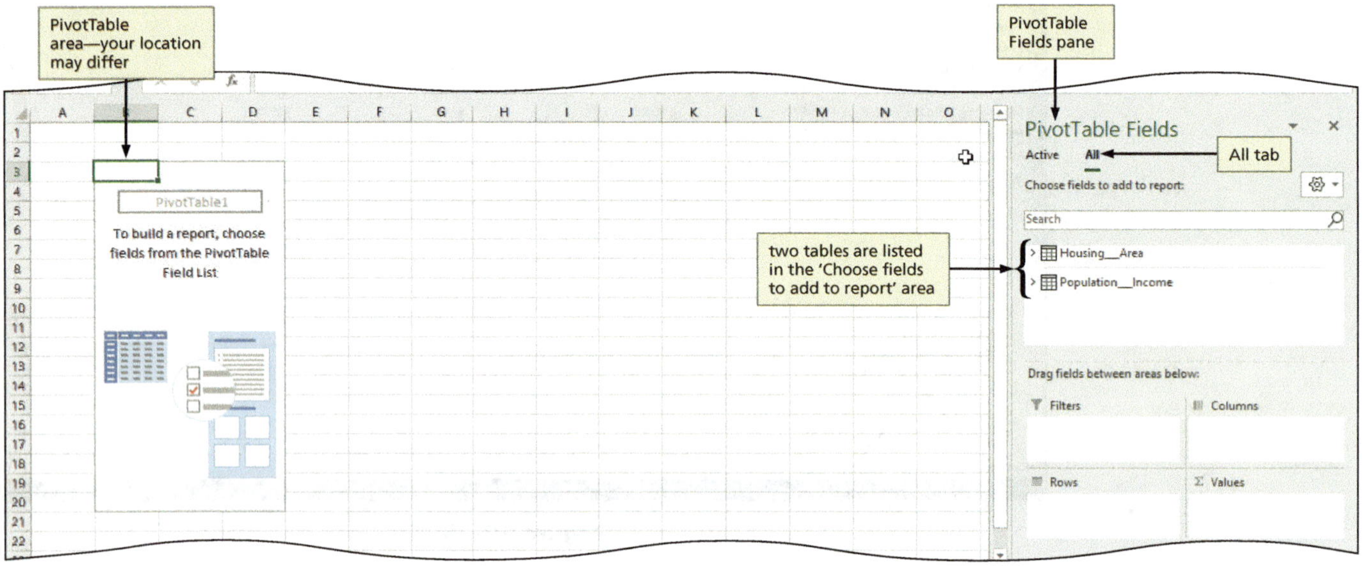

Figure 10–27

3

- In the PivotTable Fields pane, click Population__Income to display the fields from the query table.
- Click the check boxes beside State and County to add the fields to the Rows area.
- Click the Population check box to add the field to the Values area (Figure 10–28).

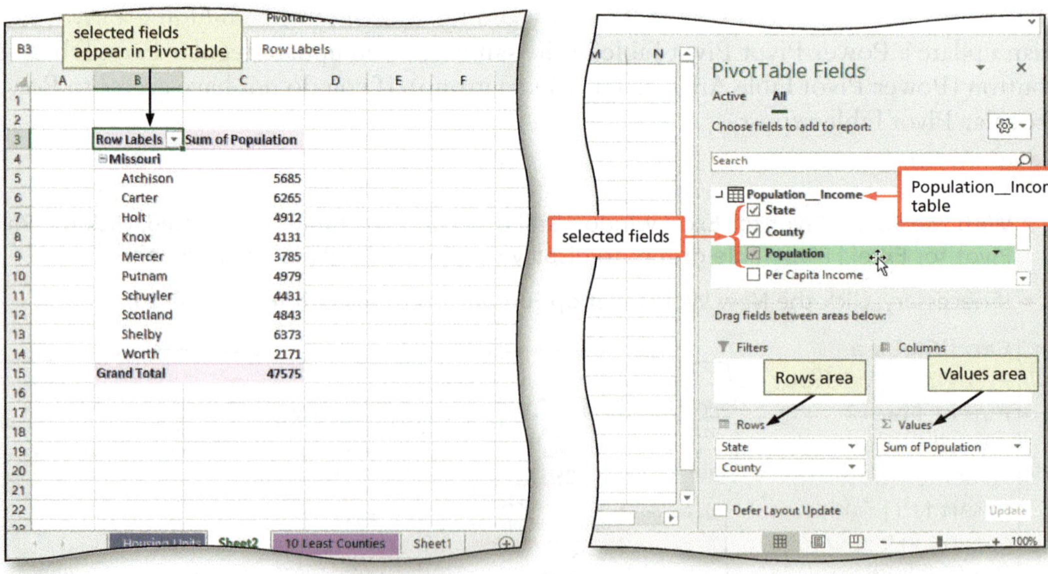

Figure 10–28

Q&A **Why do the query tables use two underscore symbols in their name?**
Database structures rarely allow spaces in the names of files or fields. Excel wants to make sure the data can be used in many kinds of databases.

4

- Scroll up in the 'Choose fields to add to the report' area (PivotTable Fields pane) and then click Housing__Area to display the fields from the query (Figure 10–29).

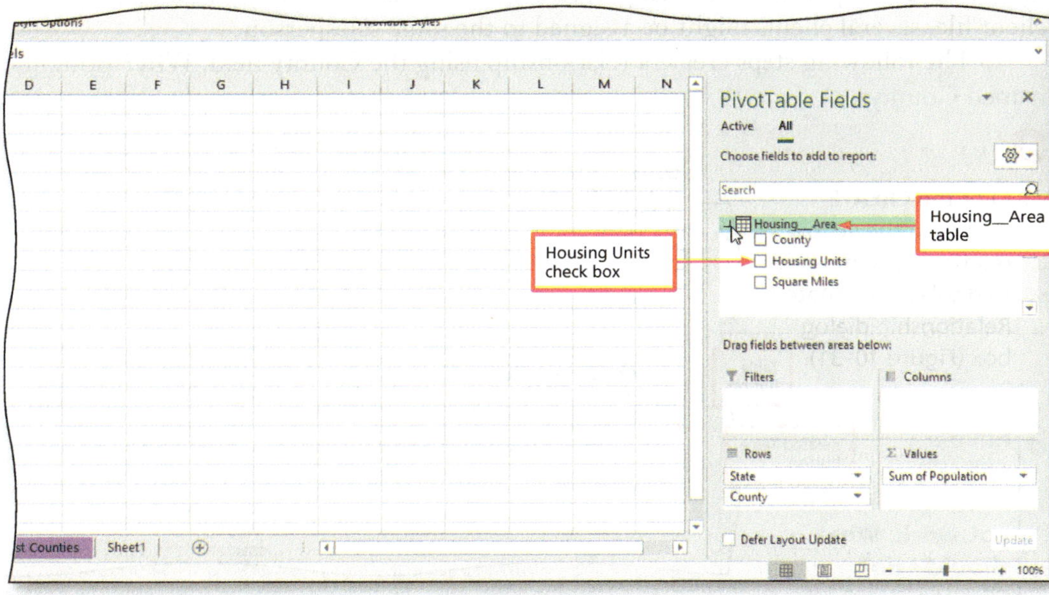

Figure 10–29

5

- Click the Housing Units check box to add the field to the Values area (Figure 10–30) and display a yellow message about table relationships.

Q&A **Why do all of the counties have the same number of housing units?**
The PivotTable does not associate the housing units with the counties automatically. You will create that relationship in the next series of steps.

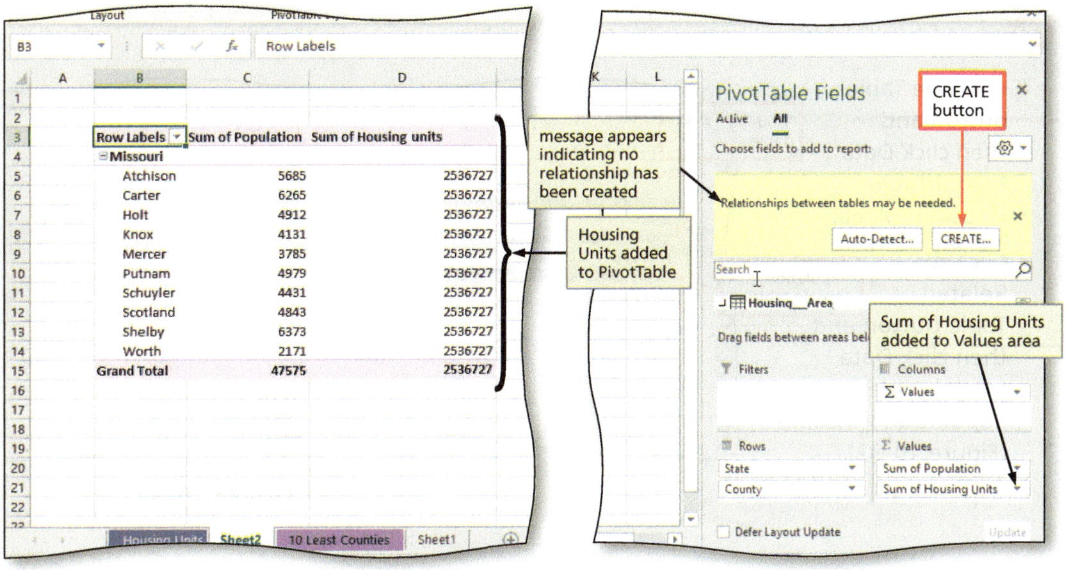

Figure 10–30

To Create a Relationship

A **relationship** is a field or column that two data sources have in common. For example, a payroll file and a human resource file might each have a field named employee_number. Sometimes that field is named identically in the two files and has the same number of rows; other times the name is different. One file might use the field name last_name and another file might call it LastName. Those two fields would have to be manually associated.

When the number of rows is different, the relationship is said to be **one-to-many**; in that case, the relationship between two tables is created by a common field that links the tables together, and one table value can have many options from another table. For example, both a client file and an employee file might have a field named salesperson. In the employee file, there is only one record for each salesperson; however, in the client file, several clients might be assigned to the same salesperson.

The following steps create a relationship using the County field. **Why?** Both query tables have a column named County.

1

- Click the CREATE button in the yellow relationships message to display the Create Relationship dialog box (Figure 10–31).

Q&A **I do not have a CREATE button, or it did not work. What should I do?**
Click the Relationships button (Data tab | Data Tools) to display the Manage Relationships dialog box. Click the New button.

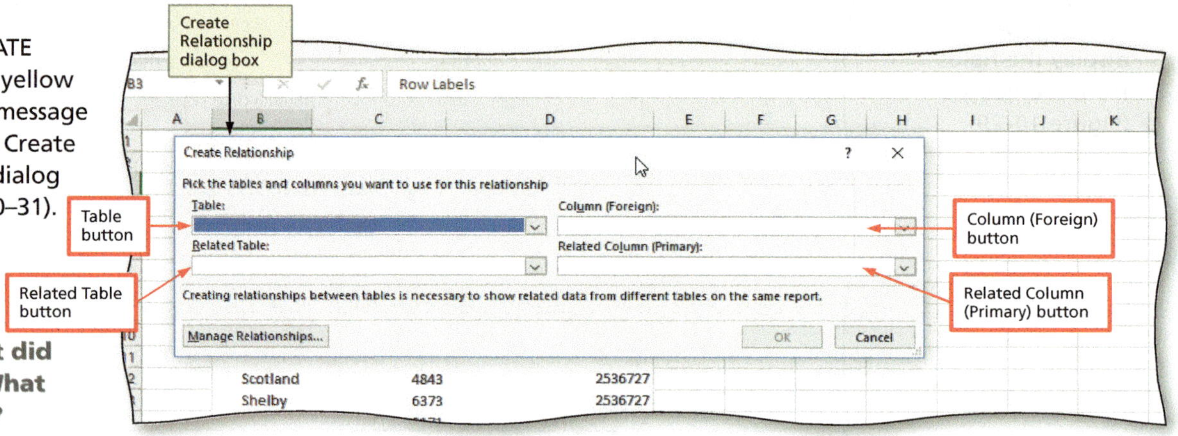

Figure 10–31

2

- Click the Table button and then click Data Model Table: Housing__Area.
- Click the Related Table button and then click Data Model Table: Population__Income (Figure 10–32).

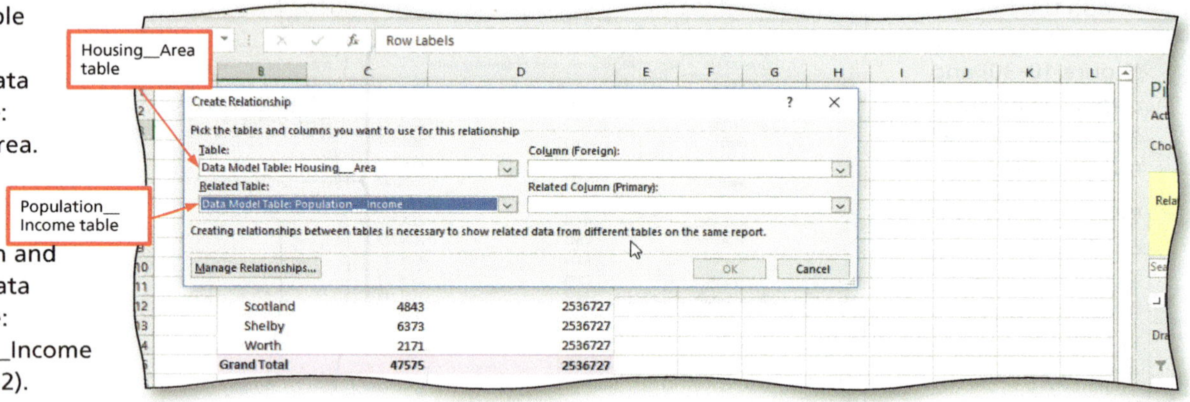

Figure 10–32

3

- Click the Column (Foreign) button and then click County (Figure 10–33).

Q&A **Why is it called a foreign column?**
Foreign, or foreign key, refers to a field in one table that uniquely identifies a row in a different table. Even though the names may be the same, the field is foreign to the second table. For most Excel purposes, it does not matter which table you use for the foreign versus primary key.

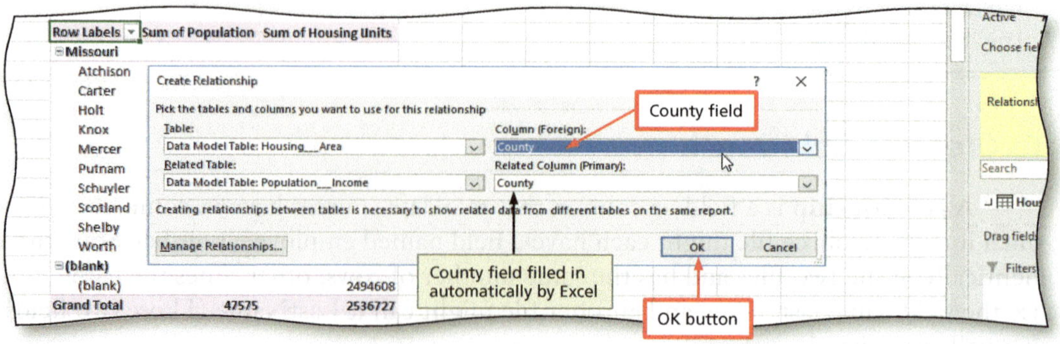

Figure 10–33

4

- Click OK (Create Relationship dialog box) to create the relationship between the tables and adjust the numbers in the PivotTable.

Other Ways

1. Click Detect Relationships button (Power Pivot tab | Relationship group), select relationships

To Manage Table Relationships

The following steps graphically display the relationship that you created in the previous steps using the Power Pivot window. **Why?** Sometimes looking at a picture makes the concept clearer. If you do not have Power Pivot, simply read these steps.

1

- Click the Manage button (Power Pivot tab | Data Model group) to make the Power Pivot for Excel window active.
- Click the Diagram View button (Home tab | View group) to see a visual display.
- Resize each of the table views to display all of the data, drag the tables by their title bars to show the relationship, and then click the Square Miles item, as shown in Figure 10–34. Your field order may differ.

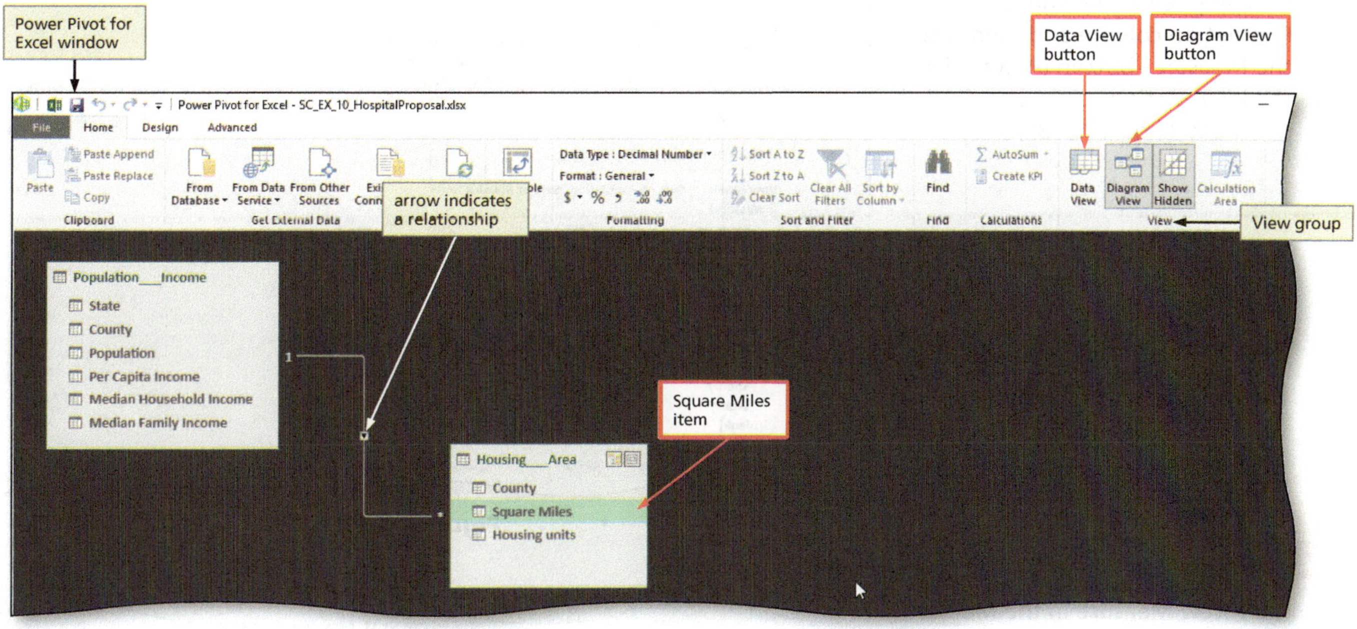

Figure 10–34

2

- Click the Data View button (Home tab | View group) to return to the Data View.

To Manage Relationships

You may need to add, edit, or delete relationships at some point. You can set up multiple relationships using Power Pivot. To do this, you would use the Manage Relationships command in the Power Pivot window, as shown in the following steps.

1. Click the 'Go to the Power Pivot window' button (Power Pivot tab | Data Model group) to make the Power Pivot for Excel window active.
2. Display the Design tab and then click the Manage Relationships button in the Power Pivot for Excel window (Design tab | Relationships group) to display the Manage Relationships dialog box.

3. Use the Create, Edit, or Delete button to make changes to the selected relationship and then click Close (Manage Relationships dialog box) to close the dialog box.
4. Minimize the Power Pivot for Excel window.

To Create a Measure

A **measure** is a calculated, named field in Power Pivot. Measures are created by a special set of functions and commands called **data analysis expressions (DAX)**. Measures have several advantages over simple formulas and other calculated fields. **Why?** With measures, you can create aggregate formulas that use one or multiple rows from multiple sources, which will adjust as you rearrange the pivot. You can format measures as you create them for global formatting benefits. Measures become fields in pivot field lists and can be used in multiple reports and across multiple worksheets. In regular PivotTables, you cannot create calculated fields using multiple data sources.

The following steps create a measure to calculate the average number of people in each household. If you do not have Power Pivot, simply read these steps.

1

- If necessary, minimize the Power Pivot for Excel window.
- Click any cell in the Sum of Population column and then click the Measures button (Power Pivot tab | Calculations group) to display the menu (Figure 10–35).

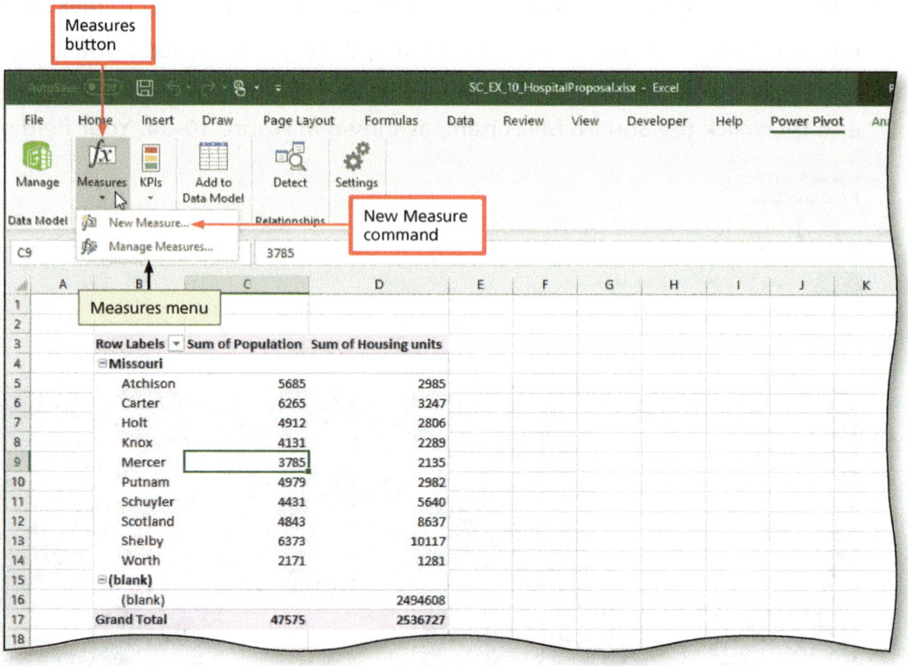

Figure 10–35

2

- Click New Measure in the Measures menu to display the Measure dialog box. If necessary, click the Table name arrow and then click Population__Income in the list.
- In the Measure name box, select any default text and then type `Occupancy Rate` to name the column.
- In the Description box, select any default text and then type `number of people per housing unit` to create a description.
- In the Formula box, following the equal sign, type `[` (left bracket) to prompt Excel to display the available fields that exist in the PivotTable (Figure 10–36).

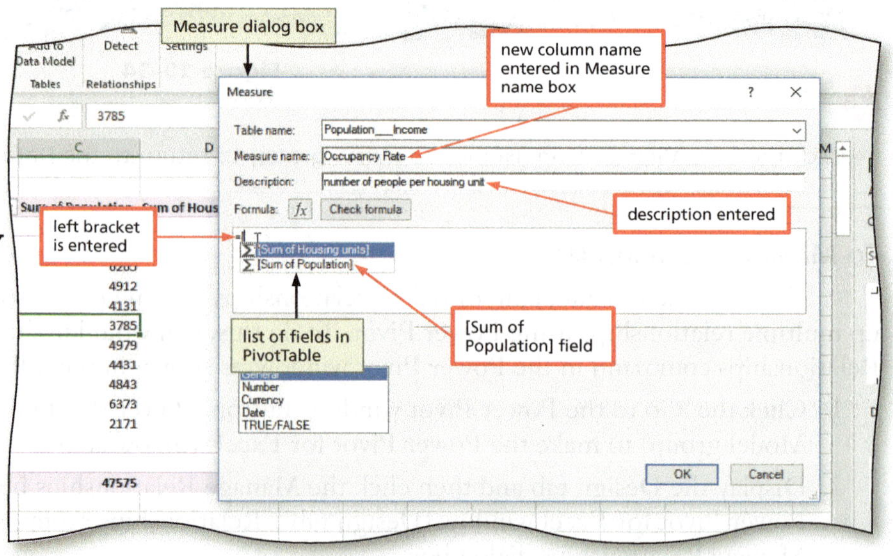

Figure 10–36

3

- Double-click the [Sum of Population] field to insert it into the formula.
- Type / [to enter the division symbol and to display again the available fields.
- Double-click the [Sum of Housing Units] field to insert it into the formula.
- In the Category box, click Number (Figure 10–37).

Experiment

- Click the Format button and then look at the various number formats that are available.

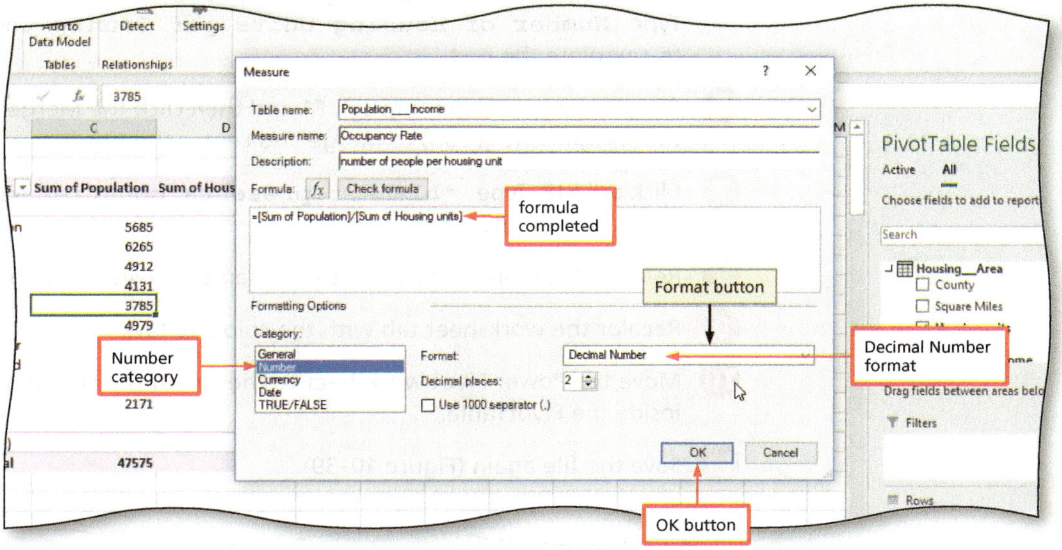

Figure 10–37

Q&A **Could I obtain the same result by creating a calculated field in the PivotTable?**
No. The Calculated Field option is unavailable to PivotTable data with multiple data sources.

4

- Click OK (Measure dialog box) to create the measure and display the new column (Figure 10–38).

Q&A **How do I edit or manage the measures I have created?**
Click the Measures button (Power Pivot tab | Calculations group) to display the Manage Measures dialog box. Then select the measure and click the Edit button.

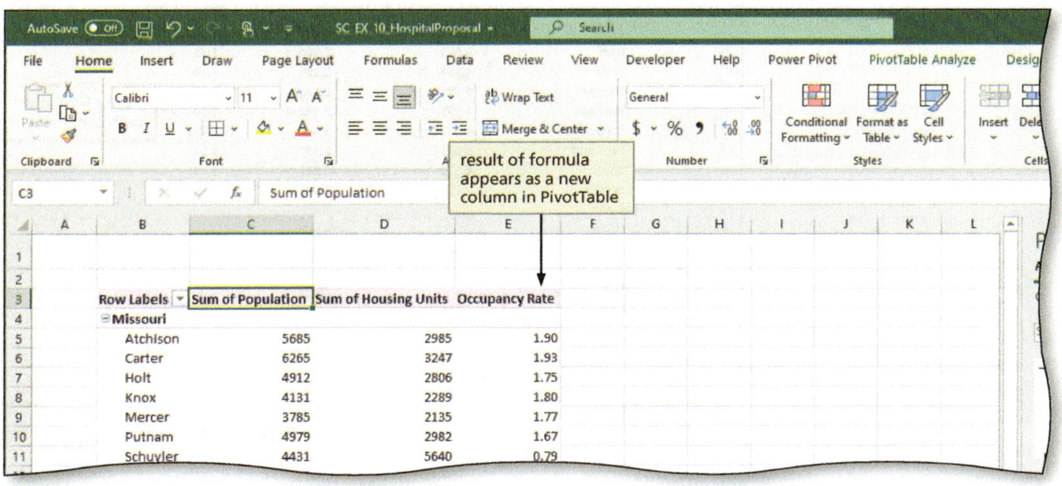

Figure 10–38

To Finish Formatting the PivotTable

The following steps format the other columns of numbers, insert a heading for the page, add a footnote, and save the file.

1 Right-click any number in the 'Sum of Population' column and then click Number Format on the shortcut menu to display the Format Cells dialog box.

2 In the Category area (Format Cells dialog box), click Number. Change the decimal places to 0 and then click to select the 'Use 1000 Separator' check box.

3. Click OK (Format Cells dialog box) to return to the PivotTable.
4. Repeat Steps 1 through 3 for the numbers in the Sum of Housing Units column.
5. Click cell A1. If necessary, change the font color to black. Change the font size to 20. Type **`Number of Housing Units per County`** and then press the ENTER key to complete the text.
6. Drag through cells A1 through F1 and then click the Merge & Center button (Home tab | Alignment group) to merge and center the title.
7. Click cell F18. Type **`*blank represents counties not in the lowest 10`** to create a footnote.
8. Rename the worksheet tab with the name, **`Power Pivot`**.
9. Recolor the worksheet tab with the color, Yellow.
10. Move the Power Pivot worksheet to the left of the Housing Units worksheet and click inside the PivotTable.
11. Save the file again (Figure 10–39).

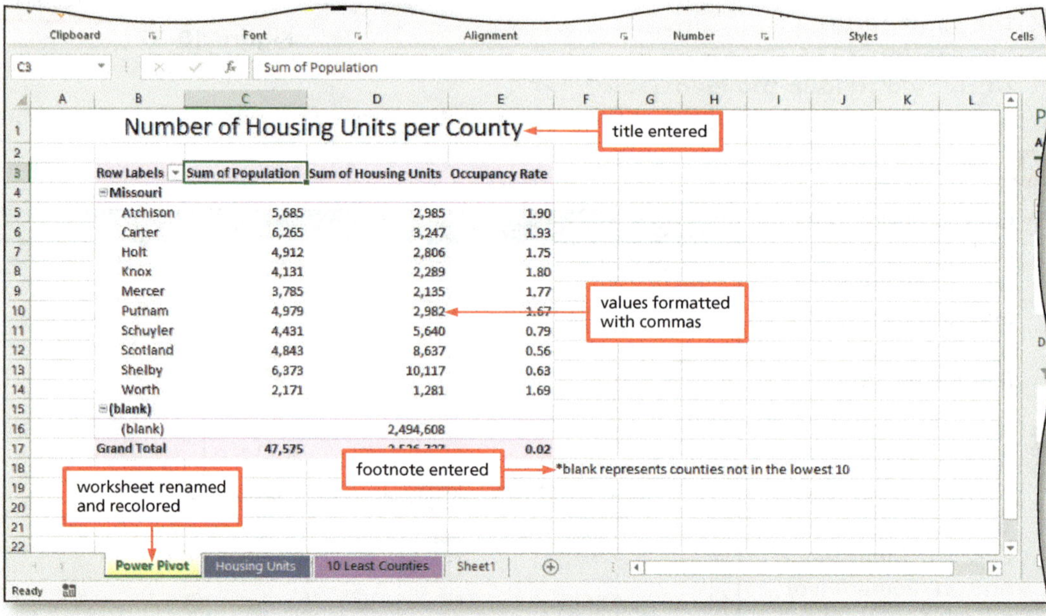

Figure 10–39

BTW
The COUNTIFS Function
The COUNTIFS function is an easy way to count data using multiple criteria sets. For example, in the 10 Least Counties worksheet, you could count the number of cities in York county with more than 1000 housing units by entering=COUNTIFS (A2:A395, "York", C2:C395, ">1000"). Criteria that includes operands or text must be enclosed within quotations marks.

Cube Functions

Normally if you want to reference a piece of data, you use a cell reference such as B4. If the data in that cell changes, your reference will reflect that change as well. And when you want to replicate a formula containing a reference that should not change, you use an absolute reference, such as $B$4. In PivotTables, however, neither of those cell references work. The data is prone to change dramatically, from numeric to text, from field to field, or even to blank. Formulas or other references to that data immediately become invalid or display errors when the data is pivoted.

The solution to that problem is to use cube functions. **Cube functions** are a set of advanced analytic functions that you can use with multidimensional data, also called **data cubes**. A Power Pivot report is considered a data cube because of its 3-D cube-like structure. With a cube function, you can reference any piece of data in the PivotTable to use in formulas or in other functions or merely to display the data in other places in the workbook. The cube function will adjust automatically if you change the way your data pivots.

Table 10–2 lists the cube functions.

Table 10–2 Cube Functions

Function	Return Value	Purpose
CUBEKPIMEMBER	Returns the name of a key performance indicator (KPI)	Produces a quantifiable measure such as net income
CUBEMEMBER	Returns a member or tuple from the cube	Validates that the member or tuple exists in the cube
CUBEMEMBERPROPERTY	Returns the value of a member property from the cube	Validates that a member name exists within the cube and returns the specified property for this member
CUBERANKEDMEMBER	Returns the nth, or ranked, member in a set	Returns one or more elements in a set, such as the top salesperson or the top 10 athletes
CUBESET	Defines a set of members by sending an expression to the cube	Identifies sets for use in other cube functions
CUBESETCOUNT	Returns the number of items in a set	Finds how many entries are in a set
CUBEVALUE	Returns an aggregated value from the cube	Displays values from the cube

The cube functions use a variety of arguments in their construction. Recall that an argument refers to any piece of information that the function needs in order to do its job. Arguments are placed in parentheses following the function name. Arguments are separated by commas. Table 10–3 lists some of the arguments used in the construction of cube functions.

For example, the following CUBEMEMBER function includes a reference to the connection or data model and then the name of the table followed by the name of the value. The function would return the calculated sum from the PivotTable.

```
=CUBEMEMBER("ThisWorkbookDataModel","[Measures].[Sum
                    of Housing Units]")
```

The reference to "ThisWorkbookDataModel" and the reference to Measures are standard references called constants; they should be entered exactly as written above. The reference to Sum of Housing Units is a variable and would be changed to match the field name in the PivotTable.

BTW
The AVERAGEIFS Function
Like its single-criteria counterpart AVERAGEIF, the AVERAGEIFS function averages all arguments that meet multiple criteria.

Table 10–3 Cube Function Arguments

Argument	Definition
Caption or property	An alternate text to display in the cell that is perhaps more user-friendly than the database, field, or row name
Connection	Names the table, query, or data model
Key performance indicator (KPI)	A quantifiable measurement, such as net profit, used to monitor performance
Measures	A pivot calculation such as sum, average, minimum, or maximum
Member expression	Uses database field-like references to the data rather than cell references
Rank	An integer to represent which piece of data to return in an ordered list
Set	A string to represent a set of values that has been defined or returned by another cube function
Sort by	A field name to sort by when a function returns a set of values
Sort order	An integer to represent how the data should be ordered when a function returns a set of values
Tuple	A row of values in a relational database

To View Cube Functions

The following steps use the 'Convert to Formulas' command. **Why?** The command converts the cells in a Power Pivot report or a PivotTable report to cube references, allowing you to see the functions behind the scenes.

1

- Click cell E3 in the Power Pivot PivotTable.
- Display the PivotTable Analyze tab.
- Click the OLAP Tools button (PivotTable Analyze tab | Calculations group) to display the menu (Figure 10–40).

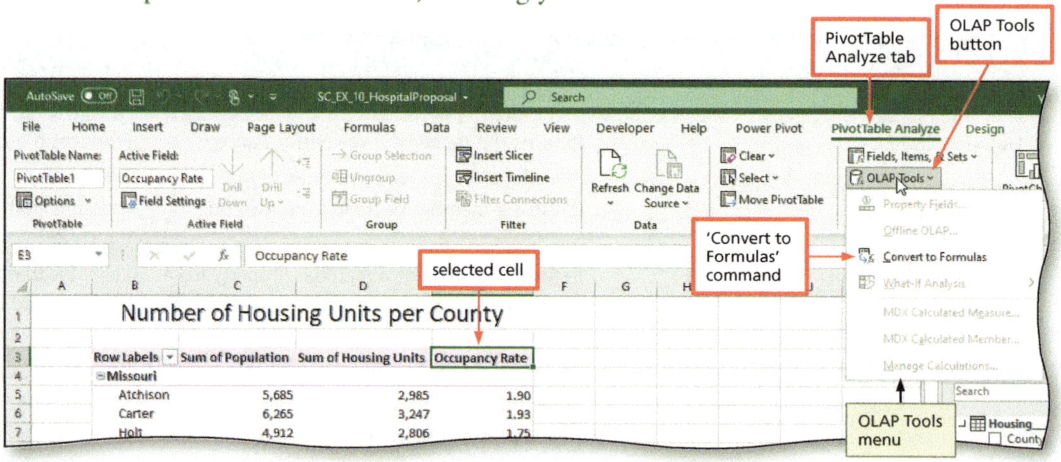

Figure 10–40

Q&A **What does OLAP stand for?**
OLAP stands for Online Analytical Processing, which is an advanced analytic tool to assist users in data warehousing and data mining, especially with multidimensional data such as a PivotTable with two outside sources.

2

- Click 'Convert to Formulas' on the OLAP Tools menu to view the cube function in the formula bar. If a Microsoft Excel dialog box is displayed, click OK (Figure 10–41).

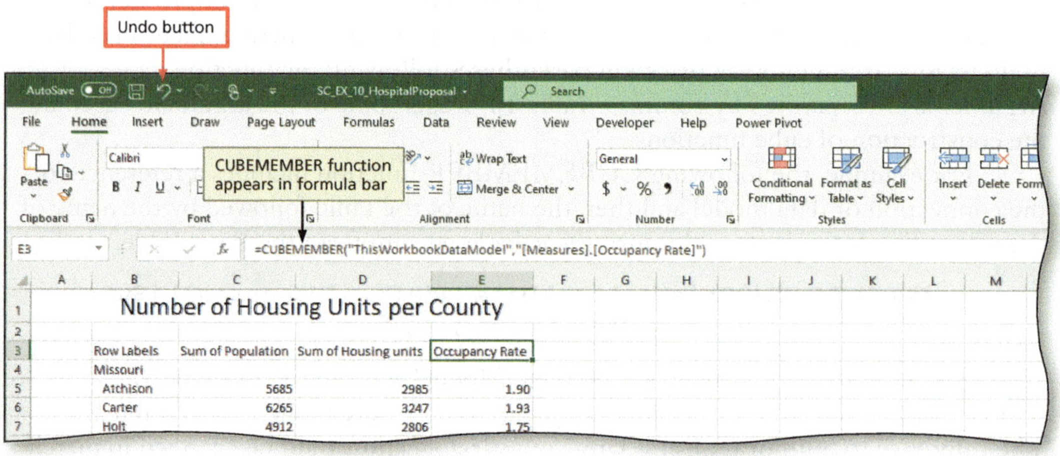

Figure 10–41

Experiment

- Click various cells in the table, including the row and column headings, while watching the formula bar. Note the various cube functions that make up the PivotTable.

3

- Click the Undo button on the Quick Access Toolbar to hide the cube functions and display the PivotTable.
- Close the Hospital Proposal document.

The GETPIVOTDATA function

Another way to access data in a PivotTable is to use the GETPIVOTDATA function. The function takes the following arguments:

```
= GETPIVOTDATA (data field, location of pivot table,
              search field, search item)
```

In a regular PivotTable, an example might be:

```
= GETPIVOTDATA ("Population", $B$3, "County", "Knox")
```

The specific names of the fields are in quotation marks when not referencing a cell location.

However, because the PivotTable in this module is a Power Pivot PivotTable, based on two different imported files, the reference is more complex and must include structured references to the file, field, and data, as shown in the following:

```
=GETPIVOTDATA("[Population__Income].[Sum of Housing Units]",
    $B$3,"[Population__Income].[State].&[Missouri]",
        "[Population__Income].[County].&[Knox]")
```

The individual parts of the structured references can be cell references. For example, if you want the user to enter the county they are looking for in cell H3, you could replace [Knox] with $H$3. Excel uses a double-underscore when naming the pivot data tables.

BTW

The GETPIVOTDATA Function

Another way to extract data stored in a PivotTable is to use the GETPIVOTDATA function. The function takes at least two arguments: the name of the data field and a reference to any cell in the PivotTable report. It returns the sum of that field. An optional third argument allows you to enter a search term. The GETPIVOTDATA function also can search calculated fields.

To Create a Power Pivot Table Reference

Rather than typing in a long, complicated function, it is easier to let Excel define the reference. If you wanted to create a reference to a cell in a Power Pivot PivotTable, you would perform the following steps.

1. Choose a cell outside of the Power Pivot table.
2. Type = (equal sign).
3. Click a cell in the Power Pivot table to create the reference and then click the Enter button.
4. Replicate or copy the function if necessary.

Using Power BI

Microsoft Power BI is a business intelligence tool that helps you learn more about your data and discover the "story" it has to tell. In Power BI, you can explore, present, and share data from Excel or other data sources. Power BI lets you go beyond the capabilities of Excel to create visually compelling and interactive business insights.

What is Power BI?

Power BI is a group of tools that work together to give data analysts and business users tools to make business decisions. These tools include 1) the **Power BI Desktop application**, a free downloadable program anyone can use to connect to, analyze and report data; 2) an online tool called the **Power BI service**, where analysts can publish their Power BI reports and decision-makers can explore results, and 3) **Power BI mobile apps**, a smartphone app users can use to monitor and explore Power BI results to use in their work. The Power BI service requires a Power BI Pro or Power BI Premium subscription for a cost. However, you do not need them to complete this module, which only uses the free Power BI Desktop app.

The Power BI Desktop app can seamlessly import data from Excel and other data sources. After you import data, you create a document called a **report**, a collection of visual analyses called visualizations. A **visualization** (sometimes called a **visual**) is a chart, map, tile, data card, or other image that portrays an object, situation, or set of information. A visualization can transform large amounts of data into understandable business information. Figure 10–42 shows the Power BI Desktop screen and a report with three visualizations, a bar chart, a treemap, and a data card. These visualizations show the relationships between the ten least populated counties in Missouri and their population, area, and income.

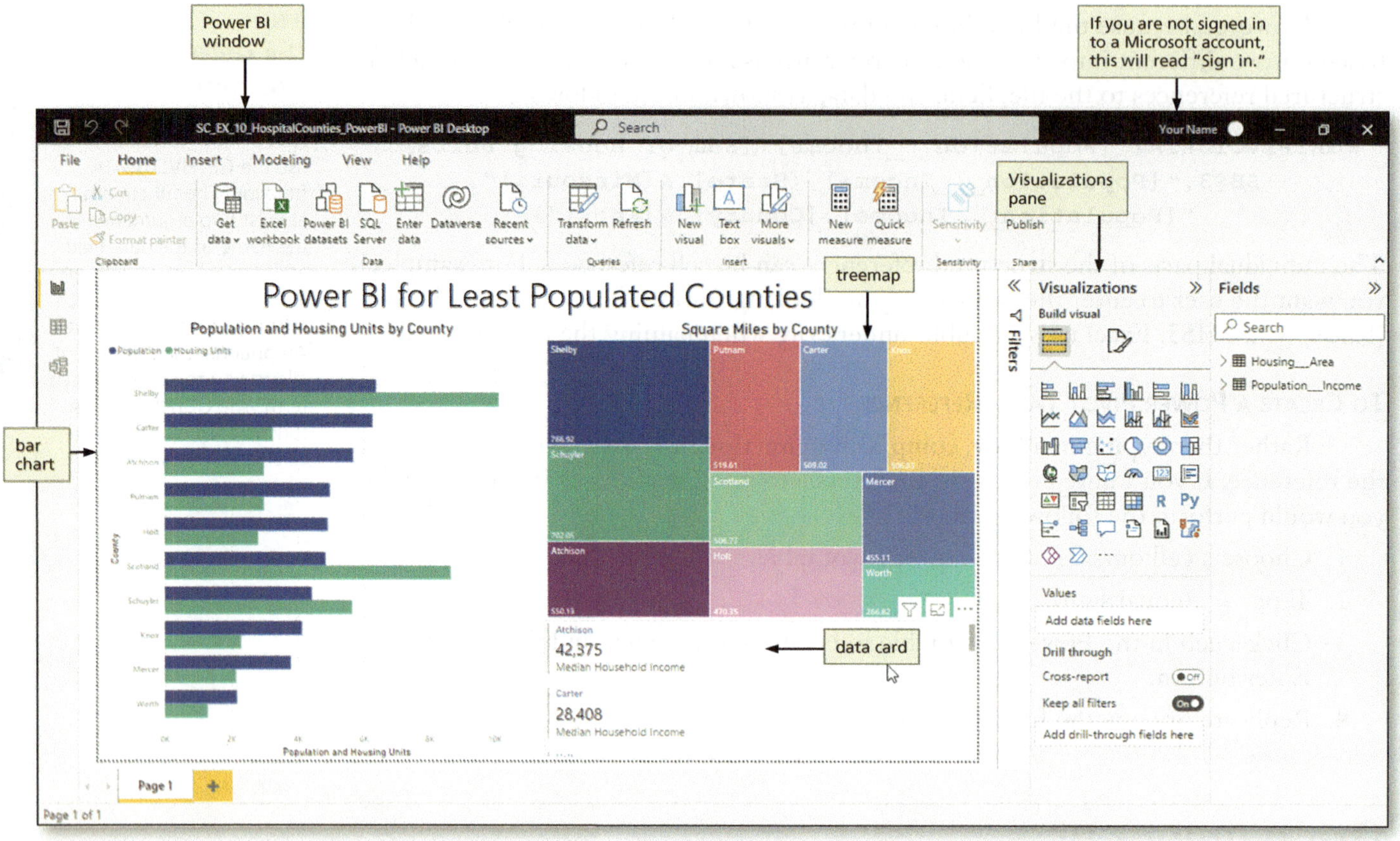

Figure 10–42

The Power BI Desktop app also lets you create data models, similar to those you created using PowerPivot. In addition, the app lets you edit data using the Query Editor, which operates similarly to the Query Editor in Excel.

A Power BI report is a file with a .pbix file extension. When you are finished with your report, you can **publish** it to the Power BI service, where you or others can create **dashboards** for presentation and further analysis.

Downloading and Installing the Power BI Desktop App

You will need to download the Power BI Desktop application and install it on your device. You must be connected to the Internet to perform these steps. **Why?** Although it can import and use the data you created in Excel, Power BI Desktop is a separate application and operates independently from Excel. If you are working in a lab situation, see your instructor or IT administration for help downloading Power BI, if it is not already installed on the lab device.

1

- Open a browser and navigate to https://powerbi.microsoft.com/desktop, to navigate to the Microsoft Store page containing a Power BI download link.
- If you have an Office 365 account, sign in. If not, you can also download Power BI Desktop for free.
- Follow the prompts to download, and then install, Power BI Desktop onto your device.

The Power BI Desktop app is updated and released monthly, with new features. This module uses Power BI Desktop March 2022. If your screen does not match the figure in this section exactly, you may be using a later version. To check your version, click the Help tab, and then in the Info group, click About. Even if you have a later version, you should still be able to complete the steps in this section successfully.

BTW
Power BI vs. Power View
Power BI was created to replace Power View, which was part of Excel and has recently been discontinued in newer versions of Excel. Power BI offers many of the same capabilities as Power View, plus many more.

To Start the Power BI Desktop App

You start the Power BI Desktop app the same way you would any app, using the Windows Start menu.

1

- Click the Start button on the Windows taskbar and then click Power BI Desktop to start the application.
- Close the Power BI Desktop startup window by clicking the close button in its upper-right corner.
- If your Visualizations pane does not appear, click the double expand arrow above Visualizations.
- If your Fields pane does not appear, click the double expand arrow above Fields (Figure 10–43).

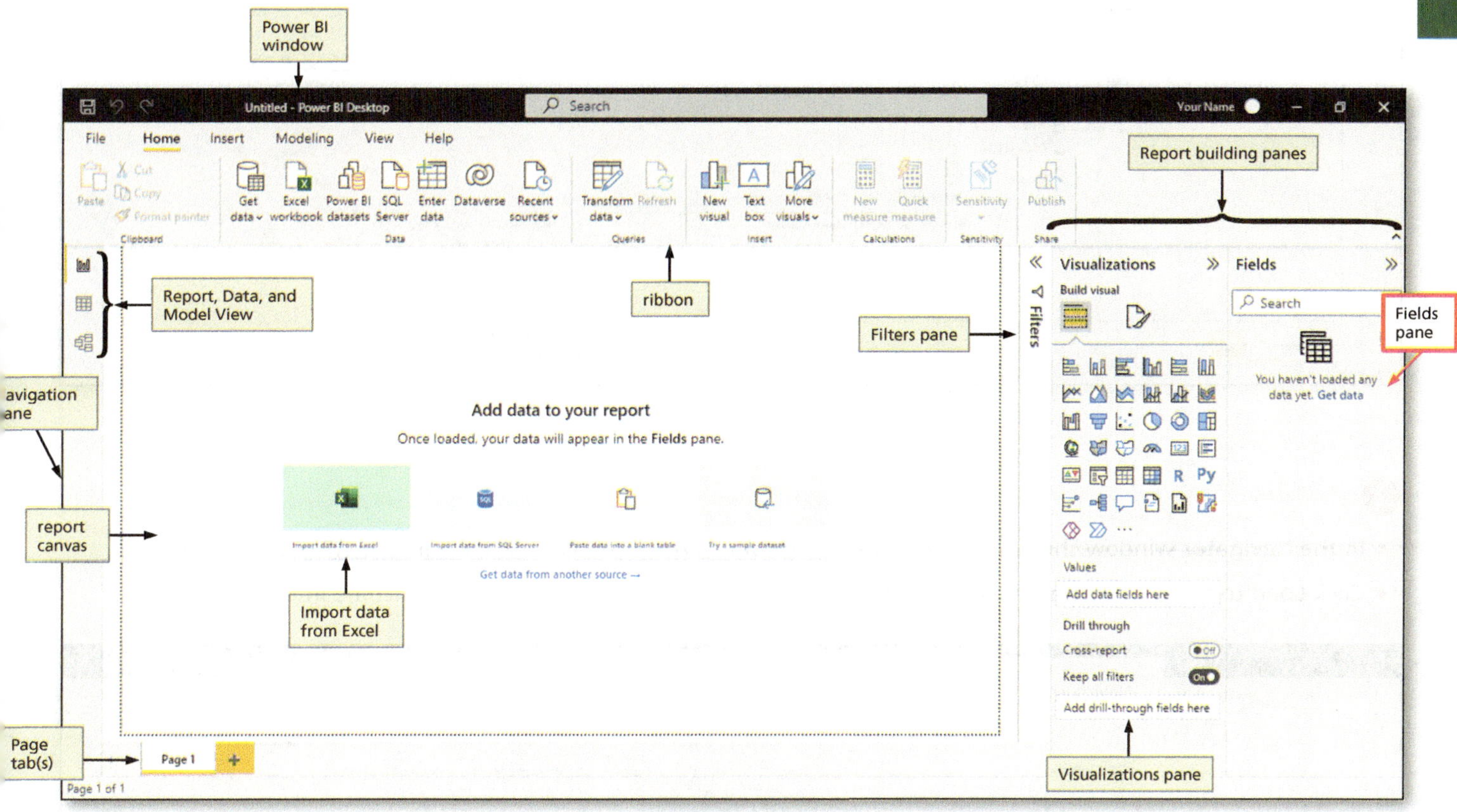

Figure 10–43

To Create a Power BI Report

Before you can create a Power BI report, you first need to import the data you want to use, in this case the Housing_Area and Population_Area tables from the hospital proposal. The following steps import these tables to the Power BI report canvas to create a Power BI table visualization that shows the 10 least populous counties and their square miles. **Why?** As with PivotTables, the report is blank until you identify data fields.

1

- Click the Import data from Excel button in the middle of the window to display the Open dialog box.
- Navigate to workbook SC_EX_10_HospitalProposal.xlsx in the file list, click the file to select it, and then click Open (Figure 10-44).

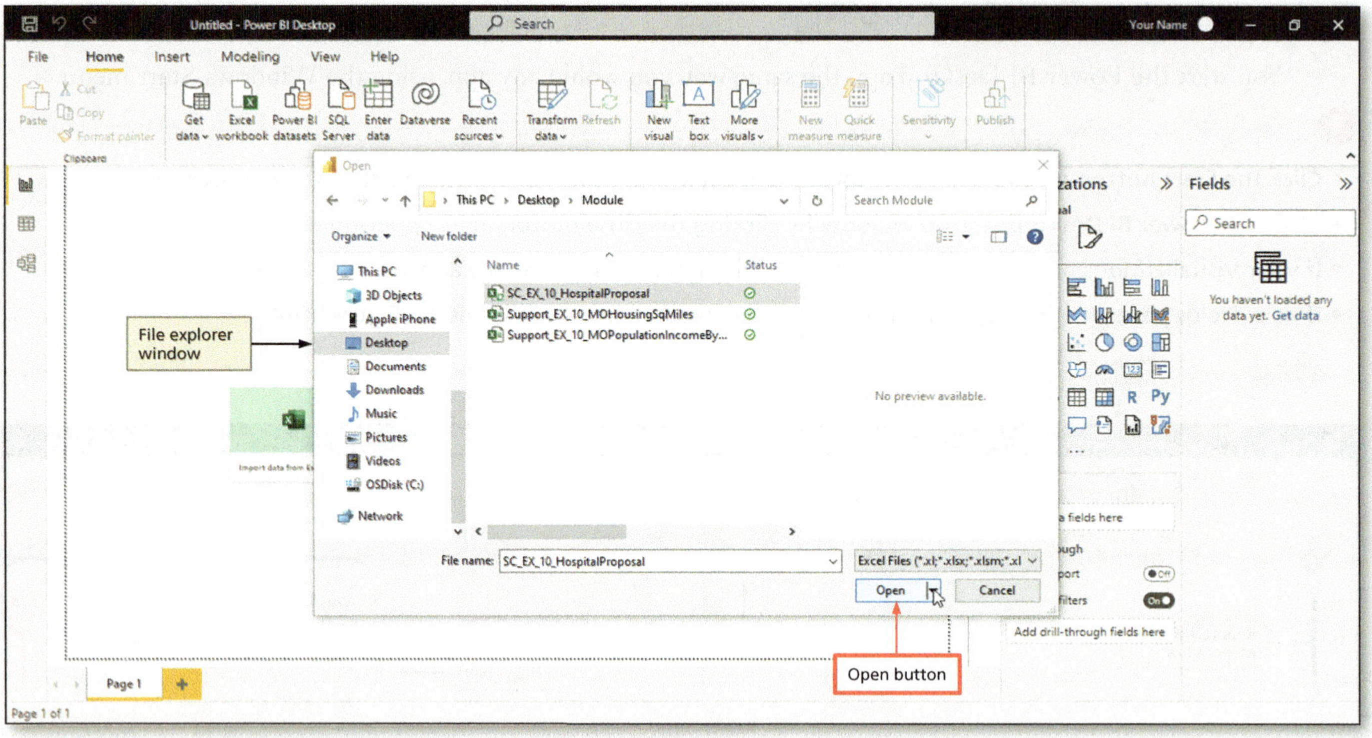

Figure 10–44

2

- In the Navigator window check the boxes next to Housing__Area and Population__Income (Figure 10–45).
- Click Load to finish importing the data and display Housing__Area and Population__Income in the Fields pane.

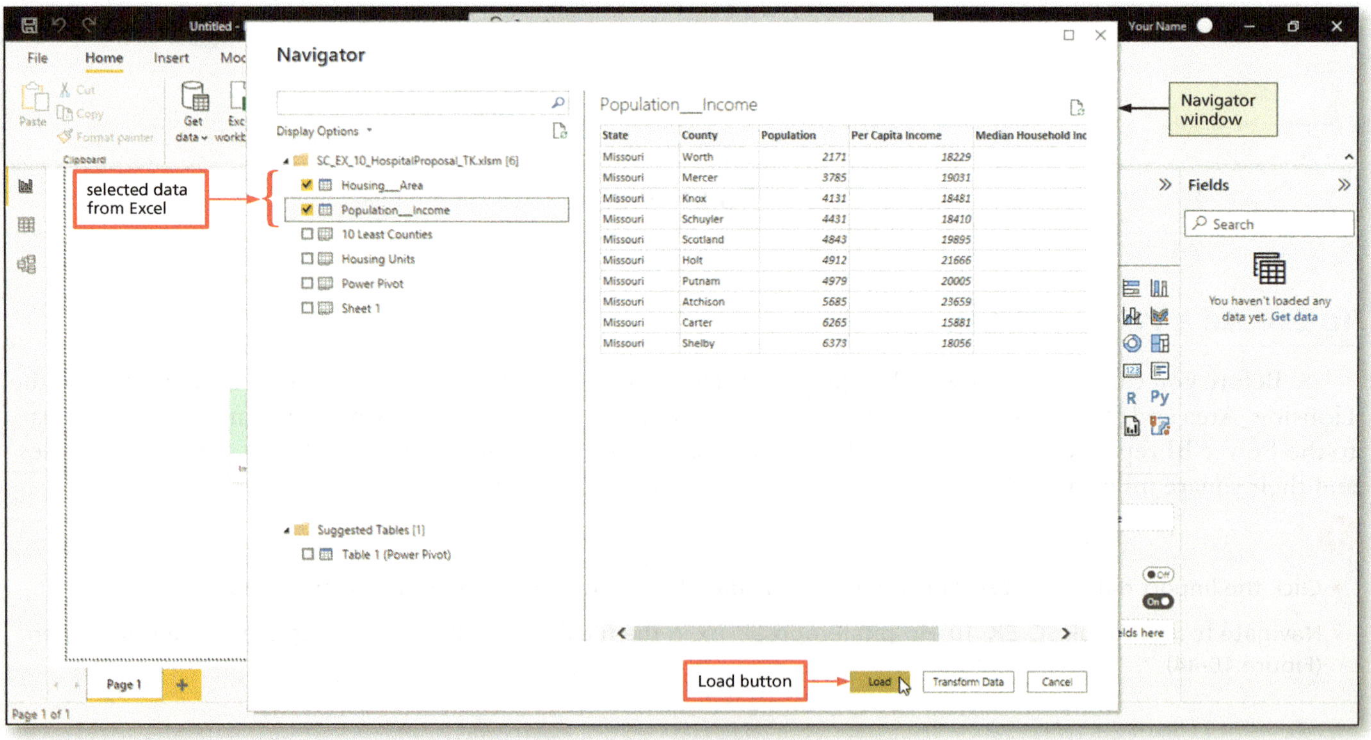

Figure 10–45

3

- In the Visualizations pane, select the Stacked bar chart icon.
- Click the expand arrow beside Population__Income in the Fields pane to display the fields.
- Click the check boxes for the County and Population fields to display them on the report canvas (Figure 10–46).

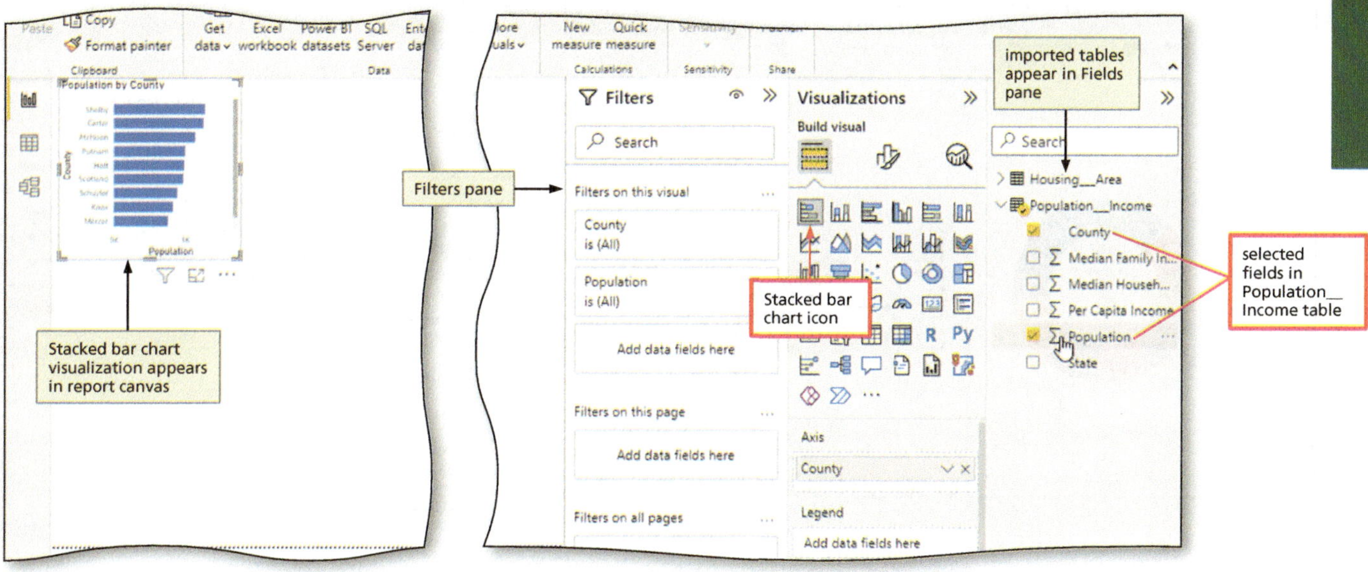

Figure 10–46

4

- In the report, drag the lower right corner of the table to fill approximately half of the pane (Figure 10-47).

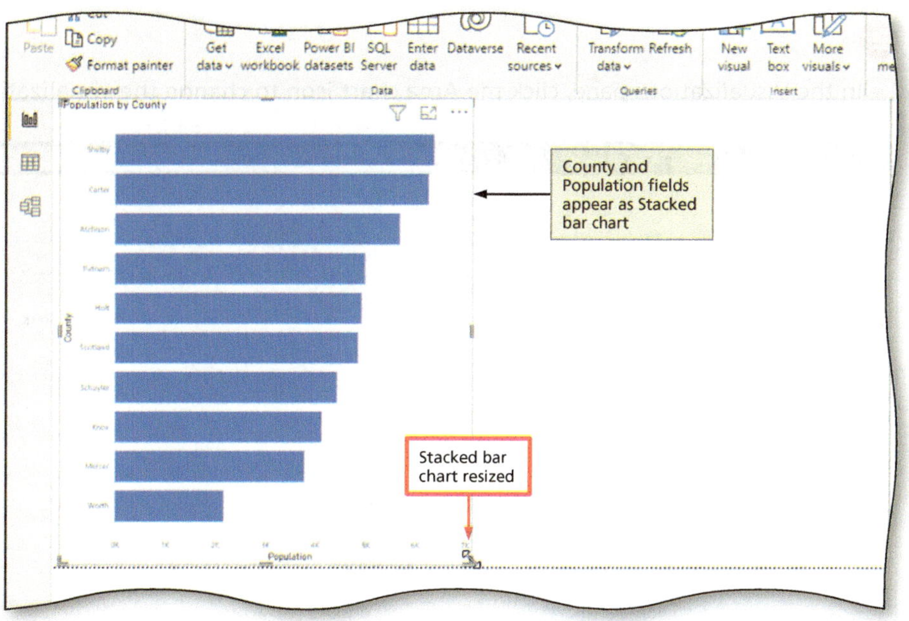

Figure 10–47

To Switch Visualizations

The following steps convert the bar chart visualization into different types of data visualizations available in Power BI. **Why?** Different kinds of visualizations can represent data more effectively. You have created various types of charts in Excel. You will examine several data visualizations in Power BI to view the data in different ways.

1

- In the Visualizations pane, click the Donut chart icon to change the visualization (Figure 10-48a).

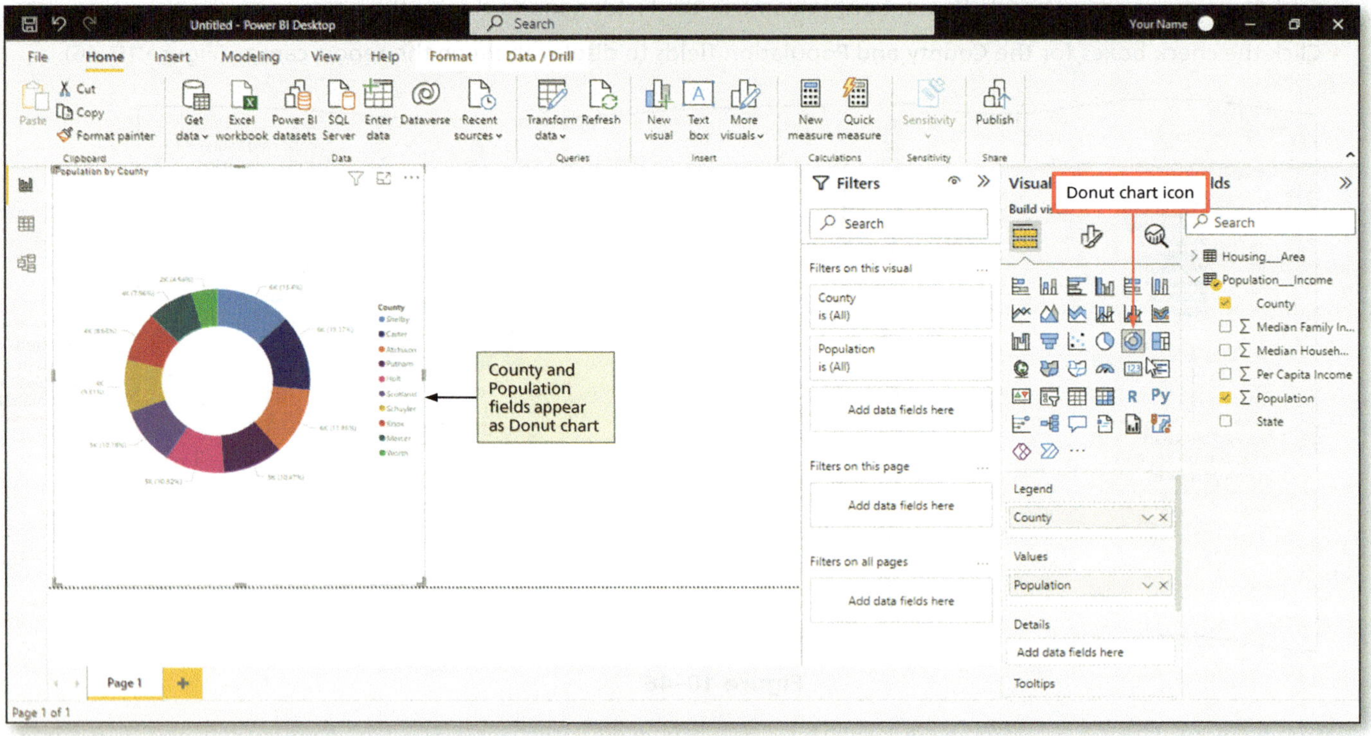

Figure 10–48a

2

- In the Visualizations pane, click the Area chart icon to change the visualization (Figure 10-48b).

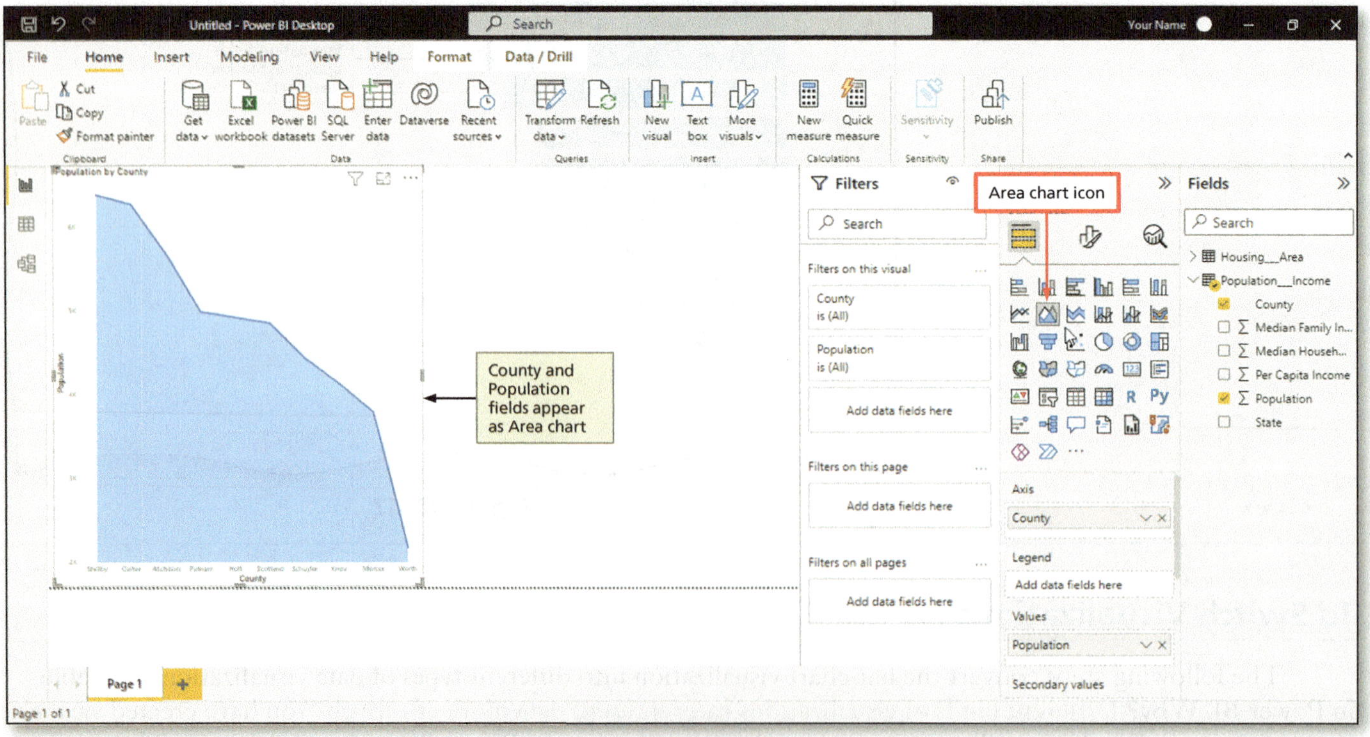

Figure 10–48b

3

- In the Visualizations pane, click the Clustered bar chart icon to change the visualization (Figure 10-48c).

Q&A

Why does the Clustered bar chart look like the Stacked Bar chart?
There is only one field, Population, in the Clustered bar chart so far. You will add another field in the next step.

Experiment

- Click on different icons in the Visualizations pane to view more data visualizations. When you are finished, click the Clustered bar chart.

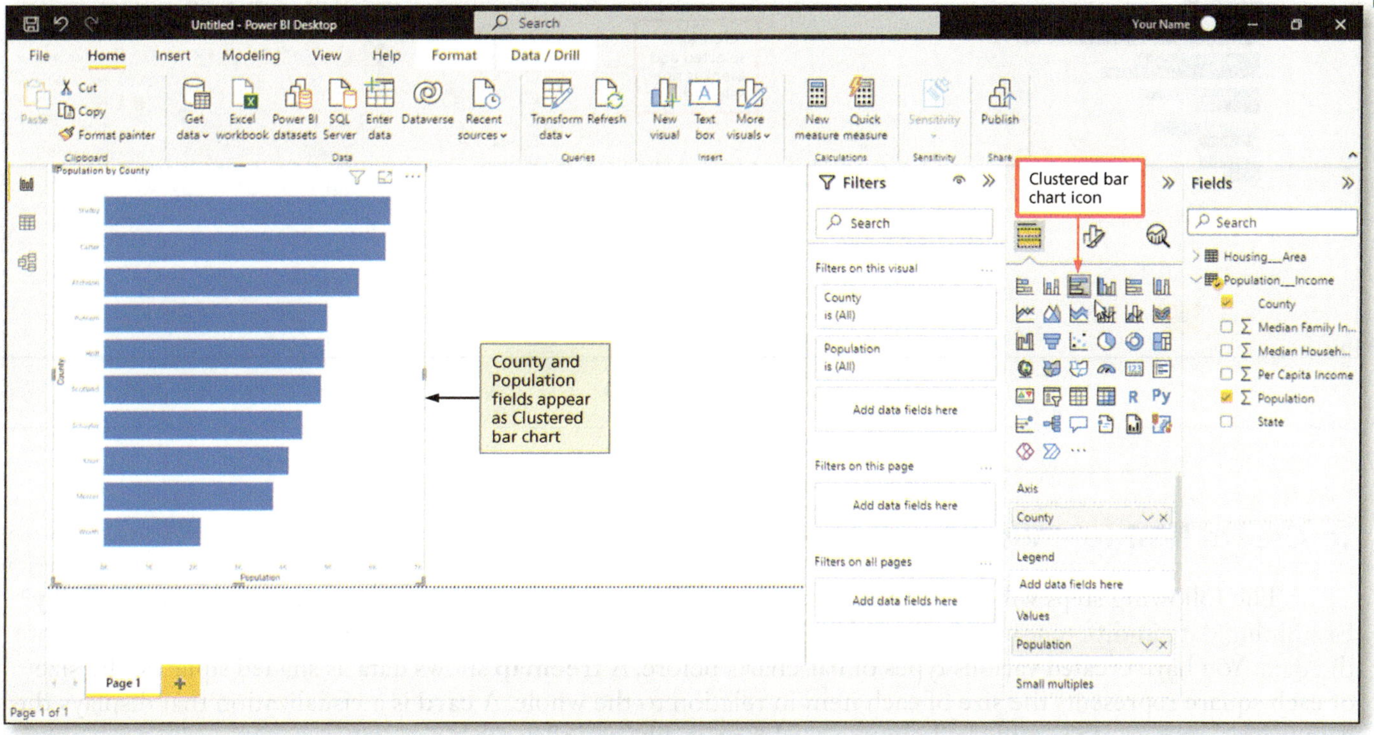

Figure 10–48c

4

- In the Fields pane, click the expand arrow next to Housing__Area to display its fields.
- Click the check box for the Housing Units field to display a new field of data in the Clustered Bar Chart.
- If your Clustered Bar Chart displays a blank county, expand the Filters pane, if necessary.
- Click the Expand arrow beside County, listed under 'Filters on this visual' to display filtering options for that field.
- Click the Select all check box to select all counties, and then click the (Blank) check box to turn off the blank county, if any (Figure 10-49).

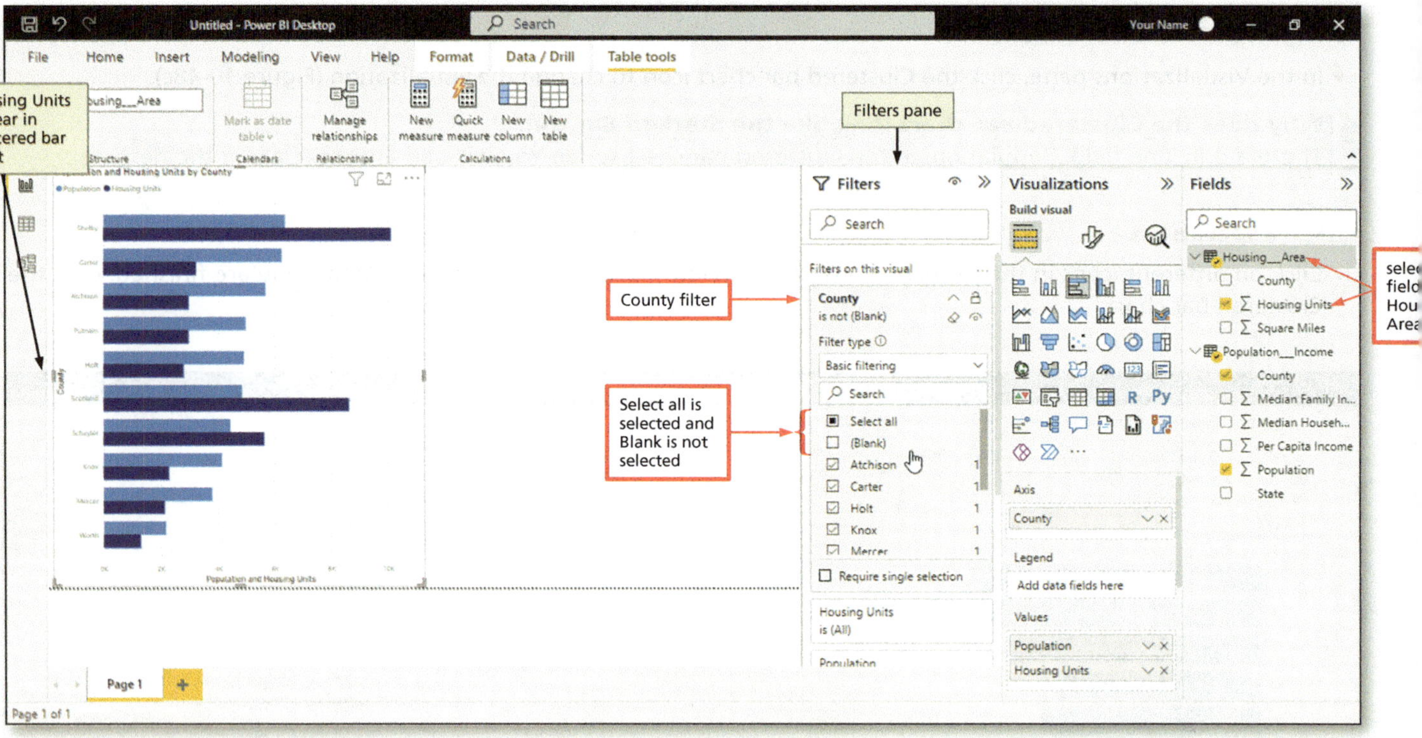

Figure 10–49

To Create Multiple Visualizations

The following steps will create different data visualizations on the same report canvas in Power BI. **Why?** Examining data in different ways in the same report is a useful tool for analyzing and drawing conclusions about the data. You have created various types of bar charts before. A **treemap** shows data as shaded squares; the size of each square represents the size of each item in relation to the whole. A **card** is a visualization that displays the data from each row of the table laid out in a card format, like an index card.

1

- On the report canvas, click outside of the clustered bar chart to deselect it.
- In the Visualizations pane, select Treemap.
- In the Fields pane, click the check box for Square Miles under Housing__Area.
- In the Fields pane, click the check box for County under Population__Income.
- In the Filters pane, remove the (Blank) county from the Treemap, if necessary (Figure 10-50).

Q&A

Why use County from Population__Income instead of Housing__Area?

We only want to compare the ten least populated counties. Housing__Area lists every county in Missouri.

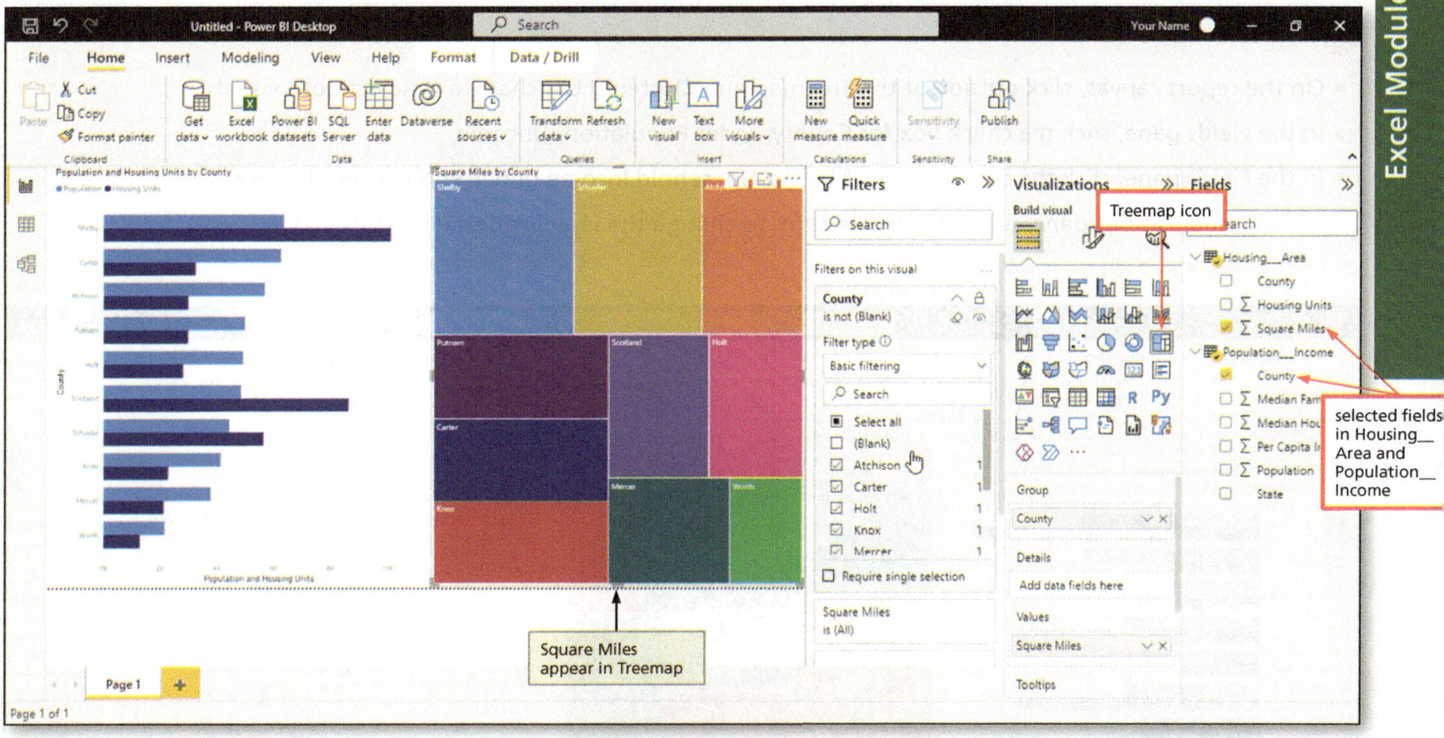

Figure 10–50

2

- Resize the Treemap to fit approximately two thirds of the remaining report canvas, making sure the boxes in the Treemap match the arrangement shown (Figure 10-51).

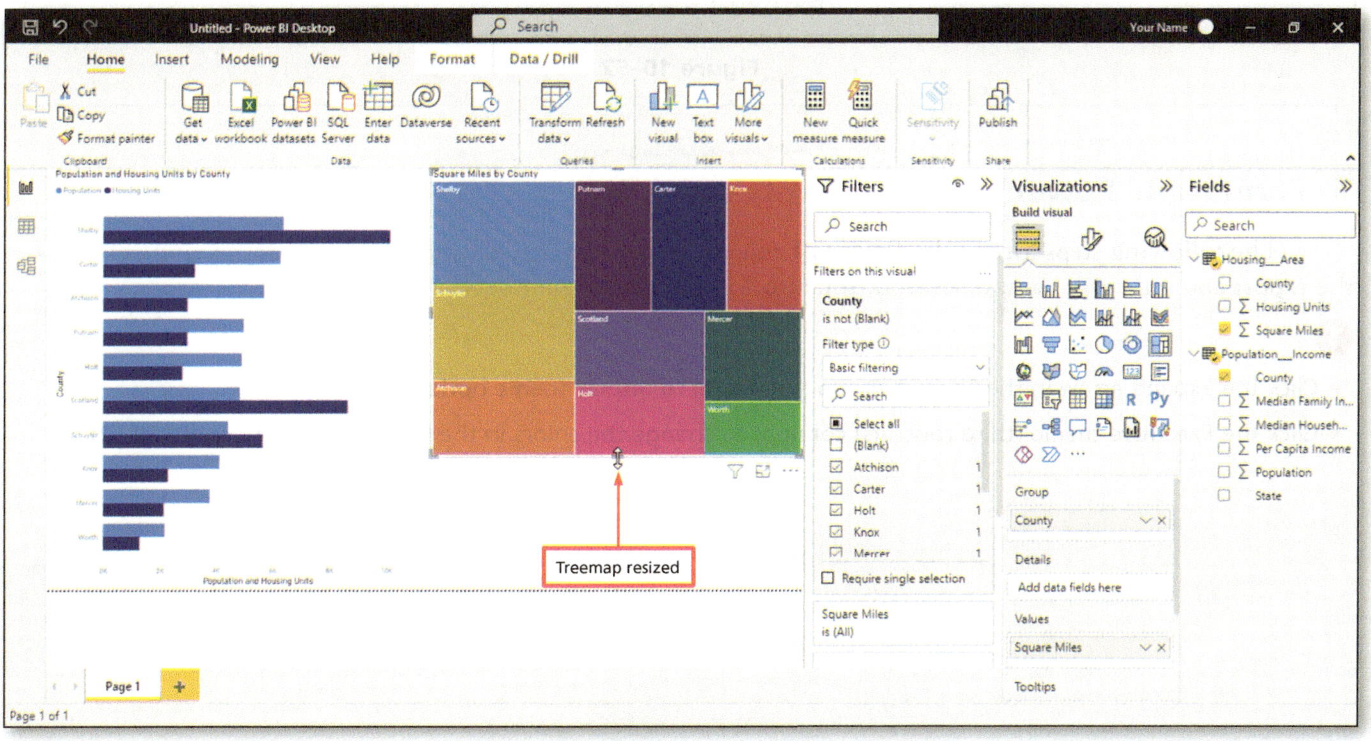

Figure 10–51

3

- On the report canvas, click outside of the Treemap and Clustered bar chart to deselect both visuals.
- In the Fields pane, click the check box for County under Population__Income.
- In the Fields pane, click the check box for Median Household Income under Population__Income.
- In the Visualizations pane, select Multi-row card to change the visualization (Figure 10-52).

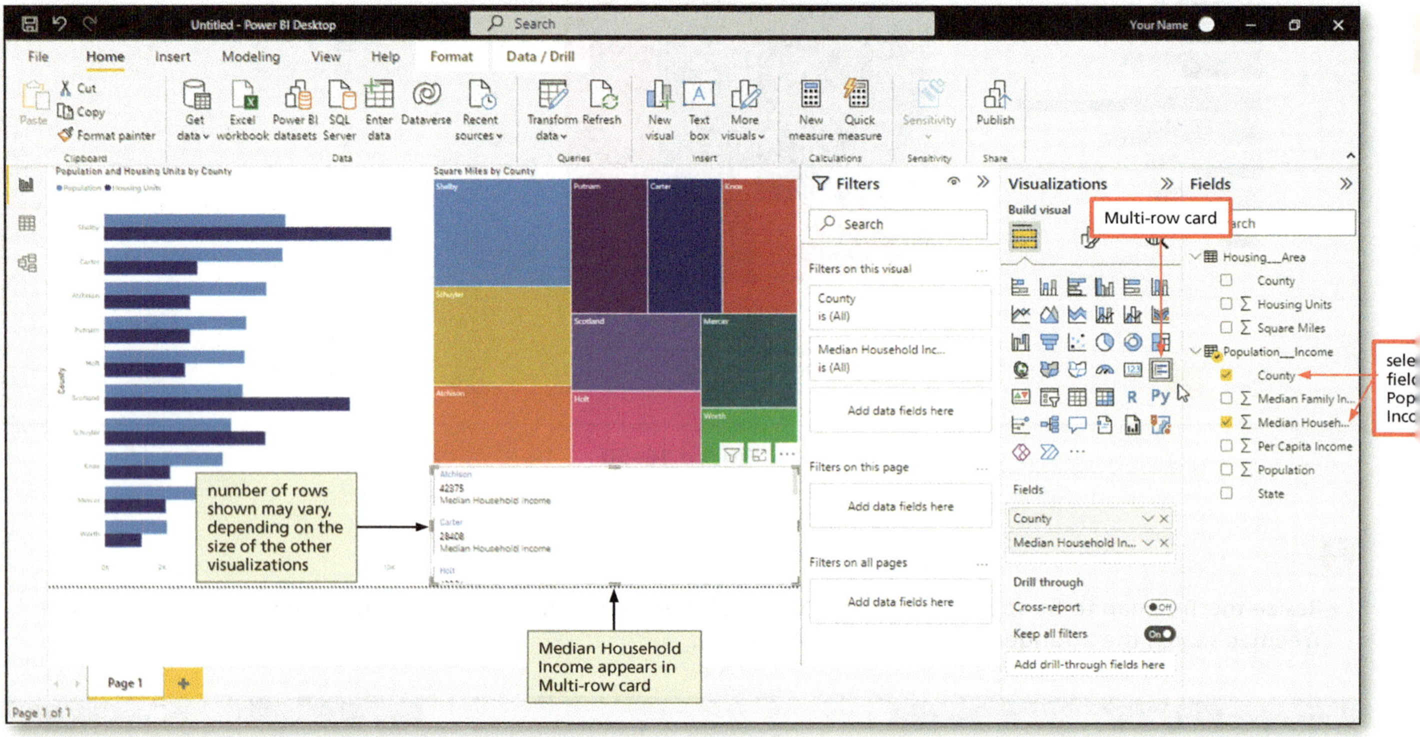

Figure 10–52

To Format the Power BI Report

The following steps format the Power BI report. **Why?** Adding a theme, title, and background enhances the report and improves comprehension. You also will format the numbers.

1

- Click the expand arrow in the Themes group (View tab) to display theme options.
- Click the Executive theme (third row, first column) to change the colors in the Power BI report (Figure 10-53).

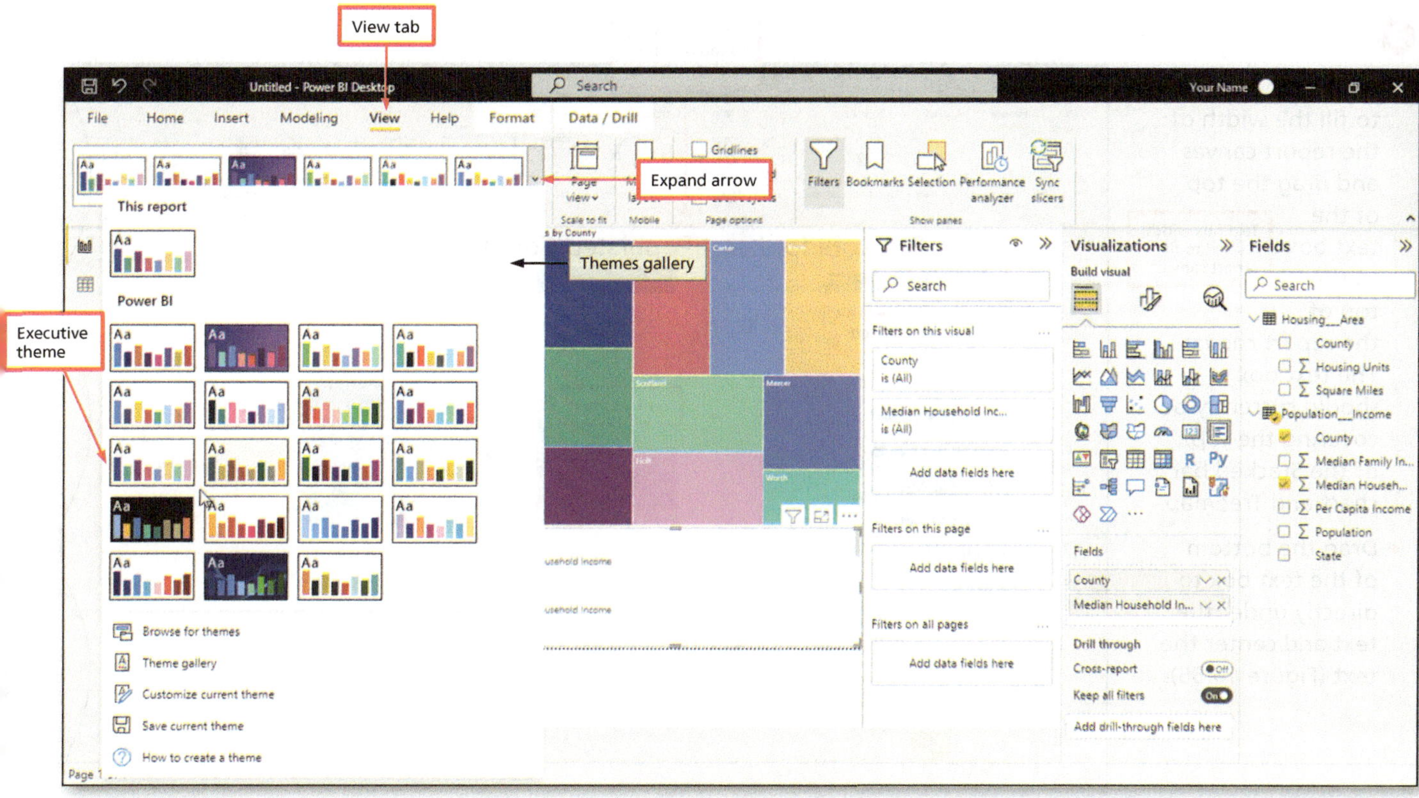

Figure 10–53

2

- Click the Text box button (Home tab | Insert group) to insert a title for the Power BI report.
- In the text box formatting window, set the font size to 36. In the Text box, type `Power BI for Least Populated Counties` to enter the title text (Figure 10-54).

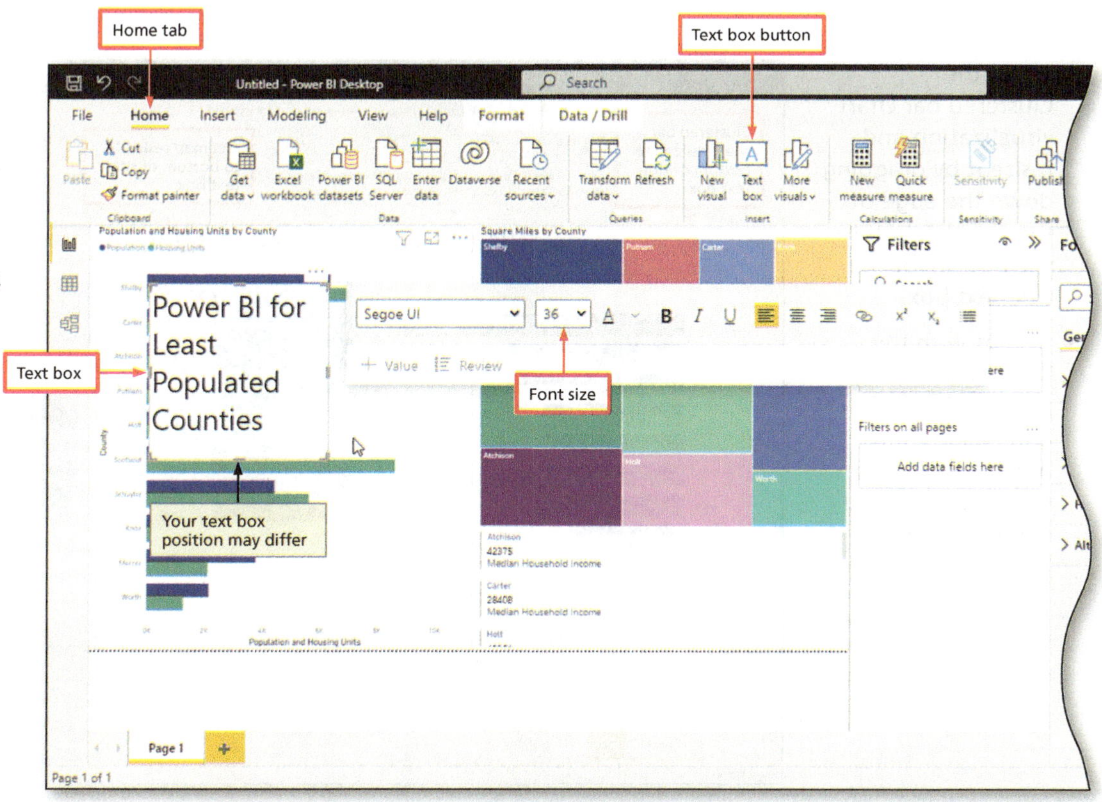

Figure 10–54

3

- Resize the text box to fill the width of the report canvas and drag the top of the text box to the top of the report canvas. The text box should currently be covering the top of the Stacked bar chart and Treemap.
- Drag the bottom of the text box to directly under the text and center the text (Figure 10-55).

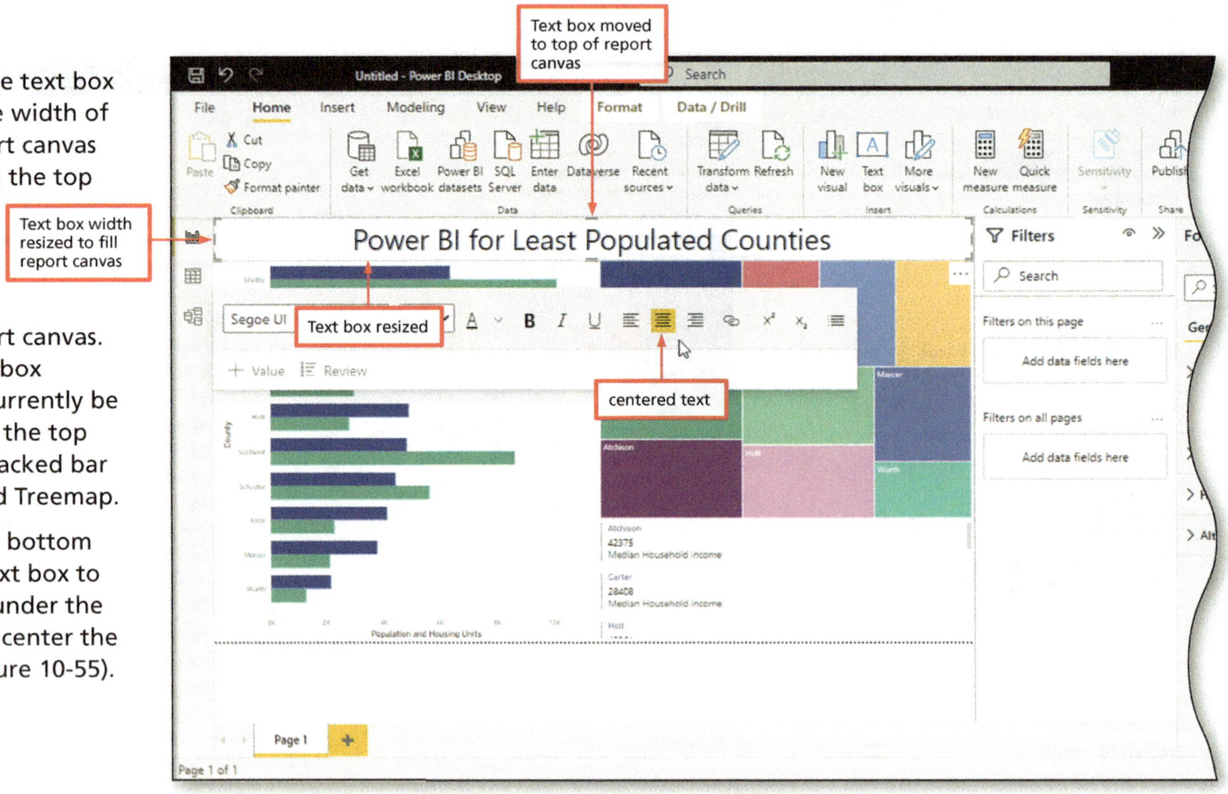

Figure 10–55

4

- Select the Clustered bar chart visualization and resize it by dragging down the edge of the visualization to the bottom of the title text box.
- Repeat with the Treemap, resizing the visualization and making sure not to overlap with the data card (Figure 10-56).

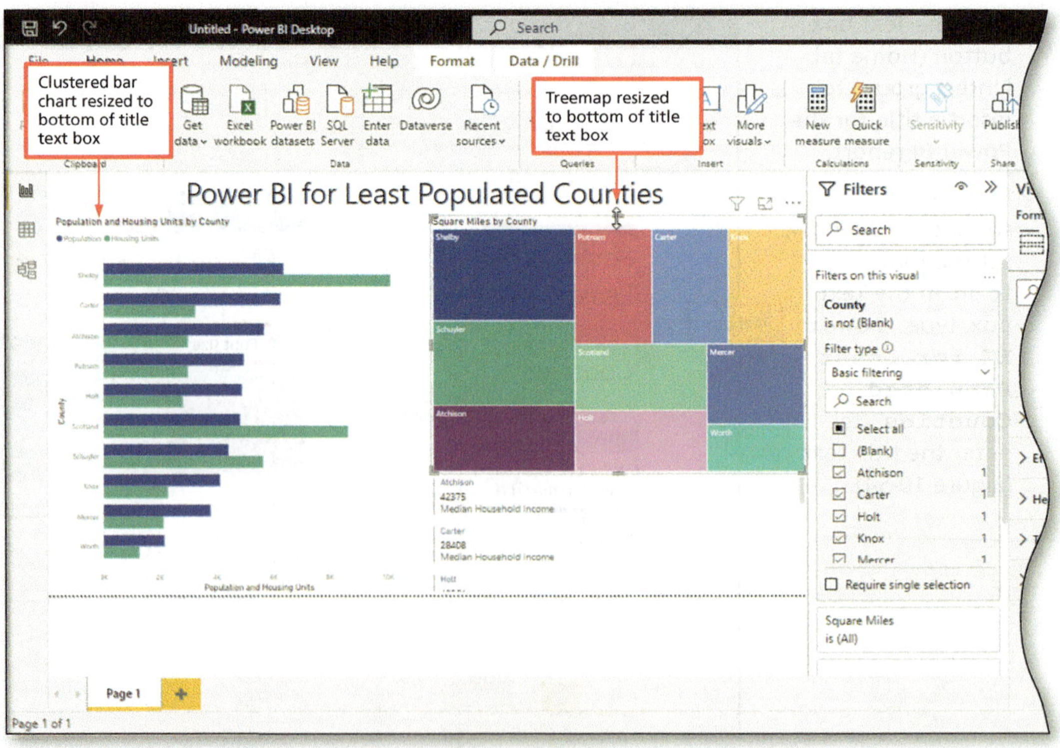

Figure 10–56

5

- Select the Treemap visual if necessary.
- In the Visualizations pane, click the Format your visual icon to display formatting options.
- Click Visual and then click the Data labels Off button to toggle Data labels to On (Figure 10-57).

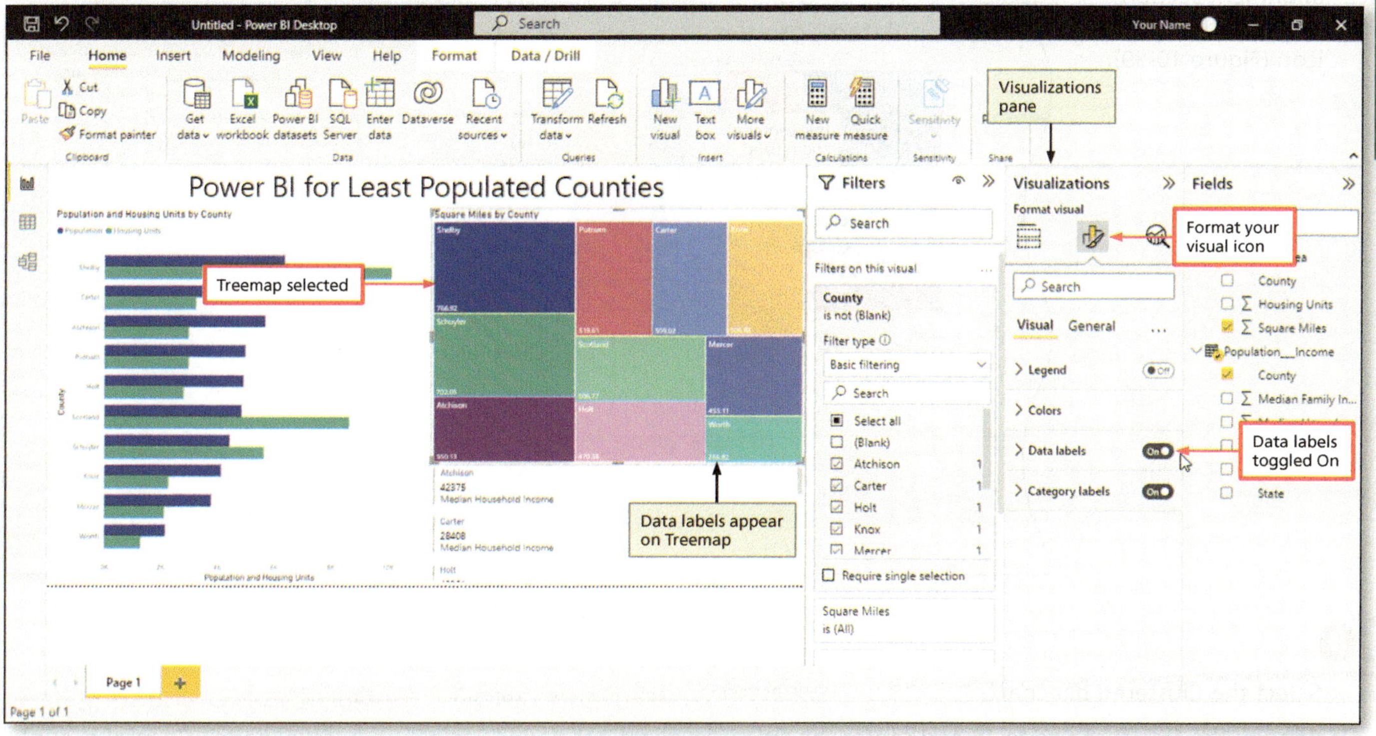

Figure 10–57

6

- Click General in the Visualizations pane to show more formatting options.
- Click the expand arrow next to Title (Visualizations pane | Format your visual pane | General group) (Figure 10-58).

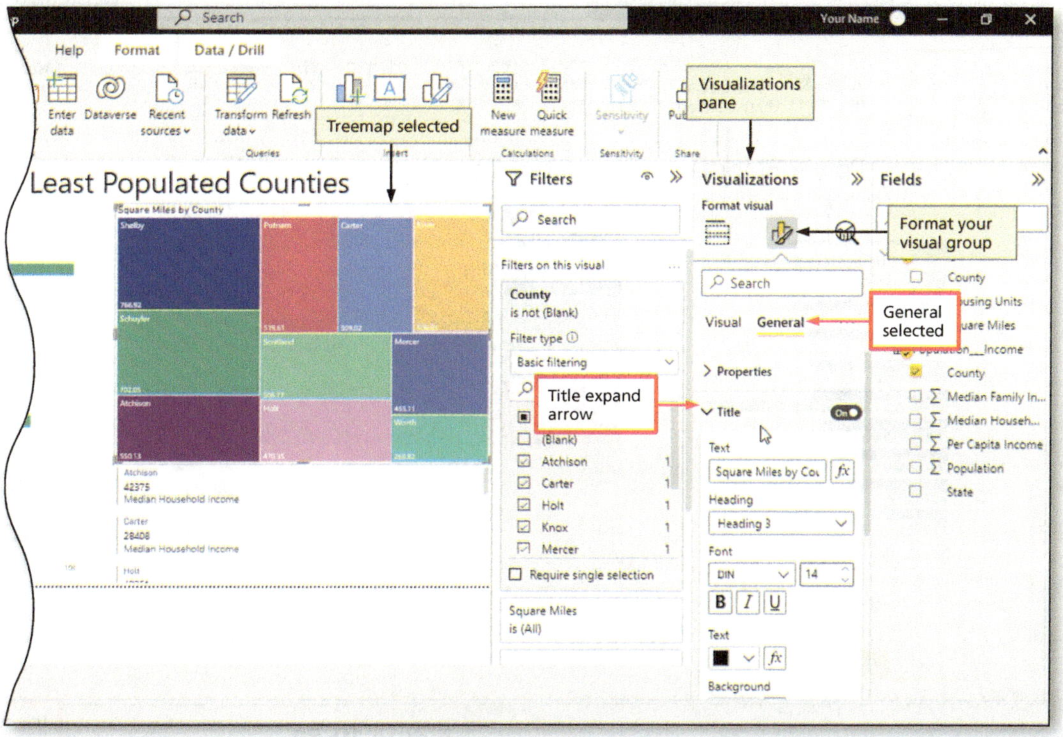

Figure 10–58

7

- Change the font size to 18 and scroll down to the Horizontal alignment section and click the Center icon (Figure 10-59).

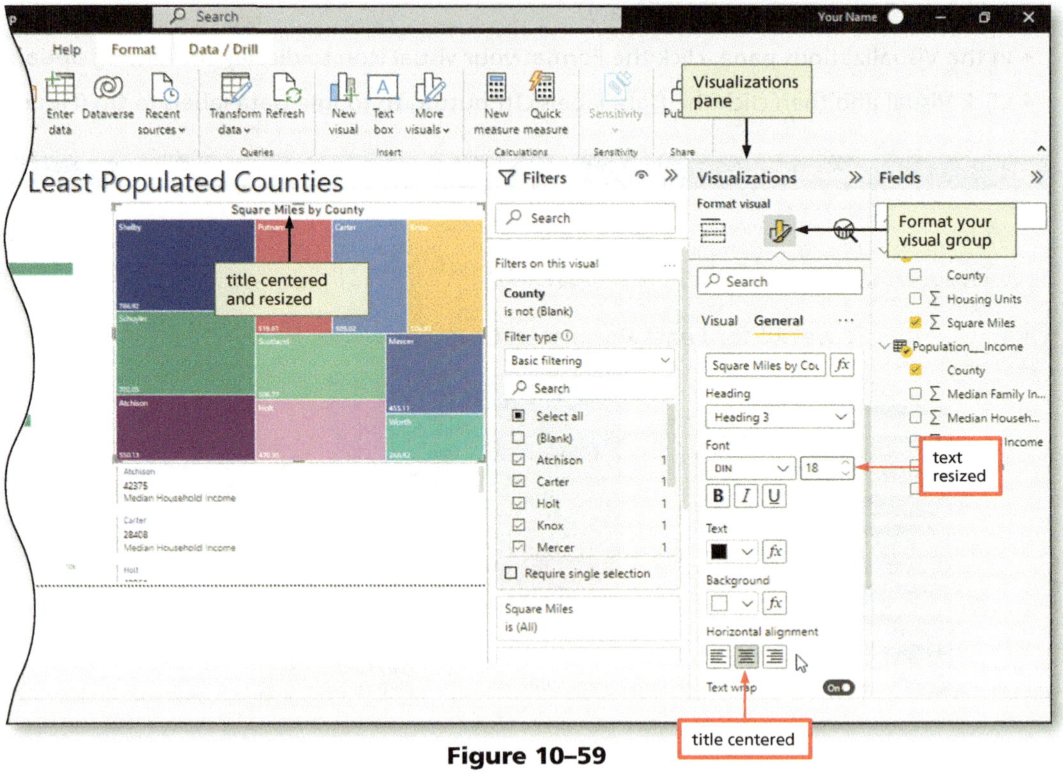

Figure 10–59

8

- Select the Clustered bar chart.
- Change the title font size to 18 and center the title (Visualizations pane | Format your visual pane | General group) (Figure 10-60).

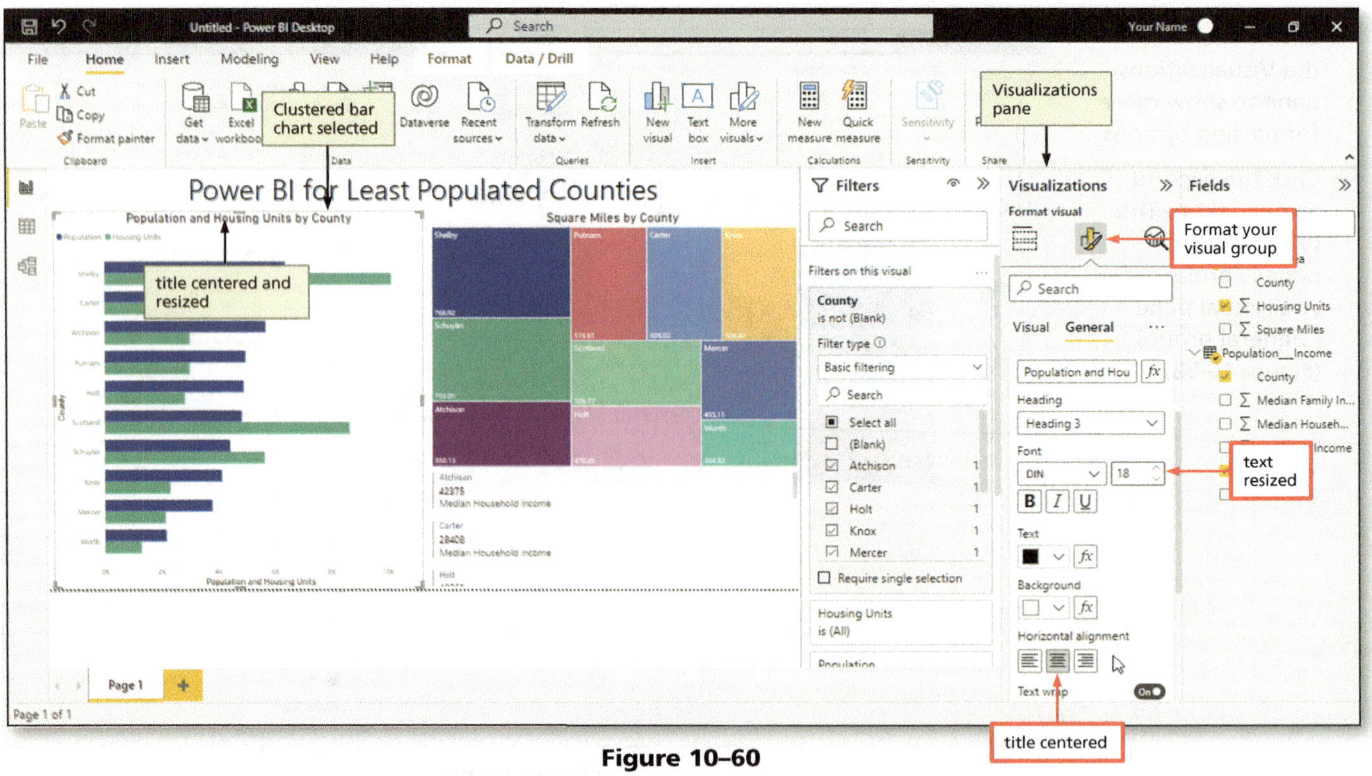

Figure 10–60

9

- Select the Multi-row card.
- Click the expand arrow next to Callout values (Visualizations pane | Format your visual pane | Visual group) and change the text size to 18 (Figure 10-61).

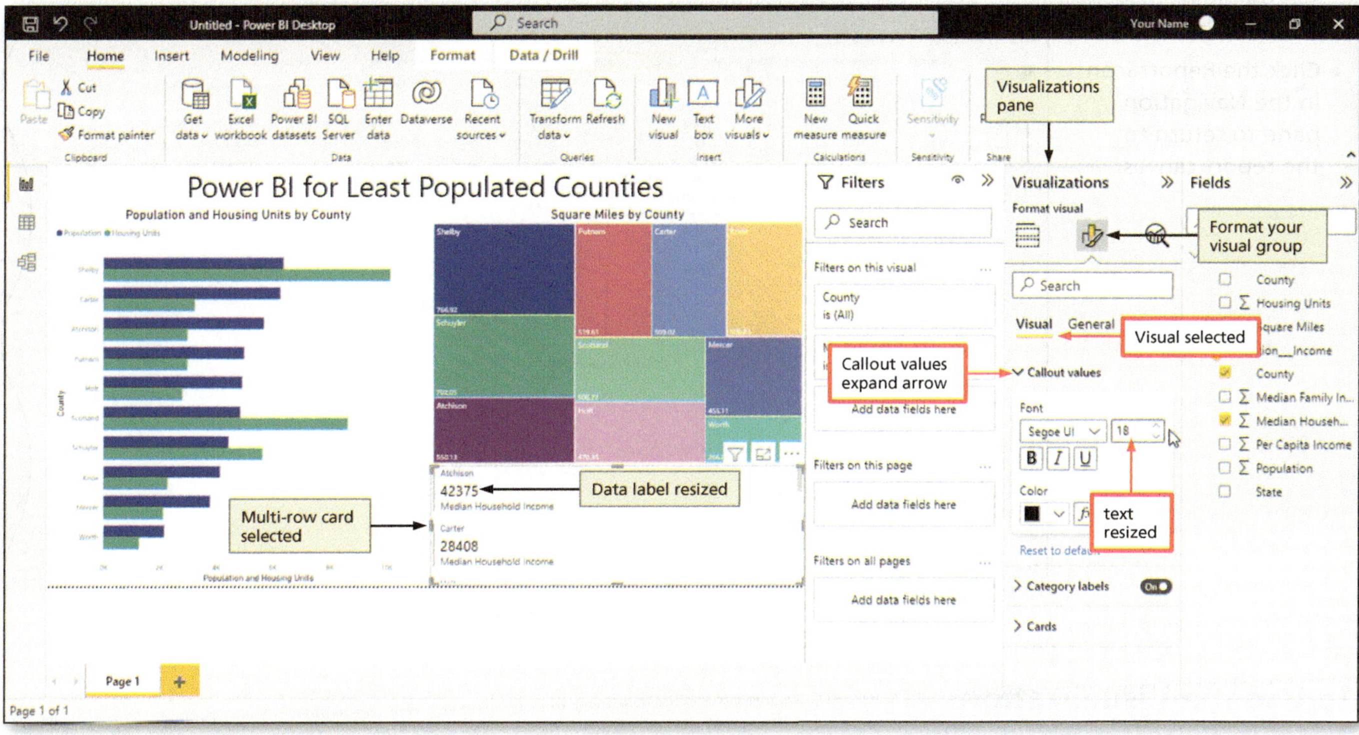

Figure 10–61

10

- Click the Data icon on the Navigation bar to view the Excel data being used in the report.
- Click the expand arrow next to Population__Income in the Fields pane and then select Median Household Income (Figure 10–62).

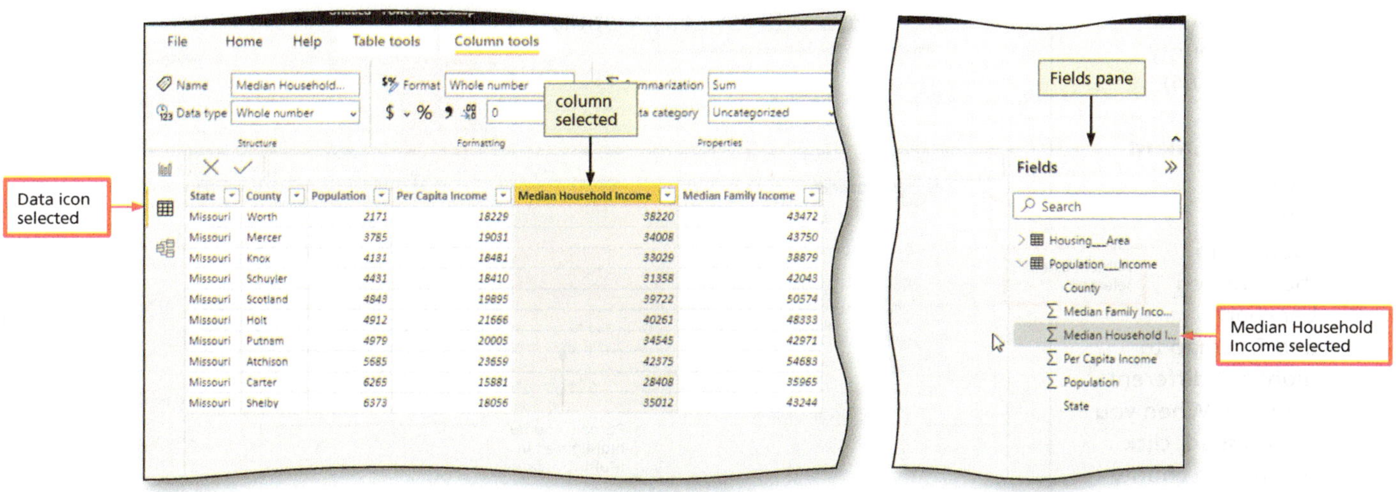

Figure 10–62

11

- Click the Comma icon (Column tools tab | Formatting group) to format the numbers (Figure 10-63).
- Click the Report icon in the Navigation pane to return to the report canvas.

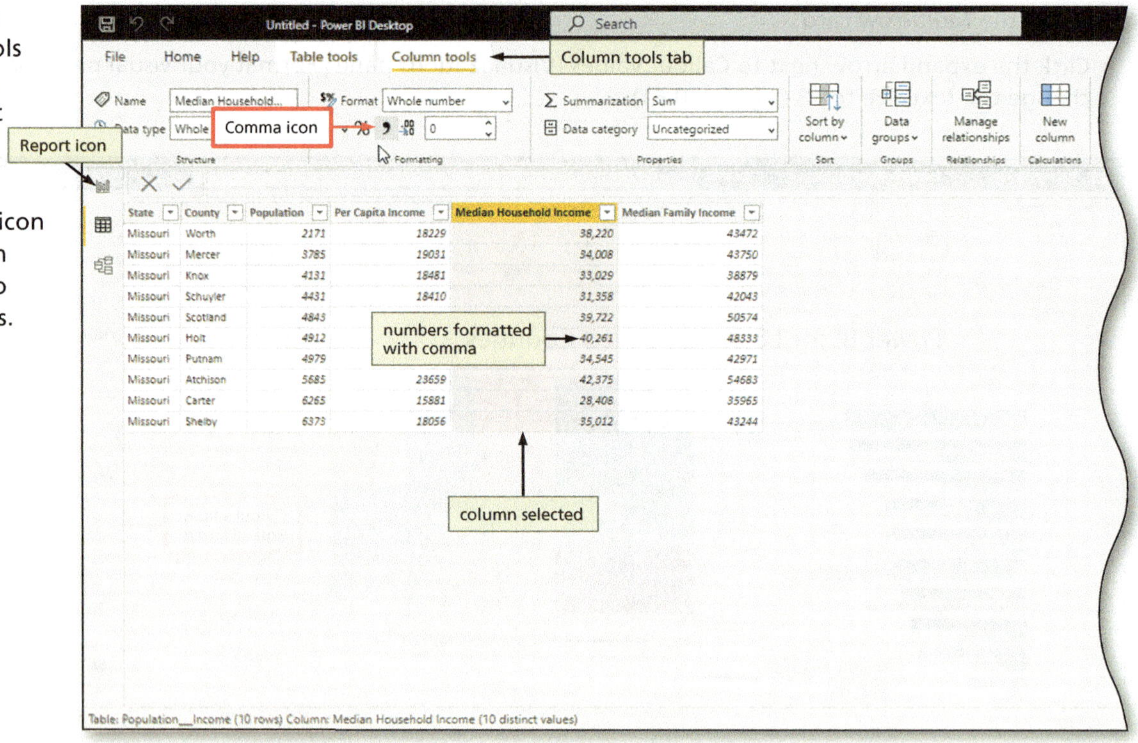

Figure 10–63

To Use the Visualizations

The following steps use the bars on the Clustered bar chart to highlight specific data items. **Why?** When presenting data, you may want to focus in on a piece of data (in this case, one county). You will also use the Treemap to highlight specific data items.

1

- In the Clustered bar chart, click the fourth set of bars to view the information for Putnam county (Figure 10-64).

Experiment

- Click on different counties in the Clustered bar chart and Treemap to highlight different counties. When you are finished, click on Putnam county in the Clustered bar chart

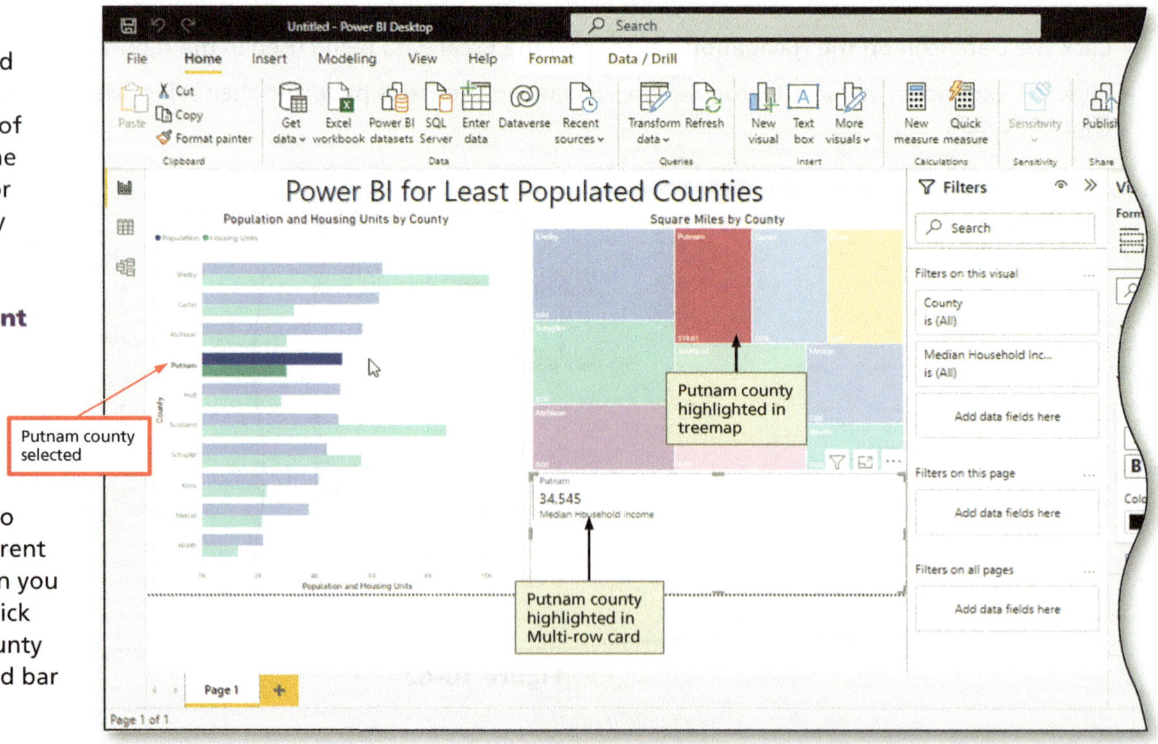

Figure 10–64

To Add a Filter in Power BI

The following steps add a filter to the Power BI report. You will filter the data to display only median household incomes greater than $35,000. **Why?** Filtering for income is another measure that the client may want to use in determining the location for the new hospital. The Filters pane has three categories: Filters on this visual, Filters on this page, and Filters on all pages. These options allow you to set specific filters for the selected visualization, the current report page, or the complete report. You will also save the file.

1

- Expand the Filters pane, if necessary. Click on Putnam county on the clustered bar chart again to deselect the individual county for all visualizations.
- Click and drag Median Household Income from the Fields pane to the box Add data fields here listed under Filters on this page (Figure 10-65).

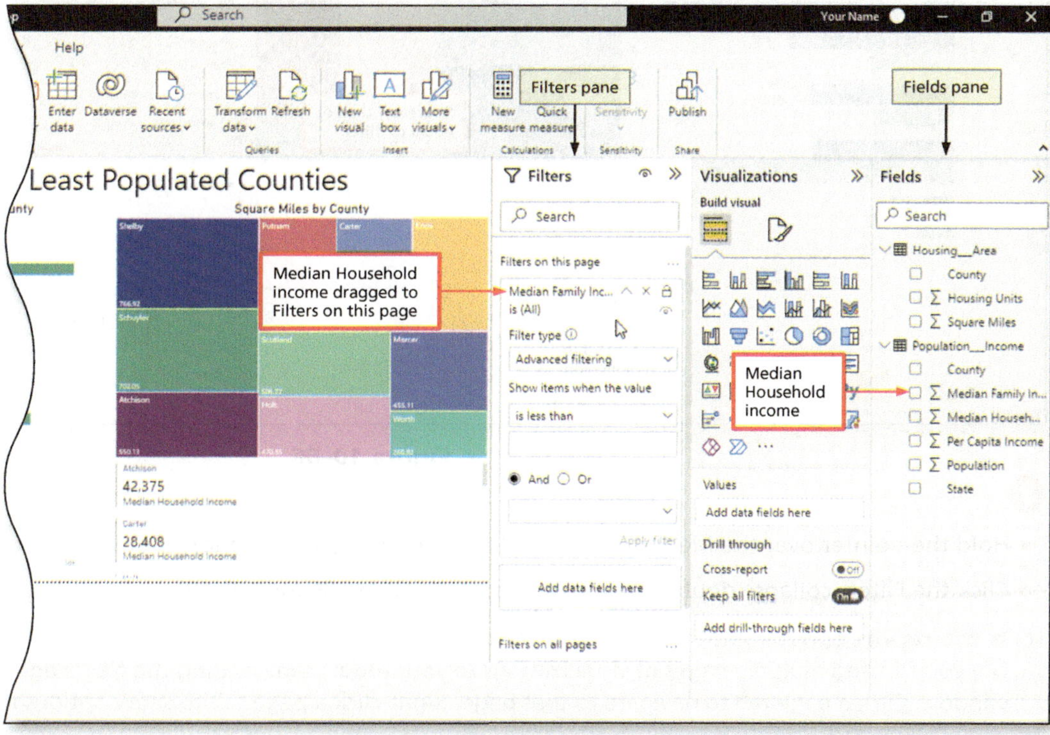

Figure 10–65

2

- Click the expand arrow to the right of the Median Household Income filter if necessary, change 'is less than' to 'is greater than or equal to' and type 35000 in the 'Show items when the value' area (Median Household income filter | Filters pane).
- Click Apply filter (Figure 10–66).

Q&A **What is the data showing?**
Power BI displays only five counties, out of 10 least populous counties, with median incomes of $35,000 or more.

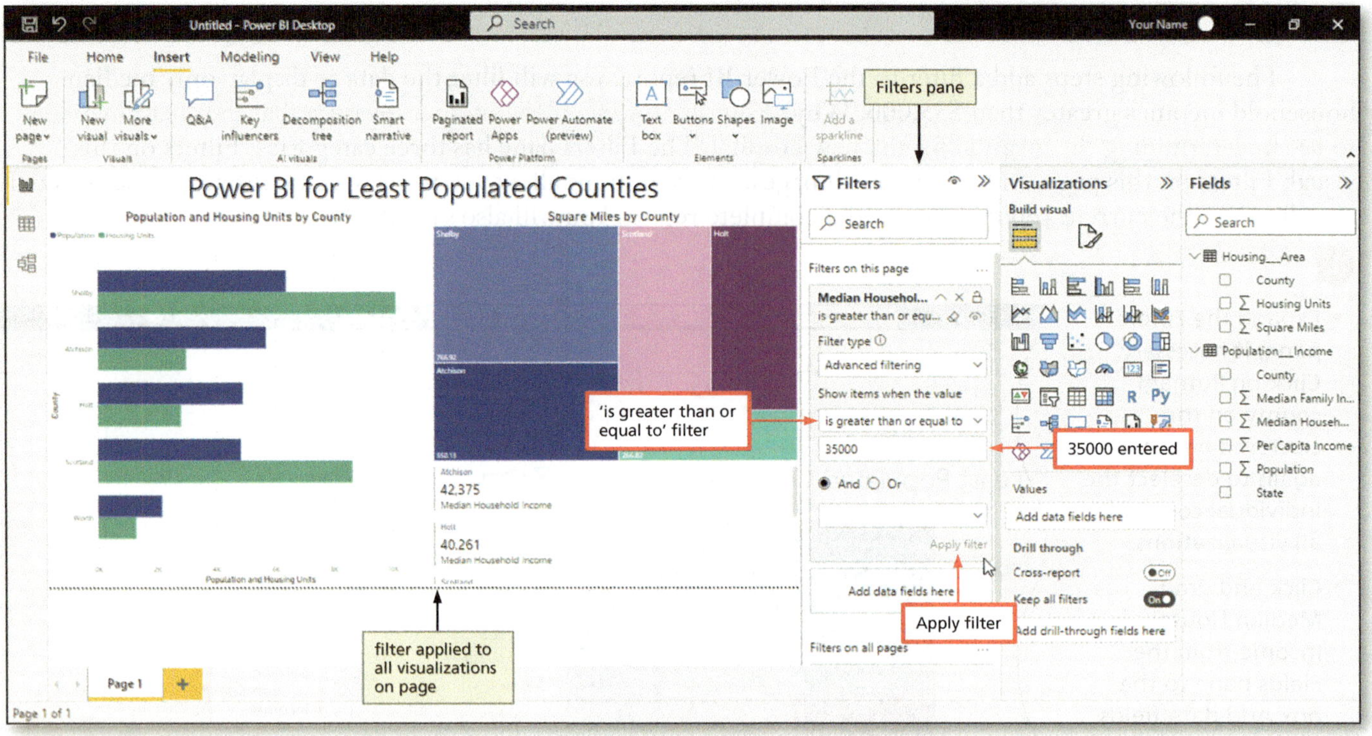

Figure 10–66

3

- Hold the pointer over the Median Household Income filter (Filters pane) and click the 'x' to remove the filter.
- Click the Filters collapse double arrow to collapse the pane (Figure 10–67).

Q&A **Is the report canvas limited to one page of visualizations?**
No, you can add multiple pages of visualizations to your report canvas using the New Page tab at the bottom left of the window. Click a page tab to navigate to that page. Right-click a page tab to show options to rename or duplicate it.

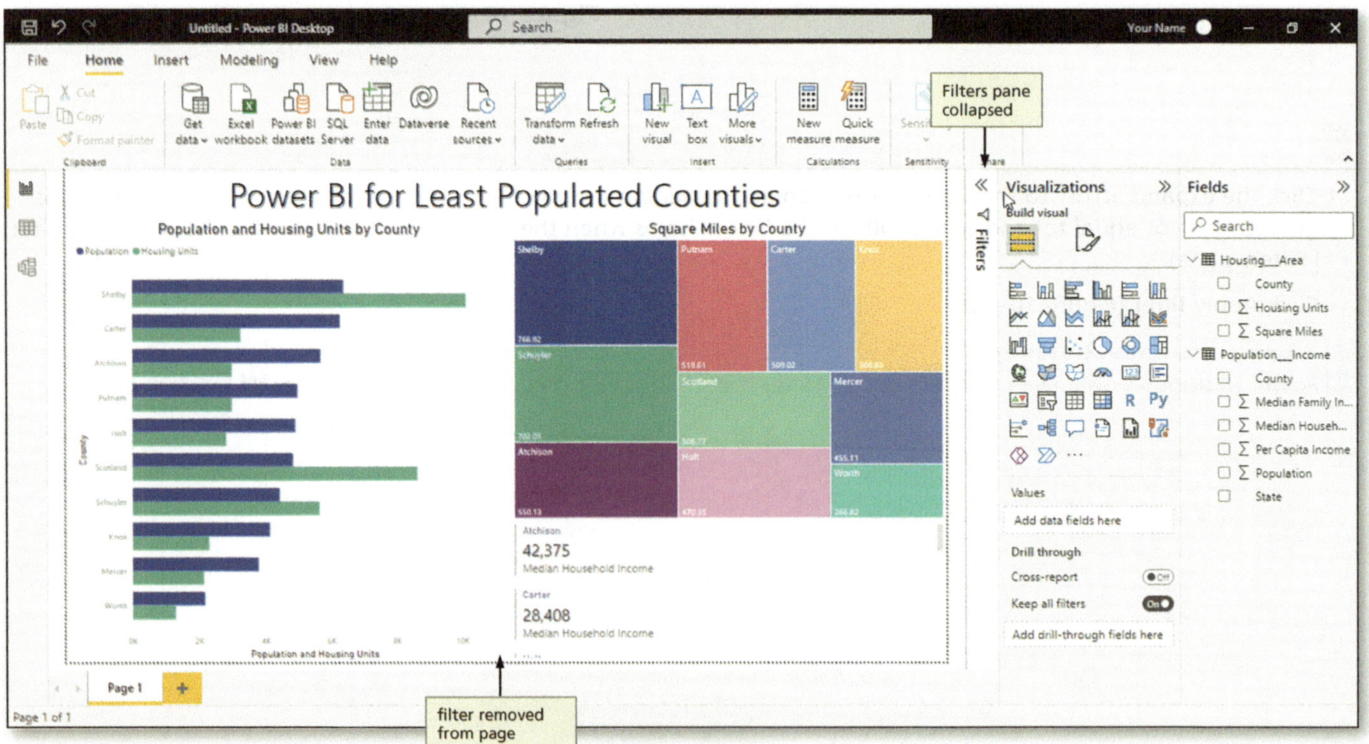

Figure 10–67

4

- Click the Save button on the title bar and save the file as SC_EX_10_HospitalCounties_PowerBI.pbix.
- Close Power BI Desktop and reopen the SC_EX_10_HospitalProposal.xlsx to continue with the module.

Q&A **How do I share my Power BI report with others?**
You can Publish (Home tab | Share group) to your workspace in the Power BI service to share your findings with others.

Break Point: If you want to take a break, this is a good place to do so. You can exit Excel now. To resume later, start Excel, open the file called SC_EX_10_HospitalProposal.xlsx, and continue following the steps from this location forward.

3D Maps

The 3D Maps power tool, formerly called Power Map, helps show your data in relation to a geographical area on a map. You can create a single map or several maps that become an animation focusing in on your data. The animation is called a tour, and each map is called a scene. If you are going to create a tour, you should plan out each scene and decide what data you want to display in each one.

The 3D Maps command opens a new window that uses a lot of your computer's resources. It is a good idea to close any apps other than Excel while working with 3D Maps.

BTW
Accessing 3D Maps
You cannot create a direct hyperlink to the 3D Maps window. You must click the 3D Map arrow (Insert tab | Tours group) and then click the 'Open 3D Maps' command on the menu. You can create a macro that opens the 3D Maps window or create a hyperlink to a saved tour.

To Open the 3D Maps Window

The following steps open the 3D Maps window. **Why?** The 3D Maps windows has the tools to create a map or tour.

1

- Click the Housing Units sheet tab and click anywhere within the data.
- Display the Insert tab (Figure 10–68).

Q&A **Do I have to be in a specific worksheet to access 3D Maps?**
No. 3D Maps can be accessed from any worksheet or window. However, if you want tables to appear in the Field List, it is best to start from a worksheet associated with the data model.

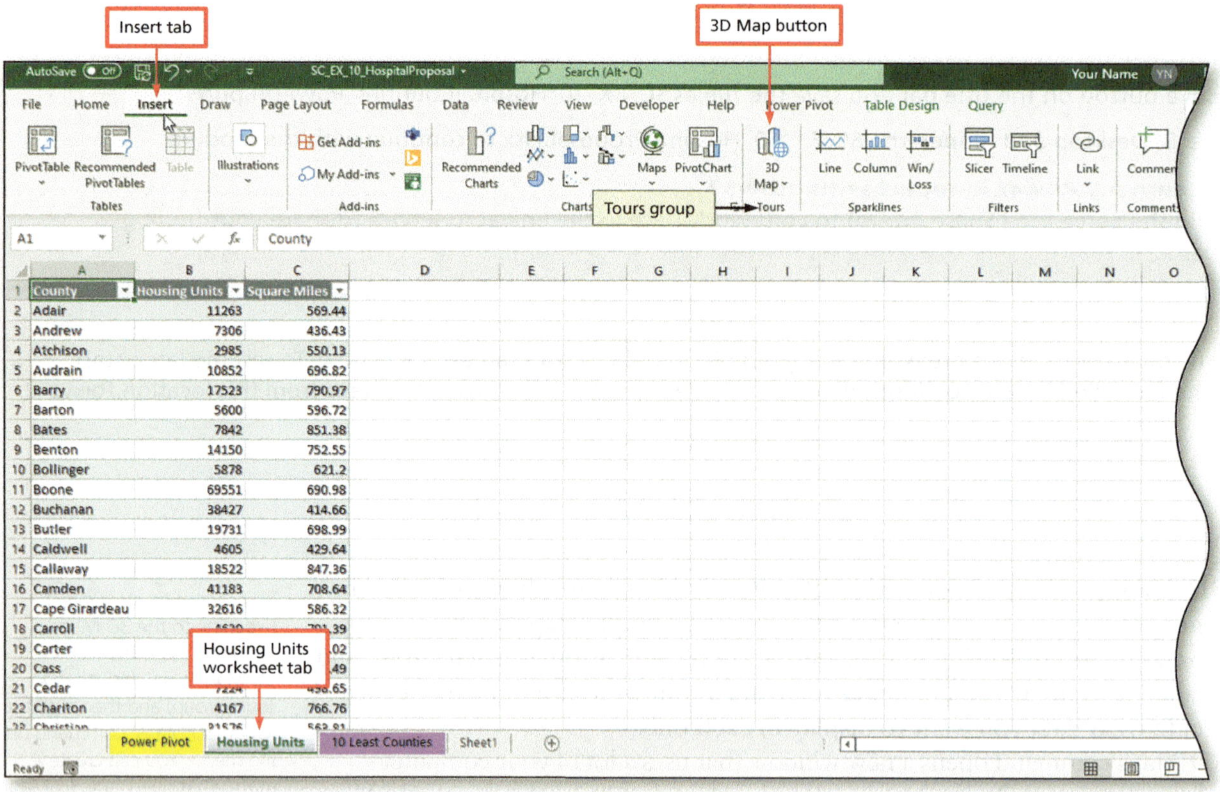

Figure 10–68

2

- Click the 3D Map button (Insert tab | Tours group) to open the 3D Maps window (Figure 10–69).

Q&A

I do not see two tables in my field list. What should I do?

It is possible that the second table was not added to the data model. Minimize the 3D Maps window and return to the main Excel window. Click the sheet tab of the missing data and click any cell in the table. Click the 3D Map arrow (Insert tab | Tours group) and then click 'Add the Selected Data to 3D Maps' on the menu.

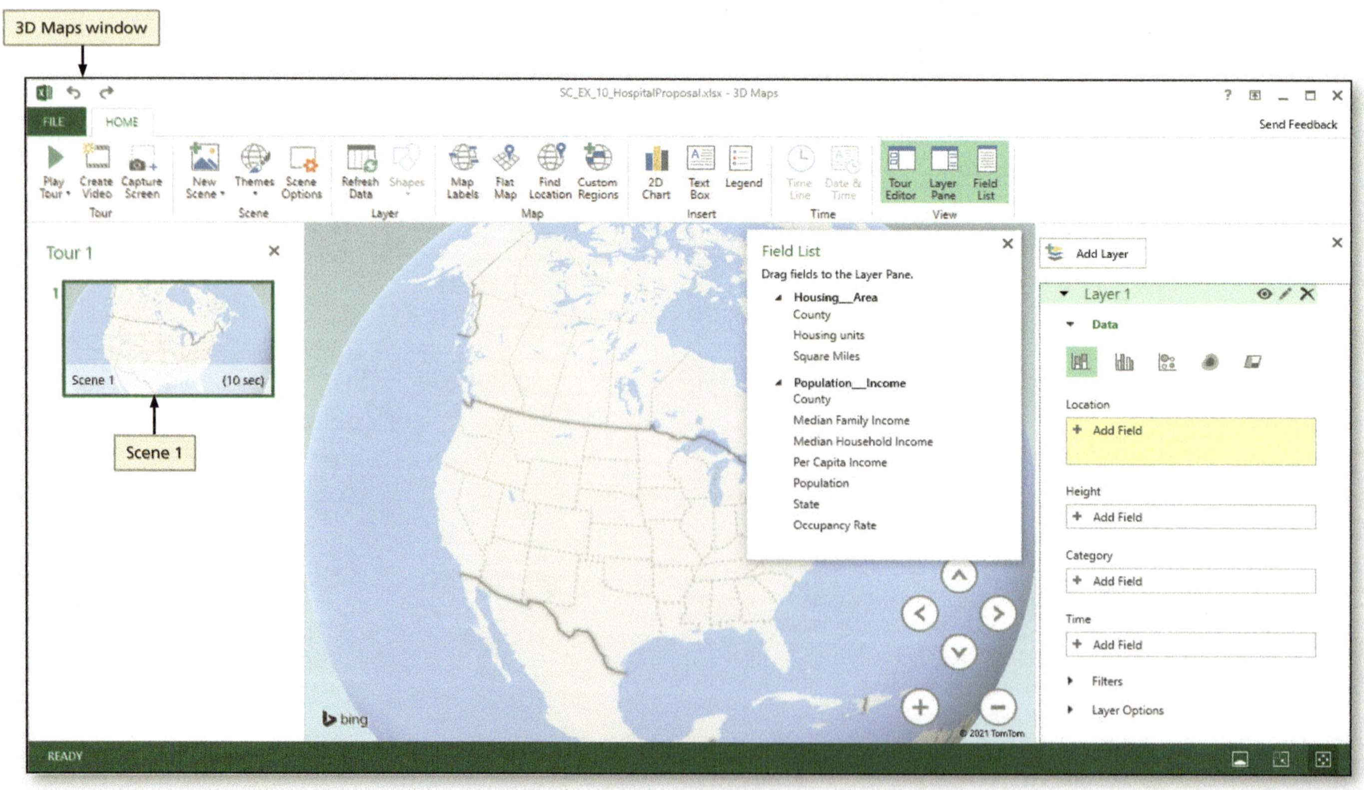

Figure 10–69

To Create Scenes

If you want to create more than just a single static map, you must add scenes to the tour. The following steps add four scenes to the tour. **Why?** The first scene will focus in on the state, the second one will focus on the counties, the third will display the population for each of the 10 least populous counties, and the fourth will annotate the chosen county for the new hospital. When you add a new scene, it temporarily duplicates the previous scene until you customize its settings.

1

- In the 3D Maps window, click the New Scene button (3D Maps Home tab | Scene group) to add Scene 2 to the tour.
- In the Field List, drag the State field from the Population__Income table to the Location area in the Layer 1 pane to focus in on the state.
- Click the Map Labels button (3D Maps Home tab | Map group) to display state labels on the map (Figure 10–70).

Q&A **Does the map have its own worksheet tab in Excel?**
3D Maps opens in a new window accessible only via the 3D Map button. If you close the window without saving, you will have to start over. To revisit a saved map, click the 3D Map button (Insert tab | Tours group). Excel will display a 3D Map dialog box from which you can choose the specific map you have created.

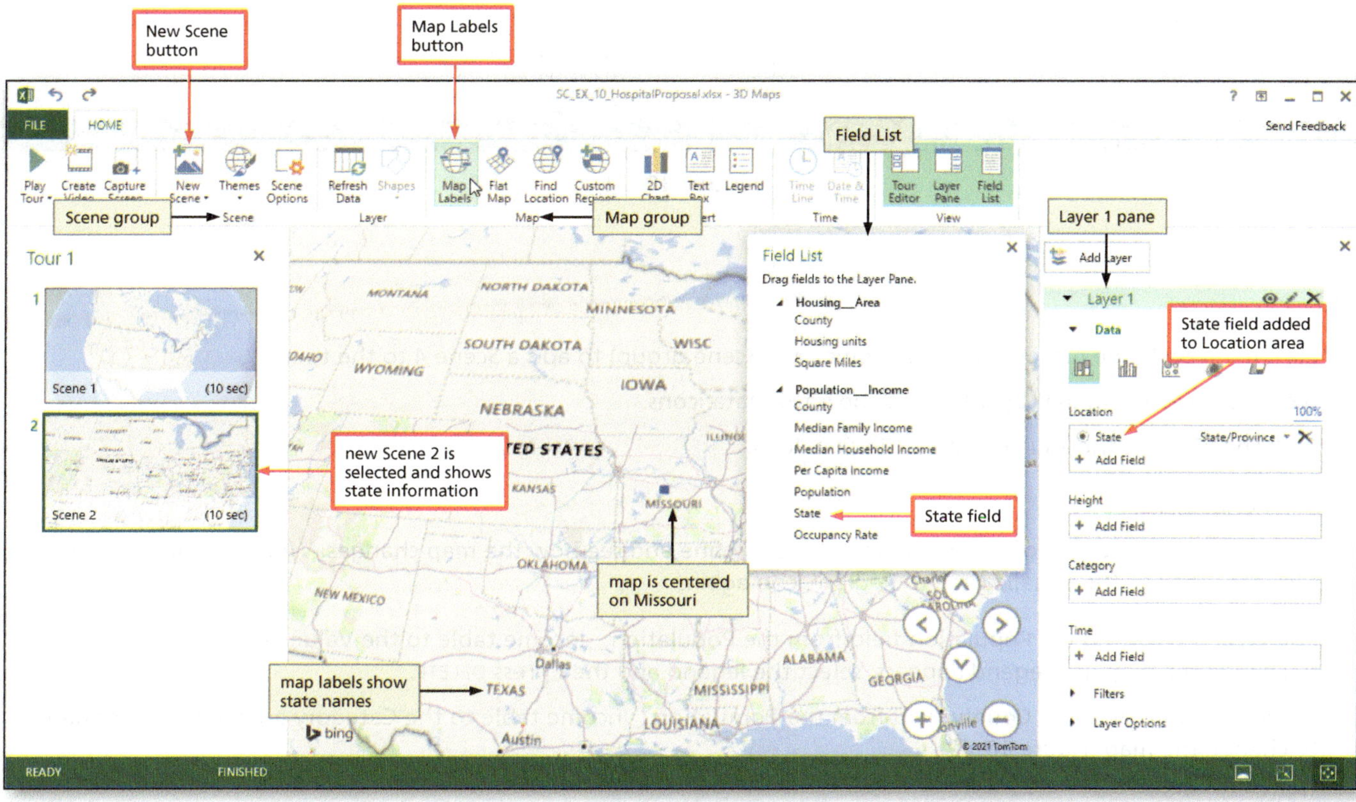

Figure 10–70

2

- Click the New Scene button (3D Maps Home tab | Scene group) to add a Scene 3 to the tour.
- In the Field List, drag the County field from the Population__Income table to the Location area in the Layer 1 pane, below State, to display the counties on the map.

Q&A **Does it make any difference which County field I choose?**
Yes. The County field from the Population__Income table has only 10 records. The County field from the Housing__Area table has 117. If you chose the latter, all counties would be indicated on the map.

- Click the Zoom in button several times to zoom in on the state of Missouri.
- If necessary, drag in the map and use the tilt buttons to better position the state (Figure 10–71).

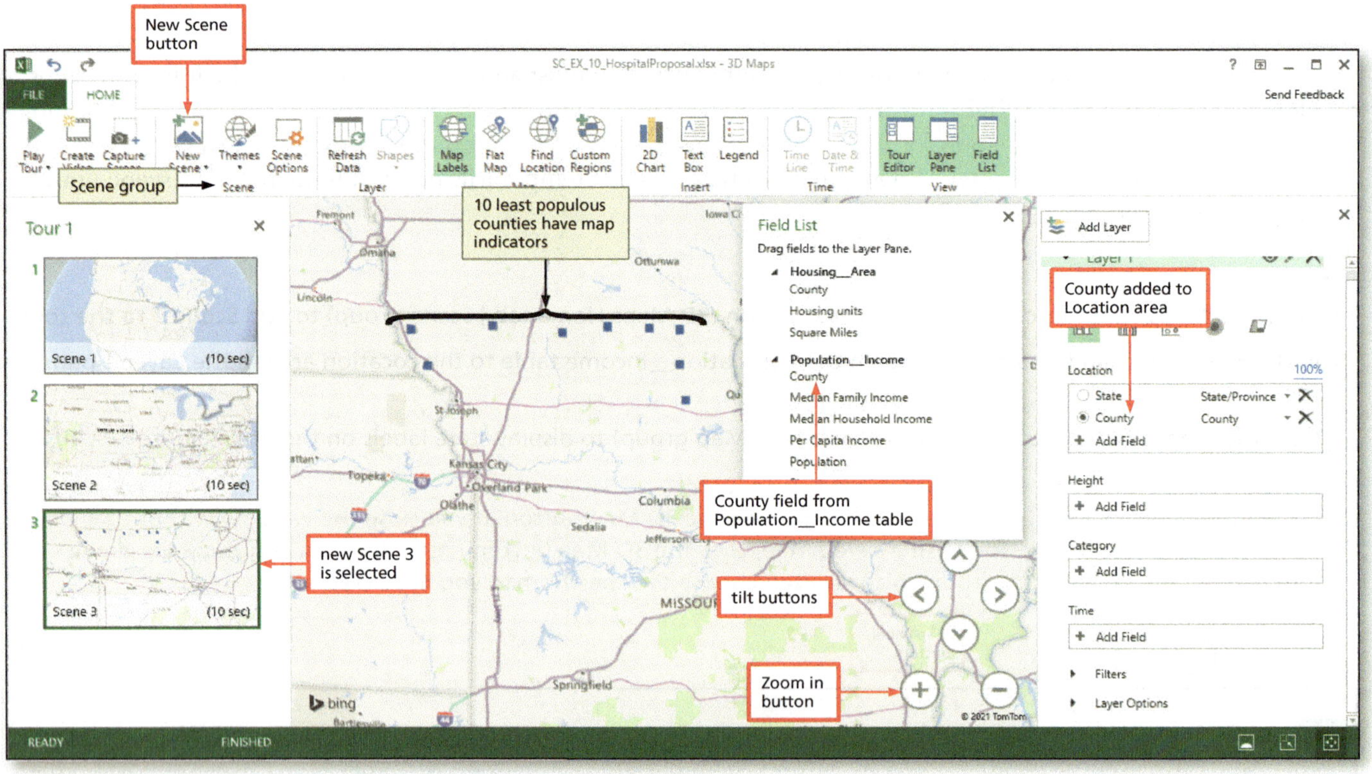

Figure 10–71

3

- Click the New Scene button (3D Maps Home tab | Scene group) to add a Scene 4 to the tour.
- Scroll as necessary in the Layer Pane to show the Data icons.
- Click the 'Change the visualization to Region' icon.

Experiment

- One at a time, click each of the icons in the Layer 1 pane and see how the map changes. When you are finished, click the 'Change the visualization to Region' icon again.

- In the Field List, drag the Population field from the Population__Income table to the Value area in the Layer 1 pane to change the map. If a legend appears, select the legend and then press DELETE.
- In the Field List, drag the County field from the Population__Income table to the Category area in the Layer pane to change the map (Figure 10–72).

Experiment

- On the map itself, point to any of the colored county regions to display its data card.

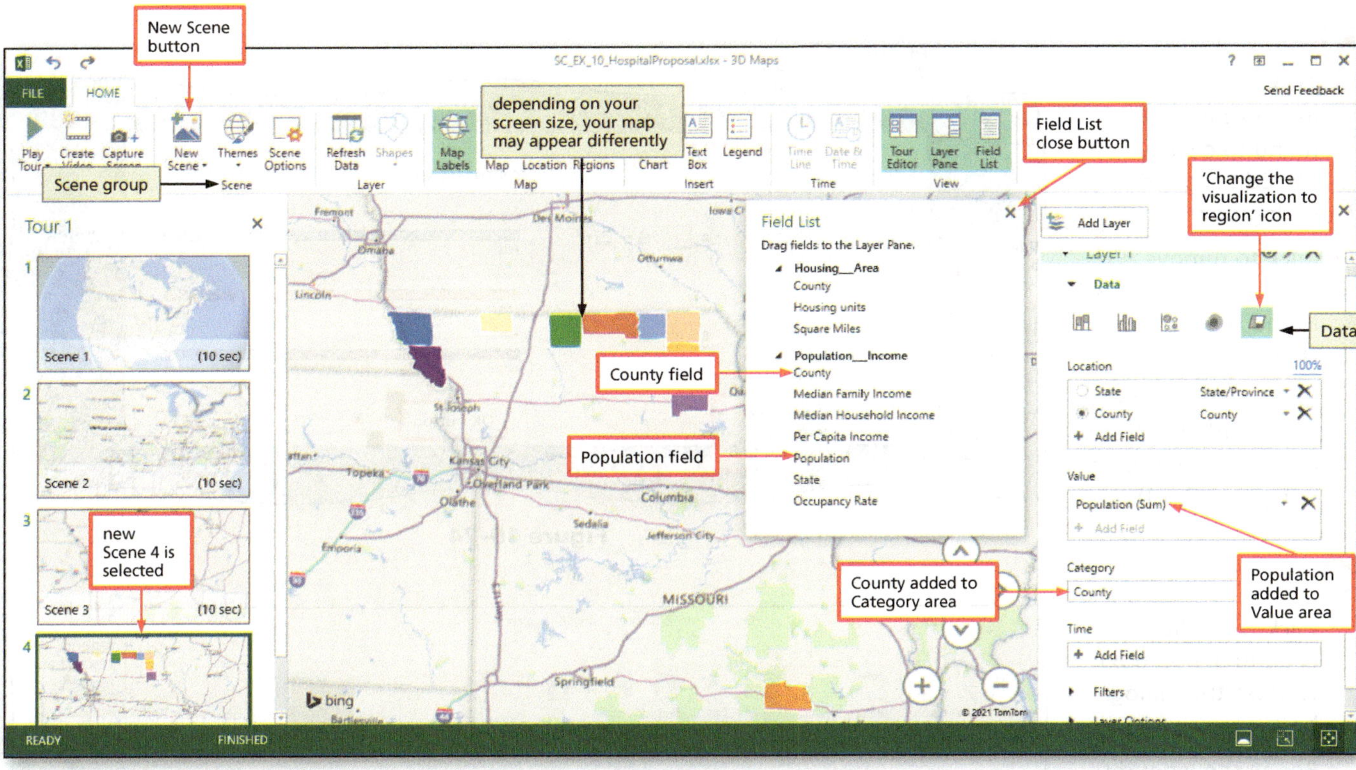

Figure 10–72

4

- Click the Field List button (3D Maps Home tab | View group) to close the Field List.
- Click the Layer Pane button (3D Maps Home tab | View group) to close the Layer 1 pane.

Q&A **My 3D Maps window suddenly closed. What should I do?**
In the Excel window, click the 3D Map button (Insert tab | Tours group) and continue with these steps.

- Drag in the map to position the state slightly to the left of center. Make sure you can see all the edges of the state outline.
- Click the Legend button (3D Maps Home tab | Insert group) to display the legend.
- Right-click the legend to display the shortcut menu (Figure 10–73).

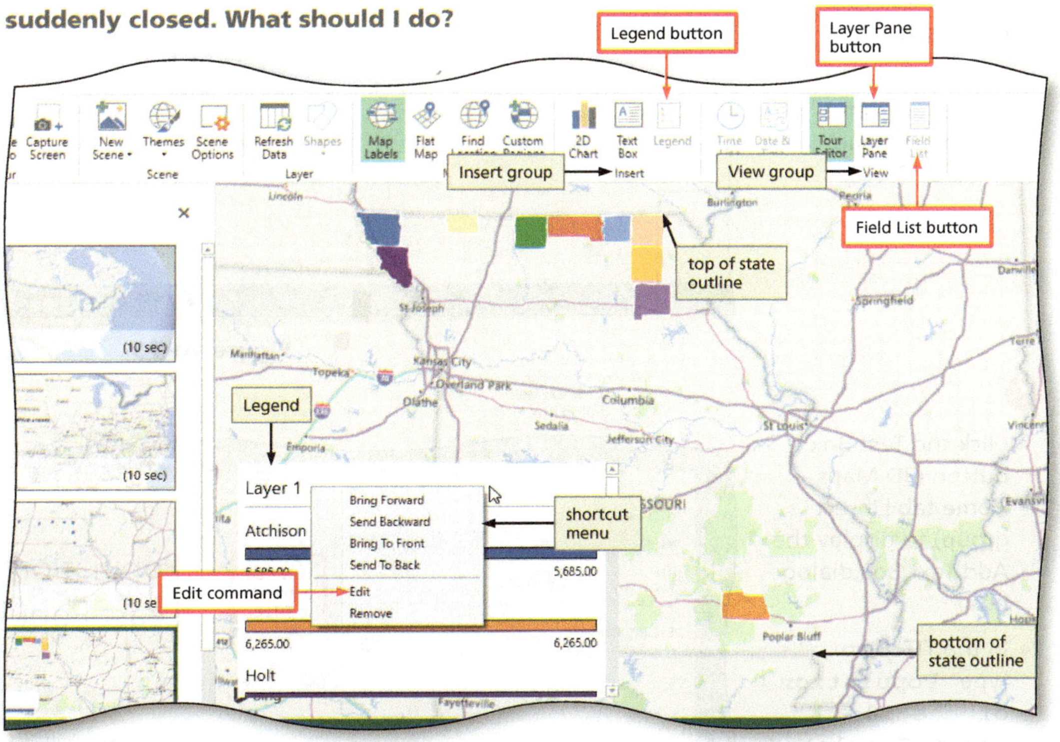

Figure 10–73

5

- Click Edit on the legend shortcut menu to display the Edit Legend dialog box.
- Click to remove the check mark in the Show Title check box.
- Change the font size of the Title to 10 and of the Categories to 8 (Figure 10–74).

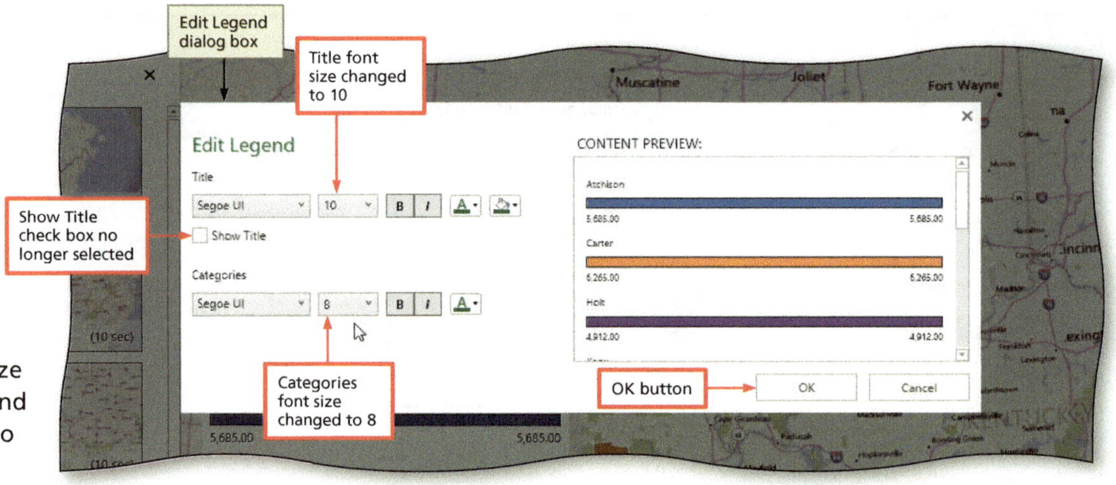

Figure 10–74

6

- Click OK (Edit Legend dialog box) to close the dialog box.
- Resize the legend to make it very narrow, just wide enough to see the name of the county and the population.
- Resize the legend to be as tall as the map itself.
- Drag the legend to the far-right side of the map (Figure 10–75).

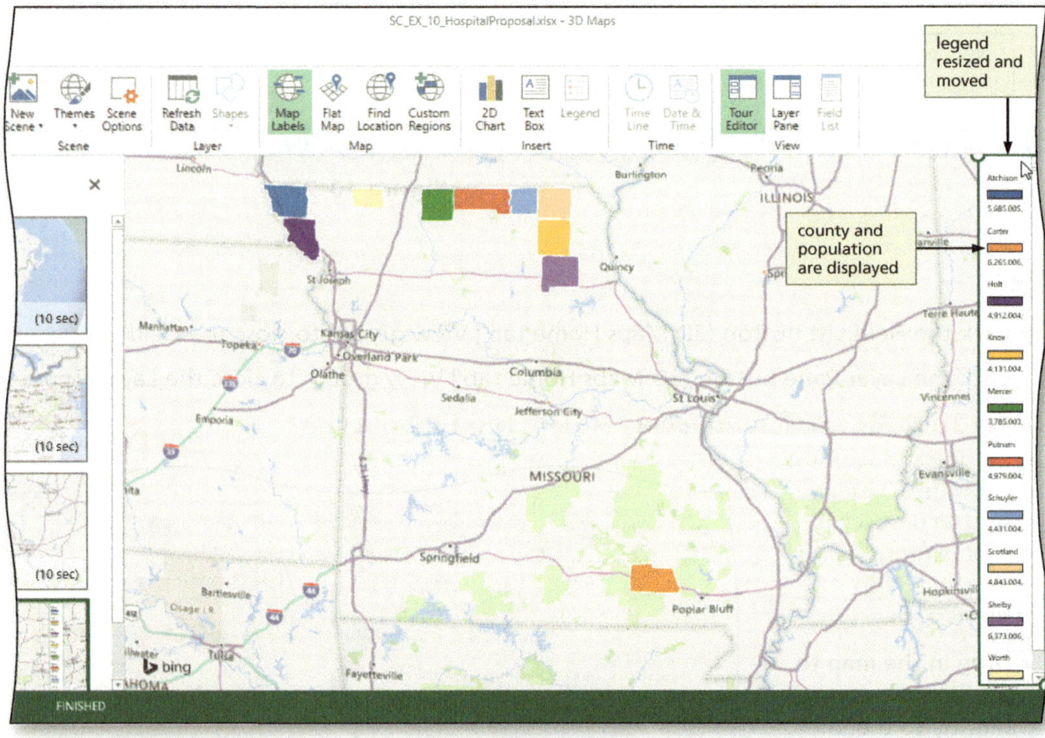

Figure 10–75

7

- Click the Text Box button (3D Maps Home tab | Insert group) to display the Add Text Box dialog box.
- In the TITLE box, type **`Population of the 10 Least Populated Counties`** to enter the title (Figure 10–76).

Figure 10–76

8

- Click the Create button (Add Text Box dialog box) to create a text box title for the map.
- Resize the text box so the title appears on one line.
- Drag the text box to the center of the map.
- Adjust the size of the map and center as necessary (Figure 10–77).

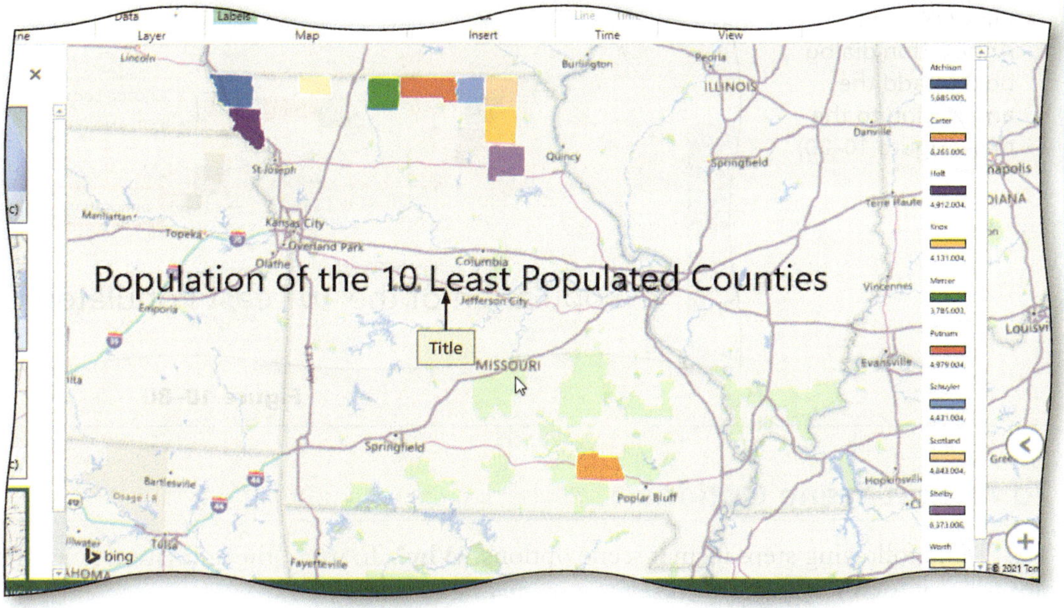

Figure 10–77

9

- Click the New Scene button (3D Maps Home tab | Scene group) to add a Scene 5 to the tour.
- Right-click the tan-colored county in the top right corner to display the shortcut menu (Figure 10–78).

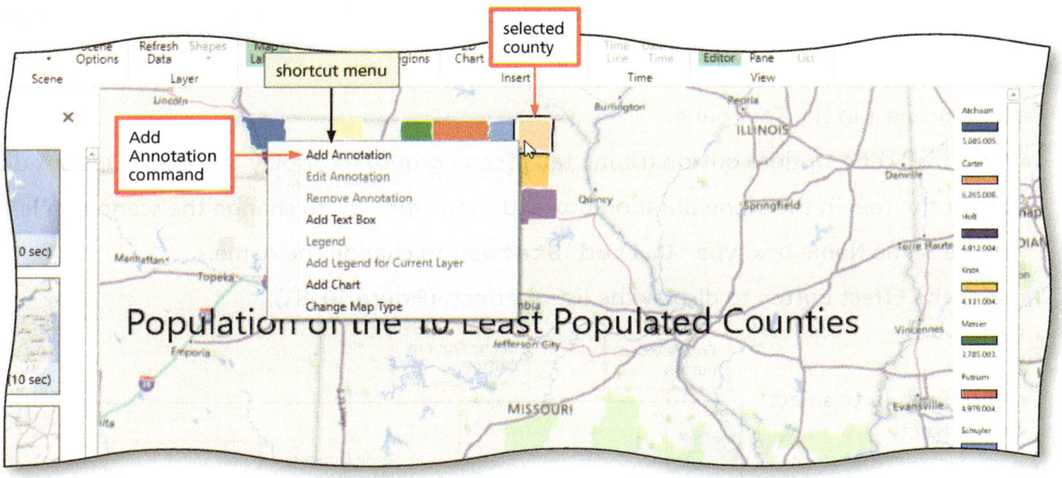

Figure 10–78

10

- Click Add Annotation to display the Add Annotation dialog box.
- Type `Chosen Location` in the TITLE box. Type `SCOTLAND COUNTY` in the DESCRIPTION box (Figure 10–79).

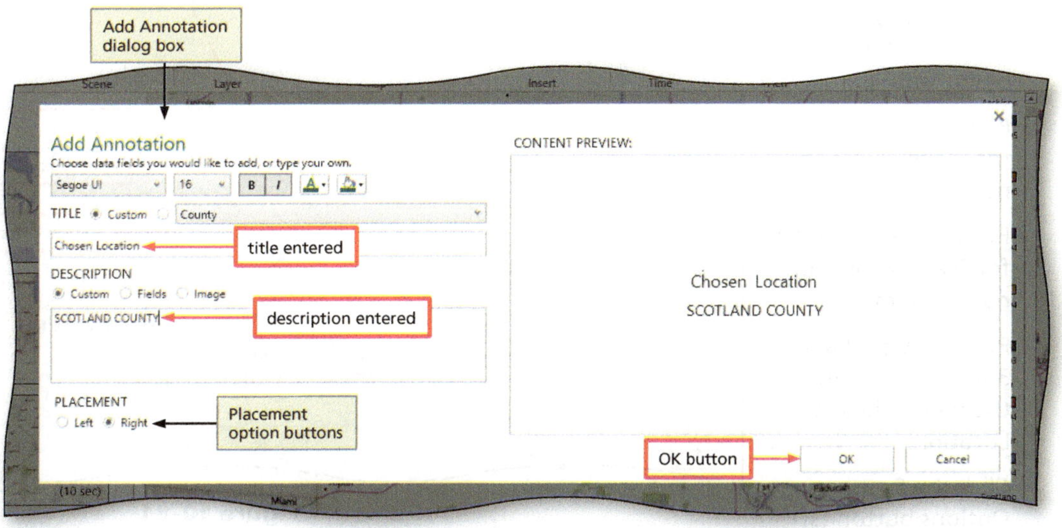

Figure 10–79

Q&A **What do the PLACEMENT option buttons do?**

You can choose on which side of the selected item the annotation will appear.

11

- Click OK (Add Annotation dialog box) to add the annotation to the map (Figure 10–80).

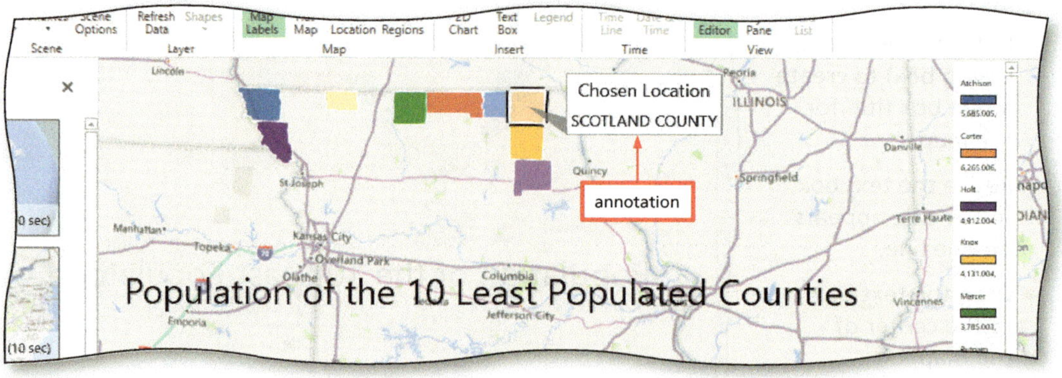

Figure 10–80

To Format Scene Options

The following steps format scene options. **Why?** To make the animation smoother, you will change the duration of each scene and then select a scene effect.

1

- Select the text, Tour 1, at the top of the Tour pane. Type `Chosen Location` to replace the text.

2

- Click Scene 1 in the Tour pane.
- Click the Scene Options button (Home tab | Scene group) to display the Scene Options dialog box.
- Select the text in the Scene duration box and then type `2` to change the scene to a length of two seconds.
- In the Scene Name box type `United States` to change the name.
- Click the Effect button to display the list of effects (Figure 10–81).

3

- Click Push In to select the effect.

4

- Repeat Steps 2 and 3 for Scene 2. Use the name State.
- Repeat Steps 2 and 3 for Scene 3. Use the name Region.
- Repeat Steps 2 and 3 for Scene 4. Use the name County.
- Repeat Steps 2 and 3 for Scene 5. Use the name Chosen Location.
- Click the Scene Options button (3D Maps Home tab | Scene group) to close the Scene Options dialog box.

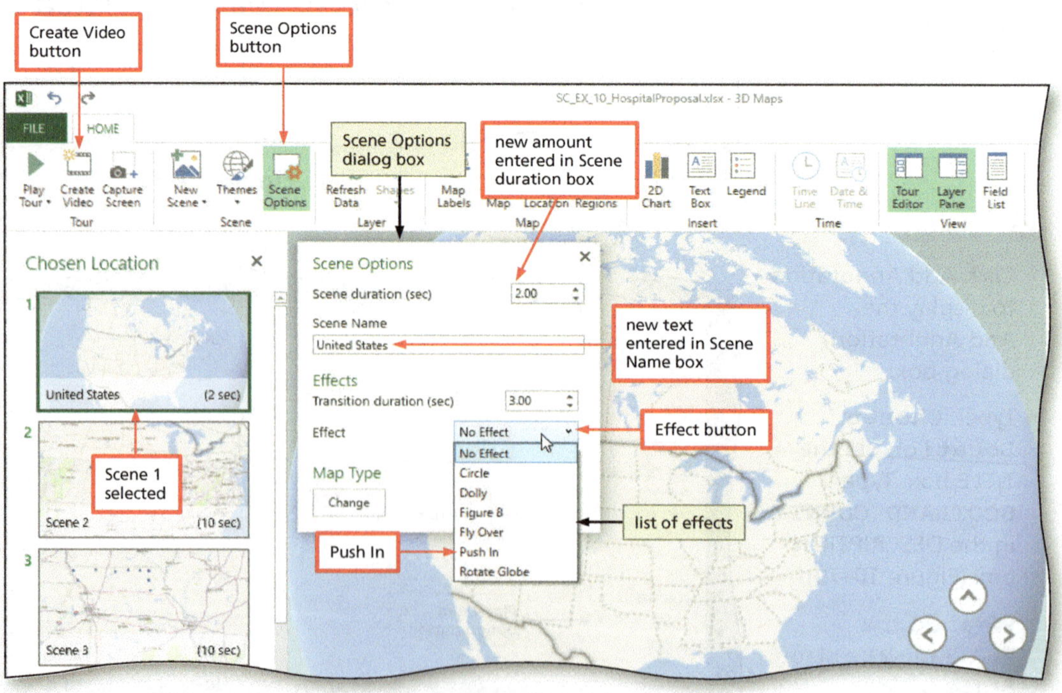

Figure 10–81

To Finish the Animation Steps

The following steps play the tour, save a copy of the tour, and take a screenshot of the final map. **Why?** You will paste the screenshot to Sheet1 in preparation for creating a home page for the workbook. You also will save the file.

1

- Click the Play Tour button (Home tab | Tour group) to play the animation. When the animation is finished, click the 'Go back to Edit view' button in the lower-left corner of the animation window to return to the 3D Maps window.
- Adjust any of the maps as necessary.
- Click the Create Video button (Home tab | Tour group) to display the Create Video dialog box.
- Click the 'Quick Export & Mobile' option button (Figure 10–82).

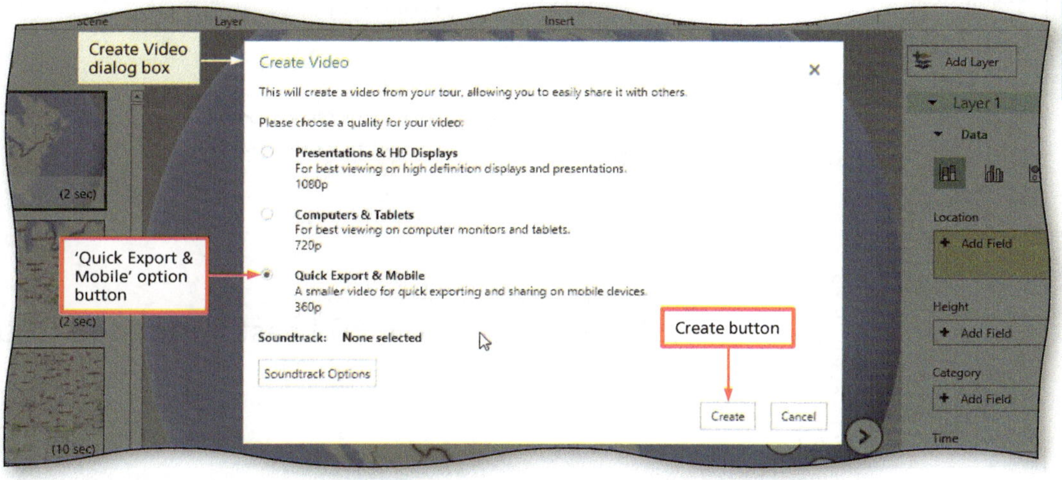

Figure 10–82

2

- Click the Create button (Create Video dialog box) to display the Save Movie dialog box.
- Type `SC_EX_10_ChosenHospitalLocation` in the File name box and then navigate to your storage location (Figure 10–83).

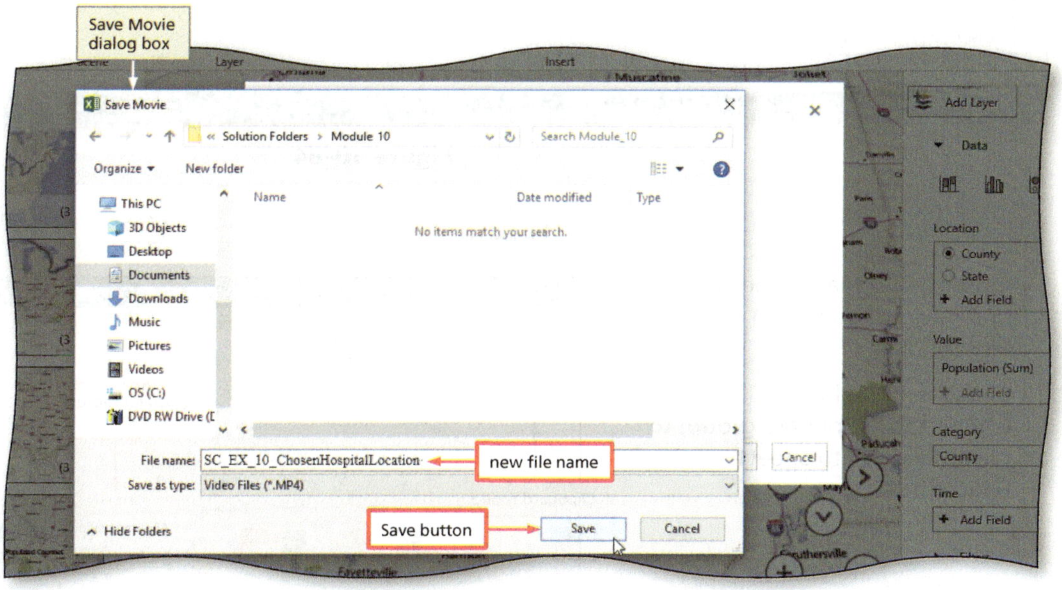

Figure 10–83

3

- Click Save (Save Movie dialog box) to save the video. When Excel has finished saving the video, click the Close button, if necessary.

Q&A
Can I play the video?
Yes, if you wish to view the video, open File Explorer, navigate to the storage location, right-click the file, and then click Open or Play on the shortcut menu. When the video is finished, click the Close button in the video window.

To Capture a Screen

The following steps capture a screen. **Why?** A screen capture is a picture that can be used in other places in the workbook and in other applications because it is stored on the clipboard.

1

- If necessary, click the Close button of any open dialog boxes. Close the Field List.
- If necessary, select Scene 5 and then click the Capture Screen button (Home tab | Tour group) to place a copy of the map on the clipboard (Figure 10–84).

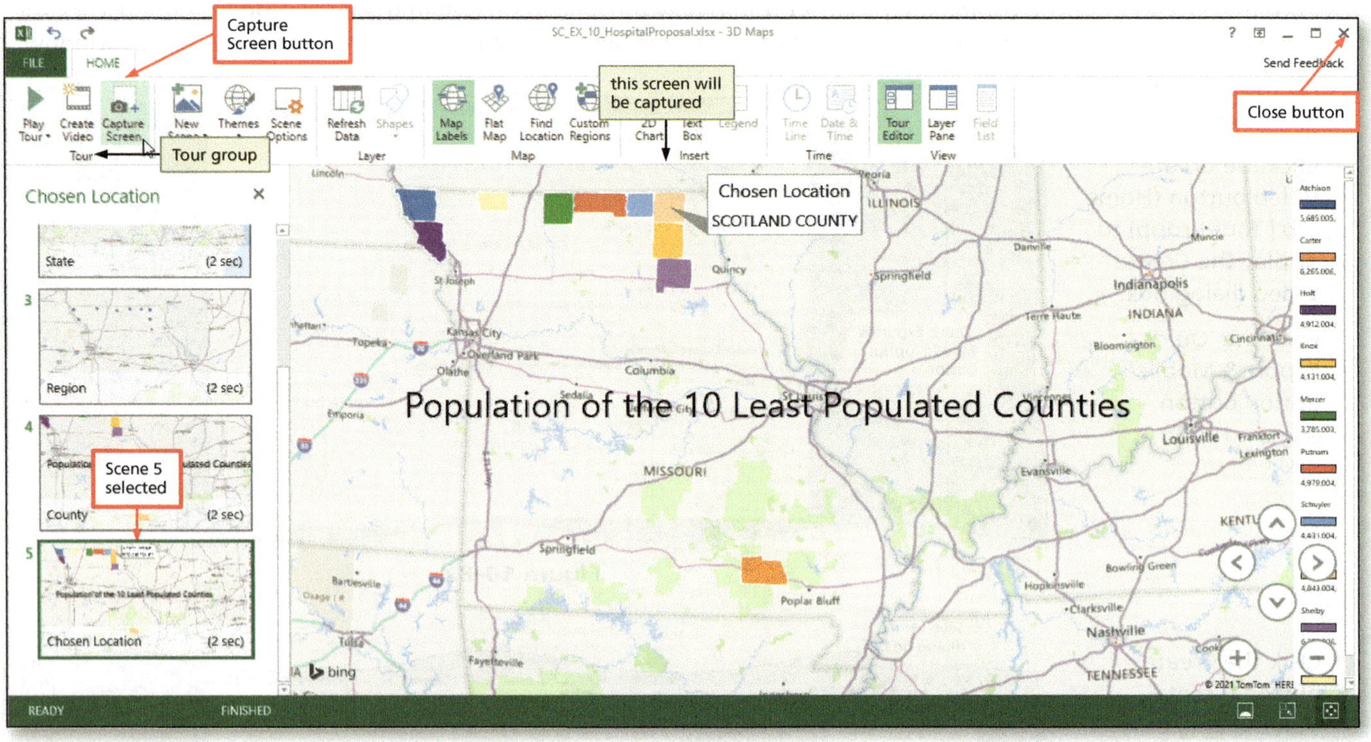

Figure 10–84

2

- Close the 3D Maps window and navigate to Sheet1 in the workbook.
- Click the Paste button (Home tab | Clipboard group) to paste the map to Sheet1 (Figure 10–85).

3

- Save the file.

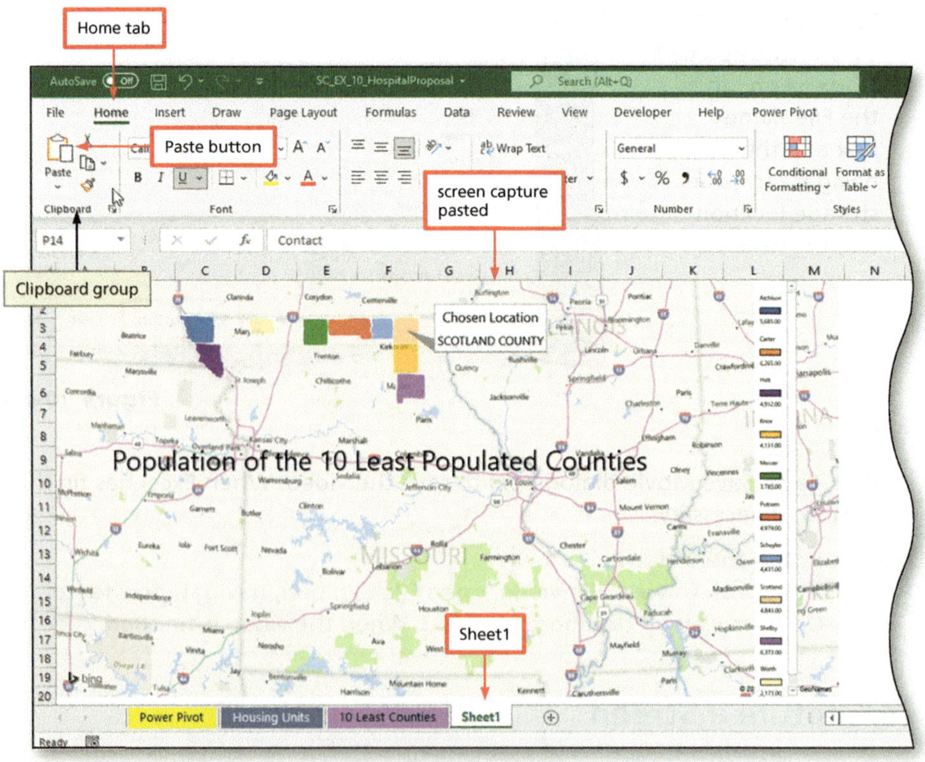

Figure 10–85

BTW
Email Hyperlinks
You can create a hyperlink that will open the user's default email app such as Outlook or Gmail, allowing them to send an email message to a specified email address. Click the Email Address button in the Insert Hyperlink dialog box (shown in Figure 10–83) and enter an email address and subject.

Formatting a Home Page with Hyperlinks and Symbols

Some Excel users create a home page or introductory worksheet to help with navigation, especially when novice users of Excel may need to interact with complex workbooks. A home page should display a title, links to other worksheets or pertinent materials, and perhaps a graphic.

A **hyperlink** is a specially formatted word, phrase, or graphic which, when clicked or tapped, lets you display a webpage on the Internet, another file, an email, or another location within the same file; also called hypertext or a link. Users click links to navigate or browse to the location. In Excel, hyperlinks can be created using cell data or linked to a graphic.

To Format the Home Page

1. If necessary, change the magnification to 100%.
2. Scroll down until you can see the lower-right corner sizing handle of the screen capture. Resize the graphic through column M to fill the left two-thirds of the screen.
3. Turn off gridlines.
4. Change the name of the worksheet tab to `Homepage.` Change the tab color to Orange. Drag the tab to the far left so it becomes the first page.

To Insert a Hyperlink

To create a hyperlink in Excel, you select the cell or graphic and then decide from among four type of hyperlinks: links to places in the workbook, links to files or webpages, a link to create a new file, or links to email addresses. Table 10–4 displays the text and hyperlinks that you will enter on the home page of the SC_EX_10_HospitalProposal workbook.

Table 10–4 Homepage Text and Hyperlinks

Cell	Text	Hyperlink location	Hyperlink
O6	Missouri Demographics	<none>	<none>
O8	Links:	<none>	<none>
P9	10 Least Counties by Population and Income	Place in This Document	10 Least Counties
P10	Housing Units	Place in This Document	Housing Units
P11	Power Pivot	Place in This Document	Power Pivot
P12	Power BI	Existing File or Web Page	SC_EX_10_HospitalCounties_PowerBI.pbix
P13	Map Animation	Existing File or Web Page	SC_EX_10_ChosenHospitalLocation.mp4
P14	Contact	E-mail Address	businessanalytics@missouri.biz

The following steps create hyperlinks on the home page. **Why?** Creating links to other tabs, files, and websites will help users navigate through the workbook.

1

- Change the width of column P to 40.
- Enter the text from the Text column in Table 10–4 into the appropriate cells. Change cell O6 to Title Style.
- Change cells O8:P14 to be font size 14.
- Bold the title in cell O6 (Figure 10–86).

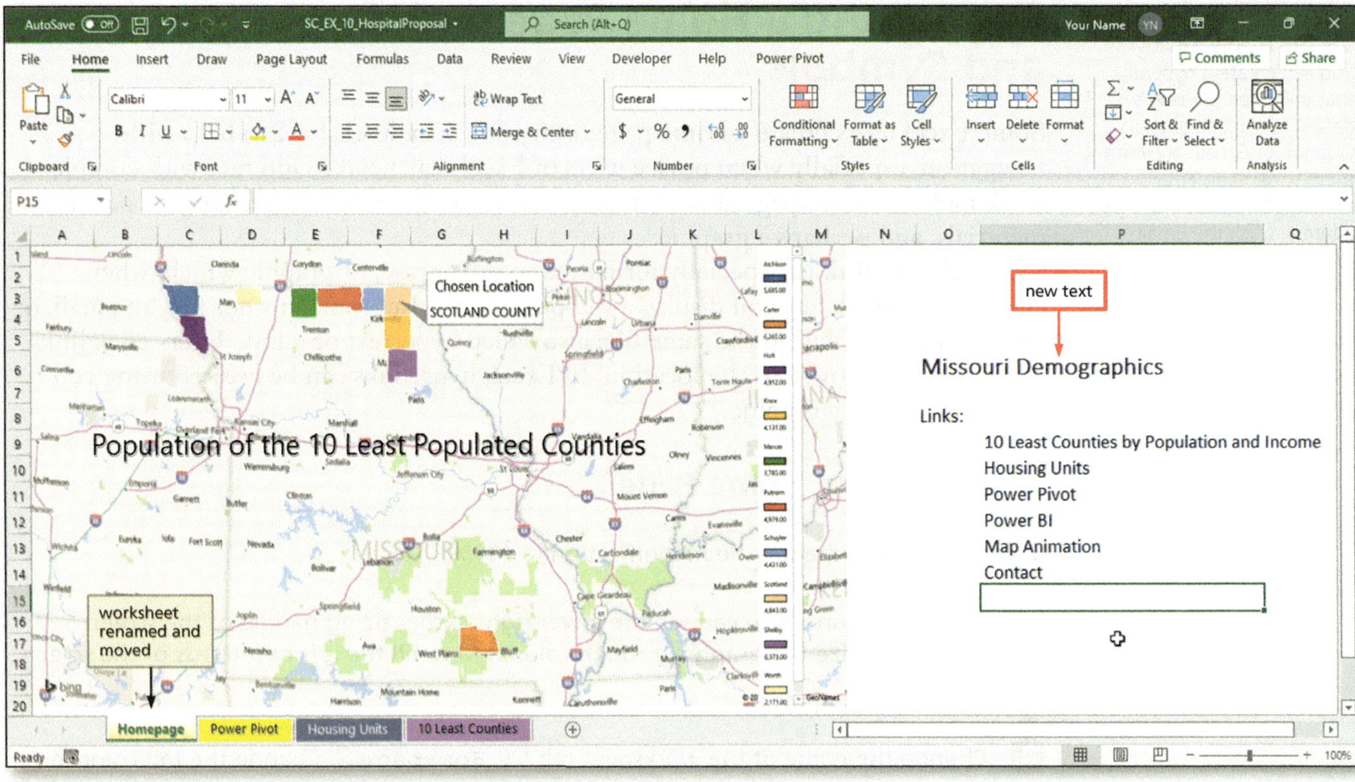

Figure 10–86

2

- Display the Insert tab.
- Select the cell you wish to make a hyperlink (in this case, cell P9) and then click the Link button (Insert tab | Links group) to display the Insert Hyperlink dialog box.
- In the Link to area, click the 'Place in This Document' button to identify the type of hyperlink.
- In the 'Or select a place in this document' area, click '10 Least Counties' (Figure 10–87).

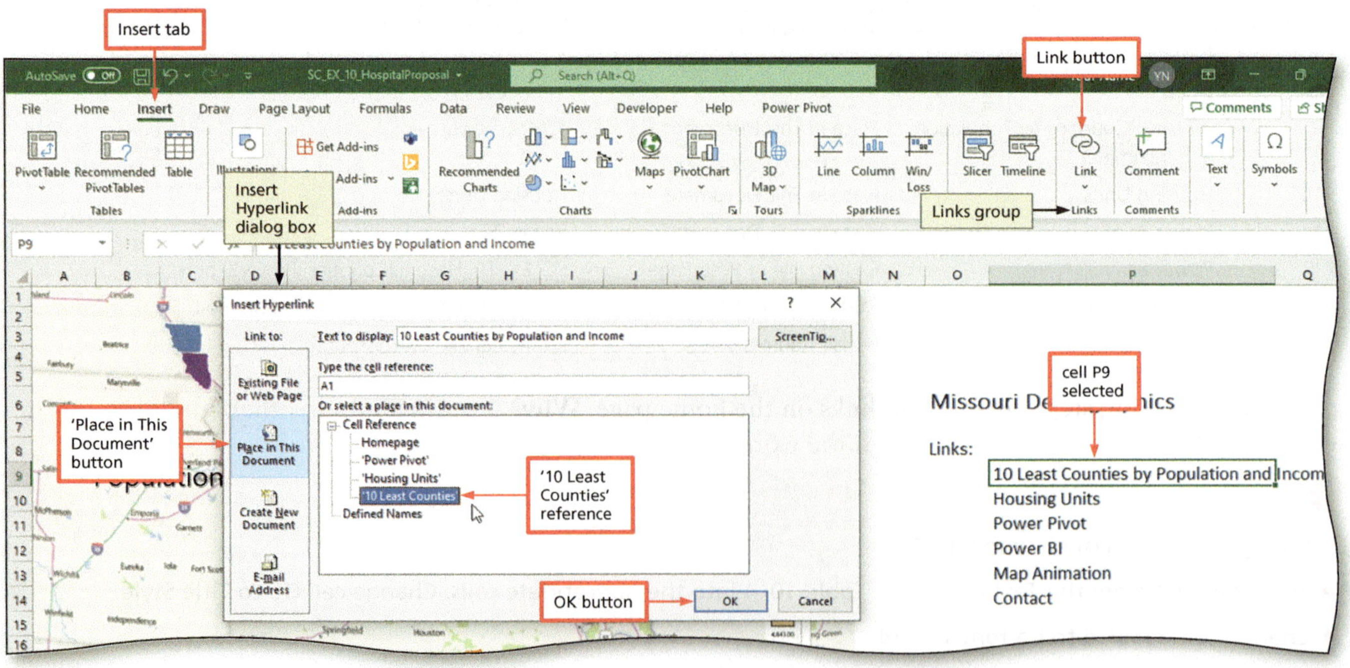

Figure 10–87

3

- Click OK (Insert Hyperlink dialog box) to assign the hyperlink.
- Repeat the process for cells P10 and P11, referring to Table 10–4 as necessary.
- Click cell P12 to select it (Figure 10–88).

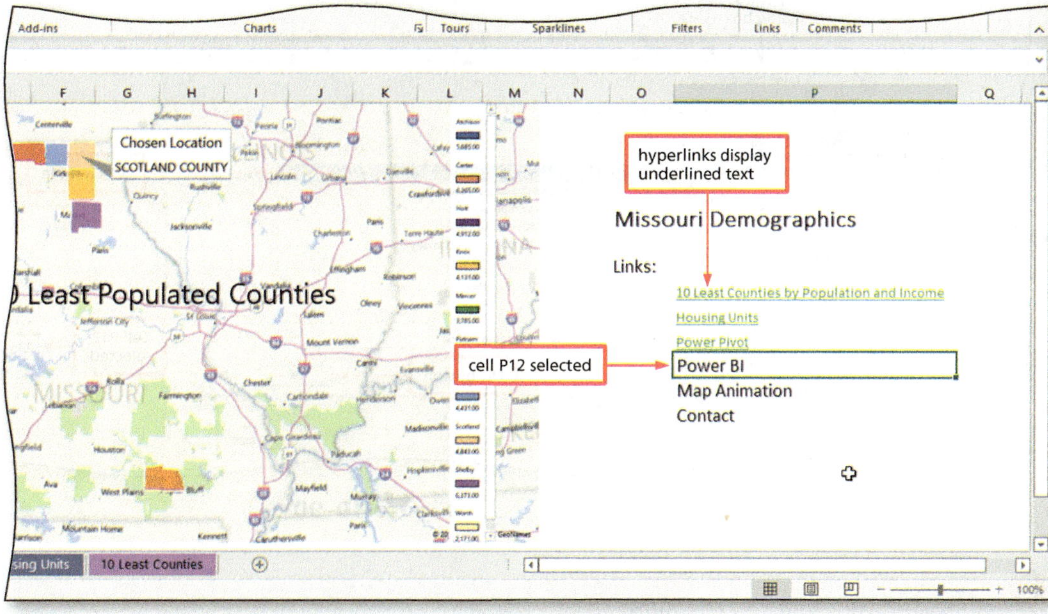

Figure 10–88

Q&A

How can I tell if a cell is hyperlinked?
Excel will underline a hyperlink, and, when a user holds the pointer over a hyperlink, the pointer will appear as a hand.

How do I edit a hyperlink if I make a mistake?
Right-click the hyperlink to display the shortcut menu and then click Edit Hyperlink to display the Edit Hyperlink dialog box.

4

- Click the Link button (Insert tab | Links group) again and then click the 'Existing File or Web Page' button to identify the type of hyperlink.
- If necessary, click Current Folder in the Look in area.
- Click SC_EX_10_HospitalCounties_PowerBI.pbix to select the file (Figure 10–89).

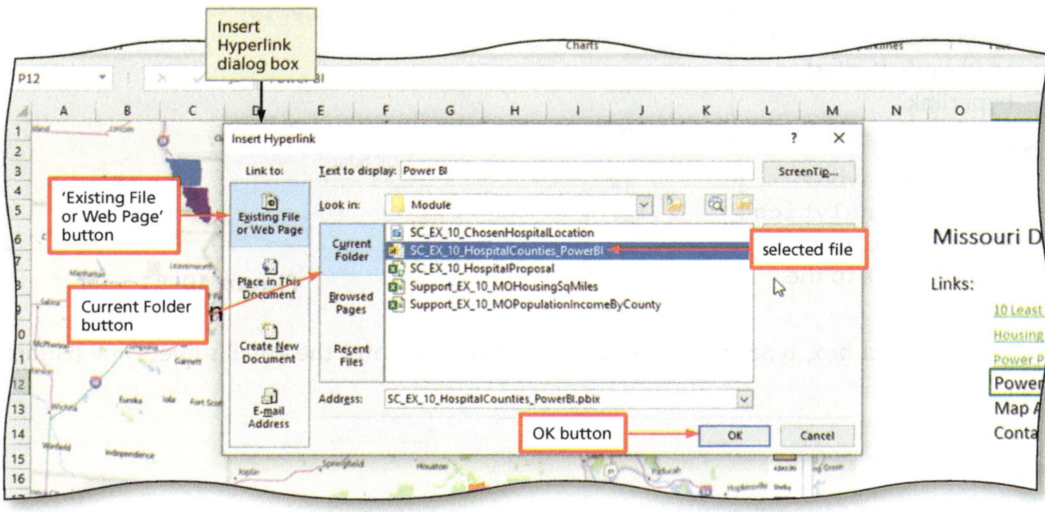

Figure 10–89

5

- Click OK (Insert Hyperlink dialog box) to apply the hyperlink.
- Click cell P13, click the Link button (Insert tab | Links group), and then click 'Existing File or Web Page' to identify the last hyperlink.
- Click SC_EX_10_Chosen HospitalLocation.mp4 to select the file (Figure 10–90).

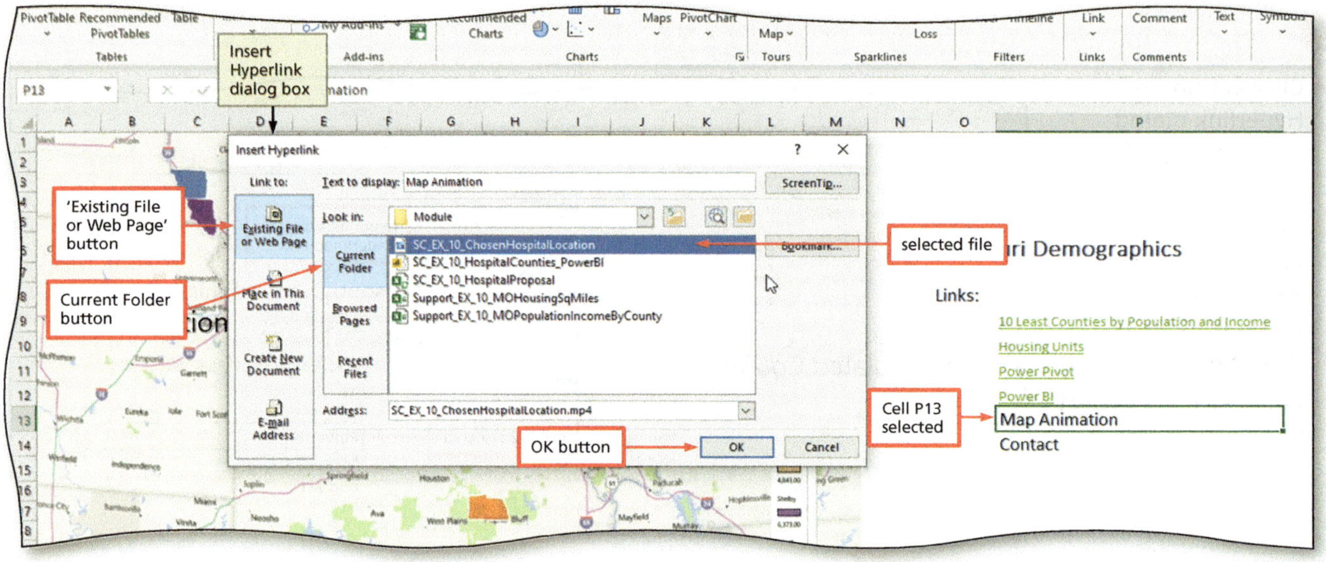

Figure 10–90

6

- Click OK (Insert Hyperlink dialog box) to apply the hyperlink.
- Click cell P14, click the Link button (Insert tab | Links group), and then click the E-mail Address button to identify the last hyperlink.
- In the E-mail address box, type **`businessanalytics@missouri.biz`** to enter the link to the email.
- In the subject box, type **`presentation link`** to enter the email subject line (Figure 10–91).

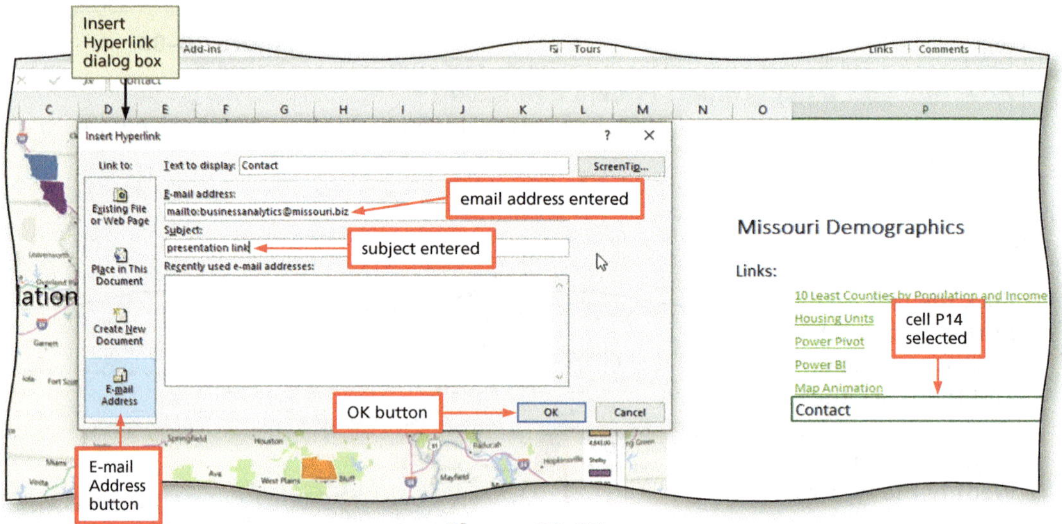

Figure 10–91

7

- Click OK (Insert Hyperlink dialog box) to apply the hyperlink.
- Select cells P8:P14. Change the font size to 14 and the font color to Blue.

Q&A **Why am I selecting P8:P16 rather than just the hyperlink cells?**
If you click cell P9 to start the selection, the hyperlink is clicked; it will transfer you to another worksheet.

- One at a time, point to each of the hyperlinks to view the ScreenTip and then click the hyperlink to verify its functionality.

Other Ways

1. Right-click cell, click Link, enter settings and hyperlink address (Insert Hyperlink dialog box), click OK
2. Press CTRL+K, enter settings and hyperlink address (Insert Hyperlink dialog box), click OK

To Customize a Hyperlink's ScreenTip

When you point to a hyperlink, Excel displays a ScreenTip with the name or location of the hyperlink and instructions for clicking or selecting. **Why?** Users are accustomed to seeing ScreenTips on hyperlinks in browsers, sometimes beside the hyperlink, other times on the browser status bar. The following steps change or customize the ScreenTip.

1

- Right click the Map Animation hyperlink and then click Edit Hyperlink on the shortcut menu.
- Click the ScreenTip button (Edit Hyperlink dialog box) to display the Set Hyperlink ScreenTip dialog box.
- In the ScreenTip text box, type `Click to play this MP4 movie.` to enter the new text (Figure 10–92).

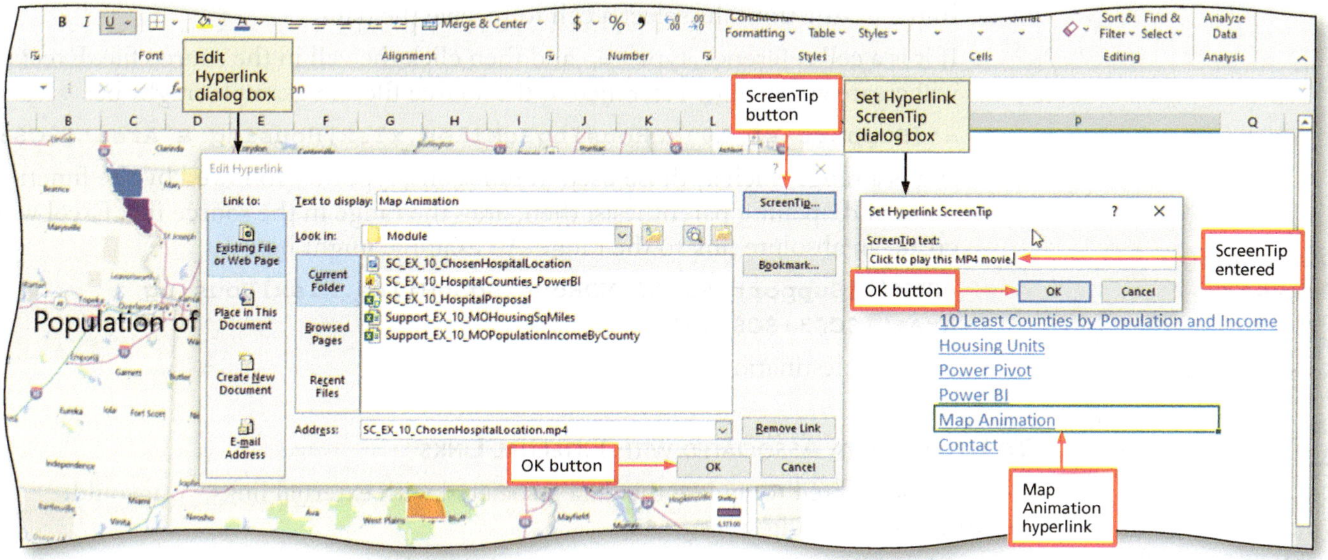

Figure 10–92

2

- Click OK (Set Hyperlink ScreenTip dialog box).
- Click OK (Edit Hyperlink dialog box).
- Copy the text formatting from one of the other hyperlinks to the Map Animation hyperlink.
- Point to the hyperlink to display the new ScreenTip (Figure 10–93).

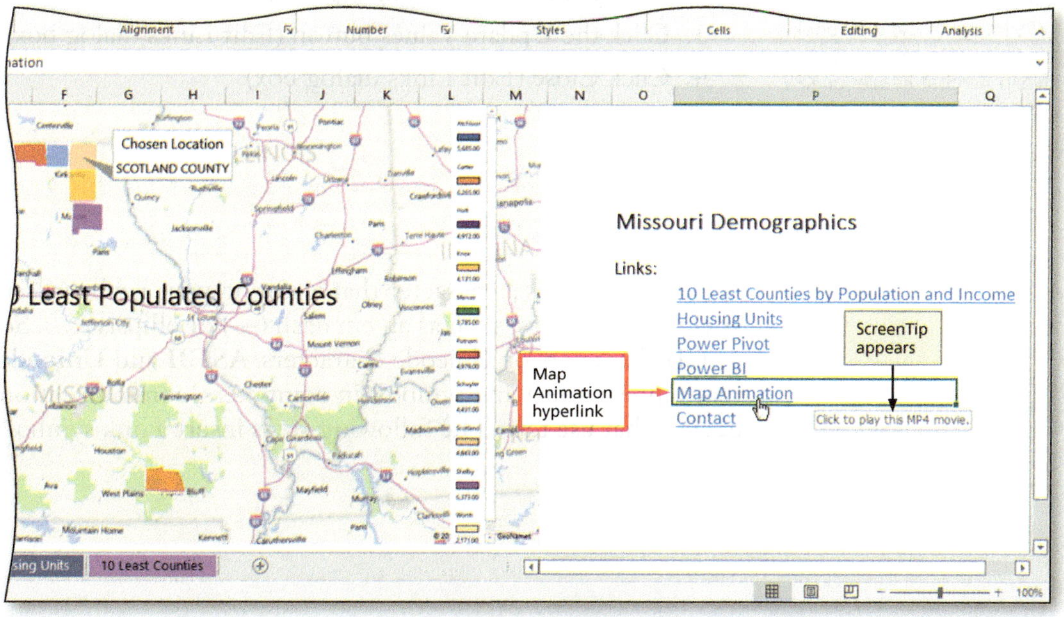

Figure 10–93

To Remove a Hyperlink

If you wanted to delete a hyperlink, you would perform the following steps.

1. Right-click the hyperlink you wish to delete.
2. On the shortcut menu, click Remove Hyperlink.

To Create an External Link

If you wanted to create an external link to the data, rather than a query or connection, you would perform the following steps. (If you have created earlier modules, you already may have learned to create an external link.)

1. Open both the source and destination files.
2. In the destination file, select a cell to receive the data.
3. If it is a cell reference, type `=` and then click the cell in the source file. Excel will create an absolute reference to the source file. An example might be:

   `='[Support_EX_10_MOHousingSqMiles.xlsx]Housing & Area'!$C$3`
4. If it is a range, such as those used in functions, type `=` followed by the function name and opening parenthesis; then, drag the range in the source file. Excel will create an absolute link to the range. An example might be:

   `=SUM('[Support_EX_10_MOHousingSqMiles.xlsx]Housing & Area'!$C$3:$C$116)`
5. Save the destination file.

To Update Data Associated with External Links

If you wanted to update the data associated with external links, you would perform the following steps.

1. Close all workbooks and then open only the destination workbook, such as SC_EX_10_HospitalProposal.xlsx.
2. Click the Edit Links button (Data tab | Queries & Connections group) to display the Edit Links dialog box.
3. Click the Update Values button (Edit Links dialog box).
4. Click Close (Edit Links dialog box).

BTW
Distributing a Workbook
Instead of printing and distributing a hard copy of a workbook, you can distribute the workbook electronically. Options include sending the workbook via email; posting it on cloud storage (such as OneDrive) and sharing the file with others; posting it on a social networking site, blog, or other website; and sharing a link associated with an online location of the workbook. You also can create and share a PDF or XPS image of the workbook, so that users can view the file in Acrobat Reader or XPS Viewer instead of in Excel.

To Insert a Symbol

A **symbol** is a character that is not on your keyboard, such as ½ and ©, or **special characters**, such as an em dash (—) or ellipsis (…). Some special symbols use ASCII characters or Unicode characters. **ASCII** and **Unicode** are coding systems that represent text and symbols in computers, communications equipment, and other devices that use text. The following steps insert a link symbol on the homepage.

1

- Select cell P8. Click the Symbols button (Insert tab | Symbols group) to display the gallery (Figure 10–94).

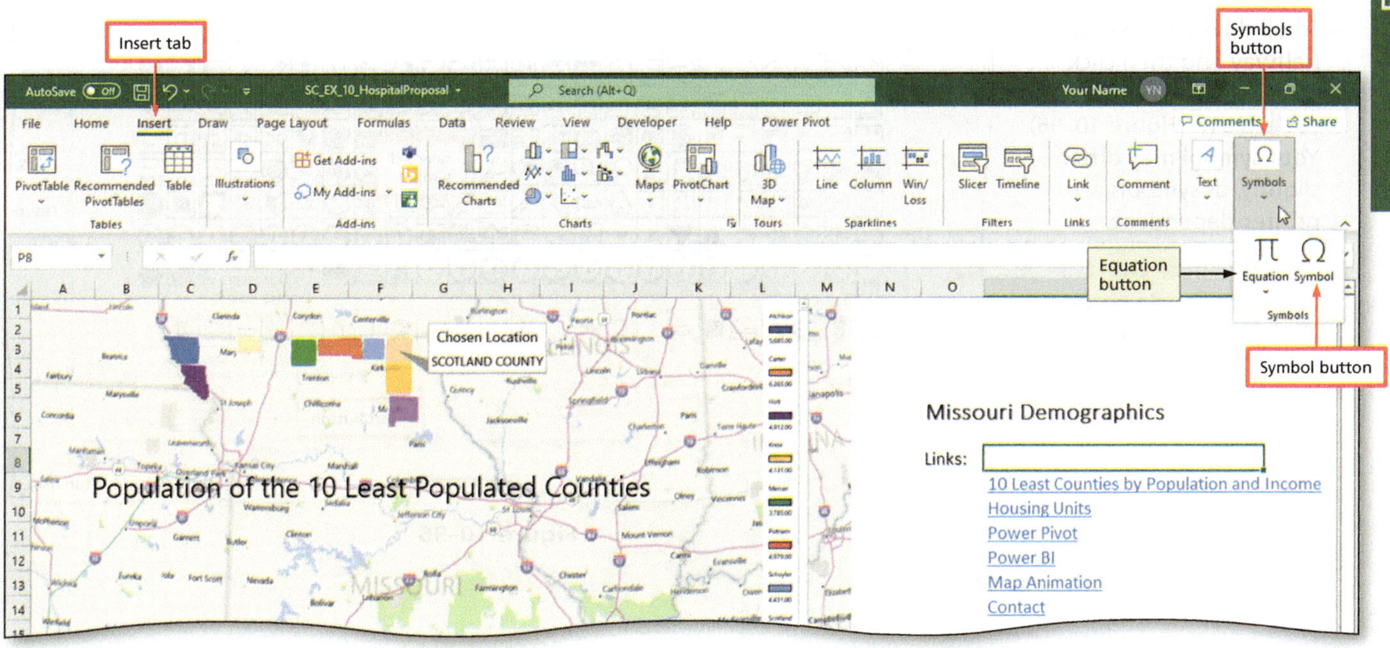

Figure 10–94

2

- Click the Symbol button in the gallery to display the Symbol dialog box.
- Click the Font arrow (Symbol dialog box) to display the list (Figure 10–95).

Figure 10–95

Q&A

What does the Equation button do?

The Equation button opens the Equation tab that displays mathematical, statistical, and other symbols to help you with formulas and scientific equations.

3

- Scroll as necessary and then click 'Segoe UI Emoji' in the list.
- Scroll down more than halfway and then click the Link Symbol, character code 1F517 (Figure 10–96). Your symbol may differ slightly, as symbols are printer-dependent.

Q&A **Could I enter the character code to find the character faster?**
Yes.

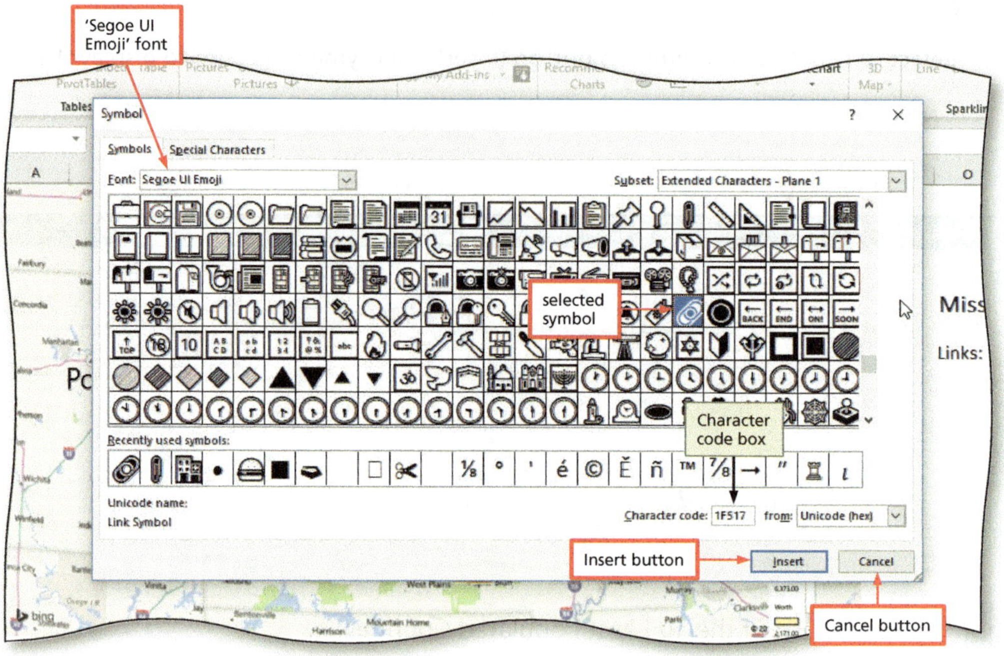

Figure 10–96

4

- Click the Insert button (Symbol dialog box) to insert the symbol and then click Close (Symbol dialog box) to return to the worksheet (Figure 10–97).

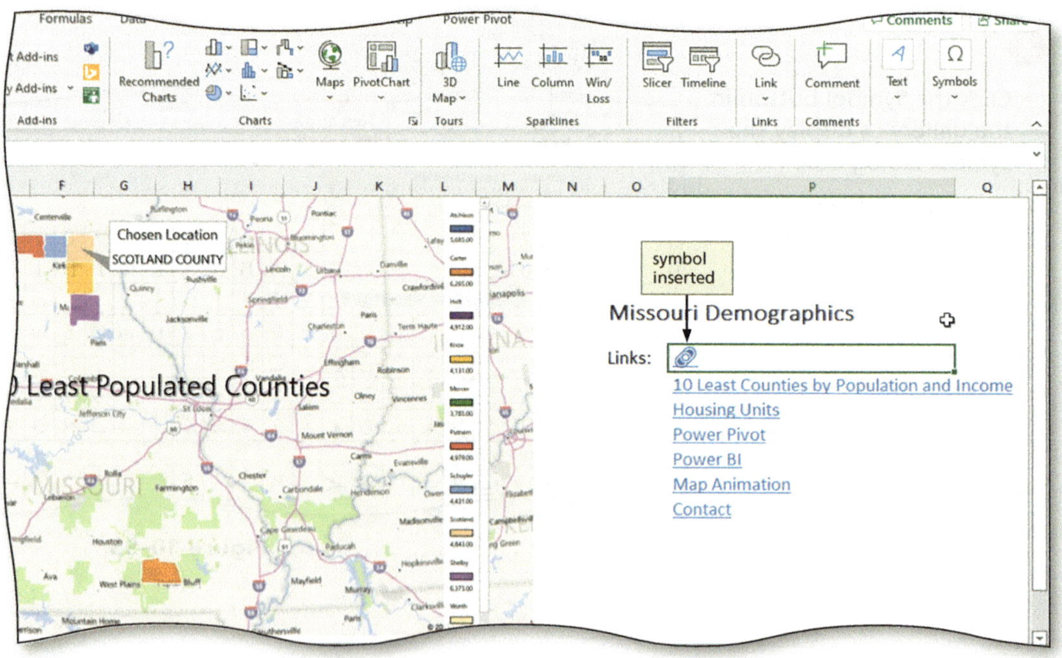

Figure 10–97

5

- With the Homepage sheet selected, save the file.

Break Point: If you wish to take a break, this is a good place to do so. Exit Excel. To resume later, start Excel, open the file called SC_EX_10_HospitalProposal, and then continue following the steps from this location forward.

Macros

A **macro** is a named set of instructions, written in the Visual Basic programming language, that performs tasks automatically in a specified order. It is a set of commands and instructions grouped together to allow a user to accomplish a task automatically. Because Excel does not have a command or button for every possible worksheet task, you can create a macro to group together commonly used tasks, which then can be reused later. People also use macros to record commonly used text, to ensure consistency in calculations and formatting, or to manipulate nonnumeric data. In this module, you will learn how to create a macro using the macro recorder. After recording a macro, you can play it back, or execute it, as often as you want to repeat the steps you recorded with the macro recorder.

Three steps must be taken in preparation for working with macros in Excel. First, you must display the Developer tab (which you did earlier in the module). Second, a security setting in Excel must be modified to enable macros whenever you use Excel. Finally, Excel requires that a workbook which includes macros be saved as an Excel Macro-Enabled Workbook file type; the file extension is .xlsm.

BTW

Naming Macros

If you use an uppercase letter when naming a macro, the user will have to use the SHIFT key when executing the macro.

BTW

Enabling Macros

Excel remembers your decision about enabling macros. If you have enabled macros in a worksheet, Excel will not ask you about enabling them the next time you open the worksheet, but will open the worksheet with macros enabled.

Consider This

Should you customize applications with macros?

Casual Microsoft Office users do not know that customization is available. Creating special macros, events, or buttons on the ribbon can help a user to be more productive. Creating a macro for repeating tasks also saves time and reduces errors. If you understand how to do so, customization is an excellent productivity tool.

To Enable Macros

The following steps enable macros in the workbook. **Why?** Enabling macros allows the workbook to open with executable macros.

1

- Click the Developer tab to make it the active tab.
- Click the Macro Security button (Developer tab | Code group) to display the Trust Center dialog box.
- Click 'Enable all macros' to select the option button (Figure 10–98).

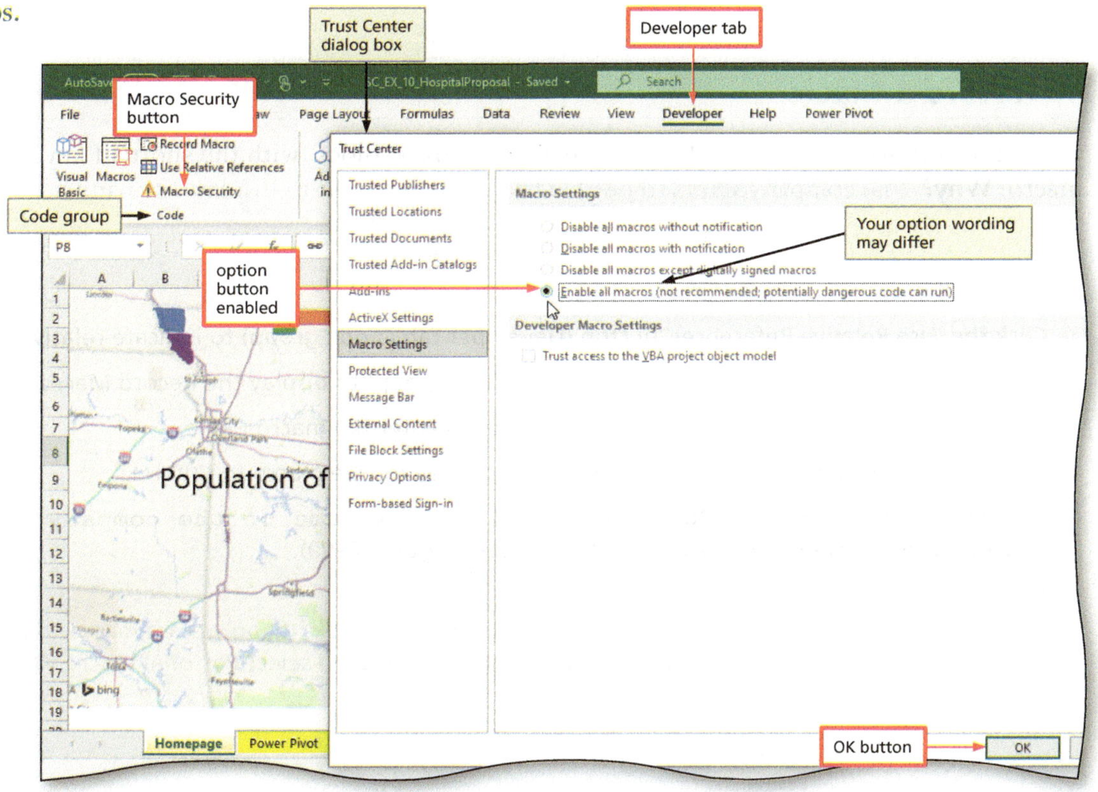

Figure 10–98

2

- Click OK (Trust Center dialog box) to close the dialog box and enable macros.

Recording Macros

A macro is created by recording a set of steps as they are performed. The steps and their order should be determined and rehearsed before creating the macro. When you create a macro, you assign a name to it. A macro name can be up to 255 characters long; it can contain numbers, letters, and underscores, but it cannot contain spaces or other punctuation. The name is used later to identify the macro when you want to execute it. Executing a macro causes Excel to perform each of the recorded steps in order.

Entering a cell reference always directs the macro to that specific cell. Navigating to a cell using keyboard navigation, however, requires the use of relative cell addressing. If you will be using keyboard navigation, you must ensure that the 'Use Relative References' button (Developer tab | Code group) is selected so that the macro works properly. For example, suppose you record a macro in cell C1 that moves to cell C4 and enters text. If the 'Use Relative References' button is not selected, the macro will always move to C4 and enter text; C4 would be considered an absolute reference. If the 'Use Relative References' button is selected while recording, the macro will move three cells to the right of the current position (which will not always be cell C4) and enter text.

As you record a macro, you do not have to hurry. The macro executes by keystroke, not the time between keystrokes during the creation process.

You can copy macros to other workbooks by copying the macro code. You will learn more about coding in the next module.

BTW

Starting Macros

Before recording a macro, you should select your starting cell. If you select it after you begin recording the macro, the macro always will start in that particular cell, which may limit the macro's usefulness.

BTW

Shortcut Keys

Macro shortcut keys take precedence over existing Excel shortcut keys. If you assign an existing shortcut key to a macro, it no longer will work for its original purpose. For instance, assigning CTRL+C to a macro means that you no longer will be able to use that shortcut key to copy content.

To Record a Macro

The following steps record a macro named Address_Block, with the shortcut key CTRL+M to execute the macro. **Why?** The company wants to be able to use the shortcut to display company information.

1

- Select cell P16.
- Click the 'Use Relative References' button (Developer tab | Code group) to indicate relative references.
- Click the Record Macro button (Developer tab | Code group) to display the Record Macro dialog box.
- In the Macro name box, type `Address_Block` to enter the macro name.
- Type `m` in the Shortcut key box to set the shortcut key for the macro to CTRL+M.
- In the Description box, type **`This macro prints the name of the company and the address in a block of three cells.`** to enter the text (Figure 10–99).

Q&A

Where are macros stored?

In this module, the macro will be stored in the current workbook. If you want a macro to be available in any workbook, you would click the 'Store macro in' button and then select Personal Macro Workbook.

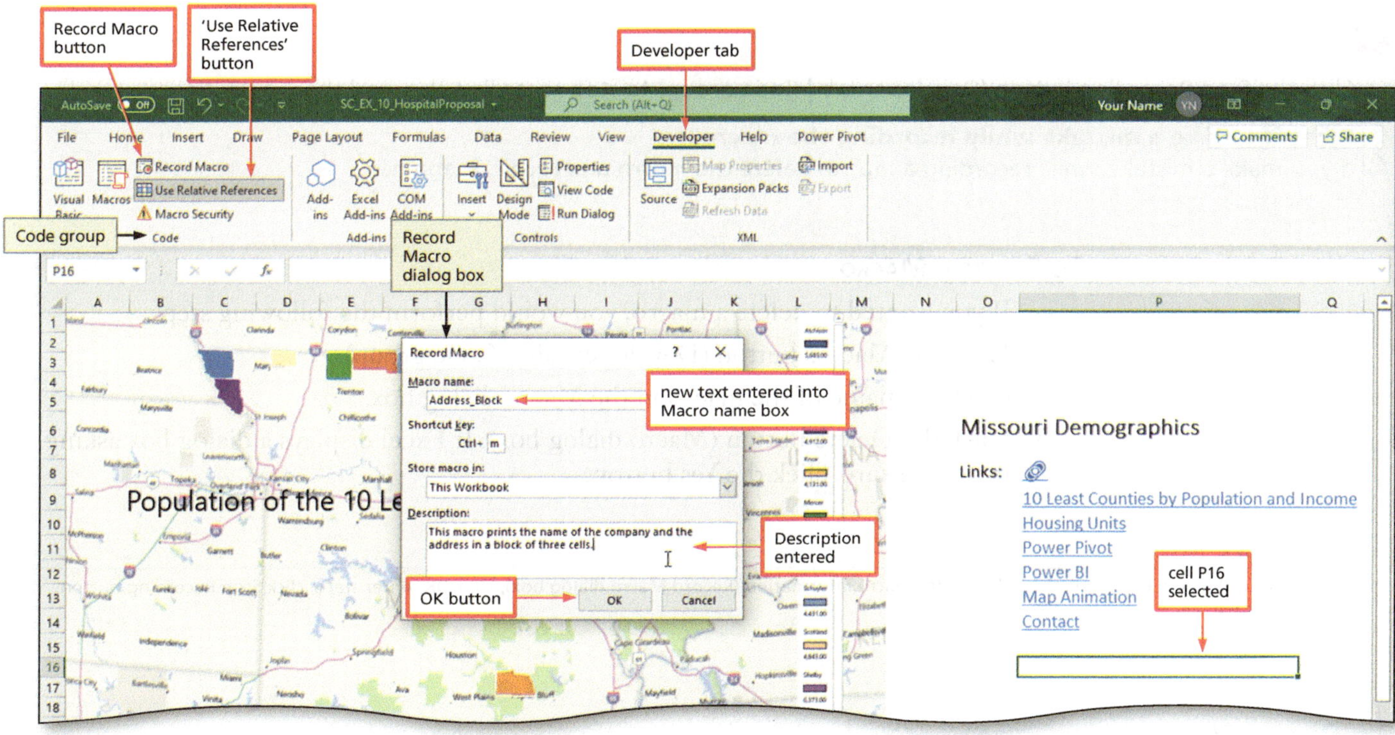

Figure 10–99

2

- Click OK (Record Macro dialog box) to begin recording the macro and to change the Record Macro button to the Stop Recording button

Q&A

What will be included in the macro?
Any task you perform in Excel will be part of the macro. When you are finished recording the macro, clicking the Stop Recording button on the ribbon or on the status bar ends the recording.

What is the purpose of the Record Macro button on the status bar?
You can use the Record Macro button on the status bar to start or stop recording a macro. When you are not recording a macro, this button is displayed as the Record Macro button. If you click it to begin recording a macro, the button changes to become the Stop Recording button.

- Type **`Business Analytics`** and press the DOWN ARROW key.
- Type **`8325 N. Broadway`** and press the DOWN ARROW key.
- Type **`Rossburg, MO 64115`** and press the DOWN ARROW key to complete the text (Figure 10–100).

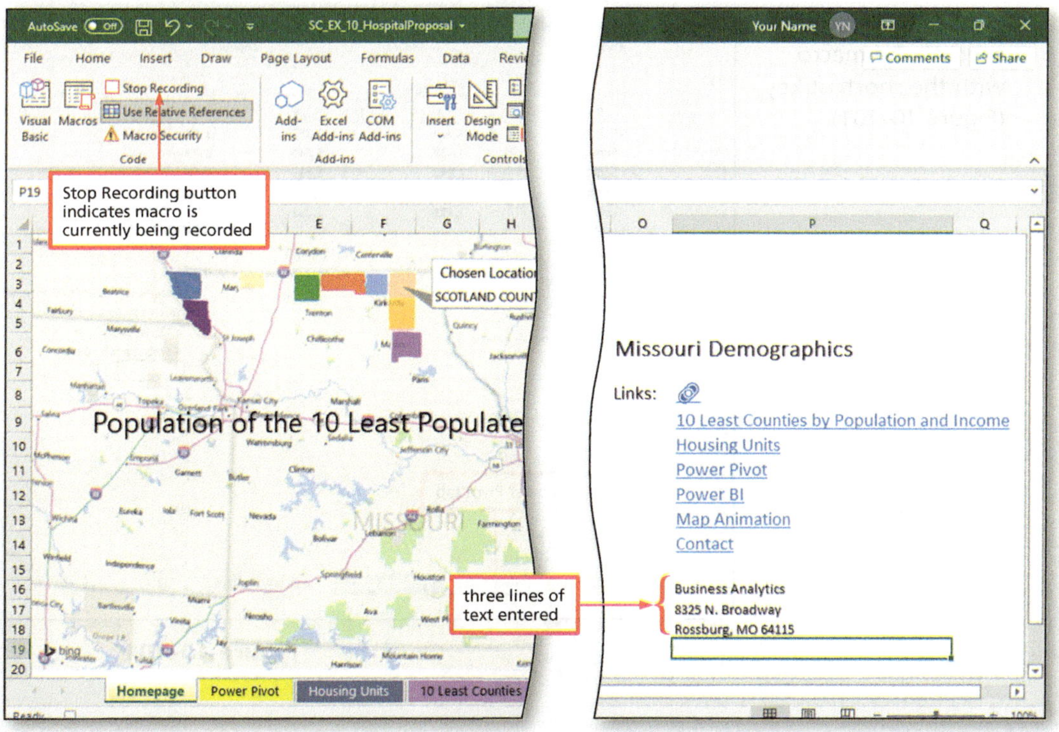

Figure 10–100

3

- Click the Stop Recording button (Developer tab | Code group) to stop recording the worksheet activities.

Q&A **What if I make a mistake while recording the macro?**
If you make a mistake while recording a macro, delete the macro and record it again.

To Delete a Macro

If you wanted to delete a macro, you would perform the following steps.

1. Click the Macros button (Developer tab | Code group).
2. Click the name of the macro in the Macro dialog box.
3. Click the Delete button (Macro dialog box). If Excel displays a dialog box asking if you are sure, click the Yes button.

Other Ways

1. Click Record Macro button on status bar, enter macro information (Record Macro dialog box), click OK, enter steps, click Stop Recording button on status bar

To Run a Macro

The following steps run (or execute) or play back the macro on the other worksheet pages. **Why?** The company wants their name and address on each sheet. You will use the shortcut key to execute the macro on the Power Pivot worksheet. You will use the View Macros button to execute the macro for the 10 Least Counties worksheet.

1

- Click the Power Pivot sheet tab and then click cell F19.
- Press CTRL+M to execute the macro with the shortcut key (Figure 10–101).

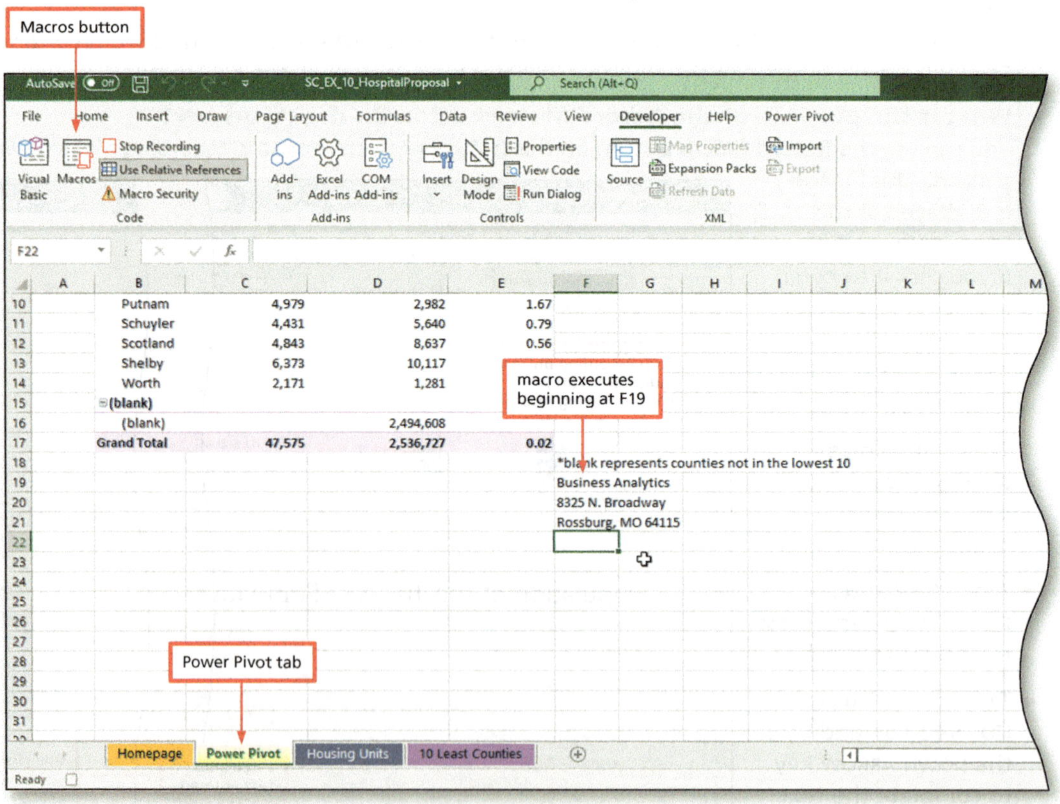

Figure 10–101

2

- Click the '10 Least Counties' sheet tab and then click cell A14.
- Click the Macros button (Developer tab | Code group) to display the Macro dialog box (Figure 10–102).

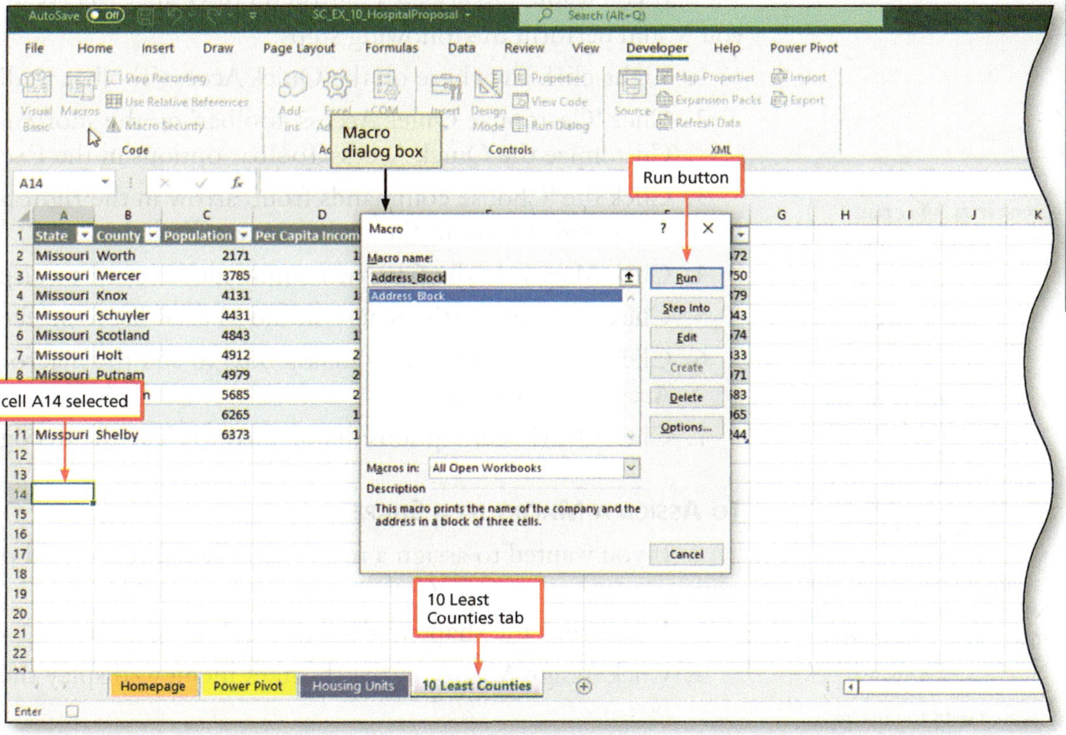

Figure 10–102

3

- Click Run (Macros dialog box) to execute the macro (Figure 10–103).

4

- Repeat the process for cell E1 on the Housing Units tab.

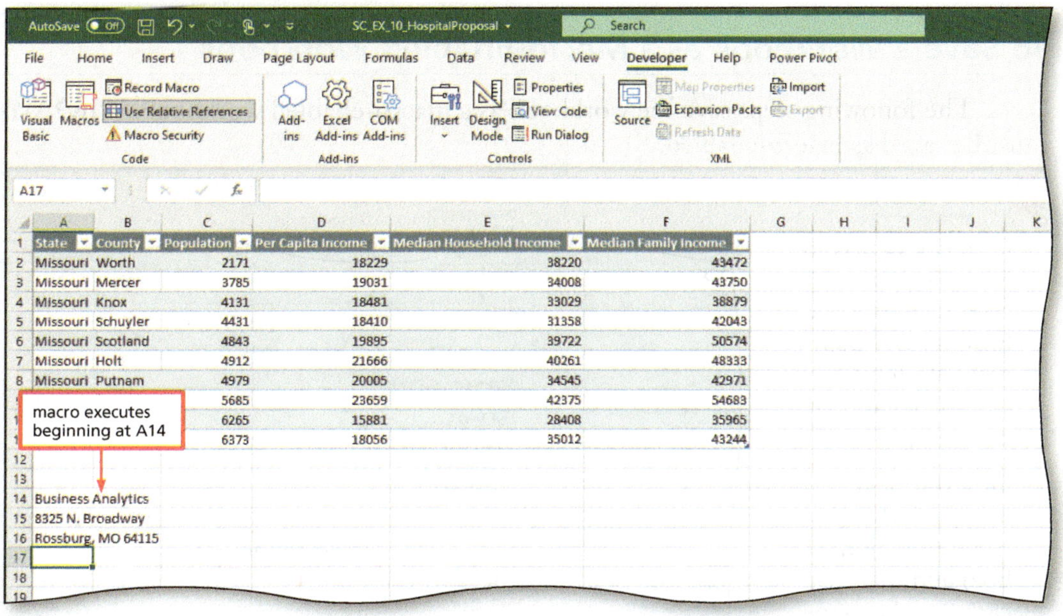

Figure 10–103

Other Ways

1. Press ALT+F8, select macro, click Run (Macro dialog box)

To Create a Macro Button on the Quick Access Toolbar

If you wanted to create a button on the Quick Access Toolbar to run the macro, you would perform the following steps.

1. Right-click anywhere on the Quick Access Toolbar to display the shortcut menu.
2. Click 'Customize Quick Access Toolbar' on the shortcut menu to display the Customize the Quick Access Toolbar options in the Excel Options dialog box.
3. Click the 'Choose commands from' arrow in the right pane to display a list of commands to add to the Quick Access Toolbar.
4. Click Macros in the Choose commands from list to display a list of macros.
5. Click the name of the macro in the Macros list to select it.
6. Click Add (Excel Options dialog box) to add the macro to the Customize Quick Access Toolbar list.
7. Click OK (Excel Options dialog box) to close the dialog box.

BTW
Storing Macros
In the Record Macro dialog box, you can select the location to store the macro in the 'Store macro in' box. If you want a macro to be available to use in any workbook whenever you use Excel, select 'Personal Macro Workbook' in the 'Store macro in' list. This selection causes the macro to be stored in the Personal Macro Workbook, which is part of Excel. If you click New Workbook in the 'Store macro in' list, then Excel stores the macro in a new workbook. Most macros created with the macro recorder are workbook-specific and thus are stored in the active workbook.

To Assign a Macro to a Shape

If you wanted to assign a macro to a shape, you would perform the following steps.

1. Right-click the shape to display the shortcut menu.
2. Click Assign Macro on the shortcut menu to display the Assign Macro dialog box.
3. Click the desired macro.
4. Click OK (Assign Macro dialog box).

To Save a Workbook as a Macro-Enabled Workbook

The following steps save the workbook as a macro-enabled workbook. **Why?** Workbooks with macros must be saved as macro-enabled.

1

- Click File to display Backstage view, click Save As, click Browse, and then navigate to your storage location if necessary.
- Click the 'Save as type' button (Save As dialog box) and then click 'Excel Macro-Enabled Workbook (*.xlsm)' to select the file format (Figure 10–104).

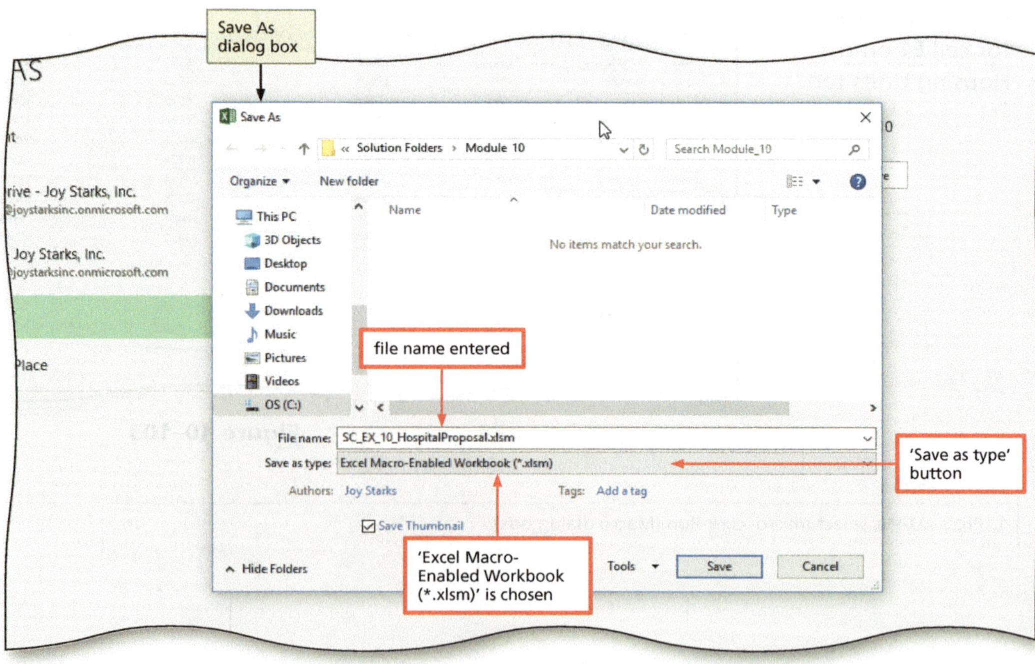

Figure 10–104

2

- Click the Save button (Save As dialog box) to save the workbook as an Excel Macro-Enabled Workbook file.

To Reset the Ribbon

It is a good idea to reset the ribbon when you are finished using the customized tools. **Why?** Other Excel users may not expect to see new tabs and new button groups, especially in lab situations. The following steps reset the ribbon, removing all customization, and then exit Excel.

1

- Right-click a blank area of the ribbon and then click 'Customize the Ribbon' on the shortcut menu to display the Excel Options dialog box.
- Click the Reset button to display its menu (Figure 10–105).

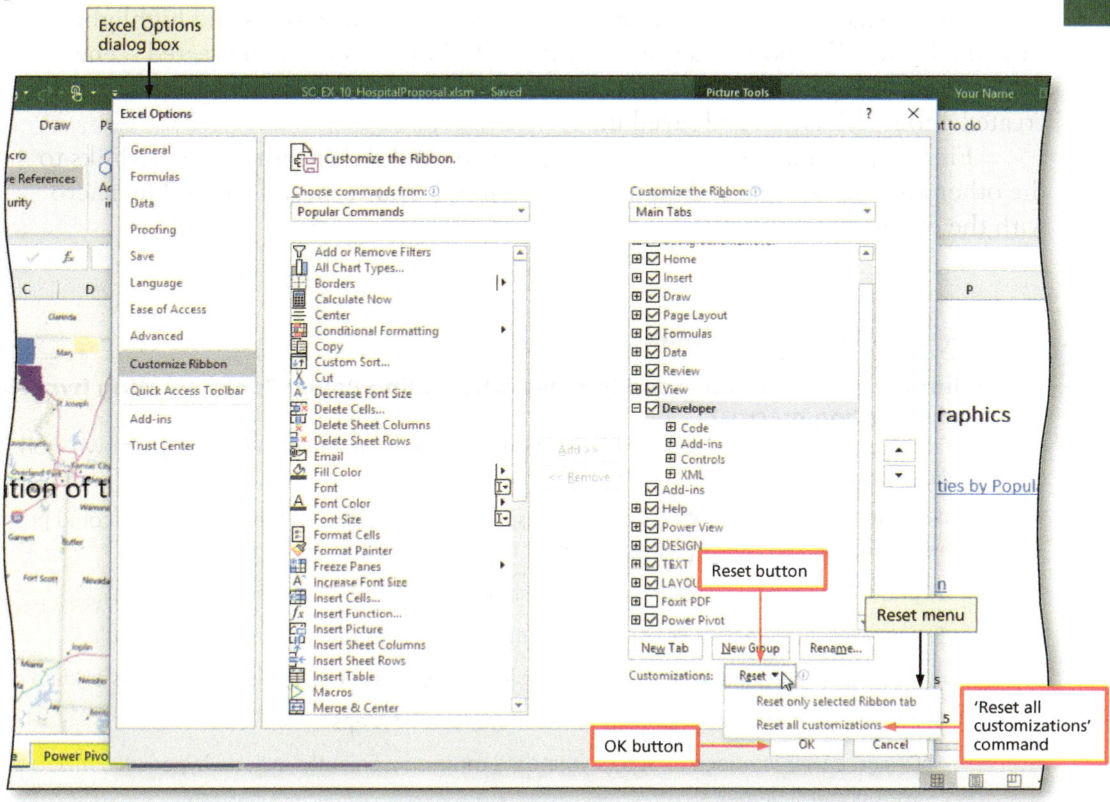

Figure 10–105

2

- Click 'Reset all customizations' in the Reset menu.
- When Excel displays a Microsoft Office dialog box asking if you want to delete all customizations, click the Yes button.
- Click OK to close the Excel Options dialog box.
- **sam** Exit Excel. If the Microsoft Office Excel dialog box is displayed, click the Don't Save button.

Summary

In this module, you learned how to use Excel power tools. You learned how to enable data analysis in workbooks and customize the ribbon to display different tabs. You imported data by using the Get & Transform commands to create query tables. You used the Power Query Editor window to make changes to the data before using it as a table. Using Power Pivot, you added tables to the data model, created a PivotTable with relationships, and used a measure to create a calculated column. You also viewed the cube functions in Power Pivot.

You learned that Power BI is a tool that is used to create visualizations of your Excel data to share online. You learned how to switch visualizations and highlight data in a Power BI report. After opening the 3D Maps window, you created scenes with different map views and map labels and displayed data related to geography. You created a tour animation and saved it.

Finally, you created a home page with a captured screenshot and hyperlinks to the other tabs and webpages. You inserted a symbol. You recorded a reusable macro with the company information.

Consider This: Plan Ahead

What decisions will you need to make when using Power Tools, creating hyperlinks, inserting symbols, and recording macros?

Use these guidelines as you complete the assignments in this module and create your own worksheets for evaluating and analyzing data outside of this class.

1. Select your data carefully. Make sure it is in a tabular format. If the original data could possibly move, copy the data in a new folder and create your spreadsheet in that folder.
2. Choose the kind of visualization you wish to create.
3. If you want to create a PivotTable from multiple sources of data, use Power Pivot.
4. If you want to create a chart with multiple data sources or to use interactive tiles or data card visualizations, use Power BI.
5. If you have data that is geographic in nature, use 3D Maps.
6. Design a user interface to access your data more conveniently. Include hyperlinks, macro instructions, screen captures, symbols, and graphics.
7. Determine any actions you want to automate and create a macro. The steps and their order should be determined and rehearsed before creating the macro.
8. Test the user interface. The final step in creating a user interface is to verify that the interface behaves as designed and as a user expects.

Apply Your Knowledge

Reinforce the skills and apply the concepts you learned in this module.

Using Power Pivot

Note: To complete this assignment, you will be required to use the Data Files. Please contact your instructor for information about accessing the Data Files.

Instructions: Start Excel and open a blank workbook. You are to create a Power Pivot PivotTable from two data files related to locations and occupancy of residence halls at a local college.

Perform the following tasks:

1. If necessary, customize the ribbon as described in the module to include the Power Pivot tab. Save the file on your storage location with the file name SC_EX_10_ResidencePivotTable.
2. Using File Explorer, copy the Data Files named Support_EX_10_Halls.xlsx and Support_EX_10_Locations.xlsx, and paste them to your storage location.
3. Use the Get Data button (Data tab | Get & Transform Data group) to import the workbook named Support_EX_10_Halls.xlsx and load the Halls table.
4. If necessary, rename the tab `Halls.`
5. Use the Get Data button (Data tab | Get & Transform Data group) to import the workbook named Support_EX_10_Locations.xlsx and load the Locations table.
6. Click Edit (Query tab, Edit group) to open the Power Query Editor window. Click the 'Use First Row as Headers' button (Power Query Editor Home tab | Transform group). Close and load.
7. If necessary, rename the tab Locations.
8. Create a Power Pivot PivotTable as follows:
   a. Display the Power Pivot tab. Click the 'Add to Data Model' button (Power Pivot tab | Tables group) to add the Locations table to the data model. Close and load, if necessary.
   b. Click the Halls tab and then click the 'Add to Data Model' button (Power Pivot tab | Tables group) to add the Halls table to the data model. Use the Power Pivot for Excel window to create a Power Pivot PivotTable on a new worksheet.
   c. In the Excel window, in the PivotTable Fields pane, place check marks in the Residence, # of Rooms, and Max Occupancy check boxes from the Halls table. Drag the Location field from the Locations table to the Filters area. Create a relationship using the Residence field common to both tables.
   d. Click the Measures button (Power Pivot tab | Calculations group) and then click New Measure on the menu. Apply the new measure to the Halls table. Name the new measure, Total Occupancy, and use the left bracket key ([ ) to help you multiply the Number of Rooms times the Max Occupancy per Room. If Excel displays a Relationships yellow box, close it.
   e. Format the grand total with a comma and no decimal places.
   f. Format the PivotTable with the Dark Yellow, Pivot Style Dark 5. Use the Value Field Settings dialog box to rename the columns to remove the words, 'Sum of', and the space after. Name the sheet tab, Power Pivot (Figure 10–106).
   g. Experiment with the filter buttons.

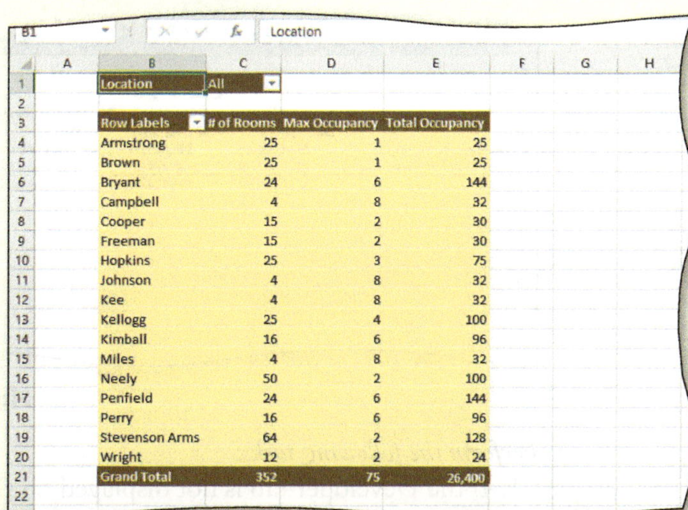

Location	All		
Row Labels	**# of Rooms**	**Max Occupancy**	**Total Occupancy**
Armstrong	25	1	25
Brown	25	1	25
Bryant	24	6	144
Campbell	4	8	32
Cooper	15	2	30
Freeman	15	2	30
Hopkins	25	3	75
Johnson	4	8	32
Kee	4	8	32
Kellogg	25	4	100
Kimball	16	6	96
Miles	4	8	32
Neely	50	2	100
Penfield	24	6	144
Perry	16	6	96
Stevenson Arms	64	2	128
Wright	12	2	24
Grand Total	352	75	26,400

Figure 10–106 Power Pivot PivotTable

Continued >

Apply Your Knowledge *continued*

9. On Sheet 1, in cell A1, insert the title Halls, Locations, and Pivot Table, apply the Title style, and bold it. Insert hyperlinks in the range B3:B5 to each of the other sheets, using the sheet name as the hyperlink text. Format the hyperlinks to be blue, and with a font size of 18, if necessary. Rename the sheet, Homepage. Arrange all tabs from left to right as Homepage, Power Pivot, Locations, and Halls.

   If instructed to do so, create another home page with a picture of your school, and your name and course number.
10. On the original homepage, click cell A1. Save the workbook. Remove the ribbon customization. Submit the revised document in the format specified by your instructor.
11. What other measure might you create with this data? How would the housing office use this data to manage room assignments?

Extend Your Knowledge

Extend the skills you learned in this module and experiment with new skills. You may need to use Help to complete the assignment.

Creating a Macro, Editing a Macro, and Assigning It to a Button

Note: To complete this assignment, you will be required to use the Data Files. Please contact your instructor for information about accessing the Data Files.

Instructions: Start Excel. Open the workbook SC_EX_10-1.xlsx from the Data Files and then save the workbook as an Excel Macro-Enabled Workbook file type using the file name, SC_EX_10_CoolPools.xlsm.

In the following steps, you are to create a macro to add a column to a worksheet, assign the macro to a button on the Quick Access Toolbar, and then execute the macro. Figure 10–107 shows the completed worksheet.

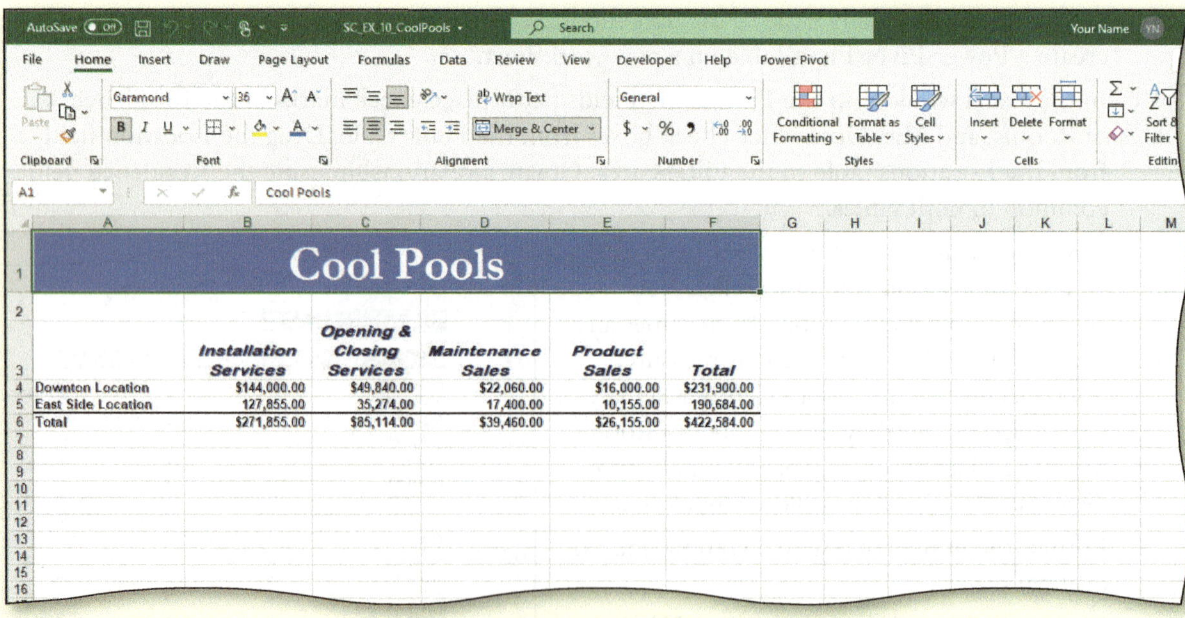

Figure 10–107

Perform the following tasks:

1. If the Developer tab is not displayed on the ribbon, display Backstage view, click Options in the left pane to display the Excel Options dialog box, click Customize Ribbon, click the Developer check box in the Customize the Ribbon area, and then click OK (Excel Options dialog box).

2. Create a macro that adds a column before the Product Sales column by doing the following:
   a. Click the Record Macro button (Developer tab | Code group).
   b. When the Record Macro dialog box appears, name the macro, AddColumn, and assign the keyboard shortcut CTRL+N. Store the macro in this workbook, enter your name in the Description box, and then click OK (Record Macro dialog box) to start the macro recording process.
   c. Select cell C3, click the Insert arrow (Home tab | Cells group), and then click the 'Insert Sheet Columns' command from the Insert Cells menu.
   d. Select cell C6, sum the cell range C4:C5, set the column width to 15, and then click the Stop Recording button (Developer tab | Code group).
3. In the newly added column, enter **`Maintenance Sales`** in cell C3, **`22060`** in cell C4, and **`17400`** in cell C5.
4. Right-click anywhere on the Quick Access Toolbar and then click 'Customize Quick Access Toolbar' on the shortcut menu. When the Excel Options dialog box is displayed, click the 'Choose commands from' arrow and click Macros. Click AddColumn, click the Add button, and then click OK to add a Macro button to the Quick Access Toolbar.
5. While still in column C, run the macro by clicking the AddColumn button on the Quick Access Toolbar. Enter the following data: **`Opening & Closing Services`**, **`49840`**, and **`35274`**. Adjust the width of column D to 17.

   If requested by your instructor, add the following text to the end of the text in cell A1: **`(EST. <year of birth>)`**, replacing <year of birth> with your year of birth.
6. Right-click the AddColumn button on the Quick Access Toolbar and then click 'Remove from Quick Access Toolbar' on the shortcut menu.
7. Use Help to learn how to access the VBA window. In the VBA window, click File on the menu bar and then click Print to print the AddColumn macro.
8. Save the workbook. Submit the revised workbook and the macro printout in the format specified by your instructor.
9. How would using the 'Use Relative References' button when recording your macro change how you insert columns using the AddColumn macro?

Expand Your World

Create a solution that uses cloud or web technologies by learning and investigating on your own from general guidance.

Creating a Report in Power BI Desktop and the Online Service

Note: To complete this assignment, you must be connected to the Internet. You will need to download the Power BI Desktop application from https://powerbi.microsoft.com/desktop and install it on your device. If you are working in a lab situation, see your instructor or IT administrator for help downloading Power BI, if it is not already installed on the lab device. You will also need Internet access to use the Power BI online service.

Instructions: Start the Power BI Desktop app. In the following steps you will create a report in Power BI Desktop and publish to the online tool called Power BI service.

Perform the following tasks:

1. On the report canvas, select Try a Sample Dataset and then click Load sample data.
2. Load the data from the financials table.
3. Save the report using the file name, SC_EX_10_Manufacturing.

Continued >

Expand Your World *continued*

4. Examine the table in Data view. Analyze the possible connections that can be made within the data.
5. Navigate to the Report canvas and perform the following analysis:
   a. Create a Clustered bar chart visualization using the fields Country, Product, and Units Sold. Change the value of Units Sold from Sum to Count (Visualizations pane | Build visual) (Figure 10-108).
   b. Create a Donut chart visualization using the fields Month Name and Sales. Change the value of Sales from Sum to Count.
   c. Create a third visualization of your choice using three fields.
   d. Apply the theme of your choice.
   e. Experiment by selecting different fields and highlighting various pieces of data.
   f. Deselect all visualizations and save your work.

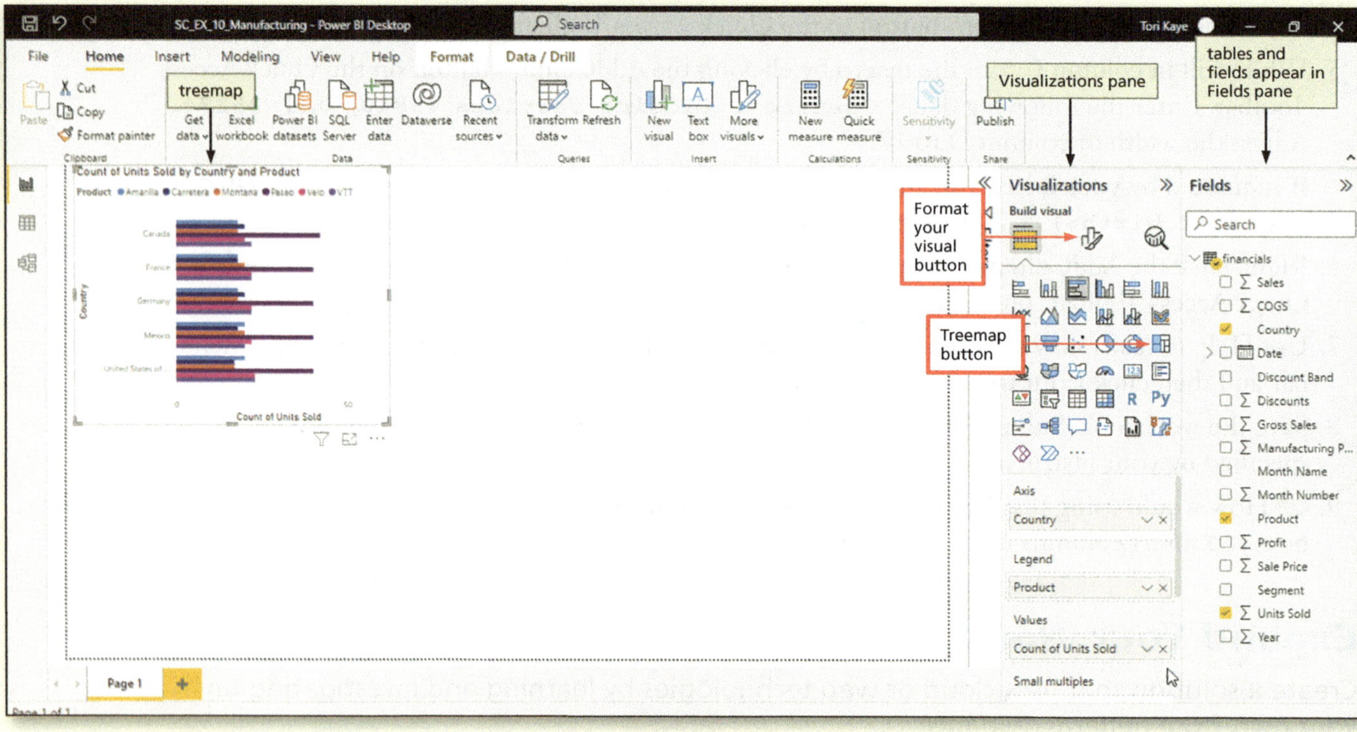

Figure 10–108

6. You will now publish your report to the Power BI service.
7. Select Publish (Home tab | Share group).
8. Save your changes, if prompted, and select My workspace in the Publish to Power BI window.
9. Click 'Open 'SC_EX_Manufacturing.pbix' in Power BI' to open the report in the Power BI online service. The application will open in your browser. (If you are unable to publish to the Power BI service, skip to Step 16.)
10. Click the More Options button (the three dots in the Power BI menu bar) and select Edit on the dropdown list. The online service will now show the Filters, Visualizations, and Fields panes and allow you to edit the report.
11. In the navigation bar on the left, select Datasets. Click SC_EX_10_Manufacturing.

12. Note the different options presented on this page. You could elect to Visualize this data and create a new report from scratch using the financials data table, or you could Auto-create a report. You could also Share this data and collaborate with others.
13. Click Create a report, select Auto-create from the menu and follow any prompts if necessary.
14. Analyze the report created by Power BI. Write a paragraph answering these questions: How does this report differ from the one you created in Power BI Desktop? How could you use this automatically-generated report to make edits and help shape the report you created?
15. Exit the Power BI online service and navigate back to Power BI Desktop.

    Save the report and submit the document to your instructor.
16. If you were unable to access the Power BI service in Step 9 above, follow the alternative directions here:
    a. Search the web to research how research the Power BI service. Microsoft has many resources available.
    b. What differences can you find between Power BI Desktop and the Power BI service?
    c. What is a Power BI dashboard?
    d. What sharing capabilities are available with the Power BI service?
    e. Write a paragraph sharing your findings. Include a Power BI service screenshot that you copy from a Microsoft website.
17. In your SC_EX_10_Manufacturing.pbix report, what visualization did you decide to create and what fields did you use? Did you use any data labels? How might you change your visualizations to improve their formatting or make them more informative?

In the Lab

Design and implement a solution using creative thinking and problem-solving skills.

Create a Visual Report and Video

Note: To complete this assignment, you will be required to use the Data Files. Please contact your instructor for information about accessing the Data Files.

Problem: The State of Utah wants a visual report displaying the number of visitors to its five large national parks in a recent year. They also would like to be able to access the National Park Service website within the report. You decide to create a workbook with a home page and 3D Map.

Perform the following tasks:

Part 1: Using File Explorer, copy the Data File named Support_EX_10_UtahParks.xlsx and paste it to your storage location. Start Excel and open a blank workbook. Save the file on your storage location with the name, SC_EX_10_UtahParksComplete. Get the data from Support_EX_10_UtahParks.xlsx and the Parks table. Using the Power Query Editor window, make the next row the header row. Close and load the query. Format the data. Click the 3D Map button (Insert tab | Tours group) to open the 3D Maps window and create the scenes shown in Table 10–5. Rename the sheet tab with an appropriate name.

Continued >

In the Lab *continued*

Table 10–5 Utah National Parks

Scene	Scene Name	Layer Pane	Instructions	Zoom & Position	Scene Options
1	United States	Remove any locations		Zoom to entire United states	3 seconds duration, 1 second Fly Over effect
2	Utah	Add State field	Create a text box with the word UTAH	Zoom to Utah	3 seconds duration, 1 second Fly Over effect
3	Parks	Click the 'Change the visualization to Region' icon. Add the Postal Code field to the Location area. Add the Visitors in 2017 field to the Value area. Add the National Park field to the Category area. Right-click the Legend and then click Remove.	Remove the Utah text box and turn on Map Labels. One at a time, right click each region on the map and then click Add Annotation. Click Fields button (Add Annotation dialog box), and then select National Park. Change the font size to 12 if necessary.	Zoom in as close as possible, while keeping all of the regions on the map.	3 seconds duration, 1 second Fly Over effect

Play the tour and then make any adjustments necessary. Capture a screenshot of scene 3. Save a video of the tour, using the 'Quick Export & Mobile' option, with the name, SC_EX_10_UtahParks.

Create a homepage with your screen capture. Add a hyperlink to your National Parks sheet. Add a hyperlink to your saved video of the map animation. Add a hyperlink to the appropriate website on the National Park Service (http://www.nps.gov/state/ut/index.htm).

Part 2: Would you use Excel for a presentation? What are the advantages and disadvantages of using visualizations in Excel versus apps like PowerPoint or Prezi?

11 User Interfaces, Visual Basic for Applications (VBA), and Collaboration Features

Objectives

After completing this module, you will be able to:

- Create custom color and font schemes and save them as an Excel theme
- Add and configure worksheet form controls
- Record user input to another location on the worksheet
- Understand Visual Basic for Applications (VBA) code and explain event-driven programs
- Explain sharing and collaboration techniques
- Use passwords to assign protected and unprotected status to a worksheet
- Compare workbooks
- Review a digital signature on a workbook
- Insert and edit comments in a workbook
- Format a worksheet background
- Enhance charts and sparklines
- Save a custom view of a worksheet

Introduction

This module introduces you to user interface design using form controls and ActiveX controls in a worksheet, the Visual Basic for Applications (VBA) programming environment, sharing and collaboration features of worksheets and workbooks, the use of comments in Excel, and the process of finalizing workbooks.

With Excel, you can design a user-friendly interface that permits users to enter information into the workbook easily, regardless of their experience with the app. Form controls include interface elements such as option buttons, check boxes, and group boxes. ActiveX controls, including the label and command button controls used in this module, provide the same core functionality as the form controls but allow you, as the designer, greater power to customize the appearance of the control. The VBA programming environment is used to program the functionality of the ActiveX controls.

When you are working on a team, the sharing features of Excel make it easy to provide team members access to worksheet data and protect information as necessary. Distributing a workbook through OneDrive, Exchange, Office 365, or SharePoint maintains ownership of the file while providing all members of the team access to the most current version of the data at all times. Commenting features of Excel encourage feedback on specific content within the worksheet.

Additional collaboration tools permit users to view multiple versions of the same workbook side by side for comparison.

Project: National Injection Molding Sales Analysis

The project in this module follows proper design guidelines and uses Excel to create the workbooks shown in Figure 11–1. National Injection Molding (NIM) develops and markets large, injection-molded products such as prefabricated steps, trays, chairs, and casings for the transportation industry. Because NIM's reach is national, members of the sales team are located in offices throughout the United States. The head of sales wants to use advanced features of Excel to share information about NIM's prospective clients and projected revenue among the sales team. The NIM Sales Analysis workbook consists of three worksheets—Prospect Recorder, Sales Data Analysis, and a hidden Prospect List. The NIM Events workbook consists of two worksheets—Event Expenses and Prior Years.

The Prospect Recorder worksheet (Figure 11–1a) in the NIM Sales Analysis workbook provides a framework for recording information about sales prospects. You will add form controls and ActiveX controls to finish the interface development. You then will create VBA code to add functionality to the command button controls added to the worksheet. The functionality added through the VBA programming environment will present a series of dialog boxes instructing the salesperson to enter the prospect's contact information, and then will copy the prospect's information into the Prospect List worksheet (Figure 11–1b), which will be hidden from casual users.

The Sales Data Analysis worksheet (Figure 11–1c) in the NIM Sales Analysis workbook provides production details for 2020 and 2021 related to the three production lines (production facilities are located in Oklahoma, Florida, and Louisiana) and four product types (trays, steps, chairs, and casings). You will co-author the workbook and add comments.

The Event Expenses worksheet (Figure 11–1d) in the NIM Events workbook contains estimated costs for three sales events throughout the year 2021. You will add a watermark to this worksheet.

The Prior Years worksheet (Figure 11–1e) in the NIM Events workbook contains attendance figures for prior events (2014 through 2020) and a chart representing the data. You will add a background to this worksheet. You will add finishing touches to the existing chart and add sparklines for each event. You also will create a custom view for the worksheet and prepare the workbook for distribution to users of older versions of Excel.

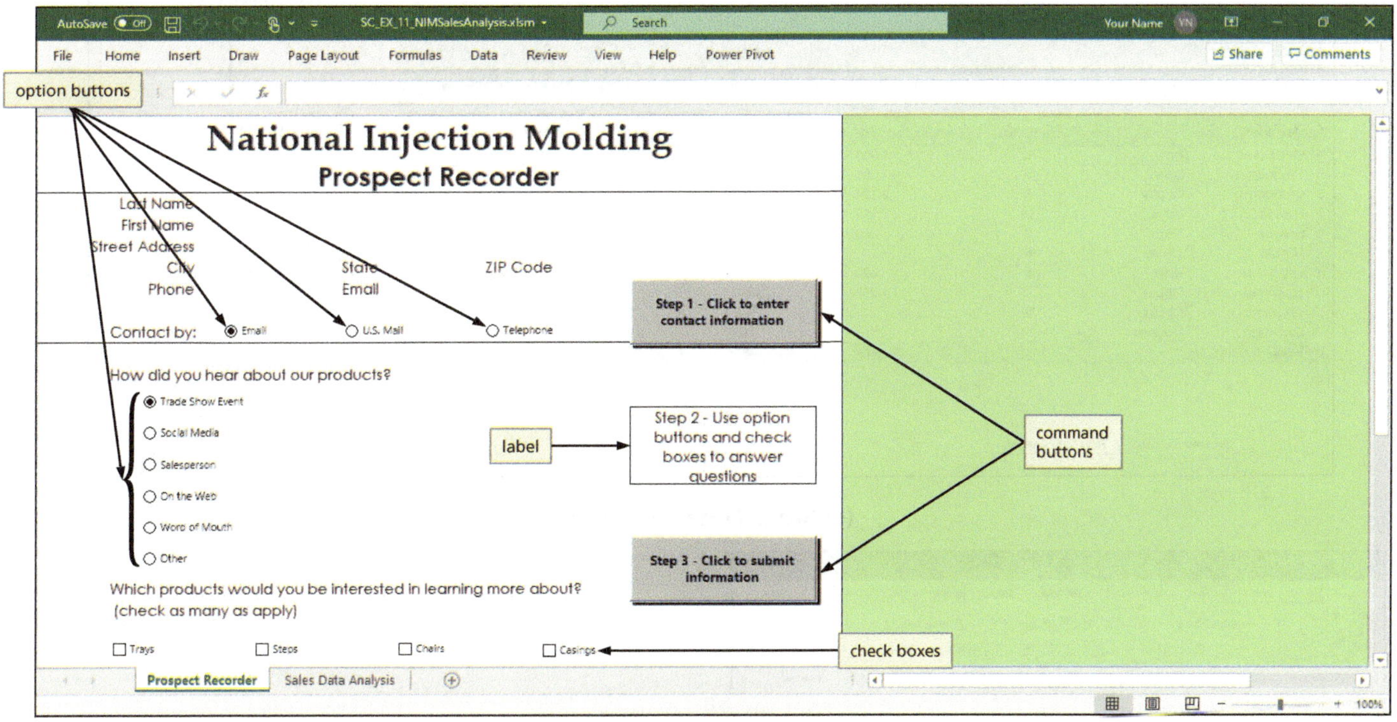

(a) Prospect Recorder Form

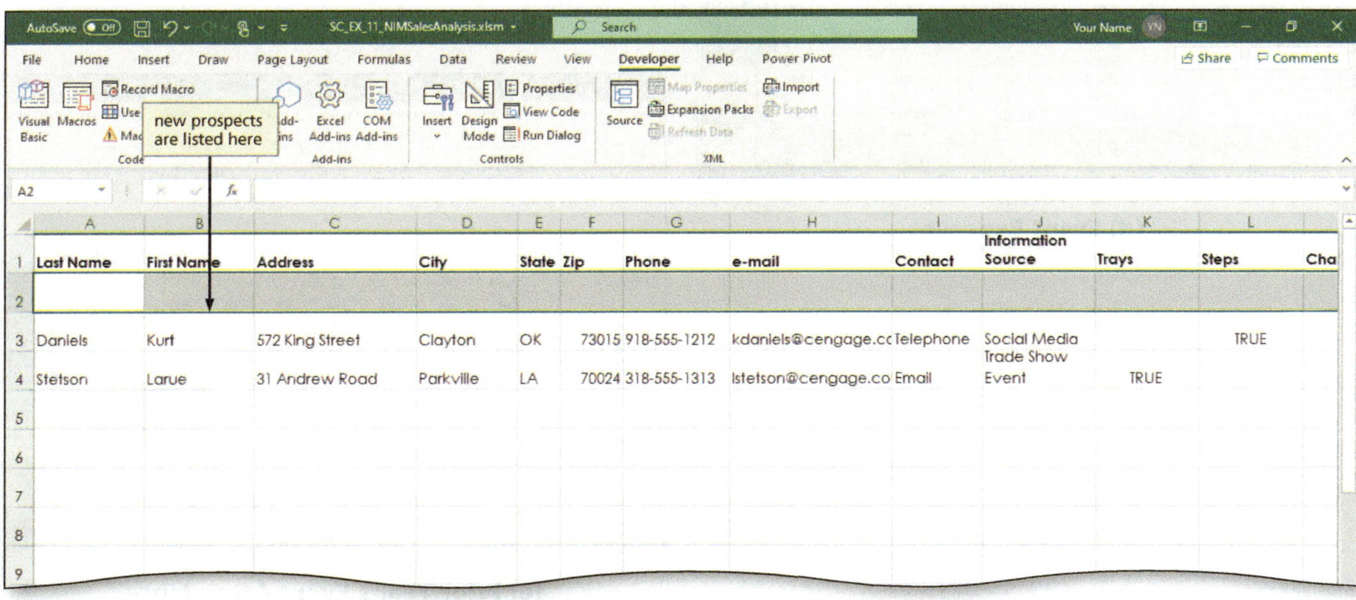

(b) Hidden Prospect List

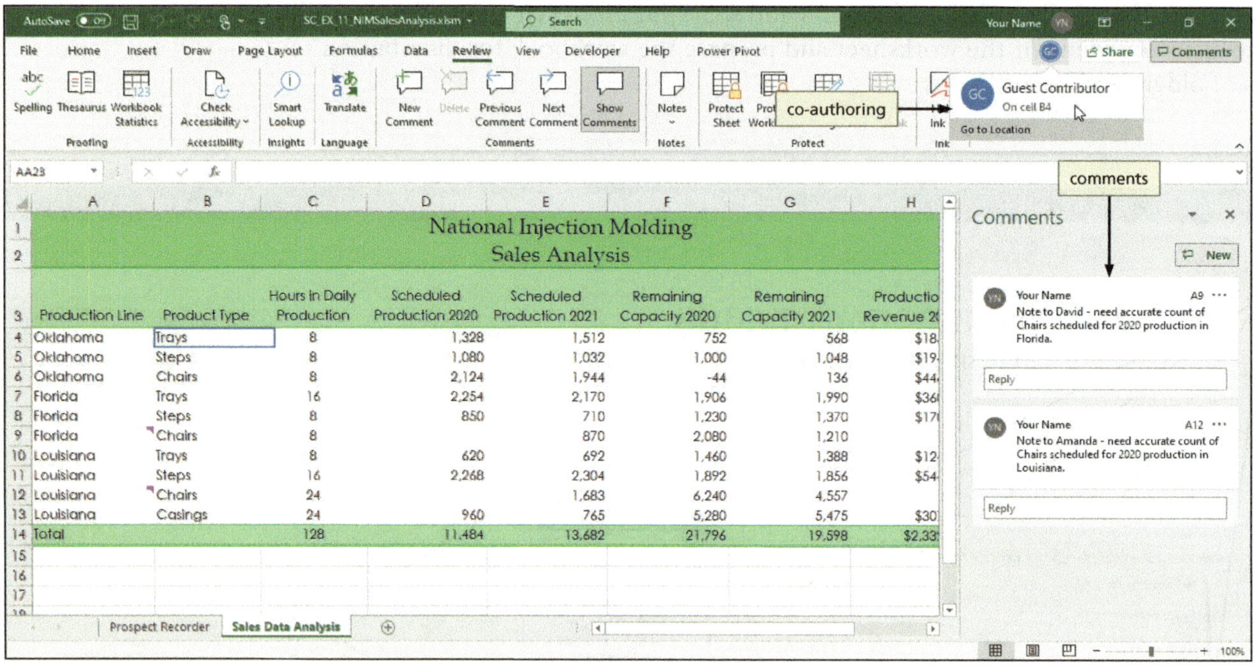

(c) Sales Data Analysis

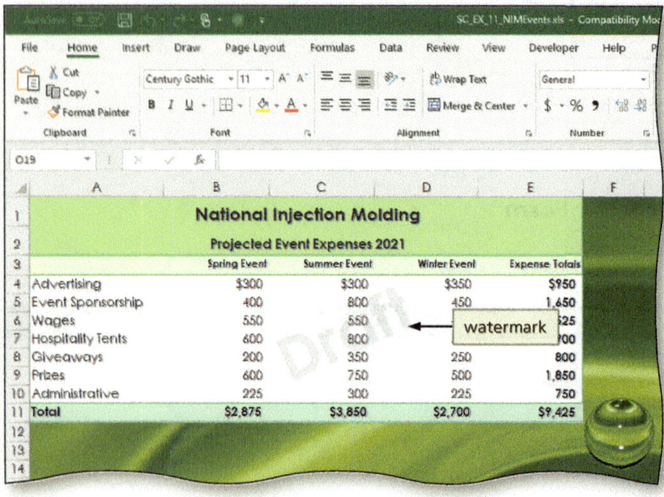

Skitterphoto/2058 images/Pixabay

(d) Event Expenses

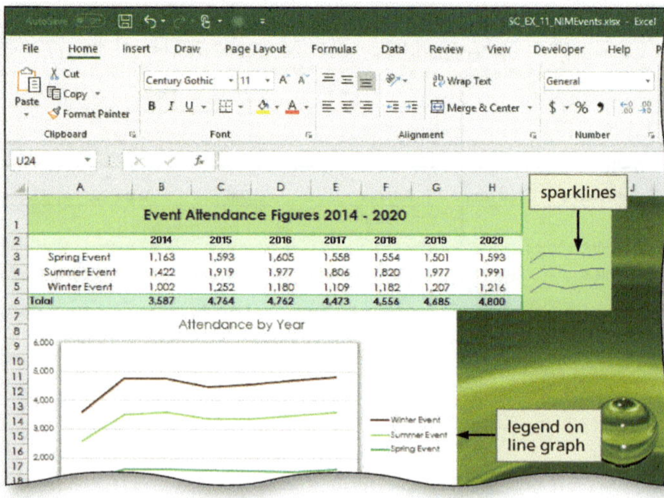

Skitterphoto/2058 images/Pixabay

(e) Prior Year's Event Attendance

Figure 11–1

The requirements document for the National Injection Molding Sales Analysis and Events workbooks is shown in Figure 11–2. It includes the needs, source of data, calculations, and other facts about the worksheets' development.

Worksheet Titles	Prospect Recorder, Sales Data Analysis, Event Expenses, and Prior Years
Needs	National Injection Molding (NIM) develops and markets four types of large injection molding items (trays, steps, chairs, and casings) to the transportation industry nationwide. NIM has three production facilities in Oklahoma, Florida, and Louisiana. The company would like a workbook to record information about sales prospects and maintain current information regarding scheduled production and sales. Additionally, a second workbook is needed to maintain current data on the upcoming 2021 sales events and consolidate historic attendance information on events held from 2014 through 2020. The information recorded from the prospects has been structured in a hidden Prospect List worksheet, but the sales manager wants a form created to make data entry easier. Changes need to be made to sales analysis data in a shared copy of the workbook. Finally, three copies of the shared events workbook exist with different cost values for the events. These values need to be merged into a single workbook, and visual enhancements to the worksheets are desired for presentation purposes.
Source of Data	A workbook has been developed with Sales Data Analysis and the start of a form. A master copy and two employee copies of the Events workbook exist.
Calculations	All formulas are set up in the workbooks. The worksheets in each workbook should be reviewed to familiarize yourself with the calculations.
Other Requirements	None.

Figure 11–2 Requirements Document

To Start Excel and Open a Workbook

The following steps start Excel and open a workbook named SC_EX_11-1.xlsx. To complete these steps, you will be required to use the Data Files. Please contact your instructor for information about accessing the Data Files.

1. sam Start Excel.
2. Open the file named SC_EX_11-1.xlsx from the Data Files.
3. If the Excel window is not maximized, click the Maximize button on its title bar to maximize the window.
4. Save the workbook on your hard drive, OneDrive, or other storage location as a macro-enabled workbook (.xlsm format) using SC_EX_11_NIMSalesAnalysis as the file name (Figure 11–3).

BTW

Create and Modify Custom Themes

Custom themes allow for personalization of workbooks with a custom set of colors, fonts, and effects. Use the Customize Colors option on the Colors menu (Page Layout tab | Themes group) or the Customize Fonts option on the Fonts menu (Page Layout tab | Themes group) to create custom options and select the desired effect setting from the Effects gallery. After selecting your desired options, click the Themes button and then click Save Current Theme to save your custom theme.

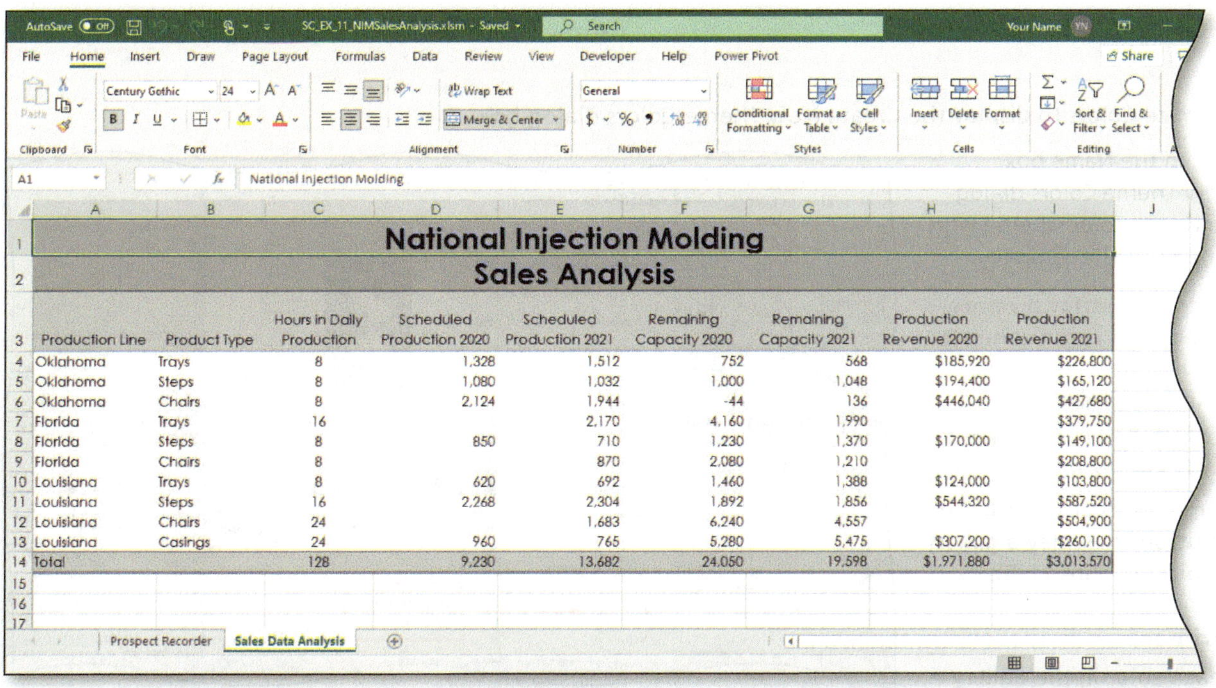

Figure 11–3

BTW
Touch Mode Differences
The Office and Windows interfaces may vary if you are using Touch Mode. For this reason, you might notice that the function or appearance of your touch screen differs slightly from this module's presentation.

Creating a Custom Theme

Excel provides an option for users to create color and font schemes rather than using one of the predefined sets. The chosen colors also will appear in the galleries related to formats, shapes, fills, and outlines. The chosen fonts will appear in the font box and in cell styles. Creating a **custom theme** means saving your own color and font schemes.

To Create a New Color Scheme

The following steps create a custom color scheme. **Why?** NIM wants to use its company colors of green and brown.

1

- Click the Colors button (Page Layout tab | Themes group) to display the Color Scheme gallery (Figure 11–4).

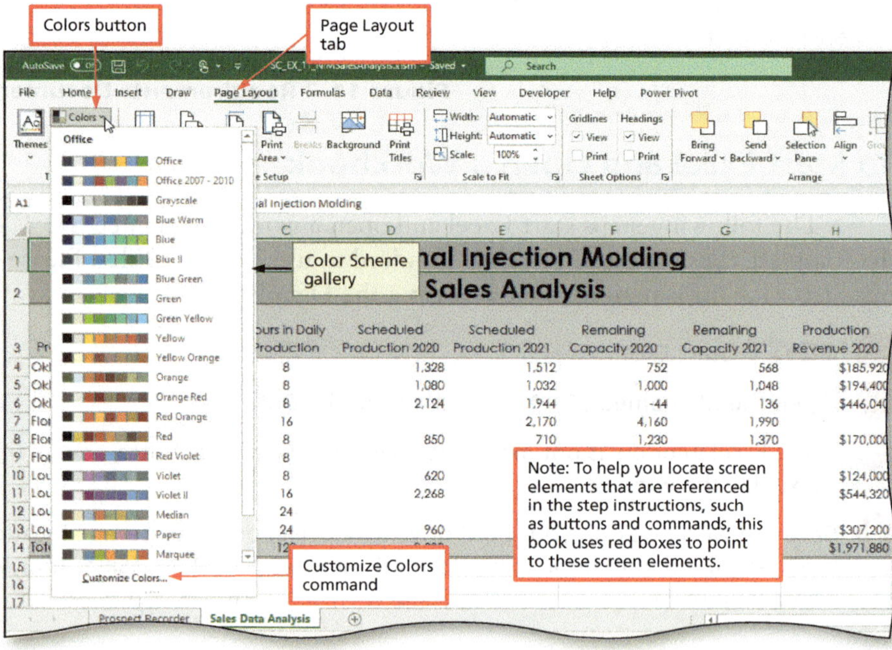

Figure 11–4

2

- Click Customize Colors to display the Create New Theme Colors dialog box.
- Type **NIM** in the Name box (Create New Theme Colors dialog box) to name the color scheme with the same name as the company.

Q&A **What if I do not enter a name for the modified color scheme?**
Excel will save your color scheme with a name that begins with the word, Custom, followed by a number (e.g., Custom 8).

- In the Theme colors area, click the Accent 1 button to display a gallery of color choices (Figure 11–5).

Experiment

- Point to each color in the gallery to display its name.

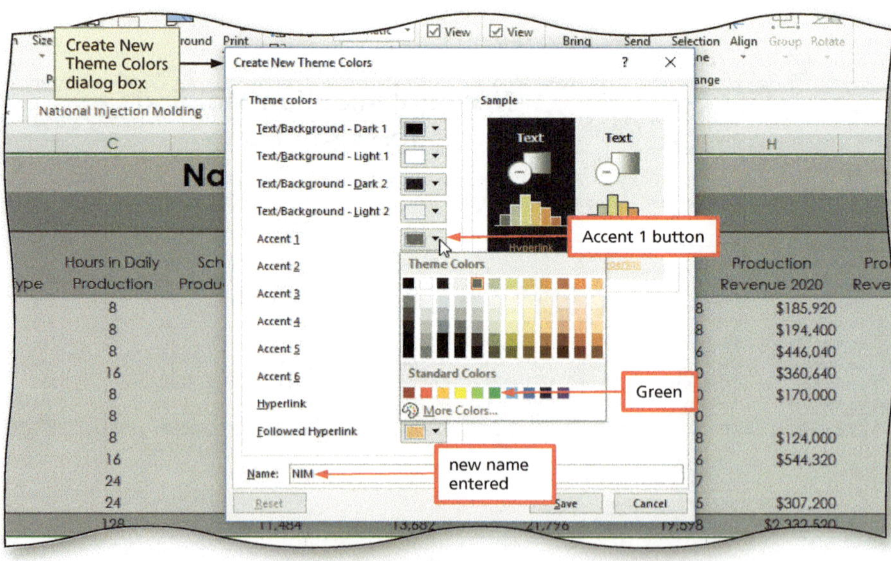

Figure 11–5

3

- Click Green in the Standard Colors area to select the Accent 1 color.
- Click the Accent 2 button, and then click Light Green in the Standard Colors to select the Accent 2 color.
- Click the Accent 3 button, and then click 'Orange, Accent 6, Darker 50%' (in the last row of the Theme colors area, column 10) to select the Accent 3 color (Figure 11–6).

Q&A **Can I delete a color scheme once I create it?**
Yes. To delete a color scheme, first display the list of color schemes, right-click the custom color scheme, and then click Delete Scheme on the shortcut menu.

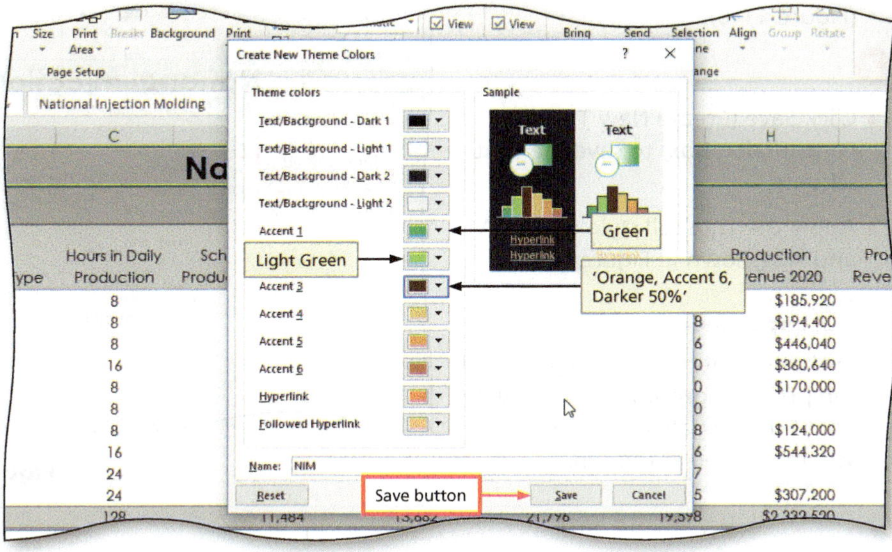

Figure 11–6

4

- Click Save (Create New Theme Colors dialog box) to save the color scheme.

Experiment

- Click the Colors button (Page Layout tab | Themes group) to display the Color Scheme gallery. The new color scheme will be in the Custom area at the top.

Q&A **Why did the colors change immediately?**
The cell styles were set previously to gray and dark gray. The new color scheme takes effect and changes all formatted cells.

To Create a Custom Font Scheme

The following steps create a custom font scheme. **Why?** Some companies associate certain fonts with branding; in this case, the NIM company wants to use the Book Antiqua font.

1

- Click the Fonts button (Page Layout tab | Themes group) to display the Font Scheme gallery and then click Customize Fonts to display the Create New Theme Fonts dialog box (Figure 11–7).
- In the Name box, type **NIM** to name the font scheme.
- Click the Heading font arrow and then click Book Antiqua in the list to choose a heading font.

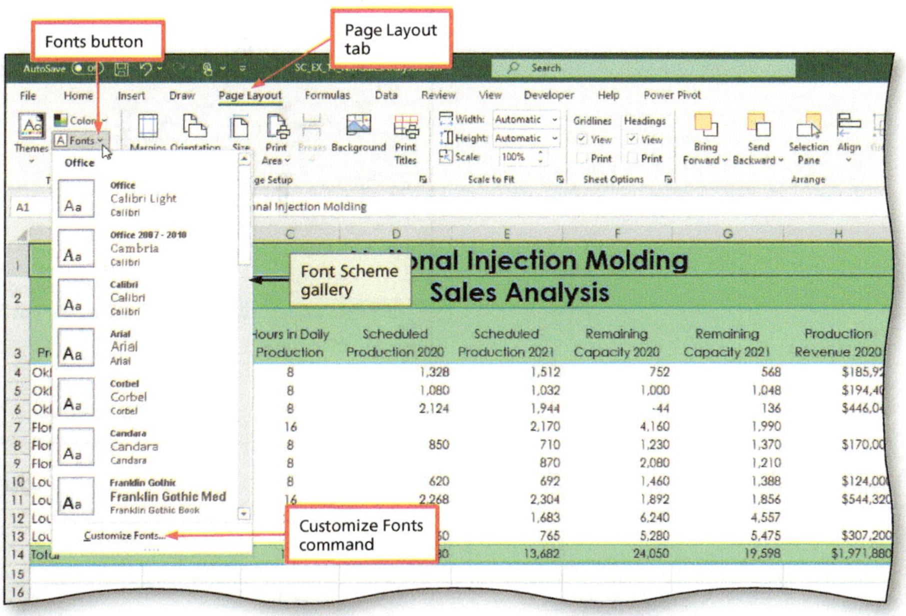

Figure 11–7

- If necessary, select Century Gothic in the Body font box (Figure 11–8).

2

- Click Save (Create New Theme Fonts dialog box) to save the font scheme.
- Apply the Title cell style to cells A1 and A2 (shown in Figure 11–9).

Experiment

- Click the Fonts button (Page Layout tab | Themes group) to display the Font Scheme gallery. The new font scheme will be at the top.

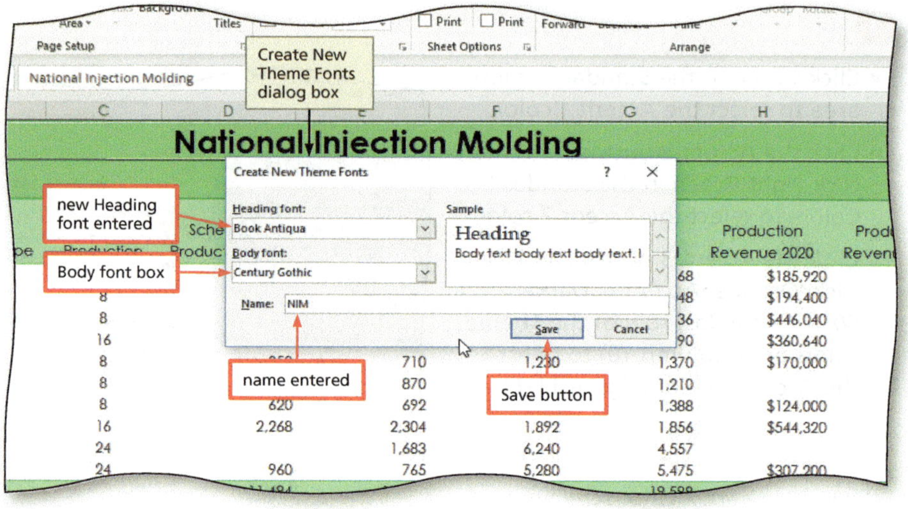

Figure 11–8

To Save a Custom Theme

The following steps save the newly created color and font schemes as an Excel theme. **Why?** Saving them as a theme makes future use easier as you would not have to choose the color and font schemes individually. Excel saves themes with the extension, .thmx. If the theme is stored in the default storage location, Microsoft Themes, the new theme will appear in the list of themes. If you are working in a lab situation, you should save new themes on your storage device. You can browse for the theme when you need it.

1

- Click the Themes button (Page Layout tab | Themes group) to Themes gallery (Figure 11–9).

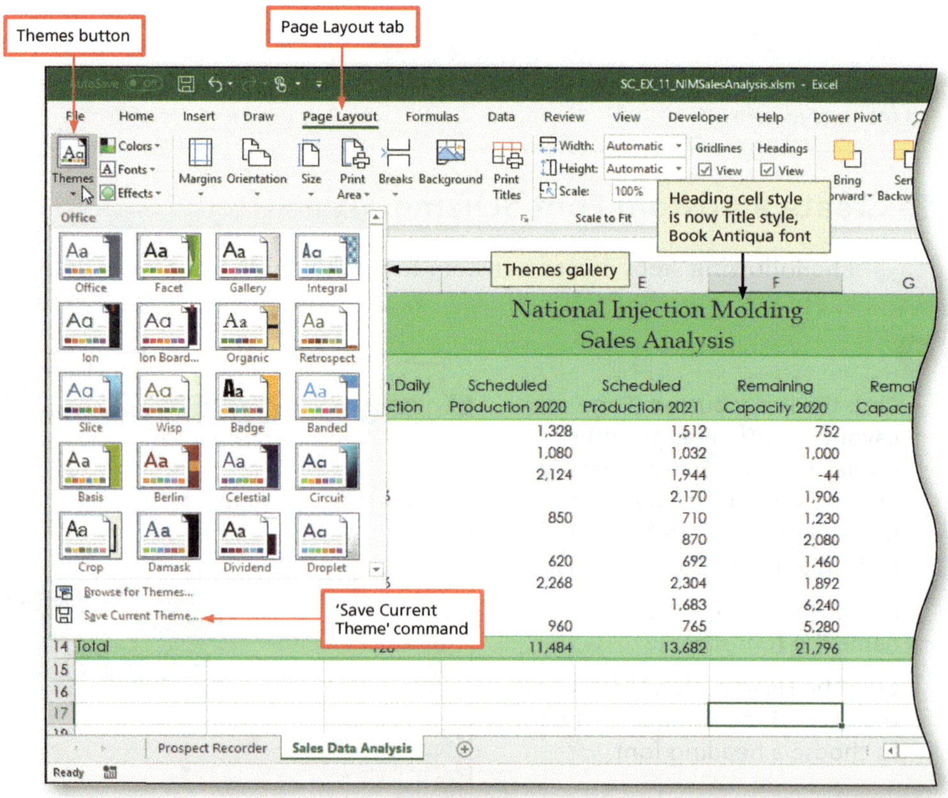

Figure 11–9

2

- Click Save Current Theme to display the Save Current Theme dialog box.
- In the File name box, type **NIM** and then browse to your Data File storage location (Figure 11–10).

Q&A **Where are themes usually stored?**
By default, Microsoft themes are stored at C:\Users\Your Name\AppData\Roaming\Microsoft\Templates\Document Themes. You should save the NIM theme in your Data File storage location.

3

- Click Save (Save Current Theme dialog box).

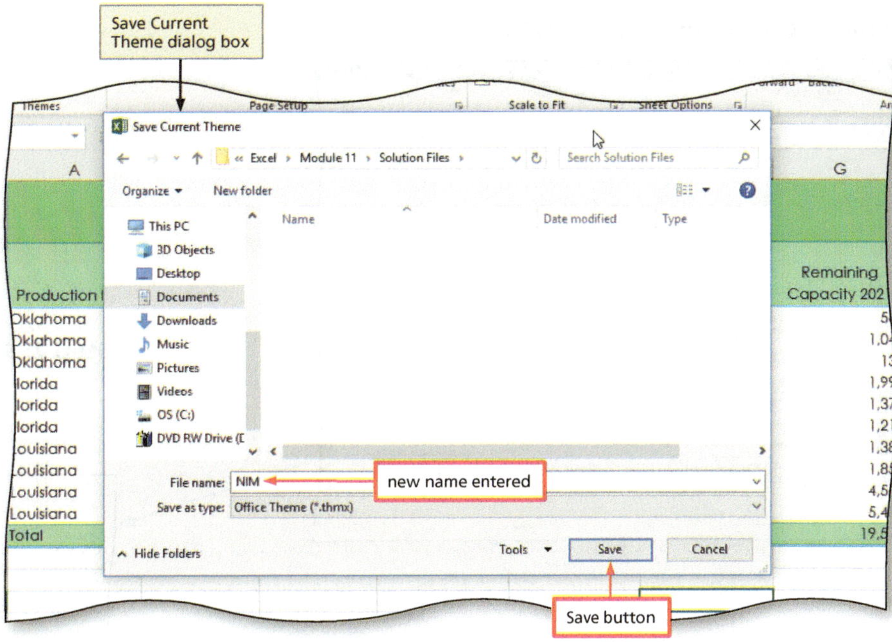

Figure 11–10

Designing the User Interface

The NIM sales team is using Excel to maintain information on prospects and their product interests. The head of sales has requested a simple user interface that can be used by salespeople to record details about prospects in the workbook. A **user interface (UI)** is a collective term for all the ways you interact with a software program. Also called a **form**, in Excel, it is an object that provides an easy-to-use data entry screen. A form is convenient for people with little or no knowledge of Excel, who might not know which cells to select or how to navigate the worksheet. Figure 11–11 shows the approach you use to create the user interface and how the Prospect Recorder worksheet will look when complete.

When a user clicks the 'Step 1 - Click to Enter Contact Information' command button, code will trigger Excel to display a series of input dialog boxes to capture contact information. The remaining data (the prospect's preferred method of communication and how they heard about NIM's products) will be entered using check boxes and option buttons to help reduce input errors that can be caused by mistyped data. Multiple check boxes can be selected for product interests. Unlike check boxes, option buttons restrict users to one selection per group, in this case to one preferred method of contact and one source of information. Because all of the data entry will use controls and input dialog boxes, you can protect the workbook restricting the user's interaction with the worksheet to those controls and dialog boxes.

BTW
Managing Theme Fonts
Each theme includes two font settings: one for body text and one for headings. To manage the fonts used for each, click the Fonts button (Page Layout tab | Themes group) and then click Customize Fonts to display the Create New Theme Fonts dialog box. Select the desired heading and body font options, enter a name for the theme, and then click Save to update and apply the font selections.

BTW
Ribbon and Screen Resolution
Excel may change how the groups and buttons within the groups appear on the ribbon, depending on the screen resolution of your computer. Thus, your ribbon may look different from the ones in this book if you are using a screen resolution other than 1366 × 768.

Planning Controls in the Form Design

You create a user interface or form by inserting form controls. **Form controls** are objects such as buttons and boxes that display data or make it easier for users to enter data, perform an action, or make a selection. Two types of controls are used to create the user interface: form controls and ActiveX controls. Form controls and ActiveX controls look identical in the Controls gallery. They do have functional

Step 1: Design the User Interface

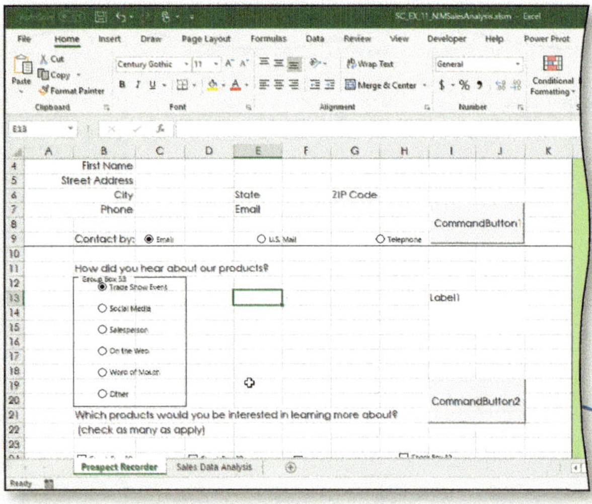

Step 2: Set Properties

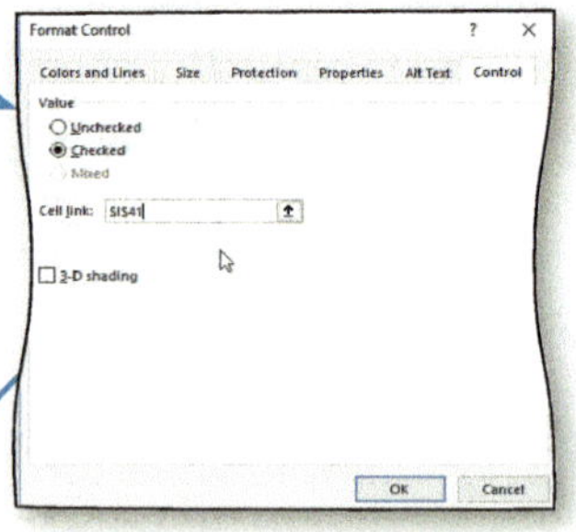

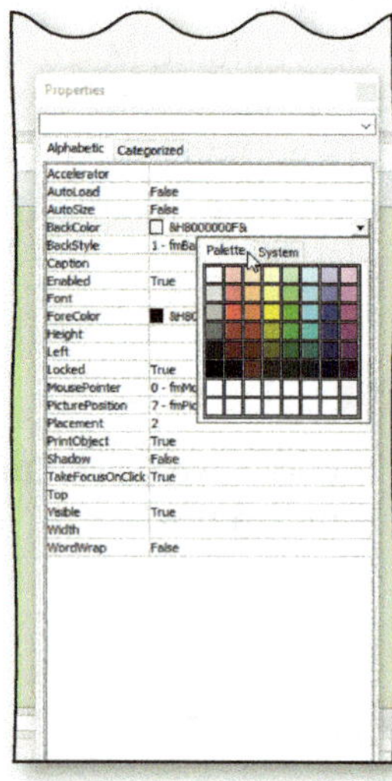

Step 3: Write the VBA Code

Step 4: Test the Final Product

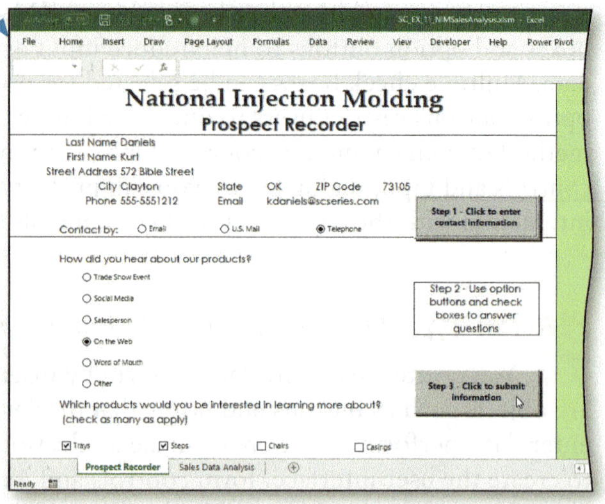

Figure 11–11

differences, however, that can help determine which one is the best choice for an object. Form controls require no knowledge of VBA to use. You can assign an Excel macro directly to a form control, allowing the macro to be run with a click. Form controls also allow you to reference cells easily and use Excel functions and expressions to manipulate data. You can customize their appearance at a rudimentary level.

ActiveX controls are controls that use a small program to enhance a user's experience or to help with tasks. ActiveX controls provide greater design flexibility than form controls. They have extensive properties used to customize their appearance. ActiveX controls cannot be assigned to an Excel macro directly. The macro code must be part of the VBA code for the control.

To create the Prospect Recorder interface, you will use form controls for the check boxes and option buttons, because of their ease of use and ability to use Excel functions with no additional code. You will use ActiveX controls for the command button and label controls to provide a more visually appealing interface than would be possible just using form controls. Figure 11–12 displays the gallery of available controls when constructing a user interface.

BTW
Copying Macros Between Workbooks
Macros consist of VBA code that can be edited or copied between workbooks using the Visual Basic Editor. To copy macros between workbooks, open the workbook containing the existing macro and the destination workbook. Open the Visual Basic Editor. In the Project pane, drag the module that you want to copy to the destination workbook.

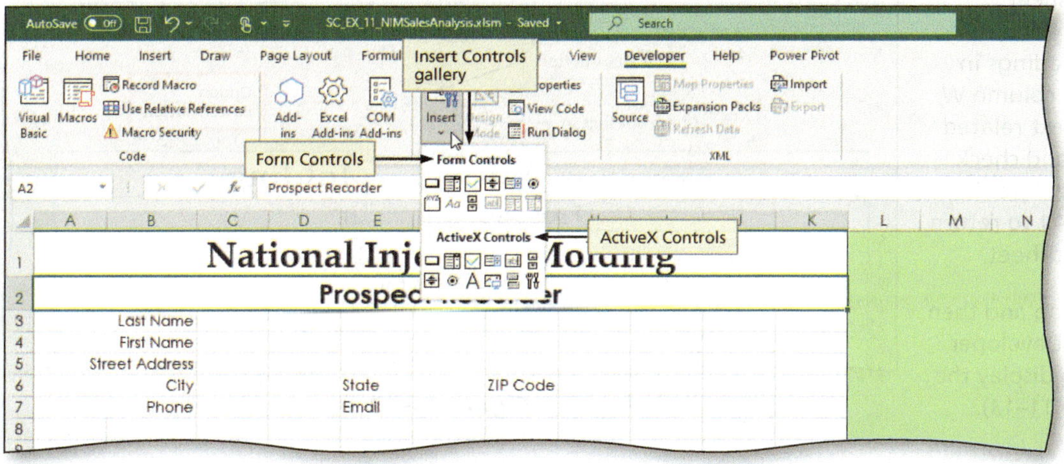

Figure 11–12

Finally, the user interface will store input in several places. It will place user input temporarily in row 40 of the Prospect Recorder worksheet, which is out of sight when the user interface is visible. It will display inputted data in the interface itself. Once the user input is recorded in row 40, an ActiveX control will display inputted data in the interface itself and then copy the input to a hidden worksheet, Prospect List. When testing the interface, you will verify the data recorded in the hidden worksheet.

To Display the Developer Tab

When you create a form, the Developer tab provides access to various VBA controls. The following steps display the Developer tab on the ribbon. If you already have the Developer tab on the ribbon, you may skip these steps.

1. Display Backstage view.
2. Click Options in the left pane to display the Excel Options dialog box.
3. Click Customize Ribbon in the left pane (Excel Options dialog box) to display the Customize the Ribbon tools.

4. Click the Developer check box in the Main Tabs list to select the Developer tab for display on the ribbon.

5. Click OK (Excel Options dialog box) to close the dialog box.

To Add Option Buttons to a Worksheet

Why? You will use option buttons not only to ensure consistent data entry but also to make the final interface one that someone unfamiliar with Excel will be able to use easily. The following steps create the option buttons. Do not be concerned about the exact placement of controls on the form. The option buttons will be aligned later in the module.

1

- Display the Prospect Recorder worksheet.

Experiment

- Look around the worksheet to view what has been added already. Look at the headings in row 39 and the data in column W, which displays stored text related to the option buttons and check boxes. You will use both later in the module. Click Cell A1 to return to the top of the spreadsheet.

- Display the Developer tab and then click the Insert button (Developer tab | Controls group) to display the Controls gallery (Figure 11–13).

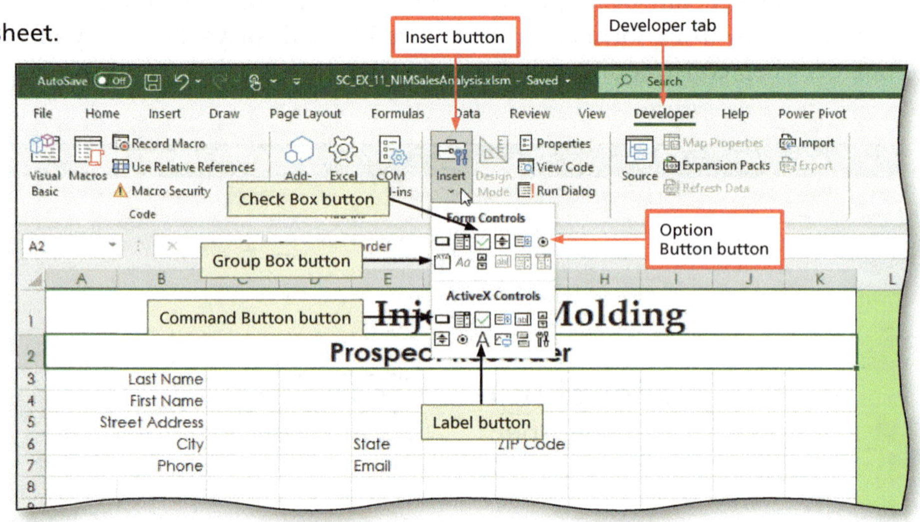

Figure 11–13

2

- Click the Option Button button in the Form Controls area (column 6, row 1) in the Controls gallery.
- Drag in the worksheet to create an option button control in cell C9 (approximately), as shown in Figure 11–14.
- Repeat to place eight additional option buttons (Figure 11–14).

Q&A

Why does my option button have more or less label text showing than in the figure?
The amount of text visible is determined by the size of the control. Dragging through a larger space on the worksheet will result in more label text being displayed. You can adjust the amount of visible label text by resizing the control.

My option buttons have numbers. Is that OK?
Yes, Excel may add a number in the caption or text beside the option button. You will change the caption later in the module.

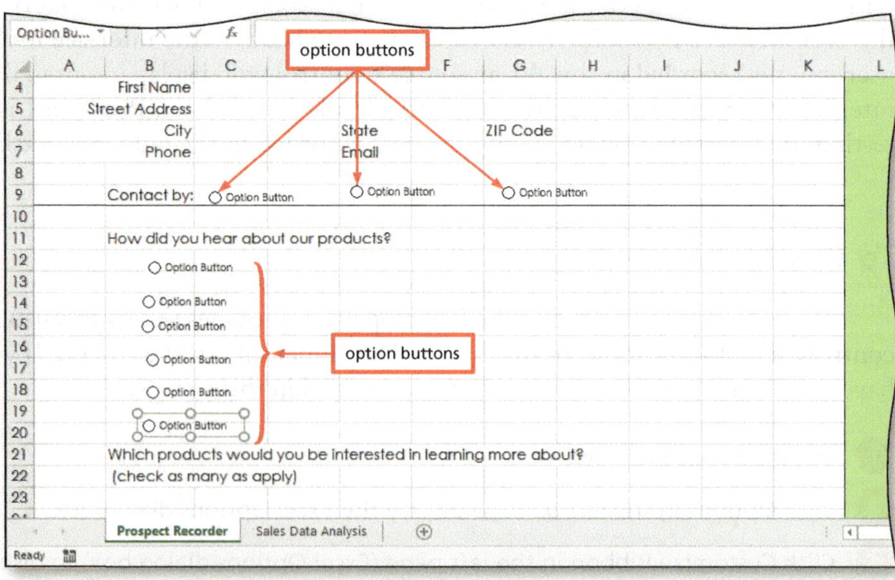

Figure 11–14

To Add Check Boxes to a Worksheet

1

- Click the Insert button (Developer tab | Controls group) again to display the Controls gallery, as shown in Figure 11–13.
- Click the Check Box button in the Form Controls area (column 3, row 1) in the Controls gallery.
- Drag in the worksheet to create a check box control in cell B24 (approximately), as shown in Figure 11–15.
- Repeat to place three additional check boxes (Figure 11–15).

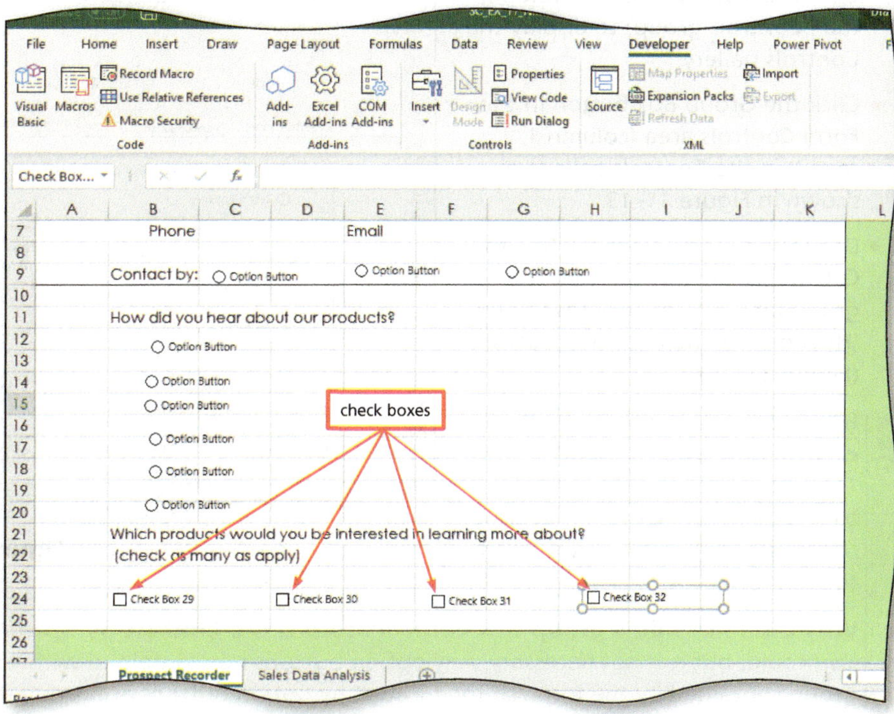

Figure 11–15

Q&A

What if I placed a control incorrectly?
If you want to reposition a control, right-click the control to select it and then drag it to its new location. You can delete a control by right-clicking the control and selecting Cut on the shortcut menu.

The check box is not the size I need it to be. What can I do?
Check boxes are resized easily. The check boxes here will be resized after the captions are changed later in this module.

To Group Option Buttons Using a Group Box

You have grouped Excel objects, such as text boxes, pictures, and shapes for the purpose of keeping them together as they are moved, edited, or deleted. Grouping form controls has a different purpose, especially with regard to option buttons. An **option button** is a control used to display a limited list of mutually exclusive choices. In other words, users can choose only one in a set of option buttons. In the Prospect Recorder form, users should be able to choose one from the upper three 'Contact by' options buttons, as well as one from the lower six 'How did you hear' option buttons. **Why?** NIM wants to know how customers would like to be contacted and how they heard about NIM products.

To make a set of option button choices mutually exclusive, you need to group them together using the Group Box form control. In this project, you will group the lower set; users will be able to choose only one from those six option buttons. Because the lower buttons will be grouped, the upper options buttons do not need a Group Box form control to keep them together and mutually exclusive because the form itself acts as their group.

The following step first creates the Group Box form control, and then groups option buttons inside it.

1

- Click the Insert button (Developer tab | Controls group) to display the Controls gallery.
- Click the Group Box button in the Form Controls area (column 1, row 2) in the Controls gallery, as shown in Figure 11–13.
- Drag the pointer from cell B12 to C20, approximately, so that the group box control encloses the six 'How did you hear' option buttons (Figure 11–16).

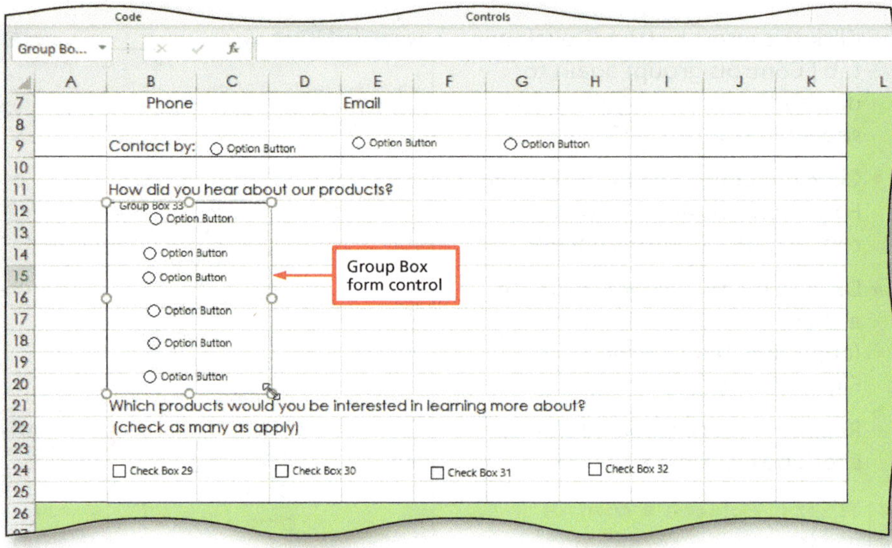

Figure 11–16

Q&A

How accurately do I have to draw the group box?
The Group Box control needs to enclose in the Option Button controls completely in order for it to work correctly.

Why did I not add a group box control around the Contact by option buttons?
You could, but it is not necessary. Any option buttons not contained within a group box are treated as their own group contained by the form, so the Contact by option buttons are grouped by default. In this project, at least one group is necessary, however. Without the addition of at least one group box on the form, the user would only be able to select only one option button out of the nine option buttons.

Labels and Text Boxes

Most forms contain text: Option buttons usually need text labels that describe each option. In addition, users need to enter text information in response to question. There are two types of text controls you can add to a form. A **Label ActiveX control** (also called a label) is a box with text used to display a message, such as identifying the purpose of a cell or text box. A label can also display descriptive text, such as titles, captions, or brief instructions on the form. A label can also display a descriptive picture.

A **Text Box ActiveX control** is a rectangular box in which the user can view, enter, or edit data. A Text Box ActiveX control is different from a regular text box that you would insert using the Text Box command (Insert tab | Text group). A Text Box ActiveX control is a special text box used for data entry, programmed with code to move the data from the text box to a specific location or into a formula on the worksheet. While you are creating a Text Box ActiveX control, Excel turns on Design Mode, allowing you to set properties and write code. After you are finished, you can turn off Design Mode, allowing users to enter text in the text box. You also can use a text box to display or view text that is independent of row and column boundaries, or free-floating, preserving the layout of a grid or table of data on the worksheet.

To Add a Label Control to the Worksheet

You have added many option buttons and check boxes to the form so far, and now you need to identify them. **Why?** Labels are an important part of a user interface because they guide users to select the correct controls as they enter their information. The following step adds a label control to the worksheet.

1

- Click cell G12 or another cell to deselect the group box.
- Click the Insert button (Developer tab | Controls group) to display the Controls gallery.
- Click the Label button in the ActiveX Controls area (column 3, row 2) of the Controls gallery (shown in Figure 11–13).
- Drag in the worksheet from cell I13 through the lower-right corner of cell J15 to create a Label form control (Figure 11–17).

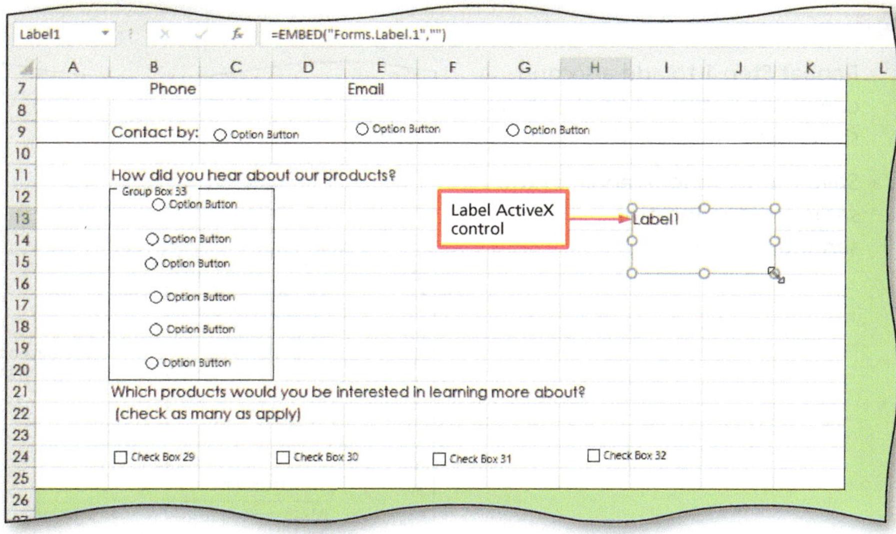

Figure 11–17

To Create a Text Box ActiveX Control

In this project, you will not use a Text Box ActiveX control; the data entry will be supplied by a series of Input Boxes that you will learn about later. If you wanted to create a Text Box ActiveX control, you would do the following:

1. Click the Insert button (Developer tab | Controls group) to display the Controls gallery.
2. Click the Text Box button in the ActiveX Controls area (column 5, row 1) in the Controls gallery.
3. Drag in the worksheet to create a text box.
4. Set properties and write code as necessary.
5. Before releasing the workbook to the public, click the Design Mode button (Developer tab | Controls group) to turn it off, making the text box active.

To Add Command Buttons to the Worksheet

The use of command buttons gives the user control over the execution of each step of the process when entering data into the form. There is a difference between a Command Button form control and a Command Button ActiveX control. **Why?** A Command Button ActiveX control can have Visual Basic code associated with it that accomplishes more complex actions than a macro or a Command Button form control can accommodate. The two buttons are created in a similar manner, however. The following steps add two Command Button ActiveX controls to the worksheet.

1

- Click the Insert button (Developer tab | Controls group) to display the Controls gallery.
- Click the Command Button button in the ActiveX Controls area (column 1, row 1) of the Controls gallery.
- Drag in the worksheet from cell I7 through the lower-right corner of cell J9 to create a Command Button ActiveX control.

2

- Repeat Step 1 to add a second command button in the location shown in Figure 11–18.
- Save the workbook again in the same storage location with the same file name.

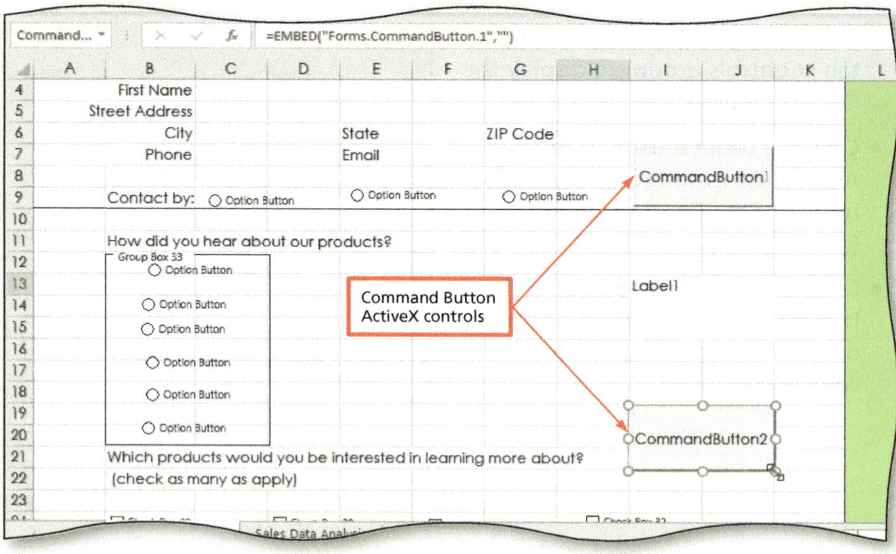

Figure 11–18

Break Point: If you want to take a break, this is a good place to do so. You can exit Excel now. To resume later, start Excel, open the file called SC_EX_11_NIMSalesAnalysis.xlsm, and continue following the steps from this location forward.

Setting Form Control Properties

Each form control in the Controls gallery has many properties, or characteristics, that can be set to determine the form control's appearance and behavior. You set these properties using the Format Control dialog box, which can be accessed by right-clicking the form control and selecting Format Control from the shortcut menu or by selecting the control and clicking the Control Properties button (Developer tab | Controls group) on the ribbon.

The next step is to set the properties for the 13 form controls (check boxes and option buttons) in the user interface. The group box, while technically a form control, will not be formatted here; it will be formatted using VBA later in the module. The three ActiveX controls also will be formatted later in the module.

To Format the Option Buttons

Why? The Option Button form controls must be formatted to identify their purpose for the user. Other formatting options can be used to make the controls and the worksheet itself easier to use. The following steps change the text associated with the option button controls and resize the controls.

1

- Right-click the first option button control in the Contact by area to display the shortcut menu (Figure 11–19).

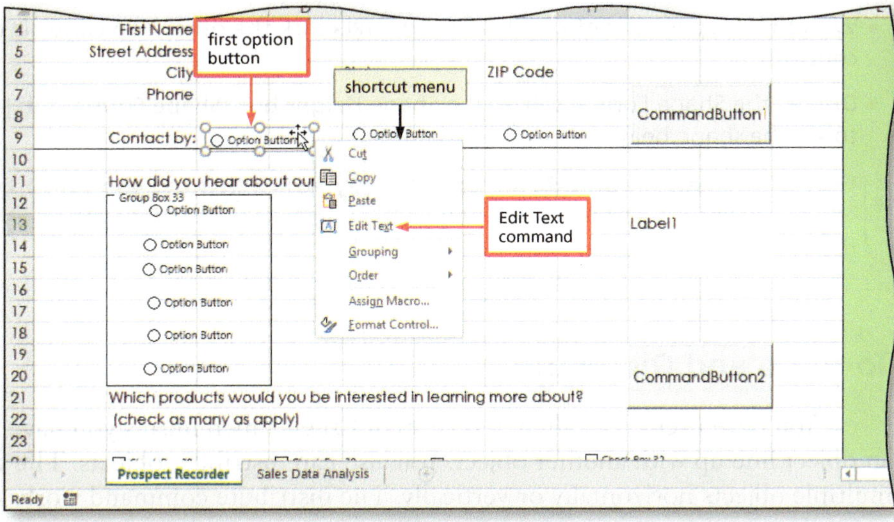

Figure 11–19

2

- Click Edit Text on the shortcut menu to edit the control text.
- Delete the text in the control and type `Email` to replace the text.
- Resize the control so that it just encloses the new text (Figure 11–20).

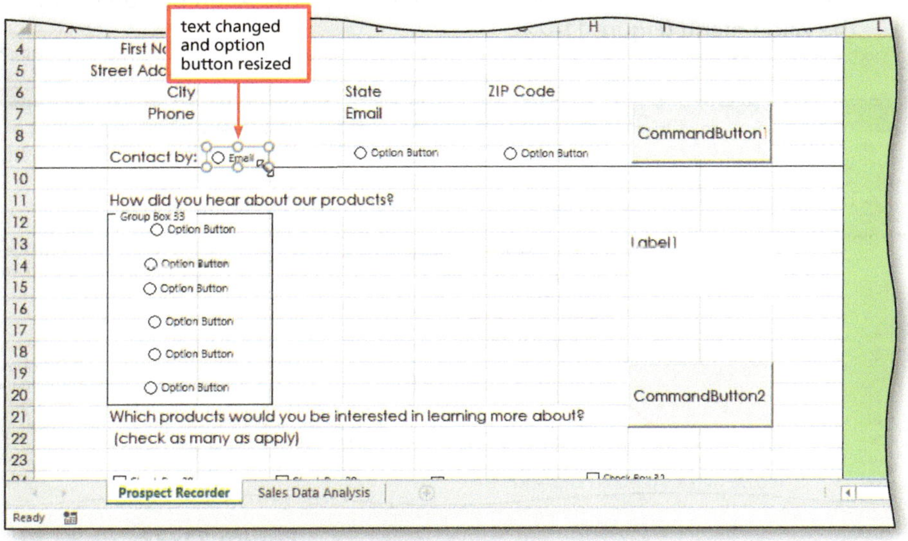

Figure 11–20

3

- Repeat Steps 1 and 2 to rename and resize the other two contact controls, with the names U.S. Mail and Telephone, respectively.
- If necessary, right-click the Telephone control to select it.
- ALT+drag the control until the right edge is aligned with the right edge of column H (Figure 11–21).

Q&A **Why did I hold down the ALT key while positioning the Telephone control?**
Using the ALT key aligns the controls to the Excel gridlines, making it easier to place items on the form.

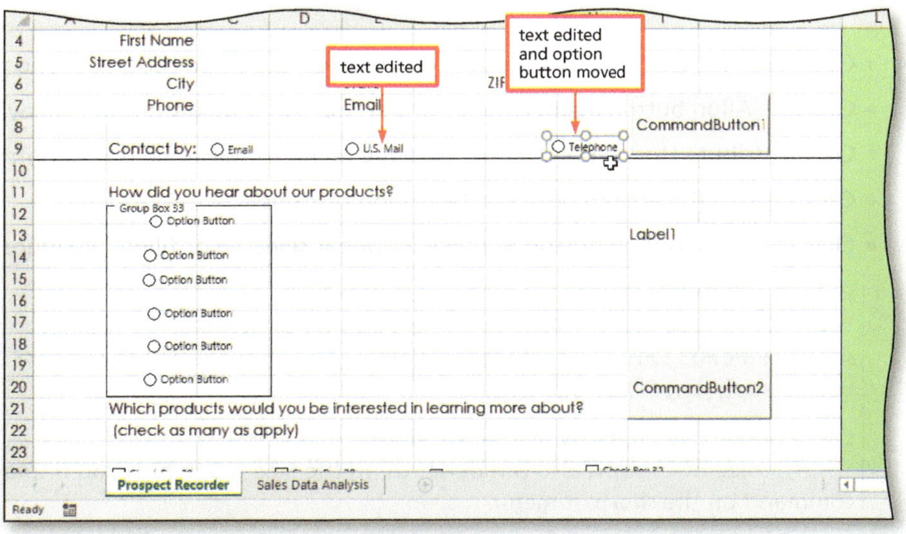

Figure 11–21

4

- With the Telephone control still selected, CTRL+click the other two controls to select all three option button controls.
- Display the Shape Format tab. In the Shape Height box (Shape Format tab | Size group), type .2 and press ENTER to set the shape height.

Q&A **Why did I need to hold down the CTRL key while clicking the other two controls?**
The CTRL key adds additional controls to the selection so that formatting and alignment options can be adjusted on the set of controls rather than individually.

To Align and Distribute

You have previously aligned objects in Excel, which means you have made either an edge or center of an object line up with another object. You also can distribute objects. The **distribute** command evenly spaces multiple objects horizontally or vertically. The distribute command works on three or more objects.

1

- With the three option buttons still selected, click the Align button (Shape Format tab | Arrange group) to display the Align menu (Figure 11–22).

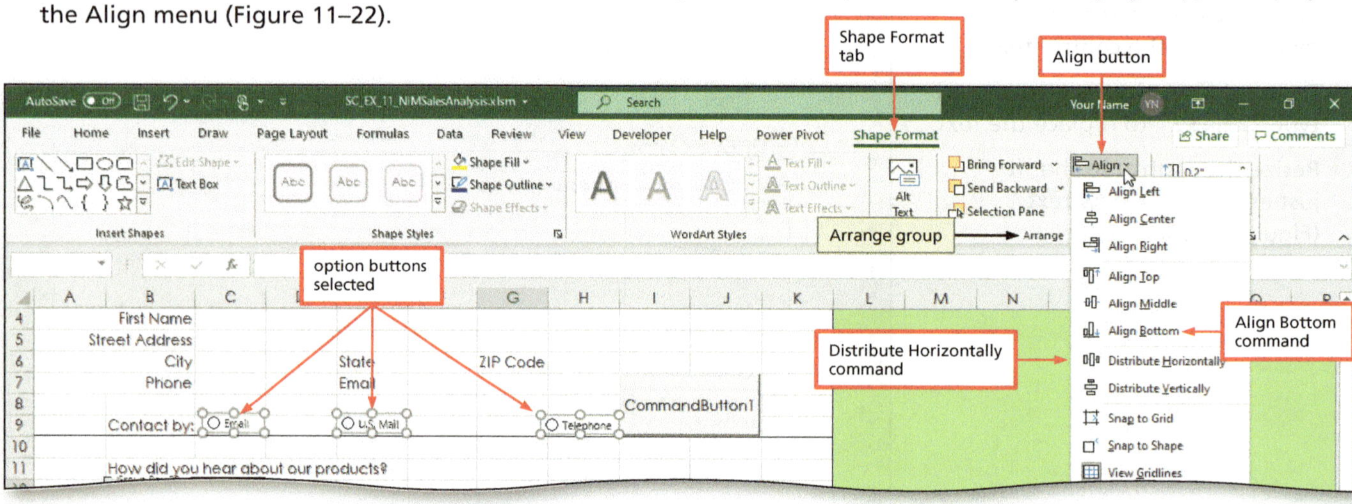

Figure 11–22

2

- Click Align Bottom on the Arrange menu to align the three controls along their bottom borders.
- Click the Align button again (Shape Format tab | Arrange group) to display the alignment options.
- Click Distribute Horizontally on the Arrange menu to space the three controls evenly between columns C and H.
- Click outside the area to deselect the option buttons.
- Click the Email option button to make it appear selected or filled in (Figure 11–23).

Q&A **How can I make the controls more visible?**
You can format the controls with borders and fill colors to make them stand out from the background. From the shortcut menu, you can select Format Control and then use the Colors and Lines tab in the Format Control dialog box to apply colors and patterns.

Can I make the controls a specific size?
Yes. The size of controls also can be set using the Size tab, which you display by selecting the Format Control command on the shortcut menu.

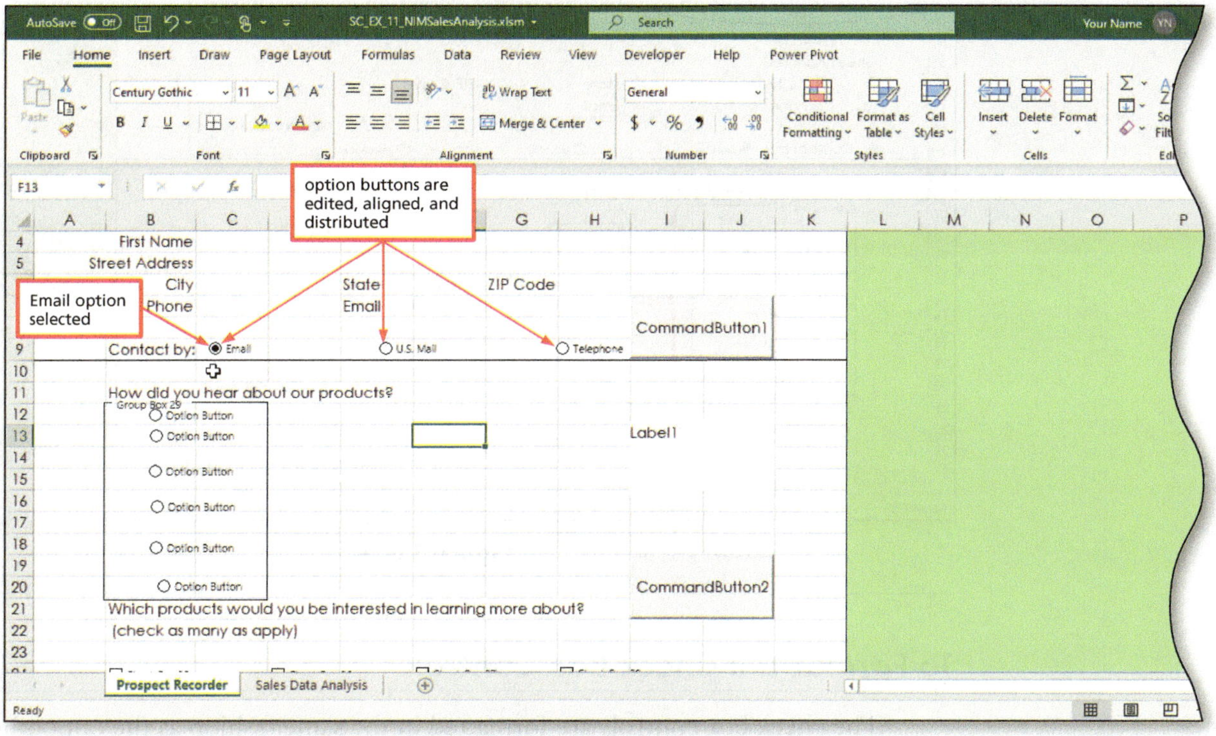

Figure 11–23

To Format the Option Buttons in the Group Box

The following steps format the option buttons in the group box control.

1. One at a time, right-click each of the six option buttons in the group box and edit the text to match the following:

   Trade Show Event

   Social Media

   Salesperson

   On the Web

   Word of Mouth

   Other

2. Select all six controls, and using the Shape Height and Shape Width boxes (Shape Format tab | Size group), set the height to 0.2" and the width to 1.1".

3. With the six controls still selected, click the Align Objects button (Shape Format tab | Arrange group), and then click the Align Left button.

4. Click the Align Object button again and then click Distribute Vertically to distribute the objects.

5. Click outside the option buttons to deselect them.

6. Click the Trade Show Event option button to make it appear selected or filled in (Figure 11–24).

Q&A **Can I format the Group Box control?**
No. You can edit the text along the top of the group box, but to change it in any other way requires writing code, which you will do later in the module.

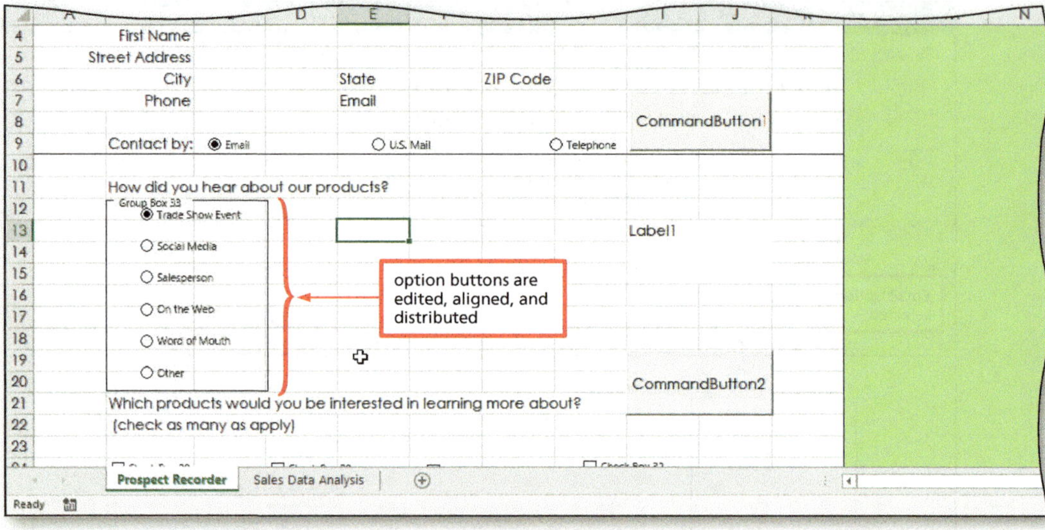

Figure 11–24

To Format the Check Box Controls

The check box controls are formatted in the same fashion as the option button controls. The following steps format and align the check box controls.

1. Select each of the four check box buttons, and in turn, type the following: **`Trays`**, **`Steps`**, **`Chairs`**, and **`Casings`**.
2. Move the leftmost check box button so that its upper-left corner aligns with the upper-left corner of cell B24, and move the rightmost check box button so that its upper-right corner aligns with the upper-right corner of cell H24.
3. Select all four controls and then, using the Shape Height and Shape Width boxes (Shape Format tab | Size group), set the height to 0.2" and the width to 1.2".
4. If necessary, select all four controls and then, using the Align Objects button (Shape Format tab | Arrange group), apply the Align Top and Distribute Horizontally formats to the group. Deselect the check box controls (Figure 11–25).

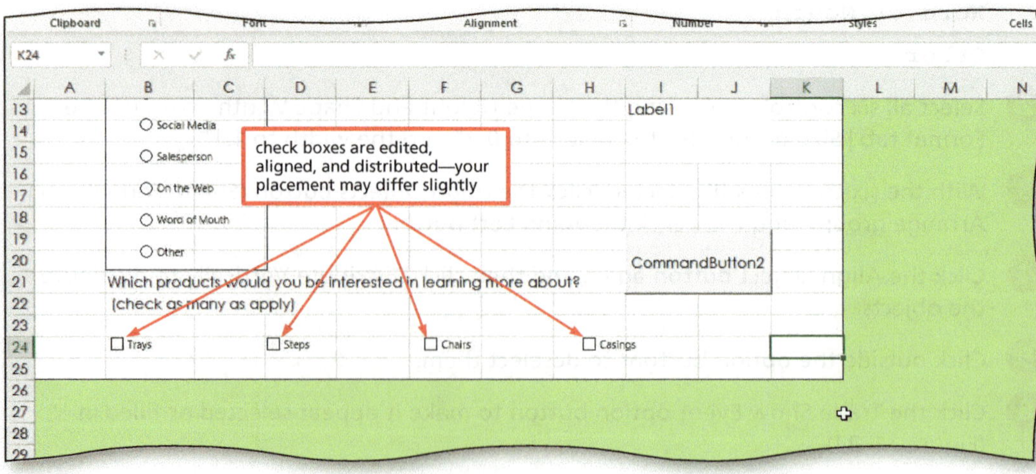

Figure 11–25

Setting ActiveX Control Properties

As with form controls, each ActiveX control in the Controls gallery has many properties that determine the control's appearance and behavior. You set these properties in Design Mode, which displays automatically in most cases. If you need to enter Design Mode, click the Design Mode button (Developer tab | Controls group). **Design Mode** allows the use of various tools including the Properties pane, where control properties can be set or edited. Turning off Design Mode makes the form and the command buttons ready to execute.

The Properties pane shows the name of the property on the left and the setting, text, or value on the right. When you click a property, some have an arrow button that displays a list of choices; some display an ellipsis button that opens a dialog box. For detailed information about each format property, select the property, and then press F1 to display a VBA Help topic.

The user interface contains three ActiveX controls: two command buttons and a label. The color, font, and effects for these controls will be modified by applying property values.

To Set Command Button Properties

Why? Text on the command button helps users know what to do in the form. You can add color, font formatting, shadow properties, and detailed captions to Command Button ActiveX controls in order to draw a user's attention. You also can give both controls user-friendly names using the Properties window. The following steps set the command button properties.

1

- Select the two command button controls.
- Display the Developer tab and then click the Properties button (Developer tab | Controls group) to open the Properties window.
- Click the BackColor property and then click the BackColor arrow to display the BackColor options.
- Click the Palette tab to display the color options (Figure 11–26).

Q&A **Why does the Properties window look different from other dialog boxes in Excel?**
The Properties window is part of the VBA interface and is used to manage ActiveX controls in Excel.

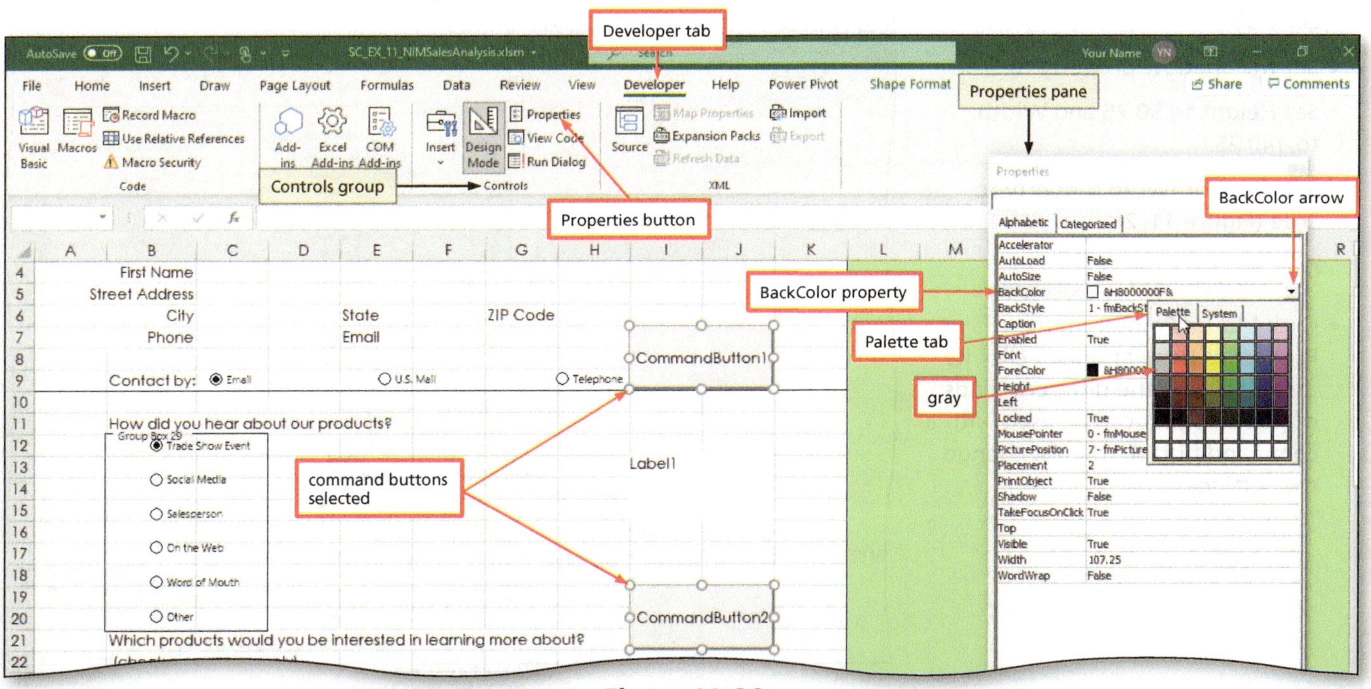

Figure 11–26

2

- Click gray (column 1, row 3) to add a gray background to the command buttons.
- Click the Font property to display the ellipsis button.
- Click the ellipsis button to display the Font dialog box.
- Select Segoe UI in the Font list, Bold in the Font style list, and 10 in the Size list to change the font on the command buttons and in the label (Figure 11–27).

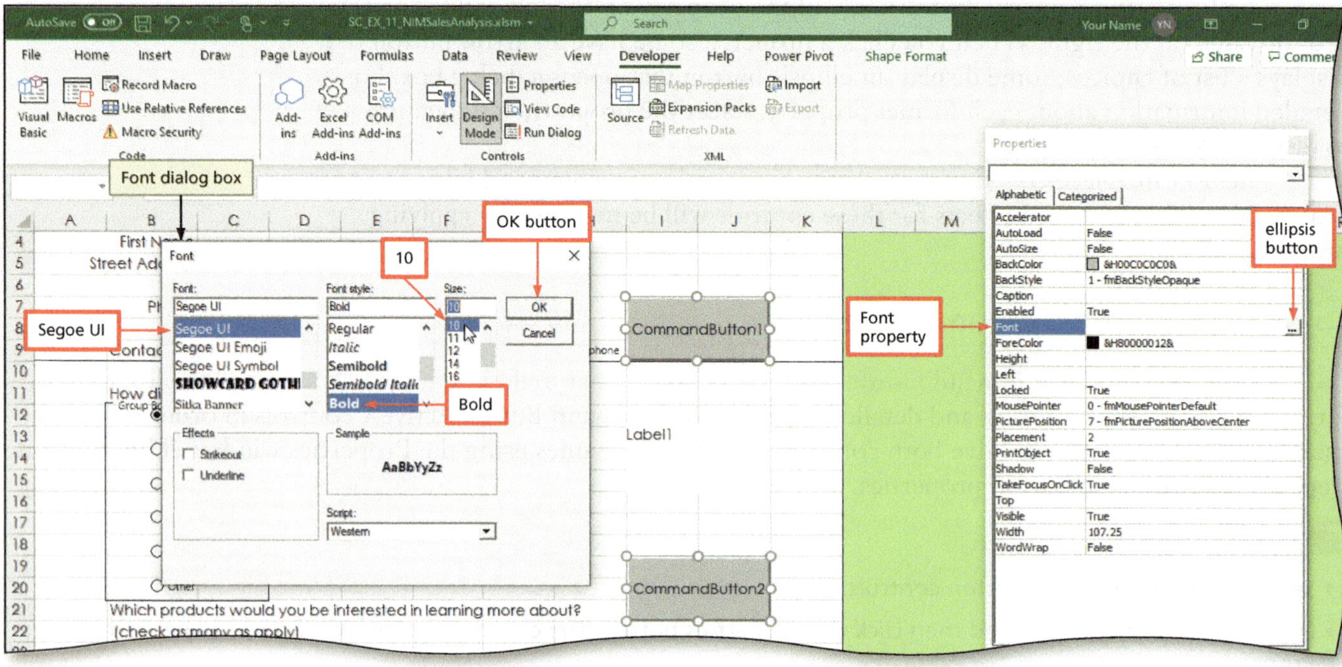

Figure 11–27

3

- Click OK (Font dialog box) to apply this font to the text in the controls.
- Set the Shadow property to True
- Set Height to 50.25 and Width to 140.25.
- Set the WordWrap property to True (Figure 11–28).

Experiment

- Click Mouse Pointer in the Properties pane and then click its arrow to view the different kinds of pointers that can be used with a command button. Do not change the setting.

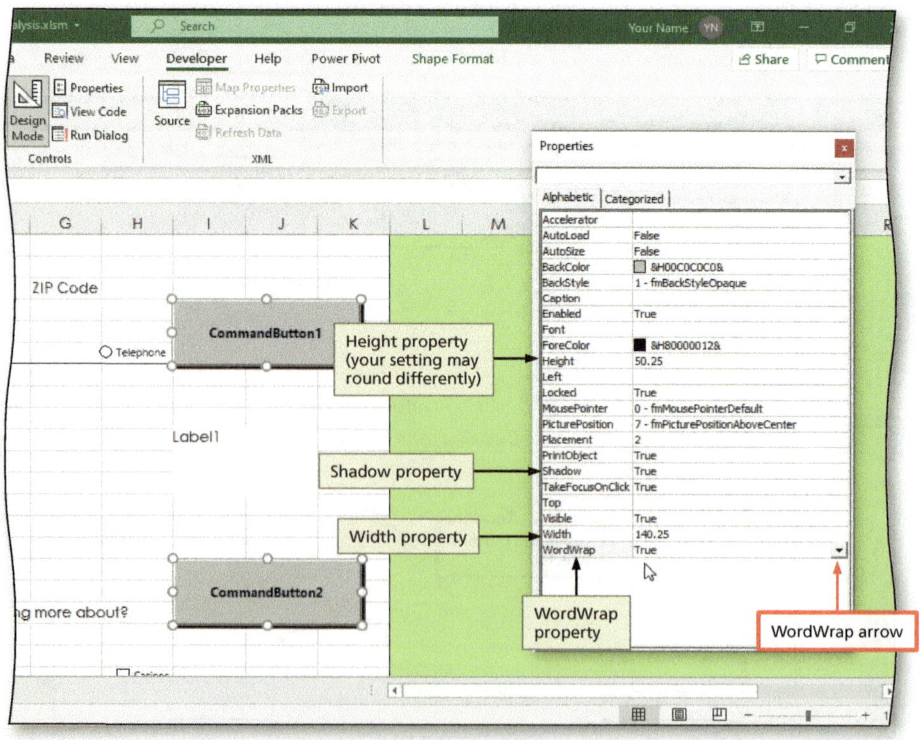

Figure 11–28

4

- Select the first command button only.
- In the Properties pane, click Name and then type `cmdStep1` to rename the control.
- Click Caption, and then type `Step 1 - Click to enter contact information` to enter the caption (Figure 11–29).

Q&A **What are the letters, cmd, before the name, Step1?**
It is common practice for developers to use a prefix with control names to indicate the type of control.

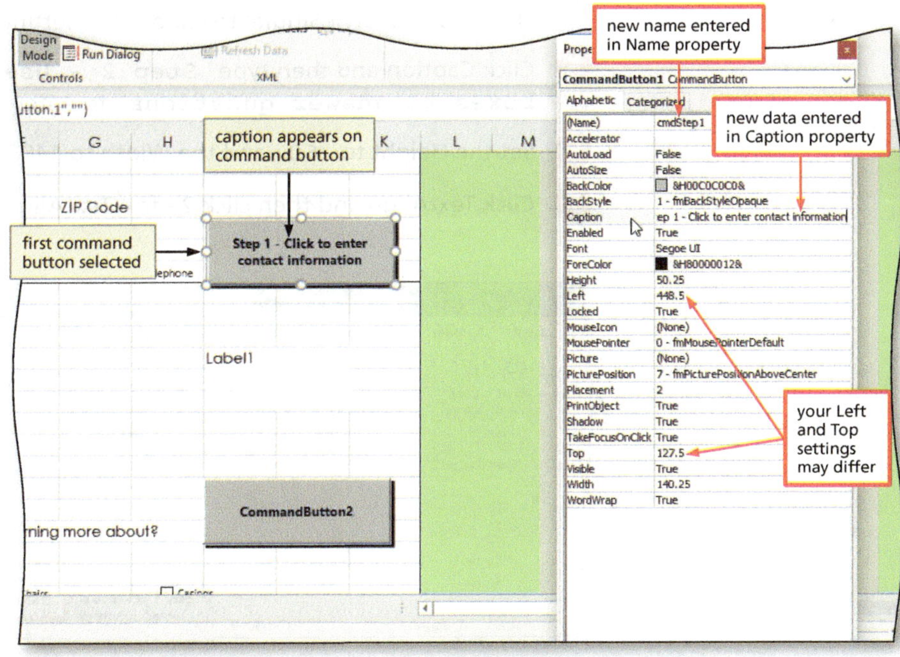

Figure 11–29

5

- Select the second command button only.
- In the Properties pane, click Name and then type `cmdStep3` to rename the control.
- Click Caption, and then type `Step 3 - Click to submit information` to enter the caption (Figure 11–30).

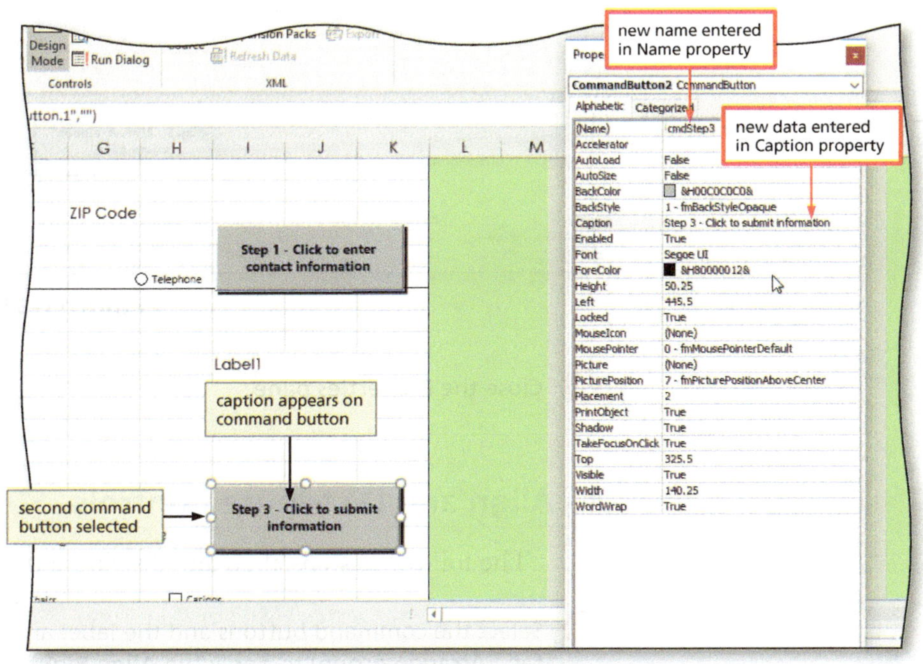

Figure 11–30

To Set Label Properties

The following steps set properties for the Label ActiveX Control.

1. Select the label control.
2. In the Properties pane, click Name and then type `lblStep2` to rename the control.
3. In the Properties pane, click BorderColor and then click the BorderColor arrow to display the BorderColor options. Click the Palette tab to display the color options. Click black (column 1, row 6) to add a black border to the label.

4. Click BorderStyle and then click the BorderStyle arrow. In the list, click '1 - frmBorderStyleSingle' to choose the setting for the border.

5. Click Caption and then type `Step 2 - Use option buttons and check boxes to answer questions` to enter the caption.

6. Set the Height to `60` and the Width to 140.25.

7. Click TextAlign and then click 2 - frm TextAlignCenter (Figure 11–31).

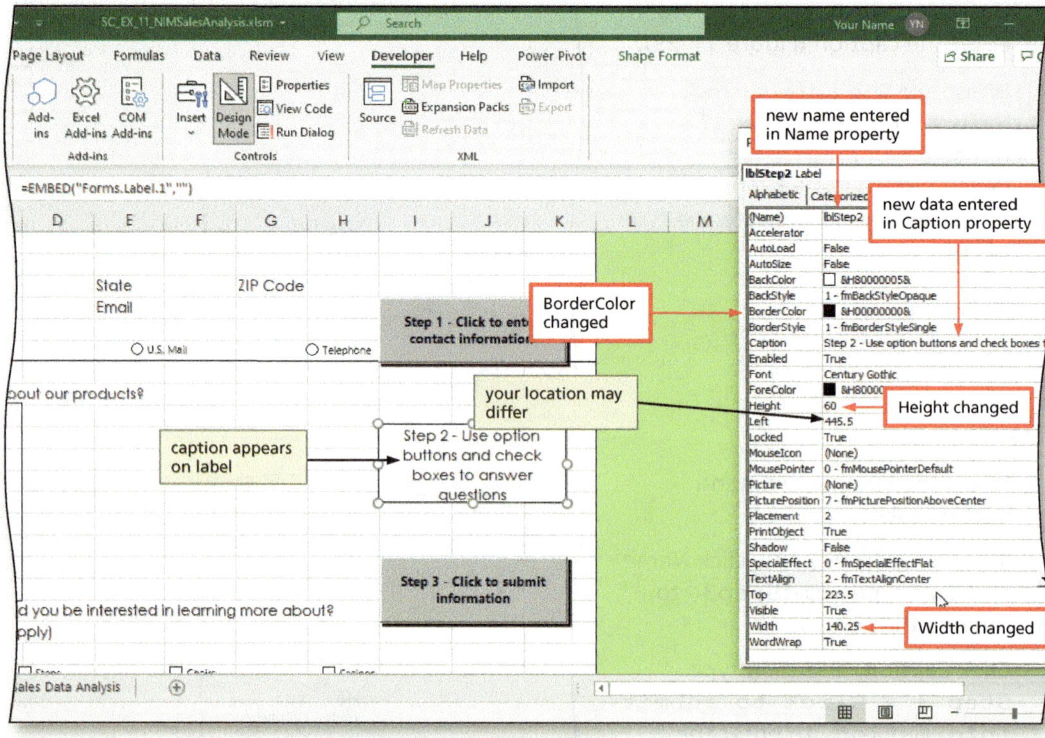

Figure 11–31

8. Close the Properties pane.

To Align and Distribute Controls

The following steps align and distribute the two command buttons and the label.

1. Select the command buttons and the label and use the Align button (Shape Format tab | Arrange group) to apply the Align Right and Distribute Vertically formats to the group.

2. Save the workbook again in the same storage location with the same file name.

Storing User Input

Once you have added the controls to the worksheet, consider where the inputted information will be stored or recorded. In most cases when you use an Excel form, you must store the information within the workbook, but it is a good idea to store it away from the form itself. You want the data to be accessible to experienced users but not distracting to users simply entering data in the form. For this project, you will store data input in row 40 of the worksheet. You then will copy that information into a hidden Prospect List worksheet for long-term retention.

Users will be entering their name, address, and other information into the form. In this module, entering and storing data will be a three-part process. Part 1: Rather than having the users try to move to specific cells and type in data, which may or may not fit in the cell, you will program a VBA function called INPUTBOX to collect their data. Users will click option buttons and check boxes to indicate their responses. Part 2: You will program Excel to transfer the data from the INPUTBOX collection to the temporary storage location in row 40 and display it on the form. Excel also will place the values for option buttons and check boxes in row 40. Part 3: When the user clicks the Submit button, Excel will transfer the data from the temporary location in row 40 to the hidden worksheet, Prospect List, and clear the form for the next entry.

To Create from Selection

In order to make the process more user-friendly, you will name specific cells and ranges. The 'Create from Selection' command names cells based on headings or adjacent cells. Excel uses the heading to name the cell, replacing any spaces with underscores. The following steps use the headings in row 39 to name the cells in row 40. **Why?** Row 40 will be the temporary storage location for inputted data.

1

- Select the range A39:H40.
- Click the 'Create from Selection' button (Formulas tab | Defined Names group) to display the Create from Selection dialog box.
- Because the headings are at the top, click the Top row check box, if necessary (Figure 11–32).

Q&A **Why am I not including columns I through N in the selection?**
I40:N40 will contain formulas or functions and do not need names.

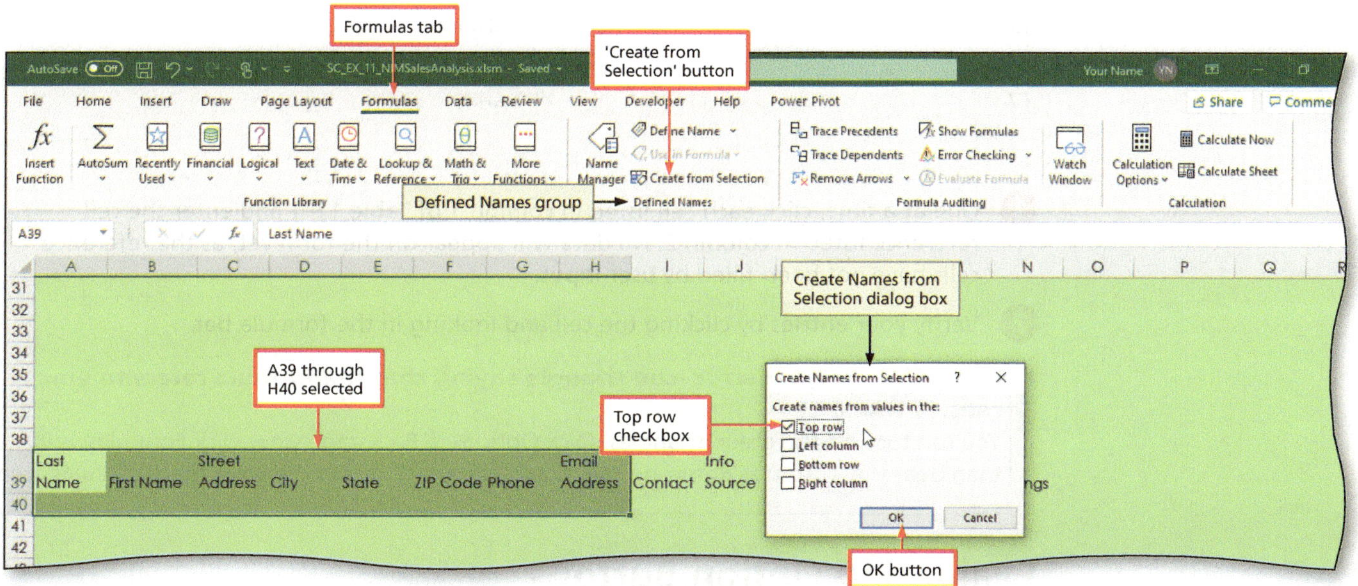

Figure 11–32

2

- Click OK (Create Names from Selection dialog box) to name the cells.

Experiment

- Click various cells in row 40 to verify their names in the Name Box on the formula bar.

To Assign Other Range Names

The following steps assign names to specific ranges in the form. The two ranges are in column W, which displays the captions of the option buttons.

1. Select the range W3:W5.
2. Click the Define Name button (Formulas tab | Defined Names group) to display the New Name dialog box.
3. Type `Contact_Options` in the Name text box.
4. Click OK (New Name dialog box).
5. Repeat steps 1 through 4 to name the range W7:W12 as `Source_Options`.

To Enter Cell References

The following steps enter cell references in the form. These cell references will display user input from programming later in the module. The cells and references to enter are listed in Table 11–1.

Table 11–1 Cell References

Cell	Reference to Enter
C3	=A40
C4	=B40
C5	=C40
C6	=D40
F6	=E40
H6	=F40
C7	=G40
F7	=H40

1. One at a time, click each cell listed in column 1 of Table 11–1 and enter the cell reference listed in column 2. No data will appear on the form yet, as the reference cells have not been filled by user input.
2. Verify your entries by clicking the cell and looking in the formula bar.

Q&A

My cells display an error icon triangle saying that the formula refers to empty cells. Is that OK?

You can turn off the green triangles: Click Options in Backstage view, click Formulas, and then clear the 'Formulas Referring to Empty Cells' check box in the Error checking rules area.

Evaluating Option Buttons

Recall that form users will click an option button in each group to select it. The first option button is already selected to be the default value in each group. Because those selections must be stored, you need to determine which option button of the group was clicked.

Excel maintains an index number behind the scenes for each option button; that index number is 1, 2, 3, and so on. To retrieve the option button index number, you use the Format Control dialog box to link to a cell reference that will display the index number. For example, if you link an option button to cell Z100, then during data input when the user clicks an option button, cell Z100 will display a 1, 2, or 3 to indicate which option button was selected. Excel only requires you to create a cell link for one option button per group; the cell link will work for all option buttons in the group.

Determining the caption of a selected option button is a separate process, however. Once you obtain the index number, you can look up the caption in column W, using the INDEX() function. Recall that the INDEX() function takes two arguments, a range and an index number. The function returns the cell value at that location in the range. For example, if your captions are located in cells A1, A2, and A3, you might type

```
=INDEX(A1:A3, $Z$100)
```

The INDEX() function would look in range A1:A3 for the specified index represented by Z100. It then would return, or display, the text at that location. Naming the range, A1:A3, would make it more user friendly.

```
=INDEX(My_Captions, $Z$100)
```

To Evaluate Option Button Selection

In this module, there are two option button groups: the prospect's preferred method of contact and how the prospect heard about NIM's products. In the first group, by using the INDEX function, you will have Excel record the user's selection as one of the captions stored in W3:W5, Email, U.S. Mail, or Telephone, rather than the numerical values (1, 2, or 3). **Why?** User input has to be changed from a numerical value to one that salespeople can understand. Likewise, in the second option button group, Excel will return one of the captions stored in W7:W12 rather than a number 1 through 6.

The following steps store the user's option button selections. The cell link will be established using the Form at Control dialog box. The INDEX() function, entered in row 40, will use the previously named range and the index number. The function will return a caption from the range in column W.

1

- Right-click the Email option button control to display the shortcut menu.
- Click Format Control to display the Format Control dialog box.
- If necessary, click the Control tab (Format Control dialog box) to display the Control sheet.
- Type **$I$41** in the Cell link box (Format Control dialog box) to link the option button index number to cell I41 (Figure 11–33).

Q&A **Why did I link only one of the option buttons to cell I41?**
Option buttons work collectively as a group with a single identity assigned to the set of options. The specific value of the selected option button will be assigned an out-of-the-way cell, I41.

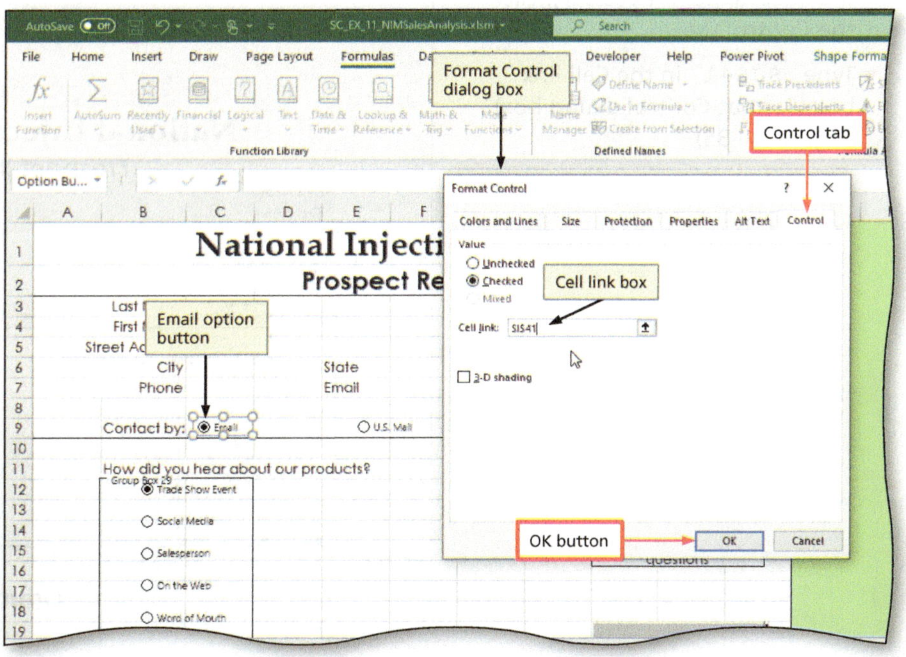

Figure 11–33

2

- Click OK (Format Control dialog box) to close the dialog box.
- If necessary, scroll down and then click cell I40 to make it the active cell.
- Type `=@INDEX(Contact_Options,$I$41)` to record text from the named range Contact_Options rather than numbers in cell I40 (Figure 11–34).
- Click the Enter button.

Q&A

How does the INDEX function work here?

In this instance, the INDEX function looks at the value in cell I41, which identifies which option button was selected, and returns the entry associated with that value from the named range, Contact_Method. The named range is found in column W in this worksheet. The @ symbol means to return a single value rather than all the values in the named range.

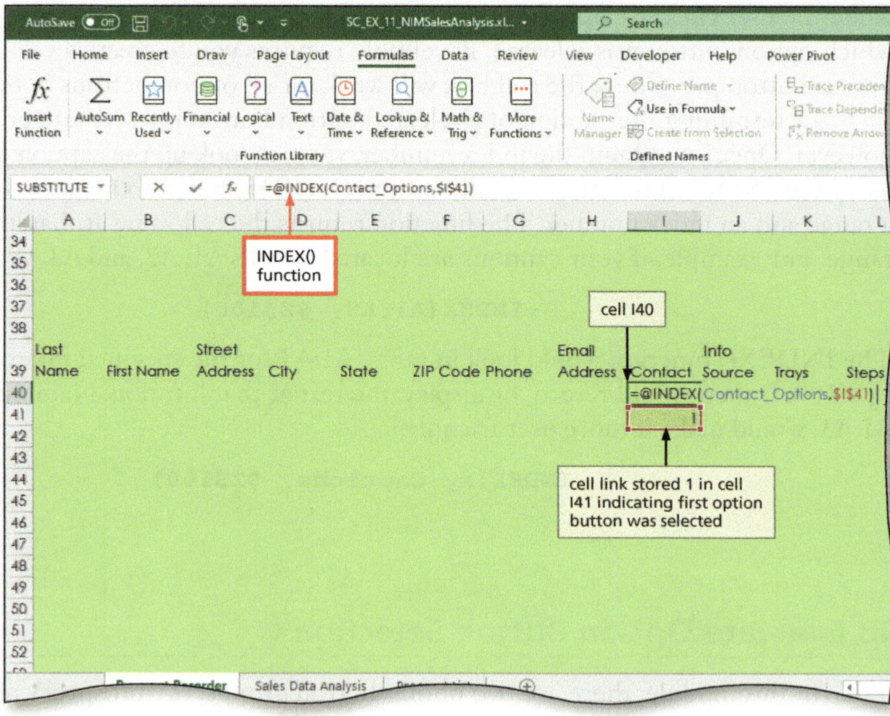

Figure 11–34

3

- Right-click the Trade Show Event option button control and then click Format Control on the shortcut menu. If necessary, click the Control tab.
- Type `$J$41` in the Cell link box (Format Control dialog box) (Figure 11–35).

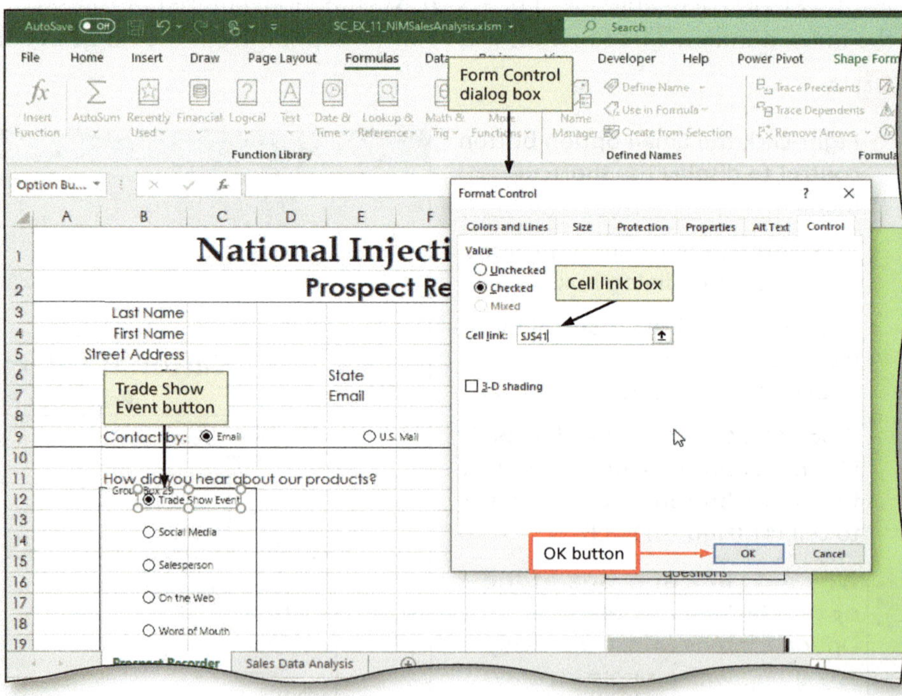

Figure 11–35

4

- Click OK (Format Control dialog box).
- Click cell J40.
- Type **=@INDEX(Source_Options,$J$41)** to enter a function that returns the caption from the named range Source_Options at the index number (Figure 11–36).

5

- Click the Enter button.

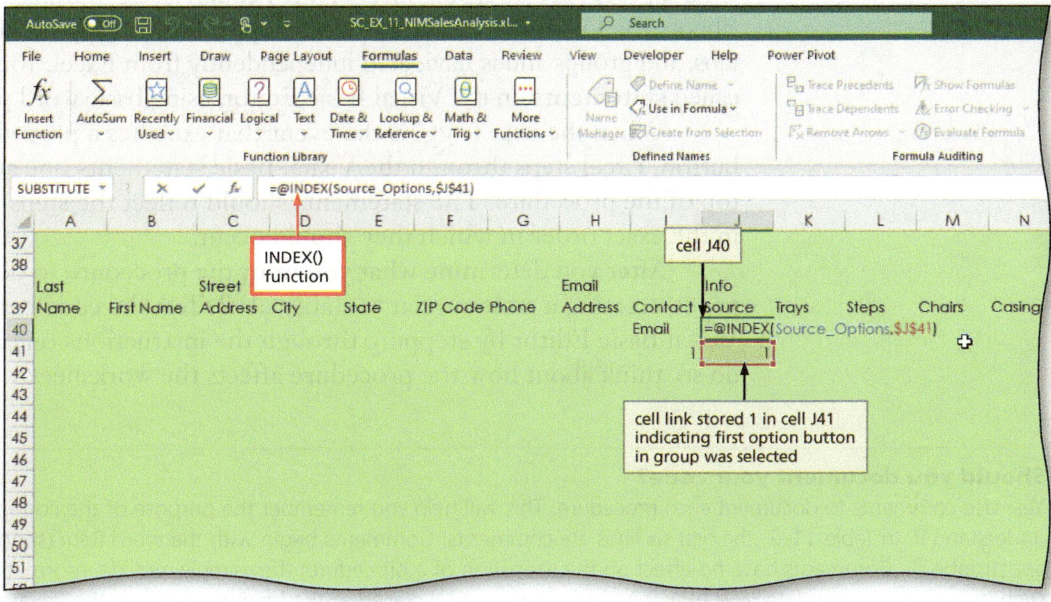

Figure 11–36

To Evaluate Check Box Control Selection

The following steps evaluate the check box selections by assigning each check box a cell link.

1. Right-click the Trays check box control. Use the shortcut menu to display the Format Control dialog box.
2. Type **$K$40** in the Cell link box (Format Control dialog box, Control tab).
3. Click OK (Format Control dialog box).
4. Repeat Steps 1 through 3 for each of the remaining three check box controls, using cells $L$40, $M$40, and $N$40 for the cell links.
5. Save the workbook again on the same storage location with the same file name.

Q&A **Why do I have to link each check box control to a specific cell?**
Unlike option buttons that work in groups, check box controls can each be either checked or unchecked, representing TRUE or FALSE values. Each one needs to be evaluated.

Writing Code for a Command Button

Earlier you placed two command buttons on the form. To make a button trigger an action when a user clicks it, you must write VBA code that tells Excel what to do after the command button is clicked. VBA is a vast subject; in this module, you will learn only a few of its many commands and techniques.

In this section, you will write the procedure that will execute when the user clicks the 'Step 1 - Click to Enter Contact Information' button. A **procedure** is a series of statements that performs an operation or calculates an answer in response to a triggered event.

You will be using the **Visual Basic Editor**, which is a full-screen editor that lets you enter a procedure by typing lines of VBA code. Accessed from the Developer tab on the ribbon, the Visual Basic Editor is like an app within an app because it has its own ribbon, tabs, and groups and is navigated independently from Excel. You type lines of code, also called **statements**, in the Visual Basic Editor, using basic word processing techniques.

When the user triggers the event that executes a procedure, such as clicking a button, Excel steps through the Visual Basic statements one at a time, beginning at the top of the procedure. The statements should reflect the steps you want Excel to take, in the exact order in which they should occur.

After you determine what you want the procedure to do, write the VBA code on paper, creating a table similar to Table 11–2. Test the code before you enter it in the Visual Basic Editor by stepping through the instructions one at a time yourself. As you do so, think about how the procedure affects the worksheet.

Consider This

Should you document your code?

Yes. Use comments to document each procedure. This will help you remember the purpose of the code or help somebody else understand it. In Table 11–2, the first six lines are comments. Comments begin with the word Rem (short for Remark) or an apostrophe ('). Comments have no effect on the execution of a procedure; they simply provide information about the procedure, such as name, creation date, and function. Comments can be placed at the beginning before the Private Sub statement, in between lines of code, or at the end of a line of code, as long as each comment begins with an apostrophe ('). It is good practice to place comments containing overall documentation and information at the beginning, before the Sub statement.

The Enter Prospect Button Procedure

Table 11–2 displays the VBA code executed when users click the first command button. Lines beginning with a single quote are called comments. In VBA, a **comment** is a statement in the code that documents it. Comments are not executed, nor are they visible to form users; they are seen only by programmers and other form developers.

Table 11–2 Enter Prospect Button Procedure

Line	Code
1	'Enter Prospect Button Procedure
2	'Author: SC Series
3	'Date Created: 11/12/2020
4	'Run from: Prospect Recorder worksheet by clicking Step 1 button
5	'Function: When executed, this procedure enters contact information for the prospect
6	'
7	Range("Last_Name").Value = InputBox("Last Name?", "Enter", , 800, 6000)
8	Range("First_Name").Value = InputBox("First Name?", "Enter", , 800, 6000)
9	Range("Street_Address").Value = InputBox("Street Address?", "Enter", , 800, 6000)
10	Range("City").Value = InputBox("City?", "Enter", , 800, 6000)
11	Range("State").Value = InputBox("State?", "Enter", , 800, 6000)
12	Range("ZIP_Code").Value = InputBox("Zip Code?", "Enter", , 800, 6000)
13	Range("Phone").Value = InputBox("Telephone Number?", "Enter", , 800, 6000)
14	Range("Email_Address").Value = InputBox("Email Address?", "Enter", , 800, 6000)

The rest of the procedure uses a VBA function named InputBox(). During Execution, the function displays a dialog box for user entry (Figure 11–37). The InputBox() function takes four arguments: a label or prompt, the title of the dialog box, the default value in the text box, the width, and the height. The dialog box automatically contains a text box, OK button, Cancel button, and Close button. The InputBox() function returns whatever the user enters in the text box.

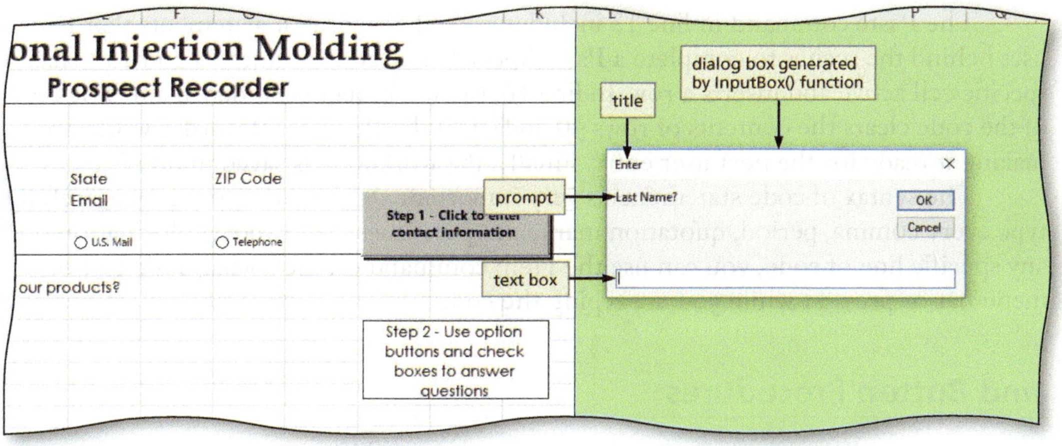

Figure 11–37

In VBA, as in other programming languages, the function and its arguments are placed to the right of an equal sign; the return location is on the left. This kind of code, that sets or resets a value, object, or location, is called an **assignment statement**. In Table 11–2, the return location is the value in a named range, in this case the single cells that were named earlier in the module.

BTW

Printing VBA Code

Some people find it easier to review and edit code by working with a printout. To print out VBA code while using the Visual Basic Editor, click File on the menu bar and then click Print on the File menu.

The Submit Button Procedure

Table 11–3 displays the VBA code executed when users click the first command button. This procedure copies the information to the hidden worksheet named Prospect List. A range is selected and copied; in this case, the range is row 40, where the user information was temporarily stored. The procedure then sets various properties of the Sheets object, short for worksheet. The code makes the worksheet visible, then active, then selects a range (lines 9–11).

Table 11–3 Submit Button Procedure

Line	Code
1	'Submit Button Procedure
2	'Author: SC Series
3	'Date Created: 11/12/2020
4	'Run from: Prospect Recorder worksheet by clicking Step 3 button
5	'Function: When executed, this procedure submits new information to the prospect list
6	'
7	Range("A40:O40").Select
8	Selection.Copy
9	Sheets("Prospect List").Visible = True
10	Sheets("Prospect List").Activate
11	Sheets("Prospect List").Range("A2:N2").Select
12	Selection.PasteSpecial Paste:=xlPasteValues, Operation:=xlNone, SkipBlanks:=False, Transpose:=False
13	Selection.Font.Bold = False
14	Sheets("Prospect List").Range("A2").Activate
15	ActiveCell.EntireRow.Insert
16	Sheets("Prospect List").Visible = False
17	Sheets("Prospect Recorder").Select
18	Range("I41:J41").ClearContents
19	Range("A40:H40").ClearContents
20	Range("K40:N40").ClearContents
21	Range("J8").Activate
22	ActiveWorkbook.Save

The Paste command in line 12 includes several assignment statements that Excel uses behind the scenes to complete a Paste Special. The code in lines 14 and 15 makes a specific cell active and inserts a row. In line 16, the worksheet is hidden again. The rest of the code clears the contents of rows 40 and 41 in the Prospect Recorder worksheet, making it ready for the next user entry. Finally, the workbook is saved in line 22.

The syntax of code statements is very important. As you enter the code, carefully type every comma, period, quotation mark, and parenthesis. For more information on any specific line of code, you can use the Help command on the Visual Basic Editor menu bar or press F1 while you are typing the code.

To Enter the Command Button Procedures

Why? To enter a procedure, you use the Visual Basic Editor. Each command button has a separate procedure. The following steps activate the Visual Basic Editor and create a procedure for each of the two command buttons.

1

- If necessary, display the Developer tab and then click the Design Mode button (Developer tab | Controls group) to make Design Mode active.
- Right-click the Step 1 button on the worksheet to display the shortcut menu (Figure 11–38).

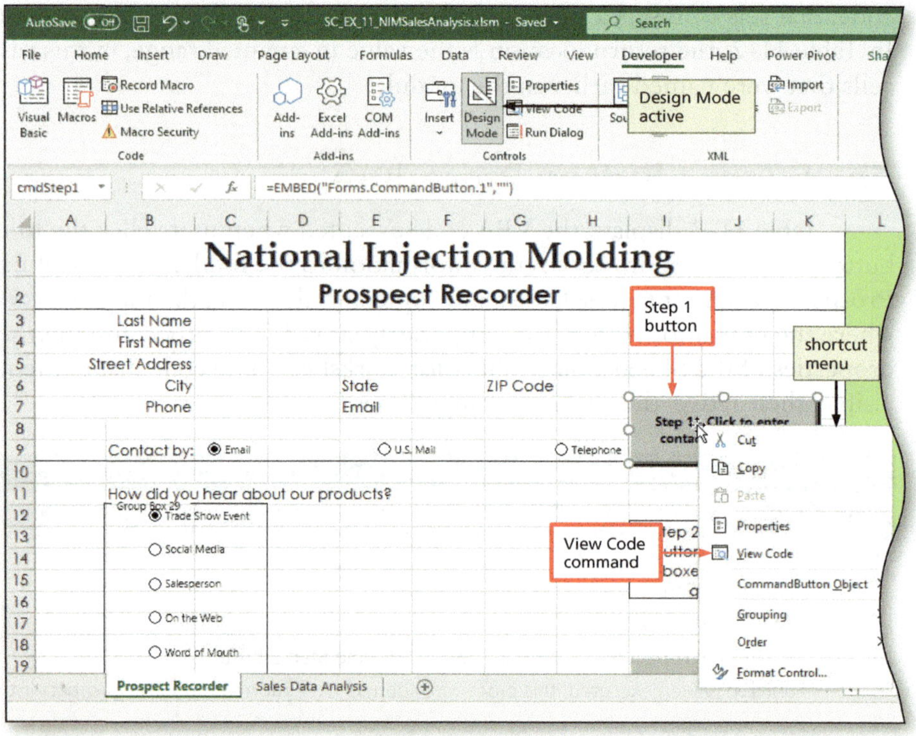

Figure 11–38

2

- Click View Code to display the Microsoft Visual Basic for Applications editor and then, if necessary, maximize the window.

Q&A **What is displayed in the code window on the right?**
The beginning and the end of the procedure is created for you already.

- If necessary, click the blank line between the beginning and end lines of code.
- Press TAB before you enter the first line of VBA code from Table 11–2. Do not enter the line numbers from the table (Figure 11–39).

Q&A **What is the purpose of the two commas in lines 9 through 15?**
Commas must separate each argument in a function. In Lines 9 through 15, the third argument is the default text for the text box. Placing nothing between the commas indicates that nothing will appear in the text box.

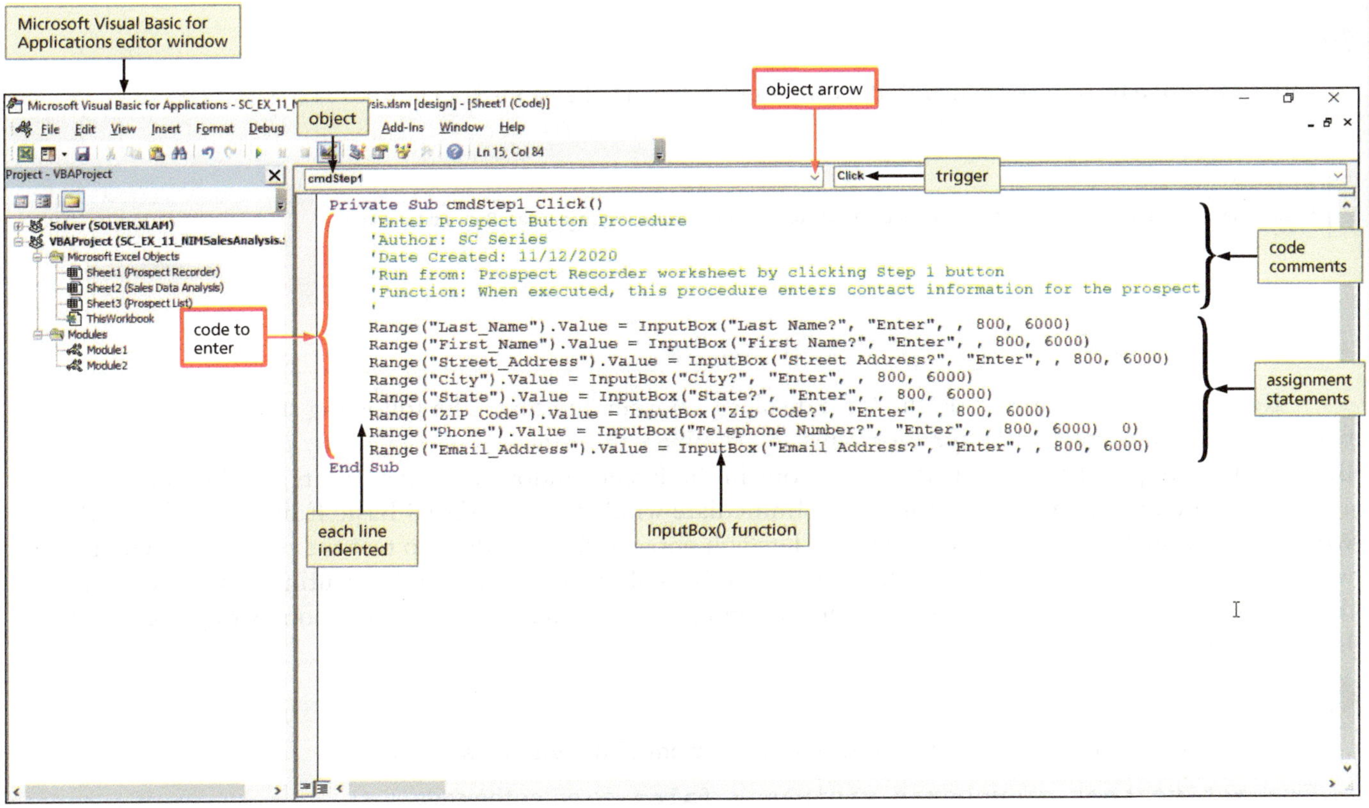

Figure 11–39

3

- Click the Object arrow and then click cmdStep3 in the list to display the beginning and ending code for the Submit button.
- Enter the VBA code shown in Table 11–3, pressing TAB at the beginning of the first line (Figure 11–40).

Q&A

Do I have to press the TAB key?

No, but it is a common programming practice to do so because it improves readability.

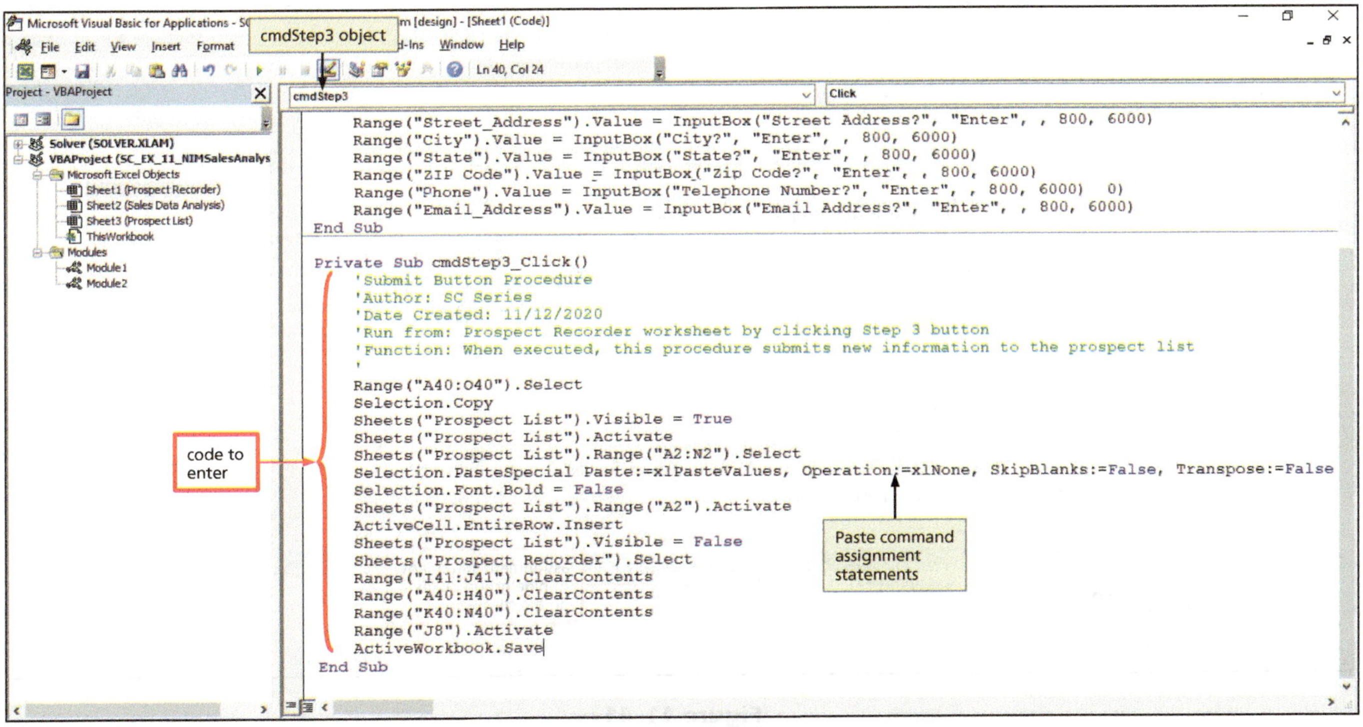

Figure 11–40

4

- Verify your code by comparing it with the content of Tables 11–2 and 11–3.

Other Ways

1. Click View Code button (Excel Window | Developer tab | Controls group), enter code in Visual Basic Editor window

To Remove the Outline from the Group Box Control

Recall that the group box on the form displays a border and text. The following steps remove those from the group box control. **Why?** Removing the outline will result in a more visually pleasing user interface. Because the group box has no formatting options in the Excel window, you must set its visibility property with a line of VBA code. You will enter this in the Immediate window in the Visual Basic Editor. The **Immediate window** is a Visual Basic Editor window that lets you enter different values to test the procedures you create without changing any data in the database and often is used for debugging and executing statements during design. As its name suggests, code entered in this window is executed immediately upon exiting the Visual Basic Editor.

1

- Press CTRL+G to open the Immediate window at the bottom of the Visual Basic Editor.
- Type **activesheet.groupboxes.visible = false** to enter the code.
- Press ENTER to execute the code, which hides the box around the group control (Figure 11–41).

Q&A **What does the code mean?**
The assignment statement code assigns the value false to the visible property of the group boxes on the active sheet.

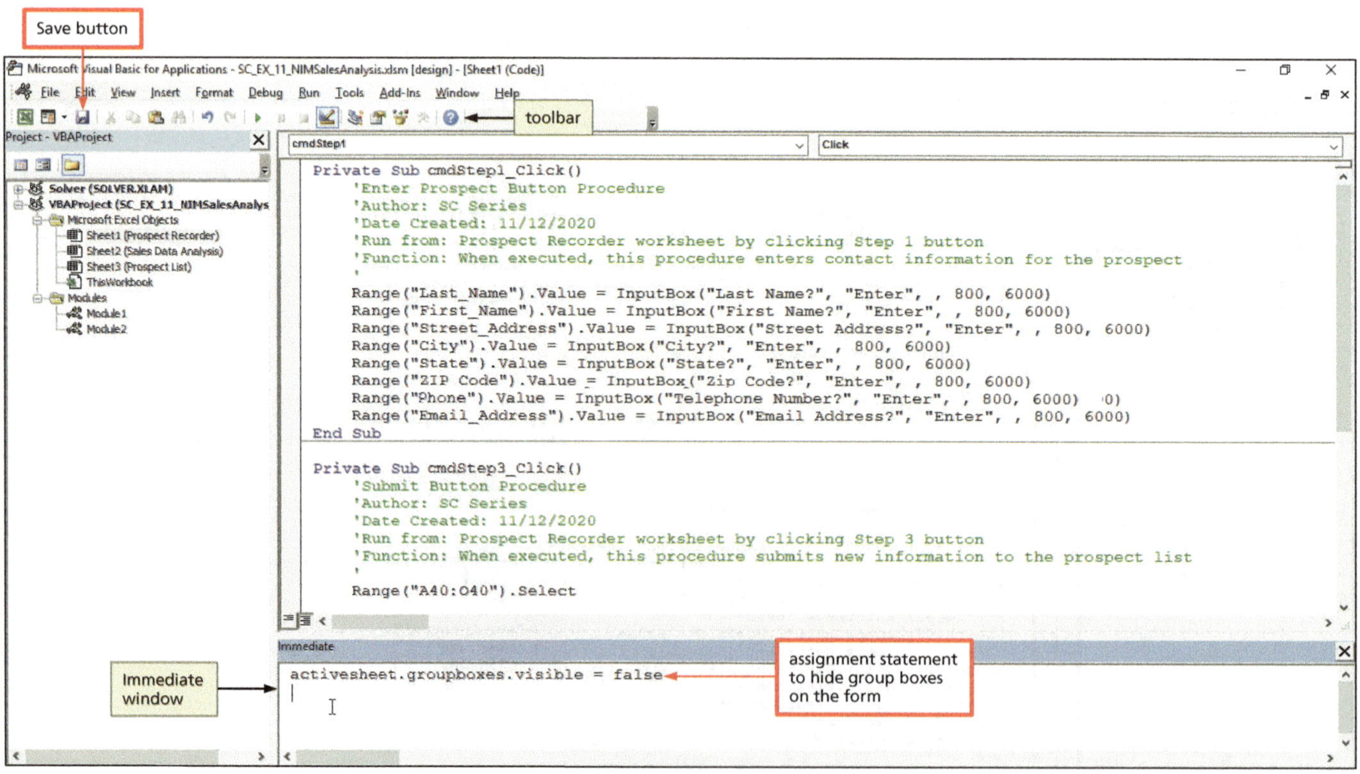

Figure 11–41

2

- Click the Save button (Visual Basic Editor toolbar).
- Close the Visual Basic Editor window.
- Save the workbook again in the same storage location with the same file name.

Other Ways

1. Click View on menu bar, click Immediate window, enter code

Break Point: If you wish to take a break, this is a good place to do so. You can now exit Excel. To resume at a later time, start Excel, open the file called SC_EX_11_NIMSalesAnalysis.xlsm, and continue following the steps from this location forward.

Preparing, Protecting, and Testing Worksheets

With any worksheet that you will distribute to others, you should consider how to prepare, protect, and test it. Excel provides several ways to prepare and protect worksheets. You can turn features on or off such as page breaks, zero values, gridlines, the formula bar, or headings. You also can limit distractions for the user by hiding the ribbon, hiding row and column headers, and hiding the active cell. It is a good idea to password protect worksheets that contain forms to prevent other users from accidentally or deliberately changing, moving, or deleting data. With worksheet protection, you can make only certain parts of the sheet editable so that users will not be able to modify data in any other region in the sheet or workbook. And, of course, before sharing a document, you must thoroughly test its functionality.

To Prepare Worksheet for Distribution

In the following steps, you prepare the worksheet for distribution to others. You will hide the ribbon, row numbers, and columns from view to restrict what the user can do in this worksheet. **Why?** You only want users to fill out the form and select options, not alter the sheet.

1

- If necessary, click the Design Mode button (Developer tab | Controls group) to exit Design Mode.
- Display Backstage view.
- Scroll as necessary and then click Options to display the Excel Options dialog box.
- Click the Advanced tab (Excel Options dialog box) to display the advanced options.
- Scroll to the 'Display options for this worksheet' area in the right pane.
- As necessary, click to clear the 'Show row and column headers' check box, the 'Show page breaks' check box, and the 'Show a zero in cells that have zero value' check box (Figure 11–42).

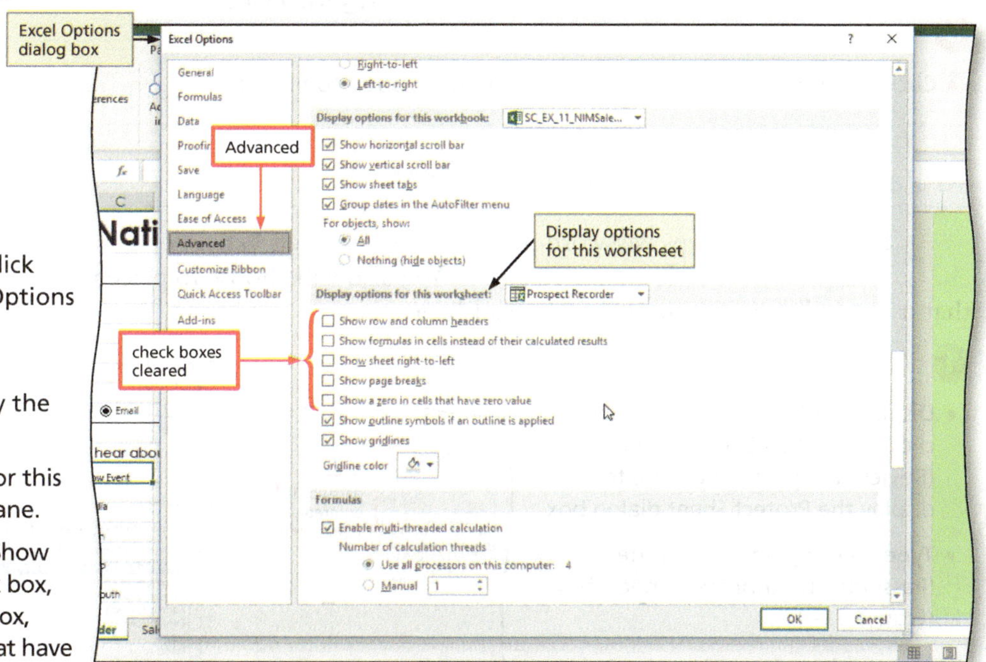

Figure 11–42

Q&A **What does clearing the 'Show row and column headers' check box do?**
It turns that feature off, hiding the display of the row numbers and the column letters on this worksheet only. Users will see only the edges of the form.

2

- Click OK to close the Excel Options dialog box.
- Display the View tab.
- As necessary, click to clear the Gridlines, Formula Bar, and Headings check boxes (View tab | Show group) to remove those features from the worksheet (Figure 11–43).

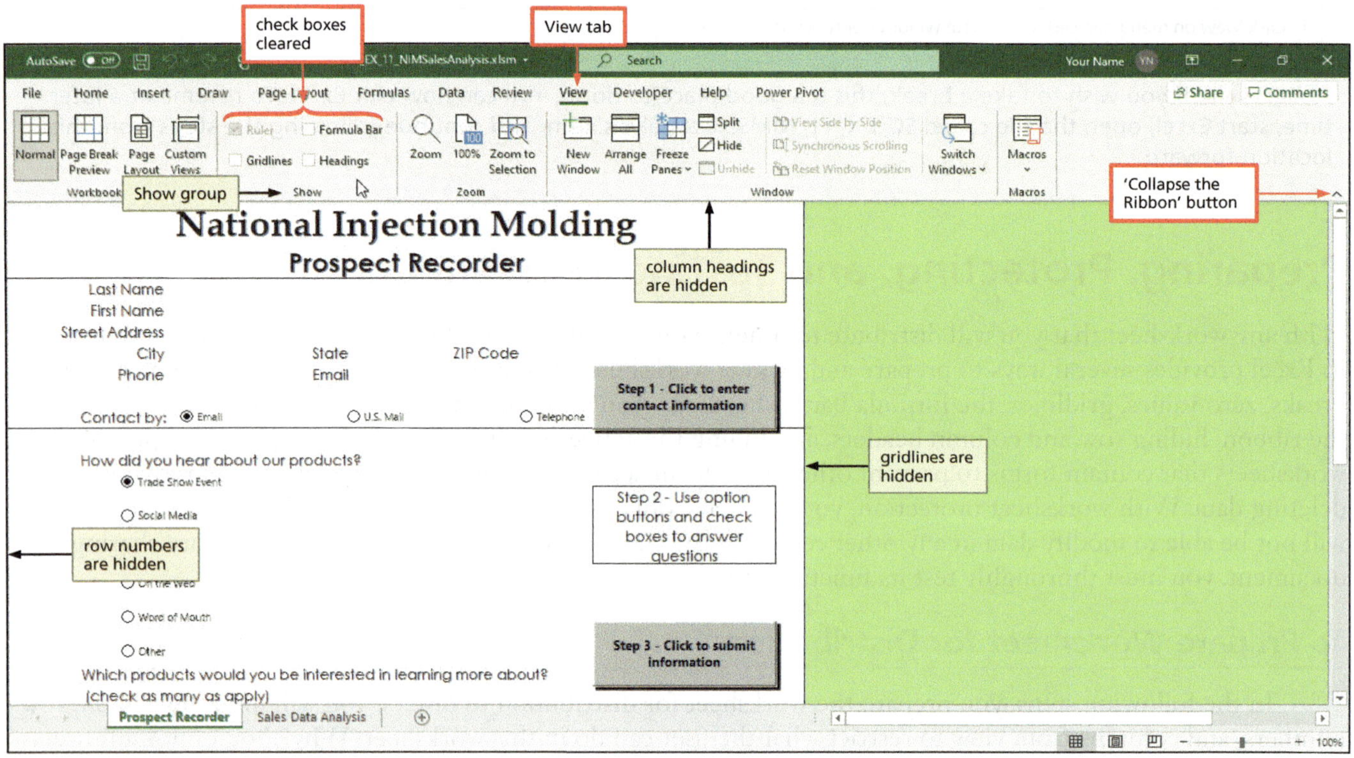

Figure 11–43

3

- Click the 'Collapse the Ribbon' button on the ribbon to hide it.

To Password Protect the Worksheet

The following steps password protect the worksheet. **Why?** A password prevents users from making changes to your VBA code and calculations. You also will choose to place the active cell in a hidden location so that it won't distract inexperienced spreadsheet users.

1

- Display the Review tab and then click the Protect Sheet button (Review tab | Protect group) to display the Protect Sheet dialog box.
- Type `Prospect19` in the 'Password to unprotect sheet' box (Figure 11–44).

Q&A **Should I password protect the entire workbook?**
No. You will edit other sheets later in the module.

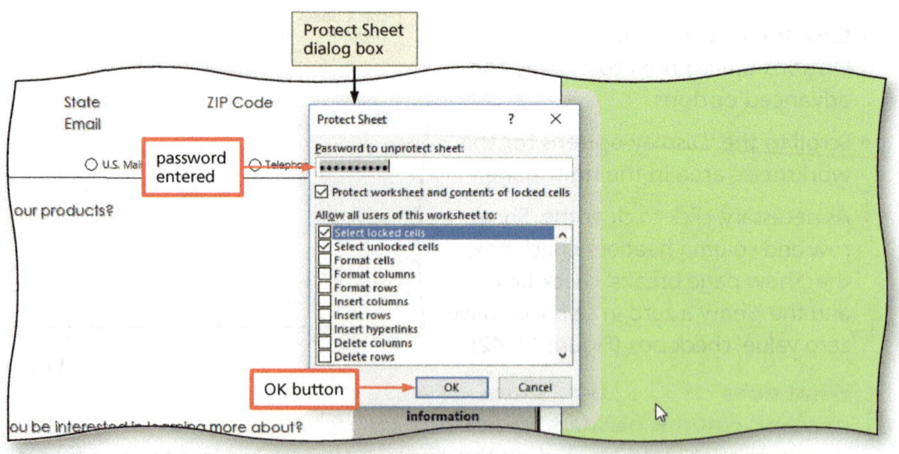

Figure 11–44

Q&A **What is the purpose of the check boxes?**
You can click those check boxes to allow all users of the worksheet to edit, insert, and change various kinds of cells, even when the worksheet is password protected.

2

- Click OK (Protect Sheet dialog box) to display the Confirm Password dialog box.
- Type `Prospect19` in the 'Reenter password to proceed' box (Figure 11–45).

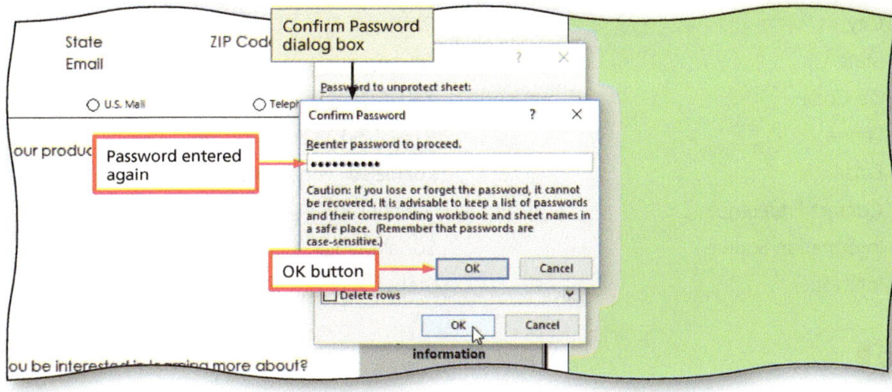

Figure 11–45

Q&A **Do any rules apply to passwords?**
Yes. Passwords in Excel can contain, in any combination, letters, numbers, spaces, and symbols, and can be up to 15 characters long. Passwords are case sensitive. If you decide to password-protect a worksheet, make sure you save the password in a secure place. If you lose the password, you will not be able to open or gain access to the password-protected worksheet.

3

- Click OK (Confirm Password dialog box) to close the dialog boxes.
- Press CTRL+G to display the Go To dialog box.
- Type `J8` in the Reference box (Go To dialog box) to enter the destination (Figure 11–46).

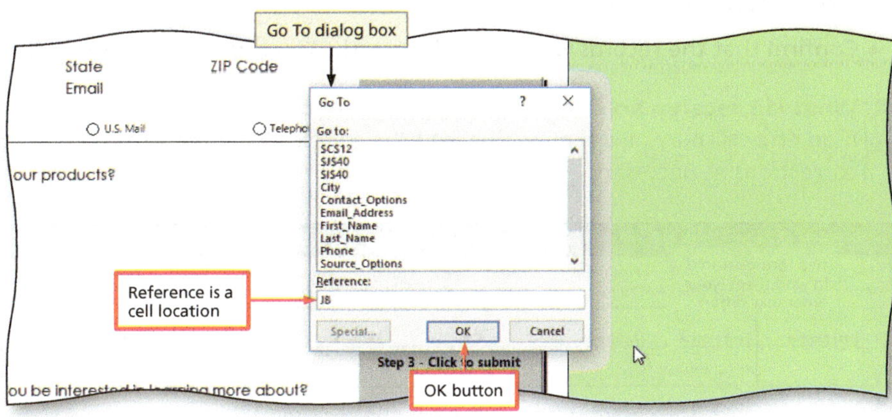

Figure 11–46

Q&A **Why use J8 as the new active cell?**
The J8 cell is hidden behind the first command button, out of the way, so as not to elicit data entry for inexperienced users.

4

- Click OK (Go To dialog box) to make cell J8 the active cell and close the dialog box.
- Save the workbook again in the same storage location with the same file name.

To Test the Controls in the Worksheet

Why? Before distributing the workbook for use, you should test the controls and verify the proper functionality of the VBA code. The following steps test the controls in the Prospect Recorder worksheet using the data shown in Table 11–4.

Table 11–4 Prospect Records

Field	Record 1	Record 2
Last Name	Daniels	Stetson
First Name	Kurt	Larue
Address	572 King Street	31 Andrew Road
City	Clayton	Parkville
State	OK	LA
Zip Code	73015	70024
Phone	918-555-1212	318-555-1313
Email	kdaniels@cengage.com	lstetson@cengage.com
Contact Preference	Telephone	Email
Information Source	Social Media	Trade Show Event
Interest(s)	Steps	Trays & Casings

1

- Click the Step 1 button on the form. Answer the prompts using the data from the first record in Table 11–4.
- Check the option buttons and check boxes as shown in the table.
- Click the Step 3 button on the form to submit the data.
- Repeat the process for the second record.
- Right-click the Prospect Recorder worksheet tab, click Unhide, and then click OK (Unhide dialog box) to display the Prospect List worksheet.
- Confirm that the records were copied correctly. The order of your records may differ (Figure 11–47).

Q&A

What if I receive an error while testing the controls?

If an error displays, Excel may highlight the code causing the error. Check your code for accuracy and make corrections as necessary.

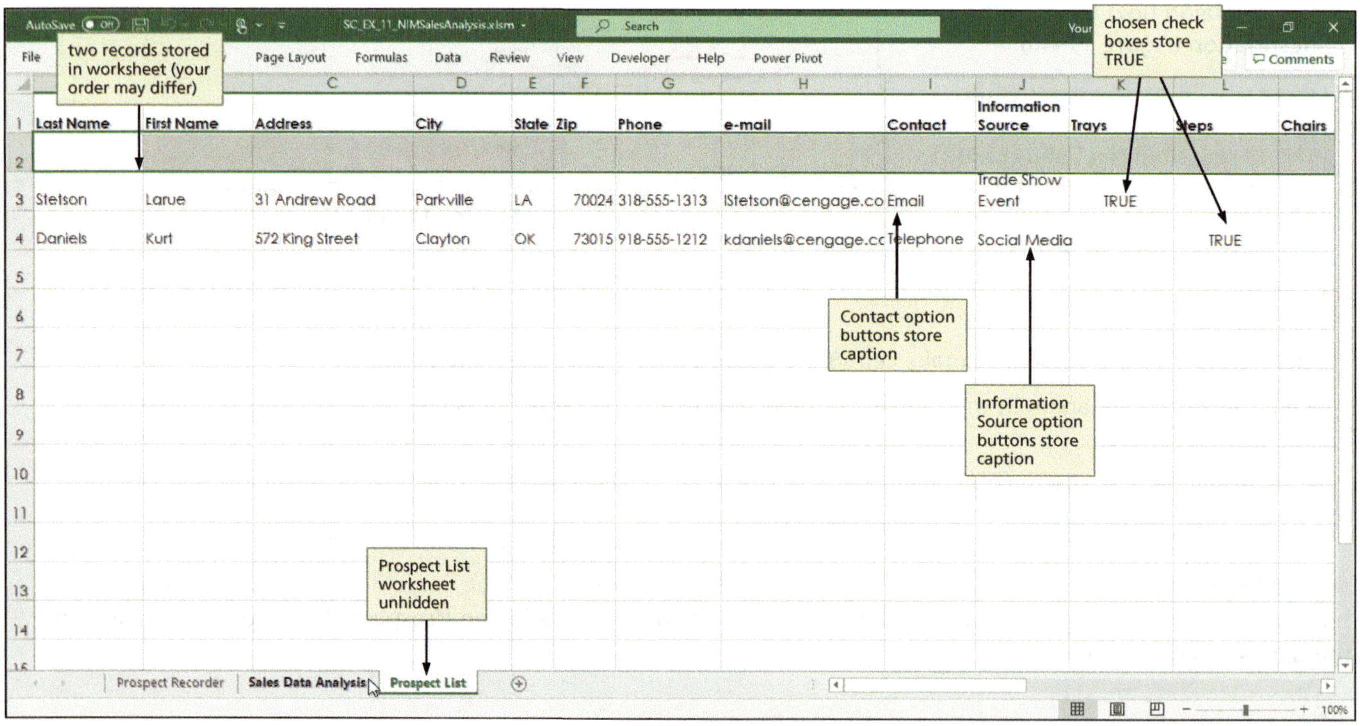

Figure 11–47

2

- Right-click the Prospect List worksheet tab and then click Hide on the shortcut menu.
- Make the Sales Data Analysis worksheet active.
- Save the workbook again in the same storage location with the same file name.

Sharing and Collaborating

Collaboration is the practice of sharing files with others, providing comments, and collecting feedback. Excel provides several ways to collaborate. As you have seen, you can physically distribute the workbook to others on storage media or through email using an attachment. In addition, you can save files in a variety of formats using OneDrive, Power BI, SharePoint, or other networked sites. Your storage locations commonly are listed when you click Save As or Publish in Backstage view.

In Excel you also can **co-author** or collaborate on the same workbook at the same time. When you co-author, you can see each other's changes quickly—in a matter of seconds. And with certain versions of Excel, you will see other people's selections in different colors. To co-author, rather than simply saving the file on OneDrive, you use the Share button on the Excel ribbon to distribute or save your file in a manner which allows others to access it.

BTW

Copying Comments

You can copy comments from one cell to other cells using the Paste Special command. Select the cell that contains the comment you need to copy, click the Copy button (Home tab | Clipboard group), select the cell or cells to which you want to apply the comment, click the Paste arrow, and then click Paste Special. In the Paste Special dialog box, in the Paste list, select Comments, and then click the OK button.

To Save a Copy of a Worksheet

The following steps save a copy of the Sales Data Analysis work to share with others.

1. Right-click the Sales Data Analysis worksheet tab. Click 'Move or Copy' on the shortcut menu.
2. Click the To book arrow (Move or Copy dialog box) and then click (new book).
3. Click the 'Create a copy' check box.
4. Click OK (Move or Copy dialog box) to move a copy of the worksheet to a new workbook.
5. Save the workbook with the name, SC_EX_11_Collaborate.xlsx.

Q&A **My workbook looks different. What should I do?**
Depending on how you saved the color and font schemes, your new workbook may not have those schemes. Choose the NIM color scheme and the NIM font scheme (Page Layout tab | Themes group) and save again.

To Distribute via OneDrive

You can use OneDrive to distribute workbooks. Colleagues can make changes and then save the workbook on OneDrive for review. Saving workbooks for distribution on OneDrive does not differ from using OneDrive to save your own files, although you do need to make the workbook available to others by saving it in an accessible location. **Why?** You may need to have a workbook reviewed by someone who does not share network access with you. The following steps distribute the workbook via OneDrive. If you cannot access OneDrive, simply read the steps.

1

- If necessary, display any tab on the ribbon and then click the 'Pin the ribbon' button in the lower-right corner of the ribbon.
- In the upper-right corner of the ribbon, click Share to open the Share dialog box (Figure 11–48). Your sharing options may differ.

Q&A

What happened to the Protect and Share Workbook command?
That command, and the Changes group on the Review tab, have been replaced by co-authoring.

What are the buttons at the bottom of the Sharing dialog box?
Those commands are shortcuts to send the file as an attachment, both as an Excel file and as a PDF file. The same commands are available in Backstage view.

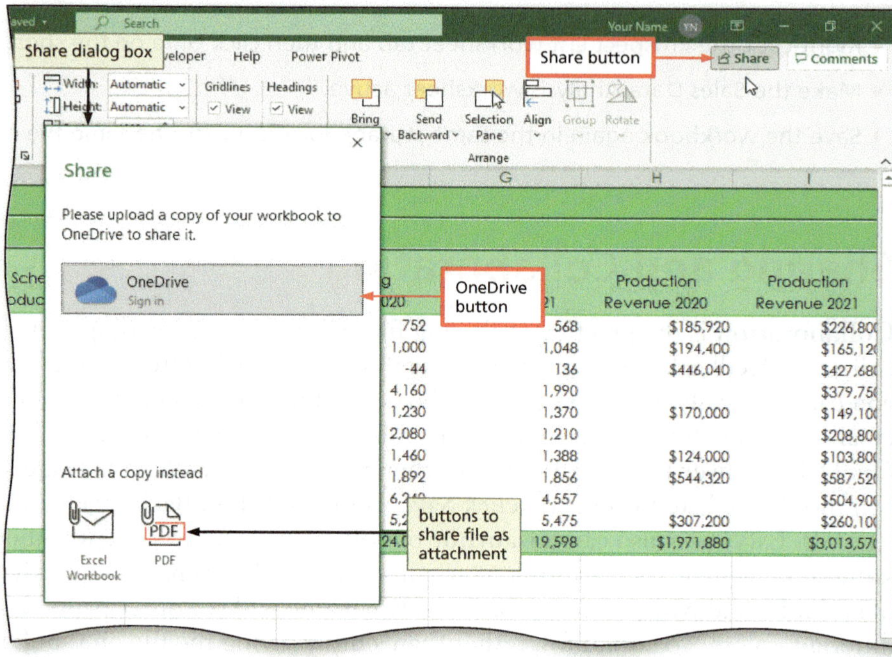

Figure 11–48

2

- Click the OneDrive button (Share dialog box) and sign in if necessary. Or, if you have access to another network, click its button and sign in.
- When Excel displays the Send Link dialog box, enter a recipient's email address above the blue line (Figure 11–49).

Q&A

Can I add a message?
Yes. Click below the blue line and type a brief message.

Experiment

- Click the 'Anyone with this link can edit' button to open the Link Settings dialog box. Look at the various groups to whom you can give permission to edit the file. Click Cancel (Link Settings dialog box) when you are finished.

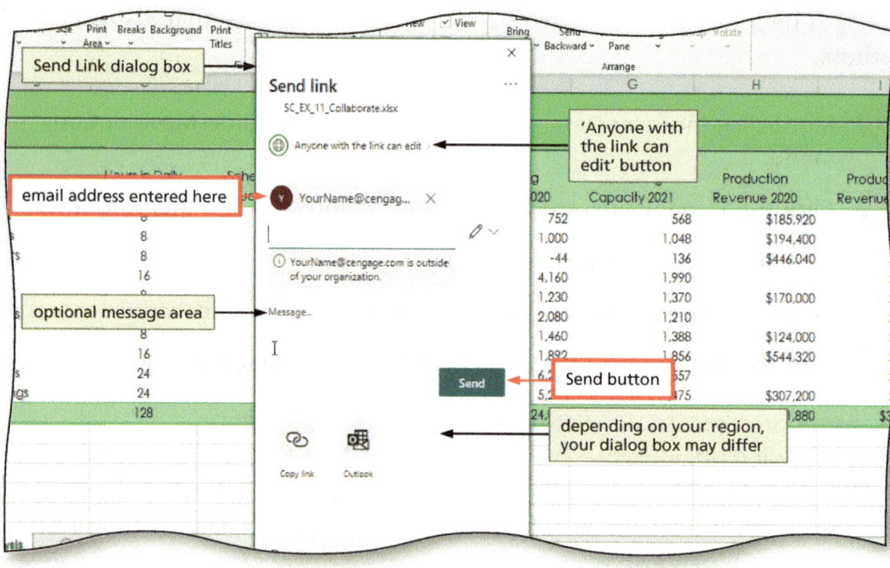

Figure 11–49

3

- Click the Send button (Send Link dialog box).
- Close the Link Sent dialog box, if necessary.

Q&A

How does the link work?
The recipient will receive an email message inviting them to open the file. They can click the link to open the workbook. A web browser will open, and the workbook will open in Excel Online.

Other Ways

1. Click Share in Backstage view, enter email address, click send.

To Co-Author a Workbook

Working together in the same workbook at the same time can improve efficiency in networked team environments. **Why?** Co-authoring a workbook can provide you with a timely, interactive editing process with colleagues. The following steps assume you have distributed the workbook to someone and that co-author has opened the file.

1

- Make sure that AutoSave is on in the upper-left corner of the title bar.
- Ask the second workbook user to click the link you sent.
- When the second user comes online, click the picture or initials in the upper-right corner of the ribbon (Figure 11–50a).
- Ask the user to click cell D7 and enter 2254 as the new value, and then save the workbook (Figure 11–50b).

Q&A **Can I track the changes made by the co-author?**
Excel no longer supports tracking changes; however, you can save a separate copy and compare workbooks, which you will do later in the module.

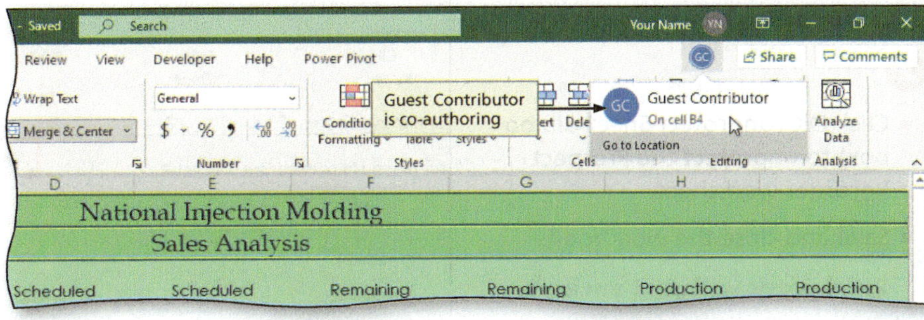

(a) Co-author information

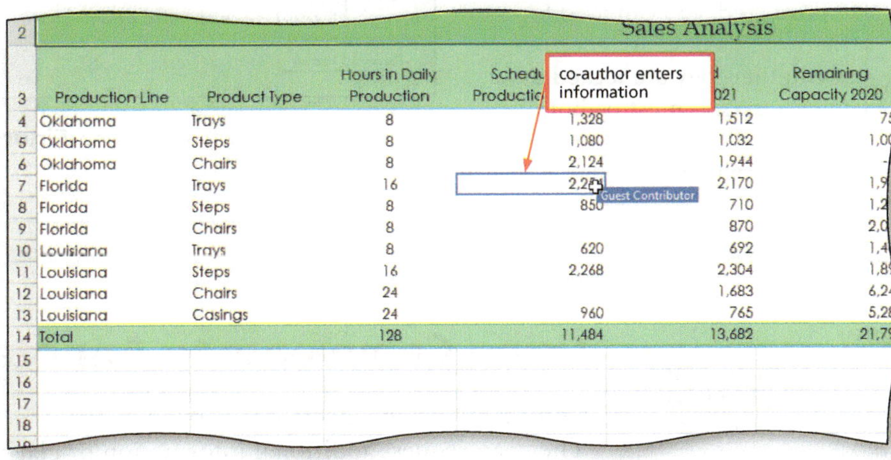

(b) Co-author editing

Figure 11–50

2

- In your copy of the workbook, point to the Save button on the Quick Access Toolbar to display a ScreenTip indicating that the workbook has been updated with changes saved by another user, and then click the Save button to save your work.
- Close the workbook and ask the second user of the workbook to close his or her workbook.

To Unprotect a Password-Protected Worksheet

The Prospect Recorder worksheet in the NIM Sales Analysis workbook is protected, which restricts the changes you can make to the worksheet to unlocked cells only. You cannot make changes to locked cells or modify the worksheet itself. You will unprotect the worksheet. **Why?** Unprotecting allows changes to locked cells and the worksheet itself. Recall that a password ensures that users cannot unprotect the worksheet simply by clicking the Unprotect button. The password for the worksheet is Prospect19. The following steps unprotect the password-protected Prospect Recorder worksheet.

1

- If necessary, open the file named SC_EX_11_NIMSalesAnalysis.xlsm.
- Display the Prospect Recorder worksheet.
- Click the Formula Bar check box (View tab | Show group) to redisplay the formula bar.

- If necessary, display the Review tab, and then click the Unprotect Sheet button (Review tab | Protect group) to display the Unprotect Sheet dialog box.
- When the Unprotect Sheet dialog box appears, type `Prospect19` in the Password box (Figure 11–51).

2

- Click OK (Unprotect Sheet dialog box) to unprotect the Prospect Recorder worksheet.
- Save and close the workbook.

Q&A **Can I work with the entire worksheet now?**
Yes. With the worksheet unprotected, you can modify the contents of cells, regardless of whether they are locked or unlocked. Cells must be both locked and the worksheet protected to restrict what users can do to cell contents.

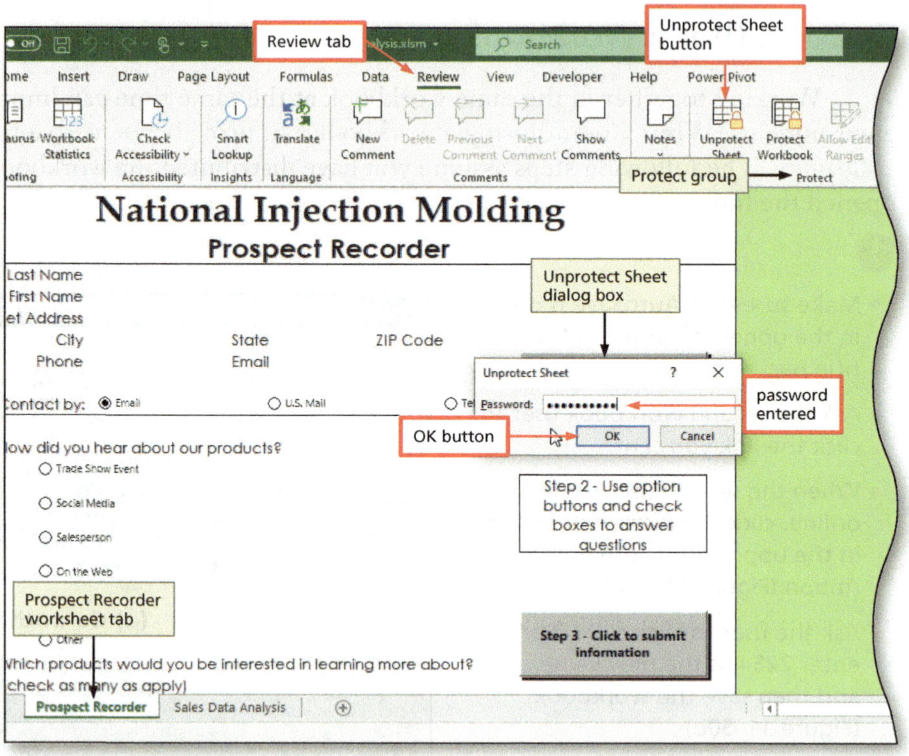

Figure 11–51

BTW
Comments and Notes
In some versions of Excel, comments are threaded, allowing you to have discussions with other people about the data. Those versions include notes for annotating the data, and they work like comments used from other versions of Excel.

Using Comments to Annotate a Worksheet

Comments are the electronic version of sticky notes or annotations in the margin. They can request additional information or clarification of existing information. Comments can provide direction to the reader about how to interpret content or describe what type of content to add. You can add a comment to any cell in a worksheet. Once you add comments, you can edit, format, move, copy, or resize them. You can choose to show comments in a worksheet, to display only a comment indicator, or to hide comments. Comments work well when multiple people are collaborating on a worksheet. Comments added by each user are identified by a name in the comment, set by the user.

Depending on the nature of the comments, you may decide to delete some or all comments after reading them and making edits to the worksheet, if appropriate.

To Add Comments to a Worksheet

Why? Comments in Excel can be used to remind the user of material that needs to be added or updated. The Sales Data Analysis worksheet in the NIM Sales Analysis workbook has some missing data. The following steps add comments to the worksheet in cells A9 and A12.

1

- Open the SC_EX_11_NIMSalesAnalysis.xlsm workbook and then, if necessary, click the Enable Content button in the yellow Security Warning bar below the ribbon.
- If necessary, display the Sales Data Analysis worksheet.

- Enter **2254** in cell D7.
- Display the Review tab and, if necessary, click the Show Comments button (Review tab | Comments group) to toggle the option off and hide all comments in the workbook.
- Right-click cell A9 to display the shortcut menu (Figure 11–52).

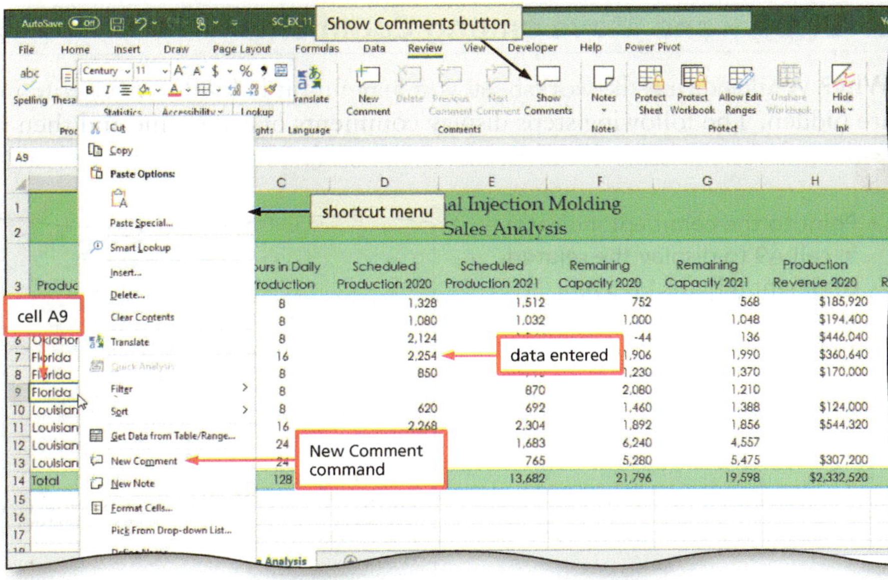

Figure 11–52

2

- Click New Comment on the shortcut menu to open a comment box next to the selected cell and display a comment indicator in the cell.
- Enter the text **Note to David - need accurate count of Trays scheduled for 2020 production in Florida.** in the comment box (Figure 11–53).

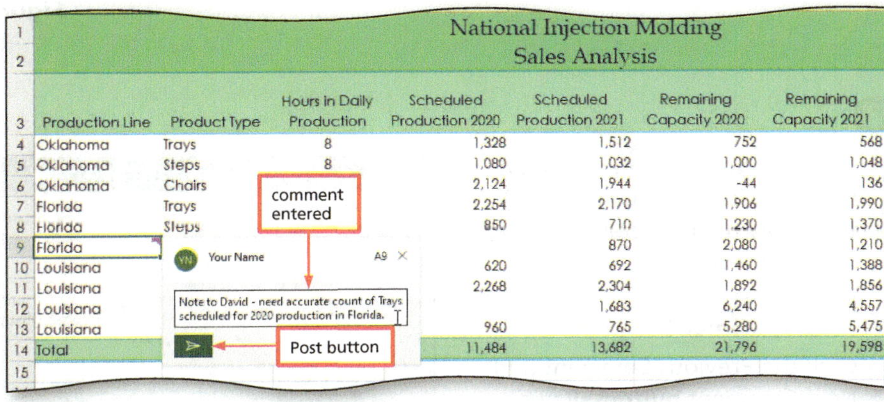

Figure 11–53

3

- Click the Post button, and then click outside the comment box to close the comment box and display only the purple comment indicator in cell A9.
- Enter a comment in cell A12 with the text **Note to Amanda - need accurate count of Trays scheduled for 2020 production in Louisiana.** (Figure 11–54).

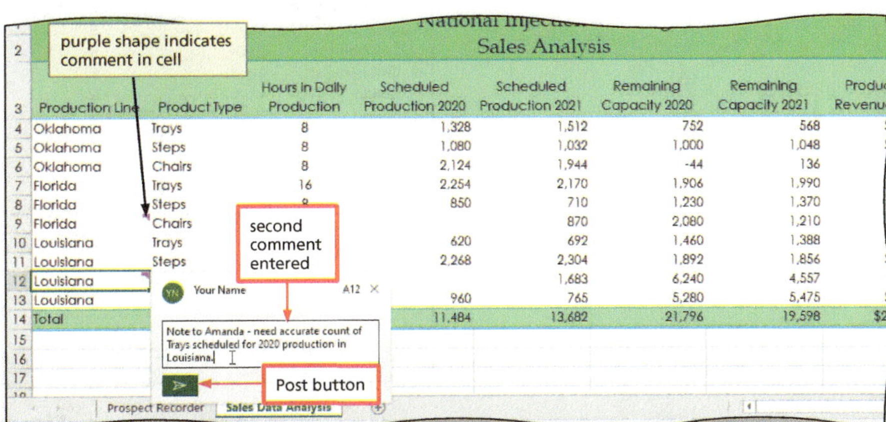

Figure 11–54

Q&A **My comment boxes do not close when I click outside the comment box. Why?**
Turn off the showing of comments by clicking the Show Comments button (Review tab | Comments group).

- Click the Post button, and then click outside the comment box to close the comment box and display only the purple comment indicator in cell A12.

Other Ways

1. Click New Comment (Review tab | Comments group)
2. Click Comments on title bar, click New

To Display and Move among Comments

Why? While editing the worksheet, you may find it helpful to have comments visible. The comments currently are hidden. The following steps display comments one at a time and then make all comments visible.

1

- Point to the comment indicator in cell A9 to display the related comment (Figure 11–55).

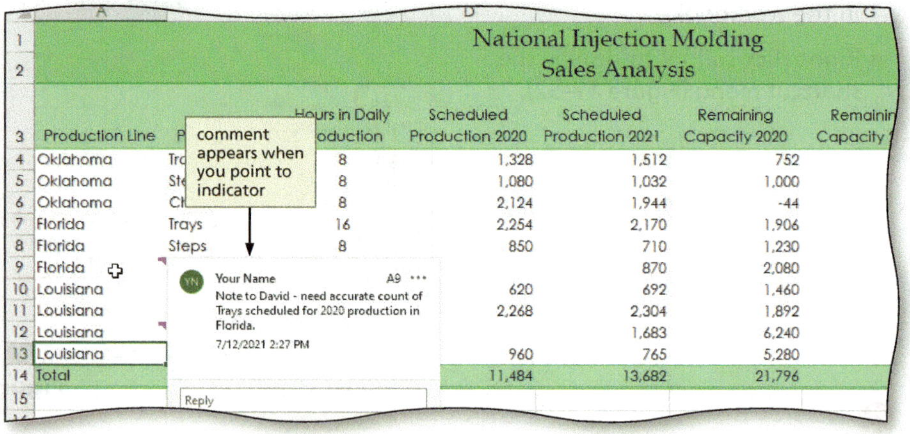

Figure 11–55

2

- Click the Next Comment button (Review tab | Comments group) to display the next comment (Figure 11–56).

Experiment

- Click the Previous Comment and Next Comment buttons (Review tab | Comments group) to move back and forth among comments.

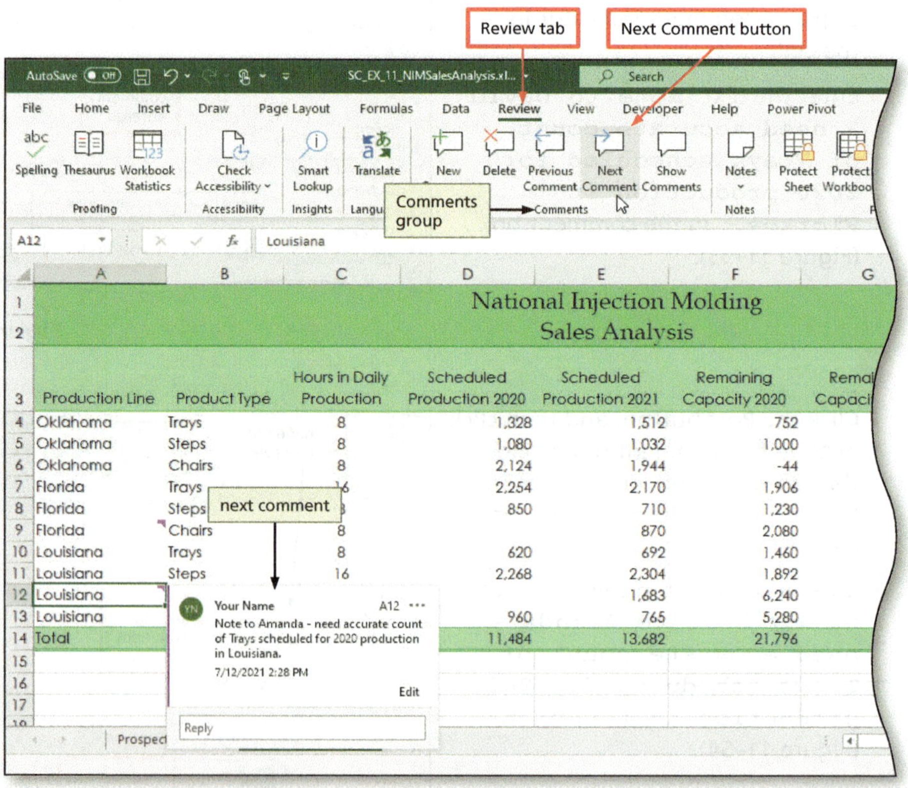

Figure 11–56

3

- Click the Show Comments button (Review tab | Comments group) to open the Comments pane and show all comments in the workbook (Figure 11–57).

Q&A **Can I print comments?**
Yes. You can print a list of comments separately using the Sheet tab in the Page Setup dialog box. To do so, click the Page Setup Dialog Box Launcher (Page Layout tab | Page Setup group), click the Sheet tab (Page Setup dialog box), click the 'Comments and notes' arrow, and then click 'At end of sheet' in the 'Comments and notes' list.

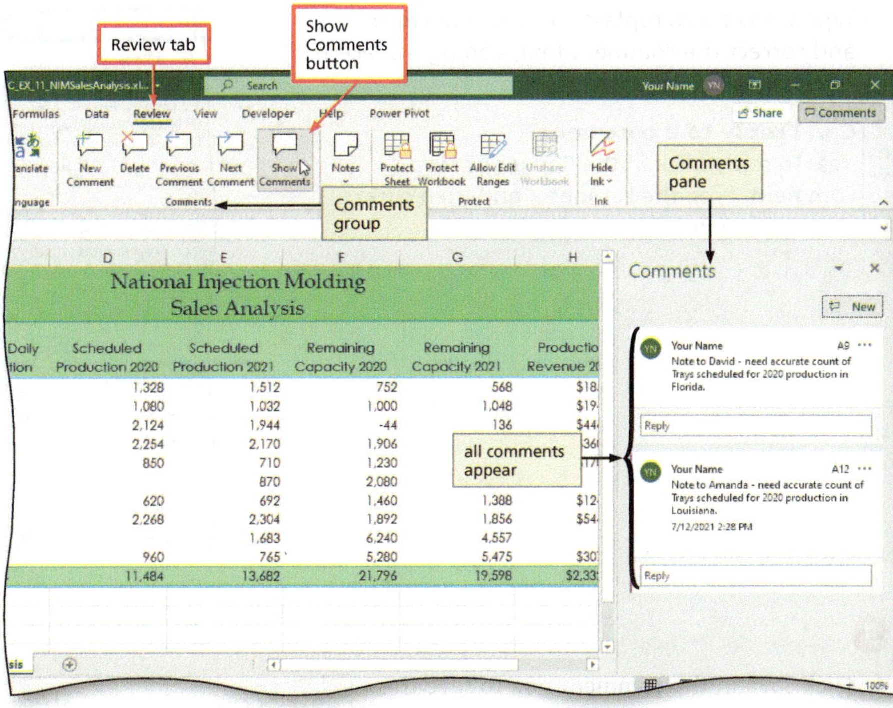

Figure 11–57

To Edit Comments on a Worksheet

You want to correct errors in the comments to David and Amanda. **Why?** After adding comments to a worksheet, you may need to edit them to add or change information. The following steps edit the comments in cells A9 and A12.

1

- Click the comment for cell A9 to select the comment in the Comments pane.
- Click Edit in the comment box to open the comment for editing.
- Select the word, Trays, in the comment (Figure 11–58).

Q&A **Can I delete the text?**
Yes, but if you want to delete the entire comment, click Cancel, click the More threaded actions button (...), and then click Delete thread.

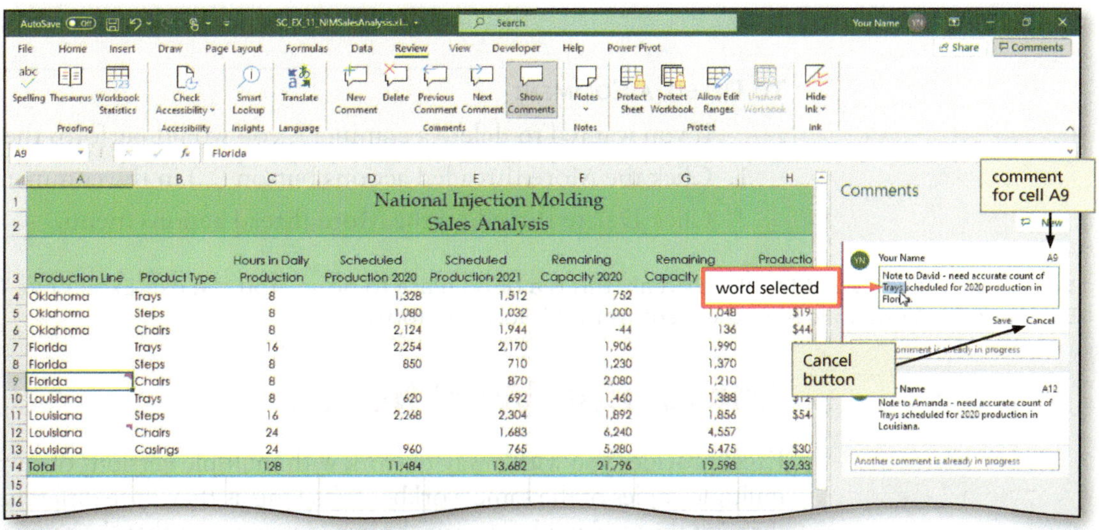

Figure 11–58

- Type **Chairs** to replace the selected word and correct the comment text, adding a space if necessary (Figure 11-59).

Q&A

Can I reply to a comment?
Yes. To reply, click in the Reply box for a comment, type the response, and then click the Post button.

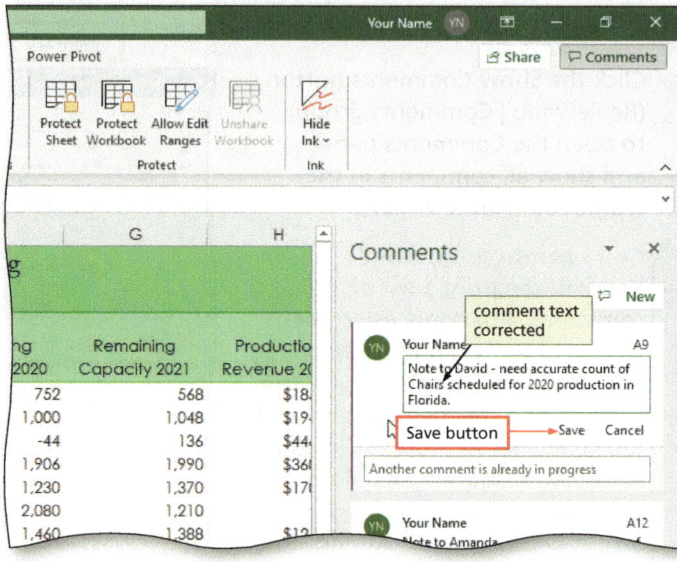

Figure 11–59

3

- Click Save in the comment box to save the correction.
- Click the Show Comments button (Review tab | Comments group) to close the Comments pane and hide all comments.
- Point to cell A12, point to the comment, click Edit, and then change the word, Trays, to Chairs to correct the second comment (Figure 11–60).
- Click Save to save the comment, and then click outside the comment box to close the comment.
- Save the workbook again in the same storage location with the same file name and close it.

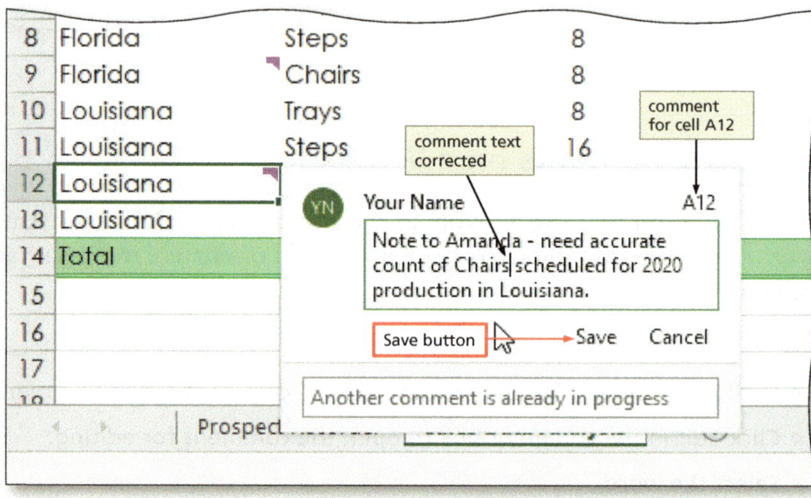

Figure 11–60

To Delete a Comment

If you wanted to delete a comment, you would perform the following steps.

1. Click the More threaded actions button (...) in the comment.
2 Click Delete thread on the More thread actions menu.

Break Point: If you want to take a break, this is a good place to do so. You can exit Excel now. To resume later, start Excel and continue following the steps from this location forward.

Comparing Workbooks

Excel provides you with a way to work with multiple versions of a workbook. You can open multiple copies of the same workbook (as long as they have different names) and move through the workbooks in a synchronized manner so that the same area of each workbook is always in view. For example, as a user scrolls down a worksheet, Excel automatically updates the view of the second worksheet to show the same rows as the first worksheet. This functionality allows for a side-by-side visual comparison of two workbooks.

To Compare Workbooks Side by Side

National Injection Molding plans to participate in three sales events. Proposed event expenditures are saved in a workbook that has been shared and copied to another member of the staff for review. To verify that there were no changes, the workbooks must be compared. **Why?** They should be compared visually to note the changes made by different users. The following steps open the master workbook, SC_EX_11-2.xlsx, and a workbook edited by a staff member, SC_EX_11-3.xlsx. The two workbooks will be compared side by side.

1

- Open the file SC_EX_11-2.xlsx from the Data Files.
- If the file opens in a maximized state, click the workbook's Restore Down button to resize the window.
- Open the file SC_EX_11-3.xlsx from the Data Files.
- If the file opens in a maximized state, click the workbook's Restore Down button to resize the window.
- Display the View tab and then click the 'View Side by Side' button (View tab | Window group) to display the workbooks side by side (Figure 11–61).
- Use the scroll bar in the active window to scroll the SC_EX_11-2.xlsx worksheet.

Q&A

How should the workbooks be arranged after clicking the 'View Side by Side' button?
Depending on how previous Excel windows were arranged on your computer, the workbooks may appear next to each other left to right, or with one window above the other. To change how the windows are positioned, drag one workbook window to the desired screen edge to dock it. Dock the second workbook window on the opposite edge.

What happens when I scroll the worksheet?
Because the Synchronous Scrolling button is selected, both worksheets scroll at the same time so that you can make a visual comparison of the workbooks.

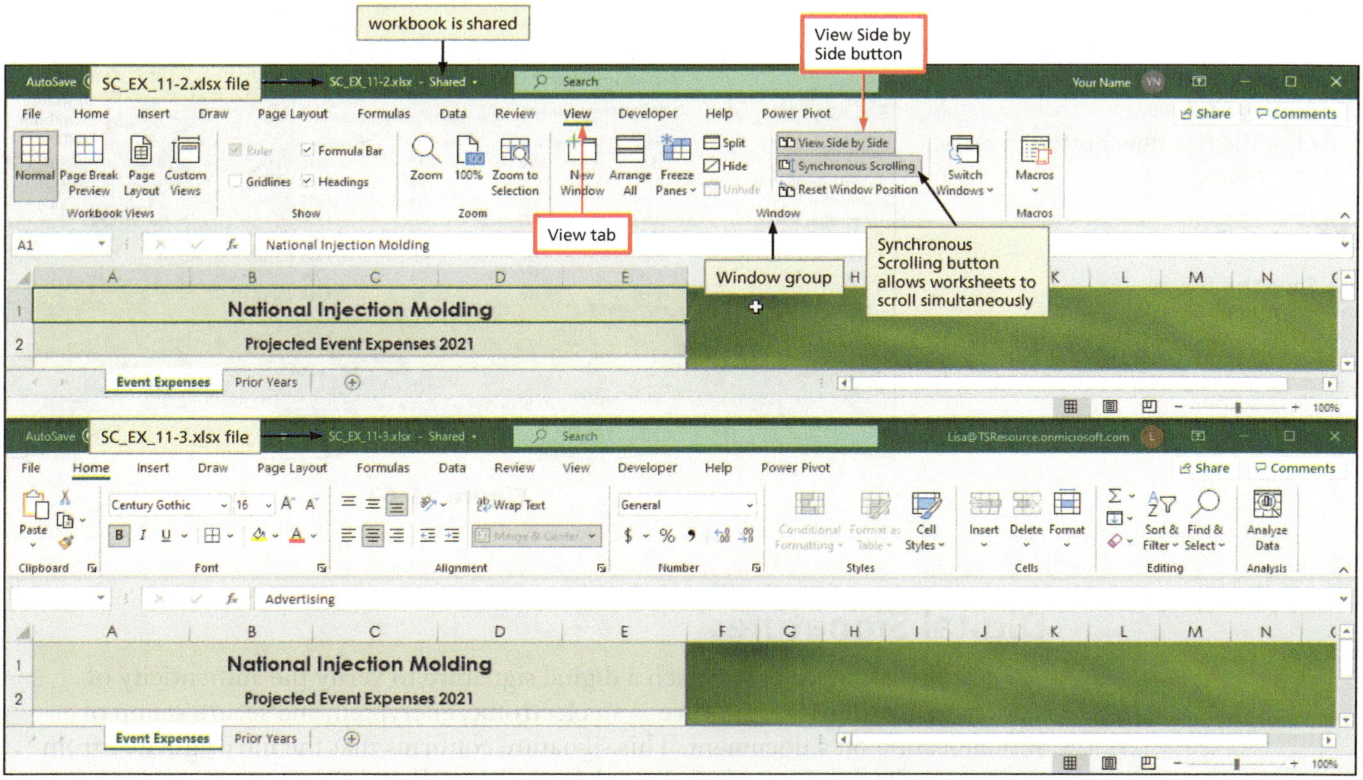

Figure 11–61

Skitterphoto/2058 images/Pixabay

2

- Click the 'View Side by Side' button (View tab | Window group) again to display the windows separately and turn off synchronous scrolling.
- Close the SC_EX_11-3.xlsx workbook.
- If Excel displays a Microsoft Excel dialog box, click the Don't Save button.
- Click the Maximize button in the SC_EX_11-2.xlsx window to maximize the window.

Q&A **What happened to the Compare and Merge commands?**
Those commands are now legacy commands; Microsoft recommends using co-authoring instead.

To Turn Off Workbook Sharing

You have shared a workbook using OneDrive. However previous versions of Excel used a workbook sharing feature that changed the status of workbook from unshared to shared. This capability is no longer included in Excel, but you may use a workbook that was shared using an earlier version, and you can unshare it. **Why?** Sometimes, turning off workbook sharing is a good idea so you will have access to all Excel features. The following steps unshare or turn off workbook sharing so that the data can be manipulated.

1

- With the SC_EX_11-2.xlsx still open, display the Review tab and then click the Unshare Workbook button (Figure 11–62).

Q&A **What if an 'Improve your collaboration' message appears after I click the Review tab?**
Click the Not now button to close the message.

2

- Save the file as SC_EX_11_NIMEvents.

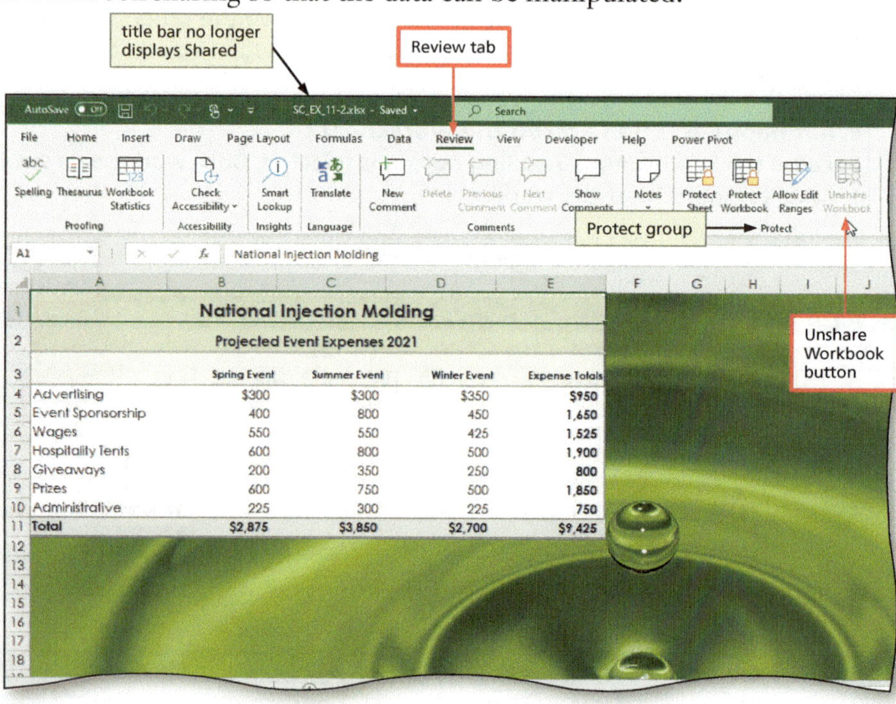

Skitterphoto/2058 images/Pixabay

Figure 11–62

Digital Signatures

Some users prefer to attach a digital signature to verify the authenticity of a document. A **digital signature** is an electronic, encrypted, and secure stamp of authentication on a document. This signature confirms that the file originated from the signer (file developer) and that it has not been altered.

A digital signature may be visible or invisible. In either case, the digital signature references a digital certificate. A **digital certificate** is code attached to a file that verifies the identity of the creator of the file. A digital certificate vouches for the file's authenticity, provides secure encryption, or supplies a verifiable signature. Many users who receive files containing macros enable the macros based on whether they are digitally signed by a developer on the user's list of trusted sources.

You can obtain a digital certificate from a commercial certificate authority (CA), from your network administrator, or you can create a digital signature yourself. A digital certificate you create yourself is not issued by a formal certification authority. Thus, signed macros using such a certificate are referred to as self-signed projects. Certificates you create yourself are considered unauthenticated and still will generate a warning when opened if the user's security level is set to very high, high, or medium. Many users, however, consider self-signed projects safer to open than those with no certificates at all.

To Add a Signature Box and Digital Signature to a Workbook

After adding a digital signature, Excel will display the digital signature whenever the document is opened. If you wanted to add a digital signature to an Excel workbook, you would perform the following steps.

1. Open the SC_EX_11_NIMSalesAnalysis.xlsm workbook and, if necessary, unprotect the Prospect Recorder worksheet using the password, Prospect19.
2. Click the Insert tab and then click the Signature Line arrow in the Text group to display the list.
3. Click the 'Microsoft Office Signature Line' command.
4. Enter your name in the Suggested signer box (Signature Setup dialog box) and then click OK to add the signature box to the workbook.
5. Right-click the signature box and then click Sign on the shortcut menu to display the Sign dialog box. If necessary, you will be prompted to get a digital ID from a Microsoft Partner.
6. In the Sign dialog box, enter your name in the signature box or click the Select Image link to select a file that contains an image of your signature.
7. Click the Sign button (Sign dialog box) to digitally sign the document. If Excel displays a dialog box, click Yes.

BTW

Adding Alternative Text for Accessibility

Alternative text is used to increase accessibility in the workbook. To set alternative text on form controls, right-click the control, click Format Control on the shortcut menu, and then enter the desired alternative text on the Alt Text tab of the Format Control dialog box.

To Review a Digital Signature on a Workbook

Excel will display the digital signature whenever the document is opened. When you open a digitally signed document, Excel displays a message announcing the signature on the status bar while the file opens. After the file is opened, Excel displays a certification icon on the status bar. You can click the icon to find out who digitally signed the document. The word, Signed, may also appear on the title bar in parentheses, indicating the document is signed digitally. If you wanted to review a digital signature on an Excel workbook, you would perform the following steps.

1. Display Backstage view. If necessary, click the Info tab and then click View Signatures to open the Signatures pane.
2. Select a name from the Valid signature list (Signature pane), click the arrow to display the shortcut menu, and then click Signature Details to display the certificate.
3. When you are finished reviewing the certificate, click the Close button (Signature Details dialog box) and then close the workbook.

BTW
Save a Chart as a Template
Chart objects can be saved as templates for reuse. To save a chart as a template, right-click the chart, click Save as Template on the shortcut menu, enter a file name for the template in the Save Chart Template dialog box, and then click Save.

Finalizing a Workbook

Once a workbook functions in the manner for which it was designed, final touches can be added to the worksheets to make them more attractive and easier to use. Excel provides several ways of finalizing a workbook that include enhancing existing objects and data, preparing custom views for multiple users, protecting your privacy, and saving the workbook in other formats. As you finalize the workbook, you should consider enhancements to charts and data that can make the information more visually appealing or easier to interpret.

For example, to improve the appearance of the Event Expenses worksheet, you will add a watermark identifying the content on the Event Expenses worksheet as a draft, to ensure that the salespeople understand that the details are subject to change. A watermark is semitransparent text overlaid on the worksheet that is used to convey something about the state of the worksheet, such as Draft or Confidential status. You will also add a background to the Prior Years worksheet. Worksheet backgrounds place an image behind the data in cells of a worksheet.

When preparing the workbook for distribution, consider establishing a custom view so that the content will display in your preferred way when you access the workbook after others have used it. In addition, regional settings in Excel allow for support of global users, so you might want to change the language settings (Excel Options dialog box), for example.

Before distributing your workbook to others, you should consider what hidden information might be in your workbook. As you learned in previous modules, rows and columns can be hidden from view, as can worksheets and workbooks. Cells also can be protected. You can use the Document Inspector to inspect and report such information, and then choose to remove the hidden information or leave the information in the workbook.

Furthermore, before distributing a workbook, you should consider whether the intended recipients have the most recent version of Excel. If this is not the case, Excel allows you to save a workbook for use in previous versions of Excel, such as Excel 97-2003. When you save a workbook in the Excel 97-2003 Workbook file format, Excel will enable the Compatibility Checker, which notifies you if any of the content of the workbook cannot be saved in that format. Additionally, the Compatibility Checker will inform you if any content will appear differently in the Excel 97-2003 Workbook format, such as cell or chart formatting.

To Add a Watermark to a Worksheet

Why? A watermark can be used to provide a reminder to the user. In this case, it will remind the users that the worksheet contains draft content. Excel does not have a watermark function, but you can use WordArt to mimic one. The following steps add a watermark to the Event Expenses worksheet.

1

- With the SC_EX_11_NIMEvents.xlsx workbook open, make Event Expenses the active worksheet.
- Display the Insert tab and then click the WordArt button (Insert tab | Text group) to display the Insert WordArt gallery (Figure 11–63).

Q&A
I don't see a WordArt button. What should I do?
Click the Text button to expand the Text group as shown in Figure 11–66. The buttons in the Text group then should appear.

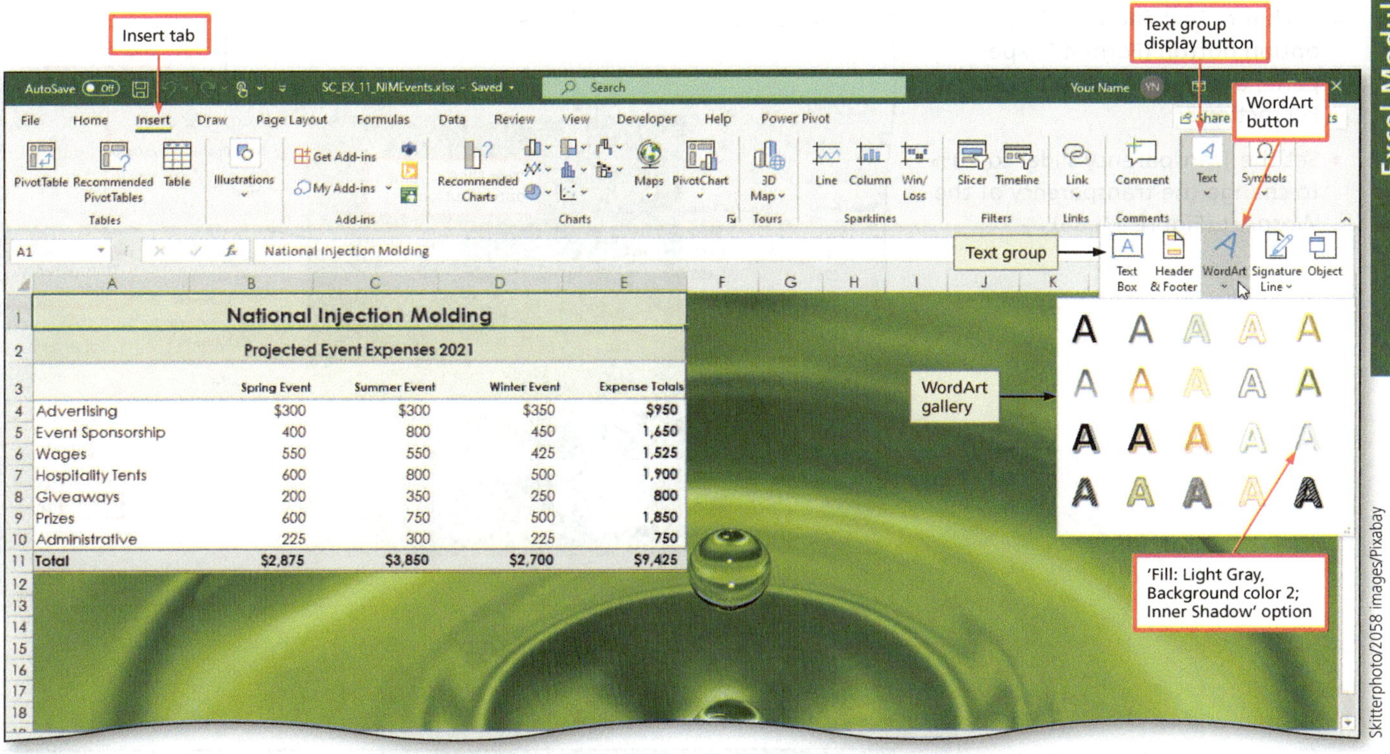

Figure 11–63

2

- Click 'Fill: Light Gray, Background color 2; Inner Shadow' (column 5, row 3 of the Insert WordArt gallery) to insert a new WordArt object.
- If necessary, select the text in the WordArt object and then type Draft as the watermark text.
- Point to the border of the WordArt object, and when the pointer changes to a four-headed arrow, drag the WordArt object to the center of the worksheet content, as shown in Figure 11–64. Your WordArt object may appear differently.
- With the WordArt text selected, right-click the WordArt object text to display a shortcut menu (Figure 11–64).

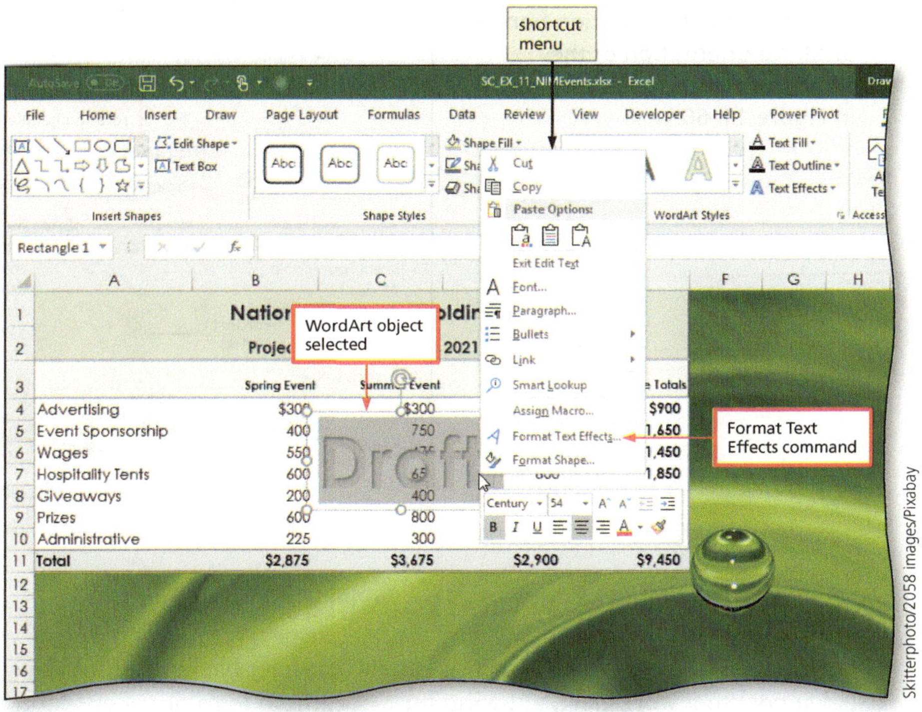

Figure 11–64

3

- Click 'Format Text Effects' on the shortcut menu to open the Format Shape pane.
- If necessary, click the Text Options tab (Format Shape pane) to display the text options.

- Click the 'Text Fill & Outline' option button (Format Shape pane) and then expand the Text Fill section.
- Set the Transparency slider to 80% to change the transparency of the WordArt (Figure 11–65).

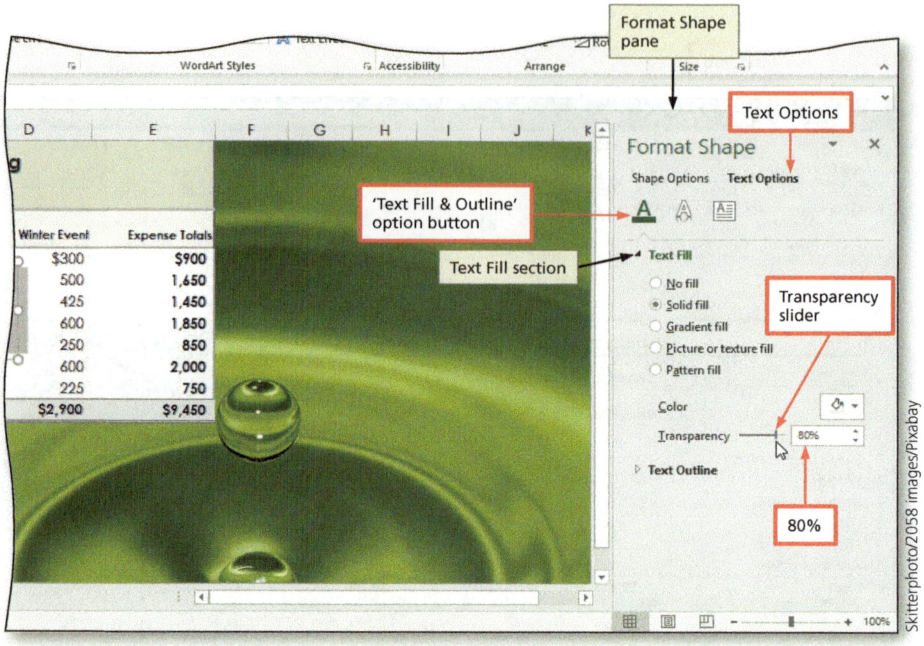

Figure 11–65

4

- Click the Close button in the Format Shape pane to close it.
- With the WordArt object still selected, drag the rotation handle until the orientation of the WordArt object appears as shown in Figure 11–66.

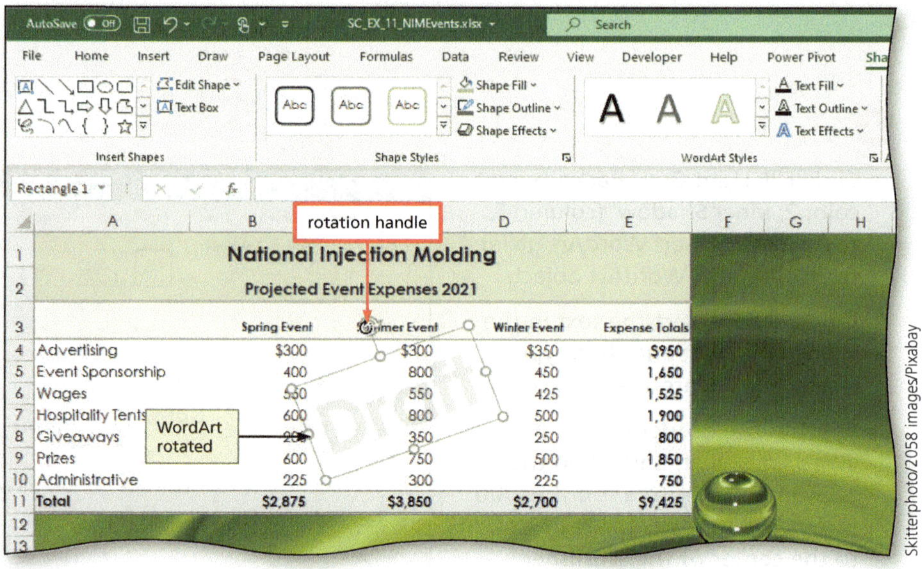

Figure 11–66

To Format a Worksheet Background

Excel allows an image to be used as a worksheet background. **Why?** Worksheet backgrounds can provide visual appeal to a worksheet, allowing for a corporate logo or other identifying image to serve as the background for an entire worksheet. Currently the Event Expenses worksheet has a background. The following steps add the same image as a worksheet background to the Prior Years worksheet.

1

- Display the Prior Years worksheet.
- Display the Page Layout tab and then click the Background button (Page Layout tab | Page Setup group) to display the Insert Pictures dialog box (Figure 11–67).

Q&A **Why do I have additional locations listed in my Insert Pictures dialog box?**
If you are logged in to your Microsoft account, you may have additional, cloud-based locations listed.

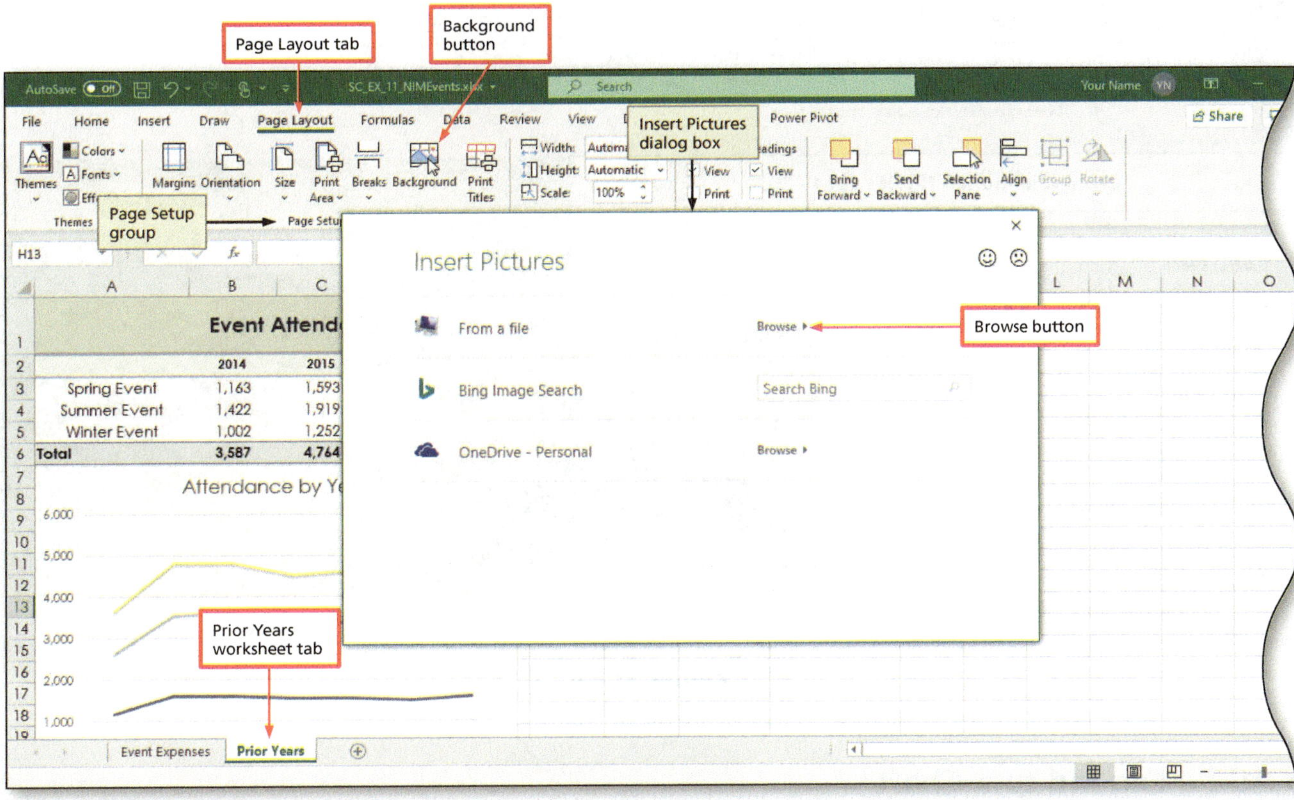

Figure 11–67

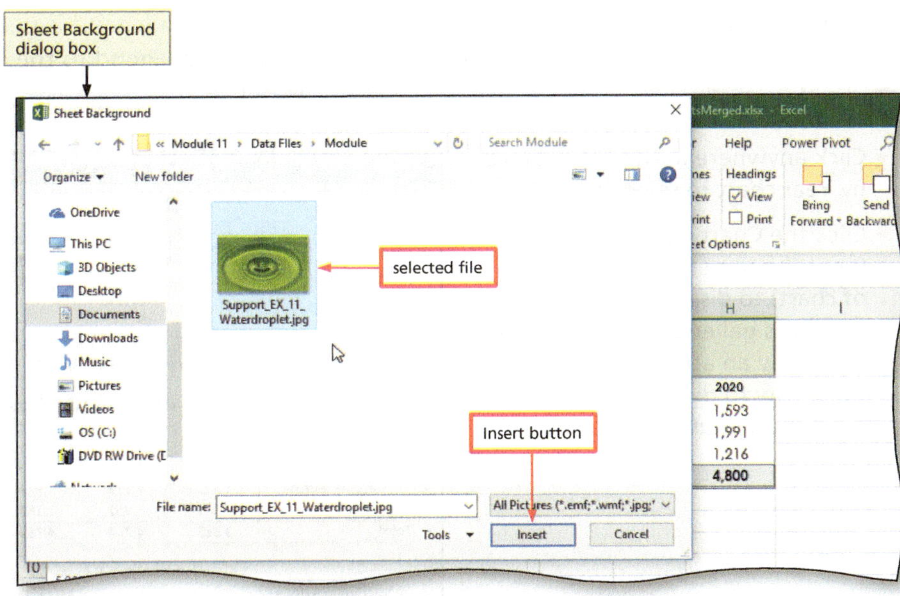

Figure 11–68

2

- Click the Browse button in the From a file area to display the Sheet Background dialog box.
- Navigate to the location of the Data Files, and then select the Support_EX_11_Waterdroplet.jpg file (Figure 11–68).

3

- Click the Insert button (Sheet Background dialog box) to display the image as the worksheet background.
- If gridlines are displayed, click the View Gridlines check box (Page Layout tab | Sheet Options group) to remove the checkmark and turn off gridlines (Figure 11–69).

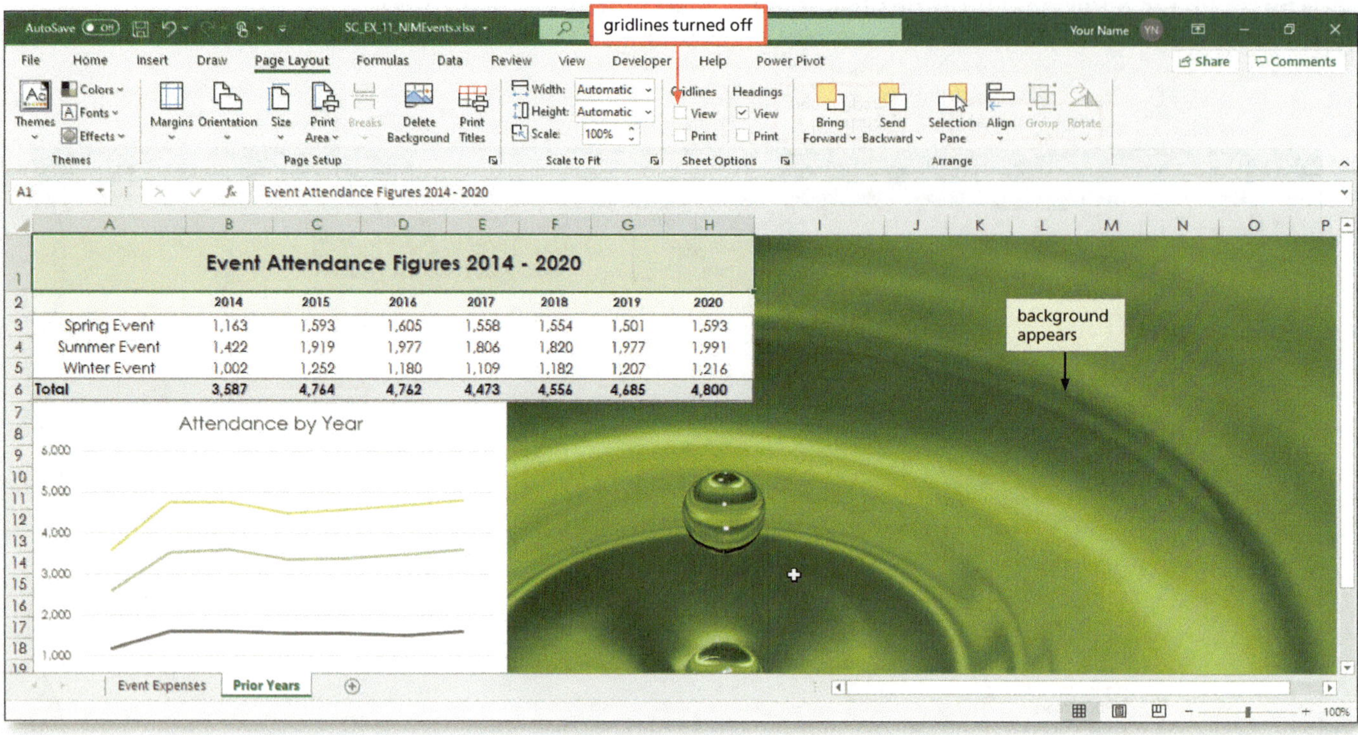

Skitterphoto/2058 images/Pixabay

Figure 11–69

To Add a Legend to a Chart

Adding a legend to the chart will improve the readability of the chart by identifying which event each line represents. **Why?** With line charts containing multiple lines, a legend is necessary for the reader to be able to understand the chart information. The following steps add a legend to the chart and apply a color scheme.

1

- Click anywhere in the Attendance by Year chart to select it.
- Click the Chart Elements button (near the upper-right corner of chart) to display the Chart Elements gallery. Point to Legend to display an arrow and then click the arrow to display the Legend submenu (Figure 11–70).

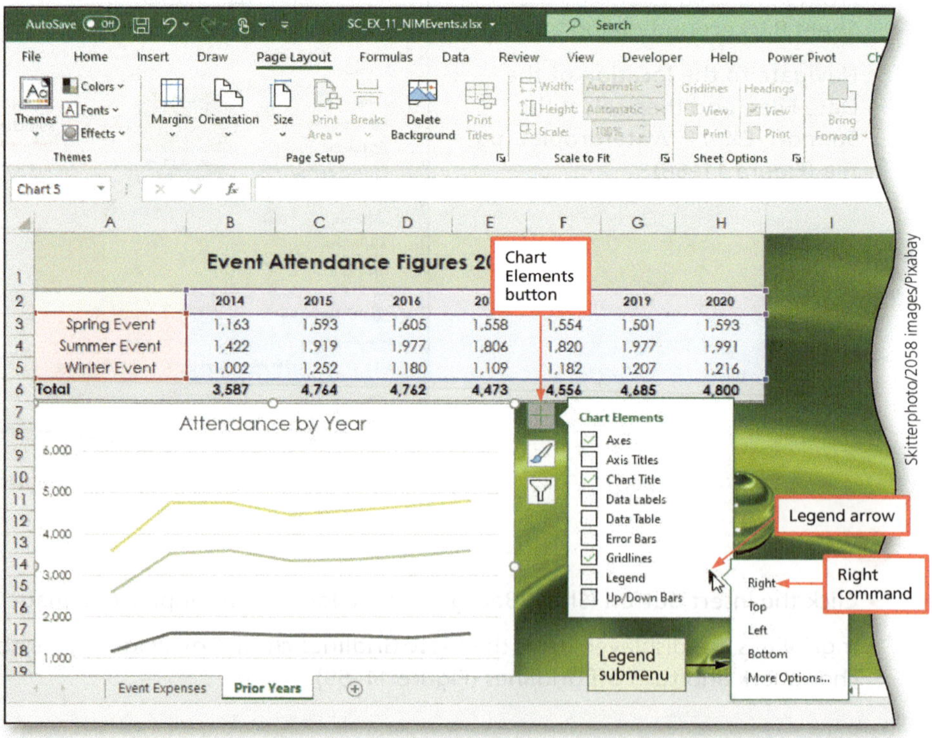

Skitterphoto/2058 images/Pixabay

Figure 11–70

2

- Click Right (Legend submenu) to add a legend to the right side of the chart.
- Click the Chart Elements button again to close the gallery.
- Click the Colors button (Page Layout tab | Themes group) and then click the NIM color scheme (Figure 11–71).

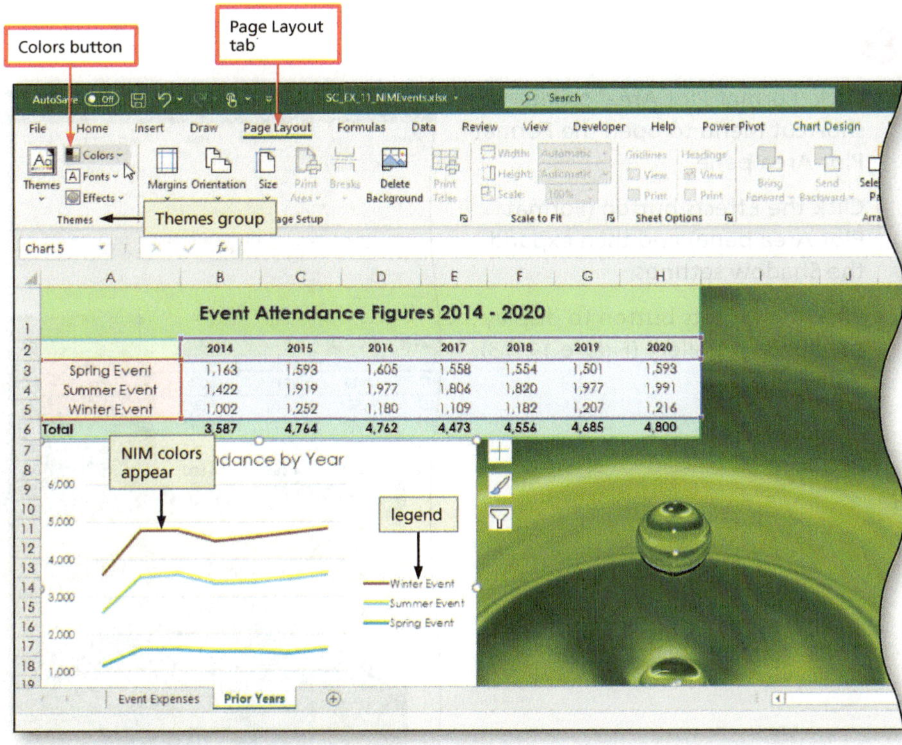

Figure 11–71

To Add a Shadow to a Chart Element

Adding a shadow to the plot area separates it from the other chart elements and improves the visual appeal of the chart. **Why?** Shadows and other design features can add depth and a more professional look to your charts. The following steps add a shadow to the plot area of the chart.

1

- Click anywhere in the plot area to select it. Do not click any of the plot lines.
- Right-click the plot area to display a shortcut menu (Figure 11–72).

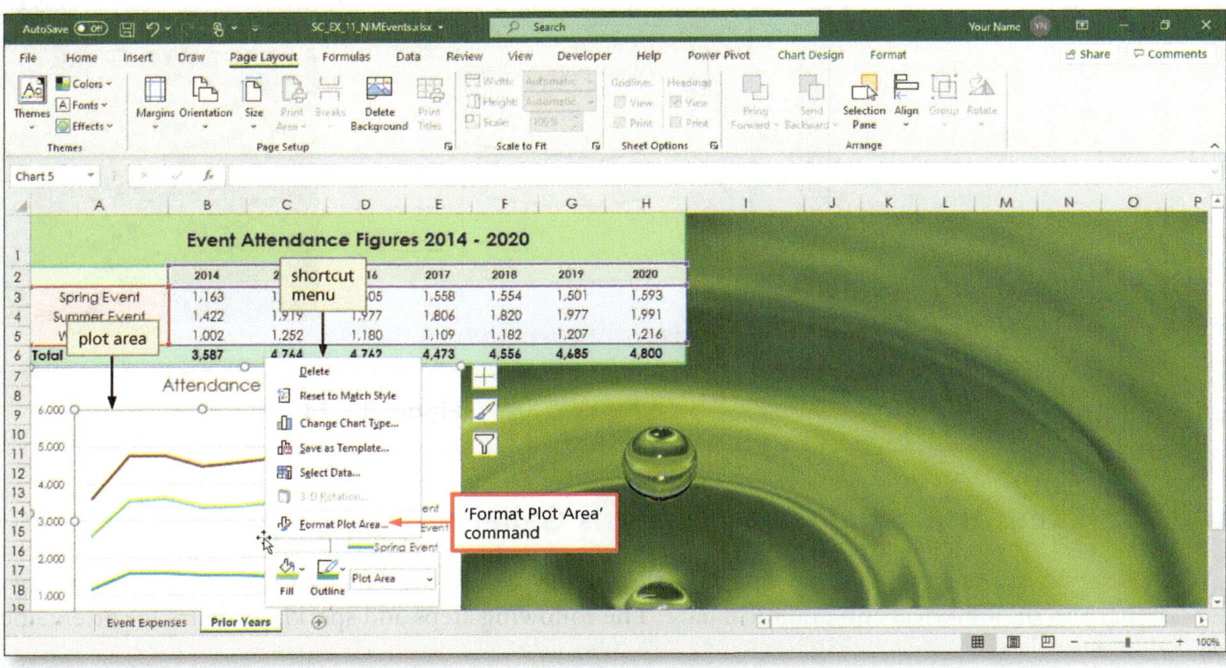

Figure 11–72

2

- Click 'Format Plot Area' on the shortcut menu to open the Format Plot Area pane.
- Click the Effects button (Format Plot Area pane) and then expand the Shadow settings.
- Click the Presets button to display the Shadow gallery (Figure 11–73).

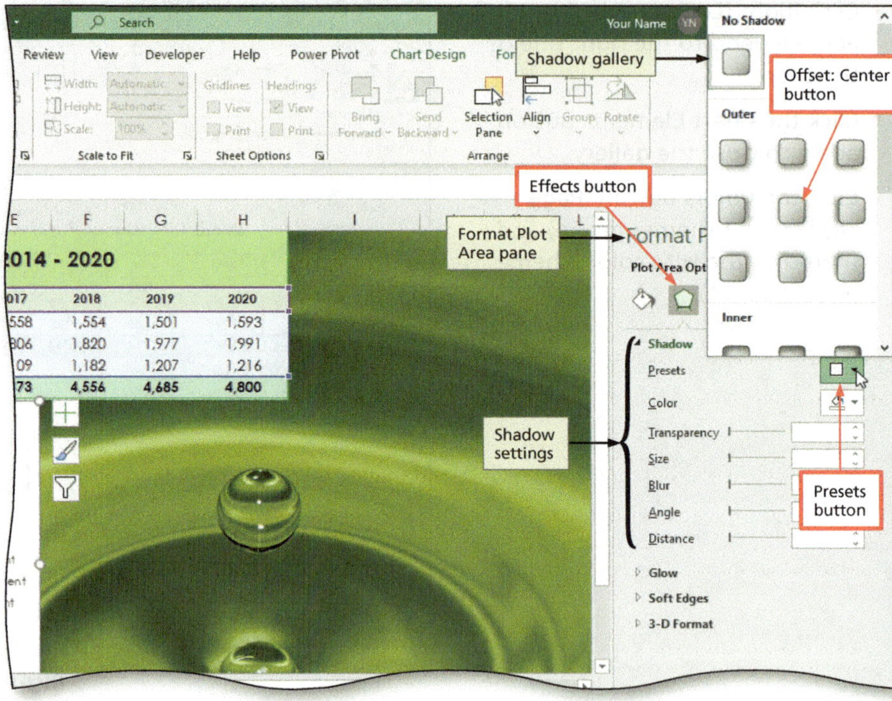

Figure 11–73

3

- Click the Offset: Center button (Outer area) to apply a shadow effect to the plot area of the chart.
- Close the Format Plot Area pane and then deselect the plot area (Figure 11–74).

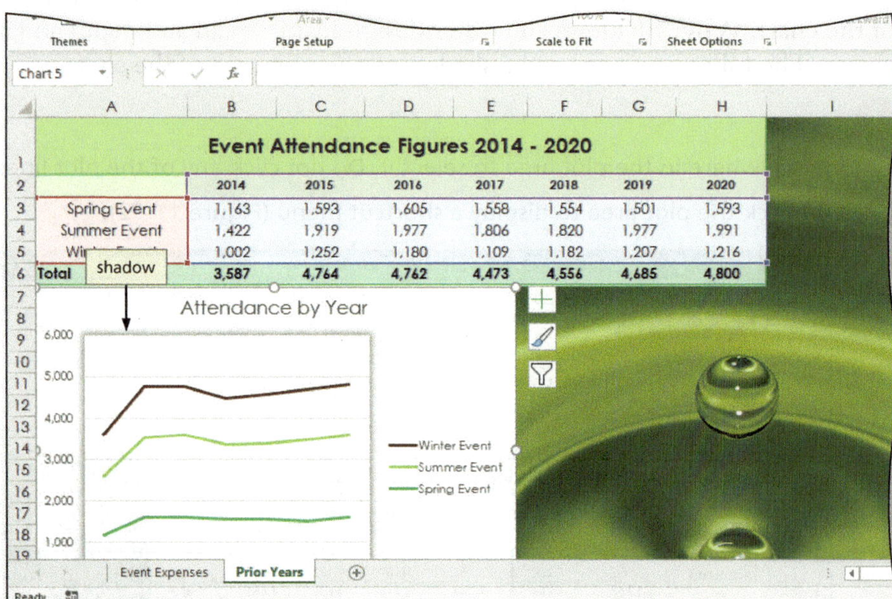

Figure 11–74

To Add Sparklines Using the Quick Analysis Gallery

Why? Sparklines are charts that are inserted immediately beside the data that creates them, allowing for easy comparison of numerical and graphical data. The following steps add sparkline charts for attendance figures.

1

- Select the range B3:H5.
- Click the Quick Analysis button to display the Quick Analysis gallery.
- Click the Sparklines tab to display the Quick Analysis gallery related to sparklines (Figure 11–75).

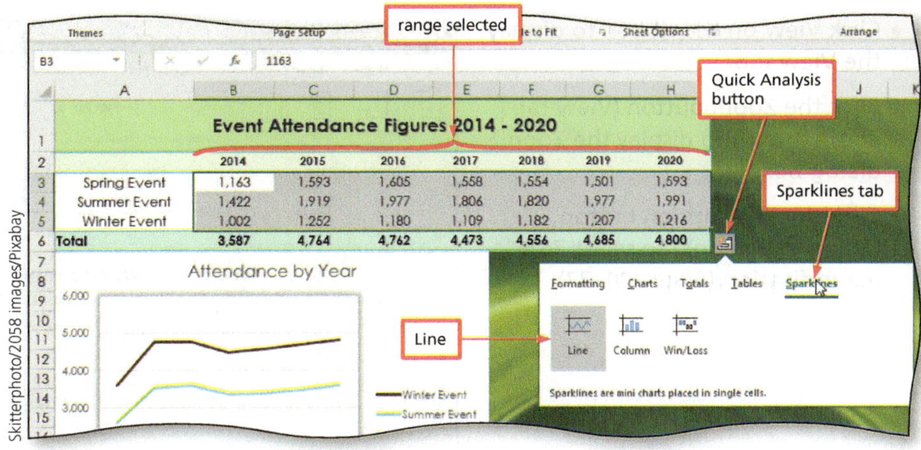

Figure 11–75

2

- Click the Line button (Quick Analysis gallery) to insert sparklines in cells I3:I5.
- Select the range I1:I6. Click the Fill Color arrow (Home tab | Font group) to display the Fill Color gallery. Click 'Lime, Accent 2, Lighter 40%' to choose a fill color.
- Make cell A1 the active cell to deselect the range (Figure 11–76).
- Save the file.

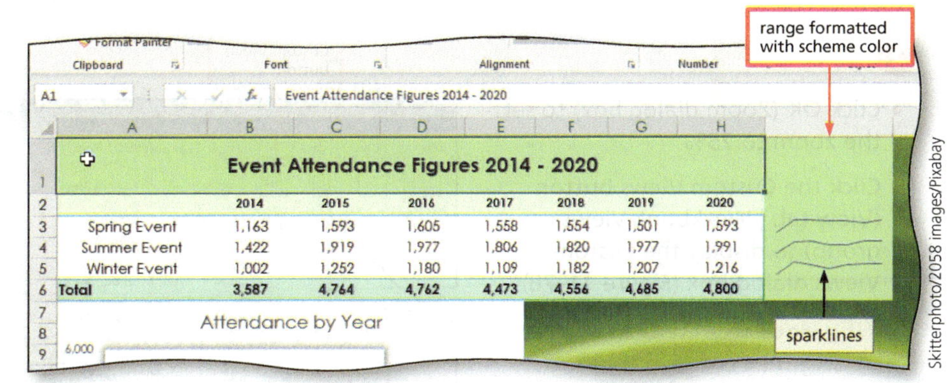

Figure 11–76

Saving Custom Views

A **custom view** allows certain layout and printing characteristics of a workbook to be saved and then used later. When a custom view of a workbook is saved, Excel stores information about the workbook's current window size and print settings. Before saving a custom view, make sure the workbook reflects the desired layout and print settings.

The Custom Views button on the View tab is used to save, delete, and display custom views. When a user saves a custom view, Excel also stores the name of the current worksheet. When a user displays a custom view by clicking the Show button in the Custom Views dialog box, Excel switches to the worksheet that was active in the workbook when the custom view was saved.

To Save a Custom View of a Workbook

Why? If a workbook requires that you customize certain layout and printing settings to use it effectively, using a custom view allows you to save those settings with the workbook. Whenever the workbook is opened, it will be opened with those settings active. The following steps create and save a custom view of the SC_EX_11_NIMEvents workbook.

1

- Click View on the ribbon to display the View tab.
- Click the Zoom button (View tab | Zoom group) to display the Zoom dialog box.
- Click the 75% option button (Zoom dialog box) to select 75% magnification (Figure 11–77).

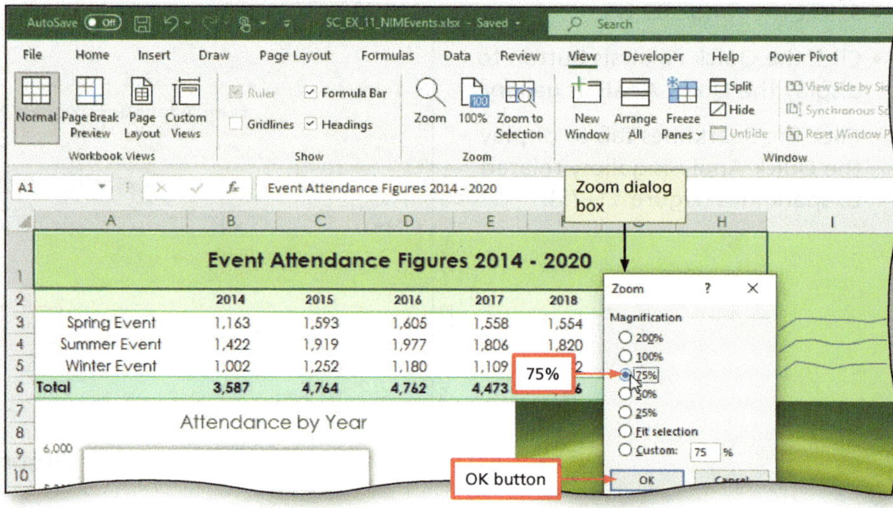

Skitterphoto/2058 images/Pixabay

Figure 11–77

2

- Click OK (Zoom dialog box) to set the zoom to 75%.
- Click the Custom Views button (View tab | Workbook Views group) to display the Custom Views dialog box (Figure 11–78).

Q&A **Why does my Custom Views dialog box contain a list of views?**
The views listed will reflect the authors of any open documents as well as any users signed in to Windows.

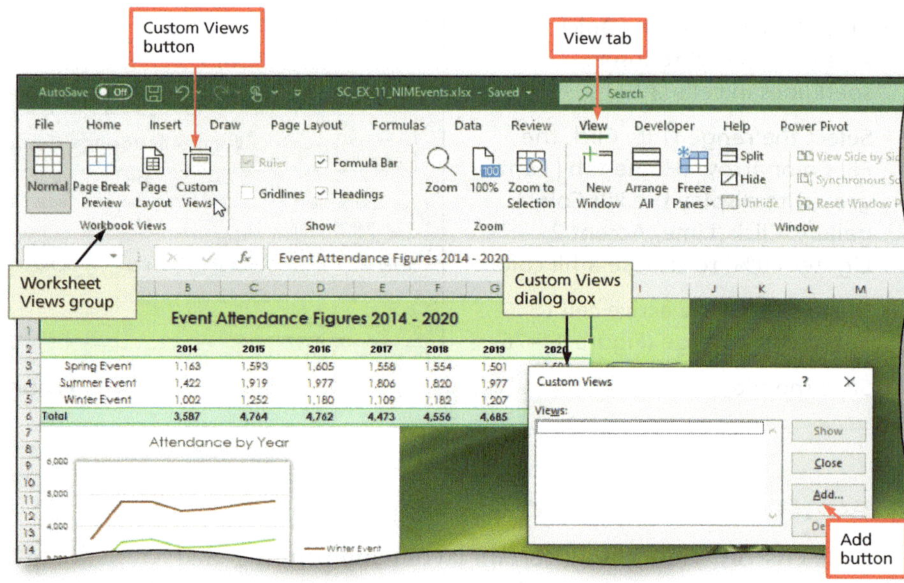

Skitterphoto/2058 images/Pixabay

Figure 11–78

3

- Click the Add button (Custom Views dialog box) to display the Add View dialog box.
- Type `Event Attendance` in the Name box to provide a name for the custom view (Figure 11–79).

4

- Click OK (Add View dialog box) to close the dialog box.

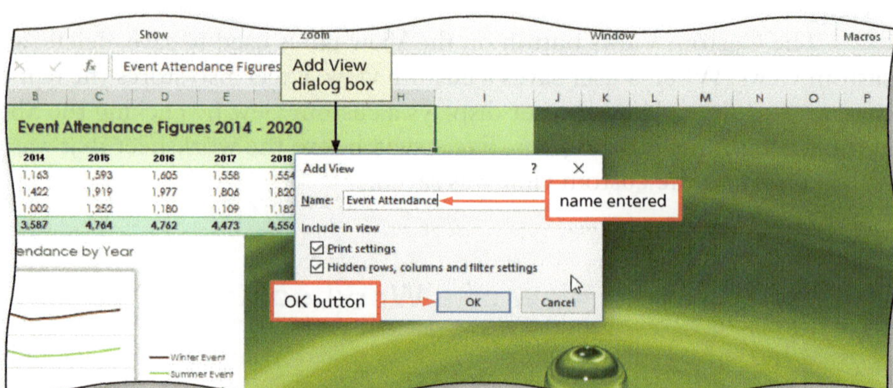

Skitterphoto/2058 images/Pixabay

Figure 11–79

To Test the Custom View

The following steps test the previously created custom view named Event Attendance.

1. Click the Prior Years worksheet tab if necessary.
2. Click the 100% button (View tab | Zoom group) to set the zoom to 100%.
3. Click the Custom Views button (View tab | Workbook Views group) to display the Custom Views dialog box. (Your dialog box may contain additional views.)
4. Click Event Attendance in the Views list and then click the Show button (Custom Views dialog box) to display the Event Attendance view, which includes a zoom to 75%.
5. Click the 100% button (View tab | Zoom group) to set the zoom back to 100%.
6. Save the workbook again on the same storage location with the same file name.

Q&A
Can I delete a custom view?
Yes. To delete custom views, select the view you want to delete, and then use the Delete button in the Custom Views dialog box shown in Figure 11–78.

To Customize Headers and Footers

If you decide to print the final version of your workbook, Excel offers many ways to customize the headers and footers. Not only can you include page numbers, but you can create custom headers and footers that include built-in elements such as text, graphics, and other spreadsheet data. To see the various built-in elements, click the Header & Footer button (Insert tab I Text Group) to display the Header & Footer tab. The elements are located in the Header & Footer Elements group. For a more exact and formatted customization, use the Header/Footer sheet in the Page Setup dialog box (Figure 11–80).

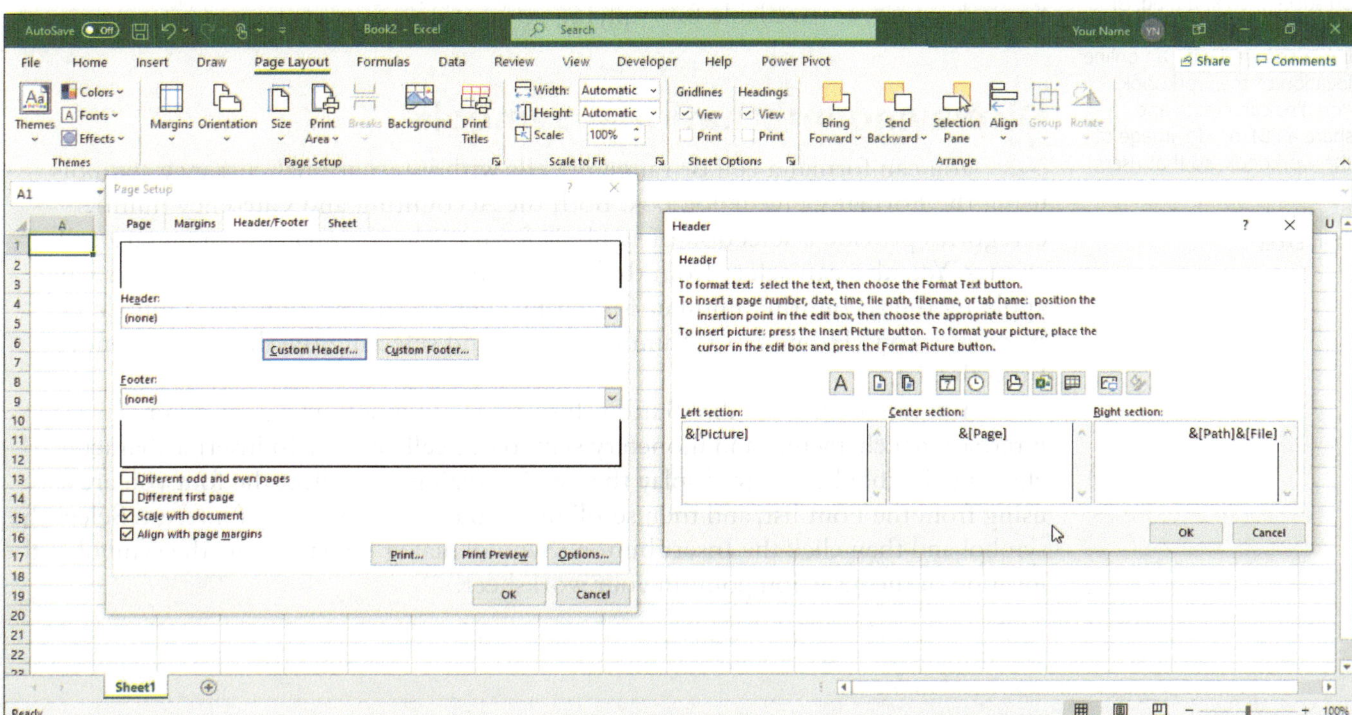

Figure 11–80

If you wanted to customize your header or footer, you would perform the following steps:

1. Click the Page Setup dialog box launcher (Page Layout tab | Page setup group).
2. On the Header/Footer tab, click the Custom Header button or Custom Footer button (Page Setup dialog box).
3. Click in the desired section box and then type text or click the appropriate button to insert a built-in element code.
4. Highlight the text or code and then click the Format Text button to display the Font dialog box. Select any format changes.
5. If you have inserted a picture, highlight the &[Picture] placeholder, and then click the Format Picture button to display the Format Picture dialog box. Select any format changes.
6. Click OK (Header dialog box or Footer dialog box). Click OK (Page Setup dialog box).

Setting Internationalization Features

BTW
Distributing a Document
Instead of printing and distributing a hard copy of a workbook, you can distribute the workbook electronically. Options include sending the workbook via email; posting it on cloud storage (such as OneDrive) and sharing the file with others; posting it on social media, a blog, or other website; and sharing a link associated with an online location of the workbook. You also can create and share a PDF or XPS image of the workbook, so that users can view the file in Acrobat Reader or XPS Viewer instead of in Excel.

Excel provides internationalization features you can use when creating workbooks. Use of these features should be determined based on the intended audience of the workbook. For instance, if you are creating a workbook that will be used in Asian countries where decimal notation differs from that used in North America, consider setting up the workbook to use the appropriate notation by creating custom number formats or changing the symbol used with the Currency or Accounting number formats.

By default, workbooks use formatting consistent with the country or region selected when installing Windows. Situations exist where a workbook will need to contain text or number formatting consistent with a different country or region. Several options are available for applying international formats to content.

Displaying International Symbols

You can format a cell or range of cells with international currency symbols using the Format Cells dialog box. Both the Accounting and Currency number categories provide a selection of symbols for use when formatting monetary cell entries. You also can select from the more commonly used currency symbols when applying the accounting number format by clicking the 'Accounting Number Format' arrow (Home tab | Number group) and selecting the desired currency from the list.

You can use the Symbol button (Insert tab | Symbols group) to enter international characters and monetary symbols as cell entries. To insert a character, click the Symbol button to display the Symbol dialog box, select the font you are using from the Font list, and then scroll until you see the symbol of interest. Select the symbol and then click the Insert button (Symbol dialog box) to insert the symbol at the location of the insertion point in your worksheet.

Displaying Data in Multiple International Formats

Data formatting varies from country to country and region to region, including the use of different characters to separate decimal places and differing date formats. If preparing a workbook for use in another region, consider changing the location setting in Windows to the region of your audience. Use the Windows search box to search for Region to access the Region & Language settings to set format options for a specific region. In Excel, you can click Options in Backstage view and then click Language in the left pane. In the 'Office authoring languages and proofing' area in the right pane, click the 'Add additional editing languages' button. Choose the language you are interested in. The Editing language is the language in which you type and edit your content. The lower part of the right pane offers ways to change the display language, which is used for all of the buttons, menus, and controls in Excel.

Excel has other language-specific features. For example, if you want to use a European style date, you can right-click a date and click Format Cells on the shortcut menu. In the Format Cells dialog box, click Date in the left pane. On the right, click the Locale button and then choose your language or region. You also can change the proofing language by clicking Options in Backstage view. Click Proofing in the Excel Options dialog box, click the Custom Dictionary button, and then choose your language.

Collaborating with Users Who Do Not Use the Same Version of Excel

It is not unusual to collaborate with others who are using different software versions, or different software entirely, to do their work. You even can find different versions of software being used within the same company. When collaborating with others, you should make decisions about how to save and distribute files after considering how your colleagues will be using the workbooks you create. In instances where people are working with earlier versions of software or different software, you need to provide workbooks in formats that they can use.

Before sharing a workbook with others, you can mark the workbook as being final. When another user of your workbook opens the workbook, he or she will be notified that you have marked the workbook as final. The workbook can still be edited, but only if the user clicks a button to indicate that he or she wants to edit the workbook.

To Save a Workbook in an Earlier Version of Excel

Why? You occasionally need to save a workbook for use in previous versions of Excel. Each version of Excel includes varying features, so you can use the Compatibility Checker to determine if the features used in your workbook are compatible with earlier versions of Excel. The following steps check the compatibility of the workbook while saving the workbook in the Excel 97-2003 Workbook file format.

1

- Display Backstage view, click Save As, and then navigate to the location where you store your files.
- Click the 'Save as type' arrow (Save As dialog box) to display the list of file types (Figure 11–81).

Q&A **Would saving the file using the same name overwrite the original version of the workbook?**
No. It is not necessary to save the workbook with a new file name. The 'Excel 97-2003' version of the workbook will have a file extension of .xls, while the original has a file extension of .xlsx.

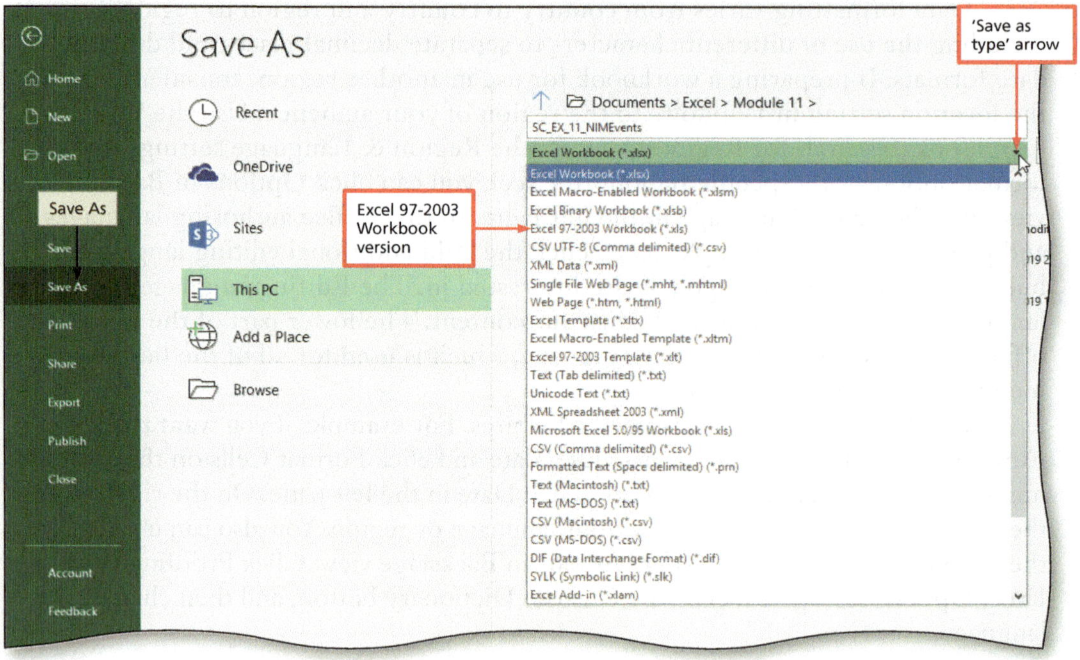

Figure 11–81

2

- Click 'Excel 97-2003 Workbook' to select the file format.
- Click the Save button (Save As dialog box) to display the Microsoft Excel - Compatibility Checker dialog box.
- Resize the dialog box so that it displays all the issues (Figure 11–82).

Q&A **What is shown in the Microsoft Excel - Compatibility Checker dialog box?**
The Summary states that some of the chart elements and the sparklines used on the Prior Years worksheet are not compatible with previous versions of Excel. While the workbook still will be saved in the Excel 97-2003 file format, the sparklines will not be saved. In addition, some cell formatting is unique to Excel 2019 and later releases. These formats will be converted to the nearest approximation in the earlier version of Excel.

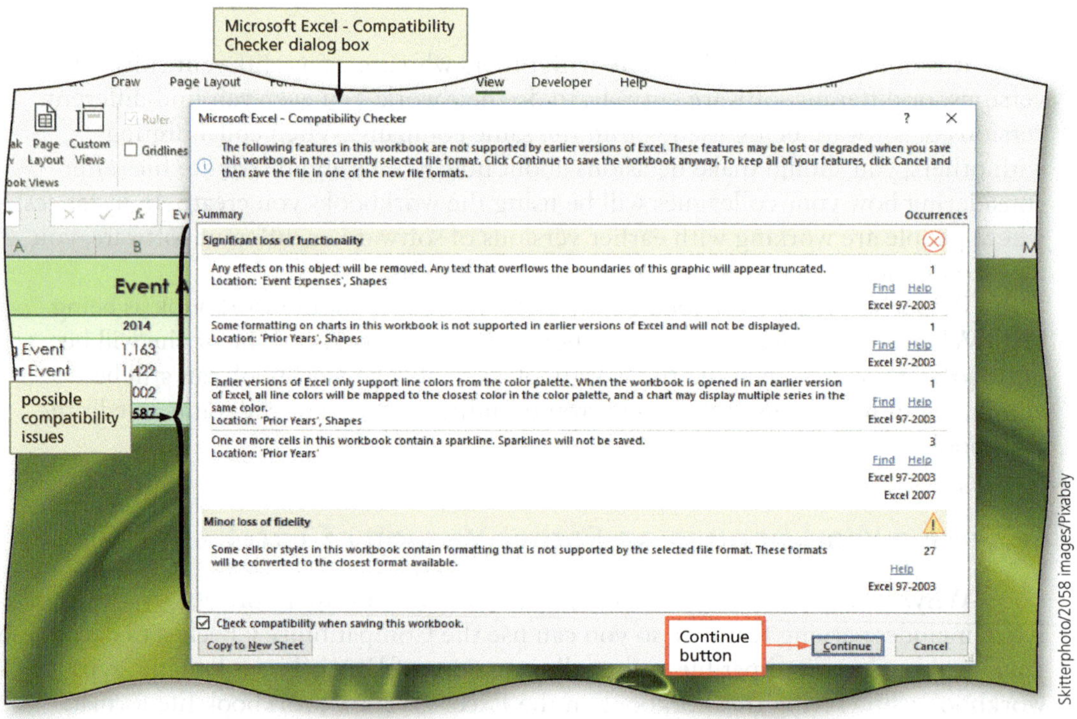

Figure 11–82

3

- Click the Continue button (Microsoft Excel - Compatibility Checker dialog box) to save the workbook in the Excel 97-2003 Workbook file format.

To Mark a Workbook as Final

The following steps mark the workbook as final. **Why?** The workbook is complete; marking it as final will prevent users from accidentally changing anything.

1

- Display Backstage view.
- Click Info in the navigation bar, and then click the Protect Workbook button in the Info gallery to display the Protect Workbook menu (Figure 11–83).

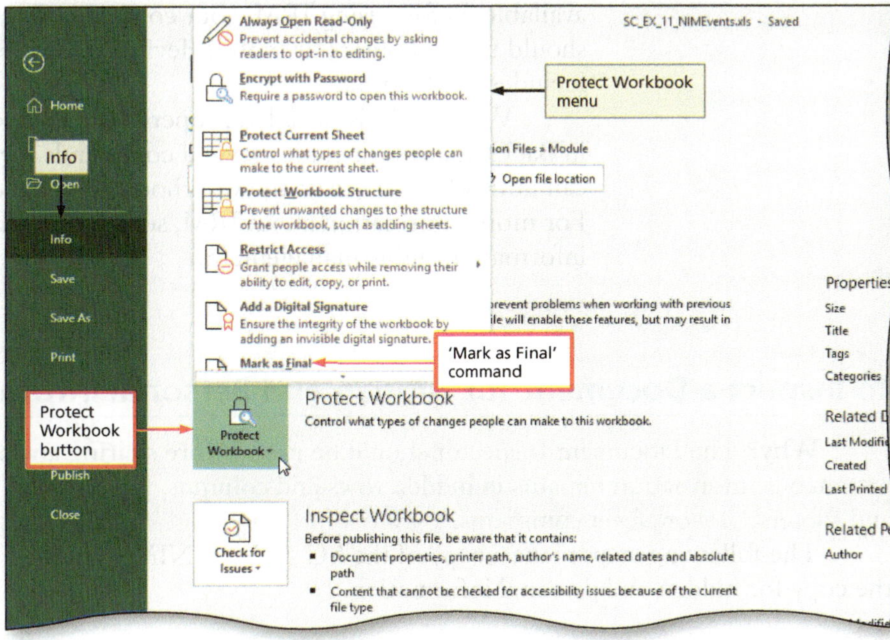

Figure 11–83

2

- Click 'Mark as Final' on the Protect Workbook menu to display the Microsoft Excel dialog box.
- If necessary, click OK on the Microsoft Excel dialog box.
- If necessary, click the Continue button on the Microsoft Excel - Compatibility Checker dialog box.
- Click OK (Microsoft Excel dialog box) to indicate you want to mark the workbook as final (Figure 11–84).

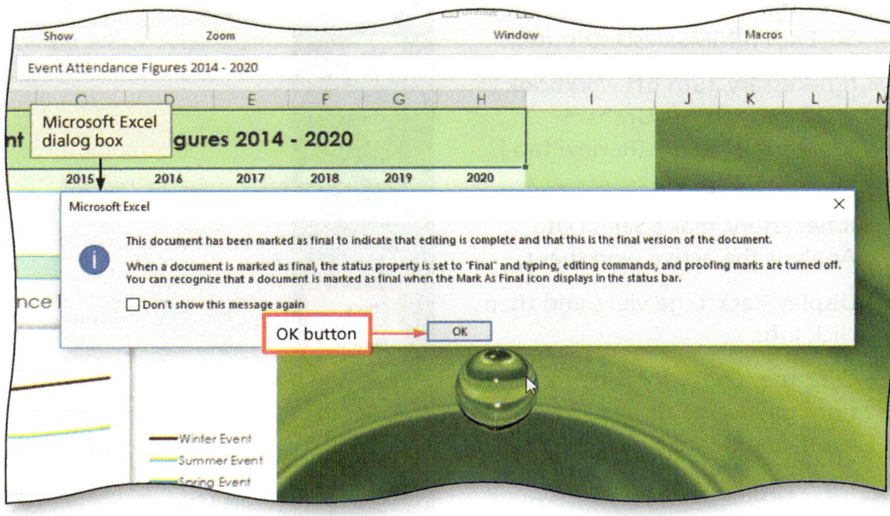

Figure 11–84

Q&A **I have saved the workbook in .xls format, but the sparklines are still showing. Why?**
Although the .xls format does not support newer features such as sparklines, more recent versions of Excel do. If you close the file and reopen the workbook saved in the older format, the sparklines will be missing.

3

- Click OK to close the Microsoft Excel dialog box and mark the workbook as final. Excel will display a MARKED AS FINAL yellow bar below the ribbon tabs.
- Close the workbook.

Information Rights Management

Information Rights Management (IRM) is a feature of Excel that allows you to restrict access to workbooks. With IRM, you can restrict who can view, modify, print, forward, and copy a workbook. The types of restrictions include a variety of options. For example, expiration dates for reading or modifying a workbook are available. Before using IRM, your computer first must be configured with IRM, as should the computers or mobile devices of anyone attempting to use a document that includes IRM features.

When IRM is installed properly, the Protect Workbook menu in the Info screen in Backstage view includes several commands for limiting access to the workbook. You can limit who can access the workbook and who can make changes to the workbook. For more information about IRM, search Excel Help using the search string, information rights management.

To Inspect a Document for Hidden and Personal Information

Why? The Document Inspector should be used before sharing a workbook publicly or when you suspect extraneous information remains in hidden rows and columns, hidden worksheets, document properties, headers and footers, or worksheet comments.

The following steps make a copy of the SC_EX_11_NIMSalesAnalysis.xlsm workbook and then inspect the copy for hidden and personal information.

1

- If necessary, open the file named SC_EX_11_NIMSalesAnalysis.xlsm and save the workbook with the file name, SC_EX_11_NIMSalesDistribute.
- If necessary, turn off workbook sharing using the Unshare Workbook button (Review tab | Protect group).
- If necessary, make Sales Data Analysis the active worksheet.
- Display Backstage view, and then click Info.
- Click the 'Check for Issues' button (Info gallery) to display the Check for Issues menu (Figure 11–85).

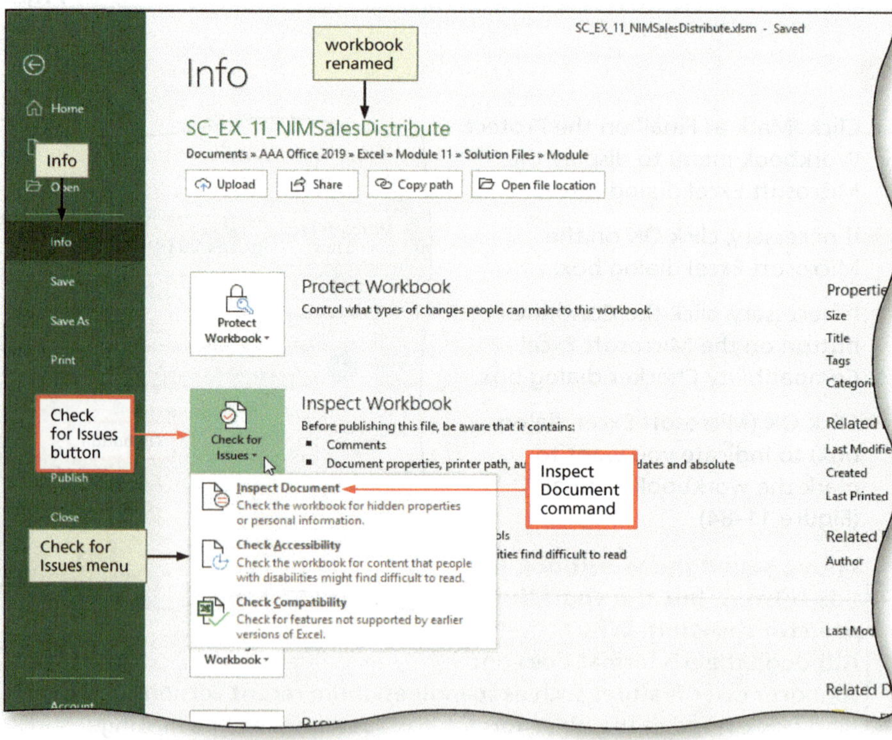

Figure 11–85

Q&A **Why did I save this workbook with a different file name?**
When preparing a workbook for distribution, you may decide to use the Document Inspector to make changes to the document. Saving the workbook with a different file name ensures that you will have a copy of the workbook with all of the original information intact for your records.

2

- Click Inspect Document (Check for Issues menu) to display the Document Inspector dialog box. If prompted, click the Yes button to save the document (Figure 11–86).

Q&A

What is shown in the Document Inspector dialog box?

The Document Inspector dialog box allows you to choose which types of content to inspect. Typically, you would leave all of the items selected, unless you are comfortable with some types of content not being inspected.

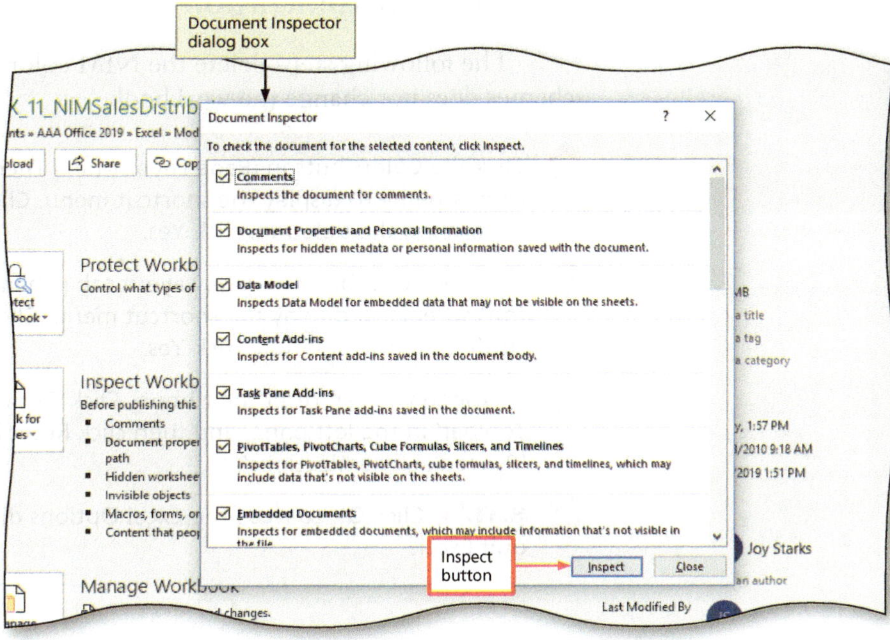

Figure 11–86

3

- Click the Inspect button (Document Inspector dialog box) to run the Document Inspector and display its results (Figure 11–87).

Experiment

- Scroll in the Document Inspector to view the issues.

Q&A

What did the Document Inspector find?

The Document Inspector found the hidden Prospect List worksheet, comments, and personal information (Figure 11–87), including document properties, author information, related dates, absolute path to the workbook, and printer properties. The Remove All button in the dialog box allows you quickly to remove the items found if needed. In many instances, you may want to take notes of the results and then investigate and remedy each one separately. In this workbook, all of these items found by the Document Inspector are expected and do not need to be remedied.

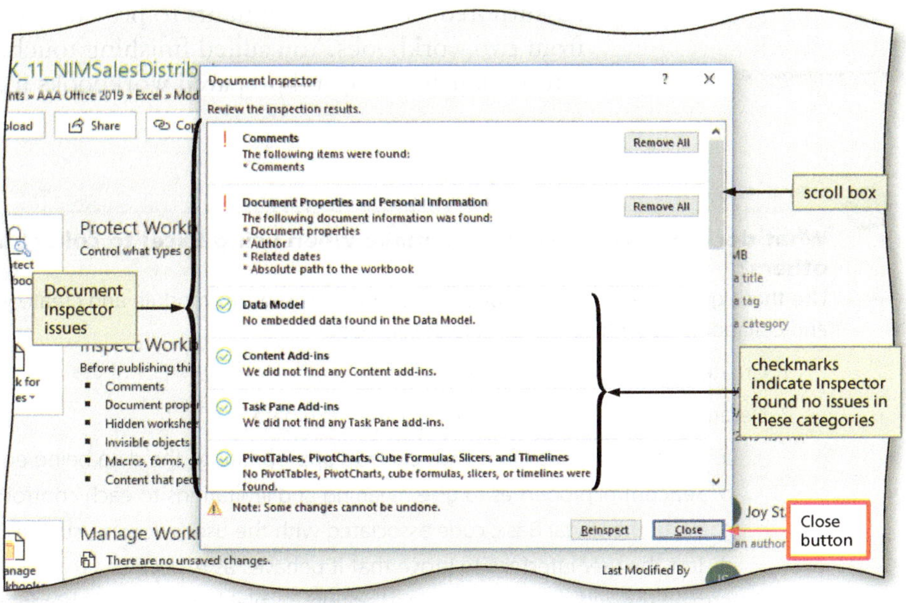

Figure 11–87

4

- Click the Close button (Document Inspector dialog box) to close the dialog box.
- Return to the worksheet.

To Delete Customization

The following steps delete the NIM color and font schemes. Deleting the schemes does not change the workbook.

1. Click the Colors button (Page Layout tab | Themes group) and then right-click the NIM color scheme to display the shortcut menu. Click Delete. If Excel displays a dialog box confirming the deletion, click Yes.

2. Click the Fonts button (Page Layout tab | Themes group) and then right-click the NIM font scheme to display the shortcut menu. Click Delete. If Excel displays a dialog box confirming the deletion, click Yes.

3. If desired you can reset the ribbon. Click Options in Backstage view, click 'Quick Access Toolbar' in the left pane, and then click Reset button (Excel Options dialog box). Click 'Reset all customizations'.

4. sam Click OK to close the Excel Options dialog box. Save the file and then quit Excel.

Summary

In this module, you developed a custom form for accepting user input, using form controls, ActiveX controls, and VBA code. You shared workbooks on OneDrive and co-authored. You used comments to provide feedback and compared worksheet data from two workbooks. You added finishing touches to worksheets, learned about internationalization, and prepared workbooks for distribution.

Consider This: Plan Ahead

What decisions will you need to make when using Excel to collect information or collaborate with others?

Use these guidelines as you complete the assignments in this module and create your own worksheets for creating Excel forms and collaborating with others outside of this class.

1. Create custom fonts, schemes, and themes as necessary.
2. Determine the purpose and needs of the form data.
   a. Design a user interface with controls appropriate to the data being entered.
   b. Set control properties to give meaning and limitations to each control's use.
   c. Write the Visual Basic code associated with the user's actions, such as clicking a button.
   d. Test the user interface to prove that it behaves as expected.
3. Determine the audience, purpose, and options available for the collaboration.
4. Evaluate changes made by colleagues.
   a. With a single distributed workbook, use co-authoring.
   b. With multiple workbooks, compare workbooks side by side.
5. Add worksheet enhancements.
   a. Add watermarks and worksheet backgrounds as appropriate.
   b. Enhance charts if appropriate.
6. Prepare workbook(s) for distribution.

Apply Your Knowledge

Reinforce the skills and apply the concepts you learned in this module.

Creating a Form

Note: To complete this assignment, you will be required to use the Data Files. Please contact your instructor for information about accessing the Data Files.

Instructions: Start Excel. Open the workbook SC_EX_11-5.xlsx, which is located in the Data Files. The spreadsheet you open contains the start of a form to gather information about visitors to a museum that will display on a kiosk on the way out of the museum. Figure 11–88 shows the completed form.

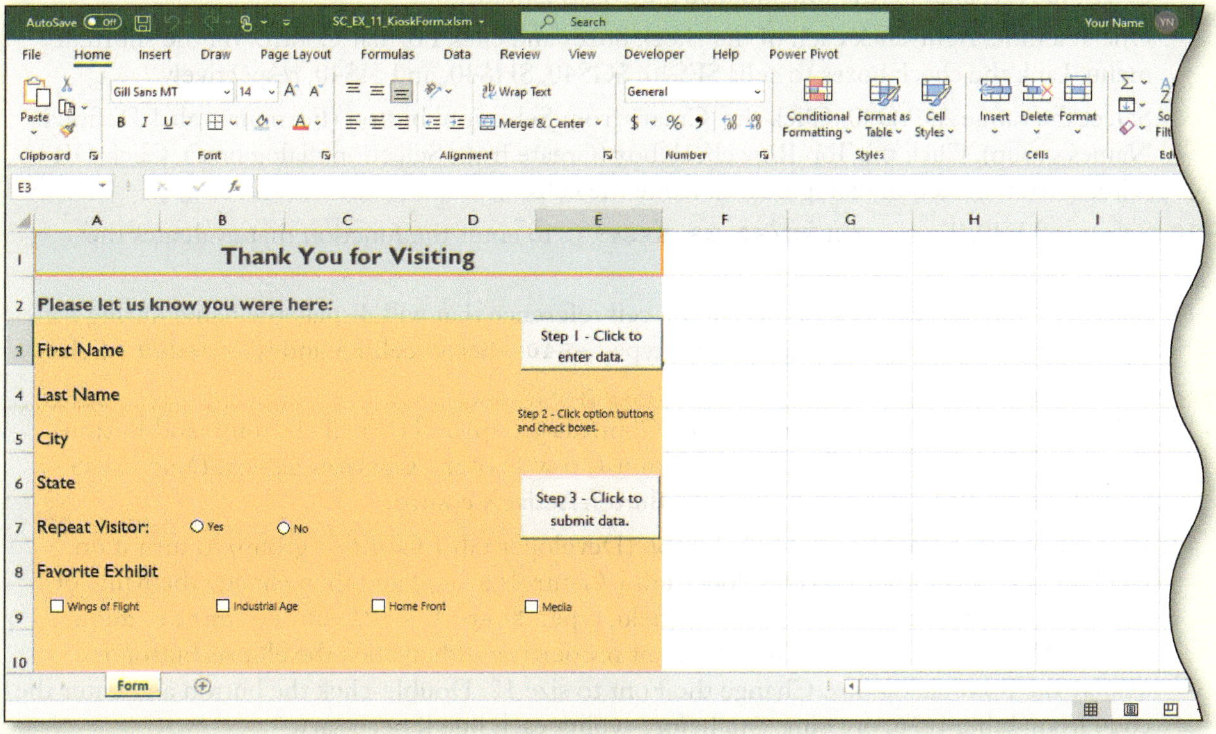

Figure 11–88

Perform the following tasks:

1. Save the workbook using the file name, SC_EX_11_KioskForm.xlsm (the macro enabled format). Examine row 39 and column W.
2. If necessary, add the Developer tab to the ribbon as described in the module.
3. Click the Insert button (Developer tab | Controls group) and then click the Option Button button in the Form Controls area (column 6, row 1) in the Controls gallery. Drag in the worksheet to create an option button control in cell B7 (approximately). Right-click the option button and click Edit Text. Change the existing text to say Yes. Resize the control as necessary.
4. Repeat Step 3 to create an option button control in cell C7 with the text No. Select both option buttons and then click the Align button (Shape Format tab | Arrange group). Align the two option buttons on the top.

Continued >

Apply Your Knowledge *continued*

5. Right-click either option button control and then click Format Control on the shortcut menu. If necessary, click the Control tab (Format Control dialog box) and then type $E$41 in the Cell link box (Format Control dialog box) to link the option button index number to cell E41.
6. Click the Insert button (Developer tab | Controls group) and then click the Check Box button in the Form Controls area (column 3, row 1) in the Controls gallery. Drag in the worksheet to create a check box control in cell A9 (approximately). Change the existing text to Wings of Flight. Resize so the check box is only slightly bigger than the text.
7. Repeat Step 6 to create a check box with the text Industrial Age in cell B9. Repeat Step 6 to create a check box with the text Home Front in cell C9. Repeat Step 6 to create a check box with the text Media in cell D9. Select all four check boxes, right-click, and then chose Format Object on the shortcut menu to open the Format Control dialog box. On the Size tab, set the height to .19. Align on the top and distribute horizontally.
8. One at a time, right-click each of the check boxes and click Format Control on the shortcut menu. Link the check boxes to cells $F$40, $G$40, $H$40, and $I$40, respectively.
9. Select the range A39:D40. Click the 'Create from Selection' button (Formulas tab | Defined Names group). Click the Top Row check box (Create from Selection dialog box). Click OK (Create from Selection dialog box) to name the cells.
10. Select cell E40. Type `=INDEX(W2:W3,$E$41)` to enter the function that evaluates the option buttons.
11. Select cell B3 and type `=A40` to enter a cell reference that will display the name during execution of the code. Select cell B4 and type `=B40`. Select cell B5 and type `=C40`. Select cell B6 and type `=D40`.
12. Click the Insert button (Developer tab | Controls group) and then click Command Button button in the ActiveX Controls area (column 1, row 1) of the Controls gallery. Drag in the worksheet in cell E3 create a Command Button ActiveX control.
13. If necessary, click the Design Mode button (Developer tab | Controls group) to turn it on. Click the Properties button (Developer tab | Controls group) and then change the name of the button to cmdStep1. In the Caption field, type `Step 1 - Click to enter data`. Change WordWrap to True. Click the Font property and then click the ellipsis button to display the Font dialog box. Change the Font to size 12. Double-click the button and enter the code from Table 11–6, pressing TAB before typing each line if necessary.

Table 11–6 Code for cmdStep1 Button
'Author: SC Series
'Date Created: 11/12/2020
'Run from: Form Worksheet, cmdStep1 Button
'Function: When executed, this procedure enters contact information for the prospect.
Range("First_Name").Value = InputBox("First Name?", "Enter", , 800, 6000)
Range("Last_Name").Value = InputBox("Last Name?", "Enter", , 800, 6000)
Range("City").Value = InputBox("City?", "Enter", , 800, 6000)
Range("State").Value = InputBox("State?", "Enter", , 800, 6000)

14. Close the VBA window.
15. Click the Insert button (Developer tab | Controls group) and then click the Command Button button in the ActiveX Controls area (column 1, row 1) of the Controls gallery. Drag in the worksheet in cell E6 create a Command Button ActiveX control.
16. If necessary click the Design Mode button (Developer tab | Controls group) to turn it on. Click the Properties button (Developer tab | Controls group) and then change the name of the button to cmdStep3. In the Caption field, type `Step 3 - Click to submit data`. Change WordWrap to True. Change the Font to size 12. Double-click the button, enter the code from Table 11–7, pressing TAB before typing each line, as necessary.

Table 11–7 Code for cmdStep3 Button

```
'Author: SC Series
'Date Created: 11/12/2020
'Run from: Form Worksheet, cmdStep3 Button
'Function: When executed, this procedure submits new information to the prospect list
Range("A40:I40").Select
Selection.Copy
Sheets("Data Sheet").Visible = True
Sheets("Data Sheet").Activate
Sheets("Data Sheet").Range("A2:I2").Select
Selection.PasteSpecial Paste:=xlPasteValues, Operation:=xlNone, SkipBlanks:=False, Transpose:=False
Selection.Font.Bold = False
Sheets("Data Sheet").Range("A2").Activate
ActiveCell.EntireRow.Insert
Sheets("Data Sheet").Visible = False
Sheets("Form").Select
Range("E41").ClearContents
Range("A40:D40").ClearContents
Range("F40:I40").ClearContents
Range("E3").Activate
ActiveWorkbook.Save
```

17. Create a Label form control between the two command buttons that says Step 2 - Click option buttons and check boxes.
18. Turn off Design Mode and test the form. Unhide the Data Sheet and check to make sure the data was recorded. If there were errors, double-check the VBA code you entered.
19. When everything runs correctly, hide the Data Sheet. Password protect the Form sheet. Save the workbook and then submit the revised workbook as specified by your instructor, along with the password. If you are working in a lab situation, delete all customization.
20. What other things could you do to this workbook to make it look more attractive or be more functional on a kiosk?

Extend Your Knowledge

Extend the skills you learned in this module and experiment with new skills. You may need to use Help to complete the assignment.

Writing VBA Code

Note: To complete this assignment, you will be required to use the Data Files. Please contact your instructor for information about accessing the Data Files.

Instructions: Start Excel. Open the file called SC_EX_11_NIMSalesDistribute.xlsm that you created earlier in this module. If you did not create the file, see your instructor for ways to complete this assignment. The document contains the Sales Data Analysis worksheet and Prospect Recorder. You are to create VBA code that will execute upon closing the file. It will include a message box shown in Figure 11–89.

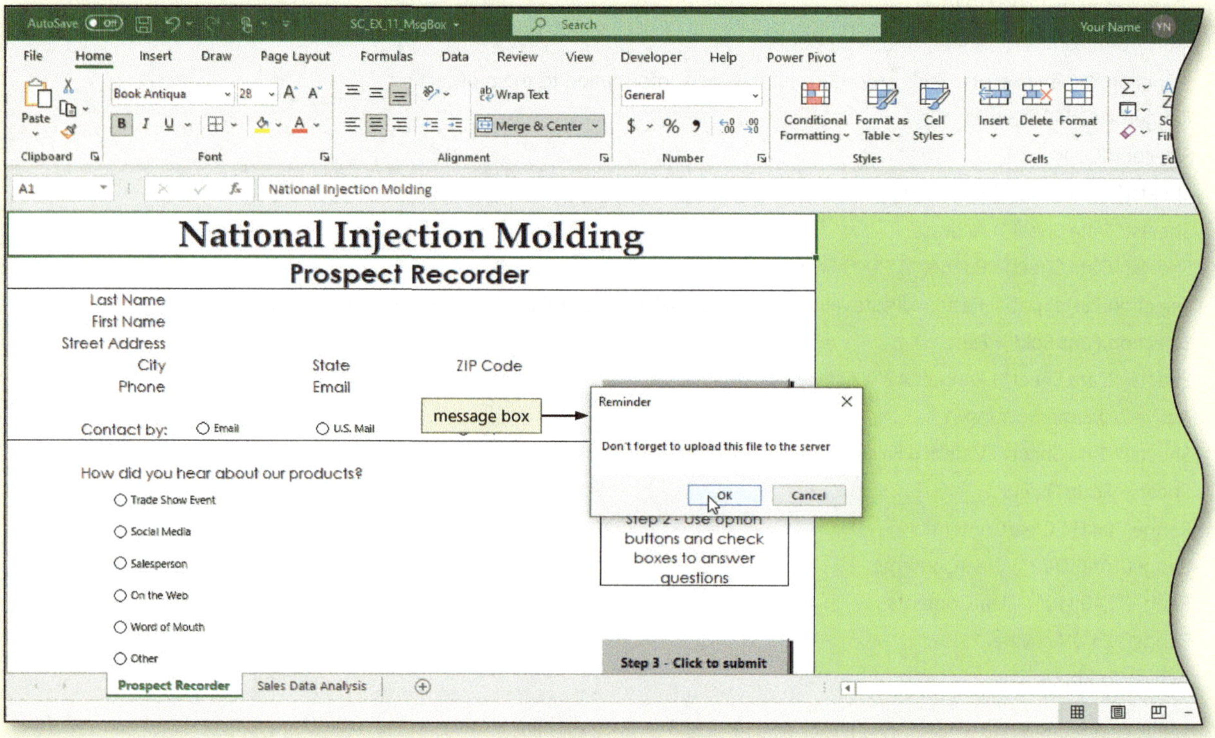

Figure 11–89

Perform the following tasks:

1. Save the file in the macro-enable format with the name, SC_EX_11_MsgBox.xlsm.
2. With the Sales Data Analysis sheet displayed, click the Visual Basic button (Developer tab | Code group) to display the Microsoft Visual Basic for Applications editor.
3. On the menu bar, click Help, and then click Microsoft Visual Basic for Applications Help in the list. Click the link for Excel VBA Reference. In the Filter by Title box in the upper-left corner, search for information about BeforeClose. Click BeforeClose in the list on the left and read about the event. Search again for information about MsgBox. Read about the MsgBox function.
4. In the Project pane (the left pane of the VBA window), double-click ThisWorkbook, so the code will apply to the entire workbook.
5. In the main window, click the Object arrow and then click Workbook. Click the Procedure arrow and then click BeforeClose. Excel will create two procedures; if necessary, click in the procedure labeled, Workbook_BeforeClose.

6. Press TAB and then type **`'This procedure displays a message box when the user closes the workbook`** to enter a code comment. Press ENTER to move to the next line. Enter another comment with your name and the date.
7. Create a message box by typing the code, **`MsgBox "Don't forget to upload this file to the server", vbOKCancel, "Reminder"`** and press ENTER.
8. Enter other comments explaining the purpose of the various parts of the MsgBox statement.
9. Save the workbook.
10. Test the workbook by clicking the Close button in the title bar. When Excel displays the message box, click the Cancel button. Test the VBA code again and this time click the OK button. If there are errors, review the VBA code and edit as necessary.
11. Submit the revised workbook in the format specified by your instructor.
12. The MsgBox function, when used with an equals sign, returns a value based on which button the user clicks in the message box (access the previous Help page and scroll down to the Return Values and Examples areas). What do you think VBA programmers do with that response value?

Expand Your World

Create a solution that uses cloud and web technologies by learning and investigating on your own from general guidance.

Preparing Surveys

Instructions: Start Excel and open a blank workbook. You are to create a survey related to either education or employment to illustrate how to use form controls and ActiveX controls in Excel to create a survey and record responses.

Perform the following tasks:

1. Open a browser and navigate to http://zoho.com/survey. Search the website for a survey template in either education or employment that you can create in Excel with form controls. Select a template that contains at least 10 questions. Right-click and print a copy, if desired.
2. Using the skills you learned in this module, use Excel to create a survey that includes at least three of the questions from the survey you found on zoho.com. You should use more than one type of control in creating your survey.
3. Create a sheet named Prospect List and hide it.
4. Write a VBA procedure to collect the entered data each time the survey is completed and store it on a separate, hidden worksheet. (*Hint*: Use the code from Tables 11–6 and 11–7.)
5. Use worksheet protection and formatting to set up your survey so that a user can answer questions but not gain access to the hidden worksheet or areas on the current worksheet outside of the survey.
6. Save the file in the macro-enabled format as SC_EX_11_SurveyComplete.xlsm and submit it in the format specified by your instructor, along with the password so the instructor can view the hidden worksheet.
7. What was the hardest thing about this assignment? Why? Did you use Help at any time? If so, what did you look up?

In the Lab

Design and implement a solution using creative thinking and problem-solving skills.

Create Schemes and Themes

Problem: You have been asked to create a custom color scheme, font scheme, and workbook theme for your school or place of employment.

Perform the following tasks:

Part 1: Start Excel and open a blank workbook. Click the Colors button (Page Layout tab | Themes group) and then click Customize Colors to open the Create New Theme Colors dialog box. Click the Accent 1 color button and then click More Colors. When Excel displays the Colors dialog box, click the Standard tab. Choose the color most closely associated with your school or business. Repeat the process for Accent 2 and Accent 3 using different colors. If your school does not have three colors, choose colors that complement the Accent 1 color. Before closing the dialog box, press ALT+PRT SC (print screen) to capture the dialog box in the clipboard. Enter a name for your color scheme. Click Save (Create New Theme Colors dialog box) and then paste the screen capture onto the worksheet.

Click the Fonts button (Page Layout tab | Themes group) and then click Customize Fonts to open the Create New Theme Fonts dialog box. Choose a heading font and body font that closely matches the fonts used in your school or company headline or logo. Before closing the dialog box, press ALT+PRT SC (print screen) to capture the dialog box in the clipboard. Enter a name for your font scheme. Click Save (Create New Theme Fonts dialog box) and then paste the screen capture onto the worksheet.

Click the Themes button (Page Layout tab | Themes group) and then click Save Current Theme to open the Save Current Theme dialog box. Enter a name of your theme and then navigate to your Data File storage location. Before clicking Save, press ALT+PRT SC (print screen) to capture the dialog box in the clipboard. Click Save (Save Current Theme dialog box) to save the theme. Paste the screen capture onto the worksheet.

Arrange the three screen captures side by side and then save the workbook with the file name SC_EX_11_Schemes. Submit the file along with your answers to the critical thinking questions in Part 2 as directed by your instructor.

Part 2: How did you decide on the sources to use for the color and font schemes? How would your school or company use these saved schemes and themes?

Index

D

E

G

H

N

O

Q

R

S

T

U

V

W